Redeemed

The Unauthorized Guide to Angel

Lars Pearson + Christa Dickson

mad norwegian press

Also available from Mad Norwegian Press...

Dusted: The Unauthorized Guide to Buffy the Vampire Slayer
by Lawrence Miles, Pearson and Christa Dickson

I, Who: The Unauthorized Guide to the Doctor Who Novels and Audios
by Lars Pearson (vols. 1-3)

Running Through Corridors: Rob and Toby's Marathon Watch of Doctor Who
by Robert Shearman and Toby Hadoke (Vol. 1: The 60s) and (Vol. 2: The 70s)

Space Helmet for a Cow: The Mad, True Story of Doctor Who
by Paul Kirkley (Vol. 1: 1963-1990) and (Vol. 2: 1990-2013)

Wanting to Believe: A Critical Guide to The X-Files, Millennium and the Lone Gunmen
by Robert Shearman

The AHistory Series by Lance Parkin and Lars Pearson
AHistory: An Unauthorized History of the Doctor Who Universe [3rd Edition]
AHistory: An Unauthorized History of the Doctor Who Universe [2012-2013 Update]
(ebook only)
Unhistory: Stories Too Strange for Even Ahistory: An Unauthorized History of the Doctor Who Universe
(ebook only)

The About Time Series by Tat Wood and Lawrence Miles
About Time 1: The Unauthorized Guide to Doctor Who (Seasons 1 to 3)
About Time 2: The Unauthorized Guide to Doctor Who (Seasons 4 to 6)
About Time 3: The Unauthorized Guide to Doctor Who (Seasons 7 to 11) [2nd Ed]
About Time 4: The Unauthorized Guide to Doctor Who (Seasons 12 to 17)
About Time 5: The Unauthorized Guide to Doctor Who (Seasons 18 to 21)
About Time 6: The Unauthorized Guide to Doctor Who (Seasons 22 to 26)
About Time 7: The Unauthorized Guide to Doctor Who (Series 1 to 2)
About Time 8: The Unauthorized Guide to Doctor Who (Series 3, forthcoming)
About Time 9: The Unauthorized Guide to Doctor Who (Series 4, The Specials, forthcoming)

Essay Collections
Chicks Dig Comics: A Celebration of Comic Books by the Women Who Love Them

Chicks Dig Gaming: A Celebration of All Things Gaming by the Women Who Love It

Chicks Dig Time Lords: A Celebration of Doctor Who by the Women Who Love It
2011 Hugo Award Winner, Best Related Work

Chicks Unravel Time: Women Journey Through Every Season of Doctor Who

Companion Piece: Women Celebrate the Humans, Aliens and Tin Dogs of Doctor Who

Queers Dig Time Lords: A Celebration of Doctor Who by the LGBTQ Fans Who Love It

Whedonistas: A Celebration of the Worlds of Joss Whedon by the Women Who Love Them

First Edition: November 2006. Second Printing: March 2017.

Table of Contents

Table of Contents

Season Five

Sidebars

The Total Kill-Count

How to Use This Book

Quite some time ago, information about any given series was so scarce, almost any program guide that did little more than provide story summaries seemed like a blessing. Now, in a world where the bare-bones facts about a show are readily accessible, the bar is set much higher. With that in mind, we've attempted to craft *Redeemed* with much greater detail about *Angel* than any online source provides. In short, we set out to compile a text that addresses every single issue (or near enough) with *Angel* that's worth addressing. Although we're living in the Information Age, there's still value in a team of researchers tunneling their way through piles of evidence—including interviews and articles that aren't available anywhere online—then putting their findings, theories and conclusions into a single, pull-off-your shelf volume.

Crucially, in addition to looking at areas of interest in *Angel* that you've hopefully never considered, *Redeemed* seeks to hold a discussion / debate / meeting of the minds between us—your tireless *Angel* researchers—and you, the *Angel* fan. Please understand that we don't expect to sway all your opinions or compel you to buy every theory we put on the table. Rather, we're making an effort to explore every facet of Angel that seems interesting ("Interesting" being our guiding watchword in all this), and provide arguments that at least sound plausible. On that note...

Of critical importance: Everything presented as "fact" by the series is in normal text, but everything inside of square brackets [like this] is either our speculation or an act of cross-referencing. Remember: If it's not in brackets, you can be confident it's information given on screen, while the bracketed material is our attempt to rationalize ambiguous details in the show, or to reconcile the *Angel*-verse against itself. It's our means of "speaking" to the reader. However, we only apply the brackets in the meat-and-potatoes continuity sections (chiefly **Character Notes** through **Magic**), and forego them in the more casual areas (such as **Points of Discussion**, etc.).

Most of the categories are self-explanatory, but a few warrant further explanation...

• **Story Summaries:** Admittedly available from a wealth of sources online, but provided as a refresher course. Some readers undoubtedly have an encyclopedic knowledge of *Angel*, but many fans are conversant in the series, yet can't remember every plot-point on command, and tend to name episodes using the *Friends* method ("The One Where Angel Becomes a Puppet," etc.) Thus, summaries are provided to jog your memory before we pile on the detail.

• **Points of Discussion:** Something of a slush-pile category, where we deliberate on anything that seems of interest to a particular episode. Topics discussed range from hardcore continuity issues to purely whimsical observations.

• **Things That Don't Make Sense:** A type of reader seems offended by this category's existence, and deems it an affront to the show to scrutinize its flaws so heavily. However, the intent here isn't to mock *Angel* or to tear it down. We might sometimes reference a logic hole or visual mistake that—if we're being truthful—genuinely impedes on the story at-hand. But often, we're just citing perfectly understandable errors, the unavoidable kind that arise when you're creating an ongoing sci-fi / drama series for network TV.

In fact, this category is something of a necessity, because any guide that thinks it can iron out every single wrinkle from every single episode is probably deluding itself. For instance, no amount of continuity glue can account (say) for Cordelia literally becoming a mannequin in 2.10, "Reunion." All of that said... please understand that this is done with love and respect for *Angel*. We're laughing ***with*** the series, not at it. And we'll try to differentiate between what's a weighty, over-riding glitch, and when we're just being nit-picky. We'll also address when commonly repeated complaints about the series don't hold up on close analysis.

• **The Lore:** The "Behind-the-Scenes" section, detailing anything pertinent to *Angel*'s creative choices, casting, broadcast issues, finances, etc. In this, we've called upon a myriad of interviews (see the **Bibliography**), plus online postings from the production team and actors. Suffice to say, if the likes of Joss Whedon posted something, we took notice.

By the way, you might notice that creators such as Whedon, Tim Minear, etc., commented far more often in Season One than in later years, and one suspects that their ever-growing workload simply left them less time for socializing with fans. For instance, let's not forget that Whedon had *three* shows in play by the time *Angel* Season Four rolled around, and became a father in 2002 to boot. Casually spending time on *The Bronze*, the main *Angel*/ *Buffy* discussion forum, probably didn't seem as much of a priority.

Sometimes, **The Lore** takes into account the official shooting scripts, many of which have information that's not given on screen (minor characters' names, etc.) or dialogue or entire scenes that were changed before broadcast. We sourced these from the now-defunct Official Angel Fan Club, and sometimes Script City (www.scriptcity.com), although IDW Publishing has released a few in illustrated script format.

Lars and Christa; Des Moines, IA

THE EPISODES

1.01: "City Of"

"It's not about saving lives, it's about saving souls. Possibly your own in the process."

Air Date: Oct. 5, 1999; **Writers:** Joss Whedon, David Greenwalt; **Director:** Joss Whedon

SUMMARY Having relocated to Los Angeles, the heroic vampire named Angel finds himself rudderless until a half-demon named Doyle suddenly shows up in his apartment. Doyle offers himself as Angel's liaison to "the Powers-That-Be," a benevolent higher body that gives Doyle visions of people in danger. As proof, Doyle directs Angel to investigate Tina, a coffee shop waitress.

Angel finds Tina stalked by Russell Winters, a multimillionaire, and accompanies her to a party. There, Angel happens upon Cordelia Chase, a Sunnydale associate who's floundering in her acting career. Unfortunately, Tina flees upon learning that Angel's a vampire, enabling Russell – who's similarly a vamp – to murder her. Russell later invites Cordelia to his mansion, hoping to snack on her too, but Angel arrives and saves Cordy.

The next day, Russell meets with his attorney, a member of the Wolfram and Hart law firm. Without ceremony, Angel interrupts the proceedings and kicks Russell out a window in broad daylight, dusting him. For an encore, Angel opens "Angel Investigations" – a detective agency that "helps the helpless" – with Cordelia as his assistant and Doyle as his contact with the Powers.

THE OPENING CREDITS The show antes-up with the lead trio of David Boreanaz (Angel), Charisma Carpenter (Cordelia) and Glenn Quinn (Doyle), yet there's glimpses of characters to come. A shaded blonde woman levels a gun (it's Kate Lockley, taking aim at Angel in 1.02, "Lonely Hearts"), a silhouetted figure flees from someone (it's Angel again, running from Spike, 1.03, "In the Dark"), and one of the – shall we say – "mournful people slathered in a pit of despair" is actually the doomed Dennis Pearson. He's destined to become Cordelia's roommate, of sorts, in "Rm w/a Vu" (1.05) – but as a fixture of the opening credits, he'll be sighing and gasping his near-to-last breath until the end of the series, 110 episodes hence.

FIRSTS AND LASTS In order of appearance, it's the debut in *Angel* of... the city of Los Angeles, Angel and his spiky hair, Angel's leather trenchcoat, Angel's vamp face, the *Angel* theme song, the office space that will house Angel Investigations, Angel's apartment, Doyle, Angelus (in flashback), Buffy (in flashback), Angel's black 1968 Plymouth GTX convertible and Cordelia Chase. Christian Kane also debuts as attorney Lindsey McDonald, but the script dubs him "Smart Young Lawyer" and the character isn't named until "Five by Five" (1.18).

First mention of Angel's benefactors, the Powers-That-Be, but also the group that's effectively their opposite number: the Senior Partners who oversee the Wolfram and Hart law firm.

First script by *Angel* co-creators Joss Whedon and David Greenwalt, who are going to write and direct some of the most instrumental stories. Angel becomes the first hero to dust a vampire (two, actually) with a spring-loaded wrist stake – the heroes' weapon of choice. Sunlight scorches a harried Angel as he desperately tries to follow someone outside for the first time, Angel gets to down a cup of coffee – a staple drink of Season One – and it's the first occasion in which he chews a bullet (four actually, while shielding Cordelia).

Inevitably, it's the first hint of Doyle's attraction to Cordelia, chiefly because she's the only good-looking woman on the planet who'll actually speak to him, however contemptuously. In terms of visual motifs, it's our first fast-moving view of the L.A. cityscape, and the first time that washed-out rapid cuts signal a scene change (you'll know it when you see it). The teaser entails Angel's first venture into a back alley and – as that's where the heroes end up in 5.22, "Not Fade Away" – serves as a neat little bookend to the entire series. Angel gets the series' first line, which simply amounts to: "Los Angeles."

Angel dons one of Doyle's dorky Hawaiian shirts (regrettably, we'll revisit this in 1.06, "Sense and Sensitivity"). Cordelia first proposes charging the agency's clients, thus sparking an ongoing debate about the morality of saving people's lives and stuffing an invoice into their hands afterward.

If we're being ludicrously technical, it possibly marks the first *Angel* appearance of a Mac computer – long a prized product placement on *Buffy*, and the tool of benevolent witches, etc.. Judge for yourselves, but when Angel here visits the public library, his computer screen displays Netscape 4 for the Mac (although the computer itself might be a PC).

POINTS OF DISCUSSION ABOUT "City Of":

1. Let's begin with the shift in tone from *Buffy,* starting with how the Mutant Enemy team (that's Joss Whedon's production company) likely seduced the WB into making *Angel*. As has been noted elsewhere, when *Smallville* was in the hopper, its producers, trying to keep things simple, probably pitched the show as "*Superman* meets *Dawson's Creek*." It seems pretty evident, as Greenwalt revealed in a 2003 *Zap2It.com* interview, that *Angel*'s remit at the beginning was simply: "*Buffy*, if you're in your twenties." It's hard to believe that something as complex as *Angel* hailed from such humble beginnings, yet this description fits *Angel* Season One as good as any. (Still, if you're going to emulate success, then adopting the *Buffy* pattern is a damn good way of going about it.)

In 1999 when *Angel* launched, the Sunnydale characters were just hitting their college years, meaning the "adult" trauma of *Buffy* Seasons Five to Seven was some distance away. That being the case, *Angel* Season One probably seemed like fertile ground to explore the awkwardness, depression and confusion with "adult" issues that hits people post-high school. To this end, *Angel* centered on the adults living in L.A., 1999-2000 – Whedon later commented that the city was intended as a character itself – and this real-world location colors the show quite a bit. Inherently, it's plausible that all sorts of dangers lurk in the back alleys of America's second biggest city – but by contrast, it's quite the conceit in "small-town" Sunnydale when literally 30 students and eight high school staff perish in less than three years and the townsfolk barely seem to notice.

Not without reason does *Buffy* open with a murder in the high school, and *Angel* conversely begin with a panning shot of L.A. One of the authors of this book actually lived in L.A. throughout 2000, and can attest that some of *Angel*'s metaphors for adult life there are pretty apt.

2. To prove the above point, the heroes here fight a vampire, albeit one entirely unlike the *Buffy* variety. Setting aside a few ambitious members of the undead (such as the Master, Spike and even Angelus), most of Sunnydale's vamps acted almost as an underclass, barely worrying about anything beyond scoring their next meal. The elitist bloodsucker Russell, on the other hand, ranks among the wealthy L.A. businessmen, meaning he can throw money at problems and thinks he can get away with anything. Smugly shielded behind his lawyers, of course. (And see **It's Really About...**)

3. Ah, now here's a fun little game we're going to play during the show's early years. In 1999, *Angel*'s producers and designers probably couldn't conceive of a DVD-flush world in which fandom would freeze-frame the show with mind-bending precision. After all, *The X-Files* helped to pioneer the seasonal DVD box set model and Season One of that show didn't surface on DVD until May 2000. Allowing for *Angel*'s production schedule, we're about a year before that.

Thus, in *Angel* Seasons One to Two (but dropping off sharply later on, probably as the designers took to the Internet and recognized fandom's crazed adherence to detail), there are several uses of dummy text, chiefly in newspaper articles. These flash past too quick for the naked eye but are visible if you pause the DVD with some precision. In "City Of," a masterful example occurs when Angel reads an on-screen article entitled "Murder Victim Trashed in Dumpster" – but the article itself discusses recycling and the difference between rhino, cattle, sheep and antelope horns. The next article bears the headline "Hiker Finds Body in Angeles Crest Forest," yet expands on the recycling information in a Swiss-cheesed fashion.

The **Things That Don't Make Sense** category will catalog future installments of this, but if you feel like skipping ahead, one of the funniest examples occurs in "Eternity" (1.17).

4. Angel's library excursion also entails a facet of the Whedon-verse that's become so familiar, you almost can't call it a goof: As was the case in Sunnydale, every single government document, autopsy photo or classified record imaginable is, apparently, available on the Internet where any boob with know-how can see it. Here, Angel identifies a murder victim in part by going to "Find-a-Loved-One.com" – a website the police evidently never frequent – and performing sophisticated word searches such as "Murders, Young Women." Using such breathtaking research, Angel pulls up a coroner's photo with the dead woman's rose tattoo. If only the real Internet were so useful, the murder arrest rate would skyrocket overnight.

5. Sharp-eyed *Buffy* viewers might notice that the vampires here sport forehead bumps that're a lot more rounded and pronounced than those of Sunnydale's undead. This is deliberate, as the *Angel* producers viewed the *Buffy* vamps as too minimalistic, and were striving instead for a more classical horror feel. The result was judged – as Whedon later expressed – "a little too Kabuki mask," and it's only a few episodes before the *Angel* vamps come into synch with their *Buffy* brethren.

Still, that leaves us with something of a pickle in terms of continuity. We could nearly cite the "rounded bump" vampires as a hither-to unseen species, save that Angel himself sports the rounded bumps. As matters stand, though, you've got to wonder if something in the water is physically altering L.A.'s vampires. Or perhaps it's the smog.

6. We've got to mention it somewhere, so... it seems a bit of an oddity that Angel uses an elaborate and amazingly sanitary sewer system to move about L.A. during the day-

time. The cleanliness, though, probably owes to the fact that metropolitan areas often have two tunnel systems: one for human waste, and one for runoff water. (Both are commonly called "sewers" but we'll sometimes make reference to "storm drains" in this volume.) Angel probably uses the latter, which is probably better for all concerned.

7. The teaser features the definitive shot of Angel walking down the alley, and – awkwardly – shows his reflection in a puddle. Once this gets co-oped into the credits, it creates the bizarre contradiction that a series featuring a reflection-less vampire shows his reflection at the start of all 110 episodes. However, see **Why Don't Vampires Cast Reflections?** for why we don't consider incidental vampire castings (in puddles, shiny desktops, name plates, doorknobs, whatever) as goofs. Ditto with anything that relies on reflected images, such as photographs and video recordings.

CHARACTER NOTES *Angel:* As the TNT syndication promos proudly point out: "He's the heroic vampire with a soul..." yadda yadda yadda. For a quick rundown of Angel's activities prior to this, see **Previously on Buffy the Vampire Slayer....**

Angel last drank human blood from Buffy [a few months ago, in *Buffy* 3.22, "Graduation Day," to save his life from poisoning], and this has apparently rekindled his bloodlust. Doyle suggests that if Angel doesn't find a mission, he will eventually take to feeding off the innocent. [Similar concerns get raised from time to time, especially in 2.08, "The Shroud of Rahmon," 4.15, "Orpheus" and to a lesser degree 3.16, "Sleep Tight." However, this never becomes a problem, suggesting that Angel's work for the Powers really does grant him greater clarity, and Buffy's blood eventually purges from his system.]

Angel drinks coffee. [He told Buffy's mom in *Buffy* 3.20, "The Prom," that he avoided coffee because it made him jittery, but he drinks the stuff like a fish throughout Season One. His vampire metabolism surely doesn't require coffee or caffeine, so he probably develops a taste for it for social reasons.]

Doyle encourages Angel to empower people's souls in addition to saving their lives. [This is surely to help develop Angel's own sense of self-empowerment.] Angel lives in an apartment beneath the Angel Investigations office. His weapons collection there includes at least two double-sided battle-axes, a knife and a sai [never used, sadly]. It's implied that Angel hasn't heard of the Powers-That-Be before now. The license plate on his convertible fuzzily looks a bit like IM0 714 [it's clearly visible as NK0 714 in loads of stories such as "She" (1.13)].

His kitchen contains tea and refrigerated pig's blood, but no sugar, milk or beer. Angel is sometimes adorned with silver rings on both hands, plus a metal necklace with a pendant. [The pendant is never terribly distinctive, but at its most visible in 1.05, "Rm w/a Vu."] He moves fast enough to catch a falling cup underhanded with the coffee still in it.

Angel claims he's witnessed "14 wars" – not including Vietnam, because hostilities there were never formally declared. He visited Missoula, Montana, during the Great Depression. He here breaks into the L.A. Public Library to research a murder victim. [It's unclear if Angel doesn't own a computer yet, simply lacks Internet access or needs to directly loot the library's archives. At the very least, this proves he can work a computer – so he's not a total Luddite whatever the show wants to claim about his cell phone conniptions – and he's said to use e-mail in "I Fall to Pieces" (1.04).]

Angel scales walls with a grappling hook and towline (used again in "She"), and has access to explosives with a timing mechanism. [He'll use them a lot more sparingly from here, but see 3.10, "Dad."] He doesn't dispute Cordelia's claim that in [more than] 200 years of life, he's never developed an investment portfolio [and he doesn't seem to worry much about it until Connor comes along in Season Three].

Angel presently believes there is "nobody left that he cares about." [That'll change.]

• *Cordelia:* Previously the "rich bitch" of Sunnydale [again, see **Previously on Buffy**...], now living the L.A. life of near-poverty because her parents didn't file taxes "in like... forever." [*Buffy* 3.20, "The Prom," specifies they didn't pay taxes for 12 years. Cordelia's mother phones in "Sense and Sensitivity (1.06), but the original draft of "City Of" (see **The Lore**) suggested her folks did some prison time and might now reside in Bimini.] She's tactless enough to ask Angel if he's still "evil" and out to "bite people." [A rather pointless question, when you think about it.]

Cordy lives in a tatty apartment, can barely afford food and resorts to snitching little sandwiches from a dinner party. Her acting agent, Joe, claims the networks have "seen enough of her." It's implied that she auditioned to play the hands in a Liqui-Gel commercial, and she already seems disillusioned with the supposed glamour of acting in L.A. [Not for nothing is it called "The City of Broken Dreams."]

She's currently studying *Meditation for a Bountiful Life* by Amanda Smith. [This book re-appears in "I Fall to Pieces," and it's not titled *Meditation for a Successful Life* as some sources claim.] She's intuitive enough to quickly peg Russell as a vampire, but also impulsive enough to blurt out, "Hey, you're a vampire!", when they're alone together.

Cordelia didn't know that Angel was living in L.A. [This implies she's completely lost touch with Buffy's group.] She's friends with a redheaded party host named Margo [who's never seen again].

• *Doyle:* Half-demon, half-human on his mother's side. He somehow knows the gist of Angel's history and recent events in Sunnydale. [Doyle must have independently researched Angel's past, because the Powers are never so chatty with their visions. But if so, a small problem exists; see **Organizations**.]

Doyle says the Powers' visions wrack him with blinding pain, enough to knock him out. [That said, neither Doyle nor his successor ever lose consciousness to standard visions on screen, so perhaps he's exaggerating a bit.] Doyle's streetwise, knowing the location of some illegal chop shops. He drinks beer and bets on the [Minnesota] Vikings. He's not trained as a warrior, and considers – but refrains from – running out on Angel during a gunfight.

Doyle's demon aspect features facial spikes, and it's possible that sneezing manifests it. [More likely, Doyle shows his demon face to Angel by deliberately sneezing as a joke. Otherwise, Doyle could hardly show his face in public – certainly not during ragweed season. For more on sneezing, see 1.07, "The Bachelor Party."]

Doyle claims he has something to atone for [see 1.09, "Hero"]. He wears a silver ring on his left hand [presumably explained in "The Bachelor Party"], and casually carries a deck of playing cards [used again in "I Fall to Pieces"].

Doyle enters Angel's apartment uninvited, and cites this as proof that he's not a vampire. [But as Angel is also a demon, vamps don't need an invitation to enter his abode. Streetwise Doyle shouldn't be so ignorant of the vampire invitation rule, so he's probably just making small-talk here.]

Doyle charmingly labels Cordelia "a stiffener."

• *Russell Winters:* Vampiric investment tycoon who owns Russell Winters Enterprises. He recently furthered a merger with Eltron after "negotiating with" [i.e. "gobbling like a ripe tomato"] the company CEO. Russell targets young girls without any ties; he forms sadistic friendships with some of these victims, but views other women (such as Cordelia) simply as a quick meal.

Russell's "vamp face" looks greener and somewhat lumpier than most vampires. [Whedon suggests on the DVD commentary that Russell's "more of a diseased, depraved vampire," but there could also be a better explanation. The *Buffy* series established that older vampires take on animalistic attributes, morphing into bat-like or goat-like humanoids. Examples include the Master from *Buffy* Season One, Kakistos from *Buffy* 3.03, "Faith, Hope and Trick" and presumably the Prince of Lies from *Angel* 5.13, "Why We Fight." It's entirely possible, then, that Russell is "middle aged" for a vampire – making him older than Angel, hence his ability to hold his own in combat with him. Who knows? Perhaps Russell's turning into a giant lizard, a praying mantis (shades of *Buffy* 1.04, "Teacher's Pet") or even a giant frog.]

ORGANIZATIONS *Angel Investigations:* It's left unstated how Angel affords such spacious office and apartment space in L.A. ["I Fall to Pieces" establishes that he doesn't own the building, and other tenants are in residence as of "Somnambulist" (1.11) and "To Shanshu in L.A." (1.22). Angel must've called in a favor or two, because L.A. rent is simply too heinous otherwise.] The office space appears full of boxes. [Probably left by the previous tenants; Angel was homeless a mere three years ago and the office looks spartan in Season One.] The street number of the Angel Investigations building: 627.

• *Wolfram and Hart:* Lindsey's business card says that the firm operates branches in New York, London, Paris, Cairo and Los Angeles. [Episodes such as 2.15, "Reprise" reiterate this. Insofar as can be determined, the card also gives the firm's contact numbers as phone: (323) 565-0044, fax: (323) 565-0633, and Telex: 8XZ BRB.]

Lindsey claims the local authorities possess no information on Angel, but that the firm has retained several top investigators to research him. [The firm seems in the dark about Angel for much of Season One, which is terribly odd considering they here learn that he's a vampire named "Angel." Honestly, how hard can it be to figure out? Doyle somehow knows Angel's history – probably through his own means – and Kate figures it out by visiting an occult bookshop in "Somnam-bulist." It's possible that Lindsey is less than forthcoming with Russell; either way, it seems that the firm didn't have Angel on its radar until he arrived in L.A. And see 1.21, "Blind Date."]

• *The Powers-That-Be:* Doyle claims the Powers want to recruit Angel because of his "potential" to do good. [Probably true, but the Powers might already know about Angel's great importance regarding the apocalypse; see 2.12, "Blood Money" and **When Do the Powers Intervene?** for more.]

DEMONOLOGY *Vampires:* Can enter a home without invitation if the residents are dead [reiterated in 1.03, "In the Dark"; 1.15, "The Prodigal," etc]. It's possible, but by no means certain, that vampires can enter homes they own without invitation. [Tina and Russell have a prior relationship, so she probably invited him inside at *some* point, and he only says, "I own the building," by way of explaining his pass-key to her apartment. But compare with Angel and Fred in 3.01, "Heartthrob," and see **How Does the Invitation Rule Work?** for the debate about vampire landlords.]

When sunlight grazes Angel, it triggers his vamp face [an instinctive reaction]. The vamps that Angel approaches in the teaser don't appear to recognize him as being among their number. [Several episodes – running as late as 5.21, "Power Play" – prove that vamps can instinctively recognize other vamps. But as the series is never consistent about this, perhaps it's an ability they learn over time.]

BEST LINE Cordelia to Angel, at a party: "I better get mingly. I really should be talking to people that are somebody."

THINGS THAT DON'T MAKE SENSE When a pair of Russell's goons abduct Tina in the parking garage, a second set of thugs manhandles Angel into an elevator. Nothing too odd about that, save that the goons with Tina haven't a clue that Angel represents a threat to them in any way, shape or form. Yet instead of simply driving away in a brisk but casual "We've got everything under control, nothing to see here" manner, they insist on racing off in a tire-screeching, teeth clenched and generally frothing-at-the-mouth fashion anyway. The bed-wetting panic on the driver's face looks especially amusing, both *before* and after he realizes that Angel's after them.

Tina tells Angel that her Girl Scout training allows her to live out of the small bag she's carrying for days. But instead of just skipping town with said bag in tow, she bizarrely runs to her own apartment to pack a second bag, thus conveniently allowing Russell to find and slaughter her. It's also weird that once Tina erroneously thinks Angel is in Russell's employ – and therefore shouldn't believe a damn thing he's said – she still gives lip-service to Angel's claim that Russell murdered her friend Denise.

Angel insists on checking Tina's pale and obviously dead body for a pulse, thus leaving his fingerprint on a murder victim, right by the wound that killed her. Only by virtue of L.A. cops in the *Angel*-verse being dumb as turnips does this go unnoticed. (Worse, they evidently fail to cross-check the fingerprint after booking Angel in 1.19, "Sanctuary.")

Cordelia's escape from Russell's office, carried out between scenes, seems wholly miraculous considering she's confronted by a shut door, he's got vampire speed *and* she's wearing heels. (Later episodes such as "Somnambulist" suggest that fear makes humans taste sweeter, so perhaps Russell is simply toying with Cordy to whet his appetite. It's also possible that by now, Cordelia has loads of experience running in heels – weirdly, we'll return to the point in 3.14, "Couplet" and 4.03, "The House Always Wins.")

Lindsey never tells Angel his name, and hands him a business card that only lists the firm's telephone numbers, nothing else. Just how useful is *that*? "Um... I'm calling for... that smart-ass young lawyer." Are psychics manning the phones at Wolfram and Hart?

Angel's car has a license plate on the front, but not the back as California law requires. Finally, fans usually mention – and they've got a point – that the combatants in the Angel/Russell fight don't remotely look like David Boreanaz or Vyto Ruginis. Mind, it also looks dodgy when "Angel" (obviously Mike Massa, Boreanaz's stunt double) leaps atop the wall surrounding Russell's estate.

POP CULTURE Doyle: "Let's go treat me to a Billy Dee." *Star Wars* actor Billy Dee Williams appeared in ads for Colt .45 malt liquor, with the marketing slogans, "Colt .45, works every time" and "Don't let the smooth taste fool you."

IN RETROSPECT Angel tells Cordelia that no cure exists for vampirism – which is ironic, considering the show will present three different methods for vampires becoming human before Season One ends (the Mohra demon blood in 1.08, "I Will Remember You," plus Darla's resurrection and the promise of the Shanshu Prophecy in "To Shanshu in L.A.").

After Tina's death, Angel rigidly informs Doyle: "I don't want to share my feelings." Five episodes from now, in "Sense and Sensitivity," he'll do little *but* share his feelings.

IT'S REALLY ABOUT... In its most basic form, it's about the hurdles that adults face in truly communicating with one another. Angel is the most heroic and noble character onhand, but even with the best of intentions, he looks awkward if not downright creepy while approaching Tina in the coffee shop. Notably, he's forced to concoct a reason for his interest in her, as if perfectly ordinary human contact along the lines of, "Hello, how are you?", isn't good enough. And even allowing that he can't say, "My friend had a psychic vision and thought you were in trouble, so I thought I'd hang out here and stalk you," it's starkly clear – and will get re-emphasized throughout Season One – that engaging someone in conversation can seem as difficult as decapitating a five-headed dragon.

The story is also about obsession, of course, particularly the kind owing to money and power. Russell's probably set for life and runs a large corporation, yet as a vampire, he feels compelled to ruin/end the lives of helpless young women just for kicks. His twisted compulsion best demonstrates itself when, after killing Tina, he watches a video of her and wistfully says, "She had something...", thus becoming one of the very few vamps in the *Angel*-verse to mourn the passing of their lunch.

CROSS-OVERS A pining Angel calls Buffy in her college dorm room, but hangs up before saying anything. The Slayer answers this call in *Buffy* 4.01, "The Freshman."

CRITIQUE Debut episodes usually prove problematic – you need only look at *Star Trek: The Next Generation* to see how it can go tragically wrong – so in some respects, let's cut "City Of" some slack. It primarily exists to explain the series' concept, placing the major players on the chessboard: Angel's the broody hero, Doyle's the disheveled sidekick and Cordelia's the tactless rich bitch who's fallen from grace, with Wolfram and Hart threatening to litigate the crap out of everyone. In terms of making us want to see more, "City Of" succeeds beautifully. More to the point, it readily distinguishes *Angel* from the *Buffy*-verse that spawned it, particularly with regards to the dynamics of L.A. versus Sunnydale. So far, so good.

There's a strange problem, though: Unless you're a hard-core fan, try to remember the overall plot. Whereas viewers might readily recall "that one where Angel eats his parents" or "that one where Buffy comes back and dribbles ice cream on Angel's chest," the story to "City Of" simply doesn't stick in the mind. Because ultimately, Angel does little more than, er, well, take out a vampire. It's admittedly a vampire who's different from the Sunnydale breed, but he's still a vampire. It's a fairly mundane undertaking – save for that great bit where Russell falls several stories and becomes a screaming torch, of course, because you'd have to be near-comatose to forget *that*.

It's a "pilot story" in the grand sense, then, in that it sells you on the premise at the cost of the story's individual needs – but perhaps that's no bad thing. You have to learn to walk before you can run, and the producers do know what they're doing. But oddly enough, even if it seems like the next story, "Lonely Hearts," is a bit more troubled than this outing, it's a far more seminal work that galvanizes the show into action.

THE LORE As with *Buffy*, the Mutant Enemy team crafted a six-minute *Angel* "pilot," purely to tease the suits at the WB into green-lighting the show. We're using the term "pilot" rather loosely, because it's really just a glorified advertisement, and more commonly referred to as the *Angel Demo Reel*. With *Buffy* already a hit, spending the money to film an entire *Angel* mini-story – along the lines of the unbroadcast *Buffy* "pilot" – presumably wasn't viewed as necessary.

The *Buffy* "pilot" entails a vastly compressed version of the story that became *Buffy* 1.01, "Welcome to the Hellmouth" (the Master and Angel don't appear in it, which gives you some clue about the severity of the cuts), but it retains most of the major plot-beats. By contrast, the *Angel Demo Reel* has little more than Angel recounting his origin. (Strangely enough, it's actually more informative than Doyle's rushed info-dump in "City Of.") The *Demo Reel* also allowed executives and producers to (however briefly) vet Boreanaz, Carpenter and Quinn as the potential *Angel* leads – let's not forget that Willow was played by Riff Regan in the *Buffy* "pilot," but the part went to Alyson Hannigan for the series.

In addition to originating the "quick flash" effect used to cut between scenes, the *Demo Reel* featured some brief shots that were recycled into "City Of" – notably in the opening credits (chiefly Angel driving his car, and the three leads standing in place looking stoic), the teaser (the woman in the blue jacket getting into the car, and the demon girl who's snogging someone) and the ending shots with Angel on the roof. (Debating the *Demo Reel*'s canonicity, by the way, hardly seems worth the bother because it entails Angel chatting directly with the viewer. Besides, there's barely any story to worry about.)

Oh, and Angel in the *Demo Reel* claims he was vamped "244 years ago" [meaning 1755] at age 27. "The Prodigal" (1.15) later tosses this dating, definitively claiming that Angel became a vampire in 1753, age 26.

• The original script for "City Of" – as everyone seems to now know – underwent a decent amount of revision as the producers figured out how *Angel* was going to work. In particular, the original script featured Whistler (from *Buffy* 2.21 and 2.22, "Becoming") in Doyle's place. (In the producers' defense, Whistler worked fine in "Becoming," but it's hard to see the part as played by Max Perlich – unless the idea was to re-cast the character – holding the charisma required for one of the *Angel* leads. Certainly, it's harder to view Whistler as a potential love interest for Cordy, when compared to Glenn Quinn.) Creating a new character also helped to clean up the script, removing the need to explain – or awkwardly ignore – Angel and Whistler's back history.

Notable details from the original script, but removed from the filmed episode: Angel opens the story playing darts in the bar, not just drunkenly going on about women... Whistler claims he's from Philadelphia, wants a beef dip (as opposed to Doyle fetching a "Billy-D") and says one of his visions got crossed with the Internet, resulting in him seeing a nudie picture... Cordelia's agent tells her the glove commercial went away because "they didn't believe your hands really wanted the gloves"... Tina claims that Russell "likes to... beat girls up" (making her look even more the fool for cavorting with him)... Angel phones 911 after discovering Tina's bloodied corpse... Margo re-assures Cordelia that she won't have to sleep with Russell, claiming, "I don't think he enjoys sex at all"... the penniless Cordelia doesn't respond much when Russell's assistant (William) offers her cheese and crackers, prompting him to mention that the cook has also made a roast, potatoes, asparagus and bread pudding.

Notable details missing from the original draft, but included in the broadcast version: Angel's opening narration, Doyle's far more direct explanation of Angel's time on *Buffy* (the studio execs specifically requested the heavy use of flashbacks) and Angel mistakenly leaping into the wrong convertible.

Other amendments: The coffeehouse scene was scripted a lot tighter and more convincingly the second time around; the term "Powers-That-Be" was used more generically at first; Tina's friend went from being "Shanise" to "Denise"; Lindsey was only in the boardroom scene, with Russell's assistant William (deleted entirely) taking his other lines; and Angel's explosives trigger a blackout *before* Cordy flees from Russell (thus making more sense than what's on screen).

• Whedon and Greenwalt considered it a seminal moment when Angel failed to save Tina, establishing that nearly anything could happen on this show. Concerned about the series' tone, however, they filmed but later struck out a bit where Angel leans over Tina's corpse and yields to his bloodlust. To read the script, it sounds rather gruesome: "[Angel] stares and stares... until he can't stand it anymore and suddenly thrusts one of his hands in his mouth, lapping up the blood ravenously, instinctively – until he utters some deep, inhuman sound and rips his hand out of his mouth." Producer Tim Minear approved of the deletion: "I don't think you needed him licking her dead body." (*Fandom.com*, Aug. 14, 2000)

• As the visionary/creator behind *Buffy*, *Angel* and *Firefly*, Joss Whedon probably needs no introduction to anyone who's reading this. Greenwalt wrote some of the definitive *Buffy* scripts, including "Angel" (*Buffy* 1.07) the first stab at the character's origins; "School Hard" (2.03), Spike and Dru's debut; and "Faith, Hope and Trick" (3.03), Faith's debut. Greenwalt's other scripts are more of a mixed bag, running the gamut of "Teacher's Pet" (1.04), the one with the giant preying mantis; "Reptile Boy" (2.05), the one with the frat house and the giant snake; "Ted" (2.11), the one with the evil John Ritter; the surprisingly standard "Nightmares" (1.10) and "Homecoming" (3.05), the one where Buffy does in a vamp with a spatula. Greenwalt also directed – among others – "The Wish" (3.09), made infamous for vamp Willow and her padded bra.

• No study of *Angel* can get very far without mentioning stuntman Mike Massa, who served as Boreanaz's stunt double on *Buffy* (that's him performing Angelus' swordplay in the Season Two finale), and who'll undertake a great deal of Angel's stunts. Jeff Pruitt – later dismissed as a stunt coordinator on *Buffy*, but who presumably would've known about such things at the time – posted in 1999 that Massa knocked himself out for a bit while using an AIR RAM (a device used to fling stuntmen onto car windshields and the like) during production on an early *Angel* story. According to Pruitt's account, Massa subsequently went to New York to work on another film, but this coincided with Boreanaz coincidentally injuring his hand and dinging his car in a fender-bender. The conjunction of events generated rumors that Massa had injured Boreanaz during a botched rehearsal, and that Massa had fled to stay with relatives in New York (odd, as his family lived in Florida) until the show's lead cooled his jets. Boreanaz and Massa returned to the set shortly afterward, and were a bit surprised to hear they'd apparently been feuding. (Jeff Pruitt, *The Bronze*, Oct. 9, 1999) Massa's impressive credits by now range from *The Matrix Reloaded* (doubling for Agent Smith), *Miss Congeniality*, *Spider-Man 2*, *The Punisher* and *Superman Returns*, where he's the lead stunt double.

• Tracy Middendorf (Tina) had recurring roles on *Beverly Hills 90210*, *Days of Our Lives*, *24* and *Alias*, although *Star Trek: Deep Space Nine* fans might recognize her as one of three actresses to play Tora Ziyal, Gul Dukat's daughter (Middendorf's the one in the *DS9* Season Four finale). Josh Holloway, here blandly credited as "Good-Looking Guy," stars as James "Sawyer" Ford on *Lost*.

• The party scene where the agent Oscar the agent approaches Angel and sizes up Our Hero as an actor is probably designed to echo Boreanaz's real-life "discovery." He was out walking his dog when his future manager spotted him – they started chatting, and next thing Boreanaz knew, he'd been launched into the acting profession. Still, he did surprisingly little work before netting the role of Angel on *Buffy*, although he entertainingly played "vampire's victim" in *Macabre Pair of Shorts* (1996).

• Four and a half years after "City Of" broadcast, Vyto Ruginis (Russell) appeared in the *Law and Order* story "Nowhere Man" as a decidedly evil attorney who squares off against Assistant DA Serena Southerlyn, played by Elisabeth Röhm (Kate Lockley). It's a safe bet that only *Angel* fans spotted the irony in this.

Previously on 'Buffy the Vampire Slayer'

Unlike most essays in this volume, which strive for comprehensive thought, this one is deliberately by-the-numbers. It's simply an intro course for anyone who watches *Angel* but not *Buffy*, or who watches *Buffy* but needs a refresher anyway. At the very least, this should help to alleviate the confusion caused by criss-crossed syndication schedules, which have baffled many a newcomer as to why Angel is heroic on his own show, yet sometimes runs around like a brutal serial killer over on *Buffy*.

To state the obvious, this sidebar is limited to events on *Buffy* that impact the *Angel* lead characters.

• **"Welcome to the Hellmouth / The Harvest" (*Buffy* 1.01, 1.02):** Sophomore Buffy Summers, having been mystically "called" / "empowered" as the newest in a long line of Vampire Slayers, arrives to attend high school in Sunnydale, California. Buffy becomes friends with classmates Xander and Willow and a mysterious stranger named Angel, and finds a nemesis (later turned ally) in the "rich bitch" Cordelia Chase. Rupert Giles – the school librarian, but secretly a member of the Watchers, a group devoted to training the Slayers – mentors Buffy.

Buffy and her allies first come into conflict with the Master, a formidable vampire who's trapped in "The Hellmouth," a center for mystical energy that's located in Sunnydale. They also encounter one of the Master's chief lieutenants, a skirt-wearing vampire named Darla.

• **"Angel" (*Buffy* 1.07):** Buffy has become enamored of

Angel, but learns he became a vampire about 240 years ago in Ireland. With Darla, he terrorized humanity as the vampire Angelus ("the one with the angelic face"), but eventually killed a young gypsy girl in Romania, 1898. The girl's family cursed him with a soul, whereupon "Angel" (as he became known) felt massive guilt, traveled to America and spent most of the twentieth century in solitude until meeting Buffy. Darla targets Angel and Buffy on the Master's behalf, but Angel kills her with a stake to the heart.

• **"Prophecy Girl" (*Buffy* 1.12) and "School Hard" (*Buffy* 2.03):** Buffy slays the Master. The vampires Spike and Dru, who ran with Angelus and Darla back in the day, take command of the Master's minions. They also learn that Angel now possesses a soul and cannot be trusted.

• **"Surprise / Innocence" (*Buffy* 2.13, 2.14) and "Passion" (*Buffy* 2.17):** Angel and Buffy consummate their relationship, but the gypsy curse – specifically tailored that Angel might know suffering – breaks when the liaison grants him with "perfect happiness." Angel consequently loses his soul and re-becomes Angelus, then allies himself with Spike and Dru and terrorizes Buffy. Angelus later murders Jenny Calendar, Giles' lover.

• **"Becoming (Parts One and Two)" (*Buffy* 2.21, 2.22):** In flashback, Darla sires Angel as a vampire in a back alley in 1753. In the modern day, Angelus instigates a ritual that will awaken the demon Acathla and bring about Earth's destruction. Willow magically restores Angel's soul, mere moments before Buffy consigns her lover to Hell to prevent Acathla's revival. Spike and Dru leave town.

• **"Faith, Hope and Trick" (*Buffy* 3.03):** Angel mysteriously returns from Hell. In episodes to come, he takes up residence in a Sunnydale mansion and maintains an uneasy friendship with Buffy. Events in "Prophecy Girl" and "Becoming" culminate in the creation of a second Vampire Slayer, a thrill-seeker named Faith.

• **"Amends" (*Buffy* 3.10):** An entity known as "the First Evil" takes credit for bringing Angel back from Hell, and tries to make him lose his soul yet again. Buffy thwarts the First, but Angel becomes suicidal and tries to fry himself in the morning sun. He's saved when a "Christmas miracle" presents itself in the form of a sun-blotting snowstorm.

• **"Helpless" and "Bad Girls" (*Buffy* 3.12, 3.14):** The Watchers' Council dismisses Giles as Buffy and Faith's Watcher, replacing him with the hapless Wesley Wyndham-Price. Wes and Cordelia become smitten in the episodes to follow, but the relationship fizzles.

• **"Graduation Day (Parts One and Two)" (*Buffy* 3.21, 3.22):** Angel realizes his relationship with Buffy cannot progress and leaves town. Cordelia's friend Harmony gets sired as a vampire and Cordelia herself, broke due to her parents' crime of tax evasion, opts to move to Los Angeles. Wesley ends his tenure as Buffy's Watcher.

1.02: "Lonely Hearts"

"I'm just trying to make a connection. The more I come to places like this, the harder it gets."

Air Date: Oct. 12, 1999; **Writer:** David Fury; **Director:** James A. Contner

SUMMARY The Powers direct Angel to investigate D'Oblique, a nightclub connected to a recent series of murders. While looking into the matter, Angel chats up a blonde club-goer named Kate, who's actually an undercover police officer researching the killings. Angel pins the crimes down to Talamour, a burrowing, worm-like demon that takes human hosts – jumping from person to person through sexual contact as its bodies start to burn out. Angel nearly corners Talamour after the demon body-swaps, but the creature escapes, leading Kate to suspect Angel as the murderer.

Cordelia and Doyle hit the books, identifying fire as Talamour's chief vulnerability. Talamour tries to host itself in Kate, but Angel intervenes and tosses Talamour onto a homeless person's trashcan fire. Talamour writhes in agony, dying as Kate shoots it for good measure. Afterward, Kate forges an uneasy truce with Angel.

FIRSTS AND LASTS Even more *Angel* traditions get set in motion here. Angel broods in the dark for the first time and Doyle gets his first on-screen vision, forcing Glenn Quinn to act out an epileptic seizure in the finest Shakespearean tradition. The fictional *Los Angeles Globe-Register*, a steady source of information on mysterious deaths and the like, makes its debut. "Lonely Hearts" also unveils the Angel Investigations business cards, complete with the company's blobby logo (actually an angel, but respectively mistaken by Angel, Doyle and Kate as a butterfly, an owl and a lobster).

Naturally, this story introduces Detective Kate Lockley, and weirdly it's the first but not the last time she'll catch Angel standing near a corpse in an incriminating fashion (see 1.15, "The Prodigal"). Cordelia invites Angel and Doyle into her apartment for the first time, although they've only got three episodes to revel in its squalor before she gets better, albeit haunted, accommodations. It's also the first script by stalwart *Angel* writer David Fury, who'll contribute to every season and also write the second-to-last episode (5.21, "Power Play"), making this story something of a bookend for him.

For the first time, Angel's manhood comes under attack (see **Points of Discussion**...), and he seems oblivious to a slutty-looking woman's advances in the nightclub, marking the first time (on *Angel*, at least) that he looks clueless about romance. And more spectacularly, someone (Angel again) dives out a window and lands on a parked car. (For the most impressive example of this, see 4.13, "Salvage," also by Fury. The man can't help himself.)

POINTS OF DISCUSSION ABOUT "Lonely Hearts":

1. Any long-running detective agency series – even an urban fantasy-flavored one such as *Angel* – will inevitably entail a character who serves as the "the police contact." It's curious, though, how much the casting of Elizabeth Röhm as Kate has colored our perceptions since "Lonely Hearts" first broadcast in 1999. As many of you doubtless know, Röhm later played Serena Southerlyn on *Law and Order*, where she set a record as the longest-serving Assistant DA on the show (she lasted three and a half seasons).

Funnily enough, Kate here says one of the least accurate statements in the entire series, although she's admittedly undercover at the time. Her comment to Angel that, "I prefer those cool bars that are hard to get into, but I can't get into them," seems utterly inconceivable considering Kate looks like Röhm, i.e. like a complete and total bombshell. It's all the more laughable, in fact, if you've seen the 1998 *Fantasy Island* episode "We're Not Worthy," in which a plain-Jane woman gets magically transformed into a smoldering temptress and readily gets into any club she damn well pleases. As you might have guessed, Röhm plays the smoldering temptress.

2. Whedon-verse shows love ripping established TV/film conventions to itty-bitty shreds, so with Angel officially dubbed "Our Hero," we're treated to the first assault on his masculinity. As Angel asks the bar patrons if they need his help, we join the scene just as he backpedals and tells this big bruiser, "Seriously, I wasn't hitting on you..." It's far more subtle than the barbs against Angel's manhood to follow, and for some choice examples, see also Angel's abhorrent dancing ability in 1.13, "She"; his Barry Manilow rendition in 2.01, "Judgment"; the prolific eunuch jokes in 2.06, "Guise Will Be Guise"; all the confusion with Angel maybe dating "Wesley" and "Fred" in 3.04, "Carpe Noctem" and much, much more.

CHARACTER NOTES *Angel:* Went to bars in his youth [as seen in *Buffy* 2.21, "Becoming"]. He's durable enough to dive out a multi-story window, land on a parked car and walk away with little difficulty. [Later episodes such as "Reprise" (2.15), "Apocalypse Nowish" (4.07) and "Time Bomb" (5.19) have him surviving drops from the tops of buildings, or close enough.] He appears to recognize, without turning around and after a savage pummeling by Talamour, that Kate has just entered the room [put it down to acute vampire senses].

Angel politely declines to "recommend" Doyle to Cordelia as boyfriend material, given that he hardly knows the man.

• *Cordelia:* In the debut *Buffy* episode, the Slayer singled out a vampire thanks to his appalling fashion sense. This being the second *Angel* story, Cordelia similarly tries to judge people by their appearance – save that Cordy gets it completely wrong, and lets the demonic serial killer walk right out the door.

Cordy is currently bigoted toward demons, wholesale regarding them as "disgusting." [She's surprisingly justified at this point, given that the early *Buffy* seasons characterized nearly all demons – barring the odd exception such as Whistler (*Buffy* 2.21-2.22, "Becoming") and eventually Anya – as abhorrent and worthy of a crossbow bolt to the throat.]

Cordelia passes out business cards with all the subtlety of a hatchet swing, asking one club-goer: "Hey, you look troubled... or is that just your lazy eye?" Her typing skills are utterly woeful. [They'll improve, somewhat, by 1.05, "Rm w/a Vu."] She disavows any notion of romance between her and Doyle, yet looks disappointed when he mentions that he's downloaded pictures of naked women. Her post-high school plan was ideally "home, hotel, hotel, husband."

• *Doyle:* He's encouraging Angel to socialize with him and Cordelia, chiefly so he can consequently spend more time with Cordy. Doyle conceals his demon aspect from Cordelia, suggesting from experience that "women tend to get a bit funny about that" [see 1.07, "The Bachelor Party" for why]. He's used to visiting taverns. When Cordelia's mistaken for a hooker [see **The Lore** for the irony in this], Doyle defends her honor by instigating a bar fight. He fares well, but his human aspect can be bruised. He types far faster than Cordelia, unsurprisingly.

• *Kate Lockley:* Independent-minded enough to prowl around dance clubs undercover, without back-up, offering herself as bait to catch a gruesome serial killer. She also doesn't have a problem searching Angel's apartment without a warrant. [The common opinion is that Kate starts out as a regular citizen and that Angel's supernatural lifestyle starts to change her worldview. That's not without justification, but consider Kate's actions *before* she gets sucked into Angel's world and you'll find that she didn't exactly start out as a wallflower.]

• *Talamour:* Wormlike demon that seems to nestle in human chest cavities. Angel theorizes that Talamour needs some kind of sex act to facilitate a body-swap, probably owing to an exchange of fluids. [Sex might allow Talamour to phermonally "prep" its target body. Yet it's probably more helpful rather than essential, given that Talamour tries to jump into Kate's body without having sex with her. This presumes – sorry to mention the possibility – that "he" didn't force "himself" upon her during the commercial break, but there's no real evidence of that.]

Cordelia's research implies that Talamour is a singular individual, not part of a larger species. She says Talamour has been around since "the dawn of time." [Cordelia's probably simplifying, and maybe we shouldn't look any harder than that. But it's possible that Talamour dates from the period of the Old Ones, the original demons (first mentioned in *Buffy* 1.02, "The Harvest"). 5.17, "Underneath," after all, claims that Nightmares once walked the land during the same period, and are now shadows of their former selves. So it's not impossible that Talamour hails from the same era, and its power has greatly diminished over the millennia.]

Talamour mimics human behavior exceptionally well, recognizing pop culture references such as Ken and Barbie. It's uncertain if it can tap the memories of its hosts. [Bartender-Talamour knows Kate's usual drink, but the demon could've previously observed this in another body.]

Talamour's former host decays rapidly after a body-swap. The new host rapidly gains super-strength, endurance and the prerequisite martial arts skills needed to fight Angel. Talamour claims it's looking for a permanent host, one that resists burn-out. [It's apparently looking for an individual with a compatible set of genetics that would prevent decay, although it's questionable if such a person even exists, as Talamour's presumably been around for a long time and never found one. The worm-component must require hosting in a biological entity, as it never considers bonding with a vampire's immortal form. Curiously, that puts it among the few body-swapping demons that *don't* invariably try to take over Angel's form: see *Buffy* 2.08, "The Dark Age."]

THE LIBRARY Angel's texts contain information on eviscerating demons, including the varieties that prey on young singles. A book illustrates a demon that wears a wreath of intestines around its head, and quite festively too.

ORGANIZATIONS *Angel Investigations:* The business cards list the office phone number as 555-0162. [Angel's thumb obscures the area code, but it appears to end in a "3." Fury's original script for this story, "Corrupt," listed the phone number as (213) 555-3462, but that's apocryphal. Let's also mention that while Cordelia's hardly the brightest bulb on the tree, the business cards don't mention the agency's address or even its name. As with Lindsey's card last episode, you have to wonder how this helps anyone.] Cordelia has a work computer, and the office also sports a new Angel Investigations sign [it's engraved, not painted as Cordelia suggested last episode].

- *The Powers-That-Be:* Their latest vision mainly provides a sense of location – the D'Oblique nightclub, which he recognizes. [Focusing on the locale makes some sense, as the Powers want Angel to track a creature that switches bodies on a daily basis. Or perhaps the Powers genuinely don't know the demon's current form.] It's already obvious that the Powers' visions are – as Cordelia puts it – "nice and vague." Yet they also [as future episodes confirm] entail an almost precognitive element, as Doyle's left with the feeling that something's going to happen. [That's accurate enough, even if predicting that Talamour will continue killing people isn't *so* hard.]

BEST LINE Angel, describing the Talamour demon: "It's a burrower." Cordelia, mired in research: "It's a donkey? We didn't see any donkey demons."

THINGS THAT DON'T MAKE SENSE Let's start with the big one. The climactic battle leaves the body of Talamour's final host – the D'Oblique bartender – eviscerated, severely torched and shot multiple times by Kate. Even allowing that Angel and Kate probably dispose of the Talamour worm itself, how on Earth does Kate even begin to explain the state of the bartender's corpse to her superiors? Claiming she shot him in self-defense is out, given that the man's chest was torn apart and he was *engulfed by flames*. It's also enormously unfair, although not an actual goof, that the bartender apparently gets the blame for Talamour's killing spree. Heaven knows what the poor man's family must make of all this.

The fire that does in Talamour seems extremely odd, too. It's a trashcan fire used by homeless people to stay warm – note how the vagrants wear caps and what looks like warm clothing – yet everyone seen outside the club has on short sleeves, casual shirts or revealing dresses. And this takes place in L.A., for pity's sake! It's surely not *that* cold right now.

Given the wealth of pick-up joints in L.A., why does the demon keep taking its victims from the same nightclub time and again, thus increasing the risk of discovery, or at the very least making the patrons unduly cautious about picking up strangers there? Indeed, even before Talamour knows it's being followed and its need for disguise increases, it appears to be body-swapping at a rate of once every 24 hours. Granted, we're talking about L.A., but it seems rather ludicrous that nobody – aside from Kate, perhaps – haven't noticed such a trail of bodies near the same locale. (The *Angel* and *Buffy*-verse talent for denial: always at your service.)

A problem that's hopefully self-evident: Kate uses her real first name while performing dangerous undercover work. (The aborted "Corrupt," at least, had Kate using an alias; see **The Lore**.) Worse, her independent streak compels her to rather idiotically meet the person who's newly atop her list of murder suspects – Angel – without any back-up whatsoever. Plus, while searching Angel's apartment, Kate peers into his refrigerator and entirely fails to spot the jars of pig's blood that're normally sitting there. (Perhaps Angel needs to visit his butcher, and hasn't restocked in all the Talamour brouhaha? That's certainly more plausible than Kate swallowing Angel's fib that he's a veterinarian.)

The morning after Talamour's bodyswap, his female host is wearing a fresh new set of clothes... even though she's just spent the night in the apartment of Talamour's previous host, who was male. It's almost feasible that Talamour keeps clothes for both genders onhand, but can it really guess the dress size of its new host in advance? And it's left unexplained why bartender-Talamour wants to host itself into Kate at all, given she can't identify him once he's bodyswapped and doesn't pose much of a threat. (Perhaps Talamour wants to get the drop on Angel using Kate's body, but the story never says this.)

POP CULTURE Cordelia refers to the doomed club-goer Sharon as "Sarah, Plain and Tall," perhaps referring to the children's book by Patricia MacLachlan, and the 1991 TV movie (starring Glenn Close as Sarah) it spawned. The story entails a widower in Kansas publicly advertising for a wife – an odd comparison, as Cordy deems Sharon as the sort of girl who's already got money and beds "Calvin Klein models."

IN RETROSPECT Doyle calls the visions his "gift," and Cordelia says: "If that was my gift, I'd return it." If only she knew.

IT'S REALLY ABOUT... The shallowness of the Los Angeles club scene, the loneliness of its patrons and the painfully poor odds of making a connection with "that special someone" in such a joint. It's a message that's remarkably encapsulated in Act Three, when a random club-goer hits on Kate. By that point, the audience is sweating to wonder if he's the newest host for the inhuman villain of the story... but then learns that he's really just a pathetic creep in an overpriced business suit, trolling about L.A. looking for cheap sex. All things considered, it's nearly impossible to tell the difference.

By extension, it's also about the dangers of meaningless sex in such an environment, as anyone who indulges in such an act winds up permanently altered with a (phallic-shaped, of course) demon inside them. The point holds a lot of merit, even if it's bizarrely inverted in the eleventh hour when Talamour dies because it *fails* to have meaningless sex.

CRITIQUE Surprisingly, it's far more emulative of *Angel* Season One – at least, as we now recognize it – than the opening story. Once Angel, Cordelia and Doyle have settled into their various roles, then it falls to Episode No. 2 to get about the actual business of the show. Or rather, invent what the hell the business of the show actually entails.

Heaven knows it's not a perfect effort, but let's also credit "Lonely Hearts" for boldly latching onto the notion of rendering life in L.A. as a metaphor and running with it. Considering Fury had to scrap his first script and bang out this version instead, the show is coming together – either by happy accident or design – as one might hope.

All of that said, parts of it feel tremendously awkward. Well, of course. It's paving new ground. But if you're watching this story in isolation, then the opening nightclub scenes drag something fierce, the cocktail of sex and violence might seem a bit shallow, and you can often hear the gears grinding in the twists to follow. A quick glance over the rather abundant Things That Don't Make Sense category should demonstrate how many problems that lurk beneath the surface – a discerning viewer will probably take stock of all this, and a casual viewer might feel ill at ease, even if they can't identify the problem. Fortunately – perhaps miraculously, given how the producers are working with a nearly clean slate – it all adds up to become more than the sum of its parts. Bonus points for starting the demon creature afire, by the way... it's hard to get enough of that sort of thing.

"Lonely Hearts": It's far from perfect, but at least it's trying hard, and it's much more of a trailblazer than we like to admit.

THE LORE By now, it's no secret that the WB higher-ups rejected Fury's first stab at this story – entitled "Corrupt" – as being too bleak and adult in tone. In essence, "Corrupt" entailed the Powers directing Angel to protect a prostitute named "Chrystal," actually an undercover detective named Kate (her last name wasn't given). The heroes soon discover that cultist pimps (sweet mercy, that's not a misprint) who worship a demon named T'Purok have been tricking hookers into wearing a magical pendant. This enables T'Purok – who exists as a sort of demon mold – to manifest in their bodies and commit double-homicides. Kate has somewhat "gone native" and taken to the life of sleeping with men for money, goes completely off her gourd when T'Purok possesses and kills her friend Janie. Angel stops in, saves the day and does in T'Purok's demon-mold body with an axe. The end.

In fairness to the studio execs, if you read "Corrupt"... well, there's quite a few passages that raise one's eyebrows in alarm. As "Chrystal," Kate attempts to seduce Angel in rather blunt terms ("How do you want me? On the bed? The chair?... Don't you like me? Don't you want to taste the fruit?"), and later tries to kill the cult leader in cold blood. Failing on that score and ignoring Angel's counsel in the process, she then proceeds to murderously line up the cultists execution-style, as if she were The Bandit Queen of India. She ends the story, rightly or wrongly, pretty much looking like a homicidal lunatic.

Similarly worrying elements: Cordelia goes undercover as a prostitute named "Cookie" (although she at least gets the amusing line, "So, how's tricks, fellow hookers?"). While possessed by T'Purok, Janie morphs into a beast, tears her victim to shreds and grotesquely rips her own face off – "with one ghastly motion and accompanied by a horrific tearing sound," the script says. Oh, and Angel, as scripted, would've used "Bat-Fu" to fight off six pimps armed with baseball bats.

Other notable, but mercifully less worrying, elements from "Corrupt"... Angel uses a throwing star, for once; the agency's business cards were originally *cut* to look like a blobby angel; and T'Purok is described as a "proxy-inhabitor," a demon who can only experience sensations by possessing individuals who've hit rock bottom. (Meaning they're inherently corrupt, hence the title. When you think about it, it's a rather judgmental way of looking at prostitutes – suggesting that by default, they're among the basest form of humanity, and the ideal vessels for demonic possession – not that Fury probably intended it that way.)

• Obi Ndefo (the doomed Bartender) has a recurring role on *Stargate SG-1* as Rak'nor, a Jaffa advisor to Teal'c. He also logged ten episodes as Bodie on *Dawson's Creek*. Jennifer Tung (Neil's Pick-Up Girl) was crowned "Miss Chinatown USA" at age 17, performed stunts for *Armageddon* (1998) and was an ensign on *Star Trek: Insurrection*. Johnny Messner (Kevin) later starred on the 2005 FOX drama *Killer Instinct* – he played a detective who's, according to the press release, "intense and private," "haunted by personal demons" and investigates bizarre crimes in the sunny climes of California. (Nothing like *Angel* at all, then.) It lasted nine episodes.

1.03: "In the Dark"

"You hid the ring, Angel. You could be walking in the light right now. So I have to wonder: What do you want, if not the ring?"

Air Date: Oct. 19, 1999; **Writer:** Douglas Petrie; **Director:** Bruce Seth Green

SUMMARY Without preamble, Angel's associate Oz arrives to give Angel "the Gem of Amarra" – a magical ring that renders any vampire wearing it impervious to physical harm and sunlight. Soon after, the vampire Spike comes calling to claim the ring, captures Angel and hires Marcus – an exceptionally vicious vampire torturer – to shish-ka-bob Angel with red-hot pokers. Doyle and Cordelia agree when Spike offers to swap Angel's life for the ring. They also arrange for Oz to storm Spike's hideout and free Angel, but Marcus grabs the ring in the resultant brouhaha. Thwarted, Spike returns to Sunnydale.

Protected from sunlight, Marcus heads for a nearby pier to indulge in his vampire fetish and stalk children. Oz nails Marcus with his van, enabling Angel to briefly leap through the sunlight and body-tackle Marcus into the pier's shady underbelly. Angel stakes Marcus, then yanks the protective ring off his hand – dusting the villain. Later, Angel worries that the ring would too much make him a creature of the day, thus hampering his ability to aid people in L.A.'s underworld, and smashes the artifact with a brick.

FIRSTS AND LASTS First appearance of Doyle's apartment, which funnily enough – dirty laundry aside – seems more livable than Cordelia's place. We also see the fashionable "sewer tunnels" (or rather, storm drains) that let Angel travel about L.A. in the day hours for the first time (although he presumably used them, off screen, as early as the first episode). Oh, and it's indirectly the first appearance of a werewolf in *Angel*. Not that you'd know it to look at Oz.

Cordelia and Doyle wield crossbows for the first time, and it's the first instance on *Angel* of the title character performing tai-chi exercises (he formerly practiced this in Sunnydale, starting with *Buffy* 3.06, "Band Candy"). Of overriding importance to slobbering James Marsters fans across the globe, it's the first appearance of Spike on *Angel*, and the first direct *Angel/Buffy* cross-over (the next occurs in 1.08, "I Will Remember You"). Indeed, when Angel chases Spike down a darkened alley, we finally learn the identity of the silhouettes who've been frantically running in the opening credits for two episodes now.

POINTS OF DISCUSSION ABOUT "In the Dark":

1. As with "I Will Remember You," it's an early episode that doesn't easily join with some of the show's themes to come. Here, it's down to the Gem of Amarra, an artifact that threatens to ramp up Angel's power levels and render a host of threats meaningless. Not to mention that a show about a vampire who struts about in broad daylight seems considerably at odds with the series' intent of focusing on L.A.'s underworld. So you can see why Angel's made to destroy the ring.

Tragically – and we're debating it at length here rather than choking the hell out of **Things That Don't Make Sense** – this comes at the cost of the episode's logic. A number of perfectly viable reasons exist why Angel might crush the ring, such as, "The ring would make me over-confident in battle," "Every A-level vampire in the world will attack us to get the damn thing..." or "I'm toast if I'm out in the sunlight and an enemy smashes the ring, or hacks off my hand." Producer Tim Minear, interviewed for *Fandom.com* (Aug. 14, 2000), alternatively said: "If [Angel] has the power to be invincible, what would happen if he spent eternity as Angelus? It's too dangerous... the only person that could possibly wear that ring would be Angel, and Angel knows that he can't be trusted."

All good and fine, save that "In the Dark" chooses... none of these options. Instead, it goes for the comparatively limp justification that Angel needs to remain a creature of the night. Good grief... couldn't his mandate to help the helpless *sometimes* entail working during the day? Couldn't he keep it for emergencies? How many people will die if Angel is incapable of going into the daylight? Because as it stands, going by what's said on screen, you're more than entitled to holler, "You dipshit! You should've kept the Gem of Amarra!!" every time sunlight impairs Angel's activities (see especially 3.14, "Couplet" and 3.20, "A New World").

2. On display here is Spike, whose relentless campaign against Angel looks all the more berserk in syndication, especially once the schedule resets after the end of Season Five. If anything, Spike's crusade seems even more vicious than normal, as he here employs the services of a torturer, and personally has a go at Angel (off screen) with a pair of needle-nosed pliers. As anyone familiar with *Buffy* will know, Spike gets most of the best lines here, including his sarcastic reply to Marcus – when the torturer dithers about his choice of music rather than maiming Angel – that "Personally, I prefer Mozart's older, funnier symphonies myself." (See **Best Line** and **In Retrospect...**)

And yes, it's true: the bit in the teaser where Spike observes Angel from afar, and provides a "voice-over" in which Angel "talks" about his "Nancy-boy hairgel" and "prancing away like a magnificent poof" lives up to its reputation and is one of the funniest things in the entire series.

3. Small point of order here: different sources variously spell "Gem of Amarra" with one R or two, so we've favored the style used in the Official Shooting Script. And finally...

4. Cordelia's reaction upon seeing Oz is about as forced, fake and shallow as... most former high school classmates who run into one another.

CHARACTER NOTES *Angel:* Previously got cast into a hell dimension in *Buffy* 2.22, "Becoming," and here tells Doyle, "I was brought back for a reason." [In *Buffy* 3.03, "Faith, Hope and Trick." This is a very curious way of putting things, especially since *Buffy* 3.10, "Amends" implied that an entity named "the First Evil" brought Angel back for purely malevolent reasons – Angel shouldn't necessarily think otherwise, but see **When Did the Powers Intervene?**]

Angel advises Rachel, a young woman that he saves, to avoid poisonous relationships. [So he's taking to heart Doyle's mission statement, from 1.01, "City Of," about saving people's souls as well as their lives.] He also mopes because Buffy didn't send a note with the Gem or deliver it herself. He knows the Gem of Amarra by sight, and using the artifact lets him feel sunlight for the first time in 200 years. [Mind, he'll find this sensation almost commonplace in Season Five.]

Marcus seems impressed that Angel's 200-year-old skin shows so little damage. [Considering all sheer number of fights and injuries Angel has sustained in the last couple centuries, his healing factor must be far above normal.] Under repeated torture, Angel says he most wants "forgiveness" for his past misdeeds. [Marcus speculates that Angel wants to *earn* such atonement, which seems fair enough.]

Angel appears to own a fair number of cooking utensils (and he puts them to good use in 1.10, "Parting Gifts").

• *Cordelia:* She's apparently lost weight by working out at a gym [although it's unclear how she affords the membership, presuming Angel's paying her at all right now]. She's naïve enough to think that invoicing a customer automatically means they'll pay up. [She hasn't fully absorbed the lessons of her parents' tax evasion, then.]

She threatens Spike with a crossbow, but never gets to shoot, so we can't gauge her accuracy. [Still, she seems pretty adept with such weaponry by 2.17, "Disharmony."] Cordelia suggests she might take a cruise to the Bahamas with Doyle... in an alternate reality where he's actor Matthew McConaughey.

• *Doyle:* Claims to know several strip clubs with tasty luncheon buffets. Doyle implies that he's defaulted on payments before, and he appears to owe several acquaintances money. [See 1.05, "Rm w/a Vu." For that matter, it's never stipulated what Doyle does for income. It's possible that Angel puts him on the agency's payroll. But going entirely by what's said on screen, Cordelia is the agency's only official employee until Wesley joins in 1.13, "She."]

Doyle recognizes the Gem of Amarra yet has never heard of Spike, a renowned Slayer-killer. [He's probably studied items of value on the black market, but hasn't researched vampire lore much.] His demon aspect enhances his sense of smell.

Doyle's associates include the human "Frankie Tripod" (who *isn't* three-legged... use your imagination), someone named Kizzy (Doyle owes him a C-note) and Manny the Pig. Doyle's books include *Iberia* and *The Pentax Way*, and he's apparently read *Angela's Ashes* [so he's quite literary, and see 1.07, "The Bachelor Party" for why]. Angel here inquires about Doyle's mother [but we never learn his response].

[A fan theory holds that Doyle palms the Gem of Amarra, and replaces it with a fake just before Angel smashes it. Glenn Quinn admittedly makes a funny little hand motion, but Doyle hardly seems so irresponsible as to sell such a powerful artifact, even presuming he could fool Angel's vampire senses at point-blank range. You could argue that Doyle kept the gem as a reserve purely for Angel's sake – meaning, tragically, that it's unguarded after 1.09, "Hero" –

but you'd also have to explain how "the gem" emits a burst of green energy when Angel smashes it, making it quite the elaborate deception on Doyle's part. Ultimately, no real evidence supports the "Doyle palmed the gem" theory, and it's never seen again.]

• *Spike:* Names Angel as his "sire." [Similar to *Buffy* 2.03, "School Hard"; the term was retconned to mean anyone in a vampire's lineage. *Buffy* 5.07, "Fool for Love," provides definitive evidence that Angel sired the wacked-out Drusilla, who in turn sired Spike. Angel is more properly Spike's "grandsire," as Spike calls him in *Angel* 5.02, "Just Rewards."]

• *Oz:* Has heard rumors about Angel's detective agency [so Buffy's crew isn't completely oblivious to Angel's activities]. Oz knows basic sixth-grade level first aid, and demonstrates the uncanny ability to pop a 180 with his van.

• *Marcus:* Expert torturer of humans, demons and politicians. He allegedly invented several "classic" torture methods. Marcus finds Mozart's *Symphony 41* an excellent accompaniment to his torture sessions. He prefers to psycho-analyze his victims, believing their pain leaves them like "innocent" children until they reveal certain truths about themselves.

ORGANIZATIONS *Angel Investigations:* A grille in Angel's apartment floor leads to tunnels that service L.A.'s sewer system [or storm drain system, as we keep saying], enabling Angel to get about in the daytime.

DEMONOLOGY *Vampires:* Water-filtered sunlight doesn't dust vampires. [1.10, "Parting Gifts" confirms that it takes concentrated sunlight to incinerate a vampire.]

• *The Gem of Amarra:* Protects its wearer against fire, sunlight and staking. [The ring seals over battle wounds rather than making its bearer invulnerable, so it's less clear how it might cope with – say – pulverization or decapitation.]

BEST LINE Marcus, examining Angel before his torture session: "His skin..." Spike: "Annoying, isn't it? Still attached."

THINGS THAT DON'T MAKE SENSE Doyle and Cordelia are relying on Oz to crash to the rescue, so there's utterly no need for them to distract Spike with the real Gem of Amarra – flinging a Crackerjack ring from the same distance would've almost surely bought them as much time, and seems far less risky. Perhaps they're concerned that Spike's vampire senses would've sensed a fake, but they only need to buy a few seconds, after all. Also, it's now entirely obvious that Doyle has a ring on his left hand, yet Cordelia, the resident fashion critic, has apparently never asked about it. (To be fair, it's not on his wedding ring finger, but see 1.07, "The Bachelor Party").

Finally, watch the bit where Oz magnificently drives his van down the pier and slams into Marcus. The shot just before impact shows the pier as being chock-full of people, all of whom Oz should've flattened.

POP CULTURE A cornered Spike to Angel: "Caught me fair and square, White Hat." Some fans mistake this as a reference to Giles' brigade of heroes in *Buffy* 3.09, "The Wish," failing to realize that the term "White Hat" stems from Westerns in which the good guys wore white hats and the villains donned black ones. (Besides, "The Wish" was an alternate reality story, so Spike couldn't know its details anyway.)

• Cordelia, confronting Spike in the office: "When you're through giving the place the full Johnny Depp-over, I hope you have the cash to pay for this." Depp apparently has a reputation for trashing hotel rooms in his free time. In 1994, the police jailed him for damaging a New York suite.

• Doyle has read and enjoyed *Angela's Ashes* (1999), Frank McCourt's memoir about growing up with a drunken, unemployed father in Brooklyn and Ireland. (Cordelia, unsurprisingly, hasn't read it.)

CROSS-OVERS Spike dug up the Gem of Amarra in *Buffy* 4.03, "The Harsh Light of Day" (and notice how that title contrasts with "In the Dark"), but the Slayer bested him and asked Oz to deliver the ring to Angel. Spike here tells Angel about Buffy's affair with a college student named Parker ("the first lunkhead who came along" as Spike puts it) in the same story. [Yet Angel strangely never pursues the point, not even when he encounters Buffy in "I Will Remember You" (1.08). Possibly he learned the releationship ended in the course of *Buffy* 4.08, "Pangs," or maybe he just blew off Spike's comment.] From here, Spike returns to Sunnydale and gets captured by the Initiative in *Buffy* 4.06, "Wild at Heart."

IN RETROSPECT Spike on Buffy: "She is cute when she's hurting, isn't she?" In a single sentence, and to an amazing degree, this prophesies the horribly twisted relationship that he'll share with the Slayer in future. Along those lines, Spike's claim that, "We all have an addiction, Angel. I believe yours is named Slutty the Vampire Slayer..." seems wildly ironic, considering that Buffy will become Spike's addiction in about a year or so.

Spike wonders if Angel, now a vampire detective, will next become a "vampire ballerina." That's not exactly what happens in 3.13, "Waiting in the Wings," but it's in the ballpark.

IT'S REALLY ABOUT... Staging a *Buffy* crossover to help market the new *Angel* series. That's not to imply that "In the Dark" isn't an effective on many levels, simply that the desperate need for Spike and Oz to visit L.A. – and give the ratings a boost – pretty much overrides everything else.

If anything, you can extract more of actual meaning from the B-plot, in which Angel's client Rachel realizes that her problem doesn't lie in her gun-toting boyfriend Lenny... it's with *her* for continually seeking out such a destructive relationship. The next episode fleshes out this notion in detail, but it's worth noting that Rachel here achieves – in one fell swoop – nearly the same level of enlightenment as the romantically confused Buffy and Spike (sorry to keep going on about it) attain in the whole of *Buffy* Season Six.

CRITIQUE It's an utterly shameless marketing stunt, practically rolling over and begging *Buffy* fans to scratch its tummy. Oh, but what the hell... even if it's doing nothing more than mining *Buffy* to give *Angel* a boost, it's a gorgeously lovable story. For dramatic tension, in fact, it ranks among the strongest Season One episodes. We should first and foremost credit the layered script, but the presence of that lovable rogue James Marsters – who could read chocolate soufflé recipes and still sound captivating – helps to put it over the top. Fans generally mention Spike's taunting of Angel as one of the funniest things they've ever seen, but Spike's coming unglued when his plans go awry – as if Angel is the Road Runner to Spike's Wile E. Coyote – is up there as well.

Sure, you can make a case that it's nothing more than formula as established on that *other* show – although few among fandom seem willing to take this as a criticism – but even if that's true, it's very, very *good* formula with a rollicking story and laugh-out-loud results. In fact, if you're trying to sell a *Buffy* fan on *Angel*, consider skipping the first two episodes and going direct to this one.

THE LORE Four days before this story aired, a whimsical Joss Whedon posted the (slightly prophetic) statement: "Good news: The network has given Angel a FIVE YEAR pick up! They are changing New Tuesday to Joss is the MAN day (or possible "da man"... their legal teams are working it out). Also the network will be called Jossyland. All executives will change their names to Joss and certain household items (soap, ziplocks, lard) will be known as Joss as well (I was against the lard). All this in testament to the fact that I am so humble and have not gotten a swelled head at all." (*The Bronze*, Oct. 15 1999)

• Boreanaz's normal stunt double, Mike Massa, was in New York during production of this story, so Chad Stahelski (Keanu Reeves' double, and that's him as "Angel" during the mall fight in *Buffy* 2.14, "Innocence") handled the bit where Angel flings himself out of Oz's van and scorches in the sun. Stahelski wore protective gel and clothes, and the fire was achieved by burning rubber cement, with the water putting out the flames once they dove off the pier. (Pruitt, *The Bronze*, Oct. 24 1999)

• Ric Sarabia ("Vendor") owns a resume that reads like a bizarre rap sheet, with roles including "Sleazy Male in Closet," "Surly Convict," "Head of Benito," "Deranged Man," "Gang Member," "Toy Robot Builder" and "Doomed Jew." On *The Weird Al Show*, he briefly appeared as "Bearded Man."

• Kevin West (Marcus) performed in such erudite fare as *Super Mario Bros.*, *Santa with Muscles* and *Killer Tomatoes Eat France!*, then turned his talents to directing commercials in 2001. He rather amusingly appeared as "Calculus" in the *Hercules* episode "Hercules and the Techno Greeks."

1.04: "I Fall to Pieces"

"What if he comes apart on you?"

Air Date: Oct. 26, 1999; **Story/Script:** David Greenwalt; **Story:** Joss Whedon; **Director:** Vern Gillum

SUMMARY The Powers direct Angel to protect Melissa Burns, an office worker who's being stalked by Dr. Ronald Meltzer, a talented surgeon. Angel eventually realizes that Meltzer has perfected a "psionic surgery" technique that allows him – through sheer willpower – to detach and mentally animate various body parts.

Angel leaves Melissa with Doyle and Cordelia for safekeeping, then infiltrates Meltzer's office. Meltzer paralyzes Angel with a tranquilizer strong enough to kill humans, then besieges Angel's apartment to get at Melissa. Meltzer pauses when Melissa harshly rebukes him, whereupon Angel recovers and overpowers the fiend. For a finale, Angel locks up Meltzer's separated parts in 12 steel boxes, then buries them in concrete.

FIRSTS AND LASTS The series never recognizes him as such, but Meltzer is potentially the first "mutant" on *Angel*. Also, without really meaning to, this story provides an early glimpse of the Hyperion Hotel entrance (see **Points of Discussion** on both counts). For the first time, Cordelia answers the phone with her infamous, "Angel Investigations. We help the hopeless..." slogan. It's also the first occasion that Our Hero saves a non-blonde (as Melissa's a brunette), and the first time Angel receives a paycheck for his good deeds.

POINTS OF DISCUSSION ABOUT "I Fall To Pieces":

1. Location shooting for Melissa's apartment was done at Los Altos Hotel and Apartments, situated at 4121 Wilshire Boulevard. The same building, notably, was later used as the exterior of the Hyperion Hotel. And before you can ask, yes, it was "I Fall to Pieces" that convinced the producers to re-

use the joint as the Hyperion. As a result, it seems eerie when a policeman dashes through Melissa's courtyard – and runs right past the Hyperion fountain that's destined to become a fixture of many nocturnal discussions/fights to the death in Seasons Two to Four. It's also interesting to note that the cop here runs into the building's genuine foyer, as opposed to Paramount Set that housed as the grandiose Hyperion lobby. (See **How Do I Take the Angel/Buffy L.A. Tour?**)

2. On *Buffy*, nearly every villainous meta-being owed to the Hellmouth's supernatural influence, an artifact, magic use or some sort of demonic inheritance. Even psionic abilities – for instance, the Slayer's telepathy in *Buffy* 3.18, "Earshot" – usually stemmed from one of these sources. Yet here we're presented with Meltzer, who gains the ability to separate his body parts simply through intense mental will, nothing else. There's no particular evidence that he possesses demon blood, so he certainly seems more akin to a mutant from *X-Men* than anything else. *Angel* will get a lot more cozy with this notion than *Buffy*, so it seems fair game – for lack of anything claiming otherwise – to declare certain characters as mutants, not demons. Potential mutants include the Wolfram and Hart telepaths (1.21, "Blind Date"); the telekinetic Bethany Chaulk (2.04, "Untouched"); the psychic Aggie (2.20, "Over the Rainbow"); the electrified Gwen in Season Four (4.02, "Ground State," etc.) and possibly Fred (5.20, "The Girl in Question"). We'd rule Vanessa Brewer, the blind assassin from "Blind Date," as demonic (see that story).

3. There's admittedly room for debate here, but... we're told that Angel secures Meltzer's body parts in 12 steel boxes, and buries them beneath 20 cubic feet of concrete in L.A.'s newest subway stop. Now, it's presented as if the heroes have simply incarcerated Meltzer, but it's rather hard to believe that even someone of Meltzer's abilities could remain in a separated state *without food, water or air for the next five years if not more*. Factor in Angel's claim that Meltzer's parts will "deteriorate" for lack of blood or oxygen even after too many minutes – minutes! – apart, and it's almost impossible to imagine the goon surviving. If Meltzer is indeed a mutant rather than demonic, this would rank as the first instance on *Angel* of the title character offing a human being (not that he's without justification, in this case), and we've duly noted it as such in the **Kill-Count** at the end of Season One.

4. Fans continually question whether Meltzer's heart-stopping drug should have worked on Angel at all, given that vampires lack a moving bloodstream. It's not much of an error, however, if you factor in that *some* blood flow must occur even if the vamp's heart isn't beating, through simple movement if nothing else. Or perhaps a vampire's dead body deliberately shifts blood around at points, to "metabolize" the blood's life energy. For that matter, we've got to account for, um, vampire erections somehow. In other words, there's evidence to suggest that a vampire's body will consciously or subconsciously emulate a human one at times, even without benefit of a truly human biology.

CHARACTER NOTES *Angel:* Doyle claims that Angel has now had four cases of protecting young women – "and three of them are still alive." [He's probably counting Melissa herself to round up.] Angel believes that Meltzer's obsession stems from his own inner rage, insecurity and lack of ability to deal with a tangible woman. [Angelus never fits that profile, so Angel is presumably drawing on the experience of witnessing evildoers throughout the decades.]

Angel proves he's savvy enough to send e-mail. He's dramatically improved at approaching the helpless, and dons a non-imposing white shirt for a meeting with Melissa [but he never makes a habit of this]. As with last episode, he encourages her to vent her anger on her nutcase stalker boy.

• *Cordelia:* Acting somewhat warmer toward Doyle, but inadvertently makes him back off by decrying Meltzer's stalking tactics. Ever the fashion mercenary, Cordelia still lusts after designer "things." She's undertaking some detective work, here masquerading as a reporter for the *Journal of Diagnostic Orthopaedic Neuropathy* – her act needs polish, but her bluntness gets some results. (Cordelia to a source: "Did [Meltzer] ever strike you as a big, dangerous creep?")

• *Doyle:* Says/jokes that even *he's* a bit attracted to the way Angel stridently walks off with his coat tails billowing. Doyle hasn't experienced a vision since 1.02, "Lonely Hearts." [Thus thwarting anyone attempting to put a vision-induced adventure in this gap.] Doyle agrees with Cordy that Angel needs to start charging for his services, because letting the clients repay a debt will help them feel more assertive and independent. Doyle drinks Single Malt Scotch and keeps whiskey onhand. He's again fiddling with a deck of cards [1.01, "City Of"]. He apparently plays "Jumble," but has never gone bungee-jumping. He has a "girthful" Aunt Judy.

• *Kate:* [Last seen in "Lonely Hearts."] Now trusts Angel enough to share police information with him. She's jailed a few stalkers in her time. Kate calls Wolfram and Hart, "The law firm that Johnnie Cochran is too ethical to join."

• *Melissa Burns:* Met Meltzer on March 5, 1999; he saved her sight by operating on an infected nerve behind Melissa's right eye. They later shared a single drink, but Meltzer became overly protective of her, claiming they were engaged. [Melissa says Meltzer has been stalking her for about seven months, which roughly matches the story's date of broadcast. Angel conversely tells Kate that Melissa's "been living in terror for five [months]," but Melissa should logically know better.]

• *Ronald Meltzer:* Owns a copy of *Meditation for a Bountiful Life* [amusingly, this is the same self-help book that Cordelia studied in 1.01, "City Of"]. Meltzer specialized in orthopedics before becoming an ocular surgeon, developing nerve and blood vessel accelerants that extended the time that a severed limb could be reattached. He became renowned, but was privately criticized for not sharing his techniques.

He eventually studied the work of Dr. Vinpur Natpudan, who fronted notions about tapping the brain's unused potential. Natpudan introduced Meltzer to "psychic surgeons" – yogis who could shut down their somatic systems for "days on end" – and Meltzer honed their techniques. [Demons such as the Pockla in 2.18, "Dead End" are highly adept at molding flesh, but again, there's no evidence that Metlzer's abilities derive from demon energy or even demon worship.]

Among other things, Meltzer can separate, levitate and "see" through his eyeballs [via a psionic link, one presumes] – possibly for miles. His detached hands can throttle a man to death; one of his severed hands pulls Doyle into a sewer tunnel. [The hand can't have any purchase, so this involves a fair amount of telekinetic strength.] Meltzer can also propel his gums and teeth from his mouth, hard enough to bite someone. His separated body parts rejoin without leaving a scar.

Melissa's rebuke disrupts Meltzer's mental control, causing various parts to limply fall off his body. Meltzer has also designed a high-pressure injector capable of tranquilizing animals from a safe distance to facilitate surgery.

ORGANIZATIONS *Angel Investigations:* Cordelia mentions the rent coming due. [Again, one wonders how Angel affords such spacious accommodations in L.A. without a proper income. It's entertaining to think he sold his Sunnydale mansion to raise funds, but – presuming he ever had legal claim to the joint – he almost never demonstrates the financial ability needed to pull this off. That said, even if Angel did sell the mansion, Sunnydale's chronically depressed property values (as *Buffy* Season Six proves) probably didn't leave him with much, especially if he bought his car over the summer.]

Cordelia's lazy method of making the office coffee: pour new grounds atop the old, then tout it as espresso.

DEMONOLOGY Angel, trying to figure out if Meltzer possesses supernatural abilities, speculates that the man might be invisible, some kind of ghost or an astral projector. [All credible notions. An invisible girl turns up in *Buffy* 1.11, "Out of Mind, Out of Sight," a ghost turns up next episode, and astral projection – of a kind – occurs in 3.11, "Birthday."]

BEST LINE Cordelia: "What *is* stalking nowadays? The third most popular sport among men?" Angel: "Fourth, after luge."

THINGS THAT DON'T MAKE SENSE All right, let's think about this. Meltzer has been secretly keeping tabs on Melissa by detaching his eyeball (and possibly other organs) and using it to "view" her while she's at her office or home. Yet this glosses over a fairly obvious point: how do his organs enter such buildings, not to mention move about without detection? For instance, when the eyeball is out by its lonesome – as appears to be the case in Act One – how could it open a door? Did it then sneak past the office receptionist? Or does it flit in though a convenient open window? In fact, how come none of Melissa's co-workers spot the damn thing? The ultimate weirdness here occurs when Melissa gets ready for bed, has her back turned and fails to spy Meltzer's eyeball simply floating there in mid-air behind her. Seriously, as the story goes to commercial, how can she not turn just a little bit and notice the damn thing hovering there – as if to say, "Hello, I'm an eyeball..." – for all the world to notice?

Kate mentions the hallway outside Melissa's apartment has a security camera, but this same camera spectacularly fails to notice the police officer getting the life throttled out of him by Meltzer's disembodied hands. It's also weird that Meltzer secretly changes Melissa's PIN number – even if he correctly guesses her current one, the bank would hardly make the switch without her authorization.

After Meltzer incapacitates Angel, he immediately dashes off to attack Melissa at Angel Investigations... even though he never learned Angel's true identity and base of operations. (It's possible that Meltzer searched Angel's person and found a business card, but the agency's cards don't mention a name or address – see "Lonely Hearts" (1.02) – they're not terribly helpful.) Finally, Doyle and Angel worry that Meltzer could escape police custody by slipping his parts through the bars of a jail cell. Well, not really... if nothing else, his head and torso would never squeeze through such a gap. He could maybe detach his hands, throttle a guard and steal his keys, but it still seems far-fetched. Mind, it sounds even more absurd when Doyle claims that Meltzer "can't be killed," given that a simple bullet to the heart or brain would surely do him in.

IT'S REALLY ABOUT... The nature of stalkers and how – genuinely violent cases aside – they often possess only as much power as the victims endow them with. Meltzer's more scary than truly dangerous, and he falls in open combat with Angel in (we timed it) precisely 28 seconds.

CRITIQUE It's funny how almost nobody can watch this story without thinking it's an *X-Files* episode, and the degree to which some of the producers freely *admit* that it's an *X-Files* story in disguise... and that's why it's all so pointless. Granted, Meltzer works fairly well as a stalking metaphor, and he's the sort of villain who would've given the all-too-human Mulder and Scully some hassle. (Lest we forget, one of their early foes was Eugene Tooms, a nemesis who stretched his skin to superhuman lengths.) But once Angel finally gets the drop on Meltzer, the villain quite literally lasts less than half a minute. Perhaps we're being a little unfair, as the overall effect here certainly isn't offensive or insulting. But it's trademark "monster of the week" territory, and it's especially hard to determine if the producers planned on Meltzer's high-velocity teeth being genuinely scary or the height of silliness. Whatever their intentions, it's the latter.

THE LORE Over on *Buffy*, Andy Umberger (Meltzer) played D'Hoffryn, Anya's demon mentor. He also appeared alongside Amy Acker in the 2003 TV movie *Return to the Batcave: The Misadventures of Adam and Burt* (2003), and got a bit part in the *Firefly* pilot (as "Dortmunder Captain"). He's also a guest attorney on *Boston Legal*, where he defended a school district from the charge that Halloween was an affront to Christians and pagans alike. As we've compared "I Fall to Pieces" to *The X-Files*, it's apt that Meltzer appears in its Season Seven finale ("Requiem") as Agent Chesty Short, an FBI auditor who rummages through Mulder and Scully's books. In response, Mulder whimsically suggests that he and Scully could save expenses by sharing hotel rooms.

• Christopher Hart (Metzger's Severed Hand) portrayed Thing in *The Addams Family* films. (Well, of course.)

1.05: "Rm w/a Vu"

"It's like I'm still getting punished, for everything
I said in High School just because I could get away with it.
Oh, but this apartment... I could be me again!
I couldn't be that awful if I got to have a place like that."

Air Date: Nov. 2, 1999; **Story/Script:** Jane Espenson; **Story:** David Greenwalt; **Director:** Scott McGinnis

SUMMARY When cockroaches overrun Cordelia's already squalid apartment, a high-maintenance Cordy freeloads with Angel. Doyle finds Cordy a striking, affordable place in the Pearson Arms apartment complex, but a formidable poltergeist manifests there.

Angel and Doyle learn that in the 1950s, the building's owner, Maude Pearson, suffered a heart attack there shortly after her son Dennis disappeared. Maude's spirit subsequently influenced some of the apartment's residents to kill themselves. Maude nearly kills Cordelia, but Cordy bitches out the departed harpy – an act of defiance that causes a *second* spirit to momentarily possess Cordy. So empowered, Cordelia takes a lamp and smashes down a section of wall, exposing a skeleton – the second spirit's body – trapped inside.

The heroes realize that in life, the possessive Maude, scornful due to Dennis' love for his fiancée, bricked him up inside the apartment wall, then died from a heart attack immediately afterward. Dennis' outraged spirit dispatches his mother's spook from the mortal plane, then sticks around as Cordelia's intangible roommate.

FIRSTS AND LASTS Most obviously, this story debuts Cordelia's new apartment (she's going to live there for nearly three seasons) and her ghostly roommate Dennis, a.k.a. "Phantom Dennis." (Writer Jane Espenson picked the name as a take-off on a movie that was very popular in 1999: *The Phantom Menace*.) Fangirls will wish to note that it's the first time on *Angel* that we see David Boreanaz is shirtless... and wrapped in a towel... and dripping wet... when Cordelia's knock at the door makes Angel dash out of the shower. We consequently get our first viewing of Angel's back tattoo (first mentioned in *Buffy* 1.07, "Angel"), and shortly afterward, we get a clear glimpse of what's been hanging from Angel's necklace since 1.01, "City Of." It's... a dangly key thing.

For what it's worth, we spot Angel reading at his office desk (a habit he'll repeat throughout Season One whenever he's worn out from all the brooding) for the first time. And we get our first exposure to Cordy's "acting" talents. When Cordelia stays with Angel under perfectly innocent circumstances, she's bizarrely the first of *two* women to get peanut butter in his bed (see 1.08, "I Will Remember You").

POINTS OF DISCUSSION ABOUT "Rm W/a Vu":

1. Here's an interesting point of design: Cordelia's apartment contains a random smattering of books – presumably just for show – and most of the titles aren't visible. However, if you pause your DVD in just the right spot, one title that clearly springs to light – it's a solid black spine with large white letters – is *White Ninja* by Eric Van Lustbader. The book (a *New York Times* bestseller, no less) features crime, political intrigue and Japanese tanjian sorcery – which hardly sounds a perfect match for Cordelia's tastes. The really funny bit, however, comes when this novel mysteriously reappears in another location – check out 2.16, "Redefinition." Oh, you must.

2. An issue with sci-fi guides such as the one you're reading is that you have to judge how much to factor evidence that wasn't particularly meant to stand scrutiny. It's said that Maude and Dennis died in 1946, but a more specific date is possible if you include documents that're only legible through the magic of pausing your DVD player. The (fictional) *Los Angeles Globe-Register* ran a report of Maude's death on April 22, 1946, and since it's claimed said that her body wasn't found for three weeks, she must have died (after bricking up Dennis) sometime around April 1. That makes

the Missing Persons report on Dennis – the one that Kate procures – the odd man out, as it's dated August 14 of the same year. It seems entirely baffling that the cops would wait four months before drafting this report, especially as at least one police detective suspected Dennis of murder – but then, Heaven only knows what police procedures were like in 1946. At the very least, unlike (say) the faux article on rhino horns in 1.01, "City Of," let's credit the show designers with mocking-up dates that're roughly in the same ballpark.

3. For Doyle's benefit, Cordelia re-creates her failed audition for a trash bag commercial. As expected, she makes Pamela Anderson look like a veritable *tour de force* of acting. A nod of admiration should go to Charisma Carpenter at this point, because it's harder than you'd think to act so awfully on purpose. Also, whereas fans seem to best remember Cordelia's line of "I'm not a sniveling, whiny little cryBuffy," a special mention is warranted – while Cordy's bitching about losing the trash bag piece – to her declaration that "I was all about things leaking. How could they not pick me?"

CHARACTER NOTES *Angel:* Speaks Latin fluently, and is here found listening to Beethoven's "Symphony No. 9 in D Minor, op. 125." His apartment [logically] is bereft of mirrors. He's familiar [perhaps too familiar, given Angelus' history] with serial killers who make their prey look like suicide victims. Angel already recognizes that Cordy can't type or file, and rapidly loses faith that she can answer the phone. When Cordy helplessly blubbers during the exorcism ritual, Angel deems her: "The biggest pain I've ever seen." [He'll change that opinion in future, of course.] Angel's apartment-warming gift to Cordelia: A small cactus.

• *Cordelia:* Her resolve here runs the whole gamut – she refuses to leave her apartment under pain of poltergeists, but later devolves into a crying lump of flesh. Maude's calling Cordelia "a stupid little bitch" reminds Cordy that she *is* quite the bitch, invigorating her.

Aura, a former member of the "Cordettes," here calls Cordy to catch up. [And for more on her, see **The Lore** in 2.20, "Over the Rainbow."] Cordy initially ignores Aura's call for fear of lying about her status in life, but later phones her back to jabber about a fellow classmate who's "nasty." And clothes.

The "D" section of Cordelia's address book includes "Danielle," "David," "Doyle" and – notably – "Tom D." [What the hell kind of organizing system is *that*?] Her typing speed, at least, has improved since her plink-one-key-at-a-time method [1.02, "Lonely Hearts"]. Books on Cordelia's apartment shelf (aside from *White Ninja*, that is) include – if you squint – what looks like *Amending America* by Richard B. Bernstein, a text on the Constitution. [That clinches it – her books are there for show.] She owns some high school trophies, including one for being Queen of the Winter Ball and at least one for cheerleading. Her high school diploma is charred [due to *Buffy* 3.22, "Graduation Day"] but signed by the late Principal Snyder. She lives down the hall from [the real-life] Steve Paymer, brother of notable character actor David Paymer. [Steve shows up at Cordy's party in 1.13, "She."] Cordy drinks diet root beer, and the shithole of an apartment she vacates was No. 4B. She moves into #212 Pearson Arms.

• *Doyle:* A demon debt collector, Griff, spends much of this story trying to maul/kill Doyle for non-payment. [The name of Griff's employer is never revealed. Angel kills Griff, which should only augment the problem, yet the debt is never mentioned again.] Doyle bravely suggests that Cordelia "spend a night" with him away from her tatty apartment, and despite some initial resistance, Cordy does, in truth, try to phone Doyle before the cockroaches compel her to freeload with Angel. Amid his self-imposed irresponsible lifestyle, Doyle cites Cordelia as a bright spot in his life.

The scrawl in Cordelia's address book seems to give Doyle's phone number as (213) 555-0189. He struggles with Latin, and famously mangles Cordelia's standard phone greeting as: "Angel Investigations. We hope you're helpless."

• *Kate:* Gets fidgety when she's seated at a computer screen and Angel leans close. [She's feeling some attraction for him – the script calls for her to notice his proximity, so we're not inventing it – and see next episode.]

• *Maude Pearson:* Her spook typically scares the female residents of Cordelia's apartment into killing themselves; failing that, she sometimes does them in herself. [Maude probably haunts all the residents regardless of gender, but seems to particularly target women – clearly viewing them as the sort of strumpet who nearly took her son from her.]

Maude can throw scissors with enough force to kill, animate electrical cords to hang people, create a telekinetic whirlwind, make a glass of water boil and write the word "Die" on Cordelia's apartment wall in what looks like blood. She can short out the apartment's wiring, imitate Angel's voice and make phone calls [although it's unclear how she knows the office phone number]. She's killed at least three apartment residents over the years, respectively in 1959, 1965 and 1994.

• *Dennis Pearson (a.k.a. "Phantom Dennis"):* While he was dead and bound, his tortured face sometimes appeared in an apartment wall and a bureau. [Dennis' shade never ventures outside the apartment even when he's freed, so he's presumably bound to the place. He here possesses Cordy for a few moments, but never displays this ability again – a pity, considering all the menaces who'll traipse through the apartment in the next three years. The possession arguably grants Cordy enhanced strength, as she's able to bash in a brick wall with a commonplace lamp.] Once Cordelia exposes Dennis' body, his spirit appears as a mass of swirling white tendrils with a skull face of sorts. After dispatching his mother, Dennis' now-invisible shade can move small objects around. [But his telekinesis never becomes very formidable: note 2.03, "First Impressions," where he fails to catch a falling Cordelia.] We never learn what Team Angel does with Dennis' rotted corpse.

ORGANIZATIONS *Angel Investigations:* Angel's office includes a fireplace. [Funny how many L.A. buildings come equipped with one, considering the climate.]

DEMONOLOGY The demon Griff refers to Doyle as a "little half-breed," proving that bigotry is alive and well in the demon world (see 1.09, "Hero").

• *Vampires:* Cordelia tells Angel that he's "completely invited over" even before she knows where she's living, and this counts as an invitation. [That's acceptable; see **How Does the Invitation Rule Work?**] Nor is it necessary to grant an invitation while standing in the actual abode; giving permission at a remote location suffices (further proven in 1.17, "Eternity" and 2.17, "Disharmony"). Angel claims that vampires "don't eat." [Actually, they can eat normal food, but little – if any – nourishment from it, still requiring blood to "live."]

• *Poltergeists:* Angel states that ghosts [and by extension poltergeists] typically stem from violent deaths, not something as mundane as a heart attack. [The definitive *Angel*-verse poltergeist story, *Buffy* 2.19, "I Only Have Eyes For You," seems to confirm this. However, it's notable that Maude's death doesn't entail any violence as such; her bile keeps her going after death. It's less certain why Dennis' spook remains on the mortal plane once he's dealt with Maude, as the *Buffy* story suggests that ghosts normally depart for the afterlife after gaining catharsis.] Poltergeists apparently show up in mirrors, even if Cordelia doesn't spot Maude in hers.

MAGIC Doyle knows a guy in Koreatown who performs cleansing spells. [Another excursion there occurs in 1.10, "Parting Gifts," suggesting that part of L.A. is prone to demons and mysticism; L.A.'s Chinatown is likely much the same, going by 3.02, "That Vision Thing."] The cleansing spell that Angel and Doyle attempt entails hawthorn berries, lungwort, bile and [judging by what's in Doyle's box] toad feet. Doyle places these ingredients, some rocks, some herbs and an undefined furry thing in a "binding circle." They then proceed with a chant, whereupon someone "with a connection to the ghost" [Cordelia qualifies, as a target of Maude's aggression] needs to strike the center of the circle. Sadly, as Cordelia wimps out on the last part, we never discover if the damn spell works or not.

BEST LINE Angel, describing Cordelia's high school followers, "the Cordettes": "It was like the Soviet Secret Police, if they cared about shoes."

THINGS THAT DON'T MAKE SENSE In true Sunnydale fashion, Doyle gets onto the Internet and miraculously finds the construction bids and city inspections for the Pearson Arms. Because of course, those sorts of things are all over the web. It's also amusing that Doyle says his work "isn't easy," then takes less than two minutes to find a 50-year-old newspaper article relating to Maude's death.

The 1950s police believed that Dennis had skipped town with his fiancée, inferring that he killed his mother beforehand. But after we learn the true fates of Dennis and his mother, it begs the question: What happened to the fiancée? Did Maude kill her too? Perhaps Maude simply scared the fiancée off, although she did a damn good job of it, if the fiancée left town – without knowing what happened to Dennis – and was never seen again.

When Angel tricks Doyle into thinking that a bill collector is upstairs, Doyle abruptly ends his conversation with Cordelia and immediately races out the back door. Yet Cordelia never asks why, from her point of view, Doyle just up and ran out the door like a lunatic. (Well, she already thinks he's weird.)

How did Griff and his men track Angel and Doyle to Cordelia's place? If they trailed one of them there, they sure wait a hell of a long time, for no good reason, before bothering to enter. (Perhaps Griff is visiting Doyle's business associates at random, and blunders in at precisely the wrong moment, but that's not the impression you get on screen.)

The final scene, which entails Cordelia phoning Aura, appears to take place shortly after the whole business with Maude. Which means that Cordelia has the bashed-in wall containing Dennis' skeleton completely torn out and replaced with new support pillars in record time.

IT'S REALLY ABOUT... To some degree, it's about oppressive mothers, given that Maude's all-too-apparent tyranny toward her son leads her to literally brick him up – the ultimate form of silencing his protests. (Note also the parallel to *Buffy* 4.22, "Reckless," where a brick wall more benignly, but just as symbolically, separates Buffy from her mother.) But given that Dennis's wrathful spook later goes beyond a simple rebuke and utterly annihilates his mother's shade, it's an analogy that goes rather too far.

Yet the story's core lies with Cordelia's sense of identity, and how much materialism does/doesn't define her. When Angel suggests that Cordy doesn't need her haunted apartment because, "It's just a place. You're more than that," it's all-too telling when Cordelia responds, "How? How am I more than that?" Yet as she'll learn over the next three years, it's absurd to try to atone one's self through *stuff*.

And purely as a side note, it's also about the tortuous hell of finding viable housing in L.A. One of the authors of this present volume knows that lesson all too well, having scoped out an L.A. apartment building with large holes in the walls, a broken elevator and flies. Lots of flies.

IN RETROSPECT Cordy here bitches about losing the trash-bag commercial role to a blonde in a skintight leather catsuit. (Cordy: "She looked like Catwoman, taking out the cat-trash.") Let's then bear in mind 2.19, "Belonging," in which Cordelia's on-set in a skimpy bikini.

CRITIQUE Here's the thing about Jane Espenson scripts: Sometimes, her amazing talent for character work beautifully compensates for what's actually a lackluster plot. You see this most prominently in her *Firefly* episode "Shindig," in which the story twists aren't terribly original, but the way Espenson molds the characters comprises some of the series' meat and potatoes. With "Rm w/a Vu," Espenson isn't so much worried about Cordelia's crazed apartment search – although that's what fans tend to remember – as she's exposing the lead characters' quirks and neuroses. In Espenson's hands, Cordelia here gets more development than her counterparts on other prime-time shows get in an entire season.

So we end up with a story that – regardless of bits of it being stapled on (all the parts with the debt-collector Griff especially) – winds up being smart, funny and ultimately charming. In fact, with benefit of hindsight, it's one of the most striking Season One stories and a neat precursor to Espenson's "Guise Will Be Guise" (2.06). Oh and besides, for fangirls (and boys) around the globe, any excuse to get Boreanaz shirtless and wet is a good one.

THE LORE Espenson originally scripted that a fully clothed Angel was reading a book when Cordelia came knocking on his apartment door. She changed this on the grounds that it was "more cinematic" (uh-huh), so a towel-clad Angel was fresh out of the shower. However, the loss of the book-reading element meant that Espenson had to toss some jokes about *Wuthering Heights*. (Espenson, *The Bronze*, Oct. 29, 1999)

• Another deletion, from the actual script this time: Griff carries garlic-coated bullets for use against vampires (although it's hard to imagine these actually working).

• Beth Grant (Maude Pearson) has a history of playing housewives and mothers in films like *Speed* (penned by Whedon), *Rain Man* and *To Wong Foo, Thanks for Everything! Julie Newmar*. She's a conservative and deliberately unlikeble teacher in the surreal film *Donnie Darko*... but conversely, in the short-lived series *Wonderfalls*, she's the wholesome and memorable muffin-baking lady in the story "Muffin Buffalo."

1.06: "Sense and Sensitivity"

"You both withdraw when I go vamp. I feel you judge me. Closeness is too important to me right now."

Air Date: Nov. 9, 1999; **Writer:** Tim Minear; **Director:** James A. Contner

SUMMARY Angel helps Kate to locate and arrest the wanted mobster "Little Tony" Papazian, but Papazian phones his attorneys at Wolfram and Hart, asking them to remove Kate as a thorn in his side. The firm employs a magic-user, Allan Lloyd, to infiltrate Kate's precinct as a psychologist specializing in "sensitivity training." Allan tricks various cops into touching a magical stick that wears away at their emotional restraint, and an afflicted Kate – burdened with years of anguish at her emotionally walled-off father, who's also a cop – comes emotionally unglued at his retirement party.

The precinct degenerates into chaos, Angel also succumbs to Lloyd's "emotion" spell and Papazian escapes to go gunning for Kate. Angel maintains enough resolve to overpower Papazian, whereupon the spell's effects diminish and the firm dumps Papazian as a client. Kate apologizes to her father for her outburst, but a restored Trevor rebuffs her.

FIRSTS AND LASTS On the production side, it's the first episode credited to writer/producer Tim Minear, whose vision for the show will prove crucial to Seasons Two and Three, and start coming to bear full-force in "Somnambulist" (1.11). Story-wise, it's the first of two appearances by Kate's father Trevor. It's also the first time the firm actively interferes in Angel's affairs, and the first appearance of Lee Mercer – the first Wolfram and Hart attorney to actually get named.

Presuming we take Doyle's comment of "Not a lot of enchanted swordsmiths open on Sunday" literally, it's also the first sign that L.A. has retailers who cater to those interested in the supernatural (see also "Somnambulist"; 1.14, "I've Got You Under My Skin"; 3.14, "Couplet" and more). Fan lore loves to claim that Angel's a total nitwit with his cell phone (in no small part due to 1.13, "She"), yet he here uses it for the first time, without incident, to call Kate. And mercifully, it's the final instance of Angel wearing a silly Hawaiian shirt.

1.06, Sense and Sensitivity

POINTS OF DISCUSSION ABOUT "Sense and Sensitivity":

1. The villain gets away with it. Well, maybe. Although Angel ruins Lloyd's scheme, we've no idea what ultimately happens to him. It's unlikely that Angel kills the man at this stage (at least, not without more cause than we're shown on screen), because Lloyd seems fully human. Under Angel's current morality, he doesn't qualify for getting beheaded, but neither can he get prosecuted for black magic use. Mind, this isn't the first instance of this dilemma – remember *Buffy* 3.20, "The Prom," in which the student Tucker unleashes hellhounds on Sunnydale High, and we're never told how the Slayer deals with the bastard afterward. Angel will face this problem again in 1.12, "Expecting" and 2.14, "The Thin Dead Line" among others, and notice how it's really only in Season Five that human villains appear *so* evil that they rank as outright killable. All things considered, one begins to wish that the Watchers over on *Buffy* had created a prison for people whose supernatural-related crimes circumvent due process.

2. It's official. Judging by Kate's beefy, sweaty and altogether male co-workers, she's quite obviously the best-looking police detective in L.A. Possibly the entire nation.

CHARACTER NOTES *Angel:* While enchanted Angel deems Cordy as "precious" and reacts violently to Papazian calling him a "nancy boy." Cordelia criticizes Angel for not asking his employees questions such as, "How did the spewing tentacle killing go?" out of simple courtesy, and dismisses his efforts to better show an interest as lame. [And she's got a point.]

Angel owns night binoculars, and comments that his parents "tasted a lot like chicken." [He probably says this to rattle Lloyd's cage, but it's a lot less funny in light of 1.15, "The Prodigal."] Angel drinks the office coffee without comment. [Either Cordelia's coffee-making skills have improved since 1.04, "I Fall to Pieces," or he can't be bothered to complain. Or perhaps his vampire taste buds simply don't care.]

• *Cordelia:* Her mother leaves a phone message at the office. [This serves as the only real proof that Cordelia still talks with her parents, or her mother at least. She does, however, use her mother's brownie recipe in 1.14, "I've Got You Under My Skin."] Hyper-emotional Kate brings Doyle's attraction for Cordelia screaming into the forefront, but Cordelia immediately changes the conversation.

• *Doyle:* Fashion-sensitive enough to notice Cordy's new shoes, even if Angel isn't. Doyle's contacts include Johnny Red, an exercise nut who takes a Thursday night spinning class.

• *Kate:* She was a child when her mother died, and her father walled himself off afterward, perhaps because Kate reminded him of his late wife. Little Kate instead got some sympathy from the mother of her best friend, Joanne. Still, her father's police career inspired her to become a police detective. [Kate mentions all this while under Lloyd's influence, but it seems genuine enough.]

"Enchanted" Kate indicates she's envisioned Angel in his underwear, and that she's wondered if he acts enigmatic to increase his chances with women. Kate's dad expresses relief at seeing her out with Angel, a male, having previously speculated that she might play for the other team. [At the risk of over cross-referencing shows, Trevor's thoughts about Kate being a lesbian sound all the more amusing if you know the "big reveal" about Elisabeth Röhm's character on *Law and Order*. And see 1.15, "The Prodigal" for the follow-up to this.] "Non-enchanted" Kate isn't opposed to roughing up suspects.

One of Kate's enchanted co-workers [identified in the script as "Harlan"], admits that he spent the last two years sitting at the desk next to Kate, desperately hoping that she might love or even notice him. [We never hear of this admission again.]

Kate currently works for the L.A. Metro Precinct, and her personnel file suggests she was appointed to the LAPD in July 1994. She's not yet a lieutenant, and she's Badge No. 5767. [Well, maybe. Her personnel file (the one that Mercer takes from the fax machine) is damn fuzzy to read, and could certainly be 5787. Some sources have claimed 3747, which seems a bit off – but if nothing else, the number pretty clearly starts with a "5."]

• *Trevor Lockley:* Closed off from his daughter, and verbally undermines her regarding the Papazian arrest. His badge number is 6873. [He next appears in 1.15, "The Prodigal."]

• *Allen Lloyd:* Describes himself as a "polytheist" whose emotion-influencing spell owes to his worship of multiple demons. [This makes him roughly akin to ritualist Ethan Rayne (first seen in *Buffy* 2.06, "Halloween") who generally worships chaos with no particular affiliation.] He lives at 322 Fletcher.

ORGANIZATIONS *Wolfram and Hart:* Mercer says the firm dumps Papazian because they "can't risk exposure" by keeping him, and that the Senior Partners deem Papazian a liability. [Mercer is probably just over-simplifying, as it's unclear precisely what they're trying to cover up, or whom they're afraid of at this point. Nor does Papazian seem to warrant the Partners' personal attention.] The firm now regards Angel as a "pressing issue" [but they don't actively move against him until 1.18, "Five by Five"].

DEMONOLOGY *'The Green Tentacled Thing':* Unnamed, sewer-lurking demon that Angel fails to fully kill with his first attempt and must dispatch *again* with an enchanted sword that Doyle supplies. Killing the beast requires cutting off all its limbs and both its heads, then burying the parts separately.

MAGIC *Lloyd's "Talking Stick":* Enchanted piece of wood that gradually erodes the emotional barriers of anyone who touches it. Some of those affected become violent, others others experience an effect similar to alcohol intoxication (say, Kate waving her handgun all over the place). Emotional insecurities surface, and the victim becomes overly sensitive to the feelings of others. The stick even affects the undead; Lloyd himself appears immune.

BEST LINE Doyle to Angel: "[Cordelia] thinks you're insensitive. And, not to bring up the irony, but consider the source."

THINGS THAT DON'T MAKE SENSE Other than the dangling issue of Lloyd's fate (see **Points of Discussion**), there's only two minor points worth mentioning... prior to getting enchanted, Kate doesn't comment on – or even seem to notice – that Cordelia and Doyle are covered with sewer dirt and giant tentacle spew. Also, Angel somehow walks straight into Lloyd's house without an invite. (Either Lloyd has set up shop in a disused building – no, we don't quite buy that either – or his particular type of spell-casting has riddled him with demonic energy, thus making him less-than-human and nullifying the rule; see **How Does the Invitation Rule Work?**)

POP CULTURE Mercer threatens to expose the brutality of Kate's police force to such a degree that "Mark Fuhrman [will] look like Gentle Ben." Fuhrman was one of the most controversial figures of the O.J. Simpson trial, but with time, he's been relegated to footnote status. Simply put, he was a police officer who testified against Simpson, but in various interviews previous to the trial, he admitted membership in a secret police organization called "Men Against Women," bragged about torturing various gang members and displayed a racist streak toward African-Americans. Needless to say, this severely hampered his credibility on the stand.

IN RETROSPECT Cordelia squirms and goes "ew... ew... ew..." when an overly emotional Angel hugs her. Come Season Three, she won't find the physical contact nearly so repulsive.

IT'S REALLY ABOUT... The problems inherent with too much and too little emotion, plus the excruciating difficulty in finding a proper balance between the two. An overabundance of sensitivity causes nothing but chaos, especially when the ensorcelled police officers start coddling criminals even more than their victims. But the opposite's true as well... when Kate's dad remains closed from his daughter, their relationship looks like something of a dead husk.

Naturally, the theme of emotional balance directly applies to L.A., a city all-too-often associated with police brutality and violence (such as the Rodney King incident, not to mention Lakers fans rioting even when the team *wins*). Paradoxically, it's a touchy-feely city where psychologists – we're not making this up – offer counseling sessions for depressed parakeets. It's something of a weird contradiction, to say the least.

CRITIQUE On the one hand, this will never please serious-minded viewers who can't stand an outpouring of emotion, no matter how whimsically it's presented. But if you run with it, it's fun and probably underrated as far as Season One stories go. Besides, any series based in L.A. in 1999 will inevitably broach "touchy feely" grounds at some point. That being the case, "Sense and Sensitivity" handles the topic very well.

Plus let's give it points for the gut-wrenching final scene, in which Kate's father rejects her. On almost any other show, Kate and her dad would've ridiculously swept away years of angst and non-communication with a single, all-forgiving hug and a cheer from the studio audience. (Indeed, the script nearly went that direction before Whedon intervened.) So here, when a stubborn Trevor Lockley shuts down his daughter, it's a testament to *Angel* for not taking the path of least resistance.

THE LORE Christian Kane proved unavailable to return as Lindsey for this story, so Lee Mercer was created to fulfill his role in the short-term. Actor Thomas Burr knew someone in the casting office and had served as a casting assistant a couple of times, and was therefore awarded the part in a hurry. (Grimshaw, *CityofAngel.com*)

• Minear initially pitched this story to Whedon as dealing with "sensitivity and cops, and cops who become so sensitive that they can't do their jobs." Whedon somewhat approached the concept from an opposite political point of view, but nonetheless thought it a superb idea. As we've indicated, Minear initially capped off the story with a big TV hug between Kate and her father, but Whedon counter-suggested that they not reconcile. Minear later admitted that Whedon was correct: "If it had gone the other way, I think the whole thing would have collapsed." (*Fandom.com*, Aug. 14, 2000)

• Ken Abraham (Spivey, the goon Kate interrogates) has a history with Hollywood vampires – he served as a production assistant on the original *Dark Shadows*, and his film credits include *Vampire Knights* and *Vampires on Bikini Beach*.

1.07: "The Bachelor Party"

"Then we have the ritual eating of the first husband's brains. And then charades."

Air Date: Nov. 16, 1999; **Writer:** Tracey Stern; **Director:** David Straiton

SUMMARY Without warning, Doyle's wife Harry – from whom he separated four years ago – shows up, asking him to sign their divorce papers. Moreover, Harry plans to marry her new lover, Richard Straley, in a few days. Innately suspicious, Doyle asks Angel to investigate Straley. Angel discovers that Straley hails from a clan of Ano-Movic demons, a pacified species that's acclimated to human civilization and now owns a series of restaurants. Doyle, uneasy with the thought that perhaps Harry rejected *him* rather than his demon persona, graciously signs the divorce papers. He also accepts Richard's invitation to attend his bachelor party.

Unfortunately, the Ano-Movic clan intends to "bless" the impending nuptials with a ritual that entails Straley eating Doyle's brains out. Doyle gets captured at the party, and Straley prepares to scoop out his gray matter with a shrimp spoon. Fortunately, Angel bursts to the rescue and Harry rebukes Straley for attempting to kill her ex-husband. Harry leaves Straley and all's well – just before Doyle gets a vision showing Buffy in danger...

POINTS OF DISCUSSION ABOUT "The Bachelor Party":

1. Doyle gets a vision about the Slayer, thus facilitating Angel's return to Sunnydale (see **Cross-Overs**). Just for fun, stop to notice how gratuitously Doyle – who doesn't know what Buffy looks like – here gets shown a photograph of Buffy in the teaser. It's probably to either avoid a potential plot hole, or the need for Doyle to end the story sputtering, "There's a blonde woman... tough... hot... in a leather coat..." when everyone knows who he's talking about. Still, we'd like to extend kudos to the script writers for closing this loophole – however spuriously – because if you're writing a book like this, the accounting of such details is worth gold.

2. Amid an otherwise dreary episode (see **The Critique**), a bright spot occurs when Straley's mother moans about the stripper at the bachelor party... but later, the bridal shower women happily sit down and play pornographic Pictionary.

CHARACTER NOTES *Angel:* Doesn't speak the demonic Aratuscan language, yet repeats Uncle John's ritualistic chant with perfect recall [thanks to his photographic memory, presumably]. He drinks Scotch with Doyle, and is presently reading *Nicholas Nickleby*, using a photo of Buffy as a bookmark. Angel doesn't know that Tiffany's issues *blue* gift boxes, and doesn't bat an eye upon discovering that Doyle has a wife.

• *Cordelia:* Goes out on a date with Pierce, a rich futures markets trader. Unfortunately, Pierce's dinner conversation at *Le Petit Renard* [which translates to "the little duck"] bores Cordelia to tears, and he rabbits at the first sign of a vampire attack. Doyle subsequently saves Cordelia, making her realize that – in matters of romance – she just might be favoring heroism over money. [There's an interesting parallel with Cordy's similarly horror-struck realization that she's infatuated with the "lowly" Xander Harris in *Buffy* 2.16, "Bewitched, Bothered and Bewildered."] Harry's arrival interrupts Cordelia's attempt to ask Doyle out for coffee.

Cordelia tells Pierce that she "left her car at the office." [That's probably an excuse to end her date early, as there's no evidence that Cordy owns a car before 3.22, "Tomorrow," and see **Points of Discussion** in 2.03, "First Impressions."]

Chatting with Harry, Cordelia agrees that Straley's demon family "sounds nice." [Either she's being polite, or she's become far more open-minded since 1.02, "Lonely Hearts," when she basically labeled all demons as unspeakably evil.]

• *Doyle:* His full name is "Allen Francis Doyle." He never knew his demonic father. [The *Buffy/Angel* novel *Monster Island*, though, names Doyle's dad as General Axtius, the leader of the "Coalition of Purity," and someone who wants to destroy all half-breeds. Yes, it feels as if the authors scooped up the theme of "Hero" (1.09) and ran with it.] Doyle's mother kept silent about Doyle's lineage, waiting to see if he had inherited his father's demonic side.

Doyle met Harry while he was volunteering at a food bank. They married before age 20, with Doyle employed as a third-grade instructor. The two of them talked about having children, but – by Harry's account – Doyle drank a fair amount and started to smother her with attention.

To Doyle's surprise, his demon aspect manifested when he was 21. Harry freaked, then acclimated and encouraged Doyle to explore his demon culture. Doyle read Harry's suggestions as pity, rejected his demon side and became "a bitch to live with." Harry walked out on Doyle four years ago. More than anything else, Doyle regrets his failure to make Harry happy.

Doyle's stronger in his demon aspect [similar to vampires when they switch to "vamp face"] but prefers fighting in his weaker human form. Blunt trauma, such as a chair smashed onto Doyle's back, makes him inadvertently reveal his demon face. Sneezing makes him switch back [as with 1.01, "City Of"]. In combat, demon-Doyle "head-butts" well. [Although it's unclear if his facial spikes serve as makeshift weapons.]

Doyle's newest strategy for getting Angel to socialize: Invite him to a sports bar. [But there's no evidence they ever go.] Doyle agrees with Harry that he drinks too much. Shortly after this epiphany, he drinks up at the bachelor party.

• *"Harry":* [Short for "Harriet," according to "Hero."] She appears to hold no ill will toward Doyle [which makes her better adjusted than most divorcées on the planet]. Harry works as an "ethnodemonologist," an expert on demon culture. [It's never clarified precisely how one makes a living doing this, although 5.09, "Harm's Way" features a human working as a "demon rights activist," so perhaps there's a market for it.] Despite Harry's expertise, she fails to identify Angel as a vampire on sight [see **Why Do Catholic Objects Harm Vampires?** for the possible implications of this].

Doyle's heritage motivated Harry to study demonology. She's traveled to Kiribati, Togo and Uzbekistan, and met Straley while scouting demon clans in South America. She can translate Aratuscan, a dead demonic language, with difficulty.

• *Richard Howard Straley:* His family owns "Straley's Steak House," an establishment that serves law-skirting (but not law-breaking) delicacies such as quail's tongues, frog's legs, etc. Straley doesn't like buffalo wings. Naturally, he lets a tart in a blue dress give him a lap dance at the bachelor party.

DEMONOLOGY *Vampires:* Doyle dusts a vampire with what looks like a wooden arrow with a metal tip. [If so, perhaps the metal point helps to tear through the vampire's flesh, and the wood of the shaft does the dusting.]

• *Ano-Movic Demons:* Formerly a nomadic tribe with violent leanings, the red-skinned Ano-Movic demons allegedly gave up their orthodox teachings and language around the turn of the century. Still, Straley's family members berate Harry for not respecting their practices, and they're appalled that Doyle brings Angel, a vampire, to the bachelor party. [The clan appears to hold some racism and hypocrisy, but they're not alone in that; see "Rm w/a Vu" (1.05) and "Hero." The Ano-Movics' disdain for Angel pares with other stories that rank vampires as among the lowliest types of demons, possibly because they started out as human.]

Harry implies that the youngest of the Ano-Movic females in Straley's family are "under 370 years old." They can readily switch between a human aspect and a red-skinned demon aspect. [Straley's entire family can do this, suggesting that – like Doyle – Ano-Movics possess more human blood than most demons. Some species, such as the Brachens in "Hero," can only attain human form if they're of mixed parentage.]

The "eating of the ex-husband's brains" ritual first requires that the victim to "bless" the marriage. [It's implied that the ritual can't proceed without such a blessing, so oddly enough, Doyle could've avoided a heap of trouble if he'd simply told them, "Screw you."] Once given, the blessing can't be revoked. The ritual hasn't been performed in centuries; no Ano-Movic has apparently married a divorcée in all that time.

The intended victim gets a shot of painkiller to the scalp, and the betrothed cuts into his head with a ritually prepared knife. However, any mention of specific "former-husband-brain-eating" forks has apparently been lost to history.

The Ano-Movics only pose a threat to Angel by ganging up on him. A [mercifully] unseen Ano-Movic ritual involves spilling the blood of a she-goat. Female Ano-Movics' knees bend in more than one way.

MAGIC Richard Straley's uncle John prepares for the ritual by anointing the carving knife over a smoking bowl, while chanting in Aratuscan.

BEST LINE Cordelia's stumbling attempt to compliment Doyle: "Maybe you actually don't have zero potential."

THINGS THAT DON'T MAKE SENSE With Angel secretly watching, Straley shifts into demon face and menacingly picks up a knife. This gives Angel a handy excuse to body-tackle Straley, but as we learn that Straley was simply trying to cut open the packages from Harry's shopping spree, doesn't it seem odd that he put on his "demon face" just to cut some box strings? (It's another obscure demon ritual, perhaps.)

There's the dangling question of how, if Harry hasn't spoken with Doyle in four years, that she knows to find him at Angel Investigations. And even though we know this next bit's done for comedy... Cordelia doesn't know about Doyle's demon aspect yet, so she whacks "demon Doyle" over the head with a serving platter. It's odd, though, that Cordy – the most fashion-conscious character – never wonders why "the demon" and Doyle were wearing the same clothes.

Finally, the "accursed books" of the Ano-Movics claim that by eating the first husband's brains out, the new husband will absorb the "love" that the first couple shared. Well, *there's* a rather suspect notion. They're divorced, for pity's sake, so isn't the second hubby just as likely to absorb the bile and anger that led to the couple's break-up? That's presuming the couple held genuine love, in the first place which is hardly a given. (Then again, the "brains-eating" ritual could've undergone any number of revisions throughout the ages. Who knows? Perhaps the ritual was initially geared to eliminate the previous husband, with all the flowery language added later.)

CROSS-OVERS In response to Doyle's vision, Angel travels to Sunnydale and – working completely behind the scenes – aids the Slayer against an American Indian spirit named Hus (*Buffy* 4.08, "Pangs"). Naturally, Buffy learns of Angel's visit and pursues him to L.A. in time for next episode.

IN RETROSPECT Cordelia finds Doyle reenacting his successful vampire dusting with the horribly clichéd line: "Fangs for the memories, vamp man!" With hindsight, her labeling this a "spaz attack" seems hypocritical, as just three episodes from now, Cordelia herself will do in an empath demon while crowing, "Feel this feeling, creepo!"

Also, it's amusing to see Doyle and Angel grilling Cordelia's date, considering she'll eventually fall for both of them.

IT'S REALLY ABOUT... Not a great deal, actually. You could claim that it's about the pointlessness of family rituals, but it's more of an excuse to detail Doyle's background than anything else. There's a bit of meaning in how Cordelia's surprised to discover she's valuing a man's substance over money these days, but that fades to the background after the first act.

CRITIQUE And it was all going so well. We took time to thump "I Fall to Pieces" (1.04), but that was mainly a case of a potentially decent story that just didn't fit into *Angel*'s groove. With "The Bachelor Party," though, we unavoidably confront the first *Angel* episode that's deplorably bad. Chiefly, it's because the plot's almost non-existent and everything's predicated on the lamest mid-story twist imaginable. In short, we're told at the end of Act Two that the demon clan wants to eat Doyle's brains. Gasp! Swoon! You mean that a group of demons might want to eat someone's brains? You could've knocked us over with a feather. Even allowing that benevolent demons inhabit the *Angel*-verse (for a start, there's Doyle himself), it's nearly the most anti-climactic thing imaginable.

Unfortunately, while most of what remains decently fleshes out Doyle's character, it isn't funny, isn't entertaining and wears on one's patience like nails on a chalkboard. It's a damn pity, too, because Act One – in which Cordelia's startled to find some substance in her co-worker – seems rather promising and includes some nice bits. But it's all downhill from there, and lazily ends with Angel crashing to the rescue.

The good news is that out of the 22 episodes in this season, there's remarkably few duds – every network show will inevitably produce some, and looking at Season One overall, it's a remarkably good average. But tragically, "The Bachelor Party" is one of the lemons.

THE LORE Quinn had never seen *Buffy* before auditioning for Doyle, and watched some Angel-relevant stories such as *Buffy* 2.21-2.22, "Becoming" to play catch-up. He initially read for the part as an American, then Irish. Quinn quickly found himself doing an audition test with Boreanaz, and the two of them wound up laughing so hard that Quinn was offered the part only hours later. A *Variety* article later claimed, wrongly, that Quinn would be playing Whistler from "Becoming" (see 1.01, "City Of"). Quinn himself didn't learn his character's name until reading about it in an *Entertainment Weekly* piece. (*Starburst* #257, Jan. 2000)

• Kristin Dattilo (Harry) played the title role in Aerosmith's 1990 music video "Janie's Got A Gun." Carlos Jacott (Richard Straley) played villains on every Whedon-verse show: He's the demon overlord Ken in *Buffy* 3.01, "Anne," and the treacherous Lawrence Dobson (Captain Mal Reynolds plugs him in the head) in the *Firefly* pilot. (The latter is especially funny, because you're not supposed to know the villain's identity at first. *Angel* and *Buffy* diehards, however, immediately pegged Jacott as the baddie. What *else* could he be?)

1.08: "I Will Remember You"

"They've got the forbidden love of all time. They have been apart for months. Now he's suddenly human? I'm sure they're down there just having tea and crackers."

Air Date: Nov. 23, 1999; **Writers:** David Greenwalt, Jennifer Renshaw; **Director:** David Grossman

SUMMARY Buffy arrives at Angel Investigations, irked that Angel visited Sunnydale without telling her (*Buffy* 4.08,"Pangs"). Not long after, a samurai-armored Mohra demon attacks the pair of them. Angel dispatches the Mohra, but some of the demon's blood seeps into his wounds. Unexpectedly, the blood's regenerative properties restore Angel's dead body to life.

Angel consults with the Oracles, mystical siblings who serve as a conduit to the Powers-That-Be, but the Oracles in turn release Angel from the Powers' service. A gleeful Angel then beds Buffy with reckless abandon, but the Powers warn Doyle that the Mohra has regenerated. Human-Angel hopes to prove himself by tackling the Mohra without Buffy's help, but the Mohra gets the upper hand until the Slayer intervenes and kills it.

Angel further asks the Oracles about a reference the Mohra's made to the "End of Days," and the Oracles say that if Angel stays human, the Slayer will die. At Angel's request, the Oracles fold time back 24 hours, enabling the forewarned Angel to kill the Mohra –

which prevents his becoming human. Oblivious to Angel's sacrifice, Buffy heads home.

FIRSTS AND LASTS Buffy turns up on *Angel* in the flesh, having previously been seen in flashbacks or as a photograph. Her contribution, as it happens, also marks the first occasion of Angel – or any of the show's leads – having sex, even if Buffy doesn't remember the festivities afterward. This also entails the first sizzling glimpse of "totally naked" Angel as he fetches some post-coital ice cream from the refrigerator. (Inevitably, we'll revisit the "totally naked-ish" part in stories such as 2.03, "First Impressions" and 5.05, "Life of the Party.")

"I Will Remember You" also debuts the Oracles, the mystical duo who occasionally give Angel enigmatic/irritating advice. The male Oracle arguably supplies the first mention of *the* Apocalypse (see 5.17, "Underneath"). There's also the first "End of Days" and "Soldiers of Darkness" references that'll continue through Season One, but not much further (see **Points of Discussion**). The fact that no time (or preciously little of it) passes in our dimension while Angel consults with the Oracles provides the first evidence that time passes at a different rate in other dimensions. (*Buffy* 3.01, "Anne" already established the point, though.)

It's the first of many appearances by the cute little Byzantine axe that Cordelia here threatens to sell – presuming it's the same weapon that'll reside in her closet by "First Impressions" and be seen throughout Season Two.

POINTS OF DISCUSSION ABOUT "I Will Remember You":

1. As with "In the Dark" (1.03), we're forced to deal with an element (in this case, Angel becoming human) that later becomes a major issue, and thereby threatens to throw the entire series out of whack. To explain: At the end of Season One, the Shanshu Prophecy will declare that Angel will one day become human. Angel, upon learning this, will spend the next four years wondering if the promised reward of humanity is genuine or outright bunk. All of which seems fair enough, unless you consider that Angel spends four years striving to attain something he here gains and gives away, even with good reason, all in the space of a day. You can see why after next episode, Angel's day of humanity gets swept under the rug.

Admittedly, the circumstances are different. Angel is here told that Buffy will die if he remains human, whereas the Shanshu doesn't carry such strings. Also, it's important to Angel that he *earns* his atonement (see "In the Dark"), which better fits the Shanshu reward. Even so, reconciling "I Will Remember You" against future seasons – in which Angel agonizes over whether he'll become human via the Shanshu – will always seem awkward because he need only find a Mohra demon and slit its throat to attain such a prize.

2. Speaking of disjoins, notice how this episode foreshadows a major conflict that never comes to pass. Beginning here and throughout Season One, there's repeated mention of "soldiers of darkness" who'll usher in "the End of Days." You can almost see the writing staff sitting around a conference table, reasoning that they can't get by on stand-alone stories forever and should slowly build up to a climactic mother of a battle. So they start stripping in murky references to a grandiose threat, but this never comes to fruition.

Retroactively, you can try to make these references apply to adversaries such as Jasmine in Season Four (although it's a stretch to call her mesmerized followers "soldiers of darkness"), or the demon cadre in the series finale. But nothing well and truly fits. Perhaps we're better off assuming that in the *Angel*-verse, an "End of Days" is *always* in the works.

3. The Mohra demon mostly comes off as elaborate cannon fodder, only speaking in grunts and the like until the final act, when it spontaneously starts using perfect English and goes on about the "End of Days." It all feels forced, but let's at least admire how one of Angel's opponents has learned the value of just shutting up and getting on with the fighting – as opposed to gibbering a lot and readily getting slaughtered.

CHARACTER NOTES *Angel:* Once Angel becomes human, he and Buffy try to take things "slowly," but this chiefly entails their downing some tea and crackers before enjoying "numbing" sex. Unlike his lovemaking with the Slayer in *Buffy* Season Two, Angel doesn't appear to lose his soul as a result. [Doyle claims that Angel "isn't cursed" any more, but that's debatable. More likely, the gypsy curse unnaturally grafts Angel's soul onto his dead vampire body – making it rather easy, if the curse gets broken, for Angel to lose his soul again. Humans, on the other hand, are pre-disposed to having souls, so the curse can't forcibly rip the soul from such a vessel. For all we know, it's Angel's sex with Buffy that technically voids the curse – in the alternate timeline, that is – but with no consequence.]

Angel has never seen a Mohra demon before. Human-Angel feels back pain and regains an appetite for food, especially chocolate, peanut butter and Cookie Dough Fudge Mint Chip ice cream. He dislikes yogurt, however. He now casts a reflection. Spilt blood triggers his gag reflex.

• *Buffy:* Claims she's in L.A. to visit her father. [Hank Summers lives in L.A. right now, and it's the holiday season, but c'mon... it's the day after Angel visited Sunnydale, which seems awfully coincidental.] The Slayer says she's fantasized about Angel turning human "a zillion times," but insists that her life's going well with him out of the picture. [Relatively speaking, she's right. The corresponding point in *Buffy* Season Four is arguably one of her more stable periods.]

1.08, I Will Remember You

Buffy likes peanut butter, preferably crunchy. Her Slayer training lets her identify a Byzantine axe kept in the Angel Investigations office. [And this is a full year before the "Knights of Byzantium" show up in *Buffy* 5.12, "Checkpoint."] A post-coital Buffy becomes the second woman – in three episodes, no less – to enjoy peanut butter in Angel's bed. [Cordelia was the first, platonically, in 1.05, "Rm w/a Vu."]

• *Cordelia:* Mercurial enough to worry that Angel's become evil again, then to ask – about a second later – if he's bought a new umbrella. She's not beyond thinking that a despondent Angel might commit suicide pining for Buffy, or that the Slayer might up and dust him. Cordelia and Doyle have now advanced to the point that they're enjoying cappuccino and even bar drinks together.

Cordy's [sloppily] doing the office cleaning, and she's not happy about it. The mercenary side of her stands willing to sell the office equipment to acquire her severance pay.

• *Doyle:* First brings the Oracles to Angel's attention, and instinctively knows, just by looking at Angel, that he's become human again. He's pleased to think this might also end his service to the Powers. [Thus raising some odd questions about who'd become the next visionary, and how the vision-transfer is supposed to work. It's similarly ambiguous when Doyle says he's now "out of a job," either meaning he's done as the visionary or – perhaps more likely – that Angel was paying him from the agency funds.]

Doyle drinks margaritas and tastes salt in his latest vision. [This either suggests that Doyle experiences the visions using all of his senses, or it's simply the aftertaste of his margarita. "To Shanshu in L.A." (1.22) seems to confirm the former by describing the visions as "Scratch 'n Sniff."]

• *The Oracles:* Classical-looking brother and sister who sometimes provide information to heroic figures. Warriors such as Angel, but not messengers such as Doyle, can access the Oracles' marble-built audience chamber through a simple chanting ritual that creates a dimensional gateway, whereupon the warrior steps through and must give the female Oracle an offering. Angel's gifts here include his watch – a symbol of time – and a famille rose vase from the Ching dynasty, circa 1811. An inscription over the Oracles' outer doorway translates as "The Gateway for Lost Souls."

The Oracles consult "the auguries" to learn of the future. They cannot blatantly grant life or death [as supported by "To Shanshu in L.A."]. Emotions such as love don't concern them, and they display some telekinetic ability. They claim that Angel serves "the same thing" that they do [this presumably means the Powers, or perhaps just the general side of "good"]. They're judgmental about who constitutes a "lower being," although the female Oracle upgrades her opinion of Angel once he agrees to sacrifice his humanity. [They next appear in 1.10, "Parting Gifts."]

ORGANIZATIONS *The Powers-That-Be:* Doyle claims the Powers don't live in our reality, proving reachable only through "dangerous channels" such as the Oracles. He also comments that *only* the Powers can make Angel human. [All respect to Doyle, this seems very unsubstantiated, given future events.] The male Oracle implies that only extraordinary circumstances – say, Angel saving humanity or averting *the* Apocalypse [see "Underneath"] – would allow the Powers to make him human.

THE LIBRARY *The Book of Kelsor*, which Angel owns, supplies information about Mohra demons.

DEMONOLOGY *Mohra Demons:* Assassins who work for unspecified powers of darkness. Their luminescent green blood lets them heal major wounds, making them "ever-stronger." [Mohra blood restores Angel to human form – but in theory, it could work on soulless vampires also. Whatever else you can say about 1.14, "I've Got You Under My Skin," it proves that human beings don't need souls to live.]

Mohra demons require vast quantities of salt, but salt tossed in their eyes blinds them. Smashing their forehead jewel – sometimes colorfully referred to as "1,000 eyes" – apparently releases the demon's internal energy and incinerates it.

• *The Lone Bar:* A dive on Second near Beach in L.A., where wounded demons sometimes go to receive medical attention.

MAGIC *Temporal Folds:* Means by which the Oracles roll back time. They claim that such folds aren't "for the indulgence" of lower beings. [The Oracles can't deploy such folds on a whim, so a sacrifice – such as Angel willingly yielding his humanity for Buffy's benefit – is probably required. "Parting Gifts" seems to confirm this.]

BEST LINE If we're avoiding all the sappy dialogue, then it's probably Buffy's post-sex comment of: "I'm so glad we didn't logic ourselves out of this." If we're dealing with the romantic stuff head-on, though, then it's Buffy's tearful remark of "I felt your heart beat..." just before the day gets erased.

THINGS THAT DON'T MAKE SENSE Angel sends Cordelia out to find Buffy, but the meet-up for some reason never happens. Fair enough, as Cordy is a mere human trying to track the Slayer on foot, but it fails to explain why human-Angel later finds Buffy dreamily wandering along a sunny pier. Does she seriously think she's going to happen across the Mohra in broad daylight? Furthermore, why doesn't she return to the office, once the trail runs cold, throughout the whole of Act Two? (You could solve some of this by arguing that Angel somehow told Buffy to meet him at the pier, but it's questionable how, as she doesn't own a cell phone right now.)

The timing of the final act is also awkward. After the Mohra starts to pummel Doyle and Angel, Buffy then has her conversation with Cordelia and learns the Angel's whereabouts. This means that on screen, Buffy goes from the office to the saline plant to save Angel's rump in mere moments – impressive, even allowing for Slayer speed. (Either we see the events out of sequence, or Angel and the Mohra spend a hell of a long time running around the plant.) Cordelia mistakes a clump of dust for Angel's remains, then realizes she just forgot to sweep under the rug. Did you *see* the size of that clump? Exactly how many years' worth of dust is under the thing?

CROSS-OVERS Cordelia claims that Angel spent three days away from L.A. (between last episode and this one), but it's said that the events of *Buffy* 4.08 "Pangs" occurred last night.

POP CULTURE Doyle, when Human-Angel starts to pig out: "Orson! We're in a situation here!" Fandom has tossed out so many theories about this, you almost wish Doyle had never said it. "Orson" most likely refers to Orson Welles, the famously beefy director of such works as the "War of the Worlds" radio version and *Citizen Kane*. It's alternatively been suggested that "Orson" denotes a character from either *U.S. Acres* (the *Garfield* spin-off comic strip) or *Mork and Mindy* – neither of which sound like the sort of references that the hip, modern *Angel* writers would touch with a barge pole.

IN RETROSPECT Doyle remarks at one point that, "I'm finally free to go out and make me own mark in the world," whereupon Cordelia retorts, "We had a cat that used to do that." Come 5.05, "Life of the Party," an *Angel* character will "mark his territory" in a similarly rude manner.

Also, Cordelia consoles Angel over losing Buffy with: "You'll meet someone else." Need we say more?

IT'S REALLY ABOUT... It's about as obvious as they come: "What would happen if Buffy and Angel attained their greatest desire?" This being the *Angel*-verse, it's guaranteed that it won't exactly grant them peace and happiness, but it's an interesting scenario cut short due to lack of space. A full dissection of Buffy and Human-Angel's relationship really deserves more examination – the sort best developed over three or five episodes. But given Sarah Michelle Gellar's filming schedule on *Buffy*, the removal of Angel from Sunnydale and the inherent problems in Angel going too long without super-powers, such elaboration is obviously impossible.

CRITIQUE It's crafted as a tear-jerker, almost certainly the biggest example of a fanfic story given life on *Angel*, and so desperate to appease everyone that it features Buffy licking ice cream drops off a bare-chested Angel in bed. But the question remains: Is it any *good*?

Answering that question, unfortunately, depends on what type of viewer you ask. Some fans are so utterly ga-ga with all the Angel-Buffy romance stuff, they'll forgive almost any failing in the story itself. Conversely, there are people won't take a shine to the rather obvious set-up and resolution, the generic demon opponent and the at-times cloying love scenes. Just for the record, we're in the latter camp.

That's not to condemn the story altogether, though, because it's still a good episode even if it's a vastly overrated one. Rewatch the story without the rose-tinted glasses, and it more or less gets the job done despite itself. But does "IWRY" (as it's commonly called in shorthand) belong in the Top Ten *Angel* stories, as we're often led to believe? Oh Heavens, no. Not by a long shot, no.

Admittedly, this is precisely what a certain swathe of fandom wanted to see – which means it's decidedly void of innovation or surprise for nearly everyone else. Let's all be careful what we wish for. But suffice to say that more than any other *Angel* episode – save perhaps for 5.20, "The Girl in Question" – this story's success or failure hinges on one's personal tastes and expectations. So you decide.

THE LORE The Mutant Enemy team chatted about this episode coming as a test from the Powers-That-Be (see **When Did the Powers Intervene?**). Minear commented: "It was supposed to be sort of 'The Last Temptation of Angel.' In *The Last Temptation of Christ*, [Jesus'] whole fever dream when he's on the cross is that he comes down off it, gets to live a normal life and grow old, and at the end makes the sacrifice... there was the idea that [the Powers] were trying to see if [Angel] was worthy. There were no scenes of this shot; I think the idea just kind of fell out of the script naturally, but it was one thing we discussed at some point." (*Fandom.com*, Aug. 14, 2000)

• Gellar had visited the *Angel* set quite a bit before this story, once showing up in the middle of the night with a cake. (*Zap2It*, May 12, 2003)

• Jane Espenson wrote the corresponding *Buffy* episode (4.08, "Pangs"), and found it challenging as the *Angel* installment started filming before she'd completely worked out the *Buffy* segment. (*The Bronze*, Oct. 15, 1999) Whedon, posting after the two stories aired – and alluding to Xander's illness in "Pangs" – wrote: "Buffy doesn't remember what happened [in "I Will Remember You"]. She absolutely positively definitely never ever will. Unless there's a story in it. Jane, feel free to slump and rest on your hilarious laurels. We were right: Syphilis is ALWAYS funny. nightums, j."

1.09: "Hero"

"Is that it? Am I done?"

Air Date: Nov. 30, 1999; **Writers:** Howard Gordon, Tim Minear; **Director:** Tucker Gates

SUMMARY Again directed by the Powers, Angel, Doyle and Cordelia track down some benevolent Lister demons who're on the run from the Scourge – genetic supremacist demons intent on slaughtering other species with human blood. Soon after, Angel arranges transport with a ship captain who owes him money, hoping to relocate the Listers to Briole, an island demon sanctuary off the coast of Ecuador. Angel and his allies smuggle the Listers onto the ship, but the Scourge assault them *en masse*. Hurriedly, the Scourge lock their targets in the hold and flee, leaving behind an energy weapon named "the Beacon" – a device capable of emitting an energy pulse that will incinerate anything with human blood within a quarter-mile radius.

Angel readies to disconnect the Beacon even though close proximity to it will kill him. However, Doyle slugs his friend off a rail into the hold's lower levels. Doyle quickly kisses Cordelia and leaps onto the Beacon, severing its connections but incinerating in the process. The Listers travel onward to their safe haven, leaving a rattled Angel and Cordelia to deal with Doyle's passing.

FIRSTS AND LASTS Barring the opening credits next episode, and a videotape in 5.12, "You're Welcome," it's the final appearance of Doyle. Obviously, this makes him the "first soldier down" – as Cordelia puts it in Season Five – and he assuredly won't be the last. Thanks to the miracle of ret-con, it's also the first instance of Jasmine's interference (as we'll learn in Season Four; see **Did Jasmine Cause All This?**), and the first of three scripts credited to *Angel* contributing producer Howard Gordon (see 1.12, "Expecting").

POINTS OF DISCUSSION ABOUT "Hero":

1. First a bit of frivolity... Glenn Quinn *really* lays on the Irish accent during Doyle's "commercial," and note especially the way he says, "If you need help, then look no fur-*der*." But then, he's not the only one with eyebrow-raising dialogue. As the Scourge leader grapples with Angel on the catwalk, the villain tries to declare, "Welcome to a cleaner world!" Yet it actually sounds like he's saying: "Welcome... to a *casino* world!"

2. It's subtle, but Doyle here bequeaths the visions to Cordy with a kiss (hence the slight energy discharge between their lips, although it's only revealed what happened next episode). Perhaps it's fortunate that Season Four retcons this event – as we learn in 4.17, "Inside Out" – because it seems a rather odd way of going about the swap on a routine basis. Some fans, with crushing inevitably, latched onto smooching as the standard means of transferring the vision-power, so it's no surprise that imaginations ran hog wild as to how, in Season Three, Doyle gave the visions to an alternate-reality Angel (see 3.11, "Birthday").

At the risk of bursting the bubble of slash writers across the world, though, there's no real mention in the entire *Angel* run as to how the visionary works. Normally, we'd muse the topic over some coffee and bang out an entire essay on the topic, but there's such an utter lack of workable evidence that'd we'd have to spuriously make stuff up to an unacceptable degree. We'll argue, however, come "Birthday," that no human was *ever* meant to operate as the Powers' visionary, but that's another discussion.

3. Here we've got to deal with the notion of "demon purity" full-on, chiefly because the Scourge come off as little more than Nazi stereotypes (right down to their leader's "Heil, Hitler!" gesture while speechifying), and partly because – like a lot of fascist mentality – their philosophy is such bunk.

Generally speaking, the Scourge present themselves as "purebloods" trying to off the "half-breeds," but in *Angel* and *Buffy*-verse terms, they've got more human blood than they pretend. The litmus test is *Buffy* 3.21, "Graduation Day Part 1," which establishes that every demon on Earth – the Scourge included – are tainted with humanity to some degree. On TV, only the post-ascended Mayor ("Graduation Day Part 2") is an exception. The earliest demons, the Old Ones (first mentioned in *Buffy* 1.02, "The Harvest") also presumably qualified as purebreds, but we never meet one in its original state.

So the Scourge's crusade is based on a sham; it's doubtful the writers deliberately had this point in mind, but it's apt any-way. Shortly after "Hero" broadcast, Jane Espenson posted on this topic: "Personally, I feel that those demons in ["Hero"] only called themselves 'pure' because they were less mixed with humanity than some others – it's a matter of degree." (Espenson, *The Bronze*, Dec. 12, 1999)

4. Well, it's the end of the road for Doyle. Whedon keeps pointing out that the character wasn't all that popular when Season One first aired, but the level to which he's been mourned probably indicates the writers did something right. It's also true that it introduced some uncertainty into the show – we're referring to the "everyone is a viable target for slaughter now" angle – although funnily enough, the producers don't leap at the opportunity to repeat this. *Angel* will neatly evolve as a show where almost anything can happen, and yet it's roughly another four years before Angel's allies start dying wholesale. Still, it always takes more effort to take a pointed stick and prod a series into moving foreward, as

opposed to just maintaining the status quo. So in eliminating one of the three leads, let's credit the producers with some ambition.

5. Arguably the scariest thing on display here is... Angel's comb-over when he's infiltrating the Scourge. Evidently, these Nazi copycats use Brylcream like there's no tomorrow.

CHARACTER NOTES *Angel:* Here tells Doyle, who in turn tells Cordelia, about the "lost" day he spent with Buffy (last episode). There's a punching bag in Angel's apartment.

• *Cordelia:* Finally learns about Doyle's demon half from one of the Listers, but now mature enough to ignore the fact – as his heritage isn't as much a hurdle as his being short and poor – and encourages Doyle to ask her out to dinner. Cordelia here films a TV ad for Angel Investigations, starring herself as the victim. Failing to get Angel's cooperation, she puts Doyle in the video to represent someone "ordinary."

Cordy doesn't understand if being "in the red" or being "in the black" means you're broke. She demonstrates her ability to drive large trucks, and carries wintergreen breath freshener. She's shrewd enough to negotiate for better terms with the *Quintessa* captain, who owes Angel money.

• *Doyle:* Shortly after Doyle learned about his demon inheritance [probably between three and four years ago, judging by the chronology of 1.07, "The Bachelor Party"], a fellow Brachen Demon named Lucas approached him. Lucas represented a group of fugitive Brachen who'd fled their home in the Oregon woods, fearing the Scourge. Doyle refused Lucas' request for help, but later had his first vision from the Powers – that of the Brachen getting slaughtered. Doyle consequently tracked down the Brachen, arriving to discover their carcasses and also Lucas' body.

[The method by which Doyle acquired the visions, plus the identity of his predecessor, goes unstated. On screen, the only viable suspect is Lucas... which makes a small bit of sense, as we're never told how Lucas thought to approach Doyle in the first place. It's certainly feasible that the Powers guided him to Doyle's apartment. If so, the transfer must occur during their one and only meeting – and please note that there's no kissing between them. [All right, all right... at least, none that we see.] We're left to our own devices, then, as to whether the Powers deliberately chose Doyle as the new visionary – or whether the vision talent randomly "picked him" – and how Doyle served out his first few years in the role before meeting Angel.]

The younger Doyle claims he's friendless, but that he knows how to set up off-track betting. The present-day Doyle carries a cell phone and – predictably – he's utterly dreadful when performing in Cordy's video. Going by Cordy's estimate, Doyle's sacrifice saves 17 Lister demons, plus herself and Angel.

• *"Harry"* [seen in 1.07, "The Bachelor Party"]: Doyle's ex-wife has decided to stay in L.A., but they're apparently not in touch. Her full name is "Harriet."

• *The Oracles:* Doyle refers to their realm as the "Netherworld of Eternal Watching." [He's probably joking.]

ORGANIZATIONS *Angel Investigations:* Currently has no business license. And no clients.

DEMONOLOGY *Vampires:* The Scourge consider vampires as the lowest of the half-breeds. [They're not alone in this – see "The Bachelor Party" among other stories – and technically, they're a bit justified. Vampires start out as human and, relatively speaking, probably *are* closer to humanity than any other species.]

Vampires don't feed on demon blood. [Spike claims in *Buffy* 5.22, "The Gift" that blood equates with "life," hence why vampires consume the stuff. As most demons appear to lack souls – although there's exceptions such as Lorne's species, evidently – their blood probably doesn't contain "life" as such, making it fairly useless if you're a vampire. Half-breeds such as Doyle, at least, might provide more nourishment if you can stomach the taste.]

• *Brachen Demons:* Full-blooded Brachen apparently can't assume human form. [Doyle's mother was human, which explains why he can "pass" among humanity.] Brachen can survive getting their necks broken. [Neck-snapping kills most demon species, though, the Scourge included. Still, see 2.22, "There's No Place Like Plrtz Glrb" for a fun little exception involving decapitation.]

Brachen Demons supposedly have a good sense of direction [partly, one presumes, due to their enhanced sense of smell (1.03, "In the Dark")]. Doyle claims [possibly as a joke, but who knows?] that they're also good at basketball.

• *The Scourge:* Pattern themselves like a small army – complete with gray uniforms, jackboots and truncheons – but their bodies look like they're in some state of decay. [Physically, the Scourge greatly resemble the inter-dimensional demons seen in *Buffy* 3.01, "Anne." Perhaps they're different factions of the same species, or maybe the demons in "Anne" were, among other things, making weapons on the Scourge's behalf.]

• *Lister Demons:* The Listers' prophecies speak of a "Promised One" who, "at the end of the century," will arrive and save them from the Scourge. [It's not a goof per se, but the story somewhat inexcusably drops this element without explanation. We're probably meant to infer that Doyle was "the Promised One," as opposed to Angel, who's initially presented as the far more obvious suspect. Nobody but nobody stops to make the connection between Doyle's sacrifice and the Listers' prophecies, however, or to even imply that the latter had any bearing on events. Which makes you wonder why all the "Promised One" stuff was brought up in the first place. See **Things That Don't Make Sense** for some legitimate glitches on this point.]

BEST LINE A mercenary Cordelia, inquiring about Doyle's latest vision: "Whatever you saw just now... did it look like they could afford to pay?"

THINGS THAT DON'T MAKE SENSE Virtually everything involving the Scourge's strategy with the Beacon. No, really. The Scourge, after all, are seasoned hunter-killers on the trail of unarmed, untrained Listers who could scarcely harm a stalk of broccoli. The Scourge don't even discover they're up against Angel until late in the game, but despite what looks like a painfully easy-win scenario, they insist on all the business with the Beacon rather than – say – making plans to simply wade in and slaughter everybody. It's the equivalent of swatting mosquitoes with an elephant gun. (It's possible that the Beacon's a prototype, and the Scourge wish to test its effectiveness in combat conditions. The story doesn't mention anything along those lines, however.)

Lots of characters seem prone to incredible overstatement. The Listers' prophecy speaks of a Promised One who will "save them" from the Scourge – quite the weighty pronouncement, considering there's only about 17 Lister lives at stake. You'd hardly call this akin to Moses leading the Israelites out of Egypt, but it's treated that way. The Scourge leader isn't much better, though, because he claims the Listers' impending murder is "a giant step toward our goal" – which again, considering the Listers number only 17, sounds optimistic to say the least.

Then there's the Scourge's stupidity for taking Angel at his word that he'd like to kill other half-breeds for them. Are they *surprised* to discover he's lying? Plus, it's surely bending if not breaking the rules to use lesser species in such a fashion – when you think about it, it's rather akin to the Ku Klux Klan recruiting self-loathing African-Americans.

Not to spoil Doyle's ultimate sacrifice, but it's strange – considering he doesn't possess any technical prowess that we know about – that he inherently knows which cables on the Beacon to disconnect.

POP CULTURE Cordelia proposes getting "that bald *Star Trek* guy" to narrate her the agency's commercial. Funny how there's two choices here – Patrick Stewart or Avery Brooks – but Cordy presumably means Stewart, as he's better known.

IN RETROSPECT Doyle and Cordelia's final kiss, of course, hauntingly parallels the lip-lock that Cordy will give Angel four years hence in 5.12, "You're Welcome."

IT'S REALLY ABOUT... Never knowing if you're truly heroic until you're tested. It's a fairly overt message, and doesn't particularly run much deeper than that.

CRITIQUE So... we bid farewell Doyle, and let's make clear that it's quite the brave and bold step forward – one that admirably reverberates throughout the rest of the series, in fact. Granted, it's rather hard to imagine Doyle being part of the show's later phases – at least, not without a severe retooling – but he was a neat character, Quinn played the role with great panache, and he'll certainly be missed. In all seriousness, it certainly plucked at our heartstrings as Doyle went out.

Such a pity – and there's little way of being diplomatic about this – that nearly everything else about this episode is such crap. The Scourge come off as laughable and clichéd villains, and it's not without good reason that they're never seen again. The entire thread about the Listers' "Promised One" serves absolutely no purpose, and even the writers seem confused as hell about it. Bits of the dialogue are painfully contrived – if you didn't read spoilers about Doyle's exit, comments such as "You don't know your strength until you're tested," "You fight the good fight, whichever way you can" and more light up a frickin' beacon (no pun intended) as to what's going to happen in the final act. Honestly, we got the point. We got it.

It's all nourishing for the series, then, but in itself verges on a train wreck for most of its duration. After this, the producers will find more elegant ways of rendering their ambition, but that still leaves "Hero" as something of a blunt instrument, and simply the wrong tool for the job at hand.

THE LORE Eliminating a main character this early in the show's run inevitably generated rumors that Quinn had been summarily dismissed, but the bulk of evidence – not the least of which being Whedon's repeated interviews about this – suggests that Doyle's death was planned early on. Only the fact that quite a few scripts were intended for Doyle, then altered to include Wesley, would seem to indicate otherwise. However, it's a normal practice for new shows to comission a bushel-full of scripts at first and revise them down the road.

• Minear later went on record that Doyle's death was in play well before "The Bachelor Party": "Again, you look at the pilot and the story where Angel doesn't save the girl. You look at episode nine of a 22-episode season, and the guy who is in the main titles, the sidekick, dies... It proves anything can happen.... There was also some feeling, too, that David and Glenn's characters were very similar: They were both half human and half demon; they both had a past; they both were brooding type characters, and they were both searching for redemption." Another benefit of eliminating Doyle, according to Minear: "It made Cordelia's character more interesting." (*Fandom.com*, Aug. 14, 2000)

• Whedon went online and commented on the fan response to Doyle's passing: "A lot of people want to kill me (a little disturbing), one person wants to eat me with a spoon (less hostile, still a little disturbing) and one wants to lick me to death (very disturbing, but oddly compelling...). Yes Doyle is dead. We killed him. Sorry about that. And yes, next week Wesley will be doing a stint on the show, obviously a very different vibe than Doyle. Hope you like, cuz Alexis makes me laugh an insane amount." (*The Bronze*, Nov. 30, 1999)

• Doyle was composer Robert J. Kral's favorite character, and Kral here became something of an emotional wreck – bear in mind that he literally had to watch "Hero" dozens of times while scoring the music. (*The Bronze*, Nov. 30, 1999)

• Fury originally scripted the "commercial" that opens this story for his aborted script "Corrupt" (see 1.02, "Lonely Hearts"); it underwent revision to include Doyle.

• Sean Gunn (the butchered Lucas) happens along, sans demon make-up, as the spa guy Mars in 1.13, "She." Anthony Cistaro (Scourge Commander) voices the Ethros Demon in 1.14, "I've Got You Under My Skin."

1.10: "Parting Gifts"

"I get the impression that Doyle didn't have much by way of possessions? Seems like he gave you the most valuable thing he had."

Air Date: Dec. 14, 1999; **Writers:** David Fury, Jeannine Renshaw; **Director:** James A. Contner

SUMMARY Wracked with a vision from the Powers-That-Be, a chagrined Cordelia realizes that Doyle's vision talent passed to her during their final kiss. Meanwhile, an empath demon named Barney arrives at the agency, seeking protection from an assassin who's dogging his every move. Angel identifies the "assassin" as Wesley Wyndham-Pryce, an ex-Watcher turned rogue demon hunter, who's *not* pursuing Barney, but rather a Kungai Demon that's been carving up demons and stealing their unique body parts and attributes.

Angel and Wesley locate the Kungai, but find the creature dying and its prized tak horn missing from its head. The Kungai expires, and the heroes conclude that *Barney* has been harvesting the rare demon parts for a black-market auction. Back at the office, Barney kidnaps Cordelia, hoping to auction her seer's eyes.

Barney's auction gets underway, but Angel and Wesley interrupt the proceedings. Cordelia kills Barney with the severed tak horn, ending the auction. Afterward, Angel and Cordelia invite Wesley to stick around, and Angel cooks his friends breakfast.

THE OPENING CREDITS Despite the impediment of Doyle getting charred into nothingness last episode, Glenn Quinn logs one final appearance in the opening title sequence. The credits after the theme music, however, cite Alexis Denisof as among the guest cast – a glaring clue, to anyone familiar with *Buffy*, as to the identity of the rogue demon hunter seen in the teaser.

FIRSTS AND LASTS First appearance on *Angel* of Wesley Wyndham-Pryce – someone so instrumental to the series, it's now startling to remember that he wasn't there from the very beginning. "Parting Gifts" also marks the first time Cordelia gets a vision, and the first time viewers can glimpse Charisma Carpenter's lower back tattoo – a colorful sun – while Cordy's making the coffee. It's technically the first time that Angel and Cordelia lock lips, but it's just a shameless attempt on Cordelia's part to foist the visions off on someone else.

First mention, by Cordelia this time, that Angel drinks "O-Positive" blood. [Oh, don't get us started; see **Points of Dis-cussion** under 2.02, "Are You Now or Have You Ever Been?".] And it's the first appearance of an empath demon [which we're counting as a generic classification, not a specific demon species] a full half a season before the Host (cited as one in 5.05, "Life of the Party") enters the picture.

POINTS OF DISCUSSION ABOUT "Parting Gifts":

1. It's at this point that the production team gets fed up (not without justification) at everyone nit-picking at the number of times Angel and other vampires have been out and about in daytime settings – not standing in the hardcore sun, mind you, but in incidental sunshine. Kate's police station, for instance, probably seemed rife with secondary sunlight that should've fried Angel like a kebab. It's perhaps sobering to think that a trend among Internet posters could make the producers take notice and alter course, but that's apparently what happened here. So Angel's scripted to definitively tell Barney that vampires can run around in the daytime just fine, thank you, so long as they critically avoid direct sunlight. Thank God, or reference books such as this one would make a meal out of trying to catalog every stray ray of sun.

2. Wesley arrives on the scene, and anyone familiar with *Buffy* will observe him entering the secondary phase of his character. He's no longer got to look like a complete buffoon for benefit of making Giles look good (as was the initial point of the character), but he'll require some time to mature. Suffice to say that the bit where Wesley tapes a knife to his ankle – then fails to tear it loose and falls over – seems to epitomize the character for now. His best line here, shouted at Barney: "I am going to thrash you within an inch of your life... *and then I'm going to take that inch!*"

Oh, and a side note about Wesley's wardrobe... mid-way

through this story, he ditches his motorcycle outfit and dons a beige suit and tie. Symbolically, this helps to contrast Wesley's relative purity against Angel's darkness – or at the very least to make the distinction between Wes' academic persona and Angel's warrior profile. Tragically, however, the suit itself makes Wes look like the sort of Nazi schemer one expects to find in an *Indiana Jones* film.

CHARACTER NOTES *Angel:* Tries to undertake assignments solo after Doyle's death, unwilling to risk anyone else's neck. He speaks fluent Korean but not the Kungai language. He didn't give Wesley much thought after leaving Sunnydale. Angel keeps coffee but no creamer in his apartment.

Barney's quick to turn up at Angel Investigations [suggesting Angel's reputation is growing among underworld folk]. At one point, Angel carries a small axe [presumably the "Byzantium axe" seen in 1.08, "I Will Remember You," reused in 1.14, "I've Got You Under My Skin"]. Angel proves his culinary skills by making breakfast for Cordelia and Wesley [but see **Things that Don't Make Sense**].

• *Cordelia:* This week's information-gathering contrivance... Cordy tracks down an art piece in her vision using "ArtLocator.net." She now has no problem accepting demons as clients, and briefly becomes a kissing fiend in the hopes of passing Doyle's vision talent to someone else. She remembers Doyle as someone who drank too much, smelled weird and had the fashion sense of a Greek tragedy... but was rather sweet. She frames her sketch of her first vision, so something tangible of Doyle will remain.

Barney empathically senses – and Cordelia doesn't particularly disagree – that she feels guilt for Doyle's death, thinking she might have prevented it if she weren't so selfish. [As with 1.05, "Rm w/a Vu," she's seeing a cause-and-effect between her own character and real-world consequences.] Barney also detects that Cordelia knows she's dreadful at acting, and wears shoes she can't really afford.

Cordelia tries out for an Extra-Strength StainBeGone commercial, her first audition in weeks [her grief for Doyle, combined with her first vision interrupting the audition, means she probably doesn't get the part]. She's miserable at brewing coffee the old-fashioned, non-auto drip way [with the older equipment in Angel's apartment], and the end result is strong and, er, clumpy. Amusingly, she's still vain enough to goad the auction-goers into bidding more for her seer's eyes. [Perhaps she's just playing for time, but notice her similarly getting pissed when she only warrants a pig and a pint of liquor in 2.20, "Over the Rainbow."]

• *Wesley Wyndham-Pryce:* [See **Previously on Buffy the Vampire Slayer**.] The Watchers discharged Wesley for botching his guardianship of Buffy and Faith. He's rather inept in battle, but *can* shoot straight [consistently true in 1.12, "Expecting"; 1.16, "The Ring" and others]. He owns a Big Dog motorcycle [seen again in 2.03, "First Impressions" and 5.03, "Unleashed"], and his weapons include sai, stakes and a small knife taped to his ankle.

Wes smooches "kissing bandit" Cordelia for the second time [see *Buffy* 3.22, "Graduation Day"], and again gets nowhere. Nonetheless, the exchange [cough] makes Wes' pants tighter. Wesley can roughly translate the Kungai demon dialect. [Even so, he isn't atop his game as a former Watcher right now. He wrongly believes the Kungai committed the string of demon murders – even though the victims were eviscerated, and even though the Kungai's tak horn appears to char anyone skewered with it to ash. He'll drastically improve in future, but see next episode for his mis-diagnosis of the invitation rule.]

ORGANIZATIONS *Angel Investigations:* L.A.'s Koreatown [which Doyle visited in 1.05, "Rm w/a Vu"] is located just North of the office.

• *Wolfram and Hart:* A dark-complected, smartly dressed female attorney [who's never seen again] successfully bids for Cordelia's seer's eyes on the firm's behalf, although it's not established precisely why the firm wants them anyway. [The firm could conceivably use Cordelia's peepers to eavesdrop on the Powers' messages; 3.02, "That Vision Thing," seems to back up this theory.]

• *The Powers-That-Be:* Rather inconveniently send their first vision to Cordelia during her Extra-Strength StainBeGone audition. [Perhaps it's down to bad timing, or perhaps the Powers know Cordelia's destiny doesn't lie with her acting career, and she just fails to take the hint.]

Even by the Powers' standards, their first vision to Cordelia is maddeningly vague. [The vision features *Maiden with Urn* by Van Gieson, a sculpture located at the hotel where Barney will hold his auction. The fact that Angel, not Cordelia, can recognize the item on sight suggests a few possibilities. Perhaps Cordelia's all-too-human brain simply needs to acclimate to the visions and isn't processing images too well right now; perhaps the Powers send an image they know Angel will recognize, even if it leaves their visionary clueless; or perhaps the Powers are prophetically warning Cordelia that she's going to wind up on the auction block. This seems remarkably unhelpful, but the same snafu occurs in 2.16, "Epiphany."]

• *The Oracles:* Refuse Angel's request to roll back time again and restore Doyle to life, calling such a request "self-serving," and that it would nullify Doyle's atonement and noble death. [Personal sacrifices tend to be worth magical currency on both *Angel* and *Buffy*, and as with 1.08, "I Will Remember You," this scenario suggests the Oracles can only revert time if someone pays such a price. Angel previously qualified for a time-reversal because he surrendered his humanity, but bringing Doyle back would void his sacrifice.]

Angel appears to again offer the female Oracle a wristwatch [as with "I Will Remember You"].

DEMONOLOGY Judging by Barney's "organ harvesting" spree, some demons possess poisoned tongues, healing hands and an organ that endows telepathy. (Barney's auction also, for what it's worth, features gypsy flesh.)

• *Vampires:* An annoyed Angel refutes the notion that vampires sleep in coffins, a misconception he claims is perpetrated by an ignorant media and hack writers. [L.A.'s underworld on the whole seems smarter than this, so it's surprising that Barney might base his vampire lore knowledge off TV. Unless he *does* know the score, and he's just making small talk.]

• *Empath Demons:* Get a rush from others' feelings of terror. Barney swiftly recovers when he's kicked in the crotch. [So it's possible – sorry to dwell on this – that empath demons keep their testicles in a different place than human males.]

• *Kungai Demon:* Of Asian origin; their head-mounted "tak horn" is capable of consuming an opponent's life force. [There's no evidence that the Kungai absorbs this energy, as even a severed tak horn incinerates Barney easily enough. So it's probably a means of defense rather than nourishment.]

The Kungai seen here clings to ceilings and appears to drip yellow-green mucus. The term "Klu-[click]-ka" in the Kungai language means "caller sale" (better translated as "auction").

• *The Lotus Spa:* Korean Mineral Bath establishment that caters to demons. Angel knows Soon, a worker there.

BEST LINE Cordelia, Doyle: "I thought our kiss meant something, and instead he used that moment to pass [the visions] on to me! Why couldn't it have been mono or herpes?"

THINGS THAT DON'T MAKE SENSE It's said that the Kungai dies from getting its tak horn ripped off, not from Wesley's crossbow bolt. But as the Kungai is already missing its tak horn and therefore "dying" during its scuffle with Angel and Wesley, it's remarkable that it remains strong enough to thrash them about the room, leap out a window and run away into the night. It's also ludicrous that the Kungai apparently clings to the ceiling during Angel's entire conversation with Wesley, yet they take nearly forever to notice the damned beast. Barney likewise seems dense because he knows Angel's renowned reputation, yet seriously thinks he can kidnap Cordelia from Angel's abode without the great hero tracking him down and beating the shit out of him.

We're told over and over and *over* that seer's eyes such as Cordelia possesses are extremely rare – yet this "valuable" commodity sells at auction for a piddling $30,000, and only then with great difficulty. Hell, the bidding nearly grinds to a halt around $11,000 until Cordelia bitches the auction-goers into going higher. Even the severed tak horn sells for $20,000.

Finally, nice as it sounds that Angel's got exceptional culinary skills, we might ask when, precisely, he learned to cook. It's hard to fathom Angelus ever picking up a frying pan, or caring about much beyond human blood. Angel had no reason to cook or crave human food much during his hundred years of solitude, and he's down to eating rats in the 1990s. So unless he was cooking for the Slayer off screen (and we could make a little game out of inserting all the hidden "breakfast/lunch/dinner" scenes into *Buffy* seasons One to Three), or he's been taking cooking class in addition to "helping the helpless" since in L.A., this is damnably hard to fit on the timeline.

IT'S REALLY ABOUT... Chiefly, it's about reformatting the series to set up Cordy as the new visionary and bring Wesley into the fold. A separate message exists, however, and ironically Barney's the one who supplies it. As he notes, Doyle chose to gift – *not curse* – Cordelia with his most prized possession: the visions. It signals a shift wherein the ages-old *Spider-Man* slogan of "With great power comes great responsibility" applies to Cordy, who – as Wesley points out in 2.16, "Epiphany" – now literally can't abandon her calling.

CRITIQUE First and foremost, "Parting Gifts" is there to retool the series after Doyle's loss in "Hero," but it's a decent little romp in its own right. Or rather, it's akin to a film that Roger Ebert will invariably score higher based on sheer pacing value, while acknowledging that overall plot seems a bit befuddling and that he'd fail a test that asked him to explain what happened. Watch this story straight through, and you're likely to enjoy yourself so much, you won't see the contradictions. Try relating the action to someone else after the fact, though, and you'll realize how many cracks exist in the concrete.

No matter, though – it gets the job done whimsically enough, and more importantly, it's a beaut of an intro for Wesley. Oh, and Charisma Carpenter gets a chance to shine, which is always appreciated. The show's in a more-awkward-than-normal phase, then, but it's got a solid footing, and a knock-out punch lies around the corner with "Somnambulist."

THE LORE Denisof had been born in Quantico, Maryland, then spent a few years in Seattle, New Hampshire and Maryland again before moving to London as a teenager. He studied at the London Academy of Music and Dramatic Art and worked for the Royal Shakespeare Company. Entertainingly, his first TV job was a George Harrison video ("I've Got My Mind Set on You"), for which he was paid a princely sum of $500. He played a young man in an arcade, trying to win a fuzzy toy for a girl he'd got his eye on, but didn't actually meet Harrison. (*BBC Cult*; *IGNFilmForce*, Feb. 11, 2003)

Denisof had met Anthony Stewart Head in a production of *Rope* (1993-1994, at the Minerva Theatre, Chichester, and Wyndham's, London) that also starred John Barrowman – he's Captain Jack in the new *Doctor Who*, and the lead on the spin-off *Torchwood*. Anyone who mutually loves Whedonverse shows and *Doctor Who* is missing out if they don't google the play's publicity shots, which (when viewed from a certain mindset) feature Wesley Wyndham-Pryce and Captain Jack as two murderers, with Rupert Giles as the housemaster/impromptu sleuth trying to expose them.

• In 1998, Denisof was vacationing in L.A. and dropped by one of Head's autograph signings – at a bookstore on Sunset Boulevard – just to say hello. The meeting was fresh in Head's mind when the part of Wesley opened up, and he readily recommended Denisof for the role. After wrapping work on *Buffy* Season Three, Denisof returned to England and bizarrely played an evil American on an episode of *Randall and Hopkirk (Deceased)*. When Denisof returned to L.A., Whedon told him that they'd decided to bring Wesley onto *Angel* – they just weren't sure how or when. Denisof later said that the knowledge of what happened to Quinn's character – and the initial worry that Wesley might similarly get the chop – made him a lot more punctual and motivated him to learn his lines. "There's a lot of incentive when they start doing away with characters around you," he said. (*BBC Cult*, Aug. 22, 2001)

• Denisof suggested to Whedon that Wesley ride around downtown L.A. on a bicycle or a moped. Whedon upped the ante to a motorcycle. (*TV Guide Insider*, Jan. 16, 2001)

• Whedon jokingly posted at this point that Fury – already pulling double duty on *Buffy* and *Angel* – needed to write even more episodes. Whedon said he was less happy, however, with Fury's insistence on "wearing the little Red Riding Hood outfit" while he wrote. (*The Bronze*, Oct. 26, 1999) Fury nearly appeared in this story as one of the producers auditioning Cordy, but decided he shouldn't take the paycheck away from a working actor and begged off. (Fury, *The Bronze*, Feb. 9, 1999)

1.11: "Somnambulist"

"You were right about one thing, Angelus. The last 200 years has been about me sticking it to my father. But I've come to realize something: It's you."

Air Date: Jan. 18, 2000; **Writer:** Tim Minear; **Director:** Winrich Kolbe

SUMMARY When Angel experiences nightmares that coincide with several real-world murders – all of which display Angelus' slaughter methodology – the heroes become worried that Angel's murdering people in his sleep. However, Angel soon realizes that he's empathically witnessing the killings as committed by Penn – a vampire Angelus sired in the 1800s.

Angel learns that Penn's patterning the modern-day killings after the family members he butchered upon becoming a vampire, and consults with Kate to snare him. Kate nearly corners Penn, but a subsequent brawl allows her to discover that Angel's a vampire. Penn escapes and shifts strategies, later kidnapping Kate and hauling her into the sewers. Angel pursues and grapples with Penn, but Kate shoves a piece of wood through *both* vampires – deliberately missing Angel's heart while dusting Penn. Afterward, Kate remains shaken for her newfound knowledge of Angel's past.

THE OPENING CREDITS Denisof fully replaces Glenn Quinn in the opening credits, both as an accredited cast member and in the "heroes walking urgently forward" shot that inevitably occurs in the theme song's waning moments. (The clip shown here, and for the rest of Season One, specifically hails from 1.13, "She.")

FIRSTS AND LASTS First appearance on *Angel* of a vampire that Our Hero sired (Spike, as Angel's "grandson," doesn't count). It's also the first use, on *Angel* again, of Angel's drawing talent when he renders a picture of Penn. "Somnambulist" also marks the first occasion that Angel's friends chain him up for everyone's safety. And it's the first flashback scene in which Angelus speaks, so it's therefore David Boreanaz's first outing with his "they're after me lucky charms" Irish (if it's not insulting to Irish people to call it that) accent.

Angel easily headlocks a cross-holding Wesley during a misunderstanding, proving for the first time (again, on *Angel*) that vampires fear the cross because it burns them like a branding iron, not because it protects the bearer with a supernatural force field. On a very subtle note, Angel's recollection of Penn's slaughtered family gives the first evidence that he's got a photographic memory. And we're treated to our first excursion into an L.A. shop – in this case, the Ancient Eye bookshop that Kate peruses – specializing in texts on the supernatural. (There'll be others, see 3.14, "Couplet" and 4.14, "Release.")

POINTS OF DISCUSSION ABOUT "Somnambulist":

1. It's another Minear script, but unlike 1.06, "Sense and Sensitivity," it's seminal without really intending to be. Some of the concepts here sound like one-offs, but they'll repeatedly come into play whether the creators planned it or not.

In the first place, Minear claims that Angelus' killing technique – in this case, his marking bloody crosses on the cheeks of his victims – owed to a desire to "mock God." We'll never hear this point expressed so clearly and concisely ever again, but it sure explains a few things, such as Angelus' fetish for convents and nuns (evidenced in 2.05, "Dear Boy"). This also sounds like Minear taking his first stab at explaining where the name Angelus (and by extension "Angel") came from – something he'll elaborate on in 1.15, "The Prodigal" and 2.07, "Darla" – and even Kate reiterates that he's "a demon with the face of an angel."

Also notice that a sleeping Angel here dreams about Penn's killings as if he's committing them – a mingling of the minds that, again, is dropped like a hot potato for future episodes. Yet it could explain why vampires of the same lineage keep sensing each other's presence... Darla appears to zero in on Angel out of L.A.'s millions as if by "vampire radar" (although he can't always detect her in the same way), Drusilla knows when Angel's turned up in 2.10, "Reunion" and so forth. Angel says he dreams about Penn's activities because he "used to have a connection" with those he sired – and if vampires *do* share a residual psionic link with their "descendents," it could certainly facilitate a special awareness of one another, even if it stops well short of outright telepathy.

In this particular case, Penn's subconscious fixation with his vampire father – and more importantly his murder methodology so closely resembling Angelus' techniques – might enhance the link enough to facilitate Angel's dreams. That could explain why Angel never dreams about the activities his other "children" or "grandchildren" even when they're in town (Drusilla in Season Two; Lawson in 5.13, "Why We Fight," etc.) That's rather fortunate if correct, or we'd constantly have to witness all manner of strange/lurid dreams from Angel and Spike come Season Five.

2. Another point about vampirism... Penn definitively tells Kate that fear makes human blood taste sweeter. Thank God, because we can now rationalize so many instances where vampires playfully lollygag after their victims as opposed to just savaging them (see, for a start, 1.01, "City Of").

3. Here we're given a conflict, of sorts, in that Kate readily finds texts on Angelus in a local bookstore, yet *Buffy* 1.07, "Angel," solely conferred information of his activities through the confidential Watchers' diaries. Minear, however, took the approach that the Watchers' texts were one source among many, and posted online that the Watchers had not, in fact, pulled off a two-century cover-up of Angelus' career. He said, "It seems to me perfectly likely that other entities, not unlike the council, or former scribes like today's Whitley Strieber, wrote their own histories of people such as Angelus. He exists in this universe and one might [also] assume that some of the books Giles has on hand might be available elsewhere, yes." (Minear, *The Bronze*, Jan. 20, 1999) So there.

4. Wesley off-handedly suggests that he and Angel "raid [Penn's] icebox." It's all the more an odd statement, when you stop to consider what Penn probably keeps in his icebox. But speaking of odd statements, it's cute that when Cordelia thinks Angel has become evil again, she tells Wesley: "You stake him and I'll cut his head off." If Wesley *staked* Angel, there wouldn't exactly be a head left to sever, would there?

5. Finally, please note how Penn escapes the office by slinging a coat over his noggin and dashing out into the daytime. With Angel immobilized, it's a crying shame that Wesley is in full "klutz" mode right now, because he could've saved everyone some time and bother by simply sprinting after Penn and yanking the coat off his head.

CHARACTER NOTES *Angel:* In the late 1700s, Angelus sought to mock God and habitually "signed" his victims by carving a cross on their left cheek with a metal finger thimble ending in a point. [This suggests that Angelus – and presumably Angel too – is right-handed.] Angel claims that Angelus fed off his victims "before they could die from their fear." [A bit of hyperbole there, as otherwise healthy people don't literally die from fear *that* often.] Angel also claims to still feel Angelus' "monstrous" persona inside him [literally true, as proven by 4.14, "Release"].

Cordy says that the Powers attached the name of "Angel," not Angelus, to their latest vision. A newspaper clipping in Wesley's file on Angel dates to the Roosevelt era. [Was this Theodore or Franklin? Both were in office after Angel regained his soul, so the reading can't be all that interesting.]

• *Cordelia:* Here rehearses a sales pitch for walk-in clients. In typical Cordelia style, it's fairly intense and overwrought. Her typing skills have again improved.

More hypocrisy on Cordy's part: She criticize Wesley for bringing a stake into Angel Investigations, when the office is quite obviously stocked with them. [1.17, "Eternity," in fact, might imply that Cordy keeps a stake hidden in case Angel reverts to Angelus again. One wonders if she's rehearsed the sudden way she can open her window shades – the neat little maneuver she pulls on Penn – with Angelus in mind.]

• *Wesley:* Extensively researched Angelus' history during his time as a Watcher in Sunnydale [*Buffy* Season Three], and can recognize bits of Angelus' murder methodology on sight. He has some underground contacts, and seems fully prepared to stake a restored Angelus. Wesley here misinterprets the invitation rule on more than one level [see **Demonology**; and he's off his game as with last episode]. Wesley – bizarrely – adores Gallagher's watermelon-smashing routine.

• *Kate:* Now wearing a silver cross around her neck. [She does this before learning that vampires exist, so at first it's more for comfort than defense.] Her research educates her about the invitation rule, and she carries a small bottle of holy water [used just this one time, against Penn].

Kate's flirtatious with Angel, then wrathful upon learning he's a vampire, then winds up sparing him. No matter how distrustful their relationship gets, she never reports him for operating without a private investigator's license. Kate operates as a trained criminal profiler. [Her profile of "the Pope" – Penn's alias – is very off-target. But in all fairness to Kate, Penn doesn't exactly match the usual profiles.]

• *Penn:* Angelus sired Penn, a Puritan, as a vampire sometime in the 1700s. [There's no evidence that Penn ever met Darla, so this possibly occurred while Angelus was operating solo.] Under guidance from Angelus, Penn first killed his sister, then most of his immediate family. [Taking the flashback shots literally, Penn or Angelus – or both – must have gruesomely posed their corpses around the dinner table. The grisly tableau certainly looks like everyone just dropped from too much wine, not from being chased willy-nilly around the room by a bloodsucking vampire.] Evidently, Penn later killed his younger brother outside a drinking establishment. Penn says Angelus approved of him in ways his mortal father never did [we'll revisit this notion in 1.15, "The Prodigal"].

Penn and Angelus parted company but were scheduled to meet in Italy. Angelus failed to show up because the Romany cursed him with a soul [in 1898, according to *Buffy* 2.21, "Becoming"]. Penn waited for Angelus for a few years [or certainly past 1900], but never saw him again until now.

Kate's research indicates that Penn committed murder sprees in L.A. in October 1929 and 1963, and probably Boston in 1908. Penn rarely deviates from his killing routine, and predictably stays at the same L.A. apartment/hotel complex. He tends to look upon humanity as nothing more than food, and is surprised that Angel even knows Kate's name.

Due to Penn's "signing" a cross on his victims, the tabloids refer to him as "the Pope." He keeps a wall with taped-up newspaper clippings of his exploits, and holds modern-day music tastes. [Incidentally, it's sometimes cited as a goof that as a vampire, Penn couldn't really have assaulted school children in the daytime as his faked plan suggests. However, it's technically not an error, since the scheme doesn't fool Angel in the slightest – perhaps partly for that reason.]

Penn's comfortable with committing centuries of killing just for killing's sake. [Compare this, however, with Lawson's attitude toward virtual immortality in "Why We Fight."]

THE LIBRARY Kate researches Angelus' past using texts from the Ancient Eye Bookshop. Older newspaper clippings in Wesley's file hail from the *Los Angeles Post Herald* and the *Los Angeles Globe* [perhaps a precursor to the modern-day *Los Angeles Globe Register*].

ORGANIZATIONS *Angel Investigations:* By now, the heroes hold no delusions that they're very effective at detective work. Angel Investigations is located next to the office of Dr. Folger, a dentist [also cited in 1.22, "To Shanshu in L.A."].

DEMONOLOGY *Vampires:* In the police station, Penn moves at super-speed like the Flash. [Even allowing for super-fast reflexes, no other vampire ever demonstrates quite this amount of speed. But coupled with stories such as "Deep Down" (4.01), this serves as evidence that vampire biology contains enough variation to generate rare abilities.]

The invitation rule only applies to human abodes, not those occupied by vamps themselves. [Previously established in *Buffy* 1.07, "Angel." It's all the more curious, then, that Wesley – as an ex-Watcher – seems to misunderstand the rule entirely in his enthusiasm for battle. Wes tries dashing into Penn's hotel room and then inviting Angel inside, a futile effort for three reasons. A) Penn's a vampire, which exempts him from the invite rule, B) only an abode's resident can grant permission to enter (see *Buffy* 5.02, "Real Me"), and C) Penn's staying at a residential hotel, and the invite rule doesn't protect public accommodation (see *Buffy* 2.18, "Killed by Death," plus *Angel* 2.09, "The Trial" and 3.21, "Benediction").]

Angelus claims "there's nothing as sweet as family blood" [possibly due to the emotion of the event, or possibly because a similar genetic heritage enhances the taste].

BEST LINE Angel: "Get me a stake." An irritated Cordelia: "It's like, eight in the morning!"

THINGS THAT DON'T MAKE SENSE Central to the story is the notion that Penn's patterning his modern-day killing spree after the eighteenth century slaughter of his family. This supposedly enables Angel to deduce the age, gender and rough location of Penn's next victim, except that, um... the pattern *doesn't* match. We're plainly told that eighteenth century Penn first murdered his young sister – yet in the modern day, according to Kate, his first victim was a middle-aged male.

Yet again, and echoing 1.02, "Lonely Hearts," Kate is insanely brazen enough to try and capture a psychotic murder suspect without any back-up. The error is compounded because none of the cops surrounding Penn object to Kate going inside alone. During the same standoff, Angel never considers using the obvious strategy of impersonating Angelus long enough to drive a stake into Penn's heart – instead, Angel announces his intention to kill Penn and haphazardly brawls with him.

Once Angel has supplied Kate with a sketch of Penn, how does Kate explain to her superiors that she's miraculously acquired the killer's likeness, and by the way knows the profile of his next victim? Also, after Penn has incapacitated several police officers and abducted Kate from the police station, doesn't anyone find it strange – in the clean-up afterward – that a sharpened stake has fallen out of Kate's duffel bag? (Well, they're viewing her as peculiar anyway.) And again, you've got to wonder what lie Kate concocts to explain her "miraculous escape" from Penn, and what happened to him.

Penn claims he waited in Italy for Angelus "until the nineteenth century," but as Angelus got cursed in 1898, he actually means the *twentieth* century. (Tim Minear admitted on *alt.tv.angel* to botching the math on that one.) Even allowing that vampires' hearts are fairly easy to puncture (*Buffy* 3.19, "Choices," etc.), it seems ludicrous that Kate has enough strength to shove a piece of wood through Angel *and* Penn in one go. Never mind her astounding degree of accuracy.

Fans sometimes mention that the "newspaper clipping" which Wes produces from "today's" edition doesn't match the newspaper he allegedly took it from. Actually, it's worse than that. The newspaper that Wes has at Cordelia's desk – supposedly that morning's edition – is the same item that's yellowed and hauled out as an "older" edition archived from 1963.

POP CULTURE Wesley comments on the folly of Angel's plan with, "You'd be locked up faster than Lady Hamilton's virtue." Lady Hamilton... well, she didn't have much virtue, which is the point. She was famously the mistress of Lord Nelson, and died of alcoholism in 1815.

• Cordy to Penn: "You're him. Apt Pupil boy." That's an easy one. In the film *Apt Pupil* (1998, but originally from the Stephen King novella *Different Seasons*), a Nazi war criminal (Ian McKellan) relates his concentration camp stories to a boy down the block (Todd Bowden) and – as you'd expect – the lad helps him cover up a murder.

IN RETROSPECT Cordelia threatens to kill Angel if he ever becomes Angelus again. Which sounds strange, considering that in Season Four, Evil Cordy will facilitate the process.

IT'S REALLY ABOUT... Primarily, it's about sons seeking their fathers' approval, something that both Angel (in "The Prodigal") and Penn fail to acquire. Along those lines, it's about offspring sometimes trying to outdo than their fathers in hideous ways, given that Angel's guilty of the very atrocities that he's trying to stop Penn from committing. It's all the more ironic, then, that Angel derides Penn for sticking to a "pathetic and clichéd" murder plan for the last 200 years, yet this only serves to make Penn a more innovative killer.

CRITIQUE Sometimes fandom gets really lucky, and we're gifted with an exceptional story that (for whatever reason) nearly everyone can acknowledge is fabulous. First and foremost, "Somnambulist" succeeds because it doesn't waste time fooling around, and provides *Angel* with its sharpest and clearest sense of threat since the series began. We're into unknown territory now, and you can't entirely swear how this will end before the final act, can you?

Then there's the elegant direction, and the remarkable evolution of Kate's character, but what *really* puts it over the top is Jeremy Renner's performance as Penn. Dealing with one of Angel's offspring was probably unavoidable, and Penn's so damn charismatic, ruthless and devious that if he'd survived – and with some retooling, of course – he could've easily become a season-long adversary. As it stands, he's still among the most distinct *Angel* foes, even though he's in a single story. We'll see more of Angel's "offspring" in future (in "Why We Fight," and arguably "Heartthrob"), but they're mere shadows compared to this guy.

So once the dust clears, we've left with what's almost undeniably the strongest Season One story, and something to celebrate. Even better, it's an early taste of the muscle Tim Minear will display later in the show, filled with choice bits such as Cordelia giving her sales pitch to a potential client... then the camera revealing she's blindly chatting up the very serial killer everyone's looking for. Even now, years after its first broadcast, "Somnambulist" sends a shiver up the spine.

THE LORE This story was originally titled "The Killer I Created," but Minear shifted gears when the plot got leaked onto the Internet. He took to the *Buffy* message board and – purely to throw people off the scent – proclaimed that his next *Angel* episode was entitled "Somnambulist." He added that it was about dreams and possibly the horrible things one does in one's sleep – all technically true, but enough to cause the intended confusion. (*Fandom.com*, Aug. 14, 2000)

• Minear wrote this episode before "Sense and Sensitivity," so it initially included Doyle. Nearly every scene with him got scrapped after his demise, as Minear felt Wesley deserved better treatment than just parroting his predecessor's lines. Tellingly, the "Doyle" version didn't include the scene where Wesley enters with a stake, motivated by information procured from his time as a Watcher. However, Minear carried over the "Lady Hamilton's virtue" line from character to character. (*alt.tv.angel*, Jan. 21, 2000) The final rooftop scene was also somewhat salvaged, but rewritten with Cordy in Doyle's place.

• A scene in "Room w/a Vu" (1.05) entailed Kate commenting on Angel's singular name, adding that such people are usually popes or rock stars, not private investigators. Angel's response – "You got me. I'm a Pope." – unintentionally parallels the name the tabloids here attribute to Penn. (*Fandom.com*, Aug. 14, 2000).

1.12: "Expecting"

"Once your little one comes out, which will probably be in no time, you'll feel a lot better."

Air Date: Jan. 25, 2000; **Writer:** Howard Gordon; **Director:** David Semel

SUMMARY Cordelia takes matters with her new beau, fashion photographer Wilson Christopher, to the next level and enjoys a night of passion with him. Unfortunately, Cordy awakes the next morning to find Wilson gone – and to find that she's the equivalent of eight months pregnant.

Angel and Wesley discover that Cordelia's girlfriends Serena and Emily are similarly big with child, and that Wilson and his hotshot friends are surrogate fathers to a towering Haxil demon. With the Haxil gestating its spawn through a psychic umbilical cord, Cordelia and her friends will come to term in hours.

The Haxil's psychic influence compels the women to travel to a nearby factory and sit in a tank of vile-smelling goo, readying for the births. Angel and Wesley drench the Haxil papa in liquid nitrogen, freezing the monster to pieces. The demon offspring immediately die upon the father's demise, returning Cordy and her friends to normal. For an encore, an enraged Cordelia swings a large pulley and shatters the Haxil to pieces.

FIRSTS AND LASTS Wesley first displays a love of weaponry by showing off his "new" Bavarian fighting adze, and we're told about Cordelia's similar fetish for magazines. More obviously, it's the first mystical pregnancy on *Angel*...

POINT OF DISCUSSION ABOUT "Expecting":

1. It's a well-known point that this story serves as a precursor to Cordelia's far more elaborate childbearing in Season Four. If you stop to tally the entire series, though, you come to the surprising discovery that mystical pregnancies on *Angel* literally occur on an annual basis.

Stop and count the young'uns... there's Cordelia in this story; the unnamed mother in 2.01, "Judgment"; Darla in early Season Three; Cordelia again through much of Season Four and finally Amanda in 5.19, "Time Bomb." In the producers' defense, they didn't plan it this way. Carpenter's real-life pregnancy tipped their hand in Season Four, Darla getting knocked up seemed too good an opportunity after 2.15, "Reprise," and the rest were just incidental one-offs.

It begs the question, though, of why such pregnancies never occurred on the adolescent-flavored *Buffy*. Teenage pregnancy presents itself as a valid topic of discussion, but it'd likely prove rather traumatizing to watch a minor experience it on screen – especially if there's demon-births involved (and on *Buffy*, you know there would be). It's a delicate topic far better suited to the more adult-orientated *Angel*. And strangely enough, once *Buffy* hit its "adult" phase in Seasons Six and Seven, no riveting need to address the topic existed, what with magical childbirths piling up on *Angel* like cordwood. Besides, Buffy's forced to act as mother *and* sister to Dawn later in the show, and maybe that was enough.

CHARACTER NOTES *Angel:* Tells Cordelia that he doesn't hum [Angelus did in *Buffy* 2.18, "Killed by Death," but let's cut Angel some slack – he was evil at the time]. Angel now considers Cordelia family, but she worries he'll give her date (Wilson) the third degree [fair enough, given Angel's attempts to grill her suitor, in 1.07, "The Bachelor Party"].

Angel is befuddled by the office coffee-maker filter.

• *Cordelia:* [A cross examination of *Buffy* stories such as 2.12, "Bad Eggs" and 3.13, "The Zeppo" indicates that Cordelia never went the distance with Xander Harris, but there's no suggestion that she's a virgin before her "big night" with Wilson. So she probably *did* sleep with one of the drooling athletic hunks who lusted after her.]

Wilson makes Cordelia feel at home in L.A. for the first time. She says she's the producer's first choice for a "Max Cracks" crackers commercial [but there's no evidence that she ever gets the part]. Cordelia's abysmal filing method includes trying to put the "Mrs. Benson" folder under "F" because she's French, but the file somehow winding up under "P."

• *Wesley:* Fails to capitalize on Serena saying that his "Hugh Grant" image is "working for her," and his social bumbling convinces Cordy's friends that he and Angel are gay. In part, this owes to Wesley mistaking Cordy's date for Wilson Christopher, an ethno-archeologist from Brandeis.

Wesley's immensely fond of Cordelia, but airs concerns to Angel that Cordelia's not focusing on her job properly. Yet Wes steadfastly befriends Cordy during her ordeal, and tears up to hear Cordy's heartfelt thanks. [Wes gets similarly misty-eyed when Angel hires him next episode, which means that if you're watching these stories back-to back, Wes cries twice in the space of about five minutes.]

Wesley says he's been patrolling [almost Slayer-style] and obviously has the social life of a potted plant. Angel and Cordelia decline his gripping challenge to engage in a 3-D word puzzle. He finds demon slaying "bracing," the sad fool. He's heard of procrea-parasitic demons [see **Demonology**], but hasn't previously encountered one. As with 1.10, "Parting Gifts," Wes can shoot straight if accorded the opportunity.

• *Phantom Dennis:* Keeps the lights up in the apartment and plays a polka on the stereo, hoping to sour Cordy and Wilson's romantic mood. [Perhaps this owes to jealousy, but perhaps Dennis, as a spook, detects something supernaturally amiss about Wilson. If so, that puts him ahead of Angel, who for once doesn't sense anything odd. See "Five by Five" (1.18).] Cordelia makes Dennis behave by threatening to play *Evita* – "the one with Madonna" – around the clock.

THE LIBRARY Wesley identifies the Haxil demon from a sixteenth century rendering of the species. He claims that engravers of that period tended to exaggerate. [Given the Haxil's features, he must say this only for Cordy's benefit.]

ORGANIZATIONS *Angel Investigations:* "Mrs. Benson" is a troublesome French client who nearly drove Angel to drink.

• *The Powers-That-Be:* Conspicuously fail to send Cordelia a warning that she's about to become knocked up with demon spawn. [As ever, it's unclear how much the Powers know, and to what degree they can send messages. Even whey they do warn their visionary, their timing sucks: see 2.16, "Epiphany."]

DEMONOLOGY *Vampires:* Their eyes, as Angel implies, are sensitive to light.

• *Procrea-parasitic demons:* Include several demon species (Haxils being one of them) who reproduce by planting their seed inside a human woman. The few mothers who survive generally wish they hadn't.

• *Haxil demon (a.k.a. "Haxil beast"):* Towering inner earth demons who grant their male followers fame and money if they'll act as carriers for the Haxil's life force. [The Haxil must grant the males success up-front, because it's crucial – certainly in money/fame-worshipping L.A. – to helping them poach mates. Also, the Haxil essence must override modern birth control techniques, as Cordy comments that her liaison with Wilson was "really safe."] The Haxil seen here speaks remarkably good English.

Haxil-inseminated women come to term in less than 24 hours. [Cordelia is diagnosed as carrying seven Haxil spawn, and if that's near standard, the half-dozen pregnant women seen here could've birthed a clutch of 42 young if not more. As Haxils are towering monsters that've entirely escaped the public's attention, it seems likely (as with the giant mantis creature in *Buffy* 1.04, "Teacher's Pet") that there's a frightfully high infant morality rate in play. Perhaps the Haxil young kill each other off until one achieves dominance.]

The mothers' amniotic fluid becomes acidic enough, when removed, to eat through syringes and even the floor. [The acid doesn't harm the mothers, however, which is understandable. The young could hardly come to term if the mothers got holed like Swiss cheese beforehand.]

Haxils use a "telepathic umbilical chord" to nourish the fetuses and psionically influence the mothers, who gain a voracious appetite and – as Cordy proves – will even drink [pig's] blood. The women hone in on the Haxil "birthing shrine," a vat filled with green goo. [Wilson's group makes such a shrine at Millikan Industrial Park in Reseda, but it's unclear if it's required to summon the Haxil in the first place. The boys apparently stocked the shrine with the prerequisite white robes for the impending mothers to wear in the ooze.]

Impending Haxil mothers become sensitive to light and seem to gain some vestige of super-strength [as Cordy, even in her ballooned state, clobbers Wesley unconscious easily enough]. Haxil demons prove vulnerable to liquid nitrogen, but they're immune to fire and decapitation.

BEST LINE Angel, watching a voracious Cordelia sloppily downing his pig's blood: "I don't think I ever realized just how disgusting that was."

THINGS THAT DON'T MAKE SENSE Cordelia follows the strange TV rule that characters who indulge in what's obviously full-on, sweaty naked sex in their own bedroom miraculously wake up the next morning wearing their day clothes. As with the spell-caster Lloyd (see 1.06, "Sense and Sensitivity"), we're left to wonder what if any punishment Angel ever metes out to Wilson's crew – they're all human and therefore don't qualify for getting disemboweled, but can hardly be prosecuted for inseminating women with demon sperm. They probably revert to "loser status" upon losing their demon patron, but that hardly seems like punishment enough.

There are six pregnant women at the Haxil birthing pit, but only four men in Wilson's gang. (Let your imaginations run wild.) Finally, Angel shows amazement at Cordelia's lousy filing skills. But as there's continually a drought of clients, how much filing presently exists to *get* confusing?

IT'S REALLY ABOUT... Women going into denial about unwanted pregnancies, then coming to view their offspring as something demonic, then finally (though sheer hormones, if nothing else) developing a sort of motherly love.

Predictably, the self-serving fathers vanish from the scene, leaving the mothers-to-be to handle the horror of the gestation. Yes, that's arguably the pessimist's view, but "Expecting" isn't exactly geared to render the final birth as something laudable.

Arguably, the story's greatest insight occurs when a ballooning Cordelia comments, "Oh, God, I'm being punished." By now it's almost a staple of the *Buffy*-verse that – for better or worse – females will blame themselves whenever a romantic encounter goes sour. For instance, notice Buffy's confusion over Angel's conversion into Angelus (*Buffy* 2.14, "Innocence"), or Buffy sleeping with Parker, an obvious cad, and later thinking that *she's* done something wrong (*Buffy* 4.03, "The Harsh Light of Day"). All of that taken into account, it's particularly stirring when Wesley – with all the tenderness that Denisof can bestow on the moment – refuses to pass judgment on Cordy and insists she's not being punished. It's similarly heart-warming when Phantom Dennis gives Cordy tissues and pulls up her covers.

CRITIQUE Well, this is a weird one. You can generally pull a few high points out of an otherwise so-so *Angel* story, and the redeeming graces here include: A) The metaphor of an unexpected pregnancy being decently well thought-out, and B) The bits with Angel, Wesley and Cordelia acting as a family unit really striking home. It sounds sappy to say it, but it's true. Boreanaz, Carpenter and Denisof all prove they're capable of adding a few points to an otherwise stale script, and at times the story becomes quite really touching.

Unfortunately, a fair amount of it feels like the generic sci-fi schlock you'd expect from other shows. It probably doesn't help that the show will so heavily mine the "pregnancy" angle in later seasons, making "Expecting" look worse because it's been endlessly copied. Trying to look at this story in a vacuum, though... the implementation drags in points, there are very few surprises, and one gets the sinking feeling that whatever Howard Gordon's resume, he never – unlike, Whedon, Minear or Greenwalt – had a unique vision for *Angel*. (We'll revisit this in 1.16, "The Ring," also by Gordon.)

It's more workable than you'd think, then, but despite the cast's best efforts, it would take a special talent to craft a "woman births demonspawn" story that *didn't* include loads of horror clichés – and this certainly isn't it.

THE LORE Here's Whedon, getting cheeky on the Internet again: "But... on subjects other than my sensitive, noble and politically motivated commitment to hot girl-on-girl action, I've heard some grumblings about all the pre-marital sex on [*Angel*]. Personally, I don't see the problem. I believe that POST-marital sex is a sin (something [my wife] Kai's getting angrier and angrier about – what's her problem?)." (*The Bronze*, May 4, 2000)

• Ken Marino (Wilson) went on to play sleazy P.I. Vinnie Van Lowe on *Veronica Mars*. Daphne Duplaix (Sarina) was Playboy's Playmate of the Month in July 1997, and appeared with Nicholas Brendon in *Piñata: Survival Island* (2002). Ken Marino (Wilson) held a recurring role on *Dawson's Creek* as Professor David Wilder.

1.13: "She"

"We marry who they command, we serve without questioning. We leave behind dreaming."

Air Date: Feb. 8, 2000; **Writer:** Marti Noxon; **Writer/Director:** David Greenwalt

SUMMARY At the Powers' request, Angel looks into reports of incinerated corpses turning up across L.A. Result: Angel stumbles into a conflict between a lithe female warrior Jhiera and a pack of male warriors – the Vigories of Oden Tal – who're pursuing her.

Jhiera hails from an intensely patriarchal dimension, where the males subjugate females by plucking out their "Ko" – a spine ridge that's the embodiment of the women's personality and sexuality, thus making the females totally submissive. Jhiera, a renegade member of a royal family, has been smuggling Ko-endowed females to our reality via dimensional portals.

The Vigories attempt to round up Jhiera and three of her charges, but Angel and his allies side with the fugitives. With the Vigories forced to retreat, Jhiera shuttles her three wards to a safe location. Afterward, Angel realizes that Jhiera or her girls caused the incinerated corpses – either by accident or design – and warns Jhiera to better respect innocents in either dimension.

FIRSTS AND LASTS It's the first proof, on *Angel* anyway, that other dimensions exist (*Buffy* established the point first, particularly in 3.01, "Anne"). Along those lines, it's the first use of dimensional portals, a means of transport that'll become vitally important to the series' next three years. (With that in mind, Cordelia's declaration of "Portals? There are portals, now? When did they put in portals?" seems especially apt.)

Wesley becomes a full-fledged staff member of Angel Investigations, and there's the first hint that Wes can hold his own in a fight, even though he still gets smacked around and the Vigories take him hostage.

POINTS OF DISCUSSION ABOUT "She":

1. Say what you will about this story, it provides the unbelievable spectacle of Angel and Wesley dancing (but not

together, that is) at Cordelia's apartment party. Or rather, Angel *imagines* himself dancing, and it's just about the funniest thing imaginable. Let's give Boreanaz some applause here, because dancing that badly on purpose is quite the challenge. (Watch especially the bit where Angel gaily claps his hands together – what the hell is the fool doing?) And given that Wesley actually puts himself out there, is it a stretch to claim that he goes home alone?

2. Fandom loves to embrace the notion that Angel can't work his cell phone – confirmed in interviews with writers such as Minear – and "She" proves something of a test case for this. An on-the-run Angel experiences no end of trouble while trying to phone Cordelia, and he declares that "a bored warlock" created cell phones in the first place, even as Cordy comes to wonder how someone trained to wield an ancient Scythian short bow can't work his bloody cell phone properly. All of which is fair enough, except...

Except that the jape overshadows how many times Angel uses his cell phone properly. In truth, he uses it just fine in "Sense and Sensitivity" (1.06), "The Prodigal" (1.15) and "Blind Date" (1.21) – and that's just in Season One. He forgets to use his cell in "War Zone" (1.20) but that's almost deliberate and perfectly in keeping with his stubborn desire to punch his way out of trouble. Even in "She," Angel's worst sin lies in his forgetting to charge his cell (hands up everyone who's *never* done that). And as Cordy herself suggests, the poor reception probably owes to Angel going through a canyon – well, there's L.A. for you. It happens.

Granted, Angel hates cell phones, but he's hardly alone in that. And true enough, Angel certainly makes an easy target because of his cell phone snafus... but let's not pretend that it's as all-pervasive a failing as some people think.

CHARACTER NOTES *Angel:* It's implied that Angelus inspired "Le Vampyr" (1857) by French poet Charles Pierre Baudelaire (1821-1867). The two men presumably met in person; Angel recalls Baudelaire as being "a little taller and a lot drunker" than his rendering in the painting *La Musique Aux Tuileries* (1862) by Edouard Manet (1832-1883). Angel knows much about this piece [but it's unclear exactly how much he knows about art from this period].

Cordelia claims that Angel sucked the energy from her party like a black hole. Angel casually agrees with Jhiera's assessment that the Romany cursed him "to help people." [Blatantly untrue, as *Buffy* Season Two says the curse was designed to make him suffer above all other considerations.] Angel drinks beer and now carries *two* grappling hooks.

• *Cordelia:* Miraculously knows enough people in L.A. to throw a proper party. Her friends include the playful Laura and Diego, who drops his pants at such functions. Her neighbor Steve Paymer [mentioned in 1.05, "Rm w/a Vu"] also attends, albeit off screen. Cordelia's happy when Angel officially hires Wesley, but only if it doesn't mean a pay cut for her [see 2.04, "Untouched" for her opinion on adding Gunn to the staff]. Cordy offers Angel some blood at the party [which implies she keeps some about the place for his benefit, or she's a very thoughtful hostess].

• *Wesley:* Now broke and prone to poaching party food, showing a particular love for mini-reubens and shrimp puffs. [A cash-strapped Cordelia similarly bagged party snacks in 1.01, "City Of"; funny how many newcomers to L.A. have to forage like this.] Wesley magnificently falls to pieces when a nice, young brunette hits on him, apparently liking his [highly questionable] choice of sweaters. Here Wesley shows distinct signs of kissing up to Angel [probably because he all-too-vividly remembers the Watcher's Council sacking him]. He's apparently heard of dimensional portals before now.

• *Phantom Dennis:* Appears friendly toward Angel.

• *Jhiera:* Her family [the male members of her family, that is] rules the Oden Tal homeland. [Indeed, her facial markings might denote her as royalty, since none of her female charges bear such decoration.] Jhiera's father promised happiness for "all" his subjects, but Jhiera denounced his patriarchal rule and fled to Earth. She literally spent a few months on ice, learning to control her Ko's heat. Her family claims she's dead, but she's become a heroic figure among females of her race.

Jhiera, a swift and agile combatant, can generate heat blasts to make people combust, physically repel them or render them unconscious. [She evidently needs her hands to direct the blasts, as she seems helpless when grabbed from behind.] She's somewhat familiar with human customs and vampire characteristics, and is currently based at the Palm Ridge Spa.

THE LIBRARY Wesley's books help to identify the Vigories [so Earth texts sometimes detail beings from extra-dimensional realms, as we'll further see in 3.20, "A New World"].

ORGANIZATIONS *Angel Investigations:* The office evidently lacks a coffee grinder, but holds maps to the sewer access points in L.A. Angel doesn't offer his employees a dental plan. (Wesley's response: "Right, well... I'll floss.")

• *The Powers-That-Be:* Cordelia says she "feels" the visions in addition to witnessing them.

DEMONOLOGY *The Vigories of Oden Tal:* [First off, it's never established that the Vigories are demonic. Cordelia loosely calls them that, and Jhiera herself looks of Asian descent. Taking the standard *Angel* and *Buffy*-verse rules into account, this either owes to parallel development (a suspect notion), or to demons/demon hybrids of Asian origin fleeing Earth and seeding Oden Tal. The lore of the Old Ones mentions an exodus from Earth to other realms, and for more along these lines, check out 2.20, "Over the Rainbow."

[In all likelihood, though, Jhiera and the Vigories are half-breeds. They're not totally averse to morality – as with vampires – so they've probably got souls and the consciences those entail. Also, the Vigories phyically look very human, so they probably possess a high percentage of human blood, even if their demon side grants them super-abilities.]

The term "Vigories" apparently refers to the males of the species. A ridge on the females' backs contains their "Ko": the embodiment of their personality and sexual desire. Clipping/plucking out such ridges kills the women's will-power and much of their persona. "Pacified" females lack names. The Ko produces a fever heat as it matures; Jhiera's charages must lie in piles of ice for a number of months, and smolder their way through two tons of ice per week. [That conjures the image of a mountain of ice, but it's about the same volume as a single bed.] The Ko's aphrodisiac effect also works on vampires.

The Vigories are herbivores, eating a thick stew made from rotting plants and flowers, and consume half their body weight per day. They're similar in description to Kovitch demons from the Caucuses. [And despite the Vigories viewing Jhiera's movement as a threat to the fabric of their entire society, we never hear from them again.]

MAGIC *Inter-Dimensional Portals:* Appear as your standard energy vortex with lots of wind. The Vigories need the "proper coordinates to align" [not a condition of portal-opening in future] before they can open a portal for a limited duration.

BEST LINE Cordelia, after a vision shows a man combusting horribly: "All I felt was his fear. And the exploding eyeballs."

THINGS THAT DON'T MAKE SENSE Jhiera hails from a society in which men literally enslave their females, mutilate their bodies and neuter their personalities. So unless there's more moderation in Oden Tal than we're led to believe, it's hard to fathom why Jhiera would trust anyone of the male gender an inch. Yet she's got all sorts of male accomplices even before Angel comes into the picture. Perhaps she views the male bodyguards she hires as disposable, but her faith in Mars – the guy who hides her girls at his health spa (and who's only named in the script) – seems a bit baffling. And why don't Jhiera's pheromones make Mars irrational? (Perhaps Jhiera's Ko just doesn't peg him as a "desirable mate.")

Wes and Cordy successfully get Jhiera's girls out of the besieged health spa and into a getaway truck, which is all well and fine. But instead of simply driving away, they then leave the girls defenseless and run back into the fray, unarmed, thus allowing the Vigories to take them hostage. Just what the hell were they thinking? And if Jhiera's fugitive girls are burning with such intense heat, how can Wes and Cordelia touch them without flinching? Are they wearing invisible oven mitts? Also, L.A. is presumably home to quite a few companies that sell compost, so it's remarkably lucky that Wes and Cordy find the one that serves as the Vigories' headquarters so quickly.

Angel's cell phone says "Low Battery," yet the battery icon appears to show the phone as fully charged. Jhiera's few months on Earth, presumably spent lying feverish in a tub of ice or coordinating her underground movement, have made her so phenomenally educated about human culture that she even understands talk of gypsy curses. At the art museum, Angel takes off his trenchcoat before he has any suspicion that the museum guards are looking for someone of his description. It's night when Angel, Wes and Cordelia arrive at the health spa, yet there's sunlight visible in the spa room, and the drawn blinds are lit as if keeping out the sun of day.

POP CULTURE Cordelia to Angel on Jhiera's burning ability: "Did she *Carrie* you?" In Stephen King's *Carrie* (1976), a tormented high school student telekinetically massacres virtually everyone at her prom, psionically triggering a blaze in the school gym and her home. (Although Cordy really shouldn't expect Angel to get a reference like *that*.)

• Wesley claims that Nancy's Petticoat flowers are named for novelist/biographer Nancy Mitford (1904-1973). True, but strangely enough, Nancy isn't as interesting as some of her siblings. Two of her sisters – Diana Mosley and Unity Valkyrie Mitford – were known associates of Hitler, and British intelligence viewed Unity as "more Nazi than the Nazis." She shot herself in the head in 1939 when Britain declared war on Germany, but didn't die from the wound until 1948.

IT'S REALLY ABOUT... It's mostly about misogyny, but in all honesty, the message never gets much more complex than "Misogyny is a bad, bad thing." As the Vigories don't really equate with real-world males, it's hard to delve much deeper than that. (The previous story, "Expecting," wasn't great, but at least it convincingly made Wilson and friends emblematic of hotshots who knock up their girlfriends and pull a runner.)

"She" potentially could've entailed the notion of "female empowerment" – *the* greatest theme of *Buffy* – but Jhiera's a remarkably poor vehicle for such an admirable message. She's rather bigoted in a different fashion – i.e. she's perfectly happy to mow down innocent humans while protecting her girls, as if the fact that humans comparatively have more freedom justifies killing them. Indeed, when it comes to genuine "female empowerment," Jhiera weirdly plays second fiddle to Laura, the assertive partygoer who's got a Master's degree and runs her own sandwich cart business.

THE CLOSING CREDITS Interspersed with music from Cordelia's party, and nutty shots of Wes and Angel "dancing."

CRITIQUE The optimist in us revels in this story's riotous Angel/Wesley dancing scene, and loves the cute little bit where Angel becomes an impromptu tour guide. But even the optimistic view – with much regret – must acknowledge that almost everything else about this story is simply dire.

For better or worse, it painfully looks and feels as if the script writers don't know what the hell they're trying to say. They're trying to set up a gender conflict that's coated in ambiguity, but the supporting characters are so cardboard and the plot details so lame, it's hard to give a flying fig about most of it. Jhiera in particular is tragically mis-written – we're presumably supposed to root for her, but it's hard to cheer for a shallow bimbo of a character who's amoral enough to not really care if innocents get diced in the crossfire, so long as *her* innocents don't wind up threshed like wheat. It's tempting to blame Marti Noxon for this, as she similarly botched some misogyny themes when she was show-runner of *Buffy* Season Six, but that's possibly unfair, and the real fault could easily lie with Greenwalt – or any Mutant Enemy member who didn't realize that this story was plunging off a cliff.

In short, little about this episode rings true or makes sense, and its main selling point is a hot Asian chick whose costume shows off her cleavage. That sort of vapid sci-fi nonsense might be good enough for other series, but *Angel* deserves better. Watch the teaser alone, because it's really quite funny, then skip to the next story.

THE LORE Minear originally crafted Angel's little "dance" for "Sense and Sensitivity" (1.06). The original concept had the hyper-emotional Angel saying something along the lines of "I feel so deeply now, the only way I can express myself is through interpretive dance," then dancing a little jig. Whedon deemed it a bit much, however, and the scene got recast here to better render Angel – according to Minear – "as a complete social retard." (*Fandom.com*, Aug. 14, 2000)

• Bai Ling (Jhiera) gained a bit of notoriety as Senator Bana Breemu in *Star Wars: Revenge of the Sith* – her actual lines wound up on the cutting room floor, but were included in the DVDs. Still, even that bit part landed her on cover of *Playboy* (June 2005), where she's scantily clad and holding a lightsaber. *People* magazine named her as one of the "50 Most Beautiful People in the World" in 1998, and she later appeared as the "Mysterious Woman" in *Sky Captain and the World of Tomorrow*. Less commendably, she appeared in the VH1 show *But Can They Sing?*. You can pretty much guess the results from the title.

1.14: "I've Got You Under My Skin"

"So someone in the family's got a squatter in their head."

Air Date: Feb. 15, 2000; **Story:** David Greenwalt; **Story/Script:** Jeannine Renshaw; **Director:** Robert David Pryce

SUMMARY At the Powers' direction, Angel and his allies investigate a family named the Andersons – one of whom is possessed by an Ethros demon. Angel ingratiates himself to the family and shows up with brownies laced with psylis eucalipsis powder, a substance that exposes Ryan, the young son, as the demon's host.

Angel and Wesley perform an exorcism and expel the Ethros, then corner the creature in some nearby sea caves. But surprisingly, the demon claims that Ryan was born without a soul or conscience, meaning the demon was *trapped* inside him, longing for death. Angel kills the Ethros just as the callous Ryan douses his sister's room with gasoline and sets it alight. The heroes save the family, with social services taking Ryan into custody.

FIRSTS AND LASTS First evidence of Wesley's abusive childhood, a sub-plot that'll simmer for nearly four years and culminate in 5.07, "Lineage." Also, when Ryan telekinetically makes Wesley stab a cross into his own neck, it's the first of two throat wounds that Wes will endure this season. (Faith gives him the other in 1.18, "Five by Five,"; with hindsight, both injuries are small potatoes compared to the throat wound that awaits Wes in 3.16, "Sleep Tight.")

POINTS OF DISCUSSION ABOUT "I've Got You Under My Skin":

1. Right... let's immediately address a common misconception about this story. Some sources claim it's a goof when Angel hands Wesley a Bible, but Angel doesn't smoke from touching the Holy text. As if to drive home the potential blunder, a Bible burns Angel in "Are You Now or Have You Ever Been?" (2.02). Fine, except that... the book Angel here hands Wes *isn't* a Bible.

Setting aside that the book isn't marked anything so obvious as "Holy Bible," the text that Wesley reads from it isn't Biblical. Rather, it's part of a Catholic exorcism ritual – you occasionally find this printed in Bibles, but it's more frequently included in separate texts. The Catholic Church, in fact, often refrains from printing such rituals in Bibles, and officially discourages laymen from practicing exorcisms. All of that said, the fact that the Catholic exorcism *actually works* adds fuel to the **Why Do Catholic Objects Harm Vampires?** essay.

2. It's long been the case on *Angel* and *Buffy* that a being's conscience is dependent on their possessing a soul. But now we're presented with Ryan, who's uniquely tailored as a soulless human. Without further evidence, we've got to rule Ryan as a freak of nature – mind, this sort of "natural soul variation" among humankind opens up all sorts of possibilities that the show never seeks to explore. For instance, by extension, it might explain why certain people (certainly Amy in *Buffy* 1.03, "Witch," and to some degree Willow) seem almost genetically predisposed to wield magic. Hell, it might even explain the presence of "mutants" (debatably starting with 1.04, "I Fall to Pieces") who are super-powered without any obvious demonic help. You don't have to own good genes to indulge in the supernatural in this world, but it helps.

3. *Angel* episodes don't display their titles, but really, the very name of this story gives the game away in the DVD set: "I've Got You Under My Skin" doesn't conjure forth many possibilities, with exorcism being the obvious candidate. Anyone still uncertain about this will note the episode DVD menu, which both displays the title and demon-Ryan's sneering mug.

CHARACTER NOTES *Angel:* Has lingering guilt regarding Doyle's death [1.09, "Hero"], and mistakenly refers to Wesley by Doyle's name. Angel feels pleased that Wesley seems resolute enough, if necessary, to kill him [he expresses similar sentiments to Gunn in 3.03, "That Old Gang of Mine"]. Angel declines to eat Cordelia's brownies because, Cordy says, he's yet to "branch out into the solids." [Yet he eats dinner with the Andersons, off screen, and skillfully made breakfast in 1.10, "Parting Gifts"; again, it's not that vampires can't eat human food, it's just that they require blood to live.]

Angel doesn't mind other people smoking [see 2.02, "Are You Now or Have You Ever Been?"] and seems at ease with children. He uses the pseudonym "Angel Jones," and indicates that "beings" akin to angels watch over people. He's heard of, but never seen before now, the Mark of Kekfadlorem [see **Demonology**].

• *Cordelia:* Cooks nut-filled brownies, which Wesley claims reek like a barnyard. Cordy improvised from a recipe from her mother's [former] housekeeper. Cordy's improved at supernatural research, finding information about Ethros Boxes.

• *Wesley:* Ryan telepathically skims Wesley's mind, and charges [correctly] that Wes longs for his father's approval, and spent many hours as a child locked up under the stairs. Wesley off-handedly says, "A father doesn't have to be possessed to terrorize his children." [All of this suggests prolonged emotional (although not physical) abuse. 2.04, "Untouched" drops further hints along these lines.] Wes also doesn't challenge Ryan's claim that he's more afraid of Angel [or rather Angelus] than the Ethros demon.

Wesley doesn't know that Kek demons went extinct, and he's never attempted an exorcism before. He never lets on if Angel calling him "Doyle" bothers him. Cordelia insinuates that Wesley wears too much cologne.

He possesses no resistance to salesmen, and owns two Thighmasters – the second having been a gift with his "Buns of Steel."

• *Kate:* Back to displaying some regard for Angel [after 1.11, "Somnambulist," but see next episode].

• *Ryan Anderson:* The Ethros-hosting Ryan can mimic voices, display telekinesis and telepathically read people's anxieties. [Ryan's unique status as a soulless human must enable him to tap the Ethros' abilities, since he doesn't possess them otherwise.] The Ethros within Ryan can only move a few marbles about the place, but can seize limited control of his body while the boy sleeps. The demon fears the void within Ryan more than dying.

• *Lizzie Borden:* Historical figure whose killings, Wesley claims, were due to an adolescent Ethros demon possessing her. [On August 4, 1892, in Fair River, MA, Lizzie allegedly did in her father and stepmother with her father's hatchet. She was later acquitted on all charges after a 13-day trial. Wesley mentions Lizzie in a different context in 4.17, "Inside Out."]

ORGANIZATIONS *Angel Investigations:* We're finally given a proper view of the poster/print that's hanging in Angel's office, and it looks like an advertisement for Canadian Pacific Steamships, a company that supplies travel to the Orient.

THE LIBRARY Books in Angel's apartment have information about Ethros demons, plus directions/chants for exorcisms.

DEMONOLOGY *Vampires:* Angel proves that vampires can freely, if uncomfortably, enter churches [previously the case in *Buffy* 2.10, "What's My Line?"]. However, he displays dread upon seeing a large Christian cross. [It's possible that Angel gets uncomfortable because Angelus made such a habit of mocking God (1.11, "Somnambulist"), but it's more likely that vampires reflexively fear the cross because it can harm them.] Angel comments that he's "not a big bleeder." [That makes sense, presuming vampires contain less blood than your average human, but see 2.01, "Judgment."]

• *Ethros Demons:* The word "Ethros" denotes both the

species and the individual seen here. Ethros-possessed humans typically cause mass murder, and the one seen here claims he's corrupted "tens of thousands." It's suggested that Ethros demons must host themselves in warm bodies; vampires aren't suitable [as with 1.02, "Lonely Hearts," then]. Exorcised Ethros demons can manifest – thoughtfully with some clothing, too – by absorbing elements from a damp locale, preferably near primordial volcanic basalt.

• *"Plakticine":* A harmless but luminescent green substance, excreted by Ethros demons. [This raises an icky possibility, as Wesley finds Plakticine "all around the foundation" of the Anderson house. Did the stuff just magically manifest, or was Ryan crapping the stuff out while sleepwalking?]

• *Kek Demons:* Wesley here gives Angel a knife with the Mark of Kekfadlorem – the only thing that can kill a Kek demon. Angel points out that Kek demons went extinct, leaving Wes to hope one exists in hibernation.

MAGIC "Not many" religious officials practice exorcisms [see **Why Do Catholic Objects Harm Vampires?**].

• *Exorcism Rituals (Ethros Demons):* The Ethros must be compelled to "show itself." [Either the initial stage of the exorcism, or simply a means of identifying the possessed party.] When ingested, psylis eucalipsis powder partly manifests the demon's aspect. [By the way, it's "eucalipsis" both in the script and on screen, not "eucalyptus" as some texts have claimed.]

A "binding powder" that Wesley cobbles together from ingredients in Angel's pantry can restrain the infected person if spread in a circle around them. Stuff you need for the exorcism: a cross, holy water to flick about the place [or alternatively to scald the infected person for kicks], tremendous mental strength and a resistance to suggestion.

The standard language of choice is Latin, and the ritual contains mention of rejecting Satan, his works and his pomps. An expelled Ethros will feel disoriented, and instinctively head toward any warm body. The newly possessed rarely survives [and the demon apparently dies also]. An Ethros Box, if present, will trap the purged demon.

• *Ethros Box:* Composed of 600 species of virgin woods, and handcrafted by blind Tibetan monks. Such a box can bind Ethros demons for 1,000 years.

• *Shorshack Box:* Normally used to trap Shorshack demons, and pieced together by mute Chinese nuns. They retail for about $20 less than Ethros Boxes, but they're not available in a mahogany finish. Ethros demons are larger than the average Shorshack, so Shorshack Boxes won't contain them.

• *Rick's Majick 'n Stuff:* Magic supply store in L.A., located at the corner of Melrose and Robertson between the yogurt shop and the Doggy Dunk. Angel knows Rick himself. The store is fresh out of Ethros Boxes.

BEST LINE Cordelia, suggesting ways for Ryan's parents to pass the time: "We can watch TV or play cards. You'll get so caught up, you won't even hear your son's pain." (She really does get most of the best lines in Season One.)

THINGS THAT DON'T MAKE SENSE The heroes make the classic mistake of failing to remove Ryan's parents – or at least his overly protective, ultra-jumpy mother Paige – from Angel's apartment, predictably giving Paige the perfect opportunity to break the binding powder and free her demon son. Fools. Also, Cordelia's findings about Ethros Boxes really are remarkable, considering the arcane book she's seen studying isn't in English. (She's cross-referencing. Maybe.)

There's confusion about "Uncle Frank," a late friend of the Anderson family. Cordelia's research into the family's activities in Akron, Ohio, suggests that he's listed as missing. But Ryan's father Seth implies that Uncle Frank died in a fire. So... which is it? Did Ryan's father go so far as to somehow dispose of Frank's body? Or was the fire department so sloppy that simply failed to notice the corpse in the ruins?

Yup, we saw it too... Boreanaz is containing his laughter as he and Wesley race down the stairs, and Wes goes into his full-on exorcist routine. Ryan's sister Stephanie miraculously fails to wake up through the light streaming in from the hallway, her brother pouring gasoline in her room and her parents screaming. Plus, the bars on her window from the previous scene have disappeared.

The biggest glitch of all: When Ryan sets the house on fire, from where does he get his handy can of gasoline? Perhaps Seth keeps it in the garage to fuel his lawnmower, weed whacker, etc. – but after the mysterious fire incident in Ohio, he'd be extraordinarily stupid to do so. Maybe Ryan searched the neighbors' garages for such a can, but he's lucky to find it before Angel and Wesley return, the little weasel.

POP CULTURE Cordelia, of course, makes the obligatory *Exorcist* reference. ("Angel, are you expecting any big vomiting here? Because... I saw the movie.") That's entirely in keeping with *Buffy* 2.19, "I Only Have Eyes for You," where she declared: "I saw that movie... even the priest died!"

IT'S REALLY ABOUT... Exorcism elements aside, there's some interesting commentary – whether this story intended it or not – about bad seeds. In a society that's quick to blame violent acts among children and adolescents on the media, violent video games or pretty much *anything* other than the children and adolescents themselves (or the lackluster parenting, for that matter), there's also the somewhat worrying possibility that the kids in question are inherently, well, without conscience. It's a pity, then, that this story doesn't attempt to write a prescription, as social services haven't a prayer of rehabilitating Ryan, who's literally lacking a soul.

CRITIQUE It's "*Angel* does *The Exorcist*," holds few aspirations beyond that and seems quite happy with its station in life. Sure, it's hardly the most original of tales, but it's a pleasant enough way to kill three-quarters of an hour, and let's accept it on that level.

In truth, formula isn't automatically a bad thing so long as it's not overplayed and it's formula done well. You can also make a case that it's possible to take old formulas and breathe new life into them – *Buffy* did this all the time, and even if *Angel* here isn't nearly so subversive or colorful, it certainly gives Wesley, still the new boy, something to do and raises questions about his past. It's a story that also raises some interesting questions about the old "nurture vs. nature" debate, even if it magnificently fails to answer them. Not terribly innovative, then, but certainly worth your time and trouble.

THE LORE Here comes Whedon again, posting in response to a fan's question: "You bring up a very interesting point about vampires of different religions not fearing crooses [sic]. For my own part, I'd just like to add: SHUT UP! You think it isn't hard enough, figuring out this mythology crap, you gotta bring that up? Aggg! Stupid crosses! They were in the stories, okay, and we hadda use 'em and now I'm always worried, how do I explain crosses working on all vampires, maybe no one will notice and I can just NOT MENTION IT!!! But NOOOO, you had open your big YAP." Whedon added... "Actually, during my little rant I came up with the answer. It isn't the person who reviles the symbol of the Christian God, it's the demon that possesses them. Whew." (*The Bronze*, Apr. 28, 2000)

• Minear wrote a *Lois and Clark* episode with the same title as this story. (It's a body-swap episode, however, and actually bears more resemblance to 3.04, "Carpe Noctem.")

• As with "Somnambulist," this story was written to include Doyle – that version had the heroes recruiting a priest who'd fail, whereupon Angel would take over. Whedon suggested that Wesley should stand in as the exorcist. Minear came up with the bit where Angel mistakenly refers to Wesley as Doyle. (*Fandom.com*, Aug. 14, 2000)

• Every member of the Anderson family except the father has guest-starred on *The X-Files*. Katy Boyer (Paige Anderson) also played maternal figures in *Jurassic Park 2: The Lost World* and *Minority Report*, but her most interestingly-named role came as "Lady X the Immortal Prisoner" in the TV movie *White Dwarf* (1995).

• Patience Cleveland (Nun) portrayed another woman of the cloth, Sister Margaret, in *Psycho III* and also appeared as the mailbox-obsessed, time travel-theorizing "Grandma Death" in 2001's *Donnie Darko*.

Why Do Catholic Objects Harm Vampires?

You'd be forgiven for thinking that certain items of generically Christian manufacture could burn vampires, but that's not exactly the case on screen. Undeniably, crosses feature as part of Christian worship, but what about holy water? It patently scalds vampires, yet it's very much a Catholic tradition, and not one that you'll find in Protestant organizations such as Lutheranism. Then we come to "I've Got You Under My Skin" (1.14), an otherwise innocuous story that provides something of a litmus test, given that Wesley successfully uses a Catholic exorcism ritual to cast out an Ethros demon.

Ever since *Buffy* 2.17, "Passion" – in which Willow, who's Jewish, dithers because she's got to nail a Christian cross to the wall as protection – it's been held that items from other faiths don't harm vampires. After all, if a sizeable Star of David offered the same protection as a cross, then Willow would surely have used one. That could also explain why the "consecrated wood" in 2.08, "The Shroud of Rahmon" doesn't make Angel's skin smoke – it's consecrated enough to bind a demon corpse, but *not* consecrated in the Catholic (or even Christian) tradition.

In light of the holy water and the potent exorcism ritual, then, do vampires scorch in contact with Christian items, or just Catholic ones? If it's the latter, that would make a great deal of sense. After all, the Catholic Church is the oldest established form of organized Christianity. Protestantism by comparison didn't exist until the 1500s, and the modern-day version really didn't emerge until the twentieth century. Logically, if we're considering the history of the *Angel*-verse, Catholics would surely hold the longest, most entrenched history in combating vampires and their ilk. As if to confirm the point, a nun in "I've Got You Under My Skin" identifies Angel as a vampire on sight – as if she's well-versed in that sort of thing – whereas Harry, the supposed demon culture expert in "The Bachelor Party" (1.07), doesn't do the same.

Presuming such a Catholicism vs. vampires conflict occurred (and it seems perfectly reasonable), then it's hardly a stretch to think that at some point, a Catholic priest or group of officials called upon God – or otherwise changed "the rules" – to "charge" the major Catholic objects, making them act like branding irons against the skin of the undead. Strangely enough, there's a precedent in *Angel* and *Buffy* for this sort of thing. We know that the Shadow Men (seen in *Buffy* 7.15, "Get It Done") changed "the rules" – essentially the mystical laws governing reality – to create the Slayer line, and that Willow further amended said laws to generate multiple Slayers in the *Buffy* finale. And if a fairly lowly order of monks possesses enough raw power to turn the Key into Buffy's sister, *and* alter everyone's memories in the process (*Buffy* Season Five), then some Catholic priests should be capable of "super-charging" the major items of their own religion.

Indeed, even a Bible scalds Angel's hand in "Are You Now or Have You Ever Been?" (2.02), and we'd bet you that it's a Catholic one, even if it's never said. There's nothing to prove otherwise, and Denver – the occult bookshop owner – would surely know which version sizzles vampires the best. If the priests did their job as we've outlined, then translations of the Bible printed in the original languages that the text was written – meaning Hebrew for the Old Testament and Greek and Aramaic for the New Testament – probably burn the hottest in contact with a vampire's skin. Even if that's stretching the point, it's certainly likely that a book with only some Biblical words would harm vampires far less than a genuine Bible. Heck, the Marvel Comics adaptation of *The Life of Pope John-Paul II* probably wouldn't harm the bastards at all.

It's perhaps important to add that the authors of this volume aren't Catholic and have nothing to gain by upholding Catholicism above other Christian groups. Nonetheless, even Whedon has conceded, from time to time, that the "vampire-burning" Christian objects on *Angel* and *Buffy* stem from a Catholic tradition. Oh, and food for thought... if a group of priests *did* "rewrite the rules" to empower Catholic objects, then they might well be responsible for the invitation rule (see **How Does the Invitation Rule Work?**), which almost certainly didn't develop in nature.

1.15: "The Prodigal"

"You got any kids, Angel? Right. Then don't think you know how a father feels, or why he does the things he does."

Air Date: Feb. 22, 2000; **Writer:** Tim Minear; **Director:** Bruce Seth Green

SUMMARY When a normally passive Kwaini demon attacks a subway train, Angel dispatches the creature but finds it was actually gunning for a subway rider smuggling the demon equivalent of PCP. Worse, Angel discovers that Kate's father, Trevor Lockley, is on the drug traffickers' payroll and has been helping them conceal evidence from the police.

Angel confronts Trevor, who reports Angel's suspicions to the drug traffickers, and the "Head Demon Guy" running the operation sends his vampire minions to silence the pair of them. The vamps kill Trevor in his apartment; Angel dusts one of the assailants but the other escapes – just as Kate arrives to discover father's dead body. A vengeful Kate attacks the drug runners, but Angel helpfully decapitates the Head Demon Guy. Kate distances herself from Angel, viewing him as part of the non-human world that got her father killed.

FIRSTS AND LASTS On *Angel*, it's the first appearance of Angel's pre-vampire self and Darla, even if her name oddly never gets spoken in this story. It's also the first mention of "darling boy," one of her pet names for Angelus (see 2.05, "Dear Boy"), and Angel's human name: Liam.

Final appearance of Trevor Lockley. In donning a wig to shadow a delivery boy, Cordelia inadvertently becomes a blonde for the first time (and just wait until Season Three).

POINTS OF DISCUSSION ABOUT "The Prodigal":

1. Anyone familiar with *Angel* knows there's a berserk number of historical events to keep straight, and on *Buffy*, one got the impression that the writers fudged the dates and figures for Angel's past as they went along. Giles claimed in *Buffy* 1.07, "Angel," that Angel was about 240 years old, although future stories (including "The Prodigal," actually) lead one to conclude that it's been 240 years since Angel became a vampire, not from his human birth.

Notoriously, Angel himself couldn't keep his age straight – he said he was 241 in "Some Assembly Required" (*Buffy* 2.02), but was somehow 243 only a year later in "Earshot" (*Buffy* 3.18). The *Angel Demo Reel* (see 1.01, "City Of"), set only months after "Earshot," claimed that Angel was 244 – but the reel is apocryphal, so we can safely ignore it.

With "The Prodigal," all of that uncertainty grinds to a halt as Minear starts chiseling Angel's dates in concrete – literally, in the case of Angel's gravestone. For that matter, a sub-head that dates this story to "Galway, Ireland, 1753" as if Minear isn't afraid to draw lines in the sand. Seasons Two and Three will only build upon this and marshal out a frightful amount of flashback sequences – with the writers pondering what point in Angel's past they *haven't* covered come Season Five (see 5.08, "Destiny"). Yet let's acknowledge that Mutant Enemy does an excellent job of keeping Angel's chronology straight.

2. Kate and Angel's sister Kathy have the same name – we're probably meant to infer from this that Angel and Kate, symbolically at least, are siblings. Sneaky, sneaky.

3. It's not specified how much time passes between Angel's death and his rising as a vampire, so we don't need to specifically ponder if burials in eighteenth century Ireland, as with those in modern-day Sunnydale, take place at blazing speed. Unfortunately, 2.10, "Reunion" (also by Minear, actually) establishes beyond much doubt that at most, vampires rise from the grave the night after they're killed – which means that, connecting the dots, Liam gets slain and buried in less than 24 hours, same as nearly every other vampire we've encountered.

4. After the Head Demon Guy orders his goons to murder Angel and Trevor, he storms off and can be heard shouting "Someone get me an adrenal gland!", just as the scene cuts to commercial. Now, this line isn't in the script, and one gets the impression that Minear or someone else started worrying that capitalism alone couldn't justify the Head Demon Guy's operation, so the line got added on the fly or in post-production. From this, we're evidently meant to infer that he's trafficking in PCP – at least, in part – to make the Kwaini demons' adrenal glands become engorged like balloons, yet

it's still unclear. We can't swear on a stack of Bibles that the Head Demon Guy is eating the glands, so perhaps he's using them to moisturize?

5. Cordelia wonders if the slain Kwaini was having a "bad, skanky rag day." It's about as vulgar as she ever gets.

CHARACTER NOTES *Angel:* Angel's sister, failing to recognize him as a newborn vampire, thought he'd returned to her as "an angel." [It's unclear if Angel's sister actually said the word "angel," or if Angelus simply paraphrased her reaction and the term took his fancy. Either way, this is clearly the root of the title character's name, expanding on an early description of him as "the one with the angelic face" (*Buffy* 1.07, "Angel"). 2.07, "Darla" (also by Minear) elaborates on this, citing "Angelus" as the Latinae (sic) for "Angel" – probably denoting that Angelus latched onto his sister's reaction and corrupted it out of his desire to mock God (1.11, "Somnambulist").]

According to Liam's tombstone, he lived from 1727 to 1753; the attending priest at his funeral says that Liam was "twenty years and six." [Life expectancy among men was about 36 at the time, so in relative terms Angel was in early middle age. It's positively odd, therefore, that he wasn't married and with kids by age 26.] Angel's real name is stipulated as "Liam." [A derivation of "William." As many fans point out, this means that Angel and Spike, do, in fact, have the same first name. We never discover Liam's family name, though.]

In Galway, Ireland, 1753, Liam lived with his father, mother and much younger sister Kathy. Liam was prone to lying, brawling in bars and chasing after Anna, the family servant. His stern-minded father variously deemed him a disgrace, a nothing and "a terrible disappointment." Liam claimed he'd been "dutiful" to the man but finally left home, with his father ordering him to never return.

A short while later, the vampire Darla spotted Liam in a bar brawl and deemed him "magnificent," leading to her siring him [*Buffy* 2.21, "Becoming"]. After his funeral, Liam rose as a vampire and re-met Darla. Angelus' first victim was a cemetery groundskeeper, but he subsequently sacked his entire village [and "hardly left anyone alive," as Darla suggests in "Darla"]. Kathy offered an invite into the family home, whereupon he murdered her, his father and his mother. [He probably killed the servant too, as Angel's conversation with Lindsey in 1.21, "Blind Date" implies.] Darla concluded that Angelus would be forever tormented by his father's lack of approval [see **Demonology**]. Angel's modern-day weaponry includes throwing stars [never used, sadly] and a boot-strapped knife.

• *Angel's father [unnamed]:* Stereotypically unyielding religious man [it's unclear if he's Protestant or Catholic, however, which was an important consideration at the time]. He's got some knowledge of vampirism [but he's technically wrong to claim, "A *demon* cannot enter a home where it's not welcome," as the invite rule specifically applies to vampires].

• *Cordelia:* Happily hacksaws demon parts in the name of research. She hates trailing suspects due to L.A.'s traffic and chronic lack of parking.

• *Wesley:* Somewhat chauvinistically claims that women in particular have trouble adjusting to the underworld. Wes possesses enough knowledge of chemistry/demon biology to perform a Scully-style autopsy on Kwaini demon organs. He's not above using words like "jonesing."

• *Kate:* Seems to take to heart her father's recommendation – despite his secret agenda to pump Kate for information at the time – that "It's not good to be alone, Katie." [This is just about the biggest display of concern Trevor will ever show for his daughter, and suggests that he's nudging Kate and Angel together even if he doesn't particularly like the man.] Kate softens her approach toward Angel, but Trevor's death stops her from looking upon Angel as human. [From this point, Kate becomes bigoted against Angel because of his vampiric nature. Here, he warns Kate that her father's in danger and helps her obtain vengeance, yet she's still ready to murder him come 1.19, "Sanctuary."]

Kate finds an envelope containing some of her father's ill-gotten loot from the demon-drug runners. [So she must know about her dad's wrongdoing, even if goes unstated.]

• *Trevor Lockley:* [Last seen in 1.06, "Sense and Sensitivity."] Trevor's tombstone says he lived 1938-2000. He served 35 years on the police force. Trevor believed he was using his department connections to illicitly move untariffed auto parts for a fee. [Perhaps the auto shop gang started out as a simple mob operation, later switching to "demon PCP" trafficking under the Head Demon Guy.] Trevor implies he was socking money for Kate, so she wouldn't have to become "crooked" like him. Trevor lives in apartment No. 6 [funny how that number keeps cropping up; see 1.18, "Five by Five"]. He also appears to live on Wilcox Avenue, and likes hot dogs served by a vendor named Manny.

THE LIBRARY Wesley's books help identify Kwaini demons, and contain an illustration suggesting they pretty much always dress like homeless people.

ORGANIZATIONS *Angel Investigations:* Cordelia installs an "Enforce Guard" security system that warns when intruders enters the office. [Perhaps Penn's visit ("Somnambulist") rattled her enough to upgrade the security, but in truth he simply walked through the front door. Hardcore intrusions occurred in 1.03, "In the Dark" and 1.08, "I Will Remember You."] The system proves useless when some drugged-up Kwaini attack the office. [A fed-up Cordelia presumably disconnects it, but see **When is Cordelia's Birthday?**]

DEMONOLOGY Angel starts to tell Kate that demons are not "other-worldly." [Indeed, they originated on Earth (as first established in *Buffy* 1.02, "The Harvest"). It's even possible, given the exodus of the Old Ones described in "The Harvest" (but see also 5.15, "A Hole in the World"), that our world is responsible for all strains of demon life, even those that now reside in other dimensions.] "Standard" demon disposal techniques, here applied to a dead Kwaini, include burial in virgin soil and a Latin incantation.

• *Vampires:* Darla states that many of the desires/emotions that a vampire experienced while alive will further define them once they're undead. [This makes perfect sense, given how closely vampires emulate their human selves, but see 4.15, "Orpheus" for more.] Before rising as a vampire, a buried Angelus could hear the hearts and blood of people above him. Darla says "vampire birthing" [i.e. vampires rising from their graves] hurts, but not for long [see 2.11, "Redefinition"].

The melee in Trevor's apartment proves that inviting one vampire into your home doesn't count as an invitation for all [*Buffy* 5.02, "Real Me" confirms the point]. Simple Christian chants don't repel vampires. A certain type of herb [cited as garlic in the script] annoys but doesn't ward off the undead.

• *Kwaini Demons:* Peaceful, articulate, gentle demons who're always female and evidently look like homeless people. They're traditionally non-violent, but the demon PCP drug enlarges the Kwaini's adrenal gland from the size of a walnut to a large, inflamed organ, plus multiplies its strength by a factor of 20.

• *"Demon PCP":* Yellow, synthetic drug that's metaphysical in nature and contains Eye of Newt (added for taste, not kick).

BEST LINE Angel, on Kate's reticence after events in "Somnambulist": "Ever since she ran me through with a two-by-four, things have been different."

THINGS THAT DON'T MAKE SENSE Angel's father boards up windows in a room that's adjacent to what's apparently the abode's front door, where we spot the body of Angel's sister. However, this suggests that Angel's dad – even allowing that he's rather distracted – entirely failed to see or hear his young daughter answering the door, her presumable delight/shock at seeing her brother "alive," her inviting Angelus inside and Angelus killing her. (Angelus presumably slaughtered his sister at another entrance and simply moved her corpse for dramatic effect.) Along those lines, the body of Angel's mother magically appears in the dining room in the final scene, even though it's played as concurrent to the previous one. (Angelus must've hauled his mother into the dining room and killed her last, as his father could hardly have missed seeing his wife's body otherwise, given its location.)

Cordelia's digital camera flips between snapshots of her surveillance like no camera of that era. Wesley says he's performing a "vivisection" on the dead Kwaini, when the term actually means cutting open something that's still alive – he's really performing a "dissection." And it's rather amusing the way the "dead" Trevor Lockley blinks several times as Kate leans over him before the commercial break.

Not an outright goof, but it's certainly a huge convenience that the Head Demon Guy's goons wear their vamp faces even while milling about the garage and casually doing the paperwork – thus tipping off Kate that she can gun down everyone in sight, no problem. Were they doing *evil* paperwork?

IN RETROSPECT Much of this drives home the point that Angel doesn't have children – at least, none that aren't vampires – and therefore can't comprehend a father's actions. Which seems totally astonishing with hindsight, considering what happens in Seasons Three, Four and Five.

IT'S REALLY ABOUT... Inherently, it's about children failing to gain their father's approval, and the crushing impossibility of such regard once the father shuffles off this mortal coil. Metaphorically speaking, the constant rebuke that Angel's father offers Liam makes him undergo a complete personality transplant – literally, once Liam becomes a vampire – although one senses that something died within the boy whilst he was still alive. It's also about Kate and Angel being on the same page as regards fathers, but that's open to debate (see the **Critique**).

CRITIQUE Ah, "The Prodigal." It's frequently held up as a true *Angel* "classic" – or at the very least gets frequently named as a standout story from Season One. But does it deserve this reputation?

In the main, yes... but it's a funny beast. There's two storylines running here – Angel's origin and Kate's modern-day dilemma – and while they're both very good, some viewers will inherently gravitate to one over the other, thus finishing the story with a sense that it's less than the sum of its parts. For the record, we like and appreciate both threads (barring the out-of-a-pop-top-can demon who's running the drug operation), but they don't join nearly as well as Minear intended. Angel and Kate lose their fathers, it's true, but the similarities end there. Kate's dad dies independent of her actions, but Angelus *brutally murders* his. Their dads aren't similar in temperament (the one's a zealous patriarch; the other's just overly reserved and distant), the kids relate to them differently (Kate offers Trevor second chances; human Angel storms out and doesn't look back), and Angel's father would've perished even if he'd been a saint, whereas Kate's dad engages in criminal activity and, arguably, causes his own demise.

Still, let's look at what we're gaining here. Even though *Buffy* largely covered this phase of Angel's back story, meaning little of this is particularly new, it's important to see it play out. It's one thing to hear about Angel lunching on his family, but it's more visceral to actually witness him doing it. If you're in that group that watches *Angel* but not *Buffy* (and they're out there), and didn't see Angelus running amok in *Buffy* Season Two, then this pretty vividly gets the point across.

It's far better than it deserves to be, then, and it's a fine example of Minear taking his first step into Angel's complicated history, scoring a win in most ways that matter.

THE LORE Julie Benz had initially auditioned for the role of Buffy, but Whedon instead cast her as Darla – or "Vampire Girl," as she was then called. Sarah Michelle Gellar had met Benz before that in New York, where they'd tested together for *All My Children*, so the eventual lead actress on *Buffy* recognized Benz in vampire make-up even if nobody else did. The scene where Angel staked Darla (*Buffy* 1.07, "Angel") entailed fits of giggles between Benz and Boreanaz, plus Benz missing a mattress intended to cushion her fall at one point. Benz later claimed: "I think David and I were just amazed that there we were running around pretending to be vampires and getting paid for it." (*SMGFan.com*, Nov. 11 2003)

• Minear banged out the script for "The Prodigal" in about three days. The graveyard scene of Angel arising as a vampire was filmed at the Hollywood Forever cemetery, right behind the Paramount lot. It was a cold night, and Minear realized that the vampires' breath was visible when it really shouldn't have been, but the gaffe didn't justify the expense required to remove it. (*Fandom.com*, Aug. 14, 2000)

• The unnamed barmaid that human Angel lusts after – seen for a fleeting few seconds – might look familiar because actress Christina Hendricks later played the polygamous scam artist Saffron on *Firefly*. She's also appeared on Eliza Dushku's *Tru Calling* and MTV's *Undressed*, which helped launch J. August Richards' career. Bob Fimiani, the groundskeeper who serves as Angelus' first victim, also played a government overseer of the Initiative (Mr. Ward) in *Buffy* Season Four. He's also an Elder Gamman in the first *Firefly* episode to feature Hendricks, and he'll be along later in Season Three (3.01 and 3.18 specifically) as the Codger Demon.

1.16: "The Ring"

"What you are is a soon-to-be-dead slave."

Air Date: Feb. 29, 2000; **Writer:** Howard Gordon; **Director:** Nick Marck

SUMMARY When businessman Darin MacNamara hires Angel to locate his kidnapped brother Jack, Angel follows Jack's trail to an arena where wealthy patrons watch captive demons fight to the death. However, Angel realizes that Darin and Jack *run* the establishment, whereupon he's captured and tossed into a slave pen with several other fighters. Darin and Jack promise freedom to any demon who survives his 21st bout, and shackle the combatants with magical wrist bands that incinerate the wearer if they step over a boundary line. Angel briefly captures Jack, but Darin shoots his brother dead rather than yield to Angel's demands.

Meanwhile, Wesley and Cordelia track Angel and snitch one of the magical cuffs for study. As Angel and the demon Trepkos battle in the arena, Wesley devises a magical key to the cuffs – and accidentally looses all the other gladiators. The demons run amuck, allowing Trepkos to kill Darin. Afterward, Angel and his friends briefly pat themselves on the back, then realize they've just loosed an entire herd of demons back into the wild.

FIRSTS AND LASTS It's the debut of Stephanie Romanov as Lilah Morgan, an associate at Wolfram and Hart who'll rise to become a far more prominent face there, chiefly thanks to the continual turnover/slaughter of her colleagues throughout the next few years. Angel's brief chat in Lilah's office marks his first visit to the firm's L.A. branch, and eerily mirrors the massive paradigm shift in the Season Four finale (see **It's Really About...**). Also bearing in mind what's to occur in seasons Three and Four, "The Ring" marks the first instance of Wesley and Lilah being in the same room as one another, even if they don't speak or even appear in the same shot.

Howard Gordon's tenure as an *Angel* writer/producer ends with this story. For the first time, Cordelia puts the online "Demons, Demons, Demons" database to good use. It's also the first time that electrical prods get used to render Angel unconscious – a precursor to this exists in the electrical bolts that took out a pontificating Spike in *Buffy* 4.06, "Wild at Heart," but they'll become the weapon of choice for incapacitating Our Hero as needed in future (see 2.09, "The Trial" and 3.22, "Tomorrow" especially).

POINTS OF DISCUSSION ABOUT "The Ring":

1. It's a story where the heroes genuinely do more harm than good, but the script papers over this. Implicitly, "The Ring" seems patterned after *Spartacus* (1960) as directed by Stanley Kubrick (see **The Lore** for evidence that the cast, at least, thought of it as such) – but if you stop to think about it, the two stories only bear surface-level similarities. *Spartacus* was about the title character (played by Kirk Douglas) shouting the message of "We must live free or die!" and leading a slave revolt against Rome's tyranny. But in "The Ring," Angel is similarly trying to rally, er, a bunch of demons. Even allowing that benevolent demons inhabit the *Angel*-verse, it's hard to escape the conclusion that some, if not the majority, of the characters that Angel frees are unrepentant, wholesale and gruesome serial killers who'll happily return to the life. This isn't Angel leading a *Spartacus*-style revolt on behalf of the oppressed masses; more accurately, it's as if he's rallying genuinely guilty convicts to incite a prison riot. Best to bear that in mind, especially once we hit **The Critique**.

2. Lilah, working on behalf of the firm, buys out Angel's "contract" from the arena fights and tells him to walk free if he forgets what he's witnessed. Angel naturally gets heroic, declines the offer and returns to the slave pens, but it seems odd that the firm would spend a lot of money to liberate Angel and then just let him go. Exactly what's going on here?

It's entirely possible that, by supernatural contract law, Angel would've become the firm's pawn if he'd taken the deal. That makes this tiny little scene a potentially *huge* turning point for the series, and it's only Angel's nobility that keeps him out of the firm's bear trap. Alternatively, the firm already senses that Angel's a player in a much larger game (confirmed in 2.12, "Blood Money") and is at least exploring the possibility that he's amoral enough to compromise with them – even if the bulk of evidence suggests they don't realize his importance until later this year (see especially 1.21, "Blind Date").

CHARACTER NOTES *Angel:* Hasn't played poker in a while, and knows at least some cursory Spanish, Russian and Italian phrases. [The Italian at least makes sense, given Angelus' trips to Rome, see especially 3.07, "Offspring" and 5.20, "The Girl in Question."] He's proficient with a fighting staff [seen again in 2.06, "Guise Will Be Guise"]. Darin and Jack apparently learn about Angel through word-of-mouth [so his underworld reputation continues to grow, as with 1.10, "Parting Gifts"].

• *Cordelia:* Wears a bracelet containing horsehair from "Keanu," her palomino horse that the IRS took away due to her father's tax evasion. Cordelia does an admirable job of infiltrating the arena, adeptly passing herself and Wesley off as Detective Andrews and "Yelsew." ["Wesley" spoken backward, obviously. There's no particular reason why Cordy would pick "Andrews," as she never meets the villainous super-nerd from *Buffy*.] She apparently owns a fake police badge, and is sneaky enough to snitch a magical wrist-cuff from the arena.

Excerpts from Cordelia and Wesley's snipping at one another: She takes swipes at his lackluster social life, he colors her world as one of "high-fashion pumps and a push-up bra."

• *Wesley:* Initially fumbles with a crossbow, but later shoots it with great accuracy (as with "Parting Gifts" and 1.12, "Expecting"). Wes proves willing, while searching for Angel, to impale a crooked bookie's hand with a crossbow arrow, then twist the bolt to make the man talk. Wes displays a rudimentary knowledge of alchemy [enough to follow the directions outlined in an ancient text, at least]. He's less adept at infiltration work than Cordelia, using appalling phrases such as: "Something's going down tonight. Something with the man."

• *Kate:* Civil when Wesley calls, but seems ambivalent concerning Angel's absence [but see 1.19, "Sanctuary"].

• *Lilah Morgan:* Already knows that Angel has a soul. She bets [and presumably wins] $5,000 on the demon Cribb, but later bets $10,000 that the demon Trepkos will defeat Angel.

THE LIBRARY Wesley devises a key for the magical cuffs after translating a book on alchemy, named *The Alchemist*.

ORGANIZATIONS *Angel Investigations:* The waiting room contains a book on oceanography [it's L.A., after all].

• *Darin and Jack's Gladiatorial Matches:* Held at a location underneath Beachwood Canyon, and the slave-cells of the facility are found beneath a [disused?] Parker Bros. building. [Curiously, the same building flashes past in the teaser to 4.20, "Sacrifice," which would almost suggest the heroes make their "final stand" near there.] "Octavian matches" of this type date back to the Roman Empire, and Wesley has heard rumors about a revival for such fights. Darin and Jack's operation markets itself with the Roman numeral XXI [probably just because the slaves need 21 kills to win their freedom].

DEMONOLOGY *Vampires:* Jack claims that a vampire's teeth "reveals a lot" about the strength of their bones. Electrical prods can effectively incapacitate vampires.

• *"Demons, Demons, Demons":* Online demon database (www.demonsdemonsdemons.com, according to Cordelia's computer screen) that lists a dozen demon species as indigenous to L.A. County alone. Search categories on this site include "Demon Love," "History" and "Habitats and Maps," with cross-referencing available as to the demon's hair, skin, slime, claws/hands and smell.

The database includes Howler Demons, screeching creatures who carry a sulfuric smell, but fails to list the extra-dimensional Vigories of Oden Tal [1.13, "She"], allowing Wes to claim a victory on behalf of paper-based research. Nor is there an entry for Wolfram and Hart. [This makes sense, as the attorneys aren't themselves demons. The website sees future use on *Angel*, plus *Buffy* 7.03, "Same Time, Same Place."]

MAGIC *The Slave Wristcuffs:* Described by Wesley as "half magic, half medieval technology." Medieval sorcerers apparently forged the cuffs, which atomize any slave that crosses a specified red line. Holding the manacle directly over the line only delivers an electrical jolt, however. Wesley devises an alchemic "key" using horsehair (from Cordelia's bracelet) that threads into the locking mechanism and triggers the release.

BEST LINE Wesley: "I lead a rich and varied social life." Cordelia, sarcastic: "Oh, I know. Every night it's *Jeopardy*, followed by *Wheel of Fortune* and a cup of hot cocoa."

THINGS THAT DON'T MAKE SENSE A "bruised" Darin shows up at Angel Investigations, but we later learn he's faking the whole thing, and he later appears sans bruises. So we've got to conclude that his "bruises" were simply make-up, which makes you wonder why Angel (with his vampire senses) and Cordelia (the fashion guru) don't notice that Darin was pulling the wool over their eyes.

A glitch with regards to the scope of the series: It's suggested that Wesley knows precious little about Wolfram and Hart. This doesn't exactly pare with future episodes such as 5.07, "Lineage," which claim that the firm's atrocities are well-documented, legendary and (almost unavoidably) known to the Watchers' Council. Granted, Wes is off his game for much of Season One, but with hindsight, this is pushing it.

IT'S REALLY ABOUT... Shamelessly capitalizing on the wrestling craze of the late 90s, then cloaking it as a *Spartacus*-style story. True, "The Ring" first broadcast in the same year as Russell Crowe's *Gladiator*, but it boils down to two muscle-toned jocks thrashing each other in an arena, something that the WWF seemingly held a monopoly on for a time.

But the office scene with Angel and Lilah at least brings up many of the issues that'll pervade the series' final year, and in fact seems like the Season Four finale (4.22, "Home") in microcosm. Here, as there, Lilah stresses to Angel that he should "compromise" by making a pact with the law firm because "a lot of people need your help" and would benefit from such a Faustian deal. The main difference, though, lies in the fact that when Lilah suggests, "There's not one reason why we can't work together," Angel here tells her to get stuffed. Three years on, he won't decline so quickly.

CRITIQUE If it weren't for 4.10, "Awakening," this story would top our list of the worst *Angel* stories of all time, and it's worthy of every bit of disdain we can heap on it. Witless, dull and slightly insulting to the intelligence, the "morality" of "The Ring" is about as substantial as tissue paper, and ultimately boils down to a bunch of demons pummeling each other while Angel acts all noble about it. Arena-style fighting has long been a staple of sci-fi (the classic *Star Trek* story "The Gamesters of Triskelion" immediately springs to mind), but it's perhaps telling that this story got made when hopeless arena-fighting schlock was particularly in vogue. (Nearly a year after this story broadcast, The Rock threw down – here we go again – with Seven of Nine in *Star Trek: Voyager* 6.15, "Tsunkatse.") As such, "The Ring" has only gotten more ludicrous with age.

Yes, it introduces Lilah, and Stephanie Romanov is fabulous. Yes, Wesley gets a choice scene with his crossbow. No, there's almost nothing else redeeming about this story. To a casual viewer, it's a cornucopia of the most embarrassing elements that the sci-fi genre has to offer, and that's before the episode has the gall to joke about a pack of killers getting unleashed upon society. Someone should've pointed out to Howard Gordon that even if you acknowledge, "Well, none of this really matters for spittle," you're still left with a story that appalllingly isn't worth spittle.

Heaven help us, even the title is painfully mundane. "The Ring." It must've taken them hours to come up with that one.

THE LORE Running contrary to the above critique, Boreanaz enjoyed this story and outlined some of his favorite Season One outings in a chat on *TV Guide Insider*: "The only one I didn't like was episode two ["Lonely Hearts"]. I liked the Spartacus episode ["The Ring"]. I also liked the one where I got to be human for a day ["I Will Remember You"]... and the pilot, the one that Joss directed. And the season finale, that was fun as well." (May 22, 2000)

• On one of the demon gladiators being named "Trepkos": Gordon's script for *The X-Files* 2.09, "Firewalker," also includes a Dr. Daniel Trepkos. As if to complete the circuit, Gordon's been a producer since day one (so to speak) on *24*, and Season Two of that show features a "Trepkos" who's one of the people behind the driving events of that year (including an assassination attempt on President Palmer).

• Stephanie Romanov had attained a height of 5'9" by age 14, and quickly found herself working for John Casablancas' model agency. Her first job entailed going to Rome, Paris and Milan, doing the photo sessions for the Italian and French versions of *Harper's Bazaar*. Before *Angel*, she'd previously appeared on FOX's *Models, Inc.* as the younger sister of a character played by Carrie-Anne Moss (Trinity in *The Matrix*). Romanov went into "The Ring" thinking Lilah was a one-off appearance – the producers later promoted her into an ongoing character. (*BBC Cult*, 2002)

• Some of the "Demons, Demons, Demons" website drawings hail from the show's conceptual sketches, including the Kwaini demon (seen last episode) and Doyle's species.

1.17: "Eternity"

"You don't think she'd try to maneuver Angel into an exchange of bodily fluids in order to make herself eternally young and beautiful, thus saving her failing career? Gee, now that you mention it..."

Air Date: April 4, 2000; **Writer:** Tracey Stern; **Director:** Regis Kimble

SUMMARY Angel randomly saves a prominent actress, Rebecca Lowell, from an attempted hit-and-run, then serves as the woman's bodyguard while she's under threat from a stalker. In due course, Angel finds that Rebecca's agent, Oliver Simon (1.01, "City Of"), has been secretly organizing the "murder attempts" to boost her media profile.

Unfortunately, Rebecca learns that Angel is a vampire and, desperate to save her youthful looks, fantasizes about becoming one herself. Rebecca visits Angel in the hope of seducing him into siring her, and tries to ease the mood by slipping a drug into his drink. Tragically, the drug grants Angel an artificial feeling of bliss – making him revert to Angelus. After a terror-filled standoff, Wesley finally knocks the vampire down the office elevator shaft, rendering him unconscious. Wes and Cordelia chain Angelus up until the drug wears off, but a horror-stricken Rebecca departs and never returns.

FIRSTS AND LASTS It's the first time on *Angel* that the title character, however temporarily, becomes Angelus again. At story's end, it's also the first occasion that we see Wesley unshaven – although his stubble here seems downright tame compared to what he'll accrue in future. And it's the final story of a type that began with "Lonely Hearts" (1.02), on which point let's just say...

POINTS OF DISCUSSION ABOUT "Eternity":

1. The show ends its "anthology phase," in that the series casts off its reliance on the heroes helping any given walk-in client or helpless person. It also represents a deviation from the *Buffy* tradition of using demons, etc., to represent real-life anxieties made flesh, which means the **It's Really About...** section will appear far less metaphorical from now on.

All told, this represents the Mutant Enemy staff's dawning awareness that their lead characters yield better dividends than the walk-in clients, who inherently can't undergo much development – or make the audience care about them much – in the course of a single episode. As if to prove the point: Quick, name a truly memorable "client" from the past 17 stories. That's right... there isn't one, save perhaps Rebecca herself.

2. It's been said that here and in Season Four, Boreanaz plays Angelus as the sort of ludicrously over-the-top villain who'd seem at home on a gorier version of the Adam West *Batman* series. That's decently true, but there's a justification for it. Stories in Season Four – 4.14, "Release" and 4.15, "Orpheus" especially – establish that under normal circumstances, Angelus' consciousness is trapped like a watchful genie, aware of events as Angel goes about his do-gooding. So Angelus spends entire decades, unable to act or speak, watching Angel insufferably acting heroic – small wonder, then, that he's completely without restraint on those rare occasions when he gets loose. And let's not forget – it wasn't that long ago that Angelus threw off his shackles and terrorized Sunnydale in *Buffy* Season Two, so his subsequent re-imprisonment probably seemed even more galling than normal.

By the way, you've got to admire the scene in which Cordelia waves a water bottle in Angelus' face and convincingly claims it's full of holy water. And notice how Boreanaz uses the *perfect* pitch while evoking the Wicked Witch of the West and telling Cordy: "What are you going to do? Melt me?"

3. For fear of breaking his curse, Angel keeps his distance – romantically, that is – from Rebecca. You can contrast this against 3.07, "Offspring," in which he throws such concerns to the wind, but it's telling that Rebecca's a brunette, not a blonde, meaning she hasn't a prayer with him. (And there's much, much more on the correlation between hair color and Angel's romantic prospects to come.)

CHARACTER NOTES *Angel:* A drugged Angel claims he's "helped to save the world" a couple of times. [That's not necessarily true – the Master arguably threatened the entire world in *Buffy* Season One, but *Buffy* 3.09, "The Wish," showed a reality where the Master "succeeded" and stopped far short of exterminating humanity. Then there's *Buffy* Season Three, where Angel helped to bring down the Mayor. But as the villain mostly became a giant snake, gauging his potential for world domination is awkward. Conversely, Angel (or rather Angelus) *did*, as he also mentions, nearly send the world screaming into hell in *Buffy* Season Two.]

Doximal, a bliss-causing tranquilizer, can temporarily

make Angelus dominant. [As we learned in *Buffy* Season Two, the gypsy curse was designed to make Angel suffer, not to make him perform heroic deeds. But as magic in the *Angel*-verse chiefly relies on personal intent as much as mystical energy, it's possible that the curse might intuitively distinguish between a genuine abatement of Angel's suffering (i.e. the moment of "perfect happiness" bit) and an outside drug simulating such an effect. As Doximal represents artificial happiness, the curse isn't technically broken, but Angelus temporarily gains control.]

The Doximal makes Angel sluggish, but doesn't diminish Angelus' faculties. [It's arguably akin to a sleepwalker with multiple personality syndrome, in which one persona functions quite well while the other "sleeps." See 4.15, "Orpheus" for why this description seems all-too apt.] Angelus claims he's never killed a famous person before, and implies that he sometimes would stake his victims' heads on pikes.

Angel currently doesn't own a television [but see 1.19, "Sanctuary"] and doesn't recognize modern-day celebrities such as Rebecca. [He's not up on network shows, but he's hardly oblivious to pop culture, as he here references *Dracula* (1979). We'll discuss the point in 2.19, "Belonging."] He apparently reads *Detective* magazine, keeps champagne glasses and stores his pig's blood in squirtable plastic packets. His suit size is apparently 44 long.

• *Cordelia:* Currently acting [if you can call it that] in a small theatre performance of Henrik Ibsen's *A Doll's House*. She's very convincing, however, while bluffing Angelus in the final showdown. [It's curious that as Cordelia claims, she apparently keeps a stake in her desk and a cross in her purse. Perhaps Cordy *has* taken some precautions against Angel re-becoming Angelus – see 1.11, "Somnambulist" for more evidence of this.]

Cordy enjoys a veal filet for lunch and finally concedes (to Rebecca) that the office coffee and tea are lousy. She's more than willing, given the opportunity, to go through Rebecca's things. She doesn't recognize Doximal by name.

• *Wesley:* Cynical enough to think that Angel probably won't find "perfect happiness" with anyone other than Buffy, so he might as well romance Rebecca. Wesley owns a pager and a TV set. [But like Angel, Wesley doesn't recognize Rebecca as a celebrity, so he probably doesn't watch prime time. Doesn't he strike you as more of a History Channel man?] He also mistakes a reference to *Entertainment Tonight* ("E.T.") for Emma Thompson.

Wes acquires the preliminary forensic reports from an "attack" on Rebecca. [There's no evidence of him having a police contact right now, so he probably lifts the files himself.] Wesley shrugs off Angelus' accusation that he lacks stones [as with Angel's Doyle comment in 1.14, "I've Got You Under My Skin"]. Wes knows about Doximal's properties.

• *Rebecca Lowell:* To Rebecca's credit, she holds together remarkably well when her potential lover becomes a bloodthirsty psychopath.

Rebecca became famous at age 14; her agent is clearly fibbing to say that she's now 24. [Actress Tamara Gorski, playing Rebecca, was 30 when this story got filmed.] She played a character named Raven on the hit series *On Your Own*. The role got Rebecca nominated for an Emmy, but she failed to win. The network killed the series a season and a half ago, and Rebecca is now deemed too "mature" for many leading parts. [Ironically, of course, she's only slightly older than some of the "teenaged" actors on *Buffy*. Believe it or not, Nicholas Brendon was 25 while filming *Buffy* Season One.]

ORGANIZATIONS *Angel Investigations:* Cordelia mentions a "Father Mackie," who's apparently the local parish priest.

DEMONOLOGY *Vampires:* Rebecca's suggestion that Angel "stop by" her home for a private screening of *On Your Own* counts as an invitation. [Oh, of course it counts; see **How Does the Invitation Rule Work?** Such a pity that Angel's response of "Thanks for the invitation, but I'm..." was struck, or there wouldn't be any debate.] Rebecca says that Angel's skin feels cold [which concurs with *Buffy* 4.07, "The Initiative," on the point that vampires are room temperature].

BEST LINE Wesley to Angel: "I thought you might like to know I got the preliminary forensics report from [the attack at] the theater. The bullets were..." An astute Angel: "Blanks." Wesley, oblivious: "No, I'm afraid they were blanks."

THINGS THAT DON'T MAKE SENSE We've noted a few instances of dummy text on *Angel* before now, but here's the all-time winner (you need to pause your DVD player, but it's there): In a newspaper story headlined "Rebecca Lowell's Brush with Death," the text itself discusses President Clinton denying all reports that he took a "presidency-enhancer" drug ("My presidency has been 100 percent natural."); the characteristics of an annoying bus passenger; and a ceremony commemorating a pizza boy's ascension into "delivery manhood." (A Gino's Pizzeria owner says: "Richie, today you are a delivery man.") Anyone think the flavor of humor here sounds familiar? If so, it's because the text originates from *The Onion* (specifically, the "In Brief" section of the June 17, 1998, issue).

Angel randomly saves Rebecca when her "stalker" tries to mow her down with his car. Nothing particularly wrong with that, save that we later discover that Rebecca's agent Oscar has been rigging the "murder attempts," and that he never intended Rebecca any real harm. So exactly how would

Rebecca have avoided getting run over if Angel *hadn't* been there? Because Angel only has time to push Rebecca out of the way, meaning she'd surely have died but for his intervention. Granted, the assailant might have room to swerve, but it's a pretty feeble "murder attempt" if the driver deliberately dodges his intended victim. Plus, we're never told what happens to Oscar – or heck, if Rebecca even fires him – which means at the very least he gets away with wrongly tying up police services.

Cordelia appears to spend an entire lazy afternoon telling Rebecca about Angel's past, plus the specifics of how to make someone a vampire. Yet she entirely fails to mention that, by the way, all vampires save Angel are soulless bloodsucking fiends – leaving Rebecca with the hideously mistaken notion that getting vamped is an excellent idea. Cordy also blunders, upon deducing Rebecca's plan, by paging Wesley instead of doing something more sensible such as phoning Angel in his apartment to warn him.

In real-life, Doximal is an anti-malaria drug, not a tranquilizer. (The only reported side-effect is that the user's skin becomes more sensitive to sunburn, which doesn't really apply to Angel.) Tranquilizers typically aren't available in powder form, as it's easy to overdose from such a concoction. (Rebecca might have ground some Doximal tablets up in advance, but it certainly looks like the drug comes powdered straight out of a company packet.) Also, Doximal's presence in the *Angel*-verse will cause some festive continuity glitches come 4.10, "Awakening."

Three goofs that everyone seems to notice... Angel's digital clock keeps reading 8:25 even when several minutes pass. (His wall clock, in fact, looks as if it wrongly reads about 7:30, although it's hazy.) Angel's back tattoo isn't visible when Boreanaz takes off his shirt. And when a vase-filled cabinet comes crashing down on Angel in Rebecca's house, we hear the sound of breaking glass, but the vases themselves are made of plastic and don't shatter. Some of them even bounce.

POP CULTURE Rebecca: "Bela Lugosi, Gary Oldman, they're vampires." Angel: "Frank Langella was the only performance I believed." Lugosi appeared in a seemingly endless string of horror films, including *Dracula* (1931). Oldman played the title role in the Coppola movie *Bram Stoker's Dracula* (1992). Frank Langella was nominated a Tony for his portrayal of the vampire in *Dracula* on Broadway (1978), and re-created the role for the motion picture (1979). The *Angel*-verse version of Dracula showed up in *Buffy* 5.01, "Buffy vs. Dracula."

IN RETROSPECT "Eternity" entails one of the good guys going rogue under unusual circumstances; the problem's solved when he falls down a large hole in the heroes' headquarters and gets smacked unconscious. Sound familiar? Yup, we'll go through those paces again – only with an insane Wesley – in 3.06, "Billy."

IT'S REALLY ABOUT... The way in which a culture that reveres the likes of *Friends* later sullies any entertainer who's not entirely young and entirely beautiful. Somewhat paradoxically, such ostracized entertainers try to regain their looks by becoming *more* inhuman, making Rebecca's fleeting attempt at vampirism look for all the world like an actress scheduling her Botox injections. It's also rather telling that a fake *Global Snooper* article about Rebecca – headlined "Where Are They This Year?" – seems only marginally more of a snap-judgment piece than most tabloids on the market.

CRITIQUE Roughly thirty-five minutes of soul-numbing boredom, capped off by a genuinely pants-wetting climax. As such, it's arguably the most lopsided *Angel* story ever.

The teaser – in which Angel and Wesley squirm while Cordelia murders a live performance of *A Doll's House* – proves funny enough, but the three acts to follow are sheer predictability. It's painfully obvious that Rebecca's agent is behind her stalking (the lack of credible suspects makes matters rather transparent here) and that Rebecca will approach Angel about making her a vampire. In a story about an actress who's losing her youth, can't reclaim her glory and never gets told about the downsides of vampirism, what *else* could she want? The cast puts in their best effort, but it's a slog.

Gotta admit, though... it's almost impossible to predict Angel's conversion to Angelus. Talk about disturbing. The bit where – to all intents and purposes! – Angel suddenly squirts pig's blood into Rebecca's mouth leaps out as one of the most brutal images in the series' entire run, and we honestly couldn't fathom whether Angel was viciously trying to scare Rebecca off the whole vampirism thing, or whether he'd genuinely lost his marbles. The action whips itself into a frenzy from there, with some superb direction driving home how much Rebecca's trapped in a darkened, enclosed space with a homicidal lunatic. She's not blind, and this isn't *Wait Until Dark*, but it's close. Some points also go to Tamara Gorski as Rebecca, for delivering everything that's expected of her.

In the grand sense, it's a damn pity that none of the producers realized how much of "Eternity" was excruciatingly dull. But there's a myriad of sins we can forgive based on that extremely alarming final act.

THE LORE The first cut of "Eternity" overran by a whopping seven and a half minutes, nearly an act's worth of material. A regrettable deletion had Angel explaining to Rebecca that vampires *do* show up in photographs, with the rumor that they didn't stemming from the truth about them failing to appear in mirrors. "It's not about physics, it's metaphysics," Angel was scripted to say. (Minear, *alt.tv.angel*, Apr. 7, 2000)

• Whedon evidently came up with the idea of Angel becoming Angelus, and objected to a cozy epilogue where Rebecca came to grips with her ordeal. (*Fandom.com*, Aug. 14, 2000)

• Whedon's view of the flexible use of the invitation rule in this story: "The actress invited Angel over when she was in his office. Jeez, people! You think we'd make some blatant mistake like that? Just because Angel OCCASIONALLY can be seen sunbathing on the show doesn't mean we don't take our mythology seriously." (*The Bronze*, April 15, 2000)

• Minear suggested, regarding Angel's conversion into Angelus: "His soul didn't leave. He didn't actually 'turn' in the 'perfect happiness' way... His 'evil' was simulated. People on drugs might let their dark sides slip out, and do things they don't really mean or want to. My notion was always that Angel was just underneath." (*The Bronze*, April 4, 2000)

• Tamara Gorski (Rebecca Lowell) previously dealt with vampires when she guest-starred on *Dracula: The Series* and *Forever Knight*. She also had a recurring role on *Hercules* as assassination-prone demigod Morrigan.

1.18: "Five by Five"

"We've only done one of the five basic torture groups. We've done blunt... but that still leaves sharp, cold, hot and loud. May I take your order, please?

Air Date: April 25, 2000; **Writer:** Jim Kouf; **Director:** James A. Contner

SUMMARY Throwing down the gauntlet against Angel, three Wolfram and Hart attorneys – Lindsey, Lilah and Lee Mercer – fortuitously learn that Faith, a rogue vampire slayer, has just arrived in L.A. (after *Buffy* 4.16, "Who Are You?"). Faith accepts the lawyers' offer of a clean record and cash in exchange for offing Angel, then embarks on a terror campaign against Angel's crew.

Angel sees Faith as a screwed-up girl in need of help, but Faith goads Angel by capturing Wesley and torturing him at length. Charging to the rescue, Angel chiefly uses defensive tactics against Faith, sensing she's motivated by guilt for her crimes and *wants* him to kill her. Unable to make Angel end her suffering, a sobbing Faith collapses into his arms. [*Continued next episode.*]

FIRSTS AND LASTS Here comes Faith the Vampire Slayer, someone who's going to become *Angel*'s Slayer-in-residence for the next three years. Topping Angel's window-surfing in "Lonely Hearts" (1.02), it's the first time that someone survives what's at least a three-story drop. (For the most inspired falls, see Angel in 2.15, "Reprise," 4.07, "Apocalypse Nowish" and 5.16, "Shells," plus Faith again in 4.13, "Salvage.")

Thematically, it's the first occasion that a turning point on *Angel* occurs in a back alley during a fierce downpour. See also 3.09, "Lullaby" and most especially 5.22, "Not Fade Away" for the most spectacular examples of this. (We should also mention that Angel got vamped in a back alley in *Buffy* 2.21, "Becoming," and that other notable back-alley entanglements, sans the rain admittedly, occur in 3.08, "Quickening" and "Apocalypse, Nowish.")

The primary Wolfram and Hart attorneys conspire together for the first time, and we finally learn Lindsey's name. (Angel says "Lindsey" aloud, but an office plaque reveals his full name as "Lindsey McDonald.") The attorneys also employ demons-for-hire for the first time, making the law firm look all the more infernal. It's also the first mention of the firm's vampire detectors, although they're not seen until 1.21, "Blind Date."

A bit on the subtle side, Lilah's admission that she's been monitoring Lee's activities – plus the rapt attention that Lindsey and Lilah provide when Faith pummels Lee for acting uppity with her – gives the first nod to Wolfram and Hart's fierce inter-office competition. When Faith pushes Lilah up against a fence, we see Lilah showing fear for the first time, something Stephanie Romanov pulls off terribly well. She's going to get a lot of practice in future.

As a matter of design, the overpass that'll serve time and again for location shots gets its first outing (see especially 4.21, "Peace Out," when someone hurls a car off it at Angel).

POINTS OF DISCUSSION ABOUT "Five by Five":

1. *Angel* started off as a *Buffy the Vampire Slayer* spin-off, but notice how Buffy now doesn't fit the *Angel* mold, and it's Faith who's far better geared to this series. Like Angel but rather unlike Buffy, Faith needs redemption, and it's only when she ventures to L.A. that she gets it. Cumulatively, *Angel* is flush with females who commited heinous crimes, but there's generally a reason for it. Darla and Drusilla, as vampires, have no soul or conscience. Jasmine and (to a lesser degree) Illyria are higher beings, so it's in their nature to conquer entire civilizations. Cordelia isn't herself in Season Four, and the deranged Slayer who cuts off Spike's forearms in 5.11, "Damage" is genuinely insane. We could go on.

None of this applies to Faith, though. Unlike all those we've just mentioned, she has a choice – on that specific level, she's arguably worse than even Angelus. But at least on *Angel* she'll straighten herself out in a way that *Buffy* couldn't provide.

2. All the torture. Sweet mercy, the torture. Granted, we don't see Faith going at Wesley, but sight of Wes' injuries, coupled with Faith's waving her torture tools all about the place, doesn't leave much to the imagination. Worse, she goes about her business with common household items such as a piece of glass and a flaming can of cooking spray – if anything, that's *more* horrific than her futuristic-looking blade from *Buffy* Season Three (named the Jackal; it's the same type of knife that appeared on the posters for *Star Trek: Nemesis*).

Now, one expects a certain amount of brutality from – say – late-night cable series such as *Oz* or *The Sopranos*. Yet here we're given what's fairly eye-popping fare even if you're watching during the daytime on a lazy weekend, and it's really shocking when you stop to consider this originally broadcast on American network TV between 8 and 9 pm Central time. Indeed, now that six years have passed, Wesley's torture seems even more unthinkable in *Angel*'s original time-slot. It's curious that this didn't ring more alarm bells, but see **The Lore** under "Destiny" (5.08), for when the Parents' Television Coun-cil *did* get its feathers ruffled.

3. There's an entertaining scene when Angel, wearing a suit and infiltrating Wolfram and Hart, improvises some meaningless blather with an attorney (named Bret Folger in the script) who's never seen him before – yet the two of them immediately act like they're best chums. (Bret: "We have to close [the Gruber deal] *now* before the soft offer becomes hard and the stock goes..." Angel: "Through the ceiling..." Bret: "In the toilet!" Angel: "Right." Bret, pleased: "Keep me in the loop." ... and that's just a sample.) Again, anyone who's spent even a small amount of time in Hollywood can tell you that a frightful amount of random conversations sound just like this.

4. In the 1898 flashbacks, Darla pauses to wonder if the newly-ensouled Angel is acting so weird because he's met someone else. It's an amusing assertion, given that vampires – owing to a total lack of conscience – are about as randy as dolphins and hardly monogamous at the best of times. Note especially 5.08, "Destiny" and 5.20, "The Girl in Question," the latter of which proves that Darla's hardly one to talk.

CHARACTER NOTES *Angel:* Elaborating on events detailed in *Buffy* 1.07, "Angel"... Back in 1898, Darla gave a [17-year-old, according to the script] gypsy girl to Angelus for his "birthday." [Vampires tend to number their age from their rebirth as a vampire, so this presumably happened 145 years to the day after Angelus rose from his grave (1.15, "The Prodigal").] Angelus slaughtered the girl while Darla watched.

After the girl's clan cursed Angelus with a soul, Darla returned home to find Angel cowering out of guilt for his crimes. Angel implied he could remember every single person he'd killed. [His photographic memory probably didn't do him any favors.] Angel fled after Darla deemed Angel's soul "filthy" and tried to stake him. Bloodlust compelled him to attack a small party of tavern-goers, and he started to feed off a young woman before recoiling and letting her go. [2.07, "Darla" reveals more about Angel's post-ensoulment period.] Angel spoke a Slavic or Rumanian dialect during this period [or so the script claims].

The modern-day Angel holds a slight advantage in battle against Faith. [As with Buffy herself, the title character tends to come out ahead.] He's quick enough to spin around and catch Faith's crossbow bolt [although she's not shooting to kill]. He neglects to carry cash to a lunch meeting [possibly a habit, although there's no sign that he carries plastic either].

• *Cordelia:* Off-handedly mentions that "Hell will freeze over before I have sex with [Wesley]," for which Wes seems suitably thankful. Cordy seems to believe that evildoers don't change [Angelus' resurgence last episode might be on her mind], although Angel does, to Cordelia's surprise, get a street punk to do the right thing and turn state's evidence.

• *Wesley:* Gets upset that Giles didn't phone him about Faith's awakening from her coma. He initially views Faith as a "sick, sick girl" in need of help, but revises his opinion to say that her "real self" is "a piece of sh – " while getting tortured. Angel in part blames Wesley for their previous failure to avert Faith's life of crime [which is rather unfair, but see *Buffy* 3.15, "Consequences"]. Wesley weathers Faith's torture remarkably well, and later seems prepared to settle matters with Faith with a knife – relenting when she breaks down in Angel's arms.

• *Faith:* Fairly psychotic, beating people up on the slightest or no provocation. [She demonstrates the havoc a single rogue Slayer can wreck, which makes the dozens if not hundreds generated after *Buffy* 7.22, "Chosen" a major concern.] Faith likes the color black. Cappuccino keeps her up at night. She carries a switchblade and apparently doesn't ponder such concepts such as "fate" and "destiny." She's offered the princely sum of $15,000, plus expenses, for killing Angel.

• *Lindsey:* Has a scheduling assistant named Jesse.

• *Lilah:* Lilah's favorite color is green, and she wears a diamond-decorated watch, believing that diamonds suit her. She also loves riding in limos.

• *Phantom Dennis:* Seems to warn Cordelia that Faith's inside her apartment by slamming the door. [As with 1.12, "Expecting," Dennis must sense Faith's demeanor and attempt to alert Cordy and Wes that something's wrong. Some sources wonder why Dennis didn't bash Faith over the head with a handy piece of furniture, but that seems well beyond his telekinetic talent – note 2.03, "First Impressions," in which he can't even stop a vision-struck Cordelia from falling.]

ORGANIZATIONS *Angel Investigations:* Cordelia wonders whether she, Wesley or Angel should apply for a small business loan to cover the rough patches. For captialism's sake, she advocates the agency accepting divorce cases. Angel continues to find such cases distasteful [and see 2.05, "Dear Boy"].

• *Wolfram and Hart:* Its security system includes mystical barriers and vampire detectors. [See 1.21, "Blind Date." We're never privy to the specifics of the "mystical barriers," which never seem to amount to toffee.] Events in Lindsey's office are recorded in Hi-def video.

BEST LINE Lindsey, verbally sparring with Angel: "I remember you throwing one of my clients through a window." Angel, wistfully admiring Lindsey's office window: "Yes. I seem to remember... it was just about that size."

THINGS THAT DON'T MAKE SENSE Angel announces to a full courtroom that Lindsey's client is guilty of "that pesky drug-dealing and murder stuff," yet the judge doesn't offer any sort of rebuke or cite Angel for contempt of court. Wesley later comments, with regards to the case, that "we won" – um, does he mean the client was found guilty? Because if so, the trial went from a virtual dismissal to a conviction, based on the testimony of a witness who's presumably got a rap sheet (he's even listed in the credits as "Gang Banger," if that tells you anything) in just a few hours. (Wesley must mean "they won" by compelling the punk to testify.)

Lindsey is seen on the phone with one of his superiors, and agrees that Angel must be dealt with. Along with Lilah and Lee, he then violates orders (as we learn) by hiring Faith to kill Angel. So... errrr... what *was* Wolfram and Hart's official plan for dealing with Angel, then?

Cordelia now lives in apartment No. 6 rather than No. 212. (That was previously the case in 1.05, "Rm w/a Vu," 1.12, "Expecting" and 1.13, "She." Trevor Lockley also lived in Apt. No. 6 in 1.15, "The Prodigal," and Angel and Darla hole up in hotel Room No. 6 in 2.09, "The Trial" – all of which makes it look as if the props team is recycling the door numbers, even though that's probably not the case). In this case, the discrepancy owes to filming taking place at a difference location – Cordelia's now down the hall from Apt. 7, and she's magically gained an indoor entrance as opposed to her outdoor one.

As Lindsey hasn't ever given Angel his name, how does Angel know to snoop in his office? (He must have seen Lindsey listed as the defense attorney at the murder trial.) Plus, given all the resources at the firm's disposal, the attorneys seem oddly oblivious to the fact that Faith and Angel know one another. They know she's a Slayer who's wanted on a murder charge back in Sunnydale, so how hard can it be to figure out?

Finally, there's a glitch with the invitation rule, as Faith holes up in the apartment of a guy she beat up, yet Angel walks straight through the door, no problem. Two possibilities: Either Faith's victim died (unlikely, as he's never listed on the critical list), or Angel visited the guy in the hospital and somehow extracted an invitation (also unlikely, given the time frame involved).

CROSS-OVERS Faith fell into a coma in *Buffy* 3.21, "Graduation Day," but recently revived to torment Buffy in *Buffy* 4.15, "This Year's Girl" and 4.16, "Who Are You?" before fleeing to L.A. [Faith's reading of *Buffy* Season Three isn't quite accurate, by the way. She wonders how matters would have unfolded if Wesley had been Buffy's Watcher, ignoring the fact that that he did serve in that role, however ineptly.]

An arrest warrant has been issued for Faith in connection with a felony charge. [It's unclear, though, exactly which crime the charge names. She inadvertently killed the Sunnydale Deputy Mayor in "Bad Girls" (*Buffy* 3.14) and willingly slew a vulcanologist in "Graduation Day" (*Buffy* 3.21) but there's never any clear-cut proof of her involvement. Yet in "This Year's Girl," she's wanted for questioning in conjunction with "a series of murders."]

Angel phones Giles, who confirms that Faith left Sunnydale a week ago. [There's no corresponding call on *Buffy*.]

IN RETROSPECT Faith's torture routine with Wesley entails her turning a hairspray can into a makeshift flame-jet. See the *Buffy* motion picture, in which Buffy similarly singes the vampire Lothos, played by Rutger Hauer. [The hairspray trick finished off Lothos in Whedon's original script, going by the *Buffy: The Origin* comic. As filmed, it simply crisps his hair.]

CRITIQUE Taut, daring, unnerving and overall rather magnificent. You can make the case that the flashbacks are gratuitous, but they're so well done, it's hard to protest much.

Given the torture angle, it's almost hard to praise this story without sounding like someone who wallows in gore – yet it's not about glorifying human suffering, it's about recognizing a well-polished piece of drama when it's put in front of you. Wesley might seem like the most "happy-go-lucky" character, but "Five by Five" proves that – unlike some shows that insist on playing patty-cake the whole time – this hardly immunizes him from harm. The big difference here, as opposed to shows with truly gratuitous violence, is one of context. Faith's actions are utterly and indisputably deplorable, but we're asked to consider how much she's an abhorrent monster, and how much she's just an incredibly screwed-up human being. The end scene where a freed Wesley finds Faith sobbing – like a real person – and drops his knife speaks volumes without uttering a single word.

Of course it's disturbing. It's *meant* to be disturbing. Thank God this sort of thing doesn't occur more often, or it'd be too much to bear. But in context, take this story as a sign – however unsettling – of *Angel* becoming unpredictable.

THE LORE Denisof had originally envisioned Wesley as someone about to take a pie in the face but not realizing it. He told *Cult Times:* "Wes was in this sort of cocoon of [slips into Wesley voice] 'It's all going terribly well', whilst slipping on a banana peel." The more *Angel* went on, however, the more Denisof witnessed Wesley racking up a laundry list of horrible injuries. "I've been burnt, shot, cut, stabbed, mutilated, punched on numerous occasions and blown up. We're running out of [injury methods]. I don't know what we'll do. The show may have to stop." He added: "I haven't given birth yet, so let's hope that doesn't happen."

Bearing in mind how quickly Doyle got killed, Denisof fearfully adopted the habit of flipping to the final page of scripts that entailed Wesley taking punishment, worried that the producers would yield to the temptation of butchering the character and leaving Denisof unemployed. "I hope they'd have the decency to call me and let me know if I was killed off before I actually read it in the script, but you never know. Schedules are tough, time is tight." (Spragg, *Cult Times*, June 2002)

• The script contained a cut bit in which Cordelia, on the phone with a potential client undergoing a divorce, expresses confusion as to whether his wife slept with the dog (Shih-Tzu) or the masseur (Shiatsu). It's the latter, fortunately. Another cut line, which potentially would've undermined the torture scene's drama: Wesley resolutely tells Faith that she will "never hear him scream," then adds, "there might be a certain amount of whimpering."

• Sorry to dash anyone's hopes, but the script specifically requested that the lesbian subtext of Faith's initial conversation with Lilah remain very "sub."

• Writer Jim Kouf had worked on movies as far back as *Utilities* (1981), and apparently tended to write scenes that proved unaffordable on a TV budget. He intended the Angel/Faith showdown to take place in the rain, but the production team thought this was overreaching and struck it out. Then during shooting, while Boreanaz and Dushku were brawling, the skies opened up and it helpfully rained. (*Fandom.com*, Aug. 14, 2000) Kouf returned to write stories in Season Two, and also scripted the *Taxi* motion picture starring Queen Latifah and *National Treasure* featuring Nicholas Cage.

1.19: "Sanctuary"

"Buffy, this wasn't about you. This was about saving someone's soul. That's what I do here and you're not a part of it."

Air Date: May 2, 2000; **Writers:** Tim Minear, Joss Whedon; **Director:** Michael Lange

SUMMARY Angel takes the drained Faith back to his apartment, hoping to begin her rehabilitation, but a Watchers' Council commando team (*Buffy* 4.16, "Who Are You?") shows up to bring her into custody. The attorneys send a demon assassin to silence Faith and eliminate Angel, but the duo dispatch the killer. Angel platonically comforts Faith after the melee – just as Buffy arrives, worried about Angel after Faith's initial attack.

Angel and Buffy argue about Faith, then defeat the commandoes, but Lindsey tips off the police that Angel's harboring Faith, a wanted fugitive. A police squad quickly arrests Angel, but Faith turns herself in, taking responsibility for her actions and making a full confession. Angel gets released while Faith is incarcerated, and a steamed Buffy returns to Sunnydale.

FIRSTS AND LASTS Wesley drown his sorrows at the *Third and Long* sports bar; it's the first time that we see him playing darts. More importantly, Buffy logs her final guest appearance on *Angel*, which marks something of a paradigm shift...

POINTS OF DISCUSSION ABOUT "Sanctuary":

1. Until now, *Buffy the Vampire Slayer* characters have trumped the *Angel* cast whenever they've turned up to give the ratings a kiss. It happened in 1.03, "In the Dark," when Spike upstaged virtually everybody, and it happened in 1.08, "I Will Remember You," when the Buffy-Angel romance took precedence over everything else. And notice how it occurs here one final time, as Buffy, Faith and even the Watcher commandoes leave preciously little time for the *Angel* crew. Cordelia's in a single scene before bolting out the door, and it's a particular disservice to Wesley, who was brutally tortured last episode and here gets over his trauma with relatively blazing speed. Granted, other *Buffy*-spawned characters will appear in future – Darla, Drusilla, Spike (again), Harmony and even Andrew – but they'll be retooled to fit *Angel* rather than beating their own drums and expecting Angel's associates to march in step.

2. When Faith channel-flips on Angel's TV (see **Character Notes**), she happens upon the "credits" for a movie that's just ended. As it happens, the credits – and you need to pause your DVD player to get the full effect – contain the

name of *Angel* production members. For comletism's sake, we thought we'd try to identify them all, so we've got: Lisa Lassek (*Angel* assistant editor, *Firefly* associate editor), Josh Charson (assistant editor, *Angel* and *Buffy*), Phillip Geoffrey Hough (no known *Angel* or *Buffy* connection, but he's a guest actor on shows such as on *Homicide* and *Law and Order*, and presumably knew someone on the Mutant Enemy Staff), and Robert D. Nellans (first assistant director, *Angel* and *Buffy*).

An entire host of people are, amusingly, "credited" as Female Dancers: Mere Smith (*Angel* script coordinator/staff writer), Tamara Lewis (unknown, although a Tamara Becher and a Tamara Bosset respectively did post-production and stunts on *Buffy*), Golda Savage (assistant editor, *Buffy*), Marilyn Adams (ditto), Elyse Smith (unknown, unless it's an alias for Elyse Allan Ramsdell, production coordinator on *Angel* and *Buffy*), Elisabeth James (assistant production office coordinator, *Angel* and *Buffy*) and Jesse Stern (assistant to David Greenwalt, *Angel*).

CHARACTER NOTES *Angel:* Now owns a television. [He didn't in 1.17, "Eternity," so he probably bought one simply to stave off Cordelia's needling. It's unlikely that it survives events in 1.22, "To Shanshu in L.A."] He seems venomous with regards to Buffy's current boyfriend Riley Finn, and claims his gypsy curse prevents him from finding someone else. [But again, see how he entirely revises that opinion by 3.07, "Offspring."] Angel admits that Buffy is "a little" stronger than him. His current rift with Buffy makes him reject her help, even when Kate tries to arrange his death.

• *Buffy:* Feels victimized by Faith's actions. [She's got the moral high ground here, given that Faith recently stole Buffy's body, tied up her mother and slept with her boyfriend.] Angel believes Buffy came to L.A. more to enact vengeance on Faith than out of concern for him. [Buffy's confession that she's "entitled" to vengeance seems to confirm this.] The blonde Slayer deems her relationship with Riley as "new" because she trusts and knows him. [Somewhat unfair, as she probably knows Angel better, and he hasn't done anything since that whole business with Angelus in Season Two – okay, that was admittedly pretty nasty – to break her trust.]

• *Cordelia:* Gets Angel to authorize a paid vacation so she can avoid the office while Faith's in residence.

• *Wesley:* The Watchers' Council didn't even offer Wesley a plane ticket home upon firing him [*Buffy* 3.22, "Graduation Day"]. The commando leader, Collins, claims the Watchers will reinstate Wesley if he helps them capture Faith, whom Wes now views as a rabid animal and a murderer. However, Wes [mainly] betrays the commandoes out of respect for Angel. His questionable skill at darts improves considerably under pressure [and see 2.01, "Judgment"].

• *Faith:* She experiences psychotic flashbacks of killing the Deputy Mayor of Sunnydale [*Buffy* 3.14, "Bad Girls"], and fantasies of killing Angel with a butcher's knife. However, she expresses some remorse for torturing Wesley, and admits that she also screwed over Buffy, "the one person in all her life" who tried to be her friend. [Yet even "remorseful" Faith isn't beyond fibbing to Buffy, as she claims that Angel said Buffy would never give Faith a chance... which he didn't.]

L.A. news channels identify Faith as a wanted fugitive. She claims she can practically live off popcorn. [Faith next appears in "Judgment."]

• *Kate:* So angry at Angel [after 1.15, "The Prodigal"] that she threatens to lock him a cell with an East-facing window, facilitating his death when the sun rises. [She can't honestly believe that Angel killed her father, so she's simply lashing out at anything supernatural.] Kate serves as a public spokesperson in the manhunt for Faith, and holds outright contempt for Lindsey and his clientele.

Kate's now investigating incidents with a potentially supernatural element, even those outside her caseload. Police department rumors claim she's "gone all Scully." [They mean she's gravitating toward the supernatural, ignoring that Scully was the skeptic.] A Detective Kendrick claims he and Kate "used to be friends." She's still wearing her cross necklace [1.11, "Somnambulist"].

• *Lindsey:* Knows the circumstances behind the death of Kate's father.

• *Lilah:* Not above pouring the coffee in business meetings [but she'll rebel against this in future; see 4.12, "Calvary"].

• *Lee:* Now in a neck brace [and not looking entirely dissimilar to Gollum from *Lord of the Rings*] after Faith thrashed him last episode.

ORGANIZATIONS *Wolfram and Hart:* Lilah has only heard rumors that Angel used to date a Slayer. [Amazingly, the firm's intelligence on Angel still isn't all that detailed. Darla's knowledge must help them by leaps and bounds, as 2.05, "Dear Boy" implies.] Lindsey worries that the Senior Partners will learn about the failed gambit with Faith.

• *The Watchers:* The Watchers' "Board of Directors" [more properly called "the Council" throughout *Buffy*] includes three alchemists. The Board is extremely frugal and often makes its agents fly coach. Watchers swear sacred oaths, including one to protect the innocent.

Wesley recognizes the Watchers' commandoes – composed of Collins, Smith and Weatherby – as the "Council's elite," and they seem familiar with him. They pretty obviously want Faith dead, letting rip with machine guns at any available opportunity, and not showing a particular concern if they kill Wesley or Buffy by mistake. [There's otherwise no evidence that the Watchers have sanctioned Buffy's death, though – even if she terminated her relationship with them in *Buffy* 3.21, "Graduation Day" – as she's the incumbent Slayer. The commandoes are *really* operating outside normal parameters.]

Weatherby deems working with a vampire as a perversion [consistent with "Graduation Day," in which Watcher policy forbids aiding a vampire, even a heroic one]. The commandoes claim to have a tranquilizer powerful enough to take down a Slayer. [Yet it's not fatal to normal humans, as Wesley incapacitates Weatherby with it.] By all accounts, the defeated commandoes slink home [and they're never seen again].

BEST LINE Angel, trying to tempt a knife-holding, psychotic-looking Faith: "I have donuts..."

THINGS THAT DON'T MAKE SENSE Lindsey, Lilah and Lee are three perfectly capable attorneys who somehow think the blue-skinned demon killer they hire to kill Faith and Angel stands a snowball's chance in hell against them. The only special power the blue-skinned demon displays is the ability to scale walls, and it literally lasts 22 seconds in combat before Faith knifes it to death. What were they thinking? (Mind you, Lilah makes a similar mistake in 3.08, "Quickening.")

The police arrest Angel for "aiding and abetting a wanted felon," but he's released on his own recognizance once Faith makes her confession. If anything, this should strengthen the abetting charge, unless we're to assume that Faith lies through her teeth to cover up Angel's involvement. Also, you'd have to think the police searched Angel's apartment for evidence after his arrest, yet they fail to find the bloody corpse of the aforementioned blue-haired demon thing. (Perhaps Wesley and Buffy had the forethought to clear it away before visiting the police station?)

When Wesley chats with the commandoes in the bar, the "No Smoking" sign magically swaps places with a clearly different "No Smoking" sign. Finally, it's rather funny that Faith becomes haggard, thrashed, half-psychotic and continually hounded throughout this story, yet she apparently finds the time and presence of mind to keep her eye-liner remarkably well-applied.

CROSS-OVERS Angel goes to Sunnydale (*Buffy* 4.20, "The Yoko Factor") and reconciles with Buffy, but not before brawling with her boyfriend Riley Finn, a military operative.

IT'S REALLY ABOUT... Angel to Buffy: "You don't know me any more, so don't come down here with your great new life and expect me to do things your way." Faith issues aside, it's about Angel – both the show and the character – laying down a few boundary lines. Angel doesn't begrudge Buffy's right to vengeance per se, but he definitely rebels against her seeking it in "his city," Los Angeles. Thematically, it's also the point that Angel at least downshifts his fixation on his ex-flame, even if he never truly stops pining for her.

CRITIQUE After the riveting (and very unsettling) "Five by Five," "Sanctuary" becomes a story of diminishing returns. Faith's internal conflict provides some great material, and Whedon continues to achieve a near-perfect level of friction between Angel and Buffy. Unfortunately, the drama starts fraying the more it goes along, and it rather unimaginatively climaxes with gunplay and a motion-picture-style helicopter showdown on the roof. Action-flick elements certainly come in handy on Whedon shows, if they're used selectively – you need only look at the bazooka in *Buffy* 2.14, "Innocence" to see that – but this simply feels like Mutant Enemy trying to steal a page from John Woo flicks and coming up short.

It's not so much Part Two of the story that began last episode, then, as a separate story in most regards that matter – especially once Buffy walks onstage and everything shifts to revolve around her. Still, even if "Sanctuary" fails to achieve its potential, it's undoubtedly a good episode and wins on points. Moreover, maybe we should look on it favorably as the point that *Angel* stops doing the obligatory *Buffy* crossovers for marketing purposes, and starts to mature into a fully independent series – beginning straightaway next episode with the introduction of Gunn.

THE LORE Minear scripted most of this episode under a tight deadline (a couple of days), but found himself gun-shy about writing for an iconic character such as Buffy – whom he'd never scripted before – and asked Whedon to handle her scenes instead. Whedon also wrote the rooftop dialogue, later claiming his favorite scene was the little chat Faith and Angel share about the microwave. Asked about the possibility of Faith returning, Whedon posted: "Eliza has said she'll come back if the stories are interesting. Which is just too damn bad, 'cause I had some really DULL stuff lined up for Faith. Man, QUALITY dull. She was gonna knit, there was a whole psoriasis arc, intense dandruff – Oh! She was gonna vacuum. But, like, obsessively." (Whedon, *The Bronze*, May 6, 2000)

• Gellar's already choked schedule proved an issue, so as with the Slayer becoming a rat in *Buffy* 2.16, "Bewitched, Bothered and Betrayed" (which allowed Gellar to host *Saturday Night Live*), the production team needed a reason to facilitate her *Angel* appearance. Yes, now you know why Buffy and Riley spend so much time making the beast with two backs in *Buffy* 4.18, "Where the Wild Things Are."

1.20: "War Zone"

"I don't need advice from some middle-class white dude that's dead."

Air Date: May 9, 2000; **Writer:** Garry Campbell; **Director:** David Straiton

SUMMARY To Cordelia's delight, software mogul/ billionaire David Nabbit hires Angel Investigations regarding a blackmail case. Angel retrieves potentially incriminating photos of Nabbit, but the assignment lands him smack-dab in the middle of street warfare between a human gang – led by a brash fighter named Gunn – and a vampire nest.

Gunn finds himself reluctant to trust the vampiric Angel, but the vampire group kidnaps and sires Gunn's sister Alonna. A traumatized Gunn dusts his sister, even as his gang and the vampire pack ready for a major smackdown. Fearing massive casualties among Gunn's troops, Angel kills the vampire leader and orders his lackeys to leave town. The bloodsuckers comply, and Gunn warms to the thought of allying with Angel.

FIRSTS AND LASTS It's not just the debut of Gunn, but also his street gang, his pickup truck that's been refitted to combat vampires and the very notion of groups of L.A. street kids in a desperate fight for survival against the supernatural (with the mass public completely oblivious to the conflict). Let's pause to cover the start of a tradition – intentional or not – that a season's third-to-last episode will majorly focus on an ongoing character. (Cameos aside, you'll see this with Fred in Season Two and Connor in Season Three.)

Another character making his debut here: David Nabbit, a self-proclaimed geek who makes "klutzy" Wesley seem like a veritable John Wayne. And technically, it's the first instance an *Angel* character called "Knox" – he's the vampire gang leader, although he's only named in the script, not on screen.

First of two instances where the heroes venture into a demon brothel (the second occurs in 3.14, "Couplet").

POINTS OF DISCUSSION ABOUT "War Zone":

1. The funniest prop on display here: Gunn's gang hideout features a wall sign that says: "Safety and sanitary equipment must be worn in the sausage stuffing room."

2. Before now, *Angel* has looked at L.A.'s supernatural component through the lens of various civilians, but "War Zone" decidedly moves the action into gang territory – the sort with open warfare in disused factories and other blight-afflicted areas. The pre-"War Zone" civilians, for all their troubles, generally gained some security once the particular demon/wacko surgeon/vampire/whatever threatening them got eliminated. Gunn's gang, however, includes hardened combatants who might not outlive the week. They genuinely can't escape their fight for survival, and the contrast between their territory and the more secure world of the civilians isn't very far-fetched, if you're familiar with the breakdown of L.A.'s neighborhoods.

3. Far removed from all that, we're also asked to consider software mogul David Nabbit, who precedes the über-nerd villains in *Buffy* Season Six by more than a year and is far more affable. Nabbit's a blackmail victim, but he's also über-wealthy (he's a billionaire – that's with a *b*), so he stretches the definition of "helping the helpless." It sure looks as if the producers are fishing to see if the audience will accept Nabbit as a recurring character, even though it's hard to see him working out long-term. If nothing else, his wealth threatens to alter the show's shape, given that he could bankroll Angel's operation for years without raising a sweat. It's perhaps with good reason, then, that he only crops up twice more.

CHARACTER NOTES *Angel:* When trapped in a meat locker, Angel opts to punch his way out rather than simply phoning Wesley or Cordelia on his cell to come and open the door. [See 1.13, "She," for the bigger debate on Angel's cell phone prowess.] Angel cites himself as "Angelus" while staking Knox, the vampire leader [as a means of asserting authority]. He's nimble enough to dodge multiple crossbow bolts, but hasn't heard about Madame Dorion's demon brothel before now.

• *Cordelia:* Considers, then discards, the idea of romancing Nabbit for the sake of his money [she's showing astounding depth of character here – for Cordy, that is]. Angel implies that he's hidden money in the office just to watch Cordy sniff it out, labeling her nose for cash as "uncanny."

• *Wesley:* Has heard of Madame Dorion's demon brothel. [Dare we consider that he's visited the joint? Mind, nothing on screen particularly suggests this.]

• *Gunn:* Sometimes fights with a long sword, not relying on any particular strategy other than "Kill everything that moves!"

As kids, Gunn and his younger sister Alonna spent time in a shelter on Plummer Street. Gunn frequently crossed some rotted out planking on the second floor and dared other youngsters to attempt it. Alonna, trying to emulate her big brother, secretly tried the stunt one time and fell through the floor. Fortunately, Gunn had been watching and caught her.

Alonna – like everyone else – refers to Gunn as "Gunn." [Probably a mark of respect, even though "Gunn" is probably her last name also.] Gunn's outfitted pickup truck comes complete with a mounted stake gun and large pieces of wood (good for smashing through walls or skewering vamps) on the hood. [And see 3.18, "Double or Nothing" for the unconventional means by which Gunn acquired his truck.]

Alonna worries that Gunn's getting reckless, unable to go for long without picking a fight. [It's his central character flaw; see 2.03, "First Impressions" especially.] The gang recently spent a vampire-free three weeks until Gunn went hunting for them. He's honorable enough to feed transients who shelter with his gang, insisting that nobody goes hungry.

• *Alonna [Gunn?]:* Carries a spear [that she never puts to use]. It's implied that Knox personally turned her.

• *David Nabbit:* Rather lacking in the social skills department, and doesn't recognize most of the people at his own party. In high school, Nabbit and his friends got heavily into the demon romance element of *Dungeons and Dragons* – this led to their visiting Madam Dorion's brothel to copulate with demons. Nabbit went there 12 times. [Nabbit reappears, cape flowing in the wind, in 1.22, "To Shanshu in L.A."]

ORGANIZATIONS *Angel Investigations:* Nabbit rewards the heroes with an eye-popping check. [The unspecified amount undoubtedly helps the heroes' cash-flow. Even so, "To Shanshu in L.A." entails the office's obliteration and Cordelia and Wesley incurring sizeable medical bills. Then there's the capital needed to acquire/renovate the Hyperion Hotel after "Are You Now Or Have You Ever Been?" (1.02), so it's hardly a shock that Angel's squeezed for cash again by 2.03, "First Impressions."]

• *Gunn's Gang:* Armed with crossbows, stakes, spears and at least one flamethrower. Some of the combatants are no older than 16. A caucasian male named "Chain" appears to serve as Gunn's second-in-command. The group's underground hideout features a number of vampire snares, and the gang partly subsists by stealing food from local grocery stores and garbage bins. At least two gang members here die fighting vampires. [One gets his neck broken, and a stake-gun wielder, Bobby, is apparently body-slammed to death.]

DEMONOLOGY *Vampires:* Alonna rises as a vampire on the evening of the same day in which she's killed. [This happens awfully quick, but it's not entirely without justification – see **Points of Discussion** under 2.10, "Reunion."] Angel coerces one of Gunn's men into granting an invitation into the gang's lair. [This entails Angel reaching around the corner and snagging the man, evidently before he's at the threshold.] Knox's vampires tend to follow a pack mentality [repeatedly demonstrated over on *Buffy*], and prove that insulating outfits can protect vampires against sunlight.

• *Madame Dorion's:* Demon bordello in Bel Air that refuses to service vampires. [Indeed, it's questionable if Dorion's services demonic males *at all* for safety reasons, especially given the wide range of demon mating habits.] The Watcher's Council is rife with stories about the joint. A demon hooker, Lina, appears similar to the creature seen briefly in the "City Of" teaser. [For all we know, it's the same character.]

BEST LINE Cordelia, fawning over the independently wealthy David Nabbit: "I like 'David.' It's such a strong, masculine name. It just feels... good in your mouth."

THINGS THAT DON'T MAKE SENSE In what's potentially the most error-free *Angel* episode of all, there's only one minor quibble: The traps in Gunn's headquarters – primarily designed to kill vampires – appear to include metal crossbow bolts. Angel even tosses one such bolt on the ground, and it makes a metal clatter. Shouldn't the gang know better than to use something that's not wood? Unless, perhaps, they're running short of resources and are going for something that wounds, allowing them to deliver the *coup de grace* by hand?

IN RETROSPECT Angel off-handedly claims that he's never going to have A) love, B) family or C) a place on the planet to call his own. Yet before the series' end, depending on how you define terms, he's actually going to net all three.

IT'S REALLY ABOUT... Despite all the street gang imagery, it's really about racial/social conflicts, or any sort of "us vs. them" mentality that comes with changing demographics. Notably, Knox claims his vampire group has "ruled" the neighborhood for 70 years, and criticizes the lowly quality of victims who've recently moved into there. It's emblematic of the tension caused by shifting patterns of blue-collar workers, white-collar workers, racial trends and more over time. As with many such conflicts, it entails one side telling its people to "get tough" on their opponents, which is why Knox stakes one of his own vampires, Ty, for perceived laziness.

It's also, within these parameters, about how close in major cities the rich neighborhoods sit to poor ones, hence Cordelia's comment, "Twenty minutes ride from billionaires and crab puffs: kids going to war."

CRITIQUE Given the mandate of turning the *Angel* ship of state and crafting a new battlefront for the characters to run around in, "War Zone" goes about its work rather admirably. If anything, it's a victim of its own success, because it retools the series *so* well that with hindsight, we gloss over just how many changes it makes. Fandom-at-large seems to recall "War Zone" as "that story that introduced Gunn" and "the one where Gunn dusts his vampire sister," but that's all.

Which is something of a pity as it's quite good on its own, but that's the price you pay sometimes for shifting gears.

But most importantly of all, it superbly lays the foundation for Gunn's character. If you're going to introduce a new lead, then you've got to expend some capital on them, and in principle you really shouldn't staple their debut into the midst of an otherwise busy story. (Quinn's half-baked debut in *Stargate SG-1* Season Five immediately springs to mind.) On many levels, then, this episode subtly reinvents the show while keeping your adrenaline pumping. Well worth your time.

THE LORE J August Richards' birth name is Jaime Augusto, and he was raised in Maryland in a bilingual household – the first American-born child in his Panamanian family. He dyed his hair red before his audition for Gunn, figuring that anyone who goes around fighting vampires and demons would look a bit different, presuming they're even half-sane. Also, he sensed that some people at The WB deemed him a bit too clean-cut for the role. Whedon later recommended that Richards lose the red hair, figuring it would've too easily made Gunn a target for vampires. (Sibbald, *Zap2It.com*, March 26, 2002)

• Garry Campbell, a freelancer whose credits included *The Kids in the Hall* and *Mad TV*, pitched the idea of street kids fighting vampires in an ongoing battle that the public didn't notice. Whedon had been inclined to debut a character with a different dynamic from that of Angel or Wes, and used this as a vehicle to launch Gunn. "War Zone" marked Campbell's only contribution to *Angel*, although he later wrote for *The Jamie Kennedy Experiment*. (*Fandom.com*, Aug. 14, 2000)

• David Herman (Nabbit) served as one of *Mad TV's* original cast members – there's no real evidence that Campbell's participation helped him get the part, but it'd hardly be surprising. He's provided a bundle of voices both *Futurama* and *King of the Hill*, and he's also in the comedy *Office Space* (1999), where he plays the curiously-named "Michael Bolton."

• Mick Murray (Knox) sports a Hollywood roster that includes such unlikely pairings as *Empire of the Spiritual Ninja* and *Mrs. Santa Claus*.

1.21: "Blind Date"

"What I'm offering you, Lindsey, is the world."

Air Date: May 16, 2000; **Writer:** Jeannine Renshaw; **Director:** Thomas J. Wright

SUMMARY Wolfram and Hart assigns Vanessa Brewer, a blind assassin with heightened senses, to murder three children – powerful seers who're foretold to give the law firm great trouble in future. Unable to countenance such slaughter, Lindsey undergoes a change of heart and approaches Angel for help.

With Lindsey's assistance, Angel infiltrates the firm's main vault and steals computer disks with information on Vanessa's assignment. But once there, Angel feels strangely moved to nick an ancient relic, the Scroll of Aberjian, before escaping. The head of Lindsey's department, Holland Manners, discovers his involvement and overlooks the offense, banking on Lindsey's potential with the firm.

Angel and company use the stolen discs to locate the children, just as Vanessa makes her move. Fortunately, Angel discovers that remaining entirely still renders him invisible to Vanessa's senses, allowing him to kill her. Holland acknowledges that Lindsey bested the firm, yet offers him the choice of leaving or accepting a promotion. Ultimately, Lindsey chooses to stay with the firm.

FIRSTS AND LASTS Holland Manners (played by Sam Anderson) gets unveiled as Lindsey and Lilah's boss – technically, he's only referred to as "Holland," but his office door plaque displays his full name. He's not just the first Division Head for Special Projects to show up (even if the title isn't officially used until 2.10, "Reunion"), but the first Wolfram and Hart higher-up of any sort to appear in the flesh. Mind, he's not going to stick around for too long, as people in his job generally have the life expectancy of a depressed lemming.

Lindsey becomes a three-dimensional character for the first time – a mere 21 episodes after his debut – and this story entails the first illicit trip into the basement vaults beneath the firm's L.A. branch. On a thematic note, Wesley's initial reading of the Prophecies of Aberjian gives the first mention of an all-crucial destiny awaiting a vampire with a soul – even if the term "Shanshu Prophecy" won't come into play until next episode.

Final appearance of evil attorney Lee Mercer, whom Holland has killed for collaborating with another firm.

POINTS OF DISCUSSION ABOUT "Blind Date":

1. As opposed to the comparatively black-and-white stories presented before now, here's where matters delve into the gray area. Several notions about power start getting proffered back and forth, and particularly notice Angel's annoying realization that Wolfram and Hart's legal shenanigans might trump any hope for justice in the world. Bearing in mind what's to come, you're justified in feeling a chill when Angel comments on the firm: "[It's] their world... structured for power, not truth. It's their system, and it's one that works because there's no guilt, no torment. I remember what that

was like... sometimes I miss that clarity." The producers surely didn't intend this as a precursor to Season Five, but it's prophetic anyway.

2. Time to pause and consider Wolfram and Hart's official policy toward Angel. The firm knows little about him for most of Season One, and there's no concrete rule against killing him, or Lindsey, Lee and Lilah would surely have expressed concern about it while conspiring to off him in "Five by Five" (1.18). Events in "To Shanshu in L.A." (1.22) clearly prove the firm's opted to screw with Angel's mind as opposed to just dusting him, and no later than "Blood Money" (2.12), a company policy explicitly forbids Angel's termination.

So what changes their minds in the interim? The most straightforward answer – although it's never said – is the Scroll of Aberjian, here found in the firm's possession. It's never mentioned before, so it's entirely possible the firm unearthed it and learned about the importance of the "vampire with a soul," which prompted the new policy. We also discover – from the series finale – that someone in the Circle of the Black Thorn possesses the original Shanshu Prophecy, which is part of the Scroll, so perhaps it simply took Angel registering high enough on the firm's radar to warrant the Circle supplying the Scroll for research. Either way, the Scroll pretty clearly causes the "don't kill Angel" policy shift – fortunately for everyone concerned, since it saves the viewer from sitting through a string of assassination attempts against Angel (in the finest tradition of Inspector Clouseau, no doubt).

3. Lee has been in secret talks with "Klein and Gabler," explaining why Holland summarily has Lee's head blown off. Funny, though, how a single off-handed reference threatens to fundamentally alter the series' entire power structure. We have to assume that "Klein and Gabler" refers to a rival law firm on par with Wolfram and Hart, and an infernal one at that. After all, a standard human firm would lack the resources to protect Lee from his former employers. It's also unlikely that they're a benevolent agency, partly because Angel would surely have dealings with them at some point if such an operation existed, and partly because Lee plans on taking his clients to there and a "good" law firm would hardly have use for the sort of beings/people using Wolfram and Hart's services. Well, beyond wantonly slaughtering them, perhaps. All the evidence, then, suggests that "Klein and Gabler" holds a fairly high rank in the *Angel*-verse, yet they're never mentioned again.

4. It's frequently cited as a goof that Angel breaks into the firm's vault on Sub-Level 2, yet Lindsey leaves his pass for Angel on Sub-Level 3. But actually, when you think about it, this makes a great deal of sense. If the Sub-Levels are numbered going downward, then Sub-Level 3 lies below Sub-Level 2 – meaning Angel enters from his self-made sewer access, scoops up Lindsey's pass on Sub-Level 3 and proceeds upward to the vault on Sub-Level 2.

Why doesn't Lindsey just leave the pass on Sub-Level 2? At a guess, Sub-Level 2 is probably nothing *but* the main vault, meaning it'd look incredibly suspicious for the Lindsey to go there. Also, he'd risk running afoul of the guard demon, and only Angel is equipped to deal with it.

CHARACTER NOTES *Angel:* His father [1.15, "The Prodigal"] was a linen/silk merchant. Angel coaches Lindsey that simple guilt isn't enough and that he needs to *show* he's different. [Angel should know, given that he spent a century doing little but wallowing in guilt.]

• *Cordelia:* Seen researching "LAPD Online." [The screen reads "For Official Use," so Willow's probably been teaching Cordelia the merits of hacking.]

• *Wesley:* Can translate ancient Aramaic.

• *Gunn:* Agrees to help Angel sneak into the firm on the grounds that "it'll be extremely dangerous."

• *Holland Manners:* Clearly runs Lindsey's department. [However, future episodes such as 5.01, "Conviction" and 5.21, "Power Play" imply that Holland runs the entire L.A. branch, not just the Special Projects division. We never see or hear about the branch's C.E.O. before Season Five, so it's not impossible that Holland here "moves upstairs" to assume that position. That's a bit tricky, though, because he only acknowledges himself as a department head in 2.10, "Reunion." Alternatively, perhaps Holland was effectively if not officially running the entire branch and was generally acknowledged as such. You can certainly find colleges where the president isn't actively running the show, for instance. It'd certainly explain why the hell Special Projects keeps handling mundane fare such as fund-raisers and standard lawsuit stuff (see, respectively, 2.12, "Blood Money" and 2.18, "Dead End") – perhaps Holland co-opted other operations for his section.]

Holland knows about his attorneys' operation with Faith. [1.18, "Five by Five." It'd be hard for him *not* to know, given the extent of Lee's pummeling, but there's no evidence of any-one being disciplined over the affair.] Holland carries broad discretion, ordering Lee's execution while choosing to overlook Lindsey's sizeable offenses. [Favoritism aside, Holland comments that "disloyalty hurts him," so perhaps Lee's getting into bed with rival bad guys is more damning than Lindsey aiding the good guys.] A bald guard named Phil shoots disloyal employees at Holland's command. Holland here moves upstairs and gives Lindsey his old office space.

• *Lindsey:* Grew up in utter poverty with his five siblings, two of whom died from the flu. The family home got repossessed when Lindsey was seven, and Lindsey's "spineless" father apparently grinned like a fool while signing away the deed. Lindsey went to law school at Hastings, where Holland handpicked him, as a sophomore, to work for Wolfram and Hart [but see "Dead End"].

Lindsey has a reputation for completing work without actually researching or even reading much of anything. He retains the computer disks that were taken from the firm's vault as insurance against the firm harming him [and see "Dead End"].

• *Lilah:* The firm's mind readers fail to detect any wrongdoing on Lilah's part. [She's probably clean for now, and only starts to violate company policy in "Blood Money"; 3.15, "Loyalty" and more.] She's not afraid to get her hands dirty with research [seen again in 3.10, "Dad"].

• *Vanessa Brewer:* Wolfram and Hart's personnel file on Vanessa claims she was born July 18, 1967 in San Francisco, and entered the firm's employ as a part-time operative in 1991. She spent five years in Pajaur studying with the Nanjin, a group of cave-dwelling monks who seek enlightenment by seeing with the heart, not the mind. [The monks' goal of "enlightenment" implies a peaceful state of being, yet Vanessa's power must be demonic in nature. It's said that Vanessa blinded herself, yet her eyeballs are perfectly intact, which suggests a ritualistic blinding rather than her simply gouging her eyes out with a convenient letter opener. More to the point, Vanessa's super-fighting abilities – enough to counter Angel – certainly owe to more than extra-sensory perception, whatever the *Daredevil* motion picture might absurdly claim.]

Vanessa voluntarily blinded herself at age 21, and the monks' techniques enabled her to develop heightened senses. [As Vanessa was born in 1967, some sources take this to mean that she blinded herself in 1988 *and then* spent five years with the monks – which seems odd for someone who started working for the firm in 1991. Going by the details that Wesley relates, however, it's entirely possible she spent at least couple of years with the monks in preparation for her blinding, performed the deed in 1988, then spent another year or two with the monks before she started taking assignments from the firm. There's room to maneuver here.]

Vanessa is 5'6" tall and weighs 122 pounds. Although blind, she appears to sense targets by heat. [Vanessa can "see" the warm-blooded seers when they're sitting still, but can't sense Angel – who lacks a body temperature – when he's not in motion, i.e. creating friction of movement.] She can kill with her sharpened walking stick.

She's been arrested at least three times: in 1993 for fleeing a homicide scene (no charges brought), in 1995 for aggravated assault (never went to trial) and in 1999 as a double homicide suspect, for which she's currently on trial. [She also kills a middle-aged black man in the teaser, presumably on Wolfram and Hart's behalf, but it's never stated why.]

• *The Seers:* Three blind children from overseas, described by Wesley as a "holy triumvirate" that have been gathered together for the first time in L.A. It's foretold that their "power" [prophetic? psychic?] goes up exponentially when they're together, and will only increase as they mature. It's said they can "see into the heart of things," which somehow threatens the firm. [The kids possess extra-sensory perception, as their toys include such sight-reliant toys as an Etch-a-Sketch and a Rubik's Cube.] An unseen mentor arrives from the east and takes the kids to safety [and they're never heard from again].

ORGANIZATIONS *Wolfram and Hart:* Lindsey has knowledge of Angel's father [so the firm has progressed in their investigation of Angel since "Five by Five"]. The firm's computer disks mention Wolfram and Hart branches in Boston and Chicago. The firm has a "harvest" time of year that apparently entails disposing of under-performing employees. [It's probably a piss-ant version of the firm's 75-year review, see 2.15, "Reprise".]

The firm employs mind readers, including two African-American women [who look surprisingly like Grace Jones during her Bond girl days], to scan employees for misconduct. [It says something about the firm that the moment after Angel trips an alarm, they start mind-scanning their own personnel.] The women convey their findings to Holland though speech, not "mind-speak." [The mind-readers' origins go unrevealed, but see 1.04, "I Fall to Pieces" for some thoughts about this, and they're glimpsed again in 3.08, "Offspring."]

The firm's L.A. office has at least 30 levels.

PROPHECY *The Prophecies of Aberjian:* Contained in the "Scroll of Aberjian" [as it's called next episode]. Wesley's initial examination of the Prophecies suggests they were written in ancient Aramaic, but lost for centuries. They apparently mention the seer children. Crucially, Wes finds at least one passage that mentions a vampire with a soul, yet doesn't cite Angel by name [all of this gets elaborated on next episode]. It's unstated why Angel feels compelled to take the Scroll from the vault.

DEMONOLOGY While researching Vanessa, Wesley finds mention of one-eyed demons and 12-eyed demons (some with double vision) but no blind demons. [The Bringers of the First from *Buffy* evidently don't count.] Wesley seems willing to accept the existence of non-demons with Vanessa's abilities [but see Vanessa's entry in **Character Development**].

• *Vampire-Sensing "Shamans":* Gray and wrinkly creatures that, as the name implies, detect vampires that enter the firm. [Hell, they might even *be* vampires, magically adapted to sense their own kind.] The shaman screeches whenever a vampire crosses the building's "threshold." [Evidently, it can only sense vampires as they enter and leave the building, or it'd keep wailing after Gunn's distraction vamp gets dusted. Perhaps the shaman gives out a similar alarm – off screen – when Angel departs the firm, but it's simply too late.]

• *Preggothian Demon:* Type of demon that guards the Wolfram and Hart vault. Wesley gives Angel a pink powder that, when blown in the demon's face, immobilizes it.

BEST LINE A dispassionate Holland, commenting on the mess left by Lee's bloodied corpse: "What a pity. You can't get that out of the carpet. Believe me, we've tried."

THINGS THAT DON'T MAKE SENSE As with 1.18, "Five by Five," courtroom cases move stunningly fast in L.A. Lindsey gives what sounds like opening arguments in Vanessa's murder trial, but even if it's actually his closing statement, he still nets an acquittal the very same day, even though Vanessa gets a hung jury. Later, Angel claims that Wolfram and Hart is representing Vanessa *pro bono* – meaning without charging – when he has no real way of knowing that.

It's entirely too coincidental that Angel randomly happens across Vanessa in the teaser, which apparently occurs just to give the heroes a head-start at researching her past, so they're better prepared when Lindsey's unexpected change-of-heart arrives. Never mind that it's just too symmetrical that the blind Vanessa is here dispatched to kill three blind children.

Once Lindsey has kept the security guard from noticing Angel, why doesn't he just leave the building rather than wandering around aimlessly, thus allowing himself to get caught in the firm's employee sweep? Why wait for Angel's call telling him to "get out" when there's nothing more for him to do anyway? Speaking of judgment lapses, how on Earth did Lee expect to keep secret his meetings with Klein and Gabler, given that Wolfram and Hart uses mind-readers? Saying "he's just stupid" hardly seems adequate, considering that the fairly obvious oversight gets him shot in the head.

A minor point: Vanessa's personnel file has a section labeled "Defenses Against." Despite this, Angel doesn't have a clue about Vanessa's weaknesses until the heat of battle. And now a hopelessly minor point: Wesley arrives back at the office with coffee and Angel tells him that Cordelia's been on the phone for "an hour and 45 minutes." If it's been that long, just where did Wesley drive to get the coffee? San Diego?

CROSS-OVERS Cordelia calls Willow for help in decrypting the firm's computer files. The *Buffy* series never mentions the call, but it coincides with the Slayer's crew hacking the Initiative's files [*Buffy* 4.21, "Primeval," and see **The Lore**].

IT'S REALLY ABOUT... Holland to Lindsey: "Do you believe in love? I'm not speaking romantically, I'm speaking about the sharp clear sense of self a man gains once he truly finds his place in the world... I believe in you. Look deep enough inside, you'll find that love."

Setting aside all the business with the blind chick and the seer kids, it's about one's metamorphosis into adulthood – the butterfly finally coming out of the cocoon, if you like. Post high school or college, most people usually flounder and spasm in their actual jobs until growing to accept, with palpable certainty, where they belong. It's a surprisingly adult conundrum, as the adolescent world can't help but consist of a volcanic amount of change, whereas this entails a person choosing a path and trying, if possible, not to budge from it.

CRITIQUE For all that you can praise Season One, and for all its great stories, it's this episode that marks the start of *Angel* as we now recognize it. With the players snugly in place on the chessboard, "Blind Date" (the ghastly title notwithstanding) lets rip and moves at a pace that seems like warp speed compared to the stand-alone tales that preceded it. Lindsey's betrayal, Holland's deviousness, the mind-readers, Lee's death, the vampire shamans, the Scroll of Aberjian... so much gets explored here, it's utterly captivating.

That said, it's not exactly what you'd call flawless. Yes, it rounds out Lindsey's character, but much of this relies on a faintly ludicrous "poverty stricken childhood" story that you'd almost expect to hail from *Oliver Twist*, with a little Lindsey begging, "Please, Mr. Manners... I want some more." Also, Vanessa's been accused of being a pale *Daredevil* rip-off – probably because she *is* a pale *Daredevil* rip-off – but that's forgivable because the adventure isn't really about her.

Instead, it's about molding *Angel* into a layered series in which you can't entirely predict anyone's actions. It absolutely breathes new life into Lindsey's character (despite the cliché-filled back story, not because of it) and seeds the ambiguity that'll work so well in Season Two. It's also faintly startling how you're made to root for *Lindsey* – of all people! – when he's threatened at the mid-point cliffhanger, considering he's been nothing but a disposable (if charismatic) law stooge before now. And if we're talking unpredictable/charismatic characters, then notice how Sam Anderson, as Holland, immediately makes his stamp as the suave, riveting seducer. Hard to ignore the "Christ being tempted in the wilderness" imagery when Holland tells Lindsey, "I'm offering you the world."

At the end of the day, you're aware that "Blind Date" trips itself up at a couple of turns. But inherently, you're also aware that *Angel* just kicked up to a new level, and there's little turning back for the characters now.

THE LORE Sam Anderson (Holland) is a veteran character actor, so readily employable that his resume, at a glance, appears to include almost every network series worth mentioning. In recurring roles, he's been a doctor on *E.R.*, a principal on both *Growing Pains* and *Boston Common*, and a tail-section survivor (if you will) on *Lost*. (That show's almost become a Wolfram and Hart reunion, by the way, what with Daniel Dae Kim – *Angel*'s Gavin Park – also numbering among the cast.) Anderson appeared in four different roles on both *WKRP in Cincinnati* and *Murder, She Wrote*. On *Boston Legal*, he played a wholesome school district supervisor who fired two teachers because they wouldn't teach creationism.

• The script tailored the mind readers as a male and a female, rather than the two women seen on screen.

• It wasn't deliberate that both Angel and Buffy's crews came to be working on encrypted disks at the same time, and the producers opted to acknowledge it through the Cordelia/Willow phone call rather than eliminating it or ignoring the similarity (remember that *Angel* and *Buffy* aired back-to-back in this era). (Whedon, *The Bronze*, May 17, 2000)

• Jennifer Badger Martin (Vanessa Brewer) did quite a lot of work on *Buffy* as a stunt double for Carpenter, Dushku, Alyson Hannigan (Willow) and Emma Caulfield (Anya). Among other stunts, Martin doubles for the titular character in *Buffy* 2.04, "Inca Mummy Girl," and she's the one performing Faith's freefall into a passing truck (*Buffy* 3.21, "Graduation Day"). (Pruitt, *The Bronze*, Oct. 17, 1999)

1.22: "To Shanshu in L.A."

"All avenues to the Powers shall be cut off to him."

Air Date: May 23, 2000;
Writer/Director: David Greenwalt

SUMMARY Wesley translates some of the prophecies in the Scroll of Aberjian, and becomes horrified to read that a "heroic vampire with a soul" will *shanshu*, meaning "to die." Meanwhile, the firm summons the formidable demon Vocah to assist with a "raising" ceremony.

Vocah swiftly decapitates Angel's support system – first by murdering the Oracles, then by planting a magical sigil on Cordelia that makes her experience horrific visions round-the-clock. Moreover, Vocah steals back the Scroll – which is required for the "rising" – and obliterates the Angel Investigations office and Angel's apartment with a bomb, severely injuring Wesley.

Members of Lindsey's department gather at a mausoleum and commence the "raising," but Angel bursts in and slays Vocah. As Lindsey completes the ritual, something magically appears in a large crate and the firm's executives evacuate with their prize. Lindsey tries to spitefully burn the Scroll and ruin Angel's chances of saving Cordelia, but Angel simply hacks off Lindsey's hand and takes the ancient text.

Wesley recovers and uses the Words of Anatole – also part of the Scroll – to cure Cordelia, then re-examines the prophecy. Wes determines that he mistranslated the word *shanshu*, which simultaneously means "life" and "death" and suggests that Angel – who's already undead – will one day attain the reward of becoming human. Angel and company breathe easy, even as Lindsey, Lilah and Holland gather in a vault to view the catch from their ceremony: the newly resurrected Darla.

FIRSTS AND LASTS The Shanshu Prophecy – the mother of all prophecies where *Angel*'s concerned – gets named and detailed (well, loosely) for the first time. Simultaneously, there's an "end of an era" feel as the series disposes of many of the trappings from Season One: the Oracles, Angel's apartment and the Angel Investigations office.

It's Darla's first appearance on *Angel* in anything other than flashbacks, and the "Vocah summoning ritual" marks the first dark ritual that we see undertaken at the firm. Vocah's arrival also marks the first "ring of fire" seen on the show (4.07, "Apocalypse, Nowish" provides the most spectacular example), and Vocah is also the first – but not the last – character who's rendered as a hunk of rotting flesh covered with maggots (Jasmine is the other, later in Season Four).

Angel kills Vocah by burying one of the demon's own scythes in his noggin, and this starts a weird trend, given all the "demon head-splittings" in Season Two.

POINTS OF DISCUSSION ABOUT "To Shanshu in L.A.":

1. The villains so easily put Angel's allies to the sword that one wonders why the hell this doesn't occur more often. Fair enough that the firm expressly forbids Angel's death (see 2.12, "Blood Money" for why), but why don't they off his associates? Why not post snipers outside Wesley's apartment and pick him off from a distance? Why not send a whole pack of commandoes to eliminate Gunn when Angel isn't around to protect him? Why not rig a device that incinerates Cordelia when she's at the tanning salon?

The answer, although it's never stated on screen, is that Wolfram and Hart have decided to gradually screw with Angel, and slaughtering his teammates wholesale would be going a bit far. It'd give Angel nothing to lose, and as Marvel Comics likes to keep telling us: "A man without hope... is a man without fear." For more on this, see **The Critique**.

2. Another broad issue to consider: The Shanshu Prophecy,

the carrot-on-a-stick which tantalizingly promises Angel will become human (although see 1.08, "I Will Remember You" for why this sounds off-kilter to say). Or rather, that a "vampire with a soul" will become human, which is why matters get so complicated come what happens to Spike at the end of *Buffy* Season Six. It's an obvious question to ask whether the Shanshu Prophecy is ultimately bunk or not, and for a debatable answer, see **Points of Discussion** under the series finale.

3. Vocah claims that the Scroll, if left in Angel's hands, will "complete" his connection to the Powers. You could infer that Angel needs a conjunction of a visionary, the Oracles and the Scroll's prophecies to finalize his link to his benefactors. However, Lindsey states without qualification that it's prophesized that Wolfram and Hart will "sever all of Angel's links" to the Powers. (If this prophecy comes from the Scroll itself, then there's some heavy irony at work here.) We finish this story somewhere between the two options... Angel keeps Cordelia and the Scroll, but the Oracles perish, and perhaps explains in part why Angel's lines to the Powers are less-than-rock-solid for the next four years. Simply put, the prophecy that Lindsey mentions appears to come true.

CHARACTER NOTES *Angel:* Seems entirely unconcerned by Wesley's (erroneous) foretelling of his death. [That's entirely in keeping with Angel's character, as death would end his suffering and he's displayed suicidal tendencies before – see *Buffy* 3.10, "Amends"]. He does, however, smile when it's revealed that the Shanshu promises "a vampire with a soul" will become human [so he'd prefer redemption if possible].

• *Cordelia:* Experiences an onslaught of visions that gives her a greater appreciation for the world's suffering. [It's one of Cordelia's greatest turning points, as she's far more vested in helping others from this point. It's also the start of her becoming the group's main source of empathy in Seasons Two and Three.] A CAT scan reveals that Vocah's attack doesn't leave Cordelia with any damage [but it might exacerbate decay already in progress; see 3.11, "Birthday"]. It's implied Cordy shops in the *Penny Saver* [but probably not by choice].

• *Gunn:* Guards the hospitalized Cordelia and Wesley on Angel's behalf. [They're unaware of his presence, as next episode shows.] Milano's Italian Kitchen sometimes donates food to Gunn's gang.

• *Lindsey:* Now promoted to the rank of "Junior Partner" at the firm, with a six-figure salary and full benefits. Lindsey speaks enough Latin to complete Darla's resurrection ritual.

• *David Nabbit:* [Last seen in 1.20, "War Zone," and appears a final time in 2.03, "First Impressions."] He shows up at Angel Investigations wearing a cape and sword, just wanting to hang out. And possibly role-play. He blew off his meeting with his Board of Directors, because tonight's his night as Dungeon Master. The heroes prompt Nabbit into leaving by giving him the silent treatment. Nabbit recently made several million dollars by spinning off his digital pager network.

• *Vocah:* [See **Points of Discussion** next episode for why there's reason to believe that Vocah survives his bout with Angel.] So-called "warrior of the underworld," armed with disposable scythes that magically manifest from his body. [The scythes can't be the only means of killing Vocah, or he'd hardly be stupid enough to leave one in the Oracles' lair for Angel to pick up.] He's skilled with conventional explosives. [Vocah also likely possesses a "shrouding" effect that enables him to move with unusual stealth, as nobody at the L.A. street fair pays him the slightest attention. You could argue that he's just mistaken for a street performer, but Cordelia doesn't notice his approach either and Vocah even eludes Angel's vampire senses at close range.]

Vocah's face is revealed as a nose-less cadaver crawling with maggots. The Oracles look upon him as a lower being.

• *Holland:* Recommends *never* being prompt for a ritual, as the chanting and blood rites seemingly go on forever.

ORGANIZATIONS *Angel Investigations:* Occupies Suite 103. Fellow tenants – at least, before the building gets obliterated – include Casas Manufacturing in 101; John Folger, DDS in 104 [mentioned in 1.11, "Somnambulist"]; and Herbert Stein in 105. Cordy and Wes are treated at [the fictional] St. Matthew's Hospital.

• *The Powers-That-Be:* Have Angel save a homeless woman who's convinced that the Dental Association is spying on her.

• *The Oracles:* Shed red blood, and the female Oracle advises Angel as a ghost for a short time after her demise. Her comment on being dead: "So far, I don't like it."

The Oracles claim to not counsel "Vocah's kind" [probably meaning agents of the "dark forces"] and that "the powers of darkness" typically can't cross the threshold of their temple. [The female Oracle's shade takes Vocah's intrusion as proof that "things are unraveling," and Vocah implies that a "new order" has arrived. Couple this with Lindsey's statement in 5.17, "Underneath" that *the* apocalypse has begun without anyone noticing, and perhaps the mystical balance of power has already shifted, making the Oracles impotent.]

THE LIBRARY One of Wesley's books claims that "the beast of Amalfi," a razor toothed six-eyed harbinger of death, will arise in 2003 in Reseda. [That places the rising near Seasons Four or Five, but the show never mentions it again.]

PROPHECY Wesley claims that prophecies are "sent from on high." [This suggests a higher power hands down knowledge of the future, then, as opposed to a seer using their brain as some sort of magical/psionic time scanner.]

• *The Scroll of Aberjian:* A patchwork of prophecies and mystic texts, the Scroll contains "the Prophecies of Aberjian," which were written over the last 4000 years in a dozen different languages [including ancient Aramaic, as Wes determined last episode], some of them not human. Some Scroll-writings appear in black and red [blood?] ink [and see **Magic**].

• *The Shanshu Prophecy:* Foretells that a vampire with a soul, once "he fulfills his destiny," will ***shanshu*** – the word evidently has roots in many different languages [going by Wesley's initial assessment, these include Proto-Ugaric, descended from the ancient Magyars, but not the Phrygian language]. No English equivalent exists for ***shanshu***, but the most ancient source is a Proto-Bantu term that considers life and death as part of the same cycle. Wes conjectures from this that since Angel is technically dead, ***shanshu*** in his case would entail becoming alive/human again.

Wesley deduces that the climactic battle in which Angel will earn his reward is probably years off, after "the coming battles." It's unclear if the Shanshu Prophecy is part of the "Prophecies of Aberjian" themselves, or completely a separate text bound in the same document. [By the way, Wesley's working off a copy... the original Shanshu Prophecy surfaces in 5.22, "Not Fade Away."]

MAGIC *The Scroll of Aberjian*: In addition to containing prophecies, the Scroll includes the Words of Anatole and appears to function as a mystic artifact in its own right. Vocah indicates that Darla's raising literally can't take place without the Scroll. [It's really an amazing all-purpose tool, then, able to cure Cordelia's "mental overload" and resurrect vampires as human beings, as well as containing prophetic texts.]

• *The Words of Anatole:* "Sacred" recitation that makes reference to wounds caused by "the beast" [not the rock creature from Season Four]. When Wesley recites the Words from the Scroll in English, there's a flash of light and Vocah's mark fades from Cordelia's hand. [The Words' final utterance is: "Unbind, unbind, unbind."] The Words come accompanied with an illustration of a brown dragon breathing fire [which is curious, considering what happens in the series finale].

• *Vocah's Mark:* A black circle with a dollop that manifests on Cordelia's hand after Vocah touches it. The sigil "opens Cordelia's mind" to numerous people crying out in pain. [Arguably, the Mark simply drops Cordelia's mental defenses and lets her hear the whole spectrum of psionic channels, rather like duct-taping a stereo headset to someone's noggin and ramping up the volume on thousands of phone calls.]

• *Darla's Raising:* Performed in a mausoleum [possibly a requirement or just for show]. Five vampires are chained around a large box while Vocah's helpers – a pair of bored-sounding monks – recite and chant. Vocah (then Lindsey) reads in English, then Latin, direct from the Scroll. The vampire quintet suddenly dust and create a whirlwind around the box, climaxing in a burst of light that manifests human Darla. [The ritual refers to "raising" something from hell, and considering Darla's rejection of God – in flashback, 2.07, "Darla" – it's reasonable to think her soul resides in a hell of sorts.]

BEST LINE Lilah, goading Lindsey when his neck's on the line: "Remember when Robert Price let the Senior Partners down and they made him eat his liver?... I don't know what made me think of that."

THINGS THAT DON'T MAKE SENSE Vocah's bomb hums like an alarm clock and occasionally beeps during its countdown to detonation, helpfully giving Wesley a clue that – hello! – that there's a bomb in the weapons cabinet. Couldn't Vocah, cunning and resourceful warrior of the underworld that he is, purchase a bomb that doesn't announce itself to anyone passing by? For that matter, you have to question the heroes' wisdom for locking a valuable artifact such as the Scroll in the easily-breakable weapons cabinet, considering they must know the firm will want it back.

Stuff everyone seems to notice... the weapons stashed in Angel's cabinet change for no good reason. There's three sai when Angel shuts the cabinet, but only one sai and what's arguably a dagger when Vocah opens it moments later. (Then again, perhaps the dagger *is* a sai, and Vocah simply knocked the sai off their hooks when he broke open the cabinet. Well, maybe.) Also, Angel rips Vocah's face mask off during the crypt fight, yet it spontaneously reappears just before Vocah is killed. (Do the face masks magically regrow like Vocah's scythes?) Then there's the trick donut that Cordelia and Wesley share in the office, which thanks to slippery editing appears in various states of "being eaten" in the same shot.

Rituals are a matter of perception: Holland arrives for the rising ceremony and bemoans, "They haven't even gotten to the Latin yet," as if this takes a long time to recite. Lindsey actually needs a mere 35 seconds to do it, and over a third of that entails him shouting, *"Serge!"* (*"Arise!"*)

IN RETROSPECT Cordelia, trying to get Angel to want "something" in life, suggests: "How would you like a puppy?" It's not her fault, but it seems a bit tactless, given Angelus' history with a puppy, nails and Valentine's Day [see *Buffy* 2.16, "Bewitched, Bothered and Bewildered"].

IT'S REALLY ABOUT... Smashing some of the fixtures from Season One in readiness for next year. But to zero in on the Shanshu and its promised reward to Angel (or so the heroes hope), it's about adults struggling and struggling and *struggling* for rewards they're never sure if they're going to attain or not. (Think of the Shanshu as metaphorically paying off your home mortgage, and it starts to make sense.)

CRITIQUE Like 4.22, "Home," it's really an extended prologue for the season to come. And like "Home," it's a really commendable effort that sweetly accomplishes everything it sets out to do – finish the year with a palpable sense of urgency, and clear the decks for Season Two. If we're zeroing in on the most lackluster element, it's actually Vocah, whose overblown purple cape makes him look like he's going to leap across rooftops and duke it out with Batman after eliminating Angel. Even Vocah's a bit forgivable, though, because the scythe fight scenes in the crypt are really cool. Sure, they're a matter of the heart trumping the brain, but they're just *neat*.

But as with last episode, the story navigates fine with a so-so villain, because it's more importantly about redefining the series' flavor and Angel's place in the world. In the first episode, a solitary Angel lacked someone to care about – and given all the development in the past year, once Cordelia and Wesley go onto the critical list, he's *even more* alone. Basically, he's now got something to lose, and that's horrifically obvious when Cordelia collapses and unleashes some genuinely unsettling screams.

We've arrived at a sweet turning point, then – and as a wise man said, change is good. If you weren't spoiled about the über-twist of Darla showing up, then it should work as a delicious reveal, and it's meant to signal that the firm's crusade against Angel won't entail legions of demon troops (well, not at first...). If this doesn't make you curious about Season Two, it's possible that you're watching the wrong show. But let's appreciate this development as a sign of the producers putting their chips on the table and – rightfully – spinning the roulette wheel to get a big payout in future.

THE LORE Greenwalt says the producers had become bored with the *Angel* sets, deeming them "ugly and brown," hence the decision to blow up Angel's brownstone. He also said, with regards to Angel's inability to have sex, that he was dying to do a scene where Angel turned to a woman and proclaimed: "I can't know perfect happiness, but that doesn't mean you can't." (Seipp, *United Press International*, May 8, 2002)

• On the day of this story's broadcast, and with *Dark Angel* now on the horizon, Whedon posted: "Because of counter programming by FOX, ANGEL will now be called LIGHT ANGEL. Or possibly PLAID ANGEL. Or ANGEL WHO IS NEITHER DARK NOR TOUCHING ANYONE NOR IN ANY WAY A CITY THEREOF BUT JUST THE ONE ANGEL WHO'S LIGHT AND/OR PLAID." (*The Bronze*, May 23, 2000)

The Total Kill-Count (thru Season One)

- Angel: 11 vampires, 12 demons, 2 human.
- Doyle: 1 vampire, 1/2 demon.
- Wesley: 1 demon.
- Cordelia: 1 1/2 demons.
- Kate: 3 vampires, 1 human.

NOTES: Going straight to the issue of Angel killing two people... we've counted Dr. Meltzer (the guy who can separate his body parts, from 1.04, "I Fall to Pieces") – as human, and see **Points of Discussion** under that story for why. Also, Vanessa from "Blind Date" (1.21) is arguably coursing with demonic energy (again, see that story for more), but she was born human, so it's more akin to Angel slaying an evil magic-user than an actual demon. Still, even if we place her in the human bucket, Vanessa's status as an assassin intent on killing three children means it's hard to imagine anyone quibbling about her death too much. However, we can't award Angel a point for dealing the demon Vocah a scythe to the head – despite the rather blatant on-screen evidence – but see "Judgment" (2.01) for the explanation.

Kate shoots one of Papazian's goons with her handgun, and the wound certainly appears lethal (1.06, "Sense and Sensitivity"). Cordelia and Doyle split a point for the tentacled thing in the same story, and Doyle nets his only other kill of the series – the vamp that he dusts to save Cordy – in "The Bachelor Party" (1.07). Wesley makes the crucial shot that slays the Haxil demon in "Expecting" (1.12) – it's his only kill of the year and seems rather meager, but he'll more than make up for it in later seasons.

2.01: "Judgment"

"Ohhhhh, Mandy.
You came and you gave without taking..."

Air Date: Sept. 26, 2000; **Writers:** Joss Whedon, David Greenwalt; **Director:** Michael Lange

SUMMARY With the heroes now operating out of her apartment, Cordelia gets a vision depicting a formidable Prio Motu demon. Angel butchers the demon, then becomes horrified to learn it was valiantly trying to protect a pregnant woman. Worse, unspecified dark forces want to eliminated the woman's unborn daughter, who is prophesized to become a force for good.

Angel tries to escort the woman to the Tribunal – an otherworldly court that's powerful enough to protect the unborn child. However, the expectant mother runs off when assassins come calling. A desperate Angel goes to a demon karaoke bar named Caritas, and asks for help from "the Host" – the green-skinned club-owner, who can "read" the destiny of anyone who sings before him. Angel gives a rendition of "Mandy," enabling the Host to deduce the pregnant woman's location as 4th and Spring. The Tribunal magically appears, even as Angel arrives and bests a representative of the dark powers in a joust, thus winning protection for the woman and her child.

THE OPENING CREDITS J. August Richards (Gunn) formally gets added to the roster.

FIRSTS AND LASTS Two new locations come onto the scene: the demon karaoke bar Caritas (which will spotlight a number of spell-binding/ghastly performances over the next year or so) and the disused Hyperion Hotel, seen briefly when Angel and the pregnant woman, on the run, stumble into its dusty lobby (see next episode for more).

The Caritas owner, presently known as the Host (and not called by his proper name until 2.19, "Belonging") makes his grand entrance looking downright sinister, then performs a quiet little version of "I Will Survive" to lighten the mood. We also meet the parasite demon Merl, who'll serve as one of Angel's contacts, however reluctantly. It's also the first instance of Cordelia officially "charging" into battle with the boys, as she here drops a gym weight on a demon worshipper's head, and she'll serve as "back-up muscle" more often in Season Two.

First mention of Gunn's first name: It's Charles.

POINTS OF DISCUSSION ABOUT "Judgment":

1. When this story gets remembered at all, it's in part because of all the jousting, but mostly because it debuts the Host (a.k.a. Lorne), played with considerable style by Andy Hallett. His make-up looks crude here, and he's going to get smoother, not to mention a much brighter shade of green, as the show goes on.

The Host/Lorne also deserves mention as the No. 1 *Angel* character who's tailor-made for turning into action figures and busts. Non-humans almost always translate into merchandise better than real-life people – have you noticed that? – which explains why Sideshow Collectibles' 12-inch Faith figure could scarcely look less like Eliza Dushku. The Host and his suits, however, are easy as cake.

2. A word on the name "Caritas." Many sources claim that Angel's wrong to say that "Caritas" is Latin for "mercy," and that it's actually Greek for "charity." However, given the flexibility of the term – not to mention the fact that "caritas" isn't a Greek word at all – Angel is standing on solid ground.

In truth, the Latin term "caritas" stems from the Greek root *charis*, which variously means "grace," "beauty" or "kindness." The latter interpretation also lent itself to the English word "charity." Given that no one-to-one translation can exist in this instance, however, it's perfectly acceptable to claim that "caritas" means "mercy." (Interestingly, "charis" is also the root for "charisma" – as in Charisma Carpenter – which means "a gift of God's grace.")

3. If you accept printed evidence on *Angel* as canon, then the white board in Cordelia's apartment – the one that tallies the heroes' missions – is a strange one. Troublingly, it mentions Vocah, whose head Angel magnificently split open in "To Shanshu in L.A." (1.22), as "pending," with a lead on on him in the "downtown area." It's certainly possible that Vocah survived – even if he's never mentioned again – and throughout this guide book, we've undoubtedly based conclusions on far less evidence. So we can't really credit Angel with the kill, and hope the heroes disemboweled the bastard off-camera.

By the way, the board also lists recent opponents as "Khee Shah" (apparently mentioned in the *Book of Santhry*, vs. 21, pg. 104... "killed when building exploded?", case pending) and "SonSoo" ("likes dark scary places," pending). Five menaces are listed as killed: "Zaroh" (cited as "beheaded, reborn, torched," case closed), a Vartite monster (slain over a two-day period), a Sloth demon, an Ethros demon (almost certainly not the one from 1.14, "I've Got You Under My Skin") and some opponent named "Zaroh," who was first seen on July 10. We've dutifully added these to the heroes' **Total Kill-Count** for Season Two.

4. One of the drink-sipping Caritas demons looks like a plainer version of Archduke Sebassis from Season Five – it clearly *isn't* Sebassis, although they could belong to the same species.

5. The title of this story either gets rendered as "Judgment" or the British-preferred spelling "Judgement." Somewhat annoyingly, the Season Two DVDs have chosen the latter. The former spelling is in wider use, though, so we've run with that.

CHARACTER NOTES *Angel:* [It's never specified where Angel lives between his apartment's obliteration in "To Shanshu in L.A." and his acquisition of the Hyperion. He's not living with Wesley, because 2.16, "Epiphany" is indisputably the first time he visits Wes' apartment. Yet it seems unlikely that he's residing with Cordelia, as he's oblivious to her Bravo watching of late. Also, no matter how much Our Heroes have grown in the last year, they don't show signs of wanting to butcher one another – compare this to 1.05, "Rm w/a Vu" and their previous catastrophic attempt to room together.]

Angel here claims he doesn't tan, date or sing in public. [He also doesn't hum (1.12, "Expecting") and dance (1.13, "She").] He thinks "Mandy" by Barry Manilow is "pretty" [and see 4.15, "Orpheus" for more on Angel's "Mandy" obsession]. Angel grew up with horses, but hasn't ridden one in "a while."

• *Cordelia:* Now taking acting class [or so the script claims; on screen, and it could easily pass as a play rehearsal], and her acting's improved considerably since 1.17, "Eternity." It's implied that Cordy appeared in some Tan 'N Screen commercials. She's been watching a *film noir* festival on Bravo and she's getting better at research, recognizing that Sloth demons don't sacrifice adolescents.

Cordelia's apartment is in Silver Lake, an L.A. suburb. [Her full address is scribbled on Angel's business card, and it looks something like 141 or 241 Emburg Street, Silver Lake, 90026, phone (323) 555-0175. (Silver Lake's area code *is* 323, so that's legit enough.)] Her apartment is "in the back." Cordy owns a glass unicorn [like Harmony in *Buffy* 5.02, "Real Me" and *Angel* Season Five], but Angel accidentally breaks it.

• *Wesley:* Now far more adept in combat [he's been training over the summer] and an exceptional darts player [since 1.19, "Sanctuary"]. He seems far more self-confident, briefly flirting with a woman in a bar [on this point, see 2.05, "Dear Boy"]. He's been broadening the team's underworld contacts, and puts Angel in touch with the demon stoolie Merl.

• *Gunn:* Gets to meet Cordelia and Wesley when they're not hospitalized [see last episode]. Gunn readily accepts that the Prio Motu demon was heroic [yet it's a lesson lost on him by 3.03, "That Old Gang of Mine"]. Gunn's group now resides in a building "off Eighth," clearing the block of vampires/demons in exchange for a break on the rent.

• *The Host:* Wesley describes the Host as "anagogic," meaning "psychic," and therefore "connected to the mystic." The Host can mentally "read" beings who sing before him, gaining insight about their auras, destinies and futures.

• *Darla:* Currently in Lindsey's care at Wolfram and Hart. She remembers Angel killing her (*Buffy* 1.07, "Angel") and senses his presence in town (see **Points of Discussion** in 1.11, "Somnambulist"). Darla likes the works of Chopin (1810-1849) and Brahms (1833-1897), but isn't fond of Russian music. She here listens to Chopin's Prelude in C Minor, Op. 28, No. 20, and prefers the man's preludes and nocturnes to his waltzes. Darla recalls Chopin dying from consumption. [She next appears in 2.03, "First Impressions."]

• *Lindsey:* Now equipped with a plastic hand [after "To Shanshu in L.A."] and wants revenge on Angel for the affront.

• *Lilah:* Presently in contract negotiations with someone named Donald, and apparently threatens to have his children killed if he doesn't sign. [Perhaps she's joking, but it's hard to tell. Elements of the firm sanction the murder of children in 1.21, "Blind Date" and 5.01, "Conviction."]

• *Phantom Dennis:* Trying to help Angel and company conduct research, but this mostly entails his telekinetically hurling books at people.

• *Merl:* [Here credited as "Merl demon."] "Parasite demon" who looks vaguely reptilian and lacks a tongue. He hangs out at Caritas, accepting cash for information.

• *Faith:* Angel briefly visits the incarcerated Faith [see "Sanctuary"] to check on her rehabilitation. She's prisoner No. 43100. A fellow prisoner attacked Faith with a homemade knife, trying to bolster her reputation, but the Slayer disarmed her and took a beating from the prison guards. [Faith next appears in 4.13, "Salvage," which also involves a knife attack.]

• *Kamal:* Atypically [and for reasons unstated] heroic Prio Motu demon. His possessions, including what looks like a small Buddha statue, suggest he was religious.

• *The Pregnant Woman:* [Named "Jo" in the script.] Worked as a cashier/stock girl at Costco six months ago, but now carrying a daughter who's foretold to fight on the side of good. [The daughter's role is never clarified, but Jo wonders if she'll become a "seer," "leader" or "Joan of Arc"-type figure.]

THE LIBRARY Wesley owns a copy of *Suleman's Compendium*, which seemingly holds details about the Hindu Kush in Northern Pakistan and the Tien Shenin in Kazakhstan.

ORGANIZATIONS *Angel Investigations:* Wesley and Cordy own pagers, and the pager signal "911" means a call to action. Angel discontinues keeping track of wins and losses on the whiteboard, claiming the heroes shouldn't keep score. [So we'll do it for him; see **The Total Kill-Count**.]

• *Caritas:* Chiefly caters to demons, but with some human clientele. [The audience undoubtedly includes vampires, but episodes such as "Reprise" (2.15) and "Heartthrob" (3.01) feature what seems like genuine humans.] Customers must pass through metal detectors. Wesley implies that violence is forbidden within the club [see 3.03, "That Old Gang of Mine"].

• *The Tribunal:* Other-worldly court that adheres to an "ancient law." Wesley loosely names it as *Cabair Binse*, which roughly translates to "chair of judgment." He also cites it as "an ancient court to settle grievances," which realistically entails a fight to the death between champions. [The Tribunal seems insistent on ruling on the pregnant woman and her daughter no matter what, but it's unclear why they feel compelled to do so. Perhaps Kamal, the Prio Motu, arranged the contest before his demise.]

At a specified time, the Tribunal judges rise out of the ground on a stone platform, as a sort of "mystical event" at the mother's location, and command that her champion fight a Medieval knight of unknown origin. [Perhaps the Knight works for the "dark ones" mentioned in "To Shanshu in L.A.," or maybe he's one of the "soldiers of darkness" referenced in 1.08, "I Will Remember You."] Both combatants must present a Coat of Arms: a bronze medallion with Medieval markings. Lack of the Coat or a champion results in a forfeit. [Angel and the knight here joust, possibly owing to the Tribunal's ancient origins, or possibly because the Knight gets the pick of weaponry for some reason.]

The Tribunal judges wear eastern-style robes that cover everything but their snake-like eyes and pale skin. [In overall look and pompousness, they highly resemble the shrouded sorcerer in *Buffy* 3.17, "Enemies," not to mention Wo Pang from 4.10, "Awakening." It's possible that they all hail from the same mystical sect.] It's taken for granted that they can protect the pregnant woman and her daughter.

[The Tribunal and Angel's jousting match take place on a fairly large L.A. street without anyone particularly noticing. As some have speculated, it's perfectly feasible that the Tribunal can magically shroud the contest. Indeed, you have to wonder why some question this theory, as if it's reasonable that a mystical Tribunal could appear from nowhere and render judgment on a jousting match between a Medieval and a heroic vampire... yet, somehow, lack the power to cloud everyone else's perceptions of the event.]

DEMONOLOGY *Vampires:* Cordelia speculates that vampires don't need to exercise [but see 2.11, "Redefinition"].

MAGIC Angel and friends stop a sword-wielding Carnyss Demon from killing three adolescents at a gym, and Wes tags the event as a "Praetorian sacrifice." [It's hard to find any correlation with – say – the Praetorian Guard of ancient Rome. However, the word "praetorian" means "venal and corruptible," so perhaps Wesley's just being overly colorful, using the term to denote a "despicable act."] Angel identifies the sacrifice's location by means of "matching quadrants."

BEST LINE(s) Gunn, having discretely guarded Cordelia and Wes in the hospital, and in jest: "I've seen you before." Cordelia: "Really? The Tan 'N Screen commercials!" Gunn: "I saw you in bed." Cordelia: "What?" Wesley: "Ah, I-I can see this is none of my business..." Gunn: "You, too."

THINGS THAT DON'T MAKE SENSE After demon assassins make the pregnant woman flee Angel's company, she's next seen running straight down a large street in L.A. Even allowing that she's in a flustered panic, isn't it more sensible to run in a flustered panic down the sidewalk rather than – oh, say – into oncoming traffic? Is this down to hormones?

When Angel visits the Prio Motu's hobby hole, he finds burning candles that somehow haven't melted in all the time the Prio Motu has been gone. Cordelia's miraculously back to living in apartment No. 212 again, having lived in Apt. No. 6 in 1.18, "Five by Five." Finally, Angel defeats the evil knight *only* because he's a vampire, and the fiend's "fatal" sword blow doesn't finish him off. What, the evil knight has never heard of *any* sort of supernatural creature that can take a central sword strike, and therefore requires a proper beheading? What sort of crappy evil minions are the dark forces hiring these days?

POP CULTURE The Host to an impatient Angel: "Well. Who's a little curt? Who's a little Curt Jurgens in *The Enemy Below*?" In *The Enemy Below* (1957), Jurgens (a.k.a. Curd Jürgens) plays Von Stolberg, a German U-boat commander who plays cat-and-mouse with the *USS Haynes*, an American destroyer led by Captain Murrell (Robert Mitchum).

IT'S REALLY ABOUT... The capacity of seasoned adults to keep screwing up. Having learned that he's a candidate for the reward of becoming human, Angel flounders as to his next move. You see this time and again in people who maneuver themselves to potentially attain great success – then fall prey to over-confidence, simple nervousness or the fact that potential or no, they still have a hell of a road to walk down. It's a very adult affliction.

TONIGHT AT CARITAS The Host livens up the teaser with Gloria Gaynor's "I Will Survive." A reptilian-looking demon named "Liz" (credited as "Lizard Demon"), who's looking forward to spawning and eating its own young soon, potently sings the Pointer Sisters' "I'm So Excited." A hairy demon named "Mordar the Bentback" breathily tries out Marvin Gaye's "Sexual Healing." Durthock the Childeater feels a little bit Country and does Billy Ray Cryus' "Achy Breaky Heart." Angel painfully crawls his way through Barry Manilow's "Mandy."

THE CLOSING CREDITS Angel re-mutilates "Mandy" for benefit of anyone who missed it the first time around.

CRITIQUE It's a bewildering story in many respects, and as with "I Fall to Pieces" (1.04), you have to wonder how Whedon could've personally generated something so half-baked. The Tribunal, the pregnant woman, the bit with the horsies and more all give the palpable sense that the scriptwriters are making up everything up they go along. And yet... there's actually a lot going for this story. The gorgeous Caritas scenes render the karaoke bar as a place that, if it were real, could only exist in L.A. The leads all get some good bits. As for the horse jousting... okay, it's hardly a slam-dunk, but it's not worth getting upset about either, and at least it's *trying* to entertain.

All told, the episode isn't overwhelmingly successful, and

it's not exactly a grand launch to Season Two. But in most ways that count, it gets the job done.

THE LORE Hallett had known Whedon socially, having come to L.A. with a friend of his, Dawn, who was one of Whedon's relations. Whedon used to watch Hallett perform as singer in a Hollywood bar, and later mentioned during an airport meeting that Hallett's performance had inspired him to create a new character. Whedon encouraged Hallett to audition for the role, but couldn't make any promises as Hallett had almost zero acting experience – he'd appeared, uncredited and without any lines, as a student in the "silent" *Buffy* story "Hush" (4.10), but that was about all. (Gill, *tve.co.il*) It's been suggested that, once Hallett was cast, Whedon was a little coy to a Fox official who previewed "Judgment" and asked where he'd seen Hallett before. Whedon's diplomatic response: "We don't think you know him from anywhere." (O'Hare, *Zap2It*, Nov. 29, 2000)

• Boreanaz had learned to ride horseback as a child, but ventured up to a ranch to practice for the jousting scene. (*TV Guide Insider* chat, Oct. 3, 2000)

• Justina Machado (Jo) later became a regular on HBO's *Six Feet Under* as Vanessa Diaz, a registered nurse. Keith Campbell (Club Manager), who frequently stunt-doubles for the likes of Tom Cruise, Robin Williams and Val Kilmer, played a werewolf in *Buffy* 2.15, "Phases."

2.02: "Are You Now or Have You Ever Been?"

"It's kind of like a puzzle. The 'who died horribly because Angel screwed up 50 years ago?' game."

Air Date: Oct. 3, 2000; **Writer:** Tim Minear; **Director:** David Semel

SUMMARY In 1952, a solitary Angel lodged at the Hyperion Hotel in L.A. Events conspired to make him befriend a young fugitive named Judy Kovacs. Judy conceded that she'd robbed her employer, a Kansas bank, after officials there learned of her partly African-American heritage and fired her. Angel sympathized with Judy's plight and tried to help, but a Thesulac demon – a paranoia-causing creature that both fueled and fed off people's fear – triggered emotional distress and violence throughout the hotel.

Angel researched an exorcism ritual, but the Thesulac influenced Judy to denounce Angel as a murderer. Under the Thesulac's thrall, a mob hanged Angel in the lobby, then scattered in horror. Angel survived but took the crowd's rejection to heart and left the hotel – allowing the Thesulac to prey off everyone who remained. Judy went missing and a string of murders, suicides and unexplained deaths followed until the Hyperion finally shuttered its doors in 1979.

In the present day, Angel's brief visit to the Hyperion (last episode) motivates him to finish business there. Angel's allies perform a ritual that manifests the Thesulac, whereupon Angel electrocutes the monster with a handy junction box. Moments later, Angel finds an aged Judy – the Thesulac's main food source for the past five decades – in her hotel room. Judy apologizes for causing Angel's "death," then expires, whereupon Angel decides to make the cleansed Hyperion into his gang's new headquarters.

FIRSTS AND LASTS The Hyperion Hotel gets a proper unveiling, and it's the first of two appearances by Denver, an occult bookshop manager.

POINTS OF DISCUSSION ABOUT "Are You Now or Have You Ever Been?":

1. As we touched on in 1.01, "City Of," some sources love to detail how vampires shouldn't show up on photographs, a point we'll explore with **Why Don't Vampires Cast Reflections?** Yet here we're given the definitive proof: Wesley and Cordelia fish out a 1952 photo of Angel, and Cordelia even comments, "It's not that that vampires don't photograph, it's that they don't photograph *well*." There's little room to maneuver with this, and bear in mind that in the whole of *Angel* and *Buffy*, it's never said that vampires *can't* show up in photographs – so we're willing to take it as given that they can.

2. All right, there's just no avoiding some discussion about Angel's blood-drinking habits. Here, we see the 1950s Angel drinking from a bottle labeled "Type O," and Cordelia in the modern day hands Angel a cup of blood that she whimsically calls "O-Pos." Similarly, she claimed in "Parting Gifts" (1.10) that Angel's refrigerator contained plenty of "O-Positive" but lacked anything vaguely resembling creamer, and the Host even pauses to offer Angel some "O-Positive" blood in "Long Day's Journey" (4.09). It would seem – although it's never out-and-out stated – that Angel's blood of choice is Type O-Positive, possibly for reasons of taste. So far, so good.

It's puzzling, though, to factor in that Angel *can't* be drinking human blood in the present day. As early as "City Of," and later in "The Shroud of Rahmon" (2.08), there's much concern about Angel feeding off humans, so it seems faintly berserk that a vampire needing to maintain such rigid self-control would drink human blood on a daily basis. After all, if one is worried about eating a cow, it seems supremely stupid to go out and eat reheated steak all the time. The argument that blood from a warm body is so much more enticing than the blood Angel microwaves isn't very convincing either, and all the aforementioned "O-Pos" references aside, the show overwhelmingly claims that Angel drinks blood from animals.

So... if Angel's drinking animal blood – usually a pig (judging by stories such as 2.17, "Disharmony") – where do all the "O-Positive" comments keep coming from? Animals have blood types, it's true, but the only non-human creatures with Type O-Positive are some strains of apes. Even if by some miracle pigs had a comparable blood type, would Angel's blood source (presumably a butcher; see 3.16, "Sleep Tight") know the difference? We have to chalk all this up to Cordelia somehow knowing Angel's blood preference and getting cute about it – even as she sweetly hands him pig's blood – with the Host later adopting the habit.

By the way, O-Positive is the blood type of universal donors. Perhaps they're innately more succulent.

3. Cordelia's laptop conspicuously has a Post-It note over the Apple logo, which has led to some speculation that the studio and Apple – who constantly stocked *Angel* and *Buffy* with computers as a marketing gimmick – had a disagreement at some point. There's no particular evidence for this, however, and the spat – if one occurred – was rather short-lived, as the logo returns in 2.04, "Untouched."

4. The candle salesman shoots himself to the tune of "Hoop-Dee-Doo" by Perry Como and the Fontaine Sisters, which hit No. 1 in 1950, and features the words, "It's got me higher than a kite!" In all the excitement, people gloss over how this is just about the most bizarre suicide music imaginable.

CHARACTER NOTES *Angel:* In 1952, a solitary Angel stayed in room 217 of the Hyperion. [There's no evidence of him fretting about the weekly bill, so he's obviously into some money at this time. See 4.15, "Orpheus" for what made Angel transition between this lifestyle and living homeless in 1990s New York (seen in *Buffy* 2.21, "Becoming").] 1950s Angel smokes and doesn't subscribe to the era's racism. He claims he hasn't opened a human's veins in quite some time [presumably not since 1943, in 5.13, "Why We Fight," and not before that since 1900 in 2.07, "Darla"]. Angel helps Judy squirrel away her stolen money in the Hyperion basement, and retrieves it in the modern day. [Presuming Angel isn't moved to return the loot, Judy's money can't be worth much *now*, allowing for inflation. That could explain why Angel's still strapped for cash in 2.03, "First Impressions" and 2.05, "Dear Boy." Not to mention the Hyperion's repair bill after "Untouched."]

• *Cordelia:* Appears to have wireless access in her apartment, and still not above fetching drinks for everyone.

• *Wesley:* The Thesulac demon cites Wesley as especially paranoid. Wes and Gunn have taken to squabbling [but compare this with 2.14, "The Thin Dead Line"].

• *Judy:* [Named "Judy Kovacs" in a newspaper clipping.] The child of a black mother and a white father whom she never knew, Judy started passing for white at age 15. She worked as a teller at City Trust bank of Salina, Kansas. The revelation of her mixed heritage cost her an engagement to someone named "Peter." Judy resided in room 214 at the Hyperion.

• *Denver:* L.A. bookshop manager or possibly owner. He's reputed for his knowledge of the supernatural, and keeps magical items in the back of his shop. The 1950s Angel asked Denver's advice in dealing with the Thesulac; Denver was "just north of 30" at the time. [He next appears in 2.15, "Reprise."]

THE HYPERION It contains 68 rooms. [That initially sounds like an awfully small number of rooms in such a spacious building, save that later episodes such as 3.19, "The Price" and 4.06, "Spin the Bottle" confirm that the Hyperion includes a ballroom, a pool, an industrial kitchen, etc., which must chew up the space.]

The Hyperion was built in 1928, and located west of Cordelia's apartment in what served – at the time – as the heart of Hollywood. The Thesulac apparently "claimed" the land before the hotel was built. During the Hyperion's construction, the demon influenced a roofer to leap to his death, taking two coworkers with him. In 1952, the Thesulac talked a candle salesman into shooting himself, then influenced the hotel manager and a bellboy, Frank Gillnitz, into hiding the corpse to avoid bad publicity. Gillnitz hacked up the body and stuffed it into a meat locker, but the police later arrested him for the "murder," leading to his execution in 1954. [The police were apparently unable to explain talk of a public hanging in the hotel lobby, presuming it was ever reported.]

The hotel closed its doors on Dec. 16, 1979, when the concierge, Roland Meeks, made his morning wake-up calls with a 12-gauge shotgun. The city declared the hotel a protected historical landmark, and its owner, a property management company [presumably Melman Realty and Development, as a "For Sale" sign indicates], spent ten years trying unsuccessfully to unload it. According to Wesley, the Hyperion is designed with a California Spanish architecture and a Deco influence.

DEMONOLOGY *Vampires:* The 1950s Angel chills his blood [evidently to keep it fresh, as Darla suggests in 2.15, "Reprise"]. Angel's hands smoke when he touches a Bible that Denver tosses. [At least in this instance, the text is plainly labeled "Holy Bible." See **Points of Discussion** under 1.14, "I've Got You Under My Skin" and **Why Do Catholic Objects Harm Vampires?**]

Denver threatens to invoke the invitation rule by putting a bedroll in his bookshop. [The rule appears to distinguish between someone's living quarters and places where they're just sleeping, so it's a questionable tactic. But then, Denver otherwise seems pretty knowledgeable on supernatural matters.] Angel endures a hanging with little trouble. [Vampires must possess strong necks, even if their hearts are rather easy to penetrate, as evidenced in *Buffy* 3.19, "Choices" and 3.22, "Graduation Day."]

• *Thesulac Demons:* "Paranoia demons" capable of invisibly whispering to their victims, gradually driving them to the point of murder or suicide. The Hyperion Thesulac whips large groups of people into a frenzy, but some individuals – say, the demented bellboy – prove more susceptible than others.

Thesulacs initiate something of a feedback loop with their victims, seeding fear and paranoia, then feasting off the generated emotions and feeding it back again. In rare instances – such as with Judy – the Thesluac can feed off a particularly receptive individual for decades. [The Thesulac must in-kind sustain Judy's physical form, as she's shut in her room for 50 years, and presumably goes without food and water once the Hyperion closes in 1979. As if to confirm this theory, the aged Judy outlives the Thesulac by only a few minutes.]

To eliminate a Thesulac, first make it manifest – either by gorging it on anguished emotions or by "raising" it. The latter option requires some sacred herbs, divining powder, an Orb of Ramjarin and a specific incantation in the name of the priests of Ramjarin. Electricity's the best method of slaying a raised Thesulac, but Denver suggests a large axe might do the trick. [Tragically, Angel never gets the chance to try.] The Hyperion Thesulac sports tentacles for legs, and it's debatable, given its cloak, as to whether it's got arms.

MAGIC Wesley comments that ancient conjuring orbs are notoriously fragile. [Other such orbs presumably include an Orb of Thesulah (*Angel* 4.15, "Orpheus"; *Buffy* 2.17, "Passion" and 2.22, "Becoming" – and note the presumably coincidental name-similarity to "Thesulac") and a Dagon Sphere (*Buffy* 5.05, "No Place Like Home" and 5.22, "The Gift").] Angel leaves Denver's Orb of Ramjarin in the Hyperion in 1952. [Heaven knows what happens to it after Angel's scuffle with the mob. Wesley somehow owns or hurriedly buys another – possibly at Rick's Majick 'N Stuff; see 1.14, "I've Got You Under My Skin."]

BEST LINE Judy, after a candle salesman kills himself in his hotel room: "Can you imagine that wallpaper being the last thing you see before you go?" A sober Angel: "Maybe it was the wallpaper that drove him to it." (By the way, this is rather reminiscent of Oscar Wilde, who declared before his passing, "My wallpaper and I are fighting a duel to the death. One or other of us has got to go.")

THINGS THAT DON'T MAKE SENSE It's implied but not flat-out stated that Judy spotted the bottle (or bottles) of blood in Angel's room, so let's assume the Thesulac told her about it to fuel the mob scene. Because otherwise, even allowing that she's a fugitive, it's silly that she'd befriend a dark and foreboding stranger who keeps such stuff about the place.

Also, once a private investigator shows up on Judy's doorstep, why doesn't she skip town? It's a full day before she decides – once the candle salesman has shot himself – that leaving would arouse too much suspicion, and she can't seriously believe that the investigator won't return for her. (The Thesulac must already have its hooks in Judy, preventing her from venturing further than the L.A. observatory.) It's also convenient for the plot that the P.I. doesn't simply tell Angel, "By the way, you're harboring a wanted fugitive... here's her name and the crime she's committed," which seems reasonable under the circumstances. Judy claims she robbed City Trust Bank, but a newspaper article names it as Union National Bank. The same article has three duplicate paragraphs, also found in the article about the "murderous" bellhop.

It's understandable that the modern-day Angel feels coy about events in 1952, but it's still quite the oversight that he doesn't tell Wesley and Cordelia, "By the way, you're tracking a Thesulac Demon..." from the start, potentially halving their research time. The Thesulac's electrocution makes for a grand finale, but it's lucky that the power's still on in the Hyperion – a building that's sat dormant since 1979, and entirely failed to sell for the last ten years.

Oh... and how do the hotel residents, upon mobbing Angel, produce a hangman's noose on such remarkably short notice?

POP CULTURE An older man to a fleeing showgirl: "Come on, Honey. How do you think Lana Turner got started?" Turner was something of a Hollywood sexpot, known for such films as *The Postman Always Rings Twice* (1946) and *Peyton Place* (1957), for which she was nominated for an Oscar.

IN RETROSPECT Wesley deems the Hyperion "a house of evil" – which seems rather tame, considering where the heroes will base themselves in Season Five.

IT'S REALLY ABOUT... On the surface, it's about paranoia – the sort that gets its tentacles into everything (not for nothing does the Thesulac have such appendages) and which heavily influenced the Red Scare. It's also to some degree about racism, as evidenced when the hotel manager turns away a respectable-looking black family and when Angel knows that Judy isn't a maid because she's the wrong color.

But above all else, it's about Angel's capacity to make the

wrong decision. Before now, we've chalked up Angel's atrocities to his Angelus persona, who literally didn't own a conscience. Angel himself has no such excuse, so when he leaves Judy and the Hyperion residents to their fate, it makes him long for redemption of an entirely different kind.

CRITIQUE We're trying to go about this guide book professionally and not gush too hard, but if we *did* become slobbering fanboys, it'd be over something like "Are You Now and Have You Ever Been?" Holy cow, what a knock-out. Multiple people contributed to *Angel*'s success, but it's striking how often a Tim Minear script will bump the entire series up to a new level – it happened with "Somnambulist," and it happens again here.

Chiefly, it's because of Minear's inherent take that Angel's soul doesn't make him a saint; true, it gives him more of a conscience than other vamps, but he's still vexed with the failings of every human being. Here, it's *ensouled* Angel who callously leaves the hotel patrons to their fate, and who's to blame for Judy's half-century of serving as a demon-battery. Most of Season Two – and again, look at Minear's "Reunion" (2.10), "Reprise" (2.15) and "Epiphany" (2.16) – hinges on this point, and it's demonstrated from the get-go here.

Even better, the direction, the dialogue and the style all fuse into an elegant yet tragic whole – you honestly feel as if you're walking about in a supernatural-tainted version of 1950s Hollywood, as opposed to (say) 5.13, "Why We Fight," which painfully stuffs Spike and a bundle of WWII troops into a submarine. Here and for the next three years, the Hyperion Hotel serves as a locale of grace and beauty, but which potentially has horror lurking in every room.

It says something we're only at episode two of the season, and this story looks almost impossible to beat – and yet it happens. Just looking at this outing, it's clear we're on the cusp of something amazing, daring and strange.

THE LORE The overrun on this story actually bested "Eternity" (1.17) – a full nine minutes this time – but Whedon deemed everything so good, he became loathe to trim anything. Minear didn't so much mind the cuts, tossing two scenes with Cordelia and Wesley discussing a 1935 serial killer who made the head of his victims into decorative planters. (Cordy: "What kind of plants you gonna keep in a human head?" Wesley: "Well, ferns, one presumes.") It's just possible – although there's no proof – that the heads and planters bit got recycled into princess Cordelia's rant in 2.22, "There's No Place Like Plrtz Glrb."

The paranoid hotel residents also shed some dialogue, including a deliberately confusing exchange where the screenwriter mentions "death of the candle salesman" and the actor thinks he means *Death of a Salesman*. Minear most hated losing some lines where the detective hunting Judy leans into Angel's room and asks him, "That your lilac perfume I'm smellin'? Didn't think so." (Minear, *alt.tv.angel*, Oct. 5, 2000)

• Whedon deemed this the best *Angel* episode to date, but worried about ratings, as it was airing opposite the premiere of James Cameron's *Dark Angel* on FOX. The dip in viewership between "Judgment" hardly proved damning, though, and *Dark Angel* later collapsed after just two seasons. (Whedon, *The Bronze*, Sept. 30, 2000)

• John Kapelos (Hotel Manager) held a regular role as Don Schanke on the vampire show *Forever Knight* – he was the outrageous but charming partner to the lead character – but 80s aficionados might remember him better as Carl the Janitor in John Hughes' *The Breakfast Club*. Tommy Hinkley (Private Investigator) ranks among his credits *Confessions of a Dangerous Mind, Ray's Male Heterosexual Dance Hall* and *I Killed My Lesbian Wife, Hung Her on a Meat Hook, and Now I Have a Three-Picture Deal at Disney*, the latter directed by Ben Affleck. Brett Rickaby (Denver) played Frank Gorshin in *Return to the Batcave: The Misadventures of Adam and Burt* (2003), alongside Amy Acker. J.P. Manoux (Bellman) played yet another bellhop in the second *Austin Powers* film, but his scenes wound up on the cutting room floor. He did voiceover work for both *Scooby-Doo* films and appeared in two movies with Michelle Trachtenberg (*Buffy*'s Dawn): *Inspector Gadget* and *Eurotrip*.

How Do I Take the 'Angel'/ 'Buffy' L.A. Tour?

We can't even pretend that the following list is overwhelmingly comprehensive or complete, and if anyone feels inclined to publish a proper *Angel / Buffy* location guide, we'd certainly purchase a copy. Nonetheless, what follows are locations as personally visited by your intrepid authors in February 2004, while zooming around Los Angeles in a rental car. Bear in mind that L.A. is a *sprawling* city, and this was literally the most ground we could cover in two days, so planning ahead is recommended.

P.S. All locations are Los Angeles proper, not a suburb, unless otherwise noted.

• **The Hyperion Hotel (Los Altos Apartments, 4121 Wilshire Boulevard, 90010).** Honestly, what half-sane *Angel* fan would skip visiting the Hyperion Hotel, or rather, the real-life apartment complex that serves as the building's exterior? We can't condone unduly snooping about the place or bothering the tenants, but visiting the locale is quite the experience, because you really do feel like you're outside the Hyperion. Best of all: The front courtyard of Los Altos and the Hyperion are one and the same, right down to the fountain. You can get some exceptionally geeky photographs here, but we can't advise re-creating the courtyard fight scenes from – say – "Dad" (3.10) or "Release" (4.14), because it's a good way to get the cops called out.

• "The Pylean Gate" from 2.20, "Over the Rainbow" (Paramount Pictures Corporation, 555 Melrose Avenue, 90038): In a bit of cross-pollination between the studios, *Angel* was owned by FOX, aired on The WB and chiefly filmed at the Paramount lot. (One presumes the bigger studios aren't *too* interested in outright destroying one another these days, and will readily scratch each others' backs if there's money to be made.) Hence, the heroes "drive" through to Pylea at the Paramount entrance – not for nothing does a befuddled Angel ask, "Isn't this a movie studio?" just beforehand. Due to heavy traffic in the area and tight gate security, we highly recommend that you park on a side street and walk some blocks if you want a decent photograph. Just be sure to obey L.A.'s confusing street signs, because we picked up a parking ticket.

• The Griffith Observatory from 2.02, "Are You Now or Have You Ever Been?": The 1950s Angel has an outdoor conversation with Judy here, but it's not named on screen. Besides, unlike some of the other locations, the Griffith would be fun to visit even if it *weren't* featured on *Angel*.

• Giles' Apartment (4616 Greenwood Place, 90027): All right, we're crossing series now, but stopping by this building was convenient at the time. Giles' apartment is – as with Los Altos – a real-life dwelling that's also appeared on *Melrose Place*, so try to avoid hassling people if you visit. Unlike Los Altos, however, you can't get beyond the front gate. We peeked through and identified the courtyard outside Giles' door, but that was the extent of it. You can skip this one if you're pressed for time.

• The Orpheum Theatre from 3.13, "Waiting in the Wings" (1801 South Grand Avenue, 90015): An odd case here, as the Orpheum is apparently magnificent on the inside, but positively drab and distinctly non-opulent on the outside. We hit this locale at mid-day and couldn't imagine getting inside without buying tickets, which frankly didn't seem worth the expense. Our visit therefore consisted of driving around the Orpheum's mundane and humble exterior while thinking, "Yup, that's dull."

• Angelus-Rosedale Cemetery (1831 W Washington Boulevard, 90007): No, that's what it's really called – we nearly died laughing when we found out. There's reason to believe that some of the cemetery shooting for both *Angel* and *Buffy* took place here, but our research couldn't pinpoint the exact episodes. One section looked strikingly like the setting for Spike's song from the *Buffy* musical, but we couldn't confirm that either. Be warned, though, that pictures aren't allowed, as we discovered when a hearse pulled up and the driver chastized us.

• The original Wolfram and Hart building (Sony Pictures, 10202 W Washington Boulevard, Culver City, 90232): Another case of studio cross-pollination, one presumes. Sony Pictures is in Culver City and therefore a bit out of the way, so it's probably best combined with a trip to the cemetery or the L.A. library (see the next entry). Viewing the building in person was fairly impressive, although of course you can't go inside, and the parking situation is again complicated. Your best bet is to simply do what we did: drive around the building and take photos, even though it was raining at the time.

• Fred's lecture hall from 4.05, "Supersymmetry" and...errr...possibly some others (the L.A. Public Library, Central Branch, 630 W. 5th Street, 90071): The Central Library's publicity office helped to confirm that Fred's science lecture – the one where the tentacled thing tries to snatch her – took place in the library's Mark Taper Auditorium. It's normally locked, but we sweetly persuaded some of the publicity people to let us inside. Yup, it's definitely the same hall, and it felt eerie to stand where Acker undoubtedly reacted to the "threat" without benefit of a *real* tentacled thing to act against.

The *bad* news is that there's reason to believe that four other episodes were filmed at the library, all in the same marble room, but we couldn't confirm it. Records in the publicity office indicated that the smackdown between Illyria and Angel's crew from "Shells" (5.16) was filmed at the library, but curse it all – we couldn't figure out where. In fact, there's reason to think that scenes from *three* other episodes occurred in this very same room: Faith's initial attack on Angel in "Five by Five" (1.18), the discussion with Fred's co-worker in "Belonging" (2.19) and the "bus station" scene where Fred goes to pieces in "Fredless" (3.05). Each contains the same distinct beige / green, triangular and artistic tiling on the floor, accompanied by the occasional red column and wooden information desks. The stand-off with Illyria and Knox, in fact, is especially entertaining because there's an Information Desk right behind the villains.

We hoofed it all over the library, but – somewhat infuriatingly – couldn't establish the location (we ruled out the library's upper rotunda, however). Anyone who *does* recognize the room should please send a postcard to the Mad Norwegian offices – if we can't use the information in a Second Edition of *Redeemed*, at least you'll provide us with some personal contentment on the issue.

2.03: "First Impressions"

"Always enhances a guy's rep when some skinny white beauty queen comes to his rescue."

Air Date: Oct. 10, 2000; **Writer:** Shawn Ryan; **Director:** James A. Contner

SUMMARY While Darla makes Angel sleep for long periods and experience lurid dreams about her, Cordelia gets an ambiguous vision of Gunn in danger. Cordelia takes Angel's Plymouth and finds Gunn safe and sound, but thieves steal the car – forcing Gunn and Cordy to search the chop shops for it. Gunn's inquiries ruffle too many feathers, convincing a demon named Deevak to try and eliminate him. Wesley and Angel find their friends just as Gunn and Cordelia locate Angel's car, leading to a brawl against Deevak's vampire minions. The heroes prevail, with Angel personally dispatching Deevak. Later, Cordelia realizes her vision was trying to convey that Gunn's brashness makes him a danger to *himself*, convincing him to use better caution in future.

2.03, First Impressions

FIRSTS AND LASTS Final appearance of billionaire/would-be crusader/nerd David Nabbit. Angel lets Cordelia drive his car for the first time, although this results in it getting stolen.

POINTS OF DISCUSSION ABOUT "First Impressions":

1. The cute pink motorcycle helmet. As any good *Angel* fan knows, L.A. traffic laws compel Angel to wear a helmet as he rides on the back of Wesley's motorcycle. Yet Wesley only keeps a pink women's helmet as a spare, and needless to say, Angel doesn't look terribly masculine while wearing it. It probably warmed some fans' hearts when Diamond Select packaged a small plastic pink helmet with the Wesley "Parting Gifts" action figure, even though the helmet doesn't hail from that story.

One unanswered question, though: Why *does* Wesley own a spare women's helmet? Either a surprising number of females have been riding Wes' hog (not completely impossible... see 2.05, "Dear Boy") or we've got to examine the obvious suspects and presume it belongs to Cordelia. Which brings us to...

2. We're given ample proof that Cordelia doesn't own a car at present – a hellish state, if you're familiar with L.A.'s geography. Cordelia takes a cab in "Reprise" (2.15), and there's scant evidence of her owning an automobile anytime before 3.22, "Tomorrow." So either she's taking public transport in Seasons One and Two, or she's hitching a ride to work with Wesley each day. If Cordy does own the pink helmet, then it's probably a designer-name item, *or* perhaps Wesley bought it for her, and Cordy simply couldn't afford to replace it.

3. David Nabbit appears one final time to give Angel financial advice, then depart the series without ceremony. So it's a final chance for us to pause and wonder why Nabbit isn't funding the heroes more directly. He's been called a billionaire, so outright buying the Hyperion must be piddling change for him – especially as it's been wallowing on the market for ten years with no takers. Yet he's never seen again, and Cordelia resumes moaning about the agency's finances two episodes from now.

CHARACTER NOTES *Angel:* Evidently sleeps naked [reconfirmed next episode, although he's merely sleeping shirtless by 5.02, "Just Rewards"]. He's now experiencing lurid dreams about Darla, who's been sneaking into Angel's bedroom to writhe naked atop him. [4.10, "Awakening" entails a dream sequence overriding Angel's gypsy curse, so even though he's deliriously happy with Darla in these dreams, they're not actually having sex. For now, Darla seems more interested in befuddling Angel than making him evil again.] This fatigues Angel, and makes him so sluggish that fighting a standard vampire proves difficult. [The dreams also cloud Angel's senses, as he never registers Darla's scent in his bedroom. See next episode for more on the dream-assault.]

One of Angel's dreams suggests that he's been singing in the shower [probably true], rehearsing for his inevitable performance at Caritas. He also owns a pager.

• *Cordelia:* Displays a decent knowledge of treating wounds and emergency room procedures. She here wields a modest-size axe that she keeps in her closet [possibly the Byzantine axe seen in 1.08, "I Will Always Remember You," and seen throughout the show] and also carries Mace. Cordy knows where Gunn lives [he told her off screen] and claims she only takes orders from Angel. If he asks nicely.

David Nabbit's diatribe about tax breaks, the F.H.A. and P.M.I. and other business terms makes Cordelia feel, er, warm.

• *Wesley:* Dons his leather "rogue demon hunter" outfit and rides his motorcycle for the first time since "Parting Gifts" (1.10). A vampire skirmish wrecks Wesley's pager and makes him throw out his back "again." [He's probably referring to a more recent injury than *Buffy* 3.22, "Graduation Day."]

• *Gunn:* Still leader of his gang, yet there are signs of disobedience – one of his men [named Keenan in the script] goes to a party instead of patrolling the garment district. One of Gunn's friends, a store worker named Veronica, seems jealous of Cordelia [but who is never seen again].

Gunn possesses a very territorial sense of justice, ordering a chop shop manager to stop stealing cars from "the neighborhood," but finding it perfectly acceptable if the man takes beemers from Brentwood. [Although 2.01, "Judgment" showed Gunn saving an affluent person from danger.] Gunn knows several car thieves, but can't hotwire a car himself. He's sparring partners with an associate named Joey.

• *David Nabbit:* Was recently in Kuala Lumpur, staging a hostile takeover. Cordelia says Nabbit made his first millions by developing software that allows blind people to web-surf. His foundation apparently gives $20 million a year to charity.

• *Phantom Dennis:* Isn't strong enough to catch Cordelia when a vision makes her fall [which explains why he didn't attack Faith in 1.18, "Five by Five"].

• *Deevak:* Tall demon with limp arms, able to morph between two guises: his larger demon self and "Jameel," his human aspect. [Deevak might well be a half-breed like Doyle, or perhaps can just "pass" like the Straley family from "The Bachelor Party" (1.07).] Deevak runs an automotive chop shop; "Jameel" operates as a low-level snitch. The "Jameel" aspect displays super-strength, but he's vulnerable to Mace. Deevak doesn't revert to human form when killed.

THE HYPERION Includes a shady Valet Parking section in the back. Nabbit suggests that Angel finance the Hyperion's mortgage by A) Taking over the owner's payments and skipping the bank, B) Making a play for a preservation grant, or C) an idea so loopy, we've consigned it to **Things That Don't Make Sense**.

ORGANIZATIONS *The Powers-That-Be:* Their vision about Gunn seems more symbolic than normal. [The vision shows a scared Gunn swinging a sword, and it doesn't seem tied to a real-life event. It's arguably the most abstract vision the Powers ever send, and why they feel inclined to mention Gunn's character flaw isn't clear. It's curious that the Powers don't deliver more "character flaw warnings" in future – Heaven knows, they're given ample reason to do so.]

DEMONOLOGY *Vampires:* Can apparently walk into parties where "everyone is invited" [as with 3.01, "Heartthrob" and see **How Does the Invitation Rule Work?**]. Angel senses that a partygoer is actually a vampire. [It's further proof that vampires can somehow recognize one another, as evidenced in other stories such as "Power Play" (5.21), yet there's no evidence that the party vamp pegs Angel as a vampire in return.]

• *Ghosts:* Cordelia says they prefer cold rooms, and Dennis keeps turning the air conditioning down to about 55 degrees.

BEST LINE(s) A bumbling Cordelia, trying to be social with Veronica at a party: "I'm just here on business. I'm a working girl... that came out wrong. I mean, obviously, I'm not a 'working girl'... Not that I couldn't be if I wanted to, of course I could. God, that sounded stuck up, didn't it? I didn't mean to imply that I could be a working girl and you couldn't. Far from it. You'd make a great... Could you just point me to the hors d'oeuvres?"

THINGS THAT DON'T MAKE SENSE There's the matter of the young African-American vampire whom Angel and Wesley interrogate. Why, pray tell, is she still at the party? She apparently works for Deevak and was presumably keeping tabs on Gunn – yet she's still there long after Gunn has left the joint. (Maybe the other vamps inadvertently injured her, although you'd think anyone with vampire constitution would've recovered a lot quicker.)

Wesley dons his motorcycle gear even before he knows that Angel's car is missing. It's possible he and Angel were going to drive separately, although Wes rides in Angel's car in just about every other story. More troublingly, Wes conspicuously takes off his glasses before donning his motorcycle helmet – how, exactly, does he see to ride around? Gunn claims that Angel owns a 1967 Plymouth, when according to 1.01, "City Of," it's a 1968. (Call it an honest mistake on Gunn's part.)

Yes, she's something of a lightweight, but it's still rather silly that Cordelia smacks Gunn's associate Joey across the back of the head with the blunt part of an axe and fails to deal him some serious damage. ("I think you cracked my skull," Joey whines. Well, no fooling.) As some fans have noticed, Nabbit's suggestion that Angel could purchase the Hyperion by "applying for an F.H.A. and getting a P.M.I. in lieu of a down" makes zero sense. (We even double-checked with a mortgage officer.) FHA refers to a Federal Housing Administration loan, but PMI refers to Private Mortgage Insurance, which covers the lender's ass and has nothing to do with a down payment. Essentially, the two terns should never be spoken in the same breath. And Angel thought Nabbit was giving him expert advice. Feh! Not only that, but given how many building violations Gavin unearths about the hotel later this season, it's amazing that Angel nets a mortgage at all. The lead paint alone would probably sink the deal.

Not that we'd ever incite people to closely monitor Julie Benz's bosom, but we can't help but notice that Darla appears to be wearing a blouse when she leans over Angel in the final scene, yet she's clearly topless in the very next shot.

POP CULTURE Cordelia to Gunn: "When you find [the snitch], you might want to be a little more Guy Pearce in *L.A. Confidential* and a little less Michael Madsen in *Reservoir Dogs*." In *L.A. Confidential* (1997), Pearce plays the bespectacled, rulebook-respecting police detective Edmund Exley. *Reservoir Dogs* (1992), Quentin Tarantino's directorial debut, has Madsen as the fairly psychotic "Mr. Blonde" (sic) – who's prone to severing a captive's ear in time to music.

• Gunn says he hasn't seen a movie since Denzel Washington "got robbed" of an Oscar for his title role in *Malcolm X* (1992). (Denzel lost to Al Pacino for *Scent of a Woman*. Some critics have argued – quite persuasively, too – that the Academy gave Pacino an Oscar simply because he'd never won, not because he actually deserved it for *that* film.) Wesley agrees that *Malcolm X* was quite the performance, Cordelia also thinks Denzel's a great actor, and Angel off-handedly concurs, "Who doesn't love Denzel?" (That's not an admission that he's seen a Denzel film, but let's take it as such; see 2.19, "Belonging." Gunn himself gets dubbed "Denzel" in 4.02, "Ground State" and 4.09, "Long Day's Journey.")

IN RETROSPECT The Host, observing Angel and Darla kissing in Angel's dream: "Somebody get these two love vamps a room." You can guess what later happens in 2.15, "Reprise," and in a hotel room, no less. Also, Angel gets to ride on the back of a motorcycle with someone else – a certain bleach-blond vampire – in 5.20, "The Girl in Question."

TONIGHT AT CARITAS In what's something of a clown motif, one of Angel's dream sequences entails him singing (off screen) "Send in the Clowns" and "Tears of a Clown." The dream-Host also sings "Get Here" by Oleta Adams.

CRITIQUE Even a lowly *Angel* episode can yield a few rich nuggets – yes, we mostly mean the now-almost-iconic pink motorcycle helmet, and there are a few others – but otherwise, this story just falls to pieces.

Thin plot and shallow supporting cast aside, it's chiefly at fault for being, so to speak, all hat and no cattle. The story clearly sets out to accomplish two goals: Make Gunn less reckless and plant the seed for a Gunn/Cordelia romance. (Oh, c'mon... the producers *must* have been contemplating such a move. Among other things, notice how fast Cordelia says, "[Gunn's] not my man, he's just a friend" – practically a guarantee that there's romance afoot.) But Gunn doesn't become noticeably less reckless, and he and Cordy don't get together – hell, they're not even exceptionally chummy after next episode – why bother? Seriously, what's the point?

Sadly, this comes at the cost of making the otherwise-savvy Cordelia screw up for most of the story. She's completely out of her element in Gunn's world and – aside from a few redeeming moments, such as her treating Veronica's wound – she does little but cause problems. Cordy and Gunn prove so limp that they need Angel and Wesley to crash to the rescue at story's end. Worse, Gunn actually *thanks* Cordelia for saving his life from Deevak – when technically, it was her blunder that got him endangered in the first place. At this point in the show, Cordy deserves a lot better than this nonsense.

All things considered, 2.01, "Judgment" wasn't great, but at least, despite loads of unanswered questions and awkward twists, it ended up with a concrete beginning, middle and ending. This looks too much like a drunken golfer who's toppled over before he's even teed off.

THE LORE Benz says nobody told her Darla was human, hence her attempts to keep playing the part like a vampire, including the sniff Darla takes in "Judgment" as if she's smelling Angel in the whole of L.A. In fact, Benz remains convinced that the writers were flying by the seat of their pants, and didn't know themselves that Darla was human until they scripted "Dear Boy." (*DragonCon* 2004 panel)

• Carpenter was less-than-thrilled with some of the location shooting, claiming, "It's uncomfortable, it's stinky. We shoot down alleyways with rats as big as dogs running around. People dump pee on us out of their windows." Boreanaz added: "Homeless people scream at me all the time. Others come up and tell me their life stories. I guess they all want to be saved." (Hogan, *Glamour UK*, July 2002)

2.04: "Untouched"

"Don't make a fuss, now, Rabbit..."

Air Date: Oct. 17, 2000; **Writer:** Mere Smith;
Director: Joss Whedon

SUMMARY Lilah befriends a young telekinetic named Bethany Chaulk, hoping to recruit her as an assassin for the firm, but the Powers bring Bethany to Angel's attention. Consequently, Wesley determines that Bethany's telekinesis stems from a traumatic childhood event – the sexual abuse she suffered at her father's hands.

Meanwhile, Holland concludes that Bethany's presence is disrupting Darla's dream-offensive against Angel, and orders Lilah to extract the girl. Lilah sends Bethany's father to the hotel, hoping that Bethany will properly travel to the dark side after killing the man. An enraged Bethany telekinetically hammers out the windows on the Hyperion's upper level, but Angel convinces her to reject, not outright kill, her father. Bethany later severs ties with her father and Lilah, leaving for parts unknown.

FIRSTS AND LASTS Bethany marks the first nearly-indisputable *X-Men* style "mutant" on *Angel* (although others arguably pre-date her; see 1.04, "I Fall to Pieces"). More frivolously, this story marks the first appearance on *Angel* of a carousel (and see 3.15, "Loyalty"). It's also the first script by Mere Smith, a writer with a penchant for tormented female characters (see 3.05, "Fredless").

First appearance of the unfinished area in the Hyperion's upper level, home to stories such as 3.06, "Billy." First explicit mention that Wesley keeps a "flat" and doesn't live at the hotel. Oh, and Gunn's shiny hubcap axe gets its first outing.

POINTS OF DISCUSSION ABOUT "Untouched":

1. A little late in the game, it's one of a few stories (see 2.18, "Dead End" and 5.21, "Power Play" for other examples) where the Powers blatantly direct Angel against one of the firm's operations, as opposed to, say, just asking him to save a homeless person from a scary monster. It's perhaps understandable that the Powers don't want Angel too close to Wolfram and Hart for fear of them corrupting him, but considering the black mark this story leaves on Lilah's record (see 2.16, "Epiphany"), it's something of a shame that the Powers don't have Angel upend the firm's apple cart more often.

2. Cordelia references her getting impaled on a metal bar in *Buffy* 3.08, "Lover's Walk," which seems a bit clairvoyant, as Bethany's telekinetic storm also shoots a nail into her arm this story. Let's hope Cordy's up on her tetanus shots.

3. The Apple logo on Cordelia's computer has reappeared, having been covered up in "Are You Now or Have You Ever Been" (2.02).

CHARACTER NOTES *Angel:* Goads Bethany into finishing her business with her father [presumably to determine whether she's redeemable or too far gone to help]. He's now spending as little as three hours awake due to Darla's dream-influence. In one of Angel's lurid dreams, Angelus and Darla have sex in a Romanian house [or so the script states] with a young girl bound and gagged nearby. [It's unclear if this is the self-same gypsy girl whose murder resulted in Angelus getting cursed with a soul; see the flashback in 1.18, "Five By Five." The actress, certainly, is different.]

• *Cordelia:* Encourages Bethany to refine her talent rather than just bluntly lashing out. [It's brave of Cordelia to get tough with Bethany, who's dangerously unstable and powerful enough to mash people with a dumpster.] Cordelia keeps spare clothes at the Hyperion [presumably the ones that Angel gives away in 2.12, "Blood Money"]. She claims to have graduated in the top ten percent of her class.

• *Wesley:* Readily identifies Bethany's father as the cause of her childhood trauma. [This clearly stems from his own parental issues – hinted at in 1.14, "I've Got You Under My Skin" and illustrated in 2.19, "Becoming" – but all indicators say Wes' abuse was mental, not physical.] Wesley and Cordy can go about three minutes without devolving into name-calling. [Wes and Gunn similarly snipped at one another in 2.02, "Are You Now or Have You Ever Been?" The gang is surprisingly bitchy in this period.]

• *Gunn:* His "neighborhood" isn't far from the corner of Hollywood and Wilcox. At Cordelia's urging [and in accordance with her befriending Gunn last episode], Angel agrees to pay Gunn on a case-by-case basis.

• *Darla:* Avoids detection by Lilah in Lindsey's office, and by Angel and Bethany in the Hyperion. She's using a purple [and presumably magical] substance named "Calynthia powder," which she keeps in a small leather pouch, to invade Angel's dreams.

• *Lilah:* Lives in a gorgeous L.A. apartment (No. 102) with a totally craphole exterior. She tours U.S. high schools, giving motivational speeches as cover for her recruitment of budding super-powered assassins. Lilah's taken to snooping in Lindsey's office [and clumsily so; see 2.11, "Redefinition" for more of her questionable tactics], and believes he's doing the same to her. Lilah describes her new clients as "monsters" [literally, one presumes] and claims that folding clothes after work calms her.

• *Bethany Chaulk:* Her father's nickname for her: "Rabbit." Bethany isn't from L.A., and her accent suggests the Northeast, "possibly Ohio" [not that Ohio is generally considered part of the Northeast]. Cordy justifiably views Bethany as someone who acts like a damsel in distress, and discourages her from preying on Angel's "old-fashioned, chivalrous" sensitivities.

Bethany's childhood abuse has given her a rather unhealthy and self-deprecating sexual appetite. She alludes to relationships where she functioned like a chambermaid – her partners barely noticed her presence and left her to clean up. She claims that everyone views her as "fragile and innocent," but that she's actually a "great big slut" whose feelings don't matter. She tries and fails to seduce Angel, who believes that Bethany wants sex but not the compassion that should accompany it. [Mind, he'll change his tune in 2.15, "Reunion."]

• *Holland:* Threatens Lilah's well-being if she doesn't remove Bethany from the Hyperion.

ORGANIZATIONS *Angel Investigations:* Finally has business cards with the agency's particulars [visible in 2.05, "Dear Boy"] on the front. [Logically, the heroes reprinted the cards to reflect their move to the Hyperion.]

• *The Powers-That-Be:* Cordelia feels Bethany's fear as part of the Powers' latest vision, and instinctively knows that Angel will arrive too late [to stop her squashing her attackers].

TELEKINESIS Wes knows nothing about telekinesis beyond its general definition. [It's clearly not part of his standard Watcher training, suggesting the talent is rare. No other human telekinetics, in fact, surface in any other *Angel* story.] Wesley's research cites telekinesis as a "psychic phenomenon" that emerges during extreme emotional stress. Bethany's talent stems from her childhood abuse, and her power apparently manifested in full at puberty.

Bethany's telekinesis initially seems to function on instinct. [Her brain must subconsciously determine the best method of defense, however blunt, as she uses entirely different methods of attack.] She contains enough raw power to blow out the Hyperion's upper windows, yet learns enough finesse to manipulate one of Cordelia's scarves and to catch her plummeting father four feet off the ground. [Sight isn't always required to telekinetically snare objects, then.]

There's a glimmering effect when she uses her power [the result of heat transfer?]. Her power engages while she sleeps, with nightmares triggering her telekinesis.

DEMONOLOGY *Vampires:* A shimmering effect occurs when an uninvited vampire leans against an entryway. [The effect first appeared on *Buffy* 5.02, "Real Me," a mere two weeks before this story was broadcast.]

2.04, Untouched

BEST LINE It's not so much the line itself as the way a random cop describes the two men that Bethany flattens as "Mr. Bills." He even delivers the classic, "Oh no, Mr. Bill!" line in a high-pitched voice (and see **Pop Culture**).

THINGS THAT DON'T MAKE SENSE For a start, there's the ages-old plot contrivance that Bethany refers to Lilah as "my friend" as opposed to the more sensible, "my friend Lilah," thus preventing the heroes from exposing the villains' game about half an episode sooner.

After her encounter with the would-be-rapists, why does Bethany just scuttle into the building next door and hang around rather than – oh, say – getting as far from the crime scene as possible? Perhaps the power exertion drained her, but she seems spry enough, even after impaling Angel with a metal bar. That brings to mind another problem: the metal bar hits Angel in such a location as to likely mess up his back tattoo, yet the design seems perfectly intact in future episodes. (And no, a vampire's healing factor can't magically repaint tattoos, as whimsical as that sounds.)

Lilah seems incredibly obtuse when she just stands around, not showing the slightest bit of concern, as Bethany's telekinetic nightmare rattles the bedroom furniture. Needless to say, when a lamp finally darts out and smacks Lilah in the face, you're entitled to claim, "I *told* you so." Bethany's dad similarly fails to bat an eye when her power quakes the hotel's very foundations... are we to infer that he's witnessed her telekinesis in action before, or he's just unfazed because he's evil?

And a visual goof: Bethany blows out the Hyperion's windows in the Act Three cliffhanger, but they're later intact.

POP CULTURE A cop says that "nobody but our Mr. Bills" witnessed Bethany's dumpster attack. "Mr. Bill" is a disaster-prone little clay man from *Saturday Night Live*. In just about every Mr. Bill short, he got flattened, dismembered or otherwise tormented by the vicious Mr. Sluggo (also mentioned in 3.19, "The Price"), with help from the evil Mr. Hands.

• An obvious point... Angel's "You wouldn't like me when I'm happy" line is a reversal of the Incredible Hulk's credo.

IN RETROSPECT Cordelia's retort to a testy Angel: "You can't fire me. I'm vision girl." That defense won't exactly help her six episodes from now.

IT'S REALLY ABOUT... The repercussions of child abuse, obviously. But it's notable that this episode takes steps – especially in the "bedroom scene" at the Hyperion – to show just how much Bethany's worldview, particularly with regards to sex, lies in pieces. One moment, she's a fully functioning individual; the next, she's scarily vacillating between being a maiden in distress and – as she puts it – a "great, big slut." Angel honorably doesn't take advantage of the situation, but the "bedroom scene" between him and Bethany illustrates how the girl's got a host of issues to work through, even after she rebukes her dad.

CRITIQUE It's never easy writing about child abuse, so let's give Mutant Enemy credit for even making the attempt. Given the limitations of exploring the issue on network television, "Untouched" generally does a commendable job. The ending's rather trite, but it at least makes clear that Bethany won't solve her problems in a day, so bravo for that level of honesty.

Here's the weird thing about "Untouched," though... it plays immensely better the first time around, when the subject matter hypnotizes you. A re-watch, unfortunately, exposes just how wooden much of it is. Mere Smith's a fan-favorite in certain quarters because she focuses so heavily on relationship issues, but she simply lacks the finesse of – to name a few – Whedon, Minear or Espenson. Smith can write a scene laden with drama, a scene with comedy or a scene with action, but the best *Angel* and *Buffy* writers can do all three at once. Too often, Smith's characters say precisely what they mean and mean precisely what they say. Too often, her jokes (such as Bethany's comment to Angel: "What, are you from the eighteenth century?") take the easy path. Too often, she boils complex characters down to their basic components (Lilah seems painfully one-sided, and Holland is never more tinny than in his two scenes here).

Granted, this represents Smith's first *Angel* script, and she'll improve with time. But that still leaves "Untouched" as a story that succeeds in the grand sense, yet suffers in its detail work.

THE LORE Prior to *Angel*, Mere Smith (full name Meredyth Smith) was living in Brooklyn and obsessively watching *Buffy* on a TV set that wasn't even hers. She'd habitually arrive at work at 7 am to get in a heady round of *Buffy*-related Internet posting before starting her day, so her ascension to the post of *Angel* script coordinator in Season One makes her one of the few "hardcore fans made good." (Drew Goddard – see 5.07, "Lineage" – is another.)

• Whedon sutured parts of this story, and apparently drafted Bethany's "chambermaid" speech, plus her line about the cause for Angel's rumpled bedcovers. Smith had conceptualized the ending as Bethany pitching her father out a 50-story building, then saving him, and found the heroes' relocation to the Hyperion helpful on this score. Largely on Smith's suggestion, the writing crew rationalized that Bethany hadn't telekinetically smooshed her father before now because abuse victims sometimes look upon their abusers as a sort of omnipotent entity. (Smith, *The Bronze*, Sept. 25, 2000)

2.05: "Dear Boy"

"Imagine Bonnie and Clyde, if they had 150 years to get it right."

Air Date: Oct. 24, 2000; **Writer/Director:** David Greenwalt

SUMMARY Still obsessively dreaming about Darla, Angel spies his "dead" ex-lover posing as suburban housewife "DeEtta Kramer." However, "DeEtta" walks into sunlight, establishing that the firm returned her to life (1.22,"To Shanshu in L.A.") as a human.

A fixated Angel pursues "DeEtta" to her home, whereupon Lindsey and Darla spring a pre-arranged trap. "DeEtta" phones 911 and reports an intruder – just as a vampire minion kills "DeEtta's husband," actually an actor hired by the firm. Angel predictably confronts Darla, but the police show up, spy "DeEtta" crying over her husband's corpse and peg Angel as the killer.

Angel escapes, but Kate takes a pack of policemen and storms the Hyperion looking for him. Wesley uncovers historical evidence that identifies "DeEtta" as Darla, slowly convincing Kate to recognize the deception. Elsewhere, Angel nabs Darla and warns that her restored soul and conscience will soon make her feel guilt for her crimes. But as morning breaks, a non-repentant Darla escapes into the sunlight. Angel returns to the Hyperion, bracing himself for future conflict.

FIRSTS AND LASTS First appearance of Drusilla on *Angel*, albeit in flashback. We see the first hint of emotional current between Lindsey and Darla, and there's the first overt sign – see **Character Development** – that Wes isn't quite as pure and virtuous as one might think. First time that the Host asks for a Sea Breeze, his beverage of choice for the rest of the show.

POINTS OF DISCUSSION ABOUT "Dear Boy":

1. You wouldn't particularly guess it from the Summary, but Angel's decisions here will shape the rest of the series. Yes, it's really that important. As we'll touch on in **It's Really About...**, Angel's pursuit of Darla comes in defiance of every bit of wisdom that's handed to him on a platter. Cordy and Wes caution Angel against his own recklessness, but the true mother of warnings occurs when Angel sings for the Host, who tells him, "You're headed into trouble, with a capital TROUB. Let [Darla] go," and "I set people on their paths, and this is way off your path, sweetie." How much more blatant can he get?

Angel's reaction to anything except what he wants to hear entails willful ignorance, verging on hostility. However, the fact remains that had Angel backed off on Darla right here and right now, most of the show's remaining hideous consequences – see **Did Jasmine Cause All This?** in particular – could've potentially been avoided. That would've deprived the viewer of an intriguing series, mind, and it's the classic Greek tragedy formula of the hero's faults driving the action – which is perfectly in keeping with the "flawed" Angel as fronted in 2.02, "Are You Now or Have You Ever Been?"

2. Among other business, we're handed (in flashback) Drusilla's definitive origin. That said, Dru's back story isn't more relevant to this episode than any other Angelus/Darla atrocity you care to mention, and in large part, it only serves as a set-up for Dru's "big entrance" in 2.09, "The Trial," especially for benefit of *Angel* viewers who don't watch *Buffy*.

3. Angel's business card lists the hotel's address as Hyperion Avenue, but the street number here is rather hard to make out and might be something like 1483 or even 3482. (It's clarified as 1481 in 3.04, "Carpe Noctem.") However, that leaves us with the problem that the number on the front of the Hyperion – and the number of the real-life apartment complex that serves as its exterior – is plainly visible in stories such as 2.11, "Redefinition" (and 4.22, "Home" especially) as 4121.

Which do we believe? Logic seems to favor the business cards, as the heroes can't be using the wrong number *ad nauseam*. But if the cards are correct, why is 4121 so prominently displayed on the Hyperion front? Almost no amount of continuity glue can fix this one, so let's leave it as an enigma.

4. Two things that're often cited as goofs but which aren't... The police burst through the door "impossibly quickly" after Darla places her hysterical 911 phone call. It's fairly clear that Lindsey uses the firm's connections to arrange this in advance, hence his comment, "Just give me a few minutes to set things in motion." What *else* would he be talking about?

Also, it's been taken as a flaw that the cops that Kate assigns to watch the Hyperion don't see Angel upon his return to the hotel. Oh, c'mon, that's easy to explain... Angel either enters the hotel through the basement access *or* he's simply sneaky enough to elude the sentries. For pity's sake, this is Angel we're talking about. If he's stealthy enough to snatch Darla into a tree without anyone noticing, he can surely slip past a couple of cops.

5. Denisof drops his Wesley accent when he mocks Cordelia's comment, "The next time I talk to him, I won't weenie out like you, Wesley." Lilting tones aside, it's probably as close as he ever gets to using his real voice on the show.

6. Surprisingly, the same scene features one of the weirdest mis-delivered lines in the entire series. Cordelia sarcastically suggests that Wes should shoot her, just as he coincidentally pulls out a trank gun. Regrettably, Carpenter over-

plays Cordy's flustering to the point that her next line – "Just a joke!" – bafflingly sounds like "Shujoe!"

7. You're missing out if you don't cast your eyes over the Caritas patrons while Angel's on stage, and witness an extremely hirsute, horned, floppy-eared demon having drinks with an sweet, perfectly normal-looking human girl. The slightly pained look he shoots her, just as Angel steamrolls through Wang Chung's "Everybody Have Fun Tonight," is priceless.

CHARACTER NOTES *Angel:* Darla claims that Angelus' evil was innate, and that "darkness" formed a part of him before they even met. [This lends credence to the theory that something about Angel's human persona, when stripped of all conscience and guilt, made Angelus such a highly accomplished vampire. It's less to do with the specific vampire demon inside Angelus, then. That makes sense, given how much vampires resonate with the loves/hates/challenges of their human lives – as Darla establishes in 1.15, "The Prodigal" – suggesting that the demons themselves are blank templates, overwritten with a human persona. See 4.15, "Orpheus" for more.]

Angelus apparently had a special fondness for convents and nuns [as per his agenda to "mock God," see 1.11, "Somnambulist"]. Angel alludes to horrific events that occurred at Our Lady of Lochenbee. He also claims he "came back from the dead." [An extremely loose reading of *Buffy* 2.22, "Becoming," in which Angel was banished to a hell dimension but not outright killed.] Angel can now smell Darla. [He couldn't during the previous two episodes, so his senses must sharpen now that he's aware of her.] The sight of her makes him so hormonal, he also sniffs Cordelia (who screams out, "Personal bubble... *Personal bubble!*").

Darla claims she can smell Angel also [as suggested in 2.01, "Judgment"], and says that that "my boy" (Angelus) wants out. [She might literally be correct. 1.17, "Eternity" and 4.14, "Release" imply that Angelus lies dormant whenever Angel's in charge, silently observing events and longing for freedom.]

• *Cordelia:* Bullied Angel into making Gunn a paid employee last episode, yet now, with finances getting tight, proposes paying Wesley in chicken pot pies. [She's playing favorites, the hussy.] Like Wesley and Gunn, she's apparently willing to risk imprisonment rather than blab about Angel to Kate.

• *Wesley:* Angel sniffs out that Wes had sex last night with a bleached blonde. [Is she the woman from the bar in "Judgment"? Either way, it's quick work on Wesley's part, as he must have squeezed in this sex between the gory Thrall demon battle and work the next morning.] Cordy's comment to Wes: "That's unbelievable. I didn't think you ever had sex."

• *Gunn:* Clearly rattled to learn that Angel can become a mass murderer under certain conditions. Gunn jokes about an "Uncle Theo" that he doesn't actually have. His rap sheet includes offenses such as disturbing the peace, resisting arrest and G.T.A. assault – some of these occurred while Gunn was a minor; others happened in the past two weeks.

• *The Host:* Currently employs a bartender named "Rico" [possibly a weird nickname for "Ramone," the bartender seen next episode].

• *Darla:* Exposed, she abandons her dream-gambit against Angel [which began in 2.03, "First Impressions"]. Darla claims she's vengeful against Angel because of "missed opportunities," deeming his restored soul a waste given to a "whiny, mopey do-gooder." [Her opinion of Angel seems based on vampire Darla's assessment of his newly ensouled self in 2.07, "Darla." It's possible that her views changed little in the century to follow, which explains why she now refuses to count herself as human.]

Angel speculates that Darla was returned to life as a human because the firm doesn't think he'll kill one. [Holland implies as much in 2.10, "Reunion." Alternatively, her rebirth as a human owed to the specific type of resurrection spell used in 1.22, "To Shanshu in L.A."]

As in "Judgment," Darla claims she can innately feel Angel's presence [again, see 1.11, "Somnambulist" for an explanation]. She acknowledges Angelus' accomplishments as a vampire as greater than her own. [5.02, "Just Rewards" confirms this, but Holtz regards Darla as the more dangerous of the two; see 3.09, "Lullaby."]

Darla knows about Angel's romance with Buffy. [Wolfram and Hart presumably briefed her, suggesting the firm now knows more about Angel's past than simple rumors (1.19, "Sanctuary").] Darla claims Buffy was just "something new" and didn't represent true happiness, whereas Angel retorts that he formerly lacked a soul and literally *couldn't* feel happiness with Darla. [But see **Who is Angel's True Love?**] Darla seems interested in seducing Angel and thereby reverting him to Angelus [yet 2.07, "Darla," confirms that the firm – or Holland, at least – doesn't foresee that happening].

Shortly before Angelus sired Dru in London, Darla murdered a "Lord Nichols" (out of a deep-rooted loathing of cheap royalty) and a streetwalker who was haggling with him (simply because Darla "liked her").

• *Drusilla:* In London [circa 1860, according to both the script and *Buffy* 2.21, "Becoming"], Darla and Angelus targeted the human Drusilla partly because of her innate innocence, and more importantly because she possessed "the sight," i.e. her prophetic visions. [Some fan speculation holds that Dru's visions suggest she was a Potential Slayer, yet her on-screen visions don't seem Slayer-related, and no Slayer is ever seen to possess her level of prophetic talent.]

Angelus slaughtered Drusilla's family. [Dru is here seen,

apparently, with her father, mother and two sisters. *Buffy* 2.10, "What's My Line?", specifies one of the sister's names as "Anne," and claims that Angelus also butchered her uncle.] Angelus and Darla chased Drusilla to her nunnery, where the vampires slaughtered several nuns and had sex in front of a terrified Dru. Angelus later sired her. [Indeed, at least one version of the script claims Angelus sired Dru *while* having sex with Darla – both adding a new level of heinousness to the act and symbolically making vamp Dru their love child. Dru's classic utterance of "Snake in the woodshed! Snake in the woodshed!" isn't in the script, suggesting it was ad-libbed or added in the eleventh hour. By the way, the line – give or take – might hail from a character's constant complaint about "something nasty in the woodshed" in Stella Gibbons' comedic novel *Cold Comfort Farm* (1932), adapted for TV as late as 1995.]

Angelus sired the deluded Dru "to make her experience eternal torment." [That's a conceit on Angelus' part, as pretty much every soulless vampire takes to the life.]

• *Lindsey:* Clearly smitten with Darla and accommodating to the notion of her killing Angel, whatever company policy might dictate.

• *Kate:* Has been transferred to the downtown precinct as something of a punishment, presumably due to her fixation with strange/grotesque cases. A co-worker named Jack stood up for Kate, but is now distanced from her. "A friend" [presumably Lindsey, as with 1.19, "Sanctuary"] covertly tips off Kate as to Angel's new residence at the Hyperion.

THE HYPERION The company business cards stipulate the hotel as zip code 90036, phone number (213) 555-0162. [The real-life Los Altos Apartments zip is 90010.]

THE LIBRARY Wesley's books include a reproduction of a daguerreotype of Darla, taken over a hundred years ago [but see **Things That Don't Make Sense**].

ORGANIZATIONS *Angel Investigations:* Cordelia goads Angel into accepting an adultery case, but Angel finds the work crass and tells the adulterer to come clean with her husband. The Hyperion office contains a tranquilizer gun with presumably enough punch to take down Angel if needed [proven in 4.11, "Soulless"].

• *Wolfram and Hart:* Darla has supplied the firm with extensive information about Angel. Lindsey confirms that the firm wants Angel "dark" and yielding to his nastier urges rather than dead [see 2.12, "Blood Money" for more]. As "DeEtta," Darla comes into collision with Angel by lunching with "her husband" at the same hotel where Angel happens to be shadowing an adulterer. [This begs the question of how the villains pre-arrange this. Either the firm is monitoring Angel's caseload – although there's no evidence of that before Season Three – or the firm rigs the adultery case from the start. Along similar lines, see "Lindsey's landlord" in 2.10, "Reunion."]

• *Caritas:* Angel dithers about the cover charge. [So the heroes, for now, aren't getting in for free.]

DEMONOLOGY Wes and Cordelia instantly disbelieve the notion of space alien abductions. [And in truth, there's no evidence of extra-terrestrials on *Angel* or *Buffy*. The closest equivalent is *Buffy* 5.09, "Listening to Fear," but even that's just a "scavenging" demon called down from a "witch's moon."]

• *Vampires:* Angel cites his age as 247. [So he was "born" in 1753, the year Darla sired Angelus according to 1.15, "The Prodigal"; vampires apparently view their crawling out of the grave as a "birth," as "Reunion" clearly shows.] Angelus assesses Dru and her sisters as virgins [vampires can innately sense virginity, as 4.17, "Inside Out," seems to confirm].

• *Thrall Demon:* Blobby, wall-embedded monstrosity with a single large head and swirling tentacles. [The demon's mesmerized followers presumably tend to its needs, as it isn't exactly mobile; mind, its power can't be absolute if its followers are slaughtering one another, potentially leaving the demon to starve to death.] The Thrall Demon seen here operates from a water tank facility built upon the former site of St. Bridget's convent in Fremont. The convent was built on cursed native burial grounds, triggering eight murders in a two-year-period before the whole place burned to the ground.

BEST LINE Darla, commenting on Lindsey's prosthetic: "You don't feel anything..." Lindsey: "Not in my hand."

THINGS THAT DON'T MAKE SENSE A long-term continuity issue: Why does the warrant for Angel's arrest simply fade into the ether after this story? Even if Kate feels convinced that Darla was responsible, how would she justify dropping the manhunt for her prime suspect? "It wasn't Angel. Rather, it was a 400-year-old blonde vampire masquerading as a slutty, well-manicured housewife."

It's also odd that Kate knows virtually nothing about Darla, considering she so thoroughly researched Angelus' history in "Somnambulist." But then, Wesley claimed in the same story that he'd extensively looked into Angel's history – yet he apparently never saw a picture of Darla in the process, or remembered one well enough to realize that "DeEtta Kramer" *does* resemble Darla to a T until late in the game. And from whence does Kate produce her print-out of Gunn's rap sheet? Her S.W.A.T. team undoubtedly didn't carry a printer with them into the Hyperion, so did they conscript the heroes' equipment, even though Kate's entering from upstairs and not from the office? Or did a courier run it down to her from the station? Why, when they could just relay it over the radio?

Daguerreotypes were the products of a photographic process in the 1800s and were notoriously light-sensitive and fragile. Which would make the daguerreotype of Darla – even allowing that it's a reproduction – just about the best-preserved of its type in the world. Also, on a side note, nobody smiled in photographs of that era like Darla is seen doing.

Getting especially anal now, but a quote from this story – "That's good to hear" – that appears on a label of one of the Season Two DVDs is attributed to Cordelia. It's actually spoken by Wesley.

IT'S REALLY ABOUT... Hopelessly screwed-up romantic entanglements that live on far past their expiration date, despite all warnings from friends and colleagues to the contrary. Worse, this generally entails a personality shift in the party everyone's worried about – notice how Angel's constantly off his rocker in this and the Darla episodes to follow, yet he's back to his normally bouncy self in the intervening tales (2.06, "Guise Will Be Guise" and 2.08, "The Shroud of Rahmon"). No wonder there's so much confusion in 2.11, "Redefinition," as to whether we're dealing with Angel, Angelus or something altogether different – because even he isn't terribly sure.

TONIGHT AT CARITAS Angel "graces" the stage with Wang Chung's "Everybody Have Fun Tonight." (The script requested he sing the Allman Brothers' "Ramblin' Man," with the Host counter-suggesting he try the group's "I'm No Angel.")

CRITIQUE It's the initial thrust into this year's big story arc (or in *X-Files* terms, it's where the "Mythology" phase hits full force), and fortunately it's a striking episode in its own right. That said, if anything it's trying to coordinate too many elements, making everything seem frayed around the edges. Lindsey and Darla's plan feels forced, Kate's kinda flung into the mix and while the flashback scenes are superb, they chiefly serve to set up Drusilla's return down the road, rather than further "Dear Boy" in itself.

Still, even if the episode cumulatively feels klutzy, it's hard to really object because it's all so engrossing. Gearing up for the series' most ambitious storyline to date was bound to create a few glitches – but that's the price you pay for not playing things safe. So all told, we're left with an episode that could've been smoother, but which facilitates the stunning and almost bulletproof drama to come.

2.06: "Guise Will Be Guise"

"What is wrong with you? You've got delusions of Angel! You're not him. You can't do stuff on your own."

Air Date: Nov. 7, 2000; **Writer:** Jane Espenson; **Director:** Krishna Rao

SUMMARY With Angel craving guidance, the Host sends him to the T'ish Magev, an extremely wise swami. Meanwhile, a gunman arrives at the hotel and threatens Cordelia at gunpoint, demanding to see her employer. In Angel's absence, Wesley hurriedly masquerades as the vampire-with-a-soul, and gets "escorted" to the estate of Magnus Bryce, the head of a magic-crafting business. Bryce then hires "Angel" to safeguard his daughter Virginia from a rival magic-user/businessman named Paul Lanier. Wesley winds up bedding Virginia, but Bryce deduces Wesley's identity and – unaware of the liaison – fires him.

Angel unmasks "the T'ish Magev" as one of Lanier's men, assigned to murder the real Magev and keep Angel from Bryce's employ. The heroes compare notes and realize that Bryce intends to gain great power by sacrificing Virginia to the Davric demon Yeska. Angel's crew storms the ritual just as Yeska appears, but the demon rejects Virginia as "impure" – i.e. not a virgin – and departs. Virginia reveals that she lost her virginity years ago, then disowns her father and leaves home.

FIRSTS AND LASTS First appearance of Virginia Bryce, Wesley's first girlfriend on *Angel* (it's debatable if Cordelia even counts in *Buffy* Season Three) and the woman who will – all things considered – best weather a relationship with him. We also see the first instance of Wesley loosely acting like the team leader, and Gunn steps foot in Caritas for the first time.

POINTS OF DISCUSSION ABOUT "Guise Will Be Guise":

1. It's about this point that one senses that security at Wolfram and Hart just ain't what it used to be. Angel's incursion there in "Blind Date" (1.21) required a "Mission: Impossible"-style torching the firm's lower levels, plus a complex distraction to thwart the joint's vampire detectors. But here, Wesley and Cordelia evidently strut through the front door simply by posing as lawyers, while Angel and Gunn simply enter through a grate.

Now, fair enough that the script-writers wish to avoid a time-sucking "break-in" every other episode, and perhaps Wolfram and Hart detects the incursion and simply fail to react before the heroes vamoose. Still, just wait for stories such as 2.10, "Reunion"; 2.16, "Reprise"; 3.02, "That Vision

Thing" and many more, as it becomes evident that heroes and vampires alike can enter the law firm any damn time they please. Heck, by 5.13, "Why We Fight," Angel's making laid-back jokes about it along with the viewers.

2. We've chosen to ignore most of the discussions between Angel and the faux T'ish Magev, mostly because like a lot of psychotherapy, it's hard to separate the actual insights from the meaningless gobbledygook. Even so, given that the imposter's out to hold Angel's attention for as long as possible, it's impressive how close his blather comes to making an actual point. At the very least, let's give a shout out to his advice on Angel getting over Darla: "Go out and find yourself some small blonde thing. Bed her. Love her. Treat her like crap. Break her heart. You and your inner demon'll thank me, I promise." With some inevitability, see **Who Is Angel's True Love?**

3. It's never stated, but Virginia's name probably owes to her father viewing her as sacrifice fodder from birth. (The state of Virginia, as it happens, owes its name to Queen Elizabeth, the virgin queen.) Similarly, it's possible that "Magnus" is either Bryce's title or his real first name, possibly due to his being groomed for the family business.

4. Gunn's classic, at-a-glance assessment of Virginia: "I could have told you she wasn't no virgin."

CHARACTER NOTES *Angel:* Briefly attempts to nab Darla from the firm, but with such recklessness that even Gunn's dismayed. He's put out at Bryce's assertion that he's a "eunuch," claiming that the details about his gypsy curse "aren't even that clear" [as we're led to believe in 5.21, "Power Play" and much of Season Three].

Angel always wears black because it eliminates any worry about matching, and his lack of a body temp means donning a coat in sweaty L.A. isn't a problem. His convertible "maybe" gets 12 mpg in the city. He recognizes Yeska as a Davric Demon. [In fact, he says, "I *know* Yeska," so it's not impossible that they've met before, even if there's no time for her to register Angel's presence here.] His reputation is pervasive enough that even Lanier's goons know about him. Angel seems very proficient with a fighting staff. And a fishing pole.

• *Cordelia:* Hacks into the LAPD database with astonishing ease. [She's built on her game since 1.21, "Blind Date."]

• *Wesley:* At story's end, he attends events with Virginia and gets touted as a "private detective and bodyguard to the stars," working for the "Wyndam-Pryce Agency." [It's his first strike, inadvertently, on the "name the agency" debate that begins in 2.12, "Blood Money.] He's read about Magnus Bryce in the business pages. He doesn't recognize Yeska by name, but is familiar with Davric Demons.

• *Gunn:* In the demon-filled Caritas, Gunn wonders how he's never noticed "this weird-ass stuff going on" despite living in L.A. all his life. [See 3.18, "Double or Nothing," which appears to contradict this statement.]

• *The Host:* Sends Angel to Magev because the hero needs "more help than he can provide." The Host's treacherous bartender, Ramone [who's fired and replaced by 2.09, "The Trial"], informs Lanier about Angel's visit to Caritas.

• *Virginia Bryce:* She's 24 and has spent most of her life under lock and key, vigilantly guarded from her father's rivals. When Virginia was younger, she loved to hear her father's teachings about runic incantations, enchanted armor, magic and more – but she now thinks she's wasting her life, longing for a ho-hum occupation such as "perfume sprayer" or "tire store employee." Virginia slept with two of her father's chauffeurs, respectively at age 16 and 18. She even dated Rick, a robed minion who awkwardly slinks out of the room.

• *Yeska:* Manifests as a fat old crone with lots of frizzy hair and teeth. A saying among magicians goes, "The goddess Yeska does not give with both hands." Bryce refers to her as "Yeska, of the razor eyes and stone heart."

• *The T'ish Magev:* Lives in a cabin in Ojai. He's a personal friend of the Host – although the Host says he never writes nor calls – and Angel's heard of him.

ORGANIZATIONS *Angel Investigations:* Has wireless Internet access, judging by Cordy's laptop.

• *Magnus Bryce's Wizardry Business:* Fronts itself as a software giant and cable network. Bryce's great-grandfather started the operation, his first spell being a simple tallness illusion cast in the family garage. The business seems to specialize in custom-work, creating looks and talent. Bryce's rivals include Lanier and someone named Briggs over at Consolidated Curses.

DEMONOLOGY *Vampires:* Believing that Wesley is Angel, Bryce's goon Benny extends an invitation. Later, Angel enters Bryce's abode and private party without hindrance. [This all suggests that vampires can receive invitations by proxy, which sounds weird but actually makes sense. See **How Does the Invitation Rule Work?** Benny must actually live in Bryce's home – reasonable enough, if he's the muscle for a wealthy magic user with a frickin' big estate.] One of Lanier's lackeys casts a spell with the incantation, "Let your flesh be weakened..." [It's presumably meant to diminish vampires, but shows no effect on the human Wesley.]

• *Davric Demons:* Grant power to followers who, on their 50th birthday, provide a sacrifice – generally a young girl – for the Davric to consume. [Virgins seem to carry a lot of currency in sacrifices, see 2.08, "The Shroud of Rahmon" and 4.17, "Inside Out."]

MAGIC Wesley suggests that spell usage melts gold a lot easier than iron.

2.06, Guise Will Be Guise

BEST LINE Cordelia, bitching about Wesley's impersonation routine: "This whole 'I'm Angel' thing is a very, *very* bad idea. I mean, if I thought *that* would work, I could've been Angel because, guess what? Pretty much a girly name."

THINGS THAT DON'T MAKE SENSE Magnus Bryce tells Wesley that he's received calls and letters threatening Virginia's life. But if his competition wants her dead so badly, it seems fairly stupid of them to announce this in advance. (Bryce must invent these details, hoping to appeal to Angel's nobility.) Bryce also claims he's deployed "dozens" of protection spells about his estate, but they must be horribly feeble ones, since Angel's crew waltzes into the final ceremony without the slightest hassle.

It's fortunate for all concerned that on the very day Wesley changes his hairstyle and starts dressing (as Cordelia puts it) "like a man" for a brief incursion into the firm, he gets called upon to impersonate Angel and – barring the coat – already looks the part. Also, when Wesley spontaneously decides to impersonate Angel, how does he acquire Angel's spare coat so fast from the hotel lobby? Does Angel keep it somewhere on the ground level, rather than – say – a more obvious place like the coat rack in his office?

After Wesley sleeps with Virginia, why does he sheepishly sneak out as if he's just bagged the farmer's daughter? After all, he's impersonating Angel, who's *supposed* to stay with her at all times. (Let's put it down to nerves.) And as he's serving as her bodyguard, where on Earth is he going when he leaves her room anyway? To the bathroom? Doesn't Virginia, as Bryce's daughter, warrant her own bathroom?

The fake Magev says that it's been "eighty degrees in the shade lately," so why does the boob have a fire going in his cabin? Cordelia cries out, "Ooh! Mug shots!" as if she's had a sudden brainstorm on how to identify Bryce's gunman, yet a series of police mug shots is already running on her computer screen when she makes this declaration. (She's just over-enthused.) Then there's the amazing coincidence that Cordelia randomly owns a copy of *Bio* magazine with a photograph of both Magnus Bryce and his totally nondescript and unimportant bodyguard – the very thug she's looking for – and that she happens to flip through said magazine while taking a break from all the tiresome mug shot viewing.

Wesley's glasses magically vanish just before he assaults two of Lanier's robed lackeys. Finally, Virginia's father seems remarkably obtuse – upon discovering his daughter's sexual history – to sputter "[But] I kept you away from all men!", given that his house is full of them.

POP CULTURE The Host, when Angel describes his singing as "rocky": "You're *Rocky* and *Rocky II* and half of the one with Mister T." In *Rocky III* (1982), Rocky tries to get his self-confidence back after a defeat by Clubber Lang (Mr. T). Hulk Hogan appears in the same movie as the boxer/wrestler Thunderlips.

IN RETROSPECT The Host comments on Angel's general lack of enthusiasm, "Once more, with less feeling...", which almost sounds like a portent of the *Buffy* musical, only a year in advance.

TONIGHT AT CARITAS Two Japanese businessmen sing "I've Got You, Babe."

CRITIQUE Anyone drooling to get on with the Darla business might view this one as disposable, but "Guise Will Be Guise" features Espenson in her prime, crafting a story that's both serious and funny – oh, *hysterically* funny, even – in all the right places. Nearly every scene gets at least one moment of sheer brilliance, whether it's Wesley "dumping" his glass of blood into a clear vase, Cordelia imitating Angel's brooding ("I have to count my past sins and then alphabetize them... oh, by the way, I'm thinking about snapping completely on Friday") or the final conversation in which Angel insists he's *not* a eunuch, Virginia insists that she's *not* a virgin and Cordelia is aghast that Wesley actually got some. Even better, amidst all the silliness, Wesley's character gets bumped to a new level.

Arguably, the best comedy stories (4.06, "Spin the Bottle" and 5.14, "Smile Time") are still to come, but it's a shame that Espenson never wrote for *Angel* again, because there's nothing quite like this episode for the rest of the show. It's totally enjoyable, and suitably the calm before the storm.

THE LORE It's almost impossible to tell the story of *Angel* without touching on the romance of Alexis Denisof and Alyson Hannigan, so... Hannigan was single when Denisof arrived on the *Buffy* set. He'd previously dated Caroline Aherne, the female lead on the BBC's *Mrs. Merton and Malcolm* series, and the British press had a great deal of sport covering their break-up. (Aherne was the better-known celebrity at the time, so the coverage mainly focused on her ongoing personal troubles.) Denisof thought Hannigan was nice, but stuck to his policy of not dating co-workers. Meanwhile, Hannigan started seeing and later broke up with Ginger Fish, a drummer for Marilyn Manson. All this taken into account, Denisof and Hannigan weren't a couple during their *Buffy* days, nor when they appeared together in *Beyond the City Limits* (2001), but they'd started to flirt. They finally got married on Oct. 11, 2003; see 4.15, "Orpheus" and 5.07, "Lineage" for more. (O'Hare, *Arizona Republic*, Feb. 13, 2000; Denisof, chat transcript, Feb. 18, 2002) Denisof now guest-stars on Hannigan's sitcom *How I Met Your Mother* – Amy Acker appeared in the Season One finale, making it something of an *Angel* reunion.

• The "blood" the vampires drink in the early *Angel* seasons was a red, sweet syrupy goop – Denisof found the experience of Wesley drinking some in this episode quite "nasty," and wished for a spit bucket. Trick glasses were used later in the show, meaning the actors didn't need to actually down anything. (Denisof, chat transcript, Feb. 18, 2002)

• Art LaFleur (T'ish Magev) played the Tooth Fairy in *The Santa Clause 2*, and it happens that he regularly guest-starred on *Hyperion Bay*, which featured Brigid Brannagh (Virginia). Brannagh also served as a regular on *Kindred: The Embraced*, a mid-90s vampire series. *G.I. Joe* fans will raise their eyebrows to realize that Michael Yama (one of the businessmen singing karaoke) voiced Torpedo on that show. In a less notable capacity, Eiji Inoue (Japanese Businessman #2), appeared in *Samurai Vampire Bikers from Hell.*

2.07: "Darla"

"God never did anything for you, but I will."

Air Date: Nov. 14, 2000; **Writer/Director:** Tim Minear

SUMMARY Darla becomes near-suicidal as her restored soul starts dropping guilt on her like a ton of bricks, prompting a smitten Lindsey to take her back to the firm. An anguished Darla phones Angel for help, but Holland deems Darla too unstable and orders her termination. Lindsey helps Angel to rescue Darla, later realizing that Holland faked the execution order to facilitate Angel "saving" his former beloved and becoming even more tormented himself. Back at the Hyperion, Darla finds life as a human unbearable and implores Angel to make her a vampire again. Angel refuses, prompting Darla to flee, insisting that Angel never look for her.

FIRSTS AND LASTS It's the only appearance on *Angel* of the Master, the villain from *Buffy* Season One, although he plays quite the important role...

POINTS OF DISCUSSION ABOUT "Darla":

1. This adventure's flush with flashbacks and continuity concerns, yet "Darla" actually alleviates some lingering question marks. Until now, it'd been established that Darla sired Angel, who sired Drusilla, who sired Spike (with only Spike's comments in *Buffy* 2.03, "School Hard" causing confusion on that score, but retcon put paid to that). But the revelation here concerning Darla's own origin connects all the major *Angel* and *Buffy* vampires back to a central source: the Master.

2. Darla's siring also potentially explains an apparent contradiction in her character, given that she's one of the most assertive and vicious vampires ever made on *Angel*, yet on *Buffy*, she's shockingly submissive to the Master and lustfully struts about in a schoolgirl outfit. Evidently, she's deviously independent under normal circumstances, but simply holds a blind spot where the Master's concerned. 5.08, "Destiny," confirms this just a little, when Angelus implies that Darla goes running back to the Master whenever he calls.

3. Continuity Bump No. 1: Angel claimed in *Buffy* 1.07, "Angel," that he never killed anyone after regaining his soul, yet we here discover that he spent a short period offing rapists, murderers and the like. Still, let's consider that Angel tells this fib to Buffy, and it's perfectly understandable that he'd sugar-coat the truth in a story where the Slayer has just learned about his past atrocities as Angelus. One can hardly blame Angel for not telling the woman he loves, "I got my soul back... and then I kept slaughtering people anyway. But only bad people!" Also bear in mind that Angel's involvement in 1900 China presumably isn't well documented, so there wasn't much risk of Giles discovering the truth in one of his books.

4. Continuity Bump No. 2: The Master states in "Angel" that he misses Angel, the most vicious creature that he ever met. Yet in the "Darla" flashback, the two barely meet and generally can't stand one another. We should allow for the possibility that they reconciled some time between 1760 and Angelus' downfall in 1898, especially as Darla in "Angel" talks about Angel being brought "back into the fold," suggesting he joined the Master's Order of Aurelius at some point.

5. Continuity Bump No. 3: Angelus in 1760 thinks the world above is quite nice, doesn't want it spoiled, and desires a proper bed. But at the end of *Buffy* Season Two, he's willing to awaken the demon Acathla and end the world, leaving Spike to extol the virtues – chiefly having people to eat – of saving the planet. Well, perhaps a hundred years spent smothered in Angel's persona has simply made Angelus bonkers.

6. Bear in mind that Darla never, ever tells Spike and Dru about Angelus getting re-ensouled – probably out of a deep-rooted embarrassment about the whole affair – so they don't learn the truth until *Buffy* 2.03, "School Hard." The show will perform all sorts of somersaults, particularly in "Why We Fight" (5.13), to preserve this detail.

7. Human Darla's suffering and personality type apparently drew the Master to her, and his hanging around outside her window very much evokes *Dracula*. In turn, this makes you wonder if Bram Stoker's book in the *Angel*-verse wasn't influenced more by the Master's activities than those of the "real" Dracula (*Buffy* 5.01, "Buffy vs. Dracula").

8. Going strictly by Angel's appearance in China, 1900, the restoration of his soul and conscience also entailed the end of his unconvincing Irish accent. Perhaps bad accents don't

happen to good people.

9. Cordelia mentions that the heroes could find Darla a lot quicker if they had a website named "Ohbythewaywevegot Darlastashedhere.com" at their disposal. As rampant web-surfers know, an intrepid fan once used that very domain name, blogging on topics ranging from the 2004 *Farscape* mini-series to her inner conflict regarding her "huge" hair.

CHARACTER NOTES *Angel:* The Master cites the name "Angelus" as being the Latinate for "Angel." [See 1.15, "The Prodigal" for more.] In 1900, an ensouled Angel tracked Darla, Dru and Spike amid the Boxer Rebellion. Darla had always talked about China, and he reasoned that she couldn't avoid such mayhem. A highly conflicted Angel resumed killing with Darla, but only fed off "rapists, murderers, thieves, scoundrels and evildoers."

Darla came to sense Angel's resistance, especially when he started subsisting off vermin and lied to protect a family of missionaries. She butchered the family anyway, save for their baby. Darla ordered Angel prove his devotion by slaughtering the child, whereupon Angel took the babe and fled. [After this, there's no evidence that Angel and Darla encountered one another until 97 years later in the *Buffy* series. The child's fate goes unstated, but one imagines Angel gave it up to a nunnery or other benign agency, because he's without it upon coming to America in 1902 (4.15, "Orpheus").]

In the modern day, Angel uses his drawing talent [previously seen on *Buffy*] to obsessively render sketches of Darla.

• *Cordelia:* Doesn't like visiting "the Valley" in L.A.

• *Darla:* The term "Darla" is an Anglo-Saxon derivation meaning "dear one," but the name didn't come into use until more than 100 years after she was born. [As Angel speculates, the Master probably bestowed Darla with the name, and it later fell into common use.] Angel never knew Darla's real name, human Darla can't remember it and it's never revealed.

In 1607, in the Virginia colony, Darla worked as a prostitute until she contracted a terminal disease [specified as syphilis in 2.09, "The Trial"]. As Darla lay dying, her cries attracted the Master [see **Demonology**]. He sang to her from outside the house, then appeared the next day dressed as a priest, acknowledging Darla as an unmarried "woman of property." [Virginia was subject to English common law at the time, meaning that unwed women could own property, but it automatically went to their husband when they got married. It's entirely possible that Darla was an only child whose father died, and it's tragically obvious how she's been making an income.] After Darla rebuked God, acknowledging herself as damned, the Master turned her into a vampire.

In 1760, seven years after Darla sired Angelus [according to "The Prodigal"], the duo cut a bloody swathe through South Wales and Northern England and met with the Master in some tunnels beneath London. Angelus and the Master failed to get along, with Darla temporarily deserting her sire in favor of her lover. [Darla's future subservience to the Master might even owe, in part, to guilt from here leaving him.] Darla accepted Angelus' call for vampires to live aboveground, preferring to stay in posh accommodations with a stellar view.

In 1880, London, while traveling with Angelus and Darla, Drusilla pined for a mate. Darla inadvertently motivated Drusilla to turn the failed poet William into the vampire Spike [see **Cross-Overs**]. Dru had already taken to calling Darla "grandmother" [also used in 2.10, "Reunion" and technically correct, given how vampires measure their parentage].

In 1898, Darla directed Dru and Spike to assault the Romany band that cursed Angelus with a soul. Darla confronted the father of the young gypsy girl that Angelus killed, threatening to murder the man's family if he didn't lift the curse. Spike rashly butchered the family anyway, so Darla snapped the man's neck.

In the modern day, human Darla feels the weight of her soul and conscience [as Angel predicted in 2.05, "Dear Boy"]. She smashes every mirror in sight, unable to stand her reflection. (Angel says he avoids that inner conflict, at least, because he's reflection-less.)

Darla becomes unable to decide if she's Darla the 400-year-old vampire or someone altogether different. She says she can "feel her body dying" – something she metaphorically attributes to the "cancerous" soul inside her. [She probably senses, however indirectly, that she *is* dying, as "The Trial" reveals.] She can't remember where her soul resided after Angel staked her [*Buffy* 1.07, "Angel"].

• *Drusilla:* Refers to the absent Angelus as "my love." [A seemingly innocent term of affection, but 5.08, "Destiny," throws a completely new light on their relationship.]

• *The Master:* Already possessed bat-like features in the 1600s. By 1760, he commanded the Order of Aurelius [first mentioned in *Buffy* 1.05, "Never Kill a Boy on the First Date"]. The Master believed that vampires should live underground, only venturing to the surface world to feed and swell their ranks. [He runs the Order as a quasi-religious organization, which probably emphasizes not getting "tainted" by the human world.] He seems physically stronger than Angelus.

• *Lindsey:* Briefly makes out with Darla on his desk until she bites him. He's taken to wearing a neck cross.

• *Holland:* Removes Lindsey from the Darla project. [As part of Holland's ploy; Lindsey is still involved in "The Trial."] It's implied that Holland presumed that Darla would break up, even become suicidal, but didn't tell Lindsey. [Holland probably knows Darla's medical diagnosis, revealed in "The Trial."]

ORGANIZATIONS *Angel Investigations:* Cordelia and Wesley concur that despite running a "detective agency," the crew stinks at actually investigating things.

• *Wolfram and Hart:* Holland tells Lindsey that he doesn't foresee any prospect for physical intimacy between Angel and Darla, but that he expects Angel to try and "save her soul" instead. [This makes sense. The firm wants to sway Angel to the dark side – see 2.12, "Blood Money" – but Angelus is simply too much of a wild card (as 4.13, "Salvage" pretty much proves). The ensouled Angel is far more malleable.]

Wesley implies that the firm restored Darla as human so they had some hope of controlling her. [Possibly so, but human Darla also causes far more emotional turmoil in Angel's life than vampire Darla, who's inherently more stakeable.] The firm owns an abandoned bank on Figaro and Ninth in L.A., and sometimes conducts executions there.

DEMONOLOGY *Vampires:* A dying Darla evidently "cried out" for the Master in her delirium. [This evidently counts as an invitation, as he effortlessly enters her house the next day. But see both **Things That Don't Make Sense** and **How Does the Invitation Rule Work?**] Vampire Darla can smell both Angel's soul and the vermin he's subsisting on.

BEST LINE The Master's estimate on Darla's romance with Angelus: "I give it a century, tops."

THINGS THAT DON'T MAKE SENSE In 1607, the Master felt "drawn" to Darla when she cried out for him. Fair enough, but why'd he wait until the next day to enter the house? And how does he time his entrance, considering it looks like it's sunny outside, and the Virginia colony didn't exactly have a plot-convenient system of sewer tunnels?

Lindsey's master plan for keeping Darla out of Wolfram and Hart's clutches: turn her loose, on foot, onto the streets of L.A. Unsurprisingly, the firm re-captures her in no time flat.

CROSS-OVERS Flashbacks in this story coincide with those in *Buffy* 5.07, "Fool for Love," which details Spike's history and relates events from his point of view. The chief difference is that in "Fool for Love," Spike deludes himself into thinking that Drusilla saw the potential (for evil) in his human aspect, whereas in *this* episode, Dru acts on Darla's suggestion that she sire "the first drooling idiot that comes along." "Fool for Love" also implies that Angelus felt jealousy upon learning that Spike killed a Slayer during the Boxer Rebellion, but we here learn that Angel's ensouled and is feeling disgust.

POP CULTURE The firm leases apartments from a building owned by a client, Annapolis Olive Oil Import Export. That's the name of a traditional mob cover; see *The Godfather II*.

IN RETROSPECT In the 1880 flashback, Dru's line to Darla ("Don't be cross. I could be your mummy") is probably deliberate foreshadowing of what's to come in "The Trial." (That said, it's far more difficult to determine if this owes to Dru's "sight" registering events 120 years into the future, or if she's just being a dingbat.) Angelus' claim to the Master that, "I could never live in a rat-infested stinkhole like this," seems ironic, considering by the late twentieth century, he'll be homeless, smelly and feeding off rats in New York City.

CRITIQUE So many people have contributed to *Angel*'s success that you hate to put someone on too high a pedestal, but it's readily obvious when Tim Minear's in the captain's chair. Tight, magnificent and containing a deft amount of twists and turns, "Darla" vastly expands on *Angel*-lore while impressively clinging to established continuity as if it were flypaper. There's scarcely a scene in which we don't learn something vital, or come to view a character in a new light – indeed, other than Lindsey's rather pathetic ploy to eject Darla from the firm, there's scarcely a line or shot that's not needed in some fashion. The whole episode funnels its efforts to answer the question of "Who is Darla?" yet fails to come up with any easy answers, while the superb direction and crisp dialogue makes it a veritable feast. Not to mention that the ties between this story and "Fool For Love" make for a delicious cross-pollination that you don't see on network TV often enough.

At the risk of overstating the point – but this is one of those "hell of a good ride" stories that's easy to drone on about – students wanting to work in Hollywood should study "Darla" as an example of how to make great television, and the possibilities of the medium. We don't smoke, but suffice to say, we felt like lighting up after watching this story.

THE LORE The producers found themselves with yet another overrun – about seven minutes of material. The cuts included Wesley, upon seeing Angel's obsessive Darla drawing in the teaser, making a masturbation joke at Angel's expense. Also, during the slo-mo scene where Spike hefts up Dru, Angel was scheduled to snap the neck of the warrior who attacked him in the alley – thus dispatching an evil-doer while making himself look like a bad-ass to the other vampires. Minear later regretted cutting a reference to the doomed Roanoke colony in Virginia, 1587 – the word "Croatoan" was historically carved into a tree there, and Minear meant to suggest that this referred to the Master. Yet he struck out mention of Roanoke because the FOX show

FreakyLinks was about to begin a story arc on the colony, plus Minear worried that it over-complicated an already busy scene. (Minear, *alt.tv.angel*, Nov. 20, 2000)

• The notion of doing Spike and Darla's origin stories arose independently, but Minear figured it'd work to interweave the storytelling into what became "Fool for Love." (Gross, *Fandom.com*, Nov. 13, 2000)

• At 5'4", Benz sometimes found it challenging to play Darla as assertive – especially against the 6'1", broad-shouldered Boreanaz. Benz appreciated that her stunt double, Lisa Hoyle, went some way toward making Darla look physically strong. (*BBC Cult*, Nov. 2001)

• Composer Robert J Kral found himself with an extremely tight deadline on this episode, having to score 38 minutes of story in just four days. Minear had asked for "Big Wagnerian Horns" and got 'em. ("37 Questions with Robert J. Kral," *Miracles TV*)

• Zitto Kazann reprised his role of "Gypsy Man" from *Buffy* 2.21, "Becoming, Part 1."

Who is Angel's True Love?

No, it's not Spike. Can we move on, please?

With *Buffy the Vampire Slayer*, Whedon and his accomplices successfully craft one of the most magnificent romances in television history. It's important to state that up-front. And in truth, in *Buffy* Seasons One to Three, the dynamics of the Angel-Buffy relationship prove as compelling, intoxicating and downright *mythic* as you've been led to believe. Not for nothing does Giles declare in "Out of Mind, Out of Sight" (*Buffy* 1.11): "A vampire in love with a Slayer. It's rather poetic, in a maudlin sort of way..."

Even casual viewers appear to have bought into this relationship, especially when you consider the immediate, jolting ratings bump between "Surprise" and "Innocence" (*Buffy* 2.13 and 2.14), the two-parter where Angel and Buffy finally get horizontal and the experience makes him go rogue. On original broadcast, it seemed almost unimaginable that Angel would become a devious fiend and willfully torment his girlfriend, but the viewership simply couldn't get enough. In fact, the influx of new viewers from "Innocence" mostly carried over to the next episode, "Phases," a comparatively "normal" episode about werewolves.

In the main, and almost undeniably, the Angel-Buffy relationship worked beautifully. But here's the giant, thundering conceit that some people don't want to acknowledge: The romance largely works because we're seeing it through Buffy's eyes, and we simply don't know much about Angel himself. We're told he was once a murderous vampire, but we're *shown* preciously little of this, and details about his background are a drop in the well compared to what the *Angel* series reveals.

And once you *do* learn about Angel over the course of his show... well, it radically changes matters, particularly with regards to Darla. On *Buffy*, Darla only lasts a total of three episodes, and she's not – all respect to Julie Benz – a terribly impressive character. Her main attributes are that she's obsequious before the Master and weirdly dresses like a schoolgirl, so she's not exactly what you'd call the height of complexity. But on *Angel*, Darla in both past and present is light-years beyond the schoolgirl routine. Indeed, she's *so* focused, capable and downright devious that Holtz seems dead-on when he claims (3.09, "Lullaby") that *Darla* was far more unpredictable than Angelus. In short, she's an incredibly formidable woman who ran with Angelus for roughly 150 years. Try, just for a moment, to comprehend the intimacy they must have formed over that duration of time, occasional dalliances (5.08, "Destiny"; 5.20, "The Girl in Question"; etc) or no.

Thus, taking the grand sweep of the *Angel* series into account, Angel's actions in *Buffy* Seasons One to Three simply don't make a great deal of sense. The notion that this man, who's led an extraordinary and utterly unique life would glimpse at a teenager who kicks ass and instantly fall for her – and then *decide to hang out with her teenage friends* – seems less and less likely. Hell, with full knowledge of Angel's age and history, it's a scenario that's increasingly on the creepy side too. (By comparison, it's much easier to believe that Spike would feel captivated by the antics of a valley girl who stakes his kind, simply because, well, he's a bit shallow.)

You may have noticed that we've yet to mention Cordelia in all this. Unlike some fans, we're not particularly troubled by the thought of Angel falling for her. It's not an ideal pairing, and it's tricky to imagine it working out in the long-term, but the attraction in and of itself seems plausible. It's likely (and understandable) that Cordy's rich bitch persona in Sunnydale forever colored the perception of her to some fans, but remember that she's every bit the mature woman by the time *Angel* Season Three rolls around. She's ultimately *not* Angel's true love, but the simple virtue of her being – at that point – an extraordinarily versatile *adult* mostly answers the issue of "Why would Angel want to date Cordy?" Rather, let's return to the root (and far more telling) question of "Why the hell would he want to date Buffy?"

Allowing that nobody exactly knows why people fall in love, two explanations spring to mind. In the first place, Angel might feel drawn to Buffy's relative innocence, especially compared to what he experienced as a murderous vampire with Darla. Oh, dear, you can see where this is going. The second and far more telling rationalization is that, well, Buffy's blonde. We've made a lot of sport in this book about Angel only dating blondes, but there's some truth in it. Cordelia even admits, in "Redefinition" (2.10): "One thing you can say about Angel, he's consistent. It's always some little blonde driving him over the edge." Very true, and which blonde came first? Darla. If you bear that in mind, then Darla's comment to Angel that, "Buffy wasn't happiness. She was just new" (2.05, "Dear Boy") not only sounds rather stinging, it looks more and more like it's the case.

Angel and Darla ran together for a century and a half. They engaged in "the whirlwind [of terror]" as Darla liked to call it. She's a vexing, sultry and dynamic *woman* who indirectly motivates Angel to shack up with Buffy, and her sudden return from the dead throws him almost irrevocably off the rails. *Of course* Darla is first and foremost in Angel's heart. How could it be anyone else?

2.08: "The Shroud of Rahmon"

"So to take his mind off the torment that is Darla, we sent Angel after a box that makes you crazy."

Air Date: Nov. 21, 2000; **Writer:** Jim Kouf; **Director:** David Grossman

SUMMARY Gunn asks for Angel's help when his cousin Lester balks at the thought of participating in a museum heist, whereupon Angel dusts and assumes the identity of one of the conspirators: a flashy vampire named Jay-Don. However, Gunn refuses to stay on the sidelines and substitutes himself for Lester as the group's driver. Meanwhile, Wesley and Cordelia deduce that the group intends to steal and sell the Shroud of Rahmon – a magical artifact used to bind an insanity-causing demon. Unfortunately, the Shroud's laced with some of the demon's power, and causes madness in those within close proximity. Wesley and Cordelia try to warn their friends, but the Shroud triggers various stages of madness in all concerned.

Kate tries to thwart the robbery, but Angel – in order to protect Kate from the thieves – bites and renders her unconscious, pretending that she's dead. The madness-afflicted thieves kill one another, leaving Angel and Gunn to set the Shroud afire and break its emotional hold. The cops nab Wesley for questioning, but Kate recovers and procures his release.

FIRSTS AND LASTS It's Cordelia's first outing with what can only be properly described as her "Shannen Doherty hair," and it's something that even she will make fun of come 4.04, "Slouching Toward Bethlehem." It also marks the first time on *Angel* that something in a sarcophagus causes loads of trouble (see 5.15, "A Hole in the World," which makes Rahmon's evil shroud look like chump change).

POINTS OF DISCUSSION ABOUT "The Shroud of Rahmon":

1. It's arguably the last time we'll need to examine police procedure in a hardcore fashion (as concerns about it taper off radically after 2.16, "Epiphany"), so we're deliberating it here rather than leaving it for **Things That Don't Make Sense**. Chiefly, it's curious how much Angel's relationship with Kate has drawn all manner of attention in the last year plus change, yet the authorities have practically forgotten about it. After all... Angel has, by now, stopped by Kate's old precinct several times, attended a policeman's retirement party (1.06, "Sense and Sensitivity"), been identified as a potential murder victim (1.11, "Somnambulist"), been apprehended for harboring a fugitive (1.19, "Sanctuary") and most recently been hunted as a murder suspect (2.05, "Dear Boy"). Yet the two detectives investigating the heist members say they "couldn't make" Angel until speaking with one of Kate's colleagues, and nearly imply that he's not in the system. Has Cordelia been moonlighting as their file clerk?

2. The high priest responsible for binding Rahmon's body sacrificed seven virgins to dye the Shroud – and he's allegedly one of the good guys. Couple this with Angelus' fixation with Dru and her sisters – "all virgins" – in 2.05, "Dear Boy," the attempted virgin sacrifice in 2.06, "Guise Will Be Guise," the virgin slaughter in 4.17, "Inside Out" and the threat to virgin Xander's life in *Buffy* 1.04, "Teacher's Pet," and you realize that virginity in the *Angel*-verse is quite, quite overrated.

3. We've got to say this at some point, so... if you stare at the show long enough, you realize how much the producers recycle the exterior footage of the Hyperion. Indeed, it becomes obvious that a film crew simply shot the exterior of Los Altos Apartments (see **How Do I Take the Angel/Buffy L.A. Tour?**) in the course of a single evening, and then used this same well of footage throughout Seasons Two, Three and Four. Yup, that's right... virtually every full-frontal evening shot of the hotel over the next three years hails from the same source. You can tell because the same rooms are illuminated – notice especially the three windows on the right-hand side in the center part, top level.

Mind, this puts continuity off-kilter, as the same hotel rooms are lit no matter how many characters are in residence. Also, it's small wonder that the heroes are always strapped for cash when they could simply turn some frickin' lights off and spare their utility bill.

CHARACTER NOTES *Angel:* Doesn't hi-five. He drinks Kate's blood, renewing concern that this might reawaken his bloodlust. [This never comes to pass, and isn't an issue again until 3.16, "Sleep Tight." But in its own small way, the predator instinct triggered by Angel's feasting off Kate might contribute to his going off the rails two episodes hence.] Angel's excited that Cordy met Asian film star Chow Yun Fat [see **Pop Culture** under 2.03, "First Impressions" for more about Angel's celebrity worship] at a party, even if Wesley accidentally dumped cocktail sauce on her in front of the man.

• *Cordelia:* While under the Shroud's influence, Cordy nabs a necklace from the museum [and as far as we know, never gives it back]. Angel and Wesley appear to have just noticed the new hairstyle that she's worn for ten days. [Let's write this off as a joke, because it's hard to imagine the boys being *that* dense. Either that, or it's miraculous that they independently notice Cordy's new "do" on the same day.]

• *Wesley:* [First off... taking stock of Wesley's romantic track record to this point, his addled comment to the police that, "I'm quite good with the ladies, you know," ranks as one of the series' most erroneous statements.] Wesley laudably notices Cordy's new shoes. He hasn't heard of the Shroud before now. He's still attending celebrity galas with girlfriend Virginia Bryce [but his attendance sharply drops off after this].

• *Gunn:* Influenced by the Shroud, Gunn displays great animosity toward vampires [largely due to his sister's death; see 1.20, "War Zone"] and by extension gets hostile toward Angel. [It's starting to emerge that Gunn never gets 100 percent comfortable with Angel's status as a vampire; see 3.03, "That Old Gang of Mine," for more.]

• *Kate:* Identifies Darla as the troublemaker in 2.05, "Dear Boy," vowing to hunt her down [see 2.10, "Reunion"].

• *Jay-Don:* Vegas-based vampire; Angel and Wesley know him by reputation. Angel claims that Jay-Don "ran with the whole Sinatra rat-pack thing, and never got over it," and he sports a New York accent.

• *"M. James Menlo":* Handle of the Nitro-carrying, vault-cracking demon in the heist.

MAGIC *The Shroud of Rahmon:* Wesley's texts claim that after the demon Rahmon was "defeated," a head priest – already driven mad by Rahmon – created the Shroud as a means of preventing the creature's resurrection. The priest dyed the Shroud with the blood of seven virgin women sacrificed on the first full moon, then wrapped the demon's body with it. But the Shroud absorbed Rahmon's power. [Rahmon's body doesn't appear to pose a threat, suggesting he's assuredly deceased. Heaven only knows what Angel and company do with his desiccated husk, however.]

In 1803, the Shroud was removed from its casing and drove the entire population of El Encanto insane, with even mothers and children hacking one another to pieces. Archaeologists at the University of New Mexico recently unearthed the Shroud from a tomb. [In America? In Mexico?]

The Shroud seems to affect everyone differently, variously triggering paranoia (in Menlo), hostility (Angel and Gunn), fatigue (Vyasa) or even giddiness, almost like alcohol intoxication (Wesley and Cordelia). [Much of this is a far cry from the murderous frenzy that destroyed El Encanto, and notice that Kate, beyond a little dizziness, doesn't seem affected at all. It's easy to write off any inconsistencies because the Shroud is mystical, and simply prone to various effects.] Rahmon's shrouded body comes sealed in a box of consecrated wood, with lead lining and gold edges. Menlo claims the box weighs about a ton, and it's difficult to move even with three demons [one of them Angel, who's stronger than most] and two humans carrying it. The thieves steal the Shroud from the Southern California Museum of Natural History. Its estimated worth on the black market: $2 million.

DEMONOLOGY *Vampires:* Angel says that scared humans taste "kind of salty." [Maybe it's just due to sweat, but 1.11, "Somnambulist," counter-suggests that fear makes humans taste sweeter.] Rahmon's box is made from consecrated wood, yet this doesn't burn Angel's skin. [See **Why Do Catholic Objects Harm Vampires?** for a possible explanation.]

BEST LINE A Shroud-influenced Cordelia, goofily looking at her reflection: "My teeth are so... big! I... am... *pleasant*."

THINGS THAT DON'T MAKE SENSE It's one of those stories in which you get so caught up in its action, you fail to realize until later that the heroes don't actually have anything resembling a plan. Fair enough that Angel and Gunn want to protect Gunn's cousin and discover the thieves' intent. But once they realize they're dealing with two standard demons and a human security guard, why bother with the museum heist at all? What, Angel and Gunn suddenly think they're incapable of killing two standard demons, and hog-tying a boob of a security guard? They don't know the Shroud's dangerous until they're further along in events, so they're not intent on nabbing the item so it can't hurt anyone. In any case, if *that* were their objective, then eliminating the criminals and stealing the Shroud at their leisure would be far, far safer. So what are they waiting for? Just kill the damn demons, already.

The Shroud starts affecting Angel the moment he walks into the vault, so it's clearly active even before the thieves accidentally crack its casing. That being the case, why didn't it affect the archaeologists who unearthed it, anyone involved in its transport to the museum or even the museum curators? If Jay-Don is the successful vampire that everyone claims, why does he take a bus from Vegas to L.A.? He doesn't even own a car? And why does Wesley ask *Cordelia* if she's ever heard of the Shroud when he hasn't? Are her research skills becoming that sharp, or is he just being polite?

Menlo and company enjoy a tense moment with a vial of nitro-glycerin while he attempts to blow the museum vault. Of course, so far as we can tell, Menlo strode into the museum without a care in the world, presumably with the nitro-glycerin vial jostling around in his duffel bag like a frozen strawberry in a blender. And there's a massive oversight with the whole "let's lift the box with Rahmon's body, which weighs about a ton, by hand" strategy. If it's *that* heavy, then surely the human museum workers keep lifting equipment to move it around, which would be a hell of a lot simpler.

If Kate suspects the museum is being robbed, why does she call for back-up upon arriving at the building rather than, oh say, before she even leaves the police station? And at the risk of constantly harping about this, what line of bull does Kate feed her superiors that even starts to explain the museum mayhem, how she knew the delusional British man was innocent of any wrongdoing, and oh, yes... the identity of the person who assaulted her. She can hardly claim that she failed to see her attacker, since he *bit* her.

Finally, without getting too technical, the beheading of the museum guard looks a bit odd. The demon makes a head-twisting motion that should've just snapped the man's neck, yet it instantly pops his head off like a bottle cap instead.

POP CULTURE Angel to Gunn: "Don't you know anything else, like say MacArthur Park?" MacArthur Park is located in western L.A., named after General Douglas MacArthur. Richard Harris (he's Dumbledore in the first two *Harry Potter* films) first performed the famously awful song "MacArthur Park" in 1968 (see 4.15, "Orpheus").

IN RETROSPECT Angel burns the Shroud, which pales in comparison to the blaze he'll start just three episodes from now. Also, Cordelia, under the influence of a magical object, steals a necklace from a museum and conveniently forgets to return it. Much the same happens to Anya in *Buffy* 7.06, "Him," wherein an emotion-changing jacket motivates her to rob a bank and she "neglects" to return the loot.

CRITIQUE After such a mother of an episode as "Darla," almost any story to follow would seem substandard. "The Shroud of Rahmon" therefore gets some scorn from time to time, with critics chiefly lambasting it as "filler." Fair enough, but even if it's hardly trying to reinvent the wheel, it's akin to (say) "I've Got You Under My Skin" (1.14) in that it's a solid enough runaround that relies on your standard "evil demon relic makes everyone act goofy" element. Perhaps that sounds like damning with faint praise, but let's keep stressing that this just isn't anything to get offended about, and – chiefly – it's a pleasant enough way to kill 45-odd minutes. Indeed, if we're to accuse "Rahmon" of being below-average for *Angel*, it's still a damn sight better than most network shows.

THE LORE Tony Todd (Vyasa) holds what seems like a billion cult-TV credits, and he's probably best-known as the title character in the *Candyman* franchise, plus an enigmatic mortician in the *Final Destination* films. He appeared on *Hercules* a couple of times – once as King Gilgamesh, who gets to facilitate the death of Herc's sidekick Iolaus. And he's also appeared on *Star Trek*: as Worf's brother (Commander Kurn) on *The Next Generation* and *DS9*, plus the adult Jake Sisko in the *DS9* story "The Visitor." W. Earl Brown (Menlo) played the title role in the TV biopic *Meat Loaf: To Hell and Back*, and his film credits include *Vampire in Brooklyn*, *Being John Malkovich* and *Vanilla Sky*.

2.09: "The Trial"

"Things fall apart. Not everything can be put back together, no matter how much you want it."

Air Date: Nov. 28, 2000; **Story:** David Greenwalt;
Script: Douglas Petrie, Tim Minear;
Director: Bruce Seth Green

SUMMARY The firm presents Darla with evidence that she's dying from the syphilitic heart condition that would've ended her first life (2.07, "Darla"), and that she's got two months to live. Angel yet again locates Darla, and upon learning of her condition vows to cure her.

At the Host's suggestion, Angel takes Darla to an underground pocket dimension, accessible through a disused pool in L.A., where champions can win magical rewards. Angel encounters the Valet, a well-mannered overseer, and successfully passes three trials. However, the Valet takes pause upon attempting to cure Darla, realizing that she's *already* on her second life and therefore beyond his power to heal.

Angel and Darla return to her room at a local motel, whereupon Darla – having witnessed Angel's heroism during the trial – accepts her soul and decides to live out her remaining time as a human being. Unfortunately, a commando team, led by Lindsey, bursts into the room and incapacitates the battle-weary Angel with stun guns. As a helpless Angel watches, the vampire Drusilla – summoned by Lindsey to "save" Darla – enters, kills Darla and proceeds to re-sire her as a vampire. [*Continued next episode.*]

FIRSTS AND LASTS Darla's performance in Caritas initiates the rule that although heroes will readily humiliate themselves while onstage (most of the gang in 2.11, "Redefinition," and any and all of Angel's "performances"), villains or pseudo-villains can compete with the Rock & Roll Hall of Fame members. Harmony is the exception (2.17, "Disharmony"), but see Lindsey's guitar playing in 2.18, "Dead End."

Two references that'll become relevant later: it's the first mention of the vampire hunter Holtz (who surfaces in 3.01, "Heartthrob"), and the first mention of the jasmine flowers in the Hyperion garden (see 4.18, "Shiny Happy People"). It's the first appearance of the modern-day Drusilla on *Angel*, and it's the end of Darla as a human being.

2.09, The Trial

POINTS OF DISCUSSION ABOUT "The Trial":

1. It's clear that the firm resurrected Darla with the goal of screwing with Angel's head, thus swaying him to the dark side, but human Darla's motives in Season Two are harder to pin down. She's obsessed with Angel, sure, but her actions seem to run the whole gamut.

"The Trial," though, provides a very palpable reason for her general state of confusion, even if we're left to connect the dots. We here learn that Darla's had a form of late-term syphilis from the moment she returned to life – and a key symptom of syphilis is madness. She's not just emotionally bewildered, wantonly manipulated and struggling to come to terms with her soul, she's literally going insane. You have to feel sorry for the woman, because in addition to being pulled in so many directions, her body chemistry isn't doing her any favors.

2. Darla stays in hotel room No. 212, which – coincidentally or not – is the same number as Cordelia's apartment. There's no particular reason for the parallel here, so as with the duplication of "6" as a door number (Trevor Lockley's apartment in 1.15, "The Prodigal" and Cordelia's weirdly inconsistent apartment door in 1.18, "Five By Five") it's either down to the *Angel* props masters re-using items to save a fast buck, or a code so secret, nobody can begin to divine its meaning.

3. Some fans have speculated, even though it's unstated, that the phases of the Trial must fashion themselves according to the challenger. Otherwise, the second phase, replete with crosses and holy water, would scarcely bother anyone who's not a vampire. The wooden stakes in the third phase seem geared to vamps also, as they'd skewer humans but surely prove useless against some of the super-strong champions attempting the contest.

4. "The Trial" itself entails a champion enduring a physical challenge, with life being granted to a second party if he's successful – or taken if he fails. The forces running the show don't seem to care spittle one way or another, and the battlefield is a mystically influenced part of L.A. that nobody notices. Sound familiar? Yup... minus the jousting, unintentionally or by design, it's pretty much "Judgment" (2.01) all over again.

CHARACTER NOTES *Angel:* Claims to love warm laundry straight from the dryer, and knows the in-and-outs of ironing.

In 1765, after a sojourn in Italy, Angelus and Darla traveled to France to satiate his craving for rich food. [Angelus proposed going to Naples in 1760 (2.07, "Darla"), but it seems strange that they'd stay put in the same country for five years, so perhaps they've recently revisited; this isn't the Italian visit detailed in 3.07, "Offspring," set in 1771; nor 5.20, "The Girl in Question," set in 1894.] They lodged at the best hotels and sometimes ate the waiters, but the vampire hunter Holtz and his followers pursued them through Arles, later cornering them in a barn. Darla abandoned Angelus and escaped on horseback, suggesting they meet up in Vienna. [3.01, "Heartthrob" confirms that they did.]

The experience made Angelus hate the French and advocate visiting Romania in future. [However, this occurred more than 130 years before the Romany ensouled Angelus, so there's no real correlation here.] Angelus looked upon Holtz as "more than mortal." [Untrue, although he's exceptionally talented.]

• *Cordelia:* Sick of hearing about Darla.

• *Wesley:* Knows of Drusilla [because he's researched Angel's history, see 1.11, "Somnambulist"] but has yet to meet her. Wesley's idea of keeping Angel emotionally in check: sit him down and work out his issues over tea.

• *The Host:* Fired his bartender Ramone, famed maker of Sea Breezes, for betraying him [in 2.06, "Guise Will Be Guise"]. The Host says he's a "channel surfer" [meaning he can read Darla's singing while simultaneously observing Angel's reactions] and claims he's "prescient" [meaning he's got foreknowledge of what's going to happen; see 4.03, "The House Always Wins"].

• *Darla:* Still trying to get re-sired after Angel refused. [In 2.07, "Darla." Yet there's no evidence that in her mad rush to escape her humanity, Darla ever contemplates suicide. Subconsciously, she's probably trying to return to the undead state that she knows best. Darla's dying from a syphilitic heart condition, but the dark ritual that resurrected her in 1.22, "To Shanshu in L.A." must've endowed her with *some* short-lived vitality, as she wasn't back on her deathbed the moment she returned to life.] She's taken to wearing a cross necklace.

• *Drusilla:* Her method of siring Darla – raking a line of blood across her bosom – parallels Darla's "turning" of Angel in *Buffy* 2.21, "Becoming."

• *Lindsey:* Tapped Wolfram and Hart's connections, including his personal doctor, to confirm Darla's terminal condition. It's unclear when he learned about her illness. [The script calls for Lindsey to shake his head "No" when Darla asks if he knew about her condition, but the scene as filmed is more ambiguous. Still, Lindsey probably didn't know about Darla's illness until recently, because otherwise his lustful pursuit of a woman with syphilis – not to mention their kissing in 2.07, "Darla" – is just rather creepy.]

He doesn't particularly confirm or deny whether he actually loves Darla. [He's infatuated at the very least, but quite what sort of relationship he expects upon re-making her a soulless vampire is harder to fathom.]

• *Holland:* Tells Darla he'd never do anything to her against her will. [He's lying. Lindsey claims in 2.11, "Redefinition" that he yielded to higher orders, and Holland surely signed off on involving Drusilla.]

• *"The Valet":* [Named in the script, but not on screen; he's sometimes referred to by Angel's nickname of "Jeeves."] Accommodating gentleman, wearing Dickens-era clothing, who oversees the trial. He can teleport people about the trial area, and briefly touches Darla's forehead to let her mentally watch Angel's battles. The Valet says he's never given information to a challenger before, allegedly because nobody's ever asked him. [This suggests the Trial doesn't occur all that often, then, and see **Magic**.] He appears to have two demon-looking attendants/guards, and for all his sensory ability, doesn't realize until told that Darla is already on her second life and beyond his help.

ORGANIZATIONS *Wolfram and Hart:* Angel suggests the firm wants him to vamp Darla. [He's speculating, as the firm undoubtedly knows that Angel would never walk that route.]

MAGIC Darla doesn't remember much about the initial days after her resurrection ["To Shanshu in L.A."] and Holland claims, "No one really remembers their first days of life." [He's either read texts on this score, or perhaps the firm has previously performed such rituals. Certainly, Buffy's confused upon her return to Earth in *Buffy* 6.01, "Bargaining," and she's got the constitution of a Slayer.]

• *"The Trial":* [On an unintended consequence of Angel's victory at the Trial, see **Did Jasmine Cause All This?**] The Host describes the Trial as "a bit of a quest," and it entails three phases. The Valet claims he's no knowledge of the second and third phases because "most other" challengers haven't survived the first one. He claims, when Angel's at the 17-second mark, that he's survived twice the duration that "most others" have lasted. [If few challengers live beyond eight seconds, then either the Trial is extremely difficult, simply isn't attempted very often or – most likely – all the challengers before Angel have been total crap.]

Angel's three challenges: He defeats a sword-wielding, super-fast healing demon by carving the monster at the waist, then chaining its separate halves away from one another... he endures a gauntlet of floor crosses barefoot and pulls a key – which opens a door to freedom – from a bowl of holy water... and he valiantly agrees to "get staked" on Darla's behalf. [Once again, sacrifice or the willingness thereof holds a lot of magical currency in the *Angel*-verse; see 1.08, "I Will Remember You" and 1.10, "Parting Gifts."]

DEMONOLOGY *Vampires:* Electrical tasers again prove extremely effective at incapacitating vampires [as with 1.16, "The Ring," although Angel here is already weakened from the Trial]. The know-how on siring someone isn't completely innate to vampires, as the "Shempire" [so named in the script] that Darla recruits seems unclear about the conversion process. [He's generally stupid, but still...] Vampires can still kick down the door of an abode even without an invite. The Valet isn't aware of any vampire deities.

BEST LINE Wesley, pondering why Angel's in the basement and not recognizing the noise of the laundry machine: "I keep hearing a 'chucka-chucka' sound..."

THINGS THAT DON'T MAKE SENSE One of Gunn's photographs shows a fugitive Darla using a public telephone. Since she doesn't appear to know anyone in L.A. beyond the people she's desperately trying to avoid, whom exactly is she calling? Is she placing an order with Domino's?

The story's first line (Cordelia: "Don't you think we should check on him?") is dubbed and extremely awkward, as Cordy's lips are pretty obviously not moving. Holtz's associates in 1765 make the tactical error of attacking the holed-up Angelus and Darla before sunrise – surely, it's far better to wait until daybreak, then burn the place to the ground when the vampires can't flee. Darla takes an unnecessary chance in not telling the Shempire that she'll need to drink *his* blood to get properly sired, because God only knows if she'll be conscious enough to mention it once he's started feasting. And a goof with hindsight... Angel wonders if his possessing a soul would make a difference if he re-vamped Darla, yet he sired the vampire Lawson (5.13, "Why We Fight") in 1943, and *he* turned out evil.

The Valet starts to oversell the Trial, as he tells a victorious Angel that, "no one's ever gone that far before in terms of sacrifice," as if others have tried and failed. But as nobody's apparently survived the first trial, it's not like anyone's had the chance, have they? (The obvious out is that if the trials are mutable, then perhaps some champion got the "sacrifice yourself" gambit right off the bat – even though this means he spectacularly failed, the fool.)

Finally, there's the odd bit where embittered Angel tells Darla: "How could the Powers allow you to be brought back and dangle a second chance, then take it away like this?" Um... precisely what the hell is he talking about? Darla's return to life owed to the firm's dark rituals, and since Darla's the No. 1 factor that interrupts Angel's service as the Powers' champion, it's not like the Powers had anything to gain from bringing her back. We'll write this off as Angel venting his frustration, with the Powers as an easy target.

POP CULTURE "Shempire": Shemp was a member of The Three Stooges, often tormented by his brother Moe.

TONIGHT AT CARITAS Darla sings *Ill Wind (You're Blow-ing Me No Good)* as popularized by Ella Fitzgerald.

CRITIQUE It's not really a whole story. Indeed, it's probably the most schizophrenic *Angel* adventure ever written (even beating out 1.17, "Eternity"), and thereby works against itself. To be fair, it's engaging for about the first third, featuring some popping Angel-Darla interaction and the gorgeous sight of Benz singing in Caritas. Then there's the final cliffhanger which – presuming you were unspoiled by this point – really blasts you back in your seat. It's a little predictable insofar as from the moment Darla resigns herself to being human, you just *know* she's due for the guillotine somehow, but big deal. It's riveting in all the right places, so bravo for that.

Tragically, everything between those two extremes – namely, everything concerning the trial itself – is a wet loaf of bread. Let's check off Angel's trials: He fights a demon (as if he's never done that before), runs across some crosses and dips his hand into holy water (nothing special there), and, worst of all, is given the "dramatic" option of sacrificing his life for Darla. Is anyone watching this genuinely confused about how it's going to turn out? For pity's sake, it's Angel. What the hell do we *think* he's going to say? "I've changed my mind, let the bitch die"? Meanwhile, the dialogue in this section falls off a cliff, with poor Julie Benz forced to say chaff such as "Why don't you just kill him if you want him dead?" and "Is that how a guy like you gets his rocks off?" while making it sound natural.

The great pity here is that if you carve out all the rubbish about the trial, the show's as well-greased as ever. So it's an almost criminal shame that such a crucial turning point comes encumbered with such a clichéd adventure beforehand.

THE LORE Benz didn't consider herself a singer, so she was petrified and had sweaty hands during Darla's song in Caritas. She also got nauseous whenever fake blood made an appearance on the set, and turned positively green while sucking Drusilla's blood. (Mason, *TV Guide Insider*, Dec. 12, 2000)

2.10: "Reunion"

"Pretty lawyers all in a row. Eenie, meanie..."

Air Date: Dec. 19, 2000; **Writers:** Tim Minear, Shawn Ryan; **Director:** James A. Contner

SUMMARY Drusilla buries Darla's body in a plant nursery, allowing Darla to awaken as a vampire despite Angel's intervention. Holland encourages the female vamps to massacre innocents across L.A. – hoping such an act will further torment Angel – then prepares to hold an intimate party for members of his department in his home.

Fed up with being manipulated, Darla and Dru obtain an invite from Holland's wife. The vamps corner the assembled attorneys in Holland's wine cellar, but a chagrined Angel arrives and also procures an invitation. Holland implores Angel for help, but Angel – emotionally numbed by recent events – coldly locks the wine cellar doors from the outside. Darla and Drusilla happily butcher Holland and his colleagues while Angel simply leaves. Wesley, Gunn and Cordelia later rebuke Angel upon hearing of his role in the massacre, but Angel – acknowledging that his friends are all that stand between him and "real darkness" – fires them in one fell swoop. [*Continued next episode.*]

FIRSTS AND LASTS We're treated to the first of two massacres involving a large group of lawyers (the other being in 4.08, "Habeas Corpses"). Some people would argue that you just can't get enough of that sort of thing.

Holland formally meets Angel for the first time, although this occurs roughly an act before Darla eats him. Final appearance of Holland as someone who's on the oxygen habit, although he'll make a brief return in 2.15, "Reprise." And it's the first time that Holland's title – Division Head for Special Projects at Wolfram and Hart – gets stated for the record.

POINTS OF DISCUSSION ABOUT "Reunion":

1. Even if you're feeling charitable, *Buffy* always fronted a rather awkward timetable as to when vampires will first rise from the dead. Generally speaking, the idea was that – barring oddities such as *Buffy* 3.12, "Selfless" and 7.08, "Sleeper" – vampires rose from the grave the night after they'd been sired. This raised some worrying questions about the record speed at which funerals occur in Sunnydale, but suffice to say the Whedon-verse usually tries adhering to this rule.

"Reunion" provides something of a litmus test, in that everyone concerned doesn't for a moment doubt that Darla will rise the night after Dru bit her. As if to punctuate the point, Wesley even rattles off the exact minutes of sunrise and sunset, and sure enough – vamp Darla sits up according to schedule. There's some room to maneuver here, but not much.

There's quite a few instances, though, of vampires rising the *same* night that they're bit – some examples include Gunn's sister Alonna (1.20, "War Zone"), Holtz's daughter (3.08, "Quickening") and Aubrey's son (3.15, "Loyalty"), presuming we take her story at face value. Judging by Gunn's sister, it's possible that people sired in the afternoon stand a good chance of rising that same evening, but anyone bitten in the night hours must wait until the next day. It's also possible that vampire kids rise from the dead quicker, although there's no particular reason for this, and that's not what seems to happen to the Anointed One in *Buffy* 1.05, "Never Kill a Boy on the First Date."

Ultimately, let's conclude that the mystical nature of vampire conversion allows for some variation, meaning that the majority of newly sired people must wait until the following evening, but some rise the very same day they're sired, and they *never* rise during the daytime (as they'd immediately go up like a torch). Following that pattern should cover nearly every vampire rising we see, or close enough for comfort.

2. Special mention should go to Drusilla's over-the-top lunatic turn, because Juliet Landau really is in rare form. Antics of note include her rubbing her inner thigh while reveling in the presence of people exuding fear (see **The Lore** next episode for more thigh-rubbing), pulling up her hair into twin prongs in the boutique (the DVD episode menu includes a neat little screen shot of this) and the suggestion that Angel might "punish" her ("Yes, yes, spank us till Tuesday, we promise to be bad if you do. Grrrruffff!"). She also bobs about like a buoy behind Holland in the wine cellar and – best of all – she bizarrely thinks that she's "ringing" when the cell phone goes off while lodged in her bosom. Great stuff.

3. The moment when Angel crashes through Lindsey's office window happens so fast, it's worth re-watching simply to catch Lilah's little shriek of terror and especially the startled look on Holland's normally unflappable face. It's just about the only time we catch him off-kilter – he even endures Darla sinking her teeth into his neck with some dignity.

CHARACTER NOTES *Angel:* Mostly seems intent on staking Darla, but hesitates at a crucial point, enabling her to escape. He somehow bursts through Lindsey's office window. [No mean feat, given Lindsey isn't exactly on the ground floor. And see 2.22, "There's No Place Like Plrtz Glrb" and 2.13, "Happy Anniversary" for Angel's motives on firing his crew.]

• *Gunn:* Seems especially troubled because Drusilla ("the granddaughter") re-sired Darla ("the grandmother"). [The thought of "vampire incest" probably rattles Gunn after the bit with his vamp sister in 1.20, "War Zone."]

• *Darla:* Shortly after rising, vamp Darla asks Dru "Why?", apparently unsettled by the loss of her humanity. [Darla suggests in 2.16, "Epiphany" that losing one's soul creates a "bitterness" that quickly passes. Events here confirm that, because after just a smidge of uncertainty, Darla's back in the saddle in no time as a ruthless bloodsucker. Or perhaps she's just crabby until she snacks on her first pedestrian – "Epiphany" also suggests that drinking "hot human blood" gets a wavering vampire back on their game.]

Darla is more at ease with Dru calling her "grand-mama". [She didn't like the term in 2.07, "Darla," but it's probably preferable to Dru calling her "my daughter" right now.]

• *Drusilla:* A classicist at heart, preferring to bury an impending vampire even though it isn't necessary. She views Angelus as her "daddy," but refers to Angel as "the Angel-beast," deeming Angel's abandonment of the lawyers as more worthy of the former.

Dru spent hours in Angel's garden [*Buffy* Season Two] talking with the night sky, and claims she can hear the stars singing to her. [It's not impossible that Dru's psychic ability lets her hear planetary motion, or what the ancients called "the harmony of the spheres." But if she's *that* psychically sensitive, then no wonder she's constantly messed up.] Dru claims "the moon" encouraged her to "come into the twentieth century"... even though it's already the 21st. (As Dru puts it: "I'm still lagging.")

Drusilla's psychic ability apparently lets her hear "sirens" in Holland's wine cellar, which originally served as a bomb shelter. [This is a truly impressive sensation on Dru's part, given the cellar is fifty years old and presumably was never used during a real air raid. Maybe the implication in 2.05, "Dear Boy" that she can "see" as far as 120 years in the future isn't so far-fetched after all.] Dru says Chateau Latour tastes like lion's blood. [Even odds on whether she's really tasted lion's blood, or if she's just acting strange.] A collision with a fast-moving car doesn't harm her in the slightest.

• *Lindsey:* Uniquely unafraid during the wine cellar confrontation, claiming that while he does care whether he lives or dies, he doesn't mind much either way. [Contrast this with 1.21, "Blind Date," when he cranked out fear by the bucket-full.] He's changed apartments since last episode. Lindsey has previously met Holland's wife Catherine. Holland says the Senior Partners have noticed the caliber of Lindsey's work [as with 1.22, "To Shanshu in L.A."].

• *Holland:* Married to a much younger, elegant woman named Catherine [the script accurately pegs her as a "trophy wife"]. Holland enjoys a passion for wine and promises to uncork a special bottle of 1928 Chateau Latour [but it's unclear if he does so before getting devoured].

• *Kate:* Back to reasonably trusting Angel again [after 2.08, "The Shroud of Rahmon"], wanting him to stop Darla and Drusilla's rampage. [Kate is the arresting officer when the police haul Angel out of the firm, but it's uncertain if Lindsey directly notified her (*a la* 1.19, "Sanctuary"), or if Angel's description in the police reports made her come running.]

• *Morgog:* A human worshipper calls him the "ruler of the Universe." Angel says Morgog has a "hairy spine-hump."

ORGANIZATIONS *Wolfram and Hart:* The firm has a means of "tagging" their vampire employees, which avoids triggering the office vampire detectors. Darla's intrusion into the firm here gets detected, but she still moves fast enough to reach Lindsey's office [she uses more discretion next episode] Information provided by Lindsey's landlord helps

Angel track down Darla and Dru. Also, the landlord doesn't appear to care or notice that Angel has just kicked in the door of the apartment that she's allegedly trying to rent, and she apparently had a telling chat with Dru and lived to tell the tale. [This all sounds too convenient, frankly. As with "Dear Boy," it's possible that the "landlord" is a Wolfram and Hart agent assigned to keep Angel on a collision course with Darla and Dru. Not that he particularly needs much help on that score.]

Holland encourages Lindsey to find "healthy attachments." [Hell, the firm probably advocates close relationships to gain leverage over its employees. Lilah threatens to have a translator's family killed in 3.09, "Lullaby," and Linwood claims the Senior Partners took his children in 3.10, "Dad."] Holland reiterates [after "Dear Boy"] that the firm doesn't want Angel dead... yet [see 2.12, "Blood Money"].

Wolfram and Hart does business with a rooftop nursery [across the street from City National Bank, located at 10889 Wilshire Boulevard].

• *The Powers-That-Be:* The timing of their latest vision strongly suggests they're trying to stop Angel from confronting Darla and Dru. [The Host confirms as much in "Epiphany."]

DEMONOLOGY *Vampires:* According to Angel, a vampire's victim can't resist drinking the sire's blood. [It's possible that vampires compel their victims to drink with a mild dose of hypnosis, or perhaps a vampire's fangs induce a narcotic effect that nullifies the victim's willpower.]

Drusilla says the unrisen Darla is "dead." [In "The Prodigal" (1.15), though, the buried Angelus hears the hearts and blood of people above him. Either Dru's over-simplifying, or maybe the sensory experience varies from vampire to vampire.] Burial isn't necessary for a vampire to rise. [*Buffy* 3.12, "Helpless," proves the point, even if it's an atypical case.] Newborn vampires need to feed soon after rising ["The Prodigal" reads along those lines].

Catherine Holland's entreaty to Angel of "Help us..." counts as an invitation. [That's perfectly acceptable as she can hardly mean, "Help us... without actually coming inside the house." See **How Does the Invitation Rule Work?**] Dru comments that Holland's wife tasted, "very sweet... like clover and honey." [Fear makes people taste sweet to vampires, as with "Somnambulist."]

BEST LINE(s) Dru, examining Lilah: "You have beautiful skin." Lilah: "I moisturize." Dru, quietly: "That was very thoughtful of you."

THINGS THAT DON'T MAKE SENSE Well, friends, we've reached one of the most delightful and wonderful glitches in the entire show: As Angel yields to Cordy's demands and pops a 180 with his Plymouth, the men in the car become stunt doubles. Fair enough, but Cordelia *becomes a mannequin.* To compound the affront, you can see the mannequin, stiff as a board, zooming by as Angel hits the accelerator. ("Gunn" looks a little waxen too, but that could be a trick of the light.) We might speculate that with all the Darla and Drusilla stunts in this episode, the production team simply ran short of female stunt doubles – either way, no amount of continuity glue or rationalization can fix this one.

The opening scene entails Angel fumbling about his office looking for a stake. Okay, he's off his game, but don't the heroes keep an ample supply of the things? Besides, doesn't Angel know where the stakes reside in his own office? It's implied that the heroes called Lindsey for more information, but given what occurred in Darla's hotel room last episode, this seems an extremely fruitless thing to do. Besides, wouldn't the firm eavesdrop on the call?

Kate's neck has now entirely healed, without a hint of a scar, after Angel drank from her a mere two episodes ago. Holland praises both Lindsey and Lilah for the department's recent successes, but if he's chiefly referring to the Angel operation, Lilah actually had little to do with that. (He's just keeping Lilah and Lindsey in competition.) Darla and Dru, two highly proficient vampires with centuries of killing experience, somehow fail to outright murder Holland's wife, thus enabling her to conveniently ask Angel's help when needed. And as most eagle-eyed viewers have noted: Darla astonishingly gains a new hairstyle between the boutique slaughter and her arrival at Holland's home. (A couple of oddball possibilities... perhaps Dru carries a curling iron in her cleavage, right next to her cell phone and make-up purse. It's also not unthinkable that Darla actually stops off to get her hair done – presuming there's time, which is unclear – or maybe her hair just gets curly when she's full of blood.)

CRITIQUE Until now, the show's played by pretty steadfast rules – the heroes act heroic, the accursed lawyers are villains, and so forth. Barring a couple of blips (such as 1950s Angel in 2.02, "Are You Now or Have You Ever Been?"), that's more or less held true. As a consequence, much of what's occurred – even the good stuff – didn't have long-lasting consequences.

Suddenly and wonderfully, everything changes. The point at which Angel consigns the lawyers to their fate should beautifully turn the blood in your veins to ice – if it doesn't, take it as a sign that you're perhaps better off watching another show. Fortunately and masterfully, it's not just the finale that deserves credit here – the racing pace, the crisp writing and the loving hi-jinks (such as that bit where Angel crashes through Lindsey's window) all work themselves to the daring point in which Angel doesn't *cause* the deaths of his enemies... he just doesn't move to stop them either. Minear's clearly working toward a vision (so to speak) here, and it's paying off in spades. The cast senses something is unusual about this story too... the protagonists do fine, but Benz, Landau, Kane and Romanov have never been better as the villains, and Sam Anderson gets the appropriate ending his character deserved.

Overall, let's relish this story as a sign of *Angel* throwing down the gauntlet and daring to put everything into disarray. The producers could've sat on their laurels and pumped out "helpless maiden of the week" stories until kingdom come, but we're into unknown territory now, and if you're watching the series in order, it's infuriatingly hard to predict what's coming next. Which is a definite plus.

2.11: "Redefinition"

"That wasn't Angel. It wasn't Angelus either. Who was *that?"*

Air Date: January 16, 2001; **Writer:** Mere Smith; **Director:** Michael Grossman

SUMMARY Paramedics dig Lindsey and Lilah out from the corpses of their co-workers, identifying them as the only survivors. Darla and Dru later show up at Wolfram and Hart, declaring they spared Lindsey and Lilah so their bosses could scapegoat one of them, then promote the other to serve as their new liaison to the firm. After some consideration, the firm's officials opt to make Lindsey and Lilah co-Executive Vice Presidents of their department, promising to later decide between the pair of them.

Meanwhile, a desensitized Angel vigorously re-trains himself as a steeled warrior. Darla and Dru try to recruit a cadre of hardened demons and stage a rampage, but a vengeful Angel butchers their prospective lackeys. For an encore, Angel sets Darla and Drusilla afire, wracking them with grievous burns. The women crack open a fire hydrant and quench themselves, leaving Darla to ponder Angel's new persona. Angel resumes his training, while Wesley, Gunn and Cordelia decide to keep Angel Investigations open and help people in need.

FIRSTS AND LASTS The Host performs "Lady Marmalade," something he'll sing again, almost two years hence, in Vegas (4.03, "The House Always Wins"). "Redefinition" also provides the first view of Wesley's apartment, although it looks somewhat Spartan, considering he's a research-heavy Watcher type who needs a lot of musty books at his disposal. And for the first time, we get an overview shot of some of the lead characters going their separate directions (the prime example of this occurs in 4.06, "Spin the Bottle").

POINTS OF DISCUSSION ABOUT "Redefinition":

1. There's a moral dilemma here, with a few parallels with the Slayer's decision to spare Angelus in *Buffy* 2.14, "Innocence." Fair enough that Buffy proved reluctant to kill her psychotic ex-boyfriend, but she doesn't even try to chain him up – and hence becomes partly responsible for everyone he murders after that point.

Similarly, even allowing for Angel's confused state of mind, he puts himself in a position to permanently end Darla and Dru's reign of terror, yet doesn't. To be more specific, after he magnificently sets the women on fire, he just turns and walks away. You could argue that eliminating the girls' demon recruits sapped Angel's strength, but the fire-engulfed Darla and Dru have never, *ever* been weaker. They spend *weeks* recovering from this incident, so it's safe to say that even a fatigued Angel could've dashed out and lopped off their heads with a hatchet, no problem. Perhaps we're meant to infer that he's royally pissed off and simply wants them to suffer, but that still leaves him partly culpable for everyone they victimize henceforth. Note the train-car of people Dru eats in *Buffy* 5.14, "Crush"; Darla's bus victims in 3.07, "Offspring"; etc. Mind, Cordelia similarly blunders by letting Harmony go for overly sentimental reasons in 2.17, "Disharmony."

2. A nit-picking point... there's blood on Angel's sword after he decapitates a vampire and the creature goes to dust. Some critics have wondered why the blood survived the dusting process, but there's numerous instances of other items coming off a dying vampire and enduring. Writer Mere Smith posted her view online that: "You decapitate someone, you're bound to get some blood on your Instrument de Decapitation. Even if said decapitee turns to dust seconds later, you're still cutting through something, and that something has some blood in it." Whedon has expressed similar sentiments from time to time, stating that vampires contain a collapsible "aura" that only dusts everything within its parameter. So the blood on Angel's sword isn't a big deal.

3. The script cites the executive who announces Lilah and Lindsey's fate as "Hunt Acrey, head of the investigative committee," although he goes unnamed on screen. Most people who've seen *The Matrix* will associate his halting speech patterns and general demeanor with Agent Smith, even though Acrey isn't wearing sunglasses and doesn't bust out any fancy martial-arts moves. A pity.

CHARACTER NOTES *Angel:* Burns his drawings of Darla [from 2.07, "Darla"; you hardly need a PhD in English Lit. to see this as a symbolic parallel to his torching Darla herself]. He's quite talented at knife-throwing, and sheds one of his trademark coats [apparently the one from 2.06, "Guise Will Be Guise"] in a storm drain. After dispatching Darla's would-be minions, Angel smokes a cigarette [something he did during the 1950s, "Are You Now or Have You Ever Been?" (2.02)].

• *Cordelia:* Takes home, from the Hyperion, a box with her Graphite iBook and some [plastic] flowers. She lives 15 miles from Caritas, and considers singing something by Shania Twain or Madonna there. Cordy being Cordy, she lays the blame at Wesley's door for over-criticizing Angel [as if she's never done that]. She drunkenly deems Tequila as more evil than vampires and Sloth demons [mentioned on her white-board in 2.01, "Judgment"].

• *Wesley:* Becomes the agency's de facto leader, yet can't particularly name his occupation, or conceive of how else he might make a living. Wesley drinks a Bloody Mary at Caritas, sans the blood. [The script also called for him to down a shot of cinnamon Schnapps.] He contemplates singing something by Cat Stevens.

• *Gunn:* Intended to sing something that Wesley, a white boy, has obviously never heard of.

• *The Host:* Senses an incoming vision from the Powers to Cordelia. [He detects this without anyone singing at the time and seems especially attuned to such transmissions, as confirmed in 3.02, "That Vision Thing."]

• *Darla:* Hopes to become a "big player" in L.A. [Darla's attempt at gang-leadership suggests she's taking a page from the Master's book and re-molding herself as the founder of an ambitious terror campaign, minus religious overtones. The *old* vampire Darla never showed an interest in such a role, probably because she submissively ceded such authority to the Master.] She claims that not everything she does is fixated on Angel. [Yet her actions here speak otherwise; she can hardly expect to take a demon wrecking crew and ransack L.A. without Angel noticing.]

Dru foretells that Darla will "never be alone again." [Considering Darla's impending insemination in 2.15, "Reprise," Dru is by some measure correct.] Darla and Dru are evidently broke. [Darla further appears in "Reprise"; see **Cross-Overs** for Dru's next step.]

• *Drusilla:* Her clairvoyance shows her, as she puts it, "such pretty fire and pain, so much suffering." [It's a foretelling of Angel torching her and Darla, but Dru doesn't deduce the vision's meaning.] Dru senses Angel's presence when Darla can't. [See 1.11, "Somnambulist" for talk about the residual psionic link between vampires and their sires, but Darla's rebirth might've temporarily muddled her senses.]

• *Lindsey:* Claims his superiors [and presumably Holland] ordered him to recruit Dru in "The Trial" (2.09). The firm evaluates the rivalry between him and Lilah as "vicious, destructive and... healthy."

• *Virginia Bryce:* Undergoing lots of therapy [after "Guise Will Be Guise"], paying for it with her enormous trust fund.

• *Merl:* Tied up by Angel and dunked in a water hole for information.

THE HYPERION Graffiti in the hotel's basement includes the words, "Smiley Forever." The building's street address, 4121, is visible [see 2.05, "Dear Boy" for more].

ORGANIZATIONS *Wolfram and Hart:* It's said that Darla and Dru ate the majority of the contracts department last episode. [Yet they were clearly under Holland's supervision – see **Points of Discussion** under 2.18, "Dead End" for what this potentially says about his authority.]

Darla and Dru appear in Lindsey's office without ringing an alarm. [It was suggested last episode that Dru had been officially "tagged" for admittance, so she might've somehow extended this privilege to Darla. See "Guise Will Be Guise" for the point where the vampire detectors become as effective as damp Kleenex.]

Lindsey and Lilah's fellow employees are ostracizing them because they're the only survivors of the massacre. [It's the prevailing view that they turned traitor, or that the firm will bump them off regardless. As Lilah expresses, "(Actual) responsibility has nothing to do with it."] Lilah implies that the firm makes people disappear at a dog-food processing plant in San Pedro.

• *The Powers-That-Be:* Direct Wesley, Cordelia and Gunn to save a young woman from a demon. [The timing of the vision, the proximity of the attack to Caritas and the routine nature of the assignment suggest the Powers are deliberately trying to keep Wesley's crew together, possibly in the hopes of bringing Angel back into the fold.]

• *Caritas:* Serves real blood.

MAGIC Virginia cites the wizard community as "very progressive," and says that her father ["Guise Will Be Guise"] always used union conjurers.

DEMONOLOGY Wesley says that Beverly Hills contains several demon hideouts. A "bar and bite club" off La Cienega and Washington features a "Fight Club"-style operation for demons and vampires.

• *Vampires:* Angel begins a heavy training regimen. [It's proof that vampires *do* augment their strength through exercise, despite Cordy's suggestion in 2.01, "Judgment."]

BEST LINE(s) Darla, demeaning Angel: "[He's] probably flogging himself in a church somewhere." Drusilla (with tingles) "Oooooooh... flogging... " (grossed out) "*Ewwww... churches.*"

THINGS THAT DON'T MAKE SENSE It's undeniably dramatic, but... why precisely is Lindsey found just lying amid the corpses of his co-workers? Was he knocked unconscious? Were they pitched atop him, and he just went down without protest? Did he drink too much?

It's hard to keep making excuses for how someone as intelligent and ruthless as Lilah keeps resorting to such feeble ploys, such as her trying to "seduce" Lindsey into stealing *more* files, then strengthen her position by exposing his disloyalty. Does she believe for a moment that this will work? Because the audience doesn't. (For more of her petty stunts, see 3.08, "Quickening" and even her "whipping a gun out of her purse" gambit in 2.18, "Dead End.")

It's said that you can see Merl's tongue – he claimed he didn't have one in 2.01, "Judgment" – when he's dangling upside down, but it's not terribly obvious, and the visibility is tenuous to us. Oh, and Merl directs Angel to "the only place [Darla and Dru] ain't been" to recruit their troops, yet the ladies appear to visit another demon bar after leaving that joint.

CROSS-OVERS Dru alerts Lindsey to Darla's plight off screen, then departs for Sunnydale in time for *Buffy* 5.13, "Crush." She tries persuading Spike to come with her to L.A. and somehow make Angel evil again, but the scheme goes awry thanks to Spike's obsession with the Slayer and Buffy's intervention. Dru then leaves town but doesn't return to L.A., leaving her final fate in the *Angel* and *Buffy*-verse a dangling question-mark, even if she'll keep appearing in flashback and as the First in *Buffy* Season Seven.

IN RETROSPECT A random vampire dislikes fast-food workers because they taste "all greasy," which almost forecasts a vamp recoiling from the Slayer's burger stench a full year before the fact [*Buffy* 6.15, "As You Were"]. Speaking of *Buffy* Season Six, loads of people who've seen the *Buffy* musical can't stop from singing along after Cordelia's comment of "Where do we go from here?"

IT'S REALLY ABOUT... Cold, pure and silent rage, the kind that almost takes on a life of its own. As Darla's final confusion about Angel's identity points out, he's presently a slave to his anger, and in some respects is channeling it into a new persona.

TONIGHT AT CARITAS A squabbling Wesley, Gunn and Cordelia sing their troubles away with "We Are the Champions" by Queen. In fact, it's the only occasion that Cordelia doesn't perform "The Greatest Love of All" – see 4.04, "Slouching Toward Bethlehem" and *Buffy* 1.07, "The Puppet Show." (The script initially called for the heroes to belt out "Bridge Over Troubled Water," with an amendment dated November 8, 2000, that they should instead perform "Without You" by Nilsson.)

CRITIQUE It's Part Two of the series' big reformatting, and once again, it's a story that should make your eyes bulge like poached eggs. The script is as finely tuned as a laser, and quite impressive even before the finale in which a pissed-off Angel – in one of the series' most visceral and memorable moments – vents his frustration on Darla and Dru by burning them. He ***burns them!*** In a world where we've become desensitized to many forms of TV violence, this sticks out as one of the most potent cards the producers could've played. Light, fluffy and harmless sci-fi this ain't.

If there's a downside, it's only that it's hard to follow-up the sugar-rush of this episode and "Reunion," but even the stand-alone stories to follow are largely tailored to work within the show's new format. Events get more isolated, but you can't accuse the series of going back to business as normal and ignoring Angel's actions. When all's said and done, "Redefinition" stands as a grand payoff to anyone who's been with the show from the start, and leaves the audience with some magnificent portents of what's to come.

THE LORE The writers found themselves tongue-twisted in planning sessions, often referring to "Darla and Drusilla" as "Darcilla." Smith incorporated this into the bit where Merl refers to the girls as "Godzilla, Darcilla, whatever." The other main contender, "Droola," made Smith giggle but didn't work so well. Smith worked "Lady Marmalade" into this story because it was one of Hallett's signature songs, and she'd decided from the get-go that Angel wouldn't speak throughout this episode, symbolizing his withdrawal from humanity into a sort of death machine. She somewhat fashioned his new persona on desensitized soldiers, such as those who'd committed the My Lai massacre. Smith kicked herself, after seeing the finished episode, for scripting the demon to put a chokehold on a vampire in the "Fight Club" scene, as vampires don't need to breathe. Oh, and the random vamp that Lindsey chastises was an (ultimately flawed) attempt to demonstrate that the firm's detectors didn't pick up Darla and Drusilla because there were already vamps in the building. (Smith, *The Bronze*, Jan. 16, 2000)

• A rather scandalous line, cut from the script: When Dru luxuriously revels in her prophetic vision of flames, her dialogue about it being "like star music" was followed with the claim: "My lower tummy is all warm." Judging by the salacious dialogue in some of Whedon's scripts (see **Points of Discussion** in 3.13, "Waiting in the Wings"), it's tempting to blame him for this.

2.12: "Blood Money"

"It'll wash."

Air Date: Jan. 23, 2001; **Writers:** Shawn Ryan, Mere Smith; **Director:** R.D. Price

2.12, Blood Money

SUMMARY Continuing his crusade against Wolfram and Hart, Angel discovers ties between the firm and a runaway center operated by Anne Steele (*Buffy* 3.01, "Anne"). Angel learns that the firm intends to hold a $2 million fundraiser for the center's benefit, then swindle the proceeds. Anne finds herself torn between Angel's accusations and Lindsey's charm, even as a blue-skinned demon named Boone privately allies himself with Lindsey and Lilah to settle old scores with Angel.

Angel barges into the event, ostensibly to show a videotape that proves the firm's corruption, but Boone brawls with him. Amid the chaos, Anne seems to reach a projector with the *real* incriminating tape, but her video proves to be nothing more than Cordelia's audition footage and shots of Wesley dancing. The distraction enables Boone – who was in league with Angel from the start – to make off with the donations. Boone later arrives at the Hyperion, curious to know if he can best Angel in a fight. Angel prevails and presumably kills Boone, then gives Anne the $2 million to aid the center.

FIRSTS AND LASTS It's the debut of Nathan Reed, the second of Lindsey and Lilah's short-lived superiors, and who looks like a candidate for the part of Egghead from the Adam West *Batman* series. Angel spooks the crap out of Lilah by enigmatically appearing in the back of her car for the first time. And it's the first clear-cut instance of Lilah breaking with company policy and conspiring to kill Angel (see 3.15, "Loyalty").

POINTS OF DISCUSSION ABOUT "Blood Money":

1. Boone looks a bit like Merv from *Sin City*, only blue. And minus the Band-Aids.

2. Here we've got to examine the slightly weird notion that the vampire invitation rule should extend to someone's car, as Angel suddenly appears inside Lilah's automobile without an invite (and see **The Lore** for Mere Smith's fanciful take on this). For the record, we don't support the notion of the invite rule covering someone's vehicle. Check out **How Does the Invitation Rule Work?** for more, but suffice to say that the invite rule is geared to protect someone's residence and doesn't extend to any and all of their personal property. Notice, just for a start, vampires' ability to walk into privately owned business (see 2.02, "Are You Now or Have You Ever Been" for but one example).

We'd here like to remind everyone of *Buffy* 1.12, "Prophecy Girl," in which some vamps besiege Cordelia's car, and certainly don't act like creatures who can't get inside without her say-so. Also, Cordelia frets in *Buffy* Season Two that Angelus might enter her car uninvited, but we're talking about "high maintenance, high anxiety" Cordy here, so it's easy to discount.

3. As we touched on in "To Shanshu in L.A." (1.22), "Blood Money" provides a palpable explanation for why the firm doesn't simply marshal their every resource to kill Angel. Nathan Reed definitively announces that the Senior Partners want Angel alive because he's slated to play a major role in "the final battle" of the apocalypse – but the prophecies don't specify which side Angel will fight for. Hence, as the firm can't dust Angel (possibly not even if they *really* tried), it's their goal to befuddle, confuse and enrage him until he joins the dark side.

We'll examine this notion more in Seasons Two and Five especially, but for now consider that we're not a million miles from the *Daredevil* graphic novel "Born Again." In that adventure, the Kingpin learns Daredevil's secret identity and nearly brings him to ruin – not by sending waves of supervillains against him, but through financial and litigious means. It's impossible to think that the firm couldn't similarly crush Angel Investigations, so the "don't kill Angel" policy evidently makes them refrain from – say – ruining Cordelia, Wesley and Gunn's lives to the point that even further motivates Angel to help the downtrodden. Overall, it's about as sensible a limitation on the firm as the vampire invitation rule, which explains on *Buffy* why the Slayer doesn't fret about getting murdered in her sleep.

4. Some confusion exists over Boone's statement that he and Angel had a "disagreement over a senorita" in the 1920s. After all, the ensouled Angel largely kept to himself throughout the twentieth century, and shows no signs of worrying about romance until Buffy happens along. Well, first off, let's consider that Boone says this for Lindsey and Lilah's benefit, and he's possibly lying or over-simplifying. But even if it's true, it's never outright stated that Angel and the senorita engaged in sexual congress, so perhaps it was a simple case of chivalry that spilled over into a brawl.

5. One of the "TV celebrities" at the fundraiser gets asked, "This thing with making your character gay? Is that, like, all about ratings? Because, um, I don't get it," which echoes clueless statements made about Willow and Tara over on *Buffy*. Oh, g'wan. You know it's true.

CHARACTER NOTES *Angel:* Reed says "the prophecies" [including, one presumes, the Scroll of Aberjian (1.21, "Blind Date")] all agree that Angel will play a key role in the apocalypse. Angel recoils at Anne's suggestion that Cordelia is his ex-girlfriend [a perfectly reasonable response, but wait until Season Three]. He's stealthy enough to pick Anne's pocket. He "donates" some of Cordelia's clothes to Anne's shelter as part of a cover story [Cordy discovers this in 2.14, "The Thin Dead Line," and calls Angel on it in 2.17, "Disharmony"]. Angel's leaning on Merl for information – without paying, of course – and expresses disdain for the bean-bag chairs in Merl's digs.

• *Cordelia:* Going batty because Wes and Gunn are using

her apartment as the agency's base of operations [as with 2.01, "Judgment"] – and also to play Risk. She videotapes herself reciting the "Got Milk" slogan, plus what looks like a dramatic recitation of her acting against a coat rack. (As one observer puts it: "I sort of believe the coat rack more.")

• *Wesley:* Foul-mouthed when the occasion calls for it.

• *Gunn:* Bonds with Wes while killing a fire-farting demon.

• *Anne Steele:* Previously appeared in *Buffy* 2.07, "Lie to Me," as a vampire groupie named "Chantarelle." She briefly encountered Angel, but doesn't remember him. [See **The Lore**; Angel presumably recalls meeting Anne, given his photographic recall, yet never mentions it.] She later changed her name to "Lily" and appeared in *Buffy* 3.01, "Anne," wherein her boyfriend died and she changed her name yet again to, um, "Anne." [It's not a coincidence that "Anne" is also Buffy's middle name. The fact that Anne's driver's license reads "Anne Steele" suggests she went the whole-hog and legally changed her name this time.]

Anne claims she once saw a 14-year-old girl sitting in her own blood after "a rough trick," and that dozens of uncaring people walked right by. Merl's research indicates that Anne doesn't have a criminal record. Her driver's license is No. N10987651, and she apparently lives at 5632 Willoughby Avenue, L.A., 90001. She's 5'8", and weighs 118 pounds.

• *Lilah:* Knows where Merl lives, and that he supplies information to Angel.

• *Lindsey:* Pays for Boone's services out of his "discretionary fund." Lindsey's office is swept for bugs three times a day [although it's probably not surveillance-free, as the hi-fi company monitoring system from 2.07, "Darla" suggests].

• *Holland:* Appears in a pre-taped, dripping segment that promotes the teen shelter. A tribute lists his life as 1951-2000.

• *Merl:* Owns an iMac, and is acquainted with the works of etiquette mistress Emily Post. He appears to live in a dank room in some sort of factory. Boone calls Merl a "lizard demon." ["Judgment" alternatively calls him a "parasite demon"; possibly he's both.]

• *Nathan Reed:* Vows to not hold Holland's soft spot for Lindsey and Lilah – but then overlooks their hiring Boone to kill Angel in direct defiance of company policy.

• *Boone:* Says he is "eternal" [meaning long-lived or even immortal, but probably not unkillable], and Angel implies that Boone operates from Brazil. Metal coils can spring from Boone's wrists and curl around his fists in preparation for battle. Boone claims he encountered Angel in Juarez in the 1920s [see **Points of Discussion**]. Allegedly, a drunken Boone "called Angel out" and they fought for three and a half hours until the sun rose, whereupon Boone's personal honor compelled him to let Angel go, on the grounds that his defeat would have been "too easy."

ORGANIZATIONS *Angel Investigations:* Gunn mistakes the agency's angel logo for a "lobster with a growth" [mostly echoing Kate's guess in 1.02, "Lonely Hearts"]. Wesley, Cordelia and Gunn can't bring themselves to say Angel's name right now, resorting to cover phrases such as "The A word" [and see 3.01, "Heartthrob"], and each of them want to rename the agency after themselves. [They never come to an agreement, though, and keep the name "Angel Investigations."]

• *Wolfram and Hart:* The firm has connections to prominent TV celebrities [repeatedly confirmed throughout Season Five], recruiting stars from the hit show *Life Lessons* to appear at the fund raiser.

• *The East Hills Teen Center:* Located on Crenshaw [see "The Thin Dead Line" for more on this]. A couple of months previously, the center faced eviction before the firm intervened. Anne comments that $100,000 is more than the shelter could raise in two years.

DEMONOLOGY *Vampire Detectors:* The firm uses a vampire detector named Zorn [the only time one of them gets a name], who's allegedly capable of sensing vampires "within 100 feet" [of the building or Zorn's himself?].

BEST LINE Lindsey's sarcastic response to the notion that Boone might kill Angel: "Boo-hoo. Let me wipe away the tears with my plastic hand."

THINGS THAT DON'T MAKE SENSE Let's see if we're reading this correctly. Lindsey and Lilah are now "Co-Executive Vice Presidents" of Wolfram and Hart's Special Projects Division, a department responsible for such unsavory activities as dark rituals, resurrections and bugging the crap out of heroic vampires. Why, then, are they overseeing something as piss-ant as a charity drive scam? Can't the firm's lackey-toad lawyers rip off a charity drive to the tune of $2 million without their help? (But see **Points of Discussion** under 2.18, "Dead End" for a possible explanation.)

Boone and Angel duke it out rather loudly in the lobby of Anne's shelter, yet none of the runaways in residence get curious and emerge to see what's causing all the fuss. Anne asks Angel to "help her with a chore," then they spend some minutes making small-talk and she fails to mention the chore again. And finally, regarding the videotape of Wesley stripping, hopping about and pretending to be James Bond (years in advance of Rowan Atkinson's antics in *Johnny English*, we might add), just what exactly *is* Wes supposed to be doing? And why would he videotape it?

CRITIQUE Few reviews can occur in a vacuum, so "Blood Money" often takes some hard knocks because it's following such a dynamic two-parter and seems inferior by comparison. And it genuinely *isn't* as good as the last two stories – but then, that's hardly a crime, and it's still a solid, decent episode with a fair number of twists. If nothing else, it's rather clever in that Angel expertly shish-ka-bobs Lindsey and Lilah with their own paranoia. In that respect, we're not too far from *The Prisoner* episode "Hammer Into Anvil," in which the lead character drives his jailer totally batty simply by giving the impression that he's up to no good.

So this hardly ranks among the show's most legendary episodes, but it's a fun diversion that makes good use of everyone's new relationships, and it's an endeavor worth your time.

THE LORE The writers deliberated on whether Anne would recognize Angel from Sunnydale and finally decided that she wouldn't, reasoning that her brief exchange with him from three years ago seemed thin at best. "To tell you the truth, I have a hard time remembering people I met three days ago," Smith later claimed. She also tried to alleviate confusion about Boone's fate by posting: "As far as I know, Boone is, in the words of Beetlejuice, dead, dead, deadski." (Smith, *The Bronze*, Jan. 24, 2000)

• Fandom wrestled with the notion of how Angel could get into Lilah's car, wondering if vampires required an invite to enter someone's vehicle – some critics pointed to Cordelia's worry about Angelus getting into her car in *Buffy* Season Two, as she'd previously given Angel a lift. Smith suggested that if the Slayer's crew did an off-screen revoke spell for Cordy, it was in the interests of shutting her up, not because it actually worked for diddly-squat. With "Blood Money," Smith argued that Lilah's car wouldn't count anyway, as it's a rental and therefore not her property. Either that, Smith says, or "Lilah secretly pines after Angel and, off screen, by herself, invited him into every place she ever goes – her apartment, her car, her grocery store, her Blockbuster, whatever." (Smith, *The Bronze*, Jan. 24, 2000)

• Mark Rolston (Boone) voiced Firefly in the *Batman* and *Justice League* animated series; he's also Private Drake in *Aliens* and Bogs Diamond in *The Shawshank Redemption*.

2.13: "Happy Anniversary"

"I'm talking about removing an infinitesimal space-time aggregate from all that surrounds it."

Air Date: Feb. 6, 2001; **Story/Script:** David Greenwalt; **Story:** Joss Whedon

SUMMARY At Caritas, the Host "reads" a college student and senses that the future of everyone on Earth will end at 10 p.m. the following evening. The Host is shocked unconscious, later awakening to find the student gone, and asks Angel for help.

Meanwhile, the singer in question – physics student Gene Rainey – works on a formula to separate a shard of time from the rest of history, essentially creating a "frozen time" bubble. Gene meets with limited success, but a group of Lubber demons, viewing him as a foretold messiah who will end all human life, secretly revise the formula. Later, Gene learns that his girlfriend, Denise, plans to break up with him after their first anniversary dinner. Gene rigs some lab equipment in his bedroom, intending to forever freeze him and Denise during the height of their lovemaking. Gene's plan works, but a Lubber demon adapts Gene's apparatus to expand the effect, hoping to encompass the entire planet. The bubble starts to expand, but Angel and the Host thump the Lubbers and close down the temporal effect. Denise dumps Gene as scheduled, with Gene realizing his role in the near-global catastrophe.

FIRSTS AND LASTS It's the first time we see the Host stepping foot inside the Hyperion (or, indeed, anywhere outside of Caritas), and the first time his "sonic cry" – here used against the Lubbers – disables an opponent. "Happy Anniversary" also provides the first viewing of Wes, Gunn and Cordelia's "luxurious" new office that's slightly more serviceable than a broom closet. It won't last.

POINTS OF DISCUSSION ABOUT "Happy Anniversary":

1. When a celebratory Gene sprints across campus, try singing along the words "Nerd on the Run" to the tune of "Band on the Run." It fits like a glove.

2. The chat between Angel and the Host as they're barreling down the road both comes off as funny *and* elegantly takes stock of the show's recent changes. In a nutshell, the Host worries that Angel isn't bothered *enough* by the notion that the world might end, and that he's changed his mission of "helping the helpless" to "hunt down the guilty." The Host deems blood vengeance the luxury of "lesser beings" (echoing statements as far back as 1.08, "I Will Remember You"), even as Angel vents frustration that he's doomed to never properly attain redemption. It's entertaining stuff, and as succinct a summation of Season Two as you're likely to find.

3. Gene claims in the final act, "I had no idea... that there were all these demons" – which sounds incredibly strange coming from a man who's been singing in demon karaoke bars. As the **Things That Don't Make Sense** category is already loaded to the hilt, let's rationalize that Gene specifically means it with regards to the Lubbers, as he's unaware that they're after him until Angel and the Host mention it. If only we could pour this story's other buckets of illogic down the drain so easily.

CHARACTER NOTES *Angel:* Expresses frustration because he's expected to atone for "100 years of unthinkable evil" [actually, it's more like 145 years of unthinkable evil, but who's counting?] and doesn't believe he can *ever* erase such wrongdoing. Angel implies that he fired his friends (2.10, "Reunion") because they couldn't cope with his vendetta against Darla and the firm, and favorably says this means they're still human. [He'll reiterate the same view in 2.22, "There's No Place Like Plrtz Glrb."] The Host assesses Angel's current aura as "beige" [he deems this "weird," as if it isn't Angel's standard aura color].

• *Cordelia:* Says the new agency must work because she and the boys can't do much else for a living. [Cordy hasn't abandoned her aspirations of being an actress – see 2.19, "Belonging" – but she's a lot more practical these days.]

• *Wesley:* The Host implies that Wesley holds crucial importance to upcoming events ("the British boy is gonna be playing a *huge*... well..."), but never specifies. [See **Did Jasmine Cause All of This?** for one possibility, although by series' end, there's more than one justification for the Host's opinion. Wes tutoring Illyria, for example, or the fate of the Circle of the Black Thorn.]

• *The Host:* Would love to sing the National Anthem at a Lakers game. He senses from Gene alone that the world might end [even though the other Caritas patrons theoretically didn't have a timeline after "tomorrow night" either; Gene must hold special significance because he's at the center of it all]. The Host can pluck specific mental images from persons who sing, sensing a recollection of Gene from a bartender who recites "For He's a Jolly Good Fellow." The Host also incapacitates two Lubbers by unleashing a "sonic cry" – a high-frequency note, of sorts. [As with 3.16, "Sleep Tight," the Host shows amazing directional control with this blast, as it doesn't affect anyone else in the immediate vicinity.] He claims he can hold a note "forever." [He's exaggerating. Probably.]

He's feeling tormented because his new bartender, Elian (who replaced the treacherous Ramone from 2.06, "Guise Will Be Guise") is unable to make a Sea Breeze with juice from a real grapefruit. The Host can speak the Lubber demon language, and implies that he knows champions besides Angel – who're presently out of town or dead.

The Host's assessment of Cordelia: "Hot-o-rama! In the 'oh my sizzling loins' sense of the word." [He'll air similar sentiments in 3.13, "Waiting in the Wings."]

• *Gene Rainey:* His work on time paradox theory earned Professor Orfala [one of his mentors] a Nobel nomination.

ORGANIZATIONS *Angel Investigations:* Wes, Cordy and Gunn have rented a very modest office, complete with bad wiring and defunct phones. They're sharing a desk. They celebrate their new business by throwing a well-attended party [but see 2.15, "Reprise"].

Virginia refers a friend, Patricia Bointon, to the agency when a demon stalks her family. Wesley's trio unmasks the family's Aunt Helen [named "Dotty Aunt Helen" in the script] as a schemer using a Wainakay demon to acquire her family's fortune. This entails Wesley somehow realizing that Kevin, the family's black-sheep son, is impotent. Another client asks for help at story's end [but we never learn the details].

• *Caritas:* Some of the clientele there just sing karaoke, unaware of the Host's destiny-reading abilities. Some actually know about the Host's talent, but chicken out.

DEMONOLOGY *Lubber Demons:* Fanatical demon "sect" awaiting a "messiah" who'll end all human life. This is evidently a popular underworld theory, although many demon species don't discuss it in mixed company. The Lubbers look like sad, pasty old men, speak their own language and sometimes wield sickles. One Lubber uses a cane topped with a red jewel to magically alter Gene's mathematical equations. Another can work a G3 Mac Powerbook.

BEST LINE(s) Angel, venting: "[I've got] 200 law graduates working full time to drive me crazy... why the hell is everyone so surprised that it's working? But no, it's 'Angel, why're you so cranky?' 'Angel, you should lighten up.' 'You should smile.' 'You should wear a nice plaid...' " The Host, recoiling: "*Oh.* Not this season, honey."

THINGS THAT DON'T MAKE SENSE Pretty much the whole of Gene's "I must freeze my girlfriend and I at the moment of orgasm" scheme. Where to begin? Gene thinks he's *only* creating a time bubble in his bedroom, so he doesn't stop to think what's going to happen when someone eventually peeps in there and spots him and Denise rutting like bunnies in molasses in January. And *of course* someone's going to look, especially once he fails to pay the rent, or they get declared missing persons. Setting aside that a bystander or two might get frozen in the act of taking a peek, the discovery of this weird effect will surely draw government experts and crackpots alike, and potentially make international news, causing quite the brouhaha.

More important... is Gene just totally blind to the time bubble's continuous power requirements, or does he seriously think that nobody's going to wonder about the strange hook-up in the laundry room and pull the plug? Even if by some miracle this doesn't happen, what then? Won't he be faintly embarrassed to wake up naked and atop Denise amid rubble some time after the fall of Western civilization? (By the way, there's some debate over why cutting the electricity would halt the effect at all, given that the time-freeze should incorporate the electricity itself. Perhaps a little fortunately, we're not qualified to discuss such theoretical physics.)

2.13, Happy Anniversary

Onto moral issues now, as Gene doesn't stop to consider that gee, maybe Denise doesn't *want* to be frozen in a bubble with him mounting her for all eternity. This pretty much sounds to us like a violation of the highest order, yet it's never mentioned or even intimated. But then, we're dealing here with a college student who's so dense, he entirely fails to notice that some of the time-equation symbols on his dry-erase board have radically changed without explanation and yet are presumably still in his handwriting. Ah, and it's technically not a glitch, but it's a near-smothering case of dramatic irony when Gene randomly strolls up behind Denise just as she spills her guts to a friend about wanting to dump sorry his ass.

Now for visual concerns... At the university library, the Host hides himself in what's plainly labeled the Mystery Section, yet the book he pulls from the shelf to cower behind is actually a Russian-English dictionary. Perhaps this is down to *really* bad shelving, though – notice how the Host puts the dictionary back on a different shelf, and with the spine facing inward to boot. Also, the lab picture of Gene and Denise is framed when Gene departs, but miraculously unframed when he returns. Does he have two? The "book photo" of Gene that Angel presents to the library assistant was actually in the Host's hands in the previous shot and wasn't Gene's face at all. (Indeed, the Host, looking for pictures of Gene, flipped right past it.)

Such a weighty problem, we don't know why we saved it for last: It's said over and over that the Lubber demons want to usher in the end of human life. All well and good, but considering they hope Gene's time freeze effect will encompass the entire world, aren't they willfully consigning *all* demons – including the entire Lubber race – to the same fate? Perhaps the Lubbers are extra-dimensional, but if anything this should give them less reason to target humanity. Either way, they're taking extreme liberties with the term "end all human life" – does freezing the entire world in a time bubble even count?

IN RETROSPECT The Host says his "garden hue and horns" have shut him out of some key public performances. That won't be such an impediment once he hits Las Vegas (4.03, "The House Always Wins").

IT'S REALLY ABOUT... We've somehow catapulted into the college-flavored *Buffy* Season Four in that a bad collegiate romance could trigger the world's end – something that feels perfectly plausible when you're an overly hormonal undergrad. Speaking of Gene, he adheres to the old chestnut that "the only bad thing about sex is that it doesn't last," as he bizarrely deems being frozen at the moment of orgasm far more preferable than dealing with the world and its complicated relationships.

TONIGHT AT CARITAS Gene sings "All By Myself" by Eric Carmen. A Torto demon and his parasite (a small, secondary head that sticks out of the Torto's chest) get onstage and proceed to murder the Everly Brothers' "Bye Bye Love."

CRITIQUE As Socrates or someone equally sage once said, the line between genius and tomfoolery is very thin. Tragically, "Happy Anniversary" falls on the wrong side of the line.

Annoyingly, some of the individual elements are perfectly workable, but they create an almost laughable quagmire when fitted together. There's a despondent college student whose romance is going down in flames, there's lots of technobabble about the nature of space-time, and there's some genocidal demons who look like sickle-bearing, well-dressed senior citizens for no readily apparent reason. If you can extract a cohesive story from this, you're a better person than we are.

Weirdly, we've defaulted back into Season One territory in that a lot of weight rests on a one-off character – Gene – but he's wildly inconsistent and almost impossible to read. Depending on how you interpret his actions, he's either shockingly naïve, suffering from chronic depression (as he's the type of person who sings heartbroken songs when he thinks his relationship is going *well*) or outright evil (as he's effectively a would-be rapist) – possibly a combination of all three. Hard to see, then, how we're supposed to root for him.

The big (and possibly only) redeeming feature here is how much the Angel and the Host make a lively team-up, and their scenes together constantly carry the episode. Gossip-mongers who suggested that *Angel* would morph into "the Angel and the Host show" while Wesley and company got their own spin-off never stood a snowball's chance of being right – yet it's easy to see why they might think that, because the duo really have a lot of fun together. Set aside the bits with Boreanaz and Hallett getting chummy, however, and nearly everything that remains – as hopefully we've illustrated – is complete and total bunk, and hardly worthy of something with Whedon's name in the story credits. Egads, let's move on.

THE LORE The shots of the college campus that Gene and Denise attend hail from UC Berkeley (specifically, we're shown the facade of the Life Sciences Building).

2.14: "The Thin Dead Line"

"I don't have to tell you who used to rule these streets, detective. The scumbags did. We've got a tougher policy now."

Air Date: Feb. 13, 2001; **Writer:** Jim Kouf, Shawn Ryan; **Director:** Scott McGinnis

SUMMARY Troubled when cops start assaulting teen-agers without cause, Anne Steele (2.12, "Blood Money") calls upon her friend Gunn to investigate. Gunn suggests videotaping some policemen in the act of hassling him and his associates, Rondell and George, to prove the cops' brutal tactics. Meanwhile, with help from Kate, Angel discovers that someone has been reviving slain policemen as zombies.

Wesley tries to intervene just as a zombie cop accosts Gunn's group – but the undead officer shoots Wes in the gut. Gunn's group hauls Wesley back to the runaway shelter, but the undead cops, fearing discovery, besiege the center to silence everyone. Angel and Kate investigate the precinct from which the slain cops originated, learning that the police captain there has been channeling the zombie god Granath to animate the dead cops. Angel smashes the captain's Granath idol and voids the spell, making the zombie cops decompose. Wesley recovers in the hospital, but when Angel tries to visit his friend, a pissed-off Cordelia orders him to leave.

FIRSTS AND LASTS First appearance of Gunn's associates, Rondell and George. Also, it's the first story in which Cordelia sports some blonde highlights.

POINTS OF DISCUSSION ABOUT "The Thin Dead Line":

1. Brent Sexton plays the zombie cop that shoots Wesley, and he's presumably "reprising" his role as the policeman who got strangled by a pair of severed hands in 1.04, "I Fall to Pieces." It's always appreciated when the producers add some symmetry that the general public will ignore, but gives us geeks something to chat about.

2. It's got zombies, which strangely enough have more of a presence on the vampire/demon-soaked *Angel* and *Buffy* than you might think. The rules that govern the *Angel*-verse seem to dictate that zombies don't possess their original personalities or souls, so they're more akin to undead foot-soldiers than anything else.

If you're in a mood to cross-reference, check out similar cases of zombie-dom in *Angel* 4.08, "Habeas Corpses"; plus in *Buffy* 3.02, "Dead Man's Hand" and 4.21, "Primeval." Exceptions arguably occur in *Angel* 3.12, "Provider" and *Buffy* 2.02, "Some Assembly Required," in which the zombies' original personas seem present, but the undead seem more akin to Frankenstein's monster than the usual zombie-lore. Indeed, only *Buffy* 3.13, "The Zeppo" seems to resurrect individuals who're mentally and physically intact enough to pass as human – and even that hinges on an astrological convergence and a good amount of magic. Sticking to the usual pattern, the zombie cops make a fair amount of sense.

3. We previously touched on the cumulative nuttiness of Angel's involvement with the police (2.08, "The Shroud of Rahmon"), and yet despite his having now been at the center of at least four major police investigations, in this episode and next, he visits Kate at the police station without raising a single eyebrow. Didn't the producers give us *any* credit for paying attention?

CHARACTER NOTES *Angel:* Now using Merl to keep tabs on the firm's activities. He's also concerned enough about Cordelia's trio to monitor their new office.

• *Cordelia:* Discovers a runaway center teen wearing one of her outfits. [Off screen, Cordy realizes that Angel gave Anne a box of her clothes in 2.12, "Blood Money"; see 2.17, "Disharmony" for the result.] As with "First Impressions" (2.03), Cordy shows experience at applying pressure to wounds. She speculates that Steven Seagal only became a movie star with demonic assistance [and it's hard to disagree].

• *Wesley:* Itching for something to fight – before he takes a gunshot wound to the gut, that is.

• *Gunn:* Well acquainted with Anne, but hasn't stopped by the shelter in some time. [He must've met her after *Buffy* 3.01, "Anne," as she didn't ask him for help in that story.] Tension exists between Gunn, Rondell and George because Gunn has been spending so much time with Wesley's group. [See 2.19, "Belonging" for what becomes of this. The squabble probably explains why Gunn doesn't consult Wesley and Cordelia before embarking on his dumb scheme to videotape the renegade cops.] Gunn's knowledge of his old terrain seems outdated.

Gunn takes the injured Wesley to Anne's shelter rather than to the hospital, and in an ambulance, no less. [His innate distrust of the authorities might factor into the decision, even allowing that zombie cops are after them.]

• *Kate:* Back to collaborating with Angel [as with 2.10, "Reprise," but it goes to hell in a handbasket between them next episode]. One of the zombie cops, Peter Harkes (1965-Aug. 13, 2000), was a colleague of Kate's, and she attended his funeral six months ago. Despite all the zombies rising up, her father's grave remains undisturbed.

• *Anne:* Tells Wesley's group that Angel helped her for selfish reasons. ["Blood Money." That seems remarkably unkind, considering Angel gave her the fund-raiser proceeds.] She's aware that Gunn used to hunt vampires. [Anne next appears in the series finale.]

• *Merl:* Packing up and moving, because too many people (Angel, Lilah's crew in "Blood Money," etc.) keep waltzing in and demanding information without paying. Strangely, his possessions include not one but *two* iMacs.

• *Captain Atkinson:* Evidently never punished for raising dead cops as zombies. [The bastard causes trouble next episode, when we also learn his name.]

ORGANIZATIONS *Angel Investigations:* The temporary office includes a desk tray [taken from the Hyperion, evidently] that says "Please ring bell for service." The street address for the office reads 4521. Virginia refers her friend and fellow country-club goer, Francine Sharp, to the agency when Francine's daughter Stephanie contracts a gray-colored third eye in the back of her head. [The heroes solve this problem next episode.]

• *Wolfram and Hart:* Merl tips off Angel that the firm's having a "big meeting" with a new demon account tomorrow night, 9:30 pm, at a place called Diaghilev. [It's never revealed if he pursues this matter.]

• *The East Hills Teen Shelter:* Located at 131 Crenshaw, near but not actually in Gunn's old neighborhood. Anne doesn't admit anyone into the shelter after 10 pm. [More a curfew than a vampire defense, as the shelter likely counts as public accommodation. See **How Does the Invitation Rule Work?**]

DEMONOLOGY *Vampires:* Angel's vampire senses let him identify burial ground that looks perfectly normal to human eyes, but has been recently disturbed.

• *Zombie Cops:* Re-animated thanks to a shrine set up by Captain Atkinson. This entails pictures of the dead cops, their badges, a bowl full of entrails, some skulls and lots of candles. Crucially, the spell requires an idol of "Granath the Zombie god"; smashing this voids the spell [as with the idol of Janus in *Buffy* 2.06, "Halloween"].

The zombie cops at first drop the local crime rate without much incident, but increasingly deviate from the law, willing to arrest or slaughter people at the slightest provocation. [The spell, or the dead cops themselves, must decay with time and corrode their judgment.] Angel and Kate identify two of the zombie cops as having died in 2000. [Only a few months ago, given the time of airing. The spell presumably requires fairly fresh corpses, as there's no evidence of it animating skeletons or the like.]

BEST LINE A hospitalized Wesley, deliriously looking at his IV drip: "Is this morphine?" (Gunn nods.) "Well, it's bloody lovely!"

THINGS THAT DON'T MAKE SENSE Upon meeting Cordelia and Wesley for the first time, Anne astonishingly gives no sign of recognizing them as "that girl auditioning for a milk commercial" and "that dancing dolt who thinks he's James Bond" from the video shown on the big screen in "Blood Money." (Perhaps she's just tactful enough to refrain from announcing things such as, "By the way, I saw you prancing in your underwear in front of hundreds of people.")

Speaking purely in terms of cosmetics, Anne's runaway center looks completely different from the one in "Blood Money," even though it's presumably the same facility. (The center's located on Crenshaw in both "Blood Money" and this story, and Gunn remarks upon entering "I ain't seen this place in forever," suggesting it's the same locale. Yet it's probably more reasonable to assume that Anne used her windfall in "Blood Money" to move up the street.) Given the zombies' trigger-happy nature, it's fairly astonishing that they're only credited with roughing people up before now. And where does Kate go while Angel confronts the spell-casting police captain?

POP CULTURE On Gunn's absence of late, George comments, "You've been moving on up, dog," and Rondell adds, "deluxe apartment in the sky." Combined, it's a reference to the theme song from *The Jeffersons*, in which a formerly lower-class black couple start living among rich folks thanks to their successful dry-cleaning business.

IN RETROSPECT Wesley's gunshot wound seems an incredible juxtaposition to the proficiency with firearms that he'll display in Seasons Four and Five. On an even more sobering note – and sorry to bring this up, but it's hard to avoid – the stomach wound that Wesley here incurs seems almost feeble to the one he gets in 5.22, "Not Fade Away."

Kate tells Angel that the zombie-patrolled precinct had previously experienced a murder every two weeks, a rape every two days and a robbery every hour and a half... and that by stopping the zombies, they've just given that level of crime back to the neighborhood. In microcosm, it somewhat mirrors the end of Season Four, in which Angel and company fight on behalf of humanity's ability to rob and murder one another.

IT'S REALLY ABOUT... The nature of police brutality, which seems very apt considering how L.A.'s become renowned for it. (Notice how Gunn's crew provides the obligatory Rodney King mention.) The cops gradually lose their ability to discern between civilians and actual troublemakers, becoming more inhuman and eventually becoming as much a menace as the criminals themselves. It's rather like "Sense and Sensitivity" (1.06), in that regard, only without all the heartfelt sobbing.

And you might expect, there's also a few traces of racial tension here. Observe in particular the neighborhood thug Jackson, who calls the cops "racist pigs" yet seems more than happy to let Wesley expire simply because he's a white man.

CRITIQUE The obvious point is that it's a triumph of brawn over brains, and foregoes a potentially intellectual discussion about race relations and gang activity in favor of a slugfest with zombie cops. However, used judiciously, this sort of adrenaline-soaked story seems worse in principle than in practice. Okay, "The Thin Dead Line" chiefly exists as an excuse for the heroes/gangs of teenagers to hit something, but it largely succeeds on that score. Indeed, one of the authors of this book was in something of a foul mood on original broadcast, and found the melee downright cathartic.

If it seems odd that we'd find this story acceptable after slagging on a comparably action-driven story such as "The Ring," it's because "The Ring" proved clueless as to what the hell it was saying or doing, whereas "The Thin Dead Line" keeps everything in a proper context. A story about police brutality in L.A. was probably inevitable, and touches such as Gunn's debate about violence with Jackson keep your head in the ballgame. In fact, even if you deem everything else about this story bunk, let's concede that the gunshot wound that takes out Wesley is *totally* shocking and hits all the right buttons.

No, you couldn't accuse this story of being brain-food exactly... but it's ultimately an entertaining piece of television, and that's got to count for something.

2.15: "Reprise"

"The world doesn't work in spite of evil, Angel. It works with us. It works because of us."

Air Date: Feb. 20, 2001; **Writer:** Tim Minear; **Director:** James Whitmore Jr.

SUMMARY With the Wolfram and Hart employees running scared because a Senior Partner will soon conduct the firm's 75-year-review, Angel views the event as a window to launch a suicide mission against the firm's Home Office. Angel consults with a now-older Denver (2.02, "Are You Now or Have You Ever Been") and learns that the Partner will travel inter-dimensionally using a magical Band of Blacknil, manifesting as a Kleynach demon. Denver supplies an enchanted glove capable of killing the Kleynach, but Darla – evidently hoping to confront the Partners and obtain further power – kills Denver and steals the object.

Angel and Darla separately infiltrate the firm as the Kleynach appears, whereupon Angel retrieves the glove and slays the Kleynach. Angel puts on the Band outside Wolfram and Hart, causing an elevator door to open. The "late" Holland Manners offers to escort Angel to the firm's Home Office, and they travel in the elevator through a mystic tunnel. But much to Angel's surprise, they arrive back where they started on Earth. Holland explains that the "Home Office" is actually the whole of humanity, with the evil inherent in every single human giving the law firm definition. The firm has no intention of decisively winning the battle between good and evil, content to simply exist.

Meanwhile, Kate becomes suicidal when her superiors fire her for being too fixated on macabre/bizarre cases, then downs a bunch of pills and leaves Angel an abusive phone message. A despondent Angel returns home and ignores Kate's message, even as Darla shows up to reclaim the Band. Utterly numb, Angel yields to his baser instincts, throws Darla onto the bed and hotly has sex with her. Soon afterward, a post-coital Angel awakens screaming, then rushes out onto the balcony in pain. [*Continued next episode*]

FIRSTS AND LASTS Final appearances of Virginia Bryce, Denver the occult bookshop manager and Holland Manners (unless you count his body-double, in flashback, in 5.06, "The Cautionary Tale of Numero Cinco"). "Reprise" also marks the first and only time we see a Senior Partner onscreen, even if it's lodged in a Kleynach demon. It's also the first occasion that the firm brings an employee back from the dead, a stunt they'll repeat in the Season Four finale, also written by Minear.

First of three *Angel* appearances by writer David Fury, who's in the teaser as a would-be goat-sacrificer (and see **The Lore**).

POINTS OF DISCUSSION ABOUT "Reprise":

1. It's hard to overstate the importance of Angel's elevator ride with Holland, given that it completely subverts the usual expectation that one can attain a sweeping victory over evil. Look at *Star Wars*, where the evil Empire suffers a total defeat – as if the restored Republic will be free of corruption. Look at *Lord of the Rings*. Hell, look at *Buffy* Season Seven, in which everything's unnaturally wrapped in a neat and tidy bow. But here – presuming that we take the elevator ride at face value (and see item No. 2) – Angel discovers that you simply can't eradicate entirely evil from humanity. Once again, we're beyond the adolescence of *Buffy* and into the adulthood realization that perhaps trying to change the entire world single-handedly is unrealistic, hence the point of the next episode.

2. Over-heated conspiracy theorists might suggest that Angel never returned to Earth after entering the infernal elevator, and that – given the tragedy of the next few years – he's simply caught in a hellish unreality from this point

onward. An interesting theory, but we don't subscribe to it. You'd have to explain all the *Buffy* crossovers just for a start, so let's not walk the route of *Newhart, St. Elsewhere* or *Dallas* by ascribing chunks of the show to a dream/alternate reality unless it's vitally necessary.

3. Speaking of turning points, there's a bigger one for Wesley here than people recognize, as Virginia breaks up with him because his work's too dangerous. It's totally heroic of Wesley to stick with his job, but the flip-side is that if Wes had given up his crusading and settled down with Virginia, he could've avoided the three-and-a-half years' of heartbreak, misery and tragedy to follow.

4. Anyone actively trying to avoid spoilers would justifiably feel thwarted by Denver's appearance in the "Previously on *Angel*..." segment, which pretty clearly signaled the character's return. (Likewise, Oz's appearance in the "Previously on..." segment for *Buffy* 4.19, "New Moon Rising" declared, even to those paying moderate attention, what was to come.) Moreover, Sam Anderson's name in the credits basically give away the supposedly dead Holland's appearance in Act Four. For other instances of the producers successfully/unsuccessfully keeping a lid on characters returning, see 3.20, "A New World"; 4.21, "Peace Out"; and especially 5.08, "Destiny."

5. The Host mentions that the Senior Partner is arriving "on Friday," which undeniably sucks for the attorneys. Bad enough that most of them will probably get killed, but they've got to work through the weekend to boot.

CHARACTER NOTES *Angel:* His plan to assault the Home Office – akin to attacking Hell single-handedly – seems entirely suicidal. [Mind, this isn't the first time that Angel's displayed such tendencies; see especially *Buffy* 3.10, "Amends."] He survives a 15-story fall with little harm [it's a record for him to date, but see 4.07, "Apocalypse, Nowish"]. He rolls in the hay with Darla chiefly because he wants to "feel something besides the cold."

• *Cordelia:* Deliberately slurs her greeting of "Angel Investigations" as "Angphlm Investigations." She takes a taxi to collect payment from the Sharps [further confirmation that she doesn't own a car yet].

• *Wesley:* Pops six stitches [on wounds incurred in 2.14, "The Thin Dead Line"] while rebuking Angel.

• *The Host:* Strives for confidentiality when he "reads" other beings, but divulges to Angel what he overhears in the restroom. [That said, the Host *does* tell Angel about the Band of Blacknil, which he apparently read off the lawyers in Caritas, so he's playing fast-and-loose with the rules.] The Host intensely dislikes Andrew Lloyd Webber musicals.

• *Darla:* Fully healed after her near-incineration (2.11, "Redefinition"). Darla's motives in wanting the Band of Blacknil seem unclear, but she tells Angel, "The [Band's] not about vengeance. It's about power." [If we're trying to psycho-analyze Darla, it's notable that she's completely alone right now... she's eaten Holland, she's dismissing Lindsey and Dru has deserted her. Historically, Darla almost always acted with a partner, so it's possible she's just making a massive power play because she's at a loose end.] After incapacitating Angel by running him through with a sword, Darla refrains from killing him [see **Points of Discussion** next episode].

• *Lindsey:* Cool as a cucumber about the impending review, and always showers upon returning home from work [suggesting his job makes him feel soiled; we'll re-examine this thread in 2.18, "Dead End"]. Lindsey harbors Darla without informing the firm, and slugs at least one guard in helping her escape. [This is a really gutsy act of disobedience, considering it occurs moments before a Senior Partner manifests.] When Lilah spots Darla and orders the guards to "stake the bitch," Lindsey pops her one [but miraculously, he's never punished for any of this].

• *Lilah:* Sweating blood about the review. She regrets not heeding her mother's suggestion about having children [all the better to offer them as sacrifice, presumably]. Lilah has hired two goons for protection [after Angel's unnerving visit in 2.12, "Blood Money"], but he incapacitates them in two seconds flat.

• *Kate:* Captain Atkinson (2.14, "The Thin Dead Line") has filed a complaint against Kate because an associate of hers (Angel) beat the crap out him. Internal Affairs reviews Kate's erratic record and fires her, suspecting she never came to terms with her father's death (1.15, "Prodigal"). Kate now realizes, based on the forensic evidence, that Angel shut in the victims of the wine cellar massacre (2.10, "Reunion"). Events culminate in her shoving aside three shelves' worth of awards, then downing vodka and a lot of pills.

• *Denver:* Claimed to be "just north of 30" when he encountered Angel in 1952. ["Are You Now or Have You Ever Been"; this presumably means he's just north of 80 in the present day. Actor Thomas Kopache was around 55 when he played the part, so this is pushing it a great deal.] He's running the same bookshop, and the window lettering cites it as "Book City, est. 1913." Denver claims that Angel's heroism in 1952 convinced him there was good in the world, yet takes the revelation that Angel left everyone to die horribly in stride, particularly as Angel's now intent on assaulting the Home Office.

Darla runs Denver through with an "antique" sword. [As specified next episode. She presumably got the sword from Denver's stock.]

THE LIBRARY Denver's books helpfully offer information about Kleynach Demons (see **Magic**).

ORGANIZATIONS *Angel Investigations:* Wesley and company ritualistically kill the Skilosh spawn growing in Stephanie Sharp [last episode], but her parents believe the heroes are con artists, and refuse to pay their fee. [Mercenaries in the audience will arguably find some justice when the Skilosh brutally kill the family – symbolically, it's the price you pay for stiffing a heroic detective agency.] Angel Investigations typically doesn't accept personal checks.

• *Wolfram and Hart:* Holland tells Angel that, "We have [an apocalypse] scheduled." [That said, Holland's claims about the firm's enduring nature seem to indicate that the firm isn't actively instigating said apocalypse. It's also unclear if this is the same apocalypse of concern in the show's last half-dozen episodes.]

Holland claims that Wolfram and Hart has existed in one form or another throughout history – apparently playing a role in the Spanish Inquisition and the Khmer Rouge – going all the way back to "when the very first cave man clubbed his neighbor." The firm's "Home Office" evidently resides within the collective psyche of humanity. [This is plausible, insofar as notions such as "good" and "evil" in the *Angel*-verse appear to stem from humankind. It's entirely possible that humanity's concept of evil defined and shaped the law firm's present incarnation, even if the organization pre-dates humanity as 5.16, "Shells" suggests. For more, see **Are the Powers and the Partners Old Ones?**]

Lilah's research suggests that the firm's previous 75-year review made the notorious Christmas purge of "68" [presumably 1968, although it's hard to say] look like kid's play. Panicked employees are engaging in by-the-numbers [and pointless] dark rituals to curry last-minute favor. One such ceremony entails a pre-made kit with a blessed ceremonial dagger, a sacred offering bowl, Latin chants and *lots* of goats. An employee named Henderson ("a brown-noser," Lilah says) pulls her child out of the company daycare, presumably to sacrifice it. Angel's murder of the Senior Partner appears to scrub the review [as it's not continued in episodes to come].

Holland's contract with the firm extends "well beyond" death, meaning the firm can bring him back as a "dead person," not a ghost, for special assignments. Holland physically looks normal, save for his bearing Darla's bite marks from "Reunion." ["Restored" people bear a mark denoting how they died, as substantiated in 4.22, "Home."] The firm's elevators now require fingerprint detectors; Angel overrides this simply by coercing Lilah.

• *Caritas:* Serves yak's bile and complimentary nachos. It's located next to a building with the street number 459.

DEMONOLOGY The Host says that anything that manifests in our dimension can be killed, a necessary consequence of being here. [The Powers and the Senior Partners are presumably more unkillable in their home realities, and this mortality factor could help explain Jasmine's fate in 4.21, "Peace Out."]

• *Kleynach Demons:* "Lots" of dark entities manifest in our dimension as Kleynachs, because they don't rely on being conjured or otherwise brought forth. Even so, the firm stages a ritual – with the usual pentagram, guys in robes chanting, lots of incense, etc. – prior to the Partner's arrival. [It's all for show.]

Legend holds that seemingly invincible Kleynachs "rose up" from their demon world to rape and pillage human villages. A brave knight used a glove "fashioned and blessed by all the powers of light" to slaughter any offending Kleynach by grabbing it around the throat [see **Magic**]. The Kleynach seen here wears red robes, has hands with talons and looks like a desiccated husk.

• *Skilosh Demons:* A few of them force Mrs. Sharp to summon Cordelia into a trap [see next episode].

MAGIC Wesley concocts a "curative charm" [better identified as "de-occulation powder" in 2.16, "Epiphany"] to remove the Skilosh spawn from Stephanie Sharp's head. This evidently involves mandrake, which the heroes provide gratis.

• *Denver's Magical Glove:* Kleynach-killing item that Denver acquired in a 1975 yard sale in Covina. He's been using it as an oven mitt. [So the glove is either insulated (magically or otherwise) or just fashioned from a type of non-conducting metal. It looks silver most of the time, but curiously appears bronze after Angel's elevator ride with Holland, implying the journey to the "Home Office" somehow tainted its essence.]

Angel drops the glove in the infernal elevator, and Holland stoops as if to pick it up. [It's never seen again.]

BEST LINE Lilah, relating details about the firm's last 75-year review: "Nearly half of mid-management was sacked. And Lindsey, they used actual sacks."

THINGS THAT DON'T MAKE SENSE So Angel goes to all the trouble of launching a campaign against the Home Office single-handed, yet he doesn't take along a sword or any type of weapon. Even allowing that it's a suicide mission, what's he going to do? Throttle the Senior Partners with his bare hands? Denver's enchanted glove can't help him either, unless the Partners lounge about as Kleynachs in their home dimension for no good reason.

The firm's vampire detectors are now so sloppy that they fail to register Angel until he steps out of the elevator and arrives at the in-progress dark ritual on Floor 15. Actually, even that's unclear. Security registers a vampire on the premises, but we're left unsure if it's Angel or Darla, who got into the firm easily enough in "Redefinition" and presumably could pull the same stunt here. Also curious... we've never seen any of the firm's lawyers in Caritas before now, yet the 75-year review has droves of them thinking that hanging out in a demon karaoke bar is the best way to spend what's potentially their scant remaining time on Earth.

Cordelia says she doesn't have any friends, and Wesley claims next episode that her heroic lifestyle doesn't allow for socializing. Yet the heroes somehow rounded up enough people to throw an office party just two episodes previous in "Happy Anniversary." They presumably weren't Gunn's friends, because he got taken to task for avoiding his gang last episode, and they can't be Wesley's mates, because it's evident that he doesn't have any after Virginia dumps his sorry ass.

Oh, and it's interesting how once Angel comes to the realization that Wolfram and Hart draws its power from the evil inherent in mankind, *every* pedestrian that he subsequently spies – as if on cue – seems overly violent, evil and despicable.

POP CULTURE The Host, describing the entity who'll be overseeing the firm's review: "Let's just say it ain't Rex Reed. It's evil, it's dark, it's merciless. Actually, it sounds an awful lot like Rex, doesn't it?" Reed acted in a smattering of films (notably *Myra Breckinridge*, 1970), but is better known as a prolific movie critic. He's written an entertainment column for *The New York Observer* for decades.

CROSS-OVERS It's said that Drusilla alerted Lindsey to the wounded Darla's location before leaving L.A., and see **Cross-Overs** under "Redefinition" for what became of her.

IN RETROSPECT Denver to Angel, after learning the dire outcome of events in 1952: "Well, point is, you tried." If anything, that wholeheartedly sums up the final episode.

Angel and Darla smash a fair amount of furniture before making the vampire with two backs, but a rutting Buffy and Spike will later top this by virtually demolishing an entire building in *Buffy* 6.09, "Smashed."

TONIGHT AT CARITAS Two people (cited as lawyers in the script) sing Peaches and Herb's "Reunited."

CRITIQUE Once again, Minear gets the leeway to redefine *Angel* in nearly every capacity... and once again, he turns out a whale of a story that's truly magnificent to behold. It's an uncompromising piece that opens the bid with the villains of the series scared shitless – and yet culminates with the hero realizing he still can't best them. Nearly every character gets their chance to shine (well, barring Gunn, who takes a powder early on), and it's amazing how Minear ropes in bit-players such as Denver while keeping everything so fluid.

If it seems that we're prone to Minear-worship (a notion we'll assuredly squash come 3.03, "That Old Gang of Mine"), it's because he's somehow allowed to change our every perception about the series and make it look so easy in the process. Not to discount the contributions of Whedon, Greenwalt and more, but when you look at this episode... and Minear's "Reunion"... and "Epiphany"... we could go on... then it's funny how often Minear takes the characters and gives them new life – in the same fashion that Stan Lee and Jack Kirby might've created *The X-Men*, but it took writer Chris Claremont and cohorts to define the characters as we know them.

For sheer daring and elegance of form, this isn't just the best Season Two story, it's potentially the best *Angel* episode period. More than five years after broadcast, we're still revved to think about it.

THE LORE David Fury scored a few bit parts even prior to *Buffy* – he's a cop in the *Lois and Clark* pilot and so forth – but switched to writing mostly because it paid better. However, his flirtation with acting explains why he gets so many speaking parts in the Whedon-verse (the would-be goat sacrificer here, plus 5.14, "Smile Time"; *Buffy* 6.07, "Once More With Feeling"; and loosely *Angel* 4.03, "The House Always Wins"). Entertainingly, he was also a pizza-delivery man in an episode of *Chance*.

• Whedon had tossed out the suggestion, "Can Holland come back all dead and take Angel on an elevator ride to hell, but end up right back where he started?" and Minear worked out the details from there. (Minear, *The Bronze*, Feb. 20, 2001)

• Thomas Kopache (Denver) appeared in all four contemporary *Star Trek* series and *Generations* – nothing too memorable, save that he's Kira Nerys' father on *Deep Space Nine*.

2.16: "Epiphany"

"You think you're the first guy who ever rolled over, saw what was lyin' next to him, and went 'Gueeeyah!!'?"

Air Date: Feb. 27, 2001; **Writer:** Tim Minear;
Director: Thomas J. Wright

SUMMARY Angel retains his soul, claiming his coupling with Darla was about pure despair, not the perfect happiness required to break his curse. Acknowledging his selfish behavior, Angel orders Darla to leave, then dashes to the dying Kate's apartment and saves her with a hot shower. Kate revives and tosses Angel out, whereupon Angel consults with the Host and realizes he gravely erred in firing everyone.

A group of Skilosh demons seek vengeance against Wesley's trio for destroying one of their spawn (last episode). The Skilosh implant Cordelia with another spawn, but Angel reunites with Wesley and Gunn. Meanwhile, Lindsey learns that Darla rolled in the hay with Angel and wrathfully takes after his rival with his pickup truck and a sledgehammer. Angel thrashes Lindsey and borrows his vehicle, crashing to the rescue and slaughtering the Skilosh. For an encore, Wesley cleanses Cordelia of her infection.

Kate later thanks Angel for his aid, acknowledging the presence of a higher power because he entered her apartment without an invitation. Later still, Angel approaches his friends and offers to work for *them*, somewhat mending affairs.

FIRSTS AND LASTS Final appearance of Kate Lockley, who exits the show with no explanation about her ultimate fate. It's never stated on screen, but her salvation likely owes to the first instance – on *Angel*, that is – of the Powers-That-Be "suspending the rules." (See **When Did the Powers Intervene?**) Angel visits Wesley's apartment for the first time, and gets an invitation inside. Final appearance of the interim Angel Investigations office, as the heroes return to the Hyperion next episode.

POINTS OF DISCUSSION ABOUT "Epiphany":

1. As with Angel's questionable sparing of Darla and Dru in "Redefinition" (see **Points of Discussion** under 2.11), we're forced to confront the notion that he simply lets Darla leave the Hyperion unhindered. Fair enough that he's feeling guilty about their tawdry night of passion, but this glosses over the point that Darla's a vampire who must kill to survive, which makes Angel partly responsible for anyone she hurts between now and "Offspring" (3.07). Seriously, how many people must die for the sake of Angel's ill-thought nookie?

But then, such restraint is going around, as Darla herself didn't go for a killing strike against a helpless Angel in "Reprise" (2.15), and Cordelia's guilty of the same against Harmony next episode. Cumulatively, everyone's unwillingness to suck it up and simply finish their business – evidently preferring to go round and round with their battles instead – makes Kate's misdirected arguments about civilians getting needlessly caught in the crossfire (2.05, "Dear Boy") seem more credible.

2. When Lindsey shucks aside his business persona and shifts to "Oklahoma good-old-boy" mode, watch closely when he roots around in his closet. In the back, you'll fairly easily spot the book *White Ninja* by Eric Van Lustbader – undoubtedly a recycled prop from 1.05, "Rm w/a Vu," where it appeared in Cordelia's apartment. We never thought we'd catch ourselves saying this, but it would seem the *one* thing Lindsey and Cordelia hold in common is that they've both read *White Ninja*. Who knew?

3. For anyone keeping track of the vital issue of when Cordelia starts owning a car (you laugh, but in *Dusted*, we had to cross-reference when precisely Buffy seems to start driving), please note that here she takes a cab. See 2.03, "First Impressions" for evidence that she's been hitching rides with Wesley, and we're still a year away from concretely spotting Cordy's automobile in 3.22, "Tomorrow."

4. The Host recognizes that Angel has (shall we say) "gotten some" from the moment he walks into Caritas, and the Host will show further intuition in the next two years about who's shagging who within the heroes' circle. Some have interpreted this to mean that the Host possesses a sort of "sex-dar" that, dunno, makes his horns tingle in the presence of someone who's recently gotten laid. That, or his "reading" people carries some benefit long after the fact, enabling him to register, "Hey, you've recently had sex."

Does this owe *anything* to super-empathic senses, though? In truth, the manner by which Angel slinks into the club – looking like a shamefaced teenager who's been fooling around with his girlfriend in a baseball dugout – doesn't exactly leave much to the imagination. Hell, college students throughout the ages have watched as a friend wandered into the room, looking disheveled and seeking advice after an ill-advised coupling. For that matter, the Host runs a karaoke bar – so he's got ample opportunity to observe body-language of all types – and he doesn't need a Spider-Sense to know who's been getting it on. His knack for observation should suffice perfectly well.

5. Another item about the Host: He flat-out states that he was never Angel's link with the Powers. It's strange to say, because he seems perfect for the post, given that he's demonic, empathic, attuned to the Powers' frequencies (2.11, "Redefinition" and 3.02, "That Vision Thing") and already counseling Angel. Yet he's never called to serve in the role. We can only presume that the role of succession is so mucked up (see **Did Jasmine Cause All This?**) that the Powers' shifting the vision-talent to the Host isn't an option after mid-way through Season One.

6. Speaking of which, the Powers notoriously send vague visions – or even "symbolic" ones, going by "First Impressions" (2.03) – yet here they send Cordelia what's arguably the most useless message of all. Just after Cordy spies the Sharp family's corpses, the Powers hit her with the "warning" of a scary Skilosh demon. Literally seconds later, a Skilosh assaults her. Not only does the vision wrack Cordy with a blistering headache that might actually *hamper* her escape, but it's rather unnecessary all around – Cordy isn't always the brightest bulb on the tree, but you'd think the dead bodies strewn about the kitchen would give her a clue

to get the hell out of Dodge. Thanks for nothing, you bastards.

CHARACTER NOTES *Angel:* Comes to recognize, chiefly based on his experiences last episode, that evil *can't* be defeated in one fell swoop – so he vastly downgrades the importance he attaches to "the grand scheme of things" and recognizes that small acts of heroism and kindness are what really matter because they're attainable. [In this, he's gone back to his mandate of "helping the helpless," as opposed to just kicking the crap out of the guilty.] Angel rapidly recovers from multiple blows from a sledgehammer [admittedly, they're inflicted by Lindsey, who's one-armed and only graced with human strength].

• *Cordelia:* Wesley insists that Cordy has become extremely solitary over the last few months, taking her responsibilities as visionary extremely seriously. Angel thinks Cordy is still out partying every weekend [despite her on-screen devotion to work in Season Two; then again, see **Things That Don't Make Sense** last episode]. Wes notes that Cordelia can't walk away from the visions, but she genuinely seems concerned about easing other people's suffering [in no small part due to 1.22, "To Shanshu in L.A."]. Cordy's grumpy at Angel even when he tries to atone for his misdeeds [but see next episode].

• *Wesley:* Still recovering from his gunshot wound (2.14, "The Thin Dead Line") and getting around in a wheelchair, or sometimes supported by a cane. He keeps a shotgun [specified as a Mossberg 12-gauge in 3.17, "Forgiving"] in his apartment. [Considering guns contributed to Virginia's dumping Wes last episode, it's doubtful he ever mentioned this formidable piece of weaponry.] He lives in Apartment 105, with a "Mrs. Starns" as his upstairs neighbor.

• *Gunn:* Has bonded with Wesley. Gunn keeps a small knife, just big enough to cut rope with, in the back of his boot.

• *The Host:* Apparently sleeps at Caritas in some back quarters [confirmed in "Offspring"]. It's implied that the Host, like Angel, has rolled over, saw what was lying next to him and gone "Gueeeyah!" at some point.

• *Darla:* Claims that losing one's soul leaves a brief "bitterness" that's removed with a hot kill. ["Redefinition" corroborates this.] She concludes, based on her immense lifespan and former standing as a seventeenth century whore, that she and Angel enjoyed "perfect" sex last episode – Angel alternatively views the event as "perfect despair." During said lovemaking, Angel [how should we say this?] "plateau-ed" once. She one-upped him by "plateau-ing" three times. ["Offspring" disputes this tally, weirdly.]

Darla claims she intended to kill Angel, but their bout of sex interrupted that plan. [She's possibly misleading him, as she had the perfect opportunity to slay him last episode – while he was sword-impaled – yet refrained.] The firm has issued orders that Darla be staked on sight. [She next appears in 3.01, "Heartthrob."]

• *Lindsey:* Advises Darla to act with more discretion, and suggests she move her stuff into his bedroom. [Read into that what you will.] He seems uncertain as to what he would've done if he'd known in advance about Darla's assault on the Senior Partner last episode. Lindsey reverts to "country boy" mode [evidently a reflection of his upbringing, see 1.21, "Blind Date"] before going after Angel, ditching his attorney clothes in favor of a plaid-shirt and cowboy boot ensemble. He owns a Ford pickup truck with Oklahoma plates No. T-42633, expiration date Dec. 2001. [Actor Christian Kane grew up in Norman, Oklahoma, and studied at the University of Oklahoma. Lindsey must keep the truck in storage, and never bothered to change the plates.]

• *Kate:* Lives in apartment No. 311. Kate feels somewhat idiotic after her suicide attempt, recognizing that her entire world revolved around being a cop, but seems at ease about finding a new path in life.

ORGANIZATIONS *Angel Investigations:* Angel's offer to work for Wesley, Cordelia and Gunn pulls the group back together. For anyone who worries about such things, the agency's hours are: 10 am to 6 pm (Monday through Thursday), 10 am to 9 pm (Friday), 9 am to 9 pm (Saturday) and closed Sunday [when evil apparently takes the day off, judging by 3.19, "The Price"].

• *The Powers-That-Be:* The Host claims the lawyer slaughter in "Reunion" (2.10) was "slated" to happen, and that the Powers simply wanted it to occur without Angel. [It's hard to tell if he's speaking literally or figuratively.] The Host says the Powers told Angel over and over and *over* not to get involved [although on screen, only the vision in "Reunion" looks like a blatant attempt to alter Angel's course].

• *Caritas:* Now features a sign that proclaims, "Eating the Clientele is Strictly Prohibited." [The script for 2.01, "Judgment," suggested such a sign, but it only now appears.]

DEMONOLOGY *Vampires:* Angel has stubble [suggesting vampires need to shave, but this potentially contradicts Angel's three-month submersion; see "Deep Down" (4.01)].

• *Skilosh Demons:* Wesley describes them as a "notoriously violent" asexual breed of demon, given to grouping in "tribes," and reproduceing by injecting its spawn into a human cranium. [It's never said why the Skilosh favor might one host over another, although it's perhaps telling that the only two victims we know about – Stephanie Sharp and Cordelia – are female.] The impregnation involves a Skilosh thrusting its three-pronged tongue onto the back of the victim's head, where a demonic eye develops. Cordelia says the process hurts like hell [and it's quite gross too.] The host can see through the extra eye. Curing the condition involves sprinkling a pink "de-occulating" powder over it while speaking a Latin chant. [The script claims this translates to, "Come clean, be new, release the grip, return to nothingness..."]

The Skilosh speak both English and their own language. They know, without being present, when two of their party are killed. [Either this is a form of empathy, or they've just got someone keeping watch.] Skilosh blood looks goopy and yellow, rather like runny eggs.

MAGIC *The Band of Blacknil:* The firm held a "disenchanting" ceremony to neutralize it. A disillusioned Darla takes the Band with her upon leaving the Hyperion, and it's last seen in Lindsey's apartment.

BEST LINE Wesley, fumbling to invite Angel into his apartment as Skilosh demons crash through the window: "Yes. No. Absolutely. I invite you in. *In* I invite you!"

THINGS THAT DON'T MAKE SENSE Right, then... the producers are getting a little too clever for their own good. The final shot of last episode, and the teaser here, are obviously intended to evoke Angel's conversion into Angelus in *Buffy* 2.13, "Surprise." But as we learn that Angel *isn't* losing his soul, what was up with his jolting awake and thrashing on the balcony? Heartburn?

Cordelia believes she's stopping by the Sharp household only to collect a check. There's no need to dawdle, so why does she tell her cab ride to leave? She's got to get home somehow, and L.A. evening bus service is scant if not nonexistent in the suburbs. And why call for a second cab when she could've had the first one wait for her?

During his heart-to-heart with Angel in Caritas, the Host drops the bombshell that Wesley, Cordelia and Gunn "might not survive the night." Just how exactly does he know this, and why the hell didn't he mention it sooner? (Let's try to reason through this mess. It's possible that Angel sings for the Host shortly after arriving, and that we cut to them having drinks afterward, but nothing on screen suggests this. Or perhaps the Host "read" the impending dilemma off Wes and company on a previous occasion, but if so, it seems irresponsible that he didn't speak up sooner. Besides, what if Angel *hadn't* dropped by Caritas? Maybe the Host would've phoned him in a panic, but he sure as hell looks like he's on his way to bed. However you choose to interpret this, the Host hasn't directly received a message from the Powers, because he tells Angel, "Do I *look* like I'm hearing voices?")

Strangely, Wesley doesn't recognize Gunn's truck, even when it's driven around the block and he's accorded a view of it more than once. "Carbon copies" on Cordelia's note pad supposedly tip off the heroes as to her location, but the pad itself doesn't appear to have any carbons. Later, Gunn somehow knows that Cordelia's got three eyes, even though he doesn't appear to see the back of her head. (Well, perhaps he glimpsed her third eye before she sat down... or maybe he saw Cordy fiddling with the back of her head and made the logical conclusion.) Wesley erroneously speculates that Cordelia's Skilosh gestation period is "nearly complete," even though she's been infected a few hours at most, and the Sharp girl apparently went far longer than that with no trouble. [He's just guessing.]

POP CULTURE The Host, on Angel's "epiphany": "You've turned a corner. Well, yay you! Zuzu's petals!" In *It's a Wonderful Life*, George Bailey (Jimmy Stewart) pockets some petals shed off a rose won by his daughter Zuzu, and happens to whip 'em out when his faith needs a boost. (By the way, the script mis-spells this as "Zsu Zsu's petals.")

IN RETROSPECT Wesley and Gunn have bonded to the extent of sharing a complicated "brother shake," which now seems faintly astonishing considering how hideously wrong their relationship goes in future. Ah, and as Cordelia mentions, this marks the second time she's gotten magically impregnated with demon spawn. It's not exactly the last, either, depending on how you view Season Four.

IT'S REALLY ABOUT... Getting laid helps to lift the mental fog that hangs over most males.

Also, this story and the previous episode, "Reprise," serve to illustrate the importance of understanding the limits of what adults can accomplish. When we're young, we're blatantly told – and fool ourselves into believing – that we can single-handedly change the world. Maturity brings with it the realization that one person – for reasons of money, authority, geography, talent, physical stamina and more – can only do so much. In short, there are things you can change and there are things you can't, and being a hero means in part recognizing the line between the two.

CRITIQUE As with "Reprise," it covers a phenomenal amount of ground, and only the clinically dead could justifiably fail to appreciate it. Minear again retools everyone's relationships, yet simultaneously gives Kate an honorable send-off, throws in some lively jokes and allows Lindsey to come totally unglued, with every sledgehammer blow reverberating through the viewers' spines. Honestly, what more could a reasonable person require?

The only snag of note is that this caps off a two-parter that's clumsily scheduled. After this, you'd expect everything to work toward an explosive finale later in Season Two, with Darla and Lindsey right at the epicenter. That became impossible for reasons of scheduling (see **The Lore** in 2.19,

"Belonging"), but it's still a shame that much of the payoff got postponed until Season Three. All of that said, "Epiphany" in and of itself caps off a storyline that's a major, *major* highlight of the show, emerging as an elegant piece which sports a solid reputation, but which really deserves a *great* one.

THE LORE Neither Röhm nor the producers ruled out the possibility of Kate returning in future, but her addition to the cast of *Law and Order* – which films in New York – left the actress and the *Angel* sets on the opposite ends of the country. Röhm later told *TV Guide:* "In all perfect worlds, I think I'd like to continue, because it would be great to do two different parts at the same time. But it is a little hard geographically." (*SciFi Wire*, May 30, 2001)

• Asked by *E! Online* if he was a Buffy-Angel shipper or an Angel-Darla shipper, Minear replied, "I don't understand how you could watch 'Becoming' and not be a Buffy-Angel shipper. And I don't understand how you could watch anything I wrote, and not be a Darla-Angel shipper. But really, I'm an Angel-Lindsey shipper."

2.17: "Disharmony"

"Watch out evil... here comes Harmony."

Air Date: April 17, 2001; **Writer:** David Fury;
Director: Fred Keller

SUMMARY Cordelia becomes surprised when her high school classmate Harmony comes to visit, then is even more shocked to learn that Harmony's now a vampire. Harmony touts herself as a reformed creature of the night, whereupon the heroes reluctantly take Harmony onboard out of respect for Cordelia. Later, the heroes investigate robed vampires working on behalf of Doug Sanders – a vampire who has adopted the pyramid sales scheme he ran in life for the undead. Angel's crew sends Harmony to reconnoiter, but Harmony falls sway to Sanders' teachings and leads the heroes into a trap. The subsequent battle leads to Sanders' decapitation and the ruin of his operation, but Cordelia can't bring herself to dust Harmony, instead ordering her to leave town. Cordelia concedes the boys were correct, and reconciles with Angel once he buys her new clothes.

FIRSTS AND LASTS Harmony makes her debut on *Angel*, although it's less of a stark contrast to her function in Season Five than Spike's outing in "In The Dark" (1.03). Willow from *Buffy* also logs one of three appearances on the show (see also 2.22, "There's No Place Like Plrtz Glrb" and 4.15, "Orpheus").

POINTS OF DISCUSSION ABOUT "Disharmony":

1. Here comes Harmony, and it's funny how many people gloss over her uniqueness among *Angel*-verse vampires. Normally, a vampire's persona is loosely based on his or her human host, sans all conscience and morality. The variance between a vampire's human and demon personas is more pronounced in some cases than others – vampire Darla isn't *so* different from human Darla (judging by 2.07, "Darla"), Spike eventually leaves his "William the bloody poet" persona behind and so forth. But Harmony? She's just about the *only* vampire who doesn't change one single iota – she's a combination of vapid, ditzy and downright blonde, both in high school and as a member of the undead. You could argue that human Harmony wasn't exactly gushing with personality to start with, but it's still rather interesting how as a vampire, she's painted as a glass unicorn-collecting, rich bitch cheerleader with fangs, and works wonderfully in that capacity.

2. Cordelia doesn't know that Harmony got vamped, even though it came to light on *Buffy* a whopping 36 episodes ago, so continuity keepers should note that the Slayer's camp and Angel's group can't be chatting much. At the very least, you'd think someone in Sunnydale or L.A. would've mentioned it in their Christmas newsletter.

3. Confirming evidence from stories such as "Are You Now or Have You Ever Been?" (2.02), last episode and "Orpheus," Doug Sanders conclusively proves that vampires can grow facial hair – and ludicrous facial hair at that.

CHARACTER NOTES *Angel:* Relegated to a card table for a "desk," and slavishly forced to make the coffee. He's particularly accommodating to Cordelia's wounded feelings, yet he blatantly fibs to her by claiming he never slept with Darla [3.07, "Offspring" shows the fallout from this]. Angel's now "infamous" enough that many of L.A.'s vampires can recognize him on sight.

• *Cordelia:* Particularly offended that Angel gave away some of her clothes (2.12, "Blood Money," as she discovered in 2.14, "The Thin Dead Line"). Angel claims "[I gave them] to the needy...", to which Cordelia retorts, "I *am* the needy." Angel's offering of new clothes [and his accurately predicting Harmony's betrayal] makes everything right between them.

Cordelia hasn't seen Harm since *Buffy* 3.22, "Graduation Day." Cordy takes two sugars in her coffee, likes pineapple and Tandoori chicken on pizza and keeps red wine about her apartment. She's surprisingly adept at close-quarters fighting [allowing that Harmony outclasses her for sheer strength] and carries two small crossbows. She here searches the "Department of Justice, Division of Fraud and Bunco" website for information [her hacking skills continue to improve]. In Ninth Grade remedial Spanish, student Donnie Wray followed Cordelia everywhere and wrote a love song that [heinously] read along the lines of: "Oh, Cordelia, how I long to feel ya..."

• *Wesley:* Unquestionably the heroes' leader now, and moves into Angel's office. Wes drinks coffee and is repeatedly in favor of simply staking Harmony.

• *Gunn:* He drinks mocha Cappuccino.

• *Harmony:* Unlike Cordy, Harm last remembers being truly happy while in high school. She thinks pig's blood tastes weird, adds lots of sugar to it and worries that it'll go straight to her hips. She doesn't know what "cacophony" means, likes potato skins and has never had a job. She characterizes her short-lived romance with Spike (*Buffy* Season Four) as a "smothering relationship, where [the other person] just can't live without you." [Nothing could be further from the truth. Harmony next appears, to Angel's dismay, in 5.01, "Conviction."]

• *The Host:* "Reads" Harmony, and says Cordelia's meant to serve as her guide. The Host apparently doesn't drink the blood served at Caritas.

• *Phantom Dennis:* Senses something awry with Harmony and slams a door to warn Cordy. [He gave a similar warning about Faith in 1.18, "Five by Five"; pity that Cordy doesn't pay more attention.]

• *Doug Sanders:* Self-described "life coach" until federal agents caught up with him, whereupon Sanders disappeared/got vamped. In life, he promoted the *Win From Within* program. As a vampire, he's authored *Selective Slaughter: Turning a Blood Bath into a Blood Bank.*

THE HYPERION A victim gets snatched "two blocks over [from the Hyperion] on Sixth."

THE LIBRARY Harmony wads her gum with a page from a 1,200-year-old volume in Wesley's collection.

ORGANIZATIONS *Angel Investigations:* Now back at the Hyperion; Cordelia has a new computer. [Harmony spills a cup of blood and shorts it out, but the heroes apparently fix this off screen. As ever, even while broke, they can somehow afford computer hardware.]

• *The Powers-That-Be:* Sanders' group has been vamping people for a month now. [With the heroes united, the Powers are likely working through a back catalog of difficult assignments.] The latest vision doesn't give Cordy a sense of location, instead showing a bird-image that the heroes must drive around to identify. [This varies with other stories where she inherently knows a street address. As with "Lonely Hearts" (1.02), one suspects the visionary's mind interprets the visions as best it can, and Cordelia's in the dark because she's never visited the area.] It's an atypical vision in that it shows two disparate images: the park assault and the bird thingy.

• *Caritas:* Serves AB-negative blood [an extremely rare type; less than 1 percent of the public possesses it].

• *Sanders' Vampire Pyramid Scheme:* Its chief motto: "Turn two and the rest are food." Each vamp can "buy into" the co-op by depositing one human into the food bank. Program members wear different-colored robes according to their levels of accomplishment. In decreasing order, they are: light-blue, yellow, green, dark blue, brown(ish) and black. Sanders wears light-blue robes. Harmony instantly jumps to dark blue by betraying Angel's group.

DEMONOLOGY *Vampires:* Cordelia invites Harmony into her apartment while they're both in the Hyperion [again proving that invitations given remotely count; see **How Does the Invitation Rule Work?**]. Wesley claims that some vampires can sense Angel's soul. [It's not a widespread talent, but not apparently limited to vampires in Angel's "family tree" either.] A young woman goes limp the very moment a vampire bites her wrist. [Lending credence to the theory that vampires inject a paralyzing agent into their victims, rendering them helpless.]

Harmony claims her vampire hunger pangs make her feel "crampy." As established in *Buffy* Seasons One and Two, vampires tend to follow an assertive leader – most of Sanders' vamps rabbit shortly after he's killed.

THINGS THAT DON'T MAKE SENSE So the heroes send Harmony on reconnaissance in the theatre, and she tells them there's "a hundred" or so vampires lurking inside. In response to this declaration, they just walk right in, carrying a few crossbows, a few axes and maybe a sword between them. They don't know Harm's betrayed them, but conversely they must know she's little use in a fight, and *did they not get the memo that they're outnumbered a whopping 25 to one?* Where's the heavy artillery? Where's the flamethrower? Boy, it's lucky they're up against weenie-dog vampires who bolt easily, because they'd have been hosed otherwise.

When Harmony thumps Cordelia aside, Cordy magically produces not one but two crossbows out of thin air. Ah yes, and it's rather ludicrous that Cordelia's entire computer shorts out and smokes after Harm spills blood on the keyboard.

BEST LINE A floundering Cordelia, on the phone with Willow and unaware of developments on *Buffy*: "Oh... Harmony's a vampire? All this time, I thought she was a great big lesbo!... Oh, yeah? Well, that's great. Good for you."

POP CULTURE Cordelia: "What do I look like, the Bird Lady of Alcatraz?" The so-called "birdman of Alcatraz" – Robert Stroud, first convicted of manslaughter, then the murder of a prison guard – apparently had an interest in birds, although he never kept them during his time in the slammer. He became the subject of a 1955 book by Thomas E. Gaddis and a 1962 film starring Burt Lancaster. Stroud died in 1963 (from natural causes, it should be said).

CROSS-OVERS Willow's at college when she gets Cordelia's call, but there's no corresponding scene in *Buffy* Season Five.

IN RETROSPECT Cordelia claims that her work for the agency fills the "air pockets" trapped inside of her, and helps her "become her." It almost sounds like a fluffy precursor to the Slayer's "cookie dough" speech in the *Buffy* finale, even if it'll never get a smidgen of its acclaim.

IT'S REALLY ABOUT... What happens when a stalwart high school friend shows up and, on an intrinsic level, seems entirely different from the person you remember. In Cordy's case, she inescapably concludes that her life's better off without Harmony in it – something that is, depending on how low one's classmates go in life, an extremely mature point-of-view.

Of course, the B-plot involves the evil duplicity of pyramid schemes. The vamps go out, violently convert some people into their own number, and view the rest as little more than fodder. If you've ever sat through a pyramid sales scheme seminar, the parallels here are downright chilling, and it's amazing how well your commonplace vampire works in that metaphor.

TONIGHT AT CARITAS Harmony sings "The Way We Were," and it's about as pleasant as nails on a chalkboard. (The Host sings it with far, far greater panache in 4.06, "Spin the Bottle.") Harm threatens to also sing both versions of *Candle in the Wind*, but mercifully doesn't.

CRITIQUE As with "Harm's Way" in future, it's tailored as a bit of fluff after some balls-to-the-wall, seat-clenching action stories. Fortunately, it's utterly charming as far as fluff goes, and contains a number of gems – be it Cordy's bewildering phone call to Willow, Wesley's wonderful battle-cry of "Kill 'em all!", or the final shot where Angel buys Cordy clothes and kowtows to her shallowness. It's such a lively story that failing to love it (at least, in parts) would be like failing to love air.

If there's a downside – albeit a forgivable one – it's that the main thread with Sanders and his pyramid vampire scheme ranks among the most forgettable *Angel* plots. Viewers might recall this story as "the one with Harmony's painful singing" or simply "that one where Cordy mistakes Harmony for a great big lesbo," but they rarely remember the villains – a pity, because pyramid sales schemes really are simply ripe for such satire, and Fury wryly fillets them.

It's a lively little story that's splendid in the moment, then, but doesn't register on one's radar too much. Still, let's appreciate how *Angel*'s the type of show that can so rapidly switch between tragedy and comedy, and respect "Disharmony" as the sort of runaround you simply need once in a while.

THE LORE This story originally included an epilogue in which Harmony, having fled to Mexico, converts other vampires into the pyramid scheme fold. As scripted, the scene had her clad in a sombrero and talking to a pair of vamps using stilted high school-level Spanish. The vamps repeated Harmony's advice that they should "turn *dos*, um... the rest is food," with Harmony enthusiastically clapping and telling them, "*Muy bueno*." (It's almost a pity this scene fell through the cracks, because come the end of *Buffy* Season Six, Harmony could've recruited Andrew and Jonathan once they fled there.)

• Another deletion from the script: Cordelia's "I'm so happy to have clothes!" dance ended with Wesley suggesting to Angel, "I could use a DVD player."

• Similar to Denisof's anxiety in Season One, McNab was in the habit of racing through every new script to make sure the producers hadn't yielded to the temptation of killing off her character. (Kane and Romanov, it must be said, found themselves falling into the same practice.) McNab noticed however, that all her episodes seemed to entail: "Make Harmony as big an idiot as possible, then have her run away with her tail between her legs." (Mason, *TV Guide Insider*, May 30, 2001; Kane interview, *BBC Cult*, Nov. 2003)

2.18: "Dead End"

"Two enemies, one case, all coming together in a beautiful buddy-movie kind of way."

Air Date: April 24, 2001; **Writer:** David Greenwalt; **Director:** James A. Contner

SUMMARY The firm gets ready to choose between Lindsey and Lilah, but tip their decision by sending Lindsey to the Fairfield Clinic – a medical facility servicing the firm's employees – where doctors and a mystical shaman replace his artificial hand with an organic one. But when the hand independently displays a desire to maim and kill, Lindsey looks for the firm's body-bank.

Meanwhile, the Powers tip off Angel to a comparable transplant case, causing him to reluctantly ally with Lindsey. The pair of them find several hacked-up donors at the body-bank, then save everyone who's not beyond hope and trigger an explosion, mercy-killing the rest. The firm chooses Lindsey to become the next head of Special Projects, but he immediately resigns, tired of his career as an evil attorney. The firm promotes Lilah in his place, heeding Lindsey's suggestion that she's got enough blackmail material to bury them. Afterward, Lindsey enjoys a surprisingly cordial conversation with Angel, then leaves town in his pickup.

FIRSTS AND LASTS It's Lindsey's last appearance as an employee of the firm, and the only time that he steps foot into Caritas. Final appearance of Nathan Reed, Lindsey and Lilah's boss, who disappears without explanation. "Dead End" also gives the first overt signs that Cordelia – a mere mortal – physically and mentally can't shoulder the Powers' visions.

POINTS OF DISCUSSION ABOUT "Dead End":

1. In Seasons One and Two, Holland Manners is only said to run the firm's Special Projects Division – so it seems a continuity snafu when it's later implied in "Conviction" (5.01) and "Power Play" (5.21) that he was "running the joint" as if he were its top dog. However, bearing in mind that the L.A. branch's C.E.O. isn't ever named (until "Conviction," actually) there's mounting evidence by this point that Holland realistically was the company head, even if his title never reflected it (judging by 2.10, "Reunion").

As it happens, many companies or colleges work that way... you have a "president" or C.E.O. who's in charge on paper, with a vice-president or someone lower effectively calling the shots. So let's now consider how it's said in "Redefinition" (2.11) that Darla and Dru ate members of the "contracts department," who are clearly Holland's employees. Then we get to "Blood Money" (2.12), in which Lindsey and Lilah run a charity drive scam that seems beneath them. And now we arrive at "Dead End," where the pair of them handle such pedestrian lawsuits as a crooked utility company and a corporation accused of selling poisoned chocolate. At least there's a hefty $60 million fee at stake this time.

Cumulatively, it looks as if Holland routed many of the firm's other operations through his department, meaning that he probably did run the L.A. firm as Season Five claims. The tradition of centralizing the company's operations in Special Projects continued after Holland's demise for a time, probably up to the massive reorganization in Season Four. Continuity's preserved, and we've explained in large part why Lindsey and Lilah keep getting stuck with grunt work.

2. Lindsey's resignation has become rather infamous, especially the part where he pinches Lilah's ass and blames it on his "evil hand." Nice to see – and we say this without sarcasm – that something as simple as an ass-pinching can bring so much cheer to so many people across fandom.

3. Take a hard look at the family photo on Nathan Reed's desk, as it features him with the prerequisite trophy wife and son. The show designers really have surpassed themselves in this case, because the son (seriously, look at him) terrifyingly looks like an *evil* son, the sort you'd expect to try and slip a dagger between Harry Potter's ribs if given the opportunity.

4. Lindsey's chest, shown when he awakens in bed, is clean-shaven. Couple this with Angel's bare and hairless chest in 2.09, "The Trial," 5.21, "Power Play," etc.; Gunn's bare chest in 4.05, "Supersymmetry"; Spike and Lindsey (again) throughout Season Five; Drogyn in "Power Play" and more, and you're almost forced to conclude that most *Angel*-verse males have unnaturally smooth pectorals.

CHARACTER NOTES *Angel:* For lack of a police contact [after 2.15, "Reprise"], Angel hires a private investigator to identify a set of fingerprints. Angel tells a shifty character that he could "live off him for a month." [Possibly true, given Angelus' track record.] The Host's "reading" of Lindsey determines that he's meant to work with Angel on this caper. Angel seems to appreciate Lindsey's 1956 pickup truck, and claims that people in the 1950s believed modern-day life would resemble *The Jetsons*, complete with air cars. Angel naughtily sticks a "Cops Suck" sign on the back of Lindsey's truck as he leaves town.

• *Cordelia:* Concedes that her vision "hangovers" are lasting longer. [It's here implied that the vision reverberates in Cordelia's mind until the heroes solve the case, but no other episode supports such a cut-off point.]

• *Lindsey:* Frequently performed in Caritas as a guitar player/singer before losing his hand [in 1.22, "To Shanshu in L.A.," which explains why Lindsey never stepped foot into Caritas once the heroes started visiting there in 2.01, "Judgment"]. Everyone save Angel rates Lindsey's performance as fabulous. The Host cites Lindsey's favorite drink as T&T. [It's presumably Tanqueray Gin and tonic.]

An organ bank label suggests that Bradley Scott, a former co-worker and the original owner of Lindsey's new hand, is O-positive. [Which in turn suggests that Lindsey has the same blood type. It happens that O-positive is Angel's favorite blood type (see 2.02, "Are You Now or Have You Ever Been"), so if Lindsey *is* O-positive, he must seem exceptionally juicy to the man.] Lindsey seems genuinely sorry when he mercy-kills Scott [although he'll set aside such compassion come Season Five]. He went through the usual childhood diseases, and isn't allergic to any medication. [Lindsey is allowed to leave town without protest, so either his damning blackmail material from 1.21, "Blind Date" still holds sway, or he's exceptionally talented at going underground. He returns in 5.08, "Destiny."]

• *Lilah:* Tries to draw a pistol in the boardroom when the firm promotes Lindsey instead of her. [She's at her wit's end to attempt such a pathetic maneuver.] Lindsey claims Lilah possesses incriminating evidence against various board members. [Yet he's probably lying, as there's no concrete proof of this. Besides, if Lilah *did* have such leverage, she'd hardly need to resort to the feeble stunt with the pistol.]

Lilah's personnel file lists her as: Junior Associate, 1994; Senior Associate, 1997; Junior Partner, 2000. She graduated from Mortonson University, school of law, in 1994 with high honors. She was recruited by the firm's L.A. office, as supervised by Holland.

• *Nathan Reed:* Works on a Mac, and his computer password is "Zen." Reed's caseload files include "Shaman Recruiting," "[Michael?] Jackson Case" and "Demon Reliability." His "To-Do" list includes "Reader Negotiation" (priority: medium), "Shaman Contracts" (high) and "Europe Fact-Finding Trip" (high priority). [The last is undoubtedly in the finest tradition of the "fact-finding trips" undertaken by Mayor Quimby on *The Simpsons*.]

• *Bradley Scott:* Age 30. He illegally dumped bearer bonds on the black market while working at the firm, served two and a half years at Soledad for embezzlement, then got paroled last month and sent by his parole officer [named Sam in the script, and on the firm's payroll] to serve as body-bank fodder.

ORGANIZATIONS *Angel Investigations:* Has a new flat-screen computer [presumably to replace the one Harmony ruined last episode]. As usual, it's a Mac.

• *Wolfram and Hart:* Handling a suit against Western Pacific Power, a company that has looted $3.5 billion since de-regulation. Lindsey favors the company returning half a billion without admitting fault, with the firm taking 20 percent off the top; Lilah advocates burying it in litigation. [Given Reed's fondness for Lindsey, he probably chooses the former.]

Another case involves Lycor, a company accused of selling a tin that leached cancer-causing cytoclistomine into its chocolate goodies. Lindsey suggests pinning blame on the fictional Drizon company, a offshore corporation "that split from Lycor six years ago and is going bankrupt." Members of the board that Reed chairs include "Leon" and "Charlie."

• *Fairfield Clinic:* The primary health care provider for the firm's L.A. branch. Dr. Melman heads a surgical team there, and Fairfield sometimes uses demon healers (such as the Pockla; see **Demonology**). A body bank supplying the clinic poses as "Southern California Travel."

• *The Powers-That-Be:* Deliver one of their scariest visions to date, with an employee of the firm stabbing himself in the eye. Cordelia doesn't sense the event's location, but unusually, she can mentally replay it for details. Wes suspects that the human body wasn't meant to bear the visions, noting that Cordelia's predecessor was half-demon. [3.11, "Birthday" confirms his theory. Maybe. It's also possible that the plethora of visions Cordelia experienced in "To Shanshu in L.A." wore down her resistance.]

• *Caritas:* The Host says he doesn't allow violence in the club. [Caritas' reputation as a violence-free zone is woefully exaggerated, as the next episode demonstrates. It's not until 3.03, "That Old Gang of Mine," that the Host installs a Sanctuary Spell there.]

DEMONOLOGY *The Pockla:* Red-skinned demon shaman healers with long talons, highly skilled at regenerating flesh. The freelance Pockla that re-attaches Lindsey's hand cost $250,000. Angel is acquainted with the Pockla; Lindsey isn't.

MAGIC *Pockla Surgery:* A human medical team gives Lindsey 2 mg of Versed, whereupon a Pockla levitates/manifests and sprinkles powder on the wound, sealing the organ onto its new owner. The Pockla "bless" the illicit organ bank by hanging their banners there. [The transplanted organs' hostility and rage appears to be a magical freak side-effect – possibly because some of the original owners are still alive and suffering – although the exact reason for this isn't given.]

BEST LINE Lindsey, totally flustered when Angel tries to help him: "You've got no business... why... *why* aren't you trying to kill me?!"

THINGS THAT DON'T MAKE SENSE One of the firm's clients – Irv Kriagle – is so oblivious that he fails to spot Lindsey's evil hand scribbling "KILL KILL KILL" in large block letters even while sitting next to the man. Later, Lindsey "tests" his evil hand by stabbing it with a letter opener hard enough to draw blood... making it just about the sharpest letter opener on the planet. (Then again, perhaps your standard letter opener at the firm comes ready-made to perform a sacrifice on a moment's notice.)

Lindsey says he previously worked with Scott in the firm's mailroom, yet in "Blind Date" (1.21), it's claimed that Holland personally handpicked Lindsey while he was a sophomore in law school at Hastings. If you connect the dots, this means that Holland bestowed Lindsey with the prestigious honor... of working as a glorified mail boy. Was the firm's "mail room" a cover for something more insidious? Also, notice how the faux travel agency goons – the ones that Angel and Lindsey render unconscious – disappear from the narrative. This makes you wonder if they recovered and left, if Lindsey somehow hauled their carcasses away before the big explosion, or if he and Angel simply forgot and left them to perish.

An extremely odd visual goof: the fingerprints Lindsey leaves on his glass are completely vertical – who drinks from a glass that way? This also entails, if you're watching close, Lindsey somehow "juggling" his glass into this weird position off screen. Is he just showing off his new hand's dexterity? Oh, and speaking of visual blunders, Lindsey's angle of vision seems entirely wrong for him to spy Lilah's gun in the records room, yet he does so anyway.

POP CULTURE The Host: "Am I the only one who saw *48 Hrs?*' " In *48 Hrs.* (1982), a quintessential "buddy film," a criminal (Eddie Murphy) gets released for two days to help an alcoholic cop (Nick Nolte) find a pair of evildoers. The protagonists wind up good friends after squabbling and beating each other up for most of the movie.

IN RETROSPECT Lindsey asks the Host for guidance, and he's apparently done so before. This seems chilling with hindsight, given what occurs between them in the series finale.

IT'S REALLY ABOUT... It's a reversal of "Blind Date" when Lindsey decides he doesn't belong at Wolfram and Hart, but it's also a testament to how much the corporate lifestyle chews people up and spits them out. It's a harsh, rigorous doctrine, and sometimes you can only best it by resigning. Along those lines, Lindsey's final insight to Angel – "The key to Wolfram and Hart: Don't let them make you play their game. You gotta make them play yours." – bears fruit in Season Five, although it takes Angel a hell of a long time to follow this advice.

TONIGHT AT CARITAS Lindsey takes to the stage with his guitar and sings "L.A. Song" (with words by David Greenwalt, and see 5.15, "A Hole in the World"). Angel jokes about singing "Stairway to Heaven."

CRITIQUE It's the end of Lindsey for now, and it's a great shame that "Dead End" only rises to the heights of being average, because the character really deserved a great departure point. Christian Kane proves as marvelous as ever, but the script just doesn't hit the heights he's displayed throughout much of Season Two, or even two episodes previous in "Epiphany." Perhaps that seems an unfair comparison, but after everything that's come before, it just feels off that Lindsey would leave the firm after *these* events. It all seems rather haphazard, and sure enough – it was (see **The Lore** next episode for why).

Sure, there's some choice moments, such as Lindsey singing in Caritas, his delightful little rant when Angel unexpectedly tries to help and especially his pinching Lilah's ass while crowing, "Evil hand!" But the story as a whole simply feels too unfinished and jumbled to work properly. It's fortunate, then, that we'll return to the character and provide some proper closure – but that can't stop the so-so "Dead End" from seeming like a bump in the road.

THE LORE Age 21, Christian Kane (Lindsey) had moved to L.A. with – as he put it – "nothing but my truck and some clothes." He quickly decided he wasn't very adept at comedy, but he could at least sing – he'd performed back-up for his cousin, Brandon Hart, a country singer in Nashville. Kane happened to meet Boreanaz a couple years prior to *Angel*, when Boreanaz was just starting on *Buffy* and Kane was appearing on *Fame L.A.* They went to the same gym, became buddies, and didn't much imagine much that they'd wind up working together. Given his background, Kane wasn't surprised that the producers eventually made Lindsey a singer in "Dead End," and thought it'd be fun for his character to perform "The Devil Went Down to Georgia." (Elias, *Entertainment Weekly Online*, Dec. 19, 2000) Since 1998, he's headlined a country western band named (wait for it...) "Kane."

• Kane was quite relieved to shed the artificial hand because he couldn't remove it during lunch breaks. He conceded to *BBC Cult* that much of his portrayal of Lindsey was based on Bernard Kahil ("Bernie the Attorney"), a lawyer friend of his in Nashville. By the time Kane left *Angel*, in addition to his friendship with Boreanaz, he'd also become chummy with Marc Blucas (*Buffy*'s Riley Finn) after they filmed *Summer Catch* (2001) together.

2.19: "Belonging"

"Let's hear about the cowardice and shame.'

Air Date: May 1, 2001; **Writer:** Shawn Ryan;
Director: Turi Meyer

SUMMARY At Caritas, a magic portal opens and disgorges a Drokken demon that's native to the Host's home dimension. The Host asks Angel's crew to slaughter the beast, but a vision instructs Cordelia to investigate a related matter. The heroes learn that five years ago, a young physics student – Winifred "Fred" Burkle – worked at a public library and disappeared when a portal opened in the Foreign Language section there. Cordelia finds the last book that Winifred checked out and reads from it, and the text generates a portal that spits out Landok, the Host's warrior cousin.

The heroes kill the Drokken, but not before the beast bites Landok and poisons him, necessitating that he go home for the antidote. Cordelia instinctively opens a portal back to Landok's homeland *using Winifred's book, and Landok successfully goes through. However, the portal inexplicably snares Cordelia also, depositing her in a wooded area. [Continued next episode]*

FIRSTS AND LASTS We learn the Host's actual name (see **Character Development**). It's loosely the debut of Amy Acker as "Fred," although she's only glimpsed in Cordelia's vision and doesn't get a proper unveiling until next episode. It's also the first suggestion that Caritas is a psychic "hot spot," but again, the term isn't used until "Over the Rainbow" (2.20).

Setting aside the unusual events in "Birthday" (3.11), this story effectively marks the end of Cordelia's acting pursuits (and see **It's Really About...**). And it's the final appearance of Gunn's associate George (formerly seen in 2.14, "The Thin Dead Line"), who's cremated after being on the losing end of a vampire fight.

POINTS OF DISCUSSION ABOUT "Belonging":

1. In Season One, and particularly in "Eternity" (1.17), Angel demonstrated a woeful lack of knowledge of modern-day television. Actually, check that... he didn't even *own* a television (see 1.18, "Five by Five," for the exception to this rule). Then again, Wesley wasn't up on the current "hit shows" either, and to look at the network schedules of the last few years, can one necessarily blame them? It's curious, though, how often people interpret this to mean that Angel's never watched a TV show or a film in the whole of his existence. Along these lines, note 5.13, "Why We Fight," in which the 1940s Angel just sits around watching mold grow (or near enough).

So then we come to "Belonging," in which Angel enthusiastically displays a fondness for Lorne Greene, star of *Bonanza* – the show ran from 1959 to 1973 and racked up a whopping 432 episodes, so we don't know precisely *when* Angel tuned in, but he certainly watched it sometime. Then let's factor in Angel's gleeful anticipation over a double-billing of *The Omega Man* (1971) and *Soylent Green* (1973) in 3.04, "Carpe Noctem," and his admiration for Denzel Washington's work in "First Impressions" (2.03). Oh, and then there's Angel's hockey obsession, as noted in 3.15, "Loyalty" and 5.05, "Life of the Party." All told, we can probably dispense with the notion that Angel is some kind of monk where pop culture's concerned.

2. The heroes investigate a murder scene near a building that's labeled "Acme Wiping Materials." It's not as entertaining as the sausage stuffing sign in "War Zone" (1.20), but it's close.

CHARACTER NOTES *Angel:* Takes everyone out to dinner to celebrate Cordelia's casting in a national suntan-lotion commercial, but seems painfully uncomfortable in public, and resists the urge to penny-pinch. The concept of "power walking" befuddles Angel. Conversely, he finds descriptions of the Host's homeland – with its simplified views of good and evil – very appealing. [And sure enough, he's comfortable in his heroic role there; see 2.21, "Through the Looking Glass."] Angel has a new, apparently demonic informant who's both a "he" and an "it."

- *Cordelia:* Feels very uneasy at the thought that she's missing something, as if there's a bigger plan at work. [She's right, and it's a real pity she doesn't take the hint – see **When Did the Powers Intervene?** for a possible explanation to Cordy's apprehension, and her downright fishy arrival in Pylea.] She also feels highly exploited by the lotion commercial. [She might take this humiliation to heart, as there's no evidence that she auditions for another role ever again. Indeed, two episodes hence, she'll claim that acting made her feel like a "concubine," and see **It's Really About...**] Eating sashimi makes Cordy violently ill. In public.

- *Wesley:* Phones his father to wish him Happy Birthday, but evidently receives skepticism/criticism after mentioning that he's now the team leader. [This corroborates hints about Wesley's less-than-ideal upbringing from "I've Got You Under My Skin" (1.14) and "Untouched" (2.04). Wesley's father appears, sort of, in "Lineage" (5.07).]

Wesley carries into combat a wooden stick, with what looks like a giant diamond on the end. Wes doesn't recognize the demon language in Fred's portal-making book. [Understandable, presuming that inter-dimensional languages are less researched in Earth's reality.]

- *Gunn:* Finds the notion of eating raw fish repellent. By now, his gang has been operating without him "for months." Rondell and George (from "The Thin Dead Line"), ask to borrow Gunn's truck for an assault on a vampire nest in McKenzie Park, but Gunn promises to show up personally. He first helps Angel and Wesley slay a Haklar demon, however, and therefore shows up late – after vampires kill George.

- *Winifred "Fred" Burkle:* Physics major who worked at the Stewart Branch Public Library in L.A. According to a missing persons flier, she disappeared on May 7, 1996, while shelving books in the Foreign Language Section. [Most information in the show concurs with this, but there's some awkward joins with 4.05, "Supersymmetry." See next episode for what became of her.]

The "Missing Persons" flier claims Fred is 5'7." [But then, the same flier lists Fred as having "medium build," which seems a stretch. Fred's driver's license more definitively lists her as 5'6" in "Through the Looking Glass."]

- *The Host:* Properly known as "Krevlornswath of the Deathwok Clan." He prefers the simpler moniker of "Lorne," but avoids using it on Earth because, given his skin color, it all-too-easily evokes *Bonanza* and *Battlestar Galactica* star Lorne Greene. The Host arrived on Earth through a portal [elaborated on next episode], and his disappearance remains a great mystery to his clan. He's happy, though, to let his mother (2.21, "Through the Looking Glass") believe that he threw himself into the sacrificial canyons of Trelinsk.

The Host wants to see Elton John in concert, and claims to "get a feel for a room" before performing there [probably true, even if it's here part of a cover story]. He's tempted to show up at the library to read *Harry Potter* to the kiddies.

PYLEA [Named next episode.] The Host's homeland, described as a world of "good and evil, black and white," where champions roam the countryside fighting for justice. But there's no music or art there [they *do* have dancing, however, see "Through the Looking Glass"]. "Nobody" there admits to having feelings.

Landok accuses the Host of "cowardice" for refusing the Deathwok Clan traditions of hunting, gathering and the sacred joust; the Host claims he was too busy chatting up females at a local waterhole [possibly an exaggeration, possibly not]. Also, the Host partly sympathized with his jousting opponents' point-of-view. This dereliction of duty bestowed a great shame upon the Host's mother, who's now given to ripping "images" of him to tiny pieces, feeding them to swine, butchering said swine and scattering their remains for dogs to eat.

A poisoned Landok requests that the Host perform sacred rituals if he dies, and thereby help Landok attain glory in the afterlife. The Host steadfastly refuses, even though he's "the only one" present who can perform such rituals. [The undertaking can't be limited to blood-relatives – who surely aren't always present in cases of violent death – but human "cows" (see next episode) are probably barred from such sacred duties. By the way, the Host's refusal doesn't exactly speak well of his character. Fair enough that he doesn't believe in the rituals, but his refusing to grant Landok's dying request seems rather selfish.] Pylea has two pink-hued suns.

ORGANIZATIONS *Angel Investigations:* The office now contains what looks like a set of little wooden Revolutionary War soldiers, and a bust of Shakespeare.

• *The Powers-That-Be:* Convey the oldest vision they'll ever send Cordelia, one with five-year-old images of Fred. [Yup, they're definitely playing Cordy; see **When Did the Powers Intervene?**]

• *Caritas:* The Drokken knocks over some Caritas patrons, proving that minimal violence can occur in the building. [The Host seems to imply that only killing in Caritas is verboten. The Drokken affair might convince the Host to install the upgraded Sanctuary Spell; see 3.03, "That Old Gang of Mine."]

THE LIBRARY The Host suggests Wesley won't find any mention of the Drokken in his books. [Probably true, although 4.20, "A New World" proves that Earth texts sometimes contain knowledge of extra-dimensional beings. Yet the Host is probably correct in this case, as Wes hasn't heard of a "Drokken."]

DEMONOLOGY *The Deathwok Clan (of Pylea):* Landok can "channel his mind" to follow the Drokken's "waves of hostility" – this is evidently a different application of the Host's power to "read" people through singing. Refining this talent requires training. The Host says he's considered a "freak" because of how he uses his ability.

• *Drokken:* Piercing a Drokken with a thromite-dipped weapon will kill the beast, but thromite doesn't exist on Earth. Drokkens become stronger after feasting on flesh, and can eat lit flares with no trouble, but prove mortal in ordinary combat.

MAGIC *Fred's Portal-Opening Book:* An aged, apparently leather-bound volume with the word "SCRSQWRN" on the title page and the word "LBMCTFRGHJC" above it in red lettering. Cordelia opens a portal by reading the phrase: "Krv drpglr pwlz chkwrt strplmt dwghzn prqlrzn lffrmtplzt." ["Through the Looking Glass" further explains how this all works.] The book remains behind on Earth after creating a dimensional portal to Pylea. [For reasons explained next episode. It's never established how the book came to reside in the library in the first place, although "Supersymmetry" performs some gut-contorting retcon to try to account for this.]

BEST LINE Gunn, rounding on Rondell after George's death: "You should have waited for me." Rondell's sobering response: "We've been waiting on you for months, bro."

THINGS THAT DON'T MAKE SENSE Common sense would seem to dictate that Lorne and Landok might have told everyone *before* rushing into battle with the Drokken, "By the way, don't allow a single bite or you're horsemeat." (It's just possible that the Drokken's bite only affects Pyleans, but there's no evidence for this on screen.)

Only an error in light of the next three episodes: Landok hails from a society in which humans are dubbed "cows" and function as slaves, yet he doesn't at all question why Lorne regards such "livestock" as his dearest friends and colleagues. Oh, and Wesley should really know the danger of reading mystic texts aloud, yet he lets Cordelia yap away with Fred's book anyway. Mind, the Host merely looks troubled about this, as opposed to more sensibly – oh, say – smacking the book out of Cordy's hands or shouting, "Stop! You *don't* wanna do that!"

IT'S REALLY ABOUT... As the title implies, it's about the desire to *belong* to somebody or some thing, even though the heroes' efforts along those lines aren't particularly successful. Thus, we're made to witness Wesley's awkward phone call to his father, Angel's unease in the role of the caring champion, Gunn's guilt for failing to support his gang – thereby contributing to George's death – and the Host's disdain for his homeland (although the latter doesn't truly gel until two episodes hence).

For Cordelia's part, this interestingly enough manifests in her performing in a suntan lotion commercial, in which the pig of a director illustrates how much Hollywood actresses must prostitute themselves to get ahead. In Hollywood, performers get judged by their height, weight, age and other characteristics entirely unrelated to their talent – as Cordelia well learns, particularly when she laments, "I just wanted... them to like me because I was *good*."

TONIGHT AT CARITAS The Host gives a rendition of Stevie Wonder's "Superstition," but the Drokken's arrival through a dimensional portal interrupts the proceedings.

CRITIQUE The big issue here: "Belonging" isn't so much a whole story as a massive prologue to what's left of the season. We'll argue next episode that the Pylean storyline holds a lot of merit, but if we're being fair, it probably could've benefited from being three episodes total as opposed to four. Even if you view "Belonging" with some charity, it's a story that smells of desperation, with a bunch of random elements – Cordelia's commercial, Gunn's associate dying and the street-hunt for the Drokken – thrown together in the vague hope of filling the prerequisite 45-odd minutes. Perhaps the producers *weren't* rewriting the script up until they had the bare minimum to complete shooting, but it certainly looks that way at times.

It's a pity, too, because it's not total chaff, and at least we learn something about the characters involved. Gunn's break from his gang begged examination some time ago, and it's time that Cordelia confronted the repugnant side of Hollywood work. Lorne is always fun when he's the nervous center of attention, and Wes gets that nifty little phone call to his dad. Yes, we'd have to admit that much of what's on display is worthy... it's just that too little of it bears connection to anything else, and cumulatively, it looks like it's simply making quota.

THE LORE The producers had tentatively planned on the season's final episodes focusing on the major storylines in play, but scheduling meant that Benz and Kane weren't available after Episode 18, which put paid to any notion of doing something with Darla or Lindsey. It would appear – although it's easy to overstate this point – that "Dead End" got written just to get Lindsey out of the way in time. The producers needed to create four more episodes, and Whedon found himself proposing: "Can they go to Oz? Can we just go to Oz? Can we go through the looking glass and just get insane?" Hence, the Pylean four-parter came about. (Whedon, *About.com*)

• The script extended the conversation with Fred's co-worker Claire, who mentioned that Fred wore an apple locket to represent Newton's apple.

• Andy Hallett claims the question of Lorne's sexuality – whether he's actually gay, or simply the gayest straight man in the world – was deliberately left ambiguous. "He calls Angel 'cupcakes', but he says that to everyone. At first it was to the gals, 'Hey sweetheart, baby, darling', and then it was to Angel... I know I wasn't that butch with it, but... Lorne's got a lot of love for everybody." (*SFX*, Aug. 2003)

When Did the Powers Intervene?

By this, we more specifically mean, "When Did the Powers Flex Their Magical Muscle?" There's any number of instances where you can – if you're in the mood – attribute underlying motives to the Powers' visions (3.01, "Heartthrob" being a prime example), but we're mostly talking about incidents where they largely wave their magic wand to fix a problem.

Now, the vast bulk of the evidence suggests that the Powers reside in a reality that's separate from our own, and typically operate on Earth via agents such as Angel. It seems likely that they can directly intervene only in extremely rare circumstances. In short, if they were capable of speaking with such clarity through a Darla-image (as occurs in 4.17, "Inside Out") all the time, they would surely do it more often. Let's also recognize that of the examples to follow, the series only confirms the Powers' involvement in "Inside Out" and 5.12, "You're Welcome." The rest is conjecture, but it makes a great deal of sense... sometimes even more than what's presented on screen.

• ***Buffy* 3.10, "Amends":** Giles concludes that the First Evil was responsible for Angel's return from Hell (*Buffy* 3.03, "Faith, Hope and Trick"), and the First itself proceeds to drive Angel insane, hoping to revert him to Angelus. Failing that, the First feels satisfied when Angel becomes suicidal and attempts to fry himself in the impending sunrise. Fortunately, an unprecedented snowfall occurs over Sunnydale, California, and saves Angel's life.

There's a giant plot-hole here, insofar as that if the First wanted Angel out of the way or dead, it could've simply left him to stew in Hell rather than freeing him. It seems more likely that Giles erroneously pins Angel's return on the First, that the First lies about it to keep Angel off-balance and that Angel's return actually owes to the Powers – who also arrange the helpful snowfall. Some reasonable fan speculation holds that the First, knowing Angel's return from Hell is inevitable, ambushes the man because it knows that a vampire with a soul could somehow prove its undoing (as occurs in *Buffy* 7.22, "Chosen"). This theory doesn't explain why the First then leaves Angel alone after he moves to L.A., but either way, the Powers must arrange the snowfall.

To quickly review: The First tries to get Angel to kill himself. The Powers send snow. They're nothing if not cryptic.

• ***Angel*** **1.01, "City Of":** All right, we'll bend the rules and look for a subtext in one of the Powers' visions here, because it's such a crucial turning point. Consider that... the Powers innocently assign Angel to protect Tina, a coffee shop worker, and this leads him to stumble across Cordelia – out of all the millions of people in L.A.! – and befriend her. It's almost impossible to think that the Powers know about Cordelia's fate or later role in the Jasmine conspiracy at this juncture, but they *might* have a vague sense of her future importance. After all, if they're carefully monitoring Angel, they're probably looking for the sort of people needed to put him on, well, the path of angels. In the main, regarding Cordelia's ability to keep Angel on the straight-and-narrow, their plan succeeds.

• **1.08, "I Will Remember You":** We'd independently theorized the Powers' behind-the-scenes involvement in this episode and thought ourselves quite clever for it, then became a little annoyed to read a Minear interview and find that the producers had, in fact, discussed this as a crux of the episode. Arrrrggggg... and it seemed like such an original notion, too. (And see **The Lore** under this story for more.)

To review: A Mohra demon "randomly" attacks Angel and Buffy, and its blood miraculously makes Angel human. The Powers' vision to Doyle brings human-Angel back into conflict with the creature (oh, what luck!), and Angel then learns from the Oracles – loosely portrayed as messengers from the Powers – that Buffy will die if he retains his humanity. In a dazzling display of self-sacrifice, Angel yields his happiness to become a vampire again.

It's clearly a top priority for the Powers to keep Angel pure in spirit, so it's hard to view this story as anything other than a covert attempt to gauge Angel's character. After all, a big issue starting with Season Two is the revelation that Angel will play a pivotal role in the Apocalypse, but nobody seems to know which side he'll fight for. As we never learn who sends the Mohra after Angel, it's probably down to the Powers.

• **2.16, "Epiphany":** Somehow, in some way, the invitation rule gets suspended so Angel can dash into Kate's apartment and save her life. Yet again, it's never explained, but it *must* owe to the Powers, who're desperate to get the wayward Angel back on track. Kate's death would certainly jeopardize Angel's recovery, especially as he'd blithely ignored her phone call, arguably a cry for help. Therefore, the Powers play a card reserved for rare circumstances, and – just this one time – void the invite rule.

• **2.19, "Belonging":** So let's think about this... the Powers direct Cordelia to retrieve Fred's portal-making book from the library, and she instinctually knows how to use it, as if the information were subconsciously encoded in her vision. When she *does* open a portal, the one being it coincidentally happens to disgorge, out of all the residents in Pylea, is Lorne's cousin. And then, when the heroes open a second portal – again based on Cordelia's oh-so-handy knowledge from the Powers – she *happens* to get mysteriously sucked into Pylea. Even though Wesley is standing right beside Cordy, and failed to even notice her go.

As this is never explained, assuming interference on the Powers' part makes sense of an otherwise baffling situation. By now, the Powers must know that the succession of their visionary has gone hopelessly awry, even if they don't know *what's* wrong, or know that Jasmine lies at the root of the problem. Additionally, most evidence suggests that the visions will kill any human who shoulders them for too long, so the Powers must become fairly desperate to get the visions out of Cordy's noggin. It seems entirely feasible, then, that the Powers direct Cordy to find Fred's portal book and then goose her – when the moment arrives – through the portal to Pylea.

If so, the Powers are probably hoping that Cordy will shag the half-demon Groo and pass the visions along to him, problem solved. Except that Cordelia resolutely decides to stick it out as the visionary, and, without knowing it, foils the Powers' plans. Combine this incident a couple more instances that we'll detail in **Did Jasmine Cause All This?**, and there's at least three – *three!* – points where Cordelia ironically could've botched Jasmine's master plan if only she'd stopped being so damned noble.

• **4.17, "Inside Out":** This one's a gimmie. As Jasmine nears the culmination of her plans, the Powers dispatch a messenger wearing Darla's aspect to speak with Connor. Again, one presumes the Powers can't deploy this sort of tactic too often, and see this story for more.

• **4.22, "Home":** We'll debate the pedigree of the *deus ex machina* amulet that the firm gives to Angel under this story, and although the evidence is mixed, but it's entirely possible that the Powers created the item. As the amulet facilitates the end of the First (in *Buffy* 7.22, "Chosen") and saves the entire Slayer line, it's feasible that the Powers crafted it with an eye toward ridding the world of that Evil twerp – the one that gave them trouble four years previous in "Amends."

• **5.12, "You're Welcome":** Another gimmie. The Powers send Cordelia to help Angel, although we'll wrangle in that story about whether it's the real Cordy or a carbon copy of her, *a la* the Darla look-alike in "Inside Out." Either way, the Powers must presume that Angel isn't going to return to his street champion routine any time soon, but hand him the knowledge needed to infiltrate and destroy the Circle of the Black Thorn. After this point, Angel is bereft of a visionary and contact with the Powers... but check out "You're Welcome," where we cheekily suggest who started serving as Cordelia's replacement in 2004 (oh, g'wan... you'll never guess).

2.20: "Over the Rainbow"

"Deep down, you've always known you'd have to take that one last trip back home."

Air Date: May 8, 2001; **Writer:** Mere Smith; **Director:** Fred Keller

SUMMARY Cordelia's friends prove unable to re-open a portal and pursue her, learning that the previous portal temporarily drained Caritas of its dimensional energy. With Lorne's help, the heroes locate another dimensional "hot spot," open a portal and venture through in Angel's car so they remain together in transit. Unfortunately, Fred's book – only designed to open portals *to* Pylea – remains behind.

Meanwhile, Cordy finds herself in Lorne's home dimension of Pylea, where humans work as slaves for various demon clans. Cordelia gets enslaved and briefly encounters Fred, who's been stranded in Pylea for five years and now gets arrested as a runaway slave. Amid the brouhaha, Cordelia gets a vision that convinces a religious order to perform tests and confirm whether or not she's "cursed."

The highly xenophobic Pyleans peg Lorne as a wanted traitor and round up Angel's group. Fortunately, the authorities recognize Cordelia as the Powers' visionary and enthrone her, per a prophecy, as their princess. Angel's group prepares for judgment, only to gaze up and see Cordy in full regalia. [*Continued next episode*]

FIRSTS AND LASTS Fred appears in the flesh, and Pylea gets named and seen for the first time. Quietly, it's the launch of Daniel Dae Kim as Gavin Park – he's just another odious Wolfram and Hart attorney at present, but will become Lilah's chief inter-office nemesis in Seasons Three and Four.

POINTS OF DISCUSSION ABOUT "Over the Rainbow":

1. The question of why everyone speaks English in Pylea proves vexing, as it's never explained, and it's doubly irritating that the heroes don't even *mention* the language issue.

Still, one explanation is that English-speaking humans somehow settled in Pylea, influenced the realm and later became the slave class. Migration between dimensions is certainly feasible in the *Angel*-verse, and a "human migration" scenario – albeit under Heaven-knows-what circumstances – seems more plausible than (say) the idea that Wolfram and Hart legitimized English in Pylea to make their paperwork more compatible with Earth.

Another possibility: That old sci-fi staple of a "translation device." It's probably more mystical than technological in this case, although it's got the same flaw as most sci-fi translators – namely, that certain colloquialisms don't translate. But if a translation system *is* in place, you've got to wonder who instigated it, and that leads us back to... the Powers-That-Be. Ah, yes. See **When Did the Powers Intervene?**

2. It seems rather too coincidental that the portal that carried Lorne to Earth and the one that transported Fred to Pylea (as cited last episode) both occurred "five years ago." This poses the question: Were the portals one and the same? Some critics favor the notion, but it seems unlikely. For a start, there's no tangible proof that the portals even work two-way, and it's odd that Fred's portal opens in the library, yet Lorne's dropped off in the location that became Caritas. It's a little more workable to suggest that Fred created Lorne's portal as part of her attempts to get back home, but the tight timeframe tends to rule it out. However you massage the numbers, it would require Fred to chalk out equations and open portals almost within mere days of her arrival – not impossible, but unlikely even for someone as bright as her, especially if she's enslaved at the time. No, there's only one means by which Lorne and Fred's transits are remotely connected, and so... see **Did Jasmine Cause All This?**

CHARACTER NOTES *Angel:* Refrains from judging Gunn's reasons for wanting to remain behind on Earth.

• *Cordelia:* Enslaved, sold to a Pylean female named Vakma and made to shovel a lot of demon horse shit. As princess, Cordelia is variously referred to as "General of the Ravenous Legion," "Eater of Our Enemy's Flesh," "Prelate of the Sacrificial Blood Rites" and "Sovereign Proconsul of Death." She's empowered to pass death sentences. On Earth, Cordy reads *Marie Claire*.

• *Wesley:* [See the rather telling **Best Line** for stuff Wes apparently keeps about his apartment.] He was formerly horrified by stories about the Tower of London.

• *Gunn:* Reluctant to travel to Pylea in light of George's death last episode, feeling he needs to better help his people, but ultimately joins Angel's crew. [See 3.03, "That Old Gang of Mine" for the outcome to Gunn's inner conflict.] Gunn mistakes the word "xenophobia" as meaning a fear of Xena: Warrior Princess, who he thinks is "kinda fly."

• *Winifred "Fred" Burkle:* Fugitive slave from Earth [see last episode] who's rather unbalanced. She sometimes thinks she was born in Pylea, and sometimes forgets the meaning of certain words and what it's like to laugh. She's here re-captured.

• *Lorne:* Five years ago, a portal spontaneously opened in the Pylean woods and transported Lorne into an abandoned building in L.A. He later built Caritas on that very spot [although we're never told how he acquired the funding] and discovered what "music" was by hearing Aretha Franklin for the first time. Prior to this, Lorne claims that he alone could hear music in Pylea, even if he couldn't identify it as such. Lorne deems sitting through a junior high production of *Cats* as preferable to returning to Pylea. His psychic friend Aggie claims that deep down, Lorne has always known he'd need to take "one last trip home." [There's no evidence of him ever returning after this, so she's probably correct.] Somewhat paradoxically, Aggie claims that Lorne's internal conflict is "clouding up his aura" [see 3.13, "Happy Anniversary"], yet also generating a "big flashing neon warning light."

Lorne likes chili and sometimes has gin and tonic with a little squeeze of lime, but implies that he can't get drunk. [If so, he either drinks for taste or perhaps alcohol blurs his perceptions just a bit, keeping his "soul-reading" ability at a manageable level in Caritas.]

Blix, Lorne's childhood friend, here calls him out as a betrayer, traitor and deserter. Lorne seems generally loathed because he "betrayed the teachings of his people" by abandoning his life-giver (his mother) and consorting with "cows." [There's no particular evidence of him consorting with cows in Pylea, but it's possible.] He's here sentenced to death for his offenses. Lorne doesn't know how the portal-opening book operates. In Pylea, he's acquainted with Constable Narwek.

• *Aggie:* Lorne's genuinely psychic friend, who makes up stuff for a psychic hotline. She can locate psychic "hot spots" and seems precognitive [because she comments, with some authority, that Angel's crew will never rescue Cordy unless Lorne accompanies them].

• *Gavin Park:* Claims the firm is interested in purchasing the Hyperion, as Angel's lease expires in six months [see 3.04, "Carpe Noctem" for where this leads].

PYLEA Populated by various demon clans, including the Deathwok and the Gathwok. Human slaves (called "cows" in Pylea) are punished with hand-held devices that jolt the slaves' collars. Such collars will destroy a slave's head if removed without permission [although Fred somehow disabled hers]. Pylea appears to use the barter system; market items include flib liquor, viper's milk, queeks, hefroot and spatulas. "Flehgnas" are a type of demon horse kept in stables. Xenophobia is fairly common in Pylea. A constabulary keeps order. Gin and tonics don't exist in Pylea; neither does music, supposedly.

THE LIBRARY Wes researches portals in his texts, and finds at least three references to iron or metal [see **Magic**].

ORGANIZATIONS *Angel Investigations:* The Hyperion mortgage is under "the company name" [yet the agency isn't incorporated, judging by 3.12, "Provider"].

• *The Covenant:* [Called the "Covenant of Trombli" next episode.] Pylean religious sect, composed of robed, red-skinned demons and led by a head priest named Silas [also not named until next episode]. He confirms Cordelia as being "cursed" (i.e. the Powers' visionary) by using some probing instruments [specified as hot pokers next episode, although they don't scar Cordy].

DEMONOLOGY *Vampires:* Pylean sunlight doesn't make Angel incinerate. [For reasons explained next episode; more vampire-friendly sunlight appears in 5.17, "Underneath."]

MAGIC *Fred's Portal-Opening Book:* Fails to travel with the heroes to Pylea, and last seen in a street outside a movie studio. [One hopes Angel's crew retrieved the book later, but it's never said.] Wesley speculates that the book remains on Earth because it's only designed to open portals *to* Pylea, meaning it'd be useless in Pylea itself.

• *Dimensional Portals:* Manifest at geographic "hot spots" flush with "psychic energy" – opening a portal can drain the hot spot, necessitating a recharge period. [Such a "recharge" appears to occur naturally, although it's unclear how. The term "psychic" implies that it's energized by the ambient emotions of persons/beings in the vicinity. This might explains why hot spots occur near high-traffic locations such as Caritas and the front of a movie studio, but not in the Foreign Language Section at Fred's library (last episode).]

Portal-travelers tend to arrive at different destinations in the target reality. A binding spell might counteract this, but could fuse the travelers together. Wesley correctly realizes that enclosing the group on four sides with metal – specifically, Angel's car – should keep everyone together during transport. [However, the Vigories of Odel Tal used portals for transport in "She" (1.13), without benefit of a Plymouth Convertible.]

BEST LINE Angel: "Who do we know that has handcuffs?" Wesley, brightening: "Well, I... [stops]... wouldn't know."

THINGS THAT DON'T MAKE SENSE When the assembled Pylean crowd comes to suspect that Cordelia is "cursed," they start shouting, then wave pitchforks and swords in her face. Yet we later learn that Cordy's being "cursed" – meaning the Powers' visionary – is a *good* thing that makes them enthrone her as royalty, so what was all the rowdiness about then? Is it a long-held Pylean tradition to greet the potential arrival of a monarch by getting unruly, then waving pitchforks and swords in her face?

In looking for a dimensional "hot spot," the heroes never consider trying the location where the Vigories of Oden Tal opened a portal in "She," which likely hasn't seen use in over a year. Nor do they consider re-trying the library room from last episode, as two portals recently opened in Caritas, but only *one* recently manifested at that location. (Perhaps the heroes reject both possibilities off screen, as it'd be damn hard to wedge Angel's car into either location.) Plus, given the unpredictability of dimensional portals, the heroes get awfully lucky to land within walking distance of Cordelia's location – rather, say, than hundreds or even thousands of miles away. Even presuming that Pylea is smaller than – for instance – the United States or Russia, it's comparatively as if they've luckily arrived in the right part of Manchester as opposed to virtually anywhere in the United Kingdom.

J. August Richards amends a line of dialogue from "Wes said the trip [to Pylea] might be one way" to "Wes said the trip *was* one way," which Wesley couldn't have known and wouldn't have said. Meanwhile, Angel leaves Gunn with certain instructions so that "someone on this side has the details" in case his group never returns from Pylea. But there's apparently nobody left with all the particulars once Gunn changes his mind and joins the expedition.

Oh, and if the Pyleans call humans "cows," then what do they call their cows?

POP CULTURE Lorne on his psychic friend Aggie: "She was doing Skybar way before Brad [Pitt] and Jennifer [Aniston]." The Skybar is a celebrity watering hole, located at 8440 W Sunset Boulevard in West Hollywood. (Lorne himself ventures there in 5.13, "Why We Fight.")

IN RETROSPECT Gunn tells Angel, referring to a rambunctious Pylean mob: "I take the twenty on the left, you take the fifty on the right." In the series finale, he'll considerably up the tally.

CRITIQUE Now we're getting somewhere, although it's still drawn out – the first half of the episode seems muddled as the heroes faff about the place, but matters pick up considerably once they get to Pylea. The cream of the crop doesn't arrive until the two episodes to follow, but we're undeniably making progress.

Reviewing the Pylean stories always proves interesting, though, because we're so far from *Angel*'s norm. A certain type of viewer who expects the gritty urban fantasy that *Angel* usually pulls off will wonder what the hell's going on, and potentially tune out. So we sympathize with anyone feeling disappointed by all this, but...

For the record, we don't mind the shift of locale and think the Pylean material overall works wonderfully. Full points for Lorne looking *really* out of place in his homeland, for a good smattering of jokes, and for the way this storyline starts to adeptly shift between whimsy and being deadly serious. Yes, it's all a bit rough, but let's give props to Mutant Enemy for running this experiment and move on...

THE LORE Acker had studied ballet for 14 years (inevitably, we'll revisit this in 3.13, "Waiting in the Wings"), and she'd worked as a model in Japan. She'd also been trained in all sorts of stage combat, including scenes with hand-to-hand combat, rapiers, daggers and quarterstaffs. As *Angel* continued, she kept encouraging the producers to let her fight with a broadsword, insisting she could hold her own. Conversely, she increasingly seemed accident-prone on the set, even managing to get hit in the face by sword fights that didn't involve her. On one occasion, a huge metal bar fell on her head – she told everyone she was fine, and that no, it didn't hurt at all, before walking off-set to bawl. (*FHM*, Aug. 2003)

• Daniel Dae Kim (Gavin Park) did a wealth of bit parts prior to *Angel*, although he'd also been featured as Lt. John Matheson on the short-lived *Babylon 5* spin-off *Crusade*. *Angel* helped his career, and he later held recurring roles on *Enterprise*, *E.R.* and *24*, but true stardom didn't arrive until he started playing Jin Kwon on *Lost*. Such is his current success that *USA Today* headlined the story "Kim surfaces as sex symbol on *Lost*" (March 21, 2006) and *People* named him one of the sexiest men alive in 2005. Casual *Lost* viewers might find it interesting that Kim's character only speaks Korean, but Kim himself stopped speaking it after age six and forgot almost everything about it – he's been getting tutored for the role.

• The Pylean angle left composer Robert J. Kral in the odd position of scoring music for a world literally without it. (Kral, *The Bronze*, May 8, 2001) He managed to have fun with Fred's theme even though it only appeared in the Pylean episodes – Minear apparently loved it, but Greenwalt wasn't so keen once the action moved back to Earth. ("37 Questions with Robert J. Kral," *Miracles TV*)

• Smith pondered making "goats," not "cows," the Pylean term for humans, but changed her mind to avoid seeming repetitive after the goat scene in 2.15, "Reprise." (Smith, *The Bronze*, May 8, 2001)

• Persia White (Aggie Belfleur) had previously appeared as Cordelia's groupie/friend Aura in the very first *Buffy* episode – Aura's the one who screams as a body topples out of her locker, although she's not named on screen. Susan Blommaert (Vakma) frequently plays judges on the likes of *Law and Order*, *Ally McBeal*, *The Practice* and *Family Law*, but her credit for *The X-Files* rather uniquely reads "Mrs. Phyllis H. Paddock/Satan." William Newman (Old Demon Man) played the villainous Cape on Ben Edlund's *The Tick*.

2.21: "Through the Looking Glass"

"Everyone is very anxious for her majesty to com-shuk *with the Groosalugg."*

Air Date: May 15, 2001; **Writer/Director:** Tim Minear

SUMMARY Cordelia orders her friends' release, but the Covenant of Trombli, a religious order with sway in the kingdom, plots to replace her with someone more malleable. Lorne and Angel query Lorne's family about possible locations for a dimensional hot spot, but Lorne's clan rebukes him while adorning Angel as a champion who slew a Drokken (2.19, "Belonging").

Unfortunately, Angel refuses the "honor" of decapitating Fred as a runaway slave, fleeing with her while Lorne gets arrested for helping them. Angel calls upon his vampire aspect to fend off some pursuers, but Pylea's physics make his vampire demon overly dominant, turning him into a monster. Fred lures Demon-Angel back to her cave, whereupon he gazes into a pool of water and – horrified at his own reflection – returns to normal.

At the palace, Cordelia learns that she's expected to *com-shuk* (i.e. mate) with a "Groosalugg." Wes and Gunn escape, but human rebels mistake them for agents of the regime and capture them. Cordelia brightens when the Grooslaugg turns out to be a tall, handsome champion who pledges loyalty to her, but the Covenant "reminds" Cordelia that she's a figurehead after she pardons Lorne... by having Lorne decapitated, and his head delivered to Cordy on a platter. [*Continued next episode*]

FIRSTS AND LASTS Fred tells Angel: "Handsome man, saved me from the monsters," and it'll become a recurring phrase for her. First appearance of the Groosalugg (a.k.a. "Groo"), and the first hard evidence – worryingly – that Wolfram and Hart operates in dimensions beyond Earth's reality. It's also the first and only time on either *Angel* or *Buffy* that we see a vampire demon's true image, and it ain't pretty.

Whedon logs his first (and only, despite what some people claim about 5.21, "Power Play") *Angel* appearance as Lorne's dancing brother Numfar.

POINTS OF DISCUSSION ABOUT "Through the Looking Glass":

1. Wesley's first-ever assessment of Fred: "That strange, wild girl saved us."

2. It's usually taken that Fred was enslaved after arriving in Pylea, then escaped. But if that's the case, it's odd that she somehow held onto her glasses and California driver's license throughout that ordeal, and it's never mentioned how she de-activated her slave collar. Was Fred actually collared as a slave (as stories such as 4.05, "Supersymmetry" appear to confirm), or did she simply spend five years on the run, eating berries and desperately trying to make faux tacos from whatever was at hand? It's probably the former, but given Fred's own murky memories – by the time she meets Cordy, she's confused on whether she was even *born* on Earth – we'll probably never know for certain.

3. Another larger issue at play: Wesley, Gunn and Cordelia discover that the Covenant's texts (see **The Library**) come adorned with the markings of a wolf, a ram and a hart. We're clearly supposed to sense Wolfram and Hart's influence, but we're annoyingly left dangling as to what this weighty reveal means. After all, there's no evidence that the Covenant answers to the firm. Nor does it seem that the firm runs an actual "office" in Pylea (perhaps because they deem the Pyleans as too Medieval, if nothing else). True, it's telling proof that the Senior Partners hold sway of some degree in other dimensions, but we're left high and dry beyond that point.

4. Translation notes: *Angel* weighs in with "com-shuk," the Pylean term for "to copulate/have sex with," and a term that accordingly joins the pantheon of sci-fi substitutes for the "f-word." By now, that group includes *frak* (the new *Battlestar Galactica*), *frell* (*Farscape*), *frinx* (*Star Trek: Deep Space Nine*) and even *ch'rowl* (if you're into Larry Niven's *Known Space* series). There isn't much danger of *com-shuk* falling into common usage among mainstream fandom, but at least Cordelia gets some hysterical dialogue along the lines of, "Do I put out some kind of *com-shuk* me vibe?"

CHARACTER NOTES *Angel:* On Pylea affecting Angel's vampire attributes, see **Demonology**. Seeing his reflection makes Angel concerned about his festive hairstyle. ("Why didn't anybody tell me about this?")

• *Cordelia:* Her father's trouble with the IRS (*Buffy* Season Three) resulted in her trust fund being drained. Cordy off-handedly claims "It's been a long time since I had a really good *com-shuk*" [possibly true, presuming she hasn't been with anyone since 1.12, "Expecting"].

• *Wesley:* Keeps a wallet photo of him, Cordelia and Angel [a bigger version appears among Cordy's possessions in "Tomorrow" (3.22), "Slouching Toward Bethlehem" (4.04) and "Shiny Happy People" (4.18)].

• *Gunn:* First to identify *com-shuk* as something dirty.

• *Fred:* Sometimes thinks of her time on Earth as a dream, and similarly attributes to "a dream" the source of the mathematical formulae/theorems she's taken to scrawling in chalk all over the wall of her cave. Fred displays considerable bravery in luring Demon-Angel back to her home. [She must be eating the local wildlife, as she's got a handy supply of blood onhand to entice him.] She's never visited the Pylean palace.

Fred still possesses her Earth glasses and California driver's license. [She's lucky, actually, that her eyeglass prescription evidently hasn't changed in the last five years. But then, Fred gets around decently well without her glasses, so her eyesight can't be *that* awful.] Her driver's license identifies her as 5'6" [compare with "Belonging"], 114 lbs, with a corrective lenses restriction. [The expiration date fuzzily reads something like March 1, 1996 – if so, Fred's license expired about two months before she disappeared on May 7, 1996, the silly girl.]

- *Lorne:* His grandmother has a glass eye.
- *Lorne's Mother:* Unnamed, hulking and rather intimidating individual who's so ashamed of her son that she goes out to thorny, parched hill territory every morning before breakfast, beats her breast and curses the loins that gave birth to "such a cretinous boy-child." [Compare with the image-ripping and swine feeding in "Belonging."] She's decided that she and Lorne's father "ate the wrong son."
- *Landok:* Has recovered after his poisoning ["Belonging"].
- *Numfar:* Lorne's brother, who performed the "Dance of Joy" for three months after Lorne went missing. He can also dance the "Dance of Honor."
- *The Groosalugg (a.k.a. "Groo"):* Half-demon warrior with a human heart. Groo says his human aspect became more apparent as he matured [so he was born with demon characteristics], and people regarded him as little more than an animal. The Covenant examined Groo and confirmed that he was "polluted" by human blood. He was cast out from his village and "life givers" [parents] and sought to end his suffering by entering contests of daring. Yet he vanquished flame beasts and Drokken alike, earning the title "Groosalugg," which means "the brave and undefeated."

Groo recently vanquished the [tentacled, says the script] "Mogfan beast" that bedeviled the scum pits of Ur. A horned, lumbering and furry luggage-carrier accompanies him.

PYLEA Cordelia considers outlawing polyester in Pylea, even though it doesn't exist there yet.

Lorne claims that the Covenant of Trombli has been running the kingdom "for the last several millennia." The Powers-That-Be are known and acknowledged in Pylea; a prophecy talks of a messiah – a being of "pure sight" – who's a direct link to the Powers and will "restore the monarchy." Silas, the Covenant leader, seems inclined to have Cordelia killed after the *com-shuk* with Groo [and without evident fear of retribution from the Powers].

Nearby Pyleans suffer pain when Lorne sings "Stop! In the Name of Love." [This undoubtedly occurs because Pylea lacks music ("Belonging"), making it totally foreign to their physiognomies. Famously, Lorne's mother cries, "It burns!", at this assault.] A "bach-nal" is a public execution [for recaptured slaves, certainly, or perhaps any criminal warranting death]. The offender gets beheaded with a *crebbil* (an axe).

It's strongly implied that Pyleans sometimes *eat* humans in addition to using them as slaves. Still, warrior culture holds such importance that even a "cow" (Angel) or "half-cow" (Groo) can elevate themselves to champion status – usually by killing a formidable demon. Similarly, Cordelia's enthronement puts her above being a simple cow – to the point that the Pyleans expect she'll dine on the flesh of her own kind. Horses exist in Pylea, as do egg-gestating "hosts." Pylea has one moon.

[It's never stated how the rebels, like Fred, got their slave collars off without dying in the process. It's possible that some humans exist in the wild in Pylea – notice how one resident nabbed Cordelia last episode, as if capturing random humans like animals and selling them wasn't all that unusual.]

THE LIBRARY Wesley's familiar with certain demonic languages that resemble the words in the Covenant's sacred texts. One text comes in three volumes written in "Trionic," meaning the reader starts in one volume, picks up in the second one and finishes in the third. The rhythm of the sentence structure clues the reader on when to leap from book to book to book. [See **Organizations**, and check out **Points of Discussion** in 3.14, "Couplet" to see where one such text next shows up.]

ORGANIZATIONS *Wolfram and Hart:* Wesley says that a "hart," meaning a male red deer, and here visually associated with the firm, is often associated with rural mysticism.

- *The Powers-That-Be:* Vision-trauma sometimes makes Cordelia bleed a little from her ears.

DEMONOLOGY *Vampires:* Wesley theorizes that Pylea's physical laws have thrown Angel's aspects out of their normal balance. His human self has dominance when he arrives in Pylea, which explains why the Pylean suns didn't scorch him [last episode], and why he can see his reflection. [Yet he doesn't become fully human, as with "I Will Remember You" (1.08), as he would surely have noticed if – say – his heart were beating again.] Angel seems to enter Fred's cave without an invite. [Fred might've invited him off screen, or – more likely – the dominance of Angel's human self suspends the invite rule.]

Calling upon his vampire self allows Angel's feral vampire demon to seize control. Demon-Angel seems stronger and quicker than Angel himself. The demon aspect goes dormant upon glimpsing itself in a pool of water [see **Why Don't Vampires Cast Reflections?** for more].

• *The Deathwok Clan:* Lorne's mother is bearded and rather husky. [Perhaps Deathwok Clan females, not the males, have beards? Consider that there's never any hint that Lorne needs to shave.] The Deathwok Clan's "Dance of Honor" and "Dance of Joy"... no, words aren't sufficient.

BEST LINE The cave-dwelling, fugitive Fred, upon hearing that Cordelia was enthroned as princess: "Oh. When I got here they... they didn't do that."

THINGS THAT DON'T MAKE SENSE Last episode, the Host expressed confusion and concern regarding talk of the Covenant and Cordelia's being "cursed." Yet here, when the plot requires more exposition, he spontaneously unloads all sorts of details about the Covenant, the prophecy regarding the "Cursed One," and so forth. Mind, if Lorne *is* as acquainted with the prophecy, why hasn't it ever occurred to him that Cordelia might fit the bill?

Again, understanding that we try to ignore visual goofs, the scene where Demon-Angel jumps his pursuers holds two inescapable flaws. First, when Demon-Angel rips the guard's leg off, it somehow reappears on the man's body in a long shot (see **The Lore**). Less obviously, when Demon-Angel makes his initial leap through the air – and you gotta pause your DVD player here – you'll note a production crew member in a blue shirt and sunglasses in the bottom right-hand corner. Heaven knows whether the man's helping to propel "Angel" through the air, scurrying for cover or something else entirely.

The Covenant members express doubt that Cordelia will survive her coupling with the Groosalugg, which seems strange, as they long ago examined Groo and surely concluded – as Groo clearly knows – that he's anatomically compatible with humans. How do Wes and company learn the details of the castle's sewer layout? (Perhaps Cordelia asked a servant, although getting a detailed knowledge of the sewer workings would make for an amusing conversation.) And how do Gunn and Wesley get the sewer muck off them after escaping from the castle? Do they bathe in a convenient stream? Oh, and Wesley's plan to navigate by the Pylean suns isn't flawed just because – as Gunn points out – there's two of them. It's also awry because there's no evidence that either sun rises in the East and sets in the West, as on Earth.

Cordelia has been enthroned at most for a day or so, and we never see photographs or coinage bearing her image. Yet the rebels already know – when they glance at Wesley's wallet photo – what Cordelia looks like. And is it really feasible that Fred's been hiding within walking distance of a Pylean settlement for years, yet has never been discovered? Because Silas' captain finds her cave easily enough next episode.

POP CULTURE *The Groosalugg.* Almost certainly derivative from the comic book *Groo the Wanderer* drawn by Sergio Aragones, featuring a similarly cuddly warrior who wreaks havoc despite his best intentions.

IT'S REALLY ABOUT... To some degree, it's the episode that puts the homosexual subtext regarding Lorne front and center. He's previously displayed anxiety about his homeland, but now it becomes painfully obvious that he's simply ill-suited for life in Pylea. Notice how when he returns home, the family is having an impromptu wrestling match in their front yard and *his mother* is manhandling an opponent as if he were a pillow. It's impossible to imagine Lorne wanting to do the same – not that there's anything wrong with that.

Otherwise, much of what remains is a reversal/reflection of everyone's status on Earth, particularly as seen in "Belonging." In that story, Cordelia was cheaply degraded while wearing a cloth bikini; here, she's exalted while donning a chain-mail one. Adoring crowds here praise the normally conflicted Angel for butchering his enemies and leaving them to suffer. Lorne was previously mistaken as a performer who reads to children, but Angel here gets that privilege. It's as if the title serves as a mandate to view everyone in a mirror.

CRITIQUE Finally, we're shifting into high gear. Given the luxury of opening the story in Pylea, "Through the Looking Glass" goes about its business with great style, flipping between comedy and dead seriousness in a fantasy locale. The sets and costumes deserve a particular shout-out, considering they couldn't have been cheap, and are the sort of endeavor that'll become unthinkable in the budget-crunched Season Five. But more importantly, the story's just loads of well-polished fun, loaded with stunning shots such as a bedraggled Fred holding up a fistful of blood to get demon-Angel's attention. In short, it's lovingly geared to be interesting, with all sorts of side-diversions such as Lorne's brief visit home. And who can possibly bitch about that sequence – or indeed the story as a whole – as it gives us the fantastic sight of Whedon dancing about like a lunatic?

THE LORE The opening scene entailed the five lead characters wandering about the same room; Minear felt that trying to make this feel organic actually proved harder than coordinating the mass droves of rioting Chinese peasants in 2.07, "Darla." (*BBC Cult*, Aug. 23, 2001)

• A one-legged stuntman – who'd apparently lost his other limb as a teenager, and gone into stunt work for just this sort of occasion – was used for the "Demon-Angel" attack. The final effect proved quite macabre, featuring a chunk of gore dangling off the prosthetic leg that got "ripped" away, and the network censors objected to a bloody stump flailing so prominently in front of the camera. Minear tried to comply and redid the editing, which helps to explain why the outdoor scuffle seems off (see **Things That Don't Make Sense**). Even then, he worried they'd strike out the bits he *did* leave – the network had threatened just that on 2.15, "Reprise" – but it appears to have broadcast without further cuts.

• Minear deemed the Demon-Angel "a bit cheesy" and tried to achieve a sort of feral assault – as opposed to the show's usual Kung-Fu fights – with that weird time-effect seen at the start of the attack. It's not "slo-mo" as such, but rather your standard 24 frames per second, shot with a 45-degree shutter setting (as opposed to the normal 180). The same effect appears in *Saving Private Ryan* and *Gladiator*. In this way, Minear later said, "the action appears violent, when in essence all the actors are doing is rolling around a bit." (Minear, *alt.tv.angel,* May 19, 2001)

• Whedon concocted Numfar's dances on his own and made the fatal mistake of impulsively demonstrating them in a production meeting. A tickled Minear couldn't imagine trusting the dance to anyone else, and convinced Whedon to enact the performance himself. (Minear, *The Bronze*, May 15, 2001) Whedon tried being discreet about all this, having his make-up done in a separate trailer. Hallett, failing to realize Minear's scheme, felt bewildered as to who the hell this "Numfar" fellow was that warranted such special attention. He became even more baffled upon witnessing Numfar's deliberately ludicrous dance, thinking him total trash. Boreanaz knew the truth, however, and – a bit to Whedon's annoyance later – couldn't resist telling Hallett. (Gill, *tve. co.il*) Basically nobody else deduced Numfar's identity until Whedon sat in Minear's chair and Minear said nothing – the reason being that the "dancing demon" was his boss.

• About three weeks before this story broadcast, Whedon posted: "Yes, I will make my on-screen debut in Angel 21. No, I will not speak, and no, you will not see my face. But I will make my presence known! Just remember my watchword: Dignity. Always dignity." (*The Bronze*, April 24, 2001)

• Here's Minear, answering a string of questions about the Pylean arc on *alt.tv.angel* (May 19, 2001):

Q: "Why didn't Angel leave any phone messages for the Scoobies before going through the portal?" Minear's answer: "They didn't have the phone number for UPN."

Q: "Why didn't they put up the top to protect Angel from the sun?" A: "They hate him."

Q: "Why didn't the Fangsters disguise themselves as native Pyleans? Why didn't Lorne dress in the same clothes he was wearing when he first arrived on Earth?" A: "Because then they wouldn't have stood out like sore thumbs."

Q: "Why does Cordelia want to outlaw polyester?" A: "It doesn't breathe."

Why Don't Vampires Cast Reflections?

Let's dispense with this one quickly, shall we? *Angel* commentators generally spend a great deal of time citing every instance of incidental "vampire reflections," such as Angel's finger showing up on the Mayor's name plate in *Buffy* Season Three, vampires showing up on cameras and videotape recorders (which operate thanks to reflective devices), etc. We've generally chosen to ignore such incidental castings, and "Through the Looking Glass" provides an explanation as to why.

Simply put, Angel's vampire demon achieves dominance while he's in Pylea, but it goes dormant upon gazing upon itself in a pool of water. The conclusion that readily springs to mind is that vampire demons can't stand the sight of themselves, and their inability to show up in mirrors results from a subconscious "blanking" of the host body's reflection. Ergo, incidental castings (of fingers, whatever) that the vampire doesn't even know about should still occur, and video-recordings and photographs (as 2.02, "Are You Now or Have You Ever Been?") are perfectly feasible.

Indeed, it's for this reason that Angel was scripted to say in "Eternity" (1.17), with regards to vampire reflections: "It's not about physics, it's metaphysics." It's a pity that line got struck, or there would be little to debate. Nonetheless, his comment fits with the vast bulk of the evidence.

2.22: "There's No Place Like Plrtz Glrb"

"... and if all thy slaves offend thee, thou shalt smite them down, too, even unto every last one in the land."

Air Date: May 22, 2001; **Writer/Director:** David Greenwalt

SUMMARY Cordy freaks when Lorne's severed head calmly explains that his species can survive decapitation, so long as their bodies aren't mutilated. The Groosalugg helpfully retrieves Lorne's body, allowing Lorne's family to reattach his noggin.

Meanwhile, Silas, the Covenant leader, dispatches soldiers to kill the remainder of Cordelia's companions. The soldiers unsuccessfully try to butcher Wesley and Gunn, convincing the rebels to accept the duo as allies. Wesley becomes the group's leader, disturbed to learn that Silas possesses a fail-safe device capable of decapitating Pylea's entire slave population – via their slave collars – at the push of a button. Angel agrees to engage the Groosalugg in combat while Wesley's rebels overrun the castle. Silas as expected goes for his control device, but Cordelia kills him, restoring order.

Cordelia outlaws slavery and appoints Groo to rule in her absence. Using the Covenant's texts, the heroes open a portal back to Caritas and joyously return to the Hyperion – only to find Willow there, come to inform Angel that Buffy died in battle (in *Buffy* 5.22, "The Gift").

FIRSTS AND LASTS Final appearance of Pylea and most of its fixtures – including Lorne's mother and cousin Landok – but first mention of Fred's taco obsession.

POINT OF DISCUSSION ABOUT "There's No Place Like Plrtz Glrb":

1. It's the end of the story arc, which leaves us with little to say that hasn't been discussed before. So let's mention a fun little visual goof (no pausing of your DVD player required) rather than consign it to Things That Don't Make Sense: During the scene where Cordelia chats with her servant about the mutilation chamber, watch the door in the upper right-hand corner. It seems to close as the servant enters, but during their conversation, it's closed... then it's open... then it's closed... then it's open... then it's closed again. It's like watching Han Solo's disappearing/reappearing vest during the carbonite-freeze scene in *The Empire Strikes Back*, only with a door.

CHARACTER NOTES *Angel:* Doesn't snore, but wails while sleeping in Fred's cave. As with 2.13, "Happy Anniversary," he again claims he fired his crew [2.10, "Reunion"] because he didn't want them tainted by the darkness consuming him. As opposed to last episode, he better controls his vampire aspect.

• *Cordelia:* Stubbornly unwilling to yield her visionary power to Groo. [See **When Did the Powers Intervene?** for the consequences of this.] She now deems the visions "an honor" [so she's light-years beyond the views she expressed in 1.02, "Lonely Hearts"].

Cordelia claims she "loves" Groo, yet she leaves him behind in Pylea easily enough. The pair of them were slated for marriage, in addition to the much-anticipated *com-shuk*.

• *Wesley:* Recognizes that his battleplan will entail some of the rebels dying, but tells Gunn: "You try not to get anybody killed, you wind up getting everybody killed." Wes displays proficiency with swords [seen again in 3.13, "Waiting in the Wings"] and a good understanding of guerilla warfare.

• *Gunn:* Also fares well with a sword, and recognizes that "sayin' people are free don't make 'em free."

• *Fred:* Considers herself squirrelly and a bit of a freak. She sometimes shrieks just to "let it out." Much of her technobabble verges on the incomprehensible. She's taco-obsessed, but has yet to master her goal of making an enchilada from tree bark, and sometimes forgets how things tasted on Earth. She knows how to prepare a challenge torch, and the words spoken at such an event. [Judging by the contents of her cave, she's also learned to stitch.]

Fred's attempts to crack inter-dimensional physics generated – unbeknownst to her – several portals at various locations. [This presumably accounts for the Drokken appearing in Caritas in 2.19, "Becoming" – but again, see **When Did the Powers Intervene?** Angel also attributes the library portal in "Becoming" to Fred, even though it's surely more to do with Cordelia reading from the portal-opening book.]

• *Lorne:* Wears a French Viscose suit. He confirms Aggie's assessment [2.20, "Over the Rainbow"] that he needed to return to home one last time to realize that, well, he quite simply doesn't belong there.

• *Groo:* Betrays some vows to the Covenant by saving Lorne on Cordelia's behalf. He obviously loves Cordelia a great deal. Groo feels pain, but burns his hand in the challenge to prove his resolve. He appears stronger than Angel's human aspect, but can't best Demon-Angel's raw savagery. [He returns in "Waiting in the Wings."]

• *Lorne's Mother:* Thanks to Lorne's role in the freeing Pylea's slaves, she's labeled "Mother of the Vile Excrement" at the Hall of Drink and Chance. Her family keeps a maggot pile and lice heap, for some reason. She ends this story wishing Lorne would "burn in Tarkna!"...

PYLEA ... "Tarkna" being the Pylean version of Hell.

As champion of the realm, Groo cannot refuse a challenge and his honor largely reflects that of the kingdom. As monarch, Cordelia would shame the kingdom by entering the castle's mutilation chamber [but she secretly does so anyway]. Fred's diet partly consists of crug-grain and thistles (which she loosely deems "oatmeal"), flavored with lots of Kalla berries. Pyleans seem to thrive on mutilation because they lack for entertainment.

ORGANIZATIONS *The Powers-That-Be:* Groo flat-out confirms that humans aren't meant to bear the Powers' visions [as suspected in 2.18, "Dead End"]. The Powers try to warn Cordelia about Groo dueling with Demon-Angel [but she fails to recognize the transformed Angel, so events proceed]. The vision is clearly prophetic.

• *Caritas:* Somewhat ransacked by the heroes' return to Earth, particularly when Angel's car plows through the bar. [Lorne evidently repairs the damage over the summer break, but see 3.03, "That Old Gang of Mine."]

THE LIBRARY For all we're told, Angel's crew keeps the Covenant's portal-making books [see **Magic**]. [Fred's book remained behind in 2.20, "Over the Rainbow," but the Covenant's texts are presumably more versatile.]

DEMONOLOGY *Van-Tals:* Evidently the Pylean equivalent of vampires, acknowledged as "drinkers of blood." The traditional methods of fire, beheading and staking with a wooden spear dispatch such creatures. [Despite the similarities, Van-

Tals and Earth vampires don't necessarily belong to the same species. *Buffy* 1.02, "The Harvest" and 7.21, "End of Days" implies that the progenitor of the vampire line died on Earth, and therefore didn't spread the vampire taint to other dimensions. It's possible, however, that a vampire or two accompanied some humans who settled in Pylea, and Silas' assertion that Van-Tals have hearts in their chests suggests that Van-Tals hail from humanity.]

• *Pyleans:* Silas' captain implies that his race – and possibly the Covenant's species too – has their hearts in their rumps. [Lorne confirms that his heart's lodged in his left butt cheek in 3.05, "Fredless," so this also applies to the Deathwok Clan if not all demons in Pylea.]

• *The Deathwok Clan:* Lorne tells his mother: "See you in a millennia or three." [Taken literally, it implies a long lifespan for the Deathwok Clan. No wonder Pylean society is so rigid.] Lorne can still talk while decapitated [which raises some questions about the Clan's vocal chords]. Deathwok Clan members don't have five toes. Landok is forbidden to fight while performing a sacred duty such as taking Lorne's head home.

MAGIC *Dimensional Portals:* Fred realizes that the words contained in portal-opening texts are "consonant representations of a mathematical transfiguration formula." Her portal-technobabble includes mention of the theorist Lutzbalm, who was laughed off the stage in Zurig, 1989. [Lutzbalm appears to have no real-world equivalent, but the name is coincidentally similar to Mark Lutz, who plays Groo.]

• *Silas' Cow-Killing Device:* Amounts to a panel inset with jeweled controls in the shape of a hand. [Magic must power the device, as Pylea doesn't seem to possess technology as we know it.] Cordelia destroys the contraption.

BEST LINE Not so much a Best Line as a Best Rant, as servants offer to dispose of Lorne's "filthy head" and Cordelia improvises: "I like the filthy head. That is, ah... I want to defile it more. I just keep it... to spit upon, and, and, and when I grow tired of that, I will make it into... a planter. A traitor planter for *all* to see... Or maybe a candy dish."

THINGS THAT DON'T MAKE SENSE Well to start, we might question Silas' motives, in that he desires to obliterate each and every slave in Pylea on the grounds that a rebel victory would "destroy their way of life." Except that... wouldn't eradicating the entire slave class *also* irrevocably change the fabric of Pylean society? For that matter, Silas is portrayed as someone who's unceasingly callous regarding the enslaved humans, yet he's polite enough, after beheading a human informant, to tell a slave: "*Please* clean that up."

Groo seems remarkably well-informed that Lorne has just been beheaded, considering nobody had any particular reason to drop him a hint. Conversely, Silas and friends seem short-sighted – presuming they know about the Deathwok Clan's ability to survive decapitation – to not double-check that Lorne has well and truly kicked the bucket before presenting Cordy with his head. Their soldiers are also dense enough to swoop in on the rebel camp, hoping to kill Wesley and Gunn, when the rebels were in the process of executing the Earthers anyway. Surely, it'd be smarter to stand back, chug a pint of flib liquor and let them get on with it? Also, the admittedly cool fight scene where Wesley and Gunn use their stocks to bash their opponents seems faintly ludicrous... it's hard to see how someone of human strength could even stand in such heavy lumber for long, let alone heft it around as a weapon without toppling over.

The rebel who fails to spot Angel and Fred's approach to the rebel camp must be blind, deaf and dead, given they pass directly beneath the tree he's perched in. Also, it's a wide-open field, so it's not as if Angel could use his normal stealth tactics. And finally... once the heroes return home, how do they get Angel's convertible out of Caritas?

IT'S REALLY ABOUT... Once the dust settles, it's about the heroes re-evaluating themselves after being away from Earth's societal rules. From here onward, they'll act to some degree with their Pylean roles in mind: notice especially how Wesley gets increasingly bold as a leader, and Cordelia, having tasted the life of royalty, drops her shameless and demeaning acting career like a bad habit. The glory of travel is that you're able to consider yourself away from what's potentially a self-restricting environment, and the heroes that finally return to the Hyperion simply aren't the same people who left the hotel three episodes ago.

CRITIQUE If you're not into the Pylean arc by now, then this installment will probably leave you cold – fortunately, we're enjoying ourselves immensely, and finished this story totally satisfied. It's funny, though, how much the Pylean adventure gets cited for its comedy bits, when the finale at least slides further into darkness with every act. Yes, Cordelia gets her lively improv about turning Lorne's severed head into a planter, but events rapidly decay after that. Case in point: Wesley winds up ordering a rebel to his death – after looking the man in the eye about it – and the rebel unswervingly obeys.

It's a finely tuned pay off, then, and fair enough that you wouldn't want to see this sort of thing all the time. But it's been a clever, fun-filled endeavor, and the sort of escapade that makes you glad – whether you enjoyed it or not – to return to L.A. Excellent work all around.

THE LORE It'll surprise nobody to hear that Carpenter's "Pylean chainmail" outfit proved scandalously cold, and her having to embrace the Groosalugg – who was wearing a chilly metal plate – didn't help. Apparently all of this made Carpenter a bit more bitchy than normal, and she later conceded that the crew took to calling her "Princess" a lot.

• Carpenter's hairdos proved rather challenging throughout their transformations (she had to wear curlers a lot in Season One) and became hard to maintain continuity-wise. Sensing that the WB wasn't receptive to the notion of her cutting her hair, Carpenter went the other direction and made it longer. This created even more headaches for the make-up team, so the producers assented to her shortening her hair halfway through Season Two. But this created a darker effect that the producers didn't feel matched Cordelia's effervescent personality, whereupon they finally started moving toward "shorter and blonder." (*BBC Cult*, Aug. 22, 2001)

• A trimmed bit of the script entailed Fred mentioning her uncle, who drank himself silly every night of the week, then drove his Ranchero into a sinkhole and drowned. She judged the man "dumber than paint."

The Total Kill-Count (thru Season Two...)

• Angel: 21 vampires, 39 demons, 15 humans, 30 zombies; 1 heroic champion (demonic).
• Cordelia: 1 vampire, 2 1/2 demons.
• Wesley: 1 vampire, 7 demons.
• Gunn: 3 vampires, 8 demons.
• Kate: 3 vampires, 1 human.

NOTES: We debated whether or not Angel killed the demon Boone in "Blood Money" (2.12), but eventually fell on the side of "yea." The zombie-count was achieved by counting the pictures in the magic-using police captain's "shrine" (in 2.14, "The Thin Dead Line"). The "heroic champion (demonic)" is the Prio Motu from 2.01, "Judgment." Surprisingly, Kate doesn't kill anything this year.

Now for the most complicated issue of all: the wine-cellar slaughter in "Reunion" (2.10). You could certainly argue that Darla and Dru are more responsible – or that given the confined space, some of the lawyers would've perished in the resultant brouhaha even if Angel *had* intervened. It's even relevant (as Wesley acknowledges) that the lawyers brought this wrath down upon themselves. We'd stop short of saying, "They deserved it," but we're not exactly dealing with Mother Teresa here.

None of this, however, absolves Angel from all blame for the incident. At the very least, his actions amount to depraved indifference – the equivalent of spotting a person drowning and doing nothing to save them. Actually, it's worse than that, bearing in mind that he not only walks away but *locks the door behind him* – thus preventing any lawyers from escaping while Darla and Dru feast on their colleagues. (As a wise man once said, "I don't need to outrun the crazed vampires, I only need to outrun my co-workers.") So it's more akin to Angel spotting a group of drowning people and poking holes in the life-raft that could've saved a few them.

Tragically, the gravity of this matter rather forces us to count the corpses. A very rough head count shows a dozen casualties, including Holland and his butler, who admittedly disappears before the final bloodletting and might escape or die off screen. Darla says next episode that she sent Wolfram and Hart a "15 body memo," but she's probably rounding up, as Kate's police report definitively mentions 13 casualties in "The Thin Dead Line" (2.14). So that's the score we're awarding Angel.

By the way, none of this addresses whether Angel helps the wounded but very-much-alive Catherine Holland as he exits the Holland household. It's hard to say how much we should take his comment that he "walked, then drove away" literally, but again, we'll defer to Kate's count.

3.01: "Heartthrob"

"You think you won just because you're still alive? I lived. You just existed."

Air Date: Sept. 24, 2001;
Writer/Director: David Greenwalt

SUMMARY Angel returns after three months away mourning Buffy, whereupon the Powers send the heroes to eliminate a vampire pack. Angel consequently dusts a blonde vamp named Elizabeth – recognizing her after the fact as someone who, along with her vampire boyfriend James, ran with Angelus and Darla in eighteenth century France.

A vengeful James visits Dr. Gregson, a demon surgeon who removes James' heart and thereby renders him invulnerable. This severely diminishes James' lifespan, but he storms the Hyperion and puts Angel and Cordelia on the run, leading to a subway brawl. James runs out of time and goes to dust, making one last declaration that he knew true love. This leaves Angel worried about his comparable success at withstanding Buffy's passing.

Meanwhile, in a Nicaraguan bar, Darla obtains a lead on a shaman who can hopefully offer advice... on the fact that she's pregnant with Angel's child.

THE OPENING CREDITS Amy Acker joins the cast listings, and the arguably definitive shot of Fred – bedraggled, in rags and scribbling on her cave wall in Pylea (as seen in 2.21, "Through the Looking Glass") – will become a staple in the opening credits for the next two years.

FIRSTS AND LASTS It's the grand debut of "preggers" Darla, a revelation that – sans spoilers – seemed entirely shocking upon first viewing. Upon rewatching the story, however, the combination of the ramped-up music and Darla's bursting abdomen makes everything seem a bit overplayed, and the chief impression that comes across is "Whoa! That belly!"

It's also the formal introduction of Holtz, an eighteenth century vampire hunter who arrives on horseback on the same straw-covered street that seems to have accompanied most of the show's flashback scenes. Speaking of which, it's the final flashback to occur on just such a straw-covered street. It's also the final time that Wesley positively glows from receiving an antique weapon (a dagger, which Angel gives him), as he'll stick to more modernized hardware in the years to come.

Cosmetically speaking, it's the first appearance of the trademarked weapons cabinet where the heroes will store their arsenal for the next two years. It'll get smashed twice this season (see 3.11, "Birthday" and 3.16, "Sleep Tight"), almost leading one to conclude that the Hyperion's spare rooms are stocked with dozens of such cabinets, and that the heroes simply lug a spare downstairs whenever needed. Speaking of weapons, the heroes' trademark "sharpened baseball bat" gets its first outing.

First and only time in the whole of *Angel* that we observe a character (Cordelia) soaking in the bathtub.

POINTS OF DISCUSSION ABOUT "Heartthrob":

1. An urban legend that's sprung up – based on the fact that *Buffy* had now moved to UPN, leaving *Angel* alone on the WB – is that executives at one or both networks issued heated edicts that Buffy's name couldn't be spoken on *Angel*, presumably to avoid helping the competition. That's untrue, as Buffy's name – regardless of euphemisms such as "the B-word" – does get spoken aloud here and in episodes such as "Carpe Noctem" (3.04) and "Fredless" (3.05). It's clearly not verboten by law, and let's not forget that such skittishness is normal behavior for the heroes: They circled around mention of Angel's name in Season Two, and will do the same to Wesley later this year.

2. Most of what Fred scribbles on her bedroom walls (see **Character Development**) is pure gibberish, but two phrases are worth mentioning: "If you could square your thoughts, could you cube your questions?" and the even-more curious statement, "time, space and Plexiglass." We can't precisely know what's on Fred's mind here, but one almost presumes she's talking about the time-traveling whales in *Star Trek IV: The Voyage Home*.

3. Speaking of *Star Trek*, and bearing in mind James T. Kirk's repeatedly becoming shirtless for no readily apparent reason, this story contains one of the flimsiest excuses for getting Cordelia down to a tight-fitting shirt. As Cordy and Angel flee into the sewer tunnels, she gratuitously says, "My coat... it's stuck." Then follows a rather blatant tearing sound, even as Cordelia leaves her jacket hanging on a ladder. So liberated, Cordelia and Angel subsequently run through a crowded subway station, Cordy jiggling all the way. It's hardly what you'd call subtle.

4. If you're killing time, then stop to slo-mo Fred's elation when Angel walks into her room – specifically, the little speech with her going, "Hey there!", and bouncing around afterward. It's so entertaining to watch her happily do her little jig, we're surprised we haven't seen it online as a forum icon.

5. Upon Angel's return to the Hyperion, there's hugs all around for him, Wes, Cordy and Gunn. Enjoy this camaraderie while it lasts, because it's not going to last out the season.

CHARACTER NOTES *Angel:* Spends some of his mourning period at a Sri Lanka monastery, and fights some demon monks there. Upon returning home, he gifts Gunn with a shrunken head, Cordelia with a blue-pendant necklace and a thrilled Wesley with a dagger from [the fictional] sixteenth-century Murshan Dynasty.

In 1767, Angelus, Darla, James and Elizabeth traveled to Marseilles. [It's never stipulated that Angelus and/or Darla sired the other pair, and they're not typically prone to cavorting with vampires that aren't their offspring.] The quartet killed the Count de Leon, and James apparently burnt the man's villa to the ground. This led them into conflict with the vampire hunter Holtz and his men. [James knows little about Holtz, so perhaps he and Elizabeth were sired after Angelus and Darla ate Holtz's family, and thereby poured gasoline onto his feud with them.] The vampires escaped, but James became outraged at Angelus' willingness to save his own skin by sacrificing others. [This presumably prompts James and Elizabeth to part ways with Angelus and Darla. There's no evidence of the couples meeting each other again until this story.] Before battling Holtz, the group was supposedly on their way to Morocco [but it's unclear if Angelus and Darla ever got there]. Sometime prior to these events, Angelus and Darla ate a troubadour in Madrid [see **The Lore**].

Angelus claims he, um, "repeated" on Holtz's wife before killing her. [Yet there's no such violation depicted in "Quickening" (3.08), so we might hope that Angelus is just exaggerating to rile Holtz. 3.15, "Loyalty," though, confirms that Holtz believes Angelus' boast.]

• *Cordelia:* The visions are making Cordelia a sobbing wreck and sensitive to bright light; a really hot bath alleviates the trauma. Unsurprisingly, she misses Pylea. She's relocated some of the heroes' weapons, Angel's hurling axe included, to the hotel basement as they were collecting dust.

• *Wesley:* Takes a pair of sickles/short scythes into combat. Wesley's [seemingly innocent] assessment of Fred: "Nice girl."

• *Gunn:* Squeamish, along with Wesley, about setting rat-traps in the Hyperion basement, leaving Cordelia to get all manly and handle it. [See **The Lore** under 4.07, "Apocalypse Nowish" for the reason behind Gunn's rat-phobia.]

• *Fred:* Has mostly kept to her room in the Hyperion [apparently located across from Room No. 201] ever since returning from Pylea. The heroes provide Fred with "lots of tacos," but she only seems interested in talking to Angel [see 3.04, "Carpe Noctem" for where this is going]. As with her cave in Pylea, Fred has scribbled mathematical formulae/ theorems – including a whole treatise on time – on the walls of her room. Aphorisms leave her "a little dry."

• *Darla:* Now in Puerto Cabazas, Nicaragua. She smokes despite being big with child [naturally, as we later learn that she's trying to kill it]. Angelus claims that Darla loves hats.

• *Holtz:* [Previously mentioned in 2.09, "The Trial." It's said that Angelus and Darla murdered his family, and 3.08, "Quickening," claims this occurred in 1764. Ergo, he's seen here after trailing them for three years, including the "barn incident" (1765) in "The Trial."] By 1767, Holtz had pursued Angelus and Darla across half of Europe and killed "scores" of vampires. He seems more interested in torturing Angelus "for years" than staking him [as 3.07, "Offspring" confirms].

• *Dennis:* Telekinetically starts Cordelia's bathwater running, and proves adept with a loofah. [This will come back to haunt us in 3.13, "Waiting in the Wings."]

• *Merl:* Begrudgingly working for Wesley and Gunn. He couldn't make a living [doing what, exactly?] in Akron at one point, and moved back to L.A.

• *Dr. Gregson:* Mystical surgeon and Slod demon, who collects rare organs for an unknown purpose.

ORGANIZATIONS *Caritas:* Has several senior citizens, both human and demon, among its clientele. [Perhaps Caritas runs a weekly special. One of the elderly demon patrons, here cited as "Codger Demon," returns as "Syd" in 3.18, "Double or Nothing."] Caritas' Happy Hour special entails: "Two drinks, one song, no waiting!"

DEMONOLOGY *Vampires:* Elizabeth's vampires ransack a college apartment party that advertises, "Come one, come all!" Also, Angel appears to need an invitation to enter Fred's room at the Hyperion [see **How Does the Invitation Rule Work?** for more]. In flashback, Elizabeth claims after eating the Count de Leon that she'll be "full for a week." [If she's speaking even a bit literally, this might help measure how often vampires must feed off humans for sustenance – excluding everyone they kill for sport, of course.]

MAGIC We're not privy to the details of Dr. Gregson's "heart-removing" operation on James, but it grants him advanced healing and *lets him function without a heart*. [So it's almost certainly got a mystical component.] Wesley says, over a choppy cell phone call, that the procedure lasts "six –" before the vampire terminates. [He pretty obviously means six hours, but see **Things That Don't Make Sense**.]

BEST LINE(s) Cordelia to Angel, pondering the cause of James' newfound strength: "The ring of Amarra. When you had that, you were invincible. Does he have a ring?" Angel: "No!" Cordelia, still thinking: "Did the Amarra people make cufflinks or belt buckles?"

THINGS THAT DON'T MAKE SENSE Wesley charges into battle without his glasses. Fair enough, he probably doesn't want to risk their getting knocked off during the melee, but does this mean he's rushing into battle half-blind from the get-go? And if he's wearing contacts, then why not just wear them all the time?

Wesley claims that James will perish "six –" after his surgery, and he's surely talking about six *hours,* since James dies on the same day. Good so far, yet scarcely that amount of time seems to elapse between James' attack on the hotel and his going to dust in the subway. So... what was James doing in the hours beforehand? He hopefully wasn't inquiring as to where Angel lives, because – grief-trauma or no – he'd be ravingly stupid to embark on time-sensitive surgery without knowing Angel's address in advance. (Some possible explanations here: Perhaps James simply gets the short end of the stick time-wise, or maybe he gets caught in rush-hour traffic, the poor bastard, while en route to the hotel.)

Most viewers get so busy watching Angel grapple with Elizabeth that they fail to notice the sloppy editing with Wesley and Gunn in the background. You need to watch close, but the action goes like this: Gunn stakes his opponent, there's a vampire-dusting sound and he then tosses the stake to Wesley. Wes stakes his foe and there's a second dusting sound. Nothing awry so far... but then the camera pulls out, and we see Gunn's target still rolling around on the ground, entirely un-dusted, while Wesley stakes his rival for a second time. To make matters more surreal, the stake magically reappears in Gunn's hands, he *again* tosses the weapon to Wes, and Wes is again shown standing over his impaled target. Whoops.

Another visual goof: James gets staked in the hotel, and we're treated to a close-up of his wound sealing over. Yet there's no hole in his shirt for the rest of the episode. (And no, his ramped-up healing factor can't mend clothes.)

It's played as if Angel is confused because Cordelia has moved some of his arsenal from the weapons cabinet to the basement. Of course, from Angel's point-of-view, the cabinet itself is a new addition – it wasn't there last season, and it's doubtful that Angel paused to move furniture before taking his sabbatical to mourn Buffy. (A possible get-out: Angel *is* expressing bewilderment about the cabinet, but that's not what the script or direction implies.)

The plot hinges on the enormous coincidence that James and Elizabeth, freed of the constraints of day jobs or any obligations, have conveniently settled in Angel's city without a clue that he lives there, and despite his now-apparently widespread reputation among L.A.'s underworld. Also, similar to Angel in "City Of" (1.01), Wesley rather incriminatingly leaves his fingerprints at a murder scene when he calls for help, unless he wipes the phone clean off screen. And it's the understatement of the year – although technically not a mistake, fine, fine – when Wes describes the co-ed massacre to the 911 operator as "an accident."

Cordelia, God bless her, really lacks the strength to projectile-hurl a fire extinguisher with such force during the Hyperion scuffle. Holtz is supposed to be British, but as many have commented, his accent is very much American. (Granted, we're told virtually nothing about Holtz's history prior to 1764, but it's possible that no explanation can account for the accent that Keith Szarabajka chooses to run with.)

IN RETROSPECT James, of course, isn't the first love-struck vampire in the *Angel*-verse to fight to the death in a subway car. All he needs is a leather jacket and bleach-blonde hair.

Gunn recommends that a grieving Angel "get hammered and go to Vegas"... the heroes will head there a year from now, minus the "hammered" part. An exasperated Cordelia says, "These visions are killing me," well in advance of revelations about her condition in 3.11, "Birthday." Angelus comments on the fawning James and Elisabeth: "Young love. Give it a century...", which pretty much echoes what the Master said about Angelus and Darla (2.07, "Darla").

IT'S REALLY ABOUT... The differing ways of handling the death of your beloved. James literally gets his heart ripped out, starts living on borrowed time and eventually crumbles to nothingness. Meanwhile, Angel feels surprised when he chooses to keep living – and indeed, living well. And notice how this all occurs in an episode in which there's a drove of senior citizens in Caritas, presumably to represent love that lasts throughout the ages.

TONIGHT AT CARITAS Lorne sings the rather obvious tune of "I Left My Heart in San Francisco."

CRITIQUE Right, then. If you're watching a series in sequence, then season openers – at least, those without the need to resolve an immediate cliffhanger – can seem awkward because they're warming up a kettle that's been cold for about three months. With that in mind, "Heartthrob" just about gets the job done. Mutant Enemy's production standards remain as solid as ever, the regulars log nice performances, and even with Fred relegated to the sidelines, Amy Acker is so charming in the role, that you can sense great things to come from her.

Unfortunately, even if you're feeling charitable, "Heartthrob" fails on one major point: James and Elizabeth just aren't desperately interesting. If you made a list of Angelus and Darla's "children," then you're probably going to jot down, in rapid succession: Spike, Dru, "that creepy guy that Kate ran through" (Penn, 1.11, "Somnambulist") and "that guy in the submarine" (Lawson, 5.13, "Why We Fight"). But James and Elizabeth? You're lucky to remember them at all, because they're basically just lesser versions of Spike and Dru. Indeed, if Spike and Dru were a rich red table wine, then the watered-down James and Elisabeth would look a bit pink, nothing more.

All told, then, it's a harmless story that more or less needed to happen, especially given *Buffy*'s departure to UPN and – as a means of seeding the future – Holtz's introduction. But it probably won't stay in your memory for long, and it chiefly suffers for being too much a carbon copy of what's gone before.

THE LORE The script contained the final scene with Darla, but – in an effort to avoid spoilers – wrote her as simply departing the bar, failing to mention her pregnancy. (See 5.08, "Destiny" and 5.12, "You're Welcome" for other attempts to omit "shocking revelations" from the script.) The script also elaborated on Angelus and Darla's conversation about the poet they ate in Madrid, which would've continued with Angelus: "He sang of noble death, yet when his own came..." Darla, fondly: "Not even a rhyme, just... howling." Another omitted bit entailed Cordelia commenting on Elizabeth's desire to wear James' necklace throughout eternity... Cordy: "You see me wearing Curt Eisenthorpe's football ring or Xander's meet medallion?" Gunn: "So... what kind of meat did he have that earned him a medallion?" Cordelia: "Not that kind of meat – swim meet, he was on the swim team. Get your mind out of the gutter. All of you!"

• An "Elizabeth James" served as David Greenwalt's assistant, which probably explains how he picked James and Elizabeth's names.

3.02: "That Vision Thing"

"I think she got the message."

Air Date: October 1, 2001; **Writer:** Jeffrey Bell; **Director:** Bill Norton

Redeemed

SUMMARY Lilah hires a formidable psychic to mentally hack into Cordelia's link with the Powers, providing false visions that manipulate Angel's team into recovering a mystical key and coin. Unfortunately, as a side-effect, Cordelia begins *physically* manifesting the characteristics seen in her visions, suffering harsh claw marks on her abdomen, festering pustules about her skin, and appalling burn marks.

Exposed, Lilah offers to restore Cordelia's health if Angel will free Billy, a nondescript white male held in a prison that's apparently run by the forces of good. Angel arrives at the prison using the key and coin, liberates Billy and organizes the swap upon returning to Earth. Lilah's psychic heals Cordelia, whereupon Angel hands over Billy and kills the psychic, warning Lilah not to repeat the stratagem. Cordelia thanks Angel for his help, but the two of them feel uneasy about Billy's release.

FIRSTS AND LASTS First script credited to staff writer Jeffrey Bell, who'll become instrumental to the show's development in Seasons Four and Five. It's the first subtle hint of Gunn's attraction to Fred ("Why would I wanna walk with a cute young woman on a beautiful night..."), and the first time Angel undertakes a mission for Wolfram and Hart, albeit unwillingly. Character-wise, it's the first of two appearances from Billy, although he isn't named until, um, 3.06, "Billy."

Of fairly great import, it's the debut of the "benevolent" and rather complicated demon Skip...

POINTS OF DISCUSSION ABOUT "That Vision Thing":

1. Continuity's been decently straightforward until now, but here we're introduced to Skip, who's a guard at the other-dimensional prison run by the Powers or some such benevolent agency. In the broad sense, he's assigned to stop Billy from escaping – although Angel thumps Skip and makes off with the fiend anyway – and will return as Cordelia's "guide" (of sorts) in "Birthday" (3.11) and "Tomorrow" (3.22). Sounds relatively simple, doesn't it?

Well, no. We later learn in "Inside Out" (4.17) – unbelievably a season and a half from now – that Skip's not an agent for good, and that he's working for the higher being known as Jasmine. Such is Skip's duplicity that we're forced to re-examine every single move he's ever made – including his claim ("Inside Out" again) that he threw the fight to Angel in this story. Much of what Skip alleges actually makes a great deal of sense, although it requires some rationalization, so you might want to head straightaway to the **Did Jasmine Cause All of This?** essay for the sordid details.

One thing seems genuine, however: The prison is likely administered by some force for good. After all, if the entire prison were for show, then Skip's "employer" could've simply turned Billy loose on Earth and achieved the same results with far less hassle. The question of whether the Powers themselves oversee the prison, though, depends on whether you think they're callous enough to perpetually scorch Billy in flames, as opposed to just locking him in a dungeon somewhere. There's no evidence that they're so heartless, but there's nothing to overwhelmingly discount it either.

2. Lascivious members of fandom gravitate toward this story's double-entendres and naughty bits of dialogue, so purely out of principle, let's catalog them here: Wesley mentions a "Cantonese Fook-beast" as a demon species (which sounds a bit rude) and later mentions "one of the unwritten laws of being a dick," referring to the heroes' role as private investigators. The heroes also search the "Van Hoa Duong" herbal shop, and see **In Retrospect** for Fred's immortal line about silverware. At a stretch, you're even entitled to raise your eyebrows when a drained Cordelia says, "Once I get a little protein in me, I'll be good as new." Even the magic key that Angel retrieves is rather phallic, and fits neatly into its hole.

3. As next episode seems to suggest, the heroes aren't flush with vehicles right now, so it's a bit unclear how Fred takes Cordelia home while the gents are using Angel's car. Perhaps the spaz-prone Fred is made to drive Gunn's pickup, although that makes for a slightly odd visual.

CHARACTER NOTES *Angel:* Doesn't seem concerned – even before hearing the details about Billy – whether or not Lilah gets the magical key and coin, so long as her onslaught against Cordelia ends. Indeed, Angel hands over the items before asking function they serve. [This is a real case of Angel's heart overruling his brain. For all he knows, Lilah could slot the key and coin together and instantly slaughter thousands, or wish him dusted.] He threatens to kill Lilah if she exploits Cordelia again.

• *Cordelia:* Vacillates between accepting her physical wounds as part of her job, and admitting she can't handle the visions any more. She defaults back to wondering if the wounds occur because she's a bad person. [See 1.05, "Rm w/a Vu" and 1.12, "Expecting" for more of Cordy's self-doubt... it's a bit catching, given Fred's insecurities in 3.18, "Double or Nothing."] While mentally scanning Cordelia, Lorne vaguely comments, "you got some power of your own." Cordy appreciates Gavin's taste in suits and Gucci loafers. She likes the mountains, and clearly isn't sure what to make of Fred.

• *Wesley:* Glances through what appears to be a Chinese text [suggesting he reads the language].

• *Gunn:* His aunt reportedly got "nasty, crusty stuff" on her back every summer because she was allergic to shellfish.

• *Fred:* Now social enough to eat Chinese take-out under a table in the Hyperion office. She also wolfs down Cordy's peanut butter. The phrase "right as rain" baffles her. In the fifth grade, Fred didn't go steady with Grayson Wells, but somehow felt as if they had.

• *Lorne:* Wesley says that Lorne's ability to read people's auras "in some shape or form connects him to the Powers-That-Be." [This seems feasible, especially as the Powers have a presence in Lorne's home dimension.] Lorne rubs Cordelia's temples while "back-tracking" her visions. He can distinguish between genuine visions from the Powers and faked ones, loves *The Sound of Music* and was surprised to find that William Shatner could sing.

• *Darla:* Presently in the Yoro Mountains, Honduras. She here visits a shaman's hut for advice on her mystical pregnancy [see **Magic**]. Darla says she's "tried everything and can't get rid of" her pregnancy. The shaman is "very powerful," and it's never clear if she leaves him unharmed or simply kills him for kicks. [Darla next appears in 3.07, "Offspring."]

• *Lilah:* Now working from Lindsey's old office [it was also Holland's; see 1.21, "Blind Date"]. A golfing game on her Mac features what looks like a little Lilah taking a swing.

• *Gavin Park:* [Last seen in 2.20, "Over the Rainbow."] Has been transferred from Real Estate to Special Projects. He claims the Senior Partners moved him partly due to his knowledge of L.A.'s karmically damaged and demon-infested property. A "SureKill Exterminator" team here shows up to fumigate the Hyperion [3.08, "Quickening" explains why].

• *"Young Man in Fez":* [So credited, but named "Fez-Head" and cited as Egyptian in the script.] Levitating young mage whose fez conceals the fact that his upper head consists of an exposed, pulsing brain. [The levitation probably just aids his concentration and isn't vitally important – he could hardly levitate in Lilah's car without bumping his brain.] Fez-Head says he sends Cordelia false images by "transmitting through the celestial pipeline."

• *Skip:* Armored and allegedly benevolent demon who guards over Billy. Skip claims that his will keeps Billy in a cage made from fire, plus silences Billy's screams. [Yet Skip never displays more formidable psionic talents, such as telepathy or telekinesis.] Skip seems a nice enough bloke, commutes about 20 minutes to work, and can literally smell Angel's vampire aspect and affiliation with the Powers-That-Be. [He next appears in "Birthday."]

• *Billy:* We're never told why the firm wants him free. ["Billy" (3.06) seems to imply it's because the firm counts Billy's family among its big-time clients, but see **Did Jasmine Cause All This?**] Nor do we ever learn what he did to warrant the agonizing fire punishment, as opposed to just getting locked up. [Then again, perhaps the flames also serve to burn off the dangerous element in Billy's pheromones – again, see "Billy."]

THE HYPERION Gavin files 57 code violations – including asbestos, termites and earthquake proofing – for the hotel with the City Planning Office. [Earthquake proofing would actually benefit the heroes, considering what's coming in "Loyalty" (3.15). "Carpe Noctem" (3.04) shows the resolution to all this, but see **Things That Don't Make Sense**.] Cordelia off-handedly mentions the hotel's industrial-size kitchen [see 3.19, "The Price"]. There's a bathroom adjacent to Wesley's office.

ORGANIZATIONS *Wolfram and Hart:* Fez-Head fills out a 1099 for the firm's payroll department. Angel coerces Gavin into helping him avoid the firm's vampire detectors and stealthily enter Lilah's office. [As with – theoretically – 4.07, "Apocalypse Nowish," but points to Angel for appearing behind Lilah's desk without her noticing.]

• *The Powers-That-Be:* Fred theorizes that the Powers' transmissions to Cordelia are a form of energy. Wes implies that the Powers don't normally send Cordelia two visions in one night.

DEMONOLOGY Demon species include "Wan-shang dhole" and "Cantonese fook-beasts" (sic).

• *Vampires:* Darla walks straight into the shaman's hut without an invite [so it's the equivalent of his "office," not his home].

• *Random Benevolent Entities in Los Angeles:* A pair of guardians – looking like frail senior citizens, but versed in martial arts and sprouting formidable claws – guard the coin in one of five Chinatown herbalist shops. A human-looking key maker owns the key, accompanied by a sword-wielding, boil-faced demon. [They're undeniably agents of good, but not necessarily linked to the Powers.]

MAGIC *The Key and the Coin:* Their markings denote them as artifacts of good. When fitted together, they spin and open a doorway [not a "portal" in the traditional sense] to the dungeon-dimension holding Billy. Weapons are magically left behind. [Angel also uses the key and the coin in "Inside Out."]

• *"Pregnancy Reading Ritual":* Darla consults a shaman who draws a bit of her blood, mixes it with two kinds of powder, smears it on his palms and places them on Darla's burgeoning belly – only to get thrown backward by an unidentified force. The shaman says this method has "never failed him" before. [So he's arguably examined other mystical pregnancies, even if Darla's case is unprecedented.] As Darla enters, the shaman is rubbing small bones and throwing them onto the table, as if trying to divine something [or maybe he's just playing craps].

BEST LINE Fred to Cordelia: "You're like Angel's Lassie. Sure, he does most of the saving. But it's your visions that tell him that Timmy's trapped in a well or that the robbers are hiding in the barn."

THINGS THAT DON'T MAKE SENSE Angel needs someone to take the traumatized Cordelia home, but to whom does he entrust this important task? Fred, who hasn't driven in five years and isn't yet comfortable using a fork. And who, as it happens, has entirely the wrong skin tone for someone who's barely left her room in the last few months. (Unless you believe the Hyperion now sports a tanning bed.) Never mind that they could've just bedded Cordelia down at the hotel for the night, because Heaven knows, there's plenty of spare rooms.

Cordelia moans, "One of these days, we need to get someone in here who can cook," apparently forgetting that Angel *can* cook (1.10, "Parting Gifts"). The old man in the herbal shop clearly falls on his front during the fight with Angel, but he's next seen flat on his back when Angel snags the key. (Angel might roll him over off screen, but it's not staged that way.) The two claw marks on Cordelia's left arm – the ones she shows to her co-workers in her apartment – weren't there when she was recovering in the Hyperion bathroom. And did Gunn forget to tell Angel about "the exterminators" who showed up at the Hyperion? Because nobody seems to register that the heroes didn't order the service, which might've led them to expose Gavin's ploy about six episodes sooner.

As Vice-President of Special Projects, why is Lilah oblivious about Gavin's transfer to her department? Especially given that he's assigned to annoy Angel, her pet project? And whereas Gavin deserves a few points for exploiting the Hyperion's building code violations while it's not even open for business, his overall strategy here just seems feeble. Does he *seriously* think this will help Angel capitulate to the dark side?

Getting picky now, but something weird is going on with Cordelia's hair while she's talking to Angel in the teaser. There's one large strand of hair in front of her face... then two... then it's back to one... then when she's in the bathroom, it's magically pulled behind her ears (well, mostly).

IN RETROSPECT Fred comments, on relearning the art of silverware, that: "I've been forking with Gunn." (Not yet, but give it time.) Lorne gets blasted across the room while exploring Cordelia's subconscious; anyone else noticed that nothing good happens when he does this? (See 4.06, "Spin the Bottle.") And when Gavin mentions "termites" in the Hyperion, you weren't alone – based on "The Price" (3.19) – if you wryly declared, "Those aren't termites, you fool. They're inter-dimensional bugs!"

CRITIQUE It's a curse of being a reviewer that you're sometimes faced with a middle-of-the-road story that leaves you without something profound to say besides, "Well... that was okay." For better or worse, "That Vision Thing" is one of those cases.

It's most assuredly watchable, and it never really embarrasses itself, or crushes the viewer beneath a falling piano of illogic. But much like the last episode, it's too much a retread of what's gone before. Cordelia's vision-power goes wonky, so everyone dashes about trying to save her while she's bed-ridden. It's "To Shanshu in L.A." (1.22) with a dash of "Expecting" (1.12) thrown in. Admittedly, Cordy's injuries here are truly horrific and certainly strike a chord – then again, "Shanshu" was terrifying enough without such visual fare, entailing little more than Carpenter screaming her lungs out.

To be entirely fair, this story also introduces a couple of new characters: Skip and Billy. Except... they don't really do much here, do they? Billy doesn't even speak, and his story is left so utterly vague, it's hard to get lathered up about it. That leaves "That Vision Thing" as useful fodder for another day, but rather lackluster in itself.

THE LORE It's about this point that the rumor mill decided that Amy Acker was going to marry David Denman, who played Skip. Acker found this a rather bizarre thing to hear, as she'd never met the man. (*FHM*, Aug. 2003)

• Romanov hadn't met Kim (Gavin) before rehearsal, and her viciousness while playing Lilah apparently rattled him to the point that Romanov felt the need to apologize. She smoothed things over with something along the lines of, "I'm so sorry, it's not me. I'm paid to do that, I have to be bad," whereupon they became good friends. (O'Hare, *Zap2It.com*, May 2, 2003)

• Kal Penn (Fez Boy) played a beer-guzzling frat boy in *Buffy* 4.05, "Beer Bad". He's best-known for work on low-brow comedy films such as *Van Wilder*, and was Kumar in *Harold and Kumar Go to White Castle*.

3.03: "That Old Gang of Mine"

"If I had killed Merl, would I have brought doughnuts?"

Air Date: Oct. 8, 2001; **Writer:** Tim Minear; **Director:** Fred Keller

SUMMARY When unknown parties murder benign demons as well as homicidal ones – including Angel's informant Merl – Gunn secretly identifies the perpetrators as his old gang, now led by his friend Rondell.

3.03, That Old Gang of Mine

The gang ostracizes a conflicted Gunn due to his association with Angel, a vampire. Worse, an upstart named Gio directs the gang to attack the clientele at Caritas, capturing most of Angel's team and Lorne in the process.

Gio summons Angel, wanting Gunn to dust him as proof of his loyalty. Angel hurriedly has Cordelia contact the Transuding Furies, the three magical women who crafted the Sanctuary Spell that prevents demon violence in Caritas, and asks them to neutralize the enchantment. Gunn refuses to dust Angel, whereupon Sanctuary Spell folds and Angel engages the gang members. A free-for-all ensues, but one of the demons "hatches" into a giant reptile thing and bites Gio's head off. Rondell blows the giant reptile away, and the gang afterward agrees to better stick to its territory.

FIRSTS AND LASTS In a deck-clearing move for Season Three, it's the final appearances of Merl, Rondell, Gunn's entire gang and Caritas in a state that's even remotely open for business. It's the first use of a Sanctuary Spell, which here seems difficult to achieve, yet by "Salvage" (4.13), it will be the sort of thing you can cobble together with some chanting and a decent spice rack. It's also, unexpectedly, the first time that sweet little Fred tries to defuse a crisis by threatening someone's life at point-blank range (see also 3.08, "Quickening"). It's always the quiet ones.

POINTS OF DISCUSSION ABOUT "That Old Gang of Mine":

1. For anyone trying to work out Angel's history, the suggestion (not outright fact, mind) that Angel has enjoyed relations with the Transuding Furies causes obvious issues. (Cordelia: "You know them?" Angel: "I did." Cordelia: "And they're gonna remember you?" Angel: "They should.") Yet Angel's time on *Buffy* seems to imply that he didn't have sex with anyone between getting ensouled in 1898 and bagging the Slayer in *Buffy* 2.13, "Surprise."

A few possibilities here: He might have slept with them while he was Angelus (although in all fairness, the Furies never refer to him as such). Alternatively, perhaps he didn't go the distance with them before, but they now expect – as they lift the Sanctuary Spell on his behalf – that he'll perform any "manly duty" left unresolved with them in past. *Or* (pushing it now), it's certainly possible that an unseen adventure exists between "Epiphany" (2.16) and this story, in which Angel loses his fear about one-night stands after his dalliance with Darla, and enjoys a night of festivities with the Furies – so long as he avoids perfect happiness.

Actually, the last option seems annoyingly plausible, given how completely Angel revises his self-imposed limits on romance by "Offspring" (3.07). *Something* must've made him change his mind.

2. Less humorously, we must consider the self-proclaimed "baby-killer" in Caritas. To recap, Gio singles out a Caritas hostage as a "baby-killer," whereupon the thuggish demon goads him back with all manner of threats about how he eats babies. Unable to cope, Gunn unloads his shotgun into the demon. Now, fans have made some attempts to revise this, claiming that the demon *isn't* a baby-killer but rather a belligerent demon with a death wish. There's scant little evidence for this on screen, however, and you're within your rights to take the demon at his word and think, "Yup, he's a baby-killer." If this all sounds irrelevant, it isn't; see **The Critique**.

3. Fred's meticulous, if a bit rambling, way of describing how Gio will die if she lodges a crossbow bolt in his throat deserves a mention. ("Now if I pierce one of your carotid arteries, considering the temperature in here – 'cause I think somebody shot the thermostat – the blood loss is gonna be heavy..." and so forth.) Curious how much the scene evokes a similarly clinical discussion between Dr. McCoy and Khan in the classic *Star Trek* story "Space Seed": Pinned to the wall by a blade-wielding Khan, a non-intimidated McCoy offers helpful tips on the best way the villain can slit his throat. (Khan's response: "I like a brave man.")

4. Angel comes bearing doughnuts when he tries to apologize to Merl. He similarly tried pacifying a psychotic Faith with doughnuts in 1.19, "Sanctuary." He's apparently a big believer in pastries as part of the appeasement process, have you noticed that?

CHARACTER NOTES *Angel:* Offers an awkward, difficult and ultimately unconvincing apology to Merl for past abuses. [It's never said why Angel even makes this attempt, unless his associates view this as part of his "rehabilitation" after Season Two.] He's surprised to find he tops the agency's "enemies of Merl" list. However, to Angel's credit, he tries to give Merl a "sincere" apology before finding his body, and seems a bit remorseful that he won't get to know Merl better.

Angel allows that Gunn might need to kill him one day [not entirely unwarranted, looking ahead to 4.10, "Awakening"], and will take it as a show of loyalty if he succeeds.

- *Cordelia:* Accepts the task of bringing Fred out of her shell [because Heaven knows, the guys aren't emotionally equipped for such a task].
- *Wesley:* Threatens to fire Gunn if he subverts Wesley's authority again. [Of course, it's a bit chilling to hear Wesley lecturing Gunn on loyalty and a failure to disclose information, considering events ahead in 3.14, "Couplet."] Wes meticulously bags and sorts crime-scene evidence [although he's never seen to use this system again]. He seems instinctively protective of Fred.
- *Gunn:* At first unable to comprehend why the heroes should investigate Merl's murder [Angel, strangely, seems

almost warm and cuddly by comparison], yet grows to accept that not all demons should be killed. Yet Gunn says he'll never be proper friends with Angel because he's a vampire [see **The Critique**]. Gunn is seen sleeping in his own Spartan-looking apartment [not a Hyperion room], complete with a red motorcycle poster and a leftover pizza box. Rondell says the death of Gunn's sister (1.20, "War Zone") initiated Gunn's split from his gang. Gunn built the crossbow gear that Gio now uses.

• *Fred:* As Cordelia suggests, Fred seems to laugh at something a shrub says [see 5.20, "The Girl in Question," for a totally loopy theory on this]. Fred's taken to wearing ponytails, and overcomes her shyness (and general reluctance to leave the Hyperion) enough to sing at Caritas and to level a crossbow at Gio's throat.

• *Rondell:* Apparently founded the gang with Gunn, and hasn't seen Gunn in the "months" since they spread George's remains in the river [2.19, "Belonging"].

• *Gio:* Evidently left Miami after performing a reprehensible act on a woman there. [Lorne "reads" Gio and makes vague statements that he left "after what he did" and that "she trusted you, right up until the end," but it's all terribly unclear.]

• *Merl:* Claims he spent three months in therapy after Angel hung him upside down in a sewer. [2.11, "Redefinition." Merl is likely joking, as he could hardly afford such demon-counseling services – which probably *do* exist in L.A., mind.] Merl needs a ride home [so he doesn't drive] and spews bright green blood when he's butchered. He owed the also-slaughtered demon bookie Samuel Larch quite a lot of money. Cordelia claims that Merl accrued half his "enemies of Merl" list in the heroes' service.

• *Transuding Furies:* Three floating sisters – two brunettes (one of them Asian) and a blonde – whom Lorne hires monthly to cast the Caritas Sanctuary Spell. They finish each other's words and serve Cordelia tea. [The sisters seem a lot more benign than the traditional use of the word "furies" would suggest, and appear more magical than demonic.] Angel knows the Furies' address, and they neutralize the Sanctuary Spell for him, even though it was put in place by mutual "consent and contract."

ORGANIZATIONS *Angel Investigations:* The gang takes a taxi home from Caritas. [So it's unlikely that Cordelia and Wesley have bought their automobiles yet, seen respectively in "Tomorrow" (3.22) and "Sleep Tight" (3.16). Who knows? Perhaps when Cordelia becomes half-demonic in "Birthday" (3.11), she gets a new car too.]

• *Rondell's Gang:* Occupy territory to one side of Venice Boulevard.

MAGIC *The Sanctuary Spell:* Generates a magical force that repels any demon who physically attempts to harm someone in Caritas. [For further applications of the Sanctuary Spell and the Furies' magic, see "Lullaby" (3.09), "Dad" (3.11) and "Salvage" (4.13).]

DEMONOLOGY *Vampires:* Gio implies that vampires reside in Miami, despite the climate.

BEST LINE Angel to Gunn, pointing out splatters of Merl's blood that're *everywhere*: "So far, we've ruled out suicide."

THINGS THAT DON'T MAKE SENSE It's clear from "Lullaby" (3.09) that a human-effective Sanctuary Spell exists, yet Lorne was evidently too dense to purchase one for Caritas. Sorry, it never occurred to him that gun-totting humans might come in there looking for trouble? Especially since the likes of Wolfram and Hart employees (2.15, "Reprise") frequent the club. We formerly saw metal detectors in operation at Caritas (2.01, "Judgment"), but that hardly seems sufficient.

We'll leave most of the thematic problems for the **Critique**, but a plot hole of some note: Gio and Rondell's crew have been hot-rodding around town, eviscerating good demons and bad demons alike. Then they storm into Caritas, where the patrons include a vampire, a pink-skinned demon who at least *says* he's a baby-killer and a giant reptile thing that brutally murders Gio. Yet at story's end, the gang is somehow motivated to exercise better restraint in future. Surely, if anything, these events would *reinforce* their bigotry rather than deflate it? (Perhaps the gang is simply less bloodthirsty without Gio as their ring-leader, but there's never any mention of this.)

Amid all the gunplay, the gang shows superb discernment between deadly vampires and innocent human bystanders. And finally, Merl glances at what looks like mail when he gets home, even though he apparently lives in a disused factory or some such. Does L.A. have a demonic Post Office that we're never told about?

IN RETROSPECT Between Fred here and Harmony in 2.17, "Disharmony," you get the impression that everyone Cordelia takes to Caritas sings badly enough to curdle milk.

IT'S REALLY ABOUT... It falls under the global umbrella of racism, but it's more specifically about killing for sport. The problem with Gio and his thugs isn't that they're killing demons per se (after all, Buffy and Angel's groups have, by now, been doing the same for four and a half years), but that they're enjoying it. In short, they're taking such a delicious joy in killing, innocent bystanders are getting cut down too. Notice especially how Angel realizes the pattern of the killings is "to have fun," and how Gio gets so wrapped up in his blood-frenzy that he even seems willing to kill human "sympathizers" such as Gunn.

TONIGHT AT CARITAS Fred warbles "Crazy For You" as only she can. (She even picks out the song herself.) Gio mocks Gunn with a rendition of "Wind Beneath My Wings."

CRITIQUE There's two ways of looking at "That Old Gang of Mine." On the one hand, it's an adrenaline rush. By now, Caritas has become such a cozy fixture of the series, the sight of machine gun-bearing lunatics surging through the door and plugging everything in sight seems inherently gut-wrenching. You're entitled to bite a few fingernails as the stand-off progresses, and those in the mood for a mindless action story will almost undoubtedly enjoy themselves. On first viewing, the story seems to sail along.

But oh dear, oh dear, *oh dear*. If you apply some critical thinking and consider the story's subtext, intentional or otherwise, then the episode gets more and more deplorable. Fundamentally, it's because there's a giant, thundering disconnect between the story Minear is trying to tell – a laudable disparagement of racism – and what actually happens on screen. It's vital that we pause here to say that "That Old Gang of Mine" has good intentions, and that Minear doubtless didn't mean a single iota of harm by it. Nonetheless, this story's honorable motives wind up in a total train wreck... so let's stop and probe why that happens.

The general set-up isn't hard to work out: Gunn, a lifetime demon/vampire killer, finds himself in the odd position of arguing that whereas some demons are murderers, others are harmless and should be left alone. Very simply put, he's saying that racism is bad. Absolutely nothing off-base about that, and we're meant to watch as Gunn inwardly wrestles with his own prejudice on this topic. Fine so far.

But two enormous problems crop up. First off, some of the demons in Caritas – by default the beings that Gunn seeks to protect from Gio's crew – are genuine killers. Their ranks, lest we forget, include a vampire and a giant reptile beast that later bites Gio's head off. Even if you ignore the demon who claims to kill babies – and it's hard to see how one can just paper over that – are we *seriously* meant to believe that the giant reptile is as docile as a kitten when it's not roused? Credit us with some intelligence, please. "Hero" (1.09) was a flawed story too, but at least it painted the similarly hunted Lister demons as genuine innocents. Doyle gave his life for them, and commendably so. But here, that's not the case – Gunn's made to defend despicable characters who, on any other *Angel* story, would warrant a sword to the throat.

Then there's Gio. He's a contemptible bigot and a moron to boot, and there's soooooooo many ways of exposing him as such. Tragically, though, we're not so much meant to loathe Gio because he's a bigot as to abhor him because he's a hotshot asshole who mocks Gunn and apparently had some unspecified foulness with a woman in Miami. In short, we're meant to despise him primarily because he's such a jerk, not because he's prejudiced.

And allowing that Gio's an obvious bigot, how does he come undone? His head gets bitten off. Sorry, *that's* the best the story can do? Instead of discrediting Gio, or having more sensible heads in the gang prevail, or having someone tear his repellant prejudice to shreds... a demon slaughters him, and with such a flair for the dramatic that we're apparently supposed to cheer. Hard to see how this advances Gunn's argument of tolerance. Honestly, what're we to take away from this? If someone's a bigot, everyone applaud when they're decapitated?

As if to round everything off, Gunn ends the story believing he can never be friends with Angel solely because Angel's a vampire. Such prejudice might've seemed credible earlier on, but it's outright lunacy to think Gunn feels that way *now*, after fighting alongside Angel for more than a year. It's thrown into the mix as a final twist in an episode that deals with racism, not because it makes sense for the character any longer.

It's possible that by now, you think we've been too harsh on this story. So let's mention that Minear himself has expressed extreme unhappiness for "That Old Gang of Mine" on more than one occasion. He's been less than forthcoming about why, but there's any number of reasons for him to feel embarrassed about an episode that laudably wants to decry bigotry and racism, but in many respects winds up doing the opposite. Isn't it rather perverse that we're apparently meant to feel satisfied about all this?

THE LORE As scripted, the final battle was a lot more complicated. Wesley was supposed to stop Rondell from shooting the giant reptile thing, identifying it as a Nurbtach Demon and claiming that lead would only make it stronger. The heroes would then fall on the creature *en masse* with whatever was at hand – Angel with a machete or something similar, Gunn with a crossbow, Wes with a sword produced from Heaven-knows-where and Rondell with an axe. The four of them would have hacked, sliced and eviscerated the demon into pieces. However, Minear felt the whole affair was all action and no real drama, and that it stopped the story from easily progressing from Gio's demise to everyone's "peaceful departure." The producers accordingly canned the entire fight, wrote off the money they'd paid for the CGI monster and settled on Rondell simply plugging the bugger instead. (Minear, *uk.media.tv.angel*, Feb. 3, 2002)

3.04: "Carpe Noctem"

"I'm gonna be young, handsome and strong forever."

Air Date: Oct. 15, 2001; **Writer:** Scott Murphy; **Director:** Bill Norton

SUMMARY A nursing home resident named Marcus Roscoe – armed with a conjuring stone and a body-swapping spell – routinely switches minds with ripped males at a health club. A "renewed" Marcus beds call girls, but each body-swap proves temporary, reducing the body-builders to husks of skin while Marcus' spirit returns to his aged body. Our heroes investigate the deaths, but Marcus secretly body-swaps with Angel and returns to the Hyperion with Cordelia – leaving Angel stuck in the nursing home in Marcus' body.

As "Angel," Marcus attempts (and fails) to bag virtually every female he happens across, and eventually realizes that he now possesses the body of an immortal vampire. Wanting to stay in Angel's body forever, Marcus tries to eliminate his old body with Angel's mind still inside it. Thankfully, Angel's associates discover all and incapacitate Marcus with a stun gun. Wesley helps Angel to ritualistically swap minds with Marcus one last time, then destroys Marcus' conjuring stone, preventing his ever body-swapping again.

POINTS OF DISCUSSION ABOUT "Carpe Noctem":

1 A curious point about Fred: Despite her inherent wackiness, she's a stereotypical woman in that she takes near-forever to get ready for a date. Consider that in the time Fred requires to "get ready" to hit the town with "Angel," Lilah and Marcus have downed so many drinks that Lilah wants a taxi to drive her home. Also, looking at the spiffy little number Fred produces for her supposed date, it's fairly certain that Cordelia's been giving her some clothes or visiting Goodwill on her behalf.

2. Angel routinely faces soulless fiends who literally lack a conscience, so it's a bit ironic that Marcus, an old man, has no such excuse and therefore becomes one of Angel's most immoral opponents. Consider: Marcus knows that his body-swaps leave his victims as heaps of skin, and yet, to get some tail, he doesn't care. And upon becoming a vampire, Marcus takes to the life and nearly slaughters a girl in a club, and later lectures Angel on the merits of vampires killing people. ("Vampires don't help people, you moron – they kill 'em!") Left in Angel's body, Marcus might well have racked up a kill-count on par with that of Angelus... and he seemed like such a harmless old duffer too.

3. Fandom can't quite decide whether there's a correlation between Marcus' body-swapping and his heart attacks. We're told that Marcus has endured three heart attacks – same as his number of husked victims – before this episode. This might imply that Marcus gets a heart attack upon each "return" to his body, but Marcus' *fourth* heart attack – a tally that puts him on par with Dick Cheney – occurs while Angel's escaping the home, and when no body-swap is in progress. It seems more likely, then, that much of this is coincidence based on Marcus being so decrepit. That said, decide for yourselves if he's struck with another coronary and bites the bullet after getting kicked out of Angel's body.

4. We haven't had a proper assault on Angel's manhood in almost a year (arguably not since the "eunuch" conversation in 2.06, "Guise Will Be Guise"), so Cordelia re-broaches the topic by telling Angel: "You're handsome, brave, heroic, emotionally stunted, erratic, prone to turning evil... and, let's face it, a eunuch." As if to raise the stakes, Marcus decides – simply by looking at Angel's dress sense – that the man *must* be gay. Still, this judgment hails from a senior citizen who apparently considers himself quite the horn-dog, yet inexplicably changes into Angel's black leather pants before going clubbing.

By the way, this all occurs in the same story where Wesley announces, "There's something about brewed tea that you simply cannot replicate with a bag," which isn't terribly masculine either.

CHARACTER NOTES *Angel:* Terribly excited about a double-showing of *The Omega Man* (1971) and *Soylent Green* (1973), both starring Charlton Heston [and both sort-of "vampire movies"]. Gavin suggests that Angel has no Social Security number, no taxpayer ID and no last name. [Gunn also confirms that Angel has no last name or bank account in 3.15, "Loyalty." See 3.12, "Provider" about the company status, but there's any number of ways that Cordelia, Wesley or Gunn could handle much of the pesky paperwork (taxes, etc.) on Angel's behalf while keeping his existence anonymous. Hell, in 2.20, "Over the Rainbow," we're even told that the Hyperion mortgage is under "the company name." However, it's less clear how Angel got his driver's license.]

The body-swap doesn't free Angelus. [The gypsy curse was tailored to make Angelus suffer, so combined with the presence of Marcus' soul, it keeps the vampire demon and its Angelus persona in check.]

• *Cordelia:* Takes Marcus/Angel down with a Taser. [A pity she didn't have it onhand in 1.17, "Eternity."]

• *Wesley:* Has a contact at the coroner's office, and is translating "Fassad's Guide" from the original Sumerian. [For fun? No wonder Wes' social life could stand improvement.]

• *Fred:* Still has the big puppy love for Angel until Cordelia gives Fred "the talk" that Angel only likes her as a friend. Fred seems familiar with the works of F. Scott Fitzgerald.

• *Lilah:* Provides Angel with the documentation he needs for the hotel thus thwarting Gavin's little "building-code violation" scheme [3.02, "That Vision Thing"]. This leads to Lilah sharing a drink with Marcus/Angel, and having a quick tussle with him on Wesley's desk. [It really says something about Lilah's character that she doesn't hesitate to roll around with the vampire who's been sneaking into the back of her car (2.12, "Blood Money") and once locked her in a cellar to die horribly (2.10, "Reunion"). Apparently, the fact that Angel is sooooooo dreamy overrides all other considerations.]

The attempted coupling makes Marcus instinctively vamp out, compelling Lilah to flee the Hyperion. Lilah carries a cross in her purse. She commissions Carter Williams, a graphic artist/forger, to produce the Hyperion documents.

• *Marcus Roscoe:* A salesman for 50 years, he presently lives at Monserrat Retirement Community, Room 316. He loves Martinis and reads *Skis & Slopes* magazine. He doesn't know anything about vampires before now. [So he probably only knows about magical objects within his field of interest. A cut scene established that Marcus searched Malaysia and Tehran for a mystical artifact to keep him young.]

THE HYPERION Thanks to Lilah, it gains earthquake certification, statement of asbestos level compliance and other relevant documents.

ORGANIZATIONS *Angel Investigations:* To clarify "Dear Boy" (2.05), the agency's business cards name its particulars as 1481 Hyperion Avenue, Los Angeles, CA, 90026. Phone: (213) 555-0162. Fax: (213) 5550-0163. Cordelia is listed as a Senior Associate [presumably because she ordered the cards]. Wesley and Gunn have names on their cards; Angel doesn't.

DEMONOLOGY *Vampires:* Marcus enjoys regular food while in Angel's vampire body. [Vampires need blood to live – probably because it equates with "life," as Spike claims in *Buffy* 5.22, "The Gift," and they're basically dead creatures without an external source of the stuff. Yet Marcus' actions help to confirm that vampires can eat normal food (remember Spike's onion-blossom obsession on *Buffy*), even if they draw little sustenance from it.]

MAGIC *Algurian body-switching spell:* Marcus makes eye contact with his intended victim, then recites the words *alii permutat anima kimota* twice, whereupon they swap souls. Marcus repeats the incantation when he senses his host body degenerating. [So the return of Marcus' soul isn't automatic; in theory, failure to say the words would leave him trapped in the host body as it husks.] Marcus' victim can reverse the effect with the incantation, even while Marcus' persona is unconscious. An Algurian conjuring orb, variously referred to as a "conjuring stone," is required. [Marcus is never seen to "use" the item, so its mere proximity to the conjurer must be good enough.] Marcus also owns a Nothian herb jar.

BEST LINE Fred on the fashion models featured in Cordy's magazine: "I spent years in a cave starving to death... what's their excuse?"

THINGS THAT DON'T MAKE SENSE After Angel finds evidence that Marcus is dabbling in magic, Marcus takes off his glasses, looks him in the eye and recites a magic incantation. Angel's response, knowing full well that he's vulnerable to magic, is to stand there like a nincompoop. What the hell's he waiting for? Perhaps he's reluctant to assault a senior citizen, even though a pair of spry old folks with giant claws assaulted him a mere two episodes ago. It'd take a mere flick of Angel's super-strong finger to knock Marcus down, but nope, nope... he just stands there and lets Marcus get on with it. Patsy.

Marcus takes a hell of a long time to realize that he's in a vampire's body – perhaps he's intuitively breathing even though it's not required, but he's also failed to notice his lack of a heartbeat or body temperature. None of the ripped men that Cordelia interviews at the gym are the least bit sweaty. Purely for the sake of facilitating a good scrap, the woman that Marcus attacks in the club produces *three* jealous boyfriends.

Ah yes... and are we to presume that Marcus initiated the soul-transfer with his first three victims while they were in Pilates class? Because even allowing for L.A. denial, it's weird that nobody in the room noticed a burst of mystical energy going between the guys and the nursing home across the street. When Angel/Marcus suffers a heart attack, the nursing home officials simply put him in an infirmary room of sorts rather than doing something more sensible like, say, taking him to a hospital. But then, these are the same officials who miraculously show up in response to Marcus' groan at story's end, having previously failed to hear a scuffle featuring baseball bats, a Taser, an energy-charged magical spell and a very loud scream. To make matters worse, the orderlies barely bat an eyelid when Angel's crew walks out of the joint holding crossbows and the like.

CROSS-OVERS Willow phones, off screen, to let Angel know of Buffy's resurrection (*Buffy* 6.01, "Becoming"). *Buffy* 6.04, "Flooded" mentions that Angel phoned Buffy back, and it's made clear that he and the Slayer shared an off-screen reunion between this episode and "Fredless." The contents of the meeting are never revealed, but the Dark Horse comic *Buffy the Vampire Slayer: Reunion* by Jane Espenson entails the Sunnydale characters wildly speculating about it.

IN RETROSPECT Cordelia to Angel, regarding Fred's crush: "There's no room in the workplace for romance." Like she's one to talk. Also, anyone think that Lilah's tussle with "Angel" feels like a warm-up for the cavorting she'll do with one of his colleagues later this year? And it's rather prophetic when Lilah suggests that Angel might "rip out Gavin's throat," given the injury she incurs a year and a half from now.

IT'S REALLY ABOUT... The hell of getting older, especially when you wake up one day and feel as though you've suddenly traded bodies with a senior citizen. And fair enough that it takes a body-swap to properly illustrate this, given that Angel – as a vampire – can't age. It's also rather symbolic that Angel lacks a beating heart... yet while he's an old man, that's precisely what craps out on him.

CRITIQUE Some members of fandom continue to cite this story as a derivative, ho-hum episode, but it's actually the best stand-alone story from early Season Three, and its reputation (rightfully) has risen with time. At the very least, any story that results in Lilah getting sweaty with an old man in Angel's body deserves some benefit of the doubt. Whereas other episodes from this period falter with regards to their drama (until the profoundly disturbing 3.06, "Billy," that is), "Carpe Noctem" knows it's a comedy and largely succeeds in that regard.

Sure, the body-swap concept isn't overwhelmingly original, but it's not intended as such. It's mainly there to let Boreanaz act like a total loon, and for the viewer to laugh when his friends stupendously don't notice *that* much awry about Angel's bizarre behavior. Notice how Cordelia doesn't even find the idea of Angel rolling around with a tart in Wesley's office all that strange – "This is totally like him," she responds – and only changes her mind when she realizes the tart in question wasn't blonde.

It's a lively change of pace then, very funny in parts and nice to enjoy over drinks with friends. So let's appreciate it as such.

THE LORE Yet again, an overrun tipped the producers' hand. "Carpe Noctem" was eight minutes too long, so a subplot regarding Marcus' daughter Madeline immediately went into the bin. The gist of it involved Madeline failing to reconcile with her selfish bastard of a father, leaving Angel, in Marcus' body, to alleviate her guilt about turning her back on the old man. There's little doubt, reading the script, that it would've cast a much darker tone on the story. (Murphy, *The Bronze*, Oct. 9, 2001)

• Romanov was of the opinion from her very first episode that Lilah had a mad crush on Angel, reasoning that you couldn't hate someone that much without secretly lusting after them. She constantly used this as an internal motivation, as if Lilah were a scorned lover. Before mention of Lilah's mother in Season Three, Romanov had privately decided Lilah was an orphan and had gone off on her own, about age 13, doing odd jobs to survive. (O'Hare, *Zap2It.com*, Feb. 11, 2002)

• Boreanaz and Romanov found the Angel-Lilah snogging scene a bit difficult, as they'd worked together for some time but were both newly married. Romanov commented, "It was weird, like all of a sudden you've got to kiss your friend." (*BBC Cult*, 2002)

• Rance Howard (Marcus) is, as many readers will know, the father of director Ron Howard. His wife, Jean Speegle Howard, appeared as the real Mrs. French (not the giant praying mantis who replaced her) in *Buffy* 1.04, "Teacher's Pet." Rance Howard's wealth of performances span more than 150 films and TV shows, going all the way back to *Frontier Woman* (1956). He also played the father of John Sheridan (Bruce Boxleitner's character) on *Babylon 5*.

• Steven W. Bailey (Ryan) appeared as the cave demon that Spike consults in *Buffy* Season Six, played the title role in the reality series *My Big Fat Obnoxious Fiancé*, and is Joe the bartender on *Grey's Anatomy*.

3.05: "Fredless"

"These are Fred's very normal parents."

Air Date: Oct. 21, 2001; **Writer:** Mere Smith;
Director: Maria Grabiak

SUMMARY To everyone's surprise, shortly after Angel beheads a Durslar demon, Fred's parents – Roger and Trish Burkle – show up, having hired a private investigator to locate their missing daughter. Unfortunately, Fred recoils upon learning her parents are present, fearing that talking with them will make her five-year-exile in Pylea seem all too real. Angel and company track a fleeing Fred to the bus station, where they pause to slaughter a giant insect demon that suddenly attacks them. Fred reconciles with her parents and leaves to return home with her folks, bidding her friends farewell. Moments after she exits, though, an entire *pack* of the insect demons storm the hotel.

Fred deduces that one of the insect demons laid its eggs in the Durslar's noggin, meaning the huge insects simply want their offspring back. Dashing back to the Hyperion, Fred uses an axe-firing contraption she cobbled together to slice open the Durslar's head, causing the little insect demons inside to scuttle out and reunite with their clan. The insect horde leaves with its young, even as Fred elects to remain with Angel Investigations.

3.05, Fredless

FIRSTS AND LASTS It's the first appearance of Fred's parents, Roger and Trish Burkle, and by extension the launch of anything remotely resembling a "normal" family set-up for one of the main characters. Arguably, it's also the last time Fred uses her Texas accent so thickly and consistently throughout an entire episode.

First appearance of the Winston Churchill photograph that'll sit in the Hyperion office for much of Season Three. (One would presume it belongs to Wesley, as it's his office now. A little bizarrely, though, Minear has claimed it belongs to Angel, the justification being: "Why *wouldn't* Angel have a picture of Winston Churchill?")

POINTS OF DISCUSSION ABOUT "Fredless":

1. It was tempting to write an essay entitled **How Awful are Everyone's Parents?**, but it seemed rather mean-spirited. Nonetheless, "Fredless" contains a fun little conceit in which everyone – the audience included – thinks Roger and Trish must be overwhelmingly evil, only to find that they're just about the sweetest parents imaginable. Mind, what's really interesting is the realization that decent parents are the minority in the *Angel*-verse: There's Buffy's pleasant mother Joyce, and – for all his faults – Angel himself. But that's about it. (To be fair to *Angel* and *Buffy*, though, dreadful parenting has pretty much become a convention of most American television these days.)

With that in mind, let's quickly take stock of all the broken parent-child relationships: Angel's father was a conservative patriarch (not that this excuses Angelus eating his family, 1.15, "The Prodigal"); Wesley has continually suffered verbal abuse and put-downs from his dad (2.19, "Belonging"; 5.07, "Lineage"); Cordy lost her college money due to her parents' tax evasion (*Buffy* Season Three), and they're never seen to visit (although her mother at least phones in 1.06, "Sense and Sensitivity"); Gunn grew up an orphan (1.20, "War Zone"); Lorne finds his family unbearable, not without good reason (2.21, "Through the Looking Glass"); Kate feels ostracized from her dad, not without good reason (1.06, "Sense and Sensitivity"); Lilah's mother apparently has some form of dementia (3.15, "Loyalty"); and Lindsey's father was a jackass (1.21, "Blind Date"). "In the Dark" (1.03), at least, seems to imply that Doyle's mother is agreeable.

A similar situation exists over on *Buffy*, although it's most relevant to mention that Spike sired, then dusted his mom (*Buffy* 7.17, "Lies My Parents Told Me"), and even Buffy's mother died of a brain tumor. Fortunately, by all accounts, Fred really knows how good she's got it.

2. It's been said that Fred's wall-scribblings include a drawing of a taco accompanied by the word, "YAY." Squinting at the screen, however, the "taco" looks like a sort of physics-related doodle. There's a cute little drawing of a house, though.

CHARACTER NOTES *Angel:* Convinces the gang to inventory the weapons cabinet [owing to his confusion in 3.01, "Heartthrob"]. It's implied that he's familiar with Faulkner, and he shares Roger Burkle's reverence for the 1963 Bob Hope Desert Classic. [This is extremely odd, as golf is far too sunny a sport for vampires to enjoy; Angel later extols the virtues of hockey (3.15, "Loyalty") because it's played at night. Perhaps during the 1960s, a bored Angel (shudder) took to watching golf on TV.]

• *Cordelia:* Has never ridden in a school bus [unsurprising, given Cordy's upbringing].

• *Wesley:* Mentions with regards to Fred – but pretty obviously saying the reverse about his own parental issues – that the Burkles "didn't grind Fred down into a tiny, self-conscious nub with their constant berating and never-ending tirade of debasement and scorn." Wesley favors painting walls horizontally; Gunn likes it vertically.

• *Gunn:* Carries a bow and arrow in his truck.

• *Fred:* Secretly mailed her parents a letter a month ago. [The heroes couldn't watch Fred every second, so she probably just nipped out to a mailbox.] Yet she stressed that her parents shouldn't look for her. As part of Fred's recovery, everyone helps to paint over the wall-scribblings in her bedroom [see 3.01, "Heartthrob"].

Fred has – gulp – memorized 452 consecutive digits of pi. She's still swooning over Angel a bit [despite her chat with Cordy last episode], but paints over her storybook scribble of her with a horse-mounted "champion" as if to signal the end of her infatuation. Fred tends to navigate with mathematical precision, and here builds a spring-loaded axe-hurling device to aid anyone who loses their arms in battle. As a young girl, she took an interest in her community library.

• *Lorne:* Watches *Judge Judy*, smokes cigarettes [as with 4.06, "Spin the Bottle," sort of] and compares sitting through *Godfather III* to a massacre. He remains bitter at Gunn for the Caritas rampage [3.03, "That Old Gang of Mine," although Lorne's resentment fades after this point]. Lorne wears "only a little" eyeliner, and his heart is located in his left butt cheek [a standard of Pylean physiognomy; see 2.22, "There's No Place Like Plrtz Glrb"].

He says that Fred's aura is "practically screaming" when she asks him for help, and advises her to leave town rather than confronting her parents. [Given the Burkles' sweet nature, working out why Lorne gives such advise is a bit difficult. It's possible Lorne believes Fred needs more time, or that he instinctively senses matters will resolve themselves later (at the bus station), or perhaps his own considerable parental issues have biased him in this case.]

• *Roger and Trish Burkle:* Live in Texas, and seem remarkably stable considering their daughter has been missing for five years. Trish formerly drove a school bus. Roger enjoys disgusting alien movies, but dozed off during *Alien IV* [probably a dig at the studio for re-writing Whedon's script to the film]. They rented out Fred's room after she'd gone missing for four years, but says they'll happily boot the tenant if Fred wants to move home. They continue visiting for a few days after Fred decides to remain in L.A.

A bit disconcertingly, Roger claims they don't get a lot of guys in Texas who wear eye-liner – "not for long, anyway." [Roger and Trish next appear, in flashback, in 5.16, "Shells."]

• *Spiro T. Agnew:* Nixon's disgraced Vice-President, cited by Angel as a Grathnar Demon. [In real life, Agnew's tax evasion forced his resignation in 1973. He died in 1996. The fact that Angel claims, "I thought only I knew he was a demon," suggests a previous encounter between them.] Roger always suspected Agnew was demonic [but then, so did much of the American public].

ORGANIZATIONS *Angel Investigations:* Wesley, Cordelia and Gunn are sloppy enough to gibber about demon worship and vampires in front of potential clients who obviously have no concept of the underworld. [Didn't they learn *anything* from the Sharpes in 2.15, "Reprise"?] The heroes' weapons inventory has at least six categories, and their arsenal includes a Prothgarian broadsword, a third century ceremonial Sancteus dagger and a three-pronged Scythian death spear from Wesley's "rogue demon hunter" days. He once used it to skewer what he thought was a small Rodentius demon, but was actually a poodle.

• *Caritas:* Located next to a jewelry store (street No. 459) and what looks like an Oriental clothing shop.

DEMONOLOGY *The giant bugs:* Have glowing blue eyes, wings [although they're never seen to fly], four legs and talons for hands. Their blood/guts look purple, and evidently crystallize into eggs. Fred suspects the bugs are a hive species, gender neutral.

BEST LINE Wesley, pretending to be Angel as Cordelia plays "Buffy": "I love you so much, I almost forgot to brood!"

THINGS THAT DON'T MAKE SENSE At story's end, after Fred has happily reunited with her "Angel family," nobody even slightly dithers about the fact that *there's a swarm of giant frickin' bugs* wandering loose in L.A. Pardon our mentioning that giant bugs in the *Angel*-verse tend to be eeeevvvvilll, and "Fredless" gives us no reason to think otherwise – yet the heroes let the critters waltz right out the door. This error could've been easily rectified, too: Wesley could've pulled out a dusty book and declared, never fear, that species of giant bugs is peace-loving, prone to basket-weaving and adopting puppies. Or Angel could've delivered the token, "We'll deal with them later" line. None of that occurs, however, and it looks as if the heroes are so thrilled to have Fred back, they're overlooking the giant bug swarm that has, for all they know, just left to devour an orphanage.

In the teaser, Angel feels confident enough sending Fred back to the Hyperion by herself, so why didn't he do that before they entered the sewers after the fiendish demon beast they encountered? It's not like Fred's much help in sewer combat right now, unless she jabs her ice cream cone into the demon's eyes. Later, Wesley, Gunn and Cordelia inventory the weapons yet somehow fail to notice Fred's spring-loaded decapitation device until Cordy trips over it, even though it's sitting right in the middle of the room. Later, Angel flings back the severed Durslar head while talking with Roger and Trish and there's the sound of a window breaking – even though the Hyperion office doesn't seem to have one.

It was lovely of Trish to plow a bus into one of the giant bugs, but how did she procure the ignition key? Did the bus driver flee on foot after seeing the giant bugs, even though he could've just driven away? Because unless Trish learned the art of hotwiring vehicles during her school bus-driving days...

Bit picky now: Fred builds the axe-throwing contraption so the heroes can still do battle even if their arms get hacked off. Granted, you can fire the gizmo with your feet, but, errrrrr, how do you aim it without using your arms?

IT'S REALLY ABOUT... First and foremost, it's about how good parents are rare and to be treasured. Tangentially, it's also about mis-judging the surface, as we're made to think that Fred's parents are villains, but they're actually quite sweet. It's possible that we're meant to similarly view the giant bugs as "good parents" – but then, some of the worst predators have a strong maternal instinct, so we refer you back to **Things That Don't Make Sense**.

TONIGHT AT CARITAS(ish) Fred batters Lorne with "Row, row, row your boat."

CRITIQUE Hardly surprising that a certain slice of fandom unswervingly loves this story. It's the right time to effectively bring Fred out of her shell, and the story's deliberately designed to be – let's say – endearingly sweet. Nonetheless, from a critical point of view, "Fredless" just isn't all that.

Unfortunately, you have to wonder if Smith's history as a *Buffy* fan didn't overly influence her professional work at points. Because however you slice "Fredless," it looks and feels like a work of fan-fiction, only one that's made professionally for TV, and with some incredibly obvious jokes. Fair enough it's about Fred getting over an inner fear, but everything's so painfully contrived to this end. It *happens* that Fred keeps her bug-guts-splattered shirt out of sentiment (thus providing her with a big clue), it *happens* that she's built a catapult that's the very solution to the problem at hand, and it *happens* that she discards this piece of formidable weaponry precisely where it's needed for the big finish. Meanwhile, the other heroes are rendered so damned useless it hurts, purely to let Fred save the day. Compounding all this, there's just not enough story to fill the required 45-ish minutes, forcing the characters to chew up time by (for instance) lounging about pining for Fred.

Where this episode shines – as you've probably suspected already – is in Roger and Trish Burkle. They're a joy to behold both here and in future, and everyone should be so fortunate to have them as parents. But whatever the Burkles' legacy, they single-handedly can't prevent this story from rising above the dizzying heights of "mediocre." Nobody would argue that Fred is a tremendously wonderful character, but she's wonderful irrespective of what happens here, not because of it.

THE LORE The script made reference to Fred having two brothers and a sister. Whedon wrote the bit where Fred comes unglued in the bus station.

• Smith later posted that Lorne didn't normally smoke, but that he was going through a rough patch after the devastation to Caritas. She added: "Well, the terrycloth says it all, don't you think?" (Smith, *The Bronze*, Oct. 23, 2001)

3.06: "Billy"

"What do you tell a woman who has two black eyes? Nothing you haven't already told her twice."

Air Date: Oct. 29, 2001; **Writers:** Tim Minear, Jeffrey Bell; **Director:** David Grossman

SUMMARY Angel and company find evidence that links the liberated Billy (3.02, "That Vision Thing") to a recent murder. Meanwhile, Wolfram and Hart tries to keep Billy under control on behalf of his rich and powerful family, but Billy somehow causes Gavin to go berserk and beat the tar out of Lilah. The heroes learn that Billy's touch can endow men with a murderous misogyny – but not before Wesley touches a sample of Billy's blood and becomes contaminated, prompting him to take after Fred with an axe. After a harrowing chase in the Hyperion, Fred rigs up a "swinging fire extinguisher trap" and bashes Wesley unconscious.

Cordelia and Angel intercept Billy when the villain attempts to leave town, but Billy touches Angel, hoping to turn him against Cordelia. Angel proves immune and brawls with Billy, but Lilah suddenly shows up and – in an act of retribution for her assault – shoots Billy dead. Afterward, Fred graciously recognizes that Wesley wasn't in his right mind, but a completely shamed Wes can only weep in his apartment.

FIRSTS AND LASTS Indisputably, it's the beginning of Wesley's descent into what we'll call his "Dark Wesley" persona, and therefore the start of the most tragic character-arc in the entire Whedon-verse. As part and parcel of this, we learn about Wesley's romantic feelings for Fred, which won't abate for the rest of the series.

Cordelia starts to learn combat techniques from Angel in the Hyperion basement. Allowing that all politicians are arguably evil, Billy's uncle – a precursor to Senator Bruckner (see 5.21, "Power Play") – constitutes the first appearance of a *really we're not joking, look!, he's aligned with the forces of evil!* politician on *Angel*.

POINTS OF DISCUSSION ABOUT "Billy":

1. For an episode that focuses so heavily on Wesley and Fred, it's also – surprisingly – the next step forward in Cordelia's character. Back in "Homecoming" (*Buffy* 3.05), Cordy was a huge liability in combat, forcing the Slayer to keep Cordy out of trouble and simultaneously do battle with a spatula. But here, Cordelia *is* Buffy. Her basement-training with Angel is a very Buffy moment, and notice how Cordy takes after the villain with a crossbow. By the way, the "big showdown" only illustrates Cordelia's emotional maturity, particularly in her telling Billy that "I'm feeling superior because I have an arrow pointed at your jugular. And the irony of using a phallic-shaped weapon? Not lost on me." Granted, if you're going to fatally shoot a man with a crossbow, then "phallic" perhaps isn't exactly the first term that springs to mind – yet that detail would have been lost on the old Cordelia, who back in "Earshot" (*Buffy* 3.18) could barely form a thought more complex than "I'm cold."

2. Taking the "Cordelia is the Slayer" motif a bit further... if you swap the characters around, this would've made a great *Buffy* story. Wesley is Giles, Fred is Willow, the self-sacrificing Gunn is Xander, Angel is (um) Angel and the Hyperion is Sunnydale High. In a pinch, Faith might serve as Lilah. You'd also have to re-tailor Giles' taunts, given he's not in love with Willow (we hope) and her sexual orientation. But otherwise, it fits together scarily well.

3. A thematic issue is whether Billy's power externally taints men with misogyny or "awakens" primal feelings inherent in them. Angel favors the latter, believing that Billy's touch didn't affect him because he surrendered personal motives such as rage, hatred and misogyny during his killing days. However, Fred conversely believes it's an "infection" of sorts.

Minear and Bell don't feel particularly inclined to answer this question, but judging by the "rules" of the *Angel*-verse, Fred is probably correct. Angel's argument would explain why Billy's power wouldn't affect Angelus, who lacked both a soul and a conscience, but Angel's soul makes him prone to all of human beings' failings, misogyny included. In short, if Billy's power triggered something inherent in humans, then Angel's soul would likely render him just as vulnerable as any male. A far more likely explanation is that Billy's power – working largely through pheromones – requires a body chemistry to work and simply doesn't affect the undead.

4. Just two episodes after Cordelia lectured Angel about the importance of separating one's business and social lives, the hussy pulls a 180 and effectively pushes Wesley into Fred's arms. Really, it would appear that she isn't really opposed to inter-office romances, so long as they're the ***right*** inter-office romances. It's also not impossible to believe – if you're so inclined – that she's a bit sweet on Angel and here acts to keep contenders away from him, even though she needn't worry much about Fred after "Carpe Noctem" (3.04).

5. It's often touted as a goof that Gunn returns to the Hyperion and magically knows what's up with the lunatic Wesley and Fred. We're of the opinion that this more or less makes sense – after all, if Gunn walked into the hotel and was greeted by the sounds of fevered running upstairs and a crazed Wesley gibbering to himself about how he's a man, Fred's the weaker sex, Garden of Eden, blah blah blah, it's not *so* hard to figure out what's happening, is it?

CHARACTER NOTES *Angel:* Suggests Angelus' butchery wasn't about hating his victims, but instead about the pain/pleasure derived from such acts. [This is a major element moving forward, particularly in Season Five, and see especially 5.08, "Destiny."]

• *Cordelia:* Well-versed in Boracci shoes, and claims there's not a thing about badly applied mascara that she doesn't know. She's learning swordplay from Angel, and proves an adept learner thanks to her three years of varsity cheer squad. Cordy successfully motivates Lilah to take action against Billy, drawing on her own vision-induced trauma [3.02, "That Vision Thing"] and the helplessness it engendered. Cordelia's savvy enough to recognize Wesley's infatuation with Fred when nobody else does. [Cordy's romantic judgment worsens from this point, though; see especially 3.18, "Double or Nothing."]

• *Wesley:* Needless to say, the whole "chasing Fred about with an axe" severely dampens his romantic intentions. [And he doesn't regain his balance until "Waiting in the Wings" (3.13).] Surprisingly, Wesley owns a video game console. He lives in Apartment 105 [reiterated in stories such as 4.05, "Supersymmetry"], and buys crime scene details from someone who normally sells such stuff to the tabloids. [Oh, and we must ask: where did Wesley learn those unbelievably sexist jokes? The Watchers' Academy?]

• *Gunn:* Gets infected by Billy's blood, but noble enough to let Fred thwack him unconscious with a severed chair leg.

• *Fred:* Displays a great deal of mettle through all of this. Almost frighteningly, she rattles off population/landmass statistics about Santa Monica, Beverly Hills and Malibu.

• *Gavin:* Beats up Lilah while under Billy's influence, but apparently gets the same in kind, if not more, off screen.

• *Lilah:* Now thinks that Angel "definitely wants to kill her" [presumably due to the misunderstanding in "Carpe Noctem," yet she realizes the truth by 3.08, "Offspring"]. She wears Boracci shoes.

• *William "Billy" Blim:* [Last seen in "That Vision Thing" (3.02).] It's repeatedly suggested, but never explicitly stated, that Billy's power owes to a demon inheritance. [See **The Lore**.] Wesley and Fred claim his red-blood cells are "supercharged," but Billy can "infect" men through simple touch. [This presumably happens by contact with Billy's sweat, suggesting that his spitting on somebody would achieve the same result. Had Billy lived, it's possible that his power might've mutated and become airborne – if so, small wonder he was locked up in "That Vision Thing."] Billy's touch affects men differently, with effects manifesting instantaneously or in a matter of hours. [It's never said, but notice how the guy's personality alters the equation. As the child of a domineering father, a crazed Wesley might feel more inclined to toy with Fred before killing her. The affected policeman, by contrast, simply goes ballistic.]

Billy is the nephew of Congressman Nathan Blim. Lilah says the Blims are "the closest thing [America] has to royalty" [they even look a bit like the Kennedys] and that the family would "own half the Eastern seaboard" even if they weren't the firm's clients. The family – including Billy's cousin Dylan – have "rules" such as never letting Billy touch you, and always keeping him away from "pets." [This implies that Billy's power works on animals, or perhaps he just likes to torment pets.]

Billy possesses enhanced strength and stamina. [Cordelia zaps him ***in the nuts***, yet he's standing just a short while later.] He can thump the ground to "charge" himself with strength, but Angel is clearly stronger. Billy's never tried to use his power on a vampire before now.

THE HYPERION Parts of it – including a floor with Room 520 – remain a bit tattered and in disuse, with bits of furniture scattered everywhere.

ORGANIZATIONS *Angel Investigations:* The office owns a microscope and a police scanner. [Minear suggests it's the same scanner that Angel swiped in "Somnambulist" (1.11), but acknowledges it probably would've been destroyed with Angel's apartment at the end of Season One. Maybe Wesley took it home beforehand.]

• *The Powers-That-Be:* Their latest vision depicts a murder that took place a week ago. [This begs the question of why they didn't alert Cordelia before now, unless events in "That Vision Thing" temporarily futzed up her mental receiver.]

DEMONOLOGY *Vampires:* Billy claims that Angel has a "standing invitation" into his home, and Angel charges inside without personally receiving it. [Some cut bits from the script suggested that Billy's entire family was demonic, which voided the invitation rule. The on-screen evidence, however, supports the notion that a vampire can receive an invitation *in abstentia*; see **How Does the Invitation Rule Work?**]

BEST LINE Not so much a "Best Line" as the scene where Cordy/Lilah find a common ground. Cordy: "Please. I was you. With better shoes." Lilah: "These are Boracci." Cordy: "Fall collection?" Lilah: "Next spring." Cordy: "He's widened the heel." Lilah: "And rounded the toe." Cordy: "That won't work with pink." Lilah: "The pink is out this spring."

THINGS THAT DON'T MAKE SENSE Lilah should know about Billy's misogyny-inducing power from the get-go, yet she isn't a bit concerned to find Billy and Gavin chatting together, nor does she take the hint when Gavin starts talking to her even more belligerently than normal. Besides, why doesn't the firm have protocols to prevent Billy from infecting their employees? At the very least, they should've stringently told their staff to "avoid this guy at all cost if you're a bloke," unless Gavin somehow didn't get the memo or was simply too arrogant to heed it.

L.A.'s finest, as ever off their game: The police arrest Billy in connection with a murder case, yet they utterly ignore Angel upon hearing Billy's explanation that "he's nobody." For pity's sake, they're taking the murder suspect at his word? Nor do they find it remotely strange that Angel has just smashed in Billy's living room window with a lawn chair.

For that matter, why *does* Billy go to all the elaborate trouble of confessing to a serious crime and getting the police to haul him away? Gunn suggests that Billy did this to escape the family estate, yet Billy's already on the loose when the episode starts and only resurfaces of his own volition. This is fiendishly complicated villainy, if he's determined to return home purely so he can bust out again.

At this point in the show, Wesley should really know better than to touch the blood of someone who's probably demonic and sporting undefined super-powers. (Minear admits on the DVD commentary that this was rather contrived.) A technical goof that everyone notices: Angel comments that a convenience store photo was taken at 11:24, yet it's time-stamped at 10:52 pm. And a technical glitch that you'll need to slo-mo your DVD for: One of the "flash cuts" between scenes – specifically, the one between the bit in the taxi and the next one with the two drivers arguing – shows the *Angel* set crew milling about on location.

Right, then... ready for the cosmetics lesson? Cordelia reasons that Lilah was crying five minutes before she arrived because "there's not a thing about badly re-applied mascara that I don't know." We can't quite figure out, though, why Lilah would re-apply mascara to an eye that's swollen shut, or why she'd apply it to one eye but not the other. For that matter, if she's going to the trouble of applying mascara, couldn't she go a bit further and better conceal her injuries? (Perhaps Lilah simply isn't thinking straight after Billy's attack and only later recovers her composure – notice how she's got the presence of mind to change her clothes and do her hair before going out to shoot him.)

IN RETROSPECT Angel claims he "long ago lost his hatred and anger"... which is ironic, as we're only 11 episodes away from his vengefully attempting to smother one of his best friends with a pillow.

IT'S REALLY ABOUT... Wrathful, primal misogyny – a topic that's presented here as being so illogical and without merit that it's hard to write much in-depth about it. It's curious, though, how much the story dresses itself in signs of male aggression, including the video games that Gunn and Angel play in Act One. You might also notice how Wesley undoes his shirt slightly before taking after Fred – apparently, real men don't wear ties.

CRITIQUE Arguably, looking at *Angel* as a whole, it's one of the most important stories of all because it's the "red line" from which the show irrevocably hurtles into a dark space. So much attention gets focused (not without justification) on the three-parter to follow, or events later in the year, that we sometimes forget the seminal nature of "Billy," or how it sharply re-establishes that anything can happen in this series, and that *everyone's* a target for tragedy.

Conceptually, it's a masterstroke. Wesley is so cold and calculating while trying to bury his axe in Fred that it's all far more harrowing and interesting than the original idea of Angel going nuts (see **The Lore**). Once Wes loses his mind, the normally elegant Hyperion refashions itself into a haunted labyrinth. The direction beautifully capitalizes on this – observe as Wes' dark shadow crops up several doors down while he's pursuing Fred, and think about how it's much more horrifying that she's being chased by a skinny white guy, not a hulking demon. Amid all this chaos, Billy himself is one of the *least* innovative bits, a stock character who's portrayed as a misogynist because... well, he just is. But that's okay because he's really just the catalyst here, unintentionally galvanizing the heroes toward ruin. Hell, Billy and Wesley never even meet, yet Billy irrevocably changes Wes' story like never before.

It's a story, then, in which some of the heroes lose an innocence that they'll never regain. The "video game party" that opens this episode serves as a last stab at showing the heroes at peace with one another, and starting next episode, Angel's child – not the protagonists themselves – will serve as the show's object of "purity." It's a tremendous paradigm shift, then, but thank God the producers bravely took such risks, because that's when *really* interesting things start to happen.

THE LORE Oddly enough, one of the most interesting things on display is the disused Ambassador Hotel, the real-life L.A. location that doubles as the Hyperion's upper levels. The Ambassador, in case you didn't know, is where Robert Kennedy was killed. He made a victory speech there on June 6, 1968, but was assassinated shortly afterward in a crowded kitchen hallway. The hotel also hosted the Academy Awards for a time, but was closed to the public in 1989. A myriad of movies were filmed there over the years, including *Rocky, The Wedding Singer, The Fabulous Baker Boys, The Naked Gun, Pretty Woman, Apollo 13, L.A. Story* and *Forrest Gump*. It would appear that *Angel* was the last TV series to film in the hotel (the crew went back there for 3.19, "The Price"). Debate over whether to preserve or bulldoze the building intensified shortly afterward, and demolition of the Ambassador finally began in September 2005.

• The story as originally conceptualized had Angel getting infected and going nuts, but Whedon suggested it'd be more interesting if Wesley went off the rails instead. (We might suggest that using Angel would've been problematic, partly because it would've been Angelus and Jenny Calendar from *Buffy* Season Two all over again, and partly because it's harder to imagine Fred eluding Angel, who's superhuman.)

• Fury was initially going to write this story, then Minear decided to handle it himself, then Bell wound up writing it with him. Later, Whedon wanted Minear to stop by his house over the weekend and – as had become the tradition – recite Shakespeare with members of the cast. (These sort of get-togethers, by the way, convinced Whedon to write the *Buffy* musical.) Minear replied that he simply couldn't spare the time, so Whedon scripted the Cordelia-Lilah scenes, alleviating Minear's workload enough for him to attend. Minear ultimately wrote the teaser and the first two acts (minus Whedon's contribution), plus the final scene between Fred and Wesley. It would appear that Bell handled everything else. (Minear, *uk.media.tv.angel*, Aug. 13, 2002)

• Minear and Bell hashed through Billy's back-story but never committed it to paper: The idea was that Billy's human father raped Billy's mother, a benevolent demon, and a twist was that Billy's evil nature owed to his human inheritance.

• Censors apparently vetoed some of the violence in the scene where Gavin assaults Lilah. Another amendment: Fred initially clobbered Wesley with a paint can, but Minear realized this was too similar to *Home Alone* and swapped it out for a fire extinguisher.

3.07: "Offspring"

"I love children. I could just eat 'em up."

Air Date: November 5, 2001; **Writer:** David Greenwalt; **Director:** Turi Meyer

SUMMARY Wesley and Gunn obtain pieces of the Nyazian Scrolls, documents purported to detail a prophecy regarding the arrival of the "Tro-clan" – a person foretold to bring about the ruination of mankind. Meanwhile, a *very* pregnant Darla shows up on Angel's doorstep, desperate for help. The heroes uneasily take Darla to Caritas so Lorne can "read" her, but Darla's bloodthirst compels her to attack Cordelia. Angel fends Darla off, but Darla flees and, increasingly wanting the blood of the pure, stalks children at an amusement house. Angel pursues and brawls with Darla – then realizes that their unborn child has a heartbeat and a soul. Darla collapses in tears at this revelation, returning with Angel to the Hyperion.

Meanwhile, a demon performs a mystic rite that causes Holtz – the highly proficient eighteenth century vampire hunter – to awaken from an extended slumber. *[Continued next episode]*

FIRSTS AND LASTS It's our first sight of the tall demon Sahjhan (although he's not named until next episode) and his underground lair, and it's the series' first venture into Rome, more than two years ahead of the definitive *Angel* Italian adventure, (see 5.20, "The Girl in Question"). It's also the second and final appearance of the Furies – who'll warrant a few more mentions – and the emergence of Holtz into the modern day.

Cordelia gains highlights for the first time, starting her evolution into a blonde throughout Season Three – given Angel's romantic fetishes, can you predict where all this is going? It's hardly a surprise, then, that Cordy's hair-color change coincides with the first stirrings of an Angel/Cordelia romance. Specifically, it's the moment when Fred describes them as soulmates, and a hesitant Angel wonders if she's got a point.

First instance of Fred wearing a ridiculously short miniskirt, not that we expect to hear many complaints.

POINTS OF DISCUSSION ABOUT "Offspring":

1. We've no proof to substantiate this, but we'd swear that one of the female vamps with Darla in flashback is a stuntman in a wig. If it's a stunt*woman*, then the end result –

sorry to sound cruel – is still the most masculine female vamp that we've ever seen.

2. Angel makes his first move, however stumbling, toward a romance with Cordelia, and it's curious how far we've moved from the Season One position that Angel essentially can't date anyone for fear of becoming a homicidal maniac again. It's worth pondering that the theoretical penalty here isn't – say – a messy inter-office relationship or an STD. If Angel screws up with this, a lot of people could die hideously.

Now, many fans and professionals alike have suggested that Angel can only experience "perfect happiness" with Buffy, so his sleeping with Cordelia wouldn't attain such heights. It's funny, though, how rarely people acknowledge that this is downright insulting to Cordelia, or every member of the female race who isn't Buffy. Yet it mostly stems from people's desire to hold up the Angel-Buffy relationship on a pedestal – a view we challenge in **Who Is Angel's True Love?**

The real-world explanation for Angel's change of heart, of course, is that the producers simply went a different direction with the title character. Fair enough, but the *Angel*-verse rationale for Angel's throwing such caution to the wind is a bit harder to ascertain. Any romance with Cordelia would surely entail consummating the relationship at *some* point, unless they're planning to live like monks, or unless they're banking on the Shanshu Prophecy's reward of one day making Angel human. (Then again, there's no guarantee the Shanshu – if it's even valid – will kick in during Cordelia's lifespan.)

We've said enough on this, but perhaps – as we suggested in "That Old Gang of Mine" (3.03) – Angel's coupling with Darla facilitated his taking a further step and banging the Furies. And when that turned out okay, he's feeling more confident about this whole love thing.

3. Yup, okay... Holtz's sunglasses in the 1771 flashback really do scream "anachronism" like few other accessories. Yet we've excluded this from **Things That Don't Make Sense**, due to the possible loophole that optician James Ayscough experimented with tinted lenses – the sort designed to correct sight defects, not to function as sunglasses as such – as early as 1752. So it's not impossible that Holtz could be wearing a variant of this in 1771... even the designers were surely trying to make Holtz look cool, not because they were making a desperate stab at realism.

4. The heroes can't determine if the "Tro-clon" (redefined in the next two episodes as a convergence of events; see **Prophecy**) is something that will bring about the "ruination" or "purification" of mankind. Depending on how you define terms... yup, Jasmine nearly accomplishes both simultaneously. It's always pleasing yet odd to see this sort of symmetry, when the writers clearly didn't intend it, and see **Did Jasmine Cause All This?** for more.

5. Funny how many antagonists – in this case, Holtz – feel the urge to string Angel up in the middle of the room when they're torturing him. And speaking of that scene, you're forgiven if you felt the urge to yell "It's Zorro!" when Holtz rides into the room on horseback.

CHARACTER NOTES *Angel:* Taking Fred's belief that "gut attraction" exists between him and Cordelia to heart, and acting more awkward around Cordy than normal. [He's just not thinking clearly here; Fred spouts off something sunshiny about Angel and Cordelia's relationship, whereupon Angel becomes a goofy schoolboy.] Cordelia implies that Angel had a birthday recently, and also believes that Angel can't use his voice mail but will usually respond to his pager.

In 1771, Angelus eluded Holtz in North Africa, then returned to Rome in search of Darla. Holtz captured Angelus and tortured him for at least a day, but Darla and her vampire minions rescued him.

Angel claims to have seen three ancient-scroll prophecies of doom. [He appears to mean actual documents of doom, but this is hard to reconcile even allowing for the likes of "To Shanshu in L.A." (1.22), "Prophecy Girl" (*Buffy* 1.12), "Becoming" (*Buffy* 2.22) or "Graduation Day" (*Buffy* 3.22). There's probably an unseen adventure or two here.]

• *Cordelia:* Still training with Angel, and one of her punches appears to sting him. [As amusing as this sounds, Cordelia isn't strong enough to damage Angel, who can withstand falling off buildings. Maybe he's just surprised that it's more than a sissy punch.] Cordy initially feels sympathy for Darla's condition, and a bit of outrage because Angel lied about sleeping with her [2.18, "Disharmony"]. Her compassion drops off, though, after Darla assaults her.

• *Wesley:* Getting better at eluding alarm systems and guard-dogs, but still a bit clumsy while sneaking around. He's entirely clueless about how a vampire pregnancy is possible.

• *Gunn:* Can juggle, and fairly well, too. He's carrying a crossbow rig. [It's similar to, if not the same as, the late Gio's rig from "That Old Gang of Mine" (3.03). Gunn built it in the first place, and perhaps just reclaimed his property.]

• *Fred:* Seems to know a bit of Latin, and regards Angel and Cordelia as a couple. [So she's completely flip-flopped after her crush on him.]

• *Darla:* Arrives in L.A. wearing a track suit, pants and a white shirt, yet shows up at the Hyperion the next day with a spiffier number and a shawl. Oh, and her hair's different too. [But then, this is a woman who arguably gets her hair done before slaughtering a bunch of lawyers in 2.10, "Reunion."]

Darla claims she visited "every shaman and seer in the Western Hemisphere," all of whom said her condition was unprecedented. She's ravenously hungry, finds pig's blood repellent and lusts for the blood of the pure. [The innocent child within Darla evidently doesn't get proper nourishment from "foul" substances such as pig's blood; the fact that this compels Darla to hunt children is presumably an unfortunate side-effect.]

In 1771, Angelus said that Darla loved the Sistine Chapel and particularly Botticelli's frescoes, her favorite being *The Last Temptation of Christ* ("probably because of the leper," Angelus said).

• *Holtz:* [First seen in 3.01, "Heartthrob."] Claimed, in 1771, that he "didn't want anything" other than to learn if a creature such as Angelus could pay for his sins. [Tellingly, Holtz ponders the dichotomy between Angelus the demon and Angel the man, yet feels no sympathy for the latter – the same attitude he'll display toward Angel in the modern day.] Holtz appears to speak Italian.

• *Monsignor Rivalli:* He wed Holtz and Caroline, and lent Holtz assistance in 1771. The Monsignor had been excommunicated from the order he founded, *Inquisitori*, which adhered to "the old beliefs." He commanded a group of robed men who were fairly adept at fighting vampires.

• *Angel and Darla's child:* Wesley theorizes that Angel's offspring possesses a soul because its father does. [This is pure conjecture, but pretty much in line with what we'll discuss in **Did Jasmine Cause All This?** The child would arguably need a soul to father Jasmine, a supposed creature of "peace" who wouldn't want to spawn from a soulless being.]

• *Arney:* Demonic contractor hired to renovate Caritas. He's charging Lorne $1,200 beyond his original estimate, and compounds the offense by wearing low-hanging pants. He's able to replay people's statements, acting like a walking demonic tape recorder.

PYLEA Fred refers to Pylea as a "hell dimension" [not strictly true, but then, she's understandably biased]. The Pylean word *kye-rumption* [spelled that way in the script] denotes when two great heroes meet in a field of battle and recognize their mutual fate. The term also means a kind of grog made out of ox dung, but that use is archaic. Fred also mentions *moira*, the gut physical attraction between two larger-than-life souls. [The Earth word *moira* doesn't seem to match Fred's definition, but it's a glitch if it denotes a further Pylean term. After all, Fred claimed that *kye-rumption* is the "only nice" Pylean word she knows, and *moira* sounds pleasant enough.]

ORGANIZATIONS *Angel Investigations:* The heroes keep a chart on Angel's family tree [and with good reason].

• *The Powers-That-Be:* Send Cordelia a vision as Darla chomps into her neck. [It's unclear if they time this to distract Darla, but it does make her take pause. If so, it's unusually helpful of them.] Cordelia confusingly describes the message as "a dream, but more like a vision," and re-experiences it while dozing. [It *is* an unusual vision, a bit prophetic regarding Darla hunting kiddies, but with images of Angelus and Darla screwing for no clear reason.] Cordy suspects the Powers were signaling the innocence of Darla's child. [That's feasible, but alternatively see **Did Jasmine Cause All This?**]

• *Caritas:* According to Arney, the Caritas renovations include use of kek-bile [surely not derived from extinct Kek Demons, 1.14, "I've Got You Under My Skin," unless the creatures' bile outlived them] and bin-der glands.

DEMONOLOGY *Vampires:* In 1771, the Monsignor's tiny cross doesn't impede Darla in the slightest. Cordy's little cross in the modern day proves equally ineffective. [It's further proof that crosses burn vampires, but don't project mystical force fields.] Wes confirms, for benefit of anyone still in doubt, that vampires can't have children.

PROPHECY *The Nyazian Prophecies:* Written in what Wesley refers to as *the* lost Nyazian Scroll. [Yet it's commonly called the Nyazian Scroll*s* starting next episode, so we've arbitrarily opted to use the plural term.] The prophecies supposedly foretell the end of the world and mention the "Tro-clon," cited as the being that will either ruin or purify mankind. [The next two episodes amend this view, however.] There's mention of Tro-clon involving both a birth and "an arising," and there's a reference to being *burren* – Middle English for "to be born," "to bear." In the Scrolls, the Middle English *arezan* and the Gothic *urazan* both mean "to appear," "to spring up." [By the way, here and in episodes such as 3.09, "Lullaby," the heroes say the Scrolls foretell of something "born out of darkness to bring darkness." It sounds more like a catch-phrase they banter around, however, and might not come directly from the Scrolls.]

The text proves tough to translate. One word means "purification" in Aramaic, "ruination" in ancient Greek and both in the lost Gashundi language [re-mentioned in the next two episodes and 3.17, "Forgiving"]. It also includes Latin terminology such as *arepare*, meaning "arrive" – i.e. to come to land, or possibly to come to as from a deep sleep.

Fred calculates the time for a key event in the prophecies [evidently Holtz's arrival] by working forward from the presumed date in the ancient Roman calendar (with its 1,464 days in a four-year cycle) and the Etruscan, Sumerian and Dradian (sic) calendars (which have their own cycles). She factors in our 365-day calendar, with a three-day discrepancy every four years. [Fred's probably over-simplifying, given the oddities in historical calendar-keeping, but let's move on.]

MAGIC Holtz slumbered in a stone sarcophagus of sorts, and Sahjhan awakens him with a small chant that mentions: "... as pledged in Caladan by Cod-she, one shall awaken in the first year of the last century; that one... joined Cod-she in the great sleep." [It's presently 2001, so please let's not start the debate that the "first year" would mean 2000.]

• *The Sanctuary Spell*: Installed in Caritas when the Furies hover and chant a bit. [They're either casting the demon-only component of the spell, or they're just "priming" the location, because the enchantment's incomplete as of 3.09, "Lullaby."]

• *Cyopian conjuring spheres:* Extremely valuable, yet fragile [as with most conjuring spheres, see 2.02, "Are You Now or Have You Ever Been?"].

BEST LINE Lorne on Darla's pregnancy: "This is way beyond my ken. And my Barbie and all my action figures." The runner-up is Gunn, detailing Darla's adept escape: "We tried to stop her by hitting her fists and feet with our faces."

THINGS THAT DON'T MAKE SENSE More a glaring omission than anything else, but given that much of this four-part story arc will revolve around the Nyazian Scrolls, it's rather irritating that we're never told what made the heroes start looking for the document in the first place. One of Gunn's snitches provided information on the Scrolls' location, so did he also bring it to their attention? If so, why now?

In Caritas, it's sensible that the heroes want Darla to rest, and it's understandable that they'd tell Angel to back off. But it's ludicrous that they leave Cordelia alone with Darla – when a peckish Darla attacks her, they've only themselves to blame. Mind, it later looks like Gunn is "guarding" Darla with his back turned, which isn't terribly smart either.

Wesley claims the police might want to know why the magical artifact collector owns Muslok trancing amalgam, which chemically resembles GHB, a.k.a. Rohypnol (or so Wesley says), the "date-rape drug." GHB and Rohypnol *are* both date-rape drugs, but they're not the *same* date-rape drug and don't resemble each other chemically. (Wes is staring down the barrel of a gun at the time, and just making up stuff up.) For that matter, wouldn't the cops find the other items in the man's collection – say, the severed demon heads – rather strange?

The obvious point: Future episodes establish that Sahjhan is intangible in our dimension, yet here we see him flicking some herbs over Holtz's stone column, lighting a cigarette from a very corporeal flame, stomping out said ciggie in the dirt and glancing at a wrist-watch that he surely didn't own when he became immaterial (as related in 3.17, "Forgiving"). Perhaps the herbs are an illusion for fanfare's sake, but can Sahjhan project a wrist-watch illusion that tells time? Besides, how does one derive pleasure from an illusionary cigarette? And even if you somehow overlook all that, it arguably looks as though Sahjhan pats a recovering Holtz on the shoulder.

Skip this paragraph if you want to avoid the salacious details: Angel here says he had sexual congress "two or three times" with Darla back in Season Two, yet "Epiphany" (2.16), made abundantly clear that they only rolled in the hay but once. (Typical male, always exaggerating.) Oh, and once the heroes learn that Darla needs the blood of the pure, what's the value in handing her a mug of pig's blood? We're some distance from Angel trying out otter's blood (5.01, "Conviction"), but surely almost any critter is preferable to swine.

IN RETROSPECT Gunn wonders if Angel and Darla's kid is "some kind of über-vamp" – and well in advance of *Buffy* Season Seven, too. Also, notice how Gunn strong-arms a collector by juggling his fragile conjuring spheres. It's not as colorful as Spike threatening to decapitate the Trio's Boba Fett action figure (*Buffy* 6.09, "Smashed"), but it's a nice touch.

IT'S REALLY ABOUT... Men living up to the responsibility that it takes two people to sire a child, whatever feelings of bewilderment and betrayal accompany an unexpected pregnancy. Darla further fillets Angel with, "You so wanna play the good guy... Yeah, you're the good guy who did *this* to me," and her even more succinct accusation of "How could you put this in me?", even as Cordelia verbally skewers Angel for "going all male." Remembering that women bear the brunt of pregnancy, men aren't portrayed in a particularly flattering light here. It's also a little telling that the heroes, upon realizing that Darla wants the blood of the pure, feel convinced that she'll go after Cordelia or Fred first – as if blokes such as Gunn and even Wesley are inherently sullied and not tasty enough.

Additionally, it's about the implicit horror in letting biology take its course. Angel and Darla's offspring is the most innocent character on display here, yet everyone regards it as something dangerous, to the degree that there'll be talk of flamethrowers next episode.

TONIGHT AT CARITAS(ish) Darla croaks "Oh, Danny boy..." before grabbing Lorne's shirt and asking, "What the hell's inside me?" Hardly a surprise that he's baffled.

CRITIQUE It's important to pause and recognize the trump card TV drama holds over movies: namely, there's vastly more time to develop the characters and concepts. Movies have their advantages, but even a superb one is generally limited to two or three hours, and simply can't compete with the duration of a TV season. And that's particularly relevant here.

For "Offspring" is the glorious point when the watershed that's built up over the last 48 *Angel* episodes (never mind everything that goes down on *Buffy*) gloriously breaks loose and takes on a life of its own. We'd have to admit that the episode itself creaks in parts, but the overarching story holds a vitality that's tragically rare and deserves applause when it happens. It's as if the show is now hitting us with a fierce wind, and you'd have to be among the clinically dead to not notice.

A curious consequence, however, is that the Character Notes section gets more sparse in this era. Well, naturally... if you're in the throes of a period where the plot's crashing down like dominoes, and the characters spend so much time reacting to various crises, there's preciously little time to stop and dissect them much. That's not a criticism, you understand – we've spent the last two-plus years getting to know Angel, Cordelia, Wesley, Darla, etc., so it's perfectly acceptable to really smack them around and see how they rebound. For that matter, the sight of Angel sparring with a pregnant woman *who's holding her own* demonstrates the bizarre lengths to which the show is now going, so it's understandable that for now, it's the plot that matters.

Like "Billy," this story isn't what you'd call picture-perfect, but it's part of a master plan that initiates what we now (and rightfully so) recognize as the cream of the series. It must seem a bit off-putting to anyone starting the show at this point, but especially if you've been around from the beginning, let's celebrate this as sparking some of the best that *Angel* has to offer.

THE LORE Keith Szarabajka's agent heard that *Angel* was casting a character named Holtz and sent around the actor's tape; it helped immensely that Szarabajka had appeared on the short-lived series *Profit*, on which Greenwalt had served as executive producer. Greenwalt needed no further persuasion and immediately signed Szarabajka up to play the part – Szarabajka was guaranteed eight episodes, but wound up appearing in 11.

Prior to *Angel*, Szarabajka's most famous work had been the late 80s series *The Equalizer* – he'd played Mickey Kostmayer, an ex-Secret Service agent and an assistant to the lead. His stage career included *Doonesbury: The Musical*, and after *Angel* he wound up with the almost obligatory (or so it feels for Whedon-verse actors) recurring role on *24*. He's also logged a lot of hours doing voice work, performing as Raven's demonic father Trigon on *Teen Titans*, and he played Wolverine on the *Ultimate Spider-Man* video game.

By the way, the silky tones Szarabajka uses as Holtz actually aren't part of his normal voice. If you're used to his *Angel* role, then – as with Denisof at times – it'll raise your eyebrows to hear him speaking naturally.

• Jack Conley (Sahjhan) had previously appeared in *Buffy* 2.15, "Phases" as the werewolf hunter Cain, and his resumé seems littered (ironically) with him either playing a police officer, a detective or an FBI man. He's also a drug enforcement agent in the Oscar-winning film *Traffic* (2000).

How Does the Invitation Rule Work?

In 254 combined episodes of *Angel* and *Buffy*, a key component of both series – the means by which one can invite a vampire into one's home – isn't terribly well defined. One can hardly blame the producers for sidestepping this issue, because narrowly defining the rule would have shackled the shows with limitations as they progressed. At the very least, it would've required the writers to artificially make one-off characters follow the same exact procedure, generating all sorts of wooden circumstances. So let's recognize up-front that the *Angel*-verse never, ever claims anything as definitive as, "To invite a vampire inside your house, stand 3.4 inches back from the doorframe and swing a dead cat over your head while intoning 'I... invite... you in...' with your eyes crossed like Marty Feldman in *Young Frankenstein*." If you're looking for a hardcore set of instructions, none appear on screen.

Unfortunately, for lack of such a concrete definition, fans and commentators alike have pounced on almost *any* ambiguity as being an outright mistake. But most of these complaints, if we're being reasonable about it, don't hold much substance. For instance, you'll sometimes read that it isn't a proper invitation when Rebecca tells Angel in 1.17, "Eternity": "Well, stop by. I'll give you a private screening of the episode I didn't win an Emmy for." Oh, but honestly... it's readily clear that she's just invited Angel into her house to watch television. Where do we expect she wants them to watch the show? In the potting shed?

The same logic applies to Cordelia telling Angel in "Rm w/a Vu" (1.05) that she's going to squat at his place until she can find a new apartment, and that he is "completely invited over" once she does. Again, red flags have flown on the grounds that Cordelia can't legitimately invite someone into an apartment she doesn't yet possess. And yet, her *intent* is very clear. She's basically saying, "Angel, you are welcome in my abode"; the fact that she hasn't a clue where she's going to live is rather irrelevant.

Indeed, the more we simplify the invitation rule's application, the more things slot into place. Essentially, you can explain almost every single use of the invitation rule if you presume that it relies on two components:

• **Personal intent.** You have to *want* to invite the vampire inside, naturally (even without benefit of knowing that he / she is a vampire).

• **A spoken or written invocation *of any variety*.** The last three words are key. No specific wording is required, but you have to "declare" your invitation in some capacity.

As it happens, "Quickening" (3.08) provides a litmus test

for the last requirement. To wit, Angelus and Darla ask Holtz's young daughter for an invitation, and the little girl stands aside, quite obviously motioning with her body language, "Come on inside, you two." Yet the vampires remain bound, and they can *only* enter once Angelus casually asks for admittance and the girl says "Yes" aloud. So it's the intent and invocation combined that do the trick. And if we apply those criteria as standard, almost any word choice passes muster, be it Catherine Holland moaning "Help us..." (2.10, "Reunion"), Darla "crying out" for the Master (2.07, "Darla") or whatever. If the overall meaning boils down to "I want you to enter my home," it puts the vampire at liberty to do so.

Along those lines, there's ample reason to believe that intent and the *written* word also constitute an invite. Vampires attend parties on more than one occasion (3.01, "Heartthrob," etc.), usually when there's a sign or poster of the "Come one, come all!" variety. All right, perhaps the party organizers actually *said* off screen, "You know, let's invite everyone..." while making plans, but there's little reason to think a written note alone wouldn't suffice. After all, if someone mailed a vampire a personal note – i.e. "Please come to my house for cuddles, Love, Dianne" – yet didn't say a word aloud, their meaning is still pretty plain.

The written word, in fact, might explain why the lucrative vampire Russell can so readily enter Tina's apartment in 1.01, "City Of." The incident begs a simple question: Can a vampire landlord enter a tenant's apartment at will? The answer is probably yes, although ownership of the building alone probably wouldn't circumvent the invite rule, as there's been no assent or invocation. Rather, the overriding invite likely stems from the lease, a "contract" that spells out the conditions in which the landlord – be they vampiric or warm-blooded – can enter. Any tenant who signs on the dotted line has just given their assent and written permission, thus voiding the rule's protection.

To pick a comparable case, look at how Angel seems bound from Fred's room in "Heartthrob." You could argue that he's just being polite, but that's not how it's played on screen, and his physically being barred from her room fits the aforementioned conditions. Angel owns the Hyperion, but it hasn't functioned as public accommodation in years, and Fred almost undoubtedly didn't sign a lease. Nor does she have any reason to verbally issue an invite until he arrives at her doorstep. Ownership of the building or no, then, Angel is stuck until Fred gives the okay.

A dangling instance that's trickier to explain, going by what's on screen: Angel and Spike enter Lindsey's apartment in "A Hole in the World" (5.15) without an invite. But lo and behold... there was a bit in the script about how Lindsey's newfound super-powers are fueled by demonic energy, and that this has left him less-than-human and nullified the rule. The relevant dialogue got struck from the episode itself, but it's comforting to know it was considered. The same "demonic energy" premise, mercifully, could apply to the spell-caster Lloyd in "Sense and Sensitivity" (1.06), thus explaining why Angel walks into the man's base of operations unhindered.

One final note: The invitation rule is so mind-bendingly useful – specifically protecting the homes of human beings, but not those of demons, even if they're ensouled and benevolent – that it simply cannot have occurred in nature. In short, it looks an awful lot like a footprint. A benevolent being or organization must have brought the rule into existence by "changing the rules," as with the Shadow Men creating the Slayer line, or religious officials "charging" Catholic objects (see **Why Do Catholic Objects Harm Vampires?**). However, there's precious little information for us to guess which group is responsible – and it's a pity, because their actions probably saved the whole of humankind in the *Angel*-verse.

3.08: "Quickening"

"We'll wait for it to be born, then we'll chop its head off."

Air Date: Nov. 12, 2001; **Writer:** Jeffrey Bell; **Director:** Skip Schoolnik

SUMMARY Holtz's benefactor, the demon Sahjhan, tasks him with dusting Angel and Darla, but numerous parties take interest in their unprecedented vampire offspring. Angel's team confirms, thanks to ultrasound equipment at a nearby hospital, that Darla's baby seems human enough. But a vampire cult, wanting to claim to the child as their messiah, puts the heroes on the run.

Angel's group ponder leaving town, but Wesley recommends they first retrieve the Nyazian Scrolls from the hotel. Simultaneously, Holtz enters the Hyperion and slaughters Wolfram and Hart commandoes hoping to seize Darla's offspring. Angel leaves his friends in an alley and tries to nab the scrolls on foot, but comes face-to-face with Holtz – just as Darla's water breaks. [*Continued next episode*]

FIRSTS AND LASTS Fred's bluff that she's going to skewer Darla's baby gets foiled by the vampire cultists' enhanced hearing – it's not the last time that whispering aloud will get Fred into trouble either (see 3.21, "Benediction"). It's also the first use of the firm's eminently killable commando squad, who here rappel into the Hyperion lobby looking like black-clad paratroopers, but might as well be sporting red shirt *Star Trek* uniforms when Holtz gets through with them. More personably, it's the first appearance of Linwood – he's Lilah and Gavin's newest boss, and (although it's not stated until 3.17, "Forgiving") the head of Special Projects.

Even though *Buffy* 3.01, "Anne" established the notion, and 1.08, "I Will Remember You" hinted at it, it's still something of a conceptual first on *Angel* when Sahjhan flat-out states that time runs differently in other dimensions. You'll want to mentally jot that down, given what happens later this season (see 3.20, "A New World").

We also learn Holtz's first name, when his wife asks her soon-to-be killers, "You know my Daniel?"

POINTS OF DISCUSSION ABOUT "Quickening":

1. The story is essentially about Angel and Darla preparing to have a child, yet in the teaser – in flashback – has them murdering one. Ah-ha! Bet Minear didn't think many people would notice that sort of symmetry.

2. Dr. Fetvanovich – a paranormal surgeon employed by the firm, and whose look and attire simply scream "Gestapo" – comes equipped with a limp. More specifically, he's got little chicken feet, but viewers often overlook this due to some very silly timing at the story's climax. To summarize, the action goes A) Angel leaps into the hotel lobby and spies the butchered commandoes' corpses, B) Amusingly, he glimpses the dead Fetvanovich's little chicken feet, C) He expresses shock/dread at Holtz's presence. Can you see the problem here? It's "piles of dead bodies, chicken feet gag, jolting cliffhanger, credits." The feet have no room to breathe, so to speak.

CHARACTER NOTES *Angel:* In York, England, 1764 [specifically May, according to "Dad" (3.10)], Angelus and Darla convinced Holtz's young daughter Sarah to invite them inside the man's home. Angelus slew Holtz's wife while Darla sired Sarah as a vampire [see next episode]. One of them [likely Angelus, given the timing] also killed Holtz's other child, an infant.

• *Cordelia:* Effectively brawls against the vampire cultists. [Her basement training is yielding results, then.]

• *Wesley:* Formerly witnessed an ultrasound in 1.12, "Expecting," but here performs one. [We have to presume that Wes is somehow trained to operate ultrasounds, as it's actually more complicated than "smear goop and stick probe on belly." Perhaps it was part of his Watcher's training, as an aid to pregnant Slayers (not unprecedented, as the 1970s Slayer on *Buffy* demonstrates).]

• *Darla:* Claims she "tried to get rid of her child." [As hinted in 3.02, "That Vision Thing."] The mystical force that instigated the pregnancy seems to protect it from physical harm. It's also hinted that she's becoming more compassionate [explained next episode]. Angel claims that Darla likes pain.

• *Lilah:* Gavin knows about Lilah's foreplay with Marcus-Angel. [3.04, Carpe Noctem." Lilah isn't startled by Gavin's accusation, so she must also know the truth about those events, somehow.] Gavin claims it's the closest Lilah has had to a meaningful relationship in years. [Probably an exaggeration, although we never learn much about her romantic history.]

• *Gavin:* Suggests that nobody at the firm really cares about Lilah's little tussle [and in truth, he's never seen to exploit this information]. The "exterminators" who "fumigated" the Hyperion [3.02, "That Vision Thing"] were actually Gavin's agents, dispatched to plant surveillance devices in the hotel.

• *Daniel Holtz:* [Despite the 1764 flashback, it's never clarified what first brings Holtz into collision with Angelus and Darla. It's entirely possible that they just happened to hole up near Holtz's house, and – after an initial encounter – were driven to target the man's family.] Adept with swordplay, Holtz proves willing to butcher humans in his quest for revenge. [A head-count suggests he slays at least ten of the firm's commandoes – that includes the sentry outside, plus Dr. Fetvanovich.]

• *Sahjhan:* Says he possesses the ability to "navigate" other dimensions, even those where time passes differently. [Therefore, at least some of Sahjhan's machinations might owe to dimension-hopping, rather than time-traveling per se.] Sahjhan approached Holtz "nine years" after the murder of his family [in 1773, as confirmed in "Dad"]. They struck a bargain, and Sahjhan used "black magic and sorcery" to render Holtz inert in a stone sarcophagus for 227 years.

Sahjhan views England as a land of "warm beer, boiled meat and bad teeth," hence his relocation to L.A. Sahjhan is immaterial [see 3.17, "Forgiving" for why], but he can somehow turn off TVs with a gesture. Through unspecified means, he can alter his appearance to look human, and it's implied that he likes Thai food. He says [or rather, jokes] that he's had a little work done, mostly around the eyes. Like Angel, he's defensive about his masculinity [seen again in "Forgiving"].

• *Linwood:* It's suggested that he left his wife for a younger beauty, and took certain blood oaths. His plan, if needed, for the dealing with the Darla-pregnancy debacle: blame everything on Lilah and Gavin.

• *Cyril*: Mail delivery boy at the firm, aligned with Gavin but also a mole for a vampire cult [see **Demonology**].

• *Dr. Fetvanovich:* Attached to the firm's satellite branch in the Balkans, and touted as the world's foremost expert in paranormal obstetrics.

• *"The Assassin":* Young bloke whose sword mysteriously flips into his hand [via the Force... okay, not really]. Lilah hires the assassin to eliminate Darla, but vampire cultists kill him. [Regrettably, check out **Things That Don't Make Sense**.]

THE LIBRARY *The Nyazian Scrolls:* Include irregular verbs, which are problematic when converted to Gashundi because of the Nyazian trick of converting both nouns and verbs.

• *Tro-Clon:* Now believed to be a confluence of events [see next episode], not a specific person or persons.

ORGANIZATIONS *Wolfram and Hart:* Lilah threatens to have Cyril's skin peeled off and stapled on inside-out if he doesn't tell her what she wants to know. [This would seem like melodrama if Lilah worked anywhere other than Wolfram and Hart. Instead, it seems worryingly plausible.]

Aside from the aforementioned branch in the Balkans, the firm has branches in Berlin, Singapore and Muncie [presumably the bigger city in Indiana (pop. about 67,000) rather than the much smaller village in Illinois (pop. about 150)]. Lilah signs a contract with a pen dipped in her own blood. [The on-screen evidence suggests she only signs her first name, as with Angel signing simply "Angel" in Season Five.] The contract is dispatched to Pinderhook down in Demon Resources.

The firm doesn't have the Nyazian Scroll, or even a copy of it, on file. [So the firm's archives aren't all-inclusive as is sometimes claimed; see, to pick an example, "A Hole in the World" (5.15).] The firm uses psychics and mind-readers that include two African-American women [presumably the same characters from 1.21, "Blind Date"], a Tarot-reader, a seer-type woman with herbs and weird objects [and who looks not unlike Mistress Cleo], a hot red-haired girl, a guy with a Fez [possibly the same affiliation as the one in 3.02, "That Vision Thing"] and a bald man who correctly predicts that Linwood will order him killed, suffocated with a plastic bag.

The firm has blueprints of the Hyperion, and the leader of the Holtz-eviscerated commandoes was named Burke.

• *Vampire Cultists:* Some of them have exceptionally scary hair. As prophesied by the Great Potentate Ul-Thar, they regard Darla's offspring as a "miracle child." They wish to nourish Darla and the child with heroes' blood, then slice Darla open, wear her entrails as a belt and consume her eyeballs. All before properly worshipping the miracle child, of course.

DEMONOLOGY *Vampires:* Young Sarah Holtz granted Angelus and Darla an invitation in 1764. [This is extremely significant; see **How Does the Invitation Rule Work?**] Vampires have exceptional hearing.

PROPHECY Lilah says there's a rumor about a prophecy involving a vampire birth, but the scroll detailing it "seems to be missing." [She's presumably referring to the Nyazian Scrolls from last episode, but her comment seems odd as these were never in the firm's archive to begin with. It's also strange to think the firm, if they knew the Scrolls' location, would leave such a crucial document in the hands of a private collector.]

BEST LINE Cyril hears the following answering machine message: "[Female voice] Hi, this is the Tittles. We can't come to the phone right now. If you want to leave a message for Christine, press one... [Male voice] for Bentley, press two... [Demonic voice] or to speak to or worship Master Tarfall, Underlord of Pain, press three."

THINGS THAT DON'T MAKE SENSE Sahjhan honestly believes that the best way to "educate" Holtz about history and the modern day is to make him sit and watch television with the sound off. Presuming that a man of Holtz's era could even compute the image of the space shuttle taking off, it's little wonder that he later needs to stop and ask if England still exists in the modern day, or if people still have families. And it's a bit picky to point out, but the "twentieth century footage" seems to involve a disproportionate amount about the space program. (Probably because in the real world, NASA footage comes cheap.)

Compounding his touching various items last episode, the "intangible" Sahjhan here tosses Holtz his cloak and apparently knocks on the door of the Grappler Demons-for-hire club. (Given that Sahjhan can't touch anything, you also have to wonder who set up the televisions in his underground hidey-hole.)

During the Hyperion stand-off, the commandoes are stupid enough to surround Holtz in a circle – meaning that if they open fire, they're going to wind up shooting themselves as well as him. Also, the firm's surveillance at the hotel keeps fading out according to the whims of the plot, missing such details as, oh, an entire *two-day* period, including Darla's arrival at the Hyperion. And even allowing that interference suddenly springs up during the fight between Holtz and the commandoes – resulting in a direct-feed video mysteriously repeating itself, somehow – it's still rather strange that Linwood and company confidently believe their men are winning the melee when the audio, at least, seems to indicate the exact opposite.

While we're on the point... Gavin's elaborate set-up is apparently so shabby that he's failed to identify Darla as the "unidentified pregnant female" at the hotel until Lilah mentions it. He's targeting Angel, yet he's never seen a photo of her in the firm's files? Worse, the firm's transcripts from the Hyperion variously name Cordelia as "Female 1" or "Female One." Good grief, they must know who *she* is by now.

Holtz is an "expert vampire hunter" who's apparently never taught his family the importance of *not* inviting people into the house after dark. Fair enough that Sarah's an error-prone child, but Mrs. Holtz, certainly, should know better than to let her young daughter anywhere near the door. Because honestly, simply telling the child "don't let strangers inside" is hardly adequate, as any acquaintance of the family could get vamped and come knocking.

Nine years pass for Holtz between flashbacks, yet he doesn't look noticeably older. Oh, and it's often said that the "English" accents on display in the flashbacks are crap – probably true, although we're hardly qualified to judge.

Technically, this next bit isn't *wrong*, but what on Earth was Lilah thinking with the swordsman that she hires to eliminate Darla? It's hard to see what she hopes to gain, as killing Darla wouldn't exactly leave her off the hook with the Senior Partners, but we're chiefly bewildered because it's such a limp effort that words almost fail. To recap, Lilah brashly tells Gavin, "Watch and learn, rookie!", whereupon she hires a goober who's stupid enough to leap into a room full of vampire cultists while yelling, "Die!" Judging by our stopwatch, he's literally eaten in just a hair over 11 seconds after making his entrance. Honestly, why the hell did she even bother?

IN RETROSPECT As with 3.01, "Heartthrob," Gunn is still rooting for a trip to Vegas. Ah, and suggestions for dealing with Angel's offspring include "a flamethrower" – they'll put one of those to use two episodes hence, albeit not against Angel's kid.

CRITIQUE It's the middle of one of the most ambitious *Angel* storylines, and like a lot of middles, it sags a bit in connecting the otherwise exceptional opening and ending installments. The vampire cultists seem a bit goofy, the Gestapo-themed surgeon comes straight from stock and Lilah's swordsman seems... actually, he's so pointless, it's hard to know what precisely the producers where thinking with him.

But as with last episode, the overall thrust of the action wins the day. If a few of the individual elements don't hold up, big deal. *Angel*'s a well-oiled machine by this point, so even the less-than-satisfactory notes don't last very long. The general action proves so enthralling, you're quite likely to throw up your arms and declare, "Do whatever the hell you want... I'm there," even if you recognize that it's not beyond criticism.

By the way, a word on the flashbacks... the show sometimes takes flak for having gratuitous scenes from Angel's history, but quite often, they *do* serve a dramatic purpose. It's one thing to hear that Angelus and Darla slaughtered Holtz's family; it's entirely another to actually watch them do it. After this and the follow-up scenes next episode, we're in no doubt that Holtz is a genuinely wronged party. He's an antagonist by default, and though of course we're cheering for Angel, we can never, ever forget – as evidenced here – that Holtz is justified in wanting retribution. We're well beyond the (admittedly effective at times) simplicity of Season One now, and the show's tripping on adrenaline – and quite successfully too.

THE LORE The no-name Wolfram and Hart tech who's doing all the transcribing is Angelo Surmelis, an interior designer on TLC's home makeover series *Clean Sweep*.

• Szarabajka – whose last name roughly means "dark fairytale" in Polish – drew on his own emotions as a father in the scenes where Holtz confronts his vampire daughter. He apparently had no problem weeping, and was having to rein himself in. (Ritchie, *CityofAngel.com*)

• The script actually called for Fetvanovich to have tiny, tiny *human* feet.

3.09: "Lullaby"

"...for surely in that time, when the sky opens and the city weeps, there will be no birth. Only death."

Air Date: Nov. 19, 2001; **Writer/Director:** Tim Minear

SUMMARY Holtz snares Angel and attempts to wring Darla's location out of him, but Lilah arrives and has a surprisingly amicable chat with Angel's nemesis. Angel escapes, causing Holtz to follow, and thus allowing Lilah to snag the Nyazian Scrolls.

Angel finds that the soul of Darla's unborn child is – by extension – granting her a conscience and human emotions once more. The heroes take refuge at Caritas, relying on its newly restored Sanctuary Spell for protection, only to disturbingly realize that Darla's undead body isn't capable of giving birth.

Holtz surmounts the Sanctuary Spell by rolling an explosive canister down Caritas' stairwell, obliterating the karaoke bar as Angel's group dashes out the back. Angel and Fred wait with Darla in a back alley while their colleagues pull the car around, but Darla – loving her child, and realizing it'll die unless she acts – stakes herself. Darla immediately goes to dust, leaving her son crying on the alley floor. Angel bundles up his child, but freezes as Holtz appears with a crossbow. Holtz lets the heroes depart, viewing the baby as an opportunity to inflict revenge on Angel. [*Continued next episode*]

FIRSTS AND LASTS Darla ends her tenure as a living being, and fans simply adore pointing out that it's her fourth death. (For those keeping track, she's killed in *Buffy* 1.07, "Angel"; *Angel* 2.07, "Darla"; and *Angel* 2.09, "The Trial.") It's also the end of Caritas, and the debut of Angel's son in the flesh. Given what's come before, it's hardly startling that his arrival comes in a back alley in the rain.

POINT OF DISCUSSION ABOUT "Lullaby":

1. The heroes never adequately stop to take stock of Darla's ultimate sacrifice – hell, they don't even mention her *name* next episode – so let's pause for a moment to note it here. It only seems right, as Darla is one of the few *Angel*-verse vampires who actually gets a proper chance for redemption (Angel and Spike being the only other notable examples). Overall, Darla's character arc entails her being super, super, super evil, then getting pregnant and becoming a bit less evil, then sacrificing herself for her child. That this

falls in a story where she and Angel confront Holtz – against whom they really *can't* find redemption – makes her final moments all the more poignant.

CHARACTER NOTES *Angel:* Notably warns Lilah to duck before setting off a grenade, even though she's a mortal enemy and this probably serves to alert Holtz also.

• *Gunn:* Owns a Game Boy.

• *Lorne:* Correctly senses Holtz's intent to bomb Caritas after the man hums a few bars of a lullaby. [This doesn't bestow Lorne with detailed information, though. He never seems to register much when there's impending danger; compare with 3.16, "Sleep Tight."] Clutter in Lorne's bedroom includes a Buddha head and a hardened rhino statue.

• *Darla:* The mystical force protecting the child from harm eliminates the possibility of a C-section. [The perpetrator behind Darla's pregnancy (see **Did Jasmine Cause All This?**) is perhaps leaving something to chance here, as she needs to deliver the child somehow. Then again, if Darla's dusting was indeed foretold, it's perhaps a risk worth taking.] Darla claims she never loved anything in her 400 years of life, and says her child is the only good thing she and Angel ever did together.

• *Holtz:* [Continued from last episode...] In 1764, Holtz found his young daughter Sarah, newly sired as a vampire by Angelus and Darla, and dusted her in the morning sun. [It's quite an impressive flaming, too.] Holtz used to sing his daughter "Ar Hyd y Nos," a.k.a. "All Through the Night." [This hails from an old folk tune, and – despite what some *Angel* resources say about the version recorded in 1784 – it's perfectly feasible that Holtz would sing it.] Holtz's men addressed him as "Captain" [used again in "Sleep Tight" and 3.17, "Forgiving"]. Holtz claims that he dreamt of confronting Angelus during his 200 years of stasis. He also says he deals in God's laws [reiterated in 3.21, "Benediction"], and always considered Darla more unpredictable/dangerous than Angelus. He learns from Lilah that gypsies re-ensouled Angel, but nonetheless vows to show him "no mercy."

• *Lilah:* Says she'd gleefully have Angel killed, but for the company policy against it [consider, in fact, her actions in 3.15, "Loyalty"]. She "motivates" a Wolfram and Hart translator by threatening the man's family.

• *Sahjhan:* Implies he knew Attila the Hun, who had a heart "as big as all outdoors when it came to gift-giving." [Attila lived circa 406-453 AD.]

• *Arney:* Lorne's contractor [3.07, "Offspring"] says he's got mouths to feed – and a family. Some of them evidently have mouths too. He rats out the heroes to Holtz, and never seems to get punished for it. [Arney presumably advises Holtz on how to thwart Caritas' Sanctuary Spell.]

ORGANIZATIONS *Wolfram and Hart:* The firm doesn't crucify people, considering it too Christian. [It's almost tedious how some fans point out that the Christians themselves didn't crucify people. But, please... the image is indisputably associated with Christianity, which is good enough where the firm is concerned.] An employee named Harvey oversees a "full cleaner service" [i.e. mopping up all the dismembered corpses]. Lilah recruits a translator of ancient texts who mentions "that worm" [Heaven only knows if he's speaking literally] Forsch, who works in the Ancient Symbols and Icons division and only has one eye.

• *Caritas:* Nearly ready for its grand re-opening before getting firebombed. Lorne had ordered Gorch entrails to stock behind the bar, next to the maraschinos. There's an old loading dock door located behind Lorne's bed. The alley behind Caritas [also seen in 3.03, "That Old Gang of Mine"] has a sign for what appears to be "Pung Fae Lucy's Restaurant."

DEMONOLOGY *Vampires:* Holtz's daughter Sarah appears to rise on the same night as her siring. ["Loyalty" (3.15) would almost suggest that child vampires rise quicker than adult ones. See 2.10, "Reunion" for more elaboration.] She also has bite-marks on her neck [most newly risen vampires don't, but there's exceptions such as Lawson in 5.13, "Why We Fight"]. Vampire Sarah seems to retain the mind of a child. Flicking holy water on vampires makes them "vamp out" for a bit.

PROPHECY Lilah's translator says that reading ancient prophecies is "more an interpretation than a strict translation." [It's like reading Nostradamus... everything is so vague (the eagle will fight the bear, yadda yadda yadda) that the meaning is murky, even if the words are clear.]

• *The Nyazian Scrolls:* Lilah marks the Scrolls' most important bits with a yellow highlighter. Wesley apparently ran into translation trouble with the Scrolls because Gashundi tenses "are tricky little buggers." The Scrolls speak of the child's arrival more as an obituary [for Darla, apparently] than a birth announcement. The texts loosely [but correctly] predict that it'll be raining when the child is born.

• *The Tro-Clon:* [See "Offspring."] Fred now views this as a convergence of events, with each player unaware of the corresponding factors. She speculates that perhaps Angel's child is a Messianic figure, and that if Holtz kills it, his vengeance will somehow "trigger the end of the world."

MAGIC *The Sanctuary Spell:* [First mentioned in "That Old Gang of Mine."] Caritas has been retro-fitted to "route the new sanctuary spells together" to prevent demon *and* human violence. This spell-activation procedure seems mechanical as much as mystical, with Lorne fiddling with electronics to "balance the inter-species flux." [For a completely bizarre application of this spell, see 4.13, "Salvage."]

BEST LINE The ever-sensitive Gunn, on Darla's impending childbirth: "What we could really use right about now is some Vaseline and a catcher's mitt." (Running a close second – even though there's no actual dialogue involved – is Wesley's weird little Lamaze demonstration.)

THINGS THAT DON'T MAKE SENSE Last episode, Wesley told Angel that the Nyazian Scrolls were in the cabinet in his office. Yet in this story, they're sitting out in the Hyperion lobby, plain as day, for Lilah to readily find. Perhaps Wes made an honest mistake, but it's rather foolish to leave such an important document lying out in the open like that.

Sahjhan fails to tell Holtz that Darla is pregnant, apparently fearing that Holtz's morals might make him balk at killing her. This makes sense given Sahjhan's true agenda (see "Forgiving"), save that – what? – he doesn't think Holtz is going to *notice* Darla's lumbering belly until after he kills her?

Holtz certainly takes his sweet time striding through the flames of Caritas, given the generous amount of action the heroes experience in the meanwhile. (Minear concedes the point on the DVD commentary: "Holtz obviously would have gone and killed them, were he not moving in slow motion.") All other evidence suggests that Holtz only has four Grapplers total, yet there's simultaneously four in the alley confronting Darla's group and three in the Hyperion lobby restraining Angel. Speaking of which... after Darla smacks Angel's car into a trio of Grapplers, the demons mysteriously vanish as she accelerates out of the alley. (Minear explains that he feared the actors would get run over, and removed them from the scene.) And on a visual note... as Caritas explodes, watch the floor carefully and you can see the wires used to help bowl over the furniture.

IT'S REALLY ABOUT... The seemingly impossible nature of childbirth, which looks painful, awkward and almost supernatural even when it goes smoothly.

Additionally, it's about the insecurities of impending parents, who nonetheless suck it up and prepare to ward off a host of threats the kid will face outside the womb. Notice how Darla worries, "This world, this horrible world... Why would anyone bring a baby into it?" There's also little denying that this story is about how a mother's love – with all due respect to the guys – is arguably so much stronger because the females actually carry the child inside them for nine months. And Darla's concern that once the child is born, she won't love her baby – literally, in her case, as it will separate her from the child's soul – smacks of separation anxiety.

Finally, it's about the innocence of new life, with Angel's son shining with purity despite his demonic heritage. As if to drive home the point, who witnesses the birth alongside Angel? Fred, the most unsoiled member of the cast.

CRITIQUE The last episode warranted improvement in parts, but we stressed that this didn't matter in the final equation. Here, it's genuinely hard to find something to criticize.

"Lullaby" in some ways exemplifies all the strengths of the *Angel*-verse, masterfully displaying a mix of comedy, tragedy, whimsy and insightfulness... usually in the same scene. Minear's direction provides some of the most striking visuals in the series so far, and there's an almost record number of choice bits – from Holtz cutely flicking water into Lilah's face, to Angel setting off a grenade with his teeth, to Fred slapping Gunn to test the Sanctuary Spell. There's also Angel and Darla's touching rooftop discussion, and it's damnably pulse-thumping when Holtz rolls the dynamite-laden barrel into Caritas. Oh, and as if anyone could forget, there's the climactic final showdown and Darla's absolutely shocking suicide. Even the heroes shying away from the back seat of Angel's car – because Darla's water broke all over it – seems more memorable than it probably should.

Perhaps the real surprise is that such a cornerstone, expertly-woven episode falls not even halfway through the season; this isn't an end-of-year clearing exercise, in which the producers feel at liberty to go for broke. The manner in which the show grabs the viewers by the throat and heaves them around has now, amazingly, become par for the course. It can't last, of course, because you simply can't maintain this momentum over a 22-episode season now matter how hard you try, but more shows should strive to get this far. To quote Lorne, "Our fillings are humming."

THE LORE The final scene warranted some consideration, as Minear worried about it being too sappy. Staging Darla's last moments in the rain helped, as it made Angel look like he was crying without the need for actual sobbing. Minear took the inspiration of Darla's hand going to dust as Angel held it from the second *Invasion of the Body-Snatchers* (1978), in which Donald Sutherland's character horrifically witnesses something similar.

- Minear had previously considered dusting Darla at the end of "Reprise" (2.15), the idea being that Angel would stake her as their hot sex wrapped up, then adopt his vamp face and ask, "Was it good for you?" When Darla's return got delayed to Season Three, Whedon wondered aloud if they could "bring Darla back in a box" – Minear counter-suggested they could bring something back *in* Darla's box, hence the whole pregnancy storyline.
- That's a real baby wailing on the alley floor, only green-screened in so the child didn't catch its death of cold.

• The filming behind the Hyperion occurred at what the crew came to designate "Piss Alley," because it reeked of urine and was infested with rats.

• John Rubinstein (Linwood) has an acting career and character work stretching back to 1967. (Not without some justification did he warrant billing above even Andy Hallett, and it's funny how venerable actors keep running Special Projects – see Sam Anderson's resumé under 1.21, "Blind Date.") He played the title role in the original Broadway cast of *Pippin*, and he also composed music for several telepics, including the closing theme to *China Beach*. 1980s aficionados might remember him from *Crazy Like a Fox*, where he played the beleaguered son of a private investigator (Jack Ward). The show, if you don't recall, opened with Ward "innocently" phoning Rubinstein for a ride and asking, "What could possibly happen?", whereupon chaos would ensue.

3.10: "Dad"

"Did you know these nappies are lined with a space-age material originally designed for NASA astronauts?"

Air Date: Dec. 10, 2001; **Writer:** David H Goodman; **Director:** Fred Keller

SUMMARY Multiple factions assault the Hyperion, hoping to kidnap Angel's son, and Angel seemingly abandons his friends and flees in his convertible with the baby. Most of the villains follow and corner Angel at a mine operation outside L.A, but Angel flings up the "baby" – actually a bomb – and escapes as the explosive annihilates his rivals.

Linwood's cadre later realizes that Lorne sensed their surveillance devices in the Hyperion and tipped off Angel, meaning Angel's "abandoned" his friends as part of the ruse. Moments later, Angel bursts into the law firm and personally charges Linwood with the baby's safety – claiming that any injuries to the child will be given to Linwood in kind. Granted a respite, the heroes get the baby a check-up at the hospital, and Angel names his son "Connor."

FIRSTS AND LASTS It's the debut of Holtz's tough-as-nails associate Justine, and also the start of Holtz gathering a human cadre to move against Angel.

POINTS OF DISCUSSION ABOUT "Dad":

1. The heroes list Angel as being a "pet psychiatrist" with Connor's physicians, or at least, that's what Fred jokes. Funny, though, how we've almost come full circle from Angel claiming to be a veterinarian in 1.02, "Lonely Hearts."

2. We're apparently meant to infer, given Angel's threat to Linwood about Connor, that Linwood pulls some strings to keep the parties braying for Connor's blood at bay in future. It's a lame excuse but somewhat necessary excuse, as it'd get boring fast if vampire cultists and the like were besieging the heroes every week. Mind, a similar development exists on *Buffy*, where Dawn isn't hunted – despite her utterly unique status as the Key – after Season Five.

3. Wesley appears to fling Connor's used diaper onto the Hyperion lobby desk. How unsanitary.

CHARACTER NOTES *Angel:* Knows how to change a standard diaper with pins, but those new-fangled fasteners give him trouble. He worries rather too much about S-E-X talk around the baby, and can now reach one of the firm's conference rooms mere seconds after triggering an alarm. [He appears to rely on sheer speed, as opposed to coercing someone, in this case.]

Angel sings James Royce Shannon's "Too-Rah-Loo-Rah-Loo-Rah" to Connor as a lullaby. His heart is set on Connor one day attending Notre Dame [but he'll wind up going to Stanford (see 5.18, "Origin")]. Angel lays his trap in a mine-shaft operated by the Bailey Mining & Exploration Co. [5.08, "Destiny" suggests Angel is familiar with Death Valley and 4.03, "The House Always Wins" establishes a trip to Las Vegas, so he probably knows about the area east of L.A.]

• *Cordelia:* Suggests that Angel share responsibility for Connor, as he can hardly dash about with the lad during the daytime. [Need we say it? The Ring of Amarra (see 1.03, "In the Dark") might've alleviated some of this concern.]

• *Gunn:* Claims he helped raise his cousin since she was, "like, a week old." [The cousin is never mentioned again, although it's obviously not Gunn's cousin Lester (2.08, "The Shroud of Rahmon"). We wish they'd embargo these off-handed references to Gunn's family – such as mention of his grandmother in 4.18, "Shiny Happy People" – because they're cumulatively getting hard to reconcile against the fact that he and Alonna spent time in a shelter (1.20, "War Zone").]

Helpfully, Gunn gets a flamethrower from one of his contacts [and he probably procures the explosive that Angel requires at the same time].

• *Lorne:* Moves into the Hyperion after Caritas' obliteration last episode, and declines his standing offer to lodge with a marginally attractive Mulix demon. Lorne's acute hearing registers a hum coming from the firm's surveillance devices [3.02, "That Vision Thing"; the heroes presumably remove them after this story]. Given his complexion, Lorne tries to avoid florescent lights.

• *Lilah:* Likes takeaway from the China Palace, and her clearance number with the firm's Files and Records department is 0112773. Lilah learns through research that Angel's real name is Liam, and she seems turned on thinking of

Holtz as a bloodthirsty, single-minded vengeance machine. She favors dissecting Connor over killing him.

• *Linwood:* Likes children, in part because the Senior Partners took his away [for whatever reason – it probably wasn't as punishment, or Linwood would hardly be serving as a department head]. Linwood frets that if Angel's child is benevolent, he could grow up to hunt down and slaughter his hunters – Linwood, Lilah and Gavin included.

• *Holtz:* His murdered infant son [3.08, "Quickening"] was also named Daniel. The firm's records claim that Holtz vowed to avenge his slaughtered family in May 1764 [they presumably perished the same month], and that he racked up an "incidental" body count of 378 vampires while hunting Angelus and Darla afterward. He disappeared in 1773 [see "Quickening"], and Sahjhan claims that Holtz waited/slept "230 years" to obtain his vengeance. [No matter how you maneuver the show's dating, it's 2001 or at most 2002 right now, so Sahjhan's approximating.] Holtz here poisons his quartet of Grappler demons, claiming he needs belief-motivated warriors rather than mercenaries. Hence his recruitment of...

• *Justine Cooper:* Vampires murdered her twin sister, an interior designer named Julia Cooper, on Thursday, June 3, 2001. Holtz says this was "six months ago." Since then, Justine has become nocturnal, a heavy drinker, a smoker and someone who roughhouses with vampires. She's a decent fighter, if a bit unfocused, and lives at 7221 Spaulding.

• *Sahjhan:* Owns a Mac laptop [like everyone else on this show], and can turn the computer on with a gesture [he displayed a similar talent for turning off TVs in "Quickening"]. He boasts that he's got a [supernaturally] fast Internet connection, and refers Holtz to the "Demons, Demons, Demons" website [which isn't terribly useful, as Holtz wants to see obituaries]. Sahjhan claims he can't touch anything in "this dimension." [This suggests that he's corporeal in *another* dimension, even if he's barred from physical form in our reality; see 3.17, "Loyalty" for more.]

• *Connor:* The heroes' list of the potential threats to Connor include: the Order of Phillius, Beltar the Cremator, Piper Beast, Frank (a local mobster who specializes in kidnapping) and the Scourge [1.09, "Hero"]. There are already three websites offering cash for Connor's capture.

Angel's vamp-face effectively calms Connor's incessant crying. The boy's height and weight put him in the 90th percentile, and he here receives his Vitamin K and P.K.U. [a newborn test for phenylketonuria, an inherited condition that makes the body over-produce a type of amino acid, leading to health problems]. His birth certificate cites him as "Connor Angel," and names his daddy as "Geraldo Angel."

• *The Furies:* At Lorne's request, they place an impassible force field over the Hyperion; they leave a mystical barrier in the sewers that opens or closes in response to a code phrase: the Pylean word for hedgehog. [This apparently sounds naughty when spoken aloud, judging by Fred's reaction.]

THE HYPERION The heroes never use the hotel's main elevator, apparently.

THE FIRM'S LIBRARY *Vampiricus Conquestus* by Larson McMillan, page 412, seems to mention Holtz. Gavin thinks the Nyazian Scrolls foretold Holtz's arrival [in "Offspring" (3.07)].

ORGANIZATIONS *Wolfram and Hart:* Lurking in the firm's "basement archives" is a plucky brunette who identifies herself as "Files and Records." She doesn't freely offer information, but appears to mentally access to the firm's entire archive. When looking up an answer, her eyes flip as if scanning records or microfilm at super-speed. [She's not seen after Season Three, however, so perhaps the firm's downfall in 4.08, "Habeas Corpses" results in her death.]

The firm's records on Angel encompass 35 file cabinets' worth of information [impressive, considering they know almost nothing about him in Season One], and go back 275 years. [That would date to roughly 1726, about a year before Angel's birth according to 1.15, "The Prodigal."] The firm's agents already know about Darla's demise and Connor's birth. Wolfram and Hart has a Contracts and Negotiations department [with close ties to Special Projects; see "Dead End" (2.18) for why].

• *The Vampire Cult:* Still trying to nab Connor. They drive blacked-out cars in the daytime. [Sadly, their taste in car music isn't anywhere near as refined as Spike's.]

• *Biker gang:* Gunn recognizes this group, describing them as "humans into extortion and kidnapping." They also make a bid to kidnap Connor [and see **The Kill-Count**].

DEMONOLOGY *Lilliad Demons:* Given to making a magical broth from the bones of human children, and wonder how a vampire-child will affect the flavor. They wear hooded cloaks, drive about town in a van and use magic directly linked to the lunar cycle. Their magical energy-strike brings down the Furies' force-field [but this being L.A., nobody notices].

BEST LINE Cordelia's ever-reliable, emasculating taunt to Angel: "You don't have a woman's touch. Whatever your taste in clothing may indicate."

THINGS THAT DON'T MAKE SENSE Wes' flamethrower – while arguably one of the coolest weapons on *Angel* thus far, you understand – is selective enough to char his opponents to skeletons while leaving the Hyperion lobby carpet and wooden door frames unsigned. Besides, do we really need to point out the potential downside of unloading the flamethrower in the lobby in the first place?

Now that Connor's in residence, Cordelia proposes kid-proofing the locks on the Hyperion weapons cabinet – as if the cabinet locks are the *non*-kid-proof variety. We'll skip most instances where "baby Connor" is clearly a prop, but a fun one occurs when Lorne discretely slips the baby-holding Angel a note: the baby's "hand" is sticking out of the blanket, but his fingers noticeably aren't moving.

How do the heroes keep their stratagem secret, considering the firm has the hotel under surveillance? Lorne informs Angel that Gavin's bugs don't cover the janitor's closet, but it's weird to think the heroes either went to the closet *en masse* or one at a time without the firm noticing. Ah, yes... and then there's the curiosity that a vampire cultist runs into the hotel yelling, "Master, it's a trick! He's taken the child!", even though there's absolutely no evidence that the cultists ever breached the Hyperion. Just whom does the boob think he's hollering at, then? It's almost a case of "supernatural natural selection," given that the blunder earns the hapless vampire the business end of Wesley's flamethrower.

Lilah generically refers to Lorne as "that green houseguest"... how can the firm *not* know his identity by this point, considering they've got 35 file cabinets of information on Angel, and he's been visiting Lorne for advice for about 18 months? (And see "Loyalty," where – amazingly – Linwood is similarly baffled.) To devolve into nit-picking, Lilah orders a "full clean-up" at the Hyperion. Yet the firm's clean-up team only removes the commandoes' bodies, leaving behind all their equipment and blood. *That's* their idea of full clean-up?

POP CULTURE Wes girds for battle by imagining himself as John Wayne in *Rio Bravo* (1959). (We hope that reference is self-evident.) Gunn similarly envisions himself as Austin Stoker in *Assault on Precinct Thirteen* (1976), which was – Ah, ha! You cannot fool us! – an homage to *Rio Bravo*. It entailed Stoker's character (Lt. Ethan Bishop) taking charge of a police station that's slated to close, then defending it when gang members try to kill everyone inside.

IT'S REALLY ABOUT... Overly protective yet well-meaning fathers who're reduced to gibbering idiots by their newborns. (Notice in particular how Angel tells Connor "Here's your ba-ba. Take your ba-ba," with some smacking noises.) Connor in response does little but wail constantly, leaving Lorne to rightfully suggest that Angel just chill out and stop stressing the kid.

CRITIQUE After the whirlwind of the last four episodes, it's hardly surprising that "Dad" downshifts in quality. Mind, it still gets many things right – Wesley's flamethrower makes for a hoot and a holler, the dialogue's still rather spirited and you almost *could* believe that Angel might run out on his crew again, given everything that's come before. Also, it's all a bit of a necessity, as it's important to wipe out the various factions hoping to kidnap "the miracle child" so we can get on to better things.

In reality, though, there's only about 20 minutes of story here. Sure, the action sequences seem exhilarating, but there are too many puddles of recap and unnecessary exposition (notice how Linwood gibbers to a video of Connor that his daddy's a "vampire with a soul"... as if we didn't know that by now). Connor mainly cries his way through the episode, and too much energy gets spent on such "weighty" matters as his Vitamin K shot. (You can readily see why babies aren't front and center on dramatic series for too long.) Plus, the hardcore climax – Angel blowing up the bad guys – happens almost an act too early, leaving the episode nowhere to really go.

It's hardly a complete and total loss, but undeniably awkward compared to the stories of late, and a sign that things might get a bit bumpy before we hit the next "mythology" phase in "Loyalty."

THE LORE Laurel Holloman (Justine) made a cinematic splash as Randy Dean, a teenage lesbian in *The Incredibly True Adventure of Two Girls in Love* (1995). She was later Mark Wahlberg's girlfriend in *Boogie Nights* (1997) and Jennifer Beals' girlfriend on the Showtime drama *The L Word*.

3.11: "Birthday"

"The Powers-That-Be popped me out of my body and sent me to a mall?"

Air Date: Jan. 12, 2002; **Writer:** Mere Smith; **Director:** Michael Grossman

SUMMARY A particularly powerful vision slams Cordelia into a coma, causing her to awaken as an intangible, invisible ghost. Sometime later, the demon Skip (3.02, "That Vision Thing") appears on behalf of the Powers, informing Cordelia that her human body can't shoulder the burden of the visions any longer. Skip reveals that Cordy's next vision will kill her, suggesting that in recognition of her service, the Powers could rewrite history so Cordy never met Angel in L.A. (1.01, "City Of"), and never received the visions.

Cordelia agrees, finding herself in a timeline where she met a talent agent and enjoyed a thriving acting career. However, "actress" Cordy feels strangely compelled to investigate the last vision she experienced in the previous history. Cordy encounters the alternate versions of Gunn and Wesley, then learns that the alt-

Angel went mad after receiving the visions from Doyle. She instinctively kisses alt-Angel, thus reclaiming her memories and the vision talent.

Skip re-appears, conceding that Cordelia could bear the visions if the Powers made her part-demon. Cordelia consents, undergoing the transformation and awakening in her original timeline. For an encore, Cordy receives a painless vision.

FIRSTS AND LASTS The alt-Angel becomes the first, but not the last, person who'll get locked up in Wesley's apartment (see 4.01, "Deep Down"). Bearing in mind what's to follow, it's the first time Wesley holds Connor, although in this case he's merely taking the lad while Angel tries to rouse Cordelia. It's Lorne, though, who steps up to bat as Connor's baby-sitter, and he'll keep doing so while everyone's off killing things (or going to the ballet, as in 3.13, "Waiting in the Wings").

When Cordy's vision "blasts" her backward, it's the first example of the weapons cabinet getting smashed in. It'll get replaced, then suffer another bashing five episodes hence.

POINTS OF DISCUSSION ABOUT "Birthday":

1. No other *Angel* story is so affected by retcon – that's continuity established after the fact, if you didn't know – as this one, as it's later established (in 4.17, "Inside Out") that Skip isn't working for the Powers. Instead, he's working to a master plan crafted by the entity Jasmine (inevitably, see **Did Jasmine Cause All This?**), and their scheme entails Cordelia here getting grafted with demon DNA.

Yes, it's true – this whole episode is an elaborate ruse, designed to hoodwink Cordelia into accepting the "demon upgrade" of her own free will. Given that personal will and intent holds great weight in the *Angel*-verse, the conspirators probably need Cordelia's assent for this to work. (And as we've hinted, this arguably marks the second instance that selflessness on Cordelia's part, ironically, allows Jasmine's plans to proceed. See also 2.22, "There's No Place Like Plrtz Glrb" and 3.22, "Tomorrow.")

So, we're left with the challenge of examining this story while taking the Season Four retcon into account. Frankly, that's a bit of a blessing, as it actually explains much of this story's illogic. But as we proceed, remember that the entire dream reality – and probably even some of what's presented as the "real" timeline – is a ploy purely designed to manipulate Cordelia, nothing else.

2. We're told that the alternate reality entailed Doyle handing off the visions to Angel, and lascivious fans have spent an almost frightful amount of time wondering how this was achieved. Doyle originally gifted the visions to Cordy with a kiss, so some fans have wondered if Doyle and Angel... well, you get the idea. But in truth, there's absolutely *no* evidence that the visions are routinely passed through kissing, as entertaining as that might sound, and even though Wesley describes the alt-Doyle as, um, "Angel's only friend."

3. We can't entirely believe we're cataloging this, but those wishing to debate when/if ever Charisma Carpenter acquired breast implants usually point to this episode – and point to Carpenter's chest in particular – as proof that Cordy is looking a bit enhanced when she awakens from her coma. However, a proper examination of the scene leads one to conclude that Carpenter is simply wearing a push-up bra, the sort that leaves a "uni-boob" effect. In short, she's been augmented, but through exterior rather than interior means.

Unbelievably, we'll re-broach the topic in "Waiting in the Wings" (3.13), and we wonder if fans would've become quite so fixated on this had Carpenter refrained from doing that *Playboy* cover. You know, the one entitled, "The *Angel* star sheds her wings... and her clothes."

CHARACTER NOTES *The alt-reality Angel:* Alt-Wes says Angel came to L.A. in pain, whereupon Doyle, "his only friend," died. Angel inherited Doyle's visions, but they've eroded his sanity. He's secured in Wesley's spare room, sometimes turns violent and occasionally sends Wes and Gunn to save people he killed 200 years ago. [This all raises the question of why Angel, a full-blooded vampire, can't handle the visions. Three possibilities spring to mind... vampires are genetically closer to humanity than some demons, so perhaps they can't shoulder the visions either. Or perhaps Angel psychologically can't bear to witness such depravities in the visions, given his history as Angelus and the presence of his soul. But let's finish with the rather-obvious solution: This is all a scheme on Skip's part, tailored to let Cordelia prove her nobility by sparing Angel pain.]

- *Cordelia:* Has been taking prescription drugs (including Seltrax) to alleviate her "vision" troubles for about a year now, and she has MRIs and CAT scans dating back at least eight months. A CAT scan taken a month ago shows widespread neuro-electrical deterioration, to such an extent that Cordelia should be "a cucumber" right now. [If so, Skip exaggerates when he says the visions will soon kill Cordelia. After all, if her brain is physically on-par with a vegetable, then a mystical component of the visions – perhaps the Powers' doing – has surely protected her this far.]

Honorably, Cordelia seems more concerned about the fate of a teenager she glimpsed in her vision than the fact that she's comatose and clinging to life as a ghost. Cordelia levitates while experiencing her first post-coma vision. [The levitation is mentioned in future, but never witnessed again.] Cordy owns a green bra, and thinks Jude Law is hunky. We never learn what Cordelia's co-workers give her as birthday presents.

- *The alt-reality Cordelia:* She's the two-time Emmy winning star of *Cordy!*, a sitcom with co-stars Gregory Dunne,

Elliott Simms and Carol Wright. Persons named Phlegmont and Mendoza created it. She's slated to tape a breast cancer P.S.A. A guy named Nev ["Nevin" in the script] serves as her personal assistant. [One conceit we're prepared to accept: Cordelia was a sucky actress in Season One (see especially 1.17, "Eternity"), so if history got "written over" as Skip suggests, she should arguably still be a sucky actress in the alt-reality. Yet Cordy showed dramatic improvement as an actress in Season Two (check out 2.01, "Judgment") so given time, her alternate self probably progressed beyond "vapid pretending."]

- *The alt-history Wesley:* Lost his left arm during an encounter with a Kungai demon [1.10, "Parting Gifts," but alt-Wes wasn't necessarily wounded by the same character]. He remains a remarkably effective fighter, with the alt-Gunn serving as his investigative partner. Alt-Wes hasn't seen Cordelia since Sunnydale [meaning *Buffy* Season Three]. He's not wearing spectacles [funny how this happens every time Wes takes a turn for the dark side; see 3.17, "Forgiving"].
- *Gunn:* Presently thinks Fred is "so cool," but takes the opportunity to rifle through Cordelia's underwear drawer while searching for clues.
- *Lorne:* Touches the comatose Cordelia's temples, and thereby determines that she's "not in her body." Lorne gets a horn broken off while conducting investigative work, but says it'll regrow in a couple days.
- *Skip:* Greatly enjoyed *The Matrix*, but "didn't love" *Gladiator*. He gives off sinister laughter when needed, and magically draws on a TV-screen akin to sports announcers strategizing play. [Both of these facts imply that Skip can mimic certain sounds and visuals, if you need further proof of his ability to deceive Cordy's senses.] He's also knowledgeable about football [see "Inside Out"].

THE HYPERION Has a luxury suite [presumably the one Jasmine occupies in Season Four]. One of the standard rooms [the one Angel apparently inhabits in the real history] features wallpaper designed by renowned artist Jacques Latour.

ORGANIZATIONS *The Powers-That-Be:* Skip says the visions are "an ancient powerful force." He labels it a "big cosmic whoops" that Cordelia ever inherited the visions, and attributes this blunder to Doyle's feelings for her. ["Inside Out" provides the real explanation. That's fortunate, because if romantic love *did* transfer the visions, it would surely cause all manner of calamity.]

Skip confirms that only demons, not humans, possess the stamina to cope with the visions. An apparition of Tammy, a woman who allegedly had the visions for a year in 1630, appears to substantiate this. Tammy says the town fathers wanted to burn her as a witch, but that her last vision blew out the back of her skull. [The bulk of evidence in Season Four, though, suggests that humans never carried the visions before Cordy, so "Tammy" is simply part of Skip's deception.]

Strangely, Cordelia believes the Powers "know everything." [They don't.] Skip corrects her to say that whereas the Powers have a handle on "life and death," free will makes matters unpredictable. He says that every living thing has a connection to the Powers-That-Be – an "instinct or intuition" that means, "We all know our purpose in this world." [This is probably more BS on Skip's part, as there's no other proof that such a link exists.] He also claims that in accordance with Cordelia's wishes, the Powers will "write over history" as opposed to folding back time [1.08, "I Will Always Remember You"].

DEMONOLOGY *The Conduit:* [No relation to the White Room denizen as named in 5.01, "Conviction."] Unseen, formless beings that inhabit an underground chamber and speak in male and female voices. [Truth to tell, they sound a bit like the Borg Collective.] The Conduit claims it is "the gateway, the all-times, the ever," and only a champion [naturally] can converse with it. Lorne hopes the Conduit will help Angel contact the Powers, but it's not terribly helpful.

MAGIC *Astral Projection:* Skip says that when most people "go astral," their spiritual shapes appear somewhat idealized.

- *"The Silence Spell":* Put on Lorne to prevent his talking about the Conduit or events regarding a beating he receives. Bizarrely, this still leaves him at liberty to write down details.

BEST LINE The alt-Wesley, when Cordelia mentions how he struck out with her in Sunnydale: "Well, as much as I'm enjoying this forced death march down memory lane..."

THINGS THAT DON'T MAKE SENSE Much confusion exists about the "171 Oak" note that ghost-Cordelia wall-scribbles in Sharpie while inhabiting Angel's body. This occurs in the *real* reality, but both Angel and Wesley fail to spot it – not even when Wesley is "staring into space" at the wall in question. Then Cordelia finds the note under the wallpaper in the alternate reality, when it's got no business being there. Then Cordelia awakens in the "our" reality, and the note is gone again. As an epilogue to this farce, a post-coma Cordy tells everyone that the three-mouthed monster she saw in her vision "has been taken care of." Well, no, that defeat occurred in the alternate history, so the beast is probably at large and lunching on virgins.

Other bewilderments about the alternate history: Ghost-Cordelia impressively masters the art of "astral possession" after just reading over Wesley's shoulder for a short while, and even though his book isn't in English. Alt-Angel is sequestered in a room with very prominent windows, so it's curious that he doesn't fry in the morning sun, or escape at nighttime in a fit of vision-insanity. The Hyperion really shouldn't be operating in the alternate reality, as the traumatic events of 1952 (2.02, "Are You Now or Have You Ever Been") still would have occurred without Cordelia's involvement and left the building derelict. (Perhaps alt-Angel's crew killed the Thesulac haunting the joint anyway, but the hotel has nonetheless been purchased, renovated and reopened in a comparatively small timeframe.)

(Pause to reiterate that sooooooooo many of these anomalies must owe to Skip manipulating Cordelia by tailoring everything that she witnesses. That still leaves the problem that Cordelia amazingly doesn't sense how much of this is just *wrong*, but it at least papers over the weird plot mechanics.)

Hands up, anyone who thinks for a single second that Angel in Season Three would talk trash about Cordelia to the Conduit. His words, not ours: "She's a rich girl from Sunnydale playing superhero. Don't the Powers get that? *She's weak*!" (For our money, Skip is also warping some of what's presented to the viewer as the "real timeline." Angel probably visits the Conduit for real, but Skip distorts his comments to further goad Cordelia.)

Gunn and Fred sense a clue in that they can't find regular aspirin in Cordelia's apartment... but why doesn't she? If she goes days without a vision, doesn't she get anything as mundane as a standard headache, or keep some for guests? Or, as Fred implies, did Phantom Dennis hide Cordelia's aspirin along with her other drugs? If so, doesn't the spook realize that aspirin is hardly incriminating? And how does Dennis procure his party hat, confetti and banner in celebration of Cordelia's birthday? He can hardly go shopping at Target.

In the teaser, we're presumably meant to infer that Wesley dashes into the hotel with Cordelia's birthday cake, but it's impressive how he fits such a large item inside his grocery bags. (Then again, something about ex-Watchers always seems to throw scale out of whack. Consider Wesley's shotgun in 4.07, "Apocalypse Nowish," and how Giles implausibly stuffs a chainsaw inside his duffel bag in *Buffy* 4.04, "Fear Itself.")

Secret agenda or no, why does Skip leave ghost-Cordelia to haunt the Hyperion before finally turning up at the climax to Act One? And why does he bother to mentally recreate a mall environment "for Cordy's comfort," when he and ghost-Cordelia could just go to a real mall?

IN RETROSPECT In both this episode and *Buffy* 3.09, "The Wish," a desire on Cordelia's part causes an entire parallel timeline to spring into existence. You'd almost think she was born susceptible to alternate realities.

CRITIQUE As with Smith's previous effort with "Fredless," this is undeniably crafted as a crowd-pleaser, and probably soothing to some because it's a "safe" avenue to explore. But is it any *good*?

By absolute measures, not tremendously so. Nearly the whole story, it must be said, is an easy lob, easy serve. Cordelia gets to experience life as an actress, becomes self-actualized and reassumes her role as the visionary. That's not too surprising by now, is it? After all, she's just spent the past 18 months declaring how much she's determined to remain at her post even if it (near-enough) kills her, so "Birthday" amounts to little more than Cordelia acting out what she's been swearing for ages now. The *Cordy!* "sitcom opener" is admittedly a lot of fun, but it only lasts a couple of minutes, and Cordy's fantasy world quickly becomes surface-level after that. Plus, everything's tidily wrapped up with a lame *deus ex machina* in which Skip essentially waves his hand and makes Cordy part demon. Thank God as ever for the Season Four retcon, because if fixing Cordy's head trauma were that simple, you'd have to wonder why the hell the Powers didn't do it long ago, thus sparing the poor girl a lot of suffering.

Ultimately, "Birthday" holds enough "Cordelia wish fulfillment" to perform well with viewers who prefer this flavor of story, and aren't looking for much beyond that. For most everyone else, it's not particularly insightful or clever, and tends to just sit there.

THE LORE Greenwalt had written a fair amount of Cordy's dialogue on *Buffy*, to the extent that Whedon kept joking that his fellow producer *was* Cordelia. In fact, Greenwalt sometimes stated that he wanted to collect Cordy's best "insights" and publish a coffee-table book entitled *The Wit and Wisdom of Cordelia Chase*. (Pierce, *Deseret News*, Feb. 18, 2002)

• The episode ran a bit long, necessitating the omission of the *Cordy!* sitcom piece that's included as an extra on the DVDs. Greenwalt and *Buffy* Producer Marti Noxon (she's the woman getting ticketed in the *Buffy* musical) sang the *Cordy!* theme. The deletion means that when a youthful Cynthia York tells Cordy, "I want to be just like you and have my own design firm," it sounds like alt-Cordy herself owns such a company, when it's actually her sitcom character. (One suspects this was Mere Smith's way of poking fun at people who can't separate actors and actresses from the roles they play.)

• Max Baker (the Hyperion clerk) guest-starred in an episode of *Son of the Beach*, opposite David Boreanaz's nubile wife, Jaime Bergman, and he appeared in 2005's *Constantine* opposite the far-less-nubile Keanu Reeves. Aimee Garcia (Tammy) later landed a regular role on the WB sitcom *All About the Andersons*, but it lasted one season. She also narrated *Spanglish* (2004).

When is Cordelia's Birthday?

Fortunately for all concerned, determining Cordelia's birthday will never rank as weighty a task as other issues in this volume. That said, if we're striving for any sort of completism, reconciling comments made about Cordy's birthday in "The Prodigal" (1.15) against the actual event in "Birthday" (3.11) requires some juggling. Bizarrely, it potentially requires us to discard the evidence – the office security code in "The Prodigal" – that presents itself as the most obvious answer.

To review, in "The Prodigal," Cordelia chastises Angel for forgetting her most recent birthday, threatening to use her birthdate as the office security code as a constant reminder / form of punishment. She then insinuates that Angel will spend the next "11 and a half months" punching in the code, which suggests she had a birthday only two weeks previous.

Now, all things being equal, *Angel*'s timeframe roughly parallels the show's broadcast dates in the real world. Season Four poses some issues, but in the main, each season – like *Buffy* – opens in the fall of one year and wraps in May of the next, then skips the summer hiatus. Ample proof exists to substantiate this, but notice, for example, how Willow informs Angel of the Slayer's death (dated to May 2001 on *Buffy*) in "There's No Place Like Plrtz Glrb" (2.22). It's hard to imagine that Willow has just been lollygagging around the Hyperion for weeks on end, waiting for Angel to come home, so *Angel* Season Two (logically enough) probably ends in unison with the finale of *Buffy* Season Five. Likewise, *Angel* Season Three opens after Angel has spent three months (i.e. the summer) away, and Season Four opens after Angel has spent Summer 2002 underwater.

With that general framework in mind, it would appear that Cordelia's birthday took place two weeks previous to the broadcast of "The Prodigal" on Feb. 22, meaning somewhere around Feb. 8. So far, so good. Then we come to "Birthday," which takes place *on* Cordy's birthday and broadcast on Jan. 14. Well, there's no particular reason as to why "The Prodigal" couldn't occur a few weeks sooner than its broadcast date. If we place Cordy's birthday as mid-January (near the best option for Buffy's birthday, actually, as we discussed in *Dusted*), then "Birthday" is satisfied, and "The Prodigal" would occur in – let's say – early February. Again... so far, so good.

The fly in the ointment, however, is that Cordelia chooses "0522" for the office security code, suggesting her birthday is May 22. Oh, dear. If we're even *trying* to stick with the notion that the show runs roughly concurrent to real-time, that seems unlikely if not outright impossible. Simply put, if Cordelia's birthday *did* fall on May 22, the chronology for the latter halves of Seasons One and Three gets thrown completely off-kilter. For a start, you'd have to postpone "The Prodigal" until June 5, and run the remainder of Season One through the summer. It's not only awkward, but it blatantly contradicts one of Faith's statements in "Sanctuary" (1.19), which dates that story to February. Likewise, if "Birthday" takes place in May, then the entire last half of Season Three – allowing that Angel spends Summer 2002 sleeping with the fishes – would occur in a hellishly narrow window. Now, many of the latter Season Three episodes admittedly take place back-to-back, so this isn't an impossible scenario, but it seems like a hell of a lot of suturing – allowing for stuff such as Cordelia and Groo's Season Three holiday – purely to accommodate Cordelia's choice for the security code. Besides, even if you *can* crowbar Season Three to reconcile against the code, it's simply berserk to give Season One the same treatment.

In all probability, Cordelia threatens to make the security code her birthdate, but in a flight of fancy changes her mind. Or perhaps she fails to make the damned security system work the first time, deems her birthdate as hexed and alternatively chooses "0522" for whatever reason. Either way, it boils down to a choice of rationalizing Cordelia's choice for the code, or – as we say – unnaturally warping the dating on at least 18 episodes. All things considered, we'd favor rationalizing the code.

Charisma Carpenter's birthday, by the way, is July 23. Which is entirely unhelpful to this entire process.

3.12: "Provider"

"Please have a seat, and one of our associates will be right with you."

Air Date: Jan. 21, 2002; **Writer:** Scott Murphy; **Director:** Bill Norton

SUMMARY Angel takes his new role as a father and provider to heart, instigating a marketing campaign that leaves the heroes flush with business. An executive named Harlen Elster gives Angel a sizeable check to eliminate a vampire nest, whereupon Angel dusts three of the vamps but discovers that "Harlen" is actually Sam Ryan, one of Harlen's laid-off employees. Ryan sought revenge on seven vampires for eating his friend Jack, but the remaining vamps corner him and Angel. Chagrined for not getting paid after all, Angel dusts the vamps and lets Ryan go on his way.

Meanwhile, Wesley and Gunn protect a woman named Allison from a zombie: her ex-boyfriend Brian. The gents discover that Allison poisoned Brian in the first place, and are further stunned when she reconciles with him. Finally, Lorne accompanies Fred when some Nahdrah demons hire to her to solve a mathematical puzzle – a gift to their prince. Fred completes the task, whereupon the joyous Nahdrahs deems Fred's head worthy of replacing their leader's decaying noggin. The heroes burst to the rescue and butcher the Nahdrahs, with Angel declaring he got carried away with dreams of profit – right before everyone scoops up the Nahdrahs' cash fee.

FIRSTS AND LASTS First use of the wall safe in Wesley's office, located behind an aerial photograph of the city. (The safe is likely a new addition and not part of the hotel as it stood in 1952. Otherwise, how would Angel know the combination?)

POINTS OF DISCUSSION ABOUT "Provider":

1. Wesley mentions an Internet article that he's writing, and Lorne comments that it's "one I'm sure we can all download at I'llneverknowtheloveofawoman.com." Sadly, the real-life version of this isn't nearly as interesting as "OhbythewaywevegotDarlastashedhere.com" (2.07, "Darla"), as it's occupied by a cyber-squatter, essentially a mercenary who buys up domain names in the hopes of reselling them.

2. Fuel for the "Can Angel use his cell-phone?" debate (see 1.13, "She" in particular): The plot here dictates that Angel successfully retrieves his voice mail, albeit off screen, despite his getting mocked for it.

CHARACTER NOTES *Angel:* Frugal enough to scrape $1.83 in change from the lobby sofa, then place it in a piggy bank for Connor that's secured in the hotel safe. He's not fond of boating, as it's expensive and best done in the daytime.

• *Cordelia:* Advises the heroes' work for the Powers takes priority over their need for cash. [Who would have thought she'd ever speak such words?] Cordy hasn't levitated or had a vision since last episode. She thinks Angel is "quite the natty dresser," believes boats are fun and favors one day renting a ski condo in Aspen.

• *Wesley:* Impressed the Nahdrahs with his web articles on DNA fusion comparisons in tri-ped demon populations. He's drafting a further Internet article that posits a formula for the genome mapping of creatures who don't have genes. [This is scientific gibberish, as "genome" means "a full set of chromosomes."] He and Fred seem to read the same science journals.

• *Gunn:* Thinks Fred is a "hot mama." Gunn basically confirms that he, errrrr, hasn't "gotten any" lately. [But then, neither has Wes.]

• *Fred:* Seems adept at building websites, and is excited [nerd] at the prospect of solving the Nahdrahs' math puzzle.

• *Lorne:* Unexpectedly discovers that baby formula isn't so bad with Kahlua. He sort-of speaks the Nahdrah language and sometimes deals with the agency's non-human clients.

He loosens the tongue of one of his sources, a Gar-wawk [demon], with chanting, a bong and a special water that one lights on fire. Lorne has "rats" – two of them literally – searching L.A. for Holtz. He feels seasick on the Nahdrahs' boat [although he's already queasy from the firewater, the bong, etc.] and has never known a Nahdrah intimately. Lack of circulation makes Lorne's hands turn pink.

• *Connor:* Gets his bottle at 3 pm.

• *Justine:* Disobeyed Holtz's order to walk away from a fight. He therefore jabs a sharp instrument [an ice pick, it seems] through her hand, then makes her sit there and endure the pain, as proof of her tenacity. Later, Holtz dispatches Justine to recruit others to his cause.

• *Sam Ryan:* Formerly worked as a press foreman for Elster Printing and Graphics (1333 Ocean Avenue, L.A., 50021), but was fired six months ago after begging Elster to bankroll a scheme to dust the vamps that killed Jack. He wanted to retrieve his "first gift" to Jack, a Timex watch. [It's never stated, but Sam's obsession over a gift to his friend – even potentially at the cost of his own life – suggests that perhaps they were *more* than friends.]

ORGANIZATIONS *Angel Investigations:* Angel tells Connor that if business keeps up, "We may have to incorporate." [Arg, that rather limits the options on how Angel has been running his business without proper identification. He mentions "the company name" in 2.20, "Over the Rainbow," so perhaps he's working with a business account of some sort. Besides, his colleagues could hardly go for years without properly listing their employer on their taxes.]

The agency now has a Yellow Pages listing, and a website with the obligatory blobby angel logo. Options on the website include Agency Services and Demon Directory. The heroes distribute 6,000 fliers, but these list the agency's phone number as (213) 555-0126 – actually that of Fabrizio's Pizza. [3.04, "Carpe Noctem" and 3.14, "Couplet" say the agency's actual number is (213) 555-0162. So the typo *is* close, not that it's much consolation to the poor sap in the teaser.] Wes prints and circulates 6,000 new fliers with the correct number. Cordy can run credit reports on potential clients.

DEMONOLOGY *Nahdrah Demons:* Aren't born so much as disgorged, and don outfits with geometric shapes – each a prime number – on the front. This group of Nahdrahs lives on a marina-docked barge, and offer $50,000 for Fred's services. At one point, Lorne is unclear if the Nahdrahs have departed to "consult with the prince, or go eat a cheese monkey." [If literally true, the latter is an amusing thought.]

The Nahdrahs' crystalline puzzle fits together in some sort of algorithmic sequence. When complete, the puzzle forms a glowing crystal pyramid with a metal rod in the middle. The Nahdrahs serve hors d'oeuvres with gray-purple eyeballs and shiny green insects. A metal plate protects their groins.

MAGIC Wes' potential explanations for Brian's return from the dead: witchcraft [seen in *Buffy* 3.12, "The Zeppo"], black magic [possibly *Buffy* 5.17, "Forever"], voodoo, zombification, demon possession and of course vampirism.

BEST LINE Wesley, "comforting" his client by debunking the myth that zombies eat people: "Zombies merely mangle, mutilate and occasionally wear human flesh. So there's no reason to be frightened."

THINGS THAT DON'T MAKE SENSE "Holtz is using the Grapplers as soldiers," Angel muses as if for the first time, even though the point was made abundantly clear three episodes ago. How does Sam Ryan, a puny human, hold shut the warehouse door when there's four super-strong vampires trying to knock it down? And a fairly big moral oversight: Wesley and Gunn's response to the revelation that Allie murdered her boyfriend is to shrug and ask for payment for services rendered. Even allowing that they can hardly prove the crime – especially given the lack of a body – aren't they supposed to actively frown on this sort of thing? Couldn't they at least vigorously shake a finger at her? And how did Brian come back from the dead as a zombie, anyway?

When the Nahdrahs move to decapitate Fred, why doesn't Lorne, who's tied up, hit them with his sonic cry? (Maybe he's too hung over/stoned, and recovering from the thump on his head, to make the attempt.) The Nahdrahs' cheap computer simulation of Fred's impending decapitation seems rather accommodating, as it apparently exists purely to leave Lorne and the audience with absolutely no doubt as to their plans. For benefit of anyone still in the dark, they even have a cute little red pointer – the sort you'd expect to see Bill Cosby using during his "Picture Pages" segment on *Captain Kangaroo* – making a crude diagonal line across Fred's neck.

Angel strangely claims that Connor will be "Notre Dame, class of 2020" – the year the lad (ignoring his hyper-aging later on) should start college, not finish it. Once the Powers blatantly warn Cordelia about the Nahdrahs' homicidal intent, she seems naïve to think they'll simply take back their money and forget about the whole business. Worse, she doesn't even arm herself with something useful such as oh, say, a crossbow, as awkward as that would be while carrying Connor.

Finally, given the entire gamut of demon habits, don't the heroes vet their potential non-human clients, purely to weed out the ones known to perform nasty practices/rituals? Back in Season One, something as innocent as a demon bachelor party nearly resulted in someone getting their brains eaten out with a shrimp fork, so the heroes can't claim all that much surprise when the Nahdrahs try to lop off Fred's head.

IN RETROSPECT Justine implies that Holtz's underground chamber lacks indoor plumbing. The bucket that Wesley later provides (4.01, "Deep Down") must seem like quite the modern convenience, then.

CRITIQUE Atypically, it's an *Angel* anthology episode – and therein lies the problem, because it's a house divided against itself. There's three plotlines in play, but Angel's thread proves almost appallingly mundane, and Wesley and Gunn's dalliance with a zombie rather stupidly entails their client getting away with murder. Only Fred's business with the Nahdrahs has any color, but even that's hardly what you'd call remarkable.

By diluting its energy among these feeble storylines, the episode loses any urgency and becomes so starved for content that Cordelia recaps the state-of-affairs for baby Connor's benefit. True, there's nothing in "Provider" that'll rub your nose the wrong way, but it's simply too thin. Gadzooks, is it thin. It's far from being the worst *Angel* story... but it might number among the most pointless.

THE LORE Jeffrey Dean Morgan (Sam Ryan) later landed a rather high-profile role as Denny Duquette on *Grey's Anatomy* – he's the heart transplant patient who falls in love with model-turned-nurse Izzy Stevens.

3.13: "Waiting in the Wings"

"Tonight, we're just a couple of young sophisticates enjoying an evening of classical dance."

Air Date: February 4, 2002;
Writer/Director: Joss Whedon

SUMMARY Upon learning that the Blinnikov World Ballet Corps will perform *Giselle* in L.A., Angel – having witnessed the group dance back in 1890 – convinces his friends to attend the theatre with him. But once at the theatre, Angel recognizes the dancers as *exactly* the same people he saw nearly 112 years previous.

Angel and Cordelia investigate backstage, encountering a magical effect that warps space and makes everything resemble a late nineteenth century theatre. The two of them temporarily lose their personalities to the spell, recreating a liaison between the company's prima ballerina and her lover, Stefan. The heroes discover that the jealous company manager – Count Kurskov – objected to the affair and used a magic medallion to pull the ballerina out of time, forcing her to eternally dance for him.

Wesley suggests battling the Count's henchmen – a group of masked swordsmen, also generated by the medallion – and thus overloading the Count's power-source. Angel finds the prima ballerina and convinces her to alter her dance routine, thereby throwing the Count's temporal effect further off-balance. The ballerina complies, allowing Angel to break the Count's medallion. The spell ends, even as the ballerina, the

Giselle dancers and the swordsmen all fade to nothingness. The heroes return home afterward – only to re-meet the Groosalugg, who's returned to romance with Cordelia.

FIRSTS AND LASTS Be forewarned that it's the last "classic" line-up of Angel, Gunn, Fred, Lorne (who admittedly doesn't do much here), the real Cordelia and the pre-contacts, pre-stubble, non-royally-pissed Wesley. Groo's in the mix starting next episode, and everything goes to hell in a hand basket from there.

For Whedon-verse fans, it's the first appearance of a notable *Firefly* actor on *Angel* – see **Points of Discussion**, and also 4.17, "Inside Out," 4.22, "Home" and 5.17, "Underneath." It's also Gunn and Fred's first kiss, and it's the first glimpse of "murderous" Wesley when he spies them (although to be fair, supernatural forces attuned to jealousy are influencing him at the time).

POINTS OF DISCUSSION ABOUT "Waiting in the Wings":

1. This being a Joss Whedon script, the dialogue almost takes on a life of its own. Notice how Lorne almost comes unstopped with food references, calling Angel "crumb cake," "you big corn muffin," "strudel" and "cinnamon buns" – that's all in the same scene. It's also typical Whedon that after it's revealed that the ballet dancers are exactly the same as they were 112 years ago – *dun, dun, dun!* – Cordelia says, "Well, it's a puzzler. Are there snacks?"

2. But more to the point... and we're wondering how to politely address this... there's all the smutty talk. Whether Whedon feels at liberty to talk dirty because he's the show's head honcho, or whether he wrote Victorian erotica in a previous life, his scripts often steam up the windshield. Let's index this purely in the name of research: a possessed Cordelia tells Angel "I want you to undress me," followed by her even-more scandalous declaration "I'm only alive when you're inside me." An aroused Angel comments "it's kind of hard" with regards to opening a door, prompting Cordelia to respond "I kind of noticed" with regards to something else entirely. There's a smattering of phallic "hot iron"/"the iron is hot" references, and there's Angel's declaration that he and Cordy "hit kind of a mystical hot spot back in one of the dressing rooms." (Well, no kidding.)

A side note: We refuse to broach the topic of Cordelia, Phantom Dennis and his skill with a loofah (3.01, "Heartthrob"), simply because loofahs are too coarse for *that* sort of thing, and it's too horrifying to contemplate.

Finally, we come to the bit where a still-aroused Angel shields his groin by folding his tuxedo coat over his arm... Whedon worried about the network censors trumping in here, but the scene somehow got through. (Angel isn't the last character who needs to "adjust himself" either, as we'll learn next episode.) Mind, with hindsight, little of this should come as a surprise from the same writer who, in the *Serenity* movie, had the "sweet little" engineer-girl character announce: "Goin' on a year now, I ain't had nothing twixt my nethers weren't run on batteries."

3. The big guest-star here, of course, is Summer Glau. She's the prima ballerina, but she's also fated to portray the unbalanced girl genius River Tam on *Firefly*. Glau's grace as the ballerina will enable *Firefly* viewers to understand why River had so many spontaneous opportunities to express herself through dance (in the episode "Safe," for instance). Her ballet training also helps explain why River looks so unbelievably fluid when she's kicking the crap out of someone, and how she pulls off those amazing splits while she's hiding in the rafters in *Serenity*.

Before you can ask, Glau's *Angel* role motivated Whedon to cast her as River, although it helped that Whedon's colleague Jeph Loeb – a *Smallville* producer, comic-book writer and someone who worked on the unmade *Buffy* animated series – suggested to Whedon that he let Glau read for the part.

4. Pursuant to the "Did Charisma Carpenter get breast implants?" issue raised in "Birthday" (3.11): Please note that fancy-dress Cordelia isn't wearing a bra, not even those specifically made for the kind of outfit she's wearing. Once again, a careful consideration the on-screen evidence leads one to conclude that they're God's creations rather than lumps of silicone.

CHARACTER NOTES *Angel:* Saw the ballet company's production of *Giselle* in 1890, and wept like a baby despite his being evil. [That Angel recognizes the *Giselle* dancers 112 years later only attests to the strength of his photographic memory. By the way, when Angel enters the ballerina's dressing room and says everything is "unchanged," he probably just means that everything "looks new. After all, if Angelus had actually been backstage after the performance, he'd probably have tried to eat everyone, the ballerina included.]

Angel is cautious about going too far with Cordelia, even while influenced by the spirits of nineteenth century lovers. "Back in the day," Angelus either acquired box seats or simply ate the people holding them.

• *Cordelia:* Now using words like "aficionado" and pronouncing them correctly. [Yes, we're being cheeky, but this is so far removed from Cordelia's *Buffy* persona, it's almost as if she spent last summer hitting the thesaurus.] The ballet "thrills" Cordelia to the point that she falls asleep, and drools on Angel's shoulder. She readily lip-massages Groo upon his return. She follows the time-honored tradition of "purchasing" a dress and wearing it once, then returning it the next day.

• *Wesley:* Confides to Cordelia that he wants to ask Fred out [so he's recovered from events in "Billy" (3.06)], and is subsequently floored to spy Fred kissing Gunn. Yet rather than turning resentful, Wesley tells the pair of them to stick together during battle. He's highly adept with a sword. [This largely owes to Denisof's British stage training. In fictional terms, Wesley must have been training himself with a sword recently – even if swordplay formed part of his Watcher's training – because Season One Wesley never fought this well.]

• *Gunn:* Goes to the ballet with the greatest reluctance, but the beauty of the performance moves him to tears. His review of the show: "These guys are tight and I am tripping out." The Count's minions give Gunn a small knife wound, moving Fred to kiss him.

• *Fred:* Can shovel food into her mouth like there's no tomorrow. She loves ballet, but hasn't seen much of it. Her family used to go to *The Nutcracker* at Christmas. When Wes and Gunn both try to hold Fred's hand, it becomes obvious that their mitts positively dwarf hers. [No, seriously, take a look at the scene. They're giants compared to her.]

• *Lorne:* Hints that he'd make a play for Cordelia himself, but says "she's out of my league." [You almost think he's going to add, "Also, I'm gay."] He here "reads" Angel and learns of his infatuation with Cordelia. [As with "Offspring" (3.07), it's astonishing that the prospect of Angel romancing someone doesn't ring any alarm bells about him potentially turning into a serial killer.] Lorne stays home from the ballet, on baby-sitting duty with Connor.

PYLEA The political situation there "got sketchy" once everyone gained their freedom [2.22, "There's No Place Like Plrtz Glrb"]. Groo was deposed, and a people's republic set up. [Still, it's a step up from their previous society, with its monarch and slave class.]

DEMONOLOGY *Vampires:* Angel says he could sense, even while sitting in the back of the audience, if the ballet performers were vampires. [But then, his "vampire radar" is stronger than most.]

MAGIC *Count Kurskov's "power center":* Kurskov wears a bejeweled chest medal that maintains the ballet company's temporal flux, and forces the ballerina to re-enact the exact same performance of *Giselle* night after night. The medal extends the dimensions of the theatre's backstage to magical proportions, and renders it as a piece of the nineteenth century that's been taken out of time. [This presumably occurs at any locale where the ballet corps performs.]

Various points in this locale contain magical "hot spots" – described as "energy trapped in time" – where "spirits" can momentarily possess trespassers and make them re-enact the events behind the Count removing the ballerina from time. [This isn't entirely unlike *Buffy* 2.20, "I've Only Got Eyes for You," but seems more like a freak side effect than anything else. It's akin to an energy "echo," which explains how the ballerina and the Count's personas influence Cordelia and Wesley while the genuine articles are elsewhere.]

The jewel also creates the other *Giselle* performers (who vanish once they leave the stage) and generates masked swordsmen who enforce the Count's will. [It's possible, given that the ballerina disappears while the Count remains corporeal once the power center is destroyed, that she was merely a magical copy of the original version. Presumably, the Count relied on his power center to remain young and will age normally from now on.]

BEST LINE Gunn, appalled when Angel reneges on getting tickets for the "Mata Hari" band, and decides they should see the ballet instead: "No. No! This is not Mata Hari. This is tutus and guys with their big-ass packages jumpin' up and down."

THINGS THAT DON'T MAKE SENSE Wesley has apparently heard that the Blinnikov World Ballet Corps is "very ahead of their time" – nice foreshadowing, but an odd claim to make about a troupe that's been doing the exact same ballet for at least 112 years. Also, some members of the audience still feel the need to applaud after the performance, even though the ending of *Giselle* was oddly changed, some of the dancers literally vanished without explanation and – the most startling of all – the finale entailed a lunatic in a tuxedo (Angel) running across the stage, leaping into one of the box seats and assaulting a patron.

And as with stories such as "Sense and Sensibility" (1.06), one wonders what becomes of the all-too-human villain, unless the ruin of Kurskov's plans and his presumed loss of immortality is deemed punishment enough. Then again, for all the heroes know, he's got a second power center somewhere and can just start up all over again.

A nit-picky point: Groo hasn't visited Earth before, yet he tracks Cordelia to the Hyperion, no problem. (Then again, he *is* the Groosalugg, a hunter by nature. Or perhaps he just asked for directions, presuming Cordelia previously mentioned the hotel by name.) Ah, and it's done for dramatic effect, but notice how Wesley doesn't make a sound while crossing the Hyperion lobby to suddenly appear behind Fred.

POP CULTURE *Giselle*. Actually a terribly sad story about a lowly vineyard country girl who's courted by a duplicitous count, and dies from the stress of it all. Her ghost encounters the Willis, the spirits of women who expired between their engagement and their wedding, and who now seek vengeance on any bastard who wrongs his fiancée. (Incidentally, the Willis make their victims dance to death – not unlike the *Buffy* musical, then.) The Willis nearly do in the Count, but a merciful Giselle lets him live. In "Waiting in the Wings," the ballerina changes the dance so she doesn't "save" the Count after all.

• Cordelia: "You wanna wander around backstage like Spinal Tap for the next... ever?" In *This is Spinal Tap* (1984), a members of a heavy metal band get hopelessly lost while attempting to find the stage.

• Fred had her first sexual dream about the Mouse King, the main antagonist in *The Nutcracker*. As the name might imply, he's a giant vermin who duels the titular character and gets stabbed to death.

• Gunn desperately longs to see Mata Hari – "the tightest band in L.A." – at the Troubadour. In real life, Mata Hari is a rock band with Whedon's brother among its members.

IN RETROSPECT Wesley here looks at a drawing of Solaris, a female demon who's just ripped off someone's arm and is munching on it – in "A New World" (3.20), he'll view an illustration of the Devil wolfing down Judas Iscariot whole.

Also, "Waiting in the Wings" usually gets compared and the possession-themed *Buffy* story "I've Only Got Eyes for You," but stop to consider that it's also like "The Puppet Show" (*Buffy* 1.07) – in which something inhuman lurks backstage and cackles a lot.

IT'S REALLY ABOUT... Inherently, it's a work of beauty, in which everyone – okay, barring Cordelia, perhaps – comes to appreciate the arts. Viewers always recall how the ballet moves Gunn to tears, often forgetting that even Angelus – who started out life as a drunken Irish lout, let's not forget – apparently came to appreciate the genre. We're supposed to be spell-bound by the emotional spectacle on display here, and Minear's realization that Whedon was inherently trying to do "*Giselle* meets *Moulin Rogue*" is rather telling.

However, the "emotional spectacle," as with a lot of high art, isn't exactly what you'd call overwhelmingly satisfying for all concerned. Kurskov exacts his vengeance upon discovering the ballerina's love affair, and Wesley similarly gets his heart shredded upon seeing Gunn and Fred in a clinch. We're moved because large parts of it *aren't* pleasant, which if anything seems to substantiate the commonplace view that *Buffy* fans become the most excited whenever the Slayer is made to suffer. Almost predictably, we'll revisit this in "A Hole in the World" (5.15).

CRITIQUE Everyone tends to view this story as a visual and emotional feast. There's absolutely no better way of putting it.

Despite his glowing reputation, Whedon is hardly a bulletproof writer. But when he's got a real, bonafide vision to deploy onto the screen, then he's virtually unstoppable. So it's simply stunning how nearly every single moment of "Waiting in the Wings" justifies its existence. The dialogue is organic, lovely and erudite as few but Whedon can provide, the direction only amplifies the action (notice especially Wesley's reflection in the chrome when he sees Gunn and Fred kissing), the lustful bits between Angel and Cordelia absolutely sizzle and the sword-wielding villains seem downright creepy and wonderfully weird. From a critical point of view, there's ***so much*** of interest, and even non-discerning viewers should at least recognize they're watching something really, really sweet.

Like the *Buffy* musical, it masterfully stands on its own, yet capitalizes on the show's present set-up in the best possible way. Other stories in this era, such as "Lullaby" and "Forgiving," are indisputably A-level, but they're relying on the seasonal story arcs as their rocket-fuel. Remarkably, "Waiting in the Wings" achieves the same velocity all by its lonesome. As such, it's as opulent as the theatre itself, and deserves all the warm regard we can bestow upon it.

THE LORE The notion of an Angel-Cordelia romance rattled some of the producers, Greenwalt included, who worried that Angel's heart forevermore belonged to Buffy. Whedon took the opposing view that "people move on," and won out. (Mason, *TV Guide Inside*, Jan. 21, 2004) Greenwalt later concurred, and addressed fandom in the middle of Season Three with: "I feel less like 'Get over it' and more like 'This is what happens.' People get on with their lives... but it doesn't mean you still don't pine for that girl you knew in high school."

Holdouts among the fans, however, felt scorned and sent Greenwalt chocolate and peanut butter as a reminder of Angel and Buffy's love. He later said: "I'm afraid to open the jars because it could be anthrax." (Pierce, *Deseret News*, Feb. 18, 2002) Minear's response to the whole controversy: "It doesn't surprise me at all. Change is always difficult for fans of a show." (O'Hare, *Zap2It.com*, May 14, 2002)

• Whedon wasn't a huge ballet fan, but he'd seen *The Nutcracker* and had filmed dance recitals in college. (He's claimed, perhaps even a bit seriously, that he's a dancer wanna-be.) Acker had mentioned to Whedon that she'd done 15 years of ballet, which inspired him to write "Waiting in the Wings" as an excuse for her to dance – no small challenge, as even Whedon couldn't imagine Fred dancing ballet for real. As you probably know, a scene was filmed wherein Wesley fantasizes about himself and Fred prancing about on stage. With Minear's encouragement, Whedon realized the scene interrupted the narrative flow and struck it, but it's available as a DVD extra.

• The composers lifted the occasional excerpt from *Giselle*, but most of it was an original score. (Kral, *The Bronze*, Feb. 5, 2002)

• Glau auditioned using both Russian and English accents, but she has neither. Like Acker, she's a Texan.

• Stephanie Romanov had been trained in ballet, tap, jazz, ballroom, tango and other forms of dance, and was therefore disappointed to only hear about the ballet story after it was in the can. As Lilah didn't appear in the episode, Romanov wasn't even sent a copy of the script. (*BBC Cult*, 2002)

• Mark Harelik (Kurskov) appeared in the *Cheers* series finale as Diane's supposed husband, who's later revealed to be her gay dog groomer. He also held down recurring roles on *Hearts Afire, Wings, Almost Perfect* and *Will and Grace*. On *Star Trek: Voyager* (5.10, "Counterpoint"), he played Devore Inspector Kashyk, Captain Janeway's bumpy headed lover. Thomas Crawford (Theater Manager) later turns up in "Slouching Toward Bethlehem" (4.04) as the "Eater Demon" that chases Cordy about the Hyperion. He also appeared in *Air Force One* and *Apollo 13*, and opposite Acker in *Catch Me If You Can*.

3.14: "Couplet"

"The truth is, you and the Groosalugg are two totally different people... who look exactly alike."

Air Date: Feb. 18, 2002; **Writer:** Jeffrey Bell; **Writer/Director:** Tim Minear

SUMMARY A chagrined Cordelia refrains from piling into bed with Groo, fearing (according to 2.21, "Through the Looking Glass") that such an act would transfer her vision talent to him. Cordy subsequently gives Groo a makeover that turns him into a veritable Angel clone, and asks Angel's help in procuring a magical prophylactic. Somewhat dismayed, Angel takes Groo to a demon brothel and purchases a potion that will insulate Cordelia's vision ability.

Meanwhile, Gunn and Fred get assigned to trail Jerry, a potentially unfaithful fiancée, to a park. They find a life-sucking tree demon has been luring hapless victims there via an Internet connection, but not before the creature nabs all three of them. Angel and Groo charge to the rescue, but the tree demon skewers Groo with a tentacle and starts to drain his life energy. Angel goads the creature into impaling him instead, correctly gambling that his undead body will prove a poor source of nourishment, and make the demon go dormant.

Later, Angel selflessly tells Cordelia to take an extended vacation with Groo, and grows encouraged about his newfound responsibility as a father. Unfortunately, Wesley – privately studying texts that comment on Connor's birth – chillingly translates a prophecy that claims Angel will kill his son.

FIRSTS AND LASTS The Gunn/Fred romance gets its first proper outing after their lip-locking last episode. For the second and last time, the heroes venture into a demon brothel. It's the final occasion that Wesley sees the "real" Cordelia until two years hence (in 5.12, "You're Welcome," if indeed it's her). You'll have to trust us on that one, because it's too hideously complicated to explain here.

POINTS OF DISCUSSION ABOUT "Couplet":

1. As Angel and Wesley enter the mystical texts bookshop, check out the display case on the right-hand side. In what's undoubtedly an act of props recycling, you should observe one of the red leather-bound "Trionic" books from Pylea ("Through the Looking Glass"). Specifically, it's the one with the wolf head on the cover. Perhaps the designers just threw it in for fun, but it actually makes sense within the *Angel*-verse. After all, 4.12, "Calvary" establishes that there's an inter-dimensional book market of sorts, so seeing a Pylean text in an L.A. store isn't tremendously odd. Heck, presuming the heroes didn't use that book to get home at the end of Season Two, maybe Groo hocked it for traveling money.

2. Before you can mention it... yes, the enchanted pillow-fight in the demon brothel (see **Organizations**) looks a lot like Xander's dream about the Potential Slayers in the appropriately titled *Buffy* 7.18, "Dirty Girls," but was broadcast about 14 months before that story. So long as we're on the topic, we might ask why the door to the "enchanted pleasure" room is open. Are they exhibitionists as well?

3. Now let's chat about the agency's finances. After two years of the heroes hurting for money and clients, it would appear that they presently have a lot more financial wherewithal: Angel here helps to finance Cordelia and Groo's vacation, Wesley pays a wizard a substantial sum of cash (in 3.15, "Loyalty"), both Wesley and Cordelia own vehicles (3.16, "Sleep Tight" and 3.22, "Tomorrow" respectively), and the agency's case files appear more numerous and complicated than ever before (3.18, "Double or Nothing"). Granted, they're bereft of clients by "The Price" (3.19), and by Season Four, Gunn and Fred can't cope with the bills. But for now, it's more feast than famine.

4. Wesley gives a neat little speech about how Angel's mission animates them. It's so stirring and such a sign of Wes and Angel's brotherhood, you can kinda tell that something gut-wrenchingly awful is on the horizon. Sure enough... next up is 3.15, "Loyalty."

5. Pursuant to the discussion about Charisma Carpenter's breasts from last episode: They're still looking rather jiggly, not fake, although it's possible she's wearing a push-up bra.

We're starting to conclude that the clothes they're picking for Cordelia are making a lot of difference.

6. And to round out the smutty talk, Gunn "adjusts" himself while sitting in his pickup with Fred. This occurs only an episode after an aroused Angel folded a tuxedo coat over his arm to, shall we say, "shield himself from embarrassment." What sort of depraved show are we watching, anyway?

CHARACTER NOTES *Angel:* Says he was a solo act "for most" of his 240 years [it was more like 40 percent of it, unless Angelus snuck away from Darla more than we suspect]. Angel is gallant enough to not interfere with Groo and Cordy's relationship, even though Groo's presence threatens his self-worth.

• *Cordelia:* Again given to running in heels [see 1.01, "City Of"]. When Cordy and her cousin Timmy were kids, she practiced cutting his hair. Remarkably, she seems to research the paranormal prophylactic all by her lonesome [unless Wesley quietly made some inquiries on her behalf]. Paying for the item "nearly cleans out" her bank account. [She and Groo next appear in 3.18, "Double or Nothing."]

• *Wesley:* Better accepts that Fred chose Gunn. He also expresses "caution" about Connor's miraculous existence, hence his researching the topic.

• *Gunn:* Has shared breakfast with Fred for weeks, and has officially entered that goofy phase of love where even watching her eat seems intoxicating. They normally split the check.

• *Fred:* Claims she doesn't have much experience with romance, and says she and Wesley are "just good friends."

• *Groo:* Killed many Bleaucha monsters in Pylea. He welcomed his overthrow from the Pylean throne [mentioned last episode], having found the tedium of government almost unbearable. He here uses Angel's favorite broadsword. Cordelia estimates that Groo heals almost as fast as Angel, and that he's perhaps a little taller too. Notably, Gunn and Fred ask Groo, not Angel, to save them from the tree demon.

PYLEA Groo says that after "There's No Place Like Plrtz Glrb" (2.22), the Pylean political factions endlessly splintered until "the more radical elements, spurred by a charismatic leader, did the Dance of Revolution." [Dare we say it? You'd almost think that Pylea was now run by Numfar, Whedon's dancing character, from "Through the Looking Glass."]

THE LIBRARY Deprived of the Nyazian Scrolls [3.09, "Lullaby"], Wesley looks for commentaries and accumulate scholarship about the texts. Wes acquires a copy of *Grammaticus' Third Century Greek Commentaries*, which are apparently in the original Greek, from a specialty bookshop. [Just so we're clear, Grammaticus was writing about the Nyazian Scrolls *in* the third century.] The bookshop manager has three copies of this text.

ORGANIZATIONS *The Powers-That-Be:* The visions are now blending into Cordelia's real-world perceptions, with Cordy momentarily viewing Groo as a Senih'd demon. They still have a prophetic component, as Cordy knows the Senih'd will arise "later today."

• *Anita's demon brothel:* [Evidently not the same locale as Madame Dorian's; see 1.20, "War Zone."] Features an enchanted room that extends every touch, emotion and desire for maximum pleasure – very good for pillow fights and such. Other sights include a man in business attire happily chained to a wall, and a red-haired female with a demonic smile and three breasts talking to a weasely little guy. The brothel's madam is an imposing woman named Anita.

DEMONOLOGY *The Tree Demon:* [Cited in the script simply as "Monster."] Located under Plummer Park, and apparently a root-based demon that draws people into its underground lair, then sucks them dry. It possesses a DSL connection and a working knowledge of the Internet, and entices victims as "Hot Blonde 37159." [It's possible that demon isn't actually wood, as it skewers Angel's chest and he doesn't go to dust. You could alternatively argue that it simply missed Angel's heart – not impossible, as it similarly stabs the half-human Groo in the chest, where his heart resides.]

MAGIC *Paranormal Prophylatic:* Cordelia reasons [correctly, it seems] that she's probably not the only super-powered woman whose abilities could be lost through physical intimacy. She tracks down Anita, a peddler of love potions, elixirs, etc. Anita supplies a blue bottle with the protective potion, and advises that Cordelia must drink it all at once before commencing with the nookie.

Gunn mentions/invents the following types of magic: "Demony love spells, mojo sex chants, voodoo booty rituals." [That said, a "demony love spell" causes no end of trouble in *Buffy* 2.16, "Bewitched, Bewildered and Bothered."]

BEST LINE Groo tells Anita that he needs the protective potion "so I may *com-shuk* my princess." Angel, pointing to himself and scrambling to protect his masculinity: "Just to reiterate, *not* the princess."

THINGS THAT DON'T MAKE SENSE The Senih'd demon gets wounded and neatly leaves a blood trail for Angel and Groo to follow, but there's no explanation for how this injury happened in the first place. It occurs before the beast encounters the heroes, so they didn't inflict it. We might also ask why pedestrians joyously applaud after witnessing Groo kill the creature in broad daylight in a park, whereupon it oozes into the ground. Do they think it's a movie shoot? If so, that's a hell of an optical effect to pull off in real-time. (Then again, ILM *was* doing amazing stuff in this period.)

Wesley's notes in the finale are presumably in his own handwriting, yet some sentences look very different from one another, suggesting that – dunno – Wesley has multiple personalities, likes to write with both hands or is practicing for a lucrative career as a forger.

Take a deep breath, as the tree demon shenanigans cause no end of trouble. Gunn and Fred don't actually stand on the tree demon's branches when they start to review their hand-held video recorder, yet they're magically in the correct position when the creature snags them. Oddly, the tree demon takes its sweet time in sucking the life out of them, but perhaps they're meant as dessert after it's done with the adulterous Jerry. More glaringly, though, Angel totally lucks out with his rather unsubstantiated idea that feeding off a vampire will make the tree demon go dormant, as opposed to, say, absolutely nothing happening at all. Also, Fred claims that the tree demon lacks vital organs, but Gunn later finds a head of sorts to impale – we can probably forgive the misdiagnosis, though, as Fred is bound by tree demon tentacles at the time.

Finally, why does Fred's hair look *more* frightful after she escapes the tree demon's lair, as opposed to when she was trapped. Was it simply hell getting out of there?

POP CULTURE Lorne to Angel: "Fine, Miss Garbo. Have it your way. Be alone." In *Grand Hotel* (1932), Greta Garbo played a melodramatic Russian dancer named Grusinskaya, and uttered her signature line "I want to be alone." The film also starred John Barrymore (Drew Barrymore's granddad) and won an Oscar for Best Picture.

IT'S REALLY ABOUT... As the old cliché goes, it's about letting someone you love roam free and seeing if they return, as both Angel and Wes let their beloveds go off with someone else. Heck, Angel goes a step further and actively facilitates this. On a related note, it's not exactly hard to guess the subtext when Cordelia remakes Groo in Angel's image, is it?

In a small fashion, of course, the story's about how people you chat with online could be anyone – soul-sucking tree demons included.

CRITIQUE As with "Provider," it's yet another story that seems clueless about what it's trying to accomplish. The heroes hunt a demon here, dig up an ancient volume of mystical commentary there. They visit a demon brothel, deal with some inter-office romance and skewer a tree-demon. The episode does all the things that *Angel* tends to do, but for the viewer, the experience is more like eating reheated mashed potatoes than getting a proper meal. It advances the characters just enough to prove its worth, but never steps up to the plate and takes a proper swing. None of this damages the series, but it's not as good as some commentators pretend.

That said, "Couplet" seemed more irritating on original broadcast – on DVD, it's one of those stories that you watch, then immediately move along to something more exciting. There *are* some funny moments – such as Cordy giving Angel's favorite broadsword to Groo, thus leaving poor Angel with a little axe – and the final cliffhanger practically knocks you off your damn chair. But in critical terms, it's a story that crawls rather than walks forward, and only loosely compliments an otherwise daring Season Three.

THE LORE Mark Lutz (Groo) was born Canadian, but spent four and a half years of his teens living in Hong Kong, which motivated him to study international relations in college. Outside of acting, he'd competed on Canada's behalf in international swimming events such as the World Cup and the Olympic Trials. In the acting profession, he'd spent a year on Canadian television as the Finnish hockey player Jukka Branny-Acke on *Power Play*, and in 2001, he was Natalie's fiancé in *The Facts of Life Reunion*. During Lutz's time as Groo, Hallett e-mailed him an entertaining fan comment about the character being the love child of Fabio and Keanu Reeves. (Bundy, *Zap2It*, May 5, 2002)

• Michael Otis (the Pillow Fight Man) appeared in a *Women: Stories of Passion* episode entitled "The Lover from Another Planet."

3.15: "Loyalty"

"That the vampire will devour his child is certain."

Air Date: Feb. 25, 2002; **Writer:** Mere Smith;
Director: James A. Contner

SUMMARY Wesley looks into the prophecy that Angel will murder Connor, consulting with an oracle of sorts – the Loa – who tell him to watch for three portents: earthquake, fire and blood. Elsewhere, Holtz assembles more soldiers and tests the mettle of Angel's associates. Gunn and Fred narrowly escape a vampire ambush that Justine secretly videotapes, hoping to study their fighting techniques, and Angel and Wesley expose one of their clients, Aubrey, as a mole for Holtz.

Wesley locates and uneasily confers with Holtz, who acknowledges Wesley's concern about Angel's son and stresses that Wes must soon make a choice. Wesley convinces himself that Angel would never harm his child – but witnesses the three portents when an earthquake hits L.A., a fire breaks out in Angel's room and Angel takes a head injury that drips blood on the swaddled Connor. [*Continued next episode*]

FIRSTS AND LASTS With Wesley starting his "descent" of sorts, it's the first outing of the stubbled look that he'll more or less sport for the remainder of the show (see **Points of Discussion** under 3.19, "The Price"). Holtz and Justine display their first spark of attraction when he saves her from a falling armoire, resulting in their doing the "dramatic eye-contact thing." And we learn of Angel's hockey fixation, which he loves because it's an indoor game played at night (see also 5.05, "Life of the Party").

POINTS OF DISCUSSION ABOUT "Loyalty":

1. Cordelia's off vacationing with Groo for three episodes, and this coincides with what's arguably the biggest black hole in fandom's knowledge of the show's production workings. Some have suggested that the producers found themselves at loggerheads with a demanding Charisma Carpenter, and thought that getting her off-set for a few episodes would cool off the situation. Yet we mention this as a matter of completeness, not because there's any hardcore evidence for it. As with Glenn Quinn's departure in Season One, it's easy to see how conspiracy theories might arise about a perfectly innocent situation, and it's hardly reasonable to expect those involved to prove, beyond a shadow of a doubt, that everything was hunky-dory. We'll probably never know, and Carpenter and Whedon continue to display a good working relationship even today (such as Carpenter's campaigning to star in the *Wonder Woman* film, directed by Whedon), so let's not dwell on it.

Still... if relations with Carpenter *were* strained, then credit the Mutant Enemy team with sculpting the overarching storylines to accommodate her absence. Simply put, the next few episodes can't occur unless Wesley is isolated from everyone he trusts – that particularly includes Cordy, who was his confidant as recently as "Waiting in the Wings" (3.13). Wes can't exactly chat with Angel over the coffee about the prophecy that he'll murder his son; nor is he overly cozy with Gunn and Fred right now, for obvious reasons. Virginia dumped Wes a year ago, the Watchers practically loathe the man and he was never chummy with Buffy's crew. That leaves... Cordelia. Hence the need to remove her from the Hyperion for a while. Mind, that leaves the niggling issue of why the heroes don't simply call Cordelia for help, which will generate fodder for **Things That Don't Make Sense** in future (see especially 3.17, "Forgiving").

2. The teaser entails Wesley having a nightmare about Angel killing Connor (Angel: "I'm teaching him how to die," just before sinking his teeth into the lad), followed by a veritable fount of blood bubbling up from the book on Wesley's desk. It's not only one of the most harrowing scenes in the entire series, but – as viewers tend to miss – it's rather prophetic too. Crucially, some of the dialogue is taken almost word-for-word from Wesley's later conversation with the Loa (a.k.a. "the giant hamburger man"). Like the Loa, the dream-Angel says, "He already knows the answer. He's just looking for the question." Also, there's Gunn's low chant of "runnin' out of time," which the Loa basically reiterates.

This *can't* be coincidence, but it's never explained either. One could argue that the Powers are trying to warn Wesley; but if so, they make a piss-poor job of it, as the nightmare only keeps Wes on his tragic path. You could also suggest that it's Jasmine manipulating Wesley per her agenda (see **Did Jasmine Cause All This?**), but it's rather easy to overplay that card. Perhaps the most obvious answer is that Wesley spent time on a Hellmouth three years ago, and his decisions are causing such ripples in Jasmine's game of cosmic proportions that it's affecting his dreams. Well, that's the best explanation we can offer.

3. The Jollyburger statue – the one possessed by the Loa and turned into a giant, snarling, energy cracking hamburger man – numbers among the series' most amusing special effects, especially when you stop to consider how much the studio probably paid for it. Indeed, the "Loa Jollyburger man" remains, for our money, among the top *Angel* characters begging to be made into an action figure, preferably with a voice chip that growls, "Betrayal and agony lie in wait." We'd buy several.

4. Baby-fashion update: In the final scene, decked out in his yellow shirt, Connor looks like a little Captain Kirk.

5. We have to say it somewhere: The carousel scene with Gunn and Fred readily brings to mind *The Lost Boys* (1987), a whimsical vampire flick that takes place at an amusement park, and in many ways is a precursor to *Buffy*.

CHARACTER NOTES *Angel:* Gunn re-confirms that Angel has no bank account or official last name [3.04, "Carpe Noctem"]. Ergo, Angel uses Cordelia's credit card number when ordering stuff over the web. [Note that Angel himself places the order, so – as with 1.01, "City Of" – he's not an idiot with computers.] Angel orders Connor itty-bitty hockey sticks and a green sports shirt with "Connor 03," and thinks his son will become a center. Angel was living in Room 312 at the Hyperion until last episode.

Angel cites Holtz as "one of the good guys," and concedes that Holtz has reason to hate him. It's implied that he's discovered the art of putting babies to sleep by taping the white noise of a vacuum cleaner, then playing it low next to Connor's bed.

• *Wesley:* Pays a wizard "an obscene amount of money" [proof that the agency is more lucrative; see 3.14, "Couplet"] for information about the Loa. He's curt when Fred suggests he take Aubrey out for coffee. [Well, no wonder. The last thing Wesley needs right now is Fred playing matchmaker.]

• *Gunn:* He's been fighting vampires and demons since he was a kid [substantiated in 3.18, "Double or Nothing"], but says he'd give up the lifestyle if required for Fred.

• *Fred:* Takes Wesley's concern about inter-office romances to heart more than Gunn. It's implied Fred can commit (or *has* committed) "high-tech robbery" by hacking into a shipping database and substituting her address for someone else. [She'd have to go back later and change the particulars again, though, or the shipper would surely discover the mistake. Unless Fred's banking on them writing off the error.]

• *Lilah:* Appears to ally with Sahjhan against Angel. She doesn't mention this to the firm, outsourcing the labor on their endeavor [see next episode for details] and burying the costs. [It's sometimes read that Lilah bargains with Sahjhan in defiance of company policy, and yet her actions actually coincide with the firm's goals. After all, Angel consuming his son's blood stands a much better chance of turning him to the dark side than killing him. In all probability, Lilah is simply playing Sahjhan from the start, and reluctant to mention it to the firm – that way, she can claim credit if her scheme works, or dodge harassment from the likes of Gavin if it fails.]

Lilah drinks Scotch, 30-year-old, with two ice cubes. Her mother has some sort of dementia [confirmed next episode], and apparently doesn't live in town.

• *Connor:* The firm acquires a sample of Connor's blood from Angel's physician and determines that it's "utterly run-of-the-mill, completely normal." [This is glaring proof that Connor was born completely human, yet it's going to cause no end of trouble. See 3.20, "A New World" and especially 4.14, "Release," for all the relevant issues.]

• *Holtz:* Has at least six men at his disposal, and operates from an otherwise unoccupied house. [As with Sunnydale, L.A. apparently has no end of abandoned houses or mansions ready for occupation.] Holtz says his wife was "violated and murdered" [see 3.08, "Quickening" for clarification], and seems particularly impressed by Fred's willingness to die for her cause. He learns about Wesley's concerns for Connor thanks to Aubrey going through Wesley's records [off screen].

• *Aubrey:* Her son Timothy snuck out one night and was sired as a vampire, then burnt in the morning sun because a scared Aubrey wouldn't invite him inside. [Aubrey's never seen again, perhaps owing to her nagging doubts about fighting Angel's crew.]

• *Sahjhan:* Claims he time-skipped 133 years [from 1769] for his bar meeting with Lilah. [Sahjhan bargained with Holtz in 1773 (3.08, "Quickening"), so he's either jumping time-periods quite heavily, or the Sahjhan in the bar is a younger version who's fulfilling history to keep the timeline intact.]

Sahjhan [impishly] claims he invented Daylight Savings Time. Lilah says she can smell fear on him. [As explained in "Loyalty." By the way, Holtz arguably implies that Sahjhan is immortal ("[The urns] last a lifetime... that is, if you live forever...) – which isn't the same as unkillable – but the point is ambiguous.]

• *Justine:* Strong enough to bash vamps around. [We'll have to overlook the conceit that even with training, the all-too-human Justine really has no business over-powering super-strong vampires; Buffy and Faith are super-powered, Justine isn't. That is, unless you're willing to entertain the idea that Justine was a Potential Slayer – but is now too old to get "called" if the incumbent Slayer died – and that gives her a slight edge. She certainly fits the profile, and notice how one of the nightclub vampires in "Benediction" (3.21) comments on Justine: "She thinks she's a Slayer."]

PROPHECY The Loa claims that three portents – "earthquake, fire, blood" – will foretell the prophecy regarding Angel's son: Wesley alone seems to witness these signs at story's end. [Yet we learn in "Forgiving" that the prophecy is bunk, so it's curious that the Loa here seem to lie. Or do they? In truth, they never actually refer to Angel murdering Connor; instead, they claim: "That the vampire will devour his child is certain." That statement is implicitly correct, if you factor in (as learned next episode) that Angel has been unknowingly consuming the blood of his son. Like all too many sources of mystical knowledge, perhaps the Loa technically speak the truth, but the interpretation's open to debate, and they're impish enough to mislead/cause sorrow for the person asking the question. Outside of *Angel*, the Loa are spirits of Voudon who act according to their own whims or ends.]

ORGANIZATIONS *Wolfram and Hart:* Sahjhan says he's familiar with the firm "in this and other dimensions [further evidence, as with "Through the Looking Glass" (2.21), that the firm isn't restricted to Earth]. Lilah knows about Sahjhan thanks to her research with "Files and Records" [3.10, "Dad"], but also claims that the firm has records "on everything that's ever happened." [She's exaggerating, especially as she later admits that the firm's archives don't mention Sahjhan's motives for targeting Angel.]

DEMONOLOGY *Vampires:* Taking Aubrey's story at face value, her son arose as a vampire on the same night he was sired. [Coupled with 3.08, "Quickening," it makes you wonder if child vamps simply arise quicker than adults.]

• *The Loa:* [Described by Fred as "mystic oracles" in "Forgiving."] Using a wizard's instructions, Wesley meets with the Loa at a specific latitude and longitude ("34 degrees, 12 minutes north, 118... 21 west"). This intersects at the Jollyburger fast food joint, where Wes stands before drive-through sign (which looks like a hamburger man), pours some herbs/dust [the script calls it "orange powder"] from a bag and intones "*Mange sec, Loa, alegba*. Accept this offering, and open the gates of truth." The Loa, profoundly annoyed at being summoned, then animate the hamburger man. In this form, they can fire electrical eye-beams.

MAGIC *Resikhian urns:* Capable of trapping Sahjhan's dimensional essence "for a lifetime." [See "Forgiving."]

BEST LINE Holtz to Wesley: "When I put my son's body into the ground, I had to open the coffin, just to know that he really was in there. You also may discover that a child's coffin, Mr. Wyndam-Pryce... it weighs nothing."

THINGS THAT DON'T MAKE SENSE Angel's physician apparently isn't opposed to just leaving blood samples lying about the place unattended, which isn't exactly a ringing endorsement of health care in L.A. Episodes past (2.05, "Dear Boy") and future (4.02, "Ground State") attest to the strength of Angel's super-sniffer, yet at no point does he smell Holtz's scent on Wesley after their secret meeting. (Granted, Holtz and Wesley aren't as close as lovers – oh, please, wipe that smirk off your face – but even traces of Holtz's scent should seem familiar to Angel by now. Perhaps Angel's senses are momentarily haywire because he's consuming Connor's blood.)

Only one snag in Lilah's secret plot against Angel (see **Character Development**): She's worried about bugs in her office to the point of hand-scribbling a note to Sahjhan, so she's evidently never heard of this new-fangled thing called "video surveillance," then.

IN RETROSPECT Holtz, cautioning Wesley on Angel: "The Beast will reemerge." No, this has nothing to do with the rocky guy from Season Four, whatever some people seem to think.

IT'S REALLY ABOUT... The classic formula of "the protagonist can't go forward but must go forward," here used to usher in an entire new paradigm. Wesley spends the entire episode trying to avoid betraying one of his greatest friends, but everything – from his opening nightmare to the final portents – forces his hand. The final climax, in which an earthquake bashes the heroes' base of operations and cracks its supports, only serves to symbolize this.

For Angel, it's about men who become doting fathers and suddenly feel the urge to label everything as "cute." Notice, especially, the little hockey shirt that he buys for Connor.

CRITIQUE With "Loyalty," it's become almost commonplace to praise Wesley's discussion with Holtz, and his encounter with the giant, snarling hamburger man. All of this is justified, because let's be fair... who in their right mind could forget the giant, snarling hamburger man? But if anything, there's scenes that don't get complimented enough. Again, just look at Wesley's nightmare, when Angel sinks his fangs into his infant son. Then Wesley looks down as blood pours from the book underneath his hands. Heaven only knows how the censors let the child-eating bit slip by, but it's one of the most harrowing scenes in the entire series ***and it's just in the teaser***.

After that, the episode accelerates enough to make your heart leap into your throat every few minutes. We didn't bother to count the sheer number of twists, but it could be a record for the show so far. It's in the nature of *Angel* and *Buffy* to run their characters through the gauntlet, but here there's a palpable sense of everyone – Wesley especially – being screwed like never before. The word "epic" gets chronically over-used in reviews, but in truth, it most assuredly applies here – even better, the show's not even logging its peak performance. Some of the best is yet to come.

THE LORE A psychologist friend of J. August Richards mentioned how some people try to constantly "rewrite the script of their lives," meaning they put themselves in a formerly traumatic position to hopefully net a different outcome. Richards adopted this as part of Gunn's rationale for his budding romance with Fred, deciding that Gunn was hoping for a better result than his doomed relationship with his sister Alonna. (Reynolds, *CityofAngel.com*)

• A scene omitted from the shooting script had Gunn and Fred riding out the quake in a doorway, clinging tight to one another. The script also requested that Angel look like "a cross between Satan and an avenging angel" when he leapt over the firewall with Connor. (That's not the imagery that springs to mind on screen, but points for trying.)

• Annie Talbot (Mother #2) rather appropriately played "Lady With Baby" in *Buffy* 5.17, "Forever."

3.16: "Sleep Tight"

"I can widen the portal and you can all be swallowed up by a world you cannot begin to imagine. Or you can keep your word and kill that child. Now.*"*

Air Date: March 4, 2002; **Writer:** David Greenwalt; **Director:** Terrence O'Hara

SUMMARY Angel becomes increasingly violent and irrational, eventually learning that Lilah has been spiking his pig's blood with blood taken from Connor (last episode). Nipping the problem in the bud, Angel gives Lilah a stern warning, and is curious to find her allied with Sahjhan – a demon whom he's never met.

Meanwhile, Holtz pledges to Wesley that he'll refrain from attacking Angel for one day, giving Wes an opportunity to extract Connor. Lorne senses Wesley's treachery, prompting Wes to secretly slug him unconscious, then talk his way past the other heroes and depart with the baby. Holtz breaks his word and brings his forces to bear against the Hyperion, and worse, Justine intercepts Wesley and slits his throat – leaving him for dead in a park while making off with Angel's son.

Angel's crew defeats Holtz's soldiers, but Lorne informs Angel of Wesley's betrayal. Holtz meets up with Justine as planned, intending to hide out in Utah and raise Connor as his own child. However, Angel and Lilah's commandoes both intercept Holtz's party. Amid the stand-off, an impatient Sahjhan shows up and magically opens a tear in reality to the Quor'toth: "the darkest of the dark worlds." Sahjhan threatens to expand the rift and kill everyone present if *somebody* doesn't kill Angel's son, but Holtz unexpectedly leaps into the rift with Connor. A surprised Sahjhan deems the problem solved and closes the rift, even as Lilah's troops withdraw and Angel suffers for the loss of his son. [*Continued next episode*]

FIRSTS AND LASTS It's the final appearance of Connor as a baby, and the last appearance of Holtz as a middle-aged man (both barring flashbacks, that is). In wake of the earthquake last episode, the Hyperion lobby is now sporting glaring cracks, and they'll be prominent there up through the end of Season Four.

POINTS OF DISCUSSION ABOUT "Sleep Tight":

1. In "Quickening" (3.08), Holtz dispatched a whole cadre of commandoes off screen. So you'd be forgiven for thinking that Holtz himself takes part in the melee here, but he manifestly doesn't. By now, it's becoming apparent that much of the character's appeal lies in the fact that we never actually see him in combat, meaning that we're fooled into thinking that as an experienced vampire hunter, he's hell on wheels. The result being: We're often scared shitless of Holtz, even though he mostly just stands around saying things in that sinuous voice of his, never actually doing anything.

2. The extended scenes with Justine make you realize that... she's wearing leather. Holtz has been similarly leather-clad for some time now, and once you factor in Angel's coats, Wesley's attire for the remainder of the show and so forth, it would appear that L.A. really has the cheapest leather in the world (even though the climate is rather unsuited for it, unless you're a vampire). Hell, you almost wonder if Holtz keeps a leather showroom in his basement, as a means of financing his operation and clothing his lieutenants on the cheap.

3. The bar scene with Lilah opens with her drinking alone, her reflection cast in a large mirror. It's hard to say if the producers honestly thought they were fooling anyone, because by now, that sort of set-up *always* means a vampire is standing there, invisibly. (And sure enough... there's Angel.)

4. The fashion update: It's curious how well Lilah has dressed up to drink by herself, a point we'll re-examine once her new boyfriend comes along later this season. Meanwhile, Fred is now wearing her hair straight, has donned cute clothes and in general looks a lot more "sexed up." If she's sleeping with Gunn by this point, then it's doing wonders for her appearance.

5. Sahjhan's entry to Quor'toth is described next episode as "a tear in the fabric of reality," and sure enough – it here looks like a billowing "blanket" of hellfire. Points to the design team for that bit of parallelism, because it's not quite how the script describes it, but works beautifully anyway.

6. The direction is a bit unclear when one of the Wraithers (see **Demonology**) looks at the heroes and salaciously declares, "I got first ride on the hottie!" We'd presume he's referring to Fred, yet immediately after his statement, the camera cuts to look right at Gunn.

CHARACTER NOTES *Angel:* Ingesting Connor's blood gives Angel mood swings, sudden fits of energy and increased hunger. He here allows Wesley to take the baby over night. [This initially seems at odds with the over-protective Angel seen in 3.10, "Dad." Yet the fact that Connor smells like a Happy Meal at present probably motivates him to get the baby out of the Hyperion for a while.]

Angel's conceptualization of a truly agonizing Hell involves Nixon and Britney Spears. He's now worrying about baby-proofing the Hyperion, advocating a chain and a combination lock for the weapons cabinet. [He's over-reacting, but really... a combination lock? To keep out an infant???]

Angel implies that he learned Lilah's location by breaking the arms of her assistant. He claims that with transfusions, he could torture Lilah and keep her alive indefinitely. [As with his threat in 2.18, "Dead End," he probably has the know-how, given Angelus' history.] Angel drinks whiskey, straight, and has never seen Sahjhan before [or any of his species, presumably]. All things being equal, he'd prefer to see Connor with Holtz than dead or with the firm. Tripping on Connor's blood, Angel says, "I like nuns." [Given Angelus' "fondness" for nuns (2.05, "Dear Boy") this is more heinous than it appears.] He also wonders how the Flying Nun flew.

• *Wesley:* [We can't psycho-analyze everything running through Wesley's head, so judge for yourselves if he deserves condemnation for leaving the heroes in the lurch against Holtz's forces. Fair enough that Wes wants to spirit Connor away, but even if Holtz keeps his word, Wesley must know that Angel's company will soon come under attack. Given that Gunn, Lorne *or Fred* could easily get killed in this ambush, it seems a glaring lapse that Wesley doesn't somehow alert them in advance. Perhaps he was intending to warn everyone after he'd gotten on the road, and Justine's throat-slitting simply scuttled those plans, but we'll never know for sure.]

Wes has a station wagon at his disposal. [He owns this vehicle, as Gunn claims next episode. The license place isn't easy to read, but looks something like 3Q71895.] Wes now carries a revolver, moves quickly enough to disarm Justine when she's not resorting to trickery, and respects soldiers. His apartment is close to Drew Medical [unless he's bluffing in his haste to leave] and across the street from a park. Street numbers on his apartment building read 2337/2339.

• *Gunn:* Not so hot on Texas, thinking Texans hate the black man. He much prefers California's music and climate, plus the Lakers.

• *Fred:* Thinks Texas is the best state in the union, and compares Angel's mood swings to her "Aunt Viola and her Southern Comfort." [And for more on Fred's family and alcohol, see **The Lore** under 5.11, "Damage."]

• *Lorne:* His "sonic cry" is very directional, nailing thugs opposing Gunn but not Gunn himself. [The script had Lorne apologizing when his scream affected Gunn also.] Lorne "reads" Wesley enough to know he's kidnapped Connor, and that he's secretly met with Holtz twice, yet he doesn't register Wesley's motives.

• *Lilah:* Her mother [mentioned last episode] no longer recognizes her but has the best room at a clinic. Lilah is getting better at sensing when Angel is near, and has authority over the firm's commando squad.

• *Holtz:* Doesn't like tea in Styrofoam cups, so Justine offers to get him some china ones. Lilah addresses him as "Captain Holtz" [his eighteenth century title, and used by his minions next episode]. He's based at 2239 Santa Elena, a big Victorian house in Silver Lake. Holtz plans to rename Connor "Steven Franklin Thomas," and pledges that the boy will never know Angel existed. [The former comes to pass, the latter doesn't; see 3.20, "A New World."]

• *Justine:* Troubled by the notion of killing Angel's human associates, but eventually marks them as "enemy soldiers." [Holtz's line to Justine that "I didn't hear you leave" suggests she wasn't acting on Holtz's wishes when she snuck out for a quick chat with Wesley, but she renews her loyalty to Holtz after that.] She thinks Utah is pretty.

• *Kim:* Guitar player who visited Lorne a couple of years ago, when he suggested that she pursue her singing rather than medical school. She here asks for help when band-playing Wraither demons "infect" her. [See **Demonology**. Lorne claims he "put Kim on her path," but if anything, his advice leads to her getting infected by a spewing demon aspect.]

• *Sahjhan:* Described as an ethereal time-traveling demon. While hopping between dimensions, he's usually got visual on arrival but not always sound. Sahjhan tells Angel, when confronted about why he's targeted Our Hero: "You will pay." [He's trying to throw Angel off-track; see next episode for the truth.] Sahjhan's bargain with Lilah specified killing Connor, but she reneged.

THE HYPERION Doesn't have earthquake insurance [in California, of all places?]. The weapons cabinet takes damage a second time [the first being in "Birthday" (3.11)] when Angel tosses one of Holtz's goons against it and breaks a pane of glass. [It's fixed, somehow, by "Double or Nothing" (3.18).]

DEMONOLOGY *Vampires:* A blanket-covered Angel runs through a patch of sunlight and doesn't smoke [unlike Spike at times in *Buffy*, and Angel himself in *Buffy* 3.18, "Earshot"].

• *Wraithers:* Demons who can look human for a time (about ten days or two weeks) before reverting to their natural forms, producing half-mangled faces, spiny backs and the occasional seven-fingered hand. Wraithers "infect" humans, who then host a tormented demon face that surfaces on occasion and generates a fair amount of green spew. [Kim's demon aspect manifests while she's singing, although on the plus side, it continues to rhyme while making threats of bodily harm.] Such victims have traces of "penloxia" in their saliva, and taking 20 milligrams of cylenthiam powder [not the similar-sounding "Calynthia powder" from 2.04, "Untouched"] – a mystical antibiotic that Lorne can procure – twice a day for a month cures the condition.

The band-playing Wraithers seen here are half-demonic and exceedingly gross, yet have groupies. [Confirmed in the script. Besides, there's a precedent for this in the real-life heavy metal group Gwar, whose members have dressed like demons for years.]

3.16, Sleep Tight

MAGIC Sahjhan intones the words "Lekko najine forkahdio!" to tear open the Quor'toth rift; saying the words in reverse closes it.

BEST LINE Angel, trying to pacify baby Connor: "It's just your Uncle Wes. He loves you bunches. He's just... English."

THINGS THAT DON'T MAKE SENSE Sahjhan can tear a rift in reality that leads to Quor'toth, and he deems his mission a success when Connor is lost into it. So unless he's bluffing about his ability to widen the rift... why did he bother with all the business of bringing Holtz through time at all, when he could've simply materialized in the Hyperion and triggered the rift *there*, before anyone could react, while the pregnant Darla or baby Connor were in residence? (Then again, Sahjhan seems a lot like Spike – so wrapped up in over-complicated schemes that he can't see the simple solutions.)

The story opens with a close-up of Wesley's handwritten note that "the father will kill the son," but Wes himself is looking at something entirely different. (Dramatic license.) But worse, Wesley – of all people! – should know Angel's capabilities, yet he makes incredibly sloppy plans in trying to steal Connor. Most noticeably, after making off with the lad, Wes goes back to his apartment to load the car. For pity's sake, if you're going to take Angel's child and embark on a fugitive existence, *pack beforehand and get a proper head start*. Mind, Lorne is a little blasé about leaving the baby alone in the lobby while he's in the other room, considering all the parties who'd probably love to nab the kid when nobody's watching.

Kim's demon aspect generates green spew, but she's not wearing green spew while "displaying" her demon side for Angel and company, even though it appears Lorne first observed this in private. (All right, perhaps Lorne just "read" the problem, and only asked her to demonstrate the one time.) Also, Kim says the Wraithers at first acted all "mellow," and only switched to hard rock music once they started exhibiting their demon selves. But as the Wraithers *still* get groupies, why did they even bother with whole organic, mellow route? Why not just play hard rock from the start? Besides, the switch means they'd have to completely re-accessorize. (Why, the cost of the dog collars alone...)

Justine pretty much shoves Connor into the back seat of Wesley's car and drives away, yet the baby's magically buckled in when she arrives for the rendezvous with Holtz. Not to mention that Connor has gained a fetching hat in the interim. And a minor glitch: The training set-up in Holtz's lair entails a vampire acting like he's being "choked," when you really can't choke a vampire.

Who precisely is yelling "Noooo! Noooooooooooooo!" when Holtz jumps into the Quor'toth rift? The script claims it's Angel, but he's doesn't look like he's yelling at all, especially given that he's busy running and getting smacked about by Quor'toth lightning. Close your eyes and the scream *sounds* like it belongs to Sahjhan – but it's odd that he'd scream in protest, then literally decide seconds later that Connor getting lost to Quor'toth suits his plans after all. So it's probably Angel, but if so, it's yet again down to Our Friend artistic license... apparently denoting the scream of anguish that's ringing through Angel's mind.

Oh, and while we don't take issue with Sahjhan's breath showing in the final stand-off – even though he's supposedly intangible – we *do* wonder why nobody else's breath is visible. Is Sahjhan puffing a cigarette while Holtz is soliloquizing?

POP CULTURE Angel refers to his earthquake-bashed room as "The wreck of the Hesperus," citing the poem of the same name by Henry Wadsworth Longfellow. It's a lament-filled piece that depicts the downing of a schooner, and it's an especially tragic comparison to Angel, given that the *Hesperus* skipper's young daughter dies when the ship breaks up.

• Gunn to Angel: "You were all hyped this morning, then you went all Tyson on those demons..." Accomplished boxer Mike Tyson became at times (shall we say) rather unstable in the ring, notably in a 1997 bout against Evander Holyfield, in which he bit the man's ear not once but twice. (In that regard, Gunn's comment better fits the injury dealt to the drug dealer Tyke in 3.20, "A New World.")

IN RETROSPECT An outraged Angel, tanked on his son's blood: "What Connor needs is to grow up!" Give it three more episodes, buddy.

IT'S REALLY ABOUT... Logically, it's about the tragedy of Wesley Wyndham-Pryce. He takes Connor as an act of compassion, similarly tries to help Justine and in almost every respect tries to do the good and honorable thing. Yet for his trouble, he gets his throat slit and walks a path that'll make him the most tragic figure in the whole *Angel*-verse. Needless to say, his actions also send shockwaves through the whole of Angel Investigations, and notice the symbolism at work when Wes enters the earthquake-damaged hotel lobby. The heroes' world is well and truly cracked.

As an aside, it's about someone snapping after the initial joy of parenthood. When Angel "overdoses" on Connor – quite literally, by drinking the lad's blood – feeding, crying and diaper-changing the baby doesn't seem so appealing after all.

CRITIQUE Suddenly, everything we know about *Angel* changes *again*... If "Billy" drew a "red line" from which the show never looked back, then "Sleep Tight" even more ambitiously draws two or three, starting with the unbelievable moment when Wesley assaults Lorne. The scene to follow – in which Angel, Gunn and Fred all happily pile into the Hyperion lobby, la la la, we haven't got the single clue that anything's even slightly wrong – made us go pale on first broadcast, and hasn't lost any mettle with age. Like some of Hitchcock's best efforts (including *Rope*, in which oodles of party-guests fail to realize there's a corpse stuffed inside the buffet table), you're wracked with conflicted loyalties ("Take Connor, Wesley... wait, *don't* take Connor, Wesley!"), and Wes' goose seems utterly cooked until he resolutely walks out of the hotel with the baby.

As if that weren't enough, the lobby stand-off occurs *before* you factor in Justine slitting Wesley's throat – one of the series' finest and most startling cliffhangers – and the grand finale of Angel falling like a marionette with its strings cut. The script, the cast, the gorgeous direction and the design all fuse together to make the story simply pop off the TV screen... all told, only the demon band members seem a bit gratuitous, but they're a blip and barely matter in the grand picture.

You've probably suspected by now that "Sleep Tight" is one of the best episodes in the entire show – and that's indisputably the case. It's even more of an accomplishment because it falls halfway through the series, displaying a tenacity that will marvelously fuel the remaining 50 episodes.

THE LORE The script had Holtz originally re-naming Connor as "John Franklin Thomas," but this was later amended to "Steven Franklin Thomas." (We've no proof, but the name "John Thomas" would probably have incited too many jokes from the balcony, hence the alteration.) Angel initially ordered vodka in the bar, but this was changed to whiskey. It was also scripted that the heroes had purchased a centrifuge (a helpful device for separating blood from plasma) "a couple of weeks ago," with Gunn claiming, "The amount of blood work we do, it'll pay for itself in no time." Yet on screen there's no such centrifuge; Fred examines Angel's pig's blood with the agency's all-purpose microscope.

3.17: "Forgiving"

"You son of a bitch! You took my son!
You're a dead man, Pryce!
YOU HEAR ME!! DEAD!! DEAD!!"

Air Date: April 15, 2002; **Writer:** Jeffrey Bell; **Director:** Turi Meyer

SUMMARY Angel rashly kidnaps and threatens to torture Linwood, wanting a means of tracking down Sahjhan. In response, Linwood arranges for Angel to visit the firm's enigmatic "White Room," in which a creepy little girl provides details of a spell that'll make Sahjhan corporeal. Angel paints a pentagram in the Hyperion lobby and performs a small ritual, causing Sahjhan to manifest on an L.A. street.

Meanwhile, Gunn and Fred hunt for Wesley and corner Justine in Sahjhan's underground lair. Angel and Sahjhan both arrive, but Sahjhan reveals that he can only open the Quor'toth portal a single time without destroying the entire universe. Sahjhan further explains that he once witnessed a "true" prophecy stating that Connor would grow up to kill him; hence, his goal all along was to eliminate Connor, not Angel. To keep everyone involved off-balance, Sahjhan flitted through time and amended the prophecies to indicate Angel would murder his child – inadvertently giving Wesley reason to kidnap the lad. After a scrap, Justine bottles Sahjhan's essence in a magical urn that Holtz kept as a fail-safe.

Later, Wesley's co-workers find him recovering at a local hospital, but Angel – outraged at his friend's betrayal – tries to smother him with a pillow. A bundle of hospital orderlies restrain Angel, leaving the mute Wesley gaping for dear life.

FIRSTS AND LASTS It's the first excursion into the White Room at Wolfram and Hart, and the first of two appearances (the other being 4.08, "Habeas Corpses") by the somewhat sinister little girl who doles out advice there. Holtz and Justine's minions (sometimes referred to as the "Holtzians") make their last appearance during a failed attempt on Angel's life, after which Justine drives off without them.

Barring dream sequences or flashbacks (such as 4.01, "Deep Down" and 5.18, "Origin"), Wesley here stops wearing glasses – this presumably means he switches to contacts, although it's never explained on screen. (And why he didn't do this before now to benefit his sex appeal, we're never told.) And while it's debatable exactly when Wesley's tenure as a member of Angel Investigations comes to an end, the near-pillow-smothering in the hospital certainly seems to clinch it.

POINTS OF DISCUSSION ABOUT "Forgiving":

1. As Sahjhan here proves, prophecies can be bunk. Granted, Sahjhan is atypical because he's able to traverse time, but this holds some troubling implications for the all-important Shanshu Prophecy. Indeed, check out **Points of Discussion** under 5.22, "Not Fade Away" for more.

2. Angel tells Fred, in his bitterness, "I'd never hurt someone I care about." We'll give him a pass on that because he's so unbalanced right now, but in all truthfulness, he's inflicted plenty of harm on people he cared about. There's Buffy,

Buffy's friends (the murdered Jenny Calendar especially), Darla... the list goes on and on.

3. It's not a glitch, but notice how Wesley's hospital room comes decorated with what looks like his illuminated X-Rays on the wall. This is typical of network dramas trying to convey a sense of, "Hey! We're in a hospital!" – but for pity's sake, people. It's hardly a cheery décor to stare at hour after hour, especially if you're recovering from getting your throat slit. (Gunn also views such "decorations" in 5.17, "Underneath.")

CHARACTER NOTES *Angel:* Unwilling to forgive Wesley despite encouragement from Lorne, tacit approval from Fred and Gunn, and the realization of Wes' motives for taking Connor. [The attack on Wesley must owe, at least in part, to Angel having nobody left to vent his spleen against. With the villains absent, pickled in an urn or lying low, Wes makes an easy target. Not that this excuses the pillow-smothering.]

Sahjhan's manifestation causes a traffic accident, and Angel implicitly admits that his dabbling with black magic is responsible for collateral injuries. [Mind, the fallout from this magic-use gets someone killed in 3.19, "The Price."] Also, Angel seems willing to kill Lilah – at the White Room girl's request – if that's the price required for getting a shot at Sahjhan. [Yet it's odd how the girl *stops* Angel from offing Lilah, as it would surely continue his march toward the dark side.]

- *Cordelia:* Her filing remains chaotic, although Angel thinks Cordy was keeping a list of time-space and shifting entities. She's vacationing with Groo in Mexico.
- *Wesley:* His colleagues are evasive about using his name, and Justine's blade messed up his trachea something fierce. In preparing to flee with Connor, Wes evidently packed his toothbrush, razor [something he's using less and less these days] and the Mossberg 12-gauge [2.16, "Epiphany"] in the closet. [Presumably, all of this is lost when Justine steals his cab.]
- *Gunn:* Doesn't condemn Wesley for taking Connor, but doesn't think Angel will forgive him either. Gunn bests Justine in combat [although she's looking pretty ragged at the time].
- *Fred:* Thinks Wesley did the right thing in abducting Connor [see next episode for more on this], but seems hurt because Wesley left without saying anything to *her*. The notion of Connor disappearing down a portal freaks her out. [It was more a rift, but whatever.] Fred can't read Gashundi [first mentioned in "Offspring" (3.07)].
- *Lorne:* He's never heard of Quor'toth.
- *Lilah:* Worked at the firm for three years before even hearing about the White Room.
- *Justine:* Helps to box up Sahjhan, and admits that Holtz only cared about revenge. [But see "Benediction" (3.21), where she readily takes up Holtz's cause again.]
- *Connor:* Sahjhan says Connor has a "big" future. [He presumably read this in the prophecies, never considering or caring that this might make his attempts to kill the lad even less likely to succeed.]
- *Sahjhan:* Judging by Fred's computer, Sahjhan isn't listed on the "Demons, Demons, Demons" website. When solidified, he's strong enough to heft pickups and shrug off burning coals flung in his face. [Sahjhan re-surfaces in 5.18, "Origin."]
- *Linwood:* His last name is "Murrow," and his formal title is "Division President of Special Projects." Lilah is No. 3 on his cell phone speed-dial.

PROPHECY Sahjhan claims to have witnessed his name, all carved in blood on an "official" scroll, in a "true" prophecy which stated: "The one sired by the vampire with a soul shall grow to manhood and kill Sahjhan." In response, Sahjhan "flitted back and forth in time" (but flitted about in a *manly* way, he says) to change the prophecy that threatened him, "polish some others" and generally confuse the issue. [Sahjhan claims he's been "living with a knife over his heart for 1,100 years" due to the prophecy, which suggests he read it circa 900 AD. Mind, Sahjhan altered the texts that apparently include *Grammaticus' Third Century Greek Commentaries* (3.14, "Couplet"), which might suggest a vigorous use of his time-travel abilities.]

QUOR'TOTH Lorne equates Quor'toth's size with China [but it's probably bigger]. Talk of Quor'toth intimidates Lorne's normally un-intimidated sources.

No portals exist to Quor'toth [but see 3.20, "A New World"]. To enter the realm, one must tear through the fabric of reality – Lorne says this sort of dark magic takes centuries to acquire. [Sahjhan demonstrated such talent last episode, which again suggests that he's extraordinarily long-lived.] Sahjhan says the universe could go ka-blooey if he tried to open a Quor'toth rift more than once. [So the talent isn't innate to Sahjhan's species. If all members of his race held such power, it'd only take one particularly nihilist demon to end the universe... and we're still here.]

THE LIBRARY *Phisto's Dictionary of Demons and Dimen-sional Spirits:* Useful for cross-referencing demon nicknames, but written in Gashundi.

ORGANIZATIONS *Wolfram and Hart:* Linwood says the firm is engaged in a war they can never win [or never *plan* to win; see 2.15, "Reprise"]. The firm's tech-team [possibly the Paranormal Disturbances Division mentioned in 3.19, "The Price"] can register severe bio-plasmic disturbances, such as the one that accompanies Sahjhan's manifestation.

• *The White Room:* Accessing it entails entering an elevator at the firm and keying in Floors 18-23-20-28-27 [also used in "Habeas Corpses"], then pulling the red "Stop Elevator" lever, whereupon a glowing button appears up top. Pushing that button makes the elevator disappear in a haze of light, accompanied by a sucking noise that's not unlike the sound of Darth Vader breathing. The White Room seems to stretch a great distance, covered in fog. [The elevator comes accompanied with Muzak, but it's not, that we can tell, the same evil Muzak from "Reprise."]

The little girl there [looking like a smaller and more evil version of Eve from Season Five] loves red, answers questions, acts extremely mature and thinks Lilah's fingernails are pretty. She likes trouble, but hates chaos. [Many of the firm's actions conform to this standard, hence their willingness to dispose of unpredictable evildoers.] The little girl appears to teleport visitors [compare with "Habeas Corpses"] out of the White Room with another haze of light and more breathing from Darth Vader. A member of the firm's litigation department visited the White Room in September, but he's in an asylum now.

DEMONOLOGY *Sahjhan's Species:* The White Room girl says Sahjhan's race was all about torture and death. [A flashback implies they stirred up trouble in Medieval times, but it's unclear.] The creatures caused too much chaos, however, so the girl says "we" [presumably meaning the firm] made them incorporeal. [This means that Sahjhan has, apparently without knowing it, been bargaining with the organization that made his race intangible.]

A Resikhian urn [mentioned in 3.15, "Loyalty"] can trap these intangible demons. In flashback, some red-robed monks chant and bottle one such creature.

MAGIC Angel paints the pentagram in the Hyperion lobby with a red substance. [It's apparently blood, as Lorne hints next episode, but it's probably not human blood. After all, it would hardly be necessary for Lilah to cut her palm and supply a few drops if they had buckets of the stuff lying about the place.] Angel then intones "Corpus Granok Sahjhan demonicus," whereupon a whirlwind forms in the Hyperion and a lightning bolt manifests Sahjhan in L.A. [The mention of Sahjhan's name implies that the spell recorporealizes him and him alone, and there's no evidence of his species becoming solid en masse.]

BEST LINE Lorne: "Finding Connor [in Quor'toth] would be like looking for a needle in a haystack..." Angel, preoccupied with thoughts of torturing Linwood: "Needles. I shoulda thought of that."

THINGS THAT DON'T MAKE SENSE The ending, magnificent as it is, entails Gunn and a few burly hospital orderlies somehow restraining Angel, an enraged powerhouse vampire.

We skirted around the issue in "Loyalty," but now we can't ignore the stubborn stupidity the heroes display in refusing to phone Cordelia. They must have Cordy's number onhand, because Fred starts to call before Angel interrupts. Yet Wesley never phoned Cordy in secret, and Angel here implies he doesn't want to interrupt Cordy's vacation. Or that he doesn't want to admit he lost the baby. Or some equally silly excuse. (Maybe Angel doesn't want Cordy holding him back at this juncture, but that's not what really comes across on screen.)

For that matter – and here we run afoul of *Angel* and *Buffy* being on separate networks, which limits the cross-overs – Angel is so determined to get Connor back that he'll use black magic, yet he never thinks of, a bit more productively, calling Buffy's crew for help. Gee, the heroes would've found Wesley a lot quicker if Willow had simply performed a locator spell, which is now old hat for her.

Meanwhile, Wesley has apparently been keeping separate diaries on "major players" such as Angel, Connor and Darla, but in readying to leave town, he rather insanely throws these vital documents into the dumpster, from which Fred and Gunn later retrieve them. Wouldn't burning the diaries have been a bit more sensible? After all, there's any number of snoopy parties – the firm, for a start – who'd love to get their hands on such data. Oh, and notice how Gunn and Fred are so relieved upon learning why Wesley took Connor that they completely overlook the downside that a major prophecy has declared that Angel will kill Connor.

It's implied that Sahjhan approached Linwood for an off-screen chat (hence Linwood's sudden appearance at the firm in a tuxedo, as if he'd been out for the evening, and his comment "Sahjhan... not much of a handshake, what with being incorporeal and all..."), but we're baffled as to what Sahjhan hoped to get out of this. Mind, it's also unclear what Sahjhan thought he'd gain from spilling his guts to Angel's crew about altering the prophecies, the big blabbermouth. Lilah obviously wants the elevator code to access the White Room, so why doesn't she just memorize the five buttons that Angel presses in front of her? And why does Linwood ask who Lorne is, considering he's surely studied the firm's data on the heroes, and explicitly viewed Lorne on-camera in "Dad" (3.10)?

IT'S REALLY ABOUT... The disbelief and panic that follows the loss of a child, plus the blinding rage that accompanies an act of betrayal. The two aren't related per se, but here unite to provoke a response that isn't remotely rational. Angel goes from one act of desperation to another, ricocheting around L.A. like a hockey puck and accomplishing preciously little for his trouble. His son doesn't come home, his relationship with Wesley undeniably takes a turn for the worse, and he overall proves that some heinous acts just can't be fixed in the space of an evening.

CRITIQUE By now, we're running out of ways of saying, "Everything you know about *Angel* just changed." But still...

Everyone tends to fixate on the grand finale with the pillow-smothering – this isn't unreasonable, as it's one of the most daring twists on modern-day television. Certainly, other shows have depicted acts just as violent or even worse, but you'd be hard-pressed to find a comparable example of two formerly tight-knit lead characters falling *quite* this far out of favor with one another. Even with benefit of hindsight, and accepting just how much Angel Investigations tears itself apart, the very notion of Angel trying to murder – or near enough – Wesley *still* seems almost inconceivable. Yet happen it does.

Mind, "Forgiving" hardly pins all its hopes on the final act, and instead taps into everything that's been unfolding for at least nine episodes now. Someone on the Mutant Enemy team – Minear, Bell, Whedon, or everyone together – has a clear-cut direction in mind, even as they're handling a *lot* of elements, and that's what's the most impressive.

Thankfully, the implementation here actually matches the quality of vision. Take, for instance, the spine-chilling bits with Angel wandering around the office, quietly pondering whether to use staple removers and a desk spindle as potential instruments of torture. Then follows the stunning reveal of a bloodied Linwood, sporting a mussed-up tuxedo, all tied to a chair and ripe for the interrogation. There's also the visit to the White Room, plus the brilliant moment when you think Lilah might gut Linwood like a fish to collect human blood for the spell. We've seen this sort of conceit so many times before, yet given everything that's in play, it's almost never more convincing than here.

We're actually leaving out so much detail, but hopefully it's clear that even without the pillow-smothering, this stands among the most finely tempered *Angel* episodes. It's not just a sterling story in itself, then, but indicative of why *Angel*'s such a fantastic show.

THE LORE The script described the flashback scene with a member of Sahjhan's race as far more gory, complete with an in-your-face (so to speak) decapitation of a knight. Oh, and a bit of trimmed dialogue had the girl in the White Room adding, as Angel departs, "Can't wait to see how it turns out. You have a web site?"

3.18: "Double or Nothing"

"It was... a truck. I was 17 years old, and I sold my soul for a truck."

Air Date: April 22, 2002; **Writer:** David H. Goodman; **Director:** David Grossman

SUMMARY Cordelia and Groo return from vacation, even as Gunn quietly flips when an agent of Mr. Jenoff – a demonic, soul-sucking casino owner – approaches him. The repo-man reminds Gunn that he mortgaged his soul to Jenoff seven years ago – and that Jenoff is calling in the debt.

Gunn has one last day with Fred and then dumps her, hoping to spare her long-term pain. Gunn then heads to the casino, but Fred begs her colleagues for help and everyone charges to the rescue. Vastly outnumbered, Angel wagers his own soul in a double-or-nothing cut of the deck against Jenoff. The casino owner wins, but Cordelia stabs Jenoff's hand as a distraction while Angel chops his head off. Jenoff's healing factor begins to sprout him another head, whereupon Angel convinces the casino patrons – i.e. indebted to Jenoff – to tear the soul-sucker apart. Gunn and Fred reconcile, with Gunn admitting that he initially mortgaged his soul to get his truck.

FIRSTS AND LASTS Cordelia emerges from vacation as a full blonde, a status she'll retain for early Season Four, and which should signal to everyone who's paying attention where her love-life is headed (see **Who is Angel's True Love?**). It's also the first blatant evidence that souls can function like currency, an element that'll get re-used in the similarly casino-themed "The House Always Wins" (4.03).

POINTS OF DISCUSSION ABOUT "Double or Nothing":

1. Behold an *Angel*-verse standard that we've mentioned before: Fred's initial response, when Gunn "dumps" her, isn't to consider that Gunn's a total jackass, but rather to think that *she's* done something wrong. This sort of self-doubt among females actually started on *Buffy* (never more so than in 2.14, "Innocence," when the Slayer gets rebuked after sleeping with Angel), but Cordelia has already exuded it in episodes such as "Expecting" (1.12) and "That Vision Thing" (3.02). With Cordy feeling more assertive of late, it's presumably Fred's turn to experience such insecurity. We've nearly seen the last of this trait, though, especially once the normally formidable Fred gets tough-as-nails in Seasons Four, and commendably so.

2. Cordelia returns to the fold, but notice how her slowly evolving romance remains on the back burner. Not without

justification do some fans moan about the Angel/Cordelia love-fest, but it's healthy to remember that it's in the background for most of Season Three. (The complaint holds more water in Season Four, but even there it's overstated.)

3. It's sometimes cited as a glitch that "Gangsta's Paradise" didn't hit the charts until September 1995, and the flashback with Gunn occurs some months, if not an entire year, before that. We're more forgiving, though, on the grounds that the song is part of the incidental music – meaning it's not issuing from someone's radio or car stereo, etc. – so it's not, strictly speaking, "occurring" in the *Angel*-verse.

CHARACTER NOTES *Angel:* Realizes that Gunn and Fred are dating, a mere five episodes after the fact. After much brooding over the loss of his son, Angel dismantles the lad's crib as a means of moving on.

• *Cordelia:* Armed with festive hats after returning from Mexico with Groo. She completely misreads Gunn's anxiety as guilt about his happiness with Fred. [For all that Cordelia is the group's conscience in Season Three, she makes some staggeringly bad calls on occasion.] However, she astutely advises Angel that if he lived another 200 years, he'd never forget the loss of his son, and should go on loving the boy anyway. Cordy implies that she hasn't had a vision in quite some time [which reduces the odds that she and Groo experienced side adventures in Mexico].

• *Wesley:* Ostracized, Wes apparently has to take a cab home from the hospital. Fred gives Wesley some of his belongings from the hotel [including his china tea set from "Carpe Noctem" (3.04); this seems to re-appear in Wesley's office in 5.14, "Smile Time"] and informs him that the prophecy foretelling that Angel would kill Connor was false.

• *Gunn:* Tells Fred that he loves her. [Side note: The fact that Gunn's romance with Fred registers in the Akashic Records, see **Magic**, suggests he hasn't loved anyone like he loves Fred in the seven intervening years, or Jenoff's people would've noticed.]

Gunn was 17 when he visited Jenoff's casino "seven years ago." [Gunn is presently 24, then. J. August Richards was born in 1973, and thus was about 28 at this point.] At the time, Jenoff recognized Gunn as a "man of the streets, protector of the young and innocent." The present-day Gunn gets gooey about Syd and Monica Frzylcka, a pair of old married demons.

• *Fred:* Says she understands Wes was trying to protect Angel and the baby, and that Angel was wrong to attack him [last episode]. Yet she piles blame onto Wes for not sharing his concerns, and harshly says he mustn't return to the Hyperion lest Angel kill him. [The general sense is that Fred blames Wesley for not confiding in *her*, never considering that her romance with Gunn complicated matters.] Fred and Gunn play a game where she guesses what he's wearing in the morning; it never takes her more than two tries. [But in all fairness, how many sets of clothes do we expect Gunn owns?] She likes pancakes, waffles, Sixth Street tacos, fish sticks and Dodger Dogs. Her favorite shake is double mocha, double whip.

• *Lorne:* Performs a reading for a client in Topanga Canyon.

• *Groo:* Loosely understands the concept of business cards.

• *Connor:* Angel suspected, based on Connor's grip, that his son was left-handed. [Going by 3.20, "A New World" and other stories, the lad turns out right-handed. Unless he's secretly ambidextrous.]

• *Mr. Jenoff:* Entitled to claim the souls of persons who forge contracts with him [see **Magic**], and does so by sticking his fingers into a debtor's eyes and siphoning off their soul, which invigorates him. He generally lets his head lackey [credited as Repo Man] have the bodies afterward. Jenoff wears reading spectacles and can smell Angel's soul. The phone number of Jenoff's casino is (213) 555-2928.

Jenoff can sprout a replacement head if decapitated. [It's not entirely certain that he's finally killed off. But as he technically earns Angel and Gunn's souls, and apparently never tries to collect the debt, we'll presume he kicks the bucket.]

• *Syd and Monica Frzylcka:* [Respectively credited as "Male and Female Elderly Demon"; the accuracy of their last name depends on whether Fred reads Cordelia's handwriting correctly. Syd was previously seen, unnamed, in "Heartthrob" (3.01).] They've been married for 300 years, "ever since the mitosis," and Syd's now a single-celled organism again. Monica comments that Fred is "a 16th" of Syd's age. [If we round Fred's age off at 25, then Syd must be around 400.] Their welcome mat reads: "Gurfong Bless Our Home." They hire the agency to off a Skench Demon [see **Demonology**] who's squatting in their home. Syd has a phobia about sputum.

PYLEA Groo mentions a Pylean custom named the *shivroth*, the Vigil of the Bereaved.

THE HYPERION The weapons cabinet looks intact again [after a glass pane got smashed in 3.16, "Sleep Tight"]. Gunn gives Fred breakfast on a fancy serving platter [presumably from the disused Hyperion kitchen; see next episode].

ORGANIZATIONS *Angel Investigations:* Fred and Gunn re-examine the agency's Pending Files. [See 3.14, "Couplet" on how the size of the stack suggests Angel Investigations has really broadened its client base in Season Three.]

DEMONOLOGY *Skench Demons:* Impish, and look a bit like the Flukeman from *The X-Files*. They squat in your apartment, shriek and project phlegm. To kill one, lop off its head.

• *Leprechauns:* According to Syd, they don't exist. [5.03, "Unleashed" re-confirms this.]

MAGIC *Jenoff's contracts:* The younger Gunn must state, of his own free will, that he's prepared to "mortgage the future" for his present happiness. He then shakes Jenoff's hand, whereupon Jenoff's spiked ring draws a bit of blood. Gunn's hand (and blood) are then slammed down on a paper contract on a line reading "siginitaura." The Repo Man implies that if Gunn fails to pay up, Jenoff can take both his soul and Fred's too. [That's probably untrue, given the deal seems inherently based on one's consent and free will. However, as the Repo Man also implies, Jenoff could simply have Fred killed.]

• *The Akashic records:* Evidently a directory that logs the transactions of souls. Using this archive, Jenoff's people know when Gunn is "thinking about giving his soul to another," i.e. Fred. [In traditional Wicca, the Akashic records contain information about the life and spirituality of individual souls. Still, it seems strange in *Angel*-verse terms that a romance – or even a marriage – would entail a literal soul-transfer.]

BEST LINE Groo, when Fred sweetly reminds Gunn to take his machete into battle: "He is very fortunate to have such a woman looking after his weapon."

THINGS THAT DON'T MAKE SENSE Angel knows of Jenoff's reputation as a soul-sucker, yet he's apparently never felt inclined to try and ruin Jenoff's operation. That wouldn't fall under Angel's mandate of "helping the helpless" per se, but even if you believe that the gamblers have only themselves to blame, it still seems a little callous to simply let a demon who consumes souls like veal go about his business.

Gunn previously stated in "Guise Will Be Guise" (2.06) that he'd spent his whole life in L.A., yet never noticed "weird-ass stuff" such as the Caritas demon karaoke bar. Yet in this story, a 17-year-old Gunn bargains with a demonic casino owner. (If we've got to choose, the whole of "Double or Nothing" obviously gets more weight than a single statement. It's just possible that Gunn is referring to the karaoke bar specifically when he mentions the "weird-ass stuff," as Caritas is certainly far more cordial and less sordid than most of L.A.'s underworld, Jenoff's casino included. Well, we're trying here.)

Last – and we're sorry to keep on about this – Jenoff is yet another entity in the *Angel*-verse who hands out business cards that contain only a phone number, not an address. (He must use the same printer as the firm; see 1.01, "City Of.")

IT'S REALLY ABOUT... Lost futures. Angel has just been robbed of his son's upbringing, while Fred – knowing that something's wrong with Gunn, to the extent of worrying that he's got leukemia – fears her potential lifetime of romance and happiness with him is about to plunge screaming off a cliff. Then there's Jenoff, who forges contracts with the desperate (although admittedly of their own free will) and winds up sucking down their souls.

Most specifically, though, it's about the inability of the young to perceive that they even ***have*** a future. Teen-aged Gunn can't conceive of life in the long-term sense, and therefore barters his very soul for a short-term gain. It's almost too emblematic of the whacked-out priorities one holds at his age.

CRITIQUE It's the bit of fluff that's got the unpleasant job of sitting between the whirlwind of the previous four episodes and season's final quartet of stories. In absolute terms, though, it's actually pretty decent, and certainly kicks the crap out of other space-holders such as "Provider." Few reviews can occur in a vacuum, so had "Double or Nothing" come early in Season Three – rather than here, in a period of mostly A-level stories – it'd sport a much better reputation. But even taken in isolation, if this were the worst that *Angel* ever got, we could all throw a party.

Yes, the episode needs oil in parts, and certain threads – such as Gunn's day out with Fred – drag on too long. That said, many of the little details validate the experiment. The use of "Gangsta's Paradise" in the Gunn flashback is particularly fun; there's a decent mislead when you think Cordy's going to dust Angel if he loses his soul, but she winds up skewering Jenoff's hand instead; and the scene where Gunn dumps Fred really does seem to rip out the poor girl's heart and deposit it beating on the table in front of her. It's not quite the twisted/sadistic relationship material that Whedon's fevered brain usually generates, but it's close.

Sure, "Double or Nothing" will never top any fan polls. But it's a decent enough and – as a casino-based tale – in some ways a warm-up to the even-better "The House Always Wins."

THE LORE Jason Carter (Repo-Man) is, of course, better known as Ranger Marcus Cole on *Babylon 5*. He also voices James Bond in the *GoldenEye* video game, and in 2002, he was the sidewalk prophet in a Chevrolet Avalanche commercial. Patrick St. Espirit (Jenoff) appeared in *The X-Files* series finale as a guard, and he played five different roles on *Walker, Texas Ranger* over a period of eight years. P.B. Hutton (Female Elderly Demon) portrayed Buffy's next-door neighbor in *Buffy* 2.09, "What's My Line?" – she's the one who's murdered by a demon assassin who turns into a horde of killer maggots.

3.19: "The Price"

"I think we can handle one little slug from hell."

Air Date: April 29, 2002; **Writer:** David Fury; **Director:** Marita Grabiak

SUMMARY When a fast-moving, transparent bug creature suddenly lodges itself inside a would-be client named Phillip Spivey – gradually draining the man of moisture and crumbling him to powder – the heroes discover an entire swarm of the bugs [named "the Sluks" in 3.21, "Benediction"] and quarantine the hotel. Angel's associates discover that the Sluks are fleeing to Earth through a rift, possibly a side-effect of the spell that Angel cast to solidify Sahjhan (3.17, "Forgiving"). Worse, one of the Sluks takes refuge inside Fred. The Sluk speaks through Fred's mouth and mentions "the Destroyer" – an abomination that's both hunting the bugs and gunning for Angel.

Gunn begs Wesley for help, then on his advice makes Fred drink some vodka, dehydrating the bug and making it flee her body. As the battle intensifies, Cordelia displays the newfound demon ability to emit an energy pulse that kills the Sluks. Shortly afterward, the dimensional rift dislodges a huge monstrosity from Quor'toth, but seconds after *that*, Angel's now-teenaged son Connor – the "Destroyer" – leaps through the rift and kills the abomination with a single blow. Victorious, Connor levels a high-velocity stake gun at his father. [*Continued next episode*]

FIRSTS AND LASTS Technically, it's the debut of Vincent Kartheiser as the teenage Connor – viewed by some as the runt of Angel Investigations – although this is just a cameo before his full introduction next episode. It's also the first excursion into the Hyperion's industrial-sized kitchen (see 4.06, "Spin the Bottle"), and the first use of Cordelia's "glowy demon power" – although she'll only use it once more (see 3.21, "Benediction") before events strip her of this ability. Halfway through the series plus change, it's the last time that a walk-in client asks for help from Angel Investigations. Not a little ironically, this results in his hideous death.

POINTS OF DISCUSSION ABOUT "The Price":

1. Some would argue that TV shows are mainly for entertainment, and that we shouldn't question the morality in them too hard. Part of what makes *Angel* great, though, is that the series *does* make you think about its moral issues, and it's on those grounds that Angel and Gunn's final "understanding" seems a bit troubling. Simply put, Gunn argues that Angel's selfishness led him to "mess with scary ass mojo no sane person should be messing with." But later, Gunn has to momentarily "abandon" his colleagues while seeking help for Fred. Gunn then acknowledges that he too was "willing to go so far" in defense someone of he loved, which apparently puts him and Angel on the same level.

Well, no. That's ludicrous, primarily because Gunn's "drastic measures" don't really endanger anyone. Yes, he temporarily leaves the heroes in the lurch, but they're in a secure location when he departs to chat with Wesley, and he comes back for them. Conversely, Angel's "drastic measures" entailed a reckless use of black magic that endangered Fred's life in the first place and got someone (their client, Spivey) killed. Gunn might've been on Angel's level if he had – say – run down a senior citizen while zooming to Wesley's apartment at 107 mph. As matters stand, he's got the high ground. (But see 5.14, "Smile Time," for where Gunn morally falls on his face.)

2. Let's pause to mention Wesley's stubble, because from now until the end of the show, his lack of a clean shave is meant to reflect his fall from grace. This is hardly anything new in the history of television (Ben Browder's Wookiee-like face in *Farscape* 4.01, "Crichton Kicks" immediately springs to mind). But "The Price" is a little interesting, as it's the only *Angel* story in which Wesley has been so tumbled about by the laundry dryer of life that he's sporting a full beard, not just some whiskers. In virtually every other episode onward, he's "a bit grizzled," nothing more.

So it begs the question: How does Wesley maintain such a consistent level of stubble from story to story? Does his hair grow faster when he's depressed? Has he become so image conscious that he's using a goatee trimmer to achieve the same level of stubble each day? The more you ponder the fictional reasons for this look, the more baffling it becomes. Perhaps Wesely was so manly that he was shaving twice a day prior to this, and now can only manage it but once. Or maybe the solution comes down to a Denisof's flippant suggestion, that Wesley sits about and intones to himself: "Do not grow, my hairs."

3. The Sluks allegedly appear in the Hyperion as a result of "thaumogenesis," a term that's recycled from *Buffy* 6.03, "After Life." No doubt, the producers thought this would lend an air of continuity to the proceedings, but if anything, the re-use of the term makes sense despite the on-screen evidence, not because of it.

Let's consider: In the *Buffy* story, "thaumogenesis" was a process in which a spell (specifically, the resurrection spell used on the Slayer in *Buffy* 6.01, "Bargaining") inadvertently created a demon. Now, the demon was linked to the spell, so killing the creature could've made Buffy dead again. Ergo, Willow and Tara had to magically solidify the beast before anyone could lop the creature's head off without penalty.

Yet by all accounts in "The Price" and "Benediction," the Sluks originated in Quor'toth. Egads. There's no particular reason why the "thaumogenesis" component of Angel's spell would manifest in Quor'toth, not on Earth (unless you again want to blame it on Jasmine; see **Did Jasmine Cause All This?**), although the time differential between the two realms could explain how the Sluks grow to maturity and increase their numbers. It could also explain how Connor is accorded enough time to familiarize himself with the Sluks and shoo them down a rift to Earth, and it even better explains why the Sluks specifically home in on the Hyperion, the location of the spell that presumably created them.

That just leaves the hurdle that killing the Sluks doesn't void the spell that made Sahjhan corporeal, as he's solid upon his release in 5.18, "Origin." Okay, fine... perhaps the urn restraining Sahjhan protected him from any "ripple effect" from the Sluks' death, or it's just feasible that Cordelia's unique abilities override such considerations. It's a minor detail, though, in an already over-complicated issue.

4. Lorne is so scared that he says, "My heart is in my mouth." Considering his heart is normally located in his left buttock, this is a lot harder for him than most people.

CHARACTER NOTES *Angel:* Says, even knowing that his black magic rite resulted in Spivey's death, that he'd perform the ritual again in the interests of getting Connor back. [The firm would be downright giddy to hear such talk from Our Hero.] Angel bought baby Connor a snow globe with a bunny inside, but the Sluk-infested Fred smashes this to drink the water. Angel knows about thaumogenesis.

• *Cordelia:* [For some speculation about the cause of her energy burst, see "Benediction."] Cordelia seems to prioritize Angel's well-being above everyone else, including Groo and Wesley, and she charmingly refers to Groo as "a sexy, well-built, go-all-night puppy dog."

• *Wesley:* Claims to help Gunn because Fred's life is on the line. [This almost implies that Wesley wouldn't have helped if someone else's life had been endangered, yet he's reaching for a book – as if double-checking the solution to the problem – even before Gunn mentions Fred's name. He's probably just posturing, then.] Wes keeps vodka on hand, and tells Gunn that none of the heroes should visit him again. [They don't until Angel comes calling in 4.02, "Ground State."]

• *Gunn:* Thinks he and Fred should vacation in Baja.

• *Fred:* Tacitly understands that Angel shouldn't forgive Wesley, but concerned about Wes' pain. She becomes the team's default research expert in Wes' absence, but acknowledges she's not very good in the role. Conversely, she's a hellcat on research about wave particle dualities or the Schrödinger equation.

• *Groo:* His mother's name "was" Pomegranate [so she's no longer alive]. Nonetheless, his good color sense makes him favor Sunburst Splendor paint, rather than Pomegranate Mist, for a room being redecorated in the Hyperion. Groo has trouble pronouncing the word "purple," and starts to realize that Cordy is placing Angel's well-being ahead of his.

• *Lilah:* Reads classified e-mails by reaching into a slot behind her desk, taking out the metal box inside, removing a wooden box inside that, taking out the "magic bug" [a spider, clearly] inside and letting the critter type in her numerical password. Despite these precautions, Gavin knows about Lilah's correspondence by the time she finishes reading it.

As a result of Lilah's aid to Angel in "Forgiving," and in violation of company policy, Gavin here manipulates Lilah into mobilizing a SWAT team to assist Angel against the Sluks. However, this causes Lilah to tick off Linwood, who hasn't forgotten his torture at Angel's hands ["Forgiving" again] and now wants Angel to die. [It's implied that Linwood intends to "deal with" Lilah over this affront, and sure enough, her working relationship with him rapidly erodes from this point. Note **The Lore** in 3.22, "Tomorrow," and see 4.01, "Deep Down."]

• *Gavin:* Knows about Angel's assault on Wesley ["Forgiving"]. Gavin possesses an emergency cell phone number for Linwood that Lilah doesn't seem to have.

• *Connor:* The Fred-Sluk says its fellows are fleeing Quor'toth to elude "the Destroyer." [Stories such as 4.13, "Salvage" confirm that this denotes Connor. "Benediction" establishes that Connor "made the Sluks" show him the way out of Quor'toth, meaning he hunted them, then followed.]

PYLEA Groo compares a Sluk's elusiveness to the glass eels of the Skrag Swamp in Uxenblurg.

QUOR'TOTH [Water must exist in Quor'toth, as the Sluks are so eager to acquire some. Besides, Holtz and Connor had to drink something during their exile there.]

THE HYPERION There's a juice bar across the street. The hotel's South Wing includes a disused ballroom/meeting hall and a good-sized kitchen too.

THE LIBRARY Fred encounters words she's never heard before, such as "amulatives," while researching the Sluks. Frustratingly, she has to keep cross-referencing Chaldean with Acadian magics.

ORGANIZATIONS *Angel Investigations:* The agency is back to having no cases [despite having lots of Pending Files last episode], and no client has phoned in more than a week.

• *Wolfram and Hart:* Its Paranormal Disturbances Division detect a "bio-plasmic infection" at the Hyperion, and the preliminary psychic readings indicate "thaumogenesis" [see **Magic**], or possibly something called "megalosis."

• *The Powers-That-Be:* Here send Cordelia a vision that's

even more unclear than usual... one that entails Angel being flung across the room. [This gets realized next episode, but it's so generic that you can hardly blame Angel for blowing it off. Unless... see **Did Jasmine Cause All This?**]

DEMONOLOGY *The Sluks:* [Unnamed until "Benediction," but cited as such in the script, where it's used as shorthand for "translucent, tentacled, slug-like creature."] Persons infected with a Sluk experience a foggy memory and a tremendous thirst – Spivey drinks "about 100 peach smoothies" yet goes to dust anyway. The Sluks refer to themselves as "we," are luminescent and survive getting skewered by Angel's dagger. Sluks appear to tap their victims' vocabulary. [The one in Fred says, "To live... to drink... to be merry," which hardly seems to hail from Sluk "society."]

Drinking alcohol "dehydrates the body and gets the [Sluk] out." [At least, according to Gunn's over-simplified explanation. Fred is saved, even though there's barely time for the alcohol she drinks to take effect, so the Sluk probably nestles in the stomach and gets puked up readily enough.]

BEST LINE Cordelia, speaking metaphorically: "Poor Angel, it's eating at him." Groo: "You are having another vision, Princess?"

THINGS THAT DON'T MAKE SENSE It's amazing how *five* of the heroes are required to venture into the basement simply to shut off the lights, leaving Fred totally alone and at the mercy of a Sluk. Also, the Sluks in Fred and Spivey seem remarkably well-informed, correctly identifying Angel as the cause of all this bother, and correctly claiming that "the Destroyer" (Connor) is gunning for him. True, we learn in "Benediction" that Connor forced the Sluks down the rift to Earth, but that hardly explains how they know so much about Angel. Did Connor chat with the Sluks over the coffee about his personal problems? And what the hell's up with the towering demon in the finale? Did it just fall down the Quor'toth rift by accident? (Apparently.) And if Connor's so intent on getting revenge on Dear Old Dad, why not let the biggie demon soften the heroes up first, rather than killing it straightaway?

Furthermore... and we'll examine this more next episode... it's tremendously hard to reconcile the manner in which Connor takes down the towering demon with *one punch* against his never displaying such brute force ever again. Just for starters, he might've fared better against the Beast in Season Four (but see **The Lore**).

The Hyperion's southern wing has been vacant since 1979, so by all rights the hotel pool – left by itself for 22-odd years – should be thick with algae, yet there's none to be found. (Perhaps the Sluks thrive on the stuff.) It's also strange to consider what exactly "shutting the hotel tight" to prevent the Sluks escaping entails – it's not like there's a magical force field to seal off the joint with, as was the case in "Dad" (3.10).

Fred gets a frightfully large tear on her face in the course of dying from dehydration, yet it disappears entirely once the Sluk's out of her. The smoothie joint across from the Hyperion doesn't take credit cards, so how does the bug-infected Spivey pay for the "about 100 peach smoothies" that he downs over the course of six hours? (Unless he came prepared to pay the agency in cash.)

Cordelia says that Angel Investigations never gets walk-in clients on Sunday, which seems to pare with the agency's stated hours in "Epiphany" (2.16), but it's odd when you think about it. Is evil considerate enough to take off both Sunday and Saturday evening? Finally, a time discrepancy: Cordelia unleashes a power-burst in the kitchen that shorts out the Hyperion's lights. Yet the others barely have time to register, "Crap, it's dark," before Angel and Cordy have gone down to the basement, turned on the lights and returned to the lobby.

POP CULTURE Lorne asks if slicing and dicing the Sluks will, so to speak, "affect Mr. Sluggo." (See 2.04, "Untouched.")

CRITIQUE Yet again, we're obliged to comment how "The Price" relies on the old sci-fi cliché of people dashing about in a darkened space hacking at killer bugs, and that the ending hinges on a contrived *deus ex Cordy.* All true, but so what?

It's hardly what you'd call revolutionary – fine, fine, fine – but it's got a polished gloss anyway, and provides some lively moments such as an addled Fred drinking from the broken snow globe. It also demonstrates the new status quo – with Wesley ostracized, a stalwart Groo noticing as Cordy pushes him away, and Fred baffled in her new role as the agency's supernatural expert. Even if this episode is only a comparatively small step forward, it *is* nonetheless a step forward rather than backward, and let's acknowledge it as a decent little runaround within the *Angel* format.

THE LORE The script originally called for Connor to carve the towering demon in two with the curvy blade on his glove. This is simplified to a single punch on screen, possibly because the "cut in two" scenario would've over-loaded the effects department.

• Fury found himself overloaded writing the *Buffy* Season Six finale, so Smith got drafted to write the Lilah scenes when this episode came up short. (Fury, *The Bronze*, April 5, 2002)

3.20: "A New World"

"You'd have to be feeling like you've traded in one hell dimension for another right about now..."

Air Date: April 6, 2002; **Writer:** Jeffrey Bell; **Director:** Tim Minear

SUMMARY Connor unleashes a blistering attack against the heroes, but Angel overcomes his wayward son. A stymied Connor flees into the daylight and hops onto a passing bus, escaping. Shortly afterward, Connor saves a young drug user named Sunny from her dealer, a callous man named Tyke. Connor fights off Tyke's thugs, then accompanies Sunny to her makeshift home, where she dies of an accidental drug overdose.

Angel finds Connor, just as Tyke comes seeking revenge. The police kill Tyke's thugs in a shootout and evidently arrest the man, even as Angel saves Connor from a policeman's shotgun blast and helps him flee the scene. Angel offers Connor sanctuary at the hotel, but Connor – acknowledging that Angel saved his life – runs off. A solemn Angel returns home, just as Connor meets up with an aged Holtz, who's followed him to Earth through the rift.

FIRSTS AND LASTS The adolescent Connor gets a full-fledged introduction, which means that for the foreseeable future, a frightful amount of the "Previously On..." segment will devote itself solely to explaining how and why Angel now has a teenage son. Lilah gets her first meaningful interaction with Wesley when she shows up at his doorstep, offering him employment the firm. And the teaser entails a slow-motion, *Matrix*-inspired scrap that'll become quite fashionable in Season Four (see 4.07, "Apocalypse, Nowish" among others).

POINTS OF DISCUSSION ABOUT "A New World":

1. First, a word about Connor. Comic-book readers often (and correctly) identify his character arc is that of a superhero – or rather, that of a superhero offspring. You find this sort of "rapid aging" effect over and over again in comics, with – to pick one of the most glaring examples – the X-Men's Cyclops having an adult son under fairly similar circumstances.

It's curious, though, how the show expects the reader to connect the dots here. You'd swear, with hindsight, that one of the characters had said, "Connor went to another dimension where time runs faster than Earth, and now he's a teenager...", but there honestly isn't one, at least, not straightaway. Whether by design or oversight, the producers probably sensed the audience would inherently understand the sci-fi staple at work here, in the same manner that almost every genre show now doesn't bother to explain the concept of parallel universes.

Oh, and an aside on Connor's features: Kartheiser looks far more like Darla's son than Angel's kid. But then, that quirk happens in real-life often enough. Also, does anyone else find it uncanny how much the aged Holtz now looks like Sahjhan, only a lot shorter and minus the scar?

2. We're dead certain this was unintentional, but notice how Lilah brings up Judas Iscariot with Wesley, and the scene to follow entails Connor slicing off Tyke's ear – something of a New Testament parallel, for anyone who recalls what the apostle Peter did to a guard in the Garden of Gethsemane.

3. We say this quietly and with the greatest reluctance, but... Charisma Carpenter looks simply awful as a blonde. Our resident fashion expert judges that Carpenter's skin and eyes were tailor-made for her to be a brunette, nothing else, so she simply doesn't get away with it. A pity, because she's going to sport that look for a while yet.

4. Time for the math lesson. We're never told the ratio of how fast time passes in Quor'toth compared to Earth, but let's ballpark it. Gunn says that Connor was in diapers "a couple of weeks" ago, and Connor himself is... well, he's either 16 or 18 depending on which episode you believe, but we'll favor the latter based on 4.22, "Home." Eighteen years vs. a two-week period means that time passes in Quor'toth at a rate of roughly 7.8 minutes per second on Earth.

Now, Connor appears to spend about a day running around in L.A., as it's morning when he shows up at the Hyperion, but getting toward dusk when Cordy and Groo get zapped and Holtz comes through the rift. If we guesstimate a duration of 12 hours – roughly the time between sunrise and dusk in L.A. at that time of year – then Holtz at story's end actually hasn't seen Connor in something like 234 days (or 33.4 weeks, if you prefer).

If anything, it's a testament to the aged Holtz's prowess. If he's somehow looking through the Quor'toth rift to Earth – and that's the implication, as he only comes through the rift after Quor'toth lightning helpfully jolts Groo and Cordy (unless Holtz himself somehow instigates it) – then to Holtz's eyes, events on Earth are moving rapid-fire fast. He could scarcely blink, because if he even takes five seconds to leap through the rift after Groo and Cordy drop, then 39 minutes have passed on Earth. Not impossible, but it means they got a *really* good jolt.

5. Speaking of which, when Gunn and Fred return to find an unconscious Groo and Cordy sprawled on the lobby floor, cheeky members of the audience might feel inclined to comment: "It's the sex."

6. Lilah offers Wesley a job at Wolfram and Hart, and the deal sounds like it comes with a good number of bells and whistles (see **Organizations**) – something that's vitally

important in modern-day America. No wonder the firm has little trouble with recruitment. In fact, perhaps they should officially change the company slogan to: "Evil: Just like good, but with better benefits."

CHARACTER NOTES *Angel:* Functions decently well after taking a shotgun blast in the center of his back.

• *Cordelia:* Getting tired of all the "Days of Yore" crap that she hears from Angel and Groo.

• *Wesley:* Not remotely interested in Lilah's offer of employment. She gives him a 1500s copy of Dante's *Divine Comedy* (specifically, "The Inferno") that isn't a first edition, but is in the original Tuscan. [This isn't as impressive as it sounds. Dante died in 1321, so a copy from the 1500s is actually way after his lifetime. Plus, the "Tuscan" version is widely available now – it's actually Italian, with a Tuscan dialect. All things considered, this is almost akin to Lilah buying a new Edgar Allen Poe book from Borders, then telling Wesley, "It's not a first edition, but it is in the original Philadephian."] Wes has already read this work several times.

Lilah points out that in "The Inferno," the innermost circle of Hell was reserved for those who betray. The three-faced Devil resides there and has the greatest sinner of all – Judas Iscariot, the betrayer of Christ – in its central mouth. [By the way, the men wriggling in the Devil's other two mouths are Brutus and Cassius, the primary betrayers of Julius Caesar. Judas fares worst, as his upper torso is stuck in the Devil's maw, whereas Brutus and Cassius are "merely" swallowed up to their waists.] Wesley owns a black Apple PowerBook.

• *Fred:* Can now say the word "portal" without freaking. She wants Wesley's help in closing the Quor'toth rift; Cordelia and Gunn veto the idea. Fred unearths a text on monstrous Quor'toth demon from last episode [see **Quor'toth**, and this suggests that Fred isn't nearly as inept at research as she felt in "The Price"].

• *Lorne:* One of his contacts has 50 hands, and probably uses sign language.

• *Groo:* In Pylea, he once happened upon a herd of Burrbeasts – creatures that, when engorged, "will couple with anything that moves" – Groo stood perfectly still for 11 days and nights [a hell of a long time to go without food, water or sleep] and the Burrbeasts didn't couple with him; Groo tells Cordy, "That honor was yours, Princess." [Some have interpreted this to mean Groo was a virgin before Cordelia, but the conversation can be equally read either way.]

• *Connor:* [We'll skip the issue of why Connor doesn't have a British accent, given that he grew up with Holtz, on the grounds that many would argue Holtz doesn't exactly have a British accent either. We'll also set aside the question of where, in Quor'toth, Connor got such a stylish haircut.]

He's very cold and collected at points [even though he's later going to become a poster-child for rage] and uses the name Holtz bestowed on him: "Steven" [3.16, "Sleep Tight"]. He's dressed in animal skins, adorned with the teeth and bones of creatures he killed in Quor'toth. Connor initially displays excellent martial arts skills, moving quickly enough to deflect Groo's axe throw. He can leap onto passing L.A. buses, isn't much for modesty, and *cuts Tyke's ear off* in retribution for his shoddy treatment of Sunny.

Connor smooches with Sunny a little and doesn't look too inept at it. [This raises all sorts of questions about his sexual history in Quor'toth, a realm presumably populated by demons. Then again, there's nothing to emphatically disprove that there weren't other humans about the place either.] He somehow tracks down Holtz in L.A. [Probably due to his enhanced sense of smell, as evidenced in stories such as "Calvary" (4.12) and "Salvage" (4.13).]

• *Holtz:* Now aged, and wearing surprisingly spiffy clothes for someone who's spent years in Quor'toth. [He probably raided someone's laundry before meeting Connor.]

• *Mistress Myrna:* Blue-haired, dimensional magic expert who liberally "teleports" about the place. At Lorne's request, she magically seals the Quor'toth rift, and wears goggles while doing so to prevent getting "schmutz" in her eye.

QUOR'TOTH Mistress Myrna says, "There are no portals to Quor'toth, and for good reason." Additionally, Fred finds an illustration of the huge demon thing that Connor killed last episode, with a reference that it usually has a mate. [This would suggest that Quor'toth creatures have previously visited Earth, and that some benevolent organization – apparently deeming contact with Quor'toth as an anathema – created a series of barriers or "rewrote the rules" (yup, see **Why Do Catholic Objects Harm Vampires?**) to avert travel there. Glory's efforts in Buffy Season Five would've endangered just these sort of dimensional "walls."]

Connor's wrist-guns appear to fire wooden stakes [so Quor'toth presumably has trees of some sort, even if our only glimpse of it ("Sleep Tight") shows nothing but hellfire]. Connor also used something akin to a spoon in Quor'toth.

ORGANIZATIONS *Wolfram and Hart:* Lilah claims that the firm has the finest collection of mystical, occult and supernatural reference material in the world [see 4.22, "Home" for more]. The firm offers full medical and dental coverage, plus a 401(k) package, to its employees.

BEST LINE Not that we find this commendable, but objectively speaking the Best Line is when a deadpan Connor tells Sunny: "If parents are evil, they should be killed."

THINGS THAT DON'T MAKE SENSE If you'll recall, Connor single-handedly killed a nine-foot-tall demon-thing at the end of last episode. Yet as this story opens – literally seconds later – the creature's corpse has forevermore disappeared from the Hyperion lobby. Maybe it dissipated like a vampire, but you'd think that would leave a *hell* of a dust pile.

Even with the best rationalizing we can offer, Connor's fighting prowess is amazingly contingent on the plot. He simultaneously throws Angel, Gunn and Groo around like they were sacks of potatoes in his first fight, but later, even when he knows one of Tyke's thugs is behind him, the kid gets bashed half-senseless by a crowbar. Even allowing that he's getting more whipped as the story goes along, the ending – in which a commonplace drug dealer who's had his ear severed takes Connor hostage at gunpoint – seems rather implausible. *This* is the mighty killer of beasts in Quor'toth?

It's clearly morning when the story opens, yet this occurs "minutes" after last episode, when the Hyperion lobby was pitch-black until Angel and Cordy turned the lights on. It's also a problem that Angel doesn't smoke even the slightest bit when he dashes into the sunlight, just before Gunn and Groo haul him back into the shade. Gunn is able to cross "Police Crime Scene" tape and ferret information from the police with surprising ease. He also tells Mistress Myrna that the pentagram in the lobby was a "dark attempt to open a fissure" when it assuredly wasn't. (Although Gunn wasn't around at the time, so let's give him a break.)

Wesley had a full beard in "The Price," yet strangely he's down to stubble when Lilah knocks on his door, presumably the morning after. Okay, perhaps it's *not* the morning after, but that's how it's presented. And it's really not a glitch, but it's certainly a little hypocritical when Tyke mocks Connor for wearing "shammies" while he's sporting a leather jacket.

Last but not least... Sunny is not only the *cleanest* homeless druggie you'll ever find, she's resourceful enough to procure men's clothes in Connor's size at a moment's notice.

IT'S REALLY ABOUT... The shock of how gurgling babies sprout into walking, talking adults-in-training that're detached from the world. Front and center, obviously, is the notion that Connor and Angel seem clueless about how to communicate with each other. Angel moodily swings between compassion and believing the worst about his offspring (notice how he all but accuses Connor of doing drugs with Sunny, and even checks Connor's arm for needle marks), and his bewilderment is such that he doesn't consider that it couldn't hurt to tell Connor "I love you." Connor conversely thinks his father can't possibly understand him, and he literally views his dad as inhuman upon seeing his vamp face.

All told, it's pretty easy to see what Connor represents. He symbolizes the confusion and rage of adolescence – especially that of young males, who all-too-often want to solve problems by planting their fist in someone's face. We're drifting, just a little, back into *Buffy* territory by examining Connor as a teenager – yet *Buffy* would hardly feature Sunny, a relatively sweet drug user, up and dying from something as commonplace as an overdose. In Sunnydale, that sort of death would owe to magic or a narcotics monster of sorts. Here, it's harsher, dirtier and manifestly more real.

It's also worth mentioning Connor's identity confusion – chiefly his insistence that his name is Steven – and how as with most teenagers, everything's a new experience to him. Observe how quickly he goes from sharing cupcakes with Sunny to exploring the notion of sex with her. (Well, there's a reason that they're called "Ho-Hos.")

CRITIQUE It's sometimes unavoidable that a creative choice will shape a show's action for a bit – which is a polite way of saying that teen Connor's introduction momentarily renders *Angel* incapable of delivering a surprise. After all, there's pretty much only one way the lad's story can go: he discovers this wild world we call L.A., even as Angel makes rather bumbling efforts to bond with him. It's not exactly the sort of riveting drama that makes you dance a little jig – notice how much time, yippee, gets devoted to the scene where Connor first experiences junk food. The unusually dubious effects on display – especially the bits with Connor leaping onto and riding the downtown bus – don't exactly help the cause either.

Fortunately, for all the barbs you can level at this story, it's still rather good. It's visceral enough to keep the interest, re-establishing L.A. as the series' home by focusing on a drug-deal gone bad – as opposed to something intensely more loopy such as Connor (say) auditioning for a *Brady Bunch* remake, or singing in Caritas. The hotel slugfest is intoxicating, the cast steps up to the plate as usual and Connor himself...

Here's the thing. You've probably read how Connor sometimes receives a good kicking as the "most whiny" member of the cast. In Season Four, this isn't entirely without justification. But some fans forget that here and in the next two episodes, Connor works very, very well. He's the vehicle for teenage anger – the sort of hormonal hell that causes young males to lash out against their fathers – and he performs that role admirably. Hell, two episodes from now (excuse the spoiler), he'll kick the crap out of Dear Old Dad, drop him in the ocean and leave him there. That's hardly the act of a whiner. It's not commendable, but it's certainly more assertive than Dawn ever was at any point during three whole years. (And no, her jolting Xander in the penultimate *Buffy* episode simply isn't in the same league as this.)

Sometimes, and however much the producers try to avoid it, the audience momentarily experiences a slow-down as a series reboots itself. This isn't a mortal sin if it leads to greater things, and it's best to view "A New World" in such a light.

THE LORE Vincent Kartheiser started acting at age six, and found himself always playing creepy/intimidating roles despite his being a self-described "five-foot-six midget white boy from Minnesota" who's "105 pounds soaking wet with a rock in my pocket." He'd previously played the lead role in *Ricky 6* (2000), a film based on the real-life satanistic murders committed by Northport, NY, teenager Ricky Kasso in 1984. (Kasso, by the way, was deemed insane and locked up in the Amityville Asylum – yes, it was named that before they changed it – and killed himself two weeks later.) Also, in *Masterminds* (1997), Kartheiser played a young troublemaker who locks horns with an evil private school headmaster, played by Patrick Stewart. (The poster to that film, with Kartheiser's character skateboarding over Stewart's mustachioed and evil head, is rather surreal and worth checking out online.) (Veitch, *E! Online: Who the Hell is This?*, Feb. 2004)

• Kartheiser initially read for a role called "Street Kid" – his agents explained that the *Angel* team hoped to avoid spoilers, and the official listing didn't denote the character's importance. The more the show went on, the more Kartheiser wanted Connor's hair cut – deeming it too much like David Cassidy for his taste – but the producers resisted.

• Kartheiser had some embarrassment during the scene where Connor leapt atop the car to save Sunny from the drug dealer, as the patchwork leather outfit he was wearing ripped from the base of his rear up to his tummy. He later couldn't quite recall events from that morning, but he somehow hadn't worn any underwear, so he gathered himself up and hastily vacated the set. (Kartheiser interview, *BBC Cult*, April 2003)

• Acker expressed some relief over Kartheiser's addition to the cast, claiming she didn't look *quite* so thin now. Kartheiser himself recognized some difficulty in trying to appear masculine during his action sequences, and commented, "I'll catch myself running in a scene, and my arms are up above my head. It's like I'm a transvestite running from the police on Sunset Boulevard or something. Or running from Eddie Murphy." (Veitch, *E! Online: Who the Hell is This?*, Feb. 2004)

3.21: "Benediction"

"I'm not asking you to follow me into hell... just help send me there."

Air Date: May 13, 2002; **Writer/Director:** Tim Minear

SUMMARY The aged Holtz lodges at a local hotel. Surprisingly, he urges Connor to seek out Angel and learn about his heritage. Connor reconciles with Angel, and helps him dispatch some vampires as the Powers direct. Meanwhile, Fred rigs up a device to track objects from Quor'toth, causing her and Gunn to spy Holtz.

Gunn and Fred try to keep Connor occupied while Angel confronts Holtz, but the ex-vampire hunter surprisingly informs Angel that – out of love for Connor – he now wants the boy to live with his biological father. Holtz hands Angel a goodbye letter for Connor, promising to depart and never return.

Angel becomes thrilled at the prospect of his son coming home, but Connor overhears Gunn and Fred chatting about Angel's plans and dashes to Holtz's side. With Connor enroute, Holtz secretly meets with Justine and – as a final act of revenge – has her kill him with an ice pick to the throat, creating two puncture marks akin to a vampire bite. Justine cradles Holtz's body as Connor shows up, then claims that Angel murdered Holtz in cold blood. [*Continued next episode*]

FIRSTS AND LASTS Depending on how you define terms, it's the last time the Powers send a routine "there's demons hither yonder... go kill them"-style vision. Cordelia and Connor inadvertently get their first taste of "intimacy" through the boy's "soul colonic" (see **It's Really About**). It's also the final appearance of Holtz as a living being, although his corpse appears next episode and he's in flashback in 5.18, "Origin." And it's the final appearance of a thriving L.A. nightclub – the sort of scene that hearkens way back to "Lonely Hearts" (1.02) – although we'll view something similar in Rome in 5.20, "The Girl in Question."

POINTS OF DISCUSSION ABOUT "Benediction":

1. Bits of tawdry business: It's more than a little evident that Cordelia has strung Groo along, bedded him and has now lost interest. She's such a man. Meanwhile, please note that Lilah's IM to Wesley is *not* registered as coming from "SluttyLilah101," whatever fan-fic writers would like to claim.

2. Cordelia is wearing a red string necklace that's presumably of the type associated with the Kabbalah. (Putting it simply – nay, *extremely* simply – the Kabbalah is a system of Jewish mysticism.) The accessory was very popular in L.A. at the time, partly due to Madonna wearing one. We mention

this because there's parts of "Benediction" where the viewer might mistakenly think that Cordelia was sporting a sort of neck scar, after someone had ringed her throat with a very tiny knife.

3. We defy you to look at the guy eating snacks by the vending machine (the one Connor spies during the credits) without thinking about Wayne from *Wayne's World*.

CHARACTER NOTES *Angel:* Both refrains from killing Holtz and apologizes for massacring the man's family.

• *Cordelia:* Her latest power-burst [see 3.19, "The Price"], triggered as a bigoted Connor learns she's part-demon and draws a knife on her, allegedly flushes the taint of Quor'toth out of Connor's system. Lorne describes this as a "soul colonic." [Yet in truth, this makes little difference to Connor's emotional stability. It's possible that Cordelia's energy wave *did* cleanse the lad of any Quor'toth "taint," but that after a brief feeling of catharsis, he simply went back to being your standard screwed-up teenager who grew up in a hell dimension. Or perhaps Cordelia's energy burst – and the one from "The Price" – was symptomatic of her undergoing "demon puberty" if you will, and that Lorne simply misdiagnoses its effects; see **Did Jasmine Cause All This?** for more.]

Cordelia claims to not care if Angel kills Holtz, on the grounds that Holtz stole Connor's childhood, but strongly encourages Angel to own up to Connor about it. [This is faintly astonishing to hear from the woman who's spent three years trying to keep Angel in check. Then again, Cordelia might be banking on Angel not killing Holtz so he doesn't have to tell Connor the ugly truth, which isn't a bad strategy.] Cordy feels confident that Connor will return to Angel because "he's family." [Let's attribute this to willful blindness on Cordy's part, given that such things really are meaningless in the *Angel*-verse. If you'll recall, her parents committed tax evasion of the highest order, thus erasing her trust fund and scuttling any hopes for college.]

• *Wesley:* Attempts to maintain his dignity by having an elegant bottle of red wine with his overcooked TV dinner. [Between this and the vodka Wesley pulled out in "The Price," he must keep a well-stocked liquor cabinet.] With Wes having gone rogue, his dress sense is improving by leaps and bounds.

Lilah arranges for a vampire pack to hunt Justine, and then – as a further test of Wesley's resolve – maneuvers him into witnessing her impending death. Wes' slight indecision about whether to warn Justine or not seems to satisfy Lilah, who offers to have Justine extracted from harm's way. Tipped off by the Powers, Angel and Connor save Justine before this can occur, allowing Wes to recognize Connor as Angel's son from his fighting moves.

• *Lorne:* Claims [jokes?] that he owns an outfit made of lead. [Actually, this brings to mind the question of how Lorne has sported a new outfit since his wardrobe presumably burned to the ground with Caritas. Perhaps his freelance consulting is going better than expected, or maybe he drained his savings in the interest of fashion.]

• *Connor:* Feels extremely hostile toward demon-kind, calling Lorne a "filthy demon" and attempting to knife the half-demon Cordelia to death (resulting in his "soul colonic"). He went to Earth without telling Holtz, and here visits the ocean for the first time. [It's unsaid, but this trip probably inspires the trap he sets for Angel next episode.] Holtz claims that Connor killed "lots" in Quor'toth, but always out of necessity or survival, and that killing Angel really isn't in Connor's nature. Connor believes that Angel's "saving people" in the nightclub was a deception intended to win his trust, and it's implied that Holtz bestowed Connor with some Christian upbringing. Connor is agile enough to run over fast-moving cars from the opposite direction. It's clear, given the letter that Holtz writes for Connor, that the boy can read English. [This is quite the accomplishment, considering Holtz raised him in a hell dimension. What did they use for pencils and paper, for instance? Nonetheless, the script included a cut line where Holtz tells Angel: "[Connor] can read. He has some trouble with spelling, though he's improving."]

• *Groo:* All but acknowledges to Lorne that his relationship with Cordelia is crumbling.

• *Holtz:* Hasn't weathered his exile in Quor'toth terribly well, and has a raspy cough. [Holtz's age is indeterminate, but Keith Szarabajka was born in December 1952, and hence was about 51 while filming 3.16, "Sleep Tight." Allowing that Season Four retcons Connor as being 18, Holtz could feasibly be 69.] He's sporting what looks like scarring or burn marks on his face. [Szarabajka's make-up somewhat obscures this detail, but the script to "A New World" called for it.]

He says his hate kept him and Connor alive in Quor'toth, but he discovered that love was even more powerful [as a weapon]. Holtz claims he's getting forgetful, unable to recall if the invitation rule includes public accommodation.

• *Justine:* Has resumed dusting vampires of late, incurring grudges in the process. She readily returns to Holtz's side. [As if we lacked for proof, it's evident that Justine has serious psychological issues with men, particularly ones who treat her poorly. She came to experience little but betrayal and abandonment from Holtz, yet her attitude toward him here is one of, "I'd have followed you into hell." She's practically begging for validation and attention from someone who's never going to properly give it, and observe how she acts submissive to another dominant male in 4.01, "Deep Down."]

QUOR'TOTH Evidently doesn't have oceans; at least, none that Connor has seen. His knowledge of vampirism is based what Holtz told him, and isn't complete. [So Quor'toth presumably doesn't have any vamps. Also, Connor's bigotry implies that no benevolent demons exist in Quor'toth.]

ORGANIZATIONS *The Powers-That-Be:* Cordelia's latest vision again "blends" into her senses [even more potently than 3.14, "Couplet"]. Cordy here goes back into the vision to witness Angel and Connor fighting together. [She technically "replayed" a vision before in 2.18, "Dead End," but this more entails Cordelia using her abilities as a sort of "Cordelia cam."] The Powers deliberately send Angel to the bar where Justine is under threat. [We'll never know if this is coincidence or not. Perhaps the Powers are attempting to thwart Lilah's plans for Wesley and simply don't succeed.]

DEMONOLOGY *Vampires:* It's again confirmed that no invite is required for public accommodation.

• *The Sluks:* [From "The Price."] So-named by Connor, who states he compelled the little bugs to show him the path through the Quor'toth rift to Earth.

MAGIC *Cedrian Crystals:* About the size of a "D" battery, and said to contain "millennia of stored mystical energy." Lorne acquires one from a six-horned Lachnie hag that owes him a favor, and gets it enchanted. Fred fits this to an army surplus Geiger counter, enabling her to track the para-plasmic radioactivity of anything that came through the Quor'toth rift. This works, apparently, off the principle that everything in nature seeks a relaxed or stable state.

BEST LINE It doesn't sound like much out of context, but it's the bit where Angel shoves Holtz against the wall and declares, "You stole my son!", whereupon Holtz quietly responds: "I kept your son alive. You murdered mine."

THINGS THAT DON'T MAKE SENSE Holtz's master plan entails Connor believing that Angel has murdered him. But as Connor is only spurred to race back to the motel because of Gunn and Fred's loose lips, how did Holtz intend to maneuver Connor into witnessing his corpse? He's leaving a bit to chance if he expects Connor to simply wander back at some point, so perhaps Justine was supposed to inform Connor after the fact. Well, maybe. It's also problematic that Holtz dies from two jabs to the throat with an ice pick – this presumably makes him bleed to death, but there's a remarkable lack of blood on his body. And no, Justine doesn't have time to wash the corpse before Connor arrives.

Connor's acute hearing lets him hear Gunn and Fred's "private" conversation, even when they're some distance away on a beach with the ocean roaring nearby. That's all well and proper, save that Angel briefed his crew about Holtz while he was standing in the doorway to the hotel office, and with Connor visibly lounging around the lobby. What, Connor can hear voices from lengthy distances over the ocean's roar, yet he can't hear a conversation that's maybe a few yards away? Mind, he's not the only one with futzed-up senses, as Angel yet again (3.16, "Sleep Tight") fails to detect Holtz's scent, this time on Connor after the boy spends considerable time in the old man's company.

Minor quibbles: Fred supposedly uses a Geiger counter to construct the Quor'toth emissions detector, yet the faceplate says the device is a "Movement Analyzer." Also, Connor somehow produces a new shirt the morning after finding a motel room for Holtz. Well, perhaps Holtz kindly snatched the boy some spares, if – as we suggested last episode – he raided a laundry line.

IN RETROSPECT Cordelia, commenting on Connor's aggression: "Looks to me like he likes to talk with his hands." It's as if she knows where all of this is going. Along those lines, Lilah wryly notes that *of course* Wes came to their bar meeting alone, because, "I mean, how else would you come?" Well... she's going to find out next episode.

Angel vents his frustration on a punching bag, and it's a pity that he doesn't think to tape a doodle of Spike's head to it – as Spike conversely does to him in the *Buffy* finale.

IT'S REALLY ABOUT... The nature of revenge, especially the way in which it involves an inherent selfishness. "Benediction" is (probably unintentionally) a divorce analogy in that regard, given that one "parent" wants to screw over the other so badly that he uses their child as a tool for his revenge. Children all too often suffer the worst in divorces anyway, and it's hard to see what Connor gains from Holtz's deception except more turmoil. Tangentially, it's about how lies sound far more effective when wrapped in the truth, which is why Holtz isn't entirely off when he tells Connor "I've never lied to you," yet he's guilty of manipulating the lad anyway.

Then there's the "soul colonic" that Cordelia gives Connor. You hardly need an English degree to spot the sexual undercurrent here. Notice how Cordelia repeatedly tells the lad to just "let go," and the script describes their connecting on "some raw, complete level." Plus – and don't think we're advocating rampant teenage sex by saying this – the "darkness and confusion" that Cordelia mentions Connor experiencing sounds like the hormonal bewilderment that plagues most young males.

Finally, Angel and Connor's playful sparring is about fathers and sons bonding through violence. It's as if Angel and Connor were playing a fierce game of hockey or rugby, only with vampires.

CRITIQUE Masterful, but surprisingly quiet. Until now, Holtz has brought all sorts of weaponry and shock troops to bear against Angel and Darla, and he's stymied them like few ever will. So it feels rather poignant that now, with Holtz clearly too decrepit to dash about the place with a crossbow, he can only kill *himself* as a final act of revenge. This close to the season's end, you almost predict that he'd bring the hordes of Quor'toth to bear against the Hyperion, but nope, nope. His story ends roughly 238 years after it started – in an alley, with only a trusted associate and an ice pick to bear witness. From that point of view, "Benediction" simultaneously serves as the penultimate chapter of this story arc, and something of an extended epilogue for Holtz.

And yet, it's precisely what's required at this juncture. Again and again, you're tempted to give Holtz a bit of sympathy because – lest we ever forget – he's a genuinely wronged and sympathetic character. So it's all the more tragic when his revenge wins out, and he stabs at Angel (so to speak) with his last breath. In all of this, Minear provides a layered, twisted and above all humanistic tale that both paves the way for the tragedy to follow, and makes for sweet work in itself.

THE LORE The final juxtaposition of Angel reading, Connor running and Justine stabbing Holtz underwent a fair amount of revision between the script and filming stages, with the contents of Holtz's letter and a bit of dialogue between Holtz and Justine being added. (One suspects that Minear, as author and director, felt inclined to tinker.) Connor's last line of "Angelus" was added, probably to remove any doubt as to who the boy blames for Holtz's demise.

• Conversely, a line got struck from the scene where Cordelia mistakes Groo for Angel, with Groo commenting: "I am not Angel. But I see you know that." (It's unclear why it was cut, although it might've generated an inadvertent cliffhanger. If you mentally insert the line, it looks for all the world like a fed-up Groo is about to do in Cordelia with an axe... *continued next episode, Boys and Girls!*)

3.22: "Tomorrow"

"What you're being called to do transcends love."

Air Date: May 20, 2002;
Writer/Director: David Greenwalt

SUMMARY Connor vows revenge and "innocently" returns to the Hyperion, then trains with Angel to learn his fighting technique. Linwood directs his commandoes to kidnap Connor so the firm can dissect him, but the heroes prevail and Connor staunchly defends Angel – purely so he can exact his own vengeance.

Meanwhile, Lilah again approaches Wesley – an encounter that leads to their spontaneously winding up in bed together. Lorne bids his friends farewell and leaves for a singing gig in Las Vegas, even as Groo concedes that Cordelia's heart lies with Angel and leaves town. Acknowledging Groo's words, Cordelia asks Angel to meet her by the seashore so they can air their romantic feelings for one another. Cordelia drives to the rendezvous, but time unexpectedly grinds to a halt. Skip appears and claims that Cordelia has used her demon abilities so wisely, she's worthy of aiding the struggle for good on a higher plane. Cordelia agrees, realizing she must sacrifice her love for Angel as a final test. Moments later, Cordy glows and rises toward the heavens.

Meanwhile, Connor intercepts Angel at the rendezvous point and incapacitates him with a stun gun. Justine arrives as planned with a boat, allowing the two of them to seal Angel inside a metal crate, travel into deep waters and dump Angel overboard. Cordelia rises even higher, even as Angel sinks to the ocean bottom. Oblivious to their friends' fate, Gunn and Fred wonder why the hotel seems so empty.

FIRSTS AND LASTS Final appearance of Groo, who here exits for parts unknown. (It's tempting to think he heads back to Pylea, but that's pure speculation, and it's hard to know what place he'd hold in the new government anyway.) Last appearance of Holtz in the flesh (as Connor and Justine burn his corpse on a funeral pyre) and last time we see the red pentagram on the lobby floor, as it's presumably scrubbed clean over the summer break.

It's the first time that Wesley and Lilah sleep together. And it's the first and only *Angel* "season finale" in the traditional sense of ending on multiple cliffhangers (see **The Critique**).

POINTS OF DISCUSSION ABOUT "Tomorrow":

1. Angel claims he doesn't own a TV right now, so for those keeping track of this desperately important plot-point, the one Faith used in "Sanctuary" (1.19) must have been incinerated along with Angel's apartment at the end of Season One. Two years hence, he hasn't replaced it. What's really entertaining, though, is how Angel looks upon a television as a necessity if his teenage son is moving in.

2. The Angel cell phone update: He continues to hate the miserable things (see 1.13, "She"), and gets butterfingers to the extent of dropping his cell off a small cliff by the ocean. We would be interested to know, however, if Greenwalt was just re-using a familiar joke, or if he deliberately made Angel lose his phone as a plot-point, heading off debate about whether the water-logged thing might start ringing in Angel's pocket while he's stuck underwater. It's a small mercy, though, because getting welded into a crate and dumped in

the ocean is bad enough. Having one's cell phone going off for days on end, and being unable to answer it, would really be the limit.

3. Some commentators question how Connor and Justine appear to concoct and enact their gambit against Angel in precious little time. Setting aside the details cut from the script (see **The Lore**), remember that at least one day passes before the pair of them take action against Angel. Plenty of time for Justine to procure a boat and ready herself, with Angel's decision to meet Cordelia playing into their hands.

4. A playful Cordelia whispers a threat of some sort into Angel's ear, and we're obviously meant to view this as further evidence of their "comfortable" relationship, as opposed to her current distancing from Groo. Yet viewers tend to miss the couple of audible words – absent from the closed captioning, but confirmed in the script – in Cordy's otherwise private statement. It's "broom handle."

CHARACTER NOTES *Angel:* Outfits Connor's room with a bookcase, and some of his favorite books from when he was Connor's age. [Presumably nothing written after 1743, then.] Angel rather hopelessly thinks that 50 cents or $1 is sufficient for a weekly allowance.

• *Cordelia:* Seems a bit reluctant to have sex with Groo even before their break-up. She owns a larger version of Wesley's wallet photo of her, him and Angel [seen in 2.21, "Through the Looking Glass"]. Cordy used her glowing-demon power "only that one time as a night-lite." She implies she can occasionally blow things up [never seen on screen, unless she's loosely referring to 3.19, "The Price"]. She's always loved Point Dume, an ocean viewpoint in L.A.

• *Wesley:* Lilah yet again approaches Wesley, this time in a bar, and the two of them wind up sleeping together. Wes remains cold and distanced from her, though. His examinations of Mesopotamian, Greek and Hindi texts, Celtic myth, the Bible and Darwin all support the coming of something that wasn't possible before. [In Wesley's world, then, nearly anything is feasible.] He therefore doesn't view Connor as particularly "miraculous."

• *Fred:* Adeptly empties a jumbo tub of popcorn, sending Gunn for another and telling him not to skimp on the butter.

• *Lorne:* Departs for Vegas, as a buddy of his owns a club just off the Strip, and needs a singer and seer. Rebuilding Caritas, he thinks, would only result in its further annihilation. [Cordelia says Lorne's club was destroyed *three* times – which sounds right, if you count Angel's convertible plowing through the joint in 2.22, "There's No Place Like Plrtz Glrb."]

Lorne concludes that Angel's romantic feelings for Cordelia are mutual. [He's known about Angel's desire since at least "Waiting in the Wings" (3.13), so there's no particular reason why Lorne uses such stark terms with him now. He's probably just relying on his intuition that they belong together.] Lorne has released a CD entitled "Songs for the Love Lorne," and he says the tunes on it are good even if his publicist's name is mud now.

• *Lilah:* Able to build a rather impressive pyramid out of sugar and Equal packets. It's implied that Lilah knows about Wesley's fixation with Fred [although 4.05, "Supersymmetry" removes all doubt]. She finds Wesley's channeling of rage, frustration and hate in bed a much bigger turn-on than love.

• *Groo:* Is apparently fond of mixing tuna and ice cream.

• *Connor:* Cordelia implies that Connor is 16. [See 4.07, "Apocalypse Nowish" for why it's more likely that he's 18. Kartheiser was born May 5, 1979, and would've been approaching 23 when this was filmed.] He sets aside the name "Steven." [Chiefly to lull Angel into a false security, but he's "Connor" for the rest of the show.]

Connor occupies room 204 at the Hyperion. He appears to believe – in light of Holtz's teachings and pedigree – that he originally came from England. Angel takes Connor to see his first movie. [The footage looks like *Courage Under Fire*.]

Connor convinces Angel to train him to fight vampires, and later incapacitates him. [This surely owes to Angel's holding back and Connor's use of a Taser. The boy can't have become so adept as to defeat Angel after one day's training.]

• *Holtz:* Connor decapitates Holtz's body before cremation, on the off chance that Angel sired him.

• *Justine:* Good with a welding torch.

• *Skip:* He claims he "isn't allowed" to pass along a message to Angel from the ascending Cordelia. [Yet he's got bigger reasons for not doing so; see **Did Jasmine Cause All This?**]

PYLEA Groo makes *mock-na,* a soothing Pylean brew designed to relieve tension. It requires *plock-weed*, which doesn't exist on Earth, but creeping fig and sour grass make a rough substitute. Groo also offers to "gently and more rapidly rub" Cordelia's *schlug-tee*, her tense neck muscle.

BEST LINE Lilah, during her post-coital conversation with Wesley: "Don't be thinking about me when I'm gone." Wes: "I wasn't thinking about you when you were here."

THINGS THAT DON'T MAKE SENSE Connor knows in advance that Angel is meeting Cordelia by the ocean, but he doesn't know that Skip has delayed Cordy. So... isn't Connor taking the rather brash risk that Cordelia could show up at any moment and find it slightly suspicious that he's beating the crap out of his father? But then, Cordelia never stops to wonder why she's receiving "a vision" that entails her getting romantic advice from *herself*, even though it's never happened before now. (P.S. The vision can't stem from the Powers, so it's likely down to Jasmine's interference. Again.)

3.22, Tomorrow

Fred and Gunn walk into the Hyperion and declare the building empty, failing to consider the not-exactly-revolutionary notion that perhaps Angel is upstairs. The timeframe with Wesley and Lilah appears a little wonky in that they presumably land in bed after their bar chat, yet a whole day passes for the other characters. (So either we're witnessing events out of order, or we're viewing Wes and Lilah's second outing in bed, not their first. Heck, that might support Lilah's "several little deaths" comment.) When the firm's commandoes drop into the drive-in from a helicopter, why don't the heroes just rev up Angel's car and try to drive away, since they're sitting ducks in that location and surrounded by civilians?

Finally, Lorne says that he's taking a 9:18 flight to Vegas. Is airport security so slack in the *Angel*-verse that Lorne can board an aircraft, looking like he does? (Perhaps the casino keeps a private jet, but that's not what the script implies.)

IN RETROSPECT Angel tries to persuade Cordelia to chat with Connor about "the facts of life." Given what's fated to occur in the next year, let's say no more. Also, Connor calls Angel "the prince of lies," but the *real* Prince of Lies shows up in 5.13, "Why We Fight."

IT'S REALLY ABOUT... In the main, it's the culmination of the cold, calculating teenage rage that's been percolating ever since Connor showed up in "The Price" (3.19). The boy only comprehends the world through half-truths and distortions, yet he's supremely convinced that he's got the whole picture, and he tries to settle matters with his father through his fists. It's important to pause here and recall that he's as much a victim as anyone, not that this excuses his making Angel sleep with the fishes, of course.

Meanwhile, Cordelia achieves veritable sainthood in accordance with her character arc for the past three years and... yes, that element is pretty straightforward, isn't it?

CRITIQUE We've arrived at yet another departure point, and it's tempting to nit-pick because there's a bit too much story here and the final effect is choppy in parts. But really, it's nearly everything you could want from a season finale, and it stands as unique among Whedon-verse shows. Most *Angel* and *Buffy* seasons end with suspense, fireworks and intrigue about what's to come, but few are cliffhangers in the traditional sense. Notice how Season One dangled a carrot about Darla and the Shanshu Prophecy, but little more; Season Two wrapped up almost everything; "Home" is mostly an extended prologue to Season Five; and the series finale simply isn't a cliffhanger as some people stubbornly believe. "Tomorrow" arguably makes for the most traditional *Angel* season-capper, then, but it's marvelous in that regard, and as promised leaves you gripping your seat going, "Aiiiiiiiggggggggg!" It's almost a pity that DVDs now let anyone skip to the Season Four opener straightaway, as it deprives them of the anticipation that swelled in the summer ramp-up to "Deep Down."

Right now, the show is exuding a confidence about its future – or rather that it *has* a future, which isn't the case come the end of Season Four – and it continues to sparkle. So for now, we can only encourage everyone to stick aboard for what's proving to be a highly entertaining ride.

THE LORE Simply put, the production staff underwent its greatest rotation between Seasons Three and Four. Certainly, it can't escape comment that Whedon's workload would reach its boiling point in the next year. With *Firefly* in production on FOX, the man had three series on the air simultaneously – which isn't to claim that Whedon simply turned a blind eye to *Angel*, because that's simply untrue. But some accounting must be made for his priorities. Whedon devoted a hell of a lot of blood serum to *Firefly*, and the fact that he's credited as writer or co-writer on six of its 15 episodes – and that he directed four of them – in so short a span of time probably illustrates which show was getting most of his attention.

Also – for those of you who don't know *Firefly*'s sordid history – it didn't help that FOX kept changing direction, and decided, for instance, that they didn't want to launch with the pilot story Whedon had prepared. The usual account has the executives telling Whedon to bang out a script for a completely different *Firefly* debut episode over the weekend (or near enough), and to deliver it by Monday morning. Whedon continued to supervise *Angel*'s production throughout all this, and he wrote and directed "Spin the Bottle" (4.06), but it's fair to say that his involvement with the show waned until Season Five. More and more work was delegated to "show runners" – on *Buffy*, this meant Producer Marti Noxon, and on *Angel*...

Well, coinciding with Whedon being torn in different directions, Greenwalt and Minear decided to move on. Both men soon worked on a string of shows cursed to early cancellation (not that this should be taken as indicative of their quality). Minear joined Whedon on *Firefly* (it lasted 15 episodes, three of them unaired in America), then worked on *Wonderfalls* (13 episodes, a whopping nine unaired in America) and *The Inside* (13 episodes, six unaired). Greenwalt became head writer on ABC's *Miracles* (13 episodes, seven unaired) and then UPN's *Jake 2.0* (16 episodes, four unaired in America).

Both Greenwalt and Minear are listed as "Consulting Producers" on *Angel* throughout Season Four, meaning they gave the writing staff some input. But the influence they previously exerted on the show clearly waned, and we'll soon witness what happened to Greenwalt's replacement,

David Simkins. Minear, at least, wrote and directed the Season Four finale, and Greenwalt directed "The Girl in Question" (5.20).

• Greenwalt tried to shoehorn an awful lot into his final *Angel* script, so a healthy amount of it got struck. Of interest, Cordelia dithered about what to wear for her rendezvous with Angel, and it's akin to Buffy's wardrobe-waffling in "Welcome to the Hellmouth." (*Buffy* 1.01, you know... the monologue that includes the line "Hi, I'm an enormous slut.") Cordelia, scandalously clad in bra and panties, would have pulled out a sizzling dress or see-through blouse and said, "Angel, I just wanted you to know... I have breasts." Then she would've picked out a drab army coat and commented, "We will live together in chastity for the rest of our lives." The deliberation ended with her going, "... that settles it, I'm goin' naked."

Arguably, other deletions would've braced up the plot. To wit, Linwood and Gavin deliberately snub Lilah and hatch their own plans to apprehend Connor. (This in part explains why Lilah winds up in bed with Wesley, not that she needed much excuse, as she's more isolated from the firm than ever.) Also deleted: Justine and Connor conspire against Angel, and Justine shows Connor how to use his Taser, helpfully mentioning that it's waterproof. (Yes, it really was mentioned.)

The Total Kill-Count (thru Season Three)...

Angel: 35 vampires, 57 demons, 19 humans, 30 zombies; 1 heroic champion (demonic).

Cordelia: 1 vampire, 2 1/2 demons; hundreds of inter-dimensional bugs.

Wesley: 4 vampires, 10 1/2 demons, 2 humans.

Gunn: 6 vampires, 13 1/2 demons.

Fred: 1 vampire, 1 human.

Connor: 1 vampire, 1 demon.

NOTES: Angel and Wesley add to their "humans killed" score in "Dad" (3.10), in which they're forced to combat vampire cultists, Liliad demons, Wolfram and Hart commandoes and a human biker gang. It wasn't easy, but we labored to distinguish between those groups, ultimately concluding that Angel offs four humans in the mineshaft explosion, and Wesley kills two bikers in the lobby with his flamethrower. That's not to drag anyone's morals into question, because the bikers are deplorable, murderous thugs intent on kidnapping a newborn for God-knows-what evil purpose. It's justifiable homicide, no problem.

Also regarding human fatalities... The curious one is Fred, who until "Sleep Tight" (3.16) had only dusted a single vamp. Yet she indisputably hits one of Holtz's men square in the back with a crossbow arrow – a clear enough kill, even if she's defending Angel at the time. Fred looks quite the little Amazon when she shoots a second Holtzian in the gut, but such injuries don't kill you quickly, and we'll presume that Lorne or someone patches him up. (By the way, the script specifies that *two* of Holtz's men perish, but the melee is so confusing, it's impossible to know who gets the second kill.)

Other notes: We counted the on-screen corpses and determined that Angel offed 11 demon monks in "Heartthrob" (3.01). The swordsmen in "Waiting in the Wings" (3.13) seem more like extensions of the Count's will and probably aren't living beings, so they didn't count. We credited Cordy with "hundreds of inter-dimensional bugs" for "The Price" (3.19), because it seemed odd to count them as demons in their own right.

4.01: "Deep Down"

"How was your summer? Mine was fine... Saw some fish. Went mad from hunger."

Air Date: Oct. 6, 2002; **Writer:** Steven S. DeKnight; **Director:** Terrence O'Hara

SUMMARY Oblivious to Angel's fate and Connor's treachery, Fred and Gunn look after the lad and struggle to keep the agency running. Elsewhere, Wesley pegs Justine as culpable in Angel's disappearance, coercing her into helping him haul a starved and weakened Angel from the ocean. Wes then leaves a handcuffed Justine by the dock, encouraging her to find a new life.

Wesley alerts Gunn and Fred to Angel's return, causing Fred to incapacitate Connor with a stun gun. Angel recovers enough to toss Connor out of the Hyperion, then worries about Cordelia's whereabouts. Meanwhile, on a higher plane of existence and surrounded by swirly lights, Cordelia finds herself painfully bored.

THE OPENING CREDITS Vincent Kartheiser (Connor) joins the main credits, and Alexis Denisof now gets the "named" position at end, akin to the "and Anthony Stewart Head" crediting on *Buffy*. The credits feature some new visuals, including Wesley hacking a demon's head off (seen next episode) and a "swooping in on Angel" effect in which – for no readily apparent reason – he's looking incredibly squished.

FIRSTS AND LASTS In something of a deck-clearing exercise, it's the final appearances of Linwood (who's decapitated) and Justine (who isn't). A mere 49 episodes and three bosses after her debut, Lilah finally takes charge of the firm's Special Projects division (this might give her effective control of the whole firm, if she inherits Holland's old post). She consequently turns Gavin into her obedient lackey-toad, for what little time remains to him.

Gunn trucks out the cute little goatee he'll wear throughout Season Four. Also, Gunn and Fred are now living together in the Hyperion, so if their relationship wasn't sexual before, it certainly is now. First and only time we learn the name of a Senior Partner: It's "Mr. Suvarta." How disappointing.

POINTS OF DISCUSSION ABOUT "Deep Down":

1. In a move that'll culminate in "Supersymmetry" (4.05), there's an undercurrent of change with Fred. Gunn has merely gained some facial hair over the summer break, and Connor's just a little better at pretending that he's not evil. But Fred... she's become the agency's de facto leader. This is curious, given that Gunn actually ran his own gang, so it'd make more sense if he ran the show while Fred handled the agency's finances. Nonetheless, Fred becomes far more assertive (not to mention a precursor to her Illyria persona, whenever she's pissed off) chiefly to deal with a very real-world problem: With Cordelia sidelined, Fred is the show's female lead by default, so it's important that she's not a wallflower.

Moreover, observe that as Fred becomes more capable, she gets more tan (despite running an agency that largely works at night), dresses better, sounds even less like she's from Texas, wears more make-up and oh, yes... her hair gets straighter. It's going to get curly again in Season Five, when she really *is* the show's main female sex symbol, but it'll be a nice, ordered curly as opposed to crazy curly.

2. A quick note that they're really dolling Lilah too, now that she's sleeping with Wesley. Stephanie Romanov was never, ever what you'd call drab and homely, but throughout Season Four, you'll see Lilah at her most sultry. Oh, and tussled. Even when she's all business, she looks very tussled.

3. The heroes here dust some car-driving vamps, and thereby gain possession of an impressive red convertible. Presuming the vamps killed the owner – and bearing in mind the vampire tow truck that Connor acquires in "Slouching Toward Bethlehem" (4.04) – the heroes really should flip such vehicles at an L.A. chop-shop, because it'd help to pay the bills.

4. It's slightly disturbing that this episode's most memorable feature is, well, Wesley locking Justine in his reinforced closet with a bucket. (Indeed, it's rather relieving that none of Diamond Select's Wesley action figures came with a little plastic bucket accessory.) He's not entirely without justification, of course, but even if the cell is soundproof as Wesley hints next episode, one wonders why Lilah doesn't notice the bodily stench emanating from the closet. Is Wesley sponge-bathing Justine? Or does he keep supplying her with clothes from Goodwill? Perhaps he's not *such* the despicable jailer, then, because it certainly looks as if Justine has been washing her hair.

Oh, and right before the "reveal" of Justine in the closet, notice how Lilah gets dressed and exits without putting on any underwear. Neither, insofar as we can tell, does Wesley when he slips on his pants. How uncomfortable.

5. The tormented Wesley saves Angel and effectively gives him his life back, even sharing his blood with the man. This means that from this point, however else you view their relationship, Wes and Angel are literally blood brothers.

6. When Wesley readies to feed Angel from some jars filled with dark liquid, Justine asks, "Blood?" Our sarcastic response: "No... molasses."

CHARACTER NOTES *Angel:* While underwater, he's famished to the point of dreaming about an elaborate, highly idealized dinner in the Hyperion lobby with his friends and a well-behaved Connor. [It's a little strange, though, that Angel dreams about human food, unless he's going to suck dry the pot roast.] He later imagines meeting with, and murdering, Cordelia and Connor. [Angel still holds some anxiety about slaughtering those closest to him, whatever bravado he peddled to Fred in 3.17, "Forgiving."] Tellingly, he mistakes Wesley for Connor and utters the words: "I should have killed you." [He's delirious, and never displays murderous intent toward his son while he's awake.]

Buffy trapped Angel in a hell dimension for "a hundred years" [*Buffy* 2.22, Becoming"].

• *Wesley:* Still having it off with Lilah. He feeds a starved Angel from his own wrist when pig's blood isn't sufficient. He kept Fred and Gunn in the dark about Connor's deception until he retrieved Angel, believing that Connor probably wouldn't harm humans. He's got another car at his disposal [seen again in "Supersymmetry"].

• *Gunn:* Has apparently moved into the Hyperion. [Finally, the heroes value their budget over their independence.] He vetoes Fred's idea that they hunt for answers on Angel at Wolfram and Hart.

• *Fred:* Now venturing into battle with Angel's wrist-stakes and a crossbow [which she previously used in 3.16, "Sleep Tight"]. Gunn won't let Fred say "bro" or "dog," but lets her use "word." Fred continues to entertain the idea of asking Wesley for help, but Gunn vetoes the idea. She's sympathetic toward Connor, but threatens to seriously hurt the lad after realizing he dunked Angel underwater. [After Wesley's actions in Season Three, betrayal is probably a hot issue for Fred. She's going to stew about Connor's deception for some time yet.]

• *Lorne:* The Lorne in Angel's dream says he was called "sweet potato" – or to be more exact, "fragrant tuber" – in Pylea. [Either the real Lorne mentioned this detail, or Angel's mind invented it.] Gunn and Fred here phone Lorne in Vegas, and weirdly, he tells them to "Make sure Fluffy's get-tin' enough love" [see 4.03, "The House Always Wins" for why].

• *Connor:* Strong enough to survive a jump off a six-story building. Fred's Taser, however, takes him down. He's portrayed as a keg of gunpowder waiting to go boom, but tends to yield whenever Angel's around. Connor plays with a Game Boy [Gunn probably gave it to him]. He's got the ravenous appetite of a teenage boy, liking bologna but not tomatoes.

• *Lilah:* Responds to Linwood's unfavorable review of her work by accusing him of cowardice, claiming she never made "the mistake of fear." [There's a heck of a lot of grandstanding going on here, as part of what makes Lilah a great villain is her ability to show fear as required. She's bluffing Linwood that she's beyond fear; check out "Reunion" (2.10), "Blood Money" (2.12) and... most episodes in which she appears, frankly. Hell, she's not exactly done with fear, either, given that Angel smells it on her in 4.07, "Apocalypse Nowish."] With backing from a Senior Partner, Lilah finishes Linwood with a decapitation device installed in his chair.

Linwood and Gavin learn about Lilah's dalliances with Wesley via the firm's psychics, but Lilah claims there's no point in taking advantage of his confidence [but see "Slouching Toward Bethlehem," and particularly **Points of Discussion** under "Supersymmetry"].

• *Justine:* Acts submissive to Wesley [just as she let Holtz emotionally dominate her]. Wesley leaves the key to Justine's handcuffs nearby, and advises that she not let her inner rage enslave her. [She's never seen again, although it's tempting to think she becomes a straightened-out mentor to the newly generated Slayers after the end of *Buffy*.]

THE HYPERION The trouble-making pentagram [3.17, "Forgiving"] is absent from the hotel lobby [Gunn, Fred and Connor must've spent the summer scrubbing it away.]

ORGANIZATIONS *Angel Investigations:* Cash is tight, Gunn says they're "closing in" on an eviction. He and Fred have failed to find their missing friends. [However, they never think about phoning Buffy's crew for help. Granted, they've never met the Sunnydale cast save Willow, but Angel's three-month absence would surely count as an emergency.] As ever, despite the agency's cash-crunch, Fred owns a new Powerbook.

Angel's car "was found" by the bluffs after his disappearance. [It's in use through Season Four, so Gunn and Fred must have retrieved it from the police. Either they have some legal authority where Angel's property and the agency are concerned, or they simply stole the car back from an impound yard.]

• *Wolfram and Hart:* Linwood mentions transferring Lilah to a "less central" office than the L.A. branch; and Gavin suggests an office located in "one of the Third World dimensions." Lilah's shacking up with Wesley appears to leave her vulnerable until she eliminates Linwood. [Sleeping with the enemy could yield good dividends, though, so the firm probably keeps fluid rules regarding such conduct.] The ease with which Lilah butchers Linwood suggests assassination is par-for-the-course at the firm.

The firm's psychics identify Angel as "safe and immobilized," but can't determine his location. [Linwood and Gavin might fail to press the issue, or perhaps Angel's incoherence stymies the psychics – they're hardly going to read much through his sensory perception, after all.]

• *The Senior Partners:* The Partner that Lilah consults apparently provides great tips on office furniture. Lilah says the Partners have been working on the Apocalypse since "the beginning of time." [She's grossly over-simplifying, given the firm's philosophy as revealed in 2.15, "Reprise."]

DEMONOLOGY *Vampires:* Wesley says a vampire can survive indefinitely without feeding, but prolonged starvation can cause "catastrophic" damage to the higher brain functions. The vampire Marissa displays the ability to scale a wall like Spider-Man or – as the script puts it – a "cockroach." [No other vampire displays this ability, even though it's rather iconic; Dracula terrifyingly scampered down a wall in Bram Stoker's novel.]

BEST LINE Justine tries to thwack Wesley with a wrench, but backs down when he threatens: "I'll take away your bucket."

THINGS THAT DON'T MAKE SENSE A couple of awkward joins to the Season Three finale... Fred and Gunn never wonder where Groo has gone, even though he apparently exited town without telling anyone. Moreover, they don't find it even vaguely suspicious that Connor slipped out of the Hyperion on the very same night that Angel and Cordy went missing, which is rather hard to chalk up to coincidence.

Setting aside that the underwater sequences with Boreanaz don't look particularly convincing... Angel, in his dreams, amazingly knows about Gunn's new facial hair and the outfit Cordelia was wearing to their rendezvous. Fred and Gunn propose getting the "freezing" Angel some blankets – kind of them, except that Angel doesn't have any body heat – and they're also a bit short-sighted to tie Connor to a wooden chair considering the boy's strength levels. Angel declares that the truth sounds less nasal when Connor speaks it, thus giving his treacherous son a helpful tip about how to lie better in future.

Oh, and Gunn says, "We already asked [Wesley] for help twice." It was really just the once (3.19, "The Price"), unless there's an off-screen inquiry that we're never told about.

IN RETROSPECT Marissa tries to seduce Connor into letting her go, a victim/call girl offers the lad a good time for $50 in "Spin the Bottle" (4.06), and we all know what later happens between Connor and Cordelia. Cumulatively, you could almost entitle Season Four: "The Year Everyone Wants to Jump Connor's Bones."

A delirious Angel instinctively grabs Wesley's windpipe – between this, "Forgiving" (3.17) and "Release" (4.14), it looks as if Angel is always trying to cut off Wesley's air supply for one reason or another. Meanwhile, a bald vamp wants Marissa to return his CDs, and the drug dealer in "A New World" (3.20) threw away a handful of 'em. It's becoming funny how often underworld scum deal with CDs on this show... but then, this *was* before widespread iPod use.

CRITIQUE Oddly enough, it's a story of halves. Probably the strongest *Angel* season-opener to date, "Deep Down" stands as emulative of an exceptional series, with the interplay between Justine and the radically altered Wesley threatening to steal the show. Unfortunately – and let's deal with this criticism straightaway – info-dumps nearly consume the first couple acts. Perhaps the producers thought the admittedly lavish "Previously on *Angel*..." segment couldn't bear the load, and sought to better explain the status quo for newcomers. Whatever the intent, the episode finds new and imaginative ways of re-hashing Connor's history, Wesley's fall from grace, etc., so there's a definite sense of treading water.

And yet... that's ultimately forgivable. Wesley's efforts to save Angel, bearing in mind everything that occurred last year, prove surprisingly touching. The final confrontation between Angel and Connor is also a beaut. Romanov has rarely been better, and the continuing shift in Fred's character from "bouncy chick" to hardened leader is compelling. It takes a while to rev its engines, but "Deep Down" ultimately displays a mettle that validates the endeavor, and – even better – piques interest in what's to come.

THE LORE Following up on the producer rotation discussed last episode... with Greenwalt, Minear and (effectively) Whedon off on other series, the keys to the *Angel* kingdom were handed to David Simkins, who was basically hired as Greenwalt's replacement. Simkins had consulted/served as producer in some capacity on shows such as *Lois and Clark*, *Roswell*, *Charmed* and *Dark Angel*. A bit infamously, Whedon touted Simkins' talents at the WB's fall preview event and expressed quite a lot of faith in the man – shortly thereafter, the dreaded "creative differences" reared their ugly heads and Simkins was out of the picture, having worked on just a few episodes. His more recent work includes the critically acclaimed but short-lived *FreakyLinks*, and the "controversial" NBC show *The Book of Daniel*.

With Simkins gone, it appears that Steven DeKnight and Jeffrey Bell – respectively Co-Producer and Co-Executive Producer – became the show-runners almost by default. Indeed, in Season Four, the line between DeKnight and Bell's decisions gets blurred sometimes. By the end of this season and going into Season Five, however, they were pretty entrenched in their roles, with Bell effectively the head honcho and top writer, and with DeKnight getting an upgrade to full-on "Producer." The other player worth mentioning in this period is Ben Edlund, whom we'll cover in 4.20, "Sacrifice."

4.02: "Ground State"

"Find the Axis, and find your lost one."

Air Date: Oct. 13, 2002; **Writer:** Mere Smith; **Director:** Michael Grossman

SUMMARY Angel comes to suspect that Cordelia no longer resides in Earth's dimension, and plots with Gunn and Fred to steal the Axis of Pythia, a mystical device capable of tracking souls or entities across a myriad of realities. Simultaneously, Gwen Raiden, an electrically charged mutant and thief, accepts an assignment to swipe the Axis from an auction house. Gwen nabs the artifact, but Angel tracks Gwen through a businessman named Elliot, her employer. Elliot tries to eliminate Angel and Gwen in one fell swoop, but they escape and Gwen graciously lets Angel have the Axis afterwards. Angel views Cordelia in a Heaven of sorts, and tries to accept life without her. Meanwhile, Cordy – fed up with life as a higher power – longs to return to Earth.

FIRSTS AND LASTS It's the final appearance of Cordelia's apartment as the heroes relocate her stuff to the Hyperion, and therefore the final outing for Phantom Dennis. We're never told what happens to him, but he's presumably still haunting the joint. There's also two firsts on display: the electrified Gwen Raiden, who's a "recurring guest star" throughout Season Four, and the first instance of Wesley running his own "help the helpless" operation.

POINTS OF DISCUSSION ABOUT "Ground State":

1. Mere Smith previously focused her attention on a telekinetic in "Untouched" (2.04), so it's perhaps not surprising that she here generates the electrically charged Gwen, even if the term "mutant" never gets used on screen (but see 1.04, "I Fall to Pieces" for a list of potential mutants on *Angel*).

Commentators tend to compare Gwen to the X-Men's

Rogue, mainly because neither of them can touch anyone without drastic consequences, and they both sport a prominent hair stripe (or stripes, in Gwen's case). The similarities end there, however, and Gwen's influences are actually more muddled than all that. Admittedly, she follows the *X-Men* movie conceit that people with hyper-evolved, unprecedented mutations will wind up with unbelievably sexy bodies. But the school that young Gwen attends in the teaser simply isn't the parallel to Professor Xavier's School for the Gifted, or even Emma Frost's Massachusetts Academy (another *X-Men* locale) that some people believe, even though Emma and Gwen's headmistress are both blonde. Heck, it probably isn't even a mutant school as we're almost led to think, given that none of the other students display a lick of special powers. It's probably a private school that accepts money from Gwen's parents, and decides to take the risk of potential lawsuits.

Furthermore, Gwen is *so* "Batman" when she's strapping on equipment for the heist, complete with her own butler, even if Batman never smeared on lipstick before venturing out to hit criminals (at least, not that we're aware of). Oh, and that teaser we mentioned? The direction, the tone and the music all come straight from *The X-Files*, not *X-Men*. Hell, it even opens with a time and location marker, same as many *X-Files* stories. By the way, we should mention that Gwen's online nickname – "Lightning Lass" – belongs to a member of DC's Legion of Super-Heroes.

2. Even allowing his newfound darker persona, it's evident that Wesley *is* the rogue demon hunter he touted himself as in "Parting Gifts" (1.10). Suffice to say, Wesley divested of his insecurities seems far more effective running his crew than Angel Investigations could've ever hoped, and we're presently light-years away from the sweater-clad fool who couldn't dance in Season One.

3. It won't last, but Angel's pining for Cordy is now getting a bit thick, particularly when he ponders Fred's more assertive personality and remarks, "She reminds me of Cordy." You almost want to respond, in Angel-voice: "... that coffee mug reminds me of Cordy... that taco stand reminds me of Cordy... that prostitute reminds me of Cordy... Gunn, your goatee reminds me of Cordy..."

4. In a parallel universe, we imagine there's an alternate version of this script in which Fred tells her team: "Everyone wear black for the break-in... Angel, you're fine as you are."

5. Angel wonders whether he should appease Dinza (see **Character Notes**) with an "unholy fruit basket." It's probably a bad idea, but it's a great name for a band.

CHARACTER NOTES *Angel:* Uses a small spray-can to detect some laser-beam alarms. [It's fun to think he's using hairspray here, and the spray's powerful means of filling the room in seconds could well explain how Angel keeps his hair so spiky.] Angel loosely reconciles with Wesley, allegedly because Wes saved him last episode, but possibly just because he wants Wes' intel on Cordelia. Angel learns about Wesley and Lilah's relationship by smelling them upon one another. Yet his sniffer can't innately tell the difference between lemons and lemon polish.

Gwen's electricity repels Angel, but also momentarily jolts his heart into operation. The excitement of this makes him kiss her. [Despite this brief diversion, he's every bit in love with Cordy. Besides, Gwen is brunette, and therefore the wrong hair color for Angel's conquests.]

Angel performed heists of this nature "maybe twice" before [including 2.08, "The Shroud of Rahmon"]. He's comforted to think that ascended-Cordelia is "doing good up there" [even though she's just kinda floating around, really].

• *Cordelia:* Her car was found abandoned [and neatly parked along the side of the road, according to Wesley's picture] after 3.22, "Tomorrow." Fred and Gunn paid Cordelia's rent for a couple months, then stopped when finances got short. [They appear to take their sweet time relocating her stuff, though, possibly because nobody's eager to move into Cordy's reputedly cursed apartment.]

• *Wesley:* Running his own supernatural-investigative agency, with two men named "Jones and Hawkins" as muscle, and someone named Diana handling the paperwork. By all accounts, Wesley here does to Lilah what Willow did to Tara in the *Buffy* musical – only without the floating in mid-air.

• *Gunn:* Nearly dies from Gwen's electrical zap, but she stops to literally jump-start his heart. Gwen calls him "Denzel" [a name she'll re-use in 4.09, "Long Day's Journey"].

• *Fred:* Momentarily cracks under the strain of serving as the group's leader. [It's notable, though, that Fred didn't yield the post to Angel upon his return.] Fred seems fairly adept at hacking the auction house's security system, and carries a gizmo that opens door locks.

• *Lorne:* Has spoken with Fred and Gunn on the phone "precisely twice" since going to Vegas [once last episode, and an implied call before that].

• *Connor:* Wandering the streets and "lodging" with a homeless community.

• *Lilah:* Personally keeping tabs on Connor, with Angel warning her to stay away from the kid. He threatens to overlook Lilah's affront "this one time" if she provides him with the name of Gwen's employer. Lilah knows that Wesley locked up Justine in his apartment last episode.

• *Phantom Dennis:* Clearly misses Cordelia.

• *Gwen Raiden:* On October 28, 1985, Gwen's parents enrolled her at Thorpe's Academy, a kids' school in Gills Rock, Wisconsin. Gwen had to wear an insulating outfit. Little Gwen took off a glove to eat a pudding cup, and consequently zapped one of her classmates. [One presumes the boy died, but it's never specified.]

Adult Gwen works as a cat burglar, paid on commission. She's adept enough to lift Eliott's watch without frying him, and she employs a hot blonde female butler named Nick [who's modeled after Marlene Dietrich, according to the script] who kindly supplies Gwen with her lipstick [because nothing says "sneaky cat-burgling" like a tube of shiny red lipstick]. Gwen is super-strong – enough to counter Angel in combat – and her electrical talent lets her override electric locks and re-direct laser bars. Plexiglas and tempered Lucite insulate against her power.

Gwen attracts lightning [see 4.16, "Players"] and has been struck 14 times. She orders a redcoat in a bar, double the vodka, and owns a Mac running OS X. Gwen has iTunes, and a rather clean desktop. [She next appears in "Long Day's Journey."]

• *Eliott:* Allegedly wants to eliminate Gwen because, "The job you did for me was a train wreck. The noise, the publicity..." [Well, that's just bunk, as there's barely any noise, and certainly no publicity. The "insulated elevator" trap that he lays for Gwen wasn't exactly spur-of-the-moment either.]

• *Dinza:* Winged, veiled and possibly decaying entity that Angel consults about Cordelia, and who directs him to the Axis of Pythia. Dinza is described as a dark demigoddess of the lost, and "one of the Eleusinian Mysteries." [In mythology, there's no such entity as Dinza, and the name isn't even Greek. The Mysteries of Eleusis, however, were a kind cultish type religion in Greece around the time of Christ. It would appear the group focused on the goddess Demeter and the story of her daughter Persephone, although everything written about them comes courtesy of their foes, so historians don't know that much. Initiates drank a sort of hallucinatory drug, which is significant in an episode featuring "the Axis of Pythia." The Pythia was the lead priestess at the Oracle of Delphi, and the "seers" there produced advice by drinking a hallucinatory potion – same as with the Mysteries, although the link probably isn't more potent than that.]

Only the dead [including vampires] can enter Dinza's presence, and she often traps those that do "for eternity." Her lair seems connected to the L.A. storm drain system.

MAGIC *The Axis of Pythia:* Estimated value: $33 million. It's a metal arch set into a marble base, forged from the tripod of the Delphic oracle [who was a person, so this must have hurt, especially if "tripod" somehow alludes to the same body part as Doyle's friend "Frankie Tripod" in 1.03, "In the Dark"]. It stands approximately two feet high and weighs 18 pounds. It presently resides at Chandler's Auction House, an establishment firmly rooted in the black market.

BEST LINE The obvious choice. Fred: "I'm still working on a plan, but so far, it involves going to prison and becoming somebody's bitch." (Special addendum when Fred later remarks: "I hope I like my cellmate.")

THINGS THAT DON'T MAKE SENSE Gwen struts about dressed as a strumpet, which almost seems commendable until you recall that the smallest touch of her skin can potentially kill people. She really should cover up her shoulders and mid-riff, because one casual brush – for instance – by a waiter in a crowded elevator could fry the man into jerky.

Lilah now runs Special Projects (if not the entire firm), yet she feels the need to follow Connor around herself, on foot, in what looks like a bad part of L.A., as opposed to assigning a skilled lackey to do it. Plus, she looks so damnably conspicuous standing there in her business attire with a pair of huge binoculars, it's a miracle the lad doesn't spot her.

Now let's pause to consider "the dramatic break-in," which begins with Gwen scaling up a "towering wall" with a grappling hook, as opposed to – oh, say – simply climbing up the grating or possibly *the tree* located right next to it. (Told you Gwen thinks she's Batman.) Then Angel, Gunn and the not-exactly-athletic Fred *do* shimmy up the grating, and it becomes quite obvious that everyone involved is "climbing" over a small parking lot wall, not onto a rooftop. If you're in doubt, observe how much the L.A. architecture looms over them. At least this accords us the amusement of J. August Richards pretending to be out of breath.

What leads Wesley to conclude that Cordelia isn't in our dimension? (All right... we'll assume he consulted a psychic or magic expert who sensed some residual energy.) That Gwen's electricity can get Angel's withered, dead heart beating seems bizarre enough, but it's really odd that this makes the interior of his chest look pink and healthy. Also, during the escape from the elevator, why does Angel conduct Gwen's electricity through his body? Why not just help her up, and have her stick her hand in the mechanism? Why doesn't this power-surge knock Angel flat on his rear? It's how tasers work, after all.

Wesley decapitates a lumbering demon that looks as if it's of the fairly brainless "Hulk smash" variety – and yet has somehow kidnapped a "Mr. O'Leary" and locked him up in a hotel, the fiend. And when Phantom Dennis "lifts" some books that are right next to Fred, she fails entirely to notice this. (You'd almost think Dennis had teleported the books onto the mantle, but he can't do that.)

POP CULTURE "Raiden." Gwen's last name, and it almost pains us to mention that the word got popularized as a *Mortal Kombat* character. We'd like to remind everyone that the term originally denoted a Japanese god of thunder and lighting.

IN RETROSPECT Fred here instructs Angel and Gunn with a "doodle" presentation that's not unlike Giles' transparencies in *Buffy* 4.10, "Hush," or a couple of the basement meetings in *Buffy* Season Seven. Also, Gunn suggests: "We could've all gone to Vegas." One more episode, buddy.

CRITIQUE It's inherently an unremarkable heist story, and if anything one that contains even less excitement than "The Shroud of Rahmon" (2.08). There's a convenient mystical character to point Angel in the right direction, there are a few booby traps and there's the obligatory double-cross. Nothing particularly rings any alarm bells, but in many ways, it's just marking time.

It does at least serve to introduce Gwen, and some commentators feel the urge to praise the hot chick in leather as the main selling point. Much as we appreciate hot chicks in leather, though, the wide world of entertainment is flush with them, and we'd appreciate something more interesting than *just* that. Alexa Davalos undeniably has stage presence in the role, so we're not trying to knock the actress herself. But it's frankly hard to see what a mutant taken from stock – in this case, a sexy cat burglar who fires electrical bolts – particularly adds to the *Angel*-verse. Ultimately more geared for shows such as *Birds of Prey*, she simply looks out of place in *Angel*'s urban-fantasy setting and – in the case of "Ground State" – barely lifts an otherwise so-so episode.

THE LORE Alexa Davalos (Gwen) has surprisingly few acting credits, although she did later feature in the short-lived FOX series *Reunion*. More prominently, she's the female lead in *The Chronicles of Riddick* (2004). Rena Owen (Dinza) appeared in the last two *Star Wars* prequels, respectively, as Senator Nee Alvar and the voice of Ministerial Assistant Taun We.

• An extremely naughty bit of dialogue cut from the script: Wesley tells Lilah, "Why are you talking when your mouth can do so many other things?"

4.03: "The House Always Wins"

"This is Vegas, sunshine. Generally speaking, you lose here, you don't get it back."

Air Date: Oct. 20, 2002; **Writer:** David Fury; **Director:** Marita Grabiak

SUMMARY Angel, Gunn and Fred journey to Vegas to witness Lorne's stage show at the Tropicana casino, but soon discover that he's the prisoner of Lee DeMarco, an evil businessman. Under threat of DeMarco killing his back-up singers, Lorne has been "reading" members of the audience. Individuals he deems to have the brightest futures are recruited to play a mystical roulette wheel; this literally steals their destinies, which DeMarco sells on an infernal futures market. The destiny-void individuals become gamblers at the casino, their lives going nowhere.

Angel inadvertently falls prey to the roulette wheel, but Cordelia – working from her higher plane – influences a slot machine to give Angel a $300,000 jackpot, a supposed impossibility for anyone without a destiny. DeMarco decides to kill Gunn and Fred as troublemakers, but Angel gains *just* enough direction to brawl with DeMarco's men. Lorne then shatters a mystical orb containing the stolen futures, restoring Angel and DeMarco's other victims. Angel's quartet returns to the Hyperion afterward, stunned to find an amnesiac Cordelia in the lobby.

FIRSTS AND LASTS It's the first appearance of amnesiac Cordelia – to listen to some fans gripe, this version of Cordy occupies most of Season Four, when in fact she get her memories back three episodes from now. First mention of Emile, Wesley's weapons-supplier (see also 4.06, "Spin the Bottle," and 5.07, "Lineage"). Also, "The House Always Wins" is the only *Angel* story to credit 12 women – the "Lornettes" – as "featured dancers."

POINTS OF DISCUSSION ABOUT "The House Always Wins":

1. We're going to forego the [*Continued next episode*] tags throughout the highly serialized Season Four, as pegging almost every episode seems a waste of space.

2. Now for the continuity lesson. Numerous *Angel* and *Buffy* episodes state over and over and *over* that Angel spent almost all of the twentieth century avoiding humanity, so it's incredibly odd when he here claims that he previously visited Vegas and spent time playing tennis (at night?) with gangster Bugsy Siegel, having drinks with the Rat Pack and gate-crashing Elvis' wedding. Reconciling this with Angel's history has always proved difficult, so we'd like to submit that... Angel is just feeling impish with his friends, and making it all up. Seriously, is he *ever* this chatty when he's not putting people on?

In the first place, we'd have to accept multiple visits on Angel's part, as Siegel was plugged with a Carbine in 1947 (one bullet caught him in the eye, a death that has since become a staple of mob films), and Elvis and Priscilla got married in 1967. The Rat Pack's Vegas appearances and career burned brightest in the early 1960s (when they helped to de-segregate the town's entertainment venues), but there's room to maneuver there. Still, it's problematic – and arguably telling – when Angel claims to have attended Elvis and Priscilla's wedding reception at the Tropicana, because it was actually at the Aladdin Hotel. (The destiny-less Angel claims to recognize the alleged reception room at the Tropicana, but even that's not automatic proof that he attended the actual event.) So we'd almost bet money that he's making most, if not all, of it up.

3. Everyone somewhat implausibly changes clothes before returning home, although this presumably occurs so "amnesiac" Cordelia doesn't have to wonder why Fred is dressed like a green demon showgirl. Speaking of which, to look at Fred's Lornette costume, it's obvious that she's been taking lessons from Cordelia on running in heels. "Okay, now I'm the demon, and I'm chasing you..."

4. Many attempts have been made to analyze Wesley and Lilah's phone sex, chiefly to wonder how Lilah could... errrr... "play along" as she's in a meeting. Some judge her desk as un-conducive to that sort of thing, but we'd deem it feasible. That said, as we're only privy to Wesley's end of the conversation, we're curious as to how Lilah says aloud, "I'm wearing my red, velvet panties" (or whatever comment prompts his response of "That is my favorite pair...") without her co-workers overhearing. So we'd like to front a whimsical solution: Perhaps Wesley has a foot fetish, Lilah's "pair" actually refers to her shoes, and he's telling her to pretend to drop a pencil, take 'em off and salaciously rub her feet. Why hasn't anyone thought of this before?

CHARACTER NOTES *Angel:* Claims he wasn't invited to Elvis and Priscilla's wedding reception, but that everyone thought he was in the band because he was drunk and surly. [Again, does "drunk and surly" sound like the twentieth century Angel that we know? He's fibbing.]

Angel isn't all that interested in Lorne "reading" him, and it's not entirely explained how he shrugged off the roulette wheel's conditioning. [Lorne seems to imply, more or less, that Angel just "snapped out of it," which is impressive for someone who literally lacks a destiny. More likely, Cordelia's fiddling with probabilities accorded Angel a window to get his destiny back on track.]

• *Wesley:* Flush with enough cash to commission formidable weaponry from a dealer named Emile. Wes' organization accepts Angel's clients while he's out of town.

• *Gunn:* Fred thinks Gunn has a nice singing voice, and Gunn seems disappointed when Lorne "works the audience" but doesn't ask him to sing. He's angered at the thought of Lorne "selling out" to DeMarco, later apologizing for the wrongful judgment.

• *Fred:* Fares better at the casino than Gunn, who suggests she's counting cards.

• *Lorne:* Able to predict the audience-members' destinies as much as 12 years in advance. [Lorne is never more adept than in this story, but it's a bit hard to reason why. We've previously speculated that he's a sort of vending machine that dispenses wisdom as handed down by a higher power, if not the Powers-That-Be themselves. Yet it's odd that Lorne's benefactor would provide such detailed information, given that it results in such dire consequences for those involved.]

Lorne is presently finishing his 17th straight week at the Tropicana. His "sonic cry," when projected through a speaker system, shorts out light bulbs in the area. He kept asking about the fictional "Fluffy" whenever Fred called [4.01, "Deep Down"] as a universal code for, "I'm being held prisoner, send help."

• *Lee DeMarco:* Second-rate lounge musician who got his hands on something legitimately mystical [see **Magic**]. It appears that he now owns the Tropicana.

ORGANIZATIONS *Wolfram and Hart:* DeMarco suggests calling the firm's L.A. branch to let them know he's snagged Angel's destiny. [This implies that the firm doesn't have a Las Vegas branch, which is curious as it's such prime sin territory. Perhaps the L.A. branch simply handles all the business in Vegas, as it's not that far by shuttle.]

MAGIC *The Million Dollar Spin-To-Win Game:* DeMarco's intended victims are handed a green casino chip that imprints their futures/destinies on contact. [The Lornettes who pass out the chips aren't affected, so perhaps their body make-up mystically shields them.] The targets are enticed to play the black-magic-laced "Spin to Win" roulette game, which they inevitably lose and thereby forfeit their futures to the "black global market." Like Lorne, the roulette wheel can register someone's destiny. [This has made some commenators wonder what DeMarco needs Lorne for, although it's far more expedient for Lorne to suss out the two or three people in the audience worth snagging, as opposed to DeMarco cycling through and mentally neutering hundreds of people.]

Smashing a glowing sphere in DeMarco's office restores everyone's destiny. [So these destinies are "borrowed" or even "leased," not permanently taken.]

BEST LINE Fred realizes that the audience thinks Lorne, actually a demon, is just someone in make-up and asks, "You don't think the Blue Man Group...?" Angel: "Only two of 'em." (But how would Angel know this? Oh, the lies he's throwing out this episode.)

THINGS THAT DON'T MAKE SENSE Persons who lose their futures become condemned to lifelessly wander about the casino. Well, for a start, almost nobody goes to Vegas alone – do their friends and families just leave them there, without alerting the police? And as few of the victims ever leave, wouldn't the ranks of the "future-lost," in time, start elbowing out the legitimate patrons? Why does the conditioning of Vivian, "the chef of the future," break down to the point that she's wandering out in the road, which can only attract undue attention to the operation? Plus, do the victims maintain the presence of mind to feed themselves daily from a convenient buffet table, or does some mystical component about the whole affair allow them to them forego meals, drinks, showers and trips to the restroom?

It's rather foolish of DeMarco to keep the all-important crystal ball with the stolen destinies out in the open where anyone could break it – as opposed to, say, behind reinforced glass. As it stands, any cleaning woman with an overzealous feather duster could knock the thing over. Lorne "spot-checks" the audience members at his show and readily identifies a future Nevada senator, a future Pulitzer winner and the future owner of three five-star restaurants – quite the talent pool, when you think about it. Also, Angel lets the casino bouncers thump him for a surprisingly long time before fighting back. And notice how Fred's Lornette body paint becomes a darker shade of green as the story progresses.

As opposed to some fans, we're not *so* troubled by this story's time-frame (allowing that some time passes before Angel's trio heads to Vegas, whatever the teaser implies), and we're not *so* perplexed by the thought of everyone changing clothes before returning home. But we've left the weightier concerns about Lorne's sudden exit in the story's final minutes until next episode.

POP CULTURE A marquee touts Lorne as "the Green Velvet Fog," thus evoking the famous jazz singer Mel Tormé, who was dubbed in many circles as "The Velvet Fog."

• Angel thinks about seeing a Vegas show starring singer/comedian Danny Giles ("The Man of Many Voices"), a long-running performer at the Mirage resort.

• Oh, and the Lornettes somewhat evoke the green, dancing Orion chick from *Star Trek*, not that it's a blatant parallel.

IT'S REALLY ABOUT... Even a non-discerning viewer should spot the metaphor at work here. Casino patrons lose their futures playing a rigged game of chance, and become doomed to spend the rest of their pathetic and sorry existences mindlessly putting quarters into slot machines, and they can only win by not playing. It's not the most original of commentaries, but it's a familiar type of metaphor, considering David Fury used to write for *Buffy*. The only difference is that a demon or vampire – not a crooked businessman – would be responsible for such an operation in Sunnydale.

TONIGHT AT THE TROPICANA Lorne dazzles the audience with "It's Not Easy Being Green" and "Lady Marmalade" [previously performed in 2.11, "Redefinition"].

CRITIQUE Given the Vegas-like glitter that practically starts falling from the sky every time someone mentions this story, it certainly doesn't suffer as a forgotten *Angel* episode. Fortunately, it's also quite a kick to watch if you're in the right mood. It certainly wins points because it pulls off something different, and it's a fabulous use of the Vegas setting. Credit the producers with some timing here, because this sort of story will become nigh-impossible once the heroes focus their attention on the home-front starting next episode, so it's pleasing that they played this card while they could.

In implementation, though, it's not without hiccups. Chief among these is the lack of a notable villain: DeMarco just doesn't cut it, and it's telling that even David Fury didn't care about the character. His script, if ever you've perused it, explicitly reads, "DeMarco's bloody, smoking body hits the floor, probably dead, but who cares?" Good grief, if the writer can't muster any emotion when the villain croaks, why should the viewer? And if we're running through the complaints, then it's true that Angel spends too much time neutered and mindlessly playing slots, and that Cordelia's Help-From-On-High seems awfully contrived.

All of that said, we're still looking at a glass half-full. Much of this owes to Andy Hallett – egads, he's ***always*** good, isn't he? – with Lorne's performance at the Tropicana standing out as one of the series' most memorable undertakings. *Angel*'s two remaining years certainly have their high points, but we'll never see anything with quite this bit of master showmanship again, so let's suitably indulge it as a fun-filled and worthy diversion from the darker events to come.

THE LORE With Simkins' departure complicating the chain of command, Fury – credited as "Consulting Producer" – helped to outline the episodes from this story through "Awakening" (4.10), which he co-wrote with DeKnight, and he also wrote "Salvage" (4.13). Then he got pulled back to *Buffy*, where he's credited with writing such episodes as "Lies My Parents Told Me" (*Buffy* 7.17) during this period. Bell and DeKnight were evidently left to continue on their own. Then Fury came back to *Angel* for "Peace Out" (4.21), whereupon he needed to reorientate his thinking to a story arc that'd been running without him. (DiLullo, *CityofAngel.com*)

• A lot of the Vegas location work occurred on the stage floor at the Riviera Hotel. A show entitled *Splash* was running there, and the dancers were co-opted to appear as the Lornettes. Hallett says the dancers probably overestimated his authority and importance, although it seems he wound up calling a shot or two with regards to the choreography. (Hallett, *BBC Cult*, April 2003)

• The well-dressed man that Lorne makes sing, by the way, is Tom Schmid. He's actually an accomplished singer and performer, whose credits include *Jekyll & Hyde* and *The Phantom of the Opera*. It's therefore rather amusing that he's here required to warble a single line from "Lady Marmalade," and deliberately off-key to boot.

• An oft-repeated nugget... in the audience at Lorne's show is *Angel* script supervisor Petra Jorgenson and writer David Fury, who's holding a bobble-head fashioned after *Angel* producer Kelly Manners.

• Brittany Ishibashi (Vivian, the future master chef) acted alongside Charisma Carpenter as a jilted elf in the *Miss Match* episode "Santa, Baby."

4.04: "Slouching Toward Bethlehem"

"Was I a nun? Were we not a happy family because I was a nun?"

Air Date: Oct. 27, 2002; **Writer:** Jeffrey Bell; **Director:** Skip Schoolnik

SUMMARY Angel tries to help Cordelia slowly re-acclimate to the mortal plane, but Cordy learns about the supernatural aspects of her lifestyle and job anyway. Lorne becomes rattled to the core after "reading" Cordelia, his empathic senses registering an unspecified-yet-approaching evil. In rapid succession, Cordy realizes Angel's vampiric nature and gets chased about the Hyperion by one of Lorne's ravenous demon clients. Connor arrives and dispatches the threat, whereupon Cordelia – now at her wits' end – runs away with him.

Meanwhile, Wesley overhears Lilah give orders for Cordelia's capture and alerts Angel, enabling the heroes to thwart Lilah's commando squad. However, Wes discovers that Lilah played him, and that the "kidnap attempt" was a distraction while a second team used a demon to telepathically rip the Cordelia-relevant data from Lorne's mind. Still bewildered, Cordelia opts to stay with Connor, the one person who didn't lie to her.

FIRSTS AND LASTS It's the first installment of this season's grand story arc, which gets a lot more serialized than in previous years. Location-wise, it's the last glimpse we're accorded inside Lilah's apartment, but the debut of the disused building space – the one decorated with some taxidermied animals – where Connor squats. (Indeed, Connor admires a stuffed bear in his new digs, wishing that he'd killed the critter.)

POINTS OF DISCUSSION ABOUT "Slouching Toward Bethlehem":

1. By this point, Fred and Gunn are getting into such trouble because they're chatterboxes. Their blathering gave away Angel's game plan to Connor in "Benediction" (3.21), they here chirp about killing demons while Cordelia cowers behind the hotel registration desk, and in "Calvary" (4.12), they'll give Angelus verbal ammunition whilst jibbering away in the lobby. Honestly, they should resort to text messaging more often. Or learn sign language.

2. The teaser entails a pair of ambitious vampires running a tow truck service, apparently eating anyone who phones them for a lift. This actually puts them among the few vamps who're smart enough to succeed in the world – Russell from "City Of" (1.01) and Mr. Trick from *Buffy* Season Three being a couple other examples – although it's never clear if they service AAA. If so, it puts a whole new spin on a stranded person phoning AAA and being told, "Someone's on their way, M'am."

3. An amnesiac Cordelia flips through her Sunnydale High yearbook, and comes across references to a "giant snake" and "flaming arrows" (both seen in the showdown in *Buffy* 3.22, "Graduation Day"). It's a bit strange that Buffy's crew joyfully signed yearbooks after the battle and the bloodshed therein, but either way, the *real* pity is that amnesiac Cordy doesn't consider that the "giant snake" and "flaming arrows" indicate she used to play *Dungeons and Dragons*. Perhaps she couldn't stand the thought of being such a nerd.

4. The episode title is something of a puzzler, because it decently fits events to come this year – the arrival of the Beast, the apocalypse-flavored rain of fire, etc. – yet applies preciously little to the story itself. Bell was obviously applying some forethought when he picked it, and see **Pop Culture** for more.

5. When commandoes burst into Connor's abode after the commercial break, notice how the second goon to jump through a window slips and lands flat on his ass. We can't really label this a violation of continuity, but it's amusing anyway.

CHARACTER NOTES *Angel:* Claims that he likes ballads. He's not unwilling to consider Gunn's suggestion that Wesley betrayed them again [yet he never pursues the matter either]. Oddly, Fred implies that Angel used to caffeinate his blood.

• *Cordelia:* [One issue we'll discuss up-front: It strains credibility that Cordelia wants to live with Connor – his honesty with her or no – when he's quite obviously a creepy, unstable adolescent who's prone to mentioning things such as the fact that he'd like to kill a bear. You have to wonder if the Jasmine entity inside Cordelia isn't pre-conditioning her toward Connor just a little, although we're in danger of overplaying that card.]

Amnesiac Cordy recalls fundamentals such as her martial arts training and the art of flossing. She owns a blue teddy bear and a Sunnydale High '99 yearbook. When singing for Lorne, she mangles "The Greatest Love of All" [her song from *Buffy* 1.07, "The Puppet Show"]. Cordelia appears to own some rosaries and crucifixes [which implies that Cordy, like Charisma Carpenter, was raised Catholic]. Connor says that Cordelia likes shoes and doughnuts [he must have learned this from Gunn and Fred over the summer]. Cordelia's comment, upon seeing a photo of her Shannen Doherty hair from Season Two: "Yikes." [We'd have to agree.]

• *Wesley:* Takes Lilah to task for betraying him. [But as she points out, he's really mad at himself. "I don't care about Angel," Wesley keeps fibbing to her, then dashes out to warn Angel the first chance he gets.] Wes loses a bet to Lilah, as he's the first to call his business with her a "relationship," and he awards her a signed $1 bill as proof of the moment. There's a birthmark [or a bite mark from Lilah, perhaps] visible on Wesley's right shoulder blade as he crawls back into bed.

• *Gunn:* Insistent that he's more than a humble "sidekick." He prefers the moniker "Big Dog."

• *Lorne:* Appears to live in room 406 at the Hyperion. It's implied that Lorne snitched some of Cordelia's lingerie "for a friend" [make of that what you will].

• *Connor:* Angel enters Connor's abode without an invitation. [It's a bit of a goof that nobody questions this after the fact, but Connor's demon inheritance (judging by events in 4.14, "Release") probably negates the need for an invite.] Connor remembers that Cordelia was nice to him [3.21, "Benediction"], and apologizes for nearly murdering her on that occasion.

• *Lilah:* Says she never would've manipulated Wesley if she ever thought he would trust her. She claims [truthfully or no] that she spared Lorne's life on Wesley's account.

ORGANIZATIONS *Angel Investigations:* The office answering machine no longer bears any derivation of Cordy's "we help the helpless" greeting. Someone named Murray from "down at the spa" summons Gunn and Fred to kill a pregnant "demon broad."

• *Wolfram and Hart:* [Given that Lilah learns about Lorne's private "reading" of Cordelia in a frighteningly short amount of time, it seems reasonable to assume that the firm deployed a sophisticated means of monitoring the Hyperion during Angel's three-month absence. Mind, the firm only has four more episodes to enjoy this souped-up surveillance before its sudden regime change.]

DEMONOLOGY *Vampires:* Touching Cordelia's handful of rosaries makes Angel vamp out. [There's numerous occasions when vampires touch a crucifix and don't vamp out – hell, Angel successfully does so two episodes from now, never mind how Spike smokingly drapes himself over one in *Buffy* Season Seven – so he's probably just caught by surprise here.]

BEST LINE Lorne says that when he read Cordy, he got "a big, fat tummy-clenchin' onion from hell. The more layers you peel, the more you cry." (This can't avoid comparison with Spike's onion blossom fixation over on *Buffy* – after all, if vampires liked onions, you'd expect them to like "onions from hell" the most.)

THINGS THAT DON'T MAKE SENSE For starters, we're not too worried about the rapid-fire speed with which Lorne has procured a client upon his sudden return from Vegas, because Cordelia spends some time gathering her wits in her room, and it might've been an "emergency intervention" on Lorne's part. We're far more concerned about the enormous conceit that Lorne is counseling a demon (tellingly named "Eater Demon" in the script) who obviously gobbles humans like candy, and who – barring the plot contrivance of needing this character to chase Cordelia about the hotel – would rank as totally killable under any other circumstance. Indeed, said demon *sits in front of Lorne, sniffs the air for humans and drools*, but does Lorne summon Angel to eviscerate the creep? Nooooooooo, he deems it a much better idea to leave the demon alone so it can hungrily hound Cordelia, or any human who happens to wander its direction.

Angel describes the two commandoes who pounce on Cordelia outside the Hyperion as "lawyers," which seems like a misnomer. Besides, how do those two creeps fit into the plot anyway? Lilah had no reason to order them into action, because they make their kidnap attempt before Lorne "reads" Cordy. Yet it's also hard to believe they've been stationed outside the Hyperion for months now, with standing orders to, "Watch until Cordelia returns, then wait about 20 minutes and attack her." Perhaps they work for Gavin, who's inept and – lacking Lilah's resources – can only spare two goons.

We won't hash through all the instances where – as Cordelia mentions – the normally adept heroes are shockingly awful liars. Suffice to say, if they *wanted* to creep Cordy out, they're doing an exceptional job. Lorne misquotes the Book of *Revelation* as the Book of *Revelations*, and like most of fandom, we can't make heads or tails of where he disappeared to at the end of last episode. It appears that he hastily entered the hotel through a side door to quickly get to a bathroom, but he returns through the garden area. We can't fathom why, unless he went out of his way to pee in the bushes.

Connor is one of those lucky TV characters who gets to live in a disused warehouse with working electricity. Also, his stake disappears from the body of the Eater Demon during the commercial break, although it's possible the gawping heroes had the presence of mind to remove it off screen. Finally... what the hell is Gunn talking about when he asks an amnesiac Cordy, "You wanna know why we call him Lorne?" Uhhhhh... *because it's his name?* Perhaps Gunn intends to lighten the mood with the Lorne Greene joke from "Belonging" (2.19), but this doesn't exactly answer the question, and Cordelia didn't even understand the reference the first time around.

POP CULTURE "Slouching Toward Bethlehem": It originally hails from a Yeats poem, "The Second Coming," the one with the oft-repeated line "what rough beast, its hour come round at last,/Slouches towards Bethlehem to be born?" Since then, the phrase has made the rounds in other forms, including as the title of Joan Didion's prominent essay collection (1968) about America's social crisis at the time. More recently, Robert Bork, Reagan's failed Supreme Court justice nominate, authored *Slouching Toward Gomorrah: Modern Liberalism and American Decline* (1996). On the liberal front, sex columnist Dan Savage wrote *Skipping Toward Gomorrah* (2002), in which he indulged in each of the Seven Deadly Sins.

IN RETROSPECT Such a pity that Cordelia doesn't have her memories when she threatens to turn Gunn into vermin, because she could've said, given events on *Angel*'s parent show, "Don't make me turn you into a rat like Buffy... or Amy."

CRITIQUE You'll have noticed by now that we can usually highlight a few high points even in an otherwise ordinary *Angel* story, but here we're confronted with a tale that's incredibly sloppy, wretchedly executed and almost unbearably stupid at times. Just what the hell happened?

It's tempting to say that "Slouching Toward Bethlehem" goes awry because it needs to start setting up the big Season Four story arc, but the *real* problem lies in that it's unbearably hollow – Cordelia's amnesia being a prime example. Yes, it's a potent motivator for her actions, but half the episode consequently gets wasted while Cordy re-discovers what the viewers, in fact, already know. Meanwhile, Lorne starts issuing proclamations that "something wicked this way comes" – as if the Almanac calls for darkness and unspeakable evil this year – but it's all so maddeningly vague that it's impossible to work up even a drop of sweat about it.

On top of all the murky and boring bits, much of the story proves downright silly. Cordelia gets scared... mainly because Lorne implausibly counsels a demon client who eats humans. Then Cordelia gets upset that Angel lied to her... but this makes her want to run off and live with a grungy, unstable teenager in an abandoned warehouse. Throughout this book, we'll argue that Season Four cements together far better than its reputation, and that it's much better suited to DVD-viewing than original broadcast. We overwhelmingly adore this year, but there are at least three episodes (not a bad average, all things considered) that qualify as train wrecks – and however you parse "Slouching Toward Bethlehem," it's one of them.

THE LORE Bell claims that the producers decided early on to deal with an Apocalypse, as the show had loosely talked about it for three years. The highly serialized nature of Season Four, however, appears to have caught everyone somewhat by surprise. Bell noted that it became harder and harder to deploy stand-alone stories amidst an Apocalypse scenario, and stated, "My feeling is we became more successful when we said, 'F**k it, it's a novel.' People don't want to read a short story in the middle of a novel. They want to get to the next chapter of the big story, and I think that *Angel* is most successful when it's just balls-out operatic melodrama."

That said, *Entertainment Weekly* came to criticize the serial format, and Bell concurred by saying: "If you haven't watched from the beginning, it's like coming in at page 262 of a Stephen King novel." (Gross, *Cinefantastique*, Oct. 2003)

• The set team went to increasing lengths to cover up Carpenter's real-life pregnancy until the "big reveal" later in the season, and Hallett noted, "They raised countertops, had her carry bags, and cut a hole in the bed so her bum would go down to hide her stomach. I give her all the credit in the world, she worked until she was nine months and one week pregnant. I thought she was going to give birth on stage seven at Paramount." (Hallett, *BBC Cult*, April 2003)

When is Cordelia Cordelia?

Any proper analysis of Season Four requires that we distinguish between when Cordelia actually is Cordelia, and when the entity known as Jasmine is controlling her body. Starting with "Apocalypse Nowish" (4.07), we'll use the term "Evil Cordy" to reference when Jasmine is driving Cordelia's form. But to properly draw the line here:

• **"Deep Down" (4.01) to "The House Always Wins" (4.03):** Cordelia appears as herself, albeit while residing on a higher plane. She spends the entire summer plus change in this "Heaven," as the Jasmine entity (presumably) requires some time to impregnate itself into Cordelia's body.

• **"Slouching Toward Bethlehem" (4.04) to "Spin the Bottle" (4.06):** The Jasmine entity returns to Earth in

Cordelia's form, but the shock of transition makes it go dormant. Cordelia's mind remains in charge of her body, albeit without any memories. As proof, notice how she greatly values honesty (as with 3.21, "Benediction"), the compassion with which she address her smooching Connor (next episode) and her cautiously wondering if she and Angel were in love (ditto) – all textbook Cordelia. Oh, and Cordelia puzzles through her amnesiac state even while alone in "Bethlehem," and it's a stretch to think the Jasmine persona would do that.

• **"Apocalypse Nowish" (4.07):** The end of "Spin the Bottle" entails a futzed-up attempt to break Cordelia's memory block, which makes Cordy's personality go to sleep while the Jasmine entity seizes control. Personality-wise, "Cordelia" becomes far more manipulative, and she starts getting visions that with hindsight are clearly false. Her head minion, the Beast, makes an appearance at this point, and we doubt this is coincidence.

• **"Habeas Corpses" (4.08) to "Inside Out" (4.17):** Evil Cordy flummoxes the heroes – Connor in particular – and gives birth to itself. The genuine Cordelia stays in her body but goes comatose, and doesn't utter a peep until...

• **"You're Welcome" (5.12):** Cordelia returns – err, arguably – for one last appearance after "Spin the Bottle," and... well, check that story to see what happens next.

4.05: "Supersymmetry"

"Vengeance. Sounds good."

Air Date: Nov. 3, 2002; **Writers:** Elizabeth Craft, Sarah Fain; **Director:** Bill Norton

SUMMARY Fred stokes her waylaid academic career and renews ties with her former professor, Dr. Oliver Seidel. But when Fred presents a paper at a physics symposium, a portal opens above her head and a tentacled creature nearly sucks her inside before Angel and Gunn intervene.

Fred learns that Seidel has been dabbling with portals using mystic texts, and has apparently cast several of his assistants to other dimensions out of professional jealousy. A vengeful Fred vows to kill Seidel, realizing that he was responsible for her five-year exile in Pylea. Gunn and Angel caution that such an act would stain Fred's soul, but she takes after Seidel with a crossbow anyway. Seidel summons a demon through a portal, trying to escape in the confusion. As Angel engages the monster, Fred uses an incantation to open an energy-charged and clearly lethal portal, intending for Seidel to fall into it. Unwilling to let Fred commit murder, Gunn snaps Seidel's neck, then casts his body into the portal. The dimensional opening closes, leaving Fred and Gunn emotionally distanced from one another.

FIRSTS AND LASTS As you might have suspected, "Super-symmetry" abruptly witnesses the end of the Gunn/Fred romance, although they'll sputter along in various forms of denial and simmering turmoil for some episodes yet. It's also the first episode credited to the writing duo of Elizabeth Craft and Sarah Fain, who'll factor pretty heavily into Season Four and a bit of Season Five. It's the first and only "appearance" of Cordelia's parents, seen in one of Cordy's photographs (her mother looks blonde, albeit possibly not a natural one), and the first instance of Fred wearing a (scandalously short, in this instance) mini-skirt. Mind, she's going to get plenty of practice next season.

Ah, yes... and it's also the earliest example of Charisma Carpenter's pregnancy starting to show. At the very least, a couple of the shirts that Cordelia dons make her look a bit preggers, and we know her expanding belly was a concern a mere two episodes from now (see **The Lore** in 4.07, "Apocalypse Nowish").

POINTS OF DISCUSSION ABOUT "Supersymmetry":

1. The ease with which Fred returns to academia after being listed as a missing person seems awkward but isn't technically wrong. That said, this episode presumes that nobody in her old department – indeed, nobody attending the symposium, where she's a billed speaker – thinks to ask, "Hey, Fred, didn't I see your face plastered all over a milk carton? What the hell happened?" After all, a missing persons poster of Fred appeared in "Belonging" (2.19), so we know they were distributed. And heck... the comic shop guy in this story certainly knows about Fred's disappearance, and he didn't even know her personally.

Now, you could counter-argue that the over-sized L.A. grants some anonymity, and that Fred was a bit shy five years back, so perhaps only her library co-workers took notice when the poor girl vanished. Or perhaps, if we're being fair, Fred prepares a cover story that we never hear her use, her most obvious excuse being: "I decided to take some years off to travel the globe, and they listed me as missing. Would you believe it? I was shocked... *shocked*, I tell you."

2. All manner of glitches are rectified (but see **Things That Don't Make Sense** anyway) if we attribute Seidel as being one of those "brilliant but alarmingly careless" academic types. After all, this is a man who keeps his portal-making book in his office where any hapless undergraduate might find it, and he's doubly silly for leaving Fred – one of the few people who would recognize the book's importance – alone in there with it, particularly when he puts a book intended for her near the portal text and leaves the room, the blithering fool. Even then, Fred only notices the portal-text because Seidel "disguised" it with a plasma and fluid turbulence text cover, then mis-shelved in the section on

neutrinos. He evidently wasn't kidding when he said he "had his own system."

3. It's often the ambiguities of the Wesley-Lilah relationship that make it so intoxicating, but to look at the mass of evidence, it seems that Lilah has fallen for Wesley hard. It was telling back in "Deep Down" (4.01) when Lilah proved so defensive of Wesley to Linwood, because she could've just said, "Yeah, I'm sleeping with him for information" if that were the case. Sure, she betrayed Wes' confidence last episode, but then, Lilah can't do anything simple. Couple that with her obvious jealousy here over Fred, and it's clear that her regard for Wesley extends beyond their just being bed buddies.

Meanwhile, Lilah's treachery last episode was clearly a bucket of water in the face to Wesley, as the two of them never (on screen, at least) have sex again, save notably when Lilah pretends to be Fred ("Apocalypse Nowish").

4. As with a lot of *Angel* stories, the fashion choices give some insight to the characters. Connor, who previously displayed the dress sense of a mule, has now taken to wearing a sporty, green polo shirt. Yup, he's obviously smitten with Cordy. Meanwhile, Fred's eroding sanity throughout this story mirrors itself in the attention (or rather, lack of attention) that she gives to her hair and choice of clothes. And we finally learn what style Lilah prefers in her off-hours: Leather, of course. (Amusingly, this makes her look like the "anti-Fred" when she strolls into the auditorium to stalk Wesley.)

P.S. The member of the cast who's impossible to read through her clothes right now? Cordelia, who goes through multiple wardrobe shifts, same as ever.

5. Counting Seidel, Elliot (4.02, "Ground State") and DeMarco (4.03, "The House Always Wins"), three out of the five episodes in this season have featured one-off slimy humans as the villains. It's not a problem in itself, but no wonder the producers deployed the Beast two episodes from now, just to return a sense of "Hulk smash!" to the proceedings.

6. Mercifully, the mystical nature of dimensional portals means that we needn't worry too hard about some of the details here. Such as, oh, how Fred's cell phone comes equipped with an "ancient portal-opening glyphs" font, which she glimpses as Seidel transmits such an incantation over her phone. Then again, perhaps Fred installed such a font on her cell for research. We'd venture to say that if such a font existed, instead of "Wingdings," it'd be called "Portaldings."

CHARACTER NOTES *Angel:* Gives Fred and Gunn a ponderous look as they head up to bed. [4.12, "Calvary" claims that Angel noticed the distance between them, and correctly deduced that Seidel was murdered.] Angel here uses a variation of his photographic memory when he assembles a few chairs and internally recreates Fred's lecture, then mentally studies the attendees. [It's the equivalent of a *Star Trek* holodeck environment, but in Angel's head.] He describes this ability as an "automatic reflex" [and indeed, he's never seen to use it again].

A "comic book guy" [named Jared in the script] claims there's whole "forums on Angel in chat rooms" [which is profoundly stupid wording, frankly]. Regardless, nobody seems clear on whether or not Angel actually exists. [That's a bit implausible, but it does, at least, explain why groupies haven't besieged the Hyperion over the past two years.]

• *Cordelia:* Lip-mashes Connor after patrolling with the lad and staking a vampire, only to later tell him they shouldn't have done that. [See **When is Cordelia Cordelia?**, and compare with "Apocalypse Nowish," when Cordy's not in the driver's seat.] She and Connor are platonically sharing a bed, but Connor claims that Cordy's "always" stealing the covers.

Cordy owns fuzzy slippers because her feet get cold easily. She realizes she and Angel were close, and here approaches him to ask if they were in love [see next episode].

• *Wesley:* Enough of a man-of-action to attend Fred's symposium with a formidable knife about his person. Wesley has been keeping tabs on Fred's activities in academia, struggles [with some success it seems] to understand her physics theories *and* surrenders an afternoon of nookie with Lilah to attend Fred's physics talk. He's evidently not worried about Lilah being alone in his apartment [same as "Apocalypse Nowish"]. He reiterates Gunn and Angel's concern that Fred needs to live with the consequences of her actions, but ultimately doesn't intervene when she goes after Seidel.

• *Gunn:* Shows a good knowledge of comic books [as with 5.16, "Shells," and see **Pop Culture**], and presumably frequents the Thwack! comic store. Gunn concedes that he might've advocated vengeance against Seidel a few years ago, but now believes Fred's bloodlust deviates from their mission of helping people.

• *Fred:* Can cite important baseball players in a metaphor [again, see **Pop Culture**], and now able to open a portal by merely speaking a few words aloud. [We might imagine she obtained this talent by poring through Wesley's books, especially if they referenced texts that they brought back from Pylea. Even so, it's still a massively advanced form of generating portals; compare with her slower portal-opening speed in 4.09, "Long Day's Journey."]

Fred was going to major in history, but switched fields after taking Seidel's physics class. By the end of her first semester, Fred was impressively taking on Weakly Interactive Massive Particles (WIMPs). She dreamed about discovering a revolutionary concept in quantum particles and getting noticed. Her re-entry into academia entailed her writing *Supersymmetry and P-Dimensional Subspace* for *Modern*

Physics Review, and her experience with portals has evidently yielded some interesting insights about "string theory" and "string compactification theory."

Fred owns a Motorola cell phone, and Gunn implies that cocoa is a comfort drink for her [reiterated in dialogue cut from 4.06, "Spin the Bottle"].

• *Lorne:* Resting in bed after last episode, and refuses to read Cordelia again.

• *Connor:* Retrieves some of Cordelia's keepsakes from the Hyperion, but petty enough to omit her pictures of Angel.

• *Lilah:* Tries to appease Wesley with the gift of an ancient metal helmet, which apparently "cost a fortune." Her license plate is 3ZV0879. An information-seeking Angel rips the top off her car.

• *Dr. Oliver Seidel, BS, MS, PhD:* Full professor of Theoretical Physics. [Seidel has obviously improved his ability to generate portals over the years, far beyond what he could accomplish when he dumped Fred into Pylea. His ability to secretly open a portal while he's on-stage probably owes to his transmitting portal glyphs with a pre-programmed cell phone. Otherwise, you'd almost have to conclude that his assistant Laurie triggers the portal to give Seidel an alibi, and it complicates the story too much if he's got an accomplice.]

Seidel has consigned at least five of his talented students (including Fred) to other dimensions, but has apparently spared Laurie Drummond – the TA for High Energy Physics when Fred in school – because she's dull enough to not overshadow him. [Angel views a list of names on Seidel's web page, and these may be Seidel's other victims. If so, their names are Naoki Hara, Sadie Atkins, Nishad Suri and Marvin Eck.]

Seidel used a different grading standard for Fred in recognition of her talents, and scored her last test as an A- when she deserved an A+.

THE LIBRARY Wes' books detail some sort of torture practiced in ancient Egypt.

MAGIC Seidel opens a portal and summons a Voynok Demon by chanting *Increpito immanis barathrum copeo lacero*. Fred creates a portal to a fire-laden, hellish domain [but *not* Quor'toth, as there's no portals there (3.20, "A New World")] by chanting *Klyv mat chyvma, klvma chyt*.

BEST LINE Fred, pondering a means of torturing Seidel: "How about a flail whipping? Would that take a nice long time?" Angel: "Hours, if you do it right... Not that you should do it at all. Ever."

THINGS THAT DON'T MAKE SENSE There's a fair amount of retcon regarding Fred's exile in Pylea, meaning this story doesn't join well with "Belonging," but let's point out the big inconsistency: Seidel must have deposited the Pylean portal book in Fred's library in the hopes that Fred would stop and read aloud from it – not an inconceivable sequence of events, though not terribly convincing either. But even if you can swallow that, why on Earth would Seidel then leave such a rare and dangerous book collecting dust in the library for five years until the Powers directed Angel and company to retrieve it? The suggestion that he's a) "got his own filing system," or b) doesn't think anyone will notice the book in such a little-used section of the library hardly seems adequate. In short, has Seidel got so many portal-creating books that he can leave one lying about Los Angeles?

The story opens with Fred happily screaming that an article of hers has been published in *Modern Physics Review* as if this is a surprise, even though magazines generally inform authors ahead of publication that their work has been accepted. Angel and Gunn say they've "got to act fast" to stop Fred from murdering Seidel, yet they seem to do absolutely nothing in the span of time it takes her to leave the Hyperion, drink beer with Wesley, nearly fall into Seidel's second portal-trap and research a means of dealing with the man. As with the magic-using Marcus in "Carpe Noctem" (3.4), Angel knows he's dealing with a foe who can open dimensional portals, yet he insists on standing around like a complete baboon while Seidel reads an incantation and summons forth a formidable demon. Surely with his vampire speed, he could've smacked the book out of Seidel's hands before he got further than a syllable?

And the obvious point... the final portal exerts an exceptional pull on Seidel, yet there's hardly any suction/wind at all on Fred and Gunn.

POP CULTURE Gunn threatens a comic book geek with: "Think *Daredevil* #181. I'm Bullseye, you're Elektra. One wins, one dies." For benefit of non-comic book fans, the issue in question involved Bullseye brutally killing Elektra with a sai through the heart. (In typical fashion, Marvel resurrected her.)

Anyone perusing the comic shop décor will notice the large number of Dark Horse Comic properties – unsurprising, given that they published the *Angel* and *Buffy* comic lines – and Angel personally peruses a copy of Dark Horse's defunct *Ghost* series. Also on display is *Wizard*, essentially the *Rolling Stone* of comic books, and a giant cardboard cutout for *Shi*, the Japanese/American warrior created by Billy Tucci.

• Fred compares two physics speakers to acclaimed baseball players "Nomar Garciaparra and Sammy Sosa," but the reference – written in 2002 – has gotten more awkward with age. Garciaparra was a six-time All Star shortstop who played for the Boston Red Sox (1996-2004), then was plagued by injuries and fell out with the Chicago Cubs, only to make a comeback as the L.A. Dodgers' first baseman. Sosa was a star right-fielder for the Cubs and ranked fifth on the major leagues' all-time home run list, but he's currently out of baseball due to declining skills and steroid suspicions.

IT'S REALLY ABOUT... What happens when romantic partners grow emotionally at different rates. Gunn's love and loyalty for Fred are beyond reproach, but he stubbornly refuses to accept how much she's changed in the last year. A clearly put-out Fred sums this up, not without justification, by declaring: "Angel and Gunn want me to be all sweetness and light." But lest you think that Fred and Gunn weren't growing apart until the resolution of this story, observe how Fred doesn't acknowledge Gunn as her boyfriend when she introduces him to Seidel.

Or if you like, it's about a clash of different worlds. Fred's taking a tepid step into a life of academia that Gunn simply can't understand; nor can he relate to her rage over her time in Pylea. In some small way, her wrath almost seems like a subtext about rape... the first portal in this episode makes Fred re-live a previous crime and shatters her feelings of security, to the point that Gunn simply can't relate when she decides to confront the aggressor. As part and parcel of all this, it's obvious that Fred and Wesley are starting to speak the same language, whereas Fred and Gunn no longer are. The disconnect shows up in little ways, such as when Fred rebuffs Gunn's offer of cocoa but accepts a cold beer from Wes.

None of this, you understand, is to fault Gunn for tirelessly supporting his girlfriend. It's simply to point out that sometimes, love isn't enough if the people involved aren't on the same level.

CRITIQUE There are two main criticisms of this episode, neither of which holds much water. Continuity cops want to complain that it doesn't join well with "Becoming," and while it's certainly preferable to save continuity if possible, we'd advocate chucking it into the fireplace if it impedes a striking story. Besides, for all someone might gripe, "Supersymmetry" only trips up in a few of its details, and never does anything as overwhelmingly glaring as (say) to claim that Fred opened the Pylean portal in a bagel shop, not the library.

The second protest usually stems from fans who're incensed about the radical reformatting of Fred's character, and it's readily obvious that Gunn and Angel aren't the only ones who can't accept the changes she's been undergoing for some time now. But they're perfectly reasonable changes, especially if you consider the context here. Lest we forget, Fred is made to confront the man who exiled her to a fugitive slave existence in a demon dimension for five years, and who obviously wanted her to die in the process. Honestly, how would you expect someone to react to this? How would *you* react in such a situation? If anything, "Supersymmetry" avoids the cop-out that Fred should – in the main – overlook the offense, even though Seidel is a four-time killer (at least) and even though prosecution is utterly impossible in this case. A murderous rage on her part seems perfectly understandable – not that we're advocating or applauding it, you understand.

The simple truth is, many viewers initially fell in love with Fred because (in a nutshell) she was "sweet." But keeping her nothing but "sweet" forever would get downright boring, in the same fashion that five years of bumbling Wesley would've gotten old fast. So what's really neat about "Supersymmetry" – beyond the charming dialogue, the ripping pace and the shocking twists – is that Fred has never seemed more ***human***, and we consequently learn more about her in the first ten minutes here than we did in the whole of "Fredless." That's no small feat, and we're still glowing to think about it.

THE LORE Writers Elizabeth Craft and Sarah Fain had known each other since preparatory school, and before *Angel* they'd co-written for shows such as *Just Deal*, *All About Us* and *Glory Days*. Whedon expressed an interest in hearing a pitch from them, and they fared well in straightaway suggesting – and getting commissioned for – the main gist of this story. (Triplett, *Kansascity.com*, April 15, 2004) Minear (still onboard as Consulting Producer) and Whedon tweaked the script, with Minear suggesting that Gunn should kill the professor. Craft thought the final result was good drama, but lamented somewhat that Fred didn't kill the villain instead. (DiLullo, *CityofAngel.com*)

• The script included a pronunciation guide, enabling the actors to wrap their lips around phrases like "peau de soie" (PO de SWAH).

4.06: "Spin the Bottle"

"A memory spell that is guaranteed to get our Cordy back to the way she was... I'm telling you, Swingers, there's no way this can fail."

Air Date: Nov. 10, 2002; **Writer/Director:** Joss Whedon

SUMMARY Lorne procures instructions for a memory spell from one of his clients, hoping it will cure Cordelia's amnesia. Angel's crew, Cordelia and Wesley assemble at the hotel and begin the ritual, but the spell goes haywire. Lorne falls unconscious, and everyone else mentally reverts to their teenage years, losing all comprehension of their adult lives.

The baffled heroes conclude they're part of a test, one that entails their tracking down a vampire and killing it. Angel gets outted as a vamp, leading to much scrambling about the hotel. Connor shows up and teen-Cordelia promises him sex if he'll kill the vampire, leading to an extremely eager Connor brawling with his father. Fortunately, Lorne recovers and devises a means of undoing the spell, returning everyone to normal save...

Cordelia, who regains her memories, but recoils to see a vision of a horrific rock-covered demon. Traumatized, Cordelia acknowledges to Angel that they were in love, then flees the hotel.

FIRSTS AND LASTS It's the end of amnesiac Cordelia and the Hyperion kitchen (although it looks different to the one seen in 3.19, "The Price" – does the hotel have two?). The Jasmine entity takes charge of Cordelia's body for the next 11 episodes, and it's the first tentative glimpse of her head lackey, the Beast, who'll more properly debut next episode.

Wesley dons his upgraded wrist-stakes for the first time, it's the second and last time that Lorne smokes (the first was in 3.05, "Fredless") and it's the only example of an *Angel* character breaking the Fourth Wall with such wanton abandon. Also, it's the final instance that anyone thinks painting a supernatural symbol on the lobby floor and casting a spell is remotely a good idea.

POINTS OF DISCUSSION ABOUT "Spin the Bottle":

1. Anyone who's seen this episode will doubtlessly remember the framing sequence, which features an on-stage Lorne relating these events in a nightclub. Some effort has gone into wondering where the framing sequences occur on the *Angel* timeline, but we'd advocate viewing it as a narrative device, more of a post-modern prank on Whedon's part. The final twist, in which we discover that Lorne has been addressing an empty room despite our hearing the audience, should sufficiently prove that it's not really occurring. Also remember that Lorne asks the TV viewers at home, after a commercial break, "Well, those were some exciting products. Am I right?"

And, Cordelia's "witnessing" of the Beast is undoubtedly based on Lounge-Lorne's interpretation of events, not what actually occurs in Cordelia's head. Best to bear that in mind.

2. Teen-Cordelia isn't so much a perfect replica of her *Buffy* persona as a fusion of that character and her refined adult self of Season Three. Perhaps we're over-stating the point, but Teen-Cordy displays a much better vocabulary than we'd normally give her credit for. Examples include: "This is a clarion call for snippety," "so we've heard from the socially handi-capable," "homo-erotic buddy cop session" and "I second the motion to be really bored."

3. Teen-Wesley calls Teen-Gunn a "pugilist," and Teen-Gunn responds: "Your ass better pray I don't look that word up." For benefit of anyone who didn't bother: Pugilist, *n.* one who fights with the fists; a boxer, usually a professional.

4. Commentators often insist on citing this story as a copycat to *Buffy* 6.08, "Tabula Rasa," which also involves a memory spell that backfires, but in truth the implementation of the two stories is very different. If anything, "Spin the Bottle" holds about as many parallels to *Buffy* 4.21, "Primeval," in which the heroes pool their consciousnesses in a cross-legged ritual, with a lot of trippy effects.

5. Compared to your standard *Angel* story, there's an ever-climbing number of references to sex, drugs, hookers, breast-fondling, erection gaffes, all manner of debauchery and what's undoubtedly the show's greatest masturbation joke when Angel "tests out" his vamp face in the bathroom, complete with "stretching face" noises. Coupled with the swipe at conservatism when Cordelia states, "I know who's president, and that I sorta wish I didn't," can you tell, gentle reader, that it's a Whedon script? Of course you can. (And for more on Whedon's left-leaning views, check out Fred's office poster in 5.01, "Conviction.")

CHARACTER NOTES *Angel:* Thinks Cordelia was his dearest friend. Teen-Angel – or "Liam," as he's more properly known – is hostile to the English and thinks his conservative-minded father is a hypocrite. But he doesn't possess his father's knowledge about vampirism [see 1.15, "The Prodigal"], and – upon discovering that he *is* a vampire – almost playfully examines his newfound abilities. Teen-Angel loses his Irish accent after a few moments. [It's undoubtedly to spare everyone from suffering through Boreanaz's appalling "Irish" voice, but it's hard to cite a reason for it. After all, Teen-Fred gets considerably more Texan.]

• *Cordelia:* Remembers all the shoe stores in the Beverly Center, but possesses no personal context about her past. [It's now fairly obvious that when Cordelia returned from the higher plane, her memories went dormant along with the Jasmine entity. Lorne's spell ultimately performs a flip-flop, giving Jasmine dominance and allowing her to tap Cordelia's recollections with ease. At best, Jasmine has been a passive observer of events for three episodes, meaning she probably wasn't inside Cordelia's mind going, "Gah! Gah! I can't control her!"]

Teen-Cordelia seems taken with Angel. ["Hello, salty goodness" she tells him, echoing their first meeting in *Buffy* 1.05, "Never Kill a Boy on the First Date."] But she's hostile and cutting to Gunn, Fred, Wesley and virtually every member of the human race who isn't in her high school clique.

There's no avoiding it... Teen-Cordelia acts like a bit of a strumpet, first fixated on Angel, then readily promising Connor a BIG reward if he kills the vampire. [All told, this should eliminate all doubt that Cordelia got through high school with her virginity intact.]

• *Wesley:* The weapons-supplier Emile [4.03, "The House Always Wins"] equips Wesley with advanced wrist-cuffs that can project wooden stakes, or extend a piece of metal as a sword. A little disturbingly, when Gunn gets pushy, Wes makes him back off by leveling a wrist-stake in his face.

Teen-Wesley was "Head Boy" at the Watcher's Academy in Southern Hampshire. And no, he doesn't see the entendre in that title. He's heard stories about Slayers being tested in a vampire-laden environment [witnessed in *Buffy* 3.10, "Helpless"].

• *Gunn:* More hostile toward Wes regarding Fred, especially once he realizes that Fred asked Wes for help last episode. Gunn is concerned that he's just the muscle of the group [even though he neglected the opportunity to run the agency during Angel's three-month absence]. He's been killing vampires since he was 12.

• *Fred:* Avoids talking to Gunn while in bed with him. Fred went to [Woodrow Wilson, according to the script] high school in San Antonio. Teen-Fred is fixated on scoring weed, even while she's supposedly hunting deadly vampires. She readily believes in aliens and any number of government conspiracy theories, some of them fronted by her friend Levon. While deluded by the memory spell, Fred looks at a fern in the lobby, says, "This is important. It's so beautiful," and throws up on it [and see 5.20, "The Girl in Question" for the possible significance of this].

• *Lorne:* His "reading" of a wraith is his first since his head got drilled [4.04, "Slouching Toward Bethlehem"]. He hasn't seen Wesley since "Sleep Tight" (3.16), but evidently holds no animosity for the beating Wes dealt him in that story. [Side Note: Lorne can also play the piano, provided we accept his lounge self as anything approaching "true."]

• *Connor:* Cordelia here states that Connor is 18 [see **Points of Discussion**, next episode]. He's mostly led by his, err, groin in this story, partly due to Teen-Cordy's offer of nookie, and partly because a hooker offers him a "reward" when he saves her from a vampire (though he's left hanging when she wants to charge him $50).

THE HYPERION According to Cordy, it's got five floors. [This matches, in the main, with the exterior shots.]

PYLEA In Pylean, "Lo-lath ch-*owrng* ne bruun" [that's transcribed direct from the script] means, "I may be prepared to shout a joyful chant." Fred thinks "Kaya-No-m'tek" means "may your words please the gods," but it actually means "may you orally please the gods," owing to an inflection error.

DEMONOLOGY *Demons of the "Karathmamanyuhg family":* They're nocturnal, and feed on roots. Or possibly human effluvia. [The closed captioning spells it "Karathmamanygh," but we've favored the script.]

MAGIC *The Memory Spell:* Provided by one of Lorne's clients, a wraith who's a "sweet girl, but not overly tangible," and professionally deals in memory spells. [The script contains more gibberish about the spell, noting that six participants are needed to represent the "six spheres of consciousness, the six gifts from the Lords of Shah-teyaman, the six walls of the house of truth."] The spell boils down to a few weird ingredients, with Angel's crew sitting cross-legged and uttering a couple of sentences, so it's hardly what you'd call complex. As the script confirms, the central bottle was passed through the wraith and contains its "liquid essence" (which isn't wraith pee, as Gunn implies).

[It's possible that if Cordelia hadn't smashed the bottle, everyone would've wandered around, tripping over themselves and vomiting on plants, then recovered while Cordelia recovered her memories. Then again, the initial confusion might not be "normal" for the spell at all. The Jasmine entity's presence – or as Lorne implies, everyone's ferociously tattered relationships – might make the spell go head over arse from the start. Theoretically, Lorne's Pylean pedigree protected his memories, or more likely it's because he was unconscious when Cordy broke the bottle.

[Deciding what makes everyone revert to their teenage memories is a bit tougher, especially as it's not a uniform regression of time – in Angel's case, the spell mentally throws him back nearly 260 years... actually, more like 360, given his century of being trapped in a hell dimension on *Buffy*. We note, however, that the heroes instigate the spell at the same location where teenage Connor came through the Quor'toth rift in "The Price" (3.19). Connor's age is up for debate, but he's roughly that age, and it might've created a sort of magical "ripple effect."]

Lorne completes the spell with some goo he prepares with a mortar and pestle, then dabbles on everyone's tongues. [He's not totally voiding the spell, as nobody expects Cordelia to return to her amnesiac state.] Items used in the memory spell include what looks like a root beer bottle or two.

BEST LINE Amid all the frivolity, it's adult Wesley's matter-of-fact answer to Gunn's question of "what happened to you": "I had my throat cut, and all of my friends abandoned me."

THINGS THAT DON'T MAKE SENSE The nature of the memory spell accounts for most of the story's inconsistencies/oversights, because "It's magic!" really does solve an awful lot of questions. However, there's an inconsistency in that "Spin the Bottle" picks up immediately after the previous story, yet Angel's facial scar – the one that (ironically) Cordelia mentioned last episode – has miraculously healed in the time between Cordelia's question and Angel's answer. He's looking cleaned-up too, and he's sporting a new haircut.

Oh, and it's a bit overplayed that amnesiac Cordy can't decide if she and Angel were in love, or if he was stalking her. Granted, she's not particularly trustful of others right now, but simply making the rounds to everyone and pointedly asking, "Hey, was Angel harassing me?", should shake out some answers one way or another. And finally, allowing that everyone's feeling a bit off kilter in this story, it's weird that nobody thinks to wonder about the large scar that's slashed across Wesley's throat.

IN RETROSPECT The call girl that Connor saves tells him, "Why don't you ride home to Mama?" Given baby Connor's relationship with Cordelia, it's hideously apt.

IT'S REALLY ABOUT... How even the most accomplished of adults were once teenagers, and therefore numbered among the most messed-up people on the planet. *Buffy* touched on this in 3.06, "Band Candy," which entailed Sunnydale's adults reverting to their roots, not to mention Giles and Joyce suddenly doing it atop a police car. But here, you realize even more potently how much people change as they mature, because the heroes' well-established relationships go out the window. Moreover, their teen selves would probably find the thought of them working together as adults utterly unthinkable.

Tangentially, it's about how teenagers can't control their own biology – hence all the bits with Angel's vamp face, Wesley's "spurting" stakes and the fact that teenage guys (Connor especially) will do anything for sex.

TONIGHT AT... ? Lounge-Lorne, our narrator, sings "The Way We Were," and with far more success than Harmony in 2.17, "Disharmony."

CRITIQUE Inherently, this episode is quite the risk because it lacks a "hook" such as the puppet-themed approach of "Smile Time" (5.14), or the style of something like "Waiting in the Wings." It's chiefly just a bunch of characters acting bewildered in an otherwise empty building, with no tangible villain save confusion and miscommunication. For this reason, "Spin the Bottle," usually isn't the first episode that pops to mind when fans name their favorite *Angel* episode.

But even if it's not a show-stopper, this story proves the old chestnut that some of the best dramas can, if required, consist of two people sitting in a black room. Or in this case, six people sitting about an otherwise empty hotel lobby. There's not exactly a wealth of plot here ("A memory spell mentally reverts everyone to being teenagers, but Lorne soon clears it all up"), but in the sizzling jokes, the puberty metaphors, the innate silliness, Whedon's astounding grasp of all the character inversions and more, "Spin the Bottle" is almost unparalleled. As such, it jousts with "Smile Time" for the position of being the funniest *Angel* story, and also shows off Whedon's impressive ability to move from sheer farce to deadly seriousness at the drop of a stake. If it weren't so contingent on continuity (and the special-effect of Wesley's wrist-stakes), you could almost perform it as a stage play.

What's all the more astonishing is that Whedon sets out to relive some old elements – mainly "bitchy" Cordelia and "klutzy" Wesley – yet none of it feels like a retread. The story itself jumps from level to level too fast, even as it grounds itself in the current *Angel* set-up and keeps a safe distance from Sunnydale. If push came to shove, then, we'd concede that other *Angel* stories technically outdo this one... but perhaps no other episode exemplifies why fans adore Whedon so much. It's first and foremost because of the masterful storytelling that comes across in his scripts, with everything else being details.

THE LORE The genesis for this story, as has been widely reported, was a reminiscing conversation Whedon and Denisof had about the days of Old School *Angel* and *Buffy*, with bumbling Wesley and snarky Cordelia. The resulting script was tailored to mostly occur in the Hyperion lobby, as Whedon wanted to avoid the expense of going elsewhere. (The lavish expense that went into the next story, "Apocalypse Nowish," probably also necessitated cannibalizing the budget from other episodes.)

• Numerous lines were cut, which arguably makes "Spin the Bottle" the No. 1 *Angel* script worth purchasing, either as the illustrated IDW Publishing comic or direct from the Official Fan Club (www.angelfanclub.com). Special mention should go to Wesley's prat-fall in Act Four... it was added at the last minute, as those involved thought it'd be criminal if "buffoon" Wesley got through this story without taking a dive. (By the way, if you haven't watched Denisof's fall on slo-mo, you're missing out.)

Other notable script-deletions include... Fred gets out of bed to fetch some cocoa, and has an awkward conversation with Gunn before Angel asks for their help... Wesley test-fires his wrist-stake and breaks a vase, then comments, "Gift from my aunt. Always hated that thing."... Angel invites a towel-clad Cordelia down to the ritual with, "Come as you are. I mean, not as you are, but with clothes. Of your choosing."... Lorne quiets everyone with, "Hush, puppies."... the tied-up

Lorne bemoans the heroes' ineptitude, then tells the viewer, "Good thing that pert little Slayer's still kickin' around, am I right?"... Teen-Fred reveals that she's adept at *Dungeons and Dragons*... Teen-Cordy ducks behind the lobby sofa, and Teen-Angel menacingly says, "Don't think you'll escape notice, hiding behind that poof!" (Teen-Wesley's response: "Now see here... oh, her.")... Teen-Fred asks Lorne, "You promise you're not some alien that's been secretly probing me?" and Lorne responds, "No, honey, we're just good friends."... Lounge-Lorne starts the episode by implying that TV mogul Aaron Spelling is a demon, and wraps things up hoping that Patti LaBelle secretly wants to be his best friend.

4.07: "Apocalypse Nowish"

"Big, powerful, clawing its way up through the bowels of the earth to slaughter us all. That pretty much covers it."

Air Date: Nov. 17, 2002; **Writer:** Steven S. DeKnight; **Director:** Vern Gillum

SUMMARY Mystical occurrences in L.A. shoot through the roof, with Biblical-level plagues afflicting the citizens. Cordy gets another vision of the rocky demon she witnessed last episode, and feels drawn to the alley behind the defunct Caritas. There, Cordelia and Connor bear witness as the formidable demon, simply named "the Beast," rips itself from the ground and flies off.

The Beast ventures to the Sky Temple nightclub, then slaughters the patrons and arranges their corpses in an alchemy symbol for fire. Overwhelmingly defeating Angel's crew in battle, the Beast completes a ritual that channels energy through the bodies and shoots a column of fire aloft, making it rain fire on L.A. As the heroes recover, the rain of fire moves Cordelia to feel sympathy for Connor and sleep with him. Unfortunately, Angel checks on the pair of them and spies their coupling.

FIRSTS AND LASTS It's the tragic end of Gunn's trademark hubcap axe, which the Beast twists completely out of shape, and it's effectively the only time that Lorne accompanies the group into battle. Also, in what'll become a trend up through the series finale, it's the first time someone (Angel) gets chucked through a stone/wood column of sorts. Somewhat breathtakingly, it's Wesley's first outing with guns. Lots of guns.

With the Jasmine entity driving Cordelia's body, it's the first time it lies about getting a vision from the Powers. Oh, and it's the debut of the Beast in the flesh (so to speak).

Let's also have a moment of silence, please, for the last time that Angel eludes the firm's vampire detectors and turns up unexpectedly in Lilah's office. Come Season Five, he won't need such subterfuge, even if it seems like hosts of other characters will.

POINTS OF DISCUSSION ABOUT "Apocalypse Nowish":

1. The Beast opens its offensive against L.A., which will entail the rocky bastard performing all sorts of Apocalypse-laden stunts. It's very impressive, but curious when you wonder how this benefits the Beast's master, the Jasmine entity. The most immediate and obvious answer is that... the Beast is simply a grandiose distraction, solely tailored to keep Angel's crew from noticing anything odd about Cordelia until it's too late. Later this year, Evil Cordy will release Angelus for much the same reason.

The show never bothers to explain, however, the various plagues – mass droves of rats, snakes and birds; five reported cases of "bleeding walls," yadda yadda yadda – that precede the Beast's arrival on Earth. Is the Beast, working from its lava-flavored domain, undertaking rituals that trigger hordes of birds, rats, snakes, etc., simply for show? We tend to doubt it. However, it's possible that the plagues are effectively a "pre-shock" to the Beast's arrival. To put it another way, the Beast's arrival might displace a huge amount of localized magic in L.A., and consequently wash up all sorts of terrors (so to speak) from the magical "storm drain."

2. Cordelia's coupling with Connor looked certifiably insane on initial broadcast, and – to be fair to everyone who nearly drank hemlock over this development – it *did* seem massively out of character for Cordy. She never slept with Angel and took her sweet time with Groo, so it seemed faintly appalling that she'd roll in the hay with a teenager after a brief kiss in "Supersymmetry" (4.05), and on the flimsiest of premises. "You never had a childhood," she tells Connor, then proceeds to rob him of the last remnants of it. Re-watch the story with the Jasmine conspiracy in mind, however, and it all makes perfect sense.

It's curious, though, how much the producers evidently worried about fallout from the idea of Cordelia sleeping with jailbait. Well, that's the impression you get from Connor's variable age. Cordelia implied that Connor was 16 in 3.22, "Tomorrow," but he's cited as being 18 here. Tellingly, Whedon scripted Cordy as saying the boy was 17 in "Spin the Bottle" (4.06) – but lo and behold, this was revised to 18 on screen. As you might have suspected, then... California's age of consent is 18.

Now, to be fair, Connor's exact age will always be indeterminate, because it's impossible to accurately gauge how long he spent in Quor'toth. It's not like keeping a calendar would have topped Holtz or Connor's list of priorities, even presuming that Quor'toth – a hellfire realm – had anything like a measurable "day." Yet if the *Angel* producers *did* sweat about Connor's age, it seems a bit silly in light of *Buffy* Season Two when – lest we've forgotten – Buffy lost her virginity on her 17th birthday to a man roughly 254 years her superior. For anyone wanting to embargo unlawful sex with teenagers in the *Angel*-verse, that ship had already sailed.

Side note about Cordy's coupling with Connor: It's nice that they took time to light candles beforehand. Mood is very important.

4. The Beast hurls Angel off the Sky Temple nightclub, and Our Hero presumably falls the distance of an L.A. skyscraper to the ground... undeniably a record for the show. It's a testament to Angel's durability, although – this being L.A. – it's possible that a palm tree or some garbage breaks his fall. We note, with some amusement, that as Angel dramatically sputters and coughs up blood, there's a banana right by his head.

5. Tricks for concealing Carpenter's pregnancy: Cordelia here spends a lot of time resting and wrapped in a blanket, and she's wearing a low-cut shirt, which draws the eye away from her abdomen and toward her cleavage (no, seriously). Mind, when she paces in Connor's abode, she patently looks like a woman who's either expecting or has a beer belly.

6. Totally random observations: The Beast has awfully white teeth, which suggests they've got very good fluorides in hell... Lilah's reference to Cordelia as "Wonder Girl" is a bit ironic, as Whedon at one point was helming the *Wonder Woman* film and Carpenter wanted to play the title part... Lorne counsels a client about snakes that are tragically manifesting out of an unspecified part of the man's anatomy. It's his nose. They're in his nose.

CHARACTER NOTES *Angel:* Can't decide whether to organize his weaponry alphabetically or by the damage they inflict (Lorne recommends the latter). Angel's arsenal includes a Khopesh [the Egyptian name for a Canaanite sickle-sword]. He invites Wesley to join his crew in battle [so he's set aside any doubts about Wes from "Slouching Toward Bethlehem" (4.04)], and he's unable, in combat, to penetrate the Beast's rocky hide.

• *Evil Cordelia:* [It's never explained why – after last episode – she doesn't simply keep pretending to be amnesiac, although it's possible Jasmine doesn't think she can keep up the pretense. Also bear in mind that Jasmine is already lodged in Cordelia's form, but appears – for whatever mystical reason – to need Connor's super-sperm to facilitate the birthing process. It's as if she's a giant egg, waiting insemination.]

Evil Cordy here tells Angel that the return of her memories (last episode) caused her to recall all the suffering he'd caused as Angelus, which she witnessed while on the higher plane. [This falsehood serves two purposes. It's a ready-made excuse for Evil Cordy to distance herself from Angel and bed Connor *and* the rebuke serves as a potent psychological weapon that keeps Angel off-kilter. Think about it: Angel's love tells him, in a nutshell, that he'll never atone for his past, and that she can't love him because of it. Argg.]

Cordelia appears to experience a nightmare of the Beast. [As with Cordy's "vision" last episode, this shouldn't be taken too literally. We're probably witnessing the dream as it's related to Connor so he'll pity her.] Dream-Cordelia claims to love eating Chocodiles. Cordy's eyes now cloud over when she receives a [false] vision.

• *Wesley:* Lilah says she doesn't mind Wes' crush on Fred and [infamously, oh *so* infamously] role-plays with Wes by dressing up as the woman. Lilah starts to take off her "Fred glasses" during their consequent bout of sex, but Wesley [gasp] tells her to leave 'em on. During the final battle, Wes hauls the unconscious Gunn out of the danger zone. [We'll revisit this point next episode.]

• *Gunn:* Failing to maintain his relationship with Fred, who's keeping her distance because he robbed her of the power of choice regarding Professor Seidel. ["Supersymmetry." By the way, according to the script, Gunn's Japanese sword has mystical runes etched on it.]

• *Fred:* Implies to a waitress that she and Gunn have fallen out of love.

• *Lorne:* Senses that Fred and Gunn aren't okay. His empathy isn't useful as a "Fred detector." Angel says the information Lorne read from Cordy ["Slouching Toward Bethlehem"] would've killed him if the firm hadn't taken it.

• *Connor:* Asks Angel to talk with the sullen Cordelia, even calling Angel "Dad" in the process. Connor claims he's never suffered a broken bone before; Evil Cordelia suspects he broke a couple of ribs brawling with the Beast. [If so, add super-healing to Connor's list of attributes.]

• *Lilah:* Angel clearly smells fear on her [as with 2.10, "Reunion"] regarding the Beast, and Lilah agrees that someone is trying to horn in on the firm's Apocalypse, supplying Angel with the data taken from Lorne's head. She's already in Wesley's apartment when he returns home. [It's possible that she's got a key; then again, she actually knocks on Wesley's door next episode. Perhaps in this case, she shimmied up the drainpipe in her Fred outfit.]

Lilah says she knows Wesley "better than (Fred) ever will." [Actually, she's got a point. Part of the Wesley-Lilah attraction stems from the fact that she accepts his dark side. Yet even when Fred falls for Wes, does she ever understand his darker persona? Does he ever, say, mention that he kept Justine in a closet? Fred prefers to see Wesley as a champion, and he wants to *be* one, but his relationship with Lilah – for now – is arguably more honest.]

• *The Beast:* Probably the physically strongest opponent ever faced by Angel's crew, and proves impervious to swords, crossbows and various axes. He staggers under Wesley's shotgun blasts, but appears unharmed. [By the way, the Beast's "arrival" at Connor's birth place is presumably pre-planned and for show, intended to sabre-rattle the boy and aid Evil Cordy in manipulating him.]

THE FIRM'S LIBRARY The firm assigned "hundreds" of psychics to decipher the "protected" intel taken from Lorne's mind, and this usually resulted in their brains being blown out. Still, the firm created a print-out of the information, and this contains pieces of glyphs, archaic languages and other symbols all jumbled together. Mention of the words "shrine" and "flesh" seem to refer to the Sky Temple slaughter. [It's almost a goof that the firm doesn't think about aligning print-outs of the data like Angel's group does, but perhaps they were too busy mopping up the brain splatter.]

ORGANIZATIONS *Wolfram and Hart:* Detects a 300 percent increase in supernatural incidents prior to the Beast's arrival. Angel claims that stopping the Beast will "protect everything [the firm] set into motion for the last thousand years." [Actually, "Reprise" (2.15) says it's been much longer than that.]

DEMONOLOGY *Vampires:* Severe trauma – in this case, a stake to the throat – makes Angel de-vamp.

• *Glurgg Demons:* They're 90 percent pus.

MAGIC The locations of the various plagues that precede the Beast's arrival link to form the shape of "The Eye of Fire" – an ancient alchemical symbol (essentially an X inside a diamond) for fire and destruction.

BEST LINE Lilah, emulating Fred and her accent: "I'm good and I'm pure and science turns me on. And one day, if I pray hard enough and eat all my vegetables, I just might have hips."

THINGS THAT DON'T MAKE SENSE Not so much a problem here, but an issue moving forward: Fireballs rain on L.A., yet Buffy's crew never properly acknowledges it. Nor does Buffy phone Angel to ask, "Are you okay? *It's raining fireballs on your head!*" Indeed, the world-at-large doesn't react to this catastrophe nearly enough – Jasmine even claims in "Peace Out" (4.21) that "thousands" apparently died in the rain of fire and the subsequent ransacking of L.A. by vampires. Presumably, that's more people killed than 9-11, yet the global media regards it as a curiosity.

The agency's phones ring off the hook, with the number of supernatural incidents making *Ghostbusters* look a petting zoo, yet Angel spends an awful lot of time milling about the lobby cleaning and organizing his weapons. Also, when Gunn and Fred visit the rat-infested house, what makes the medicine cabinet door shatter? Do Biblical plagues have a sense of drama, or is there a super-strong rat in there hurling medicine bottles at the mirror? We hate to cite visual goofs, but the "lava-covered rocks" in Evil Cordy's vision look like painted Styrofoam – probably because, errr, they *are* painted Styrofoam. Another visual gaffe: the crossbow bolts that the Beast deflects into Angel look particularly fake, and the artificial ripple effect that follows in the arrows' wake doesn't help.

Where on Earth does Wesley conceal his shotgun before its big appearance in the rooftop battle? We refer you back to his "inter-dimensional" grocery bags in 3.11, "Birthday," although... okay, okay... it could just be strapped to his thigh. Even so, why does the shotgun-blasting Wes advance on the Beast, thus giving it a chance to smack him around? (Troublingly, this happens again in 5.06, "The Cautionary Tale of Numero Cinco.") Fireballs pelt the L.A. landscape, yet there's no evidence of buildings getting damaged, or fires breaking out.

Connor and Cordelia's coupling ranks among the most clinical lovemaking in the history of TV. What, no kissing?

IN RETROSPECT Connor to Cordelia: "You're not a higher being any more." All together now: "Yes... she is!"

CRITIQUE Some might complain that everything leading up to the George Lucas-style showstopper battle is fairly irrelevant, and it's true that if you study DeKnight's other stories, he seems intent on wringing out a massive slugfest out of the proceedings as often as possible. But even if everything before the rooftop fracas *was* sub-standard (which frankly it isn't), then let's at least agree that it's quite the rooftop fracas.

At this point in the season, "Apocalypse Nowish" chiefly exists to pistol-whip the heroes and make everything look bleak. As promised... yup, everything looks damnably bleak. The Beast seems like murder on wheels when he shrugs off the heroes' assaults, and the Biblical "plagues" that accompany his arrival – if not particularly original, like the Beast himself – nicely set the mood. The episodes to follow capitalize on this with varying success, but for now, Angel's world appears suitably doomed. Considering how often we've experienced such scenarios on this show and *Buffy*, we'd mark that down as a little triumph.

That just leaves us to address the lovebirds. Cordy's evil persona has admittedly become a bit dreary compared to her normally bouncy self – although it'll improve as time goes on – but disappointed viewers sometimes miss the point that her love fest with Connor is *supposed* to seem disturbing. Actually, it was a fairly daring risk, considering nobody was exactly going to cheer about this the first time around. But with the show out on DVD, and the hindsight of knowing the game plan to Season Four, let's try to forgive any repulsion that accompanied the original broadcast. Sure, it initially looks like a throw from left field, but it galvanizes some great stories, and it's a sign of *Angel* beautifully moving forward, not backward.

THE LORE The production team intended to roll out the Beast later in the season, but the WB scheduled "Apocalypse Nowish" as the final new episode before the Christmas break, so the big gun was deployed before the holiday hiatus.

• The script doesn't even pretend that the final battle wasn't modeled on *The Matrix*, and even references "Neo" at one point. An omitted bit had Lorne assaulting the Beast with his sonic cry, and the Beast smacking him with a table. Another deleted bit justified Gunn's loathing for rats by claiming that he and his sister used to live somewhere "down on Fifth," where rats chewed a hole in Alonna's leg while they slept.

• Kartheiser was a bit terrified to simulate intercourse atop Carpenter, as she was already four months pregnant. He found himself hovering a good two and a half feet over her during the sex scene, just to ensure that he didn't cause her an injury. (Kartheiser interview, *BBC Cult*, April 2003)

• Vladimir Kulich (The Beast) portrayed 1st Warrior Buliwyf in *The 13th Warrior*. In a bit of career foreshadowing, he appeared in a TV movie called *The Big One: The Great Los Angeles Earthquake* (1990).

4.08: "Habeas Corpses"

"I know they all worked for an evil company, but this –"

Air Date: Jan. 15, 2003; **Writer:** Jeffrey Bell; **Director:** Skip Schoolnik

SUMMARY Cordelia informs Connor that their sleeping together was a mistake, causing a conflicted Connor to go to Wolfram and Hart and request Lilah's help in determining his true nature. Moments later, the building's power fades as the Beast launches a full-frontal attack on the firm.

The Beast indiscriminately butchers the staff, Gavin included. Wesley evacuates a wounded Lilah, telling her to change her name and go underground. Wes rounds up Angel's group and the heroes locate Connor in the ransacked building, but they retreat to the White Room when a security feature revives the slain attorneys as zombies. The heroes then witness the Beast drawing a dark essence from the evil little girl, who – as her last act against the Beast before she dies – teleports Angel's group safely back to the Hyperion. Afterward, Angel tells Cordy that he knows about her sex with Connor.

FIRSTS AND LASTS Last, and by far the most impressive, of the show's two lawyer massacres (see 2.10, "Reunion" for the first). As part and parcel of this, it's the end of Gavin and the insidious little girl in the White Room. Effectively, it's also the end of the Wolfram and Hart regime that's been operating the L.A. branch since the series began. In terms of décor, this means it's the final appearance of Lilah's office and the main Wolfram and Hart lobby, which is here strewn with bodies.

POINTS OF DISCUSSION ABOUT "Habeas Corpses":

1. Intentionally or otherwise, watching the helter-skelter evacuation of Wolfram and Hart brings to mind the World Trade Center. Undoubtedly, we live in a time where it's easy to see 9-11 references where none exist, but the harrowing and prolonged pictures of the firm's employees briskly walking through darkened stairwells – talking on cell phones amidst the emergency, or pushing elevator buttons in the hope of exiting the building alive – sounds an awful lot like descriptions of that fateful day in September 2001.

Amplifying the drama, Bell's script pauses to focus on the nameless employees, particularly singling out an attractive, sandy-haired young woman in a business suit. She's first seen by a useless elevator door, then heads down a stairwell. She gets no lines, but it's still cutting to spy her body among the casualties, meaning the Beast butchered her off-screen without the viewer even noticing.

2. Just before she expires, the little girl in the White Room tells the heroes, "The answer is among you." With hindsight, she presumably means Evil Cordelia, but the heroes will soon mis-interpret her words to denote Angelus. Some commentators have rightfully wondered why little girl doesn't more sensibly say, "Cordelia is the evil manipulator," or "Cordelia is the master of the Beast." Unfortunately, it seems that as ever, frickin' oracles are too cryptic for their own good.

3. It's the morning after for Connor and Evil Cordy, whereupon he practically wakes up singing, "It's the end of the world as we know it... and I feel fiiiiiiiineeee!", and *she* announces that they've made a terrible error. Recognizing that Jasmine is driving Cordelia's body throughout this period, this raises the question of why she doesn't simply keep sleeping with the boy. The answer: If she withholds sex, it's a powerful manipulation tool that makes Connor more unstable and dependent on her. Along those lines, Evil Cordy needs to play Angel and Connor against one another. If you review the stories in this period, it's obvious that Angel and his son are closer to reconciling than ever before – notice their playful banter in the haunted halls of the firm

– and Evil Cordy simply can't have that, because she needs Connor under her sway. So she engineers a rift between them, and very skillfully, too.

That just leaves one anomaly: Evil Cordy's ghastly play-acting when she awakens and acts *surprised* to find herself in bed with Connor. That might work if she was drunk the night before, but she's essentially saying, "Oh shit, there was an apocalypse and I slept with Angel's son." Scandalous, yes. Shocking, no.

4. The teaser opens immediately after last episode, and features an enraged Angel charging through a rooftop door and smashing a bunch of stuff off screen. Watching this on DVD, where there's no "Previously On" segment to set the mood, it seems even more abrupt than intended. More curiously, though... try re-watching this bit, and imagining that Angel has fallen down the stairs, uttering grunts of "nnnhh-hh... nnnhhhh!..." in the finest tradition of *Looney Tunes*. The sound effects match perfectly.

CHARACTER NOTES *Angel:* Makes Cordelia stay behind because going to the firm is "too dangerous," but conspicuously has no issue exposing Fred to the same risk. [It's unsaid, but Angel presumably fears that having Cordelia around would muddle his judgment.] His strategy for dealing with the Beast: run away. He recalls the code to the White Room [3.17, "Forgiving"] thanks to his photographic memory. [Well, that and the fact that he pocketed the paper with the code on it.] He's re-claimed the Hyperion office as his own.

• *Wesley:* Attempts to end his relationship with Lilah, feeling he needs to pick a side and stick with it. [Wes cites the battle with the Beast as a turning point, but, as we suggested under "Supersymmetry," he's been distanced from Lilah since 4.04, "Slouching Toward Bethlehem." At this point, the possibility of reuniting with Angel's crew probably seems more important than cheap sex.] He stands his ground even when Lilah offers to wear Fred-style glasses again [see last episode], yet risks his life to extract her from the besieged Wolfram and Hart. A source in the firm alerted Wesley to the danger.

Wesley sometimes carries grenades. He and Gunn each vow to eliminate the other if they become zombie-fied. [Gunn's a little quicker to agree, though.] At Gunn's urging, Wesley takes Fred and flees, leaving Gunn to the zombies' mercies. [Wesley does this *awfully* fast, and worryingly cuts off Gunn's escape in the interests of keeping the zombies at bay. That said, in most regards, Wes helps Gunn when needed. Hell, if he really wanted, he could've left Gunn to die last episode.]

• *Gunn:* Compassionate enough to behead Gavin rather than leave him shambling about as a zombie.

• *Fred:* Rushes into Gunn's arms after the big battle last episode, but seems duly impressed that Wesley possesses inside information on the firm [recall that she wanted to target Wolfram and Hart in 4.01, "Deep Down"].

• *Connor:* Gets into Lilah's office without being detected [like father, like son], withstands getting slugged through a stone column and getting buried in rubble, and punches the Beast's rocky hide without tearing his fists to ribbons.

• *Lilah:* Never seems to feel genuine emotion for Wesley more than in this story. Lilah drinks coffee and keeps a 9 mm pistol in her desk. She's wounded when the Beast stabs a rocky finger into her side. [She returns in 4.12, "Calvary."]

• *Gavin:* Attempting to flee the building when the Beast kills him. His last words, spoken to the Beast: "Uh, hi..."

• *The Beast:* Able to enter the White Room. [We're never told how this occurs, although it's entertaining to imagine the Beast squeezing itself into an elevator, tapping keys.] Fred can't find any records on the Beast. [See 4.11, "Soulless" for why. Next episode partly explains the Beast's attack on the firm. Mind, it also has the benefit of simply eliminating an organization that poses a threat to Jasmine's arrival, with agents who are probably immune to her power.]

• *The Little Girl:* Last seen chanting the teleport incantation that saves Angel's crew. [We don't *see* the girl die, but she presumably does. A new entity adopts her post in 4.22, "Home."] Both Angel and Wesley, more or less, cite her as "something old and evil that likes to pretend she's a little girl." [As explained next episode. Angel probably sensed that when he met the girl in "Forgiving" (3.17), and Wesley's had inside knowledge of the firm for some time now.]

ORGANIZATIONS *Wolfram and Hart:* Lilah calls the firm "the safest place to be in case of an apocalypse" [but she says that before the Beast strides in and butchers nearly everyone in the building]. Lilah's office and the Division of Corporate Relations are located on the Seventh Floor.

Zombie protocols resurrect slain employees into a makeshift fighting force, and the firm shutters itself in case of a full-blown attack. A post-clampdown escape shaft remains open, apparently for executives of Lilah's rank; Gavin knows about it too. It's accessible through storage closets on the Third Floor and the main lobby. The shaft drops about 30 meters, and ends up in a sewer. Gavin appears to revive as a zombie before the other employees. [Do the voodoo protocols revive middle-management first?]

• *The Senior Partners:* Want the firm to cut a deal with the Beast, thinking it might hasten their intended apocalypse and save a few bucks. [Needless to say, this doesn't come to pass.]

DEMONOLOGY *Zombies:* Wesley doesn't think their bite is contagious, and the firm's breed of zombies act rather slow and stupid. [The undead attorneys are far more *Night* *of the Living Dead* than the ones in 2.14, "The Thin Dead Line" and arguably 3.12, "Provider," so there are obviously different types.] The best way of stopping them: cutting off their heads or smash in their skulls.

BEST LINE(s) Lilah, intimidating a lackey over the phone: "Find that Beast, or I swear to God, I will..." (She falters.) Gavin, helpfully: "Boil you alive..." Lilah, recovering: "Boil... you... alive."

THINGS THAT DON'T MAKE SENSE Let's dispense with the hyperbole: Lilah says there's no way back into the firm... but there is, through the storage closet shaft. Wesley says there's no way out of the firm... but there is, through the storage closet shaft.

Lilah's fall from power brings us, somewhat mercifully, to the last of her feeble gambits. To wit, she honestly seems to think a couple of her rent-a-thugs stand a snowball's chance of restraining Connor so the firm can dissect him. Besides, Connor *wants* the firm to examine him, so isn't it simpler to just escort the teen down to the firm's laboratory and – dunno – gas him unconscious when he's not expecting it? (Perhaps Lilah's just not thinking straight because Wesley dumped her. Seriously... she couldn't even think of "boil you alive!" by herself.)

Angel deliberately dons a very nice jacket before venturing into the deathtrap that the firm has become, where it's likely to get shredded. (It doesn't, but you get the point.) It's feasible that Fred can hotwire an elevator's bypass switch, but she also miraculously gets the elevator moving despite the power being out. The Beast is considerate enough to spill most of the employees' blood on pieces of paper where it'll show up on the camera; meanwhile, the corpse-strewn floor is amazingly clean. Speaking of corpses, why exactly does zombie-Gavin revive sooner than everyone else, and shamble from the Third Floor to the Seventh Floor for no readily apparent reason?

The technology goof: There's a stack of floppy disks on Lilah's desk, but she uses a Mac, and this story was filmed after Mac phased out its floppy drives. (External floppy drives were available, but it seems sub-par for the firm's resources.) And the hairstyle goof: Cordelia has been getting progressively less blonde for a while now, and it's meant to represent her romantic distancing from Angel. The symbolism works, but this suggests that amid all of her concerns, Cordy has found time in Connor's hell-hole of an apartment to re-dye her hair brunette. That is, unless being evil makes her hair darker.

Gunn opens the story by commenting on Angel, "[I] can't ever remember seeing him that down after a fight." Well, no... except for that time he locked a bundle of lawyers in a cellar to die, and then fired his best friends.

IN RETROSPECT Lorne dozes off, later claiming he was simply "asking the Inner Lorne for a little back-up." Would that be Hulk Lorne [5.05, "Life of the Party"], who emerges when Lorne doesn't sleep enough?

IT'S REALLY ABOUT... In large measure, it's about building up the Beast's stature by watching him massacre the organization that's adeptly hounded the heroes for three years now. There's also a massive injection of "you reap what you sow," but we'll leave that discussion for **The Critique**.

CRITIQUE It's engrossing, suitably nightmarish and a genuinely exhilarating turnaround, to such an extent that we're not going to entertain the notion that it's just another zombie story. Sure, it's populated with *Night of the Living Dead* rejects, but "Habeas Corpses" works because we're made to watch the central villains of the series get butchered, and actually feel pangs of sympathy for them. Granted, the firm's higher-ups probably deserved worse, but can you genuinely say that about *everyone* at Wolfram and Hart... the typists, the secretaries and the janitors included? Hell, there's a couple of dozen bodies in the lobby alone, and it's unsettling to think they *all* had it coming. The indiscriminate way with which the Beast eviscerates attorneys and tea ladies alike proves horrifying and a bit moving simultaneously, and works in every way that it should.

Beyond the slashfest, though, it's a story with a bracing number of twists: Gavin's demise; Wesley's sudden arrival to save Lilah and – moreover – the very slight uncertainty that he might actually leave Gunn to die in battle. The plot, the characters and the production values all fuse to create this claustrophobic and unexpected little tale that we love to pieces. (We're aware that sounds a little disturbing to say, given all the brutality, but it's nonetheless true.) Indeed, if the two episodes to follow had tapped the oil field created by "Apocalypse Nowish" and this story, it's fair to say that Season Four might've ranked higher in some fans' estimation.

THE LORE It's between this episode and the previous one – and there's no way of sugarcoating this – that Glenn Quinn was found dead in his North Hollywood home. His body was discovered on Dec. 3, 2002, and although many reports were discreet, he evidently died from a heroin overdose. "Habeas Corpses," broadcast some six weeks later on Jan. 15, 2003, entailed a lot of zombies, and the suggestion that this caused Quinn's "In Memory" tribute to get delayed until next episode seems plausible.

• Robert Hall, whose effects studio Almost Human created many of the monster effects for *Buffy*, *Firefly* and Tim Minear's *The Inside*, normally worked under tight deadlines but had a month to create the Beast. Bell had wisely called him early on, and Hall noticed that whereas the producers had simply trusted him on other costumes, they took a special interest in this one. (O'Hare, *Zap2it.com*, Nov. 29, 2002)

• Vladimir Kulich needed between four to five hours to gear up as the Beast – meaning that, for a six a.m. call, he and Hall would need to congregate at around two in the morning to get it all done. Kulich was a bit surprised about all the hassle, not having any clue about the prosthetics when he read for the role. One of Kulich's friends suggested that the Beast looked a bit like Tim Curry's character (the Lord of Darkness) in *Legend*, so Kulich actively avoided watching the film to avoid duplicating Curry's performance. The Beast's shoes were five-inch platforms, similar to the ones worn by KISS, and Kulich was 6'10" tall in them. (Allyson, *Scoopme.com*, Jan. 2003)

4.09: "Long Day's Journey"

"He's looking to put an end to daylight. Wants to blot out the sun permanently."

Air Date: Jan. 22, 2003; **Writer:** Mere Smith; **Director:** Terrence O'Hara

SUMMARY Working to a secret agenda, the Beast systematically eliminates members of the Ra-Tet: a mystical order whose members included the little girl in the White Room. The Beast takes either a magic totem or type of energy from each Ra-Tet member, intending to combine these as part of a spell to permanently blot out the sun. The mutant thief Gwen allies with Angel's crew in a bid to protect the last Ra-Tet member – a laid-back individual named Manny – but the Beast or one of its agents murders Manny in Gwen's stronghold. The Beast then initiates the sun-darkening ritual in Connor's lodgings, departing as the sky over L.A. goes black.

Afterward, Cordelia relates a "vision" from the past, one that showed the Beast talking to Angelus. The heroes conclude that Angel's evil aspect might know crucial information, and Wesley darkly announces they need Angelus if they're to defeat the Beast.

FIRSTS AND LASTS Final appearance of Connor's stylish warehouse digs.

POINTS OF DISCUSSION ABOUT "Long Day's Journey":

1. The heroes here decide to bring back Angelus, a central focus of Season Four. And while they're not *wrong* for doing so... well, they're certainly leaping to silly conclusions an awful lot. Wesley named Angel as a suspect in Manny's murder last episode, on the grounds that the Beast can somehow, someway, control him... even though there's no evidence of that. (Even if this were true, it's an odd way of going about getting at the truth. "We're going to turn you into a serial killer so we can question your motives.") They place an awful lot of faith in the "vision-memory retrieval" that Cordelia displays, even though she's never demonstrated such talents before now. And they put a lot of stock in the words of the little girl in the White Room, when they're cryptic at best. For these reasons and others, be advised that the rather impulsive "turn Angel into Angelus" scheme will generate – not that we're reveling in the fact – a lot of fodder for **Things That Don't Make Sense** as we go along.

2. Pregnancy concealment strategy No. 27: Cordelia wears a hot (no, literally *hot*) black outfit with a jacket, which looks like a cooker in L.A.'s climate (for anyone who's not a vampire, that is). On that note, as Cordelia sits down for her private chat with Angel, notice how Carpenter's hand instinctively goes to her swelling tummy as if to check, "Is everything okay?"

3. Angel gives his colleagues a "rousing" speech, even though they've never needed one before, everyone's on the same page, and he's not particularly good at it. Taking into account the Slayer's "we shall prevail" lectures at this point in *Buffy* Season Seven, you'd almost think that a speech-making virus was making the rounds in California.

4. Now things get complicated regarding the Beast's abilities, as the rocky demon here sneaks up behind Gwen – an experienced cat-burglar – then kills her employer and vanishes before she can peel off her glove. We might imagine that the Beast simply flies away very, very quickly, but it's harder to think that he snuck up behind Gwen on tipee-toe, or swooped in from above before she could notice. Yet there's not much evidence the Beast can teleport... even though Lilah's account of the Beast's activities (which we'll refute) in 4.12, "Calvary" would almost make you think that, and the means by which it here escapes Wesley and Fred's portal trap might be telling. Arrrrgggg.

5. Lorne, trying to motivate Angel after he loses Cordelia to Connor, says: "There's more fish in the sea." It's a rather unfortunate metaphor to use on a man who's been dunked in the ocean for three months.

CHARACTER NOTES *Angel:* Laments that the Beast has now "killed hundreds of people that I couldn't save." [He probably means those who died in the rain of fire, although he might be counting the casualties at Wolfram and Hart too. If so, it's good to hear him displaying far more compassion for evildoers after Season Two, and notice his sentiment toward Lilah in the Season Four finale.]

• *Evil Cordelia:* Here "experiences the memory" of the Beast talking to Angelus through Angelus' eyes, and attributes this as a vision from the Powers. [She's obviously faking this "vision" as a pretense for calling forth Angelus, but later episodes – particularly 4.11, "Soulless" – imply that the meeting actually took place.] She's the first to suggest that someone must've acted on the Beast's behalf and killed Manny. [It's a good double-bluff on her part; the heroes only identify Manny's killer in 4.17, "Inside Out."]

• *Gunn:* Spends a decent amount of time with Gwen [paving the way for events in 4.16, "Players"].

• *Fred:* Clearly likes bantering around various theories with Wesley. She's overcome her paralyzing fear of portals.

• *Lorne:* Claims to have sensed the fact that Cordelia's shacked up with Connor, and tells Angel to let Cordelia go. [This happens when Gwen re-surfaces, almost as if Lorne wants Angel to check her out. Gwen's profession makes this strategy somewhat suspect, but there's a precedent for it in Batman and Catwoman. Furthermore, before "Players," Angel was (potentially) one of a very few benevolent beings who could copulate with Gwen and live to talk about it.]

• *Connor:* His enhanced hearing [3.21, "Benediction"] registers a fire engine/ambulance "four blocks over." He's now sleeping separate from Cordelia, and moves with extraordinary stealth. He's feeling even more isolated than normal at present, although he's still calling Angel "Dad." He survives a five-story drop.

• *Gwen:* Now rich because Angel gave her the Axis of Pythia [4.02, "Ground State"] after using it to locate Cordelia. Gwen worked as a thief for Mr. Ashet [see **Organizations**], for six years before meeting him. Her hideout, located in a nondescript tenement downtown, has a "panic room" protected by twelve inches of solid steel. Gwen's strong enough to push the Beast, and sufficiently durable to withstand getting smacked around in return [her mutant metabolism at work, presumably]. Gwen's butler ["Ground State"] is already in Tahiti. [Gwen ventures there next episode, returning in time for "Players."]

• *The Beast:* Lets slip that he previously met Angel. [In conjunction with Evil Cordy's "vision"; they're coordinating their efforts.] In the climactic battle, Wesley and Fred create a portal using mystic texts – the Beast falls through as planned, but somehow returns to Earth moments later.

THE LIBRARY Wesley's copy of *Rhinehardt's Compendium* mentions the little girl from the White Room.

ORGANIZATIONS *Wolfram and Hart:* Wesley's sources claim that without the little girl, the earthly contingent of Wolfram and Hart is cut off from the Senior Partners, effectively neutralized. [The White Room appears to occupy its own inter-dimensional space, and is only reachable if a "bridgehead" entity is in residence; 5.08, "Destiny" appears to confirm this.]

• *The Ra-Tet:* Mystical order of five beings, each of them totems that represent a different stage in "Ra's journey across the sky." [We're told virtually nothing about Ra himself. In *Angel*-verse terms, he could be an extraordinarily powerful demon, a highly adept magic-user or – less likely – a remnant of the Old Ones; see 5.15, "A Hole in the World."]

The Ra-Tet's origins are shrouded in mystery since the dawn of time. They're ordered by their placement from "sunrise" to "sunset," with their natures correspondingly changing from benevolent to malevolent. In order, they're Ma'at, a female white-magic shaman type; the solar-charged Mr. Ashet, Gwen's employer; Manny; the skinless sabretooth Semkhet, who resided in Death Valley; and Mesektet, the evil little girl in the White Room, who kept Semkhet as a sort of "pet."

Manny was the self-described Sacred Guardian of the Shen, Keeper of the Orb of Ma'at and Devotee of Light. He apparently lived in Belize prior to these events, and drank at the Pink Pony Lounge. Manny embodies the "man, the neutral totem," and therefore possesses no super-powers. On the plus side, he's immortal unless ritually murdered [presumably true of all the Ra-Tet]. The Orb of Ma'at resided in Manny's head. [Despite being an embodiment of man, he didn't have anything approaching human physiology.]

MAGIC *The sun-blotting ritual:* Entails the Beast fitting together three pieces ripped from the Ra-Tet's bodies: the glass orb from Manny's head, which sits atop interlocking metal "wings" taken from Ma'at and Mr. Ashet. The Beast charges the orb with the little girl's black energy [stolen last episode] and drips blood from Semkhet's heart onto it. The artifact then generates black tendrils that blot out the sun over L.A. [There's no discernable reason why the Beast performs the sun-darkening ritual where Connor lives, other than the continual need to imply a connection with the boy, and make Angel's group view him with suspicion.] Upon completing the ritual, the Beast swallows the orb from Manny's head. [He presumably does this for safekeeping, which suggests the spell is linked to the orb – so aiiiiiiieeeeeee, see **Things That Don't Make Sense** – and it helps explain events in 4.13, "Salvage."]

Manny claims that left unchecked, the darkness will spread throughout California and eventually across the whole globe. [This hardly suits Evil Cordelia's long-term goals, but she prepared for this contingency; see all the bits about the Beast's rocky knife in 4.13, "Salvage."]

BEST LINE Lorne, when Gwen is startled that he's wearing lamé: "The evil ones can't pull it off. It gets camp."

THINGS THAT DON'T MAKE SENSE The heroes take skepticism to a grandiose level here, remaining unconvinced that there's a connection after the Beast offs two members of the Ra-Tet. "Two lines don't make a pattern," they insist, even though there's only five Ra-Tet members total – meaning that 40 percent of the group has already gotten the whack – and the Beast personally slaughtered these beings. It's not as if they died as incidental casualties, say while enjoying a casual bike ride in the rain of fire. For that matter, it's fortuitous that most of the Ra-Tet, an ancient Egyptian order, is congregated in or around modern-day L.A. (Mind, a similar conceit exists on *Buffy*, where archaeologists in Sunnydale unearth up all manner of ancient artifacts that have no business being there.)

Manny is careless enough to spontaneously mention that he's immortal "unless he's ritually murdered," apparently for benefit of anyone who wishes to murder him. How do Angel and Gwen find Semkhet's cave in the whole of Death Valley? How does Gunn, in all his rampant yet justifiable jealousy, not have a problem with leaving Fred and Wesley alone at the Hyperion? Given the fate of the entire frickin' world is at stake, why is Gwen one of those stereotypical thieves who withholds confidential information (in this case, the item taken from Mr. Ashet's chest) over full disclosure to the heroes? And why was Angel *so* benevolent as to give Gwen the Axis of Pythia, which sold for $33 million, instead of saying, "Look... you sell the item and give me a mere 5 percent, which still leaves you the equivalent of a lottery winner." Because Gwen would hardly miss the $1.5 million, and it would've solved a lot of the agency's cash-flow problems.

The power-cut that Evil Cordy apparently engineers is damned selective, taking out Gwen's security cameras while the rest of the electricity stays on. It also erases the tapes prior to the blackout *or* Gwen never thinks to review the recordings and thereby catch Evil Cordy leaving the premises. Also, if Evil Cordy triggered the power cut ten minutes before her watch, then shouldn't Angel find it suspicious that she left his company at that point? Especially as Gwen *couldn't* have been responsible, despite Evil Cordelia pointing the finger at her, because she was with Gunn at the time. Ah, yes... and notice how Angel touches Gwen's waist as they exit the hotel, and it *almost* sounds like there's an electrical sound effect, yet Angel never jolts back or goes "Ouch!"

On to the climactic battle, where Wesley and Fred's portal-opening is, conspicuously, the longest portal-opening we've witnessed to this point. It's certainly a far cry from the three or four words Fred required in "Supersymmetry" (4.05) and even longer than the Pylean portals in Season Two. (Possibly, this portal is tailor-made to not suck the heroes inside along with the Beast, and to go undetected by the Beast until it's too late. On screen, the portal looks more transparent and quiet-running than the previous ones.)

The orb taken from Manny's head was rolling around on the floor prior to the Beast falling down said portal, yet it's sitting atop the Ra-Tet's metal wings when the Beast re-emerges. Worse, in the moments that it takes the Beast to return, why didn't the heroes take the opportunity to smash the orb? Why doesn't Gwen melt the Ra-Tet's metal wings as she was *supposed* to do? Either action – the orb-smashing especially – would've probably ended the Beast's sun-blotting plan right then and there.

And... why on Earth is the Beast considerate enough to knock before entering Connor's apartment?

IN RETROSPECT Cordelia says that at the end of the day, "Connor's still going to be [Angel's] son..." Errrrr... sort of.

CRITIQUE We've lavished praise on the last four episodes, so it's without any joy that we cite "Long Day's Journey" as a tragic misstep, chiefly due to all the Egyptian hokum. Implicitly, series such as *Stargate SG-1* are far better suited to this "the deities of old were real" approach; *Angel*, grounded in an urban fantasy about vampires and demons, just isn't. To make matters worse, the Egyptian characters on display aren't convincing and aren't interesting in the slightest. And it's a particularly crushing disservice to the little girl in the White Room, who before now had some genuine mystique about her. That she belongs to an ancient Egyptian group called the "Ra-Tet" is an appallingly crap explanation of who or what she was, presuming we even needed to know in the first place.

Moreover, this episode just seems sloppily put together. The dialogue feels stilted (Gwen: "I understand the amulets you want acquired are very valuable." Her client: "Yes, that's because they're extremely rare and powerful."), too much of the adventure entails the heroes keeping vigil over a locked room, the effects simply don't gel (notice the woeful staging as the Beast "leaps as if to smash through the window and fly away" in Connor's apartment); too much exposition gets repeated; and the main characters act like whittled-down versions of themselves. Wesley in particular seems a pale shell of his normally astute self until the final scene.

There's also – and again, we almost hate to point this out – a certain redundancy about this the whole story. Two episodes ago in "Apocalypse Nowish," the Beast pulled off a major dark ritual that made it spectacularly rain fire. So when he pulls off *another* major dark ritual that makes the sun go out, it feels as if we've already trod this path. Leaving the sun "permanently" dark after the rain of fire would've lent a certain simplicity to everything; making the two events separate just drags out the over-arching storylines.

Mercifully, the last half of Season Four has enough content to justify its existence, so a lot of the gut-wrenching issues here will correct themselves soon enough. Unfortunately, we've got to endure "Awakening" before that happens.

4.10: "Awakening"

"Angel... haven't we waited long enough?"

Air Date: Jan. 29, 2003; **Writers:** David Fury, Steven S. DeKnight; **Director:** James A. Contner

SUMMARY The heroes prepare a cell to restrain Angelus in the Hyperion basement, even as Wesley summons a sorcerer, Wo-Pang, to revert Angel to his murderous persona. Wo-Pang magically begins the proceedings, then reveals himself as a follower of the Beast, and commits suicide after failing to slay Angel. The heroes subsequently read tattoos on Wo-Pang's corpse, which helps them determine that a benevolent organization – the Bosh M'ad – once forged a sword that could slay the Beast.

In rapid succession, Wesley apologizes for risking Angel's life, and implicitly expresses regret for past offenses; Cordelia declares her love for Angel and the heroes obtain the Beast-killing sword from a pocket realm. Angel offs the Beast and thereby restores the sun, Connor accepts that Cordy's heart doesn't belong to him, and Angel and Cordelia finally have sex, even as...

... back in the real world, Wo-Pang looks up, having completed his mental illusion that allowed Angel to achieve "perfect happiness." With Angel's soul now in a mystical jar, Angelus opens his eyes and cackles.

POINTS OF DISCUSSION ABOUT "Awakening":

1. Angel sleeps with dream-Cordelia, and at the moment of climax, he very subtly says, "Buffy." This is obviously an attempt to placate anyone of the opinion that Angel can only attain perfect happiness with Buffy because they're eternal soul mates whose love sets the stars afire, yadda yadda yadda.

We'd best define terms here, though. If anything, Angel utters the Slayer's name because he suddenly remembers what happened when he slept with her in *Buffy* Season Two, *not* because he's fantasizing that Cordelia is his ex-girlfriend. We're comfortable assuming that Angel is thinking, "Oh, crap, I'm in the painful throes of losing my soul, just like I did with Buffy..." rather than "Oh, yes, yes, Buffy! Give it to me, Buffy!", because the latter is incredibly rude. Not to mention – as we've argued – horrendously insulting to Cordelia's character.

2. Evil Cordy accompanies Angel and Wesley into a series of death traps and remarks: "I knew you two would get me in trouble someday." It's not exactly true, but it's all the more ironic that she looks at her belly while saying it.

3. The dream reality entails Angel, Wesley, Cordelia and Connor voyaging through some underground tunnels, and enduring a series of tests blatantly plundered from the *Indiana Jones* films. Commentators frequently notice Angel's line of "Wood, why did it have to be wood?" as a nod to Indy's parallel line about snakes in *Raiders of the Lost Ark*. However, it might as well read as code for the writers saying, "We're stealing from *Indiana Jones*, but we're *aware* that we're stealing from *Indiana Jones*."

To walk through the most glaring comparisons... both Angel and Indy remove an item from an "altar" of sorts, and which makes a temple collapse. There's various parallel traps with whizzing saws, shooting spears and tinkling bells, and both protagonists must pass a test by picking out the correct symbols. (Wesley helps Angel choose Hebrew letters according to the nine antediluvian patriarchs in *Genesis*; Indy must spell out the name Yahweh on floor tiles in *The Last Crusade*.) Yup, everything shamelessly owes to *Indiana Jones*... save, perhaps, for the central sword chamber, which seems reminiscent of *Star Trek: The Next Generation*.

4. One of the purposes of *Redeemed* is to rationalize contradictory elements of the *Angel*-verse against themselves, but as Angel's dream reality holds no connection whatsoever to anything else (and frankly, for reasons of space), we've omitted many of the details.

5. "She's too old for me anyway," the dream-Connor says about Cordelia, thus stoking the fire of viewers who believed he should head for Sunnydale and start dating Buffy's sister, Dawn. Objectively speaking, though, it's hard to see Connor and Dawn sharing each other's company for more than a few minutes. Why do some people believe that just because two characters are the same age, *of course* they should date?

CHARACTER NOTES *Angel:* Sings "The Night the Lights Went Out in Georgia" for Lorne. Angel recalls every atrocity Angelus performed. [Angel's photographic memory proves a detriment in this regard.] Angel tells Connor, with regards to the boy's life "sucking," that he should "get over it." [Curiously, Angel rejected the same advice from Cordelia last episode.] Angel recommends containing Angelus in a steel-reinforced cage that's ten by 12 feet, with two or three inch bars. [The benefits of involving Angel in the cage's construction must outweigh Angelus knowing facts about his cell.]

• *Evil Cordelia:* Adeptly manipulates Angel into bringing Angelus back by going on about how Angelus thinks like the Beast, and is far more ingenious than Angel. She's now changed to a long white overcoat. [This still fails to conceal her ever-progressing pregnancy, but it makes more sense than her previous outfits. After all, the sun-blotting probably made temperatures drop across L.A.; even Fred wears a stylish long coat in 4.12, "Calvary."]

• *Wesley:* Good with a blowtorch.

• *Lorne:* Not huge with the love for singer Vicki Lawrence. At this juncture, Lorne fails to "read" anything from Angel's singing. [Lorne has never functioned as a mind-reader, and the group primarily wants access to Angelus' memories. Also, Angel and Angelus' auras might be so different, any attempt to read the one while the other maintains dominance will assuredly fail.]

• *Connor:* Resentful toward Angel because everyone presumed Connor was connected to the Beast, when it now seems that the rocky bastard is linked to his dad. [Evil Cordy is really getting her psychological hooks into the boy by now.] Connor displays no reservation at the thought of killing Angel if the Angelus gambit goes awry, and he's upset that he's got "no home to go back to." [He's presumably worried about the Beast returning, because his abode wasn't damaged much beyond the commando raid in 4.04, "Slouching Toward Bethlehem."]

• *Wo-Pang:* Shaman belonging to the order of the Kun-Sun-Dai, a group of dark mystics. He appears to meditate in a room with oil drums [weirdly], speaks Chinese and likes orange zinger tea. [Wo-Pang's attire (let's call it "red ninja garb") and soul-extracting ability beg comparisons with Giles' sorcerer colleague in *Buffy* 3.17, "Enemies." It's feasible, although not certain, that they belong to the same order.]

• *The Beast:* In the dream reality, slaying the Beast triggers an energy discharge that restores the sun [see 4.13, "Salvage"].

THE HYPERION The heroes watch newscasts on a TV in the lobby. [It's unclear where the TV came from, as Angel dithered about getting Connor one in 3.22, "Tomorrow," but didn't exactly have the opportunity. Maybe the TV came from Cordelia's apartment, and someone fetched it from storage.]

MAGIC *Muo-ping:* Glass jar used to house Angel's soul. [The means by which Wo-Pang extracts souls must necessitate pickling Angel's soul for safekeeping, because Willow simply plucked Angel's free-floating soul from the mystical ether in the *Buffy* Season Two finale.]

BEST LINE Gunn: "Pretty much the only victory we can claim is that we're not dead yet."

THINGS THAT DON'T MAKE SENSE All right... some glaring oversights about the heroes' brazen plan to restore Angelus will become evident in future episodes (especially "Salvage"), but two seem relevant here. First, the heroes never consider getting a psychic to probe Angelus' memories – something which, fair enough, rarely ends well for the psychic in the *Angel*-verse, but certainly entails less risk than making Angel a mad serial killer. There's also a blatant continuity gaffe when Angel tells Wesley, "You've never had the pleasure of [Angelus]' company," even though Wes *did* encounter Angelus in "Eternity" (1.17). Even more troubling, "Eternity" conclusively established that the powerful tranquilizer Doximall can simulate bliss and make Angel revert to Angelus. Having Angel simply ingest Doximall, then, would achieve the desired result of bringing out Angelus, eliminate all the business with the sorcerer, and place an innate time limit on the process – the period required for the Doximall to burn out of his system. Yet Angel and Wes never even consider the option. Nor does Angelus, once he's loose in future, think about procuring some Doximall as a safeguard in case he's re-ensouled.

Evil Cordelia and Angel seem to agree that Angelus is "ingenious," like the Beast. Sorry... the Beast, *ingenious*? He's not exactly a Jeopardy champion. Until now, he's barely uttered anything more complex than, "Conn-orrrrrr." Fortunately, the falsified nature of Angel's dream reality lets us rationalize away any number of potential errors, such as why, in the collapsing chamber, Cordelia pitifully screams for Angel's help when it looks like there's an exit right behind her.

Some prominent visual goofs: Wo-Pang's eyes flash red in close-up, but they look normal in pulled-back shots. Worse, the faux Wo-Pang stabs himself right in the center of his chest (it's definitely his *chest*, not his tummy), yet there's no wound or knife blade showing when he's lying on the ground. And if we're being fussy, a clip with a grimacing Wesley avoiding the trap-laden bells repeats itself seconds later.

IT'S REALLY ABOUT... The promise of a trademarked, bow-wrapped "perfect life," and the near-impossibility of attaining it. This revelation strikes adults at some point (or at least, it *should*), and it's especially profound for people who realize that while they can make progress and work to improve their lives, they can't magically change everyone to make them fall in line, rank-and-file, with whatever domestic setting seems the most appealing.

CRITIQUE We can't even beat around the bush on this one: "Awakening" is, without reservation, the most excruciating and awful *Angel* story ever made. Viewers tend to evaluate this episode through their perceived success of the final twist, so let's be clear that our disdain isn't actually focused on the final minute or so. Rather, it's centered on the utterly painful 45 minutes that precede it.

Let's stop and think about this. A big part of *Angel*'s appeal – at least, as we understand it – lies in its unpredictability. Season One got away with being fairly even-keel, but the show is never better than when it avoids taking the easy way out. Angel smothering Wesley with a pillow proves that point well enough. But here... *here* we're given an episode that's nothing *but* easy outs, and the producers honestly want us to find such drivel entertaining. Angel accepting Wesley's limp and token apology? After everything that's come before, it's nonsense. The notion of Connor suddenly shaping up, and becoming a level-headed teen? Double nonsense. The oh-so-handy sword that kills the Beast? Crap. Angel and Cordelia acting like they've in a Harlequin romance entitled *Truly, Madly Vampire*? Total and complete crap. It's not so much a dream sequence as a checklist of "Things We Could Do to Drain All the Drama and Suspense from This Show."

Worse, the artificial nature of Angel's dream sequence entails some of the most ghastly dialogue in the series' entire run. It doesn't matter that it's in keeping with Angel's character, because the viewer still has to *sit* through it. Cordelia to Angel: "I can't lose you. Not now. Not when we're just starting... what it is or could be." Connor: "It's not me [she loves]. I could feel it in her touch... in her eyes." The Beast: "If you will not stand with me, then suffer the agony of my wrath." Angel, killing the Beast: "Consider your ass kicked." Make it stop. Oh please, just make it stop.

As we said, some people want to argue that the story redeems itself through the "cleverness" of the final twist. First off, let's acknowledge that Angel's conversion into Angelus should hardly seem a shock, considering the heroes declared it as their plan from the very start. If you announce "I'm going to shoot so-and-so" early in Act One, it's not much of a surprise when they shoot so-and-so dead in the final act, is it? Second, without benefit of spoilers, we sussed out an unreality was in play on original broadcast. We couldn't pinpoint precisely when it started, but the manner in which everything was going so appallingly well was a bit of a clue.

But ultimately, the would-be success or failure of the final reveal is almost irrelevant, because it simply cannot forgive the story's overall horrendousness. Simply put, 45 minutes of crap and lame developments – even with a final twist that attempts to rationalize it all – is still 45 minutes of crap and lame developments. Indeed, the *only* redeeming feature here, with regards to Season Four, is that after this story and "Long Day's Journey," the worst is now behind us.

THE LORE Fury, feeling whimsical after this story broadcast, posted that Angel's cry of "Buffy" during the, errr, climax actually referred to a character of the same name from the WB's *Family Affair* series. He then started running down the *Family Affair* character roster: "In fact, little side note... The original draft had [Angel] calling out 'Mrs. Beasley,' but it just seemed wrong. And don't even get me started on the 'Mr. French' debate DeKnight and I had. Man, it got ugly." (Fury, *The Bronze*, Feb. 3, 2003)

• Angel's group watches a newscast on the sun-outage as reported by Larry McCormick, a real-life broadcast journalist. He had a 47-year career in broadcasting, particularly in the L.A. area (spending 33 years with KTLA, whose logo you'll see on screen), and died in 2004, age 71. His work earned him a star on the Hollywood Walk of Fame.

4.11: "Soulless"

"The truth is, Angel's just something that you're forced to wear. You're my real *father."*

Air Date: Feb. 5, 2003; **Writers:** Sarah Fain, Elisabeth Craft; **Director:** Sean Astin

SUMMARY Wesley interrogates Angelus, but Angelus uses his guile to put the heroes at each others' throats, making Wes and Gunn slug each other over Fred. At an impasse, Cordelia tells Angelus that she'll give herself to him *if* he helps them stop the Beast. Angelus agrees, detailing how he encountered the Beast after a massacre in Prussia, 1789. The Beast proposed an alliance, but Angelus – never big on teamwork – refused. Moments later, a magical order descended from the Nordic priestess Svea arrived, banishing the Beast from the mortal plane. The heroes locate the descendants of the Svea in L.A., only to find the family murdered in their home. Again out-maneuvered, Wesley decides to restore Angel's soul – only to find someone has stolen it from the Hyperion safe.

POINTS OF DISCUSSION ABOUT "Soulless":

1. This episode has, undoubtedly, the most famous guest-director the series will ever employ: Sean Astin. You'll probably remember him best as Samwise in *The Lord of the Rings* films, but his career stretches back to *The Goonies* (1985) and beyond. Unfortunately... and perhaps we should've relegated this to **The Critique**, but it goes to a bigger issue... Astin's directorial work is merely average. At the very least, he doesn't deserve the spotlight that's typically cast on his name in *Angel* texts. The fact that he had to ring up a friend to get the assignment (crucially, see **The Lore**) is perhaps rather telling, but also check out – troublingly – 5.10, "Soul Purpose" for a more prominent example of the "sci-fi celebrity tries out directing" syndrome on *Angel*.

2. Whatever the character drama at work here, you'd almost swear that "Soulless" was deliberately tailored as a budget-saver – most likely to save coin on the likes of "Apocalypse Nowish" (4.07) and the Faith three-parter, not that there's anything wrong with that. Still, notice how most of the action occurs in the Hyperion lobby (an existing set) and the basement (a room with a jail cell). Also, there are very few special effects, to the point that two of the three vamps slain in the teaser go to dust off screen.

3. For all the criticism we've leveled at the plan to make Angel into Angelus, we can credit the heroes with a few sensible precautions, even though they're never mentioned. The episode opens with Connor out on patrol, so Wesley's

group – smartly enough – probably told the boy to cool his jets while his father's an ingenious madman. Also, Angelus was strapped to a bench last episode, but he's just lounging about an empty cell in this story. Under the assumption that *any* object could become a weapon in Angelus' hands, the heroes probably tranquilized him and removed everything before this episode opens. Ditto on the sharp tranquilizer darts that Wesley shoots into Angelus, and which disappear before he wakes up.

Of course, if you're further depriving Angelus of potential escape tools, then stripping him bare seems an even better precaution. Tragically, it's hard to imagine the network censors allowing Boreanaz to be buck-naked for two episodes, even allowing for James Marsters appearing without a stitch in 5.04, "Hell Bound."

4. Here's a line that's rather easy to misconstrue, and which makes Wesley seem rather naughty. Angelus: "Which do you think is worse, Wes? Stealing my kid, like you did... or banging him like Cordelia?"

5. And as long as we're being lewd, this episode contains what's arguably the most outlandish double-entendre in the entire show. We simply can't do this justice in print, but re-watch the episode and behold the considerable dramatic flair with which Wesley declares: "Angelus is unpredictable. He'll take any opening... no matter how small."

CHARACTER NOTES *Angelus:* Can't sing much better than Angel, but comes off as extremely literate (see **Pop Culture**). Angelus encountered the Beast in 1789, Prussia, while taking a shortcut to Vienna. Cordelia told Lorne about the occasion that he nailed a puppy or puppies to a wall [as cited in *Buffy* 2.16, "Bewitched, Bothered and Bewildered"]. Angelus claims that Angel could hear Fred and Gunn having sex in the Hyperion. Wesley's tranquilizer gun takes down Angelus with as few as two shots, possibly just one.

• *Evil Cordelia:* Refuses to honor her bargain with Angelus on the grounds that his intel didn't help them against the Beast. [This condition actually wasn't part of their deal, unless Evil Cordy amended it off screen. Naturally, Jasmine has absolutely no intention of letting Angelus rape and torture her. We might speculate what the real Cordelia would have done, but then, the real Cordelia would never have brokered such an appalling pact in the first place.] Angelus exposes Cordy's sleeping with Connor ["Apocalypse Nowish"] to the group.

• *Wesley:* Deems Angelus as smarter than him, despite his reading everything available about Angelus' history [see 1.11, "Somnambulist"]. As a former Watcher, he views interrogating Angelus as a high point. Angelus psychologically capitalizes on Wesley's love for Fred, his innate insecurity, his father's shame and his failure with Faith. [It's possible that Wes thinks about recruiting Faith in 4.13, "Salvage," because of Angelus' comment, not that he really needs a reminder]

Wesley saves Fred from a close-call with Angelus and – when Fred seems suitably impressed – kisses her in the Hyperion office. Gunn becomes suitably enraged to discover this, leading to a brawl that ends when Gunn accidentally elbows Fred in the face. [Had the scuffle continued, our money favors Wesley.] Wes can read Freyan runes.

• *Fred:* Appears to respond to Wesley's kiss. It's implied that she can also read Freyan runes, albeit not terribly well.

• *Lorne:* Refuses to comment on anything he "reads" off the singing Angelus.

• *Connor:* Still has family issues, finding the murder of the Svea clan hard to bear.

• *The Beast:* In 1789, the Beast staged a massacre to get Angelus' attention, wanting help in dispatching his rivals – the Svea Priestesses – whom the Beast himself couldn't touch. He offered Angelus a favor in future, but Angelus refused. [4.17, "Inside Out" reveals that Evil Cordelia slipped out and murdered the Svea family seen here, again probably because the Beast couldn't.]

THE HYPERION Depending on traffic, it's located about 25 minutes from the Svea office in Pacoima.

THE LIBRARY Contains information on Slarf demons, spell mantras and something called the "Srail'gong technique."

ORGANIZATIONS The *Los Angeles Chronicle* has "Where Did [the Sun] Go?" as the lead story.

• *Svea Priestesses (a.k.a. Svear):* Mystical order descended from the powerful Nordic priestess Svea. The priestesses in Prussia wore blue hoods and carried crystal staffs. Their modern-day descendants seem rather domestic, and run an office with day hours. [So they're probably not the sort to venture out to combat demons, which might explain why Angel's crew hasn't encountered them before now. It's unclear if this family established themselves in L.A. after sensing the Beast's return – it's feasible, but you'd hardly think they would advertise their presence. Other descendants surely exist across the globe, although they might've forgotten their magical heritage.]

DEMONOLOGY *Vampires:* Angelus claims, "Those Prussian girls, must be the pastries. All that sweetness gets into their blood." He didn't find the bodies in the 1789 Prussia massacre as appetizing. [If blood equates with life, as Spike suggests in *Buffy* 5.22, "The Gift," then vampires logically prefer living prey.] He claims the gypsy girl that he killed [1.15, "The Prodigal"] was a virgin [again suggesting that vampires can sense virginity; and see "Inside Out"].

MAGIC Wesley briefly looks for, and finds no trace of, the Beast-killing sword that Angelus mentioned from Angel's dream [last episode]. Wes finds a banishment incantation among Svea's effects. [But neither he nor Fred ever figure out how to use it.]

BEST LINE(s) Angelus, on Connor wearing Angel's shirt: "Looks good on you, Son." Connor: "So did Cordy." Angelus: "She looks good on everybody."

THINGS THAT DON'T MAKE SENSE We take no pleasure in constantly saying this, but yet again, the heroes' overall plan is frighteningly full of holes. Essentially, they turn Angel back into one of the most murderous fiends who's ever lived, yet they've no plan for making him talk. No truth serum, no magical truth spell... what, do they seriously think Angelus will just hand over the information? He's not stupid, and he surely realizes that if he helps them, they'll just shackle him beneath Angel's soul again. Evil Cordy gets him talking, but only because she's working to a dastardly master plan, and you've got to otherwise marvel at the goodies' lack of strategy.

Besides, precisely how long does everyone think Angelus' interrogation will take? Why bother to feed him at all, as this practically begs for something to go wrong, and indeed nearly gets Fred killed? This whole scenario is simply too dangerous to let drag on for days; it's a hell of a lot safer to keep Wo-Pang about the hotel, happily drinking orange zinger tea, and simply have him re-ensoul Angel after an hour or so. Instead, they let Wo-Pang go home. Perhaps they're worried that Angelus might escape and slaughter the man, but if *that's* the issue, they really should've phoned Willow a lot sooner, as she can magically zap Angel's soul back by remote. And yes... with L.A. overrun by vampires, Wesley should've thought to break Faith out of prison earlier *or* – preferably – phoned Buffy's crew for help. Because gee, a Slayer might come in handy right now. Curse WB-UPN politics for complicating such things!

We'd also take issue with Wesley's comment that he's "not gonna see coming" whatever psychological weapon Angelus chooses to deploy. Okay, but what about the incredibly obvious avenues of attack that he totally fails to consider, such as – say – Wesley's love for Fred and his dalliances with Lilah (brought to light next episode)? Even then, Gunn's jealous rage owes less to Angelus' sharp words, and more to Wesley's outright stupidity for lip-locking Fred in the office. Kiss Fred when Angel isn't evil, for pity's sake! (On the plus side, it looks as if Wes has brushed up on his kissing technique since fizzling with Cordelia in *Buffy* Season Three. Lilah probably gave him lots of practice.)

The sun has permanently gone out over Los Angeles, yet the inevitable global uproar and volcano of media activity continues to be remarkably tame. One newspaper gives a story entitled "Crime Wave Shuts Down City" equal weight as "African Leaders Pin Hopes on New Union" and something about a Vietnam veteran. Even allowing for the Whedonverse talent for denial, this is pushing it.

Some obvious points: Events in "Eternity" (1.17) are yet again ignored, as Wesley claims Angelus last got loose in Sunnydale (*Buffy* Season Two). Wesley's car is clearly parked outside the Svea office, yet it's mysteriously elsewhere when he needs to "charge to the rescue" and help Cordelia and Connor. We later learn ("Inside Out") that Evil Cordelia killed the Svea family, but everyone else here thinks it was the Beast... yet there's no sign of forced entry or any real damage. So how did the Beast, lumbering abomination that he is, get inside?

Finally, we learn next episode that all references to the Beast were blatantly erased in Earth's dimension. So what exactly is the "big, hard thing" mentioned in the text on the Svea? Is Wesley reading Norse porn by mistake?

POP CULTURE Angelus calls Gunn and Fred: "Othello and Desdemona. My favorite couple." In *Othello*, for those of you who need to brush up on your Shakespeare, the title character, a black moor, marries the white Desdemona. He's undone when his adjunct, Iago, tricks him into thinking Desdemona had an affair. Othello kills her, realizes his catastrophic error and commits suicide. As Angelus himself mentions, the comparison to Gunn and Fred doesn't really hold up because, "Desdemona wasn't in love with the other guy."

• In his cell, Angelus sings a variation of *The Teddy Bears' Picnic* ("If you go into the woods tonight," he warbles, when it's usually, "the woods *today*"). The 1932 version of the song sold a million copies, and has been performed by such singers as Bing Crosby and Leon Redbone.

• Angelus on the Prussian slaughter: "Bodies, bodies everywhere and not a drop to drink." He's swiping a passage from Coleridge's *The Rime of the Ancient Mariner*: "Water, water, every where, nor any drop to drink." (*Rime* 121-122)

IT'S REALLY ABOUT... Lies sounding so much more effective when they're laced with the truth. Notably, Angelus puts the heroes at each others' throats by pushing their buttons, not by telling outright falsehoods.

CRITIQUE Some might argue that the set-up here is a bit predictable. Angelus stands impassive in his cage while each character gets their turn confronting him, and little of this goes well. And yet, even armed with that expectation, it's genuinely unsettling to watch much of this go down. Knowing full well that Wesley and Gunn had to duke out their troubles at *some* point, for instance, doesn't make one's eyebrows rise any less when they finally go at it. You could almost look upon this as the *Buffy* musical in microcosm (sans the singing and dancing, of course) in that everyone's secrets get ripped out into the open, and there's no way to stuff the damned genie back in his bottle once that occurs.

So it's a solid story that gives the show precisely what it needs most right now: a sense of direction. We wouldn't place it on the A-list, but it's the start of a string of episodes that'll yield increasing returns for the rest of the season, and we're willing to accept it as such.

THE LORE Sean Astin had met Greenwalt socially through Dan Petrie Jr., who'd written such films as the *Beverly Hills Cop* series, *Turner and Hooch* and *The Big Easy*, plus directed Astin in *Toy Soldiers* (1991). After Astin completed work on *Lord of the Rings*, he rang up Greenwalt and said he wanted to direct *Angel*. Greenwalt accommodated him, and "Soulless" marked Astin's first gig directing a network hour-long drama. By his own admission, Astin viewed network television as something of a portal to directing bigger projects, and took his inspiration from Richard Donner – a man who ascended to direct the likes of *Superman* (the 1978 version), *The Goonies* and *Ladyhawke* after previously directing an episode of *Gilligan's Island*. (*IGN FilmForce*, Dec. 22, 2003)

• Whedon added Angelus' line to Connor of "Doin' your mom and trying to kill your dad. Hmm. There should be a play." (DiLullo, *CityofAngel.com*)

4.12: "Calvary"

"Why do you think I let him out, you stupid bitch?"

Air Date: Feb. 12, 2003; **Writers:** Jeffrey Bell, Steven S. DeKnight, Mere Smith; **Director:** Bill Norton

SUMMARY A haggard Lilah surfaces at the Hyperion, desperate because the Beast has systematically murdered everyone affiliated with Wolfram and Hart. With Lilah's help, Wesley realizes that someone has erased all trace and mention of the Beast in Earth's dimension; he theorizes that Angelus retained his memories because his personality was dormant at the time.

Cordelia receives a vision of a ritual that promises to restore Angel's soul, but the attempt fails, allowing Angelus to bust loose and flee the Hyperion. Most of the heroes follow in hot pursuit, but Angelus doubles back and assaults Cordelia and Lilah. A chase through the hotel follows, ending with Cordelia pulling Lilah aside... and killing her with a jagged knife to the throat. As Lilah slumps dead, Cordelia stands revealed as the grand manipulator who commands the Beast and arranged Angelus' release.

FIRSTS AND LASTS Last occasion in which Lilah enjoys the oxygen habit, but this being a fantasy series, Stephanie Romanov will log three more appearances (only one of those in flashback). But it's the first outing of Connor as a "bloodhound," and he'll get another chance when he sniffs out Angelus next episode.

Fred awkwardly walks into a conversation between Wesley and Lilah, which marks the second (see also 3.04, "Carpe Noctem") and last time that she'll catch Lilah doing something rather compromising in the hotel. She must think Lilah is the biggest slut.

POINTS OF DISCUSSION ABOUT "Calvary":

1. Arguably, no other *Angel* episode causes so many misinterpretations about its title. It's "Calvary," but numerous people mistake this for its anagram, "Cavalry." Oddly enough, the anagram – while wrong – actually fits the story rather well, as Lilah's arrival looks like an ironic reversal of the cavalry charging to the rescue. Also, her line that nobody's coming to save them, not even "the forty-damned-second cavalry," only makes the erroneous title seem all the more reasonable.

No, it's definitely "Calvary," as in the name of the hill where Christ was put to death, yet this actually fits the story *worse* than "Cavalry." Nothing in this episode particularly emulates Christ or the crucifixion, so the "correct" title seems totally baffling. Ah, but wait... the hill where Christ died, while commonly called "Calvary," is more properly named "Golgotha," and *that* means skull or "the place of the skull." It's cited in every one of the Gospels, although we refer you to John 19:17 (King James version), which says, "And he bearing his cross went forth into a place called the place of a skull, which is called in the Hebrew Gol'gotha." *Calvaria*, in fact, is the Latin term for Calvary and refers to the dome of the skull. And now let's remember that this story entails Gunn and Connor kill a "soul-eater" and strip the flesh from its skull, which gets placed front and center during Evil Cordelia's faux ritual.

So, there you have it. Barring some new finding or authors' interview coming to light, the title's got nothing to do with Christ or the crucifixion. It's about... a skull. "The place of the skull," even.

2. Time for a little continuity glue, as the Beast fashions a rocky blade from its own hide as a "tribute" to its master – who's later revealed as Evil Cordy, and uses the weapon to dispatch Lilah. Given that pretty much anything serrated would've sufficed for this purpose, and given that the weapon facilitates the Beast's downfall next episode, you're entitled to ask – tribute or no – precisely why the hell the Beast would freely create an instrument capable of killing it.

The answer, even though it's never stated on screen, is that Evil Cordy probably requests the rocky blade's creation with the intent of causing the Beast's downfall. After all, consider the peace-loving and tranquil Earth that Jasmine desires... what possible place could the Beast occupy in such a setting? The answer is none, meaning that *of course* Evil Cordy wants the Beast eliminated once it's done her dirty work.

3. Lilah believes that the Beast has followed up on its assault on the firm (4.08, "Habeas Corpses") by eliminating everyone who worked there – the field agents, liaisons and people out sick included. We're inclined to take this as hearsay, because honestly... Lilah couldn't have witnessed any of this, or she'd be dead.

The alternative is to believe that the Beast has systematically gone around L.A. and culled potentially hundreds of Wolfram and Hart-affiliated agents on a one-on-one basis; this isn't inconceivable, but can the Beast really get around town that quick? How does it know who's tied to the firm? Most importantly, why would it bother? Of all the priorities on the Beast's schedule, "Mop up every son-of-a-bitch who worked for Wolfram and Hart" can't rank *that* high. So yeah... Lilah's cut off from her resources; she's going off field reports and doesn't necessarily know the score.

4. By this point, it's getting rather curious how often your commonplace vampire wears a plaid shirt. There are literally plaid-wearing vampires in "Soulless" and the three episodes to follow, *and* in "Release" (4.14) *and* in a bowling alley in "Shiny Happy People" (4.18), *and* later in 5.10, "Soul Purpose"... we could go on. Cumulatively, it's as if a plaid shirt factory blew up, and the vampires and demons sifted through the rubble afterward and went on their way. Perhaps Buffy was right in the very first *Buffy* episode: You really *can* identify vampires by their awful dress sense. (And see also the rogue Slayer's garb in 5.11, "Damage.")

5. Wesley barreled through Wo-Pang's guards in 4.10, "Awakening," so it's rather entertaining when he, Connor and Evil Cordy must kick the crap out of Wo-Pang's guards *again* to get an audience with him. It's almost as if there's a sign on the door reading, "Please beat for service."

CHARACTER NOTES *Angelus:* Correctly identifies that the Beast, prone to "smash and slaughter," is working to someone else's plan. His astute hearing lets him register, even when he's jailed in the hotel basement, everything said in the lobby. He's essentially guessed what Gunn and Fred did to Professor Seidel [4.05, "Supersymmetry"] and implies that Angel figured it out some time ago. Angelus finds Wes "tasty," even though he "doesn't swing that way" [but see – oh, dear – 5.21, "Power Play"]. He can impersonate Angel exceptionally well.

• *Evil Cordelia:* Takes a crossbow arrow in the leg while fighting Angelus.

• *Wesley:* Orders everyone to kill Angelus rather than take him alive. [He'll reverse this next episode, but it's here justified. Trying to take Angelus with anything less than lethal force will simply get people killed.] He tells Lilah, "There are many reasons we wouldn't have worked out," apologizes to Fred about his scrap with Gunn [last episode], and asks her to tell Gunn the same, but she doesn't think he'll listen.

• *Gunn:* Annoyed that Fred thinks he attacked Wesley. [Except that... he *did* attack Wesley. Think back to who threw the first punch last episode. It wasn't Wes.] Gunn claims he's never fought a soul-eater before [see **Demonology**], guards Angelus with a flamethrower [presumably the one from 3.10, "Dad"] and concurs with Wesley about killing Angelus.

• *Fred:* Definitively tells Wesley that she and Gunn "aren't together anymore." [But see 4.14, "Release" for a footnote on this.] Her reaction upon learning about Wesley's liaisons with Lilah: "It's none of my business." [Yet it doesn't exactly close the distance between them.]

• *Lorne:* Has a love for humanity, but stands ready to smack Lilah if needed. He implies that under normal circumstances where people sing for him, a souled being's aura "looks" different to him that of a soul-less creature.

• *Connor:* Moves slower than the soul-eater.

• *Lilah:* Still bleeding from the injury the Beast caused ["Habeas Corpses"], and proves inept at serving everyone coffee [how far she's fallen since 1.19, "Sanctuary"]. She's got decent reflexes, enough to hurl Angelus down the stairs.

• *Wo-Pang:* Determines that the Muo-Ping containing Angel's soul is still intact – but can't discern its location – by rolling a few bone dice on the floor. He knows of no way to re-ensoul Angel without the Muo-Ping.

THE LIBRARY Lilah owns a copy of *Rhinehardt's Compendium* that she procured on the pan-dimensional black market. Wesley's copy [4.09, "Long Day's Journey"] is identical, but missing a passage on the Beast [see **Magic**].

ORGANIZATIONS *Wolfram and Hart:* Lilah implies that the firm previously wanted Angel to become Angelus. [She's grossly over-simplifying here. Stories such as 2.07, "Darla," in fact, suggest that the firm wasn't out to get Angelus back.] She also claims you're more likely to win the lottery six times running than to have divine intervention, as she evidently had the numbers run at some point.

DEMONOLOGY *Soul-Eater:* Demon creature that Cordelia says the Chumash [see *Buffy* 4.08, "Pangs"] buried a couple of hundred years ago. Once freed from its box, the creature moves super-fast like the Flash. It [apparently] starts to drain Connor's life force before Gunn beheads it. [The creature seems to devour souls almost like Mr. Jenoff from 3.18, "Double or Nothing," although that soul-gobbling was by mutual contract.]

4.12, Calvary

MAGIC All references to the Beast were magically erased in this dimension [this undoubtedly owes to Jasmine, and might have occurred at the very second she awoke in Cordelia's body in "Spin the Bottle" (4.06)]. This affected the memories of everyone except the suppressed Angelus. [This was frightfully powerful magic, then, and something of a precursor to the memory spell invoked in 4.22, "Home"]. Lilah says that the "big magic" used to take a champion's soul makes ripples, and some of her contacts register such disturbances.

• *Evil Cordelia's "Soul-Restoration" Ritual:* Entirely fails. [4.17, "Inside Out" says the ritual's real goal is to quietly muck up Lorne's senses, fooling him into misreading Angelus as Angel.] The spell entails placing a soul-eater's skinned skull in a circle of branches. Cordelia drips blood onto the skull, and everyone takes one of seven talismans built from the likes of roadkill and buffalo wings. Cordy hurls something on the ground that knocks Angelus back, Wesley chants, candles flare, the earth shakes and glowing tendrils appear to spin Angelus around for a bit.

• *Muo-Ping:* If this jar [4.10, "Awakening"] gets broken or opened, Angel's soul can be "returned or destroyed." [This suggests it can't be destroyed in the bottle; that's feasible, as 4.15, "Orpheus" says the Muo-ping is immune to magic.]

• *The Orb of Thesulah:* [Previously used in *Buffy* 2.22, "Belonging"; and see "Orpheus."] Only method Fred can find of restoring Angel's soul; but only works if the soul has moved onto an afterlife [meaning they need to release it from the Muo-ping first].

BEST LINE Evil Cordelia to Lilah: "Man, I'd love to punch your face in." Lilah: "Are you trying to turn me on?"

THINGS THAT DON'T MAKE SENSE Not very much, although Evil Cordelia's dastardly plan has a major flaw in that Angelus could kill her, right then and there, once she opens his cell door. Sure, she probably plans in advance that funky move where she dodges him and locks herself in the cell, but if she'd mis-timed her maneuver even a little, she'd have been toast. Fair enough she suspects that Angelus will probably want to string her along and torture her, but it still puts her multi-year plan at grave risk.

Whose shirt does Lilah don after cleaning herself up in the hotel? It fits her perfectly, so it can't belong to Cordelia because it's not (errrr) too big, yet it's not Fred's shirt because it's not too small. No shells fall from Lilah's pistol, even though we hear them tinkle all over the floor, and why's she trying to shoot Angelus with a gun anyway? He's survived much, much worse, so it's far better to nail him with a tranquilizer dart.

Last point, and something of a repeat complaint: Bands of vampires are roaming L.A., causing mayhem and total anarchy. But has the greater world noticed? Not that we can see.

IN RETROSPECT Angelus, failing to find any civilians to eat, complains that there's "no fast food" left in L.A. – which brings to mind Spike's characterization of people as "Happy Meals on legs" in *Buffy* 2.22, "Becoming."

IT'S REALLY ABOUT... Past liaisons coming back to haunt us, as Wesley clearly feels guilty about his shacking up with Lilah; her mere presence in the hotel causes him considerable discomfort. It also serves – once Angelus blabs about the relationship – to drive a wedge between Wes and Fred just as things started to look rosier.

CRITIQUE Once again, there's an upward tick in quality – something that's all the more remarkable, considering there are three names attached to the writing credits and that's usually asking for trouble. But with "Calvary," we're given a worthy installment that culminates in just about the most horrifying and shocking ending imaginable. We scathed "Awakening" because (among other reasons) its final twist was over-rated, but here we're given a shock that should've genuinely knocked anyone unspoiled out of their damn seat. On first broadcast, it certainly threw us to the floor.

We could quibble about some of this, such as wondering if the show's soap-opera element isn't getting a bit thick, and noting that the parts with the faux ritual and Angelus masquerading as Angel go on for rather too long. But overall, we're satisfied. Watching Lilah further upend relationships in the Hyperion was almost guaranteed to be a hoot and a holler, and as such "Calvary" makes a laudable contribution to the seasonal story arc, and suitably serves as the last stop before the Faith three-parter.

THE LORE Romanov wasn't a stranger to getting killed and then continuing to appear on a show for whatever reason. In episode No. 8 of *Models, Inc.*, her character (Teri Spencer) was murdered in a fit of jealous rage, whereupon Romanov immediately took to playing Monique Duran – someone with Teri's looks, minus the bitchy attitude. As Victoria Dahl in *Spy Hard* (1996), she's the murdered lover of Dick Steele (Leslie Nielsen), who's contacted 15 years later by Victoria's daughter (and still played by Romanov, of course). On UPN's *Seven Days* (or *7 Days*, as it's variously called), she was the sister of a lead character and got slain after stealing half a million dollars from the Russian mafia – the heroes helpfully used time travel to ensure her demise didn't happen.

4.13: "Salvage"

"Angel's gone, Faith. Angelus is back."

Air Date: March 5, 2003; **Writer:** David Fury; **Director:** Jefferson Kibbee

SUMMARY Angelus happens upon Lilah's corpse and, purely for sadism's sake, fools the heroes into thinking that *he* murdered her. The fiend again flees, leaving Wesley the thankless task of beheading Lilah on the off chance that Angelus sired her as a vampire. Wesley renews his resolve to take Angelus alive and recruits Faith, the incarcerated Vampire Slayer, to help. Faith adeptly breaks out of prison, then goes hunting for Angelus.

Unfortunately, Angelus hears about Faith's return and allies himself with the Beast, who easily thrashes Faith within an inch of her life. But to prove that he's nobody's pawn, Angel stabs the Beast with a knife made from its own rocky body. The Beast consequently explodes, canceling the spell that darkened the sun. Faith barely escapes with her life, even as Cordelia tells Connor that she's pregnant with his child.

POINTS OF DISCUSSION ABOUT "Salvage":

1. The status quo bears some consideration, because the heroes are a group of highly skilled and extremely accomplished demon hunters who are now looking for help from other people – Angelus, then Faith, then Willow – more than at any other point in the series. Certainly, Season Four entails a more epic threat than the previous years, and the triple-whammy of facing the Beast *and* Angelus *and* the Beast Master must seem absolutely daunting. But the heroes' self-confidence seems rattled more than ever, stemming from (but hardly limited to) Wesley's downfall in Season Three, Connor's upbringing in a hell dimension, Gunn and Fred's break-up, Angel's going barking mad and Lorne's life of showbiz in Vegas failing miserably. Come Season Five, Angel's band will similarly find themselves (excuse the phrasing) in the belly of the beast... but it's notable that in the end, they'll look to each other for solutions.

2. Connor's declaration that "I don't give a flying *sluk* what Wesley says..." appears to have befuddled more than one viewer, and not without good reason. If you're not reading this book in order, the term "sluk" – here used in place of the f-word – was the name of the glowing bugs from "The Price" (3.19), and which Connor was acquainted with in Quor'toth. Unfortunately, the bugs' actual name was hastily used on screen just once (in 3.21, "Benediction") and never caught on, and it's a bit strange that the writers didn't consider how few people would get the joke.

3. Wesley goes to behead Lilah, and his tormented mind imagines a final conversation with her (see **Character Development**). Unusually for *Angel* or *Buffy*, it's a slice of outright surrealism without a supernatural explanation. In most other episodes, this sort of strangeness would stem from (say) a bit of magic, an infernal contract with the firm or even a dancing demon. But here, it's the fevered delusions of Wesley's mind, nothing more.

Oh, and doesn't Wesley look extra creepy when he pulls an axe out of the wall and announces he'll "take care" of Lilah's corpse? It says something about Fred's character that she doesn't squawk in the slightest, even though the axe-hefting Wesley surely evokes "Billy" (3.06) more than a little.

4. Critics often wonder why Gunn escorts Connor back to the Hyperion, given that the boy goes on patrol all the time. Obviously, the issue isn't that Connor needs someone to hold his hand, it's that nobody trusts him to obey orders and go home, as opposed to having another go at Angelus.

5. Acker and Kartheiser look like they're having a bit too much fun as they pull the arrow out of Cordelia's thigh.

6. So Faith dives through a glass window in prison, thrashes a few guards, grabs Wesley and hurls them both through ***another*** window, whereupon they survive a three-story plunge, smash in a car roof and walk away. It's one of the wildest and most magnificent undertakings of the entire show, and we adore it. Mind, it would've sucked if Faith had gone to all that trouble... and had smashed in *Wesley's* car by sheer chance, forcing them to hitchhike back to L.A.

CHARACTER NOTES *Angelus:* In 1845, Angelus happened upon the vampire Rosaria in a little town outside Tuscany. [Angelus also visited Italy (specifically, Rome) in 1771 (3.07, "Offspring") and 1894 (5.20, "The Girl in Question"). Tuscany was essentially the birthplace of the Italian Renaissance, so perhaps Darla's love of Botticelli – and by extension Tuscan painters – made them visit. We're probably meant to infer that Angelus slept with the nineteenth century Rosaria, and it certainly looks as if – when he stakes her in the modern day – he's getting rid of a one-night stand.]

Angelus is already acquainted with Buffy's sister Dawn. [They never meet on screen, but the spell that created Dawn in *Buffy* Season Five retroactively placed her into Angel's history.] Vamps lounging in a bar know Angelus' reputation, and applaud his return to the fold. Angelus didn't expect that killing the Beast would actually restore the sun, thinking that scenario just part of Angel's fantasy [4.10, "Awakening"].

- *Evil Cordelia:* Feigns weakness owing to her arrow-wound to the thigh, incurred fighting Angelus last episode, and holes up in her room for three episodes. Evil Cordelia tells her lackey, the Beast, to "give Mama some sugar" before kissing his rocky mug. [It's unclear how far matters go between them physically, but the mind does wonder.]

Angelus doesn't sense Evil Cordy nearby as he chats with the Beast. [Jasmine's power must shield her from detection; this talent might extend to Cordelia's sweat, etc., because Angelus doesn't smell her scent on the Beast's knife either.]

• *Wesley:* Volunteers to behead Lilah rather quickly, and upon taking her body to the basement imagines her talking to him. [This "Lilah" is kindler and gentler than the genuine article, and definitely stems from Wesley's subconscious.] In this fashion, Wesley wonders if Lilah actually loved him, and seems to express regret that he couldn't save her from her own darkness. [Much of this owes to Wesley being distraught because he didn't actually sleep with Lilah in the hopes of redeeming or "saving" her. Rather, it stemmed from him thinking that *he* couldn't attain redemption, meaning it was down to self-loathing more than anything else.]

Wesley reverses course from last episode, and declares the heroes should take Angelus alive. [Having lost Lilah, Wesley can't stand the thought of being unable to save Angel either.]

• *Lorne:* The Sanctuary Spell prevents him from using violence.

• *Connor:* Complains that the heroes have over-relied on magic this year, often with tragic results. [Well, that's valid enough.] Connor has heard about vampire Slayers [either from Fred and Gunn during the summer hiatus, or from Holtz in Quor'toth]. Faith clearly turns Connor on, and she's physically able to keep the boy in his place. [Faith's skill, rather than raw strength, accounts for this. It's also possible that Connor likes her dominating him a bit.] When Connor proves unable to follow orders and exercise restraint, Faith orders him back to the hotel.

• *Faith:* Readily becomes the team's general upon entering the Hyperion. [This isn't normal behavior for Slayers, who generally act alone. Yet Faith steps right up to the plate, with just the right mix of compassion and strength.] She's currently serving 25 to life, owing to a Murder Two conviction [she certainly qualified for Murder One, but must have plea-bargained after 1.19, "Sanctuary"]. She's daring enough to think she can fight Angelus and the Beast simultaneously, and proves highly resilient when the Beast punches the living hell out of her. Faith's inmate number: 430019. [It was 43100 in 2.01, "Judgment."]

• *The Beast:* Longs to "crush Angelus' skull," but refrains at Evil Cordy's command. The Beast's death resembles the demise it suffered in Angel's dream ["Awakening"] and it crumbles to rocky pieces afterward.

THE HYPERION Evidently has a well-equipped spice rack. [It's unclear if Gunn and Fred plunder spices left behind when the hotel closed in 1979, or if Angel got domestic again – remember his cooking skill from 1.10, "Parting Gifts" – when baby Connor was in residence. If Angel went shopping and stocked up, then perhaps he *did* cook the food he served Lorne in 4.05, "Supersymmetry."]

ORGANIZATIONS Angelus patronizes a seedy bar that numbers vampires and demons among its clientele. [The exterior footage of this joint shows North Hollywood Billiards, a real-life establishment located at 11130 Magnolia Boulevard.]

DEMONOLOGY *Vampires:* [All right, the wound on Lilah's neck isn't particularly convincing, as it's a single hole as opposed to the two bite-marks you'd expect from a vamp – and which an ice pick properly simulates in 3.21, "Benediction." Seriously, the ice pick and Evil Cordy's rocky blade *both* leave wounds akin to a vampire attack? But rather than pegging this as a goof, perhaps it's simpler to think that the more vicious vampires savagely tear out hunks of flesh as opposed to a clean bite, meaning Lilah's wound looks reasonable.]

MAGIC *The Sanctuary Spell (abridged):* Lorne phones the Furies [3.03, "That Old Gang of Mine" and 3.07, "Offspring"] and gets instructions on a homemade version of the Sanctuary Spell. This requires a heck of a lot of spices. Cloves work as an acceptable substitute for bloodroot; paprika, ginger and allspice don't. After Lorne sprinkles burnt clove dust around the perimeter of the hotel, lights a few candles and incants a few phrases in English, the spell quietly activates. This neutralizes demon violence in the hotel [as with Caritas] but gives humans free rein [as Fred proves next episode].

BEST LINE(s) Wesley asks, "Feel natural?", after Faith tests her lapsed Slayer skills against some random vamps. Faith's response: "It's like riding a biker."

THINGS THAT DON'T MAKE SENSE We've taken potshots at the sloppy means by which the heroes turned Angel into Angelus, but this might rank as the ultimate oversight: All of the sudden, the heroes realize they can create a layman's Sanctuary Spell using – among other odds and ends – some bits from the hotel spice rack. But if it was *that* easy to insulate the hotel against demon violence, wouldn't it have made more sense to do this before turning Angel into Angelus? Did they *want* Angelus to get loose and slaughter them all?

We're going to forgive the suggestion that Wesley should've briefed Faith on the Beast's invulnerability – i.e. that her crossbow arrow wouldn't do any damage – on the grounds that she wasn't expecting to encounter the rocky bastard and she's doing the best she can. More erroneously, though, Evil Cordy uses her rocky blade as a lure to bring Angelus to the Beast's hideout, and strangely, Lilah's blood is still wet and dripping from the blade by the time Angelus happens upon it. As we've said, it's nearly the coolest thing ever when Faith and Wesley endure a three-story drop, but is it reasonable that the all-too-human Wesley would survive? Even presuming Faith took the brunt of the impact, Wes miraculously just walks away. Also, Faith thwarts a prison murder attempt by smacking her would-be killer in the face with a huge barbell – nice, but this probably would've caved in the woman's skull. But then, the entire murder attempt makes no sense, because...

CROSS-OVERS Faith's fellow inmate, Deb, takes after her with a ceremonial blade akin to those of the Bringers, the servants of the First Evil. The First is presently trying to massacre the entire Slayer line in *Buffy* Season Seven, and the attempt on Faith's life is presumably part of its plan. [Yet so much about this seems wrong. Deb says, "I need the money!" as if someone paid her to assassinate Faith, even though the Bringers never showed any interest in using cash – or even in conscripting someone to do their dirty work – before now. Moreover, this goes to a thundering logic flaw in *Buffy* Season Seven, which repeatedly claims that a new Slayer will be generated if Buffy dies – even though there's six seasons' worth of *Buffy* to the contrary, including Buffy's death at the end of Season Five. The bulk of evidence says that Faith's demise, not Buffy's, would generate a new Slayer. So offing Faith in prison would arguably ruin the First's plans, not aid them.]

Angelus phones Sunnydale, asks Dawn "[Is] your sister home?" and hangs up upon getting confirmation. This lets him identify Faith as the Slayer who's rumored to be in L.A. [There's no corresponding point on *Buffy* when this happens, even though it's rather strange to think Dawn never mentioned to her sister, "By the way, Angel called. He sounded a bit high and hung up on me."]

POP CULTURE Angelus: "The question is, what do you do, hotshot? What do you do?" It's a take-off of Dennis Hopper's line about a bomb in *Speed*, and wouldn't seem note-worthy if Whedon hadn't worked on that movie's script.

CRITIQUE Season Four's serialized nature makes it unique compared to the other *Angel* years, so it's a bit strange to consider how much the Faith three-parter taps into the ongoing threads, yet feels and sounds like a separate mini-series. To the writers' credit, they keep everything perfectly smooth for the *Angel* fans while providing little info-dumps (such as Faith's little recap in Wesley's car) to help any *Buffy* viewer who wandered in to see what's up with Faith. As crossovers go, Mutant Enemy pulled this one off with much finesse.

Critically speaking, there's a palpable sense of *Angel* kicking up the adrenaline, in no small part due to all the *Matrix*-inspired fight scenes, and largely because the producers – implementing the first hardcore *Buffy* cross-over since Season One – feel the need to pull out all the stops. Even so, where the story *best* shines is in the tightness of the script. Nearly every scene entails some sort of reveal or surprise, and it feels as if David Fury labored and re-labored over this script for months on end, polishing it incessantly. Even though it's far more likely that he delayed until the last minute (see **The Lore**).

Oddly enough, Faith doesn't actually appear until the second half, but it's commendable that *Angel* races along without her – particularly in Wesley's riveting "basement discussion" with Lilah's corpse. Nonetheless, once the Slayer arrives, Faith immediately bends the story around her. That's not a criticism, you realize. The character has become an absolute natural in this element, as her "step away from the glass" moment with Wesley proves, and it's like Dushku last occupied the role yesterday as opposed to more than two years ago.

So we're at the core of this season, and it's telling that when the Beast – the major nemesis until this point – kicks the bucket, you barely notice his absence because there's *sooooooo* much going on. Complain about Season Four's inter-woven plots all you like, but for now, they're layering the show with a rich texture.

THE LORE Fury, a self-proclaimed procrastinator, evidently logged a ludicrous amount of play time in a makeshift miniature golf course set up in the *Angel* offices – most notably when he was staring down a four-day deadline. Conversely, Jane Espenson could bang out an episode in 30 hours, making Fury stifle the urge to strangle her. (DiLullo, *CityofAngel.com*)

• Dushku, who's decently strong, requested a stunt double for Kartheiser in the scene where Faith has to throw Connor around, fearing she'd hurt him for real. (*BBC Cult*, April 2003)

• Faith is presently incarcerated at the Northern California Women's Facility (NCWF) in Stockton. At the time, it was the smallest of California's three prisons for women. Four days before "Salvage" was broadcast, the NCWF shut its doors as part of a budget-cutting measure that axed five correctional facilities. (Perhaps the news of a convicted brunette murderer bursting through the visitor's room glass and surviving a three-story leap to freedom didn't help the joint's reputation.)

• Alonzo Bodden, here a humble prison guard, served as co-host of *Straight Eye for the Whipped Guy* – a show with that apparently died in the pilot stage. He also voiced Thunderon in *Power Rangers Lightspeed Rescue*.

• Spice Williams (the convict Debbie)... well, she's a curious one. She appeared in *Buffy* 2.10, "What's My Line, Part 2" as an assassin disguised as a policewoman. She portrayed a vampire in Quentin Tarantino's gorefest *From Dusk 'Till Dawn*, and she's done stuntwork on a myriad of films including *Galaxy Quest* and *Spider-Man*. She's also married to Bing Crosby's grandson, and with her husband markets a vegetarian food line named "Spice of Life Meatless Meats and Jerky."

4.14: "Release"

"Nothing will ever change who you are, Faith. You're a murderer, an animal and you enjoy it... just like me."

Air Date: March 12, 2003; **Writer:** Steven S. DeKnight, Elizabeth Craft, Sarah Fain; **Director:** James A. Contner

SUMMARY Faith tends her wounds, then resumes hunting Angelus with Wesley. Meanwhile, the deep-throated "master of the Beast" – actually Cordelia – telepathically communes with Angelus, and brings him to heel by threatening to restore Angel's soul. The Beast Master directs "his" new lackey to eliminate Faith, leading Angelus into conflict with Wesley and the Slayer. A scrap ensues, with Angelus incapacitating Wes and – for a grand finale – sinking his teeth into Faith's throat.

FIRSTS AND LASTS Final appearance of Wesley's apartment, and Heaven only knows what his landlord makes of the damage Faith does to his shower. (See **Best Line**, although you almost expect Wesley to say, "Don't worry, Lilah used to do worse than that in an afternoon.") Second time and last time (the first being 3.21, "Benediction") that Connor walks into a room, anxious to find someone, and it turns out they're just in the bathroom. Last of three episodes this season (the other two being 4.02, "Ground State" and 4.05, "Supersymmetry") where Fred uses the word "bitch," when she describes what the Beast Master will make of Angelus.

THE OPENING CREDITS A mere 58 episodes after his debut, Andy Hallett gets added to the main credits. The title sequence also gets tweaked a bit, with the elimination of the weird "swooping down on a perched Angel" shot first seen in 4.01, "Deep Down."

POINTS OF DISCUSSION ABOUT "Release":

1. Fred has her hair pulled up, and when she poses, arms outstretched, with a trank-pistol, she looks uncannily like Princess Leia. Anyone who doubts this should check out Item No. 4 on the DVD scene-select; it's as if this episode guest-stars a young Carrie Fisher. But then, if we're looking for parallels to other properties, Angelus looks a bit *Masterpiece Theatre* when he dons glasses and lounges in front of a fire in an occult bookstore. All he needs is Cookie Monster, and he's ready to co-host *Monsterpiece Theatre*.

2. The Sanctuary Spell spanks Connor when he assaults Angelus, proving that Connor is at least part-demon. That's hardly a surprise, as he's the progeny of two vampires and his super-powers must come from *somewhere*, yet it's faintly amazing that the show never really addresses this revelation further. That leaves us with the task of reconciling Connor's abilities and likely demon-hood against 3.16, "Sleep Tight," in which the firm tested baby Connor's blood as run-of-the-mill human. Either Connor started out life as normal or Lilah simply lied to Sahjhan about the test results – she didn't have much reason to fib, but then, Lilah never needed one. Still, it's possible that Connor somehow become laced with demon DNA while growing up in Quor'toth. The older Holtz never displays similar super-powers, but then, we don't know Quor'toth's effects on a growing infant versus someone who's already an adult.

One other possibility: Perhaps the Sanctuary Spell is hyper-sensitive. Ideally, it'd be calibrated to allow violence from anyone who's 100 percent, Grade-A beef, indisputably and without reservation human – and to block anyone failing to meet that threshold. At the very least, the Spell would probably register Connor as "other-worldly," even if he's more human than not. It's a pity, then, that we never see if the Spell works on Dawn, a mystical key refashioned into human form.

Ultimately, we simply don't know what's up with Connor. He's certainly unique: the child of two vampires, brought into being through the reward of a mystical contest (see **Did Jasmine Cause All This?**) and tailor-made to father a higher being on the Earthly plane. Any number of possibilities about his degree of humanity could be true. In fact, it's feasible that the Shanshu Prophecy, which talks about a heroic vampire with a soul, refers to Connor – who's a vampire progeny and the owner of a soul – even if he doesn't exhibit the more unsavory characteristics of vampirism.

3. We mentioned back in Season One that Faith attains one of the Whedon-verse's greatest stories of redemption. So it's quite the juxtaposition when Wesley, Faith's former torture victim (1.18, "Five by Five"), solicits information from a witness by stabbing her in the shoulder. Moreover, he then – having tried so hard to restore Faith's humanity in Season One – seeks to strip it away in the interests of her besting Angelus. In the end, none of this soils Faith's character, given that she resorts to trickery rather than savagery in defeating Angel's evil side. However, it's something of a barometer for how much Wesley has changed.

4. In the interests of reconciling "Release" with the next

episode, Faith and Wesley must concoct their gambit with the Orpheus drug after Faith declares, "There's gotta be another way." There's no continuity breach on that score.

5. For those keeping track of such parallels, Angelus here goads with Faith with, "There's my girl; knew she was in there somewhere... dying to come out and play again." It's a reversal of Darla's similar appeal to Angel in 2.05, "Dear Boy." ("My boy is in there, and he wants out!")

6. Evil Cordy's telepathic communication as "the Beast Master" seems a bit strange, even allowing that a slip-of-the-tongue proves her undoing in 4.16, "Players," because it's arguably a goof that Angel/Angelus doesn't identify Cordy as the grand schemer much sooner. After all, whatever the Beast Master's impressively masculine voice, "his" diction is distinctly feminine and almost trademark Cordelia at times. Telling examples include, "I'm where it's warm... and soft," "Soul, soul, who has your soul? Oh, right... me!", "This isn't the way, my sweet," "so beautifully vain," "You've been a bad boy," and especially "I've had my eyes on you for some time." Honestly, does Angelus think the Beast Master is gay?

CHARACTER NOTES *Angelus:* Now drinking with dumb vampire groupies in bar. He's quick enough to dodge trank-gun darts and shotgun blasts at almost point-blank range, refuses to blow Faith's head off when given the opportunity [he's prolonging her suffering, it seems]; and, generally speaking, looks as if he's got her outclassed. [It's possible that Faith deliberately holds back due to her Orpheus drug gambit, as explained next episode, but in the main Angelus looks stronger than her.]

Angelus' persona seems to remain aware whenever Angel has dominance [confirmed next episode], and he appears to fear the thought of Angel re-gaining control more than anything else. [Some fans have questioned why Angelus doesn't call the Beast Master's threat to re-ensoul Angel, as such an action would hardly further the Beast Master's plans, but Angelus simply can't take the risk.] Angelus implies that he intends to sire Faith as a vampire.

• *Evil Cordelia:* It's revealed that she took Angel's soul [4.11, "Soulless"]. The closer her child gets to being born, the less Cordelia-like Evil Cordelia becomes. [It's possible that we're only seeing her vicious side now that we know she's the villain, but it's entirely probable that the Jasmine entity gains dominance as it gestates. And see 4.18, "Shiny Happy People" for more on her personality shifts.]

Telepathic communication with Angelus makes Cordy's eyes cloud over [same as the faux visions she's "received" this year], and entails a glowing interface in the palm of her hand. Her telepathic voice can hurt Angelus' mind a bit, and she claims she's irked at Angelus for killing the Beast [yet there's every reason to think she isn't; see 4.12, "Calvary"].

• *Wesley:* Stresses that Faith needs to take down Angelus even at the cost of Wesley's life. He trusts Gunn to guard the Hyperion and hurt Angelus if necessary.

• *Fred:* Makes one final bid to reunite with Gunn, claiming that she misses him. However, a last kiss between them fails to generate a spark. [And see 4.16, "Players" for the final nail... so to speak... in their relationship. It's fairly evident, although it's never said, that Fred's eleventh-hour effort with Gunn owes to her learning about Wesley's relationship with Lilah. After all, shortly before that, she was practically throwing herself into Wesley's arms, telling him that her relationship with Gunn was definitively over. Wesley's working so closely with Faith probably doesn't alleviate Fred's insecurity either.]

• *Lorne:* He is acquainted with Maury, a demon who peddles fake charms, and "hangs his horns" in a shop down on Olive. Lorne says he "can't get a good read" on Cordelia and Connor's relationship. [As in many instances, this owes to Lorne's intuition and ability to read body-language, not his empathic power.]

• *Connor:* Goes right back to Cordy after she says she's pregnant, and drops any lust for Faith like a bad habit.

• *Faith:* Displays an impressive vertical leap. She admits to Angelus that she doesn't want to die [as opposed to her suicidal streak in "Five by Five"].

THE LIBRARY Angelus steals the information that Wolfram and Hart pulled from Lorne's head [4.04, "Slouching Toward Bethlehem"] and Lilah's copy of *Rhinehardt's Compendium* [4.12, "Cavalry"]. Frustrated, he tosses Lilah's book into a fireplace. [On screen, the book rattles around and doesn't appear burnt, but "Players" confirms it as destroyed. It's probable, but never stated, that Angelus torches the firm's data also.]

ORGANIZATIONS *Occult Books:* Yet another magical bookshop in L.A., located at street number 1351. Conjuring candles are currently 25 percent off; aura readings are held every Tuesday. Reg, the manager or owner, luckily escapes while the Beast Master's voice distracts Angelus.

DEMONOLOGY *Vampires:* The vampire bar [seen last episode] has back rooms where humans shoot up and allow vampires to feed off them. [This sometimes entails the drug Orpheus, as we learn next episode.] The humans effectively filter whatever drug they take, resulting in intoxicating effects for all concerned. [This isn't terribly far from Riley Finn letting female vamps feed off him in *Buffy* Season Five, although so far as we know, drugs weren't involved on those occasions.] The bar vamps wear their demon faces while hanging out socially; Angelus doesn't.

• *Strom Demons:* Can survive and heal a shotgun blast to the face.

MAGIC *The Sanctuary Spell:* As promised, it allows human violence, as evidenced when Fred smashes a pitcher against Angelus' head. The spell doesn't extend as far as the Hyperion's front courtyard.

BEST LINE Wesley, after Faith vents her frustrations by punching out his shower tile: "I'm fairly sure my security deposit's a complete loss."

THINGS THAT DON'T MAKE SENSE Firearms enthusiasts will note that Wesley and Angelus combined milk seven rounds from Wes' shotgun – such a weapon normally only carries six shells. Weirdly, Fred claims that Angelus "let her live" when he visited the Hyperion, when in truth the hotel's Sanctuary Spell would've kept her safe from harm. Yet again, Connor's exceptional hearing lets him down, as he fails to hear Cordy chatting to Angelus as the "Beast Master" while he's right outside her room. Oh, and Connor seems intent on keeping the pregnant Evil Cordy warm, as if she's got a cold. (To be fair, Connor can't know much about pregnancies.)

IN RETROSPECT Wes impales a drug-addict in the shoulder, gets the information he needs and justifies this with: "I avoided the main arteries. She'll live." Unbelievably, he'll re-use the "I avoided the major organs" excuse in 5.16, "Shells."

IT'S REALLY ABOUT... The main action with Angelus, Faith and Wesley more or less continues what's come before, but there's a bit of a subtext in the Sanctuary Spell bitch-slapping Connor about. This leads to a small identity crisis for the lad – "I don't even know what I am," he tells Evil Cordy – and in a small way it's akin to the usual metaphor of a teenager's undergoing changes during his ascent into adulthood. However it's surprising, given Connor's seething demon-bigotry in "Benediction" (3.21), how much it's not about his discovering that he's part-demon himself, like someone learning they hail from a mixed heritage.

CRITIQUE It's comparatively the loosest episode of the Faith three-parter, possibly because there are three writers in the mix, or perhaps by simple virtue of being the middle installment. But in absolute terms, it remains a sharp piece of storytelling that starts with a *sweet* teaser (Faith punching out Wesley's shower), quickens as it goes along, and explodes with one of the show's best one-on-one superpowered melees. There have assuredly been other occasions (none more egregious than *Buffy* 4.21, "Primeval") when the Mutant Enemy crew clearly took *The Matrix* a bit too much to heart. But here – thanks to the direction, and we're guessing even more to DeKnight's obvious fetish for fight scenes – the Angelus/Faith fracas amid all the scaffolding looks marvelous.

There's not much to say that wasn't covered last episode, but it's overall great stuff, and capped off by one of the series' most dynamic cliffhangers. (As a bonus, it's got that wonderfully askew bit where Connor – questioning what his demon inheritance means – tries to "vamp out" in front of a mirror.)

THE LORE Fred accidentally tranquilizes Lorne in this story, meaning that – allowing for multiple takes – Hallett did little but lie on the floor of the Hyperion set for a day. (O'Hare, *Zap2It.com*, Feb. 27, 2003)

• Catalina Larranaga (Vamp Waitress) also appeared in *The Pleasure Zone, Hollywood Sex Fantasy, Voyeur Confessions, Bare Witness, Passion Cove* and even *Downward Angel*. (One suspects, just a little, that these aren't entirely wholesome films.) On the other hand, Peter Renaday (the Beast Master's booming masculine voice) has voiceover credits that include *Shrek, Teenage Mutant Ninja Turtles* (where he's Splinter), *Transformers* (where he's Grapple) and a host of Disney films including *The Cat From Outer Space* and *The Computer Wore Tennis Shoes*.

4.15: "Orpheus"

"It leads you down to hell and leaves you there."

Air Date: March 19, 2003; **Writer:** Mere Smith; **Director:** Terrence O'Hara

SUMMARY Angelus suddenly collapses, realizing too late that Faith tricked him by lacing her system with a mystical drug named Orpheus. The heroes take Angelus and Faith – both of them comatose – back to the Hyperion. However, Angelus and Faith's minds interact as a side effect of the drug, enabling them to experience events from Angel's past. The history lesson culminates in 1990s New York, where Angel lived as a homeless person. Fortunately, Angel's "homeless" persona gains enough strength to brawl with Angelus' avatar in the simulated reality.

Meanwhile, Fred summons Willow, the sorceress who formerly restored Angel's soul (*Buffy* Season Two). Willow tries to magically shatter the glass jar containing Angel's soul, prevailing despite Evil Cordelia's secret efforts to counter her. Connor attempts to murder Angelus at Cordelia's urging, but Faith awakens and stops the lad, allowing Willow to reunite Angel's liberated soul with his body. With Angelus dormant, Willow and Faith depart for Sunnydale. But afterward, Cordelia waltzes down the Hyperion stairs and tells everyone that she's big with child.

FIRSTS AND LASTS Faith takes a final bow on *Angel*, having caused quite the ruckus in her five-episodes-plus-change on the show. Final use of the Sanctuary Spell, which Evil Cordy neutralizes, and isn't in operation next episode.

POINTS OF DISCUSSION ABOUT "Orpheus":

1. There's a genuine element of oddity when Angelus and Faith's avatars wander around Angel's mental landscape, and Angel's benevolent persona rises up (in his "1990s homeless person" aspect) to duke it out with his evil self. The problem being: Given that conscience and morality are directly linked to the presence of a soul in the *Angel*-verse, an "Angel" persona shouldn't theoretically exist without one, yet the good Angel brow-beats Angelus even *before* Willow re-ensouls him. What the hell's going on?

Fandom often equates the distinction between Angel and Angelus as akin to someone with multiple personality disorder (a.k.a. dissociative identity disorder), and perhaps they're more correct than anyone knew. After all, the disorder in real life can stem from childhood abuse, and whereas there's no evidence of Angel receiving outright physical or sexual harm during his youth, his harsh conservative upbringing (as illustrated in 1.15, "The Prodigal") might have caused a minor break in his psyche. We're not psychologists, you understand, and it's a little unsettling to think that our lead character was in life a bit mentally ill, but let's run with the notion.

This could partly explain the fairly large personality gulf between the human Liam and the vampire Angelus. Most vamps emulate their human selves much more closely – Darla, Dru, definitely Harmony and even Spike (or "William") early in his vamp days – yet Angelus is extremely distanced from Liam from the get-go. Really, it's as if his getting vamped only served to enlarge a personality rift that already existed, then the highly atypical gypsy curse bestowed upon him a soul and widened it further. If you need further proof, notice how Spike is pretty much the same pre- and post-soul (barring his different morality, obviously); nobody talks about Spike having an "evil, buried persona" akin to Angelus, possibly he didn't have a personality rift when he got sired in the first place.

If this theory holds water, then we might also imagine that "Angel" simply didn't exist as a persona until that fateful day that his conscience returned in 1898. From that point, there are literally two personas whereas only a single (albeit somewhat schismed) one existed before.

... Looking back at the last few paragraphs, it's faintly terrifying to realize how much you can construe from what's probably an off-the-cuff use of Angel's two personas in "Orpheus," and written purely to give the story a big finish.

2. By now, knowledge of Denisof and Hannigan's romance wasn't exactly a secret, so you can imagine how the fangirls reacted upon seeing Wesley and Willow on screen together. Those inclined to over-glorify this team-up, however, tend to forget how the two of them trade sorrowful notes about the heinous acts they've committed in the past year or so, such as Wesley locking someone in the closet with a bucket and Willow flaying someone alive. *Sleepless in Seattle*, this ain't.

3. And yet, there's so much deliberate and totally inadvertent flirtation between Willow and Fred, you would almost think Fred had declared, "Hello, salty goodness...", upon Willow's entering the hotel. The spell-casting bit where Willow touches Fred's chin to "lift her head" as Fred cavorts about the room with a candle and a bell, in fact, seems like a variation of "the eyelash strategy." (Oh, you know... it's when you fib with someone about their having an eyelash on their cheekbone, all for the purpose of gently rubbing it away and facilitating that little spark of physical contact – the prelude to even further touching. What, you've never deployed the eyelash strategy?)

Nothing ultimately happens between Willow and Fred, but their conversation implies that Cordy never mentioned that Willow was a lesbian. Well, that can, at times, be a difficult thing to mention over the coffee.

4. Cordelia's leaf candles, the ones that previously decorated Connor's abode, have been relocated to her room at the Hyperion. Two points: It seems unlikely that Connor retrieved them for Cordy, what with all the murder and mayhem that's been going on, so she must own cases of the things. Also, in the real world, tracking official sales of *Angel* merchandise on eBay isn't easy (because the records terminate so quickly), but we'd bet that FOX later sold those candles – considering how they've made the rounds by now – for stupefying amounts of money. Still, they do look like nice candles.

CHARACTER NOTES *Angel:* In 1902, a repentant Angel arrived at the Ellis Island Immigration Station, New York. [Angel probably smuggled himself into the U.S. illegally, and this occurred two years after his meeting with Darla in China, as detailed in 2.07, "Darla."] During the trip over, he crouched in the filth with the animals just to avoid human temptation.

By the early 1920s, a cleaned-up Angel was sitting outside The Blue Mood Lounge, Chicago, in a well-tailored suit. He hadn't fed off a human in decades [again, not since 1900], but saved a dog from a fast-moving car.

At some point in the 1970s, a mullet-sporting Angel wandered into a diner. A robbery went awry and the clerk was killed; an insanely thirsty Angel fed off the man's corpse. [Manilow's "Mandy" is playing on the jukebox and didn't become a hit until 1974, so this event occurs after that point. It's possibly even a year or two later, allowing that Angel attended Manilow concerts, almost undoubtedly before becoming a homeless person. Significantly complicating matters, Donna Summer's disco version of "MacArthur Park" is also playing on the jukebox, and it didn't see release until 1978. Thus, one either needs to date this flashback accordingly, or decide that the song's inclusion owes to Lorne singing the tune to Faith in the real world, thus causing a strange ripple in the Orpheus reality. We'd opt for the latter; otherwise, it's a remarkable coincidence on Lorne's part.]

As penance for this offense, Angel sought to "disappear" and became a homeless person in Manhattan, feeding off rats. [And he stays there until Whistler convinces him to seek out Buffy, as detailed in *Buffy* 2.21, "Becoming."]

• *Evil Cordelia:* Willow, a powerful witch, doesn't sense Evil Cordelia's true nature even when they're in the same room. Evil Cordelia is rapidly gaining in magical strength as her pregnancy progresses, and says she'd have even more power "if only this were a few weeks later." [It's unclear if this refers to after the actual birth, or simply later in the child's gestation.] She can both bypass the Sanctuary Spell's restrictions and permanently neuter the enchantment, giving Connor free rein. Additionally, Evil Cordy can magically smack Willow from a distance, make the hotel tremble with a seismic shock, project the illusion of a large, floaty demon head, and halt the path of Willow's magic marble (at least, until Connor distracts her). Her telepathic voice only sounds to Angelus like a buzzing noise while he's under the Orpheus' influence. She chants in Latin while casting spells, and her eyes again go murky.

• *Wesley:* Thinks his sense of humor is trapped in a jar somewhere.

• *Gunn:* Now dialing down his taunting of Wesley. [Gunn clearly abandoned all pretense of his reuniting with Fred during their kiss last episode, depriving him of a sizeable beef against Wes.]

• *Fred:* Gets a bit more giggly and Southern when Willow shows up, and enjoys sharing her research methodology. [Fred's becoming quite the translation nerd.]

• *Lorne:* He's witnessed the fate of many Orpheus-using girls. Orpheus peddlers were the only people that Lorne ever banned from Caritas.

• *Connor:* Willow thinks his sneer is genetic. He believes that the gravely wounded Faith was "brave, and died in battle." [He almost sounds like a Klingon.] On screen, his attempt on Angel's life only earns him a rebuke from Gunn. [Although the next few episodes keep everyone reeling so much, there's no time to properly chastise the boy.]

• *Faith:* Awakens from her coma with enough strength to thrash Connor around. [Slayer stamina: Always a plus.] She apparently attended "murder rehab" while in prison.

• *Willow:* It's implied [but not outright stated] that she's previously corresponded with Fred. [They must have started trading notes after Fred re-entered the academic life earlier this season, or else Fred surely would've asked for Willow's help once Angel went missing for three months (3.22, "Tomorrow").] It's also hinted that Willow is interested in Fred [so she's not too serious about her budding relationship with Kennedy, then], but Fred's bubbliness seems to put Willow off, and causes her to mention: "I'm seeing someone."

Willow has studied the *Dabarim*, which states that "all life a container – for the heart of all life" (sic), and she's fond of things that come in jars, including peanut butter, jelly and those two-headed fetal pigs at the Natural History Museum.

THE LIBRARY Fred gives Willow a book with some interesting stuff on Hellmouths, and she wants to bend Willow's ear sometime about the *Pergamum Codex*, because she thinks some of the obscure passages are really Latin translated from a demonic tongue, and kind of a hoot.

DEMONOLOGY *Vampires:* The 1970s Angel feeds off a freshly killed corpse. [Vampires normally don't have a taste for dead people, see "Soulless" (4.11), but this man is only moments dead, and Angel's desperate.]

MAGIC *Orpheus:* An opiate of the enchanted/mystical variety. Typically, humans inject Orpheus and let it filter through their system, then allow vampires to feed off them. [With pleasurable results for both, as implied last episode.] After Angelus drinks Faith's Orpheus-tainted blood, the pair of them fall unconscious and their – shall we say – "avatars" interact in a dreamscape depicting locales from Angel's time in twentieth century America. [So much of this surely owes to the atypical interaction of a vampire drinking Orpheus from a Slayer – whose brain (let's not forget) is receptive to psionic activity, as witnessed by the "Slayer dreams" that Buffy sometimes experiences. Normal Orpheus usage presumably doesn't entail a co-mingling of minds to this degree. That said, the drug might not "activate" until shared between two parties, which helps to explain how Faith battled Angelus for so long last episode, even though her system was flush with Orpheus.]

Wesley claims that Orpheus "leads you down to hell and leaves you there." [The short-term effects are probably pleasurable, but the long-term ones seem as Wesley describes. Consider the dream locales... Angelus and Faith first witness Angel's arrival in America, and that's peaceful enough. Then Angelus "experiences hell" by re-watching Angel save a puppy. Then Faith witnesses a heart-wrenching event as Angel feeds off a dead person, and this corresponds to the neck-wound on her avatar re-opening, which denotes psychic stress.]

Faith and Angelus' avatars initially can't touch one another, but the "rules" change as the dream progresses and contact becomes possible. The damage Angelus deals to Faith's avatar manifests on her real-world body. Upon waking up, Faith knows that Connor is about to dust Angel's body. [Presumably, she sensed the danger through her mental contact with Angelus' real-world senses, meaning she recognized *a* threat, not realizing it was Connor.]

A typical Orpheus overdose entails the user entering (as Lorne puts it) "the barrens," wherein they "let go of everything that meant something" [and presumably die].

• *Delothrian's Arrow:* Spell that Willow uses to "charge" a fast-moving marble [that's able to phase through walls, it seems] that hones on the Muo-Ping and shatters it. It's helpful, in directing the spell, to choose a specific target; Willow implies that otherwise, the spell could've shattered every jar in the world. [This presumably requires a witch of Willow's now-formidable rank, or there'd be hell to pay every time a lowly magic-user gave it a go.] The spell is touted as something that's used to "protect good magics." [That's somewhat odd terminology for a spell that, in Willow's hands, entails a hyper-velocity marble. Perhaps it's normally a means of defense?]

• *The Orb of Thesulah:* Conjuring sphere Willow uses to re-ensoul Angel. [The spell's words and accoutrements pretty much pare with Angel's re-ensoulment in *Buffy* 2.22, "Becoming." Curiously, there as here, the Orb appears to vanish at the spell's peak. If the re-ensoulment spell physically destroys such a rare orb, this could explain why Willow doesn't re-ensoul vampires more often. Alternatively, as we suggested in *Dusted*, perhaps it's only useful against vampires who've offended the Romany. One difference is that Angel here recalls recent events, but he didn't remember his actions as Angelus in "Becoming." It's possible that Willow's higher skill-level as a witch makes the transition easier.]

• *Muo-Ping:* Impervious to magic, and Willow's standard locator spell fails to register it. [It's not a cheat when Willow "uses magic" to break the Muo-Ping. The jar can evidently resist a direct magical strike, but proves fragile as normal glass against Willow's hyper-marble.] Breaking the jar releases Angel's soul into "the ether" [the same plane where it resided in the last half of *Buffy* Season Two, presumably].

BEST LINE(s) Angel to Faith, after the battle: "How you feeling?" Faith: "Like I did mushrooms and got eaten by a bear."

THINGS THAT DON'T MAKE SENSE There's yet another hole in the heroes' plan to restore Angelus, in that we've got to ask why the hell they didn't call Willow sooner. (It's possible that she only knows how to restore souls, not strip them away, but surely having an expert of her magnitude onhand is a good idea.) Along those lines, it's a fairly glaring oversight that the heroes never phoned Buffy to warn her, "Your fiendish boyfriend is back, and for all we know, he's headed your way to rip your throat out."

Once Willow arrives, Evil Cordelia gets so desperate as to contemplate doing in the meddlesome redhead with a knife. Yet how, precisely, does Evil Cordy think she's going to explain this to the others? Won't they find the sight of Willow's corpse in Cordy's bedroom, complete with a knife sticking out of it, rather suspicious? It's also a little odd when Cordelia whips her blade into the door just as Willow exits the room. Why didn't Evil Cordy do that sooner – for instance, when Willow turned her back – and why doesn't Willow hear the large THUD as the knife hits the door?

Evil Cordy magically makes a large demon face appear in the lobby, but it's so unconvincing that nobody drops for cover or grabs for a weapon. Instead, Wesley and Fred look a bit bored while Connor limply asks, "What the hell is that?"

And purely for the sake of whimsy, we have to ask why there's a sub-head – "New York, 1902" – in the first flashback inside Angel's noodle, as it's a magical recreation of that location, not the genuine article. Is the series' omniscient narrator part of the Orpheus fantasy too?

POP CULTURE Lorne comforts (or tortures, depending on your point of view) the comatose Faith by singing "MacArthur Park." It was previously referenced in 2.08, "The Shroud of Rahmon," and gets a final mention in the series finale. Dave Barry once conducted a survey that picked the song's lyrics as among the worst ever written, and his respondents have a point: "MacArthur Park is melting in the dark; All the sweet, green icing flowing down...; Someone left the cake out in the rain; I don't think that I can take it; 'cause it took so long to bake it; and I'll never have that recipe again; Oh, no!"

CROSS-OVERS Willow received Fred's call for help and departed Sunnydale in *Buffy* 7.17, "Storyteller." She and Faith here leave L.A., and arrive back in in time for *Buffy* 7.19, "Bad Girls." [A dangling continuity detail... Willow upon arrival in the Hyperion identifies Connor as Angel's teenage son, but it's unclear when she learned about him, unless Fred mentioned it. Nor is there any on-screen instance of Buffy ever getting notified or reacting to the fact that her ex-boyfriend miraculously has a teenage son by way of that blonde, skirt-wearing vampire harlot who got dispatched six years ago in the Bronze. However, the fact that Buffy doesn't mention Connor during her next meeting with Angel – in the *Buffy* series finale – makes sense, given the memory revision spell in 4.22, "Home."]

IN RETROSPECT "A coma," Evil Cordy says disdainfully of Faith's condition – which is rather ironic, considering how Cordelia's going to finish out the season.

IT'S REALLY ABOUT... Re-enforcing the notion (largely pioneered in Tim Minear stories) that even with a soul, Angel was hardly a saint. The diner flashback makes that abundantly clear, but it's also about reiterating that in certain acts of wrongdoing, you never can, nor should, stop seeking redemption. At least, that's what Angel advises Faith when she thinks it'd be far easier to just lie down and die, and she thankfully takes the message to heart.

CRITIQUE The Faith three-parter wraps up, and – combined with the last two installments – makes for an intensely satisfying experience. Considering the carnage of late, it's quite the shift in tone when Faith and Angelus slump unconscious, then spend most of the story mentally tripping through Angel's memories. It's like going from a DC Comics superhero book to something from its surreal Vertigo line, but it's a plus to see the show varying its styles and tone with such confidence.

If one were to quibble, the dialogue isn't quite as sharp as before, and the showdown between Angel's two personas seems a bit hokey. But that's about the worst criticism you can level. The relief one feels when Angelus finally gets stuffed back into his cage only underscores the trauma of the last few episodes, which includes – but certainly isn't limited to – the visceral image here of Fred, Wesley and Lorne walking down a hallway with Faith's bloodied body. Indeed, pondering this storyline with hindsight, it's faintly astonishing to think that Angelus only got loose three episodes ago, not – judging by the amount of content here – ten or so.

You'll notice that we've yet to comment on Alyson Hannigan's performance as Willow. Well, she's fabulous. *Of course* she's fabulous, but it's rather telling that the No. 2 *Buffy* female can now walk in and walk out while barely disturbing the show's equilibrium. That sort of passive contribution would've been unthinkable in Season One – glance over the entry for "Sanctuary" (1.19) in case you've forgotten – but here Willow only enhances a show that's running on all cylinders, stopping well short of dominating it.

THE LORE During production for *Buffy* 3.17, "Enemies," Dushku got a bit over-zealous and didn't realize that Faith and Angelus weren't supposed to really kiss, so she went for a full-on snog while Boreanaz was decked out in vampire teeth. She consequently punctured her tongue, then paused to announce her injury and ask if the teeth could come out in long-shot. A silence fell upon the set and the director said something akin to, "Wow, so you're really using the tongue, huh Eliza?" Dushku, now a little embarrassed, tried defusing the situation with, "What do you mean? Buffy doesn't kiss like that?" (Dushku, *Wizard World Philadelphia* panel, May 2004)

• UPN flipped their schedule on original broadcast, meaning that the *Buffy* episode with Willow leaving Sunnydale (7.17, "Lies My Parents Told Me") actually went out the week after "Orpheus." Fury duly took to the web, and advised everyone to look upon the *Buffy* story as a prequel to the already resolved *Angel* adventure. (Fury, *The Bronze*, March 7, 2003)

• Hannigan had *Buffy* Season Seven and *American Wedding* (or *American Pie 3*, if you prefer) on her plate, so she and Denisof weren't seeing a lot of each other at this point. He got a bit giddy to have his girlfriend on the set, although the complexity of Wesley's lines appears to have added to his nervousness. (O'Hare, *Zap2It*, March 16, 2003)

• Adrienne Wilkinson (Flapper) regularly appeared throughout *Xena: Warrior Princess* Season Six as Xena's daughter Eve, a.k.a. Livia. (In fact, Wilkinson's period of the show coincides with Xena undergoing a mystical pregnancy, with the child being a reincarnated villain who later ages to adulthood. It's too complicted to tackle here, but *Xena* watchers have found several parallels between this and *Angel* Season Four, especially as the *Xena* story arc – like the *Angel* one – was triggered by an actress' unexpected pregnancy.)

• The armed robber in the 1970s scene is Nate Dushku, Eliza Dushku's older brother. (You can see the resemblance, if you squint past his straggly 70s hair.) Nate's celebrity status isn't anywhere near that of his sibling, but he's at least appeared on MTV's *Undressed* (opposite J. August Richards) and in the films *Antitrust*, *Wolf Girl* and *Vampire Clan*.

4.16: "Players"

"Charles, we are the secret weapons."

Air Date: March 23, 2003; **Writers:** Jeffrey Bell, Sarah Fain, Elizabeth Craft; **Director:** Michael Grossman

SUMMARY The mutant thief Gwen asks for Gunn's help in rescuing the kidnapped daughter of her employer, part of a business conflict gone bad. The two of them infiltrate a party thrown by the alleged baddie, Mr. Morimoto, but Gunn discovers that Gwen lied about the kidnap, duping him into serving as a distraction. Gwen then moves to steal LISA, a prototype covert ops device developed by Morimoto's company, and Gunn – despite his reservations – helps her succeed. Later, Gwen reveals that LISA will regulate her body's electrical discharge, enabling her to finally touch other people. Generous soul that he is, Gunn helps Gwen "test" the device by having sex with her.

Meanwhile, Lorne embarks on a ritual that will invigorate his empathic abilities, allowing him to properly "read" the magically pregnant Cordelia. Evil Cordy moves to kill Lorne in private, only to discover that Angel had already pieced together her duplicity, and – exposed as the grand villain – she now stands surrounded by a pissed-off Angel, Wesley and Fred.

FIRSTS AND LASTS Final appearance of Gwen, final dropping of all pretense that Cordelia isn't evil and final (they're really not joking this time) statement on the Fred-Gunn relationship as Gunn sleeps with the girl we like to call "Lightning Lass." It's not the first appearance of Gunn in a suit (given his tuxedo in 3.13, "Waiting in the Wings"), but this close to Season Five, it certainly looks like a precursor to his "lawyer Gunn" incarnation.

First time *The Tick* creator Ben Edlund gets credited as an *Angel* producer, but see 4.20, "Sacrifice" for more on him. And it's the first time that Fred sweetly offers Wesley some coffee (awwwwwww... see 5.14, "Smile Time" for more).

POINTS OF DISCUSSION ABOUT "Players":

1. Some fans – none more eloquent than novelist Peter David, in his "Cowboy Pete" blog entries – have argued that Gunn acts rather dense throughout this story. To quickly recap, a criminal with a track record for deceit (4.09, "Long Day's Journey") says she wants to rescue a kidnapped child. Gunn agrees to help, but barely deems it odd that the alleged kidnapper would let his "victim" wander around a well-attended party for everyone and anyone to see. Instead of asking the tranquil little girl if anything's wrong, Gunn abducts the child – only to realize he's made off with "the kidnapper's" daughter by mistake. Gwen admits her deception but lies to Gunn again, claiming she wants to steal a device for an unseen employer. Gunn doesn't take issue with stealing advanced technology on behalf of a potentially criminal organization, and helps out mainly for the thrill of it all. As David points out, this is rather like participating in a liquor store robbery because it provides an adrenaline rush.

But it's slightly worse than all that, for two reasons. First off, we've only Gwen's word as to Morimoto's villainy – he could be the *Angel*-verse equivalent of Tony Stark (minus the Iron Man armor) for all we know. Second, Gwen's final electrical discharge – concentrated due to her desperation – drops Morimoto and four of his guards, and might well kill them. Now, it's certainly true that ordinary people can survive getting struck by lightning, but if even one or two of them die horribly, Gunn is partly culpable for sanctioning the heist. Suffice to say, he can hardly excuse all of this with, "But gee... I had fun doing it."

Only two justifications keep this mess out of **Things That Don't Make Sense**. The first is that as Gunn claims, he's "the muscle," not the brains, but this sounds rather demeaning to his character. The more palatable alternative is that Gunn probably feels useless at the Hyperion, and Gwen wants him around. He can either help her, or slink back to the hotel to mope while Angel, Wesley and Fred tackle the important work. It's still not a commendable attitude on Gunn's part, but it's an understandable one.

2. Nobody has adequately explained the location that Lorne chooses for his mock mediation routine. It's clearly not in the Hyperion, and one wonders if Lorne picked the locale because of the high ceilings, which makes his voice reverberate all the better. It's a pity, however, that Evil Cordy doesn't even try to explain why she was sneaking up behind Lorne with a large knife. Really, she had nothing to lose by claiming, "Oh... I was hoping to carve some cheese."

3. Here comes the *Maxim* observation... given that the prototype LISA could fail at a *really* inconvenient moment, Gunn apparently risks death by electrocution for the sake of a booty call. (Well, at least he'd die happy.) Gwen must experience quite the sensory overload, however, given that she's spent her whole life unable to touch anyone, and – upon gaining the ability – goes straight to sex in the space of about two minutes.

CHARACTER NOTES *Angel:* Attempts to recreate the *Rhinehardt's Compendium* entry on the Beast [seen by Angelus in 4.14, "Release"] from memory, but doesn't produce a draft that Wesley can properly translate.

• *Evil Cordelia:* The thing within her lumbering belly is squirming around in there. [Jasmine appears as a tentacled thing in "Inside Out" (4.17) and "Peace Out" (4.21), so it's possible that she's a *tiny* tentacled thing at present, thrashing around in Cordelia's womb.] Evil Cordy evidently hopes to kill Lorne with a knife. [She physically slaughtered people in "Long Day's Journey" (4.09) and "Soulless" (4.11), all of which suggests that whatever her power of late, Evil Cordy can't magically fry somebody. Perhaps the nature of Jasmine's abilities means she can use magic for communication, defense, etc., but not to outright murder someone. To confirm the point, notice how the post-natal Jasmine, even at the height of her power, doesn't zap people with lightning bolts, etc.]

• *Wesley:* Broaches the topic of his relationship with Lilah to Fred, saying he empathizes with Connor and Cordelia shacking up because they were feeling lost, lonely and alienated from their loved ones. Fred expresses that she thought Wesley hated Lilah [well, that's overstating the point], and Wesley responds: "It's not always about holding hands."

• *Gunn:* Hasn't traveled much beyond L.A. He bears a large scar on his thigh from a battle in Boyle Heights, another from a piece of vamp stake that nailed him in Alhambra, and a couple of burn marks on his hip from Encino.

His entire Japanese vocabulary consists of saying "hello," and his knowledge of Japanese culture stems from Samurai movies. Yet he at least understands the value of honoring *Reishiki*, proper etiquette, and the value of a thoughtful gift. Hence, Gunn swipes Gwen's small jade tiger antique and offers it to Morimoto. He handles himself well with a fighting staff, and defeats four martial arts experts. [Fighting vampires, with their magical Kung-Fu skills, makes Gunn ideally suited against such foes.]

- *Fred:* Rattled at the thought of Cordelia and Connor – ahem – "doing stuff" with each other.
- *Lorne:* Failed to even get a tingle that Cordelia was pregnant. [That's understandable, as his circumstances weren't exactly ideal when he "read" Cordy back in "Slouching Toward Bethlehem" (4.04). Also, if Jasmine's power can shroud her from Willow's notice last episode, it can surely deceive Lorne.] Lorne claims that Wanda, a demon that Angel recommended, sold him a "cleansing abracadabra" to clear his muddled mind. [He says this as part of a deception, but Lorne's empathic sense rebounds after "Calvary" (4.12). Either his clouded judgment was temporary, or he performed Wanda's ritual before the scheme to trip up Evil Cordy.]
- *Connor:* Troubled by the notion that Cordelia sent him to kill Angelus [last episode], even though Willow was actually helping to bring Angel back. [Say what you will about Connor, he's not outright stupid, just easily led astray.] Evil Cordy says her instincts were wrong on that occasion, and sways the boy back to her side.
- *Gwen:* Attracts a lightning bolt [she'd been struck 14 times prior to 4.02, "Ground State"] even though it's not raining, and with enough conductivity that it doesn't fry a contact who's standing next to her. Gwen owns some rare and valuable trinkets, including a dolphin thingy from Tahiti [her intended destination in 4.09, "Long Day's Journey"], and a tiger made from eighteenth century jade. Gwen steals this item back after Gunn gives it to Morimoto. Scanners and metal detectors don't register her electrical abilities.
- *Takeshi Morimoto:* He's cited for all kinds of charity work, but also for bank fraud, smuggling and money laundering. [But again, all of these allegations stem from Gwen's questionable files.] He apparently loves tigers, and his daughter is the fiery Aiko Morimoto. [Oh, she's going to be a fierce one when she grows up.]

LISA (Localized Ionic Sensory Activator) Covert device meant for black ops, designed to regulate the user's body temperature, heartbeat, body chemistry, etc. It attaches to the base of the spine and performs its work by painlessly extending small metal tendrils into the user.

THE LIBRARY A passage from Lilah's copy of *Rhinehardt's Compendium* was rendered in the early Fallorian code system. It's a tricky language; an "inverted serif" (sic) can alter the meaning of an entire passage. Wesley's other books mention demon pregnancies, but it's mostly run-of-the-mill lifecycle stuff, nothing like what's happening to Cordelia.

MAGIC *The Sanctuary Spell:* Now "flop-a-palooza," Lorne says. [Evil Cordy wrecked it last episode, but the heroes presume that this herbs-based version of the spell just expired.]

BEST LINE Morimoto's shamelessly sweet daughter, after Gunn abducts her: "When my daddy finds out... he's gonna kill you." (It's funnier on screen than in print.)

THINGS THAT DON'T MAKE SENSE Cordelia's outfit – a lacy black number – appeared in the final minute or so of "Orpheus," but it's in this episode that one might question how the heroes don't notice her shocking dress sense. The real Cordelia would *never, ever* wear that outfit, pregnancy or no, and she might as well have a neon sign declaring "I Am the Villain" above her head for all anyone questions this.

There's some very impressive security at Morimoto's estate – guards, metal detectors, etc – yet the man himself is careless enough to accept a parcel from a stranger (Gunn) who lies about their meeting at a zoo benefit. To compound the error, Morimoto thanks Gunn by admitting him and Gwen into the party, as if assassins would never come bearing gifts.

Angel reveals that Angelus didn't kill Lilah, but for the time being, everyone brazenly assumes that the Beast committed the crime – even though as with the Svea family in "Soulless" (4.11), the towering, rocky Beast couldn't exactly fit through an open window, stealthily climb up the stairwell or stride down one of the Hyperion hallways without causing significant damage. Nit-picking here, but Angel says Angelus destroyed Lilah's copy of *Rhinehardt's Compendium* "after the Beast Master tried to re-ensoul him." Actually, the Beast Master only threatened that; s/he never made the attempt.

Finally, LISA is designed to regulate a person's heartbeat, body temperature, etc., yet it's an amazingly all-purpose device that can also re-reroute the potent electricity in Gwen, an undocumented mutant. (Gwen presumably did her research on LISA, but c'mon...)

IT'S REALLY ABOUT... Gunn and Gwen undertake a *Mission: Impossible*-style mission while Angel and friends bamboozle Evil Cordelia. Implicitly, it entails Gunn's desire to become something more than just the team's muscle, but even that idea isn't properly fleshed out until Season Five.

CRITIQUE Obviously, it's filler, designed to let the viewer and the characters catch their breath while the series gears up for the arc that'll last the rest of the year. In that regard, it's a simple story: Gwen asks for Gunn's help and quickly betrays him – but it's all in a good cause, so they get some conciliatory canoodles in the final act. Nothing but nothing about this proves surprising, but the production values help the story along where it's tempted to meander. It's more or less disposable entertainment, but it's arguably not worth bitching about either (unless you buy the notion that Gunn acts dumb as a post, and we're ambivalent on that topic). Calling this story "massively underwhelming" seems apt, although there's a bit of tragedy in that it's actually the best of Gwen's three appearances, and that's just not saying much.

Thankfully, the B-plot with the Hyperion crew carries things along, even if many viewers saw the trap set for Evil Cordelia (the supposed "master villain" – hah!) long before she did. But let's face it – the final act, with Cordy stalking Lorne with a knife, only to then find everyone turning a gun on her – *still* ends everything with a warm feeling, even if you forecast it early on. It's a bit of color at the end of an otherwise drab story, and a sure-fire sign that the series isn't playing patti-cakes with Evil Cordy any longer.

THE LORE Richards had never performed with a fighting staff before, but – for what it's worth – he'd twirled his sister's majorette baton when they were younger. He learned how to handle the staff as he went, and threw in a lot of Gunn's flourishes himself. (O'Hare, *Zap2It.com*, Aug. 8, 2003)

4.17: "Inside Out"

"Damn thing's been playing us right from the start... from the inside, where it can do the most damage."

Air Date: April 2, 2003,
Writer/Director: Steven S. DeKnight

SUMMARY An infatuated Connor thrashes Angel's crew and whisks Cordy away, holing up in an abandoned warehouse. With Cordelia's child due, Angel tries getting help from the Powers through their agent, the demon Skip. When Angel learns that Skip has been part of Evil Cordelia's conspiracy from the start, he overpowers the demon and interrogates him. Skip admits that Cordelia will soon birth a higher power who has manipulated a number of factors – Connor's miracle existence, Cordelia's ascension, etc. – as a means of "giving birth to itself" on the mortal plane. Skip later escapes and nearly kills the heroes, but dies when Wesley puts a bullet in his brain.

Angel sets out to kill Evil Cordelia before her "child" arrives, but Connor stands by Cordy even when the Powers send an image of his mother, Darla, to beg him to stop. Cordelia sacrifices a young virgin that Connor procures, and uses the virgin's blood to accelerate her childbirth. Angel rears back to slay Cordelia with a sword, but a glowing, tentacled creature bursts out of her stomach and reshapes itself into a beautiful, intoxicating woman.

FIRSTS AND LASTS To the undoubted exhilaration of some viewers, it's the end of "Evil Cordelia" (see **When is Cordelia Cordelia?** if you're unclear about this). First outing of Gina Torres, a *Firefly* veteran (see 3.13, "Waiting in the Wings") as Jasmine, even if she's not named until next episode. Last appearance of Skip, and last of two instances this season (the first being with Lorne in 4.14, "Release") where Fred tranquilizes someone by mistake. Here she tags Angel, albeit when Connor throws off her aim.

POINTS OF DISCUSSION ABOUT "Inside Out":

1. Julie Benz logs her second-to-last *Angel* appearance, but the inclusion of Benz's name as a guest-star gave away her participation, even for viewers trying to actively avoid spoilers. That's not such a problem here, because Benz's return forms only one facet of an otherwise complex story, but see 4.21, "Peace Out," when a similar listing of Stephanie Romanov's name blew what was intended as a major reveal.

2. So the entity within Evil Cordelia springs forth as (drum roll)... a large green tentacled thing that's bathed in a spectral light, and then condenses into a humanoid form that looks like Gina Torres. If you were thinking that the green tentacled thing looked a bit like Cthulhu, you weren't alone.

3. Fred says she can "whip up" a torture spell for use against him in about 20 minutes, and Angel darkly tells Skip to reveal, "everything you know, or she starts whipping." We wish he'd stop talking like that, because it's making us excited.

4. When Fred comments that Evil Cordy was "grooming" Connor, we instinctively thought: "She was combing his hair, she was putting moisturizer on his blemished teenage face..."

CHARACTER NOTES *Angel:* Tipped off to the Beast Master's identity when Cordelia mentioned "My sweet baby" last episode, recalling the Beast Master's similar phrasing in 4.14, "Release." Angel tells Wesley that he's genuinely sorry for Lilah's death, not for his own sake but because Wes cared about her. [It's clearly a declaration of friendship from Angel to Wesley, and they're at their closest point since Wes kidnapped baby Connor. Indeed, Angel will show even more sympathy for Lilah in 4.22, "Home."]

• *Evil Cordelia:* Hints to Angel that she's the real Cordelia. [She's just lying to throw him off-base, the strumpet.] The genuine article kept a sacred Hutamin paw in her desk, thinking it was a back-scratcher. [It initially seems odd that Evil Cordelia, with her impressive knowledge of black magic, didn't recognize the item and dispose of it, given its ability to track her (see **Magic**). But then, the real Cordelia doesn't exactly have a photographic memory, so if she mistook it for a back-scratcher, then Jasmine would have no reason to think different. Mind, it's still fishy that Lorne – who knows the truth about the item – never told the real Cordy, "Hey, that thingy you've been using to scratch those hard-to-reach places? It's actually a wizened hand, useful for casting spells."]

Skip says that slaying Cordelia in whatever fashion suits the mood will terminate the entity inside her. However, extracting the entity without harming Cordelia isn't an option, as the entity is crammed into "every hair, cell and molecule of her body." Skip predicts that the onset of labor will drain Cordelia's life force, either killing her or turning her into a head of cabbage. Additionally, Skip claims that the entity within Cordelia doesn't have a name. [We'll learn more about the entity's name starting next episode.]

• *Gunn:* Says that his cell phone's on the blink because being close to Gwen [last episode] can really "screw with your equipment."

• *Connor:* Reacts fast enough to take out Angel, Wesley, Fred and Lorne in the space of a few moments. [He's got the element of surprise, but it's still impressive.] He's stealthy enough to avoid Angel's tracking him. Evil Cordelia's trying to distance Connor from humanity, claiming that "good" and "evil" are just words. [It's unsurprising that she'd try such a twisted tactic, as the entity within Cordy – as we'll learn – hails from a time before good and evil.]

• *"Darla":* Messenger from the Powers-That-Be, who bears Darla's memories and feelings. [This is an astonishing re-creation of Darla, to such a degree that you wonder why the Powers don't play such a card more often. It's possible that the imminent "birth" of a higher being supercedes enough of the rules and limitations of reality to facilitate this. Even so, this raises a rather unsettling possibility with regards to Cordelia – see 5.12, "You're Welcome."]

Only Connor can see the Darla-messenger at first, although Evil Cordelia eventually spies her as well. The Darla-messenger seems intangible, although she casts her image onto the virgin-sacrifice at one point. The messenger implies there are "things that I can't..." tell Connor. [There's probably limits to this line of communication, meaning she literally can't explain Evil Cordelia's true nature to the boy.]

• *Skip:* Angel visits Skip's domain using the key and the coin artifacts [3.02, "That Vision Thing."]. Skip chows down on buffalo wings, and tells Angel "the game's on at five." Angel deduces Skip's duplicity because Skip was Cordy's spirit guide [3.11, "Birthday"] and saw her ascension [3.22, "Tomorrow"] yet claimed to know nothing about her return – meaning he was either duped or part of the conspiracy from the start.

Skip claims he's essentially a mercenary-for-hire, and asks for a cigarette at one point. He fares better in combat with Angel than in "That Vision Thing," but falls when Angel wraps a chain around his wrist as impromptu brass knuckles.

ORGANIZATIONS *The Powers-That-Be:* Clearly hope to scuttle Jasmine's plans, hoping that "Darla" will convince Connor to side against Evil Cordelia. [Inevitably, see **When Did the Powers Intervene?**] Angel claims that the Powers rebuffed him the last few times he asked for their help. [The business with Darla in Season Two gets cited as an example, but he's being disingenuous; the Powers were trying to keep Angel on a path of moral integrity, and his friends concurred.]

DEMONOLOGY *Vampires:* It's reiterated [after 2.05, "Dear Boy" and others] that vampires can detect virginity.

MAGIC Evil Cordy isn't due for a couple of weeks, but instigates her labor with an unspecified ritual that entails surrounding herself in a circle with candles, then chanting in a strange language. Connor dips his hand in the butchered virgin's blood and pats Evil Cordelia's belly, which absorbs the offering. Evil Cordy insists they've got to use the blood "while it's fresh." [That makes sense, given the Whedonverse attribute that "blood equals life," see *Buffy* 5.22, "The Gift." It's also likely that this ritual requires Evil Cordy to ***kill*** a virgin, as part of the whole life-for-life equation, rather than just draining a pint or so and letting the girl live.]

• *Sand of the Red Palm:* Sand circle that binds Skip. He implies that he can break the enchantment, and Angel agrees, but he couldn't get free before the heroes deploy...

• *Sphere of the Infinite Agonies:* Ritual that, at least from its name, doesn't sound terribly pleasant, and claims to make "every second a lifetime." Fred shows Skip a musty book that allegedly contains instructions for this spell, complete with an illustration of a sphere with half of a screaming man's face being torn off. [It's a bit of a relief that Wesley didn't suggest this text when Fred was hot to punish Professor Seidel, 4.05, "Supersymmetry."] The mere threat of it gets Skip talking, and Fred says she can whip such a Sphere in 20 minutes. [She never gets to make the attempt, however, so we've no idea if she's bluffing or not.]

• *Bu'shundi ritual:* Method of tracking Evil Cordy that uses a sacred Hutamin paw. This evidently entails burning the paw a bit, because it's smoking after Wesley and Lorne use it.

BEST LINE Fred searches Cordelia's room for a clue, but only discovers: "Scented candles, couple of broken pieces of the Muo-Ping, and some toiletries that smell way too pretty to be evil. As insidious lairs go, it kept Cordy's room nice and tidy. I think it even vacuumed."

THINGS THAT DON'T MAKE SENSE Connor is lucky enough to happen across a vampire who tells its intended victim, "I really love virgins"; otherwise, he would've had to wander all over L.A. asking, "Are you a virgin? Are you a virgin?"

Suddenly, the heroes produce knowledge of a magical binding spell – the Sand of the Red Palm – that secures the armored Skip in place. Because that sort of thing certainly wouldn't have helped to bind Angelus in his cell six episodes back, goodness no. (Fine... perhaps this spell only affects intra-dimensional demons such as Skip.)

With hindsight, the revelation that Evil Cordy did in Manny in "Long Day's Journey" (4.09) rather challenges that story's claim that the murder occurred "unseen and unheard." Fair enough that Evil Cordelia "pulled a Lizzie Borden" and thwacked Manny while nude, then showered his blood off her body, but it's strange that A) Nobody heard her scrubbing up, and B) She could scrub off *so* effectively as to remove all trace of telltale blood and fool Angel's enhanced sniffer.

IN RETROSPECT Skip wonders "how much you can cut off a vampire before it goes dust-bunnies." There's an answer, of sorts, a mere three episodes from now.

IT'S REALLY ABOUT... Other than the revelations about Evil Cordelia's mischief, it's about demonstrating how far Connor has gone, and in the most brutal of fashions. His desire to protect his "family" is laudable, but the virgin-girl's sacrifice blows a gaping hole in his compassionate side, and it's only going to grow in the episodes to follow.

CRITIQUE Everyone remembers this story for its massive act of retcon (and see the accompanying essay for why), so let's dispense with that first. While some look upon all acts of continuity revision with the same regard they'd hold for a pile of plague-infested blankets, it's important to keep stating that almost everything we learn about Jasmine's machinations makes some sense. Hell, stories such as "Birthday" (3.11) actually make *more* sense once you factor that in.

This is a more important consideration than you might think. Certain comic book publishers – DC Comics in particular, of late – have a depressing tendency to willfully call forth past adventures for the purpose of grafting new and totally idiotic notions onto them, and then expecting the readership to swallow it. That's not what happens here. The systematic notion of Jasmine's interference as going all the way back to "Hero" (1.09) actually fits the series like a glove. Love or leave the assertions of "Inside Out," someone on the Mutant Enemy staff has thought about them a great deal, and that makes all the difference in the world.

Looking at the episode in isolation, though... it looks better and better the more you think about it. Carpenter, despite whatever reservations she held about this story arc, puts in a grand effort as Evil Cordy. Skip is utterly fabulous as a classic Whedon-verse demon who looks scary but talks normal and is quite funny. Kartheiser has never delivered a better performance as Connor, as his character gets closer and closer to the boundaries of sheer madness. The visuals of the virgin girl's death – Connor dragging the girl to her doom, Darla making one last appeal to Connor with her eyes, Cordelia's vicious use of a meat cleaver – proves as deplorable yet compelling as *Angel* ever gets. Oh yes, and the staple dilemma of Angel needing to kill the woman he loves yields gold too.

The series has become taut as a rubber band – not to mention growing even darker, just when you thought matters couldn't get much worse – and if we're agreed that "Apocalypse Nowish" was Steven DeKnight's commendable attempt to do *Angel* as a Hollywood blockbuster, then "Inside Out" is his real masterwork.

THE LORE It almost goes without saying that Gina Torres (Jasmine) will forever be known to Whedon-verse fans as the gun-totting first mate Zoe Washburne on *Firefly*. Before *Angel*, Torres was one of the three leads on the short-lived sci-fi series *Cleopatra 2525*, which won her an American Latino Media Arts Award in 2001. Oddly enough, she also played Cleopatra herself on *Xena* and she'd regularly guest-starred on *Hercules* as Nebula. After *Angel*, she was Link's widow in the two *Matrix* sequels – she met and married Lawrence Fishburne as a result, you know – starred in *Serenity* and played Julia Milliken, who gets embroiled in a White House sex scandal, on *24*. Oh yeah... and on *Alias*, she's the Soviet spy Anna Espinosa.

• DeKnight started out with Evil Cordelia killing the virgin with a butcher's knife, but later opted for a cleaver to up the stakes. (DeKnight, *The Bronze*, April 10, 2003)

• Greenwalt found himself surprised at the depth of affection fans had for Skip, remarking that he hadn't seen people go so hog-wild for a character since Angel appeared on *Buffy*. Skip was originally called Bob, then renamed as a tribute (of sorts) to Producer Skip Schoolnik. David Denman, playing the part, had gotten used to everyone giving him a wide berth, as Skip's back spike tended to hit people when he turned around. "Trying to go to the bathroom is really exciting," he added. (O'Hare, *Zap2It.com*, March 27, 2003)

Did Jasmine Cause All This?

Manifestly, of course, she did. But let's probe a bit deeper, going point by point through her machinations during the show's first four years. In this, we're weighing statements made by Jasmine's agent Skip in "Inside Out" (4.17) and Jasmine herself in the subsequent four episodes, particularly "Shiny Happy People" (4.18). Neither of them are particularly trustworthy as sources go, but their claims fit the on-screen evidence almost alarmingly well.

Up-front, we'd better establish that while Angel, Darla, Cordela and Connor are major players here, don't underestimate Wesley's importance, particularly in 3.06, "Billy."

• **"Angel" (*Buffy* 1.07):** All right... mercifully, Jasmine had nothing whatsoever to do with the Romany cursing Angelus. However, we should mark this event as the trigger that makes Jasmine focus so much attention on the man. After all, in "Shiny Happy People," Jasmine deems it a "miracle" of sorts that Angel is a vampire with a soul, so the gypsy curse is clearly the starting point for her master plan.

• **"Becoming" (*Buffy* 2.21-2.22):** We almost hate to suggest it, but... in "Becoming," flashbacks show the benevolent Whistler finding Angel as a homeless person in New York, and bringing Buffy to his attention. Angel consequently cleans up his act and approaches the Slayer in *Buffy* 1.01, "Welcome to the Hellmouth." Now, we never discover on whose behalf Whistler is acting, nor do we learn how he knows so much about Angel and Buffy. It's entirely possible that he's working for the Powers, but there's nothing to disprove the idea that he's working (intentionally or otherwise) for Jasmine, who stands little to gain if Angel remains a vagabond. Whistler as presented in "Becoming" hardly seems like an agent of evil; but then, nothing about Skip particularly rang alarm bells before his outing as Jasmine's agent in "Inside Out" either.

• **"Hero" (*Angel* 1.09):** Doyle dies, his vision talent gets passed to Cordelia, and Skip claims in "Inside Out" that Jasmine facilitated this swap. Indeed, there's not a scrap of evidence in the entire series (barring the "vision" of Tammy in 3.11, "Birthday," which probably owes to that louse Skip) that a human ever carried the visions before. We detailed in **When Did the Powers Intervene?** how the Powers get desperate to yank the visions out of Cordelia's noggin, so they'd hardly want her to become the visionary in the first place. The claim that Jasmine meddled with the vision-transfer, then, seems perfectly feasible.

• **"War Zone" (1.20):** Skip claims in "Inside Out" that Jasmine "nudged events" and effectively created Angel's inner circle, influencing events that ranged from the death of Gunn's sister ("War Zone"), Fred opening the wrong book (2.19, "Belonging," in flashback), Lorne leaving Pylea and Wesley "sleeping with the enemy" (again, see "Billy"). It's unclear precisely how it helps Jasmine to drag Gunn and Fred into Angel's life, although Angel's support system certainly comes in handy while she's gestating in Evil Cordy. Jasmine needs pawns and protection while she's in such a state, let's remember. Lorne's contribution, at least, is easier to explain as proven by...

• **"The Trial" (2.09):** Jasmine claims in "Shiny Happy People" that she facilitated her parentage "through Lorne" on the day that Angel went into the Trial. This would suggest that she briefly hi-jacked Lorne's "empathic receiver" and directed him to send Angel to the mystical event. Most important, consider the Trial's outcome: Angel wins the right to a "new life." He wants this reward applied this reward to human Darla, who's dying of syphilis, but she's already on her second life and beyond the power of the Trial-runners to heal. No soap for Angel then, except... Angel's reward needs to go *somewhere*, and it appears that Jasmine mystically re-distributed this life-giving potential to generate Connor. The result: two sterile vampires sire a child. Yup... it's the "new life" that Angel wins in "The Trial" that leads to the creation of his son.

• **"That Vision Thing" (3.02):** Skip claims in "Inside Out" that he deliberately lost his brawl with Angel (in "That Vision Thing"). Presuming that Skip isn't bragging, we'll have to assume that Jasmine *wanted* Angel to free Billy. But there's no good reason why she'd desire that, unless...

• **"Billy" (3.06):** Skip says ("Inside Out" again) that Wesley's "sleeping with the enemy" (i.e. his affair Lilah) contributed to Jasmine's goals. This is never explained on screen, and sounds strange until you assume that... if Wesley is sleeping with Lilah, he logically – ah, and here's the kicker – isn't sleeping with Fred.

Two points on why this is important: If Wesley is in a stable relationship with Fred, it puts him in a much better position to recognize, expose and scuttle Jasmine's machinations. "Dark Wesley," needless to say, is too distracted to figure out what's taking place with Evil Cordelia. More importantly, Jasmine needs to isolate Wesley from Angel's group so that Wes can steal Connor and indirectly facilitate the baby's exile to Quor'toth. After all, if Connor doesn't mature in Quor'toth, he can hardly do the deed with Evil Cordy and enable Jasmine's birth.

Taking everything into consideration, does Jasmine arrange for Billy's release purely so the villain can infect Wesley with misogyny, and thereby ruin Wes' chances for romance with Fred? It *sounds* like it's leaving a lot to chance... but it fits the on-screen evidence strikingly well. As a higher power, Jasmine can probably foresee various probabilities and recognize Wesley's importance to future matters. Not for nothing, one presumes, does Lorne declare in "Happy Anniversary" (2.13) that Wesley is going to "play a huge – [something or other]" in events to come. If Jasmine senses the same, then she might use Billy as a means of turning Wesley from a threat into an asset. And if that's the case, her plan works beautifully.

• **"Birthday" (3.11):** Skip gains Cordelia's permission to make her part-demon, which is covertly the first step in readying her body to gestate Jasmine. Presumably, if Cordelia hadn't been so noble as to keep the visions, she could've scuttled Jasmine's plans. But as matters stand...

• **"The Price" (3.19) and "Benediction" (3.21):** Cordelia emits two power bursts that (respectively) kill the Sluk creatures and give Connor a "soul colonic." With hindsight, it looks more and more like Cordelia is flexing mystical "muscles" as granted by her demon DNA, but it's her benevolent use of this power that helps qualify her for...

• **"Tomorrow" (3.22):** Skip gives Cordelia the opportunity to "ascend"; he claims this offer comes from the Powers, but it really owes to Jasmine. Again, if Cordelia had simply refused, it might've stopped Jasmine's plans dead in their tracks. But noooooooooo, Cordelia gets noble and accepts the offer, leading to her ascension and...

• **"The House Always Wins" (4.03) to "Inside Out" (4.17):** Jasmine returns Cordelia to Earth, but not before squirreling herself into Cordy's womb and hitching a ride. The shock of the journey, however, makes Jasmine go dormant and renders Cordelia amnesiac (see **When is Cordelia Cordelia?** for more). Jasmine regains control in "Spin the Bottle" (4.06), and causes no end of murder and mayhem as Evil Cordelia. This finally leads to her "birth" in "Inside Out," and she rules L.A. until...

• **"Peace Out" (4.21):** Connor puts paid to the mighty Jasmine with a fist through the head.

...That just leaves us to consider if there are any instances (beyond the obvious one, with Lorne in "The Trial") in which Jasmine hi-jacks the celestial pipeline and sends Cordelia false visions. Two possibilities present themselves: In "Offspring" (3.07), Cordelia gets a vision that stresses that Darla's child is innocent. This actually doesn't alter the outcome, but it certainly *sounds* like something Jasmine would say. After all, her plans can hardly proceed if Angel kills both Darla and her unborn child. Also, the vision of Angel getting tossed across the room in "The Price" (3.19) seems so useless as to give the impression that Jasmine cut off the Powers' vision in mid-thought, thus preventing the heroes from anticipating adult Connor's arrival.

4.18: "Shiny Happy People"

"For so long you've all been drowning in the fighting and the pain. I'd like to help, if you'll have me."

Air Date: April 9, 2003; **Writers:** Elizabeth Craft, Sarah Fain; **Director:** Marita Grabiak

SUMMARY Cordelia goes comatose as the higher being that she's just birthed radiates a mesmeric effect that enthralls anyone who looks at her, Angel and friends included. Adopting the name "Jasmine," the entity plans on bringing about peace on Earth, wanting to spellbind humanity and end all suffering. With soulless vampires immune to Jasmine's power, Angel's brainwashed crew set about wiping out L.A.'s undead. One such scuffle brings Fred into contact with Jasmine's blood – an act that breaks her mental conditioning.

Fred makes a failed effort to assassinate Jasmine, then flees the Hyperion. Unfortunately, Jasmine takes to the airwaves, solidifying her magical charm over the L.A. populace, and leaving Fred as the only independent-minded person in America's second-biggest city.

FIRSTS AND LASTS Final outing of that cute picture of Angel, Cordelia and Wesley as first seen in Wesley's wallet in 2.21, "Through the Looking Glass." It appears at Cordelia's bedside, which also seems to feature the final glimpse (although it's hard to tell) of one of her cheerleading trophies.

It's the final dismemberment that takes place in the Hyperion basement, as Wesley and Gunn whittle Skip's body down to size with a buzz saw. Such a pity they didn't think about opening a small portal and simply dumping the corpse down it, because they could've saved themselves some sweat.

POINTS OF DISCUSSION ABOUT "Shiny Happy People":

1. A word on pre-natal Jasmine and post-natal Jasmine, because it's striking that within moments of her "birth," she's reveling in her new senses and going on about the beauty of the world – which actually, she's been a part of for months now. There's no reason for her to lie about this to Angel and Connor, who are under her thrall (albeit willingly in Connor's case), yet she very much exhibits a different persona than she did while inside Cordelia. After all, Evil Cordelia showed a lot of malice – such as, say, taunting Lilah's bleeding corpse after stabbing her in the throat. Jasmine will prove capable of outright villainy, but she and Evil Cordelia simply don't act or operate alike.

One possibility springs to mind: We'll argue in **Are the Powers and Partners Old Ones?** that Jasmine – like Illyria and arguably Glory (*Buffy* Season Five) – is an Old One stuffed inside a human shell. That being the case, it's entirely possible that "Evil Cordelia" results from Jasmine's personality being inside a human body, which innately holds the capacity for selfishness and caprice (that's no personal disrespect to Cordelia, you realize). This warps Jasmine's personality and brings out her nasty streak, and the fact that her powers are diminished while she's inside Cordelia must be doubly infuriating, helping to bring out her vicious side.

2. Wesley suggests the following names for Jasmine: "Dianthia, Iphigeneia and Aristophila," and Jasmine says the latter means "supreme lover of mankind"... all of which raises a few red flags. "Dianthia" actually makes the most sense, because it loosely translates to "by the goddess" or "through the goddess." "Aristophila" is technically suitable, but it doesn't mean "supreme lover of mankind" as Jasmine claims (actually, that would be along the lines of "Anthropophilia"). Instead, *aristophilia* roughly means "lover of all that is good or noble."

"Iphigeneia," however, is a simply diabolical name to affix

to someone you adore. For those who don't recall, Iphigeneia was the daughter of King Agamemnon, whom he sacrificed to gain a favorable wind as his troops set sail for the Trojan War. His wife Clytemnestra later killed him in his bath for the affront, which later gets *her* murdered by her son Orestes... who was then hunted by the harpies (a.k.a. the Eumenides or the Erinyes, if you prefer). A tale of tragedy all around, with plenty of corpses. Sorry, in what possible light did Wesley think this was a good idea?

3. We'll overlook the potential glitch that Jasmine restrains her troops and simply lets Fred escape from the Hyperion, on the grounds that Jasmine doesn't know what made Fred break her conditioning, and can't risk her other minions getting similarly tainted. We'll also gloss over how the "non-pregnant" Cordelia who's lying on the lobby couch is obviously a body-double, given the understandable need to balance the show's production against Carpenter's developing pregnancy.

CHARACTER NOTES *Angel:* Enthralled by Jasmine like everyone else, but tends to display more remorse and shame for his violent ways.

• *Cordelia:* Now comatose, but comfortably bedded down in one of the Hyperion rooms.

• *Wesley:* Takes a tad longer to kneel before Jasmine than everyone else [as if his willpower holds out just a hair longer], but totally enthralled afterward.

• *Gunn:* His grandmother was named Helen. [That's not to say that Gunn ever knew the woman, but see 3.10, "Dad" concerning Gunn's family.]

• *Fred:* Pre-Jasmine, as Connor enters the Hyperion, Fred proves so resentful of the boy that she declares, "Son of a bitch!" and dashes toward him with a knife. While freed from Jasmine's control, it's notable that Fred finally goes to Wesley, not Gunn, for help. She holds a knife to Lorne's throat in making her escape from the hotel, apparently steals Wesley's car, and seems adept with a crossbow. [Perhaps she's just lousy with tranquilizer guns, as we've learned this season.]

• *Lorne:* Talented with interior decorating, and prepares one of the Hyperion's luxury suites for Jasmine.

• *Connor:* Unfazed by Jasmine's arrival, claims he "finally knows why he was created" and displays what seems like genuine remorse for hurting people in the past. [It's revealed next episode that Connor isn't under Jasmine's hypnosis. That said, her voice might serve to calm him, at least, and it's feasible that Connor's "gentle nature" upon entering the hotel simply owes to relief that his child isn't a hellspawn, plus an inability to recognize Angel as being coerced.]

• *Jasmine:* Was evidently born wearing lip-gloss.

Her power instantly enthralls anyone who looks at her, but proves useless against standard vampires. [Her mojo evidently relies on the presence of a soul, as Angel and Lorne are affected, but no other vampire or demon comes under her sway.]

Jasmine relates something of her origins, saying she's been on our world, "in the beginning, before the time of man, when great beings walked the Earth." [Much of her subsequent story shouldn't be taken as literal; we'll scrutinize her beginnings in the **Are the Powers/Partners Old Ones?** sidebar.] According to Jasmine, Earth was a demon realm in those days, the malevolent among them grew stronger, and "those of us with the will to resist" left Earth, remaining watchful. Mankind emerged after their departure, and it was hoped that this new race might "restore" a balance.

Mentally freed thanks to Jasmine's blood, Fred views Jasmine as a rotting corpse with maggots falling out. [We're probably meant to infer that Jasmine actually looks like this, yet there's no evidence of her sprinkling a steady stream of invisible maggots everywhere she goes. Nor does Fred view Jasmine's "maggoty" features for long. All things being equal, Jasmine probably *does* look like Gina Torres, and the "rotted corpse" image is simply the human brain making its best effort to comprehend and visualize her inhumanity.]

A pedestrian, John Stoller, comes into contact with Jasmine's blood during a scuffle and also views her as a corpse. He's beaten by Angel after tying to kill Jasmine, then institutionalized as a madman. The left side of Stoller's face, where Jasmine touches him, becomes hideously mutated. [This is a bit hard to rationalize, as Jasmine has nothing to gain from deliberately mutilating the man, and she doesn't particularly seem to know she's even caused him injury. It's possible that Jasmine is "leaking energy" after her birth, which warps Stoller's cell structure. Or perhaps contact with a higher being physically manifests the horror Stoller displays at Jasmine's touch. *Or* his mutilation is simply yet another perception that only Stoller and Fred can see. That could partly explain why he ends up in the psych unit, if he's rambling about a facial disfigurement that nobody else can recognize.]

Jasmine claims "no one born to this Earth can choose their own name." [Jasmine appears bound to certain "rules" which actively prohibit her choosing a name; 4.20, "Sacrifice" and 4.21, "Peace Out" explain this further. Curiously, we never learn who precisely names her "Jasmine." She enters the Hyperion courtyard and asks about the smell, which Angel attributes to the Jasmine flowers (mentioned in 2.09, "The Trial"), but we're never shown the moment when one of the heroes says, "Jasmine... that sounds like a nice name." Yet she's referred to as "Jasmine" by story's end.]

Jasmine's followers can still experience anger, depression and more. [So her power doesn't constitute perfect happiness, as evidenced because it doesn't void Angel's gypsy curse.] She's got an advanced healing factor, and knows detailed personal information about her followers. [She's not as omniscient as she sometimes claims, but she probably gains intel as she brings people into her mental network.] She mysteriously disappears from Angel and Connor's company at one point. [Even though there's no real evidence that she can teleport.]

DEMONOLOGY *Vampires:* Jasmine is ambushed by a vampire with particularly sharp fingernails. [Commonplace vampires don't normally sport such talons, which supplies further proof – unless this vamp files his nails for sadism's sake – that vampire physiology exhibits natural variations, as witnessed in 4.01, "Deep Down," 1.11, "Somnambulist" and more.]

BEST LINE(s) Fred interrupts the heroes' discussion about a name for Jasmine by mentioning Clorox. Gunn then muses: "Clorox... she bleaches away the hate." Wesley: "We should probably avoid brand names."

THINGS THAT DON'T MAKE SENSE It's a comparatively clean episode, but we might ask for what reason – other than the dictates of the plot – Jasmine feels the need to personally wander into the bowling alley fracas. (Perhaps she's concerned about maintaining control over Angel's group until her power strengthens, but it still seems a bit daring after her outlandish effort to get "born" on Earth.)

Yet again, the lack of coordination between Angel's group and the Sunnydale team continues to be an issue. Utterly bereft of allies, Fred apparently never thinks to phone Willow – that fabulously adept, potent witch she personally knows (4.15, "Orpheus") – to say, "By the way, an enchantress has just brainwashed Los Angeles into doing her bidding. Can you help?" (Admittedly, the exodus from Sunnydale in *Buffy* Season Seven is either in progress or right around the corner, so perhaps the phones aren't working there. Yet there's no mention of Fred even making the attempt.)

When Fred visits Stoller at the hospital, how does she know even a rough approximation of the man's name? Why doesn't Angel's vampire hearing register Fred's clearly traitorous remarks to the comatose Cordelia as he approaches her room? And ah, yes... it's not an outright mistake, but it's curious to see large numbers of diners happily eating away outside the bowling lanes, completely oblivious to the fact that everyone inside has been butchered by vampires, with a severed-head bowling game in progress.

POP CULTURE The title, "Shiny Happy People," is a generic phrase, but might owe to a popular song by R.E.M. (1991).

IN RETROSPECT An entranced Wesley: "I can't believe Fred's evil." Just wait until Season Five.

CRITIQUE Just when the series could be lazily coasting its way to the season finale, we're given an episode where the fate of the world comes down to Fred and Fred alone. It's not just a beautifully jolting change of pace, it does wonders for Fred's character. She's done precious little for what seems like the length of a Bible now (not since 13 episodes previous in "Supersymmetry" in fact), and it's been something of a shame. So seeing her back in the game gives a nice little tingle to one's toes.

Looking at the story overall, the producers deserve quite the applause, because watching the heroes act as Jasmine's drooling lackeys should, by all rights, be dull as spit. It's not, though, because her hold lasts for precisely half an episode – whereupon Fred tries to assassinate Jasmine with a crossbow, and everything goes joyously to hell in a hand basket. There's no *time* to get bored with the set-up, and even Angel's crew at their most fawning never get as annoying as Glory's minions in *Buffy* Season Five. Here and in episodes to come, matters keep shifting so fast that it's hard to not give it your full attention.

Sure, it's continuity-heavy as some fans like to gripe. And perhaps this would've turned people off on original broadcast (the ratings, at least, weren't anything worth throwing a party over). But now that the show is freely trafficked in syndication and available on DVD, let's revel in the acute sense that we're about to hit paydirt for the seasonal story arc, and that "Shiny Happy People" is another example of what makes *Angel* one of the best shows on television.

THE LORE Lynette Romero (News Anchor) is a real-life anchor for *Business World News*. She was also an anchor in an episode of *The West Wing* (which raises curious issues about whether *Angel* and that show occur in the same universe).

4.19: "The Magic Bullet"

"Don't let her grace or gentle beauty fool you. Winifred Burkle is a monster."

Air Date: April 16, 2003; **Writer/Director:** Jeffrey Bell

SUMMARY Under constant threat of capture, Fred makes a stand at "The Magic Bullet" bookshop and lures Jasmine out into the open. As planned, Fred shoots Jasmine with a pistol, enabling some of Jasmine's blood to coat the bullet... and strike Angel, who's standing behind her. A restored Angel and Fred flee, later wondering if the comatose Cordelia – as

Jasmine's mother – might also contain blood capable of breaking Jasmine's hold. The pair of them sneak into the Hyperion and, taking a bit of Cordy's blood, quietly break Jasmine's mental grip on Wesley, Gunn and Lorne. However, after the group similarly forces "the cure" upon Connor, the lad rats out the heroes, calling for Jasmine's legions of followers to apprehend the rogues.

FIRSTS AND LASTS When Angel and Connor perform at open-mike night in celebration of Jasmine's love, it's the last rendition on *Angel* of "Mandy" (and we're faintly amazed that it's happened often enough to warrant our mentioning it). Actually, it's the last instance of Angel singing anything at all... and it's amusing that the assembled audience only finds this entertaining – they heavily sway, even – because a higher power has brainwashed them into experiencing unbridled happiness. Perhaps the WB should've marketed this episode as, "Jasmine: So malevolent, you'll even find Angel's singing a delight."

POINTS OF DISCUSSION ABOUT "The Magic Bullet":

1. Such a pity that the Season Four DVDs don't include the "Next Time On *Angel*..." segments, because the one for "The Magic Bullet" is totally charming – and totally misleading. Essentially, the segment shows Angel getting "cured" of Jasmine's influence, whereupon the narrator says, "The truth will set Angel free... and into the arms of his only ally." Cue a shot of Angel and Fred kissing. On original broadcast, after everything that had come before, an Angel-Fred hook-up seemed all too plausible. Then you watch the episode itself, and find they kiss for just a few seconds as part of a ruse, that's all. Frankly, we wish *more* promos would resort to this sort of lying, because it'd counter-balance all the blatant ones that blow the entire plot of an upcoming episode.

2. A quick fix: Fred and Angel, after getting exposed to Jasmine's blood, both had to look at her face to crack her enchantment. Yet for everyone else, the blood alone suffices. Well, that's easy enough to explain. Lorne, Wesley and Gunn are cured from Cordelia's blood, which – being the original source of Jasmine's form – proves more potent and waives the face-watching requirement.

3. The teaser seems atypical as it opens with a bright sunny L.A. day, in which everyone feels good to be alive. Along those lines, you can tell everyone's acting out of character because they're all wearing clothes with bright colors. At least Angel's reverted back to type – given his dark jacket – after the faintly berserk white and yellow shirt he wore last episode.

4. It's another turning point in Connor's story arc (as if the virgin slaughter in 4.17, "Inside Out" wasn't enough), and detractors of the character might be tempted to view his final betrayal as the ultimate proof of his stupidity. But let's consider the boy's history. He was raised in a hell dimension, then was manipulated by Holtz, then manipulated by Justine, then witnessed his father become an infamous serial killer, then was *royally* manipulated by Evil Cordelia – the love of his life, who's now as lively as a rutabaga. He's barely known a moment's peace, ever, and even Angel's group – allegedly the good-guys – must seem wildly contradictory. They heavily over-use magic, keep revising their methodology with regards to fighting demons, and only seem happy once they "embrace" Jasmine's love – then become utterly sad when they lose it.

Taking all that into account, and remembering that Connor is 18 at best, is it any wonder that he goes off the rails? By contrast, Jasmine's the only character who offers Connor unconditional love and acceptance. He's rather vicious in his supporting her – here threatening to scalp Fred, and readying to behead everyone in 4.21, "Peace Out" – but even that, however despicable, seems in keeping with the boy's frame-of-reference. Simply put, he's decided that Jasmine is good and anyone resisting her will is evil, so they must die. It's hardly what you'd call a fair view of the world – but then, Connor hasn't had a fair and balanced life. How can you not feel *some* sympathy for the lad?

CHARACTER NOTES *Angel:* Here gets Jasmine's blood in his system. [Coupled with Hamilton in the series finale, Angel absorbs a frightful amount of potentially dangerous blood in this period.]

• *Cordelia:* Still comatose, and "enshrined" in a Hyperion room as Jasmine's mother.

• *Fred:* On the run for a week, yet hasn't made the simplest of changes to her appearance, such as cutting her hair or changing her clothes. [Didn't she learn anything from Harrison Ford in *The Fugitive*? Then again, perhaps Fred deliberately keeps her normal appearance to deploy the "give her jacket to a pedestrian" trick she pulls in the teaser, and thus avoid her pursuers.]

Fred proves vicious enough, after shooting Jasmine once to free Angel, to plug her three more times. She decides that the texts at The Magic Bullet bookshop contain "some wacko theories," and seems generally dismissive of the shop's conspiracy-minded customers. [It's not an error, but it's an interesting contrast with the conspiracy-obsessed teen Fred, who in "Spin the Bottle" (4.06) claimed that the government gleaned clandestine information through personality tests about politics and one's bowel movements. Essentially, Fred *was* the very people she here doesn't seem to comprehend. Of course, it also seems odd that she'd trivialize the customers' habits, considering Fred herself reads the *Pergamum Codex* (in 4.15, "Orpheus") for fun. By now, should *anything* seem too weird for her?]

• *Lorne:* Handling bookings at the Hyperion. He carries a hip flask.

• *Connor:* Was about five or six (he's unclear of the exact age, because they didn't exactly celebrate birthdays in Quor'toth) when Holtz taught him the art of tracking. This entailed a game wherein Holtz would tie Connor to a tree and run away, expecting the lad to escape and find him. Once, it "only" took Connor five days to track Holtz down.

Connor doesn't recognize the name "Houdini," but Jasmine's mental network later gifts him with the lyrics to "People" by Barbara Streisand and presumably [judging by the open-mike session] to "Mandy" also. He is unfazed to learn that Jasmine consumes people.

• *Jasmine:* Rewards the conspiracy-minded Magic Bullet bookshop guy with the knowledge that Lee Harvey Oswald acted alone, and that no second gunman was involved in Kennedy's death. She orders the same guy to burn down the shop, thus obliterating her spilled blood inside. [Her wounds presumably seal before she returns to the Hyperion, preventing any blood loss along the way.]

By now, it's apparent that Jasmine has been consuming some of her followers whole, for sustenance and for healing. [Green light flares behind closed doors when this occurs, and "Peace Out" suggests Jasmine reverts to being the tentacled thing – in which state she burst forth from Cordelia's belly – when she eats people.] Jasmine staggers when shot four times by Fred, but survives. She says she doesn't want people's material wealth. [But c'mon... she'll be asking for a temple two episodes from now.]

Despite followers' outrage, Jasmine mandates that Fred be taken alive [probably because she doesn't realize what allowed Fred to break free, only discovering the vulnerability of her own blood in the bookshop]. The minds of Jasmine's followers are becoming more inter-connected, allowing her to instantly convey instructions. Yet she doesn't realize when Angel's group progressively breaks loose from the network. She appears to know several languages, including Mandarin and Spanish. [She presumably picks up the languages from various speakers as they're added to mental network; notice how she didn't actually speak a word in 4.17, "Inside Out" until she'd enthralled Angel, from whom she probably learned English in an instant.]

By making Angel's group hold hands and think of Fred's characteristics, Jasmine can locate Fred through the eyes of her enthralled pedestrians. One of them accidentally gets set afire while pursuing Fred, and this ripples through the network and burns Jasmine's hand. [The man in question presumably dies, as Jasmine only becomes capable of healing people next episode.]

Jasmine loves movies, including one with "magic dwarves." [Many commentators have read this to mean *The Lord of the Rings*, as *The Fellowship of the Ring* hit theatres almost a year and a half before this story broadcast, but she probably means *Snow White*.] Her website is nearing completion. Jasmine's mojo works over the radio. She claims that she doesn't just use modern technology to spread her influence to everyone because "It's not the world's time yet." [Or more likely, she needs to power-up for a stunt that big, as in "Peace Out."]

Jasmine's bliss doesn't automatically make people quit smoking.

THE HYPERION Swamped with Jasmine's followers, to such a degree that people are pitching tents in the parking lot.

ORGANIZATIONS *Angel Investigations:* Angel off-handedly refers to "Angel, Inc." [There's no such thing, unless the gang incorporated after 3.12, "Provider." But we doubt it.]

BEST LINE A deaf woman at open-mike night, expressing herself through sign language: "I wish I could be in Fred's skull... so I could explode her brain and kill her for rejecting Jasmine."

THINGS THAT DON'T MAKE SENSE Nifty as Fred's plan to cure Angel is, it has some fundamental flaws. It presumes that Jasmine will show up in person for Fred's capture, as opposed to just sending her super-powered flunkies to beat Fred up and haul her ass back to the Hyperion. Also, it requires Angel to stand directly behind Jasmine so Fred's bullet can pass through both of them. (But as we say... it's a *really* cool plan.)

As Fred escapes from a motel, it's rather convenient that a man is filling his sidewalk-parked car from a gas can, thus providing a handy fuel source when the plot requires a car crash and an explosion. One of Jasmine's followers spotted Fred before she fell into the short green demon's hidey-hole, and Fred stays there a number of hours, so why isn't the area crawling with the authorities looking for her? (Okay, fine... it's possible that the follower wasn't certain that he'd seen Fred, and he felt so infused with Jasmine's love that he just continued on his way.)

An "executive demon" that Fred stumbles across munches on what's obviously a rubber "human hand" (although if anything, this makes the comedic scene seem even funnier). Jasmine makes people strip before she consumes them, so what does she do with the ever-growing pile of clothes afterward? Donate them to Goodwill (which has undoubtedly been renamed "Jasmine's Will")? Perhaps her eating these people somehow makes their clothes disintegrate too, but if that's the case, it's strange that she'd make them get naked in the first place. Are they tastier that way?

POP CULTURE The Magic Bullet guy says he used to listen to Art Bell, an American radio broadcaster and star of *Coast to Coast AM*, which focused on paranormal phenomena, malevolent aliens, etc.

• Gunn to Lorne: "Some gift you got there, Kreskin." Alleged psychic George Kresge, a.k.a. "The Amazing Kreskin," starred in *The Amazing World of Kreskin* in the 1970s, and made a wealth of appearances on *The Tonight Show* in that decade.

IN RETROSPECT Angel expresses amazement that Jasmine knows Mandarin, and Whedon-verse fans might feel compelled to respond, given Gina Torres' resume: "Well, sure. She spoke enough Chinese on *Firefly*."

IT'S REALLY ABOUT... The manifestation of an "Us vs. Them" proposition, as Jasmine's followers declare, as an expression of their love for her, that they must "eradicate their hate." To put it another way, those under Jasmine's control tend to act all happy and light around her, but Fred's affront has them privately braying for her blood. It's assuredly a mercy, especially given today's political climate, that the story illustrates this notion without condemning religion wholesale, or presenting itself as anti-religious propaganda.

CRITIQUE Once again, it's a beaut of an episode – arguably a bit drawn out, but with enough twists (Fred's plan to "cure" Angel) to more than counter the slow parts (her being down in the hidey-hole with the little "executive demon"). It's hard to know what else to comment on, as we're essentially looking at Part 2 of a 4-part tale, which makes critiquing "The Magic Bullet" rather like trying to review the second half-hour of a motion picture. Still, even if this story constitutes part of a larger whole, it's a part that – as in all good serialized drama – keeps you begging for more. And it continues to perform miracles for Fred's character, as she's physically the weakest of the heroes (well, barring Lorne perhaps), yet here as with last episode, she's just so *capable*.

THE LORE The "open-mike" event appears to be populated with random people, but – in what's apparently a stab at authenticity – a couple of celebrities are up on stage. The musician performing "Freddie's Dead" with Lorne is Jeffery Phillip Wiedlandt, better known as Zakk Wylde, the lead guitarist in Ozzy Osbourne's band. He's also the lead in his own group, the Black Label Society, part of the Ozzfest tour, and he's immortalized on the Hollywood Rock Walk of Fame. Nearly as entertaining, the deaf woman who signs out that she'd like to explode Fred's brain is Terrylene Sacchetti, the founder and president of the Deaf Arts Council. She'd appeared as an acting coach for the deaf in *Mr. Holland's Opus* (1995), and she's guest-starred on a number of shows including *Veronica Mars*. Oh, and the kid up there saying "Why I love Jasmine..." is Michael McElroy, who had a recurring part as Timmy on *The Tonight Show*.

4.20: "Sacrifice"

"Someone who knows the truth has to live through this."

Air Date: April 23, 2003; **Writer:** Ben Edlund; **Director:** David Straiton

SUMMARY Angel's quintet flees in wake of overwhelming opposition, taking shelter outside L.A. with a small band of monster-killers, who've thus-far remained unexposed to Jasmine's taint. In the process, Wesley happens upon a huge Spider-demon, a follower of Jasmine from another dimension. The talkative Spider-demon hopes to coax Jasmine back to his world – which contains an environment that's hostile to human-life – by appeasing her with "blood magic," an undertaking that requires a complicated weaving of flesh. Wesley also learns that Jasmine is vulnerable to one word: her real name, which is kept on the Spider-demon's world.

Angel kills the Spider-demon, but Jasmine's hold spreads among the rebels, and Connor arrives with a police commando squad to apprehend Angel's crew. With Wesley's help, Angel uses the Spider-demon's magic orb to travel to its world. The remaining heroes make a final stand, but Jasmine – now more integrated to her followers than ever before – instantly heals any injury inflicted on her troops.

FIRSTS AND LASTS It's the final appearance of Angel's convertible after nearly four years of excellent service. Our last glimpse of the car is when it's illuminated by searchlights as the heroes take to the sewers, so we might imagine they retrieve it once the Jasmine crisis blows over. Either way, we needn't shed too many tears for Angel, as he'll have a veritable fleet of hot cars at his disposal come Season Five.

First script credited to Ben Edlund, who here marches to the beat of someone else's drum, but better asserts his own style in future. And when Angel nails the Spider-demon with its own pincer, it's the second and last time this season (the first being the Beast in 4.13, "Salvage") that Angel stabs a creature to death with part of its own anatomy.

POINTS OF DISCUSSION ABOUT "Sacrifice":

1. The Spider-demon here blabs that his people possess Jasmine's true name, leading to events next episode, but it's never made clear why they have such a vital piece of information. The simplest explanation, perhaps, is that Jasmine simply learns a little about her strengths and weaknesses

every time she descends from the higher plane – remember that she didn't realize her blood made her vulnerable until about a week after Fred went rogue. It's entirely likely, then, that the Spider-demon realm inadvertently fell into possession of her name, that safekeeping of said name was given to a high priest and that she was a hell of a lot more careful in future. The Spider-demons' knowledge of Jasmine's real name could partly explain why she left their world, but we'll front a different explanation next episode.

2. By the way, a matter of style: Nobody can quite agree what to call the Spider-creature-things, and the one seen here gets credited simply as "creature." We've opted for "Spider-demons," because that it as apt as anything.

3. Again, it's startlingly clear how much Wesley's character has progressed since Season One. It's unlikely that the old Wesley could stay very calm upon finding himself in a room dripping with vivisected human flesh, yet the new model merely asks the Spider-demon who's responsible: "So... not from around here, are you?"

CHARACTER NOTES *Angel:* Decides that Connor is beyond hope for now, and brutally assaults his son, facilitating the fugitives' escape from the hotel. [It's gut-wrenching to watch, but not without justification if you consider the context. There are only five people in the whole of L.A. who've escaped Jasmine's thrall, and Angel knows that he's got to decisively incapacitate Connor if all of them are to escape.]

Angel readily senses Connor as he approaches with a commando squad. [It's possible that Angel can distinguish Connor's footsteps from everyone else, *or* maybe he simply knows that Connor – as Jasmine's best tracker and warrior – will lead any party sent to capture them, *or*, as theorized back in "Somnambulist" (1.11), vampires in the same bloodline might share a residual psionic link, and this applies to Angel and his more-than-human son.]

• *Cordelia:* Jasmine now recognizes Cordelia's blood as a threat to her plans. [We learn next episode that a couple of Jasmine's followers re-locate Cordelia while Connor isn't looking. It's also speculated that Jasmine couldn't kill Cordelia even if she wanted, which seems in line with her other limitations in our reality.]

• *Wesley:* Pops a 180 in Angel's car when the need arises.

• *Gunn:* Now states that he and Fred *both* killed Professor Seidel [4.05, "Supersymmetry"] as opposed to just taking the blame himself [4.07, "Apocalypse Nowish"]. Both of them feel tormented about Seidel's death. In spite of all their differences, Gunn saves Wesley's life by snagging him when a piece of floor collapses.

• *Fred:* Finds it hard, despite Angel's advice to the contrary, to turn off her emotions regarding their present situation.

• *Lorne:* He's heard good things about Belize, and skillfully wields a hockey stick in battle. [By the way, Lorne must need to breathe like a human; else, he could've accompanied Angel into the Spider-demon dimension.]

• *Connor:* Revels in his position as Jasmine's enforcer. Jasmine claims that pain has been the only constant throughout Connor's life [and she's definitely got a point].

• *Jasmine:* Her power now acts like a virus, its influence passing from person to person. [She presumably snares the young rebel Matthew this way, as the kid doesn't really surface long enough to see one of Jasmine's TV broadcast.] By the same token, she describes the increased inter-connection between her followers as if they're "fusing together like the cells of a single body." She can "see" through her followers' perceptions, and speak through their lips.

More importantly, she can now absorb and instantly heal injuries that her followers incur. [That said, the wounds that Jasmine "heals" while standing on her balcony – meaning the cuts that Wesley's quartet deal her commando squad – are rendered on her body as a series of lesions and almost sword-like cuts. Yet Wesley and company are armed with two poles, a wrench and a hockey stick. In all probability, the injuries on Jasmine's body are more symbolic than literal.] She revels and laughs as she heals these wounds. [New sensations thrilled her after she was "born" on Earth, and she's getting them in spades here.] Prior to this, she heals Connor's injuries by consuming some followers and waiving her hand over his head and chest. [She might even clear up the boy's acne in the process.]

The mayor of L.A. [in 2003, that would've been James K. Hahn] has declared the city "the First Citadel of Jasmine," and the L.A. Archdiocese has stated it will remove all its "false images" and replace them with "those of She Who Walks Among Us." The governor [presumably Gray Davis] tells Jasmine that he's dissolving his administration. She plans on her followers building a palace that will make "the Pyramids of Giza look like the headstones in a pauper's graveyard."

• *The Spider-demon:* Says he's a messenger from those who love Jasmine. [And yet, there's never any sign of his accomplices, so he's probably acting independently.]

THE HYPERION Contains a hitherto-unseen fire escape.

ORGANIZATIONS *Randall Golden's crew:* Rag-tag team of monster-hunters. Randall's brother Tommy used to run with Gunn's gang, but later broke off to head his own crew. When Randall was 12, he stole Gunn's car [unsuccessfully, it seems]. Tommy's unit went underground when the sun went out in L.A., and they've remained there ever since. The Spider-demon killed Tommy a week ago [so he's presumably adorning the creature's flesh-wall].

Members of Randall's crew include Holly, Trip and the

13-year-old Matthew, who witnessed vampires killing his parents in a tire trap on La Brea [Avenue].

DEMONOLOGY *Vampires:* As if to answer Skip's question about vampire dismemberment from 4.17, "Inside Out," the Spider-demon here whittles a vamp down to what looks like his head, torso and arm – yet he doesn't go to dust. Not even when the Spider-demon rips out his tongue.

• *The Spider-demons:* They equate love with sacrifice, and the one here tells Wesley that, "Before your kind was, my kind loved [Jasmine]." [There's no telling if the creature's timeframe is accurate, though.]

MAGIC *Blood/Flesh Magic:* The Spider-demon creates a tapestry from human flesh, claiming this uses a blood magic "older than words" that Jasmine will hear. [Presumably, the "call" to Jasmine will activate automatically once the creature completes the arrangement.] The Spider-demon says Jasmine doesn't care about word magic [but she does, as evidenced next episode], and that telling someone your real name makes you weak [apparently a standard in the Spider-demon realm].

• *The Spider-demon's dimensional key:* A blue globe capable of opening a portal back to the Spider-demon realm, activated by smearing a bit of blood on it. [It clearly runs off blood magic, not word magic, hence the globe's lack of inscriptions, markings or moving parts.]

BEST LINE Lorne's warning to Wesley, as pedestrians besiege the heroes: "Soccer mom, 12 o'clock!"

THINGS THAT DON'T MAKE SENSE There's just no getting around this one... out of the miles upon miles of countryside surrounding L.A., the heroes happen to venture into the *one* storm drain tunnel that leads them to the *one* inter-dimensional demon who just *happens* to hold inside information about Jasmine *and* feels like chatting with Wesley – the character best suited to figure out what's going on – instead of just gutting Wes and adding him to his flesh tapestry. None of this rings particularly true, so let's just agree with Wesley's comment that the universe, indeed, gives the heroes a long-overdue break and leave it at that. (A quick aside: Buggered if we know why the Spider-demon speaks English, unless it's empathic like the Guardian of the Word next episode.)

Subsequent to the sun going out over L.A., America's second-largest city, the entire population has been consumed by Jasmine worship. But once again, the global media appears not to have noticed. And c'mon, saying, "It's just one of those strange fixations in L.A." hardly seems sufficient... even allowing that people might not remember Jasmine's thrall once all of this is over, we live in a highly recordable age, meaning that there's surely ample proof that people became jibbering Jasmine acolytes for days on end. Besides, wouldn't every publication in L.A. be churning out pro-Jasmine pieces 24-7? (One possibility, although this isn't relevant for a couple of episodes yet, is that the renewed Wolfram and Hart quells much of the fallout from Jasmine's reign, all in the interest of getting L.A. back to business.)

Now we get to marvel at the heroes' ineptitude in their attempt to refill Angel's car. Do they incapacitate someone and make off with *their* car, thus fixing the gas problem and throwing their pursuers off the scent? No. Do they put Angel's super-strength to use and steal a car from a parking garage? No. Or if they're feeling sentimental toward Angel's convertible, do they swipe a piece of rubber hose and siphon someone else's gas tank? No. Rather, they embark on a risky stop at a gas station that's almost certain (allowing for Jasmine's mental network) to get the whole of the L.A. police after them.

Golden and company twice see Angel perform entirely superhuman leaps, yet they're still shocked and amazed to discover that he's a vampire. For that matter, you've got to question Angel's "strength in numbers" mentality in bringing Golden's crew along to hunt for the Spider-demon, considering one of the "combatants" is a 13-year-old. (Angel's just not thinking clearly after events of late.) Also, Lorne, Gunn and Fred come face-to-face with the commandoes and rather implausibly outrun them by a good margin – especially Connor, who's faster than any of them. (They must've done something terribly clever off screen, and thereby gotten a head-start.)

This time around, strangely, Jasmine appears to lunch on a group of followers while they're still in their underwear. In the teaser, we see Connor punch his fist through a door, but there's no corresponding hole on his side when he grunts in the very next shot. Ah, yes, and Gunn smacks Matthew, who's 13, unconscious in the interest of getting the boy back underground. Two things wrong with this: Matthew has a bruise on the wrong side of his face when he awakens, and it's weird that instead of simply hefting the unconscious boy over his shoulder, Gunn asks Fred – who's not exactly Hercules – to help him carry the lightweight kid. Does he need a V8?

CRITIQUE The Jasmine four-parter moves into Part 3, and we're presented with the weakest installment of the bunch. In the general sense, we're given a fairly lackluster run-around with a handful of rebels who can't muster a single lump of character among them. Everything's geared for the heroes to make their "crucial discovery," and it all runs thin up to the final act. Overall, as in future with "Time Bomb" (5.19), this episode somewhat suggests that the accomplished Ben Edlund shouldn't try to write anything straight.

And yet... in many regards, this story deserves a little more slack than it's usually given. If the main thread sputters, many of the details are lovely. For instance, the teaser – which entails Angel savagely beating Connor – should leave you in a cold sweat. Edlund's wit surfaces in places, such as Lorne explaining to Golden's gang why words such as "ugly-ass" and "beastie" sound hurtful, and the hideously mangled vampire telling the Spider-demon, "Dude... stake me already." Gina Torres shines as Jasmine even in the frickin' balcony scene, where she's relegated to flailing a bit and laughing as CGI "wounds" cover her body.

Furthermore, however much the story's middle seems soggy, let's concede that everything gets on a proper footing in the last ten-ish minutes. Connor has now become genuinely dangerous; as he enters the sewers, there's a palpable sense that he's murder on wheels. The final smackdown between Angel's allies and the commandoes looks as meaty as one might hope, and even if the CGI of the Spider-demon's dimension isn't particularly convincing, it's brief enough to get the point across.

If we add the pluses and minuses, then, it's... okay, it's not particularly memorable save for the final act, but it's not the excruciatingly poor outing that some commentators would like to think. We've certainly had worse.

THE LORE Edlund first struck fame as a comic book writer and artist who, at age 17, created *The Tick*. He and Whedon had collaborated on *Titan A.E.* (2000), a rather underrated film that performed so poorly in theatres, it prompted FOX to shutter its animation department. Still, the pairing went well enough for Whedon to take Edlund on as a producer and writer on *Firefly*. After that show got canned, Edlund moved over to the *Angel* camp and started consulting on scripts with 4.16, "Players." We'll hear a lot more from him in Season Five.

• Jeff Ricketts (the Spider-demon) was the Council assassin Weatherby in *Angel* 1.19, "Sanctuary" – which makes his scenes here with Wesley seem even more odd than normal – and he appeared as a gloved member of the Blue Sun Corporation in two episodes of *Firefly*.

4.21: "Peace Out"

"Angel's ruined everything. But he can't defeat both of us. You still believe in me, don't you?"

Air Date: April 30, 2003; **Writer:** David Fury; **Director:** Jefferson Kibbee

SUMMARY Connor's forces prevail, taking the captured heroes back to the Hyperion. On the Spider-demon's world, Angel encounters the priestly "Guardian of the Word" and "the Keeper of the Name" – who will reveal Jasmine's true moniker with its final breath. Angel defeats the Keeper in combat, then returns to Earth with its severed head. Jasmine arranges a worldwide broadcast to spread her influence, but the Keeper's head whispers her true name, permanently shattering her control. L.A. descends into rioting, even as Jasmine retains enough physical strength to brawl with Angel near an overpass. Highly conflicted, Connor abandons his loyalty to Jasmine and punches his fist through her head, killing her. Connor flees, allowing a disturbed Angel to return to the hotel. But once there, Angel finds – much to his shock and that of his colleagues – that the "late" Lilah Morgan has arrived and would like a word.

FIRSTS AND LASTS Obviously, it's Jasmine's final outing. And technically, after all the trouble they've caused over the years, it's the last use of a "dimensional portal" when Angel returns to the Hyperion lobby.

POINTS OF DISCUSSION ABOUT "Peace Out":

1. So... Jasmine claims that her conquest of the Spider-demon realm was a "trial run," and that Earth is an opportunity to perform the experiment again, only more efficiently. But let's also look at her M.O. All things considered, it looks as if she comes to a world and completely dominates it, then gets bored with her subservient creatures and departs. In that respect, she acts a fair amount like Glory from *Buffy* Season Five. Also, Jasmine is incredibly strong in terms of raw strength... again, much like Glory. We're not making this comparison off-handedly, but you'll have to read **Are the Powers and the Partners Old Ones?** for what this potentially says about Jasmine's origins.

2. As with Lorne's "meditation center" in 4.16, "Players," *Angel*-commentators have tried, and not really succeeded, to better identify the hall where Jasmine gobbles her followers. It's not worth commenting on much, save that the décor seems awfully bright and doesn't really match that of the Hyperion. Then again, it's possible that Jasmine's followers repainted it on her behalf.

3. After all the talk of "incest" this year – meaning between Connor and Cordelia, even though they aren't related by blood at all – it's amazing how many people overlook the brazen smooch that Jasmine plants on Angel's lips. Lest we forget, he's technically her grandfather. Her eternally youthful and strikingly ripped grandfather, but her grandfather nonetheless.

4. Jasmine's hold gets broken, and L.A. devolves into unbridled rioting. In other words, everything's back to normal.

CHARACTER NOTES *Angel:* Chiefly fighting for his son and the woman he's already lost, according to the empathic Keeper of the Name.

• *Cordelia:* Still comatose, but now situated by Jasmine's followers in a disused church. [She can't be very comfortable, though, just lying on a slab with some fabric draped over her.]

• *Connor:* So murderous that he's ready to personally execute the heroes before Jasmine halts him. He claims he's always known what Jasmine "really looks like" [meaning the maggoty cadaver seen in "Shiny Happy People" (4.18) and "The Magic Bullet" (4.19)], but still thinks her beautiful, on the grounds that he witnessed such fare while growing up in Quor'toth. [This is bit hard to reconcile against the heightened bigotry toward demons that Connor displays (3.21, "Benediction") upon returning from Quor'toth, although it's certainly possible to facilitate a creature's death while appreciating its "innate beauty."]

Connor seeks out the comatose Cordelia, and expresses to her how *tired* he feels, plus his frustration at Jasmine's inability to purge his hate and anger. [It's impossible to overstate this point: Connor, as Jasmine's father, was largely immune to her power. It couldn't have helped his mental stability to witness everyone around him achieving "ultimate happiness," even as he retained the ability to feel misery.] He mainly seems to kill Jasmine because he recognizes that she's just another lie – and indeed, because his life has been built upon them.

• *Jasmine:* Her name, somehow spoken in a sinuous whisper by the Keeper's severed head, sounds something like: "aaaallaallllaaahhhhaaahallllahahahahahaaaaaaaaa."

Jasmine calls herself a "frail little Power-That-Was," and says she cares about humanity whereas "the other Powers don't." [Such statements are actually murkier than you might think; again, see the **Powers/Partners** essay.] There's a statue of her in the Spider-demon realm. [This stone rendering looks more like Jasmine's present form than not, which seems to imply that she wasn't "born" as a Spider-demon in that dimension. But then, the Guardian and the Keeper are both humanoid, and the Guardian is hardly surprised when someone wearing Angel's shape shows up, so it's likely that humanoids also populate the realm.]

Jasmine tells Connor that he and Cordy are "my parents, my tether to this world"; however, she readily hurts Angel, her grandfather, after her mesmeric power is broken. [Wesley conjectures that perhaps Jasmine literally couldn't harm Cordelia, but it's perhaps more accurate to say that she *could* hurt her parents, but that she's reliant on them to maintain her hold on our reality – at least for now. This begs the question of what she'd do down the road, if Connor or Cordelia aged and died of natural causes, unless she'd become independent of them by then. Along those lines, it's implied, but not said, that Connor's punch readily kills Jasmine because his status as her father makes her vulnerable.]

She claims she "murdered thousands" [presumably the rain of fire (4.07, "Apocalypse Nowish") and its aftermath] in her efforts to "save billions." Jasmine eats an entire hall-full of people to stockpile strength for her global address, and reverts to her tentacled self [4.17, "Inside Out"] while doing so. [This mini-orgy could explain why Jasmine is turbo-charged with super-strength in the final act.] Wesley suggests that Jasmine targeted Earth in part because technology spreads her message far more quickly than a comparatively primitive setting (such as that of the Spider-demons).

After the Keeper of the Name breaks her power, Jasmine becomes scabbed with sores. [It's possible that to some degree, Jasmine relied on her followers' belief to maintain her beautified physical form. Rather like the audience needing to believe in fairies and clap for Tinkerbell, then.] The populace goes into manic withdrawal for lack of Jasmine's love, but Jasmine can still mentally commune with Connor. [He "hears" her voice through an unconscious follower's lips, even though Jasmine shouldn't hold sway over the man, but it's possible that Connor's perceptions just render this as such.]

Jasmine claims she "was forged in the inferno of creation," and she merely smokes a bit when Angel nails her with a massive electrical discharge. Ultimately, Jasmine proves mortal. [2.15, "Reprise" suggested that anything which manifests in our dimension can be killed, as a necessary consequence of being here.]

DEMONOLOGY *The Spider-demons:* Jasmine claims that "a few millennia ago," their realm was stricken with war, hatred and fear, rather like Earth. She says she "kicked their evolution up a few ticks," but that her control of the domain was "a trial run" and subject to faults. The Spider-demons built a temple to Jasmine atop a plateau, and it looks a bit like a Bundt cake. [The temple, not the plateau, that is.] She's been gone from the Spider-demon dimension for "centuries" at least, and some have begun to doubt her return. Two of Jasmine's followers in this realm include...

• *The Guardian of the Word:* A small, wizened priest of sorts, upon whom Jasmine bestowed empathy – this enables him to skim Angel's mind. [And probably accounts for the Guardian speaking English. In manner and outright devotion, he isn't too unlike "Doc," the Glory-devotee from *Buffy* Season Five.] He serves as custodian to...

• *The Keeper of the Name:* Brutish demon whose mouth is stitched together. [Apparently to stop the demon from vocalizing even part of Jasmine's real name, even by accident.] The sight of the Keeper's head makes Jasmine's followers back away. [They're echoing Jasmine's own fear.]

MAGIC *The Spider-demon's dimensional key:* [From last episode.] Makes the Spider-demons back off when Angel holds it aloft. It also opens a dimensional portal that lets Angel arrive back in the Hyperion lobby. [The globe works off blood magic and probably senses Angel's desired location after he smears a bit of blood on it, same as it dropped Angel right by Jasmine's temple in the Spider-demon realm.]

BEST LINE Connor, to the non-responsive Cordelia: "I know she's a lie. Jasmine. I just... I guess I thought this one was better than the others."

THINGS THAT DON'T MAKE SENSE Jasmine orders her totally loyal/fanatical followers to kill Angel, yet this results in their simply pawing him a little until he wards them off with the Keeper's severed head.

Fred, God bless her, fares a bit too well in combat against trained commandoes, especially considering she's only armed with a wrench. And Gunn rather impressively (that is to say, unconvincingly) kicks open the cell door in the hotel basement; judge for yourselves if it's a goof because Gunn simply lacks the strength for this, *or* whether it's evidence that the heroes put Angelus in an appallingly flimsy cell. (Perhaps Angelus "loosened" the cell bars for Gunn, but there's no evidence of this.)

On the overpass, Angel miraculously knows that Jasmine eats people before he's given cause to realize that. Everyone has changed clothes by the time Angel returns to the Hyperion, which begs the question of whether the heroes took shifts keeping an eye on Lilah while they did so. (Scandal-minded fans might also ask if Wesley let Lilah watch while he changed.)

And... sigh... one more time, it's faintly astonishing how little acknowledgment the real-world displays over the whole Jasmine affair. In this episode, the Lakers disband to devote more time to worshipping Jasmine, and she undertakes a global broadcast that's interrupted when the future CEO of Wolfram and Hart teleports onto the scene with a severed head. What on Earth does the outside world make of this? (Again, we'll suggest that the restored Wolfram and Hart labored – litigiously and mystically – to contain much of the fallout from Jasmine's tenure.)

POP CULTURE Gunn, on the realization that Jasmine eats people: "It's *To Serve Man* all over again." *To Serve Man* originated as a short story by Damon Knight (for *It* magazine, Jan. 1953) and later made into one of the most infamous *Twilight Zone* episodes (1962). In both versions, some seemingly benevolent aliens – the Kanamits – arrive and proceed to help mankind eliminate all war, famine, etc. They also transport some "lucky" humans back to their homeworld (rather like Jasmine allowing some select followers into her bedroom), but their true intentions are discovered when the decryption of one of their books – *To Serve Man* – ominously reveals said text as a cookbook. (On *Buffy*, Dawn mentioned *To Serve Man* in 7.01, "Lessons.")

• Lorne deems the emptied Hyperion creepy in "a post-apocalyptic *Night of the Comet* kind of way." In *Night of the Comet* (1984), the tail of a comet washes over Earth and turns any "unprotected" (meaning not encased in metal) human and animal into red dust. The film's not exactly what you'd call a serious examination of a global disaster, though, as evidenced when a couple of characters who attempt to go shopping after the tragedy and are accosted by zombie clerks.

IT'S REALLY ABOUT... It's more a discussion about, rather than a ringing endorsement of, freewill. Jasmine seems creepy because she's taking it away, and the heroes resist her on the almost-automatic grounds that she's wrong to do so. Yet as Jasmine herself points out, freewill has also bestowed a hell of a lot of war, disease and poverty upon the world.

Curiously, the real counter-point to this argument comes from Connor, who's effectively never made his own choices. His entire life has been dictated by the intent or deeds of other people – Holtz, Justine, Evil Cordelia, Jasmine and to a lesser degree Angel – and the only tangible choice the boy ever made was to sacrifice the virgin in "Inside Out" (not that we're applauding that, of course). He's danced to everyone else's tune before now, and his brutal slaying of Jasmine is perhaps best viewed as Connor making a desperate stab toward regaining some control of his own life. Even if, tragically, this makes him go completely insane and become downright homicidal next episode.

CRITIQUE Yet again, it's a case of *Angel* performing far, far better than it perhaps looks on paper. After all, most of the main characters spend the episode in a cell, and you can see Jasmine's sudden transformation into Supergirl coming from a mile away. The producers obviously want a balls-to-the-wall finish here, in the same fashion that the misogynist Billy was spuriously gifted with "demon strength" in Season Three.

None of this, however, detracts from what's a well-oiled, well-directed, well-performed episode with a lot of ambition. Connor yet again goes from being "the whiny one" to a pivotal part of the story, and the plowing of his fist through Jasmine's head *really* makes for an electric jolt. It was probably a given that Jasmine would wind up dead by season's end, as simply stripping her powers would seem like a slap on the wrist after all the trouble she's caused. Even so, it's still a pleasure to see how her plans crumble to pieces.

In the broader sense, it's the chance to appreciate how

remarkably the "novel" format of Season Four holds together – far better than its detractors would lead you to believe – and it's an opportunity to brace for the biggest paradigm shift the heroes will ever experience. In ways large and small, then, "Peace Out" is brilliant work.

THE LORE Mention of Romanov's name in the opening credits spoiled Lilah's big entrance at the end for anyone who was paying attention – this mainly occurred because the Screen Actors' Guild rules favor credits coming up-front, even if it's not unprecedented to delay them as part of a surprise. Such a deal had been brokered with Keith Szarabajka for Holtz's sudden return in 3.20, "A New World," but it wasn't done for Romanov. Minear, off in a writing hole when "Peace Out" was scripted, doesn't know if one of Romanov's people objected to the request, or if the *Angel* producers simply didn't ask in the first place. (Minear, *uk.media.tv.angel*, May 3, 2003)

• Robert Towers (High Priest, a.k.a. The Guardian of the Word) voiced Snoopy in *You're a Good Man, Charlie Brown* (1985), and he played Albert Einstein in *Einstein's Playground* and Karg in the *Masters of the Universe* film. Angelica Castro (Telemundo Reporter) played a harlot in *The Scorpion King* (2002). Kristin Richardson (Female Reporter) had been a character amusingly named "Darla" on *Charmed*, but as a former Rockette, she also worked as a dancer on Cher's 1999 "Do You Believe" tour.

4.22: "Home"

"Just because we tried to kill or corrupt each and every one of you at one time or another... doesn't mean we can't be trusted."

Air Date: May 7, 2003; **Writer/Director:** Tim Minear

SUMMARY Lilah – summoned back from the dead as part of her contract with the firm – congratulates the heroes for overthrowing Jasmine, which consequentially scuttled all hope for world peace. As a "reward," the Senior Partners offer the firm's L.A. branch, rebuilt and restocked with personnel, to Angel's crew to do with as they see fit. Angel and company mull over whether they can use an evil organization for good without becoming corrupted themselves, but at least agree to take the office tour.

Elsewhere, a tormented Connor goes completely insane, straps himself and the still-comatose Cordelia with dynamite and takes a sporting goods store hostage. Lacking options, Angel agrees to Wolfram and Hart's terms if the firm will help him deal with Connor. Angel overpowers his son, enabling the firm to implement a spell that rewrites Connor's history, gifting him with a loving human family. Connor forgets his true past, becoming a stable teenager, even as everyone save Angel and Lilah lose all memory of the boy. With the firm arranging for Cordelia's medical care, Angel and his inner circle prepare to oversee the firm's L.A. office.

FIRSTS AND LASTS Production-wise, it's the last script from Tim Minear, who also ends his tenure as a "Consulting Producer" after this point. As part and parcel of this house-cleaning, it's the final appearance of Stephanie Romanov as Lilah Morgan (barring a flashback in 5.18, "Origin"), and the debut of Jonathan Woodward as the lab technician Knox. And it's the final sight of Gunn with chin-hair.

A moment of silence, please, for the final appearance of the Hyperion Hotel, both the interior and exterior (unless you count its back alley appearing in the series finale), and all its accoutrements, including the weapons cabinet and the lobby office. In terms of décor, it's the debut of the sprawling new Wolfram and Hart lobby... which is never seen again, as the show bases itself in the firm's executive offices starting next episode. Similarly, Fred's laboratory will be replaced with a better model for Season Five, but the "ancient prophecies wing" that Wesley tours gets another outing in 5.07, "Lineage." It's also the debut of Angel's office at the firm (well, sort of, in that it's somewhat revamped for next year), and the "template books" that access the firm's archives, and which Wesley will put to good use throughout Season Five.

It's also, a bit sadly, the definitive end of Angel Investigations. Even though the heroes have been run ragged, and unable to function as a supernatural detective agency for some time now.

POINTS OF DISCUSSION ABOUT "Home":

1. The Senior Partners' offer – ceding control of the firm to Angel – is undoubtedly the smartest thing they ever do. We can never, ever forget that, and let's probe why it's so clever.

By now, the Senior Partners must know that they can't corrupt Angel using the usual methods. Holland, Lindsey, Lilah, Linwood and Gavin all took their shot at him... yet they failed, and most of them wound up dead. Mostly stymied, the Senior Partners here decide to "give Angel everything he wants." They save Connor, and lavish Angel with material goods.

The effect is to separate the heroes – and Angel in particular – from both their mission and humanity. And it works. Angel *hopes* to use the firm for good, but from this point, much of his job will entail signing documents to fund orphanages or whatever. That's great for everyone who benefits, but what about Angel himself? The Powers' strategy of Angel saving people individually – as Doyle adeptly pointed out in the first episode – kept him connected to those who needed help. There's none of that personalized benevolence here, and it's going to dampen Angel's heroic passion as early as 5.04, "Hell Bound." Indeed, in the episodes to come, this fundamental disconnect with the common man will doom Angel's group, causing two (and more likely three) of them to lose their lives. It's a tribute to the producers that the viewership experienced the series finale with such optimism – and rightfully so – but let's not fool ourselves that Angel and company should've ever accepted Lilah's offer.

2. Backtracking a little... Jasmine's downfall only occurred a few hours ago, yet Wolfram and Hart already has a new building erected with dozens if not hundreds of employees. Even allowing that we're talking about a multi-dimensional, demonic organization here, how did the firm renew itself with such blazing speed?

One possibility is that Wolfram and Hart was being quietly rebuilt throughout the Jasmine affair, with strict protocols to prevent its employees coming under her sway. The restored firm presumably waited to see if Angel could neutralize Jasmine, and prepared to strike back if he failed. After all, "Reprise" (2.15) clearly demonstrates that the firm draws its strength and authority from the collective consciousness of humanity, meaning that if Jasmine *had* achieved global control, the firm would've probably lost its footing on Earth. The Senior Partners might have moved against her before that occurred, with the scheme to give Angel the L.A. branch serving as a contingency plan.

Sounds good, but a possible snag is how Jasmine and her cronies didn't notice a brand-spanking new building going up at the old Wolfram and Hart location. (And the new edifice must sit on the same parcel of land, because the entire plot to "Hell Bound" relies on it.)

3. In the DVD commentary on this story, Minear says that Angel's "knifing" Connor – thus triggering the magic spell that rewrites the boy's history – fulfills "the father will kill the son" prophecy from Season Three. With all respect to Minear, this is an incredibly odd thing to say, as 3.17, "Forgiving" established that the prophecy was bunk and invented by Sahjhan. Worse, Minear points out that Angel really doesn't kill Connor anyway, as the lad gets funneled into a new life.

So to review... the father *isn't* fated to kill the son, and – even if he were – he does not, in fact, kill the son. As entertaining as Minear's commentaries are, we desperately wish he'd glossed over this point.

4. Yup... we've got another *Firefly* crossover here. Jonathan Woodward (Knox) played Lt. Tracey in *Firefly* 1.15, "The Message," and some *Angel* watchers have expressed confusion as to why this gets mentioned with such prominence, given that Woodward only appeared in the one episode. The answer is simply that *Firefly* only lasted 15 episodes (the motion picture notwithstanding), so a character who's front and center in even one story stands out more than he otherwise might. Something else about Woodward that inevitably gets mentioned: He was the chatty vampire who bonded with the Slayer in *Buffy* 7.07, "Conversations With Dead People." You can tell that Woodward is the type of actor Whedon likes to keep re-using, something made easier by the fact that Woodward's characters keep dying.

5. In the scene before the heroes step into the limo, Angel leans against the Hyperion entrance, and the 4121 numbering – the real-life street address of the apartment building that serves as the hotel exterior – couldn't be more noticeable. See 2.05, "Dear Boy" on what this potentially says about Hyperion's location.

6. The scene with Connor and his new family suggests that he's drinking some wine at dinner. He's underage. That's just shocking.

CHARACTER NOTES *Angel:* Claims – despite all of his conflict with Lilah in the past 3.5 years (give or take) – that he's sorry about what happened to her. Among the firm's materialistic goodies, Angel seems most interested in the hi-def television in his office.

• *Cordelia:* Still comatose, but cared for medically and metaphysically. Lilah says Cordy is probably even getting a manicure and blow-dry. [Indeed, Cordy looks very well kept when she next appears in 5.12, "You're Welcome."]

• *Wesley:* Refers to Lilah as a loved one, then calls this as a figure of speech. He knows about the obliteration of the Watchers' Council [*Buffy* 7.09, "Never Leave Me"; although we never see Wesley receiving notification of the event]. His wrist armaments include an air-propelled grappling hook. [You almost expect him to say, "Go, go Gadget hook..." when he uses this.] Wesley swipes Lilah's contract from the firm's files, and burns it in the hope of releasing her from service. [See **Organizations** as to why he fails.]

• *Gunn:* Now undeniably cordial with Wesley. Gunn sounds like the biggest proponent of joining the firm. [A lot of this owes to Gunn's dawning awareness, particularly in "Players" (4.16) and "Spin the Bottle" (4.06), that he's "merely" the team's muscle.] The firm arranges a private meeting between Gunn and the new denizen of the White Room – who appears as a panther – and they appear to wordlessly establish some sort of rapport [that's further explored in Season Five].

• *Fred:* Accepts a semi-automatic from Lilah as protection while she tours the firm. [We can here overlook Fred's dreadful track record with projectile weapons this year... even someone who's a terrible shot should have no trouble with that piece of hardware, as she could just spray the area with bullets if needed. But see **Things That Don't Make Sense**.] Listed in the address book of Fred's cell phone: Matthew Partney at 6200 Crestwood Boulevard in Lubbock, Texas.

• *Lorne:* Gleeful to see the entertainment division's client roster includes just about every celebrity he's wanted to meet. Secrets of the universe that Lorne learns from the firm: magician/tiger-trainer Siegfried is evil, his partner Roy... not so much. [By the way, this story broadcast before Roy's infamous savaging by a tiger in October 2003.]

• *Connor:* Clearly insane, prone to assaulting people who don't show familial respect, yet simultaneously threatens to blow up several hostages. Connor withstands Angel punching him in the face with a bowling ball. The "reborn" Connor appears to live in a cabin somewhere outside L.A. with his new parents. [The "memory" magic involved seems very similar to Dawn's insertion into the Summers family in *Buffy* Season Five. That said, the exact reason Angel must trigger the spell by slicing at Connor with a knife – as appears to be the case – is elusive.] The new Connor has at least two sisters and an aunt, and scored in the top tenth percentile, meaning he's got the pick of colleges. [This appears to settle the "What is Connor's age?" argument – see 4.07, "Apocalypse Nowish" – as 18 or thereabouts, even though his real age could certainly vary with his falsified birth certificate.] He's apparently dating someone named Tracy, a vegan. [And he's next seen in 5.18, "Origin."]

• *Lilah:* Angel's senses verify Lilah's identity; apparently she returns in the same manner as the late Holland [2.15, "Reprise"]. She says she'll be "returning to Hell" once she eases Angel's crew into the firm. [Lilah seems awfully chipper for someone who's going back to Hell soon; nonetheless, it's hard to imagine Hell as a pleasant retirement community where dead lawyers reside, as opposed to a fiery pit where they're tormented for all eternity. The Senior Partners never give a particular damn for their employees while they're alive, so it's doubtful they the lawyers are anything beyond hellfire/demon chow once they've kicked it.] Lilah is resigned to this fate, but tells Wesley it "means something" when he tries to destroy her contract and thereby free her.

Like the late Holland, Lilah sports a wound that corresponds to her "fatal" injury. [Or at least, she displays the hatchet cut that Wesley provided in 4.13, "Salvage." Lilah's scarf seems to obscure Evil Cordelia's blade cut from 4.12, "Calvary."] Aside from Angel, Lilah alone appears to remember Connor's true identity and history. [Her successor also knows the truth, starting next episode.]

• *Knox:* The "MacGyver" of Wolfram and Hart, and someone who manages the science division for the department head. He's into *Dungeons and Dragons*. [Fred gives this reference a blank stare, which is entertaining if you recall her cut line about *D&D* from "Spin the Bottle" (4.06).] He's developed a Palm Pilot capable of hacking into any electronic device within 100 yards, including the address book of Fred's cell phone.

THE FIRM'S LIBRARY Rutherford Sirk, an ex-Watcher now in the firm's employ, escorts Wesley to the "Ancient Prophecies wing." It's a stately room wherein 24 over-sized books – cited as "templates" – lie. Sirk claims that the firm possesses the most comprehensive collection of prophecy archives in existence – with materials relating to omens, revelations, etc. – all of which is accessible simply by speaking the title of the text you want over one of the templates. The book renders the text on its pages, rather like a "computer terminal" calling up the requested information.

• *Devandiré Sybylline Codex.* Sirk apparently stole the only known copy of this when he left the Watchers, and it's now available in the firm's archives, either in the original Sanskrit or translated.

ORGANIZATIONS *Wolfram and Hart:* Now outfitted with necro-tempered glass that enables vampires to bask in sunlight, and which also proves 30 percent more energy efficient. The L.A. branch is swarming with employees. [We have to presume that these staffers were pooled from other Wolfram and Hart branches, as the Beast adeptly killed the L.A. personnel in "Habeas Corpses" (4.08), yet everyone seen here seems relatively experienced. It certainly doesn't feel as if interns are shouldering the burden here.]

Lilah says the Senior Partners are "ceding this territory" to the heroes, and giving them a "controlling interest" in the L.A. branch. The main lobby sports a large representation of the letters "W&H" [as if the firm is now a demonic version of *Sesame Street*, sponsored by the letters W and H]. "Files and Records," formerly in the firm's basement [judging by 3.10, "Dad"] has now moved "upstairs." Employee contracts magically reappear if destroyed, and Lilah explains Wesley's failure to burn hers with, "Flames wouldn't be eternal if they actually consumed anything." Prominent employees include Knox; Sirk [who re-appears in 5.08, "Destiny"]; Lacey Shephard, Gunn's tour guide; and Preston, a short fellow who shows Lorne around the firm's entertainment division.

According to Knox, the building has a dungeon [probably not the storage facility in "Hell Bound"]. Angel's office features a private elevator to the motor pool, where 12 cars are at his disposal [seen next episode].

• *The White Room:* Lacey escorts Gunn to the White Room, but there's no sign of her inputting the key code ["Forgiving" and "Habeas Corpses"]. The big glowing button still appears, but Lacey herself disappears during the usual haze of light. The White Room's new denizen – a panther – appears to commune with Gunn through its soulful eyes.

BEST LINE Lilah to Wesley, on his beheading her: "It's okay, Lover. I never felt a thing." Wesley, darkly: "I'm sure that's true."

THINGS THAT DON'T MAKE SENSE For starters, Wesley suggests that the firm will respect its pledge to not harm the heroes while they tour the new facility, on the grounds that, "They are honorable, in their way." Sorry... is he high? When has the firm *ever* been honorable, save for when doing so conveniently suited its nefarious purposes? Meanwhile, Fred accepts Lilah's offer of a firearm to cart about the office, never considering that, um, there's no guarantee that it actually works. To put it another way, it's a bit of an oversight to expect that a weapon you've accepted from your mortal enemy will protect you from said enemy.

In the Ancient Prophecies wing, the "template" book that Wesley holds manifests its text on the right-hand side; yet in the next shot, when he's flipping the pages, it's clearly on the left. Ah, yes... and if the episode runs in real-time, then Gunn and Lacey are in the elevator for a ludicrous amount of time, unless they stopped for a quickie in the janitor's closet beforehand. No wonder they're smiling so much.

Connor has spontaneously become a munitions expert (although he might've beat the knowledge out of whomever he obtained the batteries and explosives from). On a visual note, the explosives strapped around Connor's waist magically disappear after Angel yanks out the trigger wire. (Minear cut a shot of Angel ripping off the explosives, on the grounds that it wasn't very convincing, which generated this visual hole.) And weirdly, the limo that takes Angel to see Connor drives on the left-hand side of the road, which is rather unsafe. Unless they're passing an invisible car.

Finally... many commentators and fans have questioned how quickly L.A. transitions from massive rioting to routine business, especially given how it looks as if Connor's hostages were out shopping. (On screen, it's not that clear, but we'll probably have to fall back on the argument that the reconstituted Wolfram and Hart – magically or otherwise – calmed matters around the city and erased as much Jasmine-trauma as possible. If so, perhaps the hostages were trying to resume life as normal. Americans do love their shopping, after all.)

CROSS-OVERS Lilah gives Angel a file concerning recent events in Sunnydale, plus an amulet that's "crucial" to an impending final battle there. Angel consequently ventures to Sunnydale and meets Buffy in the waning seconds of *Buffy* 7.21, "End of Days." He gives her the amulet in the *Buffy* series finale (7.22, "Chosen") and returns to L.A. Spike saves the day with the amulet and goes to ash, but then... see 5.02, "Just Rewards." (And check out the same story for debate on the purpose of the amulet.)

IT'S REALLY ABOUT... In many ways, it's a familiar story. A group of independent-minded people (rockers, comic-book creators, whatever) set out to "make the world a better place" through their sheer inventive acts. They set themselves up as a counter-culture, declare "down with The Man!" and become hugely popular. And then, by virtue of the money, influence and success they achieve, they become The Man.

It's hardly an original insight to say that this largely owes to the system – meaning large companies tend to act a certain way, even if reasonable people are running the show. The desire to change such an organization from within is perhaps commendable, but odds are far greater that it'll change *you*, unless you simply refrain from taking the post in the first place. That's the real issue here: When Gunn asks Wesley, "How long are you gonna be satisfied, sitting there sticking pins in maps and blowing dust off your books?", the correct answer is, "as long as it takes." Instead, Wesley's suggestion that they can enter the firm "with our eyes open and our wits about us" just screams of naïvete.

A final observation: The real tragedy here is how the heroes talk themselves into this bargain, and how their downfall comes about slowly and insidiously. Concern for his son initially galvanizes Angel into signing on the dotted line, but in short order, he'll be entranced by the hi-def TV, the motor pool and all the firm's bells and whistles. And then he's virtually screwed. Yes, the heroes buy into Lilah's notion that, "People don't need an unyielding champion. They need a man who knows the value of compromise and how to best the system from inside the belly of the beast"... but let's be honest, so much of this comes down to greed.

CRITIQUE All too often, a highly innovative series will slide into stagnation, and creatively run on empty for the sake of ratings. *The X-Files* – a show that kept your nuts in a vice throughout its early years, then ran past its expiration date because FOX couldn't bear the thought of living without it – immediately springs to mind. Anyone who's acquainted with sci-fi television (or hell, television in general) can undoubtedly think of other examples.

Then we come to "Home," which arrives when *Angel* is closer to 100 episodes than not, and Mutant Enemy has been pumping out *Buffy*-related television for six years. Whedon and his compatriots could've settled for blithely cashing the paychecks while the gravy train lasted, but with one mighty effort and outpouring of sweat, they prove that *Angel* simply isn't beyond its glory days. Granted, ratings were down for Season Four, so they arguably had little to lose, but the overriding priority in moving the heroes into the law firm was probably just, "Well, this will prove interesting, no matter how insane it turns out." And thank God they took that bold step.

Amid all the rebooting, it's also a mercy that they called one last time upon Minear – someone who knows the show of old and lifts *just* enough from his own continuity, even as he spins everything off on a different path. Thanks to the show-designers and Minear's direction, the firm gets presented as something bright, modern and a sign of "progress"... precisely the sort of thing needed to create a false sense of security. Connor gets a memorable send-off (for now), and there's precisely the sort of gripping anticipation about Season Five that needs to be there. Both as a prologue for the year to come, *and* as a story in its own right, "Home" is touching, surprising and crisply told, and it's just about the best present an *Angel* junkie could hope for.

THE LORE *[Authors' note: Although this version of Redeemed reflects the text as it was published in 2006 (barring some light editing for typos, formatting errors, etc.), the Lore sections for this episode and 5.12, "You're Welcome" have been revised, solely to include comments that Carpenter made in 2009 concerning her departure from Angel. Frankly, her statements on the topic were so forthright, it would have felt a huge disservice to Angel fans to leave them out.]*

Angel's renewal for Season Five came rather late in the game – the announcement arrived in May 2003, just as Season Four took a bow – but as a gesture of faith, the WB decided to bump the show to Wednesday night to follow *Smallville*, the network's biggest series. However, Bell had some concerns that the two shows didn't share much of a common audience. "*Smallville* is a very well-done, soapy, high school melodrama, and we are a more adult, darker show, and there's not a whole lot of piney love going on. There's no way we can hold the *Smallville* lead-in, but I would love for new fans to discover us, because I think we're a very cool show." (Gross, *Cinefantastique*, Oct. 2003)

• The period following Carpenter's departure from *Angel* saw those involved being rather reserved about the topic, at times giving the impression that her leaving was something of a mutual decision. Bell, certainly, appeared to indicate as much in a *Dreamwatch* interview were he commented amongst other things, "Charisma is irreplaceable. She has a very unique ability and her character arc came through an amazingly complex roller-coaster ride." (DiLullo, *Dreamwatch* #109, Sept. 2003) For her part, Carpenter said that she never really asked Whedon as to why Cordy wasn't joining the other characters at the firm, stating that it was "really none of her business." Still, after so many years as Cordelia, she conceded that she wasn't entirely prepared for the cast resuming work for Season Five without her. She said, "[They] went back to work on July 24... On that day I thought, 'Oh, today is officially my first day of unemployment.'" (Amatangelo, *BostonHerald.com-the Edge*, Aug. 15, 2003) She more directly addressed the departure, however, years later on a panel at DragonCon 2009, where she stated that she had fully expected to return for Angel Season Five – and only learned that she wasn't after reading the trade publications.

• Carpenter had now given birth, but helped Minear out by coming in to lie comatose in the sporting goods store. She later commented that becoming a mother made her desire "the half-hour sitcom lifestyle" to balance family and work. (Coleridge, *TV Guide Insider*, Feb. 5, 2004) After *Angel* folded, she mostly did guest-spots, including three appearances on *Charmed* as "The Seer." She later became a recurring character on *Veronica Mars* – as the steamy, gold-digging Kendall Casablancas – in 2005. *Angel* and *Buffy* addicts might want to check out *Veronica Mars* 2.09, "My Mother, the Fiend," in which Carpenter and guest-star Alyson Hannigan get to share a scene. (However, it must be said that their performances scarcely evoke Cordelia and Willow.)

• Whedon felt that while the Hyperion set was beautiful, it had become a giant room full of people standing around talking. The shift to the law firm, he thought, stopped the writers from straining to accommodate that. (*Post-Gazette*, July 2003)

• Jason Winer (Preston, Lorne's guide at the firm) later wrote for *The Wayne Brady Show*. He also co-created MTV's *The Blame Game*, a show in which two ex's were pitted against one another in a courtroom setting to see who was responsible for the break-up – Winer appeared in 136 episodes, usually as the bachelor's attorney. It all sounds rather apt, considering his *Angel* character works in Wolfram and Hart's Entertainment Division, doesn't it?

The Total Kill-Count (thru Season Four)...

• Angel: 38 vampires, 61 demons, 19 humans, 30 zombies; 1 heroic champion (demonic).

• Cordelia: 2 vampires, 2 1/2 demons; hundreds of inter-dimensional bugs.

• Wesley: 6 vampires, 13 1/2 demons, 2 humans.

• Gunn: 7 vampires, 14 1/2 demons, 1 human, lots of nasty demon babies.

• Fred: 3 vampires, 1 demon, 1 human, lots of nasty demon babies.

• Connor: 12 vampires, 2 demons, 1 higher being.

NOTES: First off, it didn't seem fair to count Angelus' kills toward Angel's tally; nor did we credit Cordelia with all the mayhem that Jasmine caused as Evil Cordy. Cordelia herself earned only one kill this year – and indeed, her final kill of the series – by dusting a vampire in "Supersymmetry" (4.05).

In a single season, Connor moved into the No. 2 position for vampires dusted, even if he hasn't a hope of surpassing Angel's total. Gunn and Fred deserved *some* credit for squishing "lots of nasty demon babies" in "Slouching Toward Bethlehem" (4.04), but the babies didn't rank as full-fledged demons, hence the special notation. Along those lines, Connor scored a point for "a higher being" by eliminating Jasmine in "Peace Out" (4.21).

Human casualties this year... Gunn, notably, snaps Professor Seidel's neck in "Supersymmetry." It's possible that Connor bludgeoned to death the cop he meets on the roof in "Home" (4.22), but we don't witness the outcome. And it's possible that the human villain DeMarco dies as a consequence of Lorne smashing his mystical globe, but his fate goes unstated.

Final note: Wesley returns home after fighting some sort of "bug swarm" in "Apocalypse Nowish" (4.07), but the details were hopelessly vague. It's tempting to hypothesize that he finally got around to killing the giant bugs from 3.05, "Fredless," but even this seems like wishful thinking.

5.01: "Conviction"

"I'm pure. I believe in evil. You and your friends, you're conflicted, you're confused.... we're not. That's why you're gonna lose."

Air Date: Oct. 1, 2003; **Writer/Director:** Joss Whedon

SUMMARY The heroes take charge of the firm's L.A. branch, even as Corbin Fries, a high-powered client, finds himself facing a jail sentence. If convicted, Fries promises to "say the magic word" and detonate a bomb that will kill everyone in California. Angel's team confirms that Fries has a magical canister hidden inside his young son Matthew, and that the code phrase will unleash a retrovirus sealed within.

Unfortunately, the firm's commando squad, still playing by old school rules, sets out to "solve the problem" by slaughtering Matthew and everyone at his school. A pissed-off Angel evacuates Matthew's classroom and overpowers the commandoes, killing their leader. Back at the firm, the Senior Partners schedule Gunn for a brain upgrade that endows him with full knowledge of the law, enabling him to win Fries a mistrial. Gunn monkey-wrenches the situation so Fries will lie low, giving Wesley and Fred time to disarm the magic container. Relieved, Angel opens a piece of his mail... and out falls the magical amulet that he gave to Buffy [*Buffy* 7.22, "Chosen"], which brings the disintegrated vampire Spike back to life.

THE OPENING CREDITS James Marsters immediately replaces Carpenter in the No. 2 slot. Symbolically, this suggests that Spike – who in terms of personality will default back to his snarky *Buffy* Season Four incarnation – will fill the character void left by Cordy in more ways than one. New images in the Opening Credits include that cute little bit where Angel closes a book and a bell tolls in the soundtrack. There's also a new "heroes striding forward" shot, but it's unique because it was apparently shot separately, as opposed to hailing from episode footage. (Moreover, the amazing thing about this shot is how much Marsters simply *exudes* Spike's bravado, even when he's merely walking forward in a determined manner for all of two seconds.)

FIRSTS AND LASTS Heralding a new era for Mutant Enemy, it's the first *Angel* episode broadcast without benefit of *Buffy* or *Firefly* airing as well. Character-wise, it's the first appearances of the "lawyered-up" Gunn; of Eve, the heroes' plucky young liaison to the Senior Partners; of that curiously masked individual who delivers the mail (see 5.06, "The Cautionary Tale of Numero Cinco"); and of Harmony as Angel's secretary. It's also, of course, the debut of the ensouled Spike on *Angel*.

Décor-wise, the following are unveiled: the firm's executive level and lobby; Fred's laboratory; Wesley and Gunn's offices; and Angel's impressive array of company cars. Angel's office technically appeared last episode, but it's undergone something of a revamp.

In terms of production, Drew Goddard – who wrote some of the most celebrated *Buffy* Season Seven episodes – transfers to Angel and gets listed as "Executive Story Editor" (see 5.07, "Lineage"). And to get technical, it's the first *Angel* episode to be transmitted in high-definition (where available), as was all of Season Five.

POINTS OF DISCUSSION ABOUT "Conviction":

1. Whedon's directing this story, and anyone familiar with his work will notice the lengthy panning shot that establishes the firm's new layout. By our stopwatch, the sequence from Fred exiting the elevator to Angel encountering Eve lasts 3 minutes, 44 seconds. Accounts differ on whether this highly complicated sequence entailed 27 or 28 takes, but either way, it apparently required five hours to film. Comparisons between this shot and Mal Reynolds' walkabout in the Whedon-directed *Serenity* film are inevitable. Especially as – again, by our stopwatch – the time from Reynolds passing through the blue-rimmed door to River saying "We're going for a ride" is 3 minutes, 40 seconds.

2. For whatever baffling reason, Whedon slips into farm boy mode in Act One, unleashing four animal references in the space of (here we go again) 5 minutes, 15 seconds. To check them off: Angel accidentally phones the firm's Ritual Sacrifice department and hears, "For goats, press one... or say *goats*!"; Harmony has laced Angel's drink with otter's blood; Wesley concedes that Fries "deserves to be eaten by weasels" and Fries says he doesn't give "a ferret's anus" about the firm's new regime. (You could even, if you wished, include the subsequent scene where Angel learns that Fries' magic container could hold a golden retriever.)

3. Lilah is gone without explanation, effectively replaced by Eve. The oft-traded theory that "bringing back" dead

employees expends a great amount of energy, and isn't cost-effective in the long run, seems reasonable.

4. Speaking of Eve, the "flash sequence" that cuts between the death of the head commando (Hauser) and the epilogue in Angel's office features one of the most curious wrinkles in the entire show. Viewed in slow motion, the "quick-flash" appears to show Eve standing in the school hallway, as if pondering Hauser's splattered blood on the wall. This isn't in the episode, nor does the script mention anything along those lines, yet it certainly casts a new light on Eve's question to Angel of "How'd you do [today]?"

5. Anyone watching the lively Angel-commando slugfest, in fact, might fail to properly notice the setting. Specifically, there's an odd juxtaposition: As Angel beats the crap out of his attackers, the classroom whiteboard displays such sage advice as "bee on time" (complete with a bee doodle) and "show your work!" Anyone doubting that this was deliberate imagery on Whedon's part should observe, after Angel blows Hauser's head off and strolls away, the overhead sign that reads: "Respect: Learn it, know it, show it!"

6. It's often said that "Conviction" opens the very day after the Season Four finale, but this isn't correct. Whereas it's certainly the heroes' first day of running the firm, 18 days have passed – judging by the *Buffy* flashback and time-stamp next episode – in the interim.

7. Denisof developed Bell's palsy two weeks before this story was filmed, meaning the left side of his face was completely paralyzed. He worried about the condition becoming permanent, but was recovering nicely when "Just Rewards" rolled around. However, this explains why, in "Conviction," the camera actively works to avoid Denisof's left profile. The nearly four-minute tracking shot in the lobby becomes a lot more lively with this in mind, and notice how in the scene around Angel's conference table, the eye is distracted from Denisof's face by the prominent placement of Acker's legs.

8. Whedon's well-known loathing for the Bush administration once again (see 4.06, "Spin the Bottle") enters the fray as Fred hangs up a poster for the Dixie Chicks, who number among President's detractors. Indeed, such is Fred's dramatic flair while revealing the poster, we're obviously meant to sit up and take notice. What's *really* amusing, though, is that Fred backs up against the poster during a subsequent discussion with Knox, making her look as if she *is* the fourth Dixie Chick. Even her dress matches.

9. Two years after *Angel* folded, J. August Richards starred as a young attorney in a short-lived *Law and Order* spin-off, which now makes "lawyer Gunn" look like something a precursor. The title of the show in question? Same as this episode: "Conviction." (For that matter, Richards also played a lawyer on *CSI: Miami* in 2004.)

CHARACTER NOTES *Angel:* He's gained some weight since last we saw him. [Boreanaz's weight-gain over the seasonal hiatus actually raises a few continuity concerns. If indeed only 18 days pass between "Home" and this story, did Angel spend the intervening time visiting an all-night vampire buffet? Pig's blood is admittedly fatty, but still...] The move to the firm hasn't done his hair any favors either; it almost [and rather appallingly] looks like a pompadour. He's giddy about his newfound gaggle of company cars [which presumably come fitted with necro-tempered glass]. Oh, and he's officially designated "CEO and President of Wolfram and Hart."

• *Wesley:* Seems deflated by Fred's friendly banter with Knox, and favors cricket over basketball. Wesley acts as Angel's head of operations, giving orders to Fred and Lorne. Notably, Wesley is sent to plug Fries in the head, as a last recourse, if the jury convicts him. Ah, yes, and Wesley recognizes Spike on sight. [They've never met, but Wes briefly resided in Sunnydale, did extensive research into Angel's history (1.11, "Somnambulist") and probably broadened his efforts in Season Three.]

• *Gunn:* Has let his hair grow out a bit, and mangles the term *feng shui* as "kung pao." Eve, on the Partners' behalf, directs Gunn to the office of Dr. Sparrow [named in the script, but not on screen until 5.21, "Power Play"], and he "upgrades" Gunn's brain via a bunch of electrodes. Gunn gains a comprehensive knowledge of the law, plus a mess-load of Gilbert and Sullivan – including the whole of *Pirates of Penzance* – as an aid to elocution. [See 5.15, "A Hole in the World" for his rendition of *The Mikado*.] He also takes to smoking cigars [or fiddling with them, at the very least].

• *Fred:* Runs the Practical Science department and – as a further office decoration – owns a rubber duck on wheels.

• *Lorne:* Scheduled to lunch with Mary-Kate [Olsen], who's promised to blab about Ashley's new piercing. He gets a little over-excited upon hearing the name of Fries' mystic: "Spanky."

• *Harmony:* [Last seen in 2.17, "Disharmony."] Recently served in the firm's steno pool, then was promoted by Wesley to serve as Angel's secretary. [5.09, "Harm's Way" claims that Harmony worked in the steno pool for "four and a half weeks." She wasn't present for the Beast-slaughter in 4.08, "Habeas Corpses," so she probably left L.A. after "Disharmony" and later returned.]

• *Eve:* Serves as the heroes' liaison to Senior Partners, but stresses that she doesn't know any confidential information about them. [There's no evidence of Eve's post existing before Season Five, so the position is presumably unique. See 5.08, "Destiny" on how Eve likely got her job.] Eve jokes about whether or not she's a "young woman" [see 5.17, "Underneath"]. Like Lilah, she knows about the memory alteration performed [last episode] to help Connor.

• *Knox:* A chemistry expert as well as a gizmo-maker.

• *Corbin Fries:* Repellent enough to plant a viral bomb inside his son, yet won't let the boy read *Punisher* comics. [That makes sense, given that Fries is precisely the sort of criminal that the Punisher, an anti-hero, routinely kills.] Fries is charged with smuggling Asian girls for labor and prostitution, plus drug-dealing and gun-running. He trafficks in illegal pesticides and rodent killers. He's part of a consortium that owns Loros, Inc., which owns stock in Oriental Bay Exports; a conviction would cause the judge in Fries' case to gain a controlling interest of Oriental Bay. Gunn uses this conflict of interest to win a mistrial. [This is awfully coincidental, however, especially as the judge's holdings are in a blind trust. Lawyer-Gunn probably arranged for the judge to own the objectionable holdings in the first place, then capitalized on it.]

• *Spanky:* Freelance mystic who resides at 840 Temple, Apt. #5, and owns an impressive assortment of spanking gear. He doesn't spank men ("It's not a judgment. Men have fine, firm asses," he says), but his website talks about the work he's lavished on his own posterior.

• *"The Conduit":* Name given to the White Room entity [seen again in 5.04, "Hell Bound"].

ORGANIZATIONS *Wolfram and Hart:* Includes a Ritual Sacrifice Department: on the company phone, press one or say "goats" for goats, or press the pound key to sacrifice a loved one or pet. [The firm outsourced goat slaying in 2.15, "Reprise," so this hotline is quite the upgrade. Technology: Your friend in goat slaughter.]

The firm is located at 1127 Spring Street, Los Angeles, CA, 90008. [The Official *Angel* Fan Club stationery repeats this address, not that we'd know anything about that, Heavens no. By the way, you get a Wolfram and Hart T-Shirt – the sort Angel wears in 5.21, "Power Play" – with your membership.] The firm holds sway over major US politicians; Jack Kennedy tried to renege on his deal with them [but lest we forget, there was only a single gunman in Dallas, 1963 (4.19, "The Magic Bullet")]. George [Bush] Sr., however, "read the fine print."

Fries implies that Holland used to run the firm [see 2.18, "Dead End" for the debate about this]. Eve claims that a lot of the firm's clients are demons, and *almost* all of them are evil. The firm's executive level comprises Angel, Wesley and Gunn's offices. [It's hard to pin down the executive level's specific floor, but it's obviously an upper one. The elevator lists 21 floors and Floor 18 is twice illuminated as Fred and Angel step out, which could denote the floor they've arrived on. As further evidence, Fred's lab is located above the executive level, and Angel falls roughly 18 stories when pitched out it in 5.16, "Shells."]

The firm's Special Ops Squad (i.e. the wetworks team) operates with a large amount of autonomy. Hauser implies that Angel can't fire the commandoes, plus Hauser's group spies on their own executives without fear of reprisal, and never considers that killing Angel might outrage the Senior Partners. The Squad alerts the firm's cleaners [3.09, "Lullaby"] to an impending slaughter. [The commandoes later appear in stories such as 5.11, "Damage," so Angel doesn't give *all* of them the pink slip.]

The jury in Fries' case is tamper-proof, purportedly because one of the D.A.'s shamans has conjured a mystical shield around them. [This begs the question of which benevolent agency has been helping to guarantee the sanctity of L.A.'s judicial system.] When Angel saves a young woman at random, officials at the firm make her sign a disclosure form, including a section regarding her immortal soul.

Lorne "reads" the employees to ferret out the genuine trouble-makers, and categorizes everyone as: "Okay/On the bubble/Evil/To be fired/Yikes!" [By the way, the names on Lorne's list are fictional, not an in-house gag as with 1.19, "Sanctuary."] There's no mention of the mind readers previously used to identify traitors [last seen in 3.08, "Quickening"].

Knox claims the firm has contained more plagues than they've ever designed. [Probably true, given the firm typically (3.17, "Forgiving" and "Shells") doesn't like chaos beyond its own timetables.] However, lab technician Lopez was linked to a cult named "the Black Tomorrow," and secretly developed a retrovirus – some derivation of the phonaya strain – for Fries. The firm discovered Lopez's moonlighting and consequently set him on fire.

DEMONOLOGY *Vampires:* Harmony laces Angel's pig's blood with otter. [Vampires appear to like this taste, as Spike implies in 5.08, "Destiny".]

MAGIC *Fries' magical container:* Built by Spanky, and can contain "anything you want in it... a bomb, a curse, a golden retriever." [If he's speaking literally, then the container must be bigger on the inside than the outside, just like the TARDIS on *Doctor Who*.] The heroes speculate that Fries is immune to the virus within, but that killing him might trigger the bomb.

BEST LINE Angel uses one of Spanky's flat-paddled "accessories" to bash the man unconscious, and famously declares: "I have no problem spanking men."

THINGS THAT DON'T MAKE SENSE In the aesthetic sense, there's the unbelievably fake CGI rendering of little Angel "leaping from rooftop to rooftop" in the teaser. Seriously, pause to look at the sucker – you'd expect to see this sort of thing on a video game, not a network drama.

5.01, Conviction

With hundreds of employees at their disposal, the person that Angel and Wesley send to observe Fries' trial is... Lorne, who doesn't look at all conspicuous in his hat, gloves, trench coat and sunglasses. While fighting Angel, the "expert" vampire-killing commandoes fail to realize they'd stand a much better chance if they'd just shoot out the classroom windows, letting more sunlight inside. Plus, a visual error: Hauser's face-mask shifts from not covering his mouth... to covering his mouth... to not covering... and so forth while he grapples with Angel by the classroom door.

We'll gloss over the complications of Angel using the firm's helicopter to reach Matthew's classroom, on the grounds that it could've landed in the athletic field and a blanket-covered Angel could've dashed inside. However, we take issue with the epilogue, in which Fred wonders if the heroes are going to spend all of their time keeping their clients in check, and asks, "Is this gonna be our lives now?" Well, yes actually, it is. What the hell did they expect?

POP CULTURE Spanky, on his name: "I'm a big *Our Gang* fan." *Our Gang* was a series of Depression Era comedy shorts about "the Little Rascals," in which the gang's de facto leader earned the nickname "Spanky" due to his mother's threats about his misbehaving. Somewhat alarmingly by today's terminology, the series even birthed a motion picture entitled *General Spanky* (1936).

• Lorne, describing a new project as "*Joanie Loves Chachi* meets *The Sorrow and the Pity*." The former is a readily maligned *Happy Days* spin-off (1982-83) that lasted a big 17 episodes; the latter is a documentary about the French collaboration with the Nazis during World War II.

• Gunn gripes the magazines in Sparrow's office are so out of date, they're reporting that "Demi [Moore] might be breaking up with Emilio [Estevez]." That occurred in 1987, after they'd been engaged for three years. (And check out **The Lore** in 5.04, "Hell Bound" for more about Moore.)

• Lorne says the jury is looking at Fries: "Like he's O.J., without the commanding performance in *Towering Inferno*." Simpson indeed appears in *The Towering Inferno* (1974), a disaster film that also features Steve McQueen, Paul Newman, Fay Dunaway, Fred Astaire, Robert Wagner and Richard Chamberlain.

• Lorne again, professionally wooing an actor with "I've got a whole freezer full of horses' heads." In *The Godfather*, a stubborn producer revisits a certain casting decision when someone deposits the head of the man's racehorse in his bed.

IN RETROSPECT Angel declares that Agent Hauser is "not part of the solution" before he kills the man; a similar sentiment gets expressed just before a prominent character gets gunned down in the series finale. Oh, and Matthew Fries wants to borrow *X-Men* comics from his classmate – it almost sounds like foreshadowing, considering Whedon's work on *Astonishing X-Men*. (Hell, Whedon's negotiations with Marvel were probably in the works already, and his first issue hit stands just a few months after *Angel* folded. We can't forget, incidentally, how much Whedon based *Buffy* on the Chris Claremont X-Men, even to the point of Buffy and Cyclops having the same last name.)

IT'S REALLY ABOUT... Subsequent to last episode, it's a further examination of the perils inherent in running a major corporation. Lilah previously told the heroes that running the firm didn't entail "a catch," but Eve tells them up-front that *of course* there's a catch, which simply put is: "In order to keep this business running... you have to keep this business running." In short, managing almost any large-scale operation invariably entails participating in some scummy behavior, or at the very least overlooking it.

It's also, if we're getting more specific, about someone selling out to Hollywood – a topic clearly near and dear to the hearts of the Mutant Enemy team. That comes across most strongly in the teaser, in which Angel can't even save a pedestrian without his corporate entourage following him around, snapping publicity pics and offering him a latte.

CRITIQUE It's undeniably the strongest *Angel* season opener and goes about its business with stunning panache, but let's look at the real-world situation for why that's the case. Simply put, whereas "Judgment" (2.01), "Heartthrob" (3.01) and "Deep Down" (4.01) had the luxury of simply warming up the bench, the *Angel* producers now realize – with the show's survival on the line, ratings-wise – that Season Five better damn well have its act together from the start. So it's incumbent on Whedon to resolutely make his best effort right here, right now... and thankfully, Joss comes through.

All of the series revamping aside, where "Conviction" really triumphs is that it channels the *Angel* (and *Buffy*, to a smaller degree) stories of old and presents an intoxicating mix of comedy and drama. Love or leave Season Four – and in the main, we loved it – it definitely needed more humor. By contrast, "Conviction" juggles such horrifying topics as a schoolroom massacre, a viral bomb and a rousing "I believe in evil" speech (just before someone gets their brains blown out, even) with some extremely punchy humor. Nearly every shot sparkles with great dialogue and Whedon's usual whimsy, and the addition of Mercedes McNab to the proceedings (shortly followed by James Marsters) makes all the difference in the world.

All told, you pretty much *know* that the heroes running Wolfram and Hart will end in tears, and your senses almost want to rebel from watching it go down. But the immediate benefit, coupled with the skilled TV-making that Whedon and his cohorts display, is that *Angel* is more intoxicating than ever.

THE LORE It appears that Whedon developed the twist that the heroes would run the firm. As a ratings boost, Marsters and McNab were brought in to soak up the *Buffy* audience, who were bereft of new episodes. The WB did some research and concluded, surprisingly, that only 25 percent of *Buffy* viewers also watched *Angel*, so it seemed a viewership worth chasing.

• Whedon and Marsters, now chums, looked forward to working with each other whenever possible. It seemed a bit odd, then, that "Conviction" only entailed Marsters showing up to scream his lungs out, whereupon Whedon – as director – thanked him and Marsters went home. (Eramo, *TV Zone*, June 2004)

• Sarah Thompson (Eve) had previously portrayed a naughty schoolgirl in *Cruel Intentions 2* (1999) – the original film starred Sarah Michelle Gellar as the lead vixen. Thompson's other prominent credit was as student Dana Poole on *Boston Public* – her character kissed and blackmailed her literature teacher, then became a stripper before leveling out a bit. Michael Shamus Wiles (Spanky) played a cop in *A.I.*, a bartender in *Fight Club*, a "Black-Haired Man" in *The X-Files* movie and the also-scandalously named "Captain Muffy" in *Magnolia*. Rodney Rowland (Corbin Fries) did a stint as Lt. Bobby "Chaser" Griffin in *Pensacola: Wings of Gold*, and later performed alongside Boreanaz in both the romantic comedy *Mr. Fix It* and an episode of *Bones* (the one entitled, errrr, "The Man With the Bone"). He was also Lt. Hawkes on the short-lived *Space: Above and Beyond* series, and keeps cropping up as the criminally unstable Liam Fitzpatrick on *Veronica Mars*.

5.02: "Just Rewards"

"Bugger."

Air Date: Oct. 8, 2003; **Writers:** David Fury, Ben Edlund; **Director:** James A. Contner

SUMMARY A bewildered Spike returns to life as a ghost, even as lawyer-Gunn overhauls the firm and shuts down its grave-robbing division. This earns the animosity of necromancer Magnus Hainsley, who purchases corpses from Wolfram and Hart; Angel in response has the firm freeze Hainsley's assets. Hainsley bargains with Spike, offering to put Spike's spook essence into Angel's body – if Spike will then impersonate Angel and restore his funds. Spike ultimately collaborates with Angel against Hainsley, leading to a scuffle in which Angel kills the necromancer. Afterward, Spike approaches Fred for help, claiming that some force is "pulling him into Hell" for brief durations.

FIRSTS AND LASTS First appearance of Angel's new lodgings, a penthouse affixed to the firm. We're finally accorded an exterior view of the new Wolfram and Hart facility, and it's a shiny-skyscraper affair in what looks like downtown L.A.

POINTS OF DISCUSSION ABOUT "Just Rewards":

1. All right, let's sort out all the business with that *deus ex machina* amulet that Spike used to save everyone's hide in the *Buffy* finale. Understanding that it's never properly explained on screen, and that it's probably just a plot device to facilitate Marsters joining the *Angel* cast...

As Angel and Wesley speculate, the Senior Partners probably wanted Angel himself, not Spike, to use the amulet against the First. Had Angel done so, he would've become the firm's property (as Spike clearly does), whereupon the Partners would've just pickled him in a jar. Once the Apocalypse rolled around, the firm's "ownership" of Angel could've posed all sorts of obligations and complications for him. And yes, this means the Partners' scheme to offer Angel the L.A. branch is actually a trap within a trap, but it fits the available evidence.

Whence did the amulet originate, though? The Partners might have designed it from scratch, but it might owe to the Powers. The amulet's intervention does, after all, save the entire Slayer line, which is more the Powers' M.O. – especially as the Slayers fulfill largely the same role as Angel when he's the Powers' champion. Besides, the amulet neuters the First Evil, which probably pleases the Powers; see **When Did the Powers Intervene?**

Whatever the amulet's pedigree, it's fairly obvious that after "Chosen," Lindsey capitalized on the situation by retrieving the amulet (either by physical or mystical means) and sent it back to the firm (and see 5.08, "Destiny" for why).

2. Sharp-eyed fans will notice that the flashback to the *Buffy* finale omits Buffy's telling Spike "I love you," and his response: "No, you don't. But thanks for saying it." It's excusable, though, given how much of this season will revolve around Angel and Spike's love for Buffy. It would somewhat tilt the balance for *Angel* viewers, you must admit, if they saw an up-front, out-of-context image of Buffy declaring her love for Spike.

3. A consequence of Spike's being "a spook" is that Marsters can't touch anything, so it's entertaining watching the degree to which he avoids brushing against anything. Notice how often he stands with his arms unnaturally crossed, as if Spike is wearing an invisible straitjacket. The chill Spike feels from the "tug of Hell" probably accounts for

this continuity-wise, but it's something of a pity that we don't see "ghostly Spike" inhabiting Angel's body and trying to imitate the man. He'd never have gotten away with it – there's the accent, just for starters – but it would've been fun to watch.

CHARACTER NOTES *Angel:* Knows that Spike went mad in the Sunnydale high school basement [*Buffy* 7.01, "Lessons" to 7.03, "Same Time, Same Place"] and the outcome of Buffy's battle against the First. [There's no evidence that Angel has spoken with Buffy since "Chosen," however... indeed, such a conversation would make 5.11, "Damage" even more of a continuity nightmare. He's probably just had someone monitoring events in Sunnydale.] Angel reluctantly reveals that Buffy is now in Europe [see 5.20, "The Girl in Question"].

Among the plethora of reasons why he finds Spike annoying, Angel seems particularly irked that Spike acclimated to being re-souled within weeks, whereas Angel spent most a century tormented by "infinite remorse" that nearly killed him. That said, Angel is slow to authorize the amulet's destruction and Spike's death.

Angel here sleeps shirtless [but not in the nude; see 2.03, "First Impressions"]. Among his company cars, Angel seems to prefer driving a Viper [reiterated in "Destiny" and 5.09, "Harm's Way"]. Angel kills Hainsley's cleaver-wielding butler by hurling a teaspoon into his noggin, and beheads Hainsley himself with a serving platter. [You'd almost suspect Angel had been watching the Food Network too much of late.]

• *Spike:* In terms of personality, he's perhaps best described – for now – as "very slightly evil and overwhelmingly taunting." Spike vamps out and charges Angel upon emerging from the amulet – only to intangibly pass through him. [It's a little unclear *why* Spike rushes Angel, unless he's simply disorientated after getting magically poured back together. Or perhaps we're meant to interpret this scene as: "Angel: The Sight of Him Enrages Me!"]

Wesley cites Spike as "the second-worst vampire ever recorded," right after Angelus. Spike [definitively] names Angel as his "grandsire." As a spook, Spike doesn't fall through the floor, and it appears as if he can "sit" on chairs and in cars. [A lot of this probably owes to Spike's status as a ghostly "avatar," meaning he *looks* as if he's "riding in a car," etc., due to sheer willpower. The alternative is to believe that he's "levitating" whenever he sits, and keeps himself perfectly balanced. No, that doesn't seem likely, does it?] Spike likes to startle people by suddenly appearing next to them [but he's probably just using his intangibility to take short-cuts, as there's no evidence that he can teleport].

Spike has previously heard of Wolfram and Hart. He keeps magically appearing back in the firm [see **Magic**] if he attempts to leave the city limits. He's more interested in eternal rest – now that he's saved the world – than atonement at present. He can sense the presence of hallowed ground. Spike's electromagnetic readings are consistent with spiritual entities, but he lacks the usual ectoplasmic matrix, and he's atypically radiating heat, putting him at just above room temperature. [See 5.04, "Hell Bound" for why Spike is being "pulled into Hell."]

• *Wesley:* Previously learned, from Angel, about Spike's alliance with Buffy, but not that Spike had gained a soul, saved the world or slept with Angel's ex-girlfriend.

• *Gunn:* Hasn't met Spike, but recognizes the name. [This probably owes to the chart on Angel and Darla's "family tree," as mentioned in "Offspring" (3.07).] Gunn's "lawyer upgrade" hasn't given him detailed knowledge of the firm's clients.

• *Lorne:* Eager to sell a movie option about "the vampire Slayer both men loved, both men lost," preferably starring Johnny Depp and Orlando Bloom – both of whom Lorne sees regularly.

• *Harmony:* Seems okay with Spike treating her like a tramp, but only if they're "going out." She utters bouts of "Ugh!" upon learning that Spike slept with Buffy. [Of course, it's amusing that a soulless vampire such as Harmony would feel morally outraged by anything.]

• *Magnus Hainsley:* One of firm's oldest clients, flush with old money and "older mojo." Hainsley owns a "respectable" number of shares in the firm.

ORGANIZATIONS *Wolfram and Hart:* Wesley calls Wolfram and Hart "a multi-billion dollar firm." Gunn has instigated internal reforms and "fired 40 employees in the past two days" [but see **Things That Don't Make Sense**]. The firm has a Voodoo Division. Hainsley has Novac, an employee of the firm with a questionable yellow tie, dismembered for delivering bad news. Angel and Gunn use the firm to freeze Hainsley's bank accounts, terminate his paper assets, turn his books over to the IRS and foreclose on his house – all within ten minutes.

• *The Senior Partners:* Hainsley fears that killing Angel would offend the Partners, as they've "got plans for him."

DEMONOLOGY *Vampires:* Harmony claims Spike "treated her like day-old rat blood." Cemeteries are evidently considered "hallowed ground" [even though vampires rise in them all the time, and they don't elicit the same dread among vamps as churches].

• *Ghosts:* Generally absorb light and heat energy, making the area around them a few degrees cooler. "Ectoplasm" makes them visible to the human eye.

MAGIC *The Amulet:* The property of Wolfram and Hart, which means they "own" Spike because he's bound to it.

Normally invulnerable, the amulet can be destroyed on "hallowed ground."

• *Necromancy:* Allows Hainsley to install demons into human cadavers. This entails Hainsley chanting over a dead body, with the prerequisite pentagram on the floor. Hainsley's client de-corporealizes and "travels" through Hainsley into the now re-animated cadaver. The average demon can't afford such services.

Hainsley's power grants him "control over the dead," so he can mentally control a vampire's every movement and summon "ghosts" (Spike included) into his presence. Hainsley could dust Angel without even needing a stake. He's never instilled someone into a conscious dead body before, but it's expected this will send Angel's soul into the ether. [A final note: We're not sure what to make of Spike's comment that Hainsley can help "get his old body back," unless the necromancer is honestly capable of reconstituting a pile of ash, or possibly knows how to implement the same dark ritual that resurrected Darla in Season One.]

BEST LINE Wesley: "Do you have any memory of a strange sensation when [the amulet] released its energy?" Spike: "What, you mean my skin and muscle burning away from the bone? Organs exploding in my chest? Eyeballs melting in their sockets? No. No memory at all. Thanks for asking."

THINGS THAT DON'T MAKE SENSE For a start, there's the remarkable coincidence that Spike's return coincides with the firm offending a necromancer, one of the few people who can actually affect Spike's condition. Gunn claims that he's fired 40 employees "in the past two days," but the timeline of "Conviction" would suggest he's been operating as "lawyer" Gunn for half a day at most when this story opens. (We tried postulating that "Conviction" takes place over several days, but that simply didn't work. The only feasible alternative – that Gunn performed much of this house-cleaning while simultaneously researching the über-important Fries case – seems downright silly.)

And what about the grave-robbing division's shutdown? With all due respect to the dead, are we seriously meant to believe that out of all the murder, atrocities and ruination the firm has been causing, that ending the practice of stealing corpses is really an A-level priority for the heroes? Surely, it makes more sense to first stop the firm from ***killing*** more people, then halt the nabbing of corpses down the road?

And finally, Angel and Spike seem remarkably confident that "ghostly" Spike can thwart Hainsley's necromancy magic, as they don't consult Wesley about it. They'd have felt damned embarrassed, one presumes, if Spike had gotten stuck in Angel's body while Angel's soul went into the ether – requiring them to yet again call Willow, and tell her to warm up the Orb of Thesulah.

CRITIQUE The primary question we're apparently meant to ask – "Will Spike side with good or evil?" – seems hopelessly loopy after we've witnessed Spike resolutely playing the hero in *Buffy* Season Seven. For pity's sake, of course Spike won't sanction Angel's death – did the producers seriously believe the viewers would think otherwise?

But here's the thing: The plot of "Just Rewards" is secondary – and justifiably so – to the concern of weaving Spike into the show as seamlessly as possible. That's more difficult than you might think, given how strongly *Angel* was rolling along without him. At the end of *Angel* Season Four, it honestly was hard to see how *Buffy* characters of any sort could transfer over without upsetting the show's equilibrium, and thereby short-changing the established cast (even if Carpenter's departure admittedly freed up some screen time). Yet credit where credit is due: Mutant Enemy masterfully accomplishes the transition, giving Marsters a loving amount of attention, but not going so far as to (in spirit, if nothing else) rename the show *Spike*.

Taking all of that into account, "Just Rewards" expertly seeds Spike into the mix, but otherwise never gets beyond "average." We certainly couldn't label it as bad, but it really doesn't deserve the ratings bonanza it experienced either (see **The Lore** under 5.13, "Why We Fight").

THE LORE Marsters spent time in the theatre before joining *Buffy*, and freely admits that he first came to L.A. with one goal in mind: money. He'd done his fair share of "artistic" work in the theatre, but had reached the point that he no longer wanted to be poor, and hoped to make "a quarter million" or so before getting out of TV. Whedon had told Marsters up front that there was no tangible guarantee of Spike going long-term, as Whedon preferred to give his villains a certain complexity and ***then*** kill them off, but it didn't happen in Spike's case.

• Marsters has expressed his utter love and delight for *Buffy* in numerous interviews, and says the experience was soured only by the steamy sex scenes in Season Six. He said, "That part I did not enjoy at all. I was the only one naked. Sarah's over there, fully clothed, she's even got mittens on, it's 40 degrees on the set, I'm naked and she's making fun of me." (*TNT Drama Lounge*, April 23, 2004) Nonetheless, he claimed that joining *Angel* was fortunate because "I don't know when I will be able to do something this delightful again, so why bid it goodbye before you have to?" (Malcolm, *TV Guide*, Sept. 6, 2003)

• Victor Raider Wexler (Magnus Hainsley) played Attorney General Nash in *Minority Report*, and he had recurring roles on *Everybody Loves Raymond* and *Two Guys, a Girl and a Pizza Place* (Nathan Fillion's most notable pre-*Firefly* credit). Joshua Hutchinson (Novac, the butchered lawyer) was a computer and video effects assistant on *Lost in Space* (1998).

5.03: "Unleashed"

"Moonrise is in 15 minutes. Shortly thereafter... dinner will be served."

Air Date: Oct. 15, 2003; **Writers:** Sarah Fain, Elizabeth Craft; **Director:** Marita Grabiak

SUMMARY Angel randomly kills a werewolf, but not before it bites and infects a young woman named Nina. With some persuading, Nina agrees to stay in a cell at the firm during nights of the full moon. Unfortunately, a treacherous member of Wesley's staff, Dr. Royce, arranges Nina's abduction on behalf of Jacob Crane – a crooked businessman who hosts dinner parties featuring the flesh of super-natural creatures. Nina finds herself bound and on the menu, with the diners intending to eat her alive once she transforms.

Angel and company uncover the affair and haul Royce to the dinner party, where Nina shifts to werewolf mode and happens to bite him. Wesley tranquilizes Nina, and Angel – clearly outgunned – suggests that Crane release Nina in exchange for dining on Royce one month hence. Crane agrees, giving Angel time to take Nina home and properly shut down Crane's operation.

FIRSTS AND LASTS Last story in which Angel sketches someone/something, and last instance of Wesley riding a motorcycle. It's the first appearance of Nina, who – setting aside 5.20, "The Girl in Question" – will serve as Angel's last romantic interest in the series. No surprises, then, that she's blonde.

POINTS OF DISCUSSION ABOUT "Unleashed":

1. By now, you're entitled to question the WB's method of making Season Five "more accessible." After the highly serialized Season Four, it's understandable that the network told the production team to make *Angel* more comprehensible to newcomers. However, while the concept of Angel being "a heroic vampire with a soul" is simple enough to pick-up, nothing in the credits suggests why the hell the goodies are running a multi-dimensional, demonic law firm. If you recall *Farscape*'s opening narration ("My name is John Crichton, I'm an astronaut blah blah blah") and realize that *Angel* doesn't have any such device, you start to see the problem.

Second, the more one ponders the lack of "Previously On *Angel*..." installments this year, the more bewildering it becomes. Only "Just Rewards" (5.02), "Shells" (5.16) and "Not Fade Away" (5.22) have them, and it's almost as if the WB now fears that such segments will give the impression that pre-knowledge is required. The immediate consequence of this, however, is that the episodes themselves contain a frightful amount of info-dumps. *Angel* isn't a stranger to this strategy, but Season Four – frankly – found more elegant ways of recapping information despite the burgeoning "Previously Ons...", and it's creating a drag as characters reiterate their status for no good reason.

2. An interesting point about Fred in Season Five: The more time passes, the more she'll seem like Reed Richards of the Fantastic Four – meaning she's considered an expert on *everything* related to science, as if every scientific discipline naturally feeds into every other. Her normal specialty is physics, yet she here studies Nina's tire tracks as if she's a forensics expert. By "Lineage" (5.07) and "Harm's Way" (5.09), she'll be performing autopsies as if she's Dana Scully. For better or worse, if it's even vaguely scientific, Fred's your girl.

3. Angel's communication skills haven't improved with age. When Nina accuses him of being a psycho rapist, he responds: "I just want you to see something." This actually entails her watching a video of her reverting from werewolf form, but you get the idea.

4. The episode ends with everyone making small talk around Angel's penthouse while Fred orders take-out, even as a sappy soundtrack drones on. In terms of style, it's as close as *Angel* ever comes to other WB shows in tying off an episode. For example, take *Birds of Prey*, a series that always seemed to end with the leads looking wistfully off a clock-tower balcony.

5. Meanwhile, a jealous Wesley has become exceptionally adept at making Fred feel awkward while he clumsily airs concerns about Knox. Indeed, for a moment there, it looks as if Wes is going to rip open his shirt and reveal a giant heart that he's carved onto his chest around the word "Fred," blood pouring from the wound. It's amazing that she ever falls for him.

CHARACTER NOTES *Angel:* Invites the crew to hang at his penthouse for the first time, and buys Chinese take-out for everyone. He's now driving a gray company car, and appears to sign documents as "Angel" [or perhaps just "Ang"]. Fred says that Angel saves "girls, guys, puppies." [She's probably generalizing, unaware of Angel's puppy-love in 4.15, "Orpheus," and is hopefully also oblivious to what Angelus did to a puppy on Valentine's Day; see *Buffy* 2.16, "Bewitched, Bothered and Bewildered."]

• *Spike:* Already hooked into the Wolfram and Hart grapevine. He regards werewolf Nina as an innate killer who'll become consumed by guilt, and he frequently turns transparent while ghostily wandering about the firm.

• *Wesley:* It's implied that he likes plum sauce.

• *Gunn:* Seems to accept that his "lawyer upgrade" deal wasn't entirely benevolent [and see 5.16, "Shells"], but gets irritated by the implication that he's now a spy for the Senior

Partners. Gunn remains something of a fighter, storming into the exotic meat dinner with a shotgun.

• *Fred:* Tries to console Nina when her sister gets angry with her. [Ironically, Fred is probably the least equipped of the heroes to offer advice on family trauma, simply because her family is so nice.] She's outfitted with a gizmo that detects surveillance devices. Her aim with a tranquilizer gun has much improved since Season Four.

• *Lorne:* The herb calendula can fool Lorne's ability to "read" people. [Proceed directly to **Things That Don't Make Sense**.] He makes Cosmos for his colleagues, and owns a collection of Nancy Sinatra music on the original 45s. It's implied that Lorne likes mu shu chicken.

• *McManus:* Nina's werewolf attacker. He left his wife and kids a couple of years back and fought his werewolf instincts, but apparently yielded to his baser urges in the last year. The firm returns McManus' body to his family.

• *Nina Ash:* Lives at 2315 Harvard [not a real location, but supposedly near East Hollywood] with her sister Jill and nine-year-old niece Amanda. She's taking ceramics class – they're learning raku – and Life Drawing. She drives a 1992 Honda Civic, license number 2ABM543. She learns that Angel is a vampire [and next appears in 5.14, "Smile Time"].

• *Dr. Evan Royce:* Described as a "cryptozoologist." [Angel's group appear to shut down Crane's operation long before – as discussed – Royce becomes someone's dinner.]

ORGANIZATIONS *Wolfram and Hart:* It's implied that the heroes used to order Chinese take-out and dine together a lot. [This doesn't occur much on screen, although Wes, Gunn and Fred enjoy take-out in 3.02, "That Vision Thing."] The building's werewolf-proof holding cell requires Level A-3 clearance. The Center for Scientology is visible from Angel's penthouse.

• *Crane's Dining Society:* [The group's menu looks fuzzy on screen, but the script mentions Chilled Muclak Soup, Hearts of Goblin Salad and Werewolf Tartar.] Angel enters the event without an invite [so it's not held at a private dwelling].

DEMONOLOGY *Werewolves:* McManus (and therefore Nina, his victim) hails from *Lycantrhopus exterus*, a rare werewolf breed that's undocumented in North America. This bipedal species sports longer-than-average canines, proves vulnerable to silver and reverts to human form upon death. [The fact that we're dealing with a new werewolf species could explain all manner of contradictions with the *Buffy* werewolf episodes, starting with 2.15, "Phases." In particular, it would reconcile Wesley's over-simplified statement that "Once a werewolf dies, it reverts to its human state" against the fact that Veruca remained a werewolf upon death in *Buffy* 4.06, "Wild at Heart," and that the bounty hunter Cain collected werewolf pelts and teeth after their owners' demise in "Phases."]

Angel remarks that no cure exists for lycanthropy. [Oz blocked his change with a meditation technique in *Buffy* 4.19, "New Moon Rising," but that hardly seems like a widespread "cure," and didn't even work entirely.] Crane has eaten werewolf in Seville, where the chef used an understated mole sauce to bring out the meat's tanginess. Crane's chef hopes to serve Nina *anaise* with a light drizzle of white truffle oil. Groups that Royce cites as wanting to kidnap werewolves: sacrificers wanting to rid the world of abominations, werewolf packs looking for new recruits and paranormal sporting groups – the sort that indulge in vampire hunting in Eastern Europe.

The day after being bitten, human-Nina develops enhanced senses and a lust for meat. She disturbingly daydreams about her niece's throat getting ripped out. Royce says that the first few transformations a werewolf experiences are the worst, and that repeatedly tranquilizing the creature isn't recommended.

• *Leprechauns:* Crane says they don't exist [as with 3.18, "Double or Nothing"].

BEST LINE An oldie but a goodie. Fred, concerning Knox: "We're friendly, but he's under me. Or I'm on top of him... professionally."

THINGS THAT DON'T MAKE SENSE As with "Hero" (1.09), the villains' alleged "master plan" seems completely bonkers. To review, Dr. Royce arranges for commandoes to abduct Nina from the firm's security forces. Does he seriously believe that he'll remain anonymous once the firm's full resources come to bear on the problem? But then, the entire kidnapping business seems hopelessly risky once you realize the villains need only capture *one* werewolf, then lock it up, feed it and have it bite hapless people once a month. Result: A continual supply of werewolf flesh. It's not like Crane's people would object on moral grounds.

Also, Royce is also stupid enough to A) dispose of the telltale Calendula in his own trash can, and B) keep a pile of incriminating evidence hidden in his office, including a carving knife, a copy of Crane's menu and Polaroids – *Polaroids*! – for absolutely no good reason. Why didn't he just send Angel a memo entitled "RE: My Complicity in the Kidnapping of Werewolf Girl" while he was at it? Then there's the appalling notion that calendula can thwart Lorne's reading. It's a real-life herb with soporific and healing effects, and the comparison that it's like someone taking Valium to thwart a lie-detector test seems downright ludicrous once you remember that Lorne directly reads peoples' auras; taking a calming herb shouldn't make the slightest difference. And if calendula *does* block Lorne's reading, that would suggest that his employee-screening (5.01, "Conviction") isn't worth spittle. All manner of evildoers could pass the test simply by (say) having a calming chamomile tea beforehand, or faithfully doing yoga.

The heroes meet outside the firm to discuss the Senior Partners' intentions, because they're worried about being spied upon. Fair enough, but there's numerous instances that will occur throughout Season Five where they air extremely sensitive information at the firm – in Angel's office especially – without fear of eavesdropping. And it's awfully convenient that Wesley feels moved to show off his shiny new pen moments before Angel desperately needs something silver to skewer a werewolf with.

Finally, behold the economics of "Friends" at work as Nina (an art student) and her sister (a nurse, but also a single mother) somehow afford a luxurious amount of living space in L.A.'s killer housing market.

IN RETROSPECT Spike had a "wee spat" with a werewolf once and "almost" lost his hand as a result; a Slayer will one-up this in 5.11, "Damage." Oh, and Fred says about Knox: "All I'm saying is, he's not evil." Whoops.

IT'S REALLY ABOUT... It's hard to find much subtext here, partly because *Buffy* already dealt with the topic of werewolves in such a nuanced fashion. In Oz, lycanthropy served as a metaphor for puberty, meaning that we watched as an adolescent male descended into a hormonal hell and lost control of his biology. Nina's situation, however, feels like someone who's learned about a disease such a diabetes, hence Fred's consoling that: "Your life doesn't have to change... much."

Meanwhile, the second half – with the elite wanting to consume werewolf flesh – is just weirdness with no real underlying tone. Although seeing Nina lying amid all the lettuce and bell peppers, you can perhaps find a small parallel in the Japanese tradition of eating sushi off a nude geisha.

CRITIQUE Ultimately, it's an outing that just doesn't work, and it's regrettable that a weak stand-alone story seems more damning now than it might've done earlier in the show. Whatever their flaws, the previous two episodes capitalized upon the new set-up as established for Season Five, so it's both troubling and disappointing when we're given a limp tale that could – with a bit of tweaking – occur in almost any season. If you're handed a dazzling new premise for the show, you're within your rights to expect it that isn't ignored so quickly.

To some degree, "Unleashed" fizzles because it focuses so much energy on Nina and – although she'll work much better in future – it's hard to invest much emotionally in her right now. Oz was a neat and fleshed-out character when he became furry, but Nina is too much of a blank slate. If she'd died in this episode, she'd have ranked only slightly higher than the demise of a cardboard client from Season One. But what really makes "Unleashed" belly-flop, to be honest, is its sloppy storytelling. Too many of the scenes feel awkward, there's some painfully obvious padding (see **The Lore**) and the villains, frankly, just seem limp. Fair enough that some snobs want to dine on werewolf flesh, but does anyone honestly believe they ever stood a prayer against Angel and the firm? And that's before factoring in the sheer number of contrivances. Wesley's silver pen seems bad enough, but honestly... the fact that Fred exposes Dr. Royce by *accidentally knocking over a trash can* only serves to make him one of the most stupid *Angel* antagonists ever created. Simply put, the show should be more refined than that right now.

THE LORE The script fails to mention two exposition scenes – Fred chatting with Nina in the van, and Angel blowing off Gunn and Lorne's advice – which suggests the episode under-ran. Neither of these segments are important to the plot, so they were likely written as filler. You can tell, really.

• Fury popped up on the discussion boards to smooth over any inconsistencies about werewolf traits: "Werewolf scratches will not turn the scratchee into a werewolf. Bites, folks. Bites do it. You need a little wolf saliva mixing in with the blood, you see." (Fury, *The Bronze*, Oct. 26, 1999)

• The lingering memory of Oz's less-than-convincing werewolf suit in *Buffy* 2.15, "Phases" – the one that Whedon and others famously said wound up looking like "a gay possum" – prompted Bell to confer with costume designer Rob Hall and make sure it didn't happen again. The scene where Angel and the werewolf crash out of Nina's house and fall two stories caused the stuntman, Steve Upton, to smack his head and fall unconscious for a bit. Upon coming to, he apparently couldn't even remember where he parked his car, so the set crew yanked out his werewolf teeth and gave him some water. (O'Hare, *Zap2It,* Oct. 12, 2003)

• John Billingsley (Dr. Royce) played Doctor Phlox on *Star Trek: Enterprise*, but you needn't look hard to realize this. He'd appeared as "Timmy the Geek" in an *X-Files* episode, and he's also a regular as Egan Foote on ABC's *The Nine*.

5.04: "Hell Bound"

"The things we did. The lives we destroyed. That's all that's ever gonna count. So, yeah, surprise: You're going to Hell. We both are."

Air Date: Oct. 22, 2003;
Writer/Director: Steven S. DeKnight

SUMMARY The force tugging Spike into a hellish realm intensifies, and he witnesses the maimed souls of employees who died at the firm. Angel and his allies identify Spike's tormentor as Matthias Pavayne, a murderous eighteenth century surgeon who was sacrificed to "de-consecrate" the ground on which the firm's L.A. branch now stands. Unfortunately, Pavayne's knowledge of sorcery enabled him to live on as a ghost, adeptly sending the spirits of anyone who died inside the firm to Hell in his place.

Pavayne tries to send Spike to Hell, but Fred and Wesley cobble together a magical circle capable of making Spike corporeal again. The ghostly Spike gains enough willpower to grapple with Pavayne's spirit, but the infernal doctor threatens to kill Fred. With little option, Spike pushes Pavayne into the mystic circle – making him corporeal but irrevocably shorting out the device. Afterward, Angel and Eve lock up Pavayne in one of the firm's vaults.

FIRSTS AND LASTS Final appearance of Spike's magic amulet, but it'll get referenced from time to time. Last outing for the panther in the White Room, although Gunn will meet another aspect of the Conduit in 5.15, "A Hole in the World."

POINTS OF DISCUSSION ABOUT "Hell Bound":

1. Notoriously, "Hell Bound" was broadcast with a Parental Discretion Advisory. The marketing repeatedly cited this, meaning it was probably a stunt to boost ratings, but some might say that any endeavor to have Marsters or Acker shed their clothes is a worthy one. For those who don't recall, Acker showers off after Fred gets splattered with blood – the shower steam leaves a lot to the imagination, although her bare-naked ass is clearly visible. Additionally, Pavayne's ghostly torment results in Marsters cowering on the floor without a stitch on him, strategically covering his privates. And there's the odd assortment of brutalized dead employees – the most notable being the woman with a shard of glass in her eye – who present themselves to Spike.

All of this probably sounded like a sensible means of galvanizing *Buffy* fans to watch *Angel* – especially with Spike being front-and-center in the marketing – but it didn't pan out much; the ratings were roughly equal to those for "Unleashed." It's curious, however, to pause and consider how much the censors prioritize quantity of sex/violence, not quality. After all, the previous episode wasn't exactly what you'd call wholesome, featuring A) the camera lingering up Nina's obviously naked body as she awakens, B) Nina getting strung up, stripped topless, hosed down and given a scrub-bath in preparation for the diners enjoying her werewolf flesh, and C) the CGI-rendered delusion of her young niece's throat getting ripped out.

2. Time has made fandom forget how unusually this story starts out, with Spike being sucked into the basement and witnessing a figure who's slicing his own fingers off. Given that the story takes place at Wolfram and Hart, you honestly have to wonder if the firm has a Finger-Slicing Department ("Our clients like lady-fingers... no, they *really* like lady-fingers."), meaning this sort of thing isn't all that unusual. Still, the dead-employee ghosts that Spike encounters provide an entertaining list of credits, with guest-actors cited as playing the likes of Glass Woman, Bloody Lawyer, Hanging Man and Armless Woman.

3. Meanwhile, Spike's line, "Too much talk of fire and brimstone" almost comes out sounding like "*fiber* and brimstone"... which makes you think he's talking about the constipation of the damned.

CHARACTER NOTES *Angel:* Presently in something of a funk, feeling [without much justification, really] as though the Powers have abandoned him. He's also despondent about the odds of obtaining redemption, thinking that he's going to Hell one day and that the Shanshu Prophecy is a bunch of bull [and see **It's Really About...**]. He says he's more of a dog person than a cat person [and see 4.15, "Orpheus"].

Angel allows Fred to proceed with her plan to re-corporealize Spike, but thinks Spike is innately selfish and can't be saved. Angel claims that as Angelus, he liked Spike's poems. [This is profoundly hard to work into the timeline, as it's hard to imagine Angelus tolerating a performance of Spike's poetry for long. Perhaps he heard Spike on a couple occasions and took the opportunity to mock him, or maybe – at a stretch – he read the written poems that Spike left lying around the place.]

• *Spike:* Seems very affectionate toward Fred, and acts the gentleman by not gawking when she's in the shower. Spike knows [presumably from the office gossip] that Angel likes Barry Manilow. He learns, from Fred, about the Shanshu Prophecy [see 5.08, "Destiny"].

Spike wonders if he's intangible because it's taking all his willpower to keep from slipping into Hell. [Untrue, as he's still intangible once Pavayne is defeated.] He's been "ghosting" into the men's bathroom and making wisecracks to Gunn. He musters enough willpower to "write" on steamy glass, and to lift a cup. Spike claims he has been "knocking around the land of the lost for months now." [He's probably being figurative, with regards to events in *Buffy* Season Seven, his undergoing a potentially lethal trial the year before, etc.] Fred says Spike is "more than a common spectral disturbance," but that his radiant heat signature has dropped another .02 degrees.

• *Wesley:* Officially named as the head of Research and Intelligence. He procures a laundry list of rare magical items for Fred [see **Magic**] in the space of 20 minutes.

• *Gunn:* Has seen a decent amount of horror flicks. He knows details about the Lanterman-Petris-Short Act, with regards to involuntary committal.

• *Fred:* Acting very cordial to the evil employees and sweetly "screams" when ghost-Spike tries, and fails, to scare her. She views Spike as being a champion like Angel. Fred has become something of an expert on the interplay between hardcore physics and magic [probably aided along by the research she did on supernatural texts throughout Season Four]. However, one method that she devises for bringing Spike back would cause a feedback wave and liquefy half of Los Angeles.

• *Matthias Pavayne:* Former European aristocrat, listed in the firm's files as Dark Soul No. 182. He was nicknamed "the Reaper" for performing unnecessary surgery on his patients. Word spread of his unorthodox practices and he fled to a California under Spanish rule. Pavayne apparently engaged in ritualistic murders for the better part of 20 years, gaining knowledge of the dark arts, until the firm had him killed [see **Organizations**].

Afterward, Pavayne's spirit forestalled his journey to Hell by dispatching the souls of anyone who died within the firm in his place. [This almost makes sense in *Angel*-verse terms, given that souls are sometimes traded as currency; see 3.18, "Double or Nothing." However, it's a bothersome detail that the dispatched employees should *already* be on the fast track to Hell, so Pavayne probably isn't giving Hell something it wasn't going to get in the first place. Nonetheless, it appears that Pavayne earns a "credit" every time he sends a soul to Hell, and we might imagine that he hit the jackpot once the Beast got done in 4.08, "Habeas Corpses." ("Thank you, Mr. Pavayne, that's 377 souls in your account..." or whatever.) At the very least, the sheer number of people killed in that episode – and whose spooks aren't present – could account for why Pavayne's power levels are comparatively high right now.] Pavanye's comment that "I've cheated Hell for hundreds of years, fed it other dirty little souls" might suggest that he ritualistically extended his life even while he was alive [hence his murderous acts].

Pavayne's spirit has gone undetected, including by the firm's hourly sweeps to guard against spectral intrusion. He's become adept at warping reality within his ghostly plane of existence. [There's no evidence of his inter-acting with the physical world, save for his killing the psychic Claire via her holding a séance.]

• *Claire:* [Named in the script, which called for her to wear a low-cut dress and a velvet cloak. They gave her the low-cut dress, at least.] Blonde spiritual consultant for the firm. She's into Pilates, and dies at Pavayne's hands.

• *The Conduit:* According to Angel, it connects Wolfram and Hart to "the other dimensions" [presumably meaning all the firm's extra-dimensional branches, or even the Senior Partners' home territory]. The Conduit again manifests as the panther [from 4.22, "Home"] and somehow converses with Gunn but not Angel. Gunn "snips off" a piece of the Conduit, netting a jar of black liquid that serves as the power-source for Fred's spook-corporealizing device, but the Conduit tells Gunn he isn't getting any more power.

THE LIBRARY The firm's archives contain more than 3,200 different references to "the dark soul" [evidently an advanced level of wrongdoer]. Four of these refer to Angelus. [Angel looks at one of the citations and says, "I didn't even have a soul when I did that!", which makes you wonder if he *did* have a soul for one or two of the others.]

ORGANIZATIONS *Wolfram and Hart:* Back in the eighteenth century, the firm's representatives decided to build a new branch in the area that would become Los Angeles. Unfortunately, a Spanish mission stood on what the firm's seers cited as the ideal location. Pavayne was accordingly sacrificed to de-consecrate the grounds. [Although given what the missions did to the American Indians in the area, Wolfram and Hart might've actually been an improvement.]

Employees who've died at the firm include a self-mutilating man in a suit, who's given to chopping off his own fingers with a knife; a woman [circa 1890s, according to the script] with her arms cut off; another woman [dressed as a 1940s Girl Friday] with a large shard of glass in her eye; another suited man with half of his face bloodied; and a final suited man swinging from a noose. [Images of these people haunt Spike, but it's unclear if they're the employees' genuine spirits – pocketed by Pavayne to forestall his going to Hell in future – or are merely illusions.]

At story's end, Pavayne gets secured, totally immobile, in the firm's Permanent Storage facility. [It's unclear if this exists within the L.A. branch itself, so write your own explanation of what happens to Pavayne after the series finale.]

Fred's department has exceeded its quarterly budget by $800,000, and the quarter ain't over yet; most of this overrun owes to her trying to recorporealize Spike. Her lab comes equipped with a shower [the script suggests that it's for treating chemical burns and such].

MAGIC Fred's contraption to recorporealize Spike requires, among other things, *The Magdalene Grimoire*, *Necronomicon des Mortes* [a rather redundant and silly name, as "Necronomicon" already means "names of the dead"], and Hochstadter's treatise on Fractal Geometry in Twelve-Dimensional Space. Half the parts she needs are antiquities of the rarest order. The device supports its imbalance "with Lumirea's fourth constant." A massive surge of dark energy – "the equivalent of nuclear evil" – is needed to catalyze the process, and acquired from the Conduit 'by Gunn.

• *Spike's amulet:* Fred wonders if it's "a trans-reality amplifier capable of focusing massive quantities of mystical energy."

BEST LINE Fred, hastily scribbling inter-dimensional equations on her office window, as her colleagues enter the room: "I just ran out of white board. I'm not crazy."

THINGS THAT DON'T MAKE SENSE This isn't the last time we'll encounter this problem (see especially 5.13, "Why We Fight"), but... the firm's staff must number in the hundreds if not thousands, and all of these people work for a company with a track record for brutally killing its underperforming employees. Yet when events in "Hell Bound" go down, only five people – our principal characters – are burning the midnight oil. Perhaps the employees are more fearful of the evening dangers than of Angel's new and improved regime, but at the very least, aren't a *few* brownnosers logging extra hours?

There's a carafe of blood just sitting out in Angel's penthouse, and you'd think it would go stale that way. (All right... maybe the carafe glass is enchanted to keep it fresh. Maybe.) The "what's going on?" conversation between the heroes in the executive lobby is a bit confusing, as Wesley mentions how Spike has been unintentionally disappearing more and more, but the heroes then start rambling on about how he's intentionally doing it.

Ah, yes, and... given ample proof that there's a murderous spirit loose in the firm, it's rather astonishing that everyone feels comfortable letting Fred wander off to shower. It's a classic "Psycho" set-up, yet nobody stands guard. At the very least, don't they want to watch?

IN RETROSPECT As Claire dies, she spits blood on Fred's face. Hauntingly, it almost foreshadows what Fred will do to Wesley in "A Hole in the World" (5.15).

IT'S REALLY ABOUT... Setting aside all the gore, it's surprisingly more about Angel than Spike. Both of them feel they deserve Hell for their abhorrent crimes, but the difference is that Spike spends most of the story doing everything in his power to keep fighting. Yet Angel has almost become sullen to think about the lives he destroyed as Angelus, and can't see why he should bother trying to attain redemption. We'll revisit this notion in "The Cautionary Tale of Numero Cinco" (5.06), but suffice to say, the firm is succeeding in its goal to cut Angel off from contact with normal people. An apathetic champion: Almost as good as a villainous one.

CRITIQUE All things being equal, this story should've seemed like a con job. Whenever a series sensationalizes its "Parental Advisory" warning as this one did, you're in your rights to expect a slash and sex-fest, with only a thin strip of story to go with it. Yet to its credit, "Hell Bound" provides an atmosphere that's intense and scary (well, scary for network television) and Pavayne makes a good adversary for Spike. None of this tallies up to "Hell Bound" being a masterpiece, but it's sweetly enjoyable as a piece of horror-flavored drama – particularly due to Marsters' performance. It's always hard to talk about this sort of thing without gushing, but...

We touched on this in "Just Rewards" (5.02), yet it remains the case: Marsters is one of the few actors who never gets bored with his character. It's now the sixth season that he's portrayed Spike – and the fourth year in a row, for that matter – yet he's just as invested in the part as he was back in 1998. Even amazingly talented actors will burn out if they stay in a dramatic role too long; you can sense fatigue setting in with Duchovny and Anderson on *The X-Files*, and (God bless) with Sarah Michelle Gellar on *Buffy*. Boreanaz valiantly carried on as Angel to the end, but even he expressed (justifiable, given the work involved) a sigh of relief when the series was cancelled. Marsters, however, continues to physically endow Spike with so much energy. He also stays in shape, continues to bleach his hair – even though he's said in interviews that it hurts like hell – and keeps himself pale all for the sake of his art. He's far, far from being the only worthy character on *Angel*... but in the case of something like "Hell Bound," he's a crucial asset in lifting an episode's final tally.

THE LORE The script called for Lorne to chat on his cell phone with Demi Moore, during what sounds like a sexcapade crisis. Lorne's dialogue read: "Demi, have I ever not been there for you? Just calm down and don't move Ashton till I get there. No, he's young! I'm sure he'll bounce right back!" The finished version, however, watered this potentially litigious scene down to Lorne talking with an unnamed celebrity who's depressed because they're getting second-billing to "Gwyneth" (presumably Gwyneth Paltrow).

Two other deletions of note... the script called for Fred to drape a sheet over Claire's body (which seems un-chivalrous on the men's part, as Fred got face-splattered with Claire's blood as she kicked the bucket). Also, the scene where

Angel, Fred and Eve chat about money was trimmed a bit – Fred sarcastically described a "de-spook-o-tron" that would zap Spike into nothing, and Eve inquired, "What would something like that run us?"

• In Sept. 2003, Acker – who apparently didn't learn about her character's fate until the following month – said that if the firm could corrupt any of the heroes, her money was on Fred. "She has all this power and all of this knowledge. I know having all the stuff at the team's fingertips... is going to change a lot of people, so I'm curious to see how they decide it will change Fred." (Bernstein, *Dreamwatch* #110, Sept. 2003)

• Simon Templeman (Matthias Pavayne) appeared in ten episodes of *Just Shoot Me!* as Simon Leeds, a British rocker who dates Nina, one of the main characters. Rather appropriately, he also played the Angel of Death in two episodes of *Charmed*. Meanwhile, Dorie Barton (Claire the medium) played a young Martha Stewart in the TV movie *Martha Inc.* (And as hardcore fans will recall, Martha was variously cited as a demon and/or a witch on *Buffy*.)

5.05: "Life of the Party"

"Spike's thinking positive. Gunn is peeing all over the office. And we're a little bit drunk... because Lorne told *us to be drunk."*

Air Date: Oct. 29, 2003; **Writer:** Ben Edlund; **Director:** Bill Norton

SUMMARY Entirely over-worked, Lorne takes the radical step of having the firm remove his need for sleep. Unfortunately, this causes Lorne's empathic abilities to go haywire, compelling people to obey his every word, no matter how casually spoken. At the firm's famed Halloween Party, Lorne's off-handed remarks make Wesley and Fred feel intoxicated without their actually getting drunk, Gunn to "stake his territory" by pissing on furniture, Spike to adopt a happy-go-lucky attitude and Angel and Eve to screw like weasels. Eventually, Lorne's condition worsens to the point that his subconscious manifests as a raging, giant Hulk-Lorne demon.

A "drunken" Wesley and Fred find Lorne's bottled sleep in the firm's psyche department, then re-endow Lorne with it. Hulk-Lorne disintegrates, everyone returns to normal, Eve covers-up her inner embarrassment/anger for copulating with Angel, and Lorne finally gets some well-needed sleep.

FIRSTS AND LASTS Final time Angel saunters out of the shower (the first was 1.05, "Rm w/a Vu"). As opposed to donning a towel to answer Cordelia's knock, he's buck-naked on this occasion. Tragically – for some – it's also what's probably constitutes the final instance of "naked Angel" when he later gets steamy with Eve behind his office couch. (He's admittedly seen in bed with Nina in 5.21, "Power Play," but that occasion is far less revealing.)

It's the debut of Archduke Sebassis, and therefore the first appearance of a member of the Circle of the Black Thorn (even if the group isn't named until "Power Play.") The Elder of the Fell Brotherhood, also a member, is mentioned but not seen (he'll turn up in 5.19, "Time Bomb").

POINTS OF DISCUSSION ABOUT "Life of the Party":

1. To review... through mystical means, a character's randomly spoken words makes people act completely out-of-character. Yup, there's a definite parallel to *Buffy* 4.09, "Something Blue," in which Willow's loose-lips magically make her associates act goofy (if you'll recall, Buffy and Spike on that occassion decide to get married). Lest you think that "Life of the Party" is a mere copycat, however, the implementation is very different, and the similarities pretty much end there.

2. Grasping at straws, some commentators have claimed that Lorne's phone conversation about a new property "perfectly" describes Whedon's *Firefly* series. ("It's *Grapes of Wrath* in outer space. Oh, it's got heart. Yes, it's got laser battles. It's got a timely message of interstellar poverty.") However, while *Firefly* certainly had heart, it contained few "laser battles" and it really didn't dwell on the topic of "interstellar poverty." Moreover, as a series about a group of smugglers who misbehave against a dominating government, it didn't overly resemble *The Grapes of Wrath* – Steinbeck's Great Depression novel about a family of sharecroppers who struggle against being destitute. Indeed, when Lorne says, "*The Grapes of Wrath* in space," he apparently means just that, as he wonders if the firm can get the late Henry Fonda to play Tom Joad – a lead character in Steinbeck's book.

3. A note about Sebassis' attendant slave. He's here credited as "Demon Slave," but – in something of a misnomer – gets renamed as "Pee-Pee Demon" for 5.22, "Not Fade Away." (Regrettably, this means that *Angel*'s series finale – one of the most stunning and dramatic endings in TV history – is quickly followed by credits that amusingly speak of a "Pee-Pee Demon.") Because of this, you'd almost think that the blue fluid which the Demon Slave pours out of his wrist – and which Sebassis drinks – *is* pee-pee, owing to some weird bit of demon physiology. But no... it happens that at the party, the Demon Slave sniffs out one of Gunn's puddles and excitedly declares "pee-pee!" Evidently, the line struck such a chord as to warrant the name swap, even though his two later appearances have nothing to do with pee-pee whatsoever.

4. The corruption update: As expected, the heroes' rela-

tionships are becoming more corporate. Previously, Angel almost needed Lorne more than Lorne needed him – but now the tables have turned. Lorne must now compete for Angel's attention, and it's almost implicit that if push came to shove – in this corporate structure – Lorne is replaceable. Mind, the other heroes aren't especially chummy either, spending much of the party in their own orbits. It's becoming apparent that much of their cohesion was lost when they (say) stopped hanging around the Hyperion lobby and eating Chinese together.

5. A consequence of Angel and Eve's going at it: They not only have sex, they have sex while Spike and Lorne are in the room. Fortunately for all concerned, Super-Happy Spike is either chatting with Lorne or wistfully looking at the wall decorations.

CHARACTER NOTES *Angel:* After some recent permutations, his hair has returned its normally shorn and spiked self. [It's very reassuring.] Angel tries to dodge the party by watching hockey [see 3.15, "Loyalty"]. Still, his party-demeanor, if still rather stiff, has improved since "She" (1.13). [Crucially, there's no talk of Angel dancing or singing.] His office's "magic windows" turn opaque at the press of a button. Angel doesn't revert to Angelus after having sex with Eve. [It's far from what you'd call "perfect happiness"; nor is it "simulated bliss" either, see 1.17, "Eternity."]

• *Spike:* Deems Halloween a bunch of "claptrap over a bit of dusty old Druid nonsense" [see **Organizations**].

• *Wesley:* Suffers yet another setback when Fred confides in him about her attraction to Knox. [It's reasonable to think that Wesley should really crap or get off the pot where Fred's concerned, but we'll shelve that discussion for 5.07, "Lineage."] His drunken party-dancing is hardly perfect, but not the catastrophic embarrassment he previously exhibited [in "She"] either. Wesley never really celebrated Halloween while living in England.

• *Fred:* Hates parties and tends to end up at the hors d'oeuvres table, desperately trying to look occupied. For eight years straight, she dressed as Raggedy Ann for Halloween.

• *Lorne:* Heads the firm's Public Relations Department. [As well as the Entertainment Division? The two departments normally wouldn't be one and the same, so no wonder Lorne is cracking under the stress of his job.] Lorne says he barely made a passing grade in mystical studies and isn't a fighter [despite 4.07, "Apocalypse Nowish"], but believes his organizing a blowout Halloween party will help Angel's cause. He has a long-standing acquaintance with Archduke Sebassis. [It sounds weird that Lorne is so familiar with someone so evil, but there's a precedent – however idiotic – in the "Eater Demon" from 4.04, "Slouching Toward Bethlehem."]

Eve definitively calls Lorne an "empath demon" [short for "empathic demon," a general classification; see 1.10, "Parting Gifts"]. Lorne has an assistant named Van, whom he advises to eat a bagel because he's "looking a little waxy." Lorne's office has a vanity table, and his sleep-deprived condition makes him imagine that he's talking to himself from the mirror on it. Lorne chats over the phone in Italian with Benigni [presumably *Life is Beautiful* star Roberto Benigni], and wonders if Fred's department can "resurrect" Henry Fonda so he can do acting work for them.

• *Eve:* Claims this isn't the first time she's had sex under a mystical influence. After all, she went to U.C. Santa Cruz. [*Buffy* Producer Marti Noxon went to that school, and two dormitories in *Buffy* Season Four – Kresge and Stevenson – are the names of Santa Cruz colleges. 5.08, "Destiny" clarifies that Eve isn't *from* Santa Cruz, but went to school there.]

• *Harmony*: Lorne claims [but whimsically so, going by 5.09, "Harm's Way"] that the Fourth Floor has a crush on her.

• *Archduke Sebassis:* The living end of a "pure bloodline of demonic royalty," commanding more than "40 legions." [Said legions might be the demonic hordes in the series finale.] He calls Angel "child" at one point [indicating Sebassis is very old].

Sebassis' "Demon Slave" (a.k.a. "Pee-Pee Demon") looks like a lesser member of the same species. The Demon Slave regularly drains blue fluid – from a corked hole into his wrist – into an elegant glass for Sebassis to drink. [It's probably blood – not, repeat *not* pee-pee – owing to Sebassis' comment that "We're all blood drinkers here." Sebassis presumably needs this liquid to survive, as the Slave always accompanies him. Or it could just be a vice of his, rather like cigarettes.] The Demon Slave escapes into the firm [to surface in 5.12, "You're Welcome"] while Sebassis is distracted.

Sebassis is armed with poisoned crossbow darts, capable of slaying humans or putting Angel into a coma for a week. [It's less potent than the vampire-killing poison from *Buffy* 3.21, "Graduation Day," then.] Outraged at Artode's death [see **Demonology**], Sebassis tries to execute Angel. [It seems incredible that Sebassis would risk outraging the Senior Partners by dusting Angel, his status with the Circle of the Black Thorn or no; see 5.18, "Origin." But then, Sebassis isn't exactly the type to totally ignore offenses against his person.] Ultimately, Artode's murder is swept under the rug, as Sebassis' people like a little bloodsport with their social functions.

• *"The Thraxis":* Entity who's invited to the party, but killed beforehand by Angel. Slaying the Thraxis, it seems, was like "bashing open a demonic piñata full of rancid Tabasco."

ORGANIZATIONS *Wolfram and Hart:* Treats Halloween like the biggest holiday/event of the year. [This departs from a long-standing tradition on *Buffy* (starting with 2.06,

"Halloween"), in which most supernatural creatures deem Halloween crass and stay home.] Last year's party entailed something hideous involving a bunch of cows and a Sambuca-doused, giant wicker effigy of Krishna. [Some employees remember last year's affair, which suggests that staffers from other branches attended the event, were spared the Beast's attack in 4.08, "Habeas Corpses" and later got transferred to the firm in L.A.]

Harmony says that company morale sucks because everyone fears that Angel will kill them; RSVPs for the party were down 80 percent from last year, apparently for the same reason. Attending the party are the Britzai representatives, the Elder of the Fell Brotherhood, the human-looking Castiglio and a short green demon named Umbrigon.

The firm's Psyche Component Storage Facility can extract more than just sleep; Madeline Chu in Accounting had her ennui removed. [A text in the Psyche Department even mentions the adverse effects of removing sleep from an empath demon, yet the staff apparently never gave Lorne so much as a word of warning. Damn interns.] Lorne's sleep-removing procedure only took 20 minutes, with no scarring.

DEMONOLOGY *Empath Demons:* Lorne normally "reads" people's destinies. A month of sleep deprivation makes him "transmit" instead of receive, causing him to "write [destinies]." Phase Two of this condition is the manifestation of his subconscious – namely, "Hulk-Lorne," a super-strong behemoth. Hulk-Lorne targets and kills two demons who offend Lorne – one by wearing human skin to the party, one (Artode) by wearing the skin of a Deathwok Clan member as a jacket. [It's suggested that Hulk-Lorne is acting out the internal conflicts that Lorne's brain would normally process through sleeping. If we're playing amateur psychologists, Hulk-Lorne probably represents Lorne's id, which is full of primordial desires, and normally unexpressed because it's allowed to frolic about in Lorne's head via dreaming. We're can't, however, comment on why Hulk-Lorne smacks Lorne *himself* around at one point.]

MAGIC *Angel's grenade:* Techno-mystical affair crafted by Fred and Wesley's departments. A hand-held spell-casting robot armed with a core enchantment, it fails Angel in battle. Knox supposedly fixes the problem. [The grenade is presumably tailored to "detonate" a magical spell – rather like 5.01, "Conviction," which implies a mystical container could hold "a curse."]

BEST LINE(s) A Lorne-influenced Angel gives a round of orders, then tells Eve, "You stay here with me and we'll have more sex." Eve: "I'm on it."

THINGS THAT DON'T MAKE SENSE Bit of a glaring oversight here: Once the heroes deduce that Lorne's words have been inadvertently influencing people, nobody considers the short-term solution of simply having Lorne issue new commands, i.e. telling Gunn to stop pissing all over stuff, Spike to act normal (for Spike) and so forth. It's even more glaring that, when Sebassis storms into Angel's office with murderous intent, Lorne doesn't try to discretely influence *him* into standing down and enjoying a nice beverage. Maybe it's risky to mentally influence someone of Sebassis' stature, but then again, it's risky to let him saunter about the firm intent on executing Angel.

Lorne cautions the heroes against rushing to judgment with demon-kind, pointing out that Caritas prospered for years with its open-door policy. Well, that, and the Sanctuary Spell to keep the more rowdy demons from brutally slaughtering everyone. Nobody at the party seems to notice Gunn relieving himself by the buffet table or the elevator. (Then again, the company grunts aren't likely to complain if an executive wishes to piss in the lobby.) By the same token, Hulk-Lorne somehow murders a demon who offended Lorne, *and* lays his corpse out on the buffet table, without anyone spotting him. (There's clearly a magical component to this.)

Sebassis struts into the party and says, "Our anti-detection spells worked nicely, Artode. They won't expect us to be armed," apparently unconcerned that someone might simply read his lips and sound an alarm. (All right... perhaps the spells conceal that as well.) And finally, you can *very* briefly spy that Boreanaz is already wearing pants when Angel stands up from behind his couch and "hurriedly puts his pants on."

IT'S REALLY ABOUT... The rigors of working in Hollywood, and no other *Angel* episode nails it so exactly. Anyone who spends time in L.A. will soon witness the daunting stress that here lays claim to Lorne – who can't handle his workload even *with* his sleep removed – and notice how a wealth of executives, producers, directors and more are scarcely in control of themselves at points because they're running on pure adrenaline. This sort of killer stress particularly cuts down actors (who've got millions of dollars and potentially thousands of jobs resting on their performances), but it's also an affliction that hits people in Lorne's profession especially hard. There's an old Hollywood observation, you know, about how marketing/sales people will work like utter fiends Monday through Friday, then find themselves unable to rest and just as intensely resort to cocaine or all manner of vices on the weekend. Not for nothing does Lorne claim, "I'm the center of gravity in a town that's full of borderline-disorder celebrities and power brokers."

CRITIQUE On initial viewing, this episode might seem like a curious deviation from the central "heroes running the evil law firm" storyline. But with benefit of hindsight, it looks more and more charming, standing as proof (as we stated in 4.20, "Sacrifice") that Edlund is never better than when he's being quirky. This story doesn't reach the heights of his script for 5.14, "Smile Time" – but then, few stories do – yet it's an entirely witty, delightful and worthy endeavor anyway. Among other merits, it's the only Season Five story where Denisof gets to act very silly, and is armed with some of the series' most memorable gags (oh, honestly, who can forget Gunn peeing on Angel's chair?).

More poignantly, however... it's a final hurrah for Lorne. Granted, he'll play a crucial role in the series finale, but "Life of the Party" – a whopping 17 episodes from the end of *Angel* – marks his last tangible contribution to the show. For better or worse, he's going to spend most of Season Five in the background, often chatting on his cell phone – which thematically makes a bit of sense, because he's *so* in his element that it doesn't warrant much discussion beyond this tale. That's a shame, because *Angel* has greatly benefited from Andy Hallett's participation, but the show has other priorities moving forward.

One other issue worth mentioning: This is the *one* episode where Eve works really well. Yes... we've avoided discussing it before now, but the series has a serious liability in actress Sarah Thompson. Frankly, she just seems miscast in the part... she'd probably work fine in other roles, such as (say) an assistant to Jack McCoy on *Law and Order*, but she's downright cardboard while playing a "mysterious" character that needs to work on multiple levels. Eve's lines aren't always golden, of course, but when Thompson is handed a meaty piece of material that screams for a sense of intrigue, she displays little sense of actually registering the fact. Her character should have a sense of menace, but doesn't. Still, if we're trying to be optimistic, her sub-par performance isn't a deal-breaker in most episodes, and at least – as a sexual foil for Angel – she's very, very good in "Life of the Party."

All told, then, this episode will probably sink like a lead balloon for those (and they're out there) who think that *Angel* shouldn't ever do a comedy story, not ever. Fortunately, we're not among them, and rate this as one of the better Season Five outings. Indeed, we'd best describe it as "endearingly madcap."

THE LORE At random, Hallett once wound up in a bar chatting with Lou Ferrigno (TV's the Incredible Hulk), and they compared notes about make-up and how many times they'd been painted green. (Veitch, *E! Online: Watch With Kristin*, Dec. 12, 2003)

• Some on-screen additions that the script fails to mention... Harmony spies the dead demon on the buffet table and comments, "Somebody really dipped his chip"; Wes and Fred are amusingly standing backward as the elevator doors open; Wesley drunkenly waggles his finger and goes "Ah!" to chastise a peeing Gunn.

• Leland Crooke (Sebassis) had previously portrayed Professor Lillian, the Slayer's extremely pleasant poetry teacher, in the teaser to *Buffy* 5.19, "Tough Love" (it's almost perverse to here see him as demonic royalty). Only four months previous to playing the "Demon Slave"/"Pee-Pee Demon," Ryan Alvarez was a choir boy on *Boston Public*.

5.06: "The Cautionary Tale of Numero Cinco"

"Hope: It's the only thing that will sustain you, that will keep you from ending up like Number Five."

Air Date: Nov. 5, 2003; **Writer/Director:** Jeffrey Bell

SUMMARY With the Mexican Day of the Dead drawing near, a demon named Tezcatcatl returns to life via a demonic contract, and begins stealing heroes' hearts for sustenance. Wesley learns that 50 years ago, the demon fell in combat to a quintet of heroic Mexican wrestlers, brothers all. Four of the brothers perished, but the survivor, "Numero Cinco," became disillusioned and joined Wolfram and Hart, later becoming a mail boy there. Tezcatcatl now hopes to find a magic talisman – presently in Numero Cinco's possession – that will make him ultra-powerful.

Governed by his apparent failure as a hero, a fatalistic Numero Cinco forces a confrontation with Tezcatcatl in a cemetery. Angel rushes to help – even as No. 5's brothers rise from their graves – leading to a struggle in which the heroes skewer Tezcatcatl through the heart, permanently killing him. Numero Cinco dies from his injuries, and all of the brothers fade into nothingness.

FIRSTS AND LASTS Starting a trend, Angel's office window takes a beating when Numero Cinco pitches him through it. (See also Lawson and Angel's struggle, 5.13, "Why We Fight"; puppet-Angel shoving Spike through his office door, 5.14, "Smile Time"; etc.) It's also the final "appearance" of Holland Manners, during a 1950's flashback when the character offers the morose Numero Cinco a job, even though we can't see Holland's face. First of two instances this year (the other being the series finale) where Spike muses, "If wishes were horses..."

POINTS OF DISCUSSION ABOUT "The Cautionary Tale of Numero Cinco":

1. This episode might seem funnier to anyone who's seen an old-style wrestling movie, particularly *Samson and the Vampire Women* (1962), which was suitably scathed on *Mystery Science Theater 3000*. For anyone who hasn't seen such fare, however... well, wait for **The Critique**.

2. The dating for this story always seems odd, as "Life of the Party" (5.05) indisputably takes place on Halloween (meaning October 31), yet "the Mexican Day of the Dead" is Nov. 2 (All Souls' Day). Moreover, Tezcatcatl kills one of his victims after an All Souls' mass, yet it really shouldn't be a mere two days after the previous episode, as Lorne is up and about when he should be recovering from a month's sleep deprivation.

However... in the many places in Mexico, the "Day of the Dead" celebration begins as early as October 18 and continues until November 9. (It's like Mardi Gras... the national media always focuses its attention on the concluding "Fat Tuesday," ignoring that the celebration actually commenced two weeks previous.) Given that the story strives for a certain sense of symmetry – claiming that Tezcatcatl has returned "50 years to the day," etc. – the final battle probably occurs on November 9, the date given on the brothers' tombstone.

3. Angel happens to mention "the father will kill the son" prophecy (from Season Three) and Wesley doesn't remember it. As we'll learn in episodes to come, the memory spell that "remade" Connor (4.22, "Home") erased everything pertaining to him, but the heroes still recall everything else about that period, including Jasmine (as evidenced next episode), Angel's battle with Sahjhan (5.18, "Origin") and so forth.

4. Lorne beams at Fred: "You're Wonder Woman!" Clearly, this is a secret message from Whedon that he hopes to cast Amy Acker in the *Wonder Woman* movie. (Oh, all right... maybe not.)

CHARACTER NOTES *Angel:* Almost to the point of loathing his work at the firm, despite Gunn's assurances it allows them to facilitate benevolent operations. He's particularly rattled by the thought that Tezcatcatl seeks to collect "the hearts of heroes" yet avoids taking his. [However, this probably owes more to Angel's status as a vampire than his current attitude toward heroism. Even presuming Tezcatcatl could have taken Angel's heart without its going to dust the moment it left Angel's chest, as Numero Cinco puts it, "Who would want that dried-up walnut of a dead thing?"]

A negative-minded Angel claims that prophecies are nonsense. Nonetheless, he finally reads the Shanshu Prophecy – out of a desire to find some reason to keep going, it seems – after witnessing Tezcatcatl's reluctance to take his heart, Numero Cinco's despondency and Wesley's observation that Angel's work has lost all meaning for him. [See 5.08, "Destiny" for more.] Angel is now driving a red convertible.

• *Spike:* Wonders if he meets the criteria for the Shanshu Prophecy because he "saved the world" at the end of *Buffy* Season Seven [again, see "Destiny" for where this is going].

• *Wesley:* Can read Cuauhtitlan pictograms.

• *Gunn:* Loves his work. Nonetheless, lawyer-Gunn doesn't feel as smart as Wesley, and even feels intimidated by Fred's intelligence.

• *"Numero Cinco":* Oddly, he lives in Apt. No. 8. Seems decrepit and hunched over while delivering mail in the firm, yet surprisingly agile – given his age – when called upon to act as a hero. He wears his mask even while hanging about his apartment.

• *Tezcatcatl:* Tall Aztec demon, described as "predatory bird meets demonic gladiator." He was one of the Aztecs' most powerful warriors, and illicitly crafted a mystical talisman that would harness the power of their sun god to make him über-powerful. This was discovered, however, leading to Tezcatcatl being sentenced to die on the Aztec version of Day of the Dead. [It's never said, however, what agency of that period could restrain Tezcatcatl, never mind execute him.] However, Tezcatcatl forged a mystical deal wherein a "shaman" cursed him to return from the dead every 50 years, enabling him to keep searching for the talisman.

Precisely 50 years ago, Tezcatcatl rose in east Los Angeles and killed more than a dozen people before the brothers defeated him. Tezcatcatl wears armor, sports a shield, is strong enough to heft dumpsters, and withstands Wesley's shotgun blast at close range. He steals hearts [apparently for sustenance, although it's certainly possible that a metaphor is at work here] from heroic individuals such as a Gulf War veteran who was awarded a Bronze Star, a fireman who saved his crew, and a churchgoer who "worked with gangs" [presumably encouraging them to abandon the life]. Eating such hearts makes Tezcatcatl nigh-invulnerable, yet his own heart remains a vulnerable spot. [Angel finally gives Tezcatcatl's talisman to Wesley for safekeeping, which – as with Pavayne in 5.04, "Hell Bound" – raises some questions about what happens to it once the series folds.]

THE LIBRARY It's definitively stated that each "template book" ties to a different discipline within the Wolfram and Hart archives. [Meaning that one book isn't the same as another, although this is slightly at odds with 5.15, "A Hole in the World."] One template is linked to historical narratives, another covers prophecies. The firm's archives also contain a copy of the Shanshu Prophecy, translated into English. Wesley researches Tezcatcatl using the firm's Meso-American text and the *Xiochimayan Codex*, which is missing several key pictographs.

ORGANIZATIONS

• *Wolfram and Hart:* Copies of any contract regarding a curse, hex or otherwise supernatural deal are on-file and available to the firm's Contracts Department. [These documents include deals beyond those that the firm negotiate, it seems.] Such files go back at least as far as the Aztec era [and probably farther, actually]. Thanks to Gunn's savvy paperwork, Angel bankrupts a company that dumps raw demon waste into Santa Monica Bay, banishes a clan of pyro warlocks into a hell dimension, and starts a foster care program for the resultant orphans of vampire attacks. In-house attacks are "down 30 percent this week," and Gunn estimates they've done more good at the firm in a month than Angel Investigations did in a year.

• *Los Hermanos Numeros:* [Meaning "The Number Brothers," if you hadn't figured that out.] Fifty years ago, they were "great warriors" in the wresting ring, but also served as heroic champions – fighting monsters, gangsters, etc. They often hung out in a bar, where people in need would phone for help. After the battle with Tezcatcatl, the brothers were buried "behind San Gregorio" and Numero Cinco stopped getting phone calls. Holland Manners, then a legal associate with Wolfram and Hart, offered Numero Cinco a position with the firm. [Holland's offer smacks of the firm wanting to snitch a heroic figure from the side of good, and it's almost akin to the firm offering Angel his C.E.O. position in microcosm.] Today, the brothers are remembered only as parodies during wrestling events, their costumes worn by midgets.

The brothers' tombstones display a few relevant dates: Numero Tres was born on August 22 of an unspecified year; Numero Cuatro on Dec. 7, 1927; Numero Cinco on Sept. 15, 1929. Numero Cinco's brothers were killed on Nov. 9, 1953.

DEMONOLOGY According to Gunn, "tumescent trolls" exist in the *Angel*-verse. Demon law requires blood signatures on all legal documents. Tests that Fred proposes, given a sample of Tezcatcatl's blood: hematological, cellular RH enzymes, a full SMA-20 and some demonoid entropy patterning.

• *Vampires:* Angel smells the blood of one of Tezcatcatl's victims, even while zooming by in a car.

• *El Diablo Robotico:* A robot "built by the Devil." [In a strange parallel, Marsters once belonged to a band called "Ghost of the Robot."] *Los Hermanos Numeros* fought this menace in their heyday. Wesley has heard of the robot, but Angel hasn't [despite his actually living through the 1950s].

MAGIC [Somewhat irritatingly, it's never explained how Numero Cinco's brothers come back to life to fight Tezcatcatl, and it's played as if it's a perfectly reasonable circumstance given that it's "the Day of the Dead." If we're looking for an explanation, perhaps Tezcatcatl's resurrection pact, in conjunction with Number Five's possessing the demon's magical amulet, accords the brothers a brief opportunity to resurrect themselves. Obviously there's *some* kind of mystical component to this, as shown by the way Numero Cinco's body fades to nothingness with his brothers at story's end.]

BEST LINE Gunn to Angel, on why Tezcatcatl wouldn't want his heart: "As meat goes, your heart's a dried-up hunk of gnarly-ass beef jerky."

THINGS THAT DON'T MAKE SENSE Well, first off... it's profoundly bizarre that Lorne deems the taciturn Numero Cinco as precisely the sort of person who'd have excellent insight on which birthday card he should give someone of the female persuasion. Is it because... dunno... Numero Cinco is aged, and therefore qualified to know the mentality of – as Lorne puts it – "an aging sexpot celebrating a decade of turning 29"?

There's no explanation why Numero Cinco – if he's been working at the firm's L.A. branch for 50 years – wasn't massacred during the Beast's attack in Season Four. And we might have one of the few genuine violations of the vampire invitation rule, when Numero Cinco wordlessly pulls Angel inside his apartment to thrash him a bit. (Numero Cinco's intent is clear enough, but most other evidence – see **How Does the Invitation Rule Work?** – suggests that a spoken declaration is also required. It's not impossible that Numero Cinco and his brothers owe their super-abilities to demonic energy – which would probably void the invite rule – as Numero Cinco seems amazingly strong for someone who's in his seventies if not older. That said, in most respects, the brothers simply seem like accomplished wrestlers, nothing more.)

Why is Angel puzzled because Gunn has some of his blood available for contract signatures? Because unless Gunn has been taking blood samples from Angel without the man's knowing, one would think that Angel donated it for just such a purpose. Also, after Numero Cinco pitches Angel through his office window, Angel sits around obviously *not* covered in pieces of glass. As with 4.07, "Apocalypse Nowish," Wesley insists on walking toward Tezcatcatl while unloading a shotgun in its direction, thus giving said demon an excellent opportunity to slug him. And this from the guy who's so adept with firearms, he can expertly peg a slug into Skip's earhole (4.17, "Inside Out").

After-hours, Wesley's office door is standing wide-open when Angel walks inside – and the heroes wonder why their security keeps getting penetrated so easily. Oh, and typos are universal... in flashback, Holland Manners' business card reads "Attorney's at Law."

IT'S REALLY ABOUT... Rather bluntly, we're meant to invite comparisons between Angel's present state of depression and a washed-up older hero – Numero Cinco – who "lost the mission" some decades previous. "You made a difference to the lives you saved," Angel tells Numero Cinco, sounding terribly convincing. However, it's hard to get much mileage out of this, considering the Angel-parallel here looks so utterly ridiculous in that damn mask.

CRITIQUE Even now, viewers look at this story and remark, "What the hell were they thinking?" Admittedly, "Numero Cinco" *is* a sorry mess, but all-too-often, the aforementioned question is the wrong one to ask. Why did Mutant Enemy attempt a Mexican wrestling story? Well... why did they attempt a *Buffy* musical? Why did they attempt an *Angel* puppet episode? Why did they attempt a frickin' ballet story? In principle, some of the most successful-yet-radical *Angel* and *Buffy* episodes sound utterly ridiculous. Some allowance has to be made for experimentation, because the sad truth is, even the most talented of TV-makers often have no clue how something will turn out until it's actually made. Under those conditions, a Mexican wrestling story might have seemed worth attempting, *except*...

The success stories we just cited had ambition, charm and glorious storytelling. That's where "Numero Cinco" throws itself under a truck. It fails not because it's about Mexican wrestling, but rather that it's so crushingly lame, unfunny, drab and predictable that it can't offer anything *but* the wrestling angle. The result being: If you don't care two shits about Mexican wrestling (and we assuredly don't), you're doomed. *Totally* doomed. Even No. 5's story – if we're being brutally honest – gets more weight than it deserves. You can feel sorry for him, sure, but not overly so.

Writer Jeffrey Bell provided *Angel* with some excellent service both before and after this point, but for our money, this is the worst story in nearly a year (since 4.10, "Awakening," in fact). Worse, if you're watching these episodes in order, it's miserable enough to raise some flags about the remainder of the season. Fortunately for all concerned, everything gets neatly back on track with "Lineage," but you're within your rights to think that a wrestling network has – appallingly – interrupted *Angel*'s broadcast. We now return you to regularly scheduled programming.

5.07: "Lineage"

"I killed my father...
He pointed a gun at you, Fred. So I shot him."

Air Date: Nov. 12, 2003; **Writer:** Drew Goddard; **Director:** Jefferson Kibbee

SUMMARY Wesley's father, Roger Wyndham-Pryce, unexpectedly arrives to evaluate him for admittance into the reformed Watchers. Meanwhile, a benevolent organization of cyborg commando-ninjas storm the law offices. Roger theorizes that the cyborgs hope to steal the firm's "template books," a means of accessing the Wolfram and Hart archives. But as Wesley secures the books in his vault, Roger incapacitates his son and steals a rod – the Staff of Devosynn – from within.

Roger lures Angel onto the roof, then uses the Staff to magically steal Angel's willpower, hoping to castrate him as an agent of an evil law firm. Wesley awakens and snatches back the Staff, causing a standoff in which father and son point pistols at one another. Roger tries to break the stalemate by taking Fred hostage, but Wesley – without a moment's hesitation – unloads his clip into his father's chest. Moments later, the dead "Roger" sparks and is revealed as a cyborg in disguise, even as his collaborators flee. Wesley restores Angel, struggles to admit his feelings for Fred, and finally phones his father just to check up on him.

FIRSTS AND LASTS First script credited to Drew Goddard, who wrote or co-wrote some of the most celebrated *Buffy* Season Seven episodes (including 7.07, "Conversations with Dead People"; 7.17, "Lies My Parents Told Me," etc.) and transferred to *Angel* for Season Five. Emil, formerly mentioned in Season Four as Wesley's weapons-maker, appears just long enough for a cyborg to break his neck. Second (after 4.22, "Home") and last venture into the firm's stately Ancient Prophecies wing; after this, the template books will simply litter Wesley's office.

POINTS OF DISCUSSION ABOUT "Lineage":

1. Even before "Lineage" broadcast, some commentators wondered – not without justification – why on Earth Wesley and Fred weren't a couple by now. They're clearly unattached, share some mutual attraction and – despite Fred's seeming interest in Knox – each *can't* be blind to how the other feels. "Lineage" even entails Wes defending Fred by "shooting his father," yet strangely, they don't become boyfriend and girlfriend for seven more episodes.

In the real-world, the producers delayed coupling Wes and Fred to make the tragedy in "A Hole in the World" (5.15) all the more cutting... yet within *Angel* continuity, Wesley and Fred's reluctance makes sense also. Almost certainly, Wesley Wyndham-Pryce is the most deeply conflicted character in the entire Whedon-verse (and considering the competition includes Angel himself, that's saying something). Thus, while Wesley clearly idolizes Fred, he constantly feels unworthy of her because he's in his "Dark Wesley" phase. Dark Wesley doesn't believe he belongs in Fred's world – he thinks she wants a hero, and simply doesn't think of himself in that way. That's bullshit, naturally, but that's what's rattling through his mind.

Meanwhile, Fred is smitten with Wesley, but she isn't the sort of woman to make the first move. Her usual approach (as evidenced with Gunn, Knox and briefly Angel) is to hang around potential lovers hoping they'll take an interest. Romantically, she's the shy Texas wallflower, and it's against her style to take a megaphone and scream at the moody British fellow that she'd like to spend time with him.

The result: Knox makes Fred feel flattered purely because he shows an interest in her. That's not to criticize Fred, however... people fall prey to dating the wrong person *only* because they show attention all the time. Besides, Fred never gets very romantically involved with Knox. He's merely a distraction – but then, on a grander scale, you could say the same about her romance with Gunn.

In Fred's defense, consider: Her choice amounts to the tasty yet inwardly tormented Englishman who's desperately trying to keep his distance *or* the kinda cute scientist geek-boy who actually wants to share her company. Whom would you choose? The female co-author of this guide book thinks that while Wesley is fabulous, she'd never date him in a million years. She'd declare him damaged goods and move on. Besides, Knox represents an unknown quantity, and Fred's potential dating pool isn't exactly bursting right now. Taking all of this into account, it makes sense that Wes and Fred still have issues.

2. Drew Goddard: A man who never met a continuity reference he didn't like. He doesn't resort to "fanwank" – loosely defined as writing a story just to relive previous adventures as a sort of "continuity-gasm" – and his episodes usually stand on their own merits. Nonetheless, his love affair with continuity references runs thick in parts, so let's check off the most pertinent ones in "Lineage," shall we?

Spike conspicuously mentions that "sex with robots is more common than most people think" (denoting his fling with the Buffy-bot, first in *Buffy* 5.18, "Intervention"); Eve says that Wesley once stole Angel's son (3.16, "Sleep Tight"); and we meet Emil, forger of Wesley's collapsible swords (first mentioned in 4.03, "The House Always Wins"). We're told that Wesley was "head boy" at the Academy (4.06, "Spin the Bottle"), that Angel killed his father (1.15, "The Prodigal"), that Spike killed his vampiric mother after she tried to shag him (the Goddard-written "Lies My Parents Told Me"), that the Watchers' Council was obliterated (the Goddard-written *Buffy* 7.09, "Never Leave Me"), and that Wesley's last girlfriend met with a grisly end (4.12, "Calvary" and 4.13, "Salvage"; see **The Critique**). The firm's Ancient Prophecies wing (and mention of Spike's amulet) hails from 4.22, "Home," and when caught in a darkened elevator, Spike impulsively shouts, "You'll never take me to hell, Pavayne!" (5.04, "Hell Bound")

That's *at least* ten episodes referenced, even before factoring in Wesley's less-than-sterling relationship with his father (1.14, "I've Got You Under My Skin," 2.19, "Belonging"). As a geeky checklist of events and characters from the last few years, it's (switch to Darth Vader voice) "Impressive... *most* impressive."

3. Wesley and Fred's fathers have the same name: "Roger." Heaven only knows if was deliberate, or if the name was simply rattling around in Drew Goddard's subconscious. It's hopefully not the latter, because it's just too creepy to paint Wesley and Fred as siblings, as opposed to the more apt symbolism of this type in 1.15, "The Prodigal."

CHARACTER NOTES *Angel:* Chastises Wesley as a subordinate, after a botched scheme to identify Emil's weapons-distributor [presumably to shut him down] injures Fred. [As before, the heroes' organic relationships are becoming more and more corporate.] Eve speculates that Angel is worried – as Wesley stole Connor in Season Three – that Wes might betray him again. [This is just rampant speculation on Eve's part, as Angel doesn't appear to have doubted Wesley's loyalties for at least a year now. Indeed, Angel finishes this story by praising Wesley for making tough decisions.]

• *Spike:* Still intangible, but musters enough concentration to punch a cyborg. He senses that Eve has been keeping an eye on him [for reasons explained next episode]. On Spike's previous encounter with Roger, see **Best Line**.

• *Wesley:* Worryingly, it's implied that Wesley has been taking Fred into dangerous missions simply to spend time with her. "Roger" levels character insults at Wesley ("Your tenure as Watcher ranks as our most embarrassing failure," etc.) that seem par-for-the course. Wesley claims his father "never had any use for him as a child," can't bear the thought of him as an adult, and would fatally shoot him if given enough reason.

When Wesley was six or seven, a bird flew into his windowpane and died. He snitched a magic scroll from his father's library, intent on performing a resurrection spell on the bird, but his father intervened before he could try. Wesley's mother, at least, thought he was quite the prodigy.

As expected, Wesley's parents live in England. Troublingly, Wesley shoots his "father" nine times... the last when he's clearly riddled with holes and on the ground. Wesley throws up immediately after doing this.

• *Fred:* Knows her way around the firm's modified sniper-rifles, and seems remarkably chipper about the arm-injury a cyborg-ninja gives her.

• *Lorne:* Apparently chats on the phone with Vin Diesel, mentioning that Louis Gossett Jr. better keep his mouth zipped if he wants a "foam party" [a social event in which the participants are lathered up with suds, sometimes dispensed from a cannon] to happen, and that "nobody" – including Lorne – cared about *Iron Eagle II* (1988, and starring Gossett). Lorne [jokingly?] says his sources believe the idea of a beautiful love child between Winston Churchill and a young Richard Harris isn't all *that* ridiculous. He also mentions an incident involving his being covered in cherries, the police pounding on the door, and Judi Dench screaming, "Oh, that's *way* too much to pay for a pair of pants!" [Dame Judi would not, of course, be talking about trousers; she'd mean (male) underwear.]

• *Eve:* Implies that Spike's world-saving amulet wasn't meant for Angel. [She's lying to throw Spike off-track, the hussy... see 5.02, "Just Rewards."]

• *"Roger Wyndham-Pryce":* The Roger-döppelganger is an astoundingly accurate copy. [So we should take his factual statements as truthful, unless given reason to think otherwise.] He's good at swordplay. He and his colleagues [during his time as an operative for the Watchers] fought werewolves, vampires and the occasional swamp-man – but not proto-human, cybernetic fighters.

THE LIBRARY [A note on the "template books": We should presume they're enchanted to such a degree, the firm can't sever their connection to the archives by remote (as with their "de-enchanting" the Band of Blacknil from afar in 2.16, "Epiphany"). Otherwise, Wesley's concern about getting them into lockdown is unnecessary, unless he's worried that any number of dangerous texts could get read before the firm could de-activate the books.] The firm's archives contain the "powerful" *Saitama Codex*. Dutrovic markings on a cyborg's central processing unit indicates an Eastern origin; Wesley suggests consulting the journals of Saitama.

ORGANIZATIONS *Wolfram and Hart:* Roger says that the firm's atrocities are "quite well documented." [This clashes with earlier stories such as 1.16, "The Ring," in which Wesley – even as a failed ex-Watcher – is totally unfamiliar with the organization.] Wesley's personal/departmental vault is hidden in the Ancient Prophecies wing. His handprint is required; his password: "Elysium."

The firm has evidently made modifications to the TS-113 sniper rifle; Wesley says they've made 200 of these units. The scope works along amplified thermal wavelengths, and the delivery system has been replaced with a "Bylantine" energy charge, eliminating the need for conventional ammo.

• *The Watchers' Council:* Roger claims some former/retired Watchers [i.e. those that survived "Never Leave Me"] are re-forming the Council. [There's no evidence of this actually occurring, however; see 5.11, "Damage."]

• *Cybernetic Commando-Ninjas:* Seem like cyber-augmented humans, not demons. They number among the good-guys, having recently eliminated a demon cabal in Jakarta and "the Tanmar Death Chamber." [That said, "Roger" sword-skewers a colleague in the interest of spooking Wesley, *and* leaves said comrade behind, so the group isn't entirely heroic.]

The cyborgs' weapon of choice: hook-tipped, swinging chains. Some [possibly all] of the cyborgs have self-destruct devices, and they have excellent intelligence on the firm. Robo-Roger's plan only entails nullifying Angel's will, not capturing the man.

MAGIC The disguise-glamour that "Roger" uses is never explained, but Angel and Wesley suspect the cyborgs stole character assessments, background information and psychological profiles from the Watchers to facilitate it.

• *The Staff of Devosynn:* Funky-looking staff, either made from wood or bone, with a green jewel in the tip. The word "Atistrata" activates the artifact whereupon the item emits a sort of smoky tendril that saps Angel's will. Shattering the crystal would restore Angel [although Wesley presumably knows another means of doing so].

BEST LINE(s) Roger, chagrined to encounter the now-heroic Spike: "We've met. 1963. My colleagues and I fell upon you slaughtering an orphanage in Vienna. [You] killed two of my men before you escaped." Spike, searching for a response: "Oh... how've you been?"

THINGS THAT DON'T MAKE SENSE Given that the list of parties who'd love to mentally castrate Angel has never been greater, we don't know what to make of the Staff of Devosynn: a magical artifact capable of sapping Angel's will, that is kept at the firm. Even if the Senior Partners believe that using the device on Angel runs counter to their plans (and that's a big *if*), surely it's such a security risk – as Roger proves – that the heroes should've destroyed the damn thing prior to this? You could argue that the heroes literally *can't* destroy such a powerful item, but Wesley seems awfully confident that he can just pitch it off a rooftop and shatter it. (He might be bluffing, but still...)

Angel is serving as Wesley's back-up in the arms deal with Emil – and therefore must have collaborated with Wes beforehand – yet he's surprised that Fred is present. Never mind that Wesley and Fred fight the robo-ninjas a hell of a long time before Angel finally bothers to crash to the rescue. And why *isn't* Fred armed for a risky mission of this sort? In the same scuffle, Fred's shoulder wound seems odd, considering she somehow got nailed by a cyborg's grappling hook but *not* whisked off her feet and killed, as with Emil's associate. (Shrapnel or some other flying object probably pegged her, but it's a strange one.)

When Wesley examines a fallen cyborg's central processing unit, strange editing makes it look like female hands – not Alexis Denisof's – are near the device.

IN RETROSPECT "Roger" on Angel: "He's a puppet. He always has been." It's as if he's been reading the show's production notes (see 5.14, "Smile Time").

IT'S REALLY ABOUT... As with "The Prodigal" (1.15), it's a discussion of fathers and sons, but the difference is that "Lineage" – at least, in part – looks at how normally adept adults revert to their teenage selves whenever their parents show up. Notice how his father's arrival makes Wesley so apologetic and clumsy, you almost expect the poor sap to fall down some stairs. Later on, the episode is about one's shifting priorities upon reaching adulthood, as Wesley clearly favors Fred's safety over that of his bullying parent. Not that his gunning down Roger is what you'd call commendable, but take it as a startling indication of Wes protecting the love of his life.

CRITIQUE Well, then... nothing like a supposed act of patricide to up the dramatic stakes, is there?

With "Lineage," Drew Goddard casts his eye over the *Angel* landscape, hones in on Wesley – a character with loads of untapped potential, even this late in the game – and lets fly with an episode that's heart-wrenching and intensely compelling. Pardon that we made some friendly barbs about Goddard's continuity fetish – it was more an observation of the man's writing technique than anything else – but at this stage, he genuinely *is* the best writer to bring the show's various threads into focus, and give a sense that Season Five is hitting high gear. Moreover, amid all the gut-wrenching drama, Goddard is very, very funny at points. (Wesley: "The last girl I was with, I had to chop into little tiny pieces because a higher power saw fit to stab her in the neck." Roger: "You don't want to discuss [your love-life]. Fine. But spare me the sarcasm. It's too embarrassing.")

If there's a flaw, it's that the robo-ninjas seem like a waste of time. However, they're not really the point of the story, and as a means of easing the financial burden and making Season Five possible (see **The Lore**), they're tolerable. But in nearly every other respect, "Lineage" is as riveting and intricate as you might expect, and a smoke-'em-if-you-got-'em reward for anyone who had faith in Season Five before now.

THE LORE *Angel* incurred a sizeable budget-cut as a condition of its renewal for Season Five, and David Fury commented: "We're going back almost to *Buffy* Year One in terms of our budget! There were a lot of cool things done on *Buffy* Year One, but it's very hard when you've [previously] had a Rain of Fire." (DiLullo, *Dreamwatch* #110, Nov. 2003) For anyone paying attention in Season Five, the cash-crunch probably explains why the law firm set sees so much action – the firm is haunted (5.04, "Hell Bound"), the firm throws a Halloween bash (5.05, "Life of the Party"), the firm is broken into (this episode, 5.13, "Why We Fight," etc.) and so forth. Indeed, one suspects that a big motivation for commando-ninjas was that they're comparatively cheap, requiring only a few stuntmen, some black outfits and a few faceplates.

• Denisof eased back on Wesley's stubble in Season Five – his new wife, Alyson Hannigan, didn't care for the unshaven look and besides, he felt it fit the character's evolving status. Hannigan found it weird to see Denisof smooching his fellow cast members, but added, given Willow's tendencies on *Buffy*, "Luckily, [Alexis] hasn't had to deal with anything except me kissing women." (O'Hare, *Zap2It.com*, Jan. 20, 2004)

• The script had Wesley referring to his mother as, well, "Mother," but this got changed for broadcast to the British-favored "Mum." However, the closed captioning insists on displaying the American-ized "Mom." Mind, the captioning also spells Emil's name as "Emile," when it's documented without the "e" elsewhere.

• Roy Dotrice (Roger Wyndam Price) has – at some point or other – portrayed Abraham Lincoln, Sir Arthur Conan Doyle, Charles Dickens, King George IV, Leopold Mozart, Anaxagoras and Zeus (the last on *Hercules*). Back in 1971, he served as Storyteller for a string of Greek legends in the series *Jackanory*. Perhaps most importantly, he was a series regular on *Beauty and the Beast* (1987-1990), where he played the Beast's adoptive father.

5.08: "Destiny"

"Here we are, then. Two vampire heroes competing to wet our whistles with a drink of light, refreshing torment."

Air Date: Nov. 19, 2003;
Writer/Director: Steven S. DeKnight

SUMMARY A mysterious box arrives at the firm that, when opened, emits a flash that re-corporealizes Spike. Unfortunately, the close proximity of two vampire champions with a soul throws the Shanshu Prophecy into confusion. Consequently, reality starts to unravel and many of the firm's employees slip into madness.

With Wesley on leave, Angel and associates consult with Sirk – a member of Wesley's department. Sirk rereads the Shanshu and reveals that the fated vampire will drink from the Cup of Perpetual Torment, an item in a disused Nevada opera house, and suffer unspeakably before regaining his humanity. Angel and Spike race to drink from the cup, brawling in the opera house. Spike bests Angel and drinks from the goblet, shocked to find that it's filled with Mountain Dew.

5.08, Destiny

As Angel and Spike realize they've been duped, Sirk goes into hiding. The Senior Partners temporarily calm the universal order, delaying the question of what precisely the Shanshu indicates. Afterward, Eve reports to the mastermind who re-solidified Spike and brought him into conflict with Angel: her lover, Lindsey McDonald.

FIRSTS AND LASTS Final appearance of Sirk (see 4.22, "Home").

POINTS OF DISCUSSION ABOUT "Destiny":

1. Time to play amateur psychologist, as it's the best way of answering: Why does Spike best Angel? It's not blatantly stated, but other episodes (such as 5.11, "Damage") suggest that it's down to how Angel and Spike view their inner guilt. Both of them were monstrous vampires, but consider that Angelus was more "successful" and legendary than Spike because Angelus actively *relished* killing. By comparison, Spike was more akin to a gang member – certainly lethal, but often just along for the ride.

Now, Angel is acutely aware of these facts, and almost undoubtedly worries that his soul and its capacity for compassion aren't enough, and that his sadistic side might win out anyway. This comes out in Season Two, when he sleeps with Darla after thrashing her around a while. Oh, and there was that whole business about locking a dozen lawyers in a cellar to die horribly. In short, Angel is concerned that he's *still* evil, whereas Spike – remorseful as he is – doesn't fret about that sort of thing. Spike sees himself as a normal person who got turned into a vampire, fell in love, finally got a soul and stopped killing. As proof, look at how Spike handles getting re-corporealized: he grabs Harmony and heads off for a nooner. In a similar situation, Angel would've just brooded.

... all of which is a lengthy way of expressing that Angel is far more conflicted (and yet in some respects, more "human") than Spike – with good reason – and this indecision allows Spike to get the better of him.

2. To review... Spike re-corporealizes, which confuses the Shanshu and throws reality out of flux. The White Room vanishes, employees suffer madness and there's a big hullabaloo until the Senior Partners magically put matters right again. Seem clear enough?

Actually, it's not. There's no evidence of any "reality warping" occurring outside the firm, and the only person blathering about "the fabric of reality unraveling" is Eve, who as Lindsey's accomplice has plenty of reason to lie. Besides, if the Shanshu is as pre-destined as everyone says, it shouldn't *get* confused. So it's entirely possible that all the mayhem at the firm owes to sabotage or magic-casting on Lindsey's part, purely to keep everyone off-balance. (And for a final word on the Shanshu, check out 5.22, "Not Fade Away.")

3. Giles got knocked unconscious so many times on *Buffy*, it became a staple of the show. Yet it's funny how on *Angel*, the "getting thumped in the head" duty falls to Lorne. Here, Lorne gets head-smacked by a delusional employee who's wielding a fire extinguisher. He's bashed unconscious in 3.16, "Sleep Tight"; 4.04, "Slouching Toward Bethlehem"; and 5.09, "Harm's Way"; and he's mugged (sort of) and appears to lose a horn in 3.11, "Birthday." Maybe he's not in danger of breaking Giles' record, but he's keeping up as best he can.

4. The tail end of "Lineage" had Spike mention (as a means of empathizing with Wesley "gunning down" his father) how he dusted his incest-minded vampire mother in *Buffy* 7.17, "Lies My Parents Told Me." The curious thing being: Spike mentions the mother-dusting ***again*** in the teaser to this episode. Really, this just owes to Goddard and Fury – who co-wrote the *Buffy* story in question – drawing upon their own continuity for the sake of laughs. But for anyone watching these episodes back-to-back on DVD, this means that Spike mentions and *re*-mentions his act of matricide and near-incest in the space of a few minutes.

5. Eve gets the worst line in this episode: "We've got trouble with a capital T, and that rhymes with P, and that stands for 'prophecy'." As a rule of thumb, Lorne can quote from *The Music Man* all he likes; there ought to be a law barring evil assistants from doing so.

CHARACTER NOTES *Angel:* In 1880, England, shortly after Spike's siring [and events with his mother, "Lies My Parents Told Me"], Dru introduced Spike to Angelus at their lodgings at the Royal London Hotel. Darla had left to answer a summons from the Master, and Angelus initially became a friend and mentor to Spike, pleased to experience the slaughter of innocents with "another man." [He presumably shared such murder with Penn (1.11, "Somnambulist") and James (3.01, "Heartthrob"), but only briefly, and he never took to them like he takes to Spike.] Spike admired Angelus, but one night, Spike returned home to find Angelus having sex with Spike's beloved, Drusilla. Angelus lectured Spike about the importance of taking what he desired, whereupon Spike leapt at Angelus in a bid to reclaim Drusilla. [The end-result of this isn't shown, but Angelus, Spike and Dru run together for some time afterward, and presumably iron out their differences. There's no evidence that Angelus and Dru ever have sex again, suggesting that Spike – even with Angelus as the group's alpha male – shows enough spine to keep her in his bed, barring incidents such as 5.20, "The Girl in Question."]

In the modern day, Angel denies Spike's request for an office. [P.S. Angel's familiarity with the Columns Opera House might suggest he visited the area in the 1930s, but it's unclear.]

• *Spike:* Suggests that Angel can't stand the sight of him, because it was Angelus' mentoring that made Spike such an efficient killer. Spike says he refrained from dusting the defeated Angel because he didn't want to hear Buffy bitch about it. [Oh, but c'mon... Spike at present just isn't the type to slay such a hero as Angel.] Spike drinks from the cup partly because he wants the foretold redemption, and partly to take something away from Angel. He steals Angel's red Viper.

• *Wesley:* On leave after events last episode. [He possibly visits his parents in England, and what an awkward reunion *that* must seem after 5.07, "Lineage." By the way, Wesley's absence might prompt Lindsey to here make his move, knowing that the heroes will turn to his agent, Sirk.]

• *Gunn:* Keeps a toy robot collection in his office, and seems to take charge in Angel and Wesley's absence [as with 5.15, "A Hole in the World"].

• *Eve:* Paints her toenails red.

• *Harmony*: Resists having casual sex with Spike, then yields when he tells her: "That's a very pretty skirt you're wearing." Their "nooner" is interrupted when the reality-madness makes Harm attack Spike.

• *Lindsey:* Now has longer hair [since 2.18, "Dead End"] and an earring in his left earlobe. Weird symbols cover Lindsey's body and apartment walls [see 5.12, "You're Welcome" for why].

PROPHECY *The Shanshu Prophecy:* Angel read a translation of the Shanshu Prophecy [5.06, "The Cautionary Tale of Numero Cinco"] that Sirk claims is about as useful as reading a 12-year-old's book report. [We won't repeat everything Sirk "reads" from the Shanshu because he's obviously spewing lies on Lindsey's behalf. Besides, if the Shanshu blatantly mentioned such an all-important Cup of Perpetual Torment, etc., Wesley would surely have told Angel about it before now. The entire Cup stratagem, by the way, probably owes to Lindsey knowing that Angel can't resist "Holy Grail"/ *Indiana Jones*-type quests; see 4.10, "Awakening."] Angel is familiar with the passage, "The vampire will have his past washed clean and live again in mortal form," which presumably hails from the actual prophecy.

• *The Columns Opera House:* Located in Death Valley, but supposedly buried in an earthquake in 1938. It's accessible now, and from the outside looks like a giant sombrero.

ORGANIZATIONS *Wolfram and Hart:* "Code Black" signals that security is sealing off the building, a.k.a. "Pandora's Box."

DEMONOLOGY Spike drinks from Angel's mug, and readily identifies the taste of otter's blood [Harmony's idea, 5.01, "Conviction"].

BEST LINE An employee (Jerry) goes insane near a copy machine and beats his colleague to death with a fire extinguisher, while screaming "Nobody! Replaces! The toner!"

THINGS THAT DON'T MAKE SENSE Spike leaves the firm with a head start on Angel, and seems to maintain it during the subsequent race to the opera house. Ergo, presuming Angel and Spike's cars are equally fast, why doesn't Spike simply dash inside and gulp down "the cup" before Angel can intervene? Mind, Spike only gets his head start because Angel unwisely blurts out the cup's location as The Columns Opera House. What... Angel is *surprised* that Spike would impulsively dash off there? And are we to presume that Spike already knows the Opera House's location... or does he stop and use Yahoo Maps before leaving the firm? Ah, yes... and Angel insists on chasing after Spike in a car – a triumph of style over sense, given that he's got a helicopter ("Conviction").

Sirk chastises Angel for lowering himself to read a translation of the Shanshu Prophecy, not the genuine article, then Sirk hypocritically consults a "newly translated group of verses." Oh, and the same text is shown in Sirk's template book, even after he flips a page.

Sorry to point this out, but Spike's "nooner" with Harmony entails... not a "wardrobe malfunction" exactly, but certainly some oddball "wardrobe mechanics." It's obvious that they're rutting like weasels in heat before the commercial break, yet after Harmony bites Spike, he rears back and his pants are curiously still on – shirt tucked in and all – even though he had no time to "rearrange" himself. The fool wasn't doing his duty with *only* his zipper down, was he? (And see **The Lore**.)

IT'S REALLY ABOUT... Over-confidence, the sort that allows an underdog to win. We already covered why Spike bests Angel, but on screen, it looks at times as if Angel can't conceive of Spike scoring a victory over him. The way Angel saunters, not dashes, toward the supposed "Cup of Torment" pretty much says it all.

CRITIQUE Science-fiction fans often muse over certain "burning questions" such as "What if the *Enterprise* took on a Star Destroyer?" and so forth. And in the *Angel*-verse, dating all the way back to *Buffy* Season Two, viewers have asked themselves, "What if Angel and Spike beat the shit out of each other?" Unbelievably, "Destiny" actually tackles this legendary question head-on, and the result...

... well, without over-stating the point, the result is not just the best Season Five story so far, but probably the most satisfying one-on-one battle in the whole damn Whedon-verse. Extremely well-written, directed and enacted by two lead actors who are accomplished at stage fighting – meaning it's gotten harder to identify Boreanaz and Marsters' stunt-doubles – this episode is a shameless but deeply satisfying attempt to let the hardcore faithful know how much the producers love them. That approach can certainly backfire, but in *this* case, the long-term viewers get served what's just about the juiciest and most succulent piece of meat possible. Better still, the actual Angel-Spike brawl entails precisely the sort of cutting dialogue one might hope for (Angel: "Buffy never really loved you... because you weren't me." Spike: "Guess that means she was thinking about you... all those times I was puttin' it to her.") And as with "Lineage," it's funnier than you might suspect (such as the word TONER being wall-scrawled in blood as the firm devolves into chaos), given all the A-level drama.

Call it wish fulfillment or (arrrg, if you must) "a love letter to the fans," but this entire endeavor comes off beautifully, albeit in a wonderfully twisted sort of way. Indeed, the only danger here is in Spike upstaging Angel *too* much. But hell... it's Angel's show, so you know the title character's going to get back in the game. And rightfully so.

THE LORE Mutant Enemy had long suffered from "spoiler whores" (persons who hope to unveil confidential information about a show well before broadcast). Thus, keeping Lindsey's return secret was given top priority, and the final scene between him and Eve didn't appear in the script. The cast nonetheless sensed that "a big reveal" was in progress, and everyone started tossing out crazy ideas. Thompson learned the truth when a confidential envelope showed up at her trailer with the missing scene. (O'Hare, *Zap2It.com*, Dec. 31, 2003) Kane subsequently arrived very early in the morning and filmed this bit with a second unit – at this point, only a select few were in the know. (*Boston Herald*, Jan. 21, 2004)

However... Lindsey later appeared with Spike in the bar scene for 5.10, "Soul Purpose," and it's here that, with hindsight, Whedon realized he'd blundered. The scene was rife with extras, many of whom would've plainly seen Marsters and Kane together. Producers hold little leverage over extras once filming concludes, so news of Kane's appearance soon hit the Internet. Whedon expressed sorrow over the disclosure, claiming: "They beat me up, they took my lunch money." He also lamented the apparent death of TV's ability to surprise the viewer, stating, "[Surprise] makes you humble. It makes you small in the world, and takes you out of your own perspective. It shows you that you're wrong, the world is bigger and more complicated than you'd imagined. The more we dilute that with insider knowledge, previews that show too much, spoilers and making-of specials, the more we're robbing ourselves of something we essentially need."

However, he also acknowledged, "The only way to rid yourself of spoilers is to try to make work that people are not interested in, and that's not a method I'm going to try." (Nussbaum, *The New York Times*, May 9, 2004)

• Denisof was off getting married to Alyson Hannigan during filming of this story, hence Wesley's absence.

• The Parents Television Council – the conservative group that seems to file the overwhelming majority of FCC complaints – registered an indecency complaint against this episode's vampire sex scenes. Of some amusement, the complaint recognized that Spike and Harmony appeared to be going at it with their clothes on, yet cited "heavy breathing" as among the scene's unsavory elements. After the usual red tape, the FCC dismissed the complaint in February 2005.

While we're on the topic... *Angel* sometimes ranked on the Council's "Top 10 Worst" shows list – something compiled (theoretically) with an eye toward family viewing potential and hour of broadcast, not an absolute indication of a show's quality. *Angel* didn't rank for Season One, hit No. 8 for Season Two, fell off entirely for Season Three and achieved No. 6 for Season Four (Cordelia's sleeping with Connor – not to mention Wesley and Lilah's shenanigans – probably didn't help matters). *Angel* Season Five (somewhat surprisingly, given the complaint against "Destiny," etc.) failed to register at all.

By comparison, *Buffy* hit the list three years running... ranking No. 4 for Season Four, No. 3 for Season Five and a triumphant No. 1 for Season Six (largely due to all the sex scenes with Spike, it seems).

• Spike and Harmony's coupling wasn't anything new to McNab, as her first sex scene – as she mentioned in an *FHM* interview – had been with Marsters on *Buffy*: "All I had were Band-Aid-sized pasties and a really thin, sheer G-string. The crew normally doesn't hang out for those scenes, but everyone seemed to be needed right behind the camera. I just found out that James is 41. I had no idea. I was like 17 when we started fooling around on the show. Jailbait."

• It's about this point that Whedon whimsically commented: "I think what this show really needs is a redhead. For me, it's becoming personally offensive that we aren't representing that group. There's only one redhead in Hollywood, so naturally they should hire my wife. I just can't believe there hasn't been an organized movement." (Veitch, *E! Online: Watch With Kristin*, Dec. 12, 2003)

• Character actor Michael Halsey (Sirk) pretty much logged an appearance on every major show in the 1980s – everything from *Moonlighting* to *The Dukes of Hazzard*. Entertainingly, he portrayed the "Fairy Prince" in an episode of *Are You Being Served?* And if you're into *Blake's 7*, he's Blake's well-intentioned attorney – the one who's murdered in the first episode – and has a bit part in the story "Gambit."

5.09: "Harm's Way"

"Since I got vamped at my graduation, I've had trouble connecting with people."

Air Date: Jan. 14, 2004; **Writers:** Elizabeth Craft, Sarah Fain; **Director:** Vern Gillium

SUMMARY As the firm hosts a summit between two feuding demon clans, Harmony flirts with a random guy in a bar. Unfortunately, a befuddled Harmony awakens the next morning... to find the man naked and dead, with telltale vampire teeth-marks on his neck, in her bed. Harm worries about being staked for violating the firm's "Don't Kill Humans" policy, and worse, the dead man was Tobias Dupree – the head negotiator between the warring clans.

The negotiations fall into in disarray, but Harmony learns the vampire Tamika – a member of the steno pool – framed her. Tamika admits to being jealous because Harmony got picked as Angel's secretary, then dukes it out with her. Harmony stakes her rival, inadvertently "offering her as a sacrifice" to the feuding clans. This pleases the representatives, and negotiations continue. Angel learns of the frame job and opts to overlook Harmony's actions.

POINTS OF DISCUSSION ABOUT "Harm's Way":

1. In order for this episode to spotlight Harmony, Spike's actions – however you parse them – become rather spurious. Now corporeal, he sets off to find Buffy, only to return at story's end after essentially deciding that he'd never top his "grand sacrifice" (*Buffy* 7.22, "Chosen") if he suddenly turned up on her doorstep alive. This partly serves to keep Spike in L.A., but it also removes any possibility of Harmony turning to him for help. Hard to see how Spike could involve himself here without Harmony getting relegated to the role of sidekick, so you can see why he's made to shuffle off for a while.

2. On the topic of Buffy, Spike states: "A man can't go out in a bloody blaze of glory... then show up three months later, tumbling off a cruise ship in the south of France." Some have wondered why Spike thinks Buffy is in France, considering she's obviously in Rome come 5.20, "The Girl in Question." (Angel, let's not forget, merely said Buffy was "in Europe" in 5.02, "Just Rewards.") There's some wiggle room, however. Either Spike is generalizing and plans to *arrive* in France, then proceed to Rome, or perhaps a jealous Angel simply fed Spike bad intel. (Oh, c'mon... it'd be just like "petty Angel" to do something like that.)

3. Angel and Spike sport bruises, and we're meant to infer that they *so* beat the shit out of each other last episode, it's taking them longer to heal. The point is debatable, though, because in every other respect, the firm doesn't look like it's recently weathered a bout of employee madness and mayhem.

4. To review, Angel enforces the "no-kill policy" by, er, decapitating any employee who violates it. Perhaps he should advertise the slogan: "Nobody in this office gets away with murder... unless it's me."

CHARACTER NOTES *Angel:* Drinks from a mug that reads "No. 1 Boss." The cleaners can't remove the "Frophla slime" from one of his outfits. He tries to learn the demon languages spoken at the summit, fails miserably and gets called a "filthy man whore" for his efforts. He offers Spike a set of wheels, so long as he doesn't take Angel's Viper. [Spike naturally decides to nick the car anyway, but we're never told if he actually does.] Angel says Harmony could've talked to him about the "dead man in her bed" issue. [Who does he think he's fooling? He would've dusted her in two seconds flat.]

• *Spike:* Affectionate toward Fred because she labored to help him re-corporealize – and believed in him, too.

• *Wesley:* Currently the most unshaven he's been in eons. [See **The Lore** under 5.07, "Lineage".] The office rumor-mill appears to think that Wesley is gay.

• *Gunn:* Got command of a few demon languages with his "lawyer-upgrade."

• *Fred:* Somewhat forced to go out for drinks with Harmony, but enjoys the experience. [There's no evidence of Fred having any other girlfriends, but it's funny how she's assigned to sympathize with inhuman characters this season. First Spike, then Harmony. It makes sense, though, because Fred is probably the only cast-member with patience for either of them.] Fred suggests that in future, she and Harmony should grab some wine and jam to the Dixie Chicks. [But they apparently never do, judging by 5.16, "Shells."]

Fred is sick of Thai food, drinks white wine [according to the script], and acknowledges to Harmony that her romantic options boil down to Knox and Wesley. She's seen conducting a post-mortem on Dupree.

• *Lorne:* Has an assistant named Dan, whom he calls "Dandito" or "Dan the man." [He's mentioned again in 5.11, "Damage," but doesn't re-appear.] Shaq [meaning Shaquille O'Neal] sends Lorne muffins, but Lorne has declared his office a carb-free zone and eats a protein snack instead. [Is he on the Atkins Diet?]

• *Harmony*: [Side note to say that it's never clear how Harmony gets to work in the morning. Perhaps as Angel's assistant, she qualifies for a car with necro-tempered glass.] Harmony confirms that she was vamped at her high school graduation [3.22, "Graduation Day," which removes some ambiguity on the point in *Buffy* Season Four]. She was in the steno pool [prior to becoming Angel's assistant, 5.01, "Conviction"] for "four and a half weeks," and says she hasn't consumed human blood in eight months. [This is a little hard to reconcile against Spike's statement that "Chosen" was only three months ago.]

Harmony sometimes sleeps in a blue nightie, usually gets up [or "rises," if you prefer] at 7 am and brushes both her human and vampire teeth. [It's impressive, by the way, how she does her make-up and hair without benefit of a reflection.] She owns a stuffed horse and zebras. Harm appears to have a third floor apartment, and is neighbors with an older woman named Mrs. Jacobi – whose dog always barks at Harmony [either because she's a vampire, or the pooch just doesn't like her]. Harmony doesn't have any friends at the firm, but can't quit because she doesn't know where else to go. She offers to teach Fred better dress sense if Fred teaches her about life. [Unsurprisingly, the *Sunnydale High Yearbook* features Harmony doling out fashion advice.] She appears to drink a margarita, later has something with a lime in it, and curses the intoxicating effects of lemon drops. She wears Chanel and is fiercely protective of her desk unicorns.

• *Tobias Dupree:* Hails from the Bay Area; works as a "demon rights activist." [An odd profession, but then, an ethnodemonologist – meaning an expert on demon culture – appeared in 1.07, "The Bachelor Party."]

• *Tamika:* Spent five years in the firm's steno pool, sat next to Harmony while there, and can type 80 words a minute. Her bite marks on Dupree are 17 mm apart, 6 mm deep.

ORGANIZATIONS *Wolfram and Hart:* In accordance with the firm's new zero-tolerance, "don't kill anyone" policy, Angel beheads Eli – a demonic member of Accounts, who was dismembering virgins for his own amusement. [It's never specified if a fully human employee would warrant the same penalty, but presumably so. The heroes certainly haven't been above killing humans this season, and such a "don't kill people" rule is worthless without the will to enforce it.] The firm now mandates random blood-tests of its vampire employees, the results are transmitted to Fred's lab [presumably to confirm the data before Angel or company security is alerted]. Rudy, an employee with a six-year-old boy at home, conducts such tests.

An employee-training video touts Wolfram and Hart as "the oldest and most powerful law firm" in L.A., founded in 1791 on ground deconsecrated by the blood of Matthias Pavayne. [5.04, "Hell Bound." There were only 600 people living in L.A. at the time, and it was in Mexico.] The firm owns the LAPD, apparently. [This potentially causes all manner of continuity glitches with previous stories, but it's far, far too open-ended an issue to properly tackle.] Dave Griffin is one of the firm's contacts there.

The firm is affiliated in some fashion with News Corp. [the parent company of 20th Century Fox, which owns *Angel* and *Buffy*], Yoyodyne [featured in *The Adventures of Buckaroo Banzai*, but taken from Thomas Pynchon's books *V* (1963) and *The Crying of Lot 49* (1966)] and Weyland-Yutani [the evil corporation from the *Alien* films; Whedon wrote the fourth one, and the Weyland-Yutani logo is also seen on *Firefly*]. A "Mistress Shriva" works in Non-Human Resources. For Curses [presumably its own department], phone extension 529.

DEMONOLOGY *Vampires:* Human blood takes about two days to purge from a vampire's system [or at least, that's the duration of time until the firm's tests become valid again]. Harmony suggests that vamps refer to non-vamps as "straight." [Mind, she's the only character who ever uses the term.] She also implies that some vamps are "right-biters vs. left-biters." [Again, she's probably just being "cute," not to mention grasping for any justification – given the state of Dupree's corpse – as to why Angel shouldn't stake her.] Harmony doesn't taste the human blood that Tamika adds to her thermos. [That's consistent with 3.16, "Sleep Tight," in which Angel doesn't register that he's been drinking Connor's blood.]

• *Vinjis and the Sahrvin:* Notoriously vicious, rival demon groups who've duked it out for five generations. Before that, they shared a few hundred miles of desert, traded livestock and even partied together until a Vinji used the wrong fork at a Sahrvin bonding ceremony. [Forks are apparently important in demon-customs, as with "The Bachelor Party."] The Sahrvins took offense, leading to continual slaughter ever since.

The Vinjis seem like an all-female clan, not all that bad looking despite their demonic features. By comparison, the Sahrvin are ugly males with facial spikes, goiters and sores. Both groups prize manners – gazing at a Vinji's ankles, for instance, can lead to eye-gouging. However, both camps have agreed to a truce as negotiated by Dupree – the only party they trust. None of the negotiators speak English; the Vinjis communicate with a combination of clicks [rather like the Nahdrah demons from 3.12, "Provider"] and screaming.

Harmony's research indicates that the Vinjis and the Sahvrin think poodles are bad luck, and that they consume camel meat as a delicacy/comfort food. She orders a live camel for the conference, and says that as host, Angel will have the honor of slicing off the camel's hump and sticking a hot poker through its heart, even as demon leaders rip apart its carcass with their bare hands. Angel vetoes the idea. [Harmony says the caterer won't accept returns, but there's later an X next to "Return Camel" on her To-Do list. Actually, the remarkable thing is that Harmony tracked down a caterer in L.A. who supplies live camels. By the way, the Sahvrin reappear in the series' final two episodes.]

BEST LINE Fred, making the best of Harmony's blunder regarding the conference food: "Angel's just feeling a little... off. And he's not in the mood to – y'know – butcher a camel."

THINGS THAT DON'T MAKE SENSE Pursuant to the huge number of enemies who'd love to use the will-sapping staff from 5.07, "Lineage," Angel's personal blood supply is kept in a communal refrigerator where virtually anyone with a hidden agenda can taint or poison it. For that matter, you'd think that Harmony – as the C.E.O.'s assistant – might warrant a small private fridge and microwave, but *her* blood-filled thermos is readily accessible for Tamika to lace with human blood.

By now, the heroes' "employee-screening" protocols don't seem worth toffee, as Tamika hatches a plot against Angel's personal assistant without – oh, say – Lorne "reading" her and sensing that something is awry. And as Tamika killed Dupree herself, it's a puzzler how she planned to avoid the random blood tests over the next couple days. Also, what does Tamika mean when she says she "broke into" Harmony's apartment in order to kill Dupree... wouldn't this damage Harmony's front door, or one of her windows, in a fashion that Harm would notice in the morning? It's also remarkably convenient that the science lab empties out just before Harm needs to punch Fred's lights out, and that she can haul Fred's carcass into a storage closet without anyone noticing. Also, Rudy and Lorne aren't duct-taped when Harmony knocks them out and tosses them into the closet, yet they're hog-tied when she dumps Fred in there. Did she go back to bind them?

Harmony's "To Do at Demon Summit" list radically changes between cuts of the camera. It starts out headlined in big, friendly bubble letters, then becomes more Spartan-looking in close-up. Oh, and actor Bryce Mouer, as the dead Dupree, doesn't make a very good stiff while in Fred's lab... his eyes flicker, both in long-shot and close-up.

CRITIQUE For some viewers, this episode doesn't go down well for a couple of reasons. For one, it's a comedy story and requires something of a downshift after the balls-to-the-wall "Lineage" and "Destiny." It also didn't help that on original broadcast, "Harm's Way" went out after the Christmas hiatus, meaning it must've seemed disappointing for anyone eager to see direct progress on the main storyline. (By contrast, the after-hiatus story last season was "Habeas Corpses," in which the Beast instigated his jaw-dropping slaughter of the running villains.)

Taken on its own merits, however... it's quite the fun-filled story, good for some laughs, and one that makes you feel duly sympathetic for Harmony. The first act admittedly crawls a bit, but everything gets rolling after that, and the part where Harmony and Tamika duel with chopsticks (shades of the Harmony-Xander sissy-fight in *Buffy* Season Four) is really lovely. Okay, it's not a laugh-riot like "Smile Time" (5.14), but it's entertaining in its own way, and certainly a neat vehicle to spotlight Mercedes McNab. With that understanding, we can't help but get a warm feeling for this episode.

THE LORE Prior to Season Five, McNab was in the process of moving to New York City – among other things, she dreamed about being on *Law and Order*, her favorite show, even if it meant playing the inevitable dead body in the teaser. When Whedon phoned, McNab immediately sensed that something was up, because he'd never called her personally in all the years they'd worked together. Whedon inquired about McNab's availability, floating the possibility of Harmony joining *Angel*. McNab mentioned her oncoming move, and asked Whedon to let her know when he was a bit more certain. She took off for New York two days later, and the *Angel* office rung her up a month afterward to seal the deal, then ask her to relocate back to Los Angeles. (O'Hare, *Zap2It.com*, Oct. 18, 2003; Eramo, *Xpose* #81, Nov. 2003)

• Fury called dibs on writing Harmony episodes (he'd previously authored 2.17, "Disharmony"), but he was busy writing "You're Welcome" (5.12), so the task of writing a Harmony piece fell to Fain and Craft. They'd never done straight-out comedy, but focused on the notion that Harm just wasn't very good at being evil, and mainly wanted to fit in. The blood-test element decently pleased them, because it explained how Harmony had been clean the last few months. (DiLullo, *CityofAngel.com*)

• The script fails to mention the "training video" that opens this story, suggesting that – as with "Unleashed" (5.03) – Fain and Craft ran short on time, necessitating its inclusion as filler.

• As this book went to press, McNab became the second *Angel* actress to grace the cover of *Playboy* (the Nov. 2006 issue, if you're interested).

• Squee if you're prone to that sort of thing... McNab and Marsters had a single date during their *Buffy* days, but quickly decided they were better off as friends. (O'Hare, *Zap2It.com*, Oct. 18, 2003)

• Danielle Nicolet (Tamika) had a recurring role on *3rd Rock from the Sun* as Caryn, one of John Lithgow's students. In the *Stargate SG-1* story "Menace," she's the android girl (Reese) who's responsible for the creation of the Replicants – those seemingly indomitable metallic spiders. Best of all, in the 1996 movie *The Prince*, she appears as a "High Class Hooker."

5.10: "Soul Purpose"

"A vigilante killed two vampires, then asked the women he saved if they'd like to get a bottle of hooch and listen to some Sex Pistols records with him."

Air Date: Jan. 21, 2004; **Writer:** Brent Fletcher; **Director:** David Boreanaz

SUMMARY Lindsey introduces himself to Spike as "Doyle" – a visionary for the Powers – and who's been assigned to fashion Spike into a champion for the helpless. Directed by "Doyle's visions," Spike starts saving innocents from vampire attacks, etc. Meanwhile, Eve uses a demon-parasite slug to wrack Angel with surreal nightmares, capitalizing on his self-doubt. Lindsey directs Spike to kill the parasite, hoping to further erode Angel's self-confidence and make him fear that Spike has replaced him as a hero. However, Angel hazily recalls Eve placing the parasite on him, viewing her as more dangerous than ever.

FIRSTS AND LASTS First appearance of Spike's apartment, as provided by Lindsey.

POINTS OF DISCUSSION ABOUT "Soul Purpose":

1. Funny how much unintentional homoerotic tension is prevalent in this episode, provided one chooses to notice it. To wit, Wesley and Gunn squabble in front of Angel as if they need to get a room, Spike throws Lindsey up against wall in a very manly fashion, and when dream-Angel says to dream-Spike, "You're taking Buffy to the prom? I thought we were going to...", it almost sounds as if Angel was attending prom with *Spike*, not the Slayer.

2. Bits of continuity-business... during the aforementioned dream sequence (in which you can't actually see Buffy's face), the Slayer randomly says, "Can you say 'jumping the gun'? I kill my goldfish" and "Every time I say the word 'prom,' you get grouchy." The lines are respectively recycled from *Buffy* 2.12, "Bad Eggs" and 3.20 "The Prom." (And by the way, the former line was originally said in context of Buffy being totally unprepared to have children.)

CHARACTER NOTES *Angel:* Noteworthy bits of Angel's dream-delusions... Spike thrashes Angel and claims the Cup of Perpetual Torment [5.08, "Destiny"]... Spike saves the world, and a "Blue Fairy" makes him human while everyone celebrates; Angel slinks off, serving as the office mail-boy [see 5.06, "The Cautionary Tale of Numero Cinco"]... Angel finds himself unable to sing while his friends watch and Lorne plays piano... Angel relaxes in a recliner in a sunny field... Fred "autopsies" the still-alive Angel, pulling out various items such as his kidneys, a license plate [HUZ 332], a goldfish bowl and his heart. ["It *is* a dried-up little walnut," she says... see "The Cautionary Tale of Numero Cinco" for more heart-metaphors.]

• *Spike:* Appears to have little money at present. [He was basically broke in *Buffy* Season Four, and hasn't enjoyed a real income since then.] Under Lindsey's direction, Spike essentially fulfills the heroic street-fighter role that Angel served in Season One. He genuinely seems to gain some purpose from these missions [even if Lindsey surely prearranges many – if not all – of these "saves"].

Spike likes Brockman beer. He drinks at a bar called The Peppermint Stick, and watches a dancer there named "Sunshine." Spike's apartment has a sewer entrance for daytime travel, and a 24-hour Korean market on the corner.

• *Wesley:* Upon learning of Spike's vigilante activities, Wesley and Gunn privately approach him with an offer to "make him part of their team," and use the firm's resources to aid his efforts. They make this offer without Angel's knowledge. [It's not explicitly said why Wes and Gunn avoid telling him. Possibly they're worried that Angel already has enough insecurity where Spike is concerned, and would become unsettled to hear that Spike has taken up the heroic torch. (Although how they expect that Angel won't hear about Spike's vigilantism remains anyone's guess.) Or possibly they just deem Spike as too useful to let Angel veto the idea of bringing him onboard.] Spike declines the offer, insisting that the firm will change the heroes, not vice versa.

• *Eve:* Asks Wesley, then Fred, to examine the markings on a rock fragment that the Senior Partners are "very interested" in. [Eve tells Lindsey that the Partners' interest here is genuine, so the rock isn't simply a means of keeping the heroes distracted from Angel's plight with the parasite. Yet we're never told why the item is so important... see **The Critique**.]

• *Harmony*: Reads *Trendy* magazine, and gets the term "Machiavelli" confused with Prince Matchabelli, a perfume. She "accidentally" authorized a few "Bath of the Month" subscriptions, and now isn't allowed to talk to Accounts without Angel's approval. She's supposed to directly report anything pertaining to the Senior Partners – or anything bearing runes – to Angel. And she's not to read the runes herself, because that could start a fire. [A sensible precaution, if you recall Xander accidentally setting one of Giles' magic books alight, *Buffy* 4.17, "Superstar."]

• *Lindsey:* His tattoos [seen in "Destiny"] keep the firm – and more importantly, the Senior Partners – from detecting him. Lindsey admits to having sent Spike's amulet back to the firm [5.01, "Conviction"] and to having mailed the package that recorporealized him ["Destiny"].

• *Lucien Drake:* Evil warlock and cult leader, with over a thousand followers. Gunn suggests the followers exchanged their children for "some serious demonic mojo" [presumably on Drake's behalf]. Drake's group has been stockpiling highly dangerous weapons and black magics. Wesley advocates assassinating Drake before he and his followers go underground; Gunn favors convincing one of Drake's initiates to overthrow him. [We never learn the outcome of this... see **The Critique**.]

ORGANIZATIONS *Wolfram and Hart:* The firm has a satellite fitted with an orbital-range microwave cannon; this focuses the satellite's communication signals into a pinpoint beam. Fred believes that cannon could be used to untraceably raise the temperature of a target area by 1,000 degrees in less than five seconds. Such a beam, she says, would be untraceable because it'd register on most atmospheric scanners as simple cell phone static. [This cumulatively sounds so unbearably stupid, we can scarcely bear to think of it... see **Things That Don't Make Sense**.]

Wesley and Gunn locate Spike use a couple of the firm's psychics [but they don't sense Lindsey's involvement – naturally enough, given his tattoos].

DEMONOLOGY *Selminth Parasite:* Parasitic slug-creature that pumps an anesthetic and neurotoxins into its victims, paralyzing them while triggering hallucinations and fever dreams. The parasites can affect vampires, and – given enough time – could have put Angel into a permanent vegetative state.

BEST LINE Dream-Fred pulls a goldfish bowl out of Angel's chest cavity, hands it to an attending bear and says, "Thank you, Bear." (It's not much on paper, but it sounds really sweet on screen.)

THINGS THAT DON'T MAKE SENSE Two episodes ago, Lindsey and Eve adeptly put Angel's house into disarray. So it's bewildering when in this story, their entire scheme is designed to do simply, er, throw Angel a *little more* off-balance – even though it carries the tangible risk that Eve will come under suspicion (which she does). In other words, their plan carries such high risk for so little gain, it's barely worthy of them. Oh, and that's ignoring the point that if the mind-parasite just needed more time to put Angel into a permanent vegetative state, why didn't they let it do precisely that – thus neutralizing Angel entirely – rather than sending in Spike to squash the critter?

Also, Eve pretends to be part of Angel's dream, drops the parasite-bug on him and later changes her clothes in the hopes of suggesting that Angel confused fantasy with reality. Well, okay, except that she lets the others *see* her in both sets of clothes, enabling Fred to channel Miss Marple and expose her treachery, especially as Eve forgot to change her earrings. Wouldn't it have been smarter to change clothes (and earrings), drop the bug on Angel and change back again without anyone noticing?

Given every previous aberration in Angel's energy levels over the past few years (Darla's dream-assault in Season Two, etc.), his abnormal fatigue should throw up all manner of red flags, yet nobody gets very concerned about it. Also, Wesley and Gunn clearly go behind Angel's back in approaching Spike, so you'd think they'd treat the situation with some discretion. Yet nobody protests when Fred comes bouncing up in the lobby and asks, for benefit of anyone who might overhear, "Did you talk to Spike?"

As for that satellite that's allegedly capable of firing off death-rays... well in the first place, if the firm *does* own such a device, it's rather astonishing that this formidable piece of hardware is never mentioned again. Not even when – oh, say – it could have eliminated the threat of Illyria's demon horde overrunning the world (5.16, "Shells"). Nor, for that matter, do the Senior Partners issue orders for its deployment against Angel come the series finale, even though it'd make quick work of the Hyperion's back alley. But really, the whole *idea* of the satellite is simply ludicrous, partly because – even if it *can* be deployed "untraceably" from orbit – what kind of *amazing* pinpoint targeting is required here? Enough to – say – fry a limo with the warlock inside? Because otherwise, Wes and company would probably have to settle for liquefying an entire building, and *that* much instantaneous devastation could touch off an international crisis, "invisible" death-rays or no. Moreover, it's played as if the satellite's "microwave cannon" is basically a glorified cell phone, and the fact that it can obliterate selected target areas is almost an optional feature.

Do we *really* need to point out the inherent folly in Lindsey picking "Doyle" as his cover identity with Spike? Points for irony, but given the circles in which Spike travels, even the moniker "Hermann Göring" is likely to raise less suspicion. Ergo, it's astonishing that Lindsey – who's found out in 5.12, "You're Welcome" – isn't exposed two episodes sooner. Why on *Earth* didn't he just call himself "Ralph"?

POP CULTURE Spike refers to Gunn and Wesley as "Crockett and Tubbs," meaning the police detectives from *Miami Vice*. Also, the license plate that Fred fishes out of Angel's chest – and her line that, "Hmmmm... came up the Gulf Stream, huh?" – stems from Richard Dreyfuss similarly pulling a Flordia license plate out of a shark's stomach in *Jaws*.

IN RETROSPECT Dream-Fred, wrapping up her "autopsy" of Angel: "There's nothing left, just a shell." It's unfortunate wording, considering what's in store for Fred five episodes from now.

CRITIQUE This late in the game, and after such stunning fare as "Lineage" and "Destiny," it's honestly hard to fathom how Mutant Enemy produced a story this hollow. The main storyline, in short, boils down to the villains using a mind-parasite to give Angel weird dreams. Setting aside that this sort of thing has been to death in science fiction about 273 times, the dream-images in question are so incredibly obvious as to be downright boring. As they don't mean anything beyond the surface-level – or say anything that hasn't been said on a myriad of occasions (such as, gee, the idea that Angel craves sunlight) – the dream-sequences can only hope to look a little strange, and it's not enough. Even the episode of *Star Trek: The Next Generation* where Troi appears as a "cellular peptide" cake seemed more interesting than this.

Moreover, it's amazing how nearly every other plot-thread disappears down a black hole, with no sense of development or payoff. To wit: Wes and Gunn go behind Angel's back to offer Spike a job... Wes and Gunn dither about a malevolent warlock... Eve wants Fred to study an artifact... yadda yadda yadda... and *none* of this goes anywhere. Painfully, it looks as if Brent Fletcher got handed this episode as a punt while the other writers were busy with stuff of actual importance. Maybe that's unfair, but you'd hope an explanation exists for how something this inconsequential got made.

Also, and we genuinely feel a sense of regret in saying this, Boreanaz's directing doesn't help matters. We totally adore Boreanaz as Angel and absolutely wouldn't dream of seeing anyone else in the role, but his work as a one-time-only director is decidedly mechanical, and he milks some of the worst performances in the show's history out of himself and the normally dazzling regulars. For the first time in possibly ever, Acker, Kane and Boreanaz himself all seem terribly limp; Denisof and Richards try their best but simply have too little to do; and the only performer who seems 100 percent committed is Marsters – and he can't carry the entire episode.

At the end of the day, we could forgive "The Cautionary Tale of Numero Cinco" (5.06), just a little, because it was trying to do something different. Ditto when we get to 5.13, "Why We Fight." Unfortunately, "Soul Purpose" doesn't even look as if it's trying, and you seriously have to wonder why everyone involved even bothered. In fact, the only good news is that it's the last *Angel* story that's truly this pointless, so we mercifully won't see the likes of it again.

THE LORE Boreanaz was undergoing knee surgery during this period, so "Soul Purpose" was viewed as a means of Angel staying off his legs for a while. (It could, in fact, explain some of the script's inadequacies, if it was largely conceived as a solution to an actor's problem.) Boreanaz was slated to direct episode seven, then was switched to episode ten once the producers realized that episodes seven and eight were a bit complicated, with the latter requiring huge amounts of fighting between Angel and Spike. (Spelling, *Dreamwatch* #110, Nov. 2003)

• Kane, realizing his character had gotten thrashed by Darla, etc., had requested that Lindsey "not get beat up by chicks anymore." He amended this upon learning that Boreanaz – his old drinking pal – was going to direct, and claims he would've done taken part even if every female present had gotten to knock him about the place. (O'Hare, *Zap2It.com*, Jan. 5, 2004)

• Carmen Nicole (Lana, a pedestrian fleeing from vampires) also hosted the Game Show Network's *Video Games* – the series didn't last long, but marked the end of GSN's exclusive focus on game shows.

5.11: "Damage"

"Gather round, and attend to a most unusual tale. A tale I like to call: The Slayer of the Vampyrs."

Air Date: Jan. 28, 2004; **Writers:** Steven S. DeKnight, Drew Goddard; **Director:** Jefferson Kibbe

SUMMARY A super-strong patient named Dana escapes from an asylum. Angel's team identifies Dana as a Vampire Slayer (owing to events in *Buffy* 7.22, "Chosen") and phone Giles for help. In response, Giles dispatches one of Spike's Sunnydale associates, Andrew, to advise on Dana's capture.

The heroes find Dana was tortured as a 10-year-old, and has become psychotic as she's unable to process the violent dreams she's witnessing as part of her Slayer lineage. Spike insists on going after Dana alone, but the demented Slayer wrongly identifies Spike as the man who physically abused her years ago. Dana hacks off Spike's hands, but Angel's team finally subdues her.

Andrew demands to take charge of Dana, with 12 Slayers stepping from the shadows as his muscle. Angel gives Dana over to Andrew's group, haunted by Andrew's words that Buffy's camp – Buffy included – no longer trusts him because he works for Wolfram and Hart. The firm's shamans re-attach Spike's hands, leaving Spike troubled because while he didn't harm Dana as she believed, he's committed so many atrocities in past.

FIRSTS AND LASTS First of two appearances on *Angel* by Andrew, and the *Angel*-debut of a Slayer who's not Buffy or Faith. Oh, and it's the last occasion that somebody drops somebody else with a tranquilizer gun (it's Wesley, taking down Dana).

POINTS OF DISCUSSION ABOUT "Damage":

1. The story ends with Angel and Spike empathizing about their past crimes, and properly recognizing that they're in the same boat. Spike's encounter with Dana drives home all the people he savagely murdered and tortured. In turn, Angel concedes that Angelus couldn't take eyes off his victims, considered the destruction of a human being as "artistic" and was into the whole killing-thing not for survival, but for sadism. (And see 5.08, "Destiny" for how this affects Angel in the modern day.) This is more of a turning point than you might think, as it arrives so late in the episode. But the upshot is that from here, Angel and Spike act more like brothers and comrades than before and – petty bickering and a couple of bumps (such as 5.20, "The Girl in Question") aside – they'll march more in-step than would've previously been possible.

2. With *Buffy* off the air, any scrap of information about the Sunnydale characters seemed like manna from Heaven, so Andrew supplies a quick update. With hundreds, possibly thousands of Slayers dotting the globe after "Chosen" (and heavens, they'd be handy in the series finale, wouldn't they?), Giles and company have been rounding up and training the newly empowered girls. There's no talk of reviving the Watchers per se, but if Giles inherited the Watchers' Council's finances after its destruction (*Buffy* 7.09, "Never Leave Me"), it would certainly explain how the *Buffy* characters can afford such out-of-pocket travel and living expenses. After all, Buffy was sorely hurting for cash on her show, yet she and Dawn have somehow relocated to Rome, and Dawn is attending what's presumably a private school. None of this sounds cheap.

The *Buffy* crew is presently combing the globe for Slayers: Xander is in Africa and kindly sent Andrew an mbuna fish; Willow and Kennedy are in Brazil – they're based Sao Paulo, but in Rio every time Andrew speaks to them (mind, 5.16, "Shells" adds a footnote about Willow); Buffy has been recruiting Slayers in Europe; and Andrew mostly coordinates with Giles – both of them seem based in England.

3. This being a Goddard script, and given his aforementioned continuity-obsession, it's not surprising that the dream-influenced Dana burbles like Nikki (the 1970s Slayer) and the Chinese Slayer who served during the Boxer Rebellion, given that Spike killed both of them (*Buffy* 5.07, "Fool for Love"). Spike even tells Dana, "Sorry, don't speak Chinese, Love" – the same thing he told the Chinese Slayer before murdering her. Mind, in some regards, Goddard deserves credit for holding himself back – a cut bit of script had Angel and his comrades pouring through Dana's dream-influenced drawings, and claiming to have identified every Slayer depicted therein. One almost imagines that Goddard, in a perfect world, wanted to recite the entire list on screen.

4. Dana goes out of her way to steal a plaid shirt. Well, naturally. If vampires insist on wearing plaid as much as we suggested in "Calvary" (4.12), it stands to reason that her Slayer-dreams have her seeing little but plaid upon plaid upon plaid.

CHARACTER NOTES *Angel:* Speaks Romanian and has some knowledge of what constitutes a proper dose of medicine for institutionalized people. He goes with Gunn's suggestion that they shouldn't risk firing or confronting Eve just yet [but see next episode].

• *Spike:* Says he killed "hundreds of families" while soulless [that's probably more literal than not, given Spike's age], but also that he mainly did it for the rush, not as a means of glorifying evil. He asks Andrew not to tell Buffy's group that he's alive [but see "The Girl in Question"], and seems impressed that Andrew double-crossed them. Once Spike "locks" a scent, he can track his target for miles.

• *Gunn:* Dead certain that the heroes made the right choice coming to Wolfram and Hart. Gunn's "lawyer-upgrade" came with golfing skills [well, now we ***know*** it was evil], and he sometimes plays with the district attorney. Half of the firm's cases, apparently, get settled on the links. Gunn is presently arguing a case before Judge Braeden.

• *Fred:* Knows general details about the Slayers, and that cooking whiskey will make the room smell like molasses [see **The Lore**].

• *Andrew:* [Formerly one of the "evil nerds" from *Buffy* Season Six, but reformed in Season Seven.] Angel is informed that Giles is sending his "top guy," and Andrew shows up. [Oh honestly... some sources take the "top guy" description literally, but it's probably hyperbole, given Andrew's admittedly improved skill-level. He was probably assigned to collect Dana simply because he was in the area, hence his arrival at the firm in (more or less) the time it takes Angel and Spike to drive across town.]

Andrew's now decked out in a business suit, coughs while attempting to smoke a pipe, sees a therapist and thinks Spike has been brought back to life "more beautiful than ever." [Some take this as further confirmation that Andrew is gay – a notion repeatedly fronted on *Buffy* – although it's more likely that he's bisexual. See "The Girl in Question" for more.]

Andrew says that Giles has "been training" him, and that he's "82 percent more manly" than the last time Spike saw him. He's never tasted a penny, but does so here.

• *Dana:* Told by her Slayer-dreams to target a vampire's head or heart, yet cuts off Spike's hands because she "didn't want him to touch her." At story's end, Spike suspects that Dana's trauma has put her beyond saving.

Fifteen years ago, when Dana was ten, a man named Walter Kindel murdered her mother, father and baby sibling. [That makes Dana age 25 now, seemingly too old to get "called" as a Slayer. Then again, the cut-off point at which one stops being a Potential is never really specified, and if Willow's spell could zap a girl as young as the ball-player in "Chosen" with the Slayer-mojo, then we're dealing with some fairly wide parameters here. By the way, actress Navi Rawat was 26 when "Damage" was filmed.]

Kindel abducted Dana, and apparently tortured her for months. She was later found wandering the streets, barely functional, and was eventually institutionalized. Kindel died five years ago, shot by police while attempting to rob a liquor store.

Dana's childhood torture, combined with the Slayer-dreams, have left her – in general savagery and appearance (such as the blood smeared on her face) – akin to the First Slayer from *Buffy*. She can tap bits of memory from past Slayers (such as the two that Spike killed), and any languages they spoke. [The Slayer-dreams don't normally facilitate this, but Dana's psychosis presumably makes conscious what would normally remain subconscious.]

• *Vernon:* [Credited as "Vernon the Creepy Psychic."] Bald-shaven, robed gentleman who apparently does all of Tom Arnold's readings; Lorne recruits him to track down Dana. Vernon can pull psychic impressions from objects – such as houses, which according to Lorne "have long memories."

THE LIBRARY Wesley brushes up on his reading of demonic possessions [a wise move, after 1.14, "I've Got You Under My Skin"], which often entail multiple personalities.

ORGANIZATIONS *Wolfram and Hart:* Apparently doing flesh-surgery [2.18, "Dead End"] with parts from cadavers, not live victims. SWAT team members [presumably an offshoot of the commandoes last seen in 5.01, "Conviction"] here assist Angel and Wesley.

DEMONOLOGY Spike initially believes that Dana is "a Chinese demon... maybe a water dragon or one of those elemental thingies."

• *Vampires:* Angel and Lorne get a real estate agent to let them into Dana's childhood home, and Angel can walk inside. [This throws up all sorts of oddball questions about whether a duly empowered real-estate agent can grant an invitation. Fortunately, the house's ownership is never discussed, so the real estate company might actually own it.]

Spike notes that blood smells metallic – like a penny – to a vampire. Various drugs that Kindel used on his victims – here retrieved by Dana – also work on Spike. [As with 1.04, "I Fall to Pieces," we should presume that vampires' bodies contain enough blood for such drugs to take effect, even if their hearts aren't beating.]

• *The Slayers:* [Andrew recaps the Slayers' origin, but you can hardly watch *Buffy* without tripping over most of it. A side note, however: Andrew names the original Slayer as "the Primitive," when she's generally called "the First Slayer."] A 40 mg dose of Thorazine regularly keeps Dana – a Slayer – properly subdued. One of the Slayers that Dana imitates was Rumanian.

BEST LINE Andrew, praising Spike: "I see your senses seem to be as well-honed as your Viggo Mortensen pectorals."

THINGS THAT DON'T MAKE SENSE It's debatable whether the central pitfall in this story was avoidable – at least, not without *Angel* Season Five spending all of its time dealing with the repercussions of "Chosen." Specifically, the heroes now run Wolfram and Hart – one of the greatest intelligence-gathering sources in the world – yet they seem rather *surprised* when Andrew informs them that hundreds, more like thousands, of Slayers are now in the picture. How could they *not* know, given that legions of super-powered girls who've surely been popping up all over in the last few months? Angel knew some details about the climactic *Buffy* battle as early as "Just Rewards" (5.02), yet the "legions of Slayers" thing somehow escaped his notice. Never mind that Spike – who actually took part in that conflict – knew about the multiple Slayers, but a) never told Angel's group, and a) somehow thinks that Dana might be demonic as opposed to something rather more obvious.

Understanding the need to keep the *Buffy* cast separate from the *Angel* characters, it makes utterly no sense that Buffy now doesn't trust Angel because he works for the firm. After all, they've got years of experience together, their last meeting was perfectly cordial and Angel *did*, on that occasion, supply the all-important amulet that saved the entire Slayer line. Bearing that in mind, it's totally baffling that Buffy hasn't phoned Angel to say, "Thanks for totally saving our asses... what's up with you running an evil law firm?"

A lesser matter: It's arguably strange that Kindel's drugs – which Dana retrieves – are still potent after 15 years, but we can't really judge because the drugs are never named.

POP CULTURE Andrew makes some references to *Lord of the Rings* (Spike is "like Gandalf the White, resurrected from the pit of the Balrog," etc.), but we trust those are self-evident. Also, Andrew says the newly empowered Slayers are getting "the full *X-Men*, minus the crappy third act." He's denoting the original *X-Men* film, although this isn't the Whedon reference that some people pretend. Whedon worked on the project, but only two of his lines (Wolverine's "You're a dick" and Halle Barry's wildly over-acted bit about what happens to a toad when it's struck by lightning) survived the rewrite process.

IT'S REALLY ABOUT... Aside from the need to acknowledge the aftermath of the *Buffy* series – an issue that viewers continually raised in this period – it boils down to Angel and Spike recognizing Dana as an innocent person twisted into something truly horrible... as were they, once upon a time.

CRITIQUE It was a given that *Angel* would address the fallout from the *Buffy* finale at some point, but fortunately for all concerned, "Damage" does more than just check off an obligation. Tightly scripted, implemented with considerable mettle and simply *dripping* with malice, it's actually – and it's a little disturbing to say, given all the horrendous acts it renders – one of the more compelling stories from Season Five. In particular, the flashback scenes to Dana's childhood prove entirely harrowing – even though we don't *see* that much – and thus it's once again a case of *Angel* venturing into territory that *Buffy* probably wouldn't. Moreover, in contrast to the unconvincing doubt about Spike's intentions as pictured in "Just Rewards," "Damage" more plausibly suggests that he might have been the villain that Dana believes. Indeed, as the story drives home, he genuinely *was* that awful, just not with her.

If there's a regret, it's curiously enough down to continuity. Simply put, you can't get through this episode without pondering – or indeed, discussing over drinks afterward – the statements made about Buffy's crew in relation to the *Angel* status quo. This was almost guaranteed to be awkward, although in fairness, the producers only had so much room to maneuver. Still, if you *can* move beyond such matters, then within its own parameters, "Damage" proves as intriguing as almost any story in this period. Even Andrew's come a long away since *Buffy*, and neatly adds to the mix.

THE LORE By this point, the cast and crew were awfully fertile – Carpenter gave birth as Season Four production neared its end, Boreanaz's wife delivered a child in May 2002, and Whedon had become a father; he'd have a second child underway just after *Angel* folded. Acker was married, but she held off conceiving until after *Angel* wrapped and later delivered in January 2005. Richards realized that he now ranked amongst a dwindling number of unmarried and childless *Angel* people, and was more than happy to keep it that way. Hallett seemed even more vehement on the point: "There are so many people on this planet as it is, we don't need any more. And I can't make it to an appointment on time, so raise a child? I can't think of a worse punishment in the world." (Veitch, *E! Online: Watch With Kristin*, Feb. 6, 2004; Gill, *tve.co.il*)

• The script elaborated that Fred readily knew about the smell of molasses because her grandfather used to make hooch, and that's what whiskey smells like as you cook it. The best cut line from the script: Andrew describes the Potential Slayers as "young prepubescent nibbles." Oh, and the script called for Andrew to ponderously chew his pipe after his initial meeting with Angel – on screen, he's sucking a juice box.

• Tom Lenk (Andrew) made his motion picture debut in *Boogie Nights* as "Uncle Floyd's kid #1." He's also "Frodo Baggins" in the spoof *Date Movie* (2006), starring Alyson Hannigan. Navi Rawat (Dana) has recurring guest spots as Melanie on *24*; as the ex-girlfriend of the troubled Ryan on *The O.C.*; and as Amita Ramanujan, a resident math genius who helps with FBI work on *Numb3rs*.

5.12: "You're Welcome"

"Doyle pissed me off so righteously going out like that, but... he used his last breath to make sure you'd keep fighting. I get that now."

Air Date: Feb. 4, 2004; **Writer/Director:** David Fury

SUMMARY The heroes rejoice when the comatose Cordelia wakes up, but Cordy details a vision from the Powers that depicts strange tattoos. Cordelia helps Wesley identify the tattoos as Enochian protection runes, even as Lindsey – now threatened with discovery – pushes his plans into high gear.

Lindsey uses his runes/tattoos to shroud him from detection and infiltrates the firm. Reaching a containment cell in the firm's basement, Lindsey makes ready to free a shadowy creature (or creatures) that the Senior Partners installed as a failsafe against Angel if their deal went south. Cordelia restores the containment cell's integrity, even as Angel battles Lindsey and Wesley performs a ritual that dissipates Lindsey's tattoos. The Partners immediately register Lindsey's presence and suck him through a portal.

Cordelia later tells Angel that she can't stay, claiming the Powers owed her a favor that she used it to put Angel back on track. A confused Angel pauses to answer a phone call from the hospital, stunned to learn that Cordelia died in her sleep and never regained consciousness. Angel turns around to find Cordelia missing, then privately thanks her for helping him.

FIRSTS AND LASTS Quite a few "lasts" accompany this story... after seven years of screen-time, it's the final outing for Charisma Carpenter as Cordelia Chase. It's also the last image of Doyle (courtesy of Cordy re-playing the Angel Investigations commercial from 1.09, "Hero") and off screen, it's the last vision from the Powers-That-Be (see **Points of Discussion**). Also, it's technically the only time that the Senior Partners mystically intervene on screen, as they scoop up Lindsey like he was an action figure.

Style-wise, Angel's brawl with Lindsey in the containment chamber more or less constitutes the series' last "leaping about in a very *Matrix*-like fashion" battle. Final use of zombies in the series, although the undead commandoes standing guard over the containment chamber seem anti-climactic after the likes of "The Thin Dead Line" (2.14) and "Habeas Corpses" (4.08).

Second and last time Cordelia references "Bizarro world" (the first was *Buffy* 2.05, "Reptile Boy"). One first appearance, though: Angel's racquetball partner, the red-skinned demon Izzerial, a.k.a. "Izzy" (although he isn't named until the series finale).

POINTS OF DISCUSSION ABOUT "You're Welcome":

1. Let's backtrack and ask a simple question: Why, exactly, do the Powers awaken Cordelia *now*? It's never stated, but it's possible that Cordelia's impending death triggers the events seen here. One interpretation is that Cordy actually "dies" right before the story begins – meaning her soul departs for the great beyond – but her spirit then encounters the Powers and "cycles" back to Earth, whereupon she's gifted with a new-yet-temporary body for the duration of this episode. Funnily enough, this would explain why Cordelia has "a roommate" in the hospital – we're speaking of the bed-ridden figure about whom Cordy comments, "Yeah, that chick's in rough shape," before pulling a curtain around the figure in question. Considering the firm is surely footing the hospital bill, some fans have wondered why Cordelia didn't warrant her own room, failing to consider that the "person" Cordelia covers up is actually *her* body, albeit shrouded from Angel and Wesley's perceptions. Well, it's possible. We never see the bed-ridden person's face, after all. Cordelia must then hang around in her Powers-given form a little while after her physical body passes on, hence her being present, and disappearing, when Angel gets the phone call about her death. It sounds simple enough.

There's one other possibility, though... the "Cordelia" seen here could be a mystical carbon-copy, as with dream-Darla in 4.17, "Inside Out." There's admittedly some differences – the Darla-copy was intangible, and declared she was a messenger from the Powers. Also, "Darla" was an idealized form of Darla, whereas Cordy assuredly acts like Cordy. Still, let's remember that Cordelia spent some time on a higher plane, so it's possible that a "more complete" record of her was somehow available to the Powers – as opposed to Darla, who never ascended. You might be thinking that if the "copy" has Cordelia's personality and memories, it doesn't make much difference either way. But c'mon... it *should* alter the equation if it's not the same character we've been following for seven seasons plus change. All of that said, Cordelia's line that "the Powers owed me one" better fits with the "soul recycling" notion, so while she *might* be a copy, she's probably the real deal.

2. Now let's tackle the oddball explanation for the clawed critter(s) in the firm's basement. It's said that the Senior Partners installed the critter(s) as a "failsafe" against Angel, but this information comes from the duplicitous Eve. Ultimately, we don't know what purpose the creature serves – or if it was designed for use against Angel at all. Hell, it could just be an upgraded security feature, crafted as a response against a Beast-style attack ["Habeas Corpses"], which would explain why the employees get enough warning to empty the premises. There's nothing to claim the heroes couldn't have similarly departed, so it's pretty piss-poor as bear-traps go. Regrettably, evaluating the possibilities depends on whether the Senior Partners believe they *could* take out Angel, given the prophecies that seem to guarantee his survival until the Apocalypse, so we're stuck without further information.

3. The series never names Cordelia's successor as visionary, presuming the vision-talent isn't now so hopelessly screwed-up that it dies on the vine. So we'll make a cheeky suggestion: the new visionary is Jaye Tyler, the beleaguered gift-shop worker who's ordered about by animal-shaped items in the short-lived *Wonderfalls*. Admittedly, this possibility springs to mind because Tim Minear served as *Wonderfalls* producer after leaving *Angel*, but even that small Whedon-verse tie – and the actual evidence – means it's not as far-fetched as one might believe.

Consider that in light of the whole Jasmine debacle, the Powers might feel inclined to revamp the entire "visionary" system. They craft a form of the vision-talent that's painless and human-friendly, then bestow it upon someone who's receptive to such a gift – someone such as Jaye. ("Why do you talk to me?" Jaye wails at a bronze monkey figurine in the *Wonderfalls* story "Cocktail Bunny." "Because... you listen," says the monkey.) If you're looking for parallels, both the Powers' visions and Jaye's animals are a little prophetic and a lot cryptic. Both attempt to protect the visionary when needed (*Angel* 2.16, "Epiphany" for a start, and the *Wonderfalls* story "Caged Bird"). Most important, both the visions and the animals want their agent (effectively) to "help the helpless."

Oh, one more thing: in real-time, Jaye starts "hearing" the animals shortly after Cordelia's death. "You're Welcome" broadcast on Feb. 4, 2004, and *Wonderfalls* debuted on March 12. Close enough for our purposes.

4. "Power Play" (5.21) reveals that Cordelia's last kiss to Angel bestows upon him one last vision from the Powers. This means that Angel is henceforth working to a secret agenda, but it's not near as complex as Jasmine's machinations, and will need minimal commentary in future.

5. Yes, we know... it's hard to look at the circular dais around the containment chamber without thinking of

Stargate. Or perhaps a *Star Trek* transporter room. Your choice.

CHARACTER NOTES *Angel:* Begins this story highly discouraged after a client kills some nuns. [Given Angelus' fetish for nun-slaughter, it's understandable that this hits Angel particularly hard.] He wants to resign as C.E.O., but feels renewed after Cordelia's visit. [And again, the Powers' secret vision motivates Angel to stay at the firm.]

Angel and Cordy both think sometimes about what might've happened if they'd met up in 3.22, "Tomorrow." Angel's penthouse has a wide-screen, wall-mounted plasma TV. Angel still has a tape of the Angel Investigations commercial with Doyle. [This should've been destroyed when Angel's brownstone got decimated in 1.22, "To Shanshu in L.A.", but perhaps it was at Cordelia's apartment when that went down. Mind, even if Angel later retrieved it, the tape rather luckily escaped the countless razings, earthquakes and fire that smote the Hyperion during the last couple years.]

• *Cordelia:* She remembers everything that occurred in Season Four, even though she's wasn't in command of her body, up to the point she went comatose ["Inside Out"]. Numerous statements indicate that Cordelia knows that she has only got a limited amount of time among the living. She scolds Angel for letting the firm "seduce him," apologizes to Wesley for her role in Lilah's death [4.12, "Calvary"] and implies that she always thought Gunn was prematurely bald.

Spike briefly bites and drinks from Cordelia as a "taste test," and determines that she's "not demonic." [Naturally... Cordelia's original body became part-demon, but her Powers-given form isn't.] She's apparently willing to let Angel torture Eve to learn Lindsey's plan. [This is a far cry from the Cordelia of old, but it's not inconsistent with her telling Angel in 3.21, "Benediction," he could kill Holtz if he wished.] Cordelia arms herself with one of Angel's wall-swords [owing to her training sessions with him in Season Three]. She looks well-kept for someone who's spent months in a coma. [Lilah stated in 4.22, "Home" that Cordelia was getting a manicure, blow-dry, etc.] Cordelia doesn't like Eve, but gives thumbs-up to the woman's Manolo Blahniks.

It's never said where Cordelia's body is laid to rest.

• *Spike:* Owns a TV and a video-game system, on which he plays *Donkey Kong* [and *Crash Bandicoot*; "Power Play"] as therapy for his re-attached hands. [After their severing last episode. The TV might also enable Spike to catch up on his favorite soap opera – *Passions* – although he must be hellishly behind at this point.]

• *Wesley:* Has missed doing supernatural research with Cordelia, and reverts to his pre-Dark Wesley persona in her presence.

• *Fred:* Definitely shoots Wesley a "you're so hot when you're chanting" look.

• *Lorne:* Promises Cordelia lunch with Colin Farrell (even though Cordy doesn't recognize Farrell, whose career took off after she went comatose).

• *Lindsey:* Claims he started hatching new plots against Angel after the Senior Partners handed "that Eurotrash vampire everything I'd worked for." [This is a fairly crappy justification, as Lindsey walked away from the promise of such a reward in Season Two; see "Power Play" for more.] He demonstrates various super-abilities and fighting prowess that he somehow "picked up in Nepal."

• *Eve*: Allowed to go free, but knows the Senior Partners will be after her. [She next appears in 5.15, "A Hole in the World."]

• *Demon Slave (a.k.a. "The Pee-Pee Demon"):* Found living inside one of the firm's copiers [after escaping in 5.05, "Life of the Party"], subsisting on toner. He's apparently returned to Archduke Sebassis [and next appears in the series finale].

ORGANIZATIONS *Wolfram and Hart:* "Code 7" is issued and prompts an evacuation before the clawed creature(s) are released. [Yup, this looks more and more like a security feature against an attack.] The heroes go drinking, for the first time in a long while, at the Cat and Fiddle bar.

DEMONOLOGY *Vampires:* Spike suggests that drinking from demons has an astringent, "sort of oaky" taste.

MAGIC Cordelia remembers Connor. [As with Angelus remembering the Beast in Season Four, it seems as if reality rewrites don't affect dormant minds. Ditto with the bottled Sahjhan remembering Connor in 5.18, "Origin."]

Greenway, a racketeer, costs the firm a $10 million bond when he ritualistically murders five "holy women" (nuns) and thereby opens a pan-dimensional doorway, escaping to another dimension. Fred says that tracking Greenway could take months, possibly years.

• *Enochian Protection Runes:* Derived from the Enochian alphabet. [This was an occult language used by Queen Elizabeth I's advisor John Dee and his colleague, the self-described mystic Edward Kelley; the script mentions it as magic in use during the seventeenth century.] The runes conceal the bearer from being viewed remotely from higher powers, seers and mystics, plus any form of modern-day surveillance. [It's never explained how the Powers know about Lindsey's tattoos, but it's possible that Lindsey's tats were calibrated for use against the Partners' black magic, leaving him more visible to benevolent entities.]

Wesley's tattoo-erasing spell entails use of woodbury lichen, a danbeetle skeleton and the arterial blood of an "unclean," meaning a demon. The heroes apparently collect this blood by slitting Lorne's throat [his heart is lodged in his ass, but cutting his jugular is probably safer and easier]. The script also mentions "scent of Magtarn" – the smoky substance that Lorne is busy wafting on screen.]

BEST LINE Most viewers would favor the exchange where Angel wants to fight Lindsey solo and declares: "I'm not risking anyone I care about." Spike: "I'll go." Angel: "Okay." (Personally, though, we prefer Spike's comment as he plays *Donkey Kong*: "Feel my wrath, Gorilla-Throwing-Barrels!" It's possibly an ad lib, as the script called for "C'mon, you stupid plumber!")

THINGS THAT DON'T MAKE SENSE As with Lindsey idiotically choosing "Doyle" as his cover name in "Soul Purpose" (5.10), he here tells Spike that he once lost his hand. Nice of him to empathize with Spike's recent injury, but once Spike starts gibbering about his "visionary," Angel and Cordelia peg Lindsey as the villain in about two seconds flat. It's possible that Lindsey wanted to get discovered as a means of luring Angel to the basement to gloat (hence his comment to Angel that "and the hero arrives right on schedule..."), but he's honestly little to gain from it. Mind, it's also baffling why Eve needs to personally monitor the proceedings after Lindsey tricks Spike into attacking Cordelia. Knowing the outcome wouldn't really make a difference – given that Lindsey plans to unleash the basement critters no matter what – and it's little wonder that this gets Eve caught, as she's chatting to Lindsey on her cell phone near two metahumans with super-hearing.

During the scrap with Lindsey, there's a remarkable lack of blood on the sword that Angel pulls out of his torso. Also, it's curious that we never again see the Senior Partners sucking an opponent inside a portal, as it's an extremely handy talent. (Maybe they can only use portals against people such as Lindsey, who's a wayward employee.)

An error we'll let slide... Angel refers to Lindsey as a "Tiny Texan," whereas 2.18, "Dead End" implied he was actually from Oklahoma.

IT'S REALLY ABOUT... As you might've suspected, it's partly about taking stock of how far the characters have progressed since Day One. Cordelia's return only drives home the point that she still views her comrades as heroes, but that the firm has seduced Angel, Gunn is talking ("I believe in what we're doing") like the party-line commando from 5.01, "Conviction," and so forth. Cordelia represents unabashed honesty about everything her friends have smothered under self-delusion for some time now.

And yet, if anything it's not Cordelia but Lindsey – a villain who knows Angel of old – who gets Angel acting like a hero again. ("Who is this?" Lindsey declares as he smacks Angel down. "*Who is this?* I came to fight the Vampire with a Soul. Guess maybe you shouldn't have sold it.") That's not to say that Cordy's role isn't vital, it's just that on screen, she inadvertently motivates Angel to stay with the firm when he was on the cusp of resigning. (There's mitigating circumstances, though... again, see "Power Play.")

CRITIQUE Really, as a means of giving closure to a character we've emotionally invested in for so many years, we can hardly ask for anything more. Often these one-off "bring back a lead character" stories are spurious, deeply unsatisfying and script the returning character as almost unrecognizable from their previous self. But for anyone who's become enthralled by the Whedon-verse, "You're Welcome" is *absolutely perfect*. It's a testament to *Angel* that the show has functioned so well without Charisma Carpenter, but suddenly – and as the producers intended – there's a Cordelia-shaped hole in the proceedings. We don't even see Cordelia pass on, but everything is so astutely played, it emerges as one of the most touching TV events that the viewership will ever experience.

Indeed, you can tell that Mutant Enemy lavished a lot of time and thought into this episode, and only the climactic sword-fight seems a bit hokey. But in the main, the pacing and plotting are superb, the cast are dead-on perfect and the dialogue is just *super* in parts. (Just one example of many: Cordelia says about Spike, "I thought he had a soul." Spike: "I thought she didn't." Cordelia: "I do." Spike: "So do I." Cordelia, irked: "Well, clearly, mine's better.")

If you're watching *Angel* sporadically, then you'll have to pardon us, because many of this story's deep-rooted emotions probably won't come across. If you are a long-term viewer, however, this is just about unbeatable, and let's cherish it.

THE LORE The producers made another stab (see **The Lore** in 5.08, "Destiny") at secrecy here, meaning the script omitted to mention Angel's final phone conversation and Cordelia's fate, and instead had her simply walking out the door after kissing Angel. With it stated in advance that Carpenter was only doing the one episode, this worked better than efforts to keep a lid on Lindsey's return.

• Whedon left flowers in Carpenter's trailer when she arrived on set, along with a note saying how much her return meant to him. (Carpenter interview, *SMGFan.com*) Nearly every account at the time suggested that Whedon and Carpenter went into "You're Welcome" fully expecting it was the final Cordy story ever. Carpenter even stated in an interview that it would have been a disservice to the fans to leave Cordy in a coma, but that conversely, "I feel like Joss feels the Cordelia stories have been told. There were no other directions to go with her. I mean, they made her a higher being! First she was bitchy, then she was nice. She's matured, she's evolved, what's left to tell? Not a lot. And that's fine." (Coleridge, *TV Guide Insider*, Feb. 5, 2004)

However, Carpenter later stated on a DragonCon 2009 panel that the truth was rather more complicated than that. In Carpenter's account, she was asked to return for an episode in Season Five and agreed to do so on one condition: that they not kill Cordelia. Carpenter says that the production team agreed, she signed the contract for the episode – meaning she was now legally bound to do the story – and that it was only when she arrived on set that Bell stopped by Carpenter's trailer... to let her know that they were going to kill Cordelia. Carpenter was rattled, took a deep breath and asked Bell to summarize how, exactly, Cordelia was to die. He did so, and Carpenter was so moved as to think, "Damn... Joss is good. He's really, really good." Later still, she says, she and Whedon did somewhat bury the hatchet, and agreed that they'd be willing to work together in future.

• An on-set party for this, *Angel*'s 100th episode, entailed Whedon introducing Denisof to press with: "He's transitioned from ridiculous, poncy moron to kind of a cool guy... [pause for emphasis] "on the show." (O'Hare, *Zap2It.com*, Jan. 20, 2004)

• By now, it was becoming clear that the series' lead was envisioning life beyond *Angel*. Boreanaz commented, two days after this story broadcast: "I'm really itching to explore other characters and do other projects. I think I've been stuck in this medical school for a while, and I need to open up and get out." (Veitch, *E! Online: Watch With Kristin*, Feb. 6, 2004)

• The script called for Spike to throw a beer after going down in flames on *Donkey Kong* – on screen, he just shakes the TV furiously. Other deleted bits from the script: Cordelia identifies a piece of artwork in Angel's quarters as a Lichtenstein... Lindsey describes the containment chamber as "Dr. Strange meets Dr. Strangelove"... Lindsey screams (how undignified) as he's sucked inside the Partners' portal... when Cordelia proposes torturing Eve, Wesley was supposed to intercede with "If we sink to their level – ", but (given the character traits involved) the line was more convincingly assigned to Fred.

5.13: "Why We Fight"

"Spike's not in the SS. He just likes wearing the jacket."

Air Date: Feb. 11, 2004; **Writers:** Drew Goddard, Steven S. DeKnight; **Director:** Terrence O'Hara

SUMMARY In 1943, the Nazis rounded up some of the strongest vampires for experimentation, hoping to create an army of super-soldiers. Three vamps – including Spike – were secured aboard a T-class prototype German submarine, but American soldiers captured the vessel. Unfortunately, the vamps broke loose, leading to mayhem and the sub's grounding. In response, U.S. government operatives conscripted the solitary Angel – who could withstand depths that would crush a human being – to dive down to the sub and investigate.

Once aboard, Angel masqueraded as Angelus and dusted the other two vampires, ordering Spike to spare the remaining crew so they could run the submarine. Unfortunately, depth charges damaged the ship's engines, and worse, a German prisoner fatally wounded Ensign Sam Lawson – the only engineer present. With little choice, Angel sired Lawson as a vampire, enabling him to make repairs. Afterward, Angel kicked Lawson and Spike off the surfaced submarine, which headed for safe waters.

In the modern day, late at night, vampire-Lawson infiltrates the firm and gets Angel's attention by capturing Fred, Gunn and Wesley. Despondent, Lawson admits to finding his near-immortal existence without purpose, and forces a confrontation in which Angel stakes him.

FIRSTS AND LASTS Final Whedon-verse contribution by actor Camden Toy, a former mime who here appears as the vampiric "Prince of Lies," but previously portrayed some of the most memorable *Buffy* monsters (a Gentleman in *Buffy* 4.10, "Hush," the flesh-eating Gnarl in *Buffy* 7.03, "Same Time, Same Place" and the Über-Vamp in four episodes of *Buffy* Season Seven).

POINTS OF DISCUSSION ABOUT "Why We Fight":

1. It's suggested – but not terribly blatantly – that the presence of Angel's soul affected Lawson's siring. Lawson still becomes a murderous vampire, no doubt about that, but he can't take to the life because Angel's soul bequeaths him with, shall we say, a measure of empathy toward humanity. We needn't linger over the mystical mechanics involved, save to mention that siring a vampire entails blood-sharing – an intensely personal and metaphysical experience. If the sire had a soul, it couldn't help but "ripple" through such an intimate process, especially as we previously postulated that vampire sires share a residual psionic link with their "descendents." Thus, Lawson probably feels Angel's chronic guilt on a sub-conscious level. More importantly, Angel's siring Lawson out of a desire to save lives – i.e. not for evil's sake – might've affected Lawson's conversion also.

As vampire-Lawson himself puts it, he feels "just enough" of Angel's soul to get "trapped" between worlds – so this entire episode is geared as a means of Lawson committing suicide. If you need further proof, notice how he balances

Angel's friends on chairs with nooses made from wire, but then forces a brawl with Angel that he knows he can't win, and *actively stops himself* from bumping into Fred's chair and thereby hanging her. He's giving depraved vampires a bad name, but that's really the point of the story.

2. This being a Goddard story, everything is slathered with continuity concerns. The "Demon Research Initiative" operatives who recruit the 1940s Angel are surely a precursor to the Initiative from *Buffy* Season Four. Also, the 1940s Spike doesn't sense that Angel is now a good guy – even though Angel doesn't emulate Angelus all *that* much – because Spike can't learn about Angel's new status until the 1990s in "School Hard" (*Buffy* 2.03). You might even deem this willfully idiotic on Spike's part, although to be fair, the whole "ensoulment" angle *was* unprecedented back then, and the submarine incident might well trip Spike's suspicions in advance of "School Hard."

3. We're back to all the business with Darla and Dru in Season Two (see 2.11, "Reunion" especially), in that the 1940s Angel spares a vampire he really should've killed without hesitation. It's understandable that he'd let Spike go, as attempting to dust him would result in a huge scrap that might re-damage the submarine – or at least, hurt or kill some of the navy men. But vampire-Lawson is another case entirely. Fair enough that Angel feels sympathy for the man, but vamp-Lawson is – literally – a soulless killing-machine. By letting him go, Angel is partly responsible for the hundreds, possibly thousands of people Lawson murders over the next six decades. Indeed, presuming that vampires must kill once a week purely to live, Lawson probably butchered about 3,100 people... that's more than twice the body-count of the *Titanic*.

4. The central irony in this story, of course, is that if the modern-day Angel had just gone ahead and staked Lawson during their penthouse discussion, he could've just walked downstairs and cut his friends loose, problem solved. But it's understandable that Angel sensed Lawson had done *something* bad, and couldn't take the risk.

CHARACTER NOTES *Angel:* Says that Lawson is the only person he sired after having a soul. [Again, this contradicts his claim in *Buffy* 1.07, "Angel" that he never fed off a human being after getting ensouled – and again, it's hardly the sort of thing he'd admit to Buffy under the circumstances.]

In 1943, Angel lodged in New York City. He was staring vacantly into space one day when agents of the government and its Demon Research Initiative [see **Organizations**] recruited him for the submarine mission. Angel jumped ship as the submarine approached Maine, going underground until the war was over. [He's living L.A. by 1952 – see "Are You Now or Have You Ever Been?" (2.02) – and we might imagine that he moved coast to coast to avoid the Initiative. The business with Lawson might also explain why Angel feels moved to help Judy in that story – a pity his efforts to help people throughout the twentieth century keep going so badly.]

The 1940s Angel speaks some German, and says he never liked the ocean. [He's going to spend a lot of time there, however, between 3.22, "Tomorrow" and 4.01, "Deep Down."]

• *Spike:* It's never said why Drusilla isn't with him in 1943. Spike had black hair at the time. [He's naturally a blonde, so he must've dyed it in this era. Spike also has dark hair in the following decade; see "The Girl in Question" (5.20).] The SS nabbed Spike in Madrid after luring him with the promise of a "Free Virgin Blood Party." He doesn't speak German, and more or less submits to Angel's authority in the 1940s, thinking he's still Angelus.

• *Wesley:* Has five or six hours of "spell-detailing" to do. He's too swamped, as Gunn suggests, to go over the portal incantations "from last Monday's Mithroc retreat."

• *Gunn:* Falters slightly during a meeting [the first sign that his "lawyer-mojo" is wearing off; see next episode].

• *Fred:* Has to redo the entire "Trask experiment" because Knox dropped the ball on it.

• *Lorne:* Going to a client's party at Skybar [the real-life establishment that his friend Aggie frequents; 2.20, "Over the Rainbow"], but describes the joint as all "fratboys and television executives."

• *Ensign Sam Lawson:* He made fun of military types while growing up, but changed his mind upon seeing pictures of what the Germans were doing. He loosely speaks German. The German prisoner Heinrich fatally wounded Lawson [presumably because he didn't want Lawson to fix the sub and deliver it to Allied hands, and also to keep the Reich's "vampire soldiers" program a secret]. A bleeding Lawson killed Heinrich by smacking him with a wrench. Lawson's chief thought, as he's dying: "Wow, this really sucks."

Vampire-Lawson has checked up on Angel about every decade, although it's implied that he hasn't done so since Angel was a homeless New Yorker in the 1990s. [So Lawson has missed one of the busiest decades in Angel's entire life, then.]

• *Nostroyev:* Typical bad-ass vampire, the so-called "Scourge of Siberia" and "Butcher of Alexander Palace," and the self-proclaimed lover of Rasputin, the mad monk. The Nazis capture Nostroyev, and Angel dusts him.

• *The Prince of Lies:* Somewhat senile vampire with bat-like attributes, and who looks like Nosferatu. [The vampire, that is, not the Gothic rock band. Like the Master, the Prince is presumably so aged (hence the comment that he's "ancient as the darkness himself") that he's becoming more animalistic as he gets older.] Angel dusts him too.

ORGANIZATIONS *Wolfram and Hart:* Vampire-Lawson calls upon his engineering skills to penetrate the firm's security, and even Angel comments: "You'd be amazed at how many people break into this building on a regular basis. [It] might as well be a bus station." The firm's tactical locators cannot find Eve. [See 5.15, "A Hole in the World" for why. The heroes apparently don't consider that Eve might be making use of Lindsey's tattoos, and cast a spell to erase them – as with last episode – but perhaps such magic only works at close range.]

Gunn mentions a protocol the firm can use to establish a new liaison with the Senior Partners. What Wesley recalls from the period before the heroes got their current jobs: "lots and lots of Jenga."

• *Demon Research Initiative:* Have been aware of the 1940s Angel for some time, and know about his ensoulment. [The Initiative officers include a "Commander Petrie" – named after *Buffy* writer Doug Petrie, undoubtedly – but he's named in the script, not on screen.]

• *The submarine crew:* The vampires killed Captain Franklin, leaving Lawson in command. Angel takes charge by using Naval Op 407 to issue order Charlie Baker Oboe Victor [actually "Charlie Baker Option Victor" in the script and subtitles; the on-screen one is accurate for the Army/Navy phonetic alphabet used during the war]. His verification codeword: "Nautilus."

DEMONOLOGY *Vampires:* Lawson rises as a vampire in what seems like a few hours at most. [Most risings occur the day after the victim dies, but Lawson's siring takes place in a submarine – a locale that's far, far away from the sun, so the normal rules might not apply. It's also possible that, like Gunn's sister Alonna (1.20, "War Zone"), he's sired in the afternoon and rises the same evening – this pares with Angel booting Lawson off the ship with eight hours remaining before sunrise.] Unlike a lot of newly risen vampires, Lawson has bloody teeth-marks on his neck.

BEST LINE Nostroyev's colorful threat to Angel: "I will break you open and play 'Coachman, Spare Your Horses' on the lute of your entrails."

THINGS THAT DON'T MAKE SENSE When Lawson first confronts Fred, she asks him, "How do you know my name?"... as if he couldn't, at that point, be an employee of the law firm where she's one of the most prominent executives. As with 5.04, "Hell Bound," it amazing how nobody – save a few of the lead characters – burns the midnight oil at this multi-billion dollar company. And while it's hardly surprising that Lawson gets inside the building, it's funny how the inter-office cameras are such crap that Security doesn't notice him overpowering three of the company's highest-ranking officers, then hauling their carcasses through the building and stringing them up with wire nooses. Mind, neither does Security bother to make rounds *on foot* and discover something is amiss... say, while Lawson is upstairs chatting with Angel.

Suddenly, the heroes are concerned that Eve might be hatching a sinister plan against them. If that's the case, why the hell did they set her free last episode, especially as she was swearing revenge? (Are they worried that she'd escape from a cell at the firm, but that turning her over to the Senior Partners seems overly cruel?) Also, Gunn says the White Room is presently empty... why, given that all the other damage from 5.08, "Destiny" seems to have been accounted for? (See "A Hole in the World" for the Room's return.)

Also, is it a good idea to let Spike flick his Bic and torch Heinrich's documents? Really, starting even a small fire in a submarine hardly seems like a good policy. Finally, given the questionable mettle of the American soldiers here, is it too harsh to wonder how they captured a German submarine in the first place? Or should we suppose that the really capable soldiers died, off screen, at the vampires' hands?

IT'S REALLY ABOUT... Oddly enough, it's an almost total reversal of "The Prodigal" (1.15). In that story, Angel and his human father start out distanced, then grow farther apart once Angel becomes a vampire, resulting in the son killing the father. By contrast, human-Lawson and Angel start out on the same page, then in some respects grow closer once Lawson undergoes conversion into a loosely compassionate flavor of vampirism, resulting in the son essentially asking the father to kill him.

CRITIQUE By now, the hit-and-miss nature of Season Five is getting harder and harder to explain. Overall, it's excellent, with episodes such as "Conviction," "Life of the Party," "Destiny," "Damage" and "You're Welcome" standing as superb achievements of television. But then we come to "Why We Fight," an episode that tries hard, but just doesn't work. Now, it happens that attempting a story about a World War II submarine (plus a horrendously clichéd Nazi plot to create super-soldiers from vampires) will draw some moans from the audience no matter what you do. That said, while this set-up stood a decent chance of beating the odds and unfolding as a meaty piece of drama, it's simply too listless, predictable and uncertain of what it's saying to prove its hecklers wrong.

Thematic issues aside, a major problem – and sorry to single anyone out here – is Eyal Podell as vampire-Lawson. He's decently good as the character's human self, and fair enough, as a vampire, the character is so downcast as to almost moan, "Life... don't talk to me about life..." Regrettably, Podell latches onto the role's despondency too much, and makes him totally lifeless on screen. "Feeling without purpose" doesn't have to equal "acting as dull as watching paint peel," you know. In fact, if you read the script, it's clear that the writers marbled some real complexity into various scenes, but Podell doesn't show any sign of having noticed. The modern-day showdown between Lawson and Angel suffers the worst on this score, with Podell delivering colorful lines such as "Sixty years of blood drying in my throat like ashes..." almost as if he's reading from a cue card.

It's worth repeating that "The Cautionary Tale of Numero Cinco" (5.06) was awful, but we appreciated its desire to do something different. You could say much the same about "Why We Fight," so in *that* regard, it's superior to the lifeless "Soul Purpose" (5.10). But that's simply not saying much, and, on many levels, this story could've fared a lot better.

THE LORE It's at this point that the WB announced that it wasn't renewing *Angel* for Season Six. Official word of the cancellation broke after "Why We Fight" broadcast, while filming was underway for "Underneath" (5.17). Some members of the cast and crew deemed the torture room set in that story as rather symbolic, given the news.

• If we're looking for reasons as to the show's demise... whereas the first two episodes this season had reaped gangbuster ratings (thanks to Marsters' inclusion, presumably), and the season overall had definitely rebounded from the somewhat blah ratings of Season Four, *Angel* was still some distance from its heyday in terms of viewership. *Buffy* had already folded, which curtailed any hope of further co-opting its audience, and it's possible that the lack of a ratings bump for the 100th episode, "You're Welcome" – considering how the WB touted Cordelia's return – helped convince network executives that the show's potential was wearing thin. (That said, the heightened expectations for "You're Welcome" were arguably misguided, as Charisma Carpenter fans were likely watching *Angel* already.)

It probably didn't help matters that, in the years since *Angel*'s start, the WB had evolved/devolved (delete according to personal preference) into a network centered around teen series in the *Dawson's Creek* vein, *Smallville* included. *Angel*, an assuredly adult show, was looking more out-of-place on its home network.

• One more angle worth mentioning... David Fury has stated that Whedon feared his staffers would turn down other jobs to remain with *Angel* out of loyalty, and therefore – his confidence boosted by the improved ratings, and bearing in mind the network's habit of dragging its feet about renewal – asked the WB to render an early verdict on *Angel* Season Six. Fury believes that the WB might have felt backed into a corner and opted for cancellation, and would've renewed *Angel* come May had matters had been left alone. The immediate upshot of the early cancellation, however, was that the producers could properly plan the final *Angel* episode.

• Whedon took to *The Bronze Beta* on Feb. 14, 2004, and posted: "No, we had no idea this was coming. Yes, we will finish out the season. No, I don't think the WB is doing the right thing. Yes, I'm grateful they did it early enough for my people to find other jobs.

"Yes, my heart is breaking.

"When *Buffy* ended, I was tapped out and ready to send it off. When *Firefly* got the axe, I went into a state of denial so huge it may very well cause a movie. But *Angel*... we really were starting to feel like we were on top, hitting our stride – and then we strode right into the Pit of Snakes 'n' Lava. I'm so into these characters, these actors, the situations we're building... you wanna know how I feel? Watch the first act of 'The Body.'

"Remember the words of the poet: 'Two roads diverged in a wood, and I took the road less traveled by and they CANCELLED MY FRIKKIN' SHOW. I totally shoulda took the road that had all those people on it. Damn."

• Goddard had a thing for submarine movies, his favorite being *Das Boot* (1981), which probably explains how "Why We Fight" came about. He posted, to elaborate the point: "I love those German men. Let me say that again, just to be clear: I love German men. Anyone who tells you otherwise is lying." He also claims, jokingly or not, that he leapt out of his seat and kissed Fury right on the mouth upon seeing the first rough cut of "Destiny." (Goddard, *The Bronze Beta*, Dec. 9, 2003)

• Eyal Podell (Lawson) was in *Behind Enemy Lines: Axis of Evil* as David Barnes, and had a recurring role on ABC's *Commander in Chief* as Eli. Roy Werner (Heinrich, the Nazi) was Captain Logan on *Power Rangers: Time Force*.

5.14: "Smile Time"

"I'm gonna tear you a new puppet hole, bitch!"

Air Date: Feb. 18, 2004; **Story:** Joss Whedon, **Story/Script/Director:** Ben Edlund

SUMMARY When a string of children fall comatose after watching a popular kid's show named *Smile Time*, Angel investigates the studio and finds a secret room. Unfortunately, a large, egg-shaped magic-repository ("the nest egg") opens up and zaps Angel – turning him into a fully mobile puppet. The heroes discover that *Smile Time* producer Gregor Framkin bargained with demonic powers to lift the show's flagging ratings, and that four disguised demons are now serving as the show's puppets. The demon-puppets have been using the nest egg to turn the *Smile Time* broadcasts into a two-way conduit, allowing the leader, Polo, to drain the life-force from children. With this currency, the demon-puppets hope to become rich and set up their own Hades.

The heroes storm the studio and eviscerate the *Smile Time* puppets, putting the show out of business. Wesley and Fred destroy the nest egg and thereby return the children to normal, with puppet-Angel due to return to revert in a couple days.

FIRSTS AND LASTS Final occasion that Nina lies naked on the bottom of cell, albeit this time with a mouth-full of puppet stuffing. Only *Angel* story to list puppeteers in the credits. Last time that Wesley makes reference to "the ladies" (as in, "This [observation] comes from people who know. This comes from the ladies.") while making laddish talk with Angel (see also 1.13, "She" and tangentially 2.08, "The Shroud of Rahmon"). Also...

POINTS OF DISCUSSION ABOUT "Smile Time":

1. Writer David Fury logs his last guest-appearance as Framkin, the pleasant *Smile Time* founder. Curiously, this raises the possibility that Framkin and Fury's character in the *Buffy* musical (6.06, "Once More, With Feeling") are one and the same. Both of them even sing... Framkin briefly recites his "Courage and Pluck" song, whereas on *Buffy*, Fury is the unnamed man who sings, "They *got!* the mustarrrrrrd... ouuuuuutttttt" (cue chorus: "THEY GOT the MUS-Tarrrrrrd *OUUUUTTTTT!!!!!*"). We need only explain why Framkin was in Sunnydale, but perhaps he was already negotiating with the demon-puppets, and they decided to congregate near the Hellmouth... No?

2. Polo seems somewhat orgasmic as he drains the kids' life-force, and whereas Edlund and Whedon were probably going for "creepy" rather than "child-molesting," it does seem a bit (shall we say) predatory. Particularly with Polo telling his victims "Now get over here and touch it... *Touch it!*" in reference to the TV screen.

3. Diamond Select dutifully offered a puppet-Angel toy, although the original version quickly sold out and can go for inflated prices on the secondary market. Diamond has subsequently issued variant puppet-Angels, including a "battle-damaged" one, a "vamp face" one and even a puppet-Spike – even though the latter didn't occur on TV. (You might be wondering why Diamond didn't simply re-issue the original puppet, but upping supplies of a commodity can actually kill interest in it and – weird as it sounds – dampen sales of new products in the same range.) As Diamond has gone this far, however, you wonder if a puppet-Buffy or a puppet-Willow is far around the corner.

4. Fred decides she's had enough of Wesley's evasiveness, practically throws herself into his arms, and the episode concludes with them smooching. Even if you didn't see the upcoming WB promotional material (see **The Lore**, next episode), the kissing sent up a beacon-flare that gut-wrenching tragedy of the worst kind was headed toward the heroes. After all, it was only two seasons previous that Willow and Tara's reunion in *Buffy* Season Six was cut short by a stray bullet killing Tara, and Willow going completely off the deep end. For anyone acquainted with the Whedon-verse (or indeed, network drama), it wasn't hard to spot the oncoming train wreck.

CHARACTER NOTES *Angel:* Confides to Wesley he's nervous because Nina asked him out to breakfast, and he can't date someone because of that whole losing-his-soul-to-perfect-happiness detail. Wesley suitably chastises him, pointing out that most people make do with "acceptable" happiness, and that – generally speaking – Angel is being a weenie. At story's end, Nina and puppet-Angel indeed go out for breakfast.

As a puppet, Angel is roughly knee-high, has three-fingered hands with opposable thumbs, and is just about the cutest thing ever. Weirdly, he retains his vampire strength – enough to give Spike a good thumping – and can still "go vamp-face." He's sometimes hyper-emotional (possessing the excitability of a puppet his size), is a bit obsessed with *Smile Time* and has a detachable nose, affixed to his face by Velcro.

Werewolf-Nina's sudden attack leaves puppet-Angel with cute claw marks, and spills his entrails (or rather, stuffing) out, but he gets stitched back together.

• *Spike:* Now getting some support from the firm [pursuant to 5.11, "Damage"], and given a replacement car when his last one somehow "ends up in the drink."

• *Wesley:* Lectures Angel about heeding "signals from the ladies," but still has the libido of cabbage whenever Fred attempts to flirt with him. When Fred says [i.e. "fibs"] that her car is in the shop, and asks if Wesley can give her a lift, Wes acts like Fred is incapable of using a telephone, and calls one of the firm's drivers on her behalf. Fred sweetly shares her coffee with Wesley, and both of them start to find *Smile Time* amusing [but only after it's well into the dead of night, and they've examined the broadcast multiple times].

• *Gunn:* Becoming so inept that in the Wayburn case, he files a Motion for Change of Venue instead of a Motion to Dismiss. [This is quite the blunder... hell, even most *Law and Order* viewers know the difference.] Gunn accordingly visits Dr. Sparrow [5.01, "Conviction"], who confirms that his lawyer-upgrade is fading, the "neural path modification" being almost completely reverted.

Sparrow suggests that as the Senior Partners authorized Gunn's upgrade, they're responsible for it now going away. [Yet it's far more likely that Sparrow – as part of the Illyria conspiracy (see next episode) – makes Gunn's lawyer-mojo fade so that...] Sparrow offers Gunn the "permanent" upgrade if he clears through customs an ancient curio cabinet that Sparrow hopes to turn a profit on. Gunn agrees to this off screen [and again, see next episode]. Sparrow [rightly or wrongly] calls Gunn a "high school dropout."

• *Fred:* Evidently went out with Knox a few times, but eventually told him she wasn't interested. [This apparently occurred at some point, off screen, between 5.07, "Lineage" and now.] Fred felt that Knox didn't make her laugh, and here returns a belated Valentine's Card that he gives her. Fred lives at 511 Windward Circle [seen next episode]. She can read some Latin, and an employee named Tracy works in her department. Once again – and certainly in contrast to Season Four – Fred proves she can shoot straight.

• *Lorne:* Likes itty-bitty marshmallows in cocoa. It's implied that he's making a splash in Hollywood, with it being presumed that Lorne is "deformed," not demonic.

• *Knox:* Fred gently, but somewhat firmly, sends Knox home after he gets snarky with Wesley.

• *Nina:* Resides in cell No. G4 at the firm during nights of the full moon, and tells her sister that she's off camping in the desert. Nina dresses spiffy when visiting the firm – in order to attract Angel's attention, it seems – and thinks Angel's vampirism is kinda sexy. [She next appears in 5.21, "Power Play."]

• *Gregor Framkin:* Started out in a garage with "a couple of used couches and a glue gun," but became a rags-to-riches story when *Smile Time* hit it big. He bargained with demons when ratings hit an all-time low last year. [This almost sounds a bit metatextual, given *Angel*'s ratings drop in Season Four.] The demon-puppets convert Framkin into a sort of "human-puppet," meaning Polo can stick his hand into a hole in Framkin's back and make him talk and perform as desired. Framkin goes limp when Polo isn't "operating" him, and can only moan that he wants to die. [We'd hope that he's restored after the nest egg explodes, but it's never said.] Like many associated with the supernatural in L.A., Framkin owns an IMac.

• *Dr. Sparrow:* Able to implant X-ray vision retinas. Sparrow says that Gunn's insurance doesn't even cover what he charges to wash his hands. [He's next seen in 5.16, "Shells."]

ORGANIZATIONS Every contract signed with the lower planes is filed in the Library of Demonic Congress, and is available "if you know where to look."

• *Wolfram and Hart:* The firm's hospital contacts [as with to 3.15, "Loyalty"] supply blood samples of the afflicted children. The heroes seem to arrive for work before 7 a.m. [as Wesley, Fred and Lorne are present before *Smile Time* airs].

• *Smile Time:* Very popular show in the Southern California market, running from 7 to 7:30 am. It's filmed at KTCE Studios. Show segments include Action Math News.

DEMONOLOGY The children's stolen life-force is "pure innocence," and "carries a lot of street value in Hell." The demon-puppets hope to "build" their own Hades with such wealth. [The script alternatively says they want to "buy" a Hades, and suggests the demon-puppets also want to purchase some demon legions and get themselves a fire-lake. Mind, they'd have to abandon their felt-made bodies before using the latter. A rough parallel to this "life-force as currency" idea exists in 4.03, "The House Always Wins."]

• *The Smile Time Puppets:* Quartet consisting of a boy named Polo, a brunette girl [named in the script as Flora], a dog named Groofus and a large purple thing named Ratio Hornblower, who "talks" to the other puppets by tooting the horn that extrudes from its face. These demons have usurped TV shows for nefarious purposes before, and were responsible for the last few seasons of *Happy Days*.

Polo can work a phone, and pours himself a drink of whiskey. [His little bottle is clearly patterned after Jack Daniel's, although the label appears to read (we're pausing the DVD here) "Jim Dandee's."] Groofus has been working on a song about the difference between metaphor and analogy [and see **The Lore**].

MAGIC [The script says that the two- to three-day delay in puppet-Angel's reversion time owes to "conservation of magic" and lag time. Mind, the interim phase as Angel changes back might prove interesting.]

• *The Nest Egg:* The demon-puppets seem confused as to why it turns Angel into a puppet. [It presumably just does to Angel whatever it did to turn the demons themselves into puppets. The magic might only work on demons, so a puppet-Wesley or puppet-Fred would be unlikely, but a puppet-Spike or puppet-Lorne is probably feasible.] The nest egg radiates a cloaking spell as the demon-puppets sing/perform – this enables Polo to secretly converse with certain viewers. Polo tells his victim/s that "*Smile Time* isn't free" and gets them to touch their TV screens. The children's life-force is drained [conducted through Polo into the nest egg, it seems], the kids go comatose while grinning like the Joker, and Polo gets back into position. The victimized children have no cellular or sub-cellular indicators as to what's happened, but Knox registers a systemic endocrine dysfunction that's similar to the effects of an obscure rain forest pathogen.

During Angel's first visit to the studio, he finds Framkin – for whatever reason – sitting in front of the nest egg with a towel over his head.

BEST LINE(s) They're not much to look at on paper, but we'd vote for Spike's delighted statements to Angel that "You're a bloody puppet!" and "They're looking at the wee little puppet man..." and (to Harmony) "You heard the puppet..."

THINGS THAT DON'T MAKE SENSE Something that's fairly obvious: Framkin sings his "Courage and Pluck" song in front of Lorne, who apparently doesn't "read" Framkin, nor ever wonder why he didn't register anything off the man. (The cheeky explanation is that David Fury is playing Framkin, and a fictional character such as Lorne can't know what a show-writer is thinking.)

Fred tells Knox that 11 children have mysteriously been rendered comatose, then strangely downgrades the number to only seven when she brings the matter to Angel's attention. We should perhaps assume that the nest egg's shrouding spells prevent the public from noticing the final mayhem at the *Smile Time* studio, because otherwise, the media might wonder why Gunn – a prominent attorney with Wolfram and Hart – can be plainly seen murdering a puppet in a beloved kids' show.

Not a goof, but you have to wonder... after the nest egg turns Angel into a puppet, he presumably can't drive back to the firm, because he'd never reach the pedals. So how long did it take him to leap, puppet-sized, across the rooftops of L.A. or to travel through the storm drain tunnels?

POP CULTURE Sparrow says Gunn has acute "*Flowers for Algernon* syndrome," referencing the Hugo and Nebula award-winning story in which a mentally handicapped janitor becomes much smarter as part of an experiment, only to have his upgraded-intelligence fade. As Sparrow implies, it was adapted into the film *Charly* (1968) and Cliff Robertson won an Oscar for the title role.

IT'S REALLY ABOUT... If nothing else, it reminds anyone who grew up on a steady diet of *Sesame Street* and *The Muppet Show* that it doesn't take much of a course correction to make a lovable kids' program seem incredibly scary. Lest we forget, the Jim Henson Company – one of the greatest bastions of creativity on the planet – released the fanciful *The Great Muppet Caper* and the assuredly sobering *The Dark Crystal* in the same year (1981). And heck, you might also view the message here as being "TV is bad for kids," especially in wake of Japanese children getting seizures from *Pokemon*.

CRITIQUE The moment you start frothing at the mouth to newcomers about the greatness of "the puppet-*Angel* story," you tend to sound as if you're certifiably insane. Mercifully for all concerned, this episode *is* as incredible as you've been led to believe and – refreshingly – actually deserves its iconic status. Indeed, if you were to group the most innovative-yet-miraculously-successful stories that Mutant Enemy ever produced, you'd probably have the silent *Buffy* story (4.10, "Hush"), the *Buffy* musical and, well, "Smile Time."

Really, attempting such a puppet-flavored story could've ended in tears, but it works because Edlund and Whedon are at their most inspired. Indeed, you could look at this episode as nothing more than "spending 45-odd demented minutes with Ben and Joss," because it's honestly hard to boil down its greatness otherwise. Nearly every scene contains something that's interesting or extraordinary, the puppets themselves are *precisely* the design that's required if you're going to attempt this sort of deliberate nonsense, and so much of the dialogue sparkles like never before. (Angel to Wesley, concerning Nina's flirtation: "I... ignored it completely, changed the subject, and locked her in a cage." Lorne's romantic advice to Angel: "The signals are there, Jefe. Nina definitely wants a piece of Angel-cake." Lorne, yelling after werewolf-Nina shreds puppet-Angel: "Is there a Geppetto in the house??" And so forth, for the bulk of the episode.)

In fact, "Smile Time" out-performs the other iconic stories we mentioned in at least one important regard: You can actually show it to newcomers, provided you don't blow the sales pitch and can make them sit still long enough. The *Buffy* musical is astoundingly great, but much of the context relies on a working knowledge of the characters. "Smile Time" conversely doesn't beyond "Angel is a vampire, and his group of heroes are running an evil law firm." Thus, if you can convince the rare person who hasn't tried out *Angel* or *Buffy*, try an experiment in which you watch this story over drinks. If they deem something as super as *this* as crap... well, there's just no hope for some people, is there?

THE LORE Act One was scripted to end with puppet-Angel hauling himself up and examining himself, *then* pulling off his nose and going "What the f – ?" before commercial break. (The added detail got trimmed, and on screen he simply goes "Huh?") The script also described Polo's death being more vicious, with puppet-Angel kicking Polo in the head *Matrix*-style, then plowing a pointed railing post right through his noggin. Also, a beheaded Roofus was slated to sing his "metaphor-analogy song" as he slowly croaked. ("Metaphor is better for an abstract cup of tea... on the other hand, you understand, there's always a-nal-o-gy.") Oh, and a cut line had Gunn discouraging legal action against *Smile Time* because, "Think about the headlines: 'Big Bad Wolfram and Hart Drops Iron Heel On *Fraggle Rock*'."

• Fury, here appearing as Framkin, said he'll forever characterize himself as an out-of-work actor with writing as his day job. He commented, "As soon as I get that big acting break I've been hoping for, I won't have to write anymore... which sounds terrible to all these people who dream about having what I have. I wish I could tell you that [writing] was... my dream. It just wasn't. But I enjoy it because I'm around a bunch of funny people much like when I was with my comedy group." (DiLullo, *CityofAngel.com*)

• Abigail Mavity (Hannah, a *Smile Time* viewer) portrayed Xander and Anya's floppy-eared daughter from an alternate timeline in *Buffy* 6.16, "Hell's Bells."

5.15: "A Hole in the World"

"Tens, maybe hundreds of thousands will die in agony... if you save her."

Air Date: Feb. 25, 2004; **Writer/Director:** Joss Whedon

SUMMARY Fred examines a stone sarcophagus that's delivered to her laboratory, but the artifact emits a small gust of air in her face. Soon after, a potent infection takes hold and threatens to liquefy Fred's organs. Angel's team learns that the sarcophagus contained the essence of the long-dead Illyria, who formerly numbered among "the Old Ones" – the original demons – and who's now trying to gestate in Fred's body and live again.

Angel and Spike jet to England and locate "the Deeper Well" – a prison for the Old Ones' remains – with the scant hope of returning Illyria there. The two of them encounter the enigmatic Drogyn, the Well's guardian, who names a ritual that will draw Illyria out of Fred and re-imprison her in the Well. However, this will cause Illyria's taint to become the equivalent of an airborne virus, slaughtering thousands of people between L.A. and England. Angel and Spike find themselves unable to pay such a price to save Fred.

Back in L.A., Gunn learns that Knox is an Illyria-acolyte who arranged for Fred to become the receptacle for his god. Worse, Gunn realizes that the item he signed through customs [last episode] in exchange for another brain-boost was Illyria's sarcophagus. Elsewhere at Fred's apartment... Wesley cradles Fred as she dies. An instant later, Fred's body undergoes convulsions, completing its metamorphosis into a shell for Illyria. A renewed Illyria rises, considers her new body and says: "This will do." [*Continued next episode.*]

FIRSTS AND LASTS After 62 episodes, it's the end of Fred as a character – although she's in flashback next episode, and Amy Acker's employment prospects seem pretty good for the rest of the season. Final use in the series of a flamethrower; Fred looks surprisingly sexy (not to mention a bit like Sigourney Weaver from *Aliens*) while wielding it. Final excursion into the White Room, and final encounter with the Conduit there (see **Organizations**).

Illyria (a.k.a. "Seven of Fred") marks the first appearance of a bona-fide, no-doubt-about-it Old One in the *Angel*-verse (but see the accompanying **Powers/Partners** essay for other potential members of the group). Also, it's the first of two appearances by the mysterious hero named Drogyn.

Last stop for out-and-out "unnecessary female guilt" in the *Angel*-verse, as a dying Fred wonders if she's "sinned" or is "being punished." And officially, it's the last time Whedon sits in the director's chair (although bits of his directing work appear next episode).

POINTS OF DISCUSSION ABOUT "A Hole in the World":

1. Television drama often clings to popular characters like gold for fear of rocking the boat, so to anyone unfamiliar with Whedon's mentality, the decision to dispose of the largely beloved Fred might seem strange. However, Whedon operates on the principle that bumping off characters the viewers actually *care* about twists the emotional knife all the more deeper than those they don't. In fact, had *Firefly* survived beyond the *Serenity* motion picture, one suspects that the cute, strawberry-sucking Kaylee – almost certainly the "sweetest" member of the cast – would have eventually wound up on the chopping block. So you can see why Fred is put to the sword.

2. Sentimental/lascivious viewers will probably want to know if Wesley and Fred ever "do it." The complication is that only a week seems to pass between this episode and their lip-locking in "Smile Time," so while it's possible that they yield to two years of pent-up attraction and hit the sheets, Fred's line to Wesley that "I finally get you up to my bedroom, and all you wanna do is read..." tends to indicate otherwise.

3. It's tough to properly catalogue the "astronauts vs. cavemen" argument from Act One, so we'll summarize it here. Angel favors the astronauts, Spike says that's bollocks and that the cavemen would win, Lorne agrees with Spike, Fred thinks the astronauts should get weapons because the cavemen have fire and Wesley mainly can't believe Angel and Spike argued about this for 40 minutes.

4. Fred seems "drawn" to examine Illyria's sarcophagus, and almost involuntarily moves her hand across one of its jewels. Now, we've seen hypnotic jewels before – such as Giles "conditioning" the Slayer in *Buffy* 3.12, "Helpless" – so it's possible that Fred falls prey to a "signal" that makes her stick her face over the sarcophagus. There's an even weightier alternative, but you'll have to wait until 5.18, "Origin" for that one.

5. Lorne asks to pray for Fred, something that Wesley appreciates. Some have wondered why Whedon – who usually says he's an atheist – would allow such a religious decla-

ration. However, like *Babylon 5* creator J. Michael Stracyznski (who was in a similar boat), Whedon recognizes that it's rather unrealistic to constantly ignore religion altogether. Hence, if you'll recall, Riley Finn going to church in *Buffy* Season Four.

CHARACTER NOTES *Angel:* Looks unfavorably on his professional relationship with Spike, offering him sizeable resources if he wants to work aboard, but later admits, to Drogyn, that Spike is a champion [see next episode for more]. Angel walks around quite well with a sword through his chest. As with Fred and Gunn's relationship in "Double or Nothing" (3.18), Angel is apparently the last to know that Fred and Wesley are together.

Years ago in St. Petersburg, Angel and Spike used a strategy that entailed them holding opposite ends of a wire and decapitating their opponents. Angel has never seen *Les Miserablés*; Spike clearly loathes the show.

• *Spike:* Prefers hitting Angel with blunt objects as opposed to sword-impaling him. Spike plays poker in Accounts Receivable. Like Angel, Spike has never ridden in an airplane before now. He says he's fought plenty of mummies, but "almost none of them" as pretty as Fred. [He might not be joking, judging by *Buffy* 2.04, "Inca Mummy Girl."]

• *Wesley:* Feels as if he loved Fred even before he met her.

• *Gunn:* Graciously gives his blessing to Wesley and Fred's relationship, and gets caught singing from "Three Little Maids From School" from *The Mikado* [a Gilbert and Sullivan piece, see 5.01, "Conviction"]. He offers (without success) his life to the Conduit if it will save Fred. Upon realizing Knox's duplicity, Gunn deals him a savage beating.

• *Fred:* In flashback, Fred bids her parents farewell and sets off to attend the physics graduate program at UCLA. At the time, she drove a Chevy and stayed with someone named "Bethany" en route. [The script says this scene occurred "some eight years back," which suggests Fred spent precious little time in school before getting exiled to Pylea.]

Among Fred's prized possessions is Feigenbaum, a tattered handmade rabbit-doll with glasses, who's called "the master of chaos." [He's evidently named after mathematical physicist Mitchell Feigenbaum, who pioneered work into chaos theory.] Fred has curtailed her spontaneous purchases, ever since an unspecified "commemorative plate incident" on eBay [see next episode, if you dare].

In school, Fred "never got a B-minus before." Before passing on, Fred asks Wesley to tell her parents that she wasn't scared and died quickly. [Yet he never tells them; crucially, see 5.20, "The Girl in Question."]

• *Lorne:* Never sensed that Knox held traitorous intentions. [Yet it's confirmed next episode that Knox sang for Lorne. The simplest explanation for Lorne's oversight is that Knox's plot revolved around his love for Fred, so presumably nothing about his aura registered as "I'm going to hurt someone" on Lorne's radar.]

Fred once told Lorne over a "sinful" amount of Chinese food that, "I think a lot of people would be green if they could. Your shade, if they had the choice." He tells Eve that singing anything by Diane Warren – save for "Rhythm of the Night" – will result in her death.

• *Illyria:* Cited in Wesley's texts as "a great monarch and warrior of the Demon Age" who was murdered by rivals and "left adrift" in the Deeper Well. She still has a few acolytes, and her sarcophagus was "pre-destined" to teleport back to the base of her power, formerly in Los Angeles. However, the continents drifted and Illyria's sarcophagus – which disappeared from the Deeper Well a month ago – materialized elsewhere. Knox and his associates then conspired to get it through customs and into the firm.

After getting infected, Fred initially feels fine, but later spits blood after off-handedly singing in front of Lorne. [It's played as if Lorne's reflexive "empathic probe" of Fred catalyzes Illyria's taint.] Truthfully or no, Knox says that Illyria's sarcophagus resists spectral analysis and lasers, that her taint doesn't match any of pathogens in the firm's archives, and that freezing doesn't impede its progress in Fred's body.

• *Eve:* Holed up in Lindsey's sigil-protected apartment. She's compelled by Angel to advise on the Illyria situation, in exchange for his not reporting her position to the Senior Partners. Eve sings one of Lindsey's songs [the one from 2.18, "Dead End"], and Lorne "reads" that Eve had no part in Fred's illness. Still, Eve's future isn't "looking too bright." [He's possibly just rattling her cage, but see the series finale.]

• *Knox:* Plays dumb when a delivery boy drops off Illyria's sarcophagus. [That makes sense. Even if there aren't cameras monitoring Knox's actions in the lab, there's little profit in him standing there and going, "Excellent, my foul plan can now begin! BWAH-HAH-HAH-HAH!!!"] He knows a great deal about the Deeper Well.

• *Roger Burkle:* In typical fatherly fashion, he says he slept in a drawer until he was three.

• *Drogyn:* Seemingly from a bygone era, he's acquainted with Angel and has been the keeper of the Deeper Well for decades now. [The script says that Drogyn has met Angel twice before, and was assigned guardianship of the Well by unnamed parties.] Drogyn is incapable of lying [although it's unclear if he's obligated to answer any question put to him]. Angel believes Drogyn is capable of killing Spike.

• *The Conduit:* Says its physical form is determined by the viewer. [It presumably appeared as a panther (4.22, "Home" and 5.04, "Hell Bound") because Gunn wanted to see (so to speak) "the big cat"]. It now looks like a Gunn-döppelganger, beats the crap out of the genuine article, declares that the Senior Partners are tired of the heroes' insolence and says it "already has Gunn's life." [The latter statement is very troubling, but the point isn't pursued.]

THE FIRM'S LIBRARY Eve explains that the book templates "can conjure up anything, not just the firm's stock." [That's an overstatement, because it would ridiculously imply that the templates can call up any record in creation when they assuredly can't. She *means* to say that the archives contain information beyond the generally accessible stacks, and it's critically important to know what you're asking for. In other words, there's no handy-dandy Table of Contents entitled "Information Relevant to Fred's Illness" that Wesley can consult, and he only makes progress when Eve tips him off to look up "The Deeper Well."] The template books can indeed function outside the firm [something of a concern in 5.07, "Lineage"]. Trying to help Fred, Wesley consults *The Dread Host's Compendium of Immortal Leeches*.

ORGANIZATIONS *Wolfram and Hart:* Angel says the firm has offices in "every major city in the world and a lot more out of it." [He's generalizing; as we keep saying, there's no Vegas branch (4.03, "The House Always Wins").] The Ancient Relics Department is located two floors beneath Fred's lab. The firm's advanced jets can reach the Cotswolds from L.A. in four hours. [That's only 13 minutes short of the world record, which included a mid-air refueling. The firm must use the same magic planes as *Alias*.]

• *The Old Ones:* [Elaborating on details from *Buffy* 1.02, "The Harvest" and other stories...] According to Drogyn and Knox, the Old Ones were "demons pure," lived "millions of years ago" and endlessly warred against one another. A great number of them were "killed," but the Old Ones could live beyond death. The greater of the slain Old Ones were interred in the Deeper Well, even as some survivors were "driven out" [and left Earth's reality].

DEMONOLOGY *The Deeper Well:* Acts as a "prison for the dead." It's effectively a tunnel that starts in the Cotswolds and likely runs – as Spike estimates – through to New Zealand, literally going through the center/bowels of the Earth. [The script amusingly typos this as "the bowls of the Earth."] Sarcophagi/coffins containing dead Old Ones line the tunnel, and Angel estimates next episode that these number in the "thousands." It's unstated if there's a guardian on the New Zealand side [but it's a safe bet]. Demon soldiers at Drogyn's command help guard the Deeper Well entrance.

• *Demon egg clutch:* Torched by Fred in the teaser, and owes to a species that reproduces by vomiting up crystals that mutate the microbes around them into forming eggs. [So it's rather akin to the giant bugs in 3.05, "Fredless," then.]

MAGIC The Deeper Well can draw back the essence of an escaped Old One, but a champion must travel from the creature's sarcophagus to the Well. Such an attempt could readily occur if Illyria's essence were within her sarcophagus. But as her essence is freed, it would "claw into every soul in its path" to avoid going back into the Well.

BEST LINE Wesley to his receptionist, after drawing a .45 and kneecapping an employee who's reluctant to research Fred's illness: "Jennifer, please send anyone else who isn't working Ms. Burkle's case to me."

THINGS THAT DON'T MAKE SENSE Every warm body available is conscripted to work on Fred's case, yet the only activity in the entire Science Department is, apparently, Knox peering through a microscope while Gunn huffs and puffs a lot. Also, did anyone else think the tail-end of Gunn's assault on Knox seemed odd? Because on screen, it looks as if Gunn is so distraught that he brings down a metal canister hard enough to split Knox's head wide open. (For this reason, it's genuinely a surprise to find Knox among the living next episode.)

Furthermore, Gunn apparently never ponders a connection between the sudden arrival of Illyria's sarcophagus and the "ancient curio cabinet" that he signed through customs last episode. Did he seriously need Knox's confession to consider a link between the two?

Angel and Spike walk straight into Lindsey's apartment without an invitation. (The script included dialogue claiming that Lindsey's super-strength in 5.12, "You're Welcome" was demon-powered, meaning the invite rule is void, but this doesn't appear on screen.) Eve has been unable to leave Lindsey's apartment for weeks, so you'd think she'd be running short of groceries by now. Ah, yes, and... we've previously taken issue with Lindsey using the alias "Doyle," yet it's here said that he put his ***real name*** on his lease agreement, which if anything seems more stupid. Has the man no sense of discretion?

One last bit of puzzlement: Gunn jokingly tells Wesley that if he hurts Fred, he'll "kill him like a chicken." Has Gunn ever killed a chicken? How exactly would he go about doing so?

POP CULTURE Lorne punches Eve and refers to himself as Jake LaMotta, a middleweight boxing champion. He then tells Eve that she should "make like Carmen Miranda and *die*," denoting the Brazilian singer and motion-picture star who up and expired suddenly from a heart attack, age 46.

• Wesley reads to Fred from the children's novel *The Little Princess* by Frances Hodgson Burnett, one of Whedon's favorite books.

• The Deeper Well contains a bridge, and Drogyn looks somewhat medieval, so of course Spike winds up asking him,

"What's your favorite color?" That's from... no, it's so obvious, figure it out amongst yourselves.

IT'S REALLY ABOUT... Inherently, it's about a loss of innocence. The heroes feared that joining the firm would come at a cost, and here it's paid in the most tragic way possible. As part and parcel of this, observe how Angel's inner circle has become corrupted by violence – Wesley shoots a difficult employee in the knee, Gunn bashes Knox even after the man is unconscious, and the normally docile Lorne punches Eve. And most terrifying of all: When Angel learns that thousands could die if he saves Fred, his initial response is "To hell with the world," before common sense and decency takes hold.

CRITIQUE For a story with such a horrible outcome, it's curious how the storytelling here is so elegant. Under Whedon's writing and direction, "A Hole in the World" unfolds almost poetically, mainly because Fred's demise isn't like any other *Angel*-verse death. Previously, every big-name character who perished (count 'em: Cordelia, Doyle, Joyce, Tara, Anya and temporarily Spike and Buffy) either died quickly or without any pain whatsoever. By contrast, Fred clearly suffers for half the episode, which means we're made to view her heroism and unbelievable resolve in a truly repellent situation that ends in her death.

Like the mourning period for Joyce in "The Body" (*Buffy* 5.17), Whedon credits his audience with an awful lot of intelligence here. He plays his cards beautifully, leading – and how easily we forget this – with a first act that's sheer comedy before changing direction and systematically slaying the character with the greatest amount of empathy for her colleagues. Once Fred spits blood on Wesley's face, there's a lengthy descent that's accompanied with some superb production values (the Deeper Well in particular) and a simply amazing string of twists. It's interesting, for instance, how Knox's betrayal *still* comes as a shock even though we've been leery of the geeky bastard for months now.

Cumulatively, it's a major, major payoff to the entire setup this season, but it's also a means of Whedon using Fred's death to make us better appreciate life and yet feel so much smaller in the process. This might be over-stating the point, but ultimately, this episode's ability to run the viewer down such a decidedly unpleasant emotional gamut stands as one of *Angel*'s greatest legacies.

THE LORE Whedon asked Acker to join him for coffee in Oct. 2003, and broke the news about the fate that awaited Fred. She was relieved, at least, to hear she'd still be with the show, albeit playing a different character. The make-up and costuming required for Illyria often necessitated that Acker report for work at about 4:45 in the morning. Stylists initially sprayed her hair blue, and she thought about having it dyed to save time, but settled for wearing a wig upon hearing about the show's cancellation – judging that she'd need to audition for other roles in her natural color. (Thurlow, *Cult Times* #104, May 2004)

• For anyone paying attention to the WB's press releases, Fred's death (unlike Lindsey's return and Cordelia's demise) was basically an open secret before this episode broadcast. Combined, the press releases and pictures for "A Hole in the World" and "Shells" not only made mention of "Fred's demise," but the fact that Gunn and Knox had "played a role in it." The photos of Acker in her Illyria get-up, in particular, left little doubt about what where this was all going.

• A fair amount of dialogue was cut for time. For instance, the scenes between Wesley and Fred were expanded upon – Fred mentions that she's never been outside the U.S. (barring Pylea) and that she never worked the word "dodecahedron" into a sentence without it sounding really forced.

Also, Lorne was originally in the opening chatter between Wesley and Gunn, but the loss of his dialogue strangely doesn't alter the scene, as they simply talk around him. Lorne would have mentioned that a vent in Gunn's office led to the break room (meaning various employees could hear Gunn singing) and that the steno pool girls were hoping for a medley from *Princess Ida*. Lorne was also excited about the merchandising potential from Angel's puppet-killing spree last episode, claiming it made something of a splash.

Are the Powers and the Partners Old Ones?

For most of *Angel* and *Buffy*, you'd be forgiven for thinking that the Old Ones – "the original demons," if you will – were nothing but a complete anathema to human life, full stop. Two *Buffy* episodes serve to front this view... "The Harvest" (*Buffy* 1.02) claims that Earth was originally akin to Hell, not paradise, but that the demonic Old Ones eventually lost their grip on reality and thereby facilitated the rise of mankind. Then in "Graduation Day" (*Buffy* 3.21), Anya confirms that all vampires and demons on Earth are diluted with the blood of humanity, and are therefore some distance from the Old Ones' purebred forms. And sure enough, when the Mayor of Sunnydale sheds every scrap of his humanity and "ascends," he purportedly becomes 100 percent demon. Specifically, he's transformed into a towering frickin' snake and slithers around a little – right before Buffy and her compatriots kill the bastard by blowing up the high school.

As you've hopefully gathered, both accounts serve to illustrate the demonic Old Ones as entirely monstrous. Nothing ever particularly contradicts this view, but it perhaps doesn't tell the entire story. The turning point, curiously enough, is Illyria's arrival in Season Five. She indisputably hails from the ranks of the Old Ones, yet the change of character she undergoes before the series finale – or rather, the fact she undergoes a change *at all* – speaks volumes. Illyria at first embarks upon the typical Old One strategy of "raise an army, feast upon your enemies' livers and conquer everything." But once that fails, she emotionally softens and becomes Wesley's compatriot. Then by the time we reach the *Angel* finale, she's performing noble acts almost despite herself.

If we pool every scrap of data on the Old Ones, then it starts to become clear – and this is key to this entire essay – that they didn't lack the *capacity* for what we'd call "good." It's simply that they existed in an era when concepts such as good and evil didn't apply. Rather, they lived in a time dominated by "the survival of the fittest," in which brutally slaughtering one another was the order of the day. Notions such as "good and evil," it would appear, only come onto the scene with the rise of humanity – quite probably because the presence of a soul in the *Angel*-verse automatically conveys a sense of conscience.

Now, as the Old Ones' era drew to a close, it would seem – again, judging by *Angel* Season Five – that they did an exceptional job of killing each other off. The murdered ones (including Illyria) were imprisoned in The Deeper Well, even as some of the survivors fled Earth for other dimensions. The last Old One to walk Earth in this period mingled its blood with humanity (according to "The Harvest") and thereby created the whole vampire line, although "End of Days" (*Buffy* 7.21) suggests the vampire progenitor itself was killed afterward. So far, so good.

So now we've established that numerous Old Ones fled to other dimensions, and that (looking at Illyria) they're not *incapable* of performing "good" or "evil" acts. It's almost too symmetrical, then, to suggest that some of the surviving Old Ones clustered together in the other dimensions and eventually gave rise to the Powers-That-Be and their opposite number, the Senior Partners. Under the new status quo, both groups probably opt to stick close to home base, redirect their attention onto humanity and let their respective agents (Angel's group, the Circle of the Black Thorn, Wolfram and Hart, etc.) duke it out on Earth. As if to confirm everything we're saying, Hamilton says (in 5.19, "Time Bomb") that the Partners know Illyria because they go "way back" together.

Now for the curveball question: Other than Illyria (and theoretically the Senior Partner that stuffs itself into a Kleynach Demon in 2.15, "Reprise") how many Old Ones do we encounter? For our money, there's at least two more: Jasmine (*Angel* Season Four) and Glory (*Buffy* Season Five). Generally speaking, all three are frightfully powerful entities far beyond the level of ordinary demons – at times transcending the laws of reality, even. They're all narcissistic, desire legions of minions / worshippers and try to acquire power just for power's sake. Each of them gets put into the shell of a human – either on purpose or against their will – which greatly diminishes their power levels. Massively different personalities aside, they all fit the same pattern.

Let's go a step further, then, and ask: If Jasmine is an Old One, is she also specifically a member of the Powers-That-Be? On the whole, it's doubtful. After all, Jasmine is highly selfish and goes about her goals by killing people – rather like Illyria and Glory – yet everything we know about the Powers suggests that they're wholeheartedly concerned about the fate of humanity and the world. Jasmine's actions must seem abominable to the Powers' philosophy, so it's hard to see that she ever numbered among their ranks. Granted, in "Peace Out" (4.21), Jasmine makes a couple of ambiguous statements as if to claim that she hails from the same affiliation as the Powers, and she's referred to as "a Power-That-Was" on occasion. However, those statements *are* ambiguous at best. Besides, let's recall that Jasmine has an amazing talent for self-delusion, and isn't beyond thinking of herself as a Power just because they're benevolent and she views herself as the same.

One last question along these lines: How does the First Feeble... apologies, the First *Evil*... from *Buffy* fit into all of this? Is it a neutered Old One that adopted itself to mirror humanity's developing sense of evil? It's not impossible, but it's not terribly likely either. Illyria, Jasmine and Glory were all rigidly focused on their goals, and the First seems downright confused by comparison. (It expends a great deal of energy trying to spook the Sunnydale crew, but the tossed-out explanation in the *Buffy* finale for its behavior – that it's hoping to eventually "become flesh" – seems maddeningly vague.) It's also nowhere near their power levels, and about as harmful as tissue paper without the Bringers and Über-Vamps to do its bidding. Besides, if the "First Evil" were literally as the name implies, it would pre-suppose the existence of a "First Good"... and there's no evidence of that either. In all likelihood, then, it's just a bog-standard mystical entity that adopted the "First Evil" moniker to make itself sound more fearsome. Not very convincingly, mind.

5.16: "Shells"

"You seek to save what's rotted through."

Air Date: March 3, 2004;
Writer/Director: Steven S. DeKnight

SUMMARY Illyria escapes from Fred's apartment and collects Knox, who's implanted himself with "sacraments" that denote him as her or "Qwa'ha Xahn" – her attending priest/guide. Wesley learns about Gunn's culpability in Illyria's sarcophagus arriving at the firm and stabs him, putting Gunn in a hospital bed.

Illyria sets out to open a portal to her temple, "Vahla ha'Nesh" – which is out-of-phase with our time-stream – and makes plans to revive her demon army within. Angel, Wesley and Spike interrupt the proceedings and Wes shoots Knox dead, but Illyria gains access to her stronghold. Once within, Illyria finds that her army... long ago crumbled to dust. Illyria initially escapes, then returns to the firm and professes to Wesley that she's nowhere to go. In exchange for Illyria refraining from killing, and showing a willingness to change, Wesley agrees to help her acclimate to the modern world.

FIRSTS AND LASTS Last glimpse of the real Fred in flashback, and final "viewing" – when Illyria magically covers herself in armor – of Acker's nekkid backside. Jonathan Woodward takes a bow as Knox, and, as with his roles on *Buffy* and *Firefly*, his character-demise signals that this series is ending sooner rather than later. When the heroes rush Illyria in Fred's lab, it's the final outing for the firm's commandoes. The days of Gunn wearing high-priced-suits are also over, but he'll struggle on in "lawyer" mode for some time yet.

Final appearance of Fred's office (but not her laboratory) and of the items within, including her Dixie Chicks poster. Final mention of Willow and, for that matter, Giles. Last instance in which a superhuman survives a fall from a truly perilous height, as Illyria pitches Angel out Fred's office window. (He appears to fall a very impressive 18 stories.)

POINTS OF DISCUSSION ABOUT "Shells":

1. Thanks to the likes of Mr. Spock, Jean Grey, etc. (we could go on for several pages), death in science fiction just doesn't carry much currency, and the producers know this. Hence, in the interests of making clear that Fred isn't returning, Dr. Sparrow reveals that Fred's soul was incinerated during Illyria's resurrection. This means that her soul isn't floating in the mystical ether for anyone to retrieve – and the more you ponder this, the more ***horrible*** it becomes. After all, in the *Angel*-verse, virtually every person who's ever died has proceeded to the afterlife, but Fred's essence has uniquely been charred into nothingness. Tragically, this will factor into the series finale, so see 5.22, "Not Fade Away."

2. A note on *Angel*-verse history: Illyria claims to know humanity, and says that in her time, "the Wolf, the Ram and the Hart" were weak, "barely above the vampire." It almost seems unthinkable that humans could exist in the chaos-prone era of the Old Ones, yet the entirety of *Angel* and *Buffy* hinges on a human – or at least, a precursor to humanity – being around when the Old Ones fled our reality, and getting attacked in a fashion as to spawn the entire vampire line. Also, "Reprise" (2.15) established that the firm's creation pretty much coincided with the rise of humanity, and if they were "weaker" in Illyria's era, it's further proof that some form of humankind stretches back that far.

The only snag is to wonder about the real-life state of humanity "millions of years ago" – but then, evolution in the *Angel*-verse doesn't follow the normal rules anyway, given that a purebred-demon era precedes mankind.

3. Wesley opens this story by trying to axe Illyria in the head, which – if you'll recall what happened with Lilah in Season Four – makes it look as if one way or another, he's always trying to decapitate his ex-girlfriends.

CHARACTER NOTES *Angel:* Says he was present when Drogyn was cursed to never lie. [There's no accounting for when this occurred, although it wasn't when Drogyn became long-lived (5.21, "Power Play") and it's probably easier to think that Angel witnessed "the cursing" as Angelus.] Angel is initially upset about Wesley stabbing Gunn, but calms considerably once he realizes the context. Angel also says that even a treacherous human such as Knox warrants more protection and consideration than an Old One such as Illyria.

• *Spike:* He tortures Sparrow enough to solicit "screams, various fluids" and the name of Illyria's destination. Spike declines the offer to operate abroad [last episode], believing Fred would want him to work with Angel's inner circle.

• *Wesley:* Comparatively unstable – and just a little scary – after Fred's death. [Indeed, he'll remain as such until the series' end.]

Wesley says he can forgive Gunn not wanting to "return to who he was" [because it's a topic close to Wesley's heart, obviously]. But he stabs Gunn because he was cowardly, didn't reveal what he knew about the Illyria conspirators and "let Fred die." [That's not entirely true, as Fred would have died even if Gunn had realized his culpability much sooner, but Wes doesn't know all the facts.] As with "Release" (4.14), Wesley's excuse for stabbing Gunn is: "I avoided the major organs. He'll probably live."

Naturally, Wes' stubble is starting to return. He says he "hates Fred," just a little, for her need to examine the sarcophagus rather than putting it into containment. [Wes seems more jealous than hateful about Fred's curiosity, even though it contributed to her death.] He recognizes that shooting Knox wasn't necessarily the "right" thing to do.

• *Gunn:* Definitively states he ***knew*** someone would die if he took the brain-boost upgrade [5.14, "Smile Time"], but didn't think it'd one of the heroes, and certainly not Fred. On Angel's behalf, Harmony has the bed-ridden Gunn sign away much of his authority. [It could've been worse... Angel could've come in and shoved a pillow in Gunn's face.] Harmony knows about Gunn's misdeed [so the whole building knows, presumably].

• *Fred:* Wesley packs up Fred's belongings, including her "chaos bunny" Feigenbaum and a hideous commemorative plate. [It looks like a Roy Rogers plate, and presumably owes to the "eBay incident" mentioned last episode.]

• *Illyria:* When Fred's brain "collapsed," it appears electrical spasms were channeled into Illyria's "function system." As a result, Illyria possesses a copy of Fred's memories. [See 5.20, "The Girl in Question."]

Illyria is frightfully strong, durable and able to move like greased lightning. She can open dimensional portals [rather ironic, considering she's in Fred's body], and fight Angel, Spike and Wesley to a standstill. Her trump card in battle is her ability to project an energy-wave that slows time for anyone caught in it. Illyria initially gives off no scent that Angel or Spike can detect [this changes by 5.19, "Time Bomb"]. She shows no interest in Fred, and regards human grief as "offal in my mouth."

According to a drawing of Illyria's statue, her native form was as a towering, armored warrior-creature with tendrils and large weapons. [The statue itself might not have been accurate, if it was built to glorify Illyria's power. But if it's anything like her original body, then the Deeper Well sarcophagi must only contain the "essences" of the Old Ones, not their physical forms.]

Illyria says her last "Qwa'ha Xahn" was taller than Knox. [That's no guarantee that Knox's predecessor was human, however. In Illyria's time, it easily could've been a large tentacled thing or some such.] Knox has surgically placed something he refers to as "Illyria's sacraments" close to his heart. This enables Illyria to home on his location, and to recognize him as her Qwa'ha Xahn.

Illyria's sarcophagus generates her body-armor, which sweeps over her like an inky darkness, then solidifies. [The script describes the desired effect as "Catwoman meets H.R. Giger."]

Illyria's temple is named "Vahla ha'Nesh." [Illyria presumably put it out of phase with our time-stream to protect its resources just prior to her downfall and "death." She probably intended that time would flow more slowly within the temple, thus keeping her army "fresh," but appears to have mis-calculated.] It's implied at story's end that the heroes permanently close the gateway to Illyria's temple.

• *Lorne:* Believes he failed miserably to sense Knox's secret plan, and thinks he's not cut out for the heroic lifestyle.

• *Harmony*: Her idea of looking for clues: Sweep beakers off a table and bash things open with a crowbar. Harm says she never trusted Knox – chiefly due to his dress sense – and that she and Fred only once went out for girl-talk [5.09, "Harm's Way"].

• *Knox:* Chooses Fred to host Illyria because she was "the most beautiful and perfect woman" Knox had ever met. When Knox was 11, he stared at Illyria's image, which was "pressed between the pages of the forbidden texts," for hours. Knox's mother thought he was looking at porn. [It's never said why Knox grew up in a household that contained "forbidden texts." It's possible that one of his parents was a Watcher, although Wesley has never heard of Illyria.]

Knox writes his name with a smiley face in the "O," and his cell phone [abhorrently] has a Rick Springfield screen-saver.

• *Willow:* According to Giles, she's "in the Himalayas," and using astral projection. [It's entirely possible, though, that Giles is stubbornly making excuses about Willow to Angel.]

• *Dr. Sparrow:* Apparently knew the full extent of the plan with Fred. [It's curious that Sparrow doesn't rabbit, but he's probably confident that Gunn – owing to his own culpability – will keep their deal quiet. Wesley appears to slug Sparrow unconscious, but he's never seen again, which leaves a dangling question mark as to how – if at all – he's punished for his role in Fred's death.] Sparrow never got used to the sight of blood, and prefers non-invasive procedures.

ORGANIZATIONS *Wolfram and Hart:* Gunn puts tactical on "Code Black" after Illyria departs the firm.

DEMONOLOGY *Vampires:* Illyria calls them "half-breeds." [To her formerly pureblood eyes, however, *all* demons are probably half-breeds.]

MAGIC *Teleportation:* Results in characteristic displacement of the atmosphere.

• *Illyria's Purple Sarcophagus Gem:* Apparently the sarcophagus' focal point. Its markings refer to a series of "concussively timed intervals." Wesley says this gem is mystically "attached" to Illyria, and once removed and given to Angel, the gem protects him from Illyria's time-freeze.

• *Knox's "Skeleton Key":* Consists of piles of bones [human, according to the script] that Knox uses to open an invisible dimensional lock that the firm places on Illyria's temple.

BEST LINE(s) Illyria, at story's end: "If I abide, you will help me." Wesley, softly: "Yes." Illyria: "Because I look like her." Wes, softer still: "... yes."

THINGS THAT DON'T MAKE SENSE Yet again (as in 5.11, "Damage"), the justifications offered to keep Angel and Buffy's groups separate raise some eyebrows. To wit, Angel phones Giles to ask for Willow's help and – although we're only privy to Angel's end of the conversation – Giles apparently tells Angel to piss off because he now works for Wolfram and Hart. Really, Giles seems exceedingly dim to entirely and wholeheartedly discount that Angel's telling the truth about *an ancient goddess who's threatening to unleash demon hordes upon Los Angeles*. What, Giles is too busy training Slayers and buttering scones to give such matters any thought? And why does Angel's crew only think about calling Willow *now*, when a mystic of her caliber might've eased or cured Fred's condition?

Wesley opens this story by breaking an axe across Illyria's nigh-invulnerable skull, so even presuming he could swing with enough force to shatter the tool (as opposed to it just bouncing off Illyria's noodle), it's troubling that he doesn't advise Angel and Spike to take more than swords into battle against Illyria. (We could, at least, assume that their swords are the enchanted/unbreakable variety. Mind, as with *Buffy* 2.14, "Innocence," a bazooka might've come in useful.) This week's excuse to keep Spike on the show, as Marsters' contract is still valid: He says he's going to work with the firm because, "This is important, what's happening here. Fred gave her life for it." Actually, she didn't so much "give her life for it" as she was "totally consumed by its evil."

POP CULTURE Gunn, trying to rationalize Illyria's time-freeze ability, and getting blank stares in return: "[It was] like she was pulling a Barry Allen. Jay Garrick? Wally [West]?" He's naming the various incarnations of the Flash – the earliest being Garrick, who dates back to 1940.

• Angel also mentions "Ralph's," a supermarket chain in California.

IT'S REALLY ABOUT... Intense grief, the kind owing to the finality of death, and the realization that you will *never* speak to the dearly departed ever again. At the risk of sounding depressing, every real-life story ends in tragedy... meaning that almost every long-term relationship inevitably generates a widow or a widower, given the relentlessness of time... and it's the providence of fiction to end the story with a "happy ending" before that occurs. Yet there's no such comfort here, as Knox says that Fred "had a warmth that took you in and held you until everything cold and distant melted away," and the heroes act like they've been poisoned because they've lost precisely that.

CRITIQUE After the comparative quiet of last episode, "Shells" directly brings Illyria and Angel's forces into collision and – fortunately for the overall health of the series – produces some highly satisfying results. This two-parter was always something of a risk, because it would've fallen to ruin had Acker foundered in her new role. Mercifully, she's *astoundingly* good as Illyria, and rewards the producers' leap of faith in her ability to shift characters at the flip of a mental switch. *Angel* was especially fortunate in this regard, because playing an ancient war-goddess who's been stuffed into a human shell isn't – let's be fair – the sort of thing they teach you in acting school using the Stanislavski Method.

Amid such meaty fare, only a couple of areas disappoint... the shift in tone from last episode is admittedly awkward, because Whedon wrote "A Hole in the World" with a certain tenderness, but DeKnight is more interested in characters punching stuff. Each approach has merit, but for symmetry's sake, it's a pity that Whedon didn't handle both episodes. Suffice to say, you can assuredly tell, mid-storyline, when they shift drivers. Also, given the ensuing bleakness to follow Fred's death, the few attempts at humor here stumble. It's not DeKnight's fault, because having any sort of levity would feel rough given the situation. Still, just to pick an example, hearing Gunn detailing the different incarnations of the Flash seems at odds with the grave matter at hand.

These are minor bumps, you understand, so let's make clear that "Shells" goes about its job with immense confidence, gives nearly every member of the cast a chance to shine, and is yet another credit to the show.

THE LORE DeKnight overwhelmingly helmed this story, but Whedon's fingerprints can be found in parts. Whedon wrote and directed the opening two scenes in Fred's apartment, plus the flashback bits with Fred and her parents (undoubtedly part and parcel of scenes filmed for last episode). He also selected the music for the ending montage, co-wrote the final conversation between Wesley and Illyria, and both co-wrote and directed the scene with Angel and Spike on the plane. He also tossed in Spike's joke about "perspective" regarding his little Jack Daniel's bottles, and DeKnight posted: "All right! You caught me! Joss wrote the perspective line! WHY MUST HE TAKE EVERYTHING GOOD IN MY WORLD." (DeKnight, *The Bronze Beta*, March 4, 2004)

• Some dark humor that was cut from the script: Harmony fondles a stapler and wonders how many staples it'd take before the captive Knox yields his secrets. She added, "The B440 model only holds fifty [staples] per clip. But don't worry. I got a key to the supply closet." (As written, the scene suggests that if Harmony doesn't know anything else, she's fluent on office supplies.)

5.17: "Underneath"

"The war's here, Angel.
And you're already two soldiers down."

Air Date: April 13, 2004; **Writers:** Sarah Fain, Elizabeth Craft; **Director:** Skip Schoolnik

SUMMARY Angel consults with Eve about the Senior Partners' plans, coming to agree that Lindsey is the foremost authority on the Partners. Angel, Spike and Gunn venture to a dimensional pocket reality that's patterned after suburban America, where Lindsey has been magically influenced into living life as a "family man." As part of this punishment, a demon (named the Wrath) routinely tortures Lindsey in his basement, with his wounds magically healing afterward. Angel removes a magic medallion from Lindsey's neck and thereby restores his memories, but the residents/jailors attack the heroes with machine guns. Gunn dons Lindsey's medallion, knowing that the holding dimension will only allow a prisoner to depart if someone else stays. An escape route briefly opens, enabling Angel and Spike to flee with Lindsey in tow.

Back home, the super-strong, well-dressed Marcus

5.17, Underneath

Hamilton introduces himself as the heroes' new liaison to the Partners, compelling Eve to sign away her rights and privileges. As the dust settles, Lindsey informs Angel that *the* Apocalypse is already underway, and that Angel was made C.E.O. to keep him oblivious to it.

THE OPENING CREDITS ... undergo their final remake. More than seven years after her debut on *Buffy*, Mercedes McNab finally claims a slot in the Opening Credits. There's also some new images, notably with shots of Illyria showing up in Acker's sequence. (Fred is still seen scribbling on her office window, but it's a pity that nobody thought to put Gunn back in his street clothes.)

FIRSTS AND LASTS A *Firefly* actor joins the *Angel* cast for the last time, as Adam Baldwin debuts as Hamilton. Last appearance of Lindsey's now-sloven apartment. Final script from Fain and Craft, and last time the evidence suggests an episode of theirs ran in short on time (as the more or less superfluous bar scene with Lorne isn't in the script).

Hamilton here puts his fist straight through a security guard's chest, and you'd almost think such slayings were in fashion this season, as Illyria – in an erased timeline – similarly "punches" Lorne to death in 5.19, "Time Bomb."

POINTS OF DISCUSSION ABOUT "Underneath":

1. Three years previous in 2.15, "Reprise," Angel's elevator ride with Holland subverted the usual sci-fi expectations about a sweeping victory over evil being possible, instead casting the heroes' conflict as an ongoing struggle. And here, "Underneath" entails Lindsey telling Angel that the starting-pistol for the Apocalypse – "not *an* Apocalypse," he says, but "*the* Apocalypse" – went off some time ago but nobody noticed.

The threat, Lindsey essentially says, isn't anything as manifest as a demon horde, but instead owes to the world's slow decline toward entropy and degradation. Meanwhile, Angel has been getting lazy and going corporate, just like the Senior Partners planned. As Lindsey flatly says, heroes aren't supposed to act like that – they're supposed to envision a better world and fight for it. It's probably the most stark advice Angel will get about the nature of heroism in Season Five, and from an old adversary to boot.

All of that said, *is* the *Angel*-verse Apocalypse in progress? We'll never know for certain, but Lindsey could be lying. After all, Angel has just hauled him out of a torture dimension, and Lindsey might just be further confusing matters, especially if he still hopes to join the Circle of the Black Thorn (see 5.21, "Power Play"). But either way, Lindsey's words about the slow decay of society hold an awful lot of relevance today, especially if you're of a mind to worry about a future in which the ice caps have melted, basic freedoms have been curtailed and the terrorists have won.

2. Illyria claims she visited a world with nothing but shrimp, which likely owes to Fain and Craft channeling *Buffy* shrimp-references of old. In *Buffy* 4.17, "Superstar," Anya speculated that in all the myriad of alternate realities, one might contain a world without shrimp, or a world of nothing *but* shrimp. Then in *Buffy* 5.11, "Triangle," the Slayer and friends magically dispatch an enemy to an alternate reality they think is "the land of the trolls," but could just as easily be – Anya says – "the world without shrimp." After such wild speculation, anyone troubled by this issue must find Illyria's statement quite the comfort.

3. How do the Senior Partners locate Eve? Although Angel and Spike don't betray her, they might've outfoxed themselves. After all, if the Partners are keeping even passive tabs on the heroes, they might deduce why Angel and Spike keep "blipping off" the radar every time they enter Lindsey's rune-protected apartment, and suitably send Hamilton to collect their renegade employee.

CHARACTER NOTES *Angel:* Thinks Gunn should feel haunted over his role in Fred's demise, but that Gunn is still a good man and should seek atonement. Angel ponders how bad things always occur at the firm, prompting Spike to ask: "You're fixin' to do something stupid, aren't you?" [Sure enough... see 5.21, "Power Play."]

• *Spike:* Bemoans getting stuck with reconnaissance duty. [He's probably been accepting freelance assignments for a while now, hence his crashing a company car in 5.14, "Smile Time."] He arrives for a meeting with a suitcase that matches his coat and contains beer. Spike says he's "seen an Apocalypse or two." [See 5.20, "The Girl in Question" for his squabble with Angel about this.] Bizarrely, Spike is familiar with *Knight Rider*, but Angel and Gunn aren't.

• *Wesley:* Keeping Illyria company, but prone to drinking a good amount of whiskey, calling Illyria names (including "Smurf"), dozing off, snoring and dreaming about Fred.

• *Gunn:* Back to wearing street clothes.

• *Illyria:* Claims that she once traveled the dimensions as she pleased, walking on worlds "of smoke and half-truths, torment and unnamable beauty, opaline towers as high as small moons, glaciers that ripped with insensate lust." Wesley tries to goad Illyria into leaving Earth for another dimension, but Illyria fears her old enemies would find her present form an easy target. Illyria is somewhat claustrophobic. She also implies that her original body had "jaws," and that she [metaphorically] used to "live seven lives" at once.

• *Lorne:* Struggling to not feel despondent over Fred's death and the hollowness of his job. Lorne consoles himself in a bar, and "reads" that the demon bartender there should expect a June wedding. ("There's rain, so get a tent," Lorne counsels.) Lorne musters up his spirits and returns to the firm, and is later flummoxed to realize that one of their own

– Gunn – was left behind.

• *Eve:* Claims she is "a child of the Senior Partners," and was "created to do their bidding." [This is frustratingly vague. It's possible that Eve was literally "made" to do the Partners' bidding, but "Power Play" paints Hamilton as a former freelance agent, and there's little else to suggest that Eve wasn't born human.] Eve deviated from the Partners' trust, it seems, after falling in love with Lindsey.

Eve doesn't contradict Angel's claim that she's immortal. She signs [using a pen, not blood, it seems] away this longevity to Hamilton. ["Power Play," however, claims that Hamilton already had an extended lifespan before this. Let's also be clear... there's no proof that Eve is older than she looks; it's just that she's as mortal as anyone else now.] Unlike her replacement, Eve never displays super-strength or virtual invulnerability [see "Power Play" for more].

• *Harmony*: Says it's really hard to get a firm ETA on alternate dimension travel. (She's tried.)

• *Lindsey:* [It's never clear why the Senior Partners dump Lindsey in the holding dimension, as keeping him alive doesn't serve much purpose. The heroes suggest that the Partners didn't want Lindsey collaborating with Angel, but if that's the case, ripping out Lindsey's entrails seems a much less risky solution. In all probability, the Partners probably just want Lindsey to suffer, even though this constitutes a security risk.]

Eve claims that Lindsey has dedicated years of his life to studying the Partners. She also implies that Lindsey knows more about Angel than Angel.

• *Marcus Hamilton:* The new liaison to the Partners. [Clearly, the Partners are done with using the soft approach with Angel.] Hamilton wears an expensive suit, and his overall demeanor suggests "The Terminator."

ORGANIZATIONS *Wolfram and Hart:* The company garage, which houses Angel's fleet of cars, contains a Hummer. [So clearly... in addition to providing legal cover for evil, the firm is a soul-sucking Earth killer.]

A proviso in Angel's contract allows him, as C.E.O., to invoke a *rapio salvus* order and take custody of a wayward employee. Gunn says this isn't normally used for protection, but should give Angel custodian-ship of Eve. [Ultimately, though, the Senior Partners probably just release Eve because they've no further need for her. They surely can't be too concerned about a snip of legalese.]

• *The Wolfram and Hart Holding Dimension:* A self-contained reality pocket with a suburban setting. Like his fellow prisoners [we only see males, so perhaps there's a separate locale for females], Lindsey awakens with his spouse, collects the newspaper, waves to his neighbors/fellow prisoners, tutors his son and eventually ventures into the basement to get a stove light. A hulking demon named "the Wrath" then rips out Lindsey's heart in a medieval-style torture chamber. Lindsey's wounds seal, but his "taken" heart remains. (Number of hearts seen on the basement floor: 18.) Lindsey comments on the torture: "Turns out they can only undo you as far as you think you deserve to be undone." [Possibly, but Gunn really believes he deserves punishment at present, and he weathers the experience about as well as Lindsey.]

The holding dimension is accessible via Angel's Camero, which drives itself through L.A. and passes through a tunnel into the hellish suburbia. The Camero has vanished by the time Angel's group tries to escape in it. [The jailers must realize that a prison-break is in progress, or perhaps the Camero is pre-programmed to only remain for a limited duration.] The holding dimension's "sunlight" doesn't harm vampires.

Numerous persons in the holding dimension – the spouses, the children, the postmen, etc. – seem super-strong and come armed with Uzis. [Angel and company bash these people about as if they're not "real," but see 5.19, "Time Bomb."] Escape is possible through a fire-filled doorway in the Wrath's chamber, although someone must take the prisoner's place, and the door closes once the medallion makes them forget.

MAGIC *Enochian Protection Runes:* The ones covering the walls of Lindsey's apartment [last seen in 5.15, "A Hole in the World"] fade before Hamilton enters. It's suggested thtat Lindsey got the idea for the runes from a wayward employee at the firm's Tokyo branch.

DEMONOLOGY Spike claims, jokingly or no, that there's thousands of types of "hell," including "fire hell, ice hell and upside-down hell."

• *Vampires:* Spike proves resilient enough to shield Lindsey from an Uzi burst.

• *Nightmares:* In Illyria's lifetime, Nightmares [specifically capitalized in the script] walked and danced, "skewering victims in plain sight to make them laugh." In the modern day, Nightmares are trapped inside humans, "pitiful echoes" of themselves. Illyria wonders whom they angered to merit such a fate. [Alternatively, it's feasible that as the age of the Old Ones drew to a close, Nightmares simply lost their potency, and found they could only survive, nestled within mankind, as pale versions of themselves.]

BEST LINE Lorne, Harmony and Eve, as Hamilton *plows his fist clear through a security guard's bloody torso:* "Aaaaaaaaaaahhhhhhhhhhhhhhh!!!!!!!!!"

THINGS THAT DON'T MAKE SENSE Mainly to compensate for the lack of a "Previously On *Angel*..." segment, the teaser entails Angel wondering why nobody has shown up for a meeting. Has he somehow forgotten that Fred is dead, Wesley is attending to Illyria, Lorne is depressed and Gunn is bed-ridden with a knife wound? Has someone been pumping stupid gas into Angel's office?

Judging by one of Gunn's medical ward monitors, his heartbeat doesn't waver once from a very precise 80 beats per minute. The firm has an odd notion of security with regards to the parking garage, as all the car keys are kept in an open valet box by the elevator. And speaking of the garage, why do Angel, Spike and Lindsey "appear" there after escaping the holding dimension? Does it have anything to do with Eve being present?

The Senior Partners are never forthcoming with their schemes, so we'll have to ignore the fact that they just leave Lindsey in Angel's company, rather than telling Hamilton to reclaim him. More erroneously, couches in the holding dimension do an amazing job of stopping Uzi bullets. Also, Angel declares that he can wait until Lindsey starts talking because, "I don't need to eat, sleep or drink." Errrr... actually, he needs to do all three.

Why isn't Spike's beer extra-fizzy from jostling around in his briefcase? (And while we're asking, does he keep onion blossoms in there?) Funny how Hamilton puts his fist clear through a guard's torso, yet there's only a tiny bit of blood on his cuff afterward, as if he's got the ability to dry-clean suits with his mind. Finally – and we know we're getting cheeky at this point – Lorne "reads" Eve as truthful because, "Nobody can fake it through 'The Pina Colada Song,' not once the chorus kicks in." Maybe he's being facetious, but if not, given that employees have faked Lorne out at least three times this year (5.03, "Unleashed"; 5.09, "Harm's Way"; and 5.15, "A Hole in the World"), why didn't he make *everyone* sing "The Pina Colada Song"?

IN RETROSPECT It's funny, considering where Harmony and Hamilton wind up in the series finale, how their first meeting entails him throwing her into a desk and knocking her out.

CRITIQUE Cookie-cutter houses in suburbia. A torture chamber in each basement. Housewives, children and ice-cream salesmen with Uzis. No, it's not what you'd call subtle, is it? But in the main, "Underneath" works because (after a bit of engine-warming) it's got such a ripping pace. If this were a novel, it'd definitely be a page-turner.

Simply put, some very talented and charismatic actors – Boreanaz, Marsters, Richards and Kane – dash about suburbia while the residents spray them with lead. Meanwhile, Adam Baldwin marches through the firm like an unstoppable Terminator, bearing down on Lorne's group. It might sound lackluster to describe it on paper, but the on-screen result is a largely charming episode, one that ends with Lindsey's speech about how society is slipping into ruin while Angel twiddles his thumbs. Everything winds up with a palpable sense of doom, and if the last two episodes didn't convince you that *Angel* was hurtling toward something big, "Underneath" certainly does.

THE LORE Location filming occurred in an actual suburb and initially irked some of the residents, although they became more accommodating upon learning that all the effort was for an *Angel* episode. One resident claimed they didn't mind the hassle, so long as they "got to meet Spike." (Baronno, *Starburst* #309, May 2004)

• Adam Baldwin (Hamilton) is, of course, beloved among *Firefly* fans as the thug Jayne Cobb. However, Hamilton's nigh-invulnerability strangely parallels Baldwin's recurring role on *The X-Files*' last two seasons... he played Knowle Rohrer, one of the "alien super-soldiers." (His character supposedly died, but returned to chase David Duchovny in the series finale.)

Baldwin has appeared in more than 60 films, including *Independence Day, Wyatt Earp* and *The Patriot*. He's particularly well-known for playing the nihilistic marine "Animal Mother" in *Full Metal Jacket*. Production of that movie, as it happens, led to Baldwin regularly playing chess with the late, great director Stanley Kubrick. Baldwin claims that Kubrick whipped him about 50 times, although he beat the man once. Kubrick told him, "The only reason you won, Adam, is because I have so little respect for your game that I made a blunder," although he was wearing a little grin as he said it.

5.18: "Origin"

"I turned your son into a healthy boy. And now, I need you... to turn him back into a killer."

Air Date: April 20, 2004; **Writer:** Drew Goddard; **Director:** Terrence O'Hara

SUMMARY Angel flips when Connor and his "new" parents arrive at the firm seeking help, worried because Connor recently survived a hit-and-run incident without a scratch. Soon after, Angel learns that Cyvus Vail, an aged demon warlock, arranged the incident as a means of demonstrating Connor's abilities. The firm previously hired Vail and his associates to cast the reality spell that erased all memory of Connor (4.22, "Home"), but Vail now requires Connor to fulfill the prophecies and dispatch Sahjhan, his old nemesis.

Vail threatens to use a magical "Orlon Window" box to restore Connor's memories, motivating Angel to convince Connor to battle Sahjhan. Unfortunately, Angel's abnormal secretiveness causes Wesley to discover that Angel cut an undisclosed deal with the Senior Partners (in "Home"). At Vail's estate, Connor releases the urn-trapped Sahjhan (3.17, "Forgiving"), but Wesley and Illyria arrive and grab Vail's Orlon Window. Wesley smashes the item, erroneously believing that its destruction will void Angel's deal and bring Fred back to life.

Wesley, Illyria and Connor regain their missing memories, allowing Connor to remember his fighting skill and decapitate Sahjhan. Vail goes into hiding, even as Connor – pretending his old memories haven't returned – goes home with his "folks."

FIRSTS AND LASTS First of three appearances by Cyvus Vail, who's yet another member of the Circle of the Black Thorn. Last appearance of Sahjhan, whose beheading by Connor marks the fulfillment of a prophecy cited (in real time) two years and six days previous in "Loyalty." Last excursion into the firm's file-cabinet-laden Files and Records archive, but first of two appearances by the Wolfram and Hart training room (seen again next episode). And if we're being ludicrously technical, it's the final "appearance" – in the memory slide-show that Wesley unleashes by breaking the Window – of the likes of Lilah, Holtz, Justine, Jasmine, etc.

POINTS OF DISCUSSION ABOUT "Origin":

1. Various prophecies foretell that Connor will kill Sahjhan, but this only occurs because Connor regains his fighting prowess after Wesley breaks the Orlon Window. But *that* only occurred because Fred has died, and Wes wants her back. We're big proponents of free will (because otherwise, much of this series would be meaningless), but it's certainly possible that fate (or Fate, if you prefer) tips events one direction or another. Suffice to say, anyone scrutinizing *Angel* should probably consider the inter-connectedness of all this. *Does* Fred perish as one component of some greater prophecies? It's entirely possible, especially if you ask whether Fred felt drawn to Illyria's sarcophagus (5.15, "A Hole in the World") because she was simply curious, because the artifact magically influenced her... or because she needed to die to crush Wesley's spirit and make events play out as scheduled.

2. A word on the Circle of the Black Thorn members (even if they're not identified until 5.21, "Power Play"): They clearly answer to the Senior Partners, but seem to think they're beyond reproach at times. Some parties (such as the necromancer Hainsley, 5.02, "Just Rewards") resist targeting Angel for fear of outraging the Partners, yet the Circle members somehow think they can pull crap with Angel and weather the storm afterward. Notice how Sebassis felt moved to try and kill Angel in "Life of the Party" (5.05), and Vail (presuming he isn't simply bluffing) thinks he can bring back Connor's memories, even though this might violate Angel's contract with the firm. They're awfully sure of themselves, aren't they? But then, you don't get to join the Circle by being a wallflower.

Mind, if we're comparing Sebassis and Vail, it's funny how both of them require strange fluids to live (Vail from his IVs, Sebassis from his "Pee-Pee Demon"), and both hold audiences in large, empty rooms with a single chair against the wall. Vail's abode, in fact, looks a bit like the Black Lodge from *Twin Peaks*, only minus the dancing midget.

3. The Connor memory spell update: Sahjhan presumably remembers Connor because – as discussed in "You're Welcome" (5.12) – his mind was suppressed in the urn when Vail's reality-alteration took effect. However, it's more telling that Wesley remembers Sahjhan as being Angel's enemy. Once again, it seems that the memory spell only extracted information pertaining to Connor, and left everything else – in such a fashion, mind, that those affected don't seem to notice.

Speaking of which, the memory slide-show that's shown after Wesley breaks the Window renders images with nothing to do with Connor – such as Lilah writhing atop Wes on the couch. (4.07, "Apocalypse Nowish," etc.) Ergo, we should probably view this as representative of the deleted recollections "slotting into place" with the retained memories.

4. When Hamilton visits Gunn in the holding dimension (from last episode), the Wrath doesn't properly clean the tool it's using to carve out Gunn's heart. It's just shocking how much cutting with dirty implements has occurred this season (the Slayer hacking off Spike's hands in 5.11, "Damage," Pavayne's knife in 5.04, "Hell Bound," etc.). Can't this show teach better cleanliness?

5. Random observations: Spike and Illyria's "training session" seems an awful lot like foreplay, especially if you recall how Spike and Buffy used to smack each other around... the designers do their best, but the "beheaded Sahjhan" is clearly just someone with their head covered up, and who twitches their hands a bit before falling over... and finally, the close-up on Connor at the final scene clearly shows that Vincent Kartheiser is a little heavily made up, lipstick included.

6. Illyria declares that she'd "like to keep Spike as my pet." Well, wouldn't everybody?

CHARACTER NOTES *Angel:* Evidently signed his contract with the firm in blood. [His own, presumably. By the way, Wesley's mistaken belief that Angel traded Fred's life for Connor's safety might inspire the ruse that Angel deploys in "Power Play."] Angel says he can't really afford to have a girlfriend, but alludes to a time in France that he made out with other vampires.

On Fred's death, Angel advises Wesley: "Get over it." [This sounds rather heartless and hypocritical, considering Angel himself jaunted off to Tibet for three months to mourn

Buffy's demise (3.01, "Heartthrob"). However, "Power Play" establishes that Angel has got a secret plan, and needs Wesley level-headed and onboard to make it work, so his words are more understandable with hindsight.]

• *Spike:* Assigned to test Illyria's strength, and goes about this by smacking her around a bit, then jotting down the results on his clipboard. He can identify Wesley's 12-year-old Lagavulin Scotch by smell, and deems it a good choice.

• *Wesley:* Looking utterly haggard, clearly isn't sleeping well and seems rather fixated with Illyria. Wesley seems even more traumatized after rebuking Angel and smashing the Window, realizing the false memories were created for a reason. [The loss and return of Wesley's memories must prove more psychologically damaging than just remembering them in the first place, because Wes must confront the notion that *he* betrayed Angel's trust – the very thing he was accusing Angel of.]

• *Gunn:* Still being tortured [after last episode], with his chest magically healing – and the blood disappearing – after the Wrath cuts his heart out. (Gunn's shirt magically re-buttons itself too.) After each "session," the Wrath hands him – as requested – a stove light. Hamilton interrupts Gunn's torture and offers him liberty, but Gunn doesn't even hear the conditions of the deal, and gets back to being tortured. [After Fred, Gunn is – commendably – unwilling to make another deal that entails a price.]

• *Lorne:* Knows of Vail, but doesn't seem personally acquainted with him.

• *Illyria:* Now acting as Wesley's muscle, and seems eager to help him declare independence from Angel's leadership. Illyria is clearly stronger than Spike. Her time-freeze can affect Vail, and she [or Wesley] can evidently remove "time-frozen" items such as the Orlon Window.

Wesley speculates that Illyria can count oxygen molecules and "analyze" an entire petri dish that she somehow fits into her mouth. Wes also implies that Illyria sleeps [suggesting her human shell needs rest at times]. Spike postulates that she can talk to plants [see 5.20, "The Girl in Question"].

Illyria senses that Fred's memories were altered (by the "reality shift" to create Connor), but can't access the original recollections until Wesley breaks the Window. She can sense variations in body temperature, such as Connor's teenage lust for her. [It's a variation of Illyria's ability to scan people's health like a medical tricorder from *Star Trek*; see the series finale.]

• *Connor:* [First off, it's only said in 5.22, "Not Fade Away" that Connor has regained his old memories, but c'mon... after Wesley breaks the Window, Connor manifestly stands up with a savage look-in-his-eyes and his hair mussed up like the *old* Connor. Then Connor dispatches Sahjhan while moving like his previous self, and there's a handful of telling lines in the final scene. ("There's nothing [Vail] can show me that I haven't already seen," and, clearly, "You gotta do what you can to protect your family. I learned that from my father.") It leaves little to the imagination.]

The "new" Connor is a ridiculously well-adjusted teenage boy. [So much so, that you almost expect him to tell Angel, "Dude, you're a vampire! Rock on!"] Laurence and Colleen Reilly are his "parents." Vail considers Connor's artificial memories as "his best work." One false memory conveys that when Connor was five, he scarily got lost in a department store. He remembers screaming, his mother running toward him and his father sweeping him up. Connor is presently attending Stanford [not Notre Dame, as Angel hoped in 3.10, "Dad"]. He seems as libidinous as every teenage boy on the planet, and off-handedly mentions that he's "always had a thing for older women." Angel consequently mutters to himself: "They were supposed to fix that." [It's hardly the sort of detail Angel would've sutured into his contract, but perhaps he's just expecting the new Connor is better adjusted on this point.]

The "new" Connor thinks he hasn't participated in a brawl before now. He's got no finesse with weapons, seems overly noble in combat, and – once his memories return – can emulate his "new" self very well.

• *Hamilton:* Like Eve and Lilah before him, Hamilton knows Connor's true identity. He also knows about Angel's dalliance with Eve [5.05, "Life of the Party"] and can access the Partners' holding dimension. The Wrath is clearly subservient to him.

• *Cyvus Vail:* [It's never revealed how he came to possess Sahjhan's urn after "Forgiving." Also, while it's never said, Sahjhan's solidification in "Forgiving" might motivate Vail to here take action against him. After all, an intangible Sahjhan probably doesn't pose as much of a threat.] Vail looks like an evil, red Yoda. He's presented as an ancient demon who labors to breathe, and has an assortment of intravenous tubes supplying him with various liquids. He heads up a large demon empire [again, like Sebassis from "Life of the Party"], and supervises some of the most powerful sorcerers on the West Coast. Vail and his associates appear to specialize in memory restructuring, mind control and temporal shifts. It seems that Vail can also create force fields. Lorne says "you could buy Bolivia" for what the firm paid Vail to alter reality and create the "new" Connor. It's confirmed that this "reality shift" occurred on "the day the heroes took over the firm" [not the same day they moved into their offices, however; see 5.01, "Conviction"].

• *Sahjhan*: Experienced the passage of time while bottled, and initially seems sincere about "owing one" to the person who freed him. He's superior in combat to the "new" Connor, but quickly falls when the old version returns.

• *The Wrath:* Eventually gets around to using every torture device in the basement, including some red-hot pokers and a gibbet [generally the term for a hanging cage-like device used to display the carcasses of executed prisoners].

ORGANIZATIONS *Wolfram and Hart:* The downstairs vending machines dispense dried-up scorpions. Some of the firm's medics have claws.

DEMONOLOGY *Kith'barn demons:* Tusked demons with ponytails and Samurai swords. Those in L.A. appear to exclusively operate as Vail's henchmen.

BEST LINE A deadpan Hamilton to Angel, on how he differs from Eve: "I'm not a little girl, and you and I won't be making love on this couch any time soon." (And thousands of fan-fic writers across the globe cried out in anguish.)

THINGS THAT DON'T MAKE SENSE Somewhat glaringly, Vail all but concedes to Angel that his Orlon Window only works at close range ("if it were to break *around someone* whose mind had been altered...", he says). Ergo, if Angel were a betting man, and given that Connor isn't in the vicinity, he could've probably just broken Vail's neck right then and there, game over.

It's understandable that Angel is over-protective of Connor, yet he weirdly shows no hesitation to introduce the lad to Illyria – who's unquestionably the biggest X-factor in residence right now. It's also unclear why, if Angel's contract with the firm was so secret, a copy of the deal exists in the firm's archives and Accounts has such openly-accessible records about the firm's giant, whopping payment to Vail. (That said, there's probably mystical rules in play regarding the proper filing of such contracts, if they're to have any potency. Surely, every evildoer would like to keep their infernal deals secret, yet twice this season – 5.06, "The Cautionary Tale of Numero Cinco" and 5.14, "Smile Time" – we've seen evidence that copies of virtually every demonic pact are on file if you just know where to look.)

Sahjhan overpowers Connor, then becomes one of those villains who insists on speechifying when he should be (say) caving in the whelp's windpipe. Mind, Vail seems awfully bold in letting Connor fight Sahjhan in his home no matter what the precautions; the prophecy has enough wiggle room that Sahjhan might break loose, eliminate Vail and get killed by Connor years later. Far better, it would seem, to let Connor have a go at Sahjhan in an abandoned building in Boston or wherever. And isn't it a mistake to leave *so* many weapons lying around the combat chamber, as this just provides Sahjhan with several instruments he can use against Connor? Because even if Connor's destined to ultimately kill Sahjhan, there's nothing to say that Sahjhan can't ram a sword into Connor's lungs beforehand.

IT'S REALLY ABOUT... The repercussions of Angel tinkering with his colleagues' memories, because even allowing that he wanted to protect his son, he allowed his best friends' minds to be violated. In this, it's actually a mirroring of Wesley's dilemma in Season Three... both men seek to protect Connor, which compels them to privately handle a dilemma rather than confiding in those closest to them.

CRITIQUE Similar to "You're Welcome" (5.12), this story is needed to tie off the series, because it'd be intensely irritating for *Angel* to end without clarification on what became of the title character's son. Thankfully, Goddard rises to the challenge of getting Connor onstage – then hustling him off again – while still crafting a really, really strong piece of storytelling. Better still, with only four episodes to go now, it proves that *Angel* can still hurtle itself into previously unknown territory.

While the script clearly holds its own, however, what *really* pushes "Origin" to the A-level is the stellar performances of the regulars. Kartheiser and Acker are quite successful in unfamiliar roles, and Denisof – once again the pivotal point as Wesley – excels even as his character becomes dangerously unstable. Dennis Christopher logs a remarkable performance as the aged Vail, considering his character can seemingly only walk a couple of feet per day.

It's clear that the series is maneuvering to wrap everything up, but it's doing so in the most compelling of fashions. Better still, there's only one character-of-old to deal with now, and that'll get handled two episodes hence in "The Girl in Question."

THE LORE Goddard initially entitled this story "Nature vs. Nurture vs. Sahjhan." Shortly after this story aired, Goddard posted on-line: "If my mom calls, I may have to jump off, but I'll be back. It'll be nice to talk to her after she sees an episode about good parenting, you know, instead of an episode where she tries to have sex with me and then I kill her, or an episode where I shoot my dad in cold blood and he's British." (Goddard, *The Bronze Beta*, April 22, 2004)

• Dennis Christopher (Vail) has acted in such disparate films as *Chariots of Fire, Dead Women in Lingerie* and *Necronomicon.* But most amusingly, he's the grown-up Eddie Kaspbrak in Stephen King's *It.* We say "amusingly," because Eddie is the asthmatic character, and Vail constantly wheezes as if he needs his inhaler.

5.19: "Time Bomb"

"You can't look at her without seeing her body's previous owner. But then, what comes out of her mouth... pure, unadulterated vertigo."

Air Date: April 27, 2004; **Writer:** Ben Edlund; **Director:** Vern Gillum

SUMMARY Illyria breaks Gunn loose from the holding dimension – mainly to put Angel and Wesley in her debt – but Angel views Illyria as too much of a wild card and asks Wesley to devise a means of killing her. Simultaneously, Illyria's human shell becomes less able to contain her inner energies, threatening an explosion to rival Chernobyl. Wesley jury-rigs a "Mutari generator" gun that will siphon Illyria's energies into a pocket universe, killing her. However, a skirmish results in Illyria slaughtering Angel, Wes, Lorne and Spike.

Illyria's unstable energies yank her back and forth through time, causing her to pull a younger version of Angel in her wake. Forewarned, Angel alters history and prevents everyone's deaths, allowing Wesley to use the generator gun. Angel finds that Wesley lied about the gun killing Illyria, and that it merely drains off her excess energy instead. Illyria survives, but loses her ability to create portals or slow time.

Meanwhile, the firm represents the Fell Brethren, who want to adopt the unborn child of a woman named Amanda. Gunn objects upon learning that the Fell want to raise the child and perform "Gordobach" (sic) – a ritual sacrifice – but Angel appallingly favors the Fell, enabling them to take the child.

FIRSTS AND LASTS Final script credited to Ben Edlund, but the first appearance of the Fell Brethren (previously mentioned in 5.05, "Life of the Party"). Illyria's excursion into the "suburban hell" to rescue Gunn probably constitutes the last instance of anyone dimension-jumping. It's also the last appearance of Wesley's blue and white teapot (the one Fred returned to him in 3.18, "Double or Nothing," and also seen in 5.14, "Smile Time").

POINTS OF DISCUSSION ABOUT "Time Bomb":

1. Understanding that he doesn't need much excuse, it's interesting to consider why Angel moves against Illyria *now*. Her actions don't really suggest she's reverting to the ways of conquest (at least, no more than usual), and she opens this story by helpfully – if selfishly – rescuing Gunn. Does the sight of blue just make Angel enraged? Unless...

An explanation might lie in Angel's statement that Illyria has remained at the firm because it "reeks of influence." With benefit of knowing that Angel is plotting against the Circle of the Black Thorn (see 5.21, "Power Play"), it makes sense that he'd want Illyria leashed. After all, it's easy to see how Illyria might feel drawn to the Circle's raw power, and a shift of allegiance on her part – especially depending on when it falls – could result in fatalities all around. So it's sensible that Angel would want her defanged.

2. Edlund doesn't bother detailing most of the temporal mechanics involved in this story, which is actually fortunate, because it means we can't actually call most of it into question. It seems reasonable, at least, to assume that Illyria's time-jumps owe to her slow-time ability misfiring as her shell decays. Likewise, it's probably safe to think that Illyria – once she believes the heroes are trying to kill her – doesn't kill Angel or Wesley at an earlier juncture for fear of creating a temporal paradox. One item that's harder to explain, however, is why the younger Angel seems to "merge" with his older self outside the training room. It's a far cry from the weird "body-hosting" in *Being John Malkovich*, but it's an odd detail anyway – one that we'll happily leave for the temporal theorists in the audience.

3. Illyria saves Gunn by taking off his medallion (from 5.17, "Underneath") and putting it on the Wrath, compelling the butcher to take Gunn's place and torture himself. We therefore see the Wrath sticking a knife into his own chest, but one presumes that – off screen – the Wrath also goes through the motions of waking up in bed with his wife, going out to collect the newspaper, waiving to the neighbors, somehow teaching his son about the Earth's inner core, the outer core, etc.

CHARACTER NOTES *Angel:* Learns that Hamilton attempted to bargain with Gunn last episode, and asks Gunn point-blank if he took a deal. (Gunn truthfully says he declined.) Angel ultimately concedes that Wesley was right about the possibility of Illyria joining their team. [By the way, Angel presumably turns the child over to the Fell as a stalling tactic, knowing full well that they won't harm the kid until his 13th birthday; see **Demonology**.]

• *Spike:* Had tons of affection for Fred, yet seems happy to smack Illyria around when needed.

• *Wesley:* Now going to pieces, and seems almost maniacal as he researches the Old Ones in his office. He says he only tried to destroy Illyria [last episode] as an "unavoidable consequence" of his attempt to bring back Fred. He's even defensive about Illyria, claiming that she held no more malicious intent than a viral phage when she was reborn in Fred. [Either Wes is becoming delusional, or he's doing everything in his power to not seethe at Illyria with hatred.] He assures Angel that he's not in love with Illyria, but needs her company.

Wesley refers to the Apocalypse as "The Thousand Year War of Good vs. Evil" [but he's probably just being figurative]. He wants to apologize to Gunn for stabbing him [5.16,

"Shells"], but doesn't exactly know how. Gunn thinks that's for the best, partly because his torture in the holding dimension was far worse [and partly because Wesley wasn't entirely without cause].

• *Gunn:* Remarkably chipper for someone who's had his heart ripped out several times over the past two weeks. He says the worst part was actually the faux family, a means of hiding over the basement-horror. Gunn can barely stomach his job now, and abruptly rebukes the Brethren until Angel intervenes.

• *Illyria:* Says that in her day, humanity was called "the ooze that eats itself," but that humans were "pretty at night." She names herself as "God-King of the Primordium," "Shaper of Things" and the victor of 10,000 wars.

Spike says that Illyria now smells like Fred. [That's a change from "Shells," suggesting that Illyria's physical form is becoming more like Fred's body on a cellular level. Heck, that probably explains why her human shell is struggling to contain her inner power.] "Betrayal" was a neutral word in Illyria's day, so she's disturbed to feel bothered by Wesley's attempt to bring back Fred [again, last episode]. In fact, while Illyria readily "kills" Wesley (in the erased history) when he points a gun at her, she clearly likes Wes and wants him to "worship"/like/not kill her in some capacity.

Spike says that Illyria spent two hours yesterday "mind-melding with a potted fern" [see next episode]. He believes that her fighting style is an ancestral version of tae kwon do and the [fictional] "Brazilian ninjitsu." Estimates on the damage caused if the energy within Illyria were to go critical range from several city blocks to the entire continental shelf.

Wesley believes he provides Illyria with "some amusement," and that she might – given time – fight alongside the heroes, even if she thinks herself above them. Spike at one point calls Illyria "Grandma." [Not entirely inaccurate, as an Old One served as the progenitor of the entire vampire line.] Wes has discussed weights and measures, day-cycles, customs and world histories with Illyria. [At least he didn't make her watch TV, as with Holtz in 3.08, "Quickening."] She registers on the firm's internal scans as a "Level 4" unstable energy source.

• *Lorne:* Isn't fond of Hamilton, but likes him better than Eve. [The script called for everyone to nod in agreement.] While trailing Illyria, Lorne refers to himself as "Secret Demon"; Illyria is "Blue Bird"; Angel is "Angel ears."

• *Hamilton:* Tips off Wesley that Illyria is in danger of going critical.

• *Amanda:* Impending mother of the child the Fell Brethren want. She's strapped for cash, as her husband was brain-damaged at work and no longer recognizes her. [This seems entirely too coincidental, and probably owes to the Brethren's dirty work.] She's been told – wrongly – that the Brethren regard her child as the next Dalai Lama, or a sort of "Holy One" in accordance with a prophecy. [It's never said what trick Angel pulls to award the child to the Brethren, considering Gunn makes clear to Amanda that the Fell intend to sacrifice her child. But then, Amanda isn't painted as the brightest bulb on the tree.]

• *The Wrath:* The only words it ever speaks, while motioning to Gunn for quiet: "Shhh."

THE LIBRARY Wes commands the firm's templates to find: "All pre-Christian works dealing with the Demon Age, same for Primordium, index any mention of 'Old Ones'."

ORGANIZATIONS *Wolfram and Hart:* Illyria penetrates the holding dimension to rescue Gunn, and winds up destroying eleven torture units, two troop carriers, an ice cream truck and eight lawns. The cost of this drags the firm's L.A. branch from being the firm's No. 1 earner to jockeying at the rear. Illyria also "renders dozens of employees useless to the company." [Worryingly, that almost suggests that the gun-toting housewife and child from "Underneath" were *real*, which puts a whole new spin on the heroes smacking them about so hard.] On the plus side, the firm makes a lot off cancer, because the patent-holder is a client.

• *The Senior Partners:* "Go way back" with Illyria [see **Are the Powers and the Partners Old Ones?**] and evidently want her eliminated, but deem her as Angel and Wesley's problem.

DEMONOLOGY *The Fell Brethren:* Pasty demons who've spent decades seeking a certain type of child to raise; pamper; worship; feed a holy diet of berries, panda-meat and consecrated urine; and finally – upon the eve of his thirteenth year – prepare for the rites of Gordobach, a ritual sacrifice as part of their religion. [They appear to target Amanda's child as directed by their "seer people."] Amanda's consent is needed to "sanctify" the transaction, and the Brethren have been doting on her with shakes, special vitamins, articles from this month's *Fit Pregnancy* and black cohosh. [The latter is an herbal supplement used to ease gynecological issues, although the latest research indicates that pregnant women shouldn't take it for various reasons. The Brethren really are fiends.] The Fell claim to have hordes at their disposal.

BEST LINE(s) Illyria, posturing: "When the world met me, it shuddered, groaned. It knelt at my feet." Spike: "Dear *Penthouse*, I don't normally write letters like this..."

THINGS THAT DON'T MAKE SENSE As with his courtroom surveillance in "Conviction" (5.01), it's faintly ridiculous that Lorne – who couldn't be less conspicuous – is assigned to shadow Illyria. Small wonder she knows Lorne is on her trail, because (say) Ulysses S. Grant could've deduced much the same, in spite of his having died in 1885.

In the second run-up to the training room slaughter, Wesley and Spike seem rather dense in that they totally ignore Angel's declaration that he's been pulled back through time and has seen Illyria – whom they're readying to attack. What, is that sort of thing considered small talk these days? For that matter, the time-slipped Angel knows about Wesley's statement that his specialized gun will kill Illyria, even though *that* version of Angel wasn't privy to it. We might also question the fact that Wesley has spontaneously developed enough engineering skills to cobble together "a Mutari Generator" that creates a pinhole into a negatively charged pocket universe. Alternatively, if the firm normally has that sort of eyebrow-raising hardware just lying about the place, why didn't Wesley think about using it on Illyria back in "Shells"?

CRITIQUE Four episodes from the end, with *Angel* revamping itself almost on a week-by-week basis, "Time Bomb" is a bit peculiar. It's not particularly bad; mind, neither is it resoundingly good. In fact, it's most notable for being so patently formulaic, and therefore seems out-of-place with the stellar innovation we've enjoyed of late. If "I've Got You Under My Skin" (1.14) was "*Angel* meets *The Exorcist*," then this is "*Angel* meets one of those time-travel episodes of *Star Trek: The Next Generation*." Notice, for example, how the audience knows more about the time-travel element than the characters, and how the lead characters die horribly, only to get saved by a time-quirk. If you're a long-time sci-fi viewer, you've undoubtedly seen much of this before.

Now, we've previously argued that formula isn't automatically a sin so long as it's formula done well, so let's be clear that Edlund makes this episode interesting enough. It works, even if it's admittedly the one story where Illyria's speechifying gets truly annoying ("My power beats at the walls of this feeble shell with fists of diamond," etc.) Even so, the real failing of "Time Bomb" isn't Edlund's storytelling, but that it chiefly exists to move the series from Point A to Point B. Specifically, it's designed from the get-go to castrate Illyria and nullify her time-freeze, thereby preventing her – three episodes hence – from fixing the series finale with a wave of her hand. Working to that limitation, Edlund can only do so much.

So we're left with a story that's decent but hardly what you'd call gripping, mainly because it's got to nudge the show into a certain position. Still, given all the irons in the fire at the moment, it's hardly surprising that a bit of course correction was required.

THE LORE Amanda was played by Boreanaz's wife Jaime Bergman. (Indeed, it's almost certainly not a coincidence that Amanda mentions "her husband" while looking straight at Angel.) Bergman is a former *Playboy* Playmate, and best-known for her role the FX spoof *Son of the Beach*. She married Boreanaz in 2001 and had a son with him – Jaden – in 2002, meaning she's not really pregnant as Amanda.

• The rehash scene where Gunn and Lorne discuss Wesley and his "full strength crazy" isn't in the script and was probably added for time.

• Nicholas Gilhool (Fell Brother #1) played "Shroom" in *Dead Poets Society* (1989).

5.20: "The Girl in Question"

"Buffy would never fall for a centuries-old guy with a dark past, and who may or may not be evil."

Air Date: May 5, 2004; **Writers:** Steven S. DeKnight, Drew Goddard; **Director:** David Greenwalt

SUMMARY When the human-tolerant Capo de Familia of the Goran demon clan "dies" in Italy, Gunn requests that someone collect the Capo's head so he can be ritualistically returned to life. Simultaneously, an agent that Angel assigned to watch Buffy phones to say that Buffy is dating the Immortal, one of Angelus and Spike's old enemies.

Angel and Spike race to Rome but fail to locate Buffy. Instead, they wind up chatting with Andrew, who's rooming with her and Dawn. Meanwhile, mysterious parties steal the Capo's head and demand a ransom. Angel and Spike solicit the firm's Rome branch for help, but still fail to get the head back and continue chasing after Buffy. Andrew advises that they move on with their lives – as Buffy has evidently done – and they return home, defeated. Once back in L.A., Angel and Spike find that Immortal has generously recovered the Capo's head and sent it to them.

During Angel and Spike's absence, Wesley panics when Fred's parents show up for a surprise visit, then becomes shocked when Illyria solves the problem by shape-shifting and imitating Fred. The Burkles depart, suitably fooled, even as Fred-Illyria suggests that she and Wesley pursue a relationship. In response, Wesley orders Illyria to never impersonate Fred again.

FIRSTS AND LASTS The series' hourglass is running low on sand now, because it's the final appearances of Buffy (or rather, her blonde stand-in, seen at a Rome nightclub), Julie Benz as Darla and Juliet Landau as Drusilla. Our last-ever shot of Darla and Dru, as it happens, is of them giggling, wearing negligees and excusing themselves to have a bath. Also in flashback, it's the final appearance of Angelus and his misbegotten accent, and of Spike in his soulless "William the

Bloody" persona. For that matter, it's the final mention of Angelus' fixation with nuns, and of Spike's nickname of "Blondie Bear" (here spoken by Angel).

Last appearance of Andrew, not to mention Roger and Trish Burkle. Final instance of Angel riding on the back of a motorcycle (see 2.03, "First Impressions") and of Spike (remembering his habits on *Buffy*) riding a motorcycle at all. Final instance of the heroes peering at someone's head in a bag (see also 2.22, "There's No Place Like Plrtz Glrb," and tangentially 5.02, "Just Rewards"). Last use of Fred's laboratory, and of a dance-hopping nightclub (funny that it's located in Rome, not L.A. as you might expect).

Creatively, it's the last script from DeKnight and Goddard, and the final tangible contribution from David Greenwalt (who's directing). It's the only occasion that we view a Wolfram and Hart branch in another city, and also – believe it or not – the final instance of Angel getting de-masculinized, as the Rome C.E.O. dresses him in a "stylish" jacket that almost defies explanation.

Only TV mention of the Immortal (but check out the *Buffy* comic book series). Arguably, it's the last time we see Wesley unshaven, and the final outing for Spike's trademark coat after nearly seven years of TV service (but see **Things That Don't Make Sense**) – although he quickly acquires an exact copy.

POINTS OF DISCUSSION ABOUT "The Girl in Question":

1. For anyone trying to evaluate this story, the pendulum usually swings back to the *Buffy* finale (7.22, "Chosen") and Buffy's infamous "cookie dough" speech therein. To recap, Buffy told Angel: "I'm cookie dough. I'm not done baking. I'm not finished becoming whoever the hell it is I'm gonna turn out to be..." The general idea was that – as part of the story's "female empowerment" angle, undoubtedly *the* greatest message in the whole of *Buffy* – the Slayer had decided she needed to wait before sharing herself with another boyfriend. Fair enough, save that...

... Buffy is dating The Immortal, who more fits the Angel-Spike mold than not. Generally speaking, the fan response to this has ranged from "I'm totally cool with that" to "You've raped the character and violated the cookie dough speech" yadda yadda yadda. Such venom is usually relegated to the minority, but it's out there.

So, let's stop to think about this. First off, Buffy never said she was becoming a nun. It's probably been a solid nine months (if a year) since "Chosen," and one can hardly expect her to stay celibate forever. Nor, by this point, can she conceivably date someone who even approaches what you'd call "normal." She tried that with Riley Finn, after all, and look how that turned out. So on the surface, her dating someone like the Immortal seems reasonable.

Besides, we're told virtually nothing about the Immortal. That being the case, how on Earth can anyone claim Buffy is making a tragic mistake? Indeed, everything we're shown suggests that he's God's gift to women (and possibly men, too). Simply *everyone* in this episode (save Angel and Spike, of course) gushes with praise for the Immortal, and let's not forget that he eventually saves Angel and Spike's sorry asses. What's to say he's not a perfect match for the Slayer? Besides, he'd be a great help in Italy. Have you *been* to Italy? A single blonde American girl would be fodder for constant harassment, and a hunky immortal boyfriend would curtail all that.

So let's concede that on screen, there's nothing that rings any alarm bells about the Immortal – unless you're the type to scathe someone's romantic choice before you've actually met them.

2. There's an extremely brief 1950s flashback in this episode, one that features Spike and Dru in Rome – looking too cool for words – standing about and artfully going "Ciao." What's remarkable is the sheer amount of hassle that undoubtedly went into this scene, which lasts all of a few seconds, and forces Marsters to affect dark hair once again (in keeping with 5.13, "Why We Fight"). In what's apparently an homage to 1950s Italian cinema, this flashback is rendered in black-and-white, but this makes for an odd constrast considering the much-earlier 1894 one is in color. You almost expect Spike to say, regarding the 1950s scene: "That was the year the demon stole all the color from Italy."

3. Illyria, her power reduced after last episode, wistfully looks at a plant and remarks, "I can no longer hear the Song of the Green." No, she's not talking about Lorne. Instead, it's meant to confirm hints from the past-couple episodes that Illyria can talk to plants. But here's the curious thing... Cordelia wondered in "That Old Gang of Mine" (3.03) if Fred was talking to a shrub, and Fred nearly seemed to converse with a houseplant before vomiting on it in "Spin the Bottle" (4.06). All considered, you have to wonder if Fred was a mutant who could converse with plants, on a sub-conscious level. Illyria might've boosted this ability once she took over Fred's body, but lost the talent after her powers got curtailed. All right, maybe it's a stretch, but it's an entertaining notion to consider.

4. How you know it's a Goddard script: Angel and Spike debate which of them has saved the world more times, and quickly check off the climactic struggles from *Buffy* Seasons One, Two and Three, plus *Angel* Season Four. Of particular amusement, Angel claims he helped Buffy to save the world in Season Two, while failing to admit that as Angelus, he endangered it in the first place. Other continuity references (that we'd attribute to Goddard, but could admittedly owe to DeKnight): There's mention of Angel's time as a homeless person in New York, of how Spike got his jacket (*Buffy* 5.07, "Fool for Love") and of Pavayne (*Angel* 5.04, "Hell Bound").

5. The teaser makes for one of those rare occasions when you're reminded that J. August Richards is taller than the show's lead actor. Like Adam Baldwin, Richards is 6'4". By comparison, Boreanaz is "only" 6'1".

6. The head of the Rome office, Ilona Costa Bianchi, only features in three scenes but is so (how shall we put this?) "spirited" that she tops our list of "*Angel* Action Figures We'd Like to See But Probably Never Will." (The others are the giant Hamburger Man from 3.15, "Loyalty" and Fred in Lornette gear from 4.03, "The House Always Wins.") Carole Davis radiates an unbelievable amount of energy into the role, especially considering that Angel and Spike just stand around neutrally, meaning she's got nothing to bounce her enthusiasm off. Her notable lines include: "Spiiiiiike... you take my breath away!" (gasps) "I have no breath!!"; "I have had dealings with The Immortal many times, and I must say that the outcome is always..." (smacks down a grape) "*most* satisfactory"; and "Brute force will only get your precious head smooshed." Her best line, of course, is (all together now): "The gypsies are filthy people! Pah! And we shall speak of them no more!"

CHARACTER NOTES *Angel:* In 1894, Angelus and Spike were trussed up by the Immortal's men and locked in "The Room of Pain." They were chained up in their underwear [as in every fangirl's wildest dream], but eventually freed and ordered to leave town. They found that the Immortal had bedded Darla and Drusilla concurrently (something the girls never let Angelus or Spike do). Plus, they *really* enjoyed it. [Angelus and Spike's mutual outrage suggests they buried the hatchet after the Angelus-Dru fling in 5.08, "Destiny."] Angelus and Spike swore "Blood Vengeance" against the Immortal, but left town without attaining a lick of it.

At the time, Angelus said he'd never tried to catch arrows in mid-air. In the modern day, the thought of dancing still rattles Angel [and well it should; see 1.13, "She"]. Angel says that he's seeing Nina, but that "she's not my girlfriend." When a bomb shreds Angel's clothes, Bianchi decks him out in a ridiculous-looking Italian motorcycle jacket, insisting that it's the latest style. [Tragically, there's better odds of *this* miserable get-up inspiring an action figure than Bianchi herself.]

• *Buffy:* She's living in Apt. 34, and Andrew says that most nights, "she and the Immortal never leave the house" [although it's unclear why they can't just make out at the Immortal's digs]. Andrew insists that Buffy fell for the Immortal of her own volition. Bianchi and the kidnapper Alfonso insist that Buffy is very fortunate if she's the Immortal's lover.

• *Spike:* Never learned to speak Italian beyond a few words. He acknowledges that he doesn't have a shot with Buffy, and probably never did. Spike's previous encounters with the Immortal have resulted in him losing his girl, getting beaten by an angry mob and thrown into prison for income tax evasion.

Spike mourns the loss of his coat, here shredded by a bomb, because he's owned it for "30 years." [It's actually 27, judging by "Fool for Love," but he's probably generalizing.] Still, he perks up when Bianchi replaces it with an exact copy and sends ten more to the L.A. office, along with a fine assortment of shoes.

• *Wesley:* Oddly, he didn't honor Fred's last request [5.15, "A Hole in the World"] to speak with her parents about her death. [He presumably just found it too painful to tell them, especially with Illyria constantly occupying Fred's body. That, or up to a point, he was holding out hope that Fred would return.]

• *Illyria:* Never shows the ability to duplicate anyone beyond Fred. Illyria can also morph into Fred's clothes [probably because her body-armor was presented, in 5.16, "Shells," as being almost organic].

Illyria takes to imitating Fred, or so she says, because Wesley's grief hangs off him "like rotted flesh" and she couldn't stand the thought of Fred's parents doing the same. [Yet it's possible – especially as she ends this story wanting a romance with Wesley – that she genuinely didn't want to cause Fred's parents pain. It seems that she's developing a real sense of humanity, although it's anyone's guess if Fred's memories are affecting her. See the series finale.]

• *Darla:* After her "Really. Great. Fornication." with the Immortal, a glowing Darla awakens with a simply unbelievable case of bed-head. [This is, undoubtedly, the happiest we've ever seen vampire Darla, which suggests the Immortal really *can* satisfy her in ways that Angelus can't.]

• *Andrew:* Very pleased to see Angel and Spike. [Andrew back-stabbed Angel in 5.11, "Damage," but he was admittedly following orders at the time, and he's very much in awe of the upper-echelons of Buffy and Angel's groups. In other words, he's not going to turn away people of Angel and Spike's stature just because he doesn't always agree with them.]

Andrew's house was incinerated as part of some "cultural misunderstanding," and he's been crashing with Buffy and Dawn ever since. Andrew speaks some Italian, and he's last seen dressed in a tuxedo and escorting two gorgeous women – Caprice and Isabella [they could be Slayers] – out for the evening. [It's further proof that Andrew is bi-sexual, not gay as is often claimed.]

• *Dawn:* [There's no mention of her location during this story, which is curious, because Rome isn't a city where you should let an impressionable teenage girl run wild.]

• *Roger and Trish Burkle:* Haven't seen Angel's group [but presumably *have* seen their daughter] since 3.05, "Fredless." They're on their way to Hawaii and visit the firm during a layover. They deem the firm an improvement over the run-down Hyperion. Trish suggests that Wesley is husband material for Fred, and has a very vague sense that something's different about her daughter.

• *The Immortal:* Glimpsed in the nightclub with Buffy, and – from the back – looks like a young man in a suit. In 1894, the Immortal returned to Rome after 300 years away [and he's probably been there ever since]. Sometime prior to 1894, in Frankfurt, he hatched "the Rathrúhn egg" and provided safe passage to some nuns that Angelus wanted. At some point, the Immortal spent 150 years in a Tibetan monastery. Bianchi says she's dealt with [meaning "slept with," presumably] the Immortal many times. She insists that the Immortal doesn't use spells, deeming them "dirty tricks for dirty people."

The Immortal has written a spiritual guide book (of sorts), and Spike has heard that the Immortal has climbed Mount Everest. Several times.

• *Ilona Costa Bianchi:* Smokes and is best described as "ex-porn star turned C.E.O."

ORGANIZATIONS *Wolfram e Hart:* The firm's Rome branch features various Italian lawyers and Italian demons. [They're allowed to smoke in the lobby, whereas it's apparently banned in L.A.] The Rome executive lobby looks precisely like the L.A. one, and Bianchi's office looks exactly like Angel's save for all the erotic art. "Pietro" serves as Bianchi's assistant.

Angel and Spike venture to Italy in jet No. N3 LR.

DEMONOLOGY *Vampires:* Their constitution prevents them from getting drunk off those small airplane bottles, as Angel and Spike discover. [Mind, this occurs on a Wolfram and Hart plane, which you'd expect to be stocked with big bottles, blood, drugs and possibly hookers.]

• *Goran Demons:* Death is more of an "interim step for them." They die (or rather, their heads drop off like ripe figs), they pupate and they live again, but only if the immediate family performs the proper rituals within a certain time.

BEST LINE Angel, goading Spike: "Sleeping together is not a relationship." Spike, goading back: "It is if you do it enough times."

THINGS THAT DON'T MAKE SENSE All right, all right... the comedy here is predicated on Angel and Spike dashing about like dolts in Rome, while simultaneously attempting to recover the Capo's head and court Buffy. Fair enough, save that the set-up in the teaser is a hash. To walk through the motions... the normally hyper-jealous Angel thinks it's a good idea to send Spike to collect the Capo's head, even though Buffy lives in Rome and Spike is almost guaranteed to look her up. Then Spike shrugs off said assignment, even though it's a perfect excuse to visit Buffy. Then there's the simply astounding coincidence that Angel's agent phones while everyone is dithering about the Capo's head, meaning Angel and Spike are given not one but *two* separate reasons to visit Rome in the space of about three minutes. Then Angel is foolish enough to blurt out that Buffy has come under the Immortal's sway – or so he believes – while Spike is in the room, and he honestly thinks Spike will stay behind after a declaration like *that*.

Nice to see that Spike is so sentimental about his prized coat, even though it was *charred to ashes* in the *Buffy* finale and magically reconstituted afterward, so it's debatable whether it's the same one he acquired 27 years or not. As Alfonso flees with the Capo's head, Spike readily procures a Vespa because the owner was idiotic enough to leave their keys in the ignition. Then Angel and Spike put-put on the Vespa, yet still keep up with Alfonso's much-faster car. Then they endure an amazingly selective (but funny) crash in which the car seems to *touch* the Vespa and it comes instantly unglued.

One visual goof: Alfonso holds the bag with the Capo's head one-handed on top, then on bottom, in the same close-up. Oh, and a rather important detail that might've curtailed half the story... if Wolfram and Hart *does* have a branch in Rome, then why didn't Gunn call them from the very start and say, "Hey, can you nip out and collect our head?"

IT'S REALLY ABOUT... Angel and Spike's inability to move on from Buffy – at least, until the point that Andrew gives them the sensible advice that they'll never catch the girl if they're constantly chasing her. As you'd expect, the fact that they're so fixated with an old flame is rather immature – hell, Angel's assigning someone to watch Buffy, especially when he's got a girlfriend at home, seems downright creepy. So let's take their letting the matter rest as a sign of their developing maturity. That said, you have to wonder if they ruffled through Buffy's underwear drawer once Andrew left for the evening.

CRITIQUE Not since "I Will Remember You" (1.08) has the viewer's pre-conceptions and expectations so dictated an episode's success or failure. We've already covered how much of this boils down to everyone's personal wish list for Buffy, and this episode's placement admittedly doesn't help. With the viewership hungry for the dramatic series finale, a comedy story this close to at this point was bound to rub some people the wrong way, and "The Girl in Question" might've fared better earlier in the season. Still, if you can view this episode divested of demands that it be *this* sort of tale or *that* sort of tale...

... well then, it's just about the funniest thing ever. Angel and Spike have been petty and bitchy with each other all year, so to watch them run around Rome like love-struck frat boys proves utterly hysterical. Their scrap in the nightclub is highly amusing, Andrew puts in a great appearance and Bianchi is unbelievably entertaining. It's a well-oiled comedy piece, and the producers really couldn't play this any other way. They didn't have the luxury of ignoring the Buffy issue altogether; nor could they attempt anything serious without Sarah Michelle Gellar. A whimsical episode makes the most sense under those conditions – and if you *must* have something dramatic, then the "Fred's parents come to visit" subplot works extremely well. Indeed, watching Acker voice Illyria while wearing Fred's body is one of the most disconcerting things in the entire series.

If you ask 100 different fans about this episode's treatment of Buffy, etc., you're probably going to get 100 different opinions. Actually, check that. Knowing fandom, you're probably going to net *200* different viewpoints. For the record, however, we went into this story unconcerned about its stance on Buffy, and constantly doubled over with laughter. If possible, we recommend that you do the same.

THE LORE The producers had originally hoped to bring back Gellar as Buffy for episode twelve (the show's 100th episode) which was slated to air during sweeps. Gellar proved unavailable – it's often suggested that she was in Japan filming *The Grudge*, and literally couldn't visit the L.A. set – so Carpenter was recruited to tie off Cordelia's storyline and "You're Welcome" came into being. No later than Dec. 2003, Whedon was stating, on the record, that he didn't know if Gellar would ever play Buffy again. (And for what it's worth, Denisof commented that whereas "Sarah made all the right noises when *Buffy* wrapped up," he never for a moment thought she was going to return.) (O'Hare, *Zap2It.com*, Jan. 20, 2004)

The producers pondered using Gellar later in the season – possibly in the penultimate episode – but rejected the idea of having her in the series finale, as it'd short-change the *Angel* characters. Finally, Mutant Enemy just decided to roll without Gellar, and crafted "The Girl in Question" to give some closure to the Angel-Spike-Buffy triangle. Even then, things didn't go according to plan. The producers hoped to use Michelle Trachtenberg as Dawn – she'd have appeared in the apartment, telling Angel and Spike that they just missed her sister, etc. – but swapped her for Andrew when that didn't work out.

• DeKnight regretted not using Darla and Drusilla more in this episode, but said there simply wasn't enough time to go around. (DeKnight, *The Bronze*, May 6, 2004)

• Most of Alfonso's goons were written as being demons, but they appear as human thugs (probably because it was cheaper).

• Andrew's Italian lines were mostly unchanged from the script, but some of Bianchi's underwent revision. Her order in Italian that Pietro should get them "some coffee and something to eat" originally (and a bit more strangely) had her telling him to bring cappuccino and some cured ham. One of her amended lines originally had her telling Angel, "You are the bread of all bread, and the wine of all wines. You are gorgeous!" Oh, and if you're curious, Andrew's lines to his chickie-babes roughly translates to, "You [Caprice], are beautiful like the night. You, Isabella, you surpass even the stars."

5.21: "Power Play"

"I've seen the faces of evil. I know who the real powers in the Apocalypse are. I'm talking about killing every single member *of the Black Thorn."*

Air Date: May 12, 2004; **Writer:** David Fury; **Director:** James A. Contner

SUMMARY Angel increasingly toes the company line and hungers for power. Meanwhile, a wounded Drogyn locates Spike and details a failed attempt on his life... apparently instigated by Angel, so that Drogyn wouldn't deduce his involvement in Illyria's return. Angel's allies secretly interrogate Lindsey and learn about the Circle of the Black Thorn – the elite demon group assigned to bring about the Apocalypse on the Senior Partners' behalf. The heroes believe that Angel hopes to join the Circle, and sacrificed Fred as a prerequisite to Circle membership.

Hamilton captures Drogyn, leading to an initiation ceremony that entails Angel killing his old friend. Wesley's quartet later confront Angel, whereupon Angel uses a magic gem to cast a temporary glamour. Shrouded from surveillance, Angel reveals that his "change of heart" was a carefully crafted lie, designed so he could learn identities of the Circle members... and facilitate their deaths. Angel boldly asks his allies to help him assassinate the Circle, thus sending a signal to the Senior Partners – and evil in general – that they don't control Earth's reality. In response, Angel's colleagues – knowing they'll likely perish in the attempt – vote to bring down the Circle. [*Continued next episode*]

FIRSTS AND LASTS Final appearances of Nina, Drogyn and – in what's the last flashback of the series – Cordelia (who's kissing Angel from 5.12, "You're Welcome"). Creatively, it's the last David Fury script. The Circle of the Black Thorn finally gets introduced, and its members include Archduke Sebassis (5.05, "Life of the Party"), Cyvus Vail (5.18, "Origin"), Izzerial (5.12, "You're Welcome"), a Sahvrin demon (5.09, "Harm's Way"), the leader of the Fell Brethren

(5.19, "Time Bomb"), a few unnamed characters and Senator Brucker (here introduced).

It's debatable, but Angel's racquetball session with Izzerial probably marks the last hardcore example of that old Whedon-verse staple: a hideous-looking demon acting like a normal joe. As opposed to the Sebassis-type villains, who *act* like demons, Izzy gossips about the Fell Brethren leader, commenting: "You know the Fells. All they can talk about is the baby. The baby's doing this now. The baby's doing that. What a wonderful ritual sacrifice he'll make... yak, yak, yak."

POINTS OF DISCUSSION ABOUT "Power Play":

1. Wesley concludes that Lindsey tried to kill Angel earlier this season as a means of joining the Circle and obtaining great power, and Lindsey doesn't really contradict the point. Obviously, the producers are making some attempt to rationalize Christian Kane's return for Season Five, and while this isn't unbelievable, it's... awkward. After all, this presumes that Angel's death would please the Senior Partners enough to award Lindsey a Circle seat – as opposed to being so angered at the quashing of their plans that they separate Lindsey from his spine. For that matter, if Lindsey's plans were so in keeping with the Partners' goals, you've got to wonder why he spent the first half of this year sneaking around behind the Partners' backs and was so fearful about registering on their radar. In short, if Lindsey was aiming for Circle membership, this seems like a very reckless and haphazard way of going about it.

2. Angel's scheme contains two rather disturbing wrinkles, but the series simply lacks the time to address them in detail. The first is that Angel murders Drogyn – an A-level heroic champion. Wesley and company go into next episode's fight with their eyes wide open, but Drogyn is another matter entirely. Granted, Drogyn is *so* heroic that he might've willingly given his life for Angel's cause... and it's more than a little ironic that Angel *can't* tip Drogyn off in advance, because Drogyn cannot lie ("A Hole in the World"). Either way, even the charitable view must acknowledge that Angel willfully betrays Drogyn, who thought of him as a brother.

A side note: If Angel had any inkling that his initiation would entail his murdering someone, then it's even worse to think the Circle could've presented him with anybody – Wesley, Gunn, Lorne – and he'd have gone slaughtered them as well.

The second curiosity is that Angel sleeps with Nina. To be fair, they might have hit the sheets before this, but they didn't start dating until "Smile Time" (5.14), meaning two episodes *after* Angel's vision about the Circle. We're not privy to Angel's mentality on this, and it's understandable that he's desperate for comfort and companionship. Still, the most-obvious interpretation is that he gets involved with Nina even knowing he's going to move against the Circle, and consequently puts her in grave danger. He does the right thing by aiding her escape from L.A., but far better for Nina, in all honesty, if he'd steered well clear of her from the start.

3. The Season Five budget constraints once again become a factor, which means there's a dwindling number of extra employees at the firm, Angel's initiation takes place in an undecorated "underground" room, and all of the Circle members are demon get-ups recycled from previous episodes. The only newcomer – Senator Brucker – looks human, so that's a gimmie. Still, this is more of an observation than a criticism, because you really don't sense the penny-pinching measures in "Power Play" upon first viewing, even if hindsight suggests the producers are saving their nickels for the grand finale.

4. The best part about the Circle members unmasking is the soft-yet-lilting party-music that starts up afterward. Evidently, there's nothing evil likes more than some smooth jazz.

CHARACTER NOTES *Angel:* Finally, irrefutably and without equivocation can have sex without becoming Angelus, and does so with Nina. [Romantics will fall back on the "he can only lose his soul by having sex with Buffy" argument, but the clear implication is that Angel has learned to mentally keep himself short of perfect happiness while having it off. The loss of his soul in *Buffy* 2.13, "Surprise," after all, totally caught him off-guard and might've otherwise been prevented.]

Angel learned about the Circle's existence from the Powers [see **Organizations**], but wasn't privy to the group's membership. [When the time comes, Angel's photographic memory presumably helps him remember the Circle members' identities.] To dupe the Circle into thinking he was responsible for Fred's death, Angel fostered insurrection among his allies and arranged the "attack" on Drogyn.

Izzerial "brands" Angel's chest with the Circle's mark, which magically disappears into Angel's skin.

- *Spike:* Off-handedly says that he and Angel "have never been intimate... except that once..." [Yes, it's there, however briefly. Let your imaginations run wild.] Spike says he'd sense it if Angel had became a megalomaniacal bastard [arguably true, even if his prior record at identifying Angel's allegiances is spotty].
- *Wesley:* Has ceased talking to Illyria after her impersonation of Fred [last episode].
- *Illyria:* Seems bothered because Wesley isn't paying her any attention. Illyria is quicker to believe that Angel has been corrupted, having witnessed the familiar pattern of rulers fighting only profitable battles, becoming paranoid and turning on their intimates.

She somewhat wishes she'd never been brought out of the Deeper Well, but feels compelled to keep experiencing life in the modern day. Illyria seems determined to protect Drogyn when asked, and they play *Crash Bandicoot* on Spike's video game system. She's unable to distinguish between Earth's odors.

• *Lorne:* Angel cut loose six of Lorne's clients, four of whom were getting in shape for *Young Guns III*.

• *Lindsey:* Still the heroes' prisoner [after "Underneath"].

• *Nina:* Now sleeping with Angel. She knows about the risk of his converting into Angelus, and of his trip last episode to see Buffy. She attends [the fictional] Southern California Academy of Art and Design (SCAAD). In preparation for moving against the Circle, Angel supplies Nina with plane tickets for herself, her sister and her niece [5.03, "Unleashed"] and all but orders her to leave town. [We might hope that Angel also supplies Nina with a supply of untraceable funds, if he honestly expects the three of them to go on the run for the rest of their lives. Also remember that Nina has special needs every time the full moon rolls around.]

• *Drogyn:* Cited as "the Battlebrand, Demonbane, Truthsayer... given eternal youth a thousand years ago." Wesley read about Drogyn at the Watchers' academy.

Drogyn can track anyone who's visited the Deeper Well, be they in "this world or another." He's still bleeding after tracking Spike all the way from England. [For all we're told, Drogyn magically teleports to Spike's location, or perhaps his poison-laden cut – see **Demonology** – just doesn't heal quickly.]

It's implied that anyone "at the mercy of Drogyn's wrath" must tell the truth. He says that his cave-home is "really quite pleasant." [There's no indication of who assumes guardianship of the Deeper Well after Drogyn's demise, but the script to "A Hole in the World" suggested that the post was "assigned," meaning the Well likely won't be left unattended.]

• *Hamilton:* Acquainted with Drogyn, and not in a friendly way. [They haven't seen one another since Drogyn became the Deeper Well guardian, which was "decades" ago, according to "A Hole in the World." In all likelihood, Hamilton was a freelance meta-human, later employed by the Senior Partners and "empowered" as their agent (see next episode).]

Hamilton readily overpowers Illyria in combat. He personally attends to the visiting Senator Brucker [as with the Fell in 5.19, "Time Bomb"; Hamilton clearly puts in an appearance for the Circle members]. He seems suspicious about Angel's glamour spell [see **Magic**].

• *Senator Helen Brucker:* Circle member who "clawed her way up from Hell and got installed in a human body." She's now a national senator, almost doubtlessly representing California [since she's got an L.A. office next episode]. Ernesto, a vampire, serves as her aide. Brucker claims to go "way back with the firm" to when Holland Manners was in charge. [This is a somewhat bizarre thing to say, given that it was only three years ago.] Brucker hopes to take the White House in 2008, partly by funding from hostile governments, but she's facing a tough re-election bid from Mike Conley – a Gulf War veteran and Bronze Star recipient. Accordingly, she asks the firm to discredit Conley, brainwashing the man into thinking he's a pedophile. [This apparently happens, judging by next episode.]

• *Dr. Sparrow:* Finally mentioned by name [but there's no word on his fate since 5.16, "Shells"].

• *Izzerial:* Plays racquetball with Angel. [They obviously do this at a court that caters to demons, assuming it's not located in the firm itself. Similarly, Izzerial – horns and all – dines at a restaurant next episode.]

• *Vail:* Comes out of hiding [after 5.18, "Origin"].

THE FIRM'S LIBRARY Wesley calls up classifications and case histories relating to Boretz Demons, and Angel knows how to usurp the template system to send Wesley secret messages.

ORGANIZATIONS *The Powers-That-Be:* Bestowed upon Angel a one-time vision when he kissed Cordelia in "You're Welcome." [In flashback, there's "blue energy" moving between their lips, as with Doyle and Cordelia in 1.09, "Hero." This is an extremely atypical vision, probably facilitated by the highly unique circumstances behind Cordy's return. This doesn't, however, make Angel the next visionary.] He experienced the vision later that evening in bed. [Presumably, the Powers recognize that Angel simply isn't resuming his role as a street champion any time soon, and hand him knowledge of the Circle to get him back on a heroic path.]

• *The Circle of the Black Thorn:* Elite demon group that's supposed to "grease the wheels" of the Apocalypse and "make sure man's inhumanity to man keeps rolling along." [In addition to the Apocalypse angle, they probably also stoke the fires of mankind's cruelty, thus empowering insidious parties such as the firm; 2.15, "Reprise."] The Senior Partners exist on another plane, and the Circle serve as their chief instrument in our reality [with the firm serving as the Circle's attorneys]. The Circle members are evil, but are more notable for being power-hungry. Drogyn hasn't heard of them.

DEMONOLOGY *Vampires:* Brucker comments, when Angel registers that her aide is a vampire, "I always forget your kind can sense each other." [This trait isn't characteristic of every vampire, however.] Ernesto likes virgin blood, room temperature; Harmony counter-offers a "fruity, unassuming vole." [The script later had her emptying a blood bag into a mug and cheerily asking, "Who wants person?"]

• *The Fell Brethren:* Their Grand Potentate is named Ed.

• *Boretz demons:* Stink, dress like transients and pray on the homeless. Boretz demons have a poisonous bite. One of them kills people at the abandoned Funville amusement park, but Illyria dispatches it.

• *Sathari:* Clan of demon assassins, armed with "four blades" and a poison capable of weakening Drogyn.

MAGIC *The Glamour Crystal:* Angel holds this and chants, "Involvere!" [Latin for "to wrap up," i.e. "envelop"], whereupon the crystal generates the illusion of Angel and his colleagues shouting at one another. Angel says the effect lasts "six minutes." [Sure enough... on screen, the glamour lasts 5 minutes, 53 seconds. The crystal must cast an illusion according to the user's desire, but it's hardly foolproof, since Hamilton clearly wonders if it's a ruse. Mind, as we learn next episode, that's fine because Angel expects the Circle to view him with suspicion.]

BEST LINE Illyria's misleading comment to Spike, on Wesley giving her the silent treatment: "He and I are not having intercourse."

THINGS THAT DON'T MAKE SENSE Spike thinks it an excellent idea to introduce Illyria to Drogyn, her former jailor, apparently unconcerned that she might revert to type and want to gouge the man's eyes out. Then the heroes compound the error by asking Illyria – of all people! – to guard Drogyn while they hustle off to challenge Angel. Fine, they believe she simply isn't interested in the matters at hand, but it's leaving an awful lot to chance.

Angel feeds off Drogyn, who's been poisoned by a Sathari demon, so shouldn't this poison Angel too? (Perhaps the poison is too diluted, or doesn't work on vampires.) The Circle-logo drawing that Wesley displays in Spike's apartment looks a lot thicker than the one he scribbles in the executive lobby. Angel wants Nina and her family to go into hiding, so isn't booking plane tickets with their *real* names – as Nina indicates – something of a giveaway?

And it's puzzling that the heroes only take the usual assortment of weapons (crossbows, a shotgun, etc.) to confront Angel rather than something that's been provably more effective, such as a tranquilizer gun or a Taser.

POP CULTURE Lorne, on the corporate-minded Angel: "It's like he's started channeling Leona Helmsley." Helmsley was a famous New York City hotel operator and real estate investor who used a forceful management style, got convicted of income tax evasion in 1989 and served 18 months in the pokey.

IT'S REALLY ABOUT... How compromising your ideals in slow increments eventually swings full circle to a choice between good and villainy. It's a familiar pattern: You give a little ground, then a little more.. and then you run out of room to maneuver, and start dealing with matters of black-and-white again. Ideology falls by the wayside in the interest of simply keeping power or acquiring stuff, and you're in danger of committing actions that would've been unthinkable in past. History has provided numerous instances of such moral erosion – in politics, business, charities, etc. – so the point here is that the heroes decide (commendably) that being dead is actually preferable to being evildoers.

CRITIQUE Given the thankless job of crafting the penultimate *Angel* episode – which by its very nature entails a big wind-up with very little release – Fury delivers a story that's suitably ominous, gets your guts in a twist and proves entirely worthy as the series draws to an end. Admittedly, this episode seems like a con-job with no real "con," meaning that precious few viewers would believe that Angel has spontaneously become so corrupt. Indeed, any lingering doubt about Angel's intentions is decisively settled when he hands Nina a plane ticket, and sends her out of danger.

And yet, this story isn't about wondering which way Angel will flip. It's about examining why he hasn't become as dark and corrupt as he's pretending. Somewhat miraculously, the set-up here is genuinely unlike anything the characters have experienced in the last five years. Granted, they've previously faced mortal peril, but here they actively pick a course of redemption that will probably destroy some if not all of them. It remains the best and most important decision they'll ever take, and allows "Power Play" to usher in one of the greatest finales in the history of television.

THE LORE The *Angel* fans didn't exactly go quietly into the night – even though the WB stated it wasn't reversing its decision about cancellation, no network stepped up to take the show over, and some key people such as DeKnight (after a point) politely told fans to save their time and trouble. Nonetheless, some of the more notable "save *Angel*" campaigns are listed below.

• **The Save Angel Blood Drive...** March 17, 2004 was declared national "Give Blood for *Angel*" day, and people in 20 states participated.

• **The Save Angel Food Drive (www.angelsfood drive.com)...** *Angel* fans raised more than $14,000 for the Los Angeles Regional Food Bank, and ordered two enormous cakes (enough to serve 200 people) for the *Angel* crew. A thousand balloons with the food drive's website were sent to the 20th Century Fox offices, and...

• **The Save Angel Swag-Offerings...** 2,000 chocolate bars with wrappers bearing the "Save *Angel*" slogan were sent to various parties in the *Angel* food chain (so to speak). Additionally, WB co-C.E.O. Jordan Levin got 100 bouquets.

• **The Save Angel Rally ...** Occurred outside the WB offices on March 31. Most of the signs involved were of the standard "Renew *Angel*"/"Fight For Quality TV" variety, although there were reports of more inventive fare such as "Don't Let the Senior Partners Win," "Support the Undead" and "Impeach Bush and Renew *Angel*."

• **Save Angel Advertising...** Fans purchased a full-page ad in *The Hollywood Reporter* (March 9, 2004), another in *Variety* (March 15, 2004), and hired a billboard truck to drive around to various networks with a sign proclaiming: "We'll follow *Angel* to hell... or another network."

• Some attempt was made, it seems, at a **Save *Angel* Weight Loss Challenge.** Also, the "Save *Angel*" campaign presented Mutant Enemy with a check for $13,000 during the 2004 Saturn Awards, for benefit of the Red Cross. (Keveney, *USA Today*, April 13, 2004; *PRWeb.com*, April 14, 2004; *SaveAngel.org*, March 11, 2004; *SavingAngel.org*, March 31, 2004)

5.22: "Not Fade Away"

"What would you do if you found out that none of it matters? That it's all controlled by forces more powerful and uncaring than we can conceive, and they will never let it get better down here. What would you do?"

Air Date: May 19, 2004; **Writer/Director:** Jeffrey Bell; **Writer:** Joss Whedon

SUMMARY As proof of his loyalty to the Circle, Angel signs away his reward of humanity as stated in the Shanshu Prophecy. Later, he convinces Lindsey to stand with the heroes in battle. More importantly, Angel tells his allies that they're going to kill the Circle members that evening, and to spend to spend the day as if it's their last. Lorne sings in a lounge, Spike wildly succeeds at a poetry slam, Gunn helps Anne Steele move furniture for the homeless shelter, Wesley simply tends to Illyria's wounds and Angel briefly visits Connor.

The heroes set out to eliminate their targets, planning to meet up in the alley north of the Hyperion afterward. Angel poisons Archduke Sebassis, then kills Hamilton – with some help from Connor, who returns home. Spike, Illyria, Gunn and Lindsey slay their opponents, but – as Angel planned – Lorne shoots Lindsey dead and departs to go into hiding. Meanwhile, Wesley finds himself overpowered by Cyvus Vail's magics. Vail drives a large knife into Wesley's stomach, then staggers as Wes unleashes a final burst of magical energy. Illyria arrives, concerned for Wesley's safety, and assumes Fred's aspect to comfort Wes as he dies. Vail recovers and taunts "Fred," but Illyria punches his head off.

Angel, Spike, Illyria and a severely wounded Gunn gather behind the Hyperion, even as the Senior Partners send a demon army against them. Spike asks if Angel has a plan, and Angel responds that personally, he just wants to kill the opposing army's dragon. As the demons dash forward, Angel declares, "Let's go to work," and swings his sword.

FIRSTS AND LASTS In reverse order, it's the final appearances on *Angel* for... Angel, a back alley in the rain, Gunn, Illyria, Spike, the Wolfram and Hart building in any capacity, Eve, the firm's executive lobby, Connor, Hamilton, Cyvus Vail and his abode, Wesley Wyndam-Pryce, Lorne, the Sahrvin demons, Lindsey, Senator Brucker, Angel's office (the window of which is again smashed), the Fell Brethren, Archduke Sebassis and his "Pee-Pee Demon," Harmony, Angel's penthouse, a unicorn on Harmony's desk, Izzerial, Spike's apartment, Anne Steele, Angel's conference room, the Shanshu Prophecy document, the Opening Credits and Wesley's trademark shotgun.

Also, it's the last instance of a vampire feeding off someone (Angel, sapping Hamilton's strength), of Illyria in Fred's aspect, of a meta-human punching someone's head off (as with Connor and Jasmine; 4.21, "Peace Out"), of someone using a wrist-stake to dust a vampire (Gunn, dispatching one of Brucker's lackeys), of someone getting tossed through a column (Angel, sailing through a support beam in the lobby), of someone getting tossed out a window (Angel again, flung out his penthouse and falling through the lobby skylight), of someone having sex (Harmony, in bed with Hamilton) and of Lorne singing in a lounge.

Spike gets the last mention of the Shanshu Prophecy (he says to Angel: "What do you think all this means for that Shanshu bugaboo?") Oh, and it's the final "Previously On *Angel*..." segment, which hasn't gotten much use this season.

POINTS OF DISCUSSION ABOUT "Not Fade Away":

1. Scarcely a convention panel on *Angel* can pass without someone asking about the "cliffhanger" ending, so let's make clear that it's not the open-ended finale that some pretend. *Angel* kept fronting the notion that a single heroic champion really *can't* achieve a great sweeping victory over evil, so we're presented with a more realistic ending than (say) *Buffy*, which tied-up everything neatly into a bow. In short, this isn't about besting your opponent, it's about the heroes themselves and how – after a series of working on behalf of a despicable law firm – they're finally returning to their true calling. The point is that Angel's band will *never* stop fighting against the forces of darkness, even unto their deaths (and even beyond, where possible).

2. As you might expect, Wesley's demise is the most mov-

ing thing on display here, and it cements his position as the most tragic character ever to feature in a Whedon project. However, as we suggested before, it's worse because Fred's soul (according to 5.16, "Shells") was supposedly destroyed bringing Illyria back to life. If that's the case, then Wes probably can't even spend the afterlife with her. But then again, perhaps it's fair to imagine divine intervention on that score. It's not as if Wes and Fred haven't earned such happiness.

3. Wesley falls while fighting Vail, in what's strangely the most lopsided contest in this story. Exactly why Wesley attacks a master warlock such as Vail with magic – or how Wes has suddenly gained the ability to project magical fire blasts – goes unstated. Perhaps we should assume that Wes was searched before being admitted into Vail's presence, so blowing the sorcerer's head off with a pistol probably wasn't an option. By contrast, the knife Wesley flashes was probably easier to conceal.

4. On Gunn's fate... well, he's probably a goner. Illyria tells him, "You're fading. You'll last ten minutes at best," and that's irrespective of the demon horde bearing down on them. If we're being honest, it's hard to imagine anything human walking away from such a "Hell on Earth" scenario. Mind, we don't see Gunn die, which means he'll undoubtedly turn up in any ancillary products (heck, he's already appeared in the comics) set after the series. And see **The Lore**.

5. Two details left lingering, probably for reasons of time. After Connor helps Angel against Hamilton, Angel just tells the boy to go home. Well, fine, but the Senior Partners must know where Connor lives and – in light of Angel's revolution – will undoubtedly seek revenge by trying to off him. We might imagine that Connor is now clever enough to take his family into hiding, but it's still a lingering question mark. Ditto on the baby that Spike reclaims from the Fell and returns to its mother. Unless the heroes craft a plan for hiding her indefinitely, you'd expect the surviving – albeit more lowly – Fell to want the kid back.

6. Almost nobody can watch the oncoming demon horde without thinking of *The Lord of the Rings*, and there's even a dragon to boot (although truthfully, it doesn't much resemble Smog). A *really neat* little detail people miss, however, is that a dragon drawing (albeit a crude one) is here seen within the Shanshu Prophecy, and has been there ever since "To Shanshu in L.A." (1.22). Ultimately, we'll never know if the Shanshu has any validity. Hell, it could have nothing to do with Angel, Spike or any character we've ever met. Nonetheless, if you so choose, the dragon-drawing might indicate the climactic battle really *is* the part of the Apocalyptic struggle that's been foretold for so long. It's less likely, however, that the appearance of what looks like a coffee stain in the Shanshu document indicates that everyone involved is going to enjoy a nice latte afterward.

CHARACTER NOTES *Angel:* Convinced the heroes aren't going to make it through this struggle alive. He poisons the "Pee-Pee Demon" with a spiked ring, and this later kills Sebassis, who drinks the Pee-Pee Demon's fluids. Angel feeds off Hamilton's blood, which is charged with the Senior Partners' power. [That could have any number of consequences for Angel in future. Mind, he's been absorbing a lot of meta-human blood recently, including Jasmine's blood (4.19, "The Magic Bullet") and feeding off Drogyn last episode.] Angel has never written a resume.

• *Spike:* Spends his "last day" at "McTarnan's Poetry Slam," where he reads his ghastly love poem [the one from *Buffy* 5.07, "Fool For Love"]. Thanks to the different venue, it's here received with much applause. Spike dedicates the poem to Cecily ["Fool for Love"] and for an encore recites, "The Wanton Folly of Me Mum..." [see, if you dare, *Buffy* 7.17, "Lies My Parents Told Me"].

• *Wesley:* Wants to spend his last day with Fred, but settles for keeping Illyria company because there's no singular experience that can sum up his life. He rebuffs Illyria's offer to imitate Fred – refusing to accept a lie under normal circumstances – but allows her to do so while he's dying.

The Circle is apparently sizing Wesley up for membership, deeming him "intriguingly unstable." [It says something about Wesley's character shifts of late that the most evil organization on the planet would consider admitting him.] Wes mixes some goop that, when applied to a bandage, helps to heal Illyria's neck wound. He shakes hands with Gunn during their last meeting, and departs after giving Angel an approving nod.

• *Gunn:* As part of his "last day," he tried to look up Rondell and his gang, then swung by to help Anne. The Circle deems Gunn a great disappointment, having hoped he was more corruptible.

• *Illyria:* Markedly less selfish than before, and seems disappointed that Wesley won't let her imitate Fred for his "last day." She's a smidge bewildered when he off-handedly mentions "Mistress Spanksalot." [You almost imagine that Illyria is a little jealous, and about to declare, "Who is this Mistress Spanksalot? Tell me, that I might rip out her giblets."] She's considerate enough to tell Gunn that he should "try not to die." Vail entirely fails to sense Illyria's power while she wears Fred's aspect. [Despite Angel duping the Circle by taking credit for Fred's death, Vail has no real reason to know what she looked like.] She's consumed by grief when Wesley dies, and wants to commit violence as a means of coping.

• *Lorne:* Noticeably has difficulty trusting Angel, but eventually agrees to kill Lindsey on the heroes' behalf. Lorne's final line, as he leaves for parts unknown: "Good night, folks."

• *Lindsey:* Sides with Angel mainly to participate in such

a monumental battle, but seems intrigued that he could acquire control of the firm afterward – or pin blame on Angel's crew if needed. Lindsey never realizes that Angel and Eve had sex ["Life of the Party"]; nor does he see Angel's double-cross coming. [The clear implication is that Angel – and by extension Lorne – believe that Lindsey will eventually revert to type and number among the villains again. Indeed, with the Circle members butchered, Lindsey is the obvious candidate to head the organization. Far better to eliminate him now, as they'll never have a better opportunity.]

• *Harmony*: Supplies Hamilton with sex and information on Angel. Angel fires Harmony for betraying him, but generously writes her a recommendation. [We can let this go for reasons of comedy, but it seems that even amid Angel's scheming, he typed up a recommendation for Harmony, stuffed it in an envelope and left it on her desk – presuming (reasonably) she'd never think to read it beforehand. Less humorously, Harmony will probably resume killing again.]

• *Connor*: Admits that he possesses both his old memories [after 5.18, "Origin"] and his artificial ones. He's applying for an internship.

• *Eve:* Last seen in an office at the firm, not knowing where to go after Lindsey's death.

• *Anne Steele:* [Last seen in 2.14, "The Thin Dead Line."] Still running the East Hills Teen Center, which is moving to a new location. They've had some good donations [lawyer-Gunn was probably helping them out anonymously] and they've hired a part-time paid psychiatric staff. Rondell and his crew [3.03, "That Old Gang of Mine"] protect them from vampire attacks.

• *Nina:* Angel says that she did some great pottery. She made him a vase.

• *Hamilton:* Directly works on the Circle's behalf. [Eve never did, insofar as we know.] Hamilton is clearly stronger and more impervious than Angel, but his strength owes to his blood being "filled" with the Senior Partners' ancient power. Angel goes vamp and feeds off Hamilton – weakening him – then snaps his neck.

• *Sebassis:* Said to command 40,000 demons [it was "40 legions" in "Life of the Party"]. He acts as if he's the Circle's leader, and the other members are said to fear him.

• *"The Pee-Pee Demon":* Blindfolded [possibly denoting a punishment after his recapture in "You're Welcome"]. In death, it dibbles green blood. [The Pee-Pee Demon's wrist fluid is blue, suggesting that it's got *two* kinds of blood. Unless, as some people want to suspect, Sebassis has been drinking pee-pee all along.]

• *Izzerial:* Finally named, and murdered by Illyria.

• *Senator Brucker:* Has a campaign office in West L.A., and dies – oozing green blood – when Gunn tosses a hatchet into her head.

• *Vail:* Claims he can "bend the fabric" of reality, displays telekinesis and survives for a time without his IV drips.

PROPHECY *The Shanshu Prophecy:* The Circle possesses the original Shanshu document, although it looks identical to (and cleaner than) Angel's copy [from 1.21, "Blind Date"]. Angel is made to sign the document in blood, which revokes the document's promised reward of humanity. [Note that Angel's signature does *not* nullify the prophecy that "the vampire with a soul will perform a pivotal role in the Apocalypse...", it simply revokes Angel's right to claim any reward from it.]

ORGANIZATIONS *Wolfram and Hart:* The L.A. branch seems to collapse after Angel kills Hamilton. [It's as if the Senior Partners deliberately bring down the building, although it's unclear what they hope to gain from this beyond showmanship. Alternatively, perhaps Angel and his allies make such a display of heroism, it temporarily nullifies the firm's power connection with the negative aspects of humanity (2.15, "Reprise").]

• *The Senior Partners:* Send legions of demon hordes [presumably Sebassis' troops], and at least one dragon, against Angel's group. [It's tempting to think that the dragon is the wayward one from *Buffy* 5.22, "Chosen," but they don't look the same.]

• *The Circle of the Black Thorn:* Angel implies that they're virtually unstoppable while together, but just demons when separated. The Circle sometimes congregates around a rectangular table bearing its emblem, and the members sound bored while opening their meetings with a chant. Some of the Circle members are human [so Wesley was a candidate on sheer talent, despite his lack of power and connections].

• *Watchers:* According to Wesley, the first lesson they're taught is to separate truth from illusion, because it's the hardest thing to do in the world of magic.

DEMONOLOGY *Vampires:* Harmony says they don't get zits or dandruff.

• *Sahrvin Demons:* Bleed red blood.

BEST LINE The best dialogue almost undoubtedly hails from Wesley's final chat with "Fred," but it's hard to do it justice removed from the moment. Rather, we'll vote for Connor's explanation on how he knew to aid Angel: "Come *on*. You drop by for a cup of coffee, and the world's *not* ending? Please."

THINGS THAT DON'T MAKE SENSE Last episode, Angel was worried enough about surveillance to shroud his office in a magical glamour. So it's odd to see him later hatching plots with Lindsey in the conference room, as if they couldn't be overheard there. Mind, the heroes don't believe that Spike's apartment – which Lindsey acquired, and which Hamilton crashed into last episode – is being monitored either. Also, Angel tells Harmony that he doesn't remember what it was like to be human because it was "too long ago." Well, true... except for that "day as a human" bit in "I Will Remember You" (1.08), which was less than five years ago.

Where precisely is Sebassis telling the Pee-Pee Demon to go when he claps his hands together? Because on screen, this results in the Pee-Pee Demon just shuffling forward and getting tangled in Vail's tubes for no good reason. Maybe Sebassis wants his drink re-filled, but do we honestly think that Sebassis is so concerned about the Circle's sensitivities that he makes the Pee-Pee Demon "pour" out his bodily fluids away from them? Besides, how does the Pee-Pee Demon navigate while blindfolded?

Lindsey says he wants Eve to stay away from the fight if matters go south, yet she's waiting for him at the firm, which doesn't exactly seem like a wise choice. Angel tells Connor that he was at the first taping of *The Carol Burnett Show*, and that Tim Conway was "on fire" that night, but Conway didn't appear until the fourth episode. (He didn't even become a full cast member until 1975. Either Angel is just generalizing, or – as with "The House Always Wins" (4.03) – he's making stuff up for the sake of small talk.) One last time with the staffing issues... only Harmony is working on the executive floor when Angel confronts Hamilton.

Finally, a sign behind Spike says that the poetry slam is occurring at 4 pm. Who on Earth holds a poetry slam at that hour? (Although for anyone trying to religiously date the series, this might suggest that the final battle occurs on a weekend.)

IT'S REALLY ABOUT... You could say it's about the message of striking a blow against evil... but as we've already stated, it's really about the heroes themselves, and how they're finally done compromising their ideals. They display a heroic mettle that inherently feels right for them, and accordingly hack off the most powerful demon group imaginable at the neck. In that regard, it's entirely comforting that Angel and company wind up at the Hyperion – where they properly belonged all along – rather than at the firm, where they didn't.

CRITIQUE For anyone who's invested in the series, this is a deeply, intensely satisfying way of finishing things off. Endings are even more important than we often believe – notice how the finale to *The Prisoner* cemented its legacy in TV history, or how much *Farscape*'s abrupt cancellation seemed like an open wound until the mini-series rolled around. So it's with an immense amount of relief that *Angel* not only ends well, but makes you realize how just how much complexity and merit the series has displayed in the last five years.

Even with multiple viewings, virtually every scene in this episode seems critically important, deeply moving or both. It's actually hard to watch it unfold without a lump in your throat. There's a hellish amount of continuity and emotional issues to cover, but Whedon and Bell show a great amount of finesse and yet tackle everything of note in about 43 minutes. More impressively, it's funny how many times you might say to yourself, "Yup... it *had* to go that way," yet the story is still full of surprises. Every character – from Angel all the way down to Eve – gets a worthy ending. Indeed, the final exchange between Wesley and Fred-Illyria is probably the best thing in the entire show, but it took five-plus seasons of development to make it that way.

The only lingering regret here – ironically – owes to *Angel*'s own success, and the fact that it wasn't is one of those series that sputtered on past its expiration date until you wound up praying it would die. *Angel* Season Five held some amazingly compelling material, and it's almost certain that Season Six would've been riveting also. So we could complain that the series didn't last longer... but honestly, who are we fooling? In today's market – in which a stupendous show like *Wonderfalls* only airs four episodes – the fact that *Angel* lasted five seasons, had such a talent pool and maintained such a level of quality is almost worth throwing a party over.

To put it another way, we're lucky not just that *Angel* thrived for so long, but that it helped to form a larger block of excellent television from Mutant Enemy. All told, *Angel* – along with *Buffy* and *Firefly* – stands as proof that networks should give a talented visionary an awful lot of power and leave them alone, because these shows (and not to knock other creators' contributions) largely succeeded because Joss Whedon was at the helm. Since 2004, a couple of series (such as *Veronica Mars*, although it's not sci-fi) have come close, but we haven't *quite* seen anything like a Whedon show since *Angel* folded... and in that regard, "Not Fade Away" stands as the perfect capstone to the continually intoxicating world that Whedon created with *Buffy*. We were therefore very, very fortunate that *Angel* finished in this fashion, and we'll always reflect upon it with that in mind.

THE LORE Spoilers abounded before this story aired, and one senses that Mutant Enemy knew up front that it couldn't keep a lid on it all. In fact, the mainstream media unloaded so many details about the characters' fates – even if it deliberately avoided specific names – that you could deduce nearly everything about the finale by process-of-elimination. Spike remained a fairly sizeable wild card, but that was about all.

• Whedon had been under the restriction of making sure that *Buffy* ended on a high note, but commented on *Angel*,

"It's a darker tale, so I have more license... to make the audience miserable and excited. ["Not Fade Away"] isn't the end of all things. It's not a final grace note after a sympathy, which I think *Buffy* was. But it is a final statement about *Angel*." (Williamson, *Calgary Sun*, May 20, 2004)

• Whedon has suggested that the heroes would not have continued running the firm even if Season Six had gone forward, and there's reason to think that the finale would've more or less played out as seen... save that Wesley almost certainly wouldn't have perished. Whedon has commented on the fallout from Season Five: "When you buck the system, and do your best to make it collapse, what if it does? The next season would have been some serious chaos." (Alter, *TV Guide Insider*, May 20, 2004) Acker has frequently commented that had the show continued, Illyria would've become more Fred-like. (Indeed, one senses that almost inevitably, Wesley would've been torn between bringing Fred back or keeping Illyria around.)

• Meanwhile, Boreanaz had played Angel for so long, he was clearly looking forward to other pastures. He said, "I don't wanna sound like I was cheering, but when Joss broke the news [of the cancellation], it was almost more like the burden of pressure came off me after five years. I mean, it's a lot of responsibility [carrying a show], and you don't realize how much... until they say it's done and you can breathe." He added that he'd only consider revisiting the part of Angel for a motion picture. (Malcolm, *TV Guide Insider*, May 12, 2004)

• In 2006, it was confirmed that Whedon hoped to do a trilogy of TV movies featuring Spike, Faith and Willow, but funding for such projects remained elusive. Acker would've reprised her role as Illyria, and she's claimed that Gunn would've become a vampire and numbered among the villains. Marsters, certainly, was willing to revisit Spike, but acknowledged that the clock was ticking on how long he could keep playing an immortal character. He said, "Spike's a vampire. He's not supposed to age! So I think there's about a five-year moratorium. I don't want [Whedon] to have to come up with something like, 'Oh, if you don't drink human blood, you do age'." (Malcolm, *TV Guide Insider*, May 13, 2004)

• Best opportunities for seeing the cast post-*Angel:* Boreanaz features on the detective series *Bones* on FOX; a brown-haired Marsters puts in regular appearances as Professor Milton Fine Brainiac on *Smallville*; Denisof occasionally crops up on his wife's sitcom (*How I Met Your Mother*); Acker caused a lot of mayhem as Kelly Peyton on the last series of *Alias*; Richards was in the short-lived *Conviction*; Hallett has largely stuck to convention appearances and Kane was in Season One of the crime series *Close to Home*.

• Marsters' middle name is "Wesley." This has utterly no bearing on anything, but it's so cute, we had to mention it somewhere.

The Final and Total Kill-Count...

• Angel: 42 vampires, 76 demons, 24 humans, 30 zombies, 1 cyborg, 1 heroic champion (demonic), 5 benevolent demon warriors.

• Spike: 5 vampires, 8 demons, 4 benevolent demon warriors.

• Cordelia: 2 vampires, 2 1/2 demons; hundreds of interdimensional bugs.

• Wesley: 6 vampires, 15 1/2 demons, 3 humans, 1 cyborg.

• Gunn: 9 vampires, 17 1/2 demons, 1 human, 1 group of "nasty demon babies."

• Fred: 3 vampires, 1 demon, 1 human, 1 clutch of demon eggs, 1 group of "nasty demon babies."

• Lorne: 2 demons, 1 human.

• Connor: 12 vampires, 3 demons, 1 higher being.

• Illyria: 2 demons, 3 humans.

• Doyle: 1 vampire, 1/2 demon.

• Kate: 3 vampires, 1 human.

... and as a basis of comparison... Buffy's final tally on her series (which exceeded *Angel* by 34 episodes): 142 vampires, 74 demons, 2 humans.

NOTES: Well, it shouldn't come as a shock that the move to the firm entails the heroes killing some human evildoers. Angel slays five humans in total this year, including two from "Conviction" (5.01): Agent Hauser, and the commando that Angel uses as a human shield against a shotgun blast, then snaps the man's neck for good measure. In "Just Rewards" (5.02), Angel kills Hainsley's cleaver-wielding butler and Hainsley himself – who seems like more of a human magic-user than demonic. Angel's fifth kill is Drogyn in "Power Play" (5.21), who's described more as "cursed" than demonic, so we categorized him more as an enhanced human. The same logic applied to Lorne shooting Lindsey in the series finale, as Lindsey seems more like a superpowered human than outright demonic. The script cites Izzy's associates as human, so Illyria picks up three human kills after slaying them in the series finale. Meanwhile, Wesley shoots one of Emil's human lackeys in "Lineage" (5.07), even if the other kills in the story were cyborgs.

Other random notes: Connor only picked up a point this year for beheading Sahjhan (5.18, "Origin"). Drogyn's warriors (5.15, "A Hole in the World") are listed in the script as demonic, but they're on the side of righteousness, so we credited Angel and Spike accordingly. And the infernal puppets in "Smile Time" (5.14) seemed as good as full-fledged demons, so we counted them as such.

Selected Bibliography

"'Angel' fans try like the devil to revive show." Bill Keveney. *USA Today* (April 13 2004).

"ANGEL Viewers Raise Over $14,000 to Feed Those in Need But The WB Ignores Challenge to Meet Donations." *PRWeb.com* (April 14 2004)

"It's a Very Vampy Birthday for Angel – and You're Invited to the Party." Interview by Kristin Veitch. *E! Online: Watch With Kristin* (Feb 6 2004): http://eonline.com/

"'Save ANGEL Week' Kicks Off With LA Rally." *Saveangel.org* (Mar 11 2004)

"Viewers Across Nation 'Give Blood For Angel'." *Save Angel Campaign* (Mar 31 2004): http://savingangel.org

Acker, Amy. "Angel Interceptors." Interview by Lorraine Thurlow. *Cult Times* #104 (May 2004).

Acker, Amy. "Cosmic Girl." Interview by Abbie Bernstein. *Dreamwatch* #110 (Sept 2003).

Acker, Amy. Interview. *FHM* (Aug 2003).

Astin, Sean. Interview. *IGN FilmForce* (Dec 22 2003): http://filmforce.ign.com/

Bell, Jeff. "Angel Evolutions." Interview by Edward Gross. *Cinefantastique* (Oct 2003).

Bell, Jeff. "Raising the Stakes." Interview by Tara DiLullo. *Dreamwatch* #109 (Sept 2003).

Benz, Julie. "Angel She-Devil's Fright Night." Interview by Charlie Mason. *TV Guide Insider* (Dec 12 2000): http://tvguide.com/news/insider/

Benz, Julie. Interview. *BBC Cult* (Nov 2001): http://bbc.co.uk/cult/buffy/angel/

Benz, Julie. Interview. *SMG Fan.com* (Nov 11 2003)

Boreanaz, David. "Angel Adieu." Interview by Shawna Malcolm. *TV Guide Insider* (May 12 2004)

Boreanaz, David. "Interview With an 'Angel'." Interview. *Entertainment Tonight Online* (Feb 22 2000): http://etonline.com/

Boreanaz, David. "There Must be an Angel Playing with Wolfram and Hart." Interview by Ian Spelling. *Dreamwatch* #110 (Nov 2003).

Boreanaz, David. Chat transcripts. *TV Guide Online* (May 22 and Oct 3, 2000): http://tvguide.com/

Boreanaz, David. Interview by Michael Hogan. *Glamour UK* (July 2002).

Boreanaz, David. Interview by Kristin Veitch. *E! Online: Watch With Kristin* (Feb 6 2004): http://eonline.com/

The Bronze VIP Posting Board Archives. http://cise.ufl.edu/~hsiao/media/tv/buffy/bronze/

The Bronze Beta (Posting Board): http://bronzebeta.com/

Burr, Thomas. "The Chill Factor." Interview by Sue Grimshaw. *City of Angel* (April 27 2004): http://cityofangel.com/

Carpenter, Charisma. "See Charisma act: But not on 'Angel'." Interview by Amy Amatangelo. *BostonHerald.com - the Edge* (August 15 2003): http://theedge.bostonherald.com/

Carpenter, Charisma. "Why Angel Lacks Charisma." Interview by Daniel R. Coleridge. *TV Guide Insider* (Feb 5 2004): http://tvguide.com/news/insider/

Carpenter, Charisma. Interview. *BBC Cult* (Aug 22 2001): http://bbc.co.uk/cult/buffy/angel/

Carpenter, Charisma. Interview. *SMG Fan.com*

Denisof, Alexis. "Going Rogue." Interview by Paul Spragg. *Cult Times* (June 2002).

Denisof, Alexis. "Hannigan and Denisof Find Love in the Whedonverse." Interview by Kate O'Hare. *Zap2It* (Jan 20 2004): http://tv.zap2it.com/

Denisof, Alexis. "Newest Angel actor earns his wings." Interview by Kate O'Hare. *Arizona Republic* (Feb 13 2000).

Denisof, Alexis. Chat transcript. *TV Guide Online* (Jan 16 2001): http://tvguide.com/

Denisof, Alexis. Interview by Kenneth Plume. *IGN FilmForce* (Feb 11 2003): http://filmforce.ign.com/

Denisof, Alexis. Interview. *BBC Cult* (Aug 22 2001): http://bbc.co.uk/cult/buffy/angel/

Denman, David. "Skip Tracer." Interview by Kate O'Hare. *Zap2It* (Mar 27 2003): http://tv.zap2it.com/

Dushuku, Eliza. Convention appearance. *Wizard World Philadelphia* (May 2004).

Fain, Sarah & Craft, Elizabeth. "Angel Writers Get Their Wings." Interview by Ward Triplett. *Kansascity.com* (April 15 2004).

Fain, Sarah & Craft, Elizabeth. "From Pen & Paper We Devour." Interview by Tara DiLullo. *City of Angel* (April 22 2004): http://cityofangel.com/

Fury, David. "The Sound of the Fury." Interview by Tara DiLullo. *City of Angel* (June 24 2003): http://cityofangel.com/

Fury, David. Interview by Tara DiLullo. *Dreamwatch* #110 (Nov 2003).

Fury, David. Interview by Mike Jozic. *MEANWHILE...* (Sept 2004): http://mikejozic.com/

Greenwalt, David. "'Angel's' Cordelia grows up." Interview by Scott D. Pierce. *Deseret News* (Feb 18 2002): http://deseretnews.com/

Greenwalt, David. "Angel – Vampire with soul." Interview by Catherine Seipp. *United Press International* (May 8 2002).

Greenwalt, David. "Producer Admires 'Angel' from Afar." Interview by Kate O'Hare. *Zap2It* (May 12 2003): http://tv.zap2it.com/

Hall, Rob. "Almost Human: From Beneath They Devour." Interview by Kate O'Hare. *Zap2It* (Nov 29 2002): http://tv.zap2it.com/

Hall, Rob. "'Angel' Unleashes a Werewolf." Interview by Kate O'Hare. *Zap2It* (Oct 12 2003): http://tv.zap2it.com/

Hallett, Andy. "'Angel's' Host Speaks." Interview by Kate

O'Hare. *Zap2It* (Nov 29 2000): http://tv.zap2it.com/

Hallett, Andy. "Lovelorn." Interview by Mika Gill (July 3 2004): http://tve.co.il/

Hallett, Andy. "The Regular Guy." Interview by Kate O'Hare. *Zap2It* (Feb 27 2003): http://tv.zap2it.com/

Hallett, Andy. Interview. *BBC Cult* (April 2003). http://bbc.co.uk/cult/buffy/angel/

Hallett, Andy. Interview. *SFX* (Aug 2003).

Hannigan, Alyson. "'Angel' Calls on Faith, Gets Willow." Interview by Kate O'Hare. *Zap2It* (Mar 16 2003): http://tv.zap2it.com/

Kane, Christian. "Christian Kane Takes Direction from 'Angel'." Interview by Kate O'Hare. *Zap2It* (Jan 5 2004): http://tv.zap2it.com/

Kane, Christian. "Fists of Jury." Interview by Justine Elias. *Entertainment Weekly Online* (Dec 19 2000): http://ew.com/

Kane, Christian. "Kane keeps devilish secrets from 'Angel' fans, cast." Interview by Amy Amatangelo. *Boston Herald* (Jan 21 2004).

Kane, Christian. Interview. *BBC Cult* (Nov 2003): http://bbc.co.uk/cult/buffy/angel/

Kartheiser, Vincent. Interview. *BBC Cult* (April 2003): http://bbc.co.uk/cult/buffy/angel/

Kartheiser, Vincent. "Angel Baby." Interview by Kristin Veitch. *E! Online: Who the Hell is This?* (Feb 2004): http://eonline.com/

Kim, Daniel Dae. "Kim surfaces as sex symbol on 'Lost'." Interview by Ann Oldenburg. *USA Today* (Mar 21 2006).

Kral, Robert J. "37 Questions with Robert J. Kral." Interview. *Miracles TV* (Nov 23 2003): http://miraclestv.com/

Kulich, Vladimir. "Beastie Boy." Interview by Allyson. *Scoopme.com* (Jan 2003): http://scoopme.com/

Lutz, Mark. "'Angel's' Groosalugg Pulls a Triple Lutz." Interview by Brill Bundy. *Zap2It* (May 5 2002): http://tv.zap2it.com/

Marsters, James. "Fangs for the Memory." Interview by Margie Baronno. *Starburst* #309 (May 2004).

Marsters, James. "James Marsters on Buffy: How Spike buffed his ego." Interview. *TNT Drama Lounge* (April 23 2004): http://tnt.tv/DramaLounge/

Marsters, James. "The Big Fang Theory." Interview by Shawna Malcolm. *TV Guide* (Sept 6 2003).

Marsters, James. Interview by Steven Eramo. *TV Zone* (June 2004).

McNab, Mercedes. "Angel Gets a Blonde Transfusion?" Interview by Charlie Mason. *TV Guide Insider* (May 30 2001): http://tvguide.com/news/insider/

McNab, Mercedes. "Mercedes McNab Brings Harmony to 'Angel'." Interview by Kate O'Hare. *Zap2It* (Oct 18 2003): http://tv.zap2it.com/

McNab, Mercedes. "Vamping It Up!." Interview by Steven Eramo. *Xpose* #81 (Nov 2003).

McNab, Mercedes. Interview. *FHM* (Jan 2004).

Minear, Tim. "'Angel' Flies Solo to the Edge." Interview by Kate O'Hare. *Zap2It* (May 14 2002): http://tv.zap2it.com/

Minear, Tim. "ANGEL: Season One, Episode By Episode with Tim Minear." Interview by Edward Gross. *Fandom.com* (Aug 14 2000).

Minear, Tim. Interview by Kristin Veitch. *E! Online: Watch With Kristin* (Mar 2004): http://eonline.com/

Minear, Tim. "Writer-producer Tim Minear on directing 'Darla'." Interview by Edward Gross. *Fandom.com* (Nov 13 2000)

Minear, Tim. *alt.tv.angel* (Nov 23 1999 - May 19 2001).

Minear, Tim. Interview. *BBC Cult* (Aug 23 2001): http://bbc.co.uk/cult/buffy/angel/

Minear, Tim. *uk.media.tv.angel* (Sept 7 2001 - May 3 2003).

Richards, J. August. "Angel's Gunn, Charles Gunn." Interview by Kate O'Hare. *Zap2It* (Aug 8 2003): http://tv.zap2it.com/

Richards, J. August. "Gunn-ing for J. August Richards." Interview by Vanessa Sibbald. *Zap2It* (Mar 26 2002): http://tv.zap2it.com/

Richards, J. August. "Shooting To Success." Interview by Julie Reynolds. *City of Angel* (Aug 15 2002): http://cityofangel.com/

Rohm, Elisabeth. "Angel Women Face Future." Interview. *SciFiWire* (May 30 2001): http://scifi.com/scifiwire/

Romanov, Stephanie. "'Angel's' Lilah Is Dead and Loving It." Interview by Kate O'Hare. *Zap2It* (May 02 2003): http://tv.zap2it.com/

Romanov, Stephanie. Interview. *BBC Cult* (2002): http://bbc.co.uk/cult/buffy/angel/

Szarabajka, Keith. "Hell Hath No Fury Like Holtz Scorned." Interview by Jeff Ritchie. *City of Angel* (Mar 28 2003): http://cityofangel.com/

Thompson, Sarah. "'Angel's' Sarah Thompson Just Wants to Sing." Interview by Kate O'Hare. *Zap2It* (Dec 31 2003): http://tv.zap2it.com/

Topping, Keith. *Hollywood Vampire* (vols. 1-2), Virgin Books, 2005 and 2006.

Whedon, Joss. "Creator previews final episode - Angel's slay ride ends." Interview by Kevin Williamson. *Calgary Sun* (May 20 2004): http://fyicalgary.com/

Whedon, Joss. "Angel Creator's Finale Post-Mortem." Interview by Ethan Alter. *TV Guide Insider* (May 20 2004): http://tvguide.com/news/insider/

Whedon, Joss. "'Angel' returns." Interview. *Post-Gazette* (July 2003).

Whedon, Joss. "Joss Whedon Talks Angel Season Two." Interview by Fred Topel. *About.com* (Sep 10 2003)

Whedon, Joss. "Put On Your Party Hats for Angel's Birthday Bash." Interview by Kristin Veitch. *E! Online: Watch With Kristin* (Dec 12 2003): http://eonline.com/

Whedon, Joss. "The End of the Surprise Ending." Interview by Emily Nussbaum. *The New York Times* (May 9 2004).

PUBLISHER / EDITOR-IN-CHIEF
Lars Pearson

SENIOR EDITOR / DESIGN MANAGER
Christa Dickson

ASSOCIATE EDITOR (MNP)
Joshua Wilson

EDITORS (REDEEMED)
Lance Parkin, Lloyd Rose

ASSOCIATE EDITORS (REDEEMED)
Robert Smith?
Lynne M. Thomas
Michael D. Thomas

COPY EDITORS
Dave Gartner, Steve Manfred

COVER ART
Richard Martinez/Art Thug

The publisher would like to thank...
Lawrence Miles (for this book's title) and Shawne Kleckner.

Dedicated to **Keith Topping**... fellow *Angel* writer, trusted convention panelist and one of the nicest people on the planet.

1150 46th Street
Des Moines, Iowa 50311
info@madnorwegian.com

21023339R00198

Printed in Great Britain
by Amazon